MULTIVARIATE ANALYSIS–II

Proceedings of the Second International Symposium on Multivariate Analysis held at Wright State University, Dayton, Ohio, June 17–22, 1968

MULTIVARIATE ANALYSIS–II

Proceedings of the Second International Symposium on Multivariate Analysis held at Wright State University, Dayton, Ohio, June 17–22, 1968

Edited by *PARUCHURI R. KRISHNAIAH*

AEROSPACE RESEARCH LABORATORIES
OFFICE OF AEROSPACE RESEARCH
UNITED STATES AIR FORCE
WRIGHT-PATTERSON AIR FORCE BASE, OHIO

1969

ACADEMIC PRESS New York and London

SPONSORED BY THE AEROSPACE RESEARCH LABORATORIES, OFFICE OF AEROSPACE RESEARCH, UNITED STATES AIR FORCE, WRIGHT-PATTERSON AIR FORCE BASE, OHIO. CONTRACT NUMBER F33615-68-C-1508

ACADEMIC PRESS, INC.
111 Fifth Avenue, New York, New York 10003

United Kingdom Edition published by
ACADEMIC PRESS, INC. (LONDON) LTD.
Berkeley Square House, London W.1

LIBRARY OF CONGRESS CATALOG CARD NUMBER: 69-18351
AMS 1968 SUBJECT CLASSIFICATION 6240

PRINTED IN THE UNITED STATES OF AMERICA

List of Contributors

Numbers in parentheses indicate the pages on which the authors' contributions begin.

Anders Ågren, University Institute of Statistics, Uppsala, Sweden (543)

T. W. Anderson, Department of Statistics, Stanford University, Stanford, California (55)

Rolf E. Bargmann, Department of Statistics, University of Georgia, Athens, Georgia (567)

Robert E. Bechhofer, Department of Operations Research, Cornell University, Ithaca, New York (463)

C. B. Bell, Department of Mathematics, Case Western Reserve University, Cleveland, Ohio (3)[1]

Z. W. Birnbaum, Department of Mathematics, University of Washington, Seattle, Washington (581)

David R. Brillinger, Department of Statistics, The London School of Economics and Political Science, Aldwych, London; Department of Statistics, The University of California, Berkeley, California (331)[2]

J. Douglas Carroll, Bell Telephone Laboratories, Incorporated, Murray Hill, New Jersey (639)

P. C. Consul, Department of Mathematics, Statistics, and Computer Sciences, University of Calgary, Calgary, Alberta, Canada (171)

M. R. Dubman, Rocketdyne, a Division of North American Rockwell Corporation, Canoga Park, California (351)

Daniel Dugue, University of Paris, Paris, France (289)

K. R. Gabriel, Hebrew University, Jerusalem, Israel (67)

R. Gnanadesikan, Bell Telephone Laboratories, Incorporated, Murray Hill, New Jersey (593)

I. J. Good, Statistics Department, Virginia Polytechnic Institute, Blacksburg, Virginia (183)

N. R. Goodman, Independent Consultant, Los Angeles, California (351)

[1] Present address: Department of Mathematics, University of Michigan, Ann Arbor, Michigan

[2] Present address: Department of Statistics, The London School of Economics and Political Science, Aldwych, London

Shanti S. Gupta, Department of Statistics, Purdue University, Lafayette, Indiana (475)

Koichi Ito, Nanzan University, Nagoya, Japan (87)

A. T. James, Department of Statistics, University of Adelaide, Adelaide, South Australia (205)

G. Kallianpur, Department of Mathematics, University of Minnesota, Minneapolis, Minnesota (367)

C. G. Khatri, Indian Statistical Institute, Calcutta, India; Department of Statistics, Purdue University, Lafayette, Indiana (219, 241)[3]

P. R. Krishnaiah, Aerospace Research Laboratories, Wright-Patterson Air Force Base, Ohio (121)

Joseph B. Kruskal, Bell Telephone Laboratories, Incorporated, Murray Hill, New Jersey (639)

Eugene Lukacs, Statistical Laboratory, The Catholic University of America, Washington, D. C. (303)

Albert Madansky, Dataplan, Inc., New York, New York (261)

Sujit Kumar Mitra, Indian Statistical Institute, Calcutta, India (241)

Masashi Okamoto, Department of Statistics, Iowa State University, Ames, Iowa; Department of Applied Mathematics, Osaka University, Osaka, Japan (673)[4]

Ingram Olkin, Department of Statistics, Stanford University, Stanford, California (261)

S. Panchapakesan, Department of Statistics, Purdue University, Lafayette, Indiana (475)

Emanuel Parzen, Department of Statistics, Stanford University, Stanford, California (389)

K. C. S. Pillai, Department of Statistics, Purdue University, Lafayette, Indiana (219)

Madan Lal Puri, Department of Mathematics, Indiana University, Bloomington, Indiana; Courant Institute of Mathematical Sciences, New York University, New York, New York (33)[5]

[3] Present address: Department of Statistics, Gujarat University, Ahmedabad, India

[4] Present address: Department of Applied Mathematics, Osaka University, Osaka, Japan

[5] Present address: Department of Mathematics, Indiana University, Bloomington, Indiana

C. Radhakrishna Rao, Indian Statistical Institute, Calcutta, India (321)

M. M. Rao, Department of Mathematics, Carnegie-Mellon University, Pittsburgh, Pennsylvania (411)

M. Rosenblatt, Mathematics Department, University of California, La Jolla, California (25)

Yu. A. Rozanov, Steklov Mathematical Institute, Academy of Sciences of the USSR, Moscow, USSR (437)

Herman Rubin, Department of Statistics, Purdue University, Lafayette, Indiana (507)

M. V. Rama Sastry, Graduate School of Business Administration, University of Washington, Seattle, Washington (687)

L. Schmetterer, Mathematisches Institut, University of Vienna, Vienna, Austria (443)

Pranab Kumar Sen, Department of Biostatistics, University of North Carolina, Chapel Hill, North Carolina (33)

Paul J. Smith, Department of Mathematics, Case Western Reserve University, Cleveland, Ohio (3)[6]

Milton Sobel, Imperial College, London, England; Department of Statistics, University of Minnesota, Minneapolis, Minnesota (515)[7]

J. N. Srivastava, Department of Mathematics and Statistics, Colorado State University, Fort Collins, Colorado (145)

C. Striebel, Department of Mathematics, University of Minnesota, Minneapolis, Minnesota (367)

Gerhard Tintner, Department of Economics, University of Southern California, Los Angeles, California (687)

M. B. Wilk, Bell Telephone Laboratories, Incorporated, Murray Hill, New Jersey (593)

Herman O. Wold, University Institute of Statistics, Uppsala, Sweden (543)

[6] Present address: Department of Mathematics, Wayne State University, Detroit, Michigan

[7] Present address: Department of Statistics, University of Minnesota, Minneapolis, Minnesota

Preface

The Second International Symposium on Multivariate Analysis was held at Wright State University, Dayton, Ohio, June 17–22, 1968. The purpose of this symposium, as with the first one, was to stimulate research and disseminate knowledge in the area of multivariate analysis. Prominent statisticians from several countries presented invited papers on a broad spectrum of topics in the area of multivariate analysis. The topics covered include nonparametric methods, multivariate analysis of variance and related topics, distribution theory, characteristic functions and characterization problems, time series and stochastic processes, decision procedures, econometrics, principal components, reliability, and applications. Most of the papers present new results in the field and a few are expository in nature. This book consists of papers presented at the symposium and will generally complement the material in the earlier book entitled "Multivariate Analysis" containing the papers presented at the First International Symposium on Multivariate Analysis, held in 1965. This volume will be of interest to mathematical and applied statisticians, as well as to probabilists, and it is hoped that it will stimulate a significant amount of research in this field.

This symposium was sponsored by the Aerospace Research Laboratories (ARL) at Wright-Patterson Air Force Base, Ohio; ARL is a unit of the Office of Aerospace Research, the research agency of the United States Air Force.

While I take complete responsibility for any mistakes in the organization of the symposium and the editing of this book, I wish to express my gratitude to several persons for their valuable help. Colonel J. C. Dieffenderfer, deputy commander of the Office of Aerospace Research, was kind enough to make the opening remarks. For presiding over the different sessions, I wish to thank Professors R. L. Anderson, R. R. Bahadur, F. J. Beutler, R. A. Bradley, H. T. David, M. H. DeGroot, D. Dugue, S. Geisser, L. J. Gleser, W. Hoeffding, D. G. Kabe, L. Katz, O. Kempthorne, A. G. Laurent, F. M. Lord, P. Masani, G. H. Moore, J. S. Rustagi, R. Sitgreaves, Colonel J. V. Armitage, and Drs. H. L. Harter, F. Proschan, and L. E. Wolaver. I am also grateful to those who reviewed the papers: Professors R. E. Barlow, D. Brillinger, A. G. Constantine, M. H. DeGroot, J. N. Darroch, S. S. Gupta, D. G. Kabe, C. G. Khatri, P. K. Pathak, E. Parzen, K. C. S. Pillai, M. L. Puri, M. M. Rao, J. N. Srivastava, M. Sobel, T. Sugiyama, C. K. Tsao, P. Whittle, A. M. Yaglom, and Drs. C. W. Dunnett, N. R. Goodman, K. Jayachandran, and A. Madansky. The papers by Professors Yu. A. Rozanov and L. Schmetterer were kindly presented at the symposium by Professors M. M. Rao and G. Kallianpur, respectively.

I am indebted to Professor C. C. Maneri for his help in making the local arrangements, and to Professor M. M. Rao for his helpful suggestions in the organization of the program. Professors J. Kohler and J. A. Redden were also helpful in making the local arrangements. I wish to express my appreciation to Colonel P. G. Atkinson, Jr. and to Professor C. R. Rao for their interest and encouragement. Special thanks are due to the contributors to this book and to Academic Press for their excellent cooperation.

P. R. Krishnaiah

Wright-Patterson Air Force Base, Ohio
May 1969

Contents

Approximate Confidence Regions for Constraint Parameters

Albert Madansky and Ingram Olkin

PART IV / Characteristic Functions and Characterization Problems

Characteristic Functions of Random Variables Connected with Brownian Motion and of the von Mises Multidimensional ω_n^2

Daniel Dugue

Some Recent Developments in the Theory of Multivariate Characteristic Functions

Eugene Lukacs

Some Characterizations of the Multivariate Normal Distribution

C. Radhakrishna Rao

PART V / Time Series and Stochastic Processes

The Canonical Analysis of Stationary Time Series

David R. Brillinger

Theory of Time-Varying Spectral Analysis and Complex Wishart Matrix Processes

N. R. Goodman and M. R. Dubman

Stochastic Differential Equations in Statistical Estimation Problems

G. Kallianpur and C. Striebel

Multiple Time Series Modeling

Emanuel Parzen

Representation Theory of Multidimensional Generalized Random Fields

M. M. Rao

On a New Class of Estimates

Yu. A. Rozanov

Multidimensional Stochastic Approximation

L. Schmetterer

PART VI / Decision Procedures

Optimal Allocation of Observations when Comparing Several Treatments with a Control

Robert E. Bechhofer

Optimality of Principal Components

Masashi Okamoto

Information Theory and the Statistical Estimation of Econometric Relations

Gerhard Tintner and M. V. Rama Sastry

PART I

Nonparametric Methods

Some Nonparametric Tests for the Multivariate Goodness-of-Fit, Multisample, Independence, and Symmetry Problems

C. B. BELL[1]
and PAUL J. SMITH[2]

DEPARTMENT OF MATHEMATICS
CASE WESTERN RESERVE UNIVERSITY
CLEVELAND, OHIO

1. INTRODUCTION AND SUMMARY

For the goodness-of-fit hypothesis, a large class of distribution-free tests is constructed. These tests are strongly distribution-free in the sense of Bell (1960). Some examples are given to indicate how to construct tests which seem good against certain classes of alternatives.

The class of all distribution-free tests of the multisample, independence, and symmetry hypotheses is characterized, following the development of Bell and Doksum (1967) and Bell and Haller (1969). In the special case of total independence, the family of all rank tests can also be characterized. This general theory is related to some earlier work, particularly to the permutation rank-order tests of Sen and Puri (1966). Some new parametric and nonparametric tests of symmetry are also proposed.

Finally, some of the open problems in this field are briefly discussed.

2. PRELIMINARIES AND NOTATION

In this paper, vectors will be denoted by boldface letters, as in Anderson (1958), that is,

$$\mathbf{X} = \begin{bmatrix} X_1 \\ \vdots \\ X_p \end{bmatrix}$$

[1] Present address: Department of Mathematics, University of Michigan, Ann Arbor, Michigan.

[2] Present address: Department of Mathematics, Wayne State University, Detroit, Michigan.

so that $\mathbf{X}^T = [X_1 \cdots X_p]$ denotes the transpose of $\mathbf{X}$. All vectors will be considered column vectors. If the vector $\mathbf{X}$ is partitioned into subvectors, this will be denoted

$$\mathbf{X} = \begin{bmatrix} \mathbf{X}^{(1)} \\ \vdots \\ \mathbf{X}^{(q)} \end{bmatrix}; \qquad \mathbf{X}^{(i)} = \begin{bmatrix} X_1^{(i)} \\ \vdots \\ X_{pi}^{(i)} \end{bmatrix}.$$

If F is the distribution function of $\mathbf{X}$, then $F_i(\mathbf{X}^{(i)})$ will denote the marginal distribution of $\mathbf{X}^{(i)}$, and if $\mathbf{X}_1, \mathbf{X}_2, \ldots, \mathbf{X}_N$ is a random sample from F, then the N-fold power distribution will be written

$$F^{(N)}(\mathbf{X}_1 \cdots \mathbf{X}_N) = \prod_{\alpha=1}^{N} F(\mathbf{X}_\alpha).$$

The symbol $\Omega_2(R^p)$ will denote the class of continuous distribution functions on R^p, and $\Omega_2{}^*(R^p)$ will denote the class of continuous distributions such that $F_i(X_i)$, $F_i(X_i \mid X_j)$, $F_i(X_i \mid X_j, X_k)$, etc. are strictly increasing continuous functions of X_i.

A statistic will be considered as a measurable function T from $\Omega \times R^{pN}$ to the real line, where Ω is some family of distributions and will be written $T_F(\mathbf{X}_1 \cdots \mathbf{X}_N)$. If T does not depend on F, then the statistic will be written $T(\mathbf{X}_1 \cdots \mathbf{X}_N)$.

If a null hypothesis H_0 is being tested against an alternative H_1, $\Omega(H_0)$ will denote the class of joint sample distributions satisfying H_0, and $\Omega(H_0 \cup H_1)$ will be the class of distributions satisfying either H_0 or H_1. For example, if one considered the independence hypothesis

$$H_0\colon \quad F(\mathbf{X}) = F_1(\mathbf{X}^{(1)})F_2(\mathbf{X}^{(2)}) \cdots F_q(\mathbf{X}^{(q)})$$

for each $\mathbf{X}$ against the general alternative

$$H_1\colon \quad F(\mathbf{X}) \neq F_1(\mathbf{X}^{(1)})F_2(\mathbf{X}^{(2)}) \cdots F_q(\mathbf{X}^{(q)})$$

then

$$\Omega(H_0) = \{F^{(N)} \mid F(\mathbf{X}) = F_1(\mathbf{X}^{(1)})F_2(\mathbf{X}^{(2)} \cdots F_q(\mathbf{X}^{(q)}); \; F_i \in \Omega_2{}^*(R^{p^i})\}$$
$$\Omega(H_0 \cup H_1) = \{F^{(N)} \mid F \in \Omega_2{}^*(R^p)\}$$

for the nonparametric version of the problem.

In the treatment of multivariate problems, it will be convenient to consider the following transformation, due to Rosenblatt (1952).

Definition 2.1. *Let F belong to* $\Omega_2^*(R^p)$. *Then the transformation* $\mathbf{Z} = \tau_F(\mathbf{X})$ *is defined by*

$$\begin{aligned} Y_1 &= F_1(X_1) \\ Y_2 &= F_2(X_2 \mid X_1) \\ &\vdots \\ Y_p &= F_p(X_p \mid X_1 \cdots X_{p-1}). \end{aligned}$$

Extending the results of Rosenblatt, one can prove:

Lemma 2.1.

(i) *If* $\mathbf{X}$ *has distribution* $F \in \Omega_2^*(R^p)$, *then* $\mathbf{Y} = \tau_F(\mathbf{X})$ *is distributed uniformly on the unit hypercube* I^p. *That is, each component* Y_i *of* $\mathbf{Y}$ *has a uniform distribution on* (0, 1) *and the* Y_i *are mutually independent.*

(ii) τ_F *is a* 1–1 *transformation of* R^p *onto* I^p, *and* τ_F^{-1} *exists.*

Essentially, τ_F is an extension of the familiar probability integral transformation.

It will be worthwhile to make formal definitions of distribution-free statistics in order to facilitate the formulation of characterization theorems.

Definition 2.2.

(i) *A statistic* $T : \Omega \times R^{pN} \to R$ *is* distribution-free (*DF*) *with respect to* Ω *if there exists a distribution function* Q_T *such that*

$$P_F[T_F(\mathbf{X}_1 \cdots \mathbf{X}_N) \leq t] = Q_T(t)$$

for all F in Ω *and all real t.*

(ii) *If* $\Omega \subseteq \Omega_2^*(R^p)$, *then* $T : \Omega \times R^{pN} \to R$ *is* strongly distribution-free (*SDF*) *with respect to* Ω *if for all real t*

$$P_G[T_F(\mathbf{X}_1 \cdots \mathbf{X}_N) \leq t] = P_{G^*}[T_{F^*}(\mathbf{X}_1 \cdots \mathbf{X}_N) \leq t]$$

whenever $\tau_G \tau_F^{-1} = \tau_{G^*} \tau_{F^*}^{-1}$, *for each* $F, F^*, G, G^* \in \Omega$.

This formulation of SDF statistics applies in goodness-of-fit problems. The SDF statistics, in addition to being DF, have the additional property of partitioning $\Omega \times \Omega$ into subsets over which the power of a test (of F versus G) is constant.

In other nonparametric problems, it is often convenient to consider a group $\mathscr{G}$ of transformations of Ω onto itself, under which the constant power classes are also equivalence classes of $\mathscr{G}$. Accordingly, one provides an alternate definition of SDF statistics.

Definition 2.3. *A statistic T is SDF with respect to Ω and 𝒢 if*

$$P_G[T_F(\mathbf{X}_1 \cdots \mathbf{X}_N) \leq t] = P_{G^*}[T_{F^*}(\mathbf{X}_1 \cdots \mathbf{X}_N) \leq t]$$

whenever $G^* = G_g$ *and* $F^* = F_g$ *for some* $g \in \mathcal{G}$, *where* $\tau_{F_g} = \tau_F g^{-1}$ *and* $\mathcal{G}$ *is the group of transformations*

$$\mathcal{G} = \{g\colon \quad R^p \to R^p \mid g(\mathbf{X}) = \tau_G^{-1}\tau_F(\mathbf{X})\}.$$

Thus, $\mathcal{G}$ is some group of transformations of the data under which the problem is invariant, and the SDF statistics are related to statistics invariant under $\mathcal{G}$. For more details, see Bell (1964).

One last bit of notation is the ε-function:

$$\varepsilon(u) = \begin{cases} 1, & u \geq 0, \\ 0, & u < 0. \end{cases}$$

This is a function which counts nonnegative values, and will be used extensively in the sequel.

3. ONE-SAMPLE TESTS AND STATISTICS

In this section, DF tests of goodness-of-fit will be considered in a multivariate setting, and some SDF tests will be proposed.

Definition 3.1.

(i) *A statistic* $T = T_F(\mathbf{X}_1 \cdots \mathbf{X}_N)$ *is of* structure (d_N') *if*

$$T_F(\mathbf{X}_1, \ldots, \mathbf{X}_N) = \Psi[\tau_F(\mathbf{X}_1), \ldots, \tau_F(\mathbf{X}_N)]$$

for some measurable function Ψ.

(ii) *If T is of structure* (d_N') *and* Ψ *is symmetric, i.e.,* $\Psi(\mathbf{Z}_1, \ldots, \mathbf{Z}_N) = \Psi(\mathbf{Z}_{i_1}, \ldots, \mathbf{Z}_{i_n})$ *for every permutation* $(i_1, \ldots, i_N)$ *of* $(1, \ldots, N)$, *then T is of* structure (d_N).

The importance of the structure (d_N) statistics is that they are equivalent to SDF statistics in the following sense:

Theorem 3.1.

(i) *If T is of structure* (d_N'), *then T is SDF.*

(ii) *If T is SDF, then there exists a statistic S of structure* (d_N') *such that* $P_F T^{-1} = P_F S^{-1}$.

(iii) *If* Ω *is symmetrically complete, then T is SDF if, and only if, T is of structure* (d_N).

Proof.

(i) Let T be of structure (d_N') and let A be any Borel set. Then

$$\begin{aligned} P_G[T_F \in A] &= P_G[\Psi\{\tau_F(\mathbf{X}_1), \ldots, \tau_F(\mathbf{X}_N)\} \in A] \\ &= P_G[(\tau_F(\mathbf{X}_1), \ldots, \tau_F(\mathbf{X}_N)) \in \Psi^{-1}(A)] \\ &= P_G[(\tau_G(X_1), \ldots, \tau_G(X_N)) \in \tau_G \tau_F^{-1} \Psi^{-1}(A)] \\ &= P_U[(\mathbf{Y}_1, \ldots, \mathbf{Y}_N) \in \tau_G \tau_F^{-1} \Psi^{-1}(A)] \end{aligned}$$

where P_U represents the uniform probability measure on I^p. Since $P_G[T_F \in A]$ depends only on $\tau_G \tau_F^{-1}$, T is SDF.

(ii) If T is SDF, define $\Psi_0(\mathbf{Y}_1, \ldots, \mathbf{Y}_N) = T_{F_0}[\tau_{F_0}^{-1}(\mathbf{Y}_1), \ldots, \tau_{F_0}^{-1}(\mathbf{Y}_N)]$ and let $S_F(\mathbf{X}_1, \ldots, \mathbf{X}_N) = \Psi_0[\tau_F(\mathbf{X}_1), \ldots, \tau_F(\mathbf{X}_N)]$. Then S is of structure (d_N'). Now let A be a Borel set. Then

$$\begin{aligned} P_G[S_F \in A] &= P_G[\Psi_0[\tau_F(\mathbf{X}_1), \ldots, \tau_F(\mathbf{X}_N)] \in A] \\ &= P_G[T_{F_0}\{\tau_{F_0}^{-1}\tau_F(\mathbf{X}_1), \ldots, \tau_{F_0}^{-1}\tau_F(\mathbf{X}_N)\} \in A] \\ &= P_G[(\tau_{F_0}^{-1}\tau_F(\mathbf{X}_1), \ldots, \tau_{F_0}^{-1}\tau_F(\mathbf{X}_N)) \in T_{F_0}^{-1}(A)] \\ &= P_G[(\mathbf{X}_1, \ldots, \mathbf{X}_N) \in \tau_F^{-1}\tau_{F_0} T_{F_0}^{-1}(A)] \\ &= P_G[(\tau_G(\mathbf{X}_1), \ldots, \tau_G(\mathbf{X}_N)) \in \tau_G \tau_F^{-1}\tau_{F_0} T_{F_0}^{-1}(A)] \\ &= P_U[(\mathbf{Y}_1, \ldots, \mathbf{Y}_N) \in \tau_G \tau_F^{-1}\tau_{F_0} T_{F_0}^{-1}(A)]. \end{aligned}$$

Now $\tau_G \tau_F^{-1} = (\tau_G \tau_F^{-1} \tau_{F_0})\tau_{F_0}^{-1}$. Let $H \in \Omega_2{}^*$ be such that $\tau_H = \tau_G \tau_F^{-1} \tau_{F_0}$. Then

$$\begin{aligned} P_G[T_F \in A] &= P_H[T_{F_0} \in A] \qquad \text{since } T \text{ is } SDF \\ &= P_H[(\mathbf{X}_1, \ldots, \mathbf{X}_N) \in T_{F_0}^{-1}(A)] \\ &= P_H[(\tau_H(\mathbf{X}_1), \ldots, \tau_H(\mathbf{X}_N)) \in \tau_H T_{F_0}^{-1}(A)] \\ &= P_U[\mathbf{Y}_1, \ldots, \mathbf{Y}_N) \in \tau_G \tau_F^{-1} \tau_{F_0} T_{F_0}^{-1}(A)]. \end{aligned}$$

Thus, $P_G[T_F \in A] = P_G[S_F \in A]$, proving (ii).

(iii) Then (iii) follows immediately, from (ii) and the symmetric completeness assumption.

Theorem 3.1 indicates how to construct DF tests of the goodness-of-fit hypothesis $H_0 : F = F_0$, using the Rosenblatt transformation. Under H_0, we know that $\mathbf{Z} = \tau_{F_0}(\mathbf{X})$ is distributed uniformly over the unit cube. Therefore, testing $H_0 : F(X_1, \ldots, X_p) = F_0(X_1, \ldots, X_p)$ on R^p is the same as testing $H_0{}^* : F^*(Z_1, \ldots, Z_p) = U_p(Z_1, \ldots, Z_p) = Z_1 Z_2 \cdots Z_p$ on I^p. Furthermore, the statistics which arise in testing $H_0{}^*$ will depend on $\mathbf{Z}_\alpha = \tau_{F_0}(\mathbf{X}_\alpha)$, and thus will be SDF. That is, a test of $H_0 : F = F_0$ against $H_1 : F = G_0$ has the same power as a test of $H_0{}^* : F^* = U_p$ against $H_1{}^* : F^* = U_p \tau_{G_0} \tau_{F_0}^{-1}$, so that one can restrict attention to goodness-of-fit tests on the unit hypercube.

Furthermore, a test of F_0 versus G_0 will have the same power as F_1 versus G_1 if $\tau_{G_0}\tau_{F_0}^{-1} = \tau_{G_1}\tau_{F_1}^{-1}$.

Obviously, one can construct many tests of $H_0 : F^* = U_p$. Therefore, one chooses a test which would be "good" against some suspected alternative. This is illustrated in the following examples.

Example 3.1.

Consider

$$H_0: \quad \mathbf{X} \sim N(\mathbf{O}, \mathbf{\Sigma}_0)$$

in two dimensions against normal shift alternatives

$$H_1: \quad \mathbf{X} \sim N(\boldsymbol{\mu}, \mathbf{\Sigma}_0)$$

where

$$\boldsymbol{\mu} = (\mu_1, \mu_2)^T \qquad \text{and} \qquad \mathbf{\Sigma}_0 = \begin{bmatrix} \sigma_1{}^2 & \rho\sigma_1\sigma_2 \\ \rho\sigma_1\sigma_2 & \sigma_2{}^2 \end{bmatrix}.$$

One first calculates

$$\begin{aligned} P_{\boldsymbol{\mu}}&[Z_1 \le z_1, Z_2 \le z_2] \\ &= P_{\boldsymbol{\mu}}\left[\Phi\left(\frac{X_1}{\sigma_1}\right) \le z_1, \Phi\left(\frac{X_2 - (\rho\sigma_2/\sigma_1)X_1}{\sigma_2(1-\rho^2)^{1/2}}\right) \le z_2\right] \\ &= P_{\boldsymbol{\mu}}\left[\frac{X_1 - \mu_1}{\sigma_1} \le \Phi^{-1}(z_1) - \frac{\mu_1}{\sigma_1},\right. \\ &\qquad \left.\frac{X_2 - \mu_2 - (\rho\sigma_2/\sigma_1)(X_1 - \mu_1)}{\sigma_2(1-\rho^2)^{1/2}} \le \Phi^{-1}(z_2) - \frac{\mu_2 - (\rho\sigma_2/\sigma_1)\mu_1}{\sigma_2(1-\sigma^2)^{1/2}}\right] \\ &= \Phi[\Phi^{-1}(z_1) - \mu_1/\sigma_1] \cdot \Phi\left[\Phi^{-1}(z_2) - \frac{\mu_2 - (\rho\sigma_2/\sigma_1)\mu_1}{\sigma_2(1-\rho^2)^{1/2}}\right], \end{aligned}$$

since $(X_1 - \mu_1)/\sigma_1$ and $[X_2 - \mu_2 - (\rho\sigma_2/\sigma_1)(X_1 - \mu_1)]\sigma_2^{-1}(1-\rho^2)^{-1/2}$ are uncorrelated standard normal variables under the alternative, and thus independent. Therefore, a test of H_0 should test the uniformity of Z_1 and Z_2. Since the form of the alternative distributions of Z_1 and Z_2 is complicated, it might be better to use a nonparametric goodness-of-fit test. Therefore, one "good" test might be

$$\phi = \begin{cases} 1 & \text{if } \; D_N(Z_{11}, Z_{12}, \ldots, Z_{1N}) > D_{N,\alpha_1} \quad \text{or if} \\ & \phantom{\text{if } \;} D_N(Z_{21}, Z_{22}, \ldots, Z_{2N}) > D_{N,\alpha_2} \\ 0 & \text{otherwise} \end{cases}$$

where $D_N(Z_{i1}, \ldots, Z_{iN})$ is the Kolmogorov-Smirnov statistic applied to Z_i $(i = 1, 2)$, D_{N, α_i} is the upper $100\alpha_i$-percentile of the Kolmogorov distribution and $(1 - \alpha_1)(1 - \alpha_2) = 1 - \alpha$. Note that any test of independence of Z_1 and Z_2 would have power α against H_1.

Example 3.2.

Here, the problem is to test $H_0 : \mathbf{X} \sim N(\mathbf{0}, \mathbf{\Sigma}_0)$ against $H_1 : \mathbf{X} \sim N(\mathbf{0}, \mathbf{\Sigma}_1)$, where

$$\mathbf{\Sigma}_0 = \begin{bmatrix} \sigma_1{}^2 & \rho\sigma_1\sigma_2 \\ \rho\sigma_1\sigma_2 & \sigma_2{}^2 \end{bmatrix}, \qquad \mathbf{\Sigma}_1 = \begin{bmatrix} \tau_1{}^2 & \eta\tau_1\tau_2 \\ \eta\tau_1\tau_2 & \tau_2{}^2 \end{bmatrix}.$$

Then

$$\begin{aligned} P_{\mathbf{\Sigma}_1}[Z_1 \le z_1, Z_2 \le z_2] &= P_{\mathbf{\Sigma}_1}\left[\frac{X_1}{\sigma_1} \le \Phi^{-1}(z_1), \frac{X_2 - (\rho\sigma_2/\sigma_1)X_1}{\sigma_2(1 - \rho^2)^{1/2}} \le \Phi^{-1}(z_2)\right] \\ &= P_{\mathbf{A\Sigma}_1\mathbf{A}^T}[U_1 \le \Phi^{-1}(z_1), U_2 \le \Phi^{-1}(z_2)] \end{aligned}$$

where

$$\mathbf{A} = \begin{bmatrix} \sigma_1^{-1} & 0 \\ -\rho(1 - \rho^2)^{-1/2}\sigma_1^{-1} & \sigma_2^{-1}(1 - \rho^2)^{-1/2} \end{bmatrix}.$$

This means that in general, U_1 and U_2 are not independent (since $\mathbf{A\Sigma A}^T$ is not generally diagonal). Therefore, a test of H_0 versus H_1 could test the independence of the Z_1 and Z_2 variables. Since the form of the marginals is complicated, it might be preferable to use a nonparametric test, such as a rank correlation test.

4. MULTISAMPLE DF PROCEDURES

In this section, the multivariate c-sample hypothesis will be treated. This includes the two-sample problem $(c = 2)$ and the randomness problem $(c = N)$ as special cases. The data will be arranged in matrix form:

$$\begin{aligned} \mathbf{Z} &= [\mathbf{X}_{11} \cdots \mathbf{X}_{1n_1} \mathbf{X}_{21} \cdots \mathbf{X}_{2n_2} \cdots \mathbf{X}_{c1} \cdots \mathbf{X}_{cn_c}] \\ &= [\mathbf{Z}_1 \cdots \mathbf{Z}_N] \qquad (N = n_1 + n_2 + \cdots + n_c). \end{aligned}$$

It is assumed that $\mathbf{X}_{ij}$, the jth vector in the ith sample, has distribution function $F_i \in \Omega_2(R^p)$. The null hypothesis is then

$$H_0\colon \quad F_1 = F_2 = \cdots = F_c.$$

In other words, the columns of $\mathbf{Z}$ are independent and identically distributed under H_0.

Under H_0, the joint distribution of the data matrix is $F^{(N)}(\mathbf{Z}) = \prod_{\alpha=1}^{N} F(Z_\alpha)$, which is invariant under any permutation of the vectors $(\mathbf{Z}_1, \ldots, \mathbf{Z}_N)$. This property motivates the following definition:

Definition 4.1.

(i) $\mathscr{S}_N$ *is the group of all permutations of the columns of the data matrix* $\mathbf{Z}$.
(ii) *The* orbit *of* $\mathbf{Z}$, *denoted* $\mathscr{S}_N(\mathbf{Z})$, *is the set of matrices* $\gamma\mathbf{Z}$ *obtained by applying* $\gamma \in \mathscr{S}_N$ *to the columns of* $\mathbf{Z}$. *Thus, almost all orbits have* $N!$ *elements.*

The fundamental property of the orbit is given in the following lemma:

Lemma 4.1.

$$P_{F^{(N)}}[\mathbf{Z}^* | \mathscr{S}_N(\mathbf{Z})] = \begin{cases} 1/N! & \text{if } \mathbf{Z}^* \in \mathscr{S}_N(\mathbf{Z}) \\ 0 & \text{otherwise} \end{cases}$$

for every $F^{(N)} \in \Omega(R^p)$.

This basic property is used to characterize the family of DF statistics and tests. Before doing this, however, it is useful to define a class of functions which distinguish among the points of the orbit.

Definition 4.2. *A real-valued measurable function t is called a* basic Pitman function *(B-Pitman function) if*

$$P_{F^{(N)}}[t(\mathbf{Z}) = t(\gamma\mathbf{Z})] = 0$$

for each $F^{(N)} \in \Omega(H_0)$ *and for each* $\gamma \neq e$, *the identity element of* $\mathscr{S}_N$.

Each B-Pitman function thus assumes a different value on each of the points of a.a. orbits, and hence $N!$ values for almost all orbits.

Since under the alternative, the distribution of the data matrix $\mathbf{Z}$ is $\prod_{i=1}^{c} \prod_{j=1}^{n_i} F_i(\mathbf{X}_{ij})$, it is clear that this joint distribution is invariant under all permutations of the $\mathbf{X}_{1j}$ among themselves, of the X_{2j} among themselves, and so forth. These permutations form a group $\mathscr{S}' = \times_{i=1}^{c} \mathscr{S}_{n_i}$. It seems desirable to form a class of functions which share this same property.

Definition 4.3. *A measurable real-valued function t is called a* basic non-sequential Pitman function *(BNS-Pitman function) if*

$$P_{F^{(N)}}[t(\mathbf{Z}) = t(\gamma\mathbf{Z})] = \begin{cases} 1, & \gamma \in \mathscr{S}' \\ 0, & \gamma \in \mathscr{S}_N \backslash \mathscr{S}' \end{cases}$$

for all $F^{(N)} \in \Omega(H_0)$.

A BNS-Pitman function thus does not distinguish between points which differ only in "chronological" order. It is clear that BNS-Pitman functions assume $N!/(n_1!\, n_2! \cdots n_c!)$ values on almost all orbits.

The next step is to define a class of statistics which order the points on the orbit.

Definition 4.4.

(i) *If t is a B-Pitman function, then*

$$R_t(\mathbf{Z}) = \sum_{\gamma \in \mathscr{S}_N} \varepsilon[t(\mathbf{Z}) - t(\gamma\mathbf{Z})]$$

is the basic Pitman statistic *based on t.*

(ii) *If $\tilde{t}$ is a BNS-Pitman function, then*

$$\tilde{R}_{\tilde{t}}(\mathbf{Z}) = (n_1!\, n_2! \cdots n_c!)^{-1} \sum_{\gamma \in \mathscr{S}_N} \varepsilon[\tilde{t}(\mathbf{Z}) - \tilde{t}(\gamma\mathbf{Z})]$$

is the BNS-Pitman function *based on $\tilde{t}$.*

Note that $R(\mathbf{Z})$ assumes values $1, 2, \ldots, N!$ on almost all orbits, and that $\tilde{R}_{\tilde{t}}(\mathbf{Z})$ assumes values $1, 2, \ldots, N!/(n_1! \cdots n_c!)$ on almost all orbits. The role of the Pitman statistics is to rank the observed value of $t(\mathbf{Z})$ among the possible values of $t(\mathbf{Z})$ on the orbit.

At this point, it is possible to characterize the class of all DF tests in terms of orbits and Pitman statistics. One first needs a completeness result.

Lemma 4.2. *$\Omega(H_0)$ is symmetrically complete.*

Proof. This follows from Bell *et al.* (1960).

The next theorem gives the fundamental property which must be satisfied by all similar tests. It represents an extension to Euclidean p-space of the basic result of Lehmann and Stein (1949).

Theorem 4.1. *Let ϕ be a test function. Then*

$$\int \phi(\mathbf{Z})\, dF^{(N)}(\mathbf{Z}) = \alpha \qquad \text{for each } F^{(N)} \in \Omega(H_0)$$

if, and only if,

$$\sum_{\gamma \in \mathscr{S}_N} \phi(\gamma\mathbf{Z}) = (N!)\alpha \qquad \text{a.e.} \quad [\Omega(H_0)].$$

The theorem yields an immediate characterization of the class of all sets similar with respect to H_0, analogous to that in Bell and Doksum (1967).

Corollary 4.1.

(i) *If A is similar with respect to $\Omega(H_0)$, then $P(A) = k/N!$ $(k = 1, 2, \ldots, N!)$.*

(ii) *The following conditions are equivalent:*

(a) *A is similar of size α.*

(b) *There exists a B-Pitman function t such that*

$$A \equiv \{\mathbf{Z} \mid R_t(\mathbf{Z}) \leq N!\,\alpha\}.$$

(c) *A contains $N!\,\alpha$ points of almost all orbits.*

Corollary 4.2. *The sets $\{A_1, A_2, \ldots, A_{N!}\}$ where $A_i = \{\mathbf{Z} \mid R_t(\mathbf{Z}) = i\}$ constitute an (essentially) maximal similar partition of the sample space. This means that no A_i contains a proper similar subset of probability α, $0 < \alpha < 1/N!$*

The next theorem characterizes the set of all DF statistics in terms of Pitman statistics, as in Bell and Doksum (1967).

Theorem 4.2.

(i) *If T is a DF statistic, then the H_0-distribution of T is discrete with probabilities which are integral multiples of* $1/n!$

(ii) *T is DF with respect to $\Omega(H_0)$ if, and only if, there exists a B-Pitman function t and a measurable real-valued function ψ such that*

$$T(\mathbf{Z}) = \psi[R_t(\mathbf{Z})] \qquad \text{a.e.} \quad [\Omega(H_0)].$$

(iii) *For each discrete distribution F_0 with probabilities which are integral multiples of* $1/N!$, *there exists a DF statistic with H_0-distribution F_0.*

(iv) *Results analogous to* (i), (ii), *and* (iii) *can be proven for NS DF statistics if "$1/N!$" is replaced by "$n_1!\,n_2! \cdots n_c!/N!$" and BNS Pitman functions and statistics are used in place of their B-Pitman analogs.*

Proof. Let T be DF. Then $\{\mathbf{Z} \mid T(\mathbf{Z}) \leq t\} = A_t$ is a similar set, and by Theorem 4.1, $P(A_t) = k/N!$ ($k = 0, 1, \ldots, N!$), so that (i) is proved.

If t is a B-Pitman function, then the set $\{\mathbf{Z} \mid R_t(\mathbf{Z}) = r\}$ is similar, and so is the set $\{\mathbf{Z} \mid \psi[R_t(\mathbf{Z})] = s\}$, so that $\psi[R_t(\mathbf{Z})]$ is DF. Conversely, if T is DF, it has a discrete distribution, so that there exist real numbers $a_1 < a_2 < \cdots < a_m$, $m \leq N!$, and integers $0 < k_1 < \cdots < k_m = N!$ such that $P_{F(N)}[T < a_1] = 0$, $P_{F(N)}[T \leq a_i] = k_i/N!$. Therefore, one can order the points of almost all orbits so that $T(\mathbf{Z}_j) = a_i$ for $k_{i-1} < j \leq k_i$. Then define $t(\mathbf{Z}_j) = j$ and $\psi(j) = a_i$ for $k_{i-1} < j \leq k_i$. Then t is a B-Pitman function and $T(\mathbf{Z}) = \psi[R_t(\mathbf{Z})]$ a.e. $[\Omega(H_0)]$.

If F_0 assigns probabilities $p_1, \ldots, p_s$ to the points $a_1 < a_2 < \cdots < a_s$, with $\sum_1^s p_i = 1$, then there are integers $0 < k_1 < \cdots < k_s = N!$ such that $\sum_1^m p_i = k_m/N!$, $m = 0, 1, \ldots, s$. Let t be any B-Pitman function and let $\psi(j) = a_i$ for $k_{i-1} < j \leq k_i$. Then $\psi[R_t(\mathbf{Z})]$ is the required DF statistic.

Theorems 4.1 and 4.2 characterize the families of similar tests and DF statistics. It is clear that the similar tests are conditional tests, given the orbit $\mathcal{S}(\mathbf{Z})$, which is a complete and sufficient statistic for $\Omega(H_0)$. If the alternative is simple, and the alternative distributions are absolutely continuous with respect to some σ-finite measure μ, then one can apply the Neyman-Pearson lemma on each orbit to obtain the MPDF test. This is formalized in the following theorem, the original version of which is due to Lehmann and Stein (1949).

Theorem 4.3. *The MPDF test of H_0 against the simple alternative*

$$H_1^*: \quad G^*(\mathbf{Z}) = \prod_{i=1}^{c} \prod_{j=1}^{n_i} F_i^*(\mathbf{X}_{ij})$$

is of the form

$$\phi(\mathbf{Z}) = \begin{cases} 1 & \text{if} \quad R_t(\mathbf{Z}) > k(\alpha, n_1, \ldots, n_c) \\ \lambda & \text{if} \quad R_t(\mathbf{Z}) = k(\alpha, n_1, \ldots, n_c) \\ 0 & \text{if} \quad R_t(\mathbf{Z}) < k(\alpha, n_1, \ldots, n_c) \end{cases}$$

where t is a B-Pitman function whose ordering of the points on the orbit is consistent with the ordering induced by L_1, the likelihood function of the alternative. That is, $L_1(\mathbf{Z}) < L_1(\mathbf{Z}^*)$ implies $t(\mathbf{Z}) < t(\mathbf{Z}^*)$ and $t(\mathbf{Z}) < t(\mathbf{Z}^*)$ implies $L_1(\mathbf{Z}) \leq L_1(\mathbf{Z}^*)$. The constants k and λ are chosen to make the test of size α.

Example 4.1.
The earliest multivariate DF procedure known to the authors is a two-sample permutation test, based on $\tilde{R}_{T^2}$, where T^2 denotes Hotelling's two-sample T^2 statistic. This test was considered by Wald and Wolfowitz (1944). This is a nonsequential permutation test, since T^2 is a BNS-Pitman function.

Like all permutation tests, this one involves a great deal of computational labor. It might seem at first glance that, as in the univariate case, attention should be restricted to statistics and tests based on the matrix of ranks, $\mathbf{R} = [r_{i\alpha}]$, where $r_{i\alpha}$ is the rank of the ith components of $\mathbf{Z}_\alpha$ among all the ith components of the pooled sample. Unfortunately, such tests and statistics need not be DF, as the next lemma shows.

Lemma 4.3. *Not all statistics based on the rank matrix* **R** *are DF.*

Proof. According to Corollary 4.2, a maximal similar partition of the sample space can contain only $N!$ subsets of R^{pN}. However, the rank matrix can take on $(N!)^p$ values, since each row of **R** is a random permutation of the integers $(1, 2, \ldots, N)$. Therefore, a rank statistic T can take on as many as $(N!)^p$ values, so the sets $\{\mathbf{Z} \mid T(\mathbf{Z}) \leq r\}$ are not similar in general.

Sen and Puri (1966) have circumvented this difficulty by proposing "permutation rank-order tests" (PROT's). They define quadratic forms involving functions of the ranks and then consider tests based on permutations of the columns of **R**. Therefore, their tests are permutation tests based on these quadratic forms, which are BNS-Pitman statistics.

5. TESTS OF INDEPENDENCE

It is possible to treat the problem of independence in a way analogous to the treatment of multisample problems in the previous section. If the generic sample vector **X** is partitioned as follows:

$$\mathbf{X} = [X_1^{(1)} \cdots X_{p_1}^{(1)}; X_1^{(2)} \cdots X_{p_2}^{(2)}; \ldots; X_1^{(q)} \cdots X_{p_q}^{(q)}]^T$$
$$= [\mathbf{X}^{(1)T} \cdots \mathbf{X}^{(q)T}]^T$$

then the null hypothesis may be written

$$H_0:\quad F(\mathbf{X}) = F(\mathbf{X}^{(1)} \cdots \mathbf{X}^{(q)}) = \prod_{i=1}^{q} F_i(\mathbf{X}^{(i)}).$$

In other words, we wish to test whether the components of the p-vector **X** consist of q independent subsets. A sample of size N chosen from F will be denoted as a matrix

$$\mathbf{Z} = \begin{bmatrix} \mathbf{X}_1^{(1)} & \mathbf{X}_2^{(1)} & \cdots & \mathbf{X}_N^{(1)} \\ \mathbf{X}_1^{(2)} & \mathbf{X}_2^{(2)} & \cdots & \mathbf{X}_N^{(2)} \\ \vdots & \vdots & & \vdots \\ \mathbf{X}_1^{(q)} & \mathbf{X}_2^{(q)} & \cdots & \mathbf{X}_N^{(q)} \end{bmatrix}$$

and the joint distribution of the sample is then

$$F^{(N)}(\mathbf{Z}) = \prod_{\alpha=1}^{N} \prod_{i=1}^{q} F_i(\mathbf{X}_\alpha^{(i)}).$$

Thus, $\Omega(H_0) = \{F^{(N)} \mid F(\mathbf{X}) = \prod_1^q F_i(\mathbf{X}_i)\}$. It is clear that permutations of the rows of **Z** leave the joint distribution invariant. That is, **Z** has the same distribution as

$$\mathbf{Z}' = \begin{bmatrix} \mathbf{X}_{i_1}^{(1)} & \mathbf{X}_{i_2}^{(1)} & \cdots & \mathbf{X}_{i_N}^{(1)} \\ \mathbf{X}_{j_1}^{(2)} & \mathbf{X}_{j_2}^{(2)} & \cdots & \mathbf{X}_{j_N}^{(2)} \\ \vdots & \vdots & & \vdots \\ \mathbf{X}_{k_1}^{(q)} & \mathbf{X}_{k_2}^{(q)} & \cdots & \mathbf{X}_{k_N}^{(q)} \end{bmatrix}$$

where $(i_1 \cdots i_N), (j_1 \cdots j_N), \ldots, (k_1, \ldots, k_N)$ are permutations of $(1, 2, \ldots, N)$. These permutations form a group isomorphic to $\times_{i=1}^{q} \mathscr{S}_N$, and this group will be denoted by $\mathscr{S}^{(I)}$, and the orbit of **Z** will be denoted $\mathscr{S}^{(I)}(\mathbf{Z})$. Clearly, almost all orbits contain $(N!)^q$ points, and

$$P_{F^{(N)}}[\mathbf{Z}^* \mid \mathscr{S}^{(I)}(\mathbf{Z})] = \begin{cases} (N!)^{-q}, & \mathbf{Z}^* \in \mathscr{S}^{(I)}(\mathbf{Z}) \\ 0 & \text{otherwise} \end{cases}$$

for every $F^{(N)} \in \Omega(H_0)$ and a.a. Z.

As in the multisample case, certain permutations in the group leave both the null and alternative distribution unchanged. In this case, since the data consist of a random sample from some continuous, p-variate distribution, any rearrangement of the same vectors $\mathbf{X}_\alpha$ leaves the joint distribution invariant. These permutations form a group $\mathscr{S}'$ isomorphic to $\mathscr{S}_N$. In practice, therefore, one is led to consider procedures and statistics which share this "nonsequential" property.

Definition 5.1.

(i) *A real-valued, measurable function t is called a* B-Pitman function (*for the independence problem*) *if*

$$P_{F^{(N)}}[\mathbf{Z} = \gamma\mathbf{Z}] = 0 \qquad \text{for} \quad F^{(N)} \in \Omega(H_0) \quad \text{and} \quad \gamma \in \mathscr{S}^{(I)}, \quad \gamma \neq e.$$

(ii) *If* $P_{F^{(N)}}[\mathbf{Z} = \gamma\mathbf{Z}] = \begin{cases} 1, & \gamma \in \mathscr{S}' \\ 0, & \gamma \in \mathscr{S}^{(I)}, \quad \gamma \notin \mathscr{S}' \end{cases}$

for each $F^{(N)} \in \Omega(H_0)$, *then t is a* BNS-Pitman function. *A B-Pitman function assumes $(N!)^q$ values on almost all orbits, while a BNS-Pitman function assumes only $(N!)^{q-1}$ values.*

Definition 5.2.

(i) *The* B-Pitman statistic *generated by the B-Pitman function t is*

$$R_t(\mathbf{Z}) = \sum_{\gamma \in \mathscr{S}^{(I)}} \varepsilon[t(\mathbf{Z}) - t(\gamma\mathbf{Z})].$$

(ii) *The* BNS-Pitman statistic *generated by the BNS-Pitman function $\tilde{t}$ is*

$$\tilde{R}_{\tilde{t}}(\mathbf{Z}) = (1/N!) \sum_{\gamma \in \mathscr{S}^{(I)}} \varepsilon[\tilde{t}(Z) - \tilde{t}(\gamma\mathbf{Z})].$$

As before, the Pitman statistics are used to rank the observed data point according to the ordering induced by the function t (or $\tilde{t}$).

Before stating the main theorems characterizing DF tests and statistics, it must be shown that $\Omega(H_0)$ is complete.

Lemma 5.1. *The orbit $\mathscr{S}^{(I)}(\mathbf{Z})$ is a complete statistic with respect to $\Omega(H_0)$.*

Proof. See Bell (1967).

Now it is possible to state the main characterization theorems for the independence hypothesis.

Theorem 5.1 (Lehmann and Stein). *Let ϕ be a test function. Then*

$$\int \phi(\mathbf{Z})\, dF^{(N)} = \alpha \qquad \text{for each} \qquad F^{(N)} \in \Omega(H_0)$$

if, and only if,

$$\sum_{\gamma \in \mathscr{S}^{(I)}} \phi(\gamma\mathbf{Z}) = (N!)^q\alpha \qquad \text{a.e.}$$

Corollary 5.1.

(i) *If A is similar with respect to $\Omega(H_0)$, then*

$$P(A) = k/(N!)^q \qquad (k = 1, 2, \ldots, (N!)^q).$$

(ii) *The following are equivalent:*
(a) *A is similar of size α.*
(b) *There exists a B-Pitman function t such that*

$$A \equiv \{Z \mid R_t(\mathbf{Z}) \leq \alpha N!\}.$$

(c) *A contains $\alpha(N!)^q$ points of almost all orbits.*

Corollary 5.2. *The sets $\{A_1 \cdots A_{(N!)^q}\}$, where $A_i = \{Z \mid R_t(\mathbf{Z}) = i\}$ constitute an (essentially) maximal similar partition of the sample space.*

Theorem 5.2.

(i) *If T is a DF statistic, then the H_0-distribution of T is discrete with probabilities which are integral multiples of $(N!)^{-q}$.*
(ii) *T is DF with respect to $\Omega(H_0)$ if, and only if, there exists a B-Pitman function t and a measurable real function ψ such that*

$$T(\mathbf{Z}) = \psi[R_t(\mathbf{Z})] \qquad \text{a.e.}$$

(iii) *For each discrete distribution F_0 with probabilities which are integral multiples of $(N!)^{-q}$, there exists a DF statistic with H_0-distribution F_0.*
(iv) *Results analogous to* (i), (ii), (iii) *can be proven for NSDF statistics if $(N!)^{-q}$ is replaced by $(N!)^{-q+1}$ and BNS-Pitman functions and statistics are used in* (ii).

The proofs of these theorems are analogous to the proofs in the multisample case.

Finally, one can always construct a DF test against a simple alternative.

Theorem 5.3. *The MPDF size α test of the independence hypothesis against a simple alternative*

$$F^*(\mathbf{X}^{(1)} \cdots \mathbf{X}^{(q)})$$

is of the form

$$\phi(\mathbf{Z}) = \begin{cases} 1, & R_t(Z) > k(\alpha, N) \\ \lambda, & R_t(\mathbf{Z}) = k(\alpha, N) \\ 0, & R_t(\mathbf{Z}) < k(\alpha, N) \end{cases}$$

where t is a BNS-Pitman function whose ordering of the points of the orbit is consistent with the ordering induced by the joint density of the alternative (in the sense of Theorem 4.3), *and k and λ are chosen to make the size of the test equal to α.*

6. TOTAL INDEPENDENCE AND RANK PROCEDURES

Just as in the multisample problem, there are difficulties in constructing rank tests of the general independence hypothesis. That is, if $r_{i\alpha}$ is the rank of the ith component of $\mathbf{X}_\alpha$ among all of the ith components in the sample, then tests of independence based on $[r_{i\alpha}]$ may not be distribution-free. However, if one considers the hypothesis of *total independence*, that is

$$H_0\colon\quad F(\mathbf{X}) = F(X_1 \cdots X_p) = F_1(X_1) \cdots F_p(X_p) \qquad \text{for all} \quad \mathbf{X},$$

then all rank tests are distribution-free, and it is possible to characterize rank tests and to relate then to strongly distribution-free tests, as is done in Bell and Doksum (1967). This is the special case of the general independence hypothesis of Section 5, with $q = p$.

Definition 6.1. *Let $\delta_1 \cdots \delta_p$ be permutations in $\mathscr{S}_N$, and let $\gamma = (\delta_1 \cdots \delta_p)$ belong to $\mathscr{S}^{(I)}$. Then*

$$B(\delta_1 \cdots \delta_p) = B(\gamma) = \{\mathbf{Z} \mid X_{1,\delta_1(1)} < X_{1,\delta_1(2)} < \cdots < X_{1,\delta_1(N)};$$
$$X_{2,\delta_2(1)} < \cdots < X_{2,\delta_2(N)}; \ldots; X_{p,\delta_p(1)} < \cdots < X_{p,\delta_p(N)}\}$$

is the basic rank set (*B-rank set*) *corresponding to γ. If a set C is of the form $\bigcup_{\delta_1 \in \mathscr{S}_N} B(\delta_1 \cdots \delta_p)$, then C is called a* basic nonsequential rank set (*BNS-rank set*). *A set $A \subseteq R^{np}$ such that $\mathbf{Z} = (\mathbf{X}_1 \cdots \mathbf{X}_N) \in A$ implies $Z^* = (\mathbf{X}_{i_1} \cdots \mathbf{X}_{i_N}) \in A$ for any permutation $(i_1 \cdots i_N)$ of the integers $(1 \cdots N)$ is* nonsequential.

One notes that

$$\bigcup_{\delta_1 \in \mathscr{S}_N} B(\delta_1, \ldots, \delta_p) = \bigcup_{\delta_i \in \mathscr{S}_N} B(\delta_1, \ldots, \delta_p) \qquad \text{for} \quad i = 1, 2, \ldots, p.$$

Definition 6.2. *A function $v(\mathbf{X}_1 \cdots \mathbf{X}_N)$ is called a* rank function *if it is constant over each B-rank set, and NS-rank function if it is constant over each BNS-rank set.*

It is apparent that each B-rank set is similar of size $(N!)^{-p}$, since it contains one point of almost all orbits. Similarly, a BNS-rank set is similar of size $(N!)^{-p+1}$.

The practical reason for considering tests based on ranks is that they are invariant with respect to a "reasonable" group of transformations of the data. In this case, we define

$$\tilde{\mathscr{G}} = \{\mathbf{g} \mid \mathbf{g}(\mathbf{X}) = [g_1(X_1), \ldots, g_p(X_p)]^T\}$$

where each g_i is a continuous, strictly increasing transformation of the real line onto itself. Obviously, a maximal invariant partition of the sample space under $\tilde{\mathscr{G}}$ is the collection of basic rank sets, so that an invariant function must be a ranking function, or in other words, a function of the rank matrix $\mathbf{R} = [r_{i\alpha}]$.

At this stage, the necessary machinery has been developed to characterize the family of all rank statistics and to relate the invariance property to the strongly distribution-free property.

Lemma 6.1. *If a nonsequential similar set A is SDF with respect to $\Omega(H_0 \cup H_1)$ and $\tilde{\mathscr{G}}$, then A is almost invariant wrt $\tilde{\mathscr{G}}$ and $\Omega(H_0 \cup H_1)$.*

Proof. If A is NS and similar, then for every $\mathbf{g} \in \tilde{\mathscr{G}}$ and for every $F^{(N)} \in \Omega(H_0 \cup H_1)$,

$$P[A \mid F] = P[A \mid F\mathbf{g}^{-1}] = P[\mathbf{g}A \mid F]$$

so that

$$\int [I_A(\mathbf{Z}) - I_{\mathbf{g}A}(\mathbf{Z})]\, dF^{(N)}(\mathbf{Z}) = 0.$$

However, $(H_0 \cup H_1)$ is symmetrically complete from Lemma 4.1, so $I_A(\mathbf{Z}) - I_{\mathbf{g}A}(\mathbf{Z}) = 0$ a.e. and thus $(A \backslash \mathbf{g}A) \cup (\mathbf{g}A \backslash A)$ has measure zero for every member of $\Omega(H_0 \cup H_1)$, so that A is almost invariant.

It is impossible to strengthen Lemma 6.1 by eliminating the NS condition, as the following example shows.

Example 6.1.

Let $N = 2, p = 2$, and $A = \{\mathbf{Z} \mid X_{11} < X_{12} < 0\} \cup \{\mathbf{Z} \mid X_{12} < X_{11}; X_{11} > 0\}$. This set is not a rank set, and is clearly neither invariant nor almost invariant. Also, it depends on the "chronological" order of the two vectors $(X_{11}, X_{21})^T$, $(X_{12}, X_{22})^T$. However, for any bivariate F and any continuous strictly increasing g_1 and g_2

$$\iiiint_A dF(g_1(X_{11}), g_2(X_{21}))\, dF(g_1(X_{12}), g_2(X_{22})) = \tfrac{1}{2}$$

so that A is a SDF set.

The characterization of rank statistics is given in the following theorem.

Theorem 6.1.

(i) *T is a rank statistic iff there exists a measurable function ψ and a rank function t such that $T(Z) = \psi[R_t(\mathbf{Z})]$.*

(ii) *The following conditions are equivalent:*

(a) *T is a NS rank statistic.*

(b) *T is NS and SDF wrt $\Omega(H_0 \cup H_1)$ and $\tilde{\mathscr{G}}$.*

(c) *$T(\mathbf{Z}) = \psi[R_u(\mathbf{Z})]$ where u is a NS-rank function and ψ is measurable and real-valued.*

Proof. The proof is an extension of the bivariate version given in Bell and Doksum (1967).

Some rank tests of total independence have been proposed by Puri and Sen (1968). Their tests belong to the Chernoff-Savage class of rank-tests, and this property is exploited to prove results about asymptotic normality and asymptotic relative efficiency.

7. TESTS OF SYMMETRY

It is possible to carry out a development of DF tests for multivariate symmetry which parallels the treatment of multisample and independence problems.

For symmetry the null hypothesis is

$$H_0\colon \quad F(X_1, \ldots, X_p) = F(\gamma(X_1, \ldots, X_p))$$

for all γ in $\mathscr{S}_p$ and all $\mathbf{X}$ in R^p.

The pertinent substitutions in the development of Section 5 are

$$\text{“}S_p \wr S_N\text{”} \quad \text{for “}S^{(I)}\text{”} \quad \text{and} \quad \text{“}(N!)(p!)^N\text{”} \quad \text{for “}(N!)^q\text{”},$$

where $S_p \wr S_N$ is the wreath product (Hall, 1959) of S_p with S_N (see Bell and Haller, 1968).

The structure of wreath product groups is not of prime interest here. However, one should note that the function $\prod_{i=1}^N F(X_{i1}, \ldots, X_{ip})$ is invariant under all $p!$ permutations of each p-tuple $(X_{i1}, \ldots, X_{ip})$ as well as under the $N!$ permutations of the N p-tuples. The least group containing these permutations is the wreath product $S_p \wr S_N$ of $(N!)(p!)^N$ elements.

Definition 7.1. *Definitions* 5.1 *and* 5.2 *with the given substitutions.*

Theorem 7.1. *Theorems* 5.1, 5.2, 5.3, *and Corollaries* 5.1 *and* 5.2 *are valid for the symmetry hypothesis with the given substitutions.*

In order to construct some tests from the class characterized in Theorem 7.1, one first considers some normal theory tests.

For p-variate normals, the symmetry hypothesis becomes

$$H_0{}^*\colon \quad \mu_1 = \cdots = \mu_p; \qquad \sigma_{11} = \sigma_{22} = \cdots = \sigma_{pp};$$

and there exists ρ such that $\sigma_{ij} = \rho\sigma_{ii}$ for all i and j. In matrix notation, if $\mathbf{e} = [1, 1, \ldots, 1]^T$ and $\mathbf{E}$ is a $p \times p$ matrix all of whose entries are 1, then the null hypothesis is

$$H_0{}^*\colon \quad \boldsymbol{\mu} = \mu\mathbf{e}, \qquad \boldsymbol{\Sigma} = \sigma^2[\rho\mathbf{E} + (1 - \rho)\mathbf{I}].$$

In order to derive the maximum likelihood test of H_0, it is convenient to make a change of variable $\mathbf{Y} = \mathbf{CX}$, where $\mathbf{C}$ is an orthogonal matrix whose first row is $[1/\sqrt{p}, 1/\sqrt{p}, \ldots, 1/\sqrt{p}]$. Then under H_0, Y_1, and $\mathbf{Y}^{(2)}$ are independent and $\mathbf{Y}^{(2)}$ has a spherical $(p-1)$-variate normal distribution centered at the origin. If one defines

$$\mathbf{A} = \sum_{\alpha=1}^{n} (\mathbf{Y}_\alpha - \overline{\mathbf{Y}})(\mathbf{Y}_\alpha - \overline{\mathbf{Y}})^T = [a_{ij}] = \begin{bmatrix} a_{11} & \mathbf{a}_{(i)} \\ \mathbf{a}_{(1)}^T & \mathbf{A}_{22} \end{bmatrix}.$$

Then the maximum likelihood criterion is to reject H_0 for $\lambda \le \lambda_0$, where

$$\lambda^{2/n} = |\mathbf{R}| \frac{\prod_{i=2}^{p} a_{ii}(p-1)^{p-1}}{[\operatorname{tr} \mathbf{A}_{22} + N(\overline{\mathbf{Y}}^{(2)})^T \overline{\mathbf{Y}}^{(2)}]^{p-1}}$$

and $\mathbf{R}$ is the sample correlation matrix of $\mathbf{Y}$.

Since λ varies between 0 and 1, its distribution is determined by its moments. Now, $\mathbf{R}$ is independent of the a_{ii} and $\overline{\mathbf{Y}}^{(2)}$ under H_0, and the moments of $|\mathbf{R}|$ are known (Anderson, 1958). Therefore, one need only calculate the moments of

$$V = \frac{(p-1)^{p-1} \prod_{i=2}^{p} a_{ii}}{[\operatorname{tr} \mathbf{A}_{22} + n(\overline{\mathbf{Y}}^{(2)})^T \overline{\mathbf{Y}}^{(2)}]^{p-1}}.$$

The moments of V can be found by using the method outlined in Anderson (1958, p. 252), so that one finally obtains

$$E[\lambda^k] = (p-1)^{k(p-1)} \frac{\Gamma[N(p-1)/2]}{\Gamma[(Nk+N)(p-1)/2]} \prod_{i=2}^{p} \frac{\Gamma[(Nk+N-i)/2]}{\Gamma[(N-i)/2]}$$

and these moments in turn determine the distribution of λ uniquely.

In summary,

Theorem 7.2.

(i) *Let*

$$\phi_1(\mathbf{Z}) = \begin{cases} 1 & \text{if } \lambda^{2/N} < k(N, \alpha) \\ 0 & \text{otherwise.} \end{cases}$$

Then ϕ_1 is similar of size α wrt $\Omega(H_0{}^*)$, where

$$P\{\lambda^{2/N} < k(N, \alpha)\} = \alpha.$$

(ii) *Under $H_0{}^*$, $|\mathbf{R}|$ and V are independent.*

(iii) *Let*

$$\phi_2(\mathbf{Z}) = \begin{cases} 1 & \text{if } |\mathbf{R}| < k_1(N, \alpha_1) \quad \text{or} \quad V < k_2(N, \alpha_2) \\ 0 & \text{otherwise.} \end{cases}$$

Then $\phi_2(Z)$ is similar of size α wrt $\Omega(H_0{}^*)$, where

$$P_{H_0}[|\mathbf{R}| < k_1] = \alpha_1, \qquad P_{H_0}[V < k_2] = \alpha_2$$

and

$$(1 - \alpha_1)(1 - \alpha_2) = 1 - \alpha,$$

where α is the desired size of the test.

The critical values of $|\mathbf{R}|$ and V must be computed from the H_0-distributions, which in turn depend on the moments of $|\mathbf{R}|$ and V. The values α_1 and α_2 would be chosen to guard against certain alternatives to symmetry, which would result either in dependence between Y_1 and $\mathbf{Y}^{(2)}$ or in a shift in $\mathbf{Y}^{(2)}$ away from the origin. For more detail in the bivariate case, see Bell and Haller (1968).

In order to construct DF tests for H_0, one notes that

Theorem 7.3.

(i) *λ, $|\mathbf{R}|$ and V are BNS-Pitman functions. Therefore,*
(ii) *Each function $h[R_T]$ is DF wrt $\Omega(H_0)$ for $T = \lambda$, $|\mathbf{R}|$ or V.*

A more intuitively appealing DF test results from noting:

Lemma 7.1.

$$P_J\{W_{i_1} < W_{i_2} < \cdots < W_{i_p}\} = (p!)^{-1}$$

for all permutations $(i_1, \ldots, i_p)$ of $(1, \ldots, p)$ and for all $J^{(N)}$ in $\Omega(H_0)$.

Now let S_1 be a BNS Pitman function which is constant on each of the $p!$ sets $\{W_{i_1} < \cdots < W_{i_p}\}$ of R^p and which assumes only the values $1, 2, \ldots, p!$. Let $n(k)$ = the number of sample vectors which fall in the region $[S_1 = k]$. It follows immediately that:

Theorem 7.4.

(i) *Under H_0, each $n(k)$ has a binomial distribution with parameters N and $(p!)^{-1}$.*

(ii) *Each function $\psi[n(1), \ldots, n(p!)]$ is a statistic DF wrt $\Omega(H_0)$; and, in particular,*

(iii) *$T = \sum_{k=1}^{p!} [n(k) - N(p!)^{-1}]^2 N^{-1}(p!)$ is DF wrt $\Omega(H_0)$ and has asymptotically a chi-square distribution with $(p!) - 1$ degrees of freedom.*

Which other tests are "good" and how they are good remains to be studied. These and other open problems are discussed in the next section.

8. OPEN PROBLEMS AND CONCLUDING REMARKS

(*I*) *Which tests are "good"?* In the body of this paper the class of all DF tests for several hypotheses are given. However, as a practical matter, one needs rules for choosing good tests from among them. One method is that of constructing the MPDF test against a simple alternative. But what can be done for composite alternatives? What are other criteria for goodness?

(*II*) *What is the family of all goodness-of-fit tests?* The Rosenblatt transformation gives a "large" class of such tests, but the exact converse of Theorem 3.1 depends on the positional order of the coordinates of a data point. This leads to the following general problem.

(*III*) *How does one eliminate the effect of the coordinate system on the tests?* From the Rosenblatt transformation, one sees that different classes of tests are obtained if the measurements are (inner diameter, outer diameter, length) than if they were (outer diameter, length, inner diameter). Perhaps, some sort of averaging or mixing process can eliminate this undesirable situation. However, the mathematics, especially the defining of the pertinent transformation group, becomes intractable. There is also the problem of destroying independence in averaging.

(*IV*) *Which are the "natural" transformation groups?* Ranks tests which are quite popular can generally be characterized in terms of the appropriate transformation group. There seems to be no "natural" group and no "natural" rank sets for the symmetry hypothesis (see Bell and Haller, 1968).

(*V*) *Can singular multivariate distributions be handled by some modification of the general theory?* The transformed variables are no longer mutually independent if the distribution is concentrated on a space of lower dimension. However, one recalls that the probability transformation gives a uniform distribution for the singular continuous Cantor function. Does an analogous result hold for higher dimensions?

(*VI*) *Are multivariate DF procedures essentially univariate procedures?* One recalls that the measure algebra of any nonatomic, separable probability measure is equal to that of the uniform distribution on the unit interval. This is reflected in the fact that the orbit sizes for the two-sample, k-sample and randomness cases do not depend on the dimension of the sample space but only on the sample sizes. However, on the other hand, the orbit sizes depend strongly on the dimension for the symmetry and independence cases.

REFERENCES

1. Anderson, T. W. (1958). "Introduction to Multivariate Statistical Analysis." Wiley, New York.
2. Bell, C. B. (1960). On the structure of distribution-free statistics. *Ann. Math. Statist.* **31** 703–709.
3. Bell, C. B. (1964). Some basic theorems of distribution-free statistics. *Ann. Math. Statist.* **35** 150–156.
4. Bell, C. B. (1969). Completeness theorems for characterizing distribution-free statistics. To be published.
5. Bell, C. B., and Doksum, K. A. (1967). Distribution-free tests of independence. *Ann. Math. Statist.* **37** 619–628.
6. Bell, C. B., and Haller, H. S. (1969). Bivariate symmetry tests: parametric and non-parametric. *Ann. Math. Statist.* **39** 259–269.
7. Bell, C. B., Blackwell, D., and Breiman, L. (1960). On the completeness of order statistics. *Ann. Math. Statist.* **31** 794–797.
8. Hall, M. (1959). "Theory of Groups." Macmillan, New York.
9. Lehmann, E. L., and Stein, C. (1949). On the theory of some nonparametric hypotheses. *Ann. Math. Statist.* **20** 28–45.
10. Puri, M. L., and Sen, P. K. (1968). On a class of rank order tests for independence in multivariate distributions. To be published.
11. Rosenblatt, M. (1952). Remarks on a multivariate transformation. *Ann. Math. Statist.* **23** 470–472.
12. Sen, P. K., and Puri, M. L. (1966). On a class of multivariate multisample rank-order tests. *Sankhyā Ser. A* **28** 353–376.
13. Wald, A., and Wolfowitz, J. (1944). Statistical tests based on permutations of observations. *Ann. Math. Statist.* **15** 358–372.

Conditional Probability Density and Regression Estimators[1]

M. ROSENBLATT

MATHEMATICS DEPARTMENT
UNIVERSITY OF CALIFORNIA
LA JOLLA, CALIFORNIA

1. INTRODUCTION

Some very simple estimators of a univariate density function have been proposed and investigated in recent years (see [1, 3–5, 7, 9–10]). Similar estimators of multivariate densities have been considered by Cacoullos [2]. These estimators have a nonparametric flavor. The object of this paper is to show how the same simple ideas can be used to obtain plausible estimators of the conditional probability density and the regression in the case of sampling from a multivariate distribution.

2. PRELIMINARIES

For convenience we shall consider sampling from a bivariate distribution. The assumptions, estimates, and conclusions are similar when sampling from a k-variate distribution with $k > 2$. Let $(X_1, Y_1), \ldots, (X_n, Y_n)$ be a sample of size n (independent realizations) from a population with joint density $f(x, y) > 0$ uniformly continuous in (x, y). The marginal density of X alone is

$$g(x) = \int f(x, y)\, dy > 0. \tag{1}$$

Our object is to obtain estimators of the conditional density $f(y \mid x) = f(x, y)/g(x)$ and the conditional mean or regression $r(x) = E(Y \mid X = x)$. For this purpose, we choose a smooth positive density function $h(x, y)$ with the marginal in x

$$k(x) = \int h(x, y)\, dy > 0. \tag{2}$$

[1] This research was supported by the Office of Naval Research.

We will be a little more explicit about detailed regularity conditions to be imposed on f, g, h, and k later on. Let $b(n)$ be a bandwidth parameter depending on n that tends to zero as $n \to \infty$. Consider

$$\hat{f}_n(x, y) = n^{-1}b(n)^{-2} \sum_{j=1}^{n} h(b(n)^{-1}(x - X_j), b(n)^{-1}(y - Y_j)) \tag{3}$$

and

$$\hat{g}_n(x) = n^{-1}b(n)^{-1} \sum_{j=1}^{n} k(b(n)^{-1}(x - X_j)) = \int \hat{f}_n(x, y)\, dy \tag{4}$$

as estimators of $f(x, y)$ and $g(x)$. Then

$$\hat{f}_n(y \mid x) = \hat{f}_n(x, y)/\hat{g}_n(x) \tag{5}$$

is a plausible estimator of the conditional density function $f(y \mid x)$ that is continuous in (x, y). Of course, $\hat{f}_n(y \mid x)$ is for each x a density function in y. If

$$h(x, y) \le C(1 + x^2 + y^2)^{-5/2} \tag{6}$$

for a constant $C > 0$, then the functions

$$m(x) = \int yh(x, y)\, dy, \qquad c(x) = m(x)/k(x) \tag{7}$$

will be well defined and continuous. If f satisfies a bound like that in (6), the regression

$$r(x) = \int yf(x, y)\, dy/g(x) = E(Y \mid X = x) \tag{8}$$

will exist and be continuous. But then

$$r_n(x) = \int y\hat{f}_n(y \mid x)\, dy = \frac{b(n) \sum_{j=1}^{n} m(b(n)^{-1}(x - X_j))}{\sum_{j=1}^{n} k(b(n)^{-1}(x - X_j))} + \frac{\sum_{j=1}^{n} Y_j k(b(n)^{-1}(x - X_j))}{\sum_{j=1}^{n} k(b(n)^{-1}(x - X_j))} \tag{9}$$

is a natural estimator of the regression $r(x)$. If $h(x, y) = k(x)l(y)$ with

$$\int yl(y)\, dy = 0 \tag{10}$$

then $m(x) = 0$ and the expression for $r_n(x)$ given in (9) simplifies

$$r_n(x) = \frac{\sum_{j=1}^{n} Y_j k(b(n)^{-1}(x - X_j))}{\sum_{j=1}^{n} k(b(n)^{-1}(x - X_j))}. \tag{11}$$

3. ASYMPTOTIC BEHAVIOR OF THE ESTIMATORS

Our object will be that of describing the asymptotic behavior of the estimators locally (at a point) as $n \to \infty$. The approach will be very much in the same spirit as that given by Rosenblatt [5] for estimation of the density function. This means that a moderate amount of smoothness in terms of differentiability for f and g will be assumed. As has already been remarked by Bartlett [1], if the weight function (in our case h) is not assumed to be positive, and much greater smoothness (higher order of differentiability) holds for f and g, the asymptotic behavior of the estimators can be improved. Before we start our investigation, it is worthwhile noting that Weiss and Wolfowitz [9] have considered some related optimality questions when estimating a density function at a point. Nadarya [3] and Woodroofe [10] have looked at the maximal deviation between the estimator and the density function over an interval as $n \to \infty$. Nadarya has also considered estimation of a regression in the case of a very special model. A heuristic discussion of the estimation of a regression has been given by Watson [8].

Since the estimators we consider are ratios, it is more convenient in discussing asymptotic behavior not to compute moments of the estimators directly since they might not exist, but rather to obtain approximations (with moments) having the same asymptotic behavior. In the following discussion o and O have the usual interpretation in terms of order of magnitude statements while o_p and O_p mean that o and O hold respectively with a probability that can be chosen arbitrarily close to one. Our development of the results will be curious since assumptions will be introduced as required in the derivation. However, assumptions and conclusions will be stated in a complete form at the end of the derivation.

Let us first consider the asymptotic behavior of $\hat{f}_n(y \mid x)$. Now

$$\begin{aligned}\hat{f}_n(y \mid x) = [E\hat{f}_n(x, y) + \{\hat{f}_n(x, y) - E\hat{f}_n(x, y)\}] \\ \times [E\hat{g}_n(x) + \{\hat{g}_n(x) - E\hat{g}_n(x)\}]^{-1}.\end{aligned} \tag{12}$$

Notice that

$$\begin{aligned}E\hat{f}_n(x, y) &= b(n)^{-2}Eh(b(n)^{-1}(x - X), b(n)^{-1}(y - Y)) \\ &= \int h(\alpha, \beta)f(x - b(n)\alpha, y - b(n)\beta)\, d\alpha\, d\beta\end{aligned} \tag{13}$$

while

$$\begin{aligned}E\hat{g}_n(x) &= b(n)^{-1}Ek(b(n)^{-1}(x - X)) \\ &= \int k(\alpha)g(x - b(n)\alpha)\, d\alpha.\end{aligned} \tag{14}$$

On the other hand,

$$\sigma^2[\hat{f}_n(x, y)] = n^{-1}b(n)^{-4}\sigma^2[h(b(n)^{-1}(x - X), b(n)^{-1}(y - Y))]$$
$$\cong n^{-1}b(n)^{-2}f(x, y) \int h^2(\alpha, \beta)\, d\alpha\, d\beta \tag{15}$$

and similarly

$$\sigma^2[\hat{g}_n(x)] = n^{-1}b(n)^{-2}\sigma^2[k(b(n)^{-1}(x - X))]$$
$$\cong n^{-1}b(n)^{-1}g(x) \int k^2(\alpha)\, d\alpha \tag{16}$$

as $n \to \infty$. Therefore

$$\hat{f}_n(y \mid x) = [E\hat{f}_n(x, y) + \{\hat{f}_n(x, y) - E\hat{f}_n(x, y)\}](E\hat{g}_n(x))^{-1}$$
$$\times (1 + O_p(nb(n))^{-1/2}) \tag{17}$$

if $n^{-1}b(n)^{-1} = o(1)$. A simple computation with fourth order moments indicates that $\hat{f}_n(x, y) - E\hat{f}_n(x, y)$ is asymptotically normally distributed with mean zero and variance (15) if $n^{-1}b(n)^{-2} = o(1)$ using the Liapounov form of the central limit theorem. The asymptotic behavior of $\hat{f}_n(y \mid x)$ can be made more apparent if f and g are assumed to satisfy the following differentiability condition. We shall say that $f(x, y)$ $(g(x))$ satisfies *condition R* if

$$f(x + \alpha, y + \beta) = f(x, y) + \alpha f_x(x, y) + \beta f_y(x, y)$$
$$+ \tfrac{1}{2}\{\alpha^2 f_{xx}(x, y) + 2\alpha\beta f_{xy}(x, y) + \beta^2 f_{yy}(x, y)\}$$
$$+ p(x, y; \alpha, \beta)\{\alpha^2 + \beta^2\}^{1 + a/2} \tag{18}$$
$$(g(x + \alpha) = g(x) + \alpha g_x(x) + \tfrac{1}{2}\alpha^2 g_{xx}(x) + p(x; \alpha)\alpha^{2+a})$$

where p is a bounded function and $0 < a < 1$. Then if

$$\int uh(u, v)\, du = \int vh(u, v)\, dv = 0 \tag{19}$$

and

$$\int uk(u)\, du = 0, \tag{20}$$

it follows that

$$E\hat{f}_n(x, y) = f(x, y) + \tfrac{1}{2}b(n)^2[f_{xx}(x, y)m_{2,0} + 2f_{xy}(x, y)m_{1,1}$$
$$+ f_{yy}(x, y)m_{0,2}] + o(b(n))^2 \tag{21}$$

where

$$m_{a,b} = \int u^a v^b h(u, v)\, du\, dv \tag{22}$$

and

$$E\hat{g}_n(x) = g(x) + \tfrac{1}{2}b(n)^2 g_{xx}(x) \int u^2 k(u)\, du + o(b(n))^2. \tag{23}$$

Theorem 1. *Let the weight functions h and k satisfy* (6), (19), *and* (20). *Further assume that f and g belong to the class R. Then*

$$\begin{aligned}\hat{f}_n(y \mid x) = f(y \mid x) &+ \tfrac{1}{2}b(n)^2 g(x)^{-1}[f_{xx}(x, y)m_{2,0} \\ &+ 2f_{xy}(x, y)m_{1,1} + f_{yy}(x, y)m_{0,2}] \\ &- \tfrac{1}{2}b(n)^2 f(x, y)g(x)^{-2}g_{xx}(x) \int u^2 k(u)\, du \\ &+ o(b(n))^2 \\ &+ g(x)^{-1}\{\hat{f}_n(x, y) - E\hat{f}_n(x, y)\}(1 + O_p(nb(n))^{-1/2}) \qquad (24)\end{aligned}$$

if $n^{-1}b(n)^{-1} = o(1)$ *as* $n \to \infty$. *The term* $\{\hat{f}_n(x, y) - E\hat{f}_n(x, y)\}$ *is asymptotically normal with mean zero and variance*

$$n^{-1}b(n)^{-2}f(x, y) \int h^2(u, v)\, du\, dv \qquad (25)$$

as $n \to \infty$ *if* $n^{-1}b(n)^{-2} = o(1)$. *The deviation between* $\hat{f}_n(y \mid x)$ *and* $f(y \mid x)$ *can be made to be* $O_p(n^{-1/3})$ *as* $n \to \infty$ *by setting* $b(n) = An^{-1/6}$ *for some constant A.*

Let f be a positive continuous density satisfying (6) and assume that

$$k(x) \le C(1 + x^2)^{-3}.$$

We now consider the asymptotic behavior of the proposed regression estimate

$$r_n(x) = \frac{\sum_{j=1}^n Y_j k(b(n)^{-1}(x - X_j))}{\sum_{j=1}^n k(b(n)^{-1}(x - X_j))} = \frac{a_n(x)}{\hat{g}_n(x)}. \qquad (26)$$

It seems natural to assume that the regression function $r(x)$ to be estimated is continuously differentiable up to second order. The mean of the numerator of (26) is

$$\begin{aligned} E&\left\{\sum_{j=1}^n Y_j k(b(n)^{-1}(x - X_j))\right\} \\ &= nE\{E(Y \mid X)k(b(n)^{-1}(x - X))\} \\ &= n \int r(u)k(b(n)^{-1}(x - u))g(u)\, du \\ &= n \int r(x - b(n)\alpha)g(x - b(n)\alpha)k(\alpha)\, d\alpha\, b(n) \\ &= nb(n)\left\{r(x)g(x) + \tfrac{1}{2}b(n)^2(r(x)g(x))_{xx} \int \alpha^2 k(\alpha)\, d\alpha + o(b(n))^2\right\} \end{aligned}$$

(27)

if g is continuously differentiable up to second order and (6) and (31) are valid. Actually conditions (6) and (31) can be weakened in a more careful estimation procedure. Now

$$\begin{aligned}\sigma^2[a_n(x)] &\cong n^{-1}b(n)^{-2}E\{Yk(b(n)^{-1}(x-X))\}^2\\ &= n^{-1}b(n)^{-1}\int y^2k^2(\alpha)f(x-b(n)\alpha, y)\,d\alpha\,dy\\ &= n^{-1}b(n)^{-1}\int E(Y^2\,|\,x-b(n)\alpha)g(x-b(n)\alpha)k^2(\alpha)\,d\alpha \quad (28)\\ &\cong n^{-1}b(n)^{-1}E(Y^2\,|\,x)g(x)\int k^2(\alpha)\,d\alpha \quad (29)\end{aligned}$$

while the asymptotic behavior of the variance of $\hat{g}_n(x)$ is given to the first order by (23). A similar estimation procedure leads to the following estimate of the covariance of $a_n(x)$ and $g_n(x)$

$$\operatorname{cov}[a_n(x), g_n(x)] \cong n^{-1}b(n)^{-1}r(x)g(x)\int k^2(\alpha)\,d\alpha. \quad (30)$$

If f satisfies (6), then $E|y|^3 < \infty$ and this implies by Liapounov's form of the central limit theorem that $\{a_n(x) - Ea_n(x) - \hat{g}_n(x) + E\hat{g}_n(x)\}$ is asymptotically normally distributed if $n^{-1}b(n)^{-1} = o(1)$.

Theorem 2. *Let f be a positive continuous density satisfying (6). Assume that $r(x)$ and $g(x)$ are continuously differentiable up to second order. If the positive weight function*

$$k(x) \le C(1+x^2)^{-3} \quad (31)$$

for some constant $C > 0$, then

$$\begin{aligned}r_n(x) = r(x) &+ \tfrac{1}{2}b(n)^2g(x)^{-1}\{(r(x)g(x))_{xx} - 1\}\int u^2k(u)\,du + o(b(n))^2\\ &+ g(x)^{-1}\{a_n(x) - Ea_n(x) - \hat{g}_n(x) + E\hat{g}_n(x)\}\\ &+ O_p(n^{-1}b(n)^{-1} + n^{-1/2}b(n)^{3/2}) \quad (32)\end{aligned}$$

where $a_n(x) - Ea_n(x) - \hat{g}_n(x) + E\hat{g}_n(x)$ is asymptotically normally distributed with mean zero and variance

$$n^{-1}b(n)^{-1}E[(Y-1)^2\,|\,x]g(x)\int k^2(u)\,du \quad (33)$$

as $n \to \infty$ if $n^{-1}b(n)^{-1} = o(1)$. The deviation between $r_n(x)$ and $r(x)$ can be made to be $O_p(n^{-2/5})$ as $n \to \infty$ by setting $b(n) = An^{-1/5}$ for some constant A.

The procedures discussed here may even be of some interest in the case of a regression analysis with a fixed independent variable. Suppose the basic model is as follows. If the experiment is carried out at level x, the response is

$$Y = r(x) + Z \quad (34)$$

where r is a given smooth function of the variable x and the error term Z is a random variable with mean zero and some unknown smooth density function. The object is to estimate the unknown regression function $r(x)$. Ordinarily, one would try to do this by independent observations at a number of fixed levels and by constructing an estimator in terms of these observations. An alternative procedure would be to choose the level at random with a given smooth positive density function. Now we would have

$$Y = r(X) + Z \tag{35}$$

with Z independent of X and with mean zero. Then

$$E(Y \mid X = x) = r(x)$$

and we are in the context of Theorem 2 as long as the assumptions specified there are satisfied. Expression (33) becomes

$$n^{-1}b(n)^{-1}(r(x) - 1)^2 + \sigma^2 g(x) \int k^2(u)\, du \tag{36}$$

in this context, where σ^2 is the variance of Z and g the density of X.

In closing, I should like to mention a recent unpublished article of related interest by Schuster [6].

REFERENCES

1. Bartlett, M. S. (1963). Statistical estimation of density functions. *Sankhyā Ser. A* **25** 245–254.
2. Cacoullos, T. (1966). Estimation of a multivariate density. *Ann. Inst. Statist. Math.* **18** 179–189.
3. Nadarya, E. A. (1965). On nonparametric estimates of density functions and regression curves. *Theory Probability Appl.* **10** 186–190.
4. Parzen, E. (1962). On estimation of a probability density and mode. *Ann. Math. Statist.* **33** 1065–1076.
5. Rosenblatt, M. (1956). Remarks on some nonparametric estimates of a density function. *Ann. Math. Statist.* **27** 832–835.
6. Schuster, E. F. (1968). Simple estimates of conditional density functions and regressions. Ph.D. Thesis, Univ. of Arizona, Tucson, Arizona. Unpublished.
7. Watson, G. S., and Leadbetter, M. R. (1963). On the estimation of the probability density. *Ann. Math. Statist.* **34** 480–491.
8. Watson, G. S. (1964). Smooth regression analysis. *Sankhyā Ser. A* **26** 359–372.
9. Weiss, L., and Wolfowitz, J. (1967). Estimation of a density function at a point. *Z. Wahrscheinlichkeits-Theorie Verw. Geb.* **7** 327–335.
10. Woodroofe, M. (1967). On the maximum deviation of the sample density. *Ann. Math. Statist.* **38** 475–481.

On Robust Nonparametric Estimation in Some Multivariate Linear Models[1]

PRANAB KUMAR SEN

DEPARTMENT OF BIOSTATISTICS
UNIVERSITY OF NORTH CAROLINA
CHAPEL HILL, NORTH CAROLINA

MADAN LAL PURI[2]

DEPARTMENT OF MATHEMATICS
INDIANA UNIVERSITY
BLOOMINGTON, INDIANA

COURANT INSTITUTE OF MATHEMATICAL SCIENCES
NEW YORK UNIVERSITY
NEW YORK, NEW YORK

1. INTRODUCTION

The maximum likelihood and the least-squares methods are most frequently used for the estimation of parameters of interest in various linear models in the univariate as well as multivariate statistical analysis. The former method requires the knowledge of the form of the parent distribution and retains its (asymptotic) optimality when this requirement is satisfied; otherwise, it may lead to inefficient (or even inconsistent) estimators. Moreover, in the majority of the situations, the solution of the likelihood equation(s) requires elaborate trial and error procedures. Among the class of linear unbiased estimators, the least-squares estimators are optimum when the parent distribution possesses finite second order moments. However, among the entire class of estimators (linear as well as nonlinear, biased as well as unbiased), the optimality of the least-squares estimators requires stringent regularity conditions on the parent distribution. Furthermore, the setting of confidence intervals based on least-squares estimators requires the knowledge of the

[1] Work supported by National Institutes of Health, Public Health Service, Grant GM-12868 and The Office of Naval Research, Contract N00014-67A0467-0004.

[2] Present address: Department of Mathematics, Indiana University, Bloomington, Indiana.

form of the parent distribution. Finally, both these procedures are vulnerable to outliers and contaminated errors.

For these reasons, alternative estimators (which are not so sensitive to outliers or gross errors, and are reasonably efficient for a broad class of distributions) are often preferred. In simplest type of univariate models, robust estimators, such as the Winsorized or the Trimmed means have been considered by Tukey [32], Huber [11], and others. Often, linear functions of order statistics are also employed for estimating parameters (cf. Sarhan and Greenberg [23], for details). A third approach to the problem of robust estimation is based on suitable rank tests (which are robust for outliers and gross errors). For the univariate one-sample and two-sample location problems, robust estimators based on simple rank tests were proposed almost simultaneously by Hodges and Lehmann [8] and by Sen [24]. Generalizations of such procedures for the one-way and two-way analysis of variance (ANOVA) models are due to Bhuchongkul and Puri [2], Lehmann [12–14], Sen [25–27], and Puri and Sen [16, 17] among others. Estimation of the parameters of a simple regression line based on suitable rank tests has been considered by Theil [31], Brown and Mood [4], Adichie [1], and Sen [28] among others.

In the multivariate problems too, robust estimators are already in use. In the one-sample location problem, the work of Puri and Sen [22] covers a full multivariate generalization of Hodges and Lehmann [8], Sen [24], and includes the work of Bickel [3] as a special case. Besides, Puri and Sen [22, 19] have also considered the multivariate two-sample and multivariate analysis of variance (MANOVA) one-way layout problems. These procedures are based on a class of robust rank tests studied in detail by the authors [15, 18, 29, 30]. Very recently, the present authors [18] have also developed the theory of rank order tests for a general class of multivariate linear hypotheses testing problem.

The purpose of the present paper is to consider a general (multivariate) linear model (which includes the one-sample and two-sample location problems as particular cases), and to propose and study suitable robust estimators of the parameters in this model The procedure rests on the rank tests studied by the authors [15, 18, 29]. The allied efficiency results are also studied, and it is shown that these are very close to those of a similar class of robust estimators in the multivariate one- and two-sample problems, studied by Puri and Sen [21, 22].

2. FORMULATION OF THE PROBLEMS

Consider a sequence of stochastic matrices

$$\mathbf{E}_\nu^{p\times N_\nu} = (\mathbf{X}_{\nu 1}, \ldots, \mathbf{X}_{\nu N_\nu}), \qquad 1 \le \nu < \infty,$$

where

$$\mathbf{X}_{\nu i} = (X_{\nu i}^{(1)}, \ldots, X_{\nu i}^{(p)})', \qquad i = 1, \ldots, N_\nu$$

are independent stochastic vectors having continuous cumulative distribution functions (cdf) $F_{\nu i}(\mathbf{x})$, $\mathbf{x} \in R^p$, $i = 1, \ldots, N_\nu$, respectively. It is assumed that

$$F_{\nu i}(\mathbf{x}) = F(\mathbf{x} - \boldsymbol{\alpha} - \boldsymbol{\beta} c_{\nu i}), \qquad i = 1, \ldots, N_\nu; \quad 1 \leq \nu < \infty, \tag{2.1}$$

where $\boldsymbol{\alpha} = (\alpha_1, \ldots, \alpha_p)'$ and $\boldsymbol{\beta} = (\beta_1, \ldots, \beta_p)'$ are unknown parameters, and $c_{\nu 1}, \ldots, c_{\nu N_\nu}$ are known (scalar) constants. The purpose of the present paper is to develop the theory of robust estimation of the parameters $(\boldsymbol{\alpha}, \boldsymbol{\beta})$ based on suitable rank statistics. Specifically, the following problems will be considered:

(i) estimation of $\boldsymbol{\alpha}$ assuming $\boldsymbol{\beta} = \mathbf{0}$,
(ii) estimation of $\boldsymbol{\beta}$ treating $\boldsymbol{\alpha}$ to be a nuisance parameter,
(iii) simultaneous estimation of both $(\boldsymbol{\alpha}, \boldsymbol{\beta})$; and
(iv) confidence regions for $\boldsymbol{\alpha}$ and $\boldsymbol{\beta}$.

It may be noted that problem (i) is the multivariate one-sample location problem, studied in detail by Puri and Sen [22], while a special case of (ii), in which $c_{\nu i}$'s can assume only the values 0 or 1, is the multivariate two-sample location problem also studied by the authors [22]. Problem (iii) is the multivariate generalization of the simple regression problem studied by Adichie [1], Brown and Mood [4], Sen [28], and Theil [31].

3. PRELIMINARY NOTIONS AND BASIC ASSUMPTIONS

We assume that $c_{\nu i}$'s satisfy the following conditions:

(A)[3]
$$\sum_{i=1}^{N_\nu} c_{\nu i} = 0 \qquad \text{for every } \nu, \quad 1 \leq \nu < \infty \tag{3.1}$$

(B)[4]
$$\max_{1 \leq i \leq N_\nu} \{N_\nu c_{\nu i}^2/(C_\nu^*)^2\} = O(1), \tag{3.2}$$

where

$$(C_\nu^*)^2 = \sum_{i=1}^{N_\nu} c_{\nu i}^2, \tag{3.3}$$

(C)
$$\lim_{\nu\to\infty} N_\nu = \infty; \qquad \lim_{\nu\to\infty} C_\nu^* = \infty. \tag{3.4}$$

[3] This can always be done by reparametrization of $\boldsymbol{\alpha}$ and $\boldsymbol{\beta}$.

[4] In the univariate case (3.2) may be replaced by the weaker condition, viz., $\max_{1 \leq i \leq N_\nu}\{c_{\nu i}^2/(C_\nu^*)^2\} = o(1)$. However, in the majority of the cases, (3.2) is satisfied. If the score function $\phi_j(u)$ has a bounded first derivative, we can still work with the weaker condition (for details, see Hájek [7], Theorem 2.2).

Let $\mathscr{F}_p$ be the class of all (p-variate) absolutely continuous cdf's with finite Fisherian information, and let $\mathscr{F}_p{}^0$ ($\subset \mathscr{F}_p$) be the subclass of all diagonally symmetric cdf's. (Note that $F(\mathbf{x})$ is diagonally symmetric about $\mathbf{0}$ when its density function $f(\mathbf{x})$ remains invariant under simultaneous changes of signs of all the coordinates.) For problem (ii), we shall assume that the cdf F, defined by (2.1), belongs to $\mathscr{F}_p$, while for problems (i) and (iii), we assume that $F \in \mathscr{F}_p{}^0$. Then let $R_{\nu i}^{(j)}$ be the rank of $X_{\nu i}^{(j)}$ among the N_ν observations $X_{\nu i}^{(j)}, \ldots, X_{\nu N_\nu}^{(j)}$, $i = 1, \ldots, N_\nu$; $j = 1, \ldots, p$. (Since $F(\mathbf{x})$ is absolutely continuous, ties may be ignored, in probability.) Let now $\phi_j(u)$ be an absolutely continuous function of $u : 0 < u < 1$, and assume that it is (i) nondecreasing in u and (ii) square integrable over (0, 1). Also, let $U_{\nu 1}, \ldots, U_{\nu N_\nu}$ be the N_ν ordered random variables in a sample of size N_ν from the rectangular distribution over (0, 1). Define a set of general *scores* by

$$a_{\nu,\alpha}^{(j)} = E\{\phi_j(U_{\nu\alpha})\}, \qquad \alpha = 1, \ldots, N_\nu; \quad j = 1, \ldots, p. \tag{3.5}$$

[We may also define $a_{\nu,\alpha}^{(j)} = \phi_j(\alpha/[N_\nu + 1])$. However, it is known (cf. Hájek [6, 7]) that these scores lead to asymptotically equivalent statistics. Hence, we shall work only with the scores in (3.5).] Thus (3.5) generates a score-function $\phi_{\nu,j}(u)$ taking constant values over the intervals $[(i-1)/N_\nu, i/N_\nu]$, $i = 1, \ldots, N_\nu$. The following two conditions are satisfied by $\phi_{\nu,j}(u)$, under fairly general conditions (cf. Hoeffding [10], Hájek [6]):

(I) $$\lim_{\nu\to\infty} \phi_{\nu,j}(u) = \phi_j(u): \qquad 0 < u < 1, \quad j = 1, \ldots, p; \tag{3.6}$$

(II) $$\lim_{\nu\to\infty} \int_0^1 [\phi_{\nu,j}(u) - \phi_j(u)]^2 \, du = 0, \qquad j = 1, \ldots, p. \tag{3.7}$$

The estimators of $\boldsymbol{\beta}$ to be considered here are based on the following rank order statistics:

$$S_{\nu j} = \sum_{i=1}^{N_\nu} c_{\nu i} a_{\nu, R_{\nu i}^{(j)}}^{(j)}, \qquad j = 1, \ldots, p; \quad \mathbf{S}_\nu = (S_{\nu 1}, \ldots, S_{\nu p}), \tag{3.8}$$

where $R_{\nu i}^{(j)}$ is the rank of $X_{\nu i}^{(j)}$ among all $X_{\nu 1}^{(j)}, \ldots, X_{\nu N_\nu}^{(j)}$.

For the estimation of α, we consider the following rank order statistics:

$$\mathbf{h}_\nu{}^* = (h_{\nu 1}^*, \ldots, h_{\nu p}^*), \tag{3.9}$$

where

$$h_{\nu j}^* = (1/N_\nu) \sum_{\alpha=1}^{N_\nu} E_{\nu,\alpha}^{(j)} Z_{\nu,\alpha}^{(j)}; \tag{3.10}$$

and $Z_{\nu,\alpha}^j = 1$ if the αth smallest observation among $|X_{\nu 1}^{(j)}|, \ldots, |X_{\nu N_\nu}^{(j)}|$ is from a positive $X_{\nu i}^{(j)}$ and is 0, otherwise, and $E_{\nu,\alpha}^{(j)}$ is the expected value of the αth order statistic of a sample of size N_ν from a distribution $\Psi_j{}^*(x)$ given by

$$\Psi_j{}^*(x) = \Psi_j(x) - \Psi_j(-x) \qquad \text{if} \quad x \geq 0, \quad \text{and} \quad 0, \text{otherwise}, \tag{3.11}$$

where $\Psi_j(x)$ is an absolutely continuous (univariate) cdf symmetric about 0, i.e., $\Psi_j(x) + \Psi_j(-x) = 1$ for all x. It is further assumed that (i) $J_j(u) = \Psi_j^{-1}(u)$ is absolutely continuous and for all $0 < u < 1$,

$$J_j^{(i)}(u) = (d^i/du^i)J_j(u)$$
$$\leq K[u(1-u)]^{\delta - i - (1/2)} \qquad i = 0,1; \quad j = 1, \ldots, p, \tag{3.12}$$

where $\delta > 0$ and $0 < K < \infty$. Other notations will be introduced as and when they are necessary.

4. POINT ESTIMATION OF α WHEN IT IS ASSUMED THAT $\beta = 0$

As has been noted earlier, this is the estimation problem relating to the multivariate one-sample location problem, and is already studied in detail by Bickel [3], and Puri and Sen [22]. Hence, only the estimators will be defined and their properties will be stated; for proofs the reader is referred to Puri and Sen [22]. In this section it is assumed that $F \in \mathscr{F}_p{}^0$. Suppose now that in (3.9) and (3.10), the variables $\mathbf{X}_{\nu i}$ are replaced by $\mathbf{X}_{\nu i} + \mathbf{a}$, $\mathbf{a} = (a_1, \ldots, a_p)'$; the corresponding rank statistic is denoted by

$$h_\nu^*(\mathbf{a}) = (h_{\nu 1}^*(a_1), \ldots, h_{\nu p}^*(a_p))'. \tag{4.1}$$

It follows that $h_\nu^*(\mathbf{a})$ is nondecreasing in each element of $\mathbf{a}$. We define

$$\boldsymbol{\mu}_\nu^* = (\mu_{\nu 1}^*, \ldots, \mu_{\nu p}^*)',$$

where

$$\mu_{\nu j}^* = (1/2N_\nu) \sum_{\alpha=1}^{N_\nu} E_{\nu,\alpha}^{(j)}, \qquad j = 1, \ldots, p. \tag{4.2}$$

For each $j = 1, \ldots, p$, let

$$\alpha_{\nu j,1}^* = \sup\{a_j : \quad h_{\nu j}^*(-a_j) > \mu_{\nu j}^*\}, \tag{4.3}$$

$$\alpha_{\nu j,2}^* = \inf\{a_j : \quad h_{\nu j}^*(-a_j) < \mu_{\nu j}^*\}. \tag{4.4}$$

Then, the proposed estimator of $\boldsymbol{\alpha}$ is

$$\boldsymbol{\alpha}_\nu^* = (\alpha_{\nu 1}^*, \ldots, \alpha_{\nu p}^*)'; \qquad \alpha_{\nu j}^* = \tfrac{1}{2}(\alpha_{\nu j,1}^* + \alpha_{\nu j,2}^*), \qquad j = 1, \ldots, p. \tag{4.5}$$

It is shown by Puri and Sen [22] that $\boldsymbol{\alpha}_\nu^*$ is a translation invariant estimator of $\boldsymbol{\alpha}$, its distribution is absolutely continuous and is diagonally symmetric about $\boldsymbol{\alpha}$. Two important members of the class of estimators obtained in (4.5) [in conjunction with (3.11) and (3.12)] are (a) the Wilcoxon scores estimator $\boldsymbol{\alpha}_{\nu(R)}^*$, resulting from the use of rectangular distribution over (0, 1) for Ψ_j^* in (3.11), and (b) the normal scores estimator $\boldsymbol{\alpha}_\nu^*(\Phi)$, resulting from the use of the standard normal cdf for Ψ_j in (3.11). In (a) and (b), $\mu^*_{\nu j}$ are respectively equal to 1/4 and $(2\pi)^{-1/2}$, for all $j = 1, \ldots, p$.

For the asymptotic distribution and efficiency of $\boldsymbol{\alpha}_\nu^*$, we introduce the following notation. Let

$$B_j(J_j, F) = \int_{-\infty}^{\infty} (d/dx)J_j[F_{[j]}(x)]\, dF_{[j]}(x), \qquad j = 1, \ldots, p, \tag{4.6}$$

where $F_{[j]}$ is the marginal cdf of $X_{\nu i}^{(j)}$ and $J_j(u) = \Psi_j^{-1}(u)$, $0 < u < 1$, with Ψ_j's defined by (3.11). Also, let $F_{[j,l]}(x, y)$ be the joint cdf of $(X_{\nu i}^{(j)}, X_{\nu i}^{(l)})$, $j \neq l = 1, \ldots, p$, and define

$$\gamma_{jj}(J_j, J_j, F) \equiv \gamma_{jj}(J_j) = \int_0^1 J_j^2(u)\, du - \left[\int_0^1 J_j(u)\, du\right]^2, \qquad j = 1, \ldots, p \tag{4.7}$$

$$\gamma_{jl}(J_j, J_l, F) = \int_{-\infty}^{\infty}\int_{-\infty}^{\infty} J_j[F_{[j]}(x)]J_l[F_{[l]}(y)]\, dF_{[j,l]}(x, y) - \left[\int_0^1 J_j(u)\, du\right]\left[\int_0^1 J_l(u)\, du\right], \qquad j \neq l = 1, \ldots, p. \tag{4.8}$$

Further, let $\mathbf{J} = (J_1, \ldots, J_p)'$, and

$$\boldsymbol{\Gamma}(F, \mathbf{J}) = ((\gamma_{jl}(J_j, J_l, F)))_{j, l=1, \ldots, p}. \tag{4.9}$$

Finally, let

$$\boldsymbol{\Gamma}^*(F, \mathbf{J}) = ((\gamma_{jl}^*))$$

where

$$\gamma_{jl}^* = \gamma_{jl}(J_j, J_l, F)/[B_j(J_j, F)B_l(J_l, F)], \qquad j, l = 1, \ldots, p. \tag{4.10}$$

Then, we have the following theorem proved by Puri and Sen [22].

Theorem 4.1. *Under the conditions of Section 3 as* $\nu \to \infty$,

$$\mathscr{L}[N_\nu^{1/2}(\boldsymbol{\alpha}_\nu^* - \boldsymbol{\alpha})] \to N(\mathbf{0}, \boldsymbol{\Gamma}^*(F, \mathbf{J})). \tag{4.11}$$

Let now $\hat{\boldsymbol{\alpha}}_\nu$ be the maximum likelihood estimator of $\boldsymbol{\alpha}$. Also, let $\mathbf{I}(F) = ((I_{jl}(F)))_{j,l=1,\ldots,p}$ where

$$I_{jl}(F) = E\left\{\left(\frac{\partial \log f}{\partial \alpha_j}\right)\left(\frac{\partial \log f}{\partial \alpha_l}\right)\right\}, \qquad \text{for} \quad j, l = 1, \ldots, p. \tag{4.12}$$

Then, from the results of Wald [33], it follows that as $\nu \to \infty$,

$$\mathscr{L}[N_\nu^{1/2}(\hat{\boldsymbol{\alpha}}_\nu - \boldsymbol{\alpha})] \to N(\mathbf{0}, [\mathbf{I}(F)]^{-1}). \tag{4.13}$$

Finally, the least-squares estimator of $\boldsymbol{\alpha}$ is $\bar{\mathbf{X}}_\nu = (\bar{X}_{\nu 1}, \ldots, \bar{X}_{\nu p})$, where

$$\bar{X}_{\nu j} = (1/N_\nu) \sum_{i=1}^{N} X_{\nu i}^{(j)}, \quad j = 1, \ldots, p.$$

From the classical (multivariate) central limit theorem, it follows that if $F(\mathbf{x})$ possesses finite second order moments, then as $\nu \to \infty$,

$$\mathscr{L}[N_\nu^{1/2}(\bar{\mathbf{X}}_\nu - \boldsymbol{\alpha})] \to N(\mathbf{0}, \boldsymbol{\Sigma}), \tag{4.14}$$

where $\boldsymbol{\Sigma} = ((\sigma_{jl}))$ is the population dispersion matrix with elements

$$\sigma_{jl} = \text{Covar}(X_{\nu i}^{(j)}, X_{\nu i}^{(l)}), \qquad \text{for} \quad j, l = 1, \ldots, p. \tag{4.15}$$

Because of (4.11), (4.13), and (4.14), we can compare the matrices $\boldsymbol{\Gamma}^*(F, \mathbf{J})$, $\mathbf{I}(F)$, and $\boldsymbol{\Sigma}$ for the comparison of the asymptotic properties of the estimators $\boldsymbol{\alpha}_\nu^*$, $\hat{\boldsymbol{\alpha}}_\nu$, and $\bar{\mathbf{X}}_\nu$. This will be considered in Section 6.

5. ESTIMATION OF THE REGRESSION PARAMETER $\boldsymbol{\beta}$

In this section, $\boldsymbol{\alpha}$ will be regarded as a nuisance parameter, and it is assumed that $F(\mathbf{x}) \in \mathscr{F}_p$. Now, suppose in the definition of $\mathbf{S}_\nu$ in (3.8), we replace the variables $\mathbf{X}_{\nu i}$ by $\mathbf{X}_{\nu i} + c_{\nu i}\mathbf{b}$, $i = 1, \ldots, p$, where $\mathbf{b} = (b_1, \ldots, b_p)'$; the corresponding rank statistic (vector) is then denoted by

$$\mathbf{S}_\nu(\mathbf{b}) = (S_{\nu 1}(b_1), \ldots, S_{\nu p}(b_p)). \tag{5.1}$$

It follows from the results in Section 3 that $\mathbf{S}_\nu(\mathbf{b})$ is nondecreasing in each element of $\mathbf{b}$.

Now consider the situation in which $\boldsymbol{\beta} = \mathbf{0}$. In this situation, the distribution of the rank vectors $\mathbf{R}_{\nu i}$, $i = 1, \ldots, N_\nu$, is independent of $c_{\nu 1}, \ldots, c_{\nu N_\nu}$, but as we are considering a multivariate situation, this distribution depends on the unknown F. To overcome this problem, we proceed as follows. Under the hypothesis $H_0 : \boldsymbol{\beta} = \mathbf{0}$, $\mathbf{X}_{\nu 1}, \ldots, \mathbf{X}_{\nu N_\nu}$ are N_ν independent and identically distributed random variables (vectors), and hence, their joint distribution remains invariant under all possible ($N_\nu!$) permutations of the vectors among themselves. These permutations generate a permutational (conditional) probability distribution. Proceeding as in Puri and Sen [18], it follows that if we consider the conditional distribution of $\mathbf{S}_\nu$ generated by these equally likely permutations, then the center of gravity of this conditional distribution is $\mathbf{0}$. In order to estimate $\boldsymbol{\beta}$, based on $\mathbf{S}_\nu(\mathbf{b})$, we shall align the observations $\mathbf{X}_{\nu i}$ by taking $\mathbf{X}_{\nu i} + c_{\nu i}\mathbf{b}$, where $\mathbf{b}$ is so chosen that $\mathbf{S}_\nu(-\mathbf{b})$ is closest to its (null) center of gravity $\mathbf{0}$. With this end, we define

$$\beta_{\nu j,1}^* = \sup\{b_j : \quad S_{\nu j}(-b_j) > 0\} \tag{5.2}$$

$$\beta_{\nu j,2}^* = \inf\{b_j : \quad S_{\nu j}(-b_j) < 0\}. \tag{5.3}$$

Then the proposed estimator of $\boldsymbol{\beta}$ is

$$\boldsymbol{\beta}_\nu^* = (\beta_{\nu 1}^*, \ldots, \beta_{\nu p}^*)'; \qquad \beta_{\nu j}^* = \tfrac{1}{2}(\beta_{\nu j,1}^* + \beta_{\nu j,2}^*), \quad j = 1, \ldots, p. \tag{5.4}$$

It may be noted that in the particular case of $p = 1$, such an estimator is considered by Adichie [1], though under more restrictive conditions, namely, $F \in \mathscr{F}_1{}^0$ and $N_\nu^{-1}(C_\nu^*)^2 \to c^2 > 0$ as $\nu \to \infty$.

The property of translation invariance of $\boldsymbol{\beta}_\nu^*$ follows exactly on the same line as in the univariate case [1]; while proceeding as in the work of Puri and Sen [18] and using the results of the authors [22], the following result can be proved:

If $F(\mathbf{x}) \in \mathscr{F}_p{}^0$, the distribution of $\boldsymbol{\beta}_\nu^*$ is diagonally symmetric about $\boldsymbol{\beta}$, that is, $(\boldsymbol{\beta}_\nu^* - \boldsymbol{\beta})$ and $(\boldsymbol{\beta} - \boldsymbol{\beta}_\nu^*)$ both have the same distribution. Thus, $\boldsymbol{\beta}_\nu^*$ is unbiased for $\boldsymbol{\beta}$.

For the study of the large sample properties of $\boldsymbol{\beta}_\nu^*$, we define $B_j(\phi_j, F)$ as in (4.6) with J_j replaced by ϕ_j, $j = 1, \ldots, p$. Also, we define the marginal cdf of $X_{\nu i}^{(j)} - \beta_j c_{\nu i}$ by $F_{[j]}$, and the joint cdf of $(X_{\nu i}^{(j)} - \beta_j c_{\nu i}, X_{\nu i}^{(l)} - \beta_l c_{\nu i})$ by $F_{[j,l]}(x, y)$, for $j \neq l = 1, \ldots, p$. Then we define $\gamma_{jj}(\phi_j)$ and $\gamma_{jl}(\phi_j, \phi_l, F)$ as in (4.7) and (4.8) with J_j replaced by ϕ_j, $j = 1, \ldots, p$. Furthermore, as in (4.9), we define

$$\Gamma(F, \boldsymbol{\phi}) = ((\gamma_{jl}(\phi_j, \phi_l, F)))_{j,l=1,\ldots,p}, \quad \boldsymbol{\phi} = (\phi_1, \ldots, \phi_p). \tag{5.5}$$

Finally, we let

$$\gamma_{jl}^*(\phi_j, \phi_l, F) = \frac{\gamma_{jl}(\phi_j, \phi_l, F)}{B_j(\phi_j, F)B_l(\phi_l, F)}, \quad j, l = 1, \ldots, p; \tag{5.6}$$

$$\boldsymbol{\Gamma}^*(\mathbf{F}, \boldsymbol{\phi}) = ((\gamma_{jl}^*(\phi_j, \phi_l, F)))_{j,l=1,\ldots,p}. \tag{5.7}$$

Then we have the following theorem.

Theorem 5.1. *Under the conditions of Section* 3 *as* $\nu \to \infty$,

$$\mathscr{L}(C_\nu^*[\boldsymbol{\beta}_\nu^* - \boldsymbol{\beta}]) \to N(\mathbf{0}, \boldsymbol{\Gamma}^*(F, \boldsymbol{\phi})). \tag{5.8}$$

Proof. Because of the property of translation invariance of $\boldsymbol{\beta}_\nu^*$, we may assume without any loss of generality that $\boldsymbol{\beta} = \mathbf{0}$. We also denote by $\mathbf{x} \leq \mathbf{y}$, the coordinatewise inequalities $x_i \leq y_i$, $i = 1, \ldots, p$. Then, by definition of $\boldsymbol{\beta}_\nu^*$ in (5.2)–(5.4), we have

$$P\{\mathbf{S}_\nu(-\mathbf{a}) < \mathbf{0}\} \leq P\{\boldsymbol{\beta}_\nu^* \leq \mathbf{a}\} \leq P\{\mathbf{S}_\nu(-\mathbf{a}) \leq \mathbf{0}\}. \tag{5.9}$$

Now, consider a sequence of values of $\mathbf{a}$, namely

$$\mathbf{a} = \mathbf{a}_\nu = (C_\nu^*)^{-1}\boldsymbol{\lambda}, \qquad \boldsymbol{\lambda} = (\lambda_1, \ldots, \lambda_p), \tag{5.10}$$

where $\lambda_1, \ldots, \lambda_p$ are all real and finite. Then using the results of Puri and Sen [18], it can be shown easily that for any fixed $\boldsymbol{\lambda}$,

$$\lim_{\nu\to\infty} [P\{\mathbf{S}_\nu(-[C_\nu^*]^{-1}\boldsymbol{\lambda}) \le \mathbf{0}\} - P\{\mathbf{S}_\nu(-[C_\nu^*]^{-1}\boldsymbol{\lambda}) < \mathbf{0}\}] = 0. \quad (5.11)$$

Hence, from (5.9) and (5.10), for any $\boldsymbol{\lambda}$, we have

$$\lim_{\nu\to\infty} P\{C_\nu^* \boldsymbol{\beta}_\nu^* \le \boldsymbol{\lambda}\} = \lim_{\nu\to\infty} P_0\{\mathbf{S}_\nu(-[C_\nu^*]^{-1}\boldsymbol{\lambda}) \le \mathbf{0}\}, \quad (5.12)$$

where P_0 indicates the probability computed under $H_0 : \boldsymbol{\beta} = \mathbf{0}$. Now, the right-hand side of (5.12) can also be written as

$$\lim_{\nu\to\infty} P_{\{H_\nu\}}\{\mathbf{S}_\nu(\mathbf{0}) \le 0\}, \quad (5.13)$$

where $\{H_\nu\}$ relates to the sequence of alternative hypotheses

$$H_\nu:\quad \boldsymbol{\beta} = \boldsymbol{\beta}_\nu = -(C_\nu^*)^{-1}\boldsymbol{\lambda}, \qquad 1 \le \nu < \infty. \quad (5.14)$$

Now, it follows from the results of Puri and Sen [18] that under $\{H_\nu\}$,

$$\lim_{\nu\to\infty} \mathscr{L}([C_\nu^*]^{-1}\mathbf{S}_\nu(\mathbf{0})) = N(-\boldsymbol{\lambda}^*, \boldsymbol{\Gamma}(F, \boldsymbol{\phi})), \quad (5.15)$$

where $\boldsymbol{\Gamma}(F, \boldsymbol{\phi})$ is defined by (5.5), and

$$\boldsymbol{\lambda}^* = (\lambda_1^*, \ldots, \lambda_p^*); \qquad \lambda_j^* = \lambda_j B_j(\phi_j, F), \quad j = 1, \ldots, p. \quad (5.16)$$

Thus, (5.13) equals

$$(2\pi)^{-p/2}|\boldsymbol{\Gamma}(F, \boldsymbol{\phi})|^{-1/2} \int_{-\infty}^{\lambda_1^*} \cdots \int_{-\infty}^{\lambda_p^*} \exp\{-\tfrac{1}{2}\mathbf{t}'\boldsymbol{\Gamma}^{-1}(F, \boldsymbol{\phi})\mathbf{t}\}\, d\mathbf{t}, \quad (5.17)$$

where $\mathbf{t} = (t_1, \ldots, t_p)$. Let us now consider the transformation

$$\mathbf{U} = (U_1, \ldots, U_p)' = (t_1/B_1(\phi_1, F), \ldots, t_p/B_p(\phi_p, F))'. \quad (5.18)$$

Then using (5.6), (5.7), (5.16), and (5.18), it readily follows that (5.17) can also be written as

$$\{(2\pi)^{-p/2}|\boldsymbol{\Gamma}^*(F, \boldsymbol{\phi})|^{-1/2}\} \int_{-\infty}^{\lambda_1} \cdots \int_{-\infty}^{\lambda_p} \exp\{-\tfrac{1}{2}\mathbf{U}'\boldsymbol{\Gamma}^{*-1}(F, \boldsymbol{\phi})\mathbf{U}\}\, d\mathbf{U}. \quad (5.19)$$

The rest of the proof follows from (5.12), (5.13), (5.17), and (5.19). Q.E.D.

Remark. In the particular case of $p = 1$, Adichie [1] considered a similar theorem under the more restrictive situation in which $F \in \mathscr{F}_1{}^0$ and $N_\nu^{-1}(C_\nu^*)^2 \to C^2 > 0$. Neither of these conditions appears to be necessary. Moreover, Adichie's proof is based directly on the results of Hájek [6]. While the authors were considering the multivariate generalizations of Hájek's results, it was found that his contiguity arguments in the multivariate case introduces a number of complications. As such, the proof of Adichie's results faces considerable difficulties in the multivariate case. The present proof based on the results of Puri and Sen [18] avoids these difficulties and simplifies the situation considerably. It is also noted that in many situations Adichie's condition, namely, $N_\nu^{-1}(C_\nu^*)^2 \to C^2 > 0$ may not hold whereas the condition that $\lim_{\nu\to\infty} C_\nu^* = \infty$ holds. As an example, consider the following situation:

$$c_{\nu i}^2 = g_\nu(i), \quad i = 1, \ldots, N_\nu \tag{5.20}$$

where g_ν is a nondecreasing function of i, such that for some $\delta \geq 1$,

$$g_\nu(i)/i^\delta \geq c > 0 \qquad \text{for all} \quad i \geq i_0. \tag{5.21}$$

Here, naturally, $N_\nu^{-1}(C_\nu^*)^2$ cannot tend to any finite limit as $\nu \to \infty$. A very typical case which deserves to be mentioned is the simple regression model where

$$c_{\nu i} = c_{\nu 0} + c(i - \tfrac{1}{2}(N_\nu + 1), \quad c \neq 0, \tag{5.22}$$

which does not satisfy Adichie's condition, but satisfies ours.

Now let $\hat{\boldsymbol{\beta}}_\nu$ be the maximum likelihood estimator of $\boldsymbol{\beta}$, and we define the information matrix $\mathbf{I}(F)$ as in (4.12). Then, again using the results of Wald [33], it follows that under the conditions on $c_{\nu 1}, \ldots, c_{\nu N_\nu}$ in Section 3,

$$\lim_{\nu\to\infty} \mathscr{L}[C_\nu^*(\hat{\boldsymbol{\beta}}_\nu - \boldsymbol{\beta})] \to N(\mathbf{0}, [\mathbf{I}(F)]^{-1}). \tag{5.23}$$

Finally, the least-squares estimator of $\boldsymbol{\beta}$ is $\tilde{\boldsymbol{\beta}}_\nu = (\tilde{\beta}_{\nu 1}, \ldots, \tilde{\beta}_{\nu p})'$, where

$$\tilde{\beta}_{\nu j} = \sum_{i=1}^{N_\nu} (X_{\nu i}^{(j)} - X_\nu^{(j)})c_{\nu i}/(C_\nu^*)^2, \qquad j = 1, \ldots, p. \tag{5.24}$$

Since $\tilde{\boldsymbol{\beta}}_\nu$ is a vector of linear functions of $\mathbf{X}_{\nu i}$, $i = 1, \ldots, N_\nu$, we may again use the multivariate central limit theorem, and obtain under the conditions of Section 3 that

$$\lim_{\nu\to\infty} \mathscr{L}[C_\nu^*(\tilde{\boldsymbol{\beta}}_\nu - \boldsymbol{\beta})] \to N(\mathbf{0}, \boldsymbol{\Sigma}) \tag{5.25}$$

where $\boldsymbol{\Sigma}$ is defined by (4.15).

Stochastic comparison of the estimators is made in Section 6.

6. ASYMPTOTIC RELATIVE EFFICIENCIES (ARE) OF THE ESTIMATORS

The estimators of $\boldsymbol{\alpha}$ and $\boldsymbol{\beta}$ studied in the preceding two sections are all asymptotically normally distributed. A comparison of their asymptotic covariance matrices reveals some idea about their relative performances. To be precise, we employ the notion of "the generalized variance" by Wilks

[34], and define a measure of the asymptotic relative efficiency (ARE) based on generalized variances.

Consider two sequences of estimators $\{\mathbf{T}_{N_\nu}\}$ and $\{\mathbf{T}^*_{N_\nu}\}$, such that $N_\nu^{1/2}(\mathbf{T}_N - \boldsymbol{\theta})$ and $N_\nu^{1/2}(\mathbf{T}_N{}^* - \boldsymbol{\theta})$ both have asymptotically null mean vectors and dispersion matrices $\boldsymbol{\Sigma}$ and $\boldsymbol{\Sigma}^*$, respectively. The corresponding generalized variances are defined by $|\boldsymbol{\Sigma}|$ and $|\boldsymbol{\Sigma}^*|$, where $|\boldsymbol{\Sigma}|$ refers to the determinant of $\boldsymbol{\Sigma}$. Now, suppose that there exists a sequence of positive integers $N_\nu{}^* = N_\nu{}^*(N_\nu)$, such that $\lim_{\nu\to\infty} N_\nu{}^*/N_\nu$ exists for which the generalized variances of the statistics $N_\nu^{1/2}(\mathbf{T}_{N_\nu} - \boldsymbol{\theta})$ and $(N_\nu{}^*)^{1/2}(\mathbf{T}^*_{N_\nu{}^*} - \boldsymbol{\theta})$ are equal in the limit (as $\nu \to \infty$) [in the sense that their ratio asymptotically equals 1]. Then the ARE of $\mathbf{T}_{N_\nu}$ with respect to $\mathbf{T}^*_{N_\nu}$ is defined by

$$e_{\mathbf{T},\mathbf{T}^*} = \lim_{\nu\to\infty} N_\nu^*/N_\nu = \{|\boldsymbol{\Sigma}^*|/|\boldsymbol{\Sigma}|\}^{1/p}. \tag{6.1}$$

Thus, from Theorem 4.1 and (4.13), it follows that in accordance with the above definition of ARE

$$e_{\boldsymbol{\alpha}^*,\hat{\boldsymbol{\alpha}}} = \{|\mathbf{I}(F)|\;|\boldsymbol{\Gamma}^*(F, J)|\}^{-1/p}, \tag{6.2}$$

where $\mathbf{I}(F)$ and $\boldsymbol{\Gamma}^*(F, \mathbf{J})$ are defined by (4.12) and (4.10). Now, using the well-known results on the multivariate (multiparameter) generalization of the Rao-Cramér inequality, it follows that the characteristic roots of $\mathbf{I}(F)\boldsymbol{\Gamma}^*(F, \mathbf{J})$ are all bounded below by 1, and as a result, (6.2) is bounded above by 1. Similarly, from Theorem 4.1 and Eq. (4.14), we obtain

$$e_{\boldsymbol{\alpha}^*,\overline{\mathbf{X}}} = \{|\boldsymbol{\Sigma}|/|\boldsymbol{\Gamma}^*(F, \mathbf{J})|\}^{1/p}. \tag{6.3}$$

Now, we write

$$\boldsymbol{\Sigma} = ((\sigma_{jk})) = (([\sigma_{jj}\sigma_{kk}]^{1/2}\rho_{jk})); \qquad ((\rho_{jk})) = \mathbf{R}; \tag{6.4}$$

$$\boldsymbol{\Gamma}(F, \mathbf{J}) = (([\gamma_{jj}(J_j)\gamma_{kk}(J_k)]^{1/2}\rho_{jk}(\mathbf{J}))); \qquad ((\rho_{jk}(\mathbf{J}))) = \mathbf{R}(\mathbf{J}), \tag{6.5}$$

and define the marginal ARE's by

$$e^{(j)}_{\alpha_j^*, \bar{X}_j} = \sigma_{jj} B_j^2(J_j, F)/\gamma_{jj}(J_j), \quad j = 1, \ldots, p. \tag{6.6}$$

Then, from (6.3)–(6.6), we have

$$e_{\boldsymbol{\alpha}^*,\overline{\mathbf{X}}} = \left\{\prod_{j=1}^{p} e^{(j)}_{\alpha_j^*,\bar{X}_j}\right\}^{1/p} \{|\mathbf{R}|/|\mathbf{R}(\mathbf{J})|\}^{1/p}. \tag{6.7}$$

The first factor on the right-hand side of (6.4) is the geometric mean of the marginal ARE's while the second factor depends on the joint distributions through the correlation matrices $\mathbf{R}$ and $\mathbf{R}(\mathbf{J})$. In general, the relationship between $\mathbf{R}$ and $\mathbf{R}(\mathbf{J})$ is not so explicit as to enable us to derive suitable bounds for $|\mathbf{R}|/|\mathbf{R}(\mathbf{J})|$. On the other hand, for various commonly used rank statistics, bounds for the values of $e^{(j)}_{\alpha_j^*, \bar{X}_j}$ are available in the literature. We shall consider in detail the following cases.

(I) Wilcoxon Scores Estimator

In this case, $\alpha^*_{\nu j}$ is the median of the $\frac{1}{2}(N_\nu(N_\nu + 1))$ midranges

$$\tfrac{1}{2}(X^{(j)}_{\nu i} + X^{(j)}_{\nu i'}), \qquad 1 \le i \le i' \le N_\nu, \quad j = 1, \ldots, p.$$

Here

$$J_j(u) = 2u - 1, \qquad 0 < u < 1, \qquad \text{for} \quad j = 1, \ldots, p.$$

Hence

$$e^{(j)}_{\alpha_j^*, \bar{X}_j} = 12\sigma_{jj}\left(\int_{-\infty}^{\infty} f^2_{[j]}(x)\, dx\right)^2. \tag{6.8}$$

It is well known that

(i) $$e^{(j)}_{\alpha_j^*, \bar{X}_j} \ge 0.864 \qquad \text{for all } F_{[j]}, \quad j = 1, \ldots, p \tag{6.9}$$

(ii) $$e^{(j)}_{\alpha_j^*, \bar{X}_j} = 3/\pi \qquad \text{when } F_{[j]} \text{ is normal, and} \tag{6.10}$$

(iii) It is usually greater than one for cdf's with *heavy tails*. Consequently, if we estimate $\boldsymbol{\alpha}$, based on the coordinate-wise Wilcoxon signed rank statistics, the first factor on the right-hand side of (6.7) is bounded below by 0.864 for all F, is equal to $3/\pi$ for multinormal cdf's, and may be greater than 1 for many nonnormal cdf's. However, the second factor on the right-hand side of (6.7) depends on the product moment correlations $((\rho_{jk}))$ as well as the grade correlations $((\rho^g_{jk}))$, where

$$\rho^g_{jk} = 12\int_{-\infty}^{\infty}\int_{-\infty}^{\infty} [F_{[j]}(x) - \tfrac{1}{2}][F_{[k]}(y) - \tfrac{1}{2}]\, dF_{[j,k]}(x, y), \quad j, k = 1, \ldots, p. \tag{6.11}$$

For arbitrary continuous cdf's, the relationship between $((\rho_{jk}))$ and $((\rho^g_{jk}))$ is not so explicit as to allow us to derive suitable bounds for $|\rho_{jk}|/|\rho^g_{jk}|$. However, we note that when $\rho_{jk} = 0$ for $j \ne k$, i.e., when $X^{(1)}_{\nu i}, \ldots, X^{(p)}_{\nu i}$ are pairwise uncorrelated, $|\rho_{jk}| = 1$ whereas $|\rho^g_{jk}| \le 1$, and hence, the second factor on the right-hand side of (6.7) is bounded below by 1. [It will be exactly equal to one, when $\rho_{jk} = 0$ implies $\rho^g_{jk} = 0$, a case that arises when $X^{(1)}_{\nu i}, \ldots, X^{(p)}_{\nu i}$ are pair-wise independent.] Thus, in this case, the geometric mean of the marginal ARE's provides a lower bound to $e_{\boldsymbol{\alpha}^*, \bar{\mathbf{X}}}$. A second important case often arising in practice is the equicorrelation model, where $X^{(1)}_{\nu i}, \ldots, X^{(p)}_{\nu i}$ are symmetric dependent or interchangeable variables (when adjusted by $\alpha_1, \ldots, \alpha_p$). In this case,

$$\rho_{jk} = \rho \quad \text{for} \quad j \ne k = 1, \ldots, p \Rightarrow |\rho_{jk}| = (1 - \rho)^{p-1}[1 + (p - 1)\rho]; \tag{6.12}$$

$$\rho^g_{jk} = \rho^g \quad \text{for} \quad j \ne k = 1, \ldots, p \Rightarrow |\rho^g_{jk}| = (1 - \rho)^{p-1}[1 + (p - 1)\rho^g]. \tag{6.13}$$

Hence, in this case, the second factor on the right-hand side of (6.7) reduces to

$$[(1-\rho)/(1-\rho^g)\}^{1-1/p}\{[1+(p-1)\rho]/[1+(p-1)\rho^g]\}^{1/p} = h(\rho, \rho^g). \quad (6.14)$$

Hence, if the relationship between ρ and ρ_g is known, suitable bounds to $h(\rho, \rho^g)$ may be derived. For example, if ρ and ρ^g satisfy the following implications:

$$\rho \leq 0 \Rightarrow \rho \leq \rho^g \leq 0 \qquad \text{and} \qquad \rho \geq 0 \Rightarrow 0 \leq \rho^g \leq \rho, \quad (6.15)$$

then upon noting that $(1-\rho)^{p-1}[1+(p-1)\rho]$ is unimodal with the mode at $\rho = 0$, it follows from (6.14) and (6.15) that

$$h(\rho, \rho^g) \leq 1 \qquad \text{for} \quad -1/(p-1) < \rho \leq 1. \quad (6.16)$$

Thus, in this case,

$$e_{\boldsymbol{\alpha}^*,\bar{\mathbf{X}}} \leq \left\{ \prod_{j=1}^{p} e^{(j)}_{\alpha_j^*,\bar{X}_j} \right\}^{1/p} \quad (6.17)$$

It is to be noted that (6.15) holds for a broad class of distributions including the multinormal forms. A third important case is the situation in which $F(\mathbf{x})$ is itself a multinormal cdf. In this case, $\rho^g_{jk} = (6/\pi)\sin^{-1}(\frac{1}{2}\rho_{jk})$ [which implies (6.15)], and hence

$$\{|\mathbf{R}|/|\mathbf{R}(\mathbf{J})|\}^{1/p} = g(\rho_{jk}; \quad 1 \leq j < k \leq p). \quad (6.18)$$

In the case of $p = 2$, Eq. (6.18) is equal to

$$\{(1-\rho^2)/(1-(36/\pi^2)[\sin^{-1}\tfrac{1}{2}\rho]^2)\}^{1/2}, \quad (6.19)$$

and hence maximizing and minimizing (6.19) with respect to ρ, $(-1 \leq \rho \leq 1)$, we obtain from Eqs. (6.7), (6.18), and (6.19) that

$$0.91 \leq e_{\boldsymbol{\alpha}^*,\bar{\mathbf{X}}} \leq 0.95, \quad (6.20)$$

where the lower bound is attained as $|\rho| \to \pm 1$. For $p > 2$, it has been shown by Bickel [3] *that* $e_{\boldsymbol{\alpha}^*,\bar{\mathbf{X}}}$ *can be arbitrarily close to zero, indicating that there is no guarantee about the minimum efficiency of the estimator based on the signed rank statistics when* $p > 2$.

(II) The Normal Scores Estimator

In this case, we use the standard normal cdf for $\psi_j(x)$ in (3.11), so that $\mathbf{h}_\nu^*$ is the vector of one-sample normal scores statistics. Here, from the results of Chernoff and Savage [5], we have

$$e^{(j)}_{\alpha_j^*,\bar{X}_j} \geq 1, \quad j = 1, \ldots, p, \quad (6.21)$$

where the equality sign holds only when F is a multinormal cdf. The correlation matrix $\mathbf{R}(\mathbf{J})$ has elements (in this case) specified by (where Φ is the standard normal cdf):

$$\rho_{jk}^{\Phi} = \int_{-\infty}^{\infty} \int_{-\infty}^{\infty} \Phi^{-1}(F_{[j]}(x))\Phi^{-1}(F_{[k]}(y))\, dF_{[j,k]}(x, y) \qquad (6.22)$$

for $1 \leq j < k \leq p$. As in the Wilcoxon scores estimator, here also, the relation between $\mathbf{R}$ and $\mathbf{R}(\Phi)$ for arbitrary F is not in such a form as to allow us to derive suitable bounds for $\{|\mathbf{R}|/|\mathbf{R}(\phi)|\}^{1/p}$. However, as in the preceding case, the following results are obtained without much difficulty:

(a) If $\rho_{jk} = 0 \ \forall \ j \neq k$, then $|\mathbf{R}| = 1$, $|\mathbf{R}(\phi)| \leq 1$, and hence from (6.7) and (6.21), the ARE is bounded below by 1.

(b) If $\rho_{jk} = \rho \ \forall \ j \neq k$ and $\rho_{jk}^{\phi} = \rho^{\phi} \ \forall \ j \neq k$, and if (6.15) holds for ρ and ρ^{ϕ}, then (6.16) also holds for ρ and ρ^{ϕ}. As a result, in this case, the first factor on the right-hand side is bounded above by 1.

(c) If F is itself a multinormal cdf, $\rho_{jk}^{\phi} = \rho_{jk}$ for all $j, k = 1, \ldots, p$, and hence, from (6.7) and (6.21), we obtain that the ARE in this case equals 1 for all $\mathbf{R}$. *Thus, even for $p > 2$, the normal scores estimator cannot be inefficient whereas the Wilcoxon score estimator can, indeed, have a very low efficiency.* For the comparison of the Wilcoxon and normal scores estimators, see Puri and Sen [22].

Let us now consider the ARE of the estimators of the regression coefficients considered in Section 5. In this case, the definition of the ARE in (6.1) requires certain modifications, as here the sample size N_ν does not enter into the limiting covariance matrices of the estimates. If we look at Theorem 5.1, Eqs. (5.23) and (5.25), we note that here $(C_\nu^*)^2$ plays the role of N_ν. Consequently, some smoothness condition has to be imposed on C_ν^*. We relate $(C_\nu^*)^2$ to the sample size N_ν by a function

$$(C_\nu^*)^2 = Q_\nu(N_\nu), \qquad 1 \leq \nu < \infty, \qquad (6.23)$$

where Q_ν is a nondecreasing function of N_ν. Note that $Q_\nu(N_\nu)$ may or may not tend to a finite limit as $\nu \to \infty$. We impose the following smoothness condition on Q_ν:

Let $\{a_\nu\}$ be a sequence of real numbers such that

$$\lim_{\nu \to \infty} a_\nu = a: \quad 0 < a < \infty,$$

then

$$\lim_{\nu \to \infty} Q_\nu(a_\nu N_\nu)/Q_\nu(N_\nu) = \mathscr{S}(a) \qquad \text{(say)} \qquad (6.24)$$

exists and is a strictly monotonic function of a : $0 < a < 1$. (By definition $\mathcal{S}(1) = 1$.) This implies that $\mathcal{S}^{-1}(a)$ also exists and is monotonic in a, with $\mathcal{S}^{-1}(1) = 1$. Then, arguing as in (6.1), we obtain from Theorem 5.1 and Eq. (5.23) that the ARE of $\boldsymbol{\beta}_v{}^*$ with respect to $\hat{\beta}$ is

$$e^*_{\boldsymbol{\beta}^*, \hat{\boldsymbol{\beta}}} = \mathcal{S}^{-1}\{[|\mathbf{I}(F)|\,|\boldsymbol{\Gamma}^*(F, \boldsymbol{\phi})|]^{-1/p}\}. \tag{6.25}$$

Since, by arguments similar to those in (6.2), $|\mathbf{I}(F)|\,|\boldsymbol{\Gamma}^*(F, \boldsymbol{\phi})|$ is greater than or equal to 1, it follows that (6.25) is also bounded above by 1. Similarly, the ARE of $\boldsymbol{\beta}_v{}^*$ with respect to $\tilde{\boldsymbol{\beta}}_v$ is obtained from Theorem 5.1 and Eq. (5.25) as equal to

$$e^*_{\boldsymbol{\beta}^*, \tilde{\boldsymbol{\beta}}} = \mathcal{S}^{-1}\{[|\boldsymbol{\Sigma}|/|\boldsymbol{\Gamma}^*(F, \boldsymbol{\phi})|]^{1/p}\}. \tag{6.26}$$

Thus, we obtain that on equating $\mathbf{J} \equiv \boldsymbol{\phi}$,

$$e^*_{\boldsymbol{\beta}^*, \hat{\boldsymbol{\beta}}} = \mathcal{S}^{-1}(e_{\boldsymbol{\alpha}^*, \hat{\boldsymbol{\alpha}}}) \qquad \text{and} \qquad e^*_{\boldsymbol{\beta}^*, \tilde{\boldsymbol{\beta}}} = \mathcal{S}^{-1}(e_{\boldsymbol{\alpha}^*, \bar{\mathbf{X}}}). \tag{6.27}$$

Since $\mathcal{S}^{-1}(a)$ is a completely known, monotonic and single valued function of $a : 0 < a < \infty$, it follows that all that has been discussed following (6.3) also applies to (6.26) (with the only change that $\mathbf{J}$ is replaced by $\boldsymbol{\phi}$). In this case also the two notable estimators are based on Wilcoxon and the normal scores statistics respectively, where for the former $\phi_j(u) = u : 0 < u < 1$ and for the latter $\phi_j(u) = \Phi^{-1}(u)$, $0 < u < 1$, $\Phi^{-1}(x)$ being the standard normal cdf. As an illustration of the relation (6.27), we consider the simple model in which

$$c_{vi} = c(i - (N_v + 1)/2), \qquad c \neq 0; \quad 1 \leq i \leq N_v, \quad 1 \leq v < \infty. \tag{6.28}$$

In this case, $(C_v{}^*)^2 = c^2 N_v(N_v{}^2 - 1)/12$, and as a result, $\mathcal{S}(a)$, defined by (6.24), is equal to a^3. Thus $\mathcal{S}^{-1}(a) = a^{1/3}$. Consequently, here

$$e^* = (e)^{1/3}. \tag{6.29}$$

So the bounds for e will naturally supply the bounds for e^*. In the majority of cases, such relations are not difficult to establish, and hence, the results in (6.3)–(6.22) can be readily generalized to the regression model.

7. JOINT ESTIMATION OF (α, β)

In Section 5, we considered the estimator of $\boldsymbol{\beta}$, treating $\boldsymbol{\alpha}$ to be a nuisance parameter, and in Section 4, we considered the estimator of $\boldsymbol{\alpha}$ treating $\boldsymbol{\beta} = \mathbf{0}$. When we seek to estimate both $(\boldsymbol{\alpha}, \boldsymbol{\beta})$, the estimator of $\boldsymbol{\beta}$ therefore stands valid, whereas we have to modify the estimator of $\boldsymbol{\alpha}$, in view of the fact that the true value of $\boldsymbol{\beta}$ is now known. This demands more restrictive conditions on the scores $\mathbf{J}$ as well as on the known regression constants $c_{\nu 1}, \ldots, c_{\nu N_\nu}$. We shall now impose the following restrictions in addition to those in Section 3:

(i) $$\lim_{\nu\to\infty} N_\nu^{-1}(C_\nu^*)^2 = (C^*)^2; \qquad 0 < (C^*)^2 < \infty; \tag{7.1}$$

(ii) $$|(d/dx)J_j(F_{[j]}(x)| < K \qquad \text{for all } x \text{ and } j = 1, \ldots, p. \tag{7.2}$$

Both these conditions are assumed by Adichie [1] (in the univariate case) for the joint estimation of (α, β).

Then define

$$\hat{X}_{\nu i}^{(j)} = X_{\nu i}^{(j)} - \beta_{\nu j}^* c_{\nu i}, \quad j = 1, \ldots, p; \quad i = 1, \ldots, N. \tag{7.3}$$

Throughout Section 4, replace the variables $X_{\nu i}^{(j)}$ by $\hat{X}_{\nu i}^{(j)}$, $i = 1, \ldots, N_\nu$, $j = 1, \ldots, p$, and consider the estimators proposed there based on these variables. The rank order estimator, derived in (4.4) and (4.5), is denoted by $\boldsymbol{\alpha}_\nu^{**} = (\alpha_{\nu 1}^{**}, \ldots, \alpha_{\nu p}^{**})'$. Now, under the conditions stated above, it follows from the results of Adichie [1] that

$$|N_\nu^{1/2}(\alpha_{\nu j}^* - \alpha_{\nu j}^{**})| \xrightarrow{p} 0 \qquad \text{as} \quad \nu \to \infty \qquad \text{for all} \quad j = 1, \ldots, p. \tag{7.4}$$

Consequently, the estimator $\boldsymbol{\alpha}_\nu^{**}$ possesses asymptotically all the properties that $\boldsymbol{\alpha}^*$ has.

Now, under (7.1), $\mathscr{S}(a)$, defined by (6.24), equals a, and hence $\mathscr{S}^{-1}(a) = a : 0 < a < \infty$. Consequently, if we consider the estimates $N_\nu^{1/2}[(\boldsymbol{\alpha}_\nu^{**} - \boldsymbol{\alpha}), (\boldsymbol{\beta}_\nu^* - \boldsymbol{\beta})]$ and compare it with $N_\nu^{1/2}[(\hat{\boldsymbol{\alpha}}_\nu - \boldsymbol{\alpha}), (\hat{\boldsymbol{\beta}}_\nu - \boldsymbol{\beta})]$ according to the criterion of generalized variance [defined in Section 6], the ARE of the former with respect to the latter is deduced to be equal to

$$e_{(\boldsymbol{\alpha}^{**}, \boldsymbol{\beta}^*), (\hat{\boldsymbol{\alpha}}, \hat{\boldsymbol{\beta}})} = \{|\mathbf{I}(F)|\,|\boldsymbol{\Gamma}^*(F, \mathbf{J})|\}^{-1/p}; \tag{7.5}$$

similarly,

$$e_{(\boldsymbol{\alpha}^{**}, \boldsymbol{\beta}^*), (\tilde{\boldsymbol{\alpha}}, \tilde{\boldsymbol{\beta}})} = \{|\boldsymbol{\Sigma}|/|\boldsymbol{\Gamma}^*(F, \mathbf{J})|\}^{1/p}, \tag{7.6}$$

where in (7.5) and (7.6), we have set $\boldsymbol{\phi} = \mathbf{J}$, and the estimators $\hat{\boldsymbol{\alpha}}$ and $\tilde{\boldsymbol{\alpha}}$ are also adjusted for $\boldsymbol{\beta}$ by the substitution of its estimator $\hat{\boldsymbol{\beta}}_\nu$ and $\tilde{\boldsymbol{\beta}}_\nu$, respectively. Since (7.5) and (7.6) agree with (6.2) and (6.3), respectively, the results of Section 6 also stand valid in this case.

It may be remarked that the results of this section stand valid even if [in (7.1)] $N_\nu^{-1}(C_\nu^*)^2 \to \infty$ as $\nu \to \infty$. Then, (7.5) needs be changed to

$$\begin{aligned} e_{(\boldsymbol{\alpha}^{**}, \boldsymbol{\beta}^*), (\hat{\boldsymbol{\alpha}}, \hat{\boldsymbol{\beta}})} &= \{e_{\boldsymbol{\alpha}^*, \hat{\boldsymbol{\alpha}}} \cdot e_{\boldsymbol{\beta}^*, \hat{\boldsymbol{\beta}}}\}^{1/2} \\ &= [\{|\mathbf{I}(F)||\boldsymbol{\Gamma}^*(F, \mathbf{J})|\}^{-1/p} \mathscr{S}^{-1}\{[|\mathbf{I}(F)||\boldsymbol{\Gamma}^*(F, \boldsymbol{\Phi})|]^{-1/p}\}]^{1/2}, \end{aligned} \tag{7.7}$$

and (7.6) to

$$e_{(\boldsymbol{\alpha}^{**},\boldsymbol{\beta}^{*}),(\tilde{\boldsymbol{\alpha}},\tilde{\boldsymbol{\beta}})} = \{e_{\boldsymbol{\alpha}^{*},\tilde{\boldsymbol{\alpha}}} \cdot e_{\boldsymbol{\beta}^{*},\tilde{\boldsymbol{\beta}}}\}^{1/2}$$
$$= [\{|\boldsymbol{\Sigma}|/|\boldsymbol{\Gamma}^{*}(F, \mathbf{J})|\}^{1/p}\mathscr{S}^{-1}\{[|\boldsymbol{\Sigma}|/|\boldsymbol{\Gamma}^{*}(F, \boldsymbol{\Phi})|]^{1/p}\}]^{1/2}. \tag{7.8}$$

However, if $N_\nu^{-1}(C_\nu{}^{*})^2 \to 0$ as $\nu \to \infty$, (7.4) does not hold, and as a result, $\boldsymbol{\alpha}^{**}$ loses its rationality.

8. CONFIDENCE REGIONS FOR α AND β

The problem of attaching confidence regions for the location parameter in the multivariate one-sample problem and the difference of location parameters in the multivariate two-sample problem, based on robust rank tests, are considered in detail by the authors [21]. The results of this paper suggest that, in the multivariate case, we should either use the Bonferroni inequality to derive separate confidence statements for each component parameter or, in large samples, we may attach nonparametric Scheffé bounds for all the parameters taken together. Since the one-sample problem is already considered by Puri and Sen [21], we shall confine ourselves only to the problem of $\boldsymbol{\beta}$.

(I) Bonferroni-Bounds for β Based on Rank Tests

Define $\mathbf{S}_\nu(\mathbf{b})$ as (5.1). Under the null hypothesis $\beta_j = 0$, $S_{\nu j}(0)$ has a completely specified distribution generated by the $N_\nu!$ equally likely permutations of the observations $X_{\nu 1}^{(j)}, \ldots, X_{\nu N_\nu}^{(j)}$, among themselves. Thus, it is possible to find two values, say, $S_{\nu j}^{(1)}$ and $S_{\nu j}^{(2)}$, such that

$$P\{S_{\nu j}^{(1)} \le S_{\nu j}(0) \le S_{\nu j}^{(2)} \mid \beta_j = 0\} = 1 - \varepsilon_\nu{}^0, \tag{8.1}$$

for $j = 1, \ldots, p$. Let then $\varepsilon_\nu = p\varepsilon_\nu{}^0$. By the Bonferroni inequality, we have then

$$P\{S_{\nu j}^{(1)} \le S_{\nu j}(0) \le S_{\nu j}^{(2)}\ \forall\, j = 1, \ldots, p \mid \beta = 0\} \ge 1 - \varepsilon_\nu. \tag{8.2}$$

Define

$$\beta_{\nu j,U}^{*} = \sup\{b_j:\quad S_{\nu j}(-b_j) \ge S_{\nu j}^{(1)}\} \tag{8.3}$$
$$\beta_{\nu j,L}^{*} = \inf\{b_j:\quad S_{\nu j}(-b_j) \le S_{\nu j}^{(2)}\}. \tag{8.4}$$

Then, from (8.1)–(8.4), we have

$$P\{\beta_{\nu j,L}^{*} \le \beta_j \le \beta_{\nu j,U}^{*}\ \forall\, j = 1, \ldots, p \mid \boldsymbol{\beta}\} \ge 1 - \varepsilon_\nu, \tag{8.5}$$

which provides the desired confidence (rectangular) region for $\boldsymbol{\beta}$. It follows from the results of Puri and Sen [18] that for large ν,

$$S_{\nu j}^{(i)} \cong (-1)^i(\tau_{\varepsilon^0/2})C_\nu{}^{*}\gamma_{jj}(\phi_j), \qquad j = 1, \ldots, p; \quad i = 1, 2; \tag{8.6}$$

where $\varepsilon_\nu{}^0 \to \varepsilon^0$ and τ_α is the $100\alpha\%$ point of a standard normal distribution. Proceeding then exactly as in Theorem 1 of Sen [28] (with straightforward generalizations), it can be shown that as $\nu \to \infty$

$$C_\nu{}^*(\beta^*_{\nu j,U} - \beta^*_{\nu j,L}) \xrightarrow{p} 2\tau_{\varepsilon^0/2}[\gamma_{jj}(\phi_j)]^{1/2}/\{B_j(\phi_j, F)\}, \tag{8.7}$$

for all $j = 1, \ldots, p$. Consequently, we obtain a consistent estimator of $B_j(\phi_j, F)$ as follows:

$$\hat{B}_j(\phi_j, F) = [2\tau_{\varepsilon^0/2}(\gamma_{jj}(\phi_j))^{1/2}]/[C_\nu{}^*(\beta^*_{\nu j,U} - \beta^*_{\nu j,L})], \qquad j = 1, \ldots, p. \tag{8.8}$$

(II) Large Sample Scheffé Bounds for $\boldsymbol{\beta}$

Because of Theorem 5.1, for large samples

$$P\{(C_\nu{}^*)^2[(\boldsymbol{\beta}_\nu{}^* - \boldsymbol{\beta})'[\Gamma(\mathbf{F}, \boldsymbol{\phi})]^{-1}(\boldsymbol{\beta}_\nu{}^* - \boldsymbol{\beta})] \le \chi^2_{p,\varepsilon}\} \simeq 1 - \varepsilon, \tag{8.9}$$

where $\chi^2_{p,\varepsilon}$ is the upper $100\varepsilon\%$ point of the chi-square distribution with p degrees of freedom. Now, in (8.8), we have obtained consistent estimator of $B_j(\phi_j, F), j = 1, \ldots, p$. Also, define

$$\hat{\gamma}_{jl} = (1/N_\nu)\sum_{i=1}^{N_\nu} a^{(j)}_{\nu, \hat{R}_{ij}} a^{(l)}_{\nu, \hat{R}_{il}} \tag{8.10}$$

where $\hat{R}_{ij}$ is the rank of $X^{(j)}_{\nu i} - \beta^*_{\nu j} c_{\nu i}$ among all

$$X^{(j)}_{\nu 1} - \beta^*_{\nu 1} \cdot c_{\nu 1}, \ldots, X^{(j)}_{\nu N_\nu} - \beta^*_{\nu j} \cdot c_{\nu N_\nu}, \quad j = 1, \ldots, p.$$

Proceeding then precisely on the same line as in Theorem 4.2 of Puri and Sen [17], it follows that $\hat{\gamma}_{jl}$ is a consistent estimator of $\gamma_{jl}(\phi_j, \phi_l, F)$ for all $F \in \mathscr{F}_p, j \ne l = 1, \ldots, p$ while $\gamma_{jj}, j = 1, \ldots, p$ are all known. Consequently, we obtain the following consistent estimator for γ^*_{jl}:

$$\hat{\gamma}^*_{jl} = \hat{\gamma}_{jl}/[\hat{B}_j(\phi_j, F)\hat{B}_l(\phi_l, F)], \quad j \ne l = 1, \ldots, p, \tag{8.11}$$

and also

$$\hat{\gamma}^*_{jj} = \gamma_{jj}(\phi_j)/[\hat{B}_j(\phi_j, F)]^2, \quad j = 1, \ldots, p, \tag{8.12}$$

are consistent estimators of $\gamma^*_{jj}, j = 1, \ldots, p$. Thus, in (8.9), we estimate the unknown $\boldsymbol{\Gamma}^*(F, \phi)$ by $\hat{\boldsymbol{\Gamma}}^* = ((\hat{\gamma}^*_{jl}))$, and on substitution, we derive the desired simultaneous confidence bound for $\boldsymbol{\beta}$.

If we compare the Bonferroni bounds in (8.5) with the parametric ones based on the maximum likelihood or the least-squares principle, we again arrive at the ARE's studied in (6.25) and (6.26). The same ARE's are also obtained if we compare the corresponding Scheffé bounds.

When we seek the simultaneous bounds for $(\boldsymbol{\alpha}, \boldsymbol{\beta})$, the Bonferroni bounds follow as in (8.5) and Puri and Sen [21] where $\varepsilon_\nu{}^0$ has to be replaced by $\frac{1}{2}\varepsilon_\nu{}^0$. For the Scheffé bounds, for large ν, we have

$$P\{N_\nu[(\boldsymbol{\alpha}_\nu{}^* - \boldsymbol{\alpha})'[\boldsymbol{\Gamma}^*(F, \mathbf{J})]^{-1}(\boldsymbol{\alpha}_\nu{}^* - \boldsymbol{\alpha})] + (C_\nu{}^*)^2[(\boldsymbol{\beta}_\nu{}^* - \boldsymbol{\beta})'[\boldsymbol{\Gamma}^*(F, \boldsymbol{\phi})]^{-1}(\boldsymbol{\beta}_\nu{}^* - \boldsymbol{\beta})] \leq \mathscr{X}^2_{2p,\,\varepsilon}\} \simeq 1 - \varepsilon, \tag{8.13}$$

and we estimate Γ^* as in (8.11), (8.12), and as by Puri and Sen [21]. The rest of the procedure is simple.

REFERENCES

1. ADICHIE, J. N. (1967). Estimates of regression parameters based on rank tests. *Ann. Math. Statist.* **38** 894–904.
2. BHUCHONGKUL, S., and PURI, M. L. (1965). On the estimation of contrasts in linear models. *Ann. Math. Statist.* **36** 198–202.
3. BICKEL, P. J. (1964). On some alternative estimates of shift in the *p*-variate one sample problem. *Ann. Math. Statist.* **35** 1079–1090.
4. BROWN, G. W., and MOOD, A. M. (1951). On median tests for linear hypotheses. *Proc. Second Berkeley Symp. Math. Statist. Prob.* (J. Neyman, ed.) **1** 159–166. Univ. of California Press, Berkeley, California.
5. CHERNOFF, H., and SAVAGE, I. R. (1958). Asymptotic normality and efficiency of certain nonparametric test statistics. *Ann. Math. Statist.* **29** 972–994.
6. HÁJEK, J. (1962). Asymptotically most powerful rank order tests. *Ann. Math. Statist.* **33** 1124–1147.
7. HÁJEK, J. (1968). Asymptotic normality of simple linear statistics under alternatives. *Ann. Math. Statist.* **39** 325–346.
8. HODGES, JR., J. L., and LEHMANN, E. L. (1963). Estimates of location based on rank tests. *Ann. Math. Statist.* **34** 598–611.
9. HOEFFDING, W. (1948). A class of statistics with asymptotically normal distribution. *Ann. Math. Statist.* **19** 293–325.
10. HOEFFDING, W. (1953). On the distribution of the expected values of the order statistics. *Ann. Math. Statist.* **24** 93–100.
11. HUBER, P. J. (1964). Robust estimation of a location parameter. *Ann. Math. Statist.* **35** 73–101.
12. LEHMANN, E. L. (1963). Robust estimation in analysis of variance. *Ann. Math. Statist.* **34** 957–966.
13. LEHMANN, E. L. (1963). Nonparametric confidence intervals for a shift parameter. *Ann. Math. Statist.* **34** 1507–1512.
14. LEHMANN, E. L. (1964). Asymptotically nonparametric inference in some linear models with one observation per cell. *Ann. Math. Statist.* **35** 726–734.
15. PURI, M. L., and SEN, P. K. (1966). On a class of multivariate multisample rank order tests. *Sankhyā Ser. A* **28** 353–376.
16. PURI, M. L., and SEN, P. K. (1967). On robust estimation in incomplete block designs. *Ann. Math. Statist.* **38** 1587–1591.
17. PURI, M. L., and SEN, P. K. (1967). On some optimum nonparametric procedures in two-way layouts. *J. Amer. Statist. Assoc.* **62** 1214–1229.
18. PURI, M. L., and SEN, P. K. (1969). A class of rank order tests for a general linear hypothesis. *Ann. Math. Statist.* **40** No. 4 (in press).

19. Puri, M. L., and Sen, P. K. (1968). On a class of rank order estimates of contrasts in MANOVA. *Sankhyā Ser. A* **30** 31–36.
20. Puri, M. L., and Sen, P. K. (1968). On Chernoff-Savage tests for ordered alternatives in randomized blocks. *Ann. Math. Statist.* **39** No. 3 967–972.
21. Puri, M. L., and Sen, P. K. (1968). Nonparametric confidence regions for some multivariate location problems. *J. Amer. Statist. Assoc.* **63** 1373–1378.
22. Puri, M. L., and Sen, P. K. (1969). On the estimation of location parameters in the multivariate one sample and two sample problems. *Metrika* (in press).
23. Sarhan, A. E., and Greenberg, B. G., (eds.) (1962). "Order Statistics." Wiley, New York.
24. Sen, P. K. (1963). On the estimation of relative potency in dilution (-direct) assays. *Biometrics* **19** 532–552.
25. Sen, P. K. (1966). On a distribution-free method of estimating asymptotic efficiency of a class of nonparametric tests. *Ann. Math. Statist.* **37** 1759–1770.
26. Sen, P. K. (1966). On nonparametric simultaneous confidence regions and tests for the one criterion analysis of variance problem. *Ann. Inst. Statist. Math.* **18** 319–336.
27. Sen. P. K. (1967). On pooled estimation and testing heterogeneity of shift parameters by distribution-free methods. *Calcutta Statist. Assoc. Bull.* **16** 139–152.
28. Sen, P. K. (1968). Estimates of the regression coefficient based on Kendall's tau. *J. Amer. Statist. Assoc.* **63** 1379–1389.
29. Sen, P. K., and Puri, M. L. (1967). On the theory of rank order tests for location in the multivariate one sample problem. *Ann. Math. Statist.* **38** 1216–1228.
30. Sen, P. K., and Puri, M. L. (1968). On a class of multivariate multisample rank order tests. II. Tests for the homogeneity of dispersion matrices. *Sankhyā Ser. A* **30** 1–22.
31. Theil, H. (1950). A rank invariant method of linear and polynomial regression analysis. *Indag. Math.* **12**, *Fasc. 2*, 85–91, 173–177.
32. Tukey, J. W. (1960). A survey of sampling from contaminated distributions. *In* "Contributions to Probability and Statistics" (I. Olkin *et al.*, eds.). Stanford Univ. Press, Stanford, California.
33. Wald, A. (1943). Tests of statistical hypotheses concerning several parameters when the number of observations is large. *Trans. Amer. Math. Soc.* **54** 426–482.
34. Wilks, S. S. (1962). "Mathematical Statistics." Wiley, New York.

PART II

Multivariate Analysis of Variance and Related Topics

Statistical Inference for Covariance Matrices with Linear Structure

T. W. ANDERSON[1]

DEPARTMENT OF STATISTICS
STANFORD UNIVERSITY
STANFORD, CALIFORNIA

1. INTRODUCTION

We consider a random vector $\mathbf{X}$ of p-components with expected value $\mathscr{E}\mathbf{X} = \boldsymbol{\mu}$ and covariance matrix $\mathscr{E}(\mathbf{X} - \boldsymbol{\mu})(\mathbf{X} - \boldsymbol{\mu})' = \boldsymbol{\Sigma}$. The familiar problem of linear regression arises when the covariance matrix $\boldsymbol{\Sigma}$ is known (to within a constant of proportionality) and the mean vector $\boldsymbol{\mu}$ is assumed to be a linear combination of given vectors

$$\boldsymbol{\mu} = \sum_{j=1}^{r} \beta_j \mathbf{z}_j, \tag{1}$$

where $\beta_1, \ldots, \beta_r$ are unknown coefficients and $\mathbf{z}_1, \ldots, \mathbf{z}_r$ are known p-component vectors. For the sake of convenience in exposition, these vectors are assumed to be linearly independent. On the basis of one observation $\mathbf{x}$ on $\mathbf{X}$, the best linear unbiased estimates or Markov estimates of $\beta_1, \ldots, \beta_r$ are the solution to the "normal equations"

$$\sum_{i=1}^{r} \mathbf{z}_j' \boldsymbol{\Sigma}^{-1} \mathbf{z}_i \hat{\beta}_i = \mathbf{z}_j' \boldsymbol{\Sigma}^{-1} \mathbf{x}, \qquad j = 1, \ldots, r. \tag{2}$$

If $\mathbf{X}$ has a normal distribution, these estimates are maximum likelihood.

In this paper we shall consider statistical inference when the covariance matrix is assumed to be a linear combination of given matrices

$$\boldsymbol{\Sigma} = \sum_{g=0}^{m} \sigma_g \mathbf{G}_g, \tag{3}$$

where $\sigma_0, \sigma_1, \ldots, \sigma_m$ are unknown coefficients and $\mathbf{G}_0, \mathbf{G}_1, \ldots, \mathbf{G}_m$ are known, symmetric, linearly independent $p \times p$ matrices. It is assumed that there is at

[1] This paper was written while the author was at the Mathematics Department of Imperial College of Science and Technology, London, England. The research was partially supported by the United States Air Force under Contract F 41609-67-C-0032. Reproduction in whole or in part is permitted for any purpose of the United States Government.

least one set of coefficients for which (3) is positive definite. We consider the problem of estimating $\sigma_0, \sigma_1, \ldots, \sigma_m$ on the basis of N observations $\mathbf{x}_1, \ldots, \mathbf{x}_N$ on $\mathbf{X}$. In this case we assume that $\mathbf{X}$ has a normal distribution. ($\boldsymbol{\mu}$ is not assumed to be of the form (1).)

Since $\boldsymbol{\Sigma}^{-1} = \boldsymbol{\Psi}$, say, is the matrix of the quadratic form in the normal density

$$(2\pi)^{-p/2} |\boldsymbol{\Sigma}|^{-1/2} \exp[-\tfrac{1}{2}(\mathbf{x} - \boldsymbol{\mu})'\boldsymbol{\Sigma}^{-1}(\mathbf{x} - \boldsymbol{\mu})], \tag{4}$$

we also treat problems of inference when it is assumed that

$$\boldsymbol{\Sigma}^{-1} = \boldsymbol{\Psi} = \sum_{g=0}^{m} \psi_g \mathbf{G}_g, \tag{5}$$

where $\psi_0, \psi_1, \ldots, \psi_m$ are unknown coefficients. It is assumed that there is at least one set of coefficients for which (5) is positive definite.

In this paper we shall review the derivation of the maximum likelihood estimates in the two problems, which was carried out originally by Anderson (1966). The results are developed further here by suitable specialization. The relation between the estimation of $\sigma_0, \sigma_1, \ldots, \sigma_m$ and the Markov estimates of $\beta_1, \ldots, \beta_r$ is shown. Tests that $\boldsymbol{\Sigma}$ or $\boldsymbol{\Sigma}^{-1}$ are of the forms (3) or (5), respectively, are studied. (Tests and multiple decision problems concerning $\psi_0, \psi_1, \ldots, \psi_m$ when (5) is assumed were treated by Anderson (1963).)

Bock and Bargmann (1966) found the maximum likelihood equations when $\boldsymbol{\Sigma} = \mathbf{K}\boldsymbol{\Delta}\mathbf{K}' + \gamma\mathbf{I}$, where $\boldsymbol{\Delta}$ is diagonal, and $\boldsymbol{\Sigma} = \mathbf{K}\boldsymbol{\Delta}\mathbf{K}' + \boldsymbol{\Gamma}$, where $\boldsymbol{\Delta}$ and $\boldsymbol{\Gamma}$ are diagonal; $\mathbf{K}$ is assumed known. These cases arise from the factor analysis model $\mathbf{X} = \boldsymbol{\mu} + \mathbf{K}\mathbf{f} + \mathbf{u}$ where $\mathscr{E}\mathbf{f} = \mathbf{0}$, $\mathscr{E}\mathbf{u} = \mathbf{0}$, $\mathscr{E}\mathbf{f}\mathbf{f}' = \boldsymbol{\Delta}$, $\mathscr{E}\mathbf{f}\mathbf{u}' = \mathbf{0}$, and $\mathscr{E}\mathbf{u}\mathbf{u}' = \gamma\mathbf{I}$ and $\boldsymbol{\Gamma}$ in the two cases, respectively. These forms of $\boldsymbol{\Sigma}$ are (3), where $\mathbf{G}_0 = \mathbf{I}$ and $\mathbf{G}_g = \mathbf{k}_g\mathbf{k}_g'$ and $\mathbf{k}_g$ is the gth column of $\mathbf{K}$, $g = 1, \ldots, m$, in the first case, and where $\mathbf{G}_g$ has 1 in the $(g + 1)$st diagonal position, $g = 0, \ldots, p - 1$, and $\mathbf{G}_g = \mathbf{k}_{g-p+1}\mathbf{k}_{g-p+1}'$, $g = p, \ldots, p + m - 1$, in the second case.

The general problem is considerably simpler if $\mathbf{G}_0, \mathbf{G}_1, \ldots, \mathbf{G}_m$ are simultaneously diagonalized by the same orthogonal matrix; that is,

$$\mathbf{G}_g = \mathbf{P}\boldsymbol{\Lambda}_g\mathbf{P}', \qquad g = 0, 1, \ldots, m, \tag{6}$$

where $\mathbf{P}\mathbf{P}' = \mathbf{I}$ and $\boldsymbol{\Lambda}_g$ is diagonal. Then $\boldsymbol{\Sigma} = \mathbf{P}(\sum_{g=0}^{m} \sigma_g \boldsymbol{\Lambda}_g)\mathbf{P}'$ is diagonalized by $\mathbf{P}$. Srivastava (1966) has obtained the maximum likelihood equations in this case, but in general they are much more complicated than the equations obtained in the present paper. Graybill and Hultquist (1961) obtained some results when the $\mathbf{G}_g$'s are generated by certain components of variance models, and they obtained estimates when $m + 1$ is equal to the number of distinct characteristic roots of $\boldsymbol{\Sigma}$. Herbach (1959) treated some special cases (based on his Columbia dissertation).

2. MAXIMUM LIKELIHOOD ESTIMATES OF THE COEFFICIENTS IN THE COVARIANCE MATRIX

A sufficient set of statistics for $\boldsymbol{\mu}$ and $\sigma_0, \sigma_1, \ldots, \sigma_m$ are

$$\bar{\mathbf{x}} = (1/N) \sum_{\alpha=1}^{N} \mathbf{x}_\alpha, \qquad \mathbf{C} = (1/N) \sum_{\alpha=1}^{N} (\mathbf{x}_\alpha - \bar{\mathbf{x}})(\mathbf{x}_\alpha - \bar{\mathbf{x}})'. \tag{7}$$

The logarithm of the likelihood function is proportional to

$$(2/N) \log L = -p \log (2\pi) - \log|\boldsymbol{\Sigma}| - \operatorname{tr} \boldsymbol{\Sigma}^{-1}\mathbf{C} - (\bar{\mathbf{x}} - \boldsymbol{\mu})'\boldsymbol{\Sigma}^{-1}(\bar{\mathbf{x}} - \boldsymbol{\mu}). \tag{8}$$

Since $\boldsymbol{\Sigma}$ is assumed positive definite, $\boldsymbol{\Sigma}^{-1}$ is positive definite; (8) is maximized with respect to $\boldsymbol{\mu}$ at $\hat{\boldsymbol{\mu}} = \bar{\mathbf{x}}$ and the last term is then 0. The logarithm of the reduced likelihood function is proportional to

$$-p \log (2\pi) - \log |\boldsymbol{\Sigma}| - \operatorname{tr} \boldsymbol{\Sigma}^{-1}\mathbf{C}. \tag{9}$$

The maximization of (8) with respect to $\sigma_0, \sigma_1, \ldots, \sigma_m$ is carried out by differentiating (9) with respect to these variables. From $\sigma_{ij} = \sum_{h=0}^{m} \sigma_h g_{ij}^{(h)}$, we obtain

$$\partial\sigma_{ij}/\partial\sigma_g = g_{ij}^{(g)}, \qquad i, j = 1, \ldots, p.$$

We write these equations in matrix form as

$$\frac{\partial}{\partial\sigma_g}\boldsymbol{\Sigma} = \mathbf{G}_g, \qquad g = 0, 1, \ldots, m. \tag{10}$$

From $\mathbf{I} = \boldsymbol{\Sigma}\boldsymbol{\Sigma}^{-1}$, we find

$$\mathbf{0} = \frac{\partial}{\partial\sigma_g}\mathbf{I} = \left(\frac{\partial}{\partial\sigma_g}\boldsymbol{\Sigma}\right)\boldsymbol{\Sigma}^{-1} + \boldsymbol{\Sigma}\left(\frac{\partial}{\partial\sigma_g}\boldsymbol{\Sigma}^{-1}\right); \tag{11}$$

then

$$\frac{\partial}{\partial\sigma_g}\boldsymbol{\Sigma}^{-1} = -\boldsymbol{\Sigma}^{-1}\left(\frac{\partial}{\partial\sigma_g}\boldsymbol{\Sigma}\right)\boldsymbol{\Sigma}^{-1} = -\boldsymbol{\Sigma}^{-1}\mathbf{G}_g\boldsymbol{\Sigma}^{-1}. \tag{12}$$

We also use

$$\frac{\partial \log|\boldsymbol{\Sigma}|}{\partial\sigma_g} = \sum_{i,j=1}^{p} \frac{\partial \log|\boldsymbol{\Sigma}|}{\partial\sigma_{ij}} \frac{\partial\sigma_{ij}}{\partial\sigma_g} = \sum_{i,j=1}^{p} (\operatorname{cof} \sigma_{ij}/|\boldsymbol{\Sigma}|) g_{ij}^{(g)} = \sum_{i,j=1}^{p} \sigma^{ij} g_{ij}^{(g)}$$
$$= \operatorname{tr} \boldsymbol{\Sigma}^{-1}\mathbf{G}_g; \tag{13}$$

here cof σ_{ij} denotes the cofactor of σ_{ij} in $|\boldsymbol{\Sigma}|$ and σ^{ij} is the i, j-th element of $\boldsymbol{\Sigma}^{-1}$.

The derivatives of (9) are $-\operatorname{tr} \boldsymbol{\Sigma}^{-1}\mathbf{G}_g + \operatorname{tr} \boldsymbol{\Sigma}^{-1}\mathbf{G}_g\boldsymbol{\Sigma}^{-1}\mathbf{C}$, and the equations for the maximum likelihood estimates are

$$\operatorname{tr}\Big(\sum_{h=0}^{m} \hat{\sigma}_h \mathbf{G}_h\Big)^{-1} \mathbf{G}_g = \operatorname{tr}\Big(\sum_{h=0}^{m} \hat{\sigma}_h \mathbf{G}_h\Big)^{-1} \mathbf{G}_g\Big(\sum_{h=0}^{m} \hat{\sigma}_h \mathbf{G}_h\Big)^{-1} \mathbf{C}, \qquad g = 0, 1, \ldots, m. \tag{14}$$

There is at least one solution for which $\sum_{h=0}^{m} \hat{\sigma}_h \mathbf{G}_h$ is positive definite if $\mathbf{C}$ is positive definite; if there is more than one such solution, we take the solution that maximizes (9). In Anderson (1966), iterative solutions for (14) are obtained and the information matrix is derived.

Now let us suppose that $\mathbf{G}_0, \mathbf{G}_1, \ldots, \mathbf{G}_m$ can be diagonalized by the orthogonal matrix $\mathbf{P}$ as in (6). (A necessary and sufficient condition is that $\mathbf{G}_g \mathbf{G}_h = \mathbf{G}_h \mathbf{G}_g$, $g, h = 0, 1, \ldots, m$.) Let the jth diagonal element of $\boldsymbol{\Lambda}_g$ be λ_{jg}. Define $\mathbf{V}$ by $\mathbf{C} = \mathbf{PVP}'$ or equivalently

$$\mathbf{V} = \mathbf{P}'\mathbf{CP}. \tag{15}$$

If we substitute into (14) and use the fact that $\operatorname{tr} \mathbf{AB} = \operatorname{tr} \mathbf{BA}$, we obtain

$$\operatorname{tr}\Big(\sum_{h=0}^{m} \hat{\sigma}_h \boldsymbol{\Lambda}_h\Big)^{-1} \boldsymbol{\Lambda}_g = \operatorname{tr}\Big(\sum_{h=0}^{m} \hat{\sigma}_h \boldsymbol{\Lambda}_h\Big)^{-1} \boldsymbol{\Lambda}_g\Big(\sum_{h=0}^{m} \hat{\sigma}_h \boldsymbol{\Lambda}_h\Big)^{-1} \mathbf{V}, \qquad g = 0, 1, \ldots, m. \tag{16}$$

In other terms, we can write (16) as

$$\sum_{j=1}^{p} \frac{\lambda_{jg}}{\sum_{h=0}^{m} \hat{\sigma}_h \lambda_{jh}} = \sum_{j=1}^{p} \frac{\lambda_{jg} v_{jj}}{(\sum_{h=0}^{m} \hat{\sigma}_h \lambda_{jh})^2}, \qquad g = 0, 1, \ldots, m. \tag{17}$$

If the substitutions are made in the likelihood function, it will be seen that $\bar{\mathbf{x}}$ and $v_{11}, \ldots, v_{pp}$, the diagonal elements of $\mathbf{V}$, are a sufficient set of statistics. Iterative solutions for (16) were considered in Anderson (1966).

The equations may be reduced by taking account of the multiplicities of the roots. Write $\boldsymbol{\Lambda}_g$ as

$$\boldsymbol{\Lambda}_g = \begin{bmatrix} \nu_{1g}\mathbf{I} & \mathbf{0} & \cdots & \mathbf{0} \\ \mathbf{0} & \nu_{2g}\mathbf{I} & \cdots & \mathbf{0} \\ \vdots & \vdots & & \vdots \\ \mathbf{0} & \mathbf{0} & \cdots & \nu_{ng}\mathbf{I} \end{bmatrix}, \tag{18}$$

where the orders of the $\mathbf{I}$'s on the main diagonal are $p_1, p_2, \ldots, p_n$, respectively, and the p_k's do not depend on g. ($p_1 + p_2 + \cdots + p_n = p$.) Define $V_1, \ldots, V_n$ by

$$p_1 V_1 = \sum_{j=1}^{p_1} v_{jj}, \quad p_2 V_2 = \sum_{j=p_1+1}^{p_1+p_2} v_{jj}, \quad \ldots, \quad p_n V_n = \sum_{j=p-p_n+1}^{p} v_{jj}. \tag{19}$$

Substitution of (18) and (19) into (17) gives

$$\sum_{k=1}^{n} \frac{p_k v_{kg}}{\sum_{h=0}^{m} \hat{\sigma}_h v_{kh}} = \sum_{k=1}^{n} \frac{p_k v_{kg} V_k}{\left(\sum_{h=0}^{m} \hat{\sigma}_h v_{kh}\right)^2}, \qquad g = 0, 1, \ldots, m. \tag{20}$$

Making the substitutions in the likelihood function shows that $\bar{\mathbf{x}}, V_1, \ldots, V_n$ are a sufficient set of statistics.

Srivastava (1966) gives equations similar to (20) (Eq. (5.18) in his paper), but his definition of V_k (θ_r in his notation) is indirect; in fact, it requires augmenting $\mathbf{G}_0, \mathbf{G}_1, \ldots, \mathbf{G}_m$ by $n - (m + 1)$ other matrices. How complicated his definition is may be indicated by the fact that a second paper, Srivastava and Maik (1967), was devoted to showing $V_k > 0$ under special conditions.

An essential simplification occurs if $n = m + 1$. Then the equations

$$\sum_{h=0}^{m} \hat{\sigma}_h v_{kh} = V_k, \qquad k = 1, \ldots, n, \tag{21}$$

can be solved for $\hat{\sigma}_0, \hat{\sigma}_1, \ldots, \hat{\sigma}_m$. (Since $\mathbf{G}_0, \mathbf{G}_1, \ldots, \mathbf{G}_m$ are linearly independent, $\mathbf{\Lambda}_0, \mathbf{\Lambda}_1, \ldots, \mathbf{\Lambda}_m$ are linearly independent and the matrix of coefficients in (21) is nonsingular.) Substitution in (20) verifies that this set of values provides a solution to the likelihood equations. If we consider the transformed variable, $\mathbf{Z} = \mathbf{P}'\mathbf{X}$, the individual components of $\mathbf{Z}$ are independently distributed and $\sum_{h=0}^{m} \sigma_h v_{kh}$ is the variance of the components in the kth set of components. Since

$$\mathbf{V} = (1/N) \sum_{\alpha=1}^{N} \mathbf{z}_\alpha \mathbf{z}_\alpha',$$

$V_1, \ldots, V_n$ are the unique maximum likelihood estimates of the n variances. The set $\hat{\sigma}_0, \hat{\sigma}_1, \ldots, \hat{\sigma}_m$ is a one-to-one transformation of these estimates.

In this case it is easy to verify that Srivastava's solution (1966) is equivalent to the one given here.

3. LIKELIHOOD RATIO CRITERIA FOR THE HYPOTHESIS THAT THE COVARIANCE MATRIX IS A LINEAR COMBINATION

The likelihood ratio criterion for the hypothesis that (3) holds for some $\sigma_0, \sigma_1, \ldots, \sigma_m$ is the ratio of the likelihood function maximized under this null hypothesis to the likelihood function maximized under the hypothesis that $\mathbf{\Sigma}$ is unrestricted. In the latter case the maximized likelihood function is

$$(2\pi)^{-pN/2} |\mathbf{C}|^{-N/2} e^{-pN/2}. \tag{22}$$

(See Section 3.2 of Anderson (1958), for example.) If we multiply (14) by $\hat{\sigma}_g$ and sum over g, we obtain

$$p = \operatorname{tr}\left(\sum_{h=0}^{m} \hat{\sigma}_h \mathbf{G}_h\right)^{-1} \mathbf{C}. \tag{23}$$

Hence, the likelihood function maximized when (3) holds is

$$(2\pi)^{-pN/2}\left|\sum_{h=0}^{m}\hat{\sigma}_h \mathbf{G}_h\right|^{-N/2} e^{-pN/2}. \tag{24}$$

Thus, the likelihood ratio criterion is the $\frac{1}{2}N$th power of

$$|\mathbf{C}|\left|\sum_{h=0}^{m}\hat{\sigma}_h \mathbf{G}_h\right|^{-1}. \tag{25}$$

Under the null hypothesis $-N$ times the logarithm of (25) has a limiting χ^2-distribution with $\frac{1}{2}p(p+1)-(m+1)$ degrees of freedom.

If $\mathbf{G}_0, \mathbf{G}_1, \ldots, \mathbf{G}_m$ can be diagonalized by the same orthogonal matrix $\mathbf{P}$, the likelihood ratio criterion is the $\frac{1}{2}N$th power of

$$|\mathbf{C}|\left[\prod_{j=1}^{p}\left(\sum_{h=0}^{m}\hat{\sigma}_h \lambda_{jh}\right)\right]^{-1}. \tag{26}$$

If $\mathbf{\Lambda}_g$ has the form (18), $g = 0, 1, \ldots, m$, the likelihood ratio criterion is the $\frac{1}{2}N$th power of

$$|\mathbf{C}|\left[\prod_{k=1}^{n}\left(\sum_{h=0}^{m}\hat{\sigma}_h \nu_{kh}\right)^{p_k}\right]^{-1}. \tag{27}$$

If $n = m + 1$, the likelihood ratio criterion is the $\frac{1}{2}N$th power of

$$|\mathbf{C}|\left[\prod_{k=1}^{n} V_k^{p_k}\right]^{-1}. \tag{28}$$

As pointed out by Srivastava (1966), the null hypothesis can be considered as the hypothesis that $\mathbf{Z} = \mathbf{P}'\mathbf{X}$ has a diagonal covariance matrix and that this diagonal covariance matrix has the form $\sum_{g=0}^{m}\sigma_g \mathbf{\Lambda}_g$. The likelihood ratio criterion for the null hypothesis is the product of the criterion that the covariance matrix is diagonal and the criterion that it is of the form $\sum_{g=0}^{m}\sigma_g \mathbf{\Lambda}_g$, given it is diagonal. If the covariance matrix is diagonal, the two criteria are independently distributed. The criterion for diagonality is the criterion of independence of the components of $\mathbf{Z}$ and has been studied considerably (Anderson (1958), Chapter 9, for example). In the case of $n = m + 1$, the hypothesis that the diagonal covariance matrix has the special form is the hypothesis that the variance of the components of $\mathbf{Z}$ are equal in the sets of $p_1, \ldots, p_n$ components.

4. MAXIMUM LIKELIHOOD ESTIMATES AND MARKOV ESTIMATES

We shall now show that the likelihood equations (14) for the coefficients for covariance matrices of the normal distribution are equivalent to the normal equations (2) for the coefficients for mean vectors. If $\mathbf{X}$ has a normal distribution, the covariance between two elements of $\mathbf{C}$ is

$$\text{Cov}\,(c_{ij}, c_{kl}) = [(N-1)/N^2](\sigma_{ik}\sigma_{jl} + \sigma_{il}\sigma_{jk}). \tag{29}$$

(See Anderson (1958), Section 4.2.3, for example.) We see that the covariance is quadratic in the elements of $\mathbf{\Sigma}$.

Theorem. *If*

$$\mathbf{c} = \begin{pmatrix} c_{11} \\ c_{22} \\ \vdots \\ c_{pp} \\ c_{12} \\ \vdots \\ c_{p-1,p} \end{pmatrix}, \qquad \mathbf{g}_h = \begin{pmatrix} g_{11}^{(h)} \\ g_{22}^{(h)} \\ \vdots \\ g_{pp}^{(h)} \\ g_{12}^{(h)} \\ \vdots \\ g_{p-1,p}^{(h)} \end{pmatrix}, \tag{30}$$

each of $\frac{1}{2}p(p+1)$ *components, and* $\mathbf{\Phi}$ *is* $N^2/(N-1)$ *times the covariance matrix of* $\mathbf{c}$, *then*

$$\mathbf{g}_h'\mathbf{\Phi}^{-1}\mathbf{c} = \tfrac{1}{2}\,\text{tr}\,\mathbf{\Sigma}^{-1}\mathbf{C}\mathbf{\Sigma}^{-1}\mathbf{G}_h, \qquad h = 0, 1, \ldots, m. \tag{31}$$

Proof. The linear transformation $\mathbf{X} = \mathbf{A}\mathbf{X}^*$, where $\mathbf{A}$ is nonsingular, induces the linear transformations $\mathbf{\Sigma} = \mathbf{C}\mathbf{\Sigma}^*\mathbf{C}'$, $\mathbf{C} = \mathbf{A}\mathbf{C}^*\mathbf{A}'$, and $\mathbf{G}_h = \mathbf{A}\mathbf{G}_h{}^*\mathbf{A}'$, $h = 0, 1, \ldots, m$; the last transformations can be written as $\mathbf{c} = \mathbf{B}\mathbf{c}^*$ and $\mathbf{g}_h = \mathbf{B}\mathbf{g}_h{}^*$ for a suitable nonsingular matrix $\mathbf{B}$, and $\mathbf{\Phi} = \mathbf{B}\mathbf{\Phi}^*\mathbf{B}'$. Both sides of (31) are invariant under the transformation. Since there is a matrix $\mathbf{A}$ to make $\mathbf{\Sigma}^* = \mathbf{I}$, we need only verify (31) for $\mathbf{\Sigma} = \mathbf{I}$. Then (29) is

$$\text{Cov}(c_{ij}, c_{kl}) = [(N-1)/N^2](\delta_{ik}\delta_{jl} + \delta_{il}\delta_{jk}), \tag{32}$$

which may be summarized as

$$\mathbf{\Phi} = \begin{pmatrix} 2\mathbf{I} & \mathbf{0} \\ \mathbf{0} & \mathbf{I} \end{pmatrix}. \tag{33}$$

Then the left-hand side of (31) is

$$\mathbf{g}_h'\mathbf{\Phi}^{-1}\mathbf{c} = \tfrac{1}{2}\sum_{j=1}^{p} g_{jj}^{(h)}c_{jj} + \sum_{\substack{i,j=1 \\ i<j}}^{p} g_{ij}^{(h)}c_{ij} = \tfrac{1}{2}\sum_{i,j=1}^{p} g_{ij}^{(h)}c_{ij} = \tfrac{1}{2}\,\text{tr}\,\mathbf{G}_h\mathbf{C}, \tag{34}$$

which is the right-hand side of (31) for $\mathbf{\Sigma} = \mathbf{I}$. Q.E.D.

The analog of the normal equations (2) is

$$\sum_{f=0}^{m} \hat{\sigma}_f \operatorname{tr} \hat{\boldsymbol{\Sigma}}^{-1}\mathbf{G}_g \hat{\boldsymbol{\Sigma}}^{-1}\mathbf{G}_f = \operatorname{tr} \hat{\boldsymbol{\Sigma}}^{-1}\mathbf{G}_g \hat{\boldsymbol{\Sigma}}^{-1}\mathbf{C}, \qquad g = 0, 1, \ldots, m; \tag{35}$$

here the covariance matrix $\boldsymbol{\Sigma}$ is replaced by its estimate $\hat{\boldsymbol{\Sigma}} = \sum_{h=0}^{m} \hat{\sigma}_h \mathbf{G}_h$. The equations (35) are identical to the maximum likelihood equations (14).

In the case of linear structure for $\boldsymbol{\mu}$ with $\boldsymbol{\Sigma}$ known, the Markov estimates are the values $\beta_1, \ldots, \beta_r$ that minimize

$$\left(\mathbf{x} - \sum_{j=1}^{r} \beta_j \mathbf{z}_j\right)' \boldsymbol{\Sigma}^{-1} \left(\mathbf{x} - \sum_{j=1}^{r} \beta_j \mathbf{z}_j\right), \tag{36}$$

where $\mathbf{x}$ is replaced by $\bar{\mathbf{x}}$ if there is more than one observation. Similarly, minimization of the analog

$$\operatorname{tr} \boldsymbol{\Sigma}^{-1}\left(\mathbf{C} - \sum_{h=0}^{m} \sigma_h \mathbf{G}_h\right) \boldsymbol{\Sigma}^{-1} \left(\mathbf{C} - \sum_{h=0}^{m} \sigma_h \mathbf{G}_h\right) \tag{37}$$

with respect to $\sigma_0, \sigma_1, \ldots, \sigma_m$ (where $\boldsymbol{\Sigma}$ is not treated as a function of $\sigma_0, \sigma_1, \ldots, \sigma_m$) yields (14).

5. MAXIMUM LIKELIHOOD ESTIMATES OF THE COEFFICIENTS IN THE INVERSE OF THE COVARIANCE MATRIX

When (5) holds, it is convenient to write the logarithm of the reduced likelihood function as proportional to

$$\begin{aligned} &-p \log(2\pi) + \log|\boldsymbol{\Psi}| - \operatorname{tr} \boldsymbol{\Psi}\mathbf{C} \\ &\quad = -p \log(2\pi) + \log\left|\sum_{g=0}^{m} \psi_g \mathbf{G}_g\right| - \sum_{g=0}^{m} \psi_g \operatorname{tr} \mathbf{G}_g \mathbf{C}. \end{aligned} \tag{38}$$

It will be observed that $\bar{\mathbf{x}}$ and $\operatorname{tr} \mathbf{G}_0 \mathbf{C}$, $\operatorname{tr} \mathbf{G}_1\mathbf{C}, \ldots, \operatorname{tr} \mathbf{G}_m \mathbf{C}$ form a sufficient set of statistics for $\boldsymbol{\mu}$ and $\psi_0, \psi_1, \ldots, \psi_m$. The derivative of (38) with respect to ψ_g is $\operatorname{tr} \boldsymbol{\Psi}^{-1}\mathbf{G}_g + \operatorname{tr} \mathbf{G}_g \mathbf{C}$. The likelihood equations are

$$\operatorname{tr}\left(\sum_{h=0}^{m} \hat{\psi}_h \mathbf{G}_h\right)^{-1} \mathbf{G}_g = \operatorname{tr} \mathbf{G}_g \mathbf{C}, \qquad g = 0, 1, \ldots, m. \tag{39}$$

Because the distributions constitute an exponential family, there is a unique set of maximum likelihood estimates. Iterative solutions for (39) and the information matrix were obtained by Anderson (1966).

If $\mathbf{G}_0, \mathbf{G}_1, \ldots, \mathbf{G}_m$ can be diagonalized by the same diagonal matrix $\mathbf{P}$, the likelihood equations can be written

$$\sum_{j=1}^{p} \frac{\lambda_{jg}}{\sum_{h=0}^{m} \hat{\psi}_h \lambda_{jh}} = \sum_{j=1}^{p} \lambda_{jg} v_{jj}, \qquad g = 0, 1, \ldots, m. \tag{40}$$

If $\mathbf{\Lambda}_g$ has the form (18), $g = 0, 1, \ldots, m$, the likelihood equations reduce to

$$\sum_{k=1}^{n} \frac{p_k \nu_{kg}}{\sum_{h=0}^{m} \hat{\psi}_h \nu_{kh}} = \sum_{k=1}^{n} p_k \nu_{kg} V_k, \qquad g = 0, 1, \ldots, m. \tag{41}$$

If $n = m + 1$, the unique solution for $\hat{\psi}_0, \hat{\psi}_1, \ldots, \hat{\psi}_m$ is the solution of the set of linear equations

$$\sum_{h=0}^{m} \hat{\psi}_h \nu_{kh} = V_k^{-1}, \qquad k = 1, \ldots, n. \tag{42}$$

If $\mathbf{G}_0, \mathbf{G}_1, \ldots, \mathbf{G}_m$ can be diagonalized by the same diagonal matrix $\mathbf{P}$ and $n = m + 1$, then (3) is equivalent to (5). The variance of the components in the kth set of components of $\mathbf{Z} = \mathbf{P}'\mathbf{X}$ is

$$\sum_{h=0}^{m} \sigma_h \nu_{kh} = \left(\sum_{h=0}^{m} \psi_h \nu_{kh} \right)^{-1}, \qquad k = 1, \ldots, n. \tag{43}$$

6. LIKELIHOOD RATIO CRITERIA FOR THE HYPOTHESIS THAT THE INVERSE OF A COVARIANCE MATRIX IS A LINEAR COMBINATION

If we multiply (39) by $\hat{\psi}_g$ and sum over g, we obtain

$$p = \operatorname{tr} \sum_{h=0}^{m} \hat{\psi}_h \mathbf{G}_h \mathbf{C}. \tag{44}$$

The likelihood ratio criterion for testing the hypothesis that $\mathbf{\Sigma}^{-1}$ is a linear combination of specified $\mathbf{G}_0, \mathbf{G}_1, \ldots, \mathbf{G}_m$ is the $\frac{1}{2}N$th power of

$$|\mathbf{C}| \cdot \left| \sum_{h=0}^{m} \hat{\psi}_h \mathbf{G}_h \right|. \tag{45}$$

Under the null hypothesis $-N$ times the logarithm of (45) has a limiting χ^2-distribution with $\frac{1}{2}p(p + 1) - (m + 1)$ degrees of freedom.

If $\mathbf{G}_0, \mathbf{G}_1, \ldots, \mathbf{G}_m$ can be diagonalized by the same orthogonal matrix $\mathbf{P}$, the likelihood ratio criterion is the $\frac{1}{2}N$th power of

$$|\mathbf{C}| \prod_{j=1}^{p} \left(\sum_{h=0}^{m} \hat{\psi}_h \lambda_{jh} \right). \tag{46}$$

If $\mathbf{\Lambda}_g$ has the form (18), $g = 0, 1, \ldots, m$, the criterion is the $\frac{1}{2}N$th power of

$$|\mathbf{C}| \prod_{k=1}^{n} \left(\sum_{h=0}^{m} \hat{\psi}_h \nu_{kh} \right)^{p_k}. \tag{47}$$

If $n = m + 1$, the criterion is the $\frac{1}{2}N$th power of (28).

7. AN EXAMPLE

Olkin and Press (1969) and Srivastava (1966) have considered cases of circular symmetry. Suppose an experimenter has an apparatus surrounded by p observation posts symmetrically placed. For instance, if $p = 6$, the observations are made at the vertices of a hexagon, and the apparatus is at the center. The experimenter may wish to test the null hypothesis that the observation posts yield symmetrical observations in the sense that the correlation between observations at all adjacent posts is the same, between observations at all pairs two apart is the same, etc. If the hypothesis is true, the covariance matrix is of the form (3) with the $\mathbf{G}_g$'s as symmetric circulants. When $p = 6$, $\mathbf{G}_0 = \mathbf{I}$,

$$\mathbf{G}_1 = \begin{pmatrix} 0 & 1 & 0 & 0 & 0 & 1 \\ 1 & 0 & 1 & 0 & 0 & 0 \\ 0 & 1 & 0 & 1 & 0 & 0 \\ 0 & 0 & 1 & 0 & 1 & 0 \\ 0 & 0 & 0 & 1 & 0 & 1 \\ 1 & 0 & 0 & 0 & 1 & 0 \end{pmatrix}, \tag{48}$$

$$\mathbf{G}_2 = \begin{pmatrix} 0 & 0 & 1 & 0 & 1 & 0 \\ 0 & 0 & 0 & 1 & 0 & 1 \\ 1 & 0 & 0 & 0 & 1 & 0 \\ 0 & 1 & 0 & 0 & 0 & 1 \\ 1 & 0 & 1 & 0 & 0 & 0 \\ 0 & 1 & 0 & 1 & 0 & 0 \end{pmatrix}, \tag{49}$$

$$\mathbf{G}_3 = \begin{pmatrix} 0 & 0 & 0 & 1 & 0 & 0 \\ 0 & 0 & 0 & 0 & 1 & 0 \\ 0 & 0 & 0 & 0 & 0 & 1 \\ 1 & 0 & 0 & 0 & 0 & 0 \\ 0 & 1 & 0 & 0 & 0 & 0 \\ 0 & 0 & 1 & 0 & 0 & 0 \end{pmatrix}. \tag{50}$$

The matrices are diagonalized by the orthogonal matrix whose jth row is

$$6^{-1/2}[1, \sqrt{2}\cos(\pi j/3), \sqrt{2}\sin(\pi j/3), \sqrt{2}\cos(2\pi j/3), \sqrt{2}\sin(2\pi j/3), (-1)^j]. \tag{51}$$

The roots of $\mathbf{G}_0$ are 1, of $\mathbf{G}_1$ are 1, $\cos \pi/3$, $\cos \pi/3$, $\cos 2\pi/3$, $\cos 2\pi/3$, -1, of $\mathbf{G}_2$ are 1, $\cos 2\pi/3$, $\cos 2\pi/3$, $\cos 4\pi/3$, $\cos 4\pi/3$, 1, and of $\mathbf{G}_3$ are 1, -1, -1, 1, 1, -1. Thus $p_1 = 1$, $p_2 = 2$, $p_3 = 2$, $p_4 = 1$, and $n = 4 = m + 1$.

8. ON COMPUTATION OF ESTIMATES

It was shown (Anderson (1966)) that a possible iterative solution of (14) is $\hat{\mathbf{\Sigma}}_i = \sum_{h=0}^{m} \hat{\sigma}_h^{(i)}\mathbf{G}_h$, where

$$\hat{\sigma}_h^{(i)} = \hat{\sigma}_h^{(i-1)} + r_h^{(i)},$$

$r_0^{(i)}, r_1^{(i)}, \ldots, r_m^{(i)}$ is the solution of

$$\sum_{h=0}^{m} r_h^{(i)} \operatorname{tr} \hat{\mathbf{\Sigma}}_{i-1}^{-1}\mathbf{G}_h[2\hat{\mathbf{\Sigma}}_{i-1}^{-1}\mathbf{C}\hat{\mathbf{\Sigma}}_{i-1}^{-1} - \hat{\mathbf{\Sigma}}_{i-1}^{-1}]\mathbf{G}_g = \operatorname{tr}[\hat{\mathbf{\Sigma}}_{i-1}^{-1}\mathbf{C}\hat{\mathbf{\Sigma}}_{i-1}^{-1} - \hat{\mathbf{\Sigma}}_{i-1}^{-1}]\mathbf{G}_g, \qquad g = 0, 1, \ldots, m, \tag{52}$$

and $\hat{\sigma}_0^{(0)}, \hat{\sigma}_1^{(0)}, \ldots, \hat{\sigma}_m^{(0)}$ is a suitable set of initial values. If $\hat{\mathbf{\Sigma}}_{i-1}^{-1} = \mathbf{K}_i\mathbf{K}_i'$, the equations can be written

$$\sum_{h=0}^{m} r_h^{(i)}[2 \operatorname{tr}(\mathbf{K}_i'\mathbf{G}_h\mathbf{K}_i)(\mathbf{K}_i'\mathbf{C}\mathbf{K}_i)(\mathbf{K}_i'\mathbf{G}_g\mathbf{K}_i) - \operatorname{tr}(\mathbf{K}_i'\mathbf{G}_h\mathbf{K}_i)(\mathbf{K}_i'\mathbf{G}_g\mathbf{K}_i)] = \operatorname{tr}(\mathbf{K}_i'\mathbf{C}\mathbf{K}_i)(\mathbf{K}_i'\mathbf{G}_g\mathbf{K}_i) - \operatorname{tr}(\mathbf{K}_i'\mathbf{G}_g\mathbf{K}_i), \qquad g = 0, 1, \ldots, m. \tag{53}$$

The forward solution of $\hat{\mathbf{\Sigma}}_{i-1}\mathbf{X} = \mathbf{I}$ by any method of pivotal condensation gives $\mathbf{F}\hat{\mathbf{\Sigma}}_{i-1}\mathbf{X} = \mathbf{T}\mathbf{X} = \mathbf{F}$, where $\mathbf{F}$ is triangular with 1's on the main diagonal and $\mathbf{T}$ is triangular. Division of each row of $\mathbf{F}$ by the corresponding diagonal element of $\mathbf{T}$ yields the corresponding row of $\mathbf{K}_i'$, which is lower-left triangular. Thus, the backward solution of the inversion is not needed.

If $\hat{\sigma}_0^{(0)}, \hat{\sigma}_1^{(0)}, \ldots, \hat{\sigma}_m^{(0)}$ is a set of consistent estimate and $\hat{\sigma}_h^{(0)} = O_p(N^{-1/2})$, then $\hat{\sigma}_0^{(1)}, \hat{\sigma}_1^{(1)}, \ldots, \hat{\sigma}_m^{(1)}$ is a set of (asymptotically) efficient estimates. In fact, in the left-hand side of (52) for $i = 0$, $\hat{\mathbf{\Sigma}}_0$ may be any consistent estimate of $\mathbf{\Sigma}$. For example, such an estimate is $\mathbf{C}$ and the coefficient of r_h is $\operatorname{tr} \mathbf{C}^{-1}\mathbf{G}_h\mathbf{C}^{-1}\mathbf{G}_g$.

The matrix of coefficients on the left-hand side of (52) will be positive definite if $2\mathbf{C} - \hat{\mathbf{\Sigma}}_{i-1}$ is positive definite. (The corresponding matrix in (3.9) of Anderson (1966) for the case that $\mathbf{G}_0, \mathbf{G}_1, \ldots, \mathbf{G}_m$ are diagonalized by the same orthogonal matrix is positive definite if $2v_k > \hat{v}_k{}^0$ for each k.)

An iterative solution of (39) in the second case is

$$\hat{\mathbf{\Psi}}_i = \sum_{h=0}^{m} \hat{\psi}_h^{(i)}\mathbf{G}_h,$$

where

$$\hat{\sigma}_h^{(i)} = \hat{\sigma}_h^{(i-1)} + t_h^{(i)},$$

$t_0^{(i)}, t_1^{(i)}, \ldots, t_m^{(i)}$ is the solution of

$$\sum_{g=0}^{m} t_g^{(i)} \operatorname{tr} \hat{\mathbf{\Psi}}_{i-1}^{-1}\mathbf{G}_g\hat{\mathbf{\Psi}}_{i-1}^{-1}\mathbf{G}_h = \operatorname{tr} \hat{\mathbf{\Psi}}_{i-1}^{-1}\mathbf{G}_h - \operatorname{tr} \mathbf{C}\mathbf{G}_h, \qquad h = 0, 1, \ldots, m, \tag{54}$$

and $\hat{\psi}_0^{(0)}, \hat{\psi}_1^{(0)}, \ldots, \hat{\psi}_m^{(0)}$ is a suitable set of initial values. If $\hat{\mathbf{\Psi}}_{i-1}^{-1} = \mathbf{L}_i \mathbf{L}_i'$, the equations can be written

$$\sum_{g=0}^{m} t_g^{(i)} \operatorname{tr}(\mathbf{L}_i'\mathbf{G}_g \mathbf{L}_i)(\mathbf{L}_i'\mathbf{G}_h \mathbf{L}_i) = \operatorname{tr}(\mathbf{L}_i'\mathbf{G}_h \mathbf{L}_i) - \operatorname{tr} \mathbf{CG}_h, \qquad h = 0, 1, \ldots, m. \tag{55}$$

For an asymptotically efficient set of estimates one can replace $\hat{\Psi}_0$ on the left-hand side of (54) by any consistent estimate. If $\mathbf{C}^{-1}$ is used, the coefficient of $t_g^{(i)}$ is tr $\mathbf{CG}_g \mathbf{CG}_h$. If $\hat{\mathbf{\Psi}}_{i-1}$ is positive definite, the matrix of coefficients on the left-hand side of (54) is positive definite.

REFERENCES

Anderson, T. W. (1958). "An Introduction to Multivariate Statistical Analysis." Wiley, New York.

Anderson, T. W. (1963). Determination of the order of dependence in normally distributed time series. *In* "Time Series Analysis" (M. Rosenblatt, ed.). Wiley, New York, pp. 425–446.

Anderson, T. W. (1966). Estimation of covariance matrices which are linear combinations or whose inverses are linear combinations of given matrices. Technical Report No. 3, Contract AF 41(609)-2653, Teachers College, Columbia Univ.

Bock, R. Darrell, and Bargmann, R. E. (1966). Analysis of covariance structures. *Psychometrika* **31** 507–534.

Graybill, F. A., and Hultquist, R. A. (1961). Theorems concerning Eisenhart's Model II. *Ann. Math. Statist.* **32** 261–269.

Herbach, L. H. (1959). Properties of model II-type analysis of variance tests, A: Optimum nature of the *F*-test for model II in the balanced case. *Ann. Math. Statist.* **30** 939–959.

Olkin, I., and Press, S. J. (1969). Testing and estimation for a circular stationary model. (Unpublished).

Srivastava, J. N. (1966). On testing hypotheses regarding a class of covariance structures. *Psychometrika* **31** 147–164.

Srivastava, J. N., and Maik, R. L. (1967). On a new property of partially balanced association schemes useful in psychometric structural analysis. *Psychometrika* **32** 279–289.

A Comparison of Some Methods of Simultaneous Inference in MANOVA[1]

K. R. GABRIEL

HEBREW UNIVERSITY
JERUSALEM, ISRAEL

INTRODUCTION AND SUMMARY

A variety of techniques are available for multiple comparisons on variables and effects in MANOVA. This paper attempts a common listing of these test procedures, step-down methods, and simultaneous confidence bounds in terms of the one-way setup. Comparisons of the properties of different procedures are made mainly in terms of their power to detect the ultimate detailed divergences from the hypotheses. It is brought out that the choice of a suitable technique depends greatly on the family of hypotheses for which inferences are sought. An experimenter interested in contrastwise inferences on all linear combinations of variables does best with the maximum characteristic root statistics, but one interested merely in comparing all pairs of samples on all single variables cannot do better than with a battery of t tests.

Most comparisons can readily be extended to other MANOVA setups.

1. DATA AND NOTATION

Consider a one-way p-variate Normal MANOVA setup comparing c classes by means of samples of sizes $n_1, n_2, \ldots, n_c$, respectively. Denote the αth observation of sample k with respect to variable i by

$$y_{k\alpha}^{(i)}, \qquad i = 1, \ldots, p, \quad k = 1, \ldots, c, \quad \alpha = 1, \ldots, n_k$$

and the corresponding p-variable vector observation by

$$\mathbf{y}'_{k\alpha} = (y_{k\alpha}^{(1)}, \ldots, y_{k\alpha}^{(p)}), \qquad k = 1, \ldots, c, \quad \alpha = 1, \ldots, n_k.$$

[1] This research was supported by the National Center for Health Statistics grant NCHS-IS-1.

Next, write the kth sample mean vector as

$$\bar{\mathbf{y}}_k = n_k^{-1} \sum_{\alpha=1}^{n_k} \mathbf{y}_{k\alpha}, \qquad k = 1, \ldots, c$$

and the overall mean as

$$\bar{\bar{\mathbf{y}}} = n^{-1} \sum_{k=1}^{c} \sum_{\alpha=1}^{n_k} \mathbf{y}_{k\alpha},$$

where

$$n = \sum_{k=1}^{c} n_k.$$

Correspondingly, define the sums of squares and products between samples and within samples as, respectively,

$$H = \sum_{k=1}^{c} n_k(\bar{\mathbf{y}}_k - \bar{\bar{\mathbf{y}}})(\bar{\mathbf{y}}_k - \bar{\bar{\mathbf{y}}})'$$

and

$$S = \sum_{k=1}^{c} \sum_{\alpha=1}^{n_k} (\mathbf{y}_{k\alpha} - \bar{\mathbf{y}}_k)(\mathbf{y}_{k\alpha} - \bar{\mathbf{y}}_k)'.$$

Further, consider any subset V of p_V $(1 \le p_V \le p)$ of the variables and any subgroup G of c_G $(2 \le c_G \le c)$ of the classes. Let a superscript V on a matrix (vector) denote the $p_V \times p_V$ principal minor ($p_V \times 1$ subvector) of the rows and columns (rows) belonging to V. Thus, if, for example, $V = \{p\}$ $(p_V = 1)$ the subset consisting of the last variable only, then $\mathbf{y}_{k\alpha}^V = y_{k\alpha}^{(p)}$, $\bar{\mathbf{y}}_k{}^V = \bar{y}_k^{(p)}$, $\bar{\bar{\mathbf{y}}}^V = \bar{\bar{\mathbf{y}}}^{(p)}$, where the scalar means are defined analogously to the vector means, and also $H^V = \sum_k n_k(\bar{y}_k^{(p)} - \bar{\bar{y}}^{(p)})^2$ and $S^V = \sum_k \sum_\alpha (y_{k\alpha}^{(p)} - \bar{y}_k^{(p)})^2$. Further, let a subscript G on a matrix (vector) denote that the summation or averaging of the matrix (vector) is restricted to the samples from the classes of subgroup G. Thus $\bar{\bar{\mathbf{y}}}_G = n_G^{-1} \sum_{k \in G} \sum_\alpha \mathbf{y}_{k\alpha}$ where $n_G = \sum_{k \in G} n_k$ and $H_G = \sum_{k \in G} n_k\, (\bar{\mathbf{y}}_k - \bar{\bar{\mathbf{y}}}_G)(\bar{\mathbf{y}}_k - \bar{\bar{\mathbf{y}}}_G)'$. An example of the joint use of superscripts and subscripts for $V = \{1\}$ and $G = \{3, 4\}$, is $H_G{}^V = n_3(\bar{y}_3^{(1)} - \bar{\bar{y}}_G^{(1)})^2 + n_4(\bar{y}_4^{(1)} - \bar{\bar{y}}_G^{(1)})^2$.

For a vector space $\tilde{V}$ spanned by the variables in V and for a linear set of contrasts G^* generated by the differences in group G, the definitions of $\mathbf{y}_{k\alpha}^{\tilde{V}}, \bar{\mathbf{y}}_k^{\tilde{V}}, \bar{\bar{\mathbf{y}}}_{G^*}^{\tilde{V}}$, $H_{G^*}^{\tilde{V}}$, and $S^{\tilde{V}}$ are the same as those for V and G. For other vector spaces $\tilde{V}$ of variables and linear sets G^* of contrasts, the definitions are analogous.

In the more general nonparametric model allowing for shift alternatives, the data are ranked separately for each variable. Analogously to the within matrix S, one defines T based on the within sample rankings. Thus, if $R_{k\alpha}^{(1)}$

is the rank of observation α within sample k on variable 1, one uses vectors $\mathbf{r}'_{k\alpha} = (n_k + 1)^{-1}(R^{(1)}_{k\alpha}, \ldots, R^{(p)}_{k\alpha})$ to compute T exactly as one computes S from the vectors $\mathbf{y}'_{k\alpha}$, above. Pairwise sample comparisons are carried out by jointly ranking the observations of both samples, and comparing mean ranks. Thus, for samples k and l the ith variable comparison uses

$$\frac{\bar{R}^{(i)}_k - \bar{R}^{(i)}_l}{n_k + n_l + 1},$$

where $\bar{R}^{(i)}_k$ is the mean of the n_k kth sample i-variable observations ranks in the joint ranking with sample l. Note that $\binom{c}{2} + 1$ separate rankings are involved, one for each pair of samples and one within samples. Computationally, this may be prohibitive without use of a computer. A FORTRAN program carrying out all these rankings and obtaining the summary L statistics [6] for overall testing and simultaneous inference is available from the author. This program also allows for permutation of the data to provide randomization tests.

2. MODEL AND HYPOTHESES

Assume the Normal model $\mathbf{y}_{k\alpha} \sim \mathcal{N}(\boldsymbol{\mu}_k, \Sigma)$ independently for $1, \ldots, n_k$ $k = 1, \ldots, c$ with any $(c \times p)$ expectation matrix $M = (\boldsymbol{\mu}_1, \ldots, \boldsymbol{\mu}_c)'$ and any $(p \times p)$ positive definite variance matrix Σ. The overall MANOVA hypothesis is that of expectation equality of the c classes on all p variables,

$$\omega_0\colon\ \boldsymbol{\mu}_1 = \cdots = \boldsymbol{\mu}_c.$$

More specific hypotheses in MANOVA are those of equality within a subgroup G of classes with respect to a subset V of the variables,

$$\omega_G{}^V\colon\ \boldsymbol{\mu}_k{}^V = \bar{\boldsymbol{\mu}}_G{}^V, \qquad \text{say,} \qquad \forall\, k \in G.$$

In particular, $\omega_0 = \omega_{G_0}^{V_0}$, where V_0 is the set of all p variables and G_0 the group of all classes.

Consider the *family* of hypotheses of within subgroup expectation equality on subset variables. This may be written

$$\Omega = \{\omega_G{}^V \mid V \subset V_0, G \subset G_0\}.$$

There are $(2^c - c - 1) \times (2^p - 1)$ hypotheses in Ω, including ω_0 which is called the *total* or *intersection* hypothesis because it implies all other hypotheses of Ω. Further implication relations exist in Ω, in that $\omega_G{}^V \subset \omega_F{}^W$ whenever $W \subset V$ and $F \subset G$, as is readily seen from the above definition of the hypotheses.

The family Ω of hypotheses may be extended in two ways. First, one may consider comparisons not only on single variables but also on linear combinations of variables as well. If $\tilde{V}$ is a vector space of such combinations, then $\omega_G{}^{\tilde{V}}$ is the hypothesis that all classes of group G have equal expectations on every variable of space $\tilde{V}$. Second, one may consider contrasts between class expectations and not only differences. If G^* is a linear set of such contrasts, $\omega_{G^*}^V$ becomes the hypothesis of nullity of all contrasts in G^* on each of the variables of V. The extension to $\omega_{G^*}^{\tilde{V}}$ is obvious. Thus one obtains four families of hypotheses, as follows:

variable sets, class differences	$\Omega = \{\omega_G{}^V \mid V \subset V_0, G \subset G_0\}$,
variable spaces, class differences	$\tilde{\Omega} = \{\omega_G{}^{\tilde{V}} \mid \tilde{V} \subset \tilde{V}_0, G \subset G_0\}$,
variable sets, class contrasts	$\Omega^* = \{\omega_{G^*}^V \mid V \subset V_0, G^* \subset G_0{}^*\}$,
variable spaces, class contrasts	$\tilde{\Omega}^* = \{\omega_{G^*}^{\tilde{V}} \mid \tilde{V} \subset \tilde{V}_0, G^* \subset G_0{}^*\}$,

where $\tilde{V}_0$ is the space spanned by V_0, and $G_0{}^*$ the linear set of contrasts in G_0. Indeed, if $\tilde{V}$ is spanned by V and G^* by G, one obtains

$$\omega_G{}^V = \omega_G{}^{\tilde{V}} = \omega_{G^*}^V = \omega_{G^*}^{\tilde{V}},$$

so that the four families are seen to have the same intersection hypothesis. Yet it is important to distinguish the four families, for $\tilde{\Omega}$ contains Ω as well as hypotheses on spaces of variables not spanned by any set of the original variables, e.g., the sum of the variables, and Ω^* contains Ω as well as hypotheses on linear sets of contrasts other than those generated by a set of class differences. Similarly, $\tilde{\Omega}^*$ contains both $\tilde{\Omega}$ and Ω^* and additional hypotheses. More detailed simultaneous inferences are possible on $\tilde{\Omega}^*$ than on either $\tilde{\Omega}$ or Ω^* and least detailed on Ω. A question that arises here, but not in classical hypothesis testing, is what detail, or which atomic hypotheses, are relevant to the required inferences. The appropriate family will then be chosen accordingly ([14], Chapter 1).

The hypotheses $\omega_{G^*}^{\tilde{V}}$ of any one of these families may be classified by the dimension $p_{\tilde{V}}$ of the variables space and the degrees of freedom $c_{G^*} - 1$ of the linear set of contrasts. In particular, for V and G these become the number of variables p_V in set V and the number of classes c_G in group G. One may define

$$\text{rank } \omega_{G^*}^{\tilde{V}} = \min(p_{\tilde{V}}, c_{G^*} - 1),$$

so that rank one hypotheses are univariate, $p_{\tilde{V}} = 1$ and/or unicontrast, $c_{G^*} - 1 = 1$. Among rank one hypotheses those with $p_{\tilde{V}} = c_{G^*} - 1 = 1$ concern the nullity of a single contrast on a single linear variable combination; within Ω, they concern the equality of two classes on a single variable. These hypotheses are referred to as *atomic* in that such an *atom* implies no other hypothesis of the family, but every nonatomic hypothesis $\omega_{G^*}^{\tilde{V}}$ is equivalent to the intersection of all its atoms within the family, that is,

$$\omega_{G^*}^{\tilde{V}} = \bigcap_{\tilde{W}} \bigcap_{F^*} \{\omega_{F^*}^{\tilde{W}} \mid \tilde{W} \subset \tilde{V},\, F^* \subset G^*,\, p_{\tilde{W}} = c_{F^*} - 1 = 1\}.$$

As an alternative model, one may consider more generally independent vectors $\mathbf{y}_{k\alpha}$, $\alpha = 1, \ldots, n_k$, $k = 1, \ldots, c$, where

$$F(\mathbf{y}_{k\alpha}) = F(\mathbf{y} + \boldsymbol{\mu}_k),$$

with unspecified p-variate distribution function F and any $(c \times p)$ location matrix $M = (\boldsymbol{\mu}_1, \ldots, \boldsymbol{\mu}_c)'$. Hypotheses ω_0 and $\omega_G{}^V$ of Ω may be considered here analogously to those of the above Normal model. Indeed, the Normal model and its hypotheses in Ω might be considered special cases of these latter ones. The extension to other families of hypotheses is not available at present.

3. AVAILABLE PROCEDURES FOR SIMULTANEOUS INFERENCE

Two types of simultaneous inference procedures are available. *Simultaneous Test Procedures* (STP's) use the original variables without any ordering and allow inferences with respect to them. *Step-down* procedures, on the other hand, analyze successive deviations of the variables from their regressions on all previous variables. The order of variables entering into step-down analysis is arbitrary, and the analysis of regression residuals cannot be readily interpreted in terms of the original variables, except that a hypothesis on *all* variables corresponds to one on *all* residuals. To stress the different types of variables analyzed by step-down methods, the families of hypotheses corresponding to Ω and Ω^*, but relating to regression residuals, are denoted $\Omega(R)$ and $\Omega^*(R)$, respectively.

An STP [4, 5] uses a statistic Z_i for each hypothesis ω_i of a given family and rejects ω_i if $Z_i > \zeta$, where ζ is a critical value common to all ω_i of the family. This ζ is chosen so as to ensure a probability of at least α—the *level* of the STP—that no hypothesis of the family be wrongly rejected. A listing of STP's in MANOVA is given in Table I with some detail about the statistics used and the family of hypotheses on which it provides inferences. The table also lists some MANOVA step-down procedures.

Some of these test procedures were originally proposed as *simultaneous confidence bounds* (SCB's) and others can be inverted to provide such bounds. Table II, therefore, lists SCB's corresponding to the STP's of Table I, showing bounds on deviations from the atomic hypotheses of Ω as well as bounds

TABLE I

Procedure	Statistic $Z_G{}^V$ for samples group G on variables set V	Critical value ζ	
		Distribution	Parameters
STP's based on the original (unordered) variables			
Maximum root	$c_{\max}[(S^{\tilde{V}})^{-1}H^{\tilde{V}}_{G*}]$	$c^{e}_{\max}$	$p, c-1, n-c$
Increasing root functions[a]	$\psi[(S^{\tilde{V}})^{-1}H^{\tilde{V}}_{G*}]$	ψ	$p, c-1, n-c$
Maximum T^2 [b]	$\max\limits_{(k,l)\in G} c_{\max}[(S^{\tilde{V}})^{-1}H^{\tilde{V}}_{(k,l)}]$	χ^2 ratio[f,g]	$p, n-c-p+1$
Maximum F [c]	$\max\limits_{i\in V} [H^{(i)}_{G*}/S^{(i)}]$	χ^2 ratio	$c-1, n-c$
Maximum t^2 [d]	$\max\limits_{i\in V} \max\limits_{(k,l)\in G} H^{(i)}_{(k,l)}/S^{(i)}$	χ^2 ratio	$1, n-c$
Root ratio R	$c_{\max}[H^V_{G*}]/c_{\max}[S^V]$	—	as $c_{\max}$
B-K bounds	As max root	—	as $c_{\max}$
Symmetric gauge functions	σ : various (incl. above two)	—	as $c_{\max}$, also others
Nonparametric	$\frac{1}{2}\sum_G n_k n_l \sum_V U^{(i)}_{(k,l)} U^{(j)}_{(k,l)} T^{ij}_G$	χ^2 or permutation distribution	$p(c-1)$
Maximum W	Wilcoxon-Mann-Whitney maximum	Tables	
Methods based on successive (ordered) deviations from regressions on previous variables			
Step-down	$H^{(j)}_{G*}/S^{(j)}$ cond. on $1, \ldots, j-1$	χ^2 ratio	$c-1, n-c-j+1$
Finite-Intersection (any $c-1$ contrasts)	$\max[t^{2(j)} \mid \text{contrasts}]$ cond. on $1, \ldots, j-1$	Mult. F [h]	$c-1, 1, n-c-j+1$
Multiv. SANOVA ($c-1$ indpt. contrasts)	As above	Max $St.$ χ^2 [i]	$c-1, 1, n-c-j+1$

[a] Includes as special cases the likelihood ratio statistic, Hotelling-Lawley's trace and Pillai's trace. The distribution of ψ is not known in general.

[b] $T^2 = (n-c)c_{\max}$ when $c_G = 2$.

[c] $F = (n-c)c_{\max}/(c_G - 1)$ when $p_V = 1$.

[d] $t^2 = (n-c)c_{\max}$ when $c_G - 1 = p_V = 1$.

[e] Distribution tabulated as $\theta = c_{\max}/(1 + c_{\max})$ with parameters $\min(p, c-1)$, $(|p-c+1|-1)/2$, $(n-c-p+1)/2$.

[f] F ratio times ratio of numerator to denominator degrees of freedom.

[g] A method of getting approximate percentage points for $T^2_{\max}$ is given by Siotani [21] (in Japanese). See also Siotani [22]. Bonferroni inequalities were used by Kaskey *et al.* [7].

Test Procedures for Simultaneous Inference in One-Way MANOVA

Point	Overall rejection prob.	Family	Coherence	Consonance	Original ref. (see also Table II)	Fortran program
α	α	$\tilde{\Omega}^{*\,j}$	Yes	$\tilde{\Omega}^*$	S. N. Roy[k]	Yes
α	α	$\tilde{\Omega}^*$	Yes	—	Gabriel [5]	Yes
$\alpha/\binom{c}{2}$	$<\alpha$	$\tilde{\Omega}$	Yes	$\tilde{\Omega}$	Roy and Bose [19]	
α/p	$<\alpha$	Ω^*	Yes	Ω^*		
$\alpha/p\binom{c}{2}$	$<\alpha$	Ω	Yes	Ω		
—	$<\alpha$	$\tilde{\Omega}^{*\,j}$	No	—		Yes
—	α	$\tilde{\Omega}^*$	Yes	$\tilde{\Omega}^*$		
—	$<\alpha$	$\tilde{\Omega}^*$	Some	?		
α	$\approx\alpha$	Ω	Yes	—	Gabriel and Sen [6]	Yes
$\alpha/p\binom{c}{2}$	$<\alpha$	Ω	Yes	Ω		
$1-(1-\alpha)^{1/p}$	α	$\Omega^*(R)$	Yes	$\Omega^*(R)$	J. Roy [17]	
$1-(1-\alpha)^{1/p}$	α	$\Omega(R)$	Yes	$\Omega(R)$	Krishnaiah [12]	
$1-(1-\alpha)^{1/p}$	α	$\Omega(R)$	Yes	$\Omega(R)$	Krishnaiah [11]	

[h] Multivariate *F*, distribution tabulated by Krishnaiah and Armitage [13].

[i] Studentized largest chi-square, distribution tabulated by Armitage and Krishnaiah [1].

[j] Krishnaiah also proposed the use of this type of procedure for a more restricted family of orthogonal hypotheses [10]. However, little appears to be known about the requisite distributions.

[k] The method is implicit in Roy's writing and teaching though he does not seem to have formulated it explicitly.

TABLE II

Confidence Bounds for Simultaneous Inference in One-Way MANOVA—*Confidence at Least* $1 - \alpha$

Procedure	General: Bounds on $c_{\max}^{1/2}[\sum_{k \in G} n_k(\boldsymbol{\mu}_k^V - \bar{\boldsymbol{\mu}}_G^V)(\boldsymbol{\mu}_k - \bar{\boldsymbol{\mu}}_G^V)']$ for group G and subset V	Atomic: Bounds on $(\mu_k^{(i)} - \mu_l^i)/(n_k^{-1} + n_l^{-1})$	Original ref. (see also Table I)
Methods based on the original (unordered) variables			
Maximum root	Not available		Roy and Bose [19]
Increasing root functions	Not available		Gabriel [5]
Maximum T^2	Not available		
Maximum F	Not available		
Maximum t^2	Not available		
Roots ratio R	$c_{\max}^{1/2}[H_G{}^V] \pm \zeta^{1/2} c_{\max}^{1/2}[S^V]$	$(\bar{y}_k^i - \bar{y}_l^i)/(n_k^{-1} + n_l^{-1}) \pm \zeta^{1/2}(S^i)^{1/2}$	Roy and Gnanadesikan [20]
B-K bounds	$c_{\max}^{1/2}[S^V]\{c_{\max}^{1/2}[(S^V)^{-1} H_G{}^V] - \zeta^{1/2}\}$ lower bound, upper bound as by Roy-Gnanadesikan		Bhapkar [2], Khatri [8]
Symmetric gauge functions	Various (incl. above two)		Mudholkar [15]
Nonparametric L	Not available	See Gabriel and Sen [6]	Gabriel and Sen [6]
Maximum W	Not available	As above	
Methods based on (successive) ordered deviations from regressions on previous variables			
No bounds available on original variables except one (see Roy [17], Krishnaiah [11, 12]).			

relevant to nonatomic hypotheses, where available. Original references are cited in either Table I or II, according to whether the method was originally proposed for tests or for bounds, respectively.

Tables I and II show a number of unique STP's as well as two classes, each of which include STP's based on some of the well known MANOVA test criteria. The class of increasing root function STP's [5] includes all procedures based on functions ψ of $S^{-1}H$ such that (i) ψ is monotone increasing in all roots[2] of $S^{-1}H$, (ii) ψ is equal for any two such matrices with equal nonzero roots, irrespective of the number of zero roots either matrix may have, (iii) $\psi = c_{\max}$ if $S^{-1}H$ has only one nonzero root. Wilks's likelihood ratio as well as Hotelling-Lawley's and Pillai's traces are statistics belonging to this class. The class of σ-STP's uses symmetric gauge function of the square roots of the characteristic roots of $S^{-1}H$. For a discussion of symmetric gauge functions see Mudholkar [15].

All SCB's of Table II provide bounds for the atomic comparisons, i.e., univariate comparisons of pairs of sample means. Roy and Gnanadesikan's R procedure as well as Bhapkar-Khatri's and, more generally, Mudholkar's procedures, further provide bounds for multivariate comparisons of several (3 or more) means. Corresponding to hypothesis $\omega_{G^*}^{\tilde{V}}$, bounds are set on the noncentrality parameter $c_{\max}^{1/2}[\chi_{G^*}^{\tilde{V}}]$, where $\chi_{G^*}^{\tilde{V}}$ is related to expectations as $H_{G^*}^{\tilde{V}}$ is related to sample means, that is,

$$((\chi_G^V))_{ij} = \sum_{k \in G} n_k(\mu_k^{(i)} - \bar{\mu}_G^{(i)})(\mu_k^{(j)} - \bar{\mu}_G^{(j)}),$$

where $i \in V$ and $j \in V$.

The functions $c_{\max}^{1/2}[\chi_{G^*}^{\tilde{V}}]$ are unlikely to have physically meaningful interpretations in many practical applications. The utility of the bounds on these functions therefore seems doubtful, and, indeed, no useful application seems to be known to date. However, $c_{\max}^{1/2}[\chi_G^V]$ is positive definite in all expectation differences, that is, it is zero if, and only if, the expectations of all classes are equal. Thus, the main use of these SCB's is in determining whether $\omega_{G^*}^{\tilde{V}}$ is true according to whether the bounds for $c_{\max}^{1/2}[\chi_{G^*}^{\tilde{V}}]$ include zero. As such, the SCB's function as STP's, and are thus presented in Table I. It will be noted that the STP derived from B-K SCB's is equivalent to the $c_{\max}$ STP.

4. PROPERTIES AND COMPARISONS OF PROCEDURES

4.1. Coherence and Consonance

A method of simultaneous inference should preserve, as far as possible, the implication relations between the hypotheses of the family $\tilde{\Omega}^*$, or other

[2] This definition differs slightly from that of Gabriel [5], essentially only in that the present definition excludes $c_{\max}$ from the ψ class.

family under consideration. A basic requisite is that any such method be *coherent* in the sense that, when $\tilde{W} \subset \tilde{V}$ and $F^* \subset G^*$, i.e., when $\omega_{G^*}^{\tilde{V}} \subset \omega_{F^*}^{\tilde{W}}$, acceptance of $\omega_{G^*}^{\tilde{V}}$ is always accompanied by acceptance of $\omega_{F^*}^{\tilde{W}}$. Equivalently, $\omega_{G^*}^{\tilde{V}}$ is always rejected when $\omega_{F^*}^{\tilde{W}}$ is ([4], Section 3). A further desirable quality is *consonance* ([4]), Section 3). This means that any $\omega_{G^*}^{\tilde{V}}$ is rejected only if at least one hypothesis $\omega_{F^*}^{\tilde{W}}$ implied by it is also rejected. Thus a coherent and consonant procedure rejects a hypothesis if, and only if, at least one of the implied atoms is rejected.

An STP is coherent and consonant if its statistics satisfy Roy's union-intersection principle within the family of hypotheses considered ([4], Corollary 2). In other words, the statistic for any hypothesis must be the maximum of the statistics for all atoms it implies ([4], Theorem 3). It is well known that $c_{\max}$ satisfies this requirement for $\tilde{\Omega}^*$, and clearly max T^2 satisfies it for $\tilde{\Omega}$ and max F for Ω^*. Both max t^2 and max W obviously satisfy it for Ω. This establishes the coherence and consonance properties of STP's in Table I. Those for step-down methods similarly follow.

If a statistic is coherent for a wider family of hypotheses, it obviously is coherent also for any subfamily contained in it. Hence, each of the above statistics is coherent for Ω. Coherence of the increasing root function class of STP's was proved for $\tilde{\Omega}^*$ by Gabriel [5], and that of L for Ω by Gabriel and Sen [6]. The only incoherent procedure is that based on the ratio of roots[3] R (examples of rejecting a hypothesis implied by a nonrejected hypothesis are shown in Section 5, Table VI). Presumably, Roy and Gnanadesikan [20] intended not to test hypotheses implied by accepted hypotheses, thus avoiding incoherences by ignoring them. (The most common univariate methods of multiple comparisons proceed in the same way. [4], Section 9.)

For nonatomic hypotheses the SCB's on $c_{\max}^{1/2}[\chi_G{}^V]$ present some further difficulties. First, note that this noncentrality parameter is never smaller for an implying hypothesis than for one implied by it. Thus, if $W \subset V$ and $F \subset G$, so that $\omega_G{}^V \subset \omega_F{}^W$, then $c_{\max}[\chi_G{}^V] \geq c_{\max}[\chi_F{}^W]$. This may be proved as follows:

$$\begin{aligned}
c_{\max}[\chi_G{}^V] &= c_{\max}\left[\left(\sum_{k\in G} n_k(\mu_k^{(i)} - \bar{\mu}_G^{(i)})(\mu_k^{(j)} - \bar{\mu}_G^{(j)})\right)_{i,j\in V}\right] \\
&= \max_{\alpha}\left\{\sum_{i\in V}\sum_{j\in V}\alpha_i\alpha_j\sum_{k\in G} n_k(\mu_k^{(i)} - \bar{\mu}_G^{(i)})(\mu_k^{(j)} - \bar{\mu}_G^{(j)}) \,\middle|\, \sum_{i\in V}\alpha_i^2 = 1\right\} \\
&= \max_{\alpha}\left[\sum_{k\in G} n_k\left(\sum_{i\in V}\alpha_i\mu_k^{(i)} - \sum_{i\in V}\alpha_i\bar{\mu}_G^{(i)}\right)^2 \,\middle|\, \sum_{i\in V}\alpha_i^2 = 1\right] \\
&\geq \max_{\alpha}\left[\sum_{k\in G} n_k\left(\sum_{i\in W}\alpha_i\mu_k^{(i)} - \sum_{i\in W}\alpha_i\bar{\mu}_G^{(i)}\right)^2 \,\middle|\, \sum_{i\in W}\alpha_i^2 = 1\right] \\
&\geq \max_{\alpha}\left[\sum_{k\in F} n_k\left(\sum_{i\in W}\alpha_i\mu_k^{(i)} - \sum_{i\in W}\alpha_i\bar{\mu}_F^{(i)}\right)^2 \,\middle|\, \sum_{i\in W}\alpha_i^2 = 1\right] \\
&= c_{\max}[\chi_F{}^W].
\end{aligned}$$

[3] In terms of the definition in [4], the R procedure is not strictly an STP.

The first inequality follows since a maximum over a narrower set of α's must be no larger than over a wider set. The second inequality is clear since $\sum_{i \in W} \alpha_i \bar{\mu}_G^{(i)}$ is the mean of the values $\sum_{i \in W} \alpha_i \mu_k^{(i)}$ with weights n_k, $k \in G$ (see also Gabriel [3]). Now, note that the bounds set on $c_{\max}^{1/2}[\chi_G{}^V]$ may include lower values than those within the bounds for $c_{\max}^{1/2}[\chi_F{}^W]$, thus leading to incoherent results. This is readily seen from the following example: set

$$H_G^{(1,2,3)} = \begin{pmatrix} 9 & 0 & 0 \\ 0 & 6\frac{1}{4} & 0 \\ 0 & 0 & 4 \end{pmatrix} \quad \text{and} \quad S^{(1,2,3)} = \begin{pmatrix} 4 & 0 & 0 \\ 0 & \frac{1}{4} & 0 \\ 0 & 0 & 1 \end{pmatrix},$$

so that

$$H_G^{(2)} = 6\tfrac{1}{4} \quad \text{and} \quad S^{(2)} = \tfrac{1}{4}.$$

The following Roy-Gnanadesikan bounds will be obtained:

$$3 - \sqrt{\zeta}\,2 \le c_{\max}^{1/2}[\chi_G^{(1,2,3)}] \le 3 + \sqrt{\zeta}\,2$$

and

$$2\tfrac{1}{2} - \sqrt{\zeta}\,\tfrac{1}{2} \le c_{\max}^{1/2}[\chi_G^{(2)}] \le 2\tfrac{1}{2} + \sqrt{\zeta}\,\tfrac{1}{2}.$$

If $\sqrt{\zeta} = \frac{1}{2}$, this means that $c_{\max}^{1/2}[\chi_G^{(2)}]$ cannot be less than $2\frac{1}{4}$ whereas $c_{\max}^{1/2}[\chi_G^{(1,2,3)}]$ can be as little as 2. As the latter parameter was just proved to be no less than the former, these bounds clearly are not coherent. (For a discussion of coherence of confidence statements see Gabriel [4] Section 5). In the same example, one obtains the following B-K bounds

$$2 - \sqrt{\zeta} \le c_{\max}^{1/2}[\chi_G^{(1,3)}] \le 3 + 2\sqrt{\zeta}$$

and

$$3 - 2\sqrt{\zeta} \le c_{\max}^{1/2}[\chi_G^{(1)}] \le 3 + 2\sqrt{\zeta}.$$

Again, with $\sqrt{\zeta} = \frac{1}{2}$, $c_{\max}^{1/2}[\chi_G^{(1)}]$ may not be below 2, whereas $c_{\max}^{1/2}[\chi_G^{(1,3)}]$, which was proved to be no less, may be as low as $1\frac{1}{2}$, another incoherence.

Not only are these bounds set on functions of limited practical interest, but furthermore they are incoherent with one another. One may doubt whether there is much practical utility to them.

4.2. Numerical Comparisons

The statistics of all STP's enumerated in Table I for family Ω, are—except for the nonparametric statistics L and max W—functions of the two matrices S^V and $H_G{}^V$. It is instructive to consider the numerical relations among the various statistics. Table III has been set up for this purpose, allowing comparisons for four distinct cases: multivariate multiple comparisons ($p_V > 1$,

$c_G > 2$), multivariate single comparison ($p_V > 1$, $c_G = 2$), univariate multiple comparisons ($p_V = 1$, $c_G > 2$), and univariate single or atomic comparison, ($p_V = 1$, $c_G = 2$).

TABLE III

Numerical Comparison of Statistics[a]

Multivariate multiple $p_V > 1$, $c_G > 2$
$\psi_G{}^V > c_G{}^V > (R_G{}^V, \max_G T^V_{k,l}, \max_V f_G{}^i) > \max_{G,V} t^i_{k,l}$
Multivariate simple $p_V > 1$, $c_G = 2$
$R^V_{k,l} < \psi^V_{k,l} = c^V_{k,l} = T^V_{k,l} > \max_V f^i_{k,l} = \max_V t^i_{k,l}$
Univariate multiple $p_V = 1$, $c_G > 2$
$R_G{}^i = \psi_G{}^i = c_G{}^i = f_G{}^i > \max_G T^i_{k,l} = \max_G t^i_{k,l}$
Univariate simple $p_V = 1$, $c_G = 2$
$R^i_{k,l} = \psi^i_{k,l} = c^i_{k,l} = T^i_{k,l} = f^i_{k,l} = t^i_{k,l}$

[a] *Notation:* For group G on variable set V, $c_G{}^V = c_{\max}$, $T_G{}^V = T^2/(n-c)$, $f_G{}^V = F(c_G - 1)/(n-c)$ $t_G{}^V = t^2/(n-c)$. Max_G and $\max_V$ are short for $\max_{(k,l)\in G}$ and $\max_{i\in V}$, respectively. All inequalities are strict with probability one.

Proofs: The $R \leq c$ inequality follows from Roy's theorem $c_{\max}[H]/c_{\max}[S] \leq c_{\max}[S^{-1}H]$ [18]. It is readily seen that the inequality is strict with probability one except when H and S are scalars, and then it is obviously an equality.

The $\psi \geq c_{\max}$ inequalities are proved by Gabriel [5]. The inequality with respect to maxima over G and/or V follow from the fact that the left-hand statistics are similar maxima over the wider families G^* and/or $\tilde{V}$, respectively.

4.3. Resolution and Atomic Power

The purpose of simultaneous inference is to point out what the rejection of a hypothesis is due to, that is, to locate the atoms of the hypothesis which must also be rejected. Consonant procedures ensure that there always is some such *resolution* of rejection into rejection of atoms. In that sense, consonant procedures are the most desirable and other procedures may be compared according to the extent of resolution they do provide. If one procedure always rejects all atoms rejected by another and sometimes rejects more, it will be said to be strictly *more resolvent* than the other. If it merely has a higher chance of rejecting atoms, it will be said to have a higher *resolution probability*.

In evaluating a simultaneous inference procedure, it will therefore be necessary to consider not only the total—experimentwise—probability of rejection, i.e., the level of significance under the hypothesis and the power under the alternatives but also, one will need to consider the resolution probabilities, at least that between the total hypothesis and the atoms. The product of the total power and the resolution probability is the *atomic power*, that is, the power of a procedure to reject an atomic hypothesis under its alternative. Indeed, this atomic power may be ultimately the criterion by which a simultaneous inference procedure should be evaluated. The purpose of such a procedure being the establishment of significant detailed departures from the hypothesis, its advantages should be measured in terms of the probability of establishing such departures.

Where the distribution of the test statistics is the same for all atomic hypotheses, the atomic power may be represented by a single function $\beta(\delta)$ of a suitable noncentrality parameter δ. In that case, an evaluation of a procedure may well be made in terms of the total level α and the atomic power function $\beta(\delta)$. Contrast this with the classical testing situation in which one is concerned with the probability of rejecting the total hypothesis ω_0 if it is true—level α_0—and with total power $\beta_0(\Delta)$, where Δ is a noncentrality parameter for ω_0. The levels may well be equal—$\alpha = \alpha_0$—in both types of inference, but total power β_0 is quite a different matter from atomic power β. For a given $\alpha = \alpha_0$ a good test has large β_0 whereas a good method of simultaneous inference has large β. For confidence statements the corresponding comparison is in terms of narrowness of bounds on Δ and on δ, respectively.

Comparisons of the performance of STP's must be made with respect to a given family of hypotheses. Of all STP's of level α which use the same statistics for atomic hypotheses, the consonant STP will be the most resolvent ([4], Corollary 3), and generally one STP will be strictly more resolvent than another if its statistics for nonatomic hypotheses are smaller than or equal to those of the other ([4], Theorem 5). Such comparisons can be made among Normal procedures all of which use the common t statistics for atomic decisions.

For the most general family $\tilde{\Omega}^*$ the $c_{\max}$ STP is, therefore, the most resolvent. The other available methods are the incoherent ratio of roots R procedure, the increasing root functions ψ STP's which are less resolvent [5], and the other symmetric gauge function σ STP's which are also less resolvent than the $c_{\max}$ STP. (Mudholkar [15] shows the analogous result in terms of width of SCB's.)

For pairwise class differences family $\tilde{\Omega}$ the max T^2 STP is the most resolvent, the $c_{\max}$ STP being inferior, and, *a fortiori*, the other ones mentioned above. (The corresponding result for SCB's was shown by Krishnaiah [9].)

For contrastwise univariate family Ω^* the most resolvent STP is that using max F, $c_{\max}$ and other ones being inferior. Max T^2 is not available.

Max t^2 provides the most resolvent STP for family Ω. Less resolvent are max T^2 and max F, the $c_{\max}$ STP being less resolvent than either of these and the ψ and σ STP's even less so.

In view of Table III, the R procedure is equal to the $c_{\max}$ STP for all univariate tests, hence its atomic power is the same.

The above comparisons are strictly valid only when all the STP's are of exact level α. The max T^2, max F, and max t^2 STP's (and also that using max W) of Table I merely have the level α as an upper bound by the first Bonferroni inequality. Hence, it is not clear whether they will actually be more resolvent than the $c_{\max}$ STP of exact level α (see, however, Section 5 for a numerical illustration).

No general statements can be made about comparisons with the nonparametric STP's which use different statistics for atomic hypotheses and can be used only for family Ω.

Among step-down methods the Finite Intersection procedure is strictly more resolvent within $\Omega(R)$ than J. Roy's original procedure. (The corresponding confidence bound width comparison was made by Krishnaiah [12].) However J. Roy's procedure extends to the contrast family $\Omega^*(R)$.

This evaluation of simultaneous procedures deals exclusively with atomic hypotheses, stressing all of them equally. If decisions on other hypotheses are also taken into account, or different atoms stressed differently, the evaluation of such procedures becomes much more difficult.

4.4. Robustness

As far as robustness is concerned very little is known. All parametric procedures lean on Normality assumptions, though probably those using max T^2 and max F do so less heavily than that using $c_{\max}$, but more heavily than the max t^2 procedure. The nonparametric procedures are not distribution-free, except asymptotically, though the permutation distribution ensures robustness under the null hypothesis.

4.5. General Linear Setups

Last, generalization to other multivariate setups are immediate for the Normal parametric procedures, with all the comparisons going over as well. The nonparametric procedures, on the other hand, do not carry over to those situations.

5. AN EXAMPLE

As an illustration consider Reeve's anteater data which have a trivariate six class (localities) one-way MANOVA setup [16]. These data were analyzed in an earlier paper [5] by means of the $c_{\max}$ STP and increasing root function

STP's. For a nonparametric STP Table IV shows the L statistic for each of the 399 hypotheses of family Ω italicizing all values significant at overall level 5%. (Compare with a similar table of c_{max} by Gabriel [5].) Asymptotic theory [6] suggested a critical value from the chi-square distribution with $p_{V_0}(c_{G_0} - 1) = 15$ df. However, 230 permutations of the data showed this distribution to be unsuitable—Table V—and gave an estimated upper 5% critical value of 29.8 (as compared with 25.0 from the chi-square distribution which was exceeded by 32 out of the 230 L values).

Another nonparametric procedure is the max W STP. First, the Wilcoxon-Mann-Whitney statistic is computed for each atom, i.e., each univariate two sample comparison, and the absolute value W of the corresponding Normalized statistic noted. Then max W is obtained for all hypotheses of ω as the maximum of the W's over all atoms of the hypothesis. For a 5% level STP any hypothesis is declared significant if its max W exceeds the upper $0.025/[3 \times \binom{6}{2}] = 0.00055$ point of the Normal distribution. In the present example, however, the samples were too small to allow use of the Normal approximation, so each atomic hypothesis was tested at 0.0011 (two-sided) by means of tables of the Wilcoxon-Mann-Whitney statistic and each non-atomic hypothesis declared significant if any of its atoms was. The results of this procedure appear in Table VI.

A comparison of several of the STP's for family Ω of class differences on variable sets is presented in Table VI which shows, for each hypothesis, which of the 5% level STP's would have rejected it. (Groups of 3 and 4 localities have been omitted from the table for reasons of space.) The relation between the STP's for atomic hypotheses are as expected from the foregoing discussion, even though the latter do not attain the exact 5% level: the order of atomic power is max $t^2 >$ max $F >$ max $T^2 > c_{max} = R$. The reverse order is found for nonatomic hypotheses, with the c_{max} and max T^2 STP's showing more significant results than the max F and max t^2 STP's.

Actual calculation of the atomic power function for this set-up—Table VII—bring the comparisons out strikingly. The power of locating pairwise class differences on single variables is appreciably higher with the max t^2 STP than with the c_{max} STP. The advantage of the max t^2 *for this purpose* is stressed by recalling a similar comparison [5] showing the c_{max} STP to have considerably more atomic power than STP's with the other common MANOVA statistics, that is, the likelihood ratio determinantal ratio and Hotelling-Lawley's and Pillai's traces.

The R procedure coincides with the c_{max} STP for univariate hypotheses. For multivariate hypotheses it is clearly inferior in providing fewer rejections, and incoherent ones at that. Thus, for instance, it rejects equality of the group of localities 2, 3, 4, 5, 6 on the single variable Z but not on all three variable XYZ together.

TABLE IV *L Statistics for All Groups of Localities on All Sets of Variables*[a]

	Variables						
Localities	XYZ	XY	XZ	YZ	X	Y	Z
123456	*71.944*	*44.812*	*65.945*	*54.496*	*36.247*	*34.191*	20.709
12345	*58.571*	*35.714*	*53.300*	*42.697*	28.405	26.036	12.926
1234 6	*50.678*	*32.137*	*47.895*	*41.390*	29.755	27.155	9.741
123 56	*60.684*	*36.110*	*57.244*	*47.909*	*31.197*	29.011	17.670
12 456	*46.410*	*32.039*	*42.890*	*34.000*	26.155	23.709	15.714
1 3456	*52.599*	*36.014*	*46.995*	*42.047*	28.700	29.275	18.359
23456	18.832	7.232	15.458	9.943	0.697	1.577	8.428
1234	*38.606*	23.420	*36.456*	*30.216*	22.074	19.001	2.287
123 5	*47.789*	27.190	*44.996*	*36.347*	23.434	20.894	10.096
12 45	*35.348*	28.328	*32.542*	24.149	18.518	15.857	9.644
1 345	*40.368*	26.976	*35.456*	*31.355*	20.994	21.176	11.397
2345	13.602	6.229	10.467	6.023	0.434	1.181	5.354
123 6	*44.160*	26.684	*41.929*	*35.603*	24.889	22.158	7.448
12 4 6	*30.357*	21.184	29.282	23.713	19.671	17.162	7.268
1 34 6	*33.960*	23.994	*31.363*	*30.573*	22.211	22.415	8.745
234 6	4.951	1.131	4.656	4.065	0·422	0.730	3.475
12 56	*35.758*	23.541	*34.792*	28.000	21.266	18.732	13.251
1 3 56	*41.539*	27.471	*38.425*	*35.614*	23.707	24.224	15.451
23 56	12.806	3.445	11.588	8.164	0.294	1.024	6.763
1 456	27.282	23.389	24.074	21.579	18.629	18.794	13.384
2 456	10.486	4.676	7.996	4.559	0.381	0.581	3.594
3456	14.649	6.213	11.667	7.019	0.560	1.215	6.099
123	*32.565*	18.144	*30.888*	24.667	17.207	14.041	0.204
12 4	20.595	12.852	20.122	14.488	12.115	9.309	1.528
12 5	25.173	15.007	24.825	18.386	13.629	10.918	7.391
12 6	24.446	15.934	23.920	18.513	14.966	12.368	5.553
1 34	23.030	15.336	21.030	20.508	14.586	14.316	2.113
1 3 5	29.786	18.610	27.284	25.160	16.001	16.163	8.699
1 3 6	27.641	18.698	25.529	24.940	17.402	17.547	6.584
1 45	17.361	14.736	14.815	12.836	11.048	10.998	8.136
1 4 6	13.855	13.187	12.884	12.925	12.147	12.423	6.293
1 56	16.829	15.049	16.109	15.733	13.797	13.947	11.053
234	1.023	0.509	0.871	0.770	0.240	0.334	0.730
23 5	8.054	2.619	6.995	4.481	0.031	0.665	3.899
23 6	3.667	0.592	3.521	3.086	0.202	0.359	2.556
2 45	7.567	4.060	5.286	2.587	0.244	0.488	2.233
2 4 6	1.819	0.395	1.636	1.500	0.114	0.223	1.163
2 56	5.068	1.093	4.730	3.367	0.140	0.231	2.506
345	10.561	5.270	7.783	4.206	0.353	0.875	3.847
34 6	3.395	0.767	3.283	2.773	0.287	0.544	2.500
3 56	8.823	2.585	7.929	5.394	0.214	0.791	4.565
456	6.519	3.805	4.340	1.664	0.265	0.221	1.286

TABLE IV (*Cont.*) *L Statistics for All Groups of Localities on All Sets of Variables*[a]

Localities	XYZ	Variables XY	XZ	YZ	X	Y	Z
12	15.161	7.779	15.159	9.525	7.410	4.554	0.022
1 3	17.188	10.217	15.594	15.113	9.777	9.486	0.161
23	0.216	0.147	0.135	0.029	0.021	0.001	0.021
1 4	5.234	4.915	4.831	4.808	4.648	4.627	1.374
2 4	0.200	0.158	0.132	0.154	0.058	0.129	0.132
34	0.607	0.204	0.605	0.587	0.162	0.204	0.577
1 5	7.385	6.574	7.248	7.228	6.217	6.188	6.015
2 5	2.626	0.654	2.418	1.633	0.003	0.176	1.355
3 5	5.213	1.819	4.442	2.819	0.008	0.489	2.523
45	4.741	3.248	2.736	0.800	0.184	0.183	0.747
1 6	8.143	8.095	7.655	7.879	7.500	7.759	4.709
2 6	1.142	0.059	1.106	1.108	0.056	0.056	0.822
3 6	2.310	0.386	2.280	1.949	0.126	0.302	1.713
4 6	0.477	0.177	0.398	0.238	0.000	0.038	0.210
56	1.300	0.380	1.206	0.626	0.081	0.000	0.329

[a] 5% significant statistics set in italics. Critical value 29.8.

TABLE V

Sample Permutation Distribution of L — 230 Permutations

L	Frequency of permutations	Expected frequency under $\chi^2(15)$-asymptotic
0 —	5	11.5
7.261 —	8	11.5
8.547 —	12	23
10.307 —	15	23
11.721 —	22	23
13.030 —	22	23
14.339 —	21	23
15.773 —	20	23
17.322 —	21	23
19.311 —	29	23
22.307 —	23	11.5
24.996 —	14	5.75
27.488 —	11	3.45
30.578 —	7	2.3
	230	230.00

TABLE VI

Significance Decisions by Various Procedures for Groups of Localities on Sets of Variables[a]

Localities	Variables *XYZ*	*XY*	*XZ*	*YZ*	*X*	*Y*	*Z*
123456	*RcTFtLW*	*RcTFtLW*	*RcTFtLW*	*RcTFtLW*	*RcTFtLW*	*RcTFtLW*	*RcTFt W*
12345	*RcTFtLW*	*RcTFtLW*	*RcTFtLW*	*RcTFtLW*	*RcTFt W*	*RcTFt W*	*RcTFt W*
1234 6	*RcTFtLW*	*RcTFtLW*	*RcTFtLW*	*cTFtLW*	*RcTFt W*	*RcTFt W*	
123 56	*RcTFtLW*	*RcTFtLW*	*RcTFtLW*	*RcTFtLW*	*RcTFtLW*	*RcTFt W*	*RcTFt W*
12 456	*RcTFtLW*	*RcTFtLW*	*RcTFtLW*	*RcTFtLW*	*RcTFt W*	*RcTFt W*	*RcTFt W*
1 3456	*RcTFtLW*	*RcTFtLW*	*RcTFtLW*	*RcTFtLW*	*RcTFt W*	*RcTFt W*	*RcTFt W*
23456	*cTFt W*	*cT*	*RcTFt W*	*RcTFt W*			*RcTFt W*
12	*cTFt W*	*RcTFt W*	*cTFt W*	*cTFt*	*RcTFt W*	*TFt*	
1 3	*cTFt W*	*RcTFt W*	*cTFt W*	*cTFt W*	*RcTFt W*	*Ft W*	
23							
1 4	*cTFt*	*TFt*	*cTFt*		*Ft*		
2 4							
34							
1 5	*RcTFt W*	*cTFt W*	*RcTFt W*	*RcTFt W*	*t W*	*RcTFt W*	*RcTFt W*
2 5	*cTFt*	*cT*	*cTFt*	*cTFt*			*Ft*
3 5	*cTFt W*	*cT*	*cTFt W*	*cTFt W*			*TFt W*
45	*cT*		*cT*				
1 6	*cTFt W*	*cTFt W*	*cTFt W*	*cTFt W*	*RcTFt W*	*RcTFt W*	
2 6							
3 6							
4 6							
56							

[a] (For brevity groups of 3 or 4 localities are omitted). All procedures test at a level of 5% or less, rejections are indicated as follows: *R*-ratio of roots, *c*-maximum root, *T*-max T^2, *F*-max *F*, *t*-max t^2, *L*-nonparametric *L* and *W* for the maximum Wilcoxon-Mann-Whitney statistic.

TABLE VII

Atomic Powers of Various 5% Level MANOVA *STP's*
(6 classes, 3 variables, 42 error df)

Statistic	Noncentrality parameter $\delta = (\mu - \mu_0)/\sigma$: 0	1.6	3.2	4.8	6.4	Critical value	θ
Maximum root	<0.0001	0.004	0.116	0.592	0.951	$\theta_{0.05} = 0.3323$	0.3323
Max T^2	0.0001	0.012	0.215	0.740	0.981	$F_{(3,40)0.05/15} = 5.55$	0.294
Max F	0.0002	0.015	0.240	0.775	0.986	$F_{(5,42)0.05/3} = 3.20$	0.276
Max t^2	0.0006	0.041	0.403	0.892	0.997	$F_{(1,42)0.05/45} = 12.2$	0.225

It should be mentioned that the max t^2 STP which comes out so well in this comparison is not available for exploration either of contrasts or linear combinations of variables. The additional insight into the data brought out by exploring the sum and differences of the original variables in the earlier $c_{\max}$ STP analysis [5] could not have been obtained by the max t^2 STP. (Though the max T^2 STP would also have provided it). Clearly, the additional power on the atoms of Ω is gained by ignoring other atoms, such as those in $\tilde{\Omega}$. This illustrates the importance of proper choice of the family of hypotheses on which inferences are to be made.

The nonparametric L-STP does not come out well on detailed hypotheses. It does not show significance on any atomic hypothesis. Use of this technique in lieu of the parametric STP's results in giving up most power of resolution. (An attempt was made to obtain greater detailed power by modifying $L_G{}^V$ to $L_G{}^V N_{G_0}^{V_0}/N_G{}^V$ (see Gabriel and Sen [6], Section 4), but this resulted in a large number of incoherences.)

The max W STP performs much better. It is closely related in its structure to the max t^2 STP, and indeed the results of these two STP's in Table VI do not differ very much, though the max t^2 STP provides several more significance decisions than the max W STP.

REFERENCES

1. ARMITAGE, J. V., and KRISHNAIAH, P. R. (1964). Tables for the studentized largest chi-squared distribution and their applications. ARL 64-188. Aerospace Res. Labs., Wright-Patterson Air Force Base, Ohio.
2. BHAPKAR, V. P. (1965). Lectures in multivariate analysis. Univ. of North Carolina, Chapel Hill, North Carolina.
3. GABRIEL, K. R. (1964). A procedure for testing the homogeneity of all sets of means in analysis of variance. *Biometrics* **20** 459–477.
4. GABRIEL, K. R. (1969). Simultaneous test procedures—some theory of multiple comparisons. *Ann. Math. Statist.* **40** 224–250.
5. GABRIEL, K. R. (1968). Simultaneous test procedures in multivariate analysis of variance. *Biometrika* **55** 489–504.
6. GABRIEL, K. R., and SEN, P. K. (1968). Simultaneous test procedures for one-way ANOVA and MANOVA based on rank scores. *Sankhyā Ser. A* **30** 303–312.
7. KASKEY, G., KRISHNAIAH, P. R., and AZZARI, A. (1962). Cluster formation and diagnostic significance in psychiatric symptom evaluation. *Proc. Fall Joint Comput. Conf., Philadelphia, 1962*. Spartan Books, Washington, D.C.
8. KHATRI, G. C. (1966). A note on a MANOVA model applied to problems in growth curves. *Ann. Inst. Statist. Math.* **18** 75–86 (also, Mimeo Seri. No. 399, 1964, Inst. Statist. Univ. North Carolina, Chapel Hill, North Carolina).
9. KRISHNAIAH, P. R. (1964). Multiple comparison tests in multivariate case. ARL 64-124. Aerospace Res. Labs., Wright-Patterson Air Force Base, Ohio.
10. KRISHNAIAH, P. R. (1965). On the simultaneous ANOVA and MANOVA tests. *Ann. Inst. Statist. Math.* **17** 35–53.
11. KRISHNAIAH, P. R. (1965). On a multivariate generalization of the simultaneous analysis of variance test. *Ann. Inst. Statist. Math.* **17** 167–173.

12. KRISHNAIAH, P. R. (1965). Multiple comparison tests in multi-response experiments. *Sankhyā Ser. A* **27** 65–71.
13. KRISHNAIAH, P. R., and ARMITAGE, J. V. (1965). Probability integrals of the multivariate F distribution, tables and applications. ARL 65-236. Aerospace Res. Labs., Wright-Patterson Air Force Base, Ohio.
14. MILLER, R. G. (1966). "Simultaneous Statistical Inference." McGraw-Hill, New York.
15. MUDHOLKAR, G. S. (1966). On confidence bounds associated with multivariate analysis of variance and non-independence between two sets of variates. *Ann. Math. Statist.* **37** 1736–1746.
16. REEVE, E. C. R. (1941). A statistical analysis of taxonomic differences within the genus *Tamandua* Gray (Xenartha). *Proc. Zool. Soc. London Ser. A* **111** 279–302.
17. ROY, J. (1958). Step-down procedure in multivariate analysis. *Ann. Math. Statist.* **29** 1177–1187.
18. ROY, S. N. (1954). A useful theorem in matrix theory. *Proc. Amer. Math. Soc.* **5** 635–638.
19. ROY, S. N., and BOSE, R. C. (1953). Simultaneous confidence interval estimation. *Ann. Math. Statist.* **24** 513–536.
20. ROY, S. N., and GNANADESIKAN, R. (1957). Further contributions to multivariate confidence bounds. *Biometrika* **44** 399–410.
21. SIOTANI, M. (1959). On the range in multivariate case (in Japanese). *Proc. Inst. Statist. Math.* **6** 155–165.
22. SIOTANI, M. (1960). Notes on multivariate confidence bounds. *Ann. Inst. Statist. Math.* **11** 167–182.

On the Effect of Heteroscedasticity and Nonnormality upon Some Multivariate Test Procedures

KOICHI ITO

NANZAN UNIVERSITY
NAGOYA, JAPAN

1. INTRODUCTION AND SUMMARY

As in case of univariate analysis, a statistical hypothesis in multivariate analysis is usually tested on the assumption that the observations are (i) independently and (ii) normally distributed (iii) with a common variance-covariance (var-covar) matrix. A desirable characteristic of a test is that the significance level and the power of the test should be insensitive or "robust" to departures from the standard assumption given above.

There are numerous works in univariate analysis to examine the robustness of test procedures in which studies were made not only from the large sample but also from the small sample points of view (as for the literature, see, e.g., Scheffé [23], Chapter 10 and Plackett [20], Chapter 5). In what follows, we shall examine the magnitude of the effect on some multivariate test procedures when (i) the observations, while remaining independent of one another, are normally but heteroscedastically (hetstically) distributed; (ii) the observations, while remaining independent of one another, are not normally distributed. The small sample treatment of the problem, however, is very difficult, if not impossible, and we shall have to content ourselves in most of the cases with its asymptotic (asymp) treatment for large values of the sample sizes. Hence, most of the results shown in the present paper are merely preliminary, and need to be investigated further in the general case in which the sample sizes are not necessarily large.

In characterizing a multivariate nonnormal distribution we shall specify only the first four moments, and we shall find that the effect of nonnormality upon some usual multivariate test procedures can be asymp indicated in terms of the third and fourth cumulants of the parent populations, and that this result is considered of some value in the present status of the theory of multivariate analysis.

Different from the lines of approach followed by Srivastava [25], Yao [30], etc., the present paper is concerned with a study of the magnitude of the effect of heteroscedasticity (hetsty) and/or nonnormality upon some standard test procedures, which is a multivariate extension of univariate works due to Scheffé [23] and Box [3] along the line of study by Ito and Schull [15] and Ito [14].

In Part I, consideration will be given to testing hypotheses about mean vectors by means of four tests in the heteroscedastic (hetstic) normal case or in the nonnormal case. It is shown in Section 3 that a certain exact test, called the T_s^2 test, is a most powerful test among all tests obtainable under Scheffé's procedure [22] for the multivariate Behrens-Fisher problem, and it is fairly powerful in the homoscedastic (homstic) case as compared with the ordinary generalized Student T^2 test. For the multivariate Behrens-Fisher problem, two approximate tests called the T_u^2 test (equivalent to the Hotelling's T_0^2 test in the normal, homstic case) and the T_v^2 test which are multivariate extensions of Welch's u-test and v-test, respectively [28], are examined in Section 4. An asymp expansion of the noncentral cdf of the T_v^2 statistic is given in terms of the noncentral cdf of χ^2 statistics, and by means of this result together with Ito and Schull's results for the T_u^2 test [15], a numerical comparison is made between the T_u^2 test and the T_v^2 test. It is found that for large sample sizes the T_v^2 test is less affected than the T_u^2 test by violation of the assumption of homsty, and that if homsty is assumed, then the T_u^2 test is better than the T_v^2 test, but as soon as there exists any doubt as to whether the var-covar matrices are equal, the T_v^2 test is preferable to the T_u^2 test. This large sample conclusion may be extended to the case of k samples. In Section 5 the asymp properties of the T_u^2 test, the T_v^2 test, and the T_w^2 test (the likelihood ratio test [lrt]) are investigated in the nonnormal case, and it is found that the T_u^2 test and the T_w^2 test are asymp equivalent, and that the effect of the third and the fourth cumulants upon the three tests are broadly of the same order, with the levels of significance of the tests having no effect by the existence of the third cumulants. However, the effect of hetsty is marked upon the T_u^2 test while there is none upon the T_v^2 test.

Testing certain hypotheses about var-covar matrices of the nonnormal populations is the topic in Part II. In Section 6, the central and noncentral limiting distributions of four likelihood ratio criteria (lrc) are derived in the nonnormal case, each for testing a certain different hypothesis.

Use is made of all the above findings to give a conclusion that when sample sizes are very large, the effect of violation of the normality assumption is slight on testing hypotheses about the mean vectors but dangerous on testing hypotheses about var-covar matrices, as shown in the case of univariate analysis (Scheffé [23], p. 337).

2. PRELIMINARIES—THE MATHEMATICAL MODEL OF k SAMPLES

Let there be given k random vectors of p components, each representing a p-variate parent population

$$\mathbf{x}_t' = [x_{1t}, x_{2t}, \ldots, x_{pt}], \qquad t = 1, 2, \ldots, k, \tag{2.1}$$

whose distributions are characterized by as many moments as desired. Specifically the first four moments of $\mathbf{x}_t$ are given by (Kendall and Stuart [17], p. 319),

$$E(\mathbf{x}_t) = \boldsymbol{\mu}_t, \tag{2.2}$$

$$E(\mathbf{x}_t - \boldsymbol{\mu}_t)(\mathbf{x}_t - \boldsymbol{\mu}_t)' = \boldsymbol{\Sigma}_t, \tag{2.3}$$

$$E(x_{it} - \mu_{it})(x_{jt} - \mu_{jt})(x_{lt} - \mu_{lt}) = \kappa_{ijl}^{(t)} \tag{2.4}$$

$$\begin{aligned} &E(x_{it} - \mu_{it})(x_{jt} - \mu_{jt})(x_{lt} - \mu_{lt})(x_{mt} - \mu_{mt}) \\ &\quad = \kappa_{ijlm}^{(t)} + \sigma_{ij}^{(t)}\sigma_{lm}^{(t)} + \sigma_{il}^{(t)}\sigma_{jm}^{(t)} + \sigma_{im}^{(t)}\sigma_{jl}^{(t)}, \end{aligned} \tag{2.5}$$

where the prime denotes the transpose of a vector (or a matrix); and x_{it} and μ_{it} denote the ith components of $\mathbf{x}_t$ and $\boldsymbol{\mu}_t$, respectively, etc., $\boldsymbol{\Sigma}_t = (\sigma_{ij}^{(t)})$ is a $p \times p$ positive definite, symmetric (pds) matrix whose elements are assumed to be finite; $\kappa_{ijl}^{(t)}$ and $\kappa_{ijlm}^{(t)}$ are the third and fourth cumulants of every kind of $\mathbf{x}_t$, respectively, both assumed to be finite; $i, j, l, m = 1, 2, \ldots, p$. By a sample of size N_t of $\mathbf{x}_t$ is meant a collection of N_t mutually independent random vectors

$$\mathbf{x}_{t\alpha}' = [x_{1t\alpha}, x_{2t\alpha}, \ldots, x_{pt\alpha}], \qquad \alpha = 1, 2, \ldots, N_t, \tag{2.6}$$

each of which follows the same distribution as $\mathbf{x}_t$. Thus the k vectors of (2.1) give rise to k samples, namely, the vectors (2.6) wherein t takes the values $1, \ldots, k$, each being independently drawn from the p-variate parent population specified by (2.2)–(2.5). The total number of such vectors is

$$N = \sum_{t=1}^{k} N_t. \tag{2.7}$$

We shall also assume that two vectors belonging to two different samples are always independent. Then about the distribution of the N vectors $\mathbf{x}_{t\alpha}$ we know the following facts: (i) $\mathbf{x}_{t\alpha}$ and $\mathbf{x}_{s\beta}$ are independent if either $t \neq s$ or $\alpha \neq \beta$; (ii) for every fixed t the vectors $\mathbf{x}_{t\alpha}$, $\alpha = 1, 2, \ldots, N_t$, are identically distributed; (iii) each $\mathbf{x}_{t\alpha}$ has the first four moments given by (2.2)–(2.5). If the parent populations follow p-variate normal distributions, then not only all $\kappa_{ijl}^{(t)}$ and $\kappa_{ijlm}^{(t)}$ but also all cumulants of higher orders vanish.

In the case of one sample, i.e., $k = 1$, we shall omit the subscript t not only from all the above expressions but also from all what follows. We shall also denote the upper 100 α% point of the distribution of a statistic U by U_α and the lower 100 α% point of the distribution of a statistic W by $W(\alpha)$. If a statistic is distributed as a central chi-square with n degrees of freedom, it is denoted by $\chi^2(n)$, with its upper 100 α% point expressed as $\chi_\alpha{}^2(n)$.

PART I. TESTING HYPOTHESES ABOUT MEAN VECTORS

In testing the null hypothesis

$$H_{01}: \quad \boldsymbol{\mu}_1 = \boldsymbol{\mu}_2 = \cdots = \boldsymbol{\mu}_k \tag{$*1$}$$

against the whole class of alternatives

$$H_1: \qquad \text{not } H_{01} \tag{$*2$}$$

under the assumptions of normality of the parent populations and of homsty of var-covar matrices, there have been proposed for use, among others, the $T_0{}^2$ test, due to Lawley [18] and Hotelling [6, 7], and the W test (lrt), due to Wilks [29], both of which are defined, respectively, as follows. The critical region for the $T_0{}^2$ test of 100 α% significance level is given by

$$\{T_0{}^2: \quad T_0{}^2 > T_{0\alpha}^2(p, k-1, N-k)\}, \tag{$*3$}$$

where

$$T_0{}^2 = \operatorname{tr} \mathbf{Q}_B \mathbf{S}_0^{-1}, \tag{$*4$}$$

with

$$\mathbf{Q}_B = \sum_{t=1}^{k} N_t(\overline{\mathbf{x}}_t - \overline{\mathbf{x}})(\overline{\mathbf{x}}_t - \overline{\mathbf{x}})', \qquad \mathbf{S}_0 = \sum_{t=1}^{k} n_t \mathbf{S}_t/(N-k), \qquad \overline{\mathbf{x}}_t = \sum_{\alpha=1}^{N_t} \mathbf{x}_{t\alpha}/N_t,$$

$$\overline{\mathbf{x}} = \sum_{t=1}^{k} r_t \overline{\mathbf{x}}_t, \qquad r_t = N_t/N, \qquad \mathbf{S}_t = \sum_{\alpha=1}^{N_t} (\mathbf{x}_{t\alpha} - \overline{\mathbf{x}}_t)(\mathbf{x}_{t\alpha} - \overline{\mathbf{x}}_t)'/n_t,$$

$$n_t = N_t - 1.$$

The $T_0{}^2$ statistic follows the Hotelling's $T_0{}^2$ distribution with $(p, k-1, N-k)$ degrees of freedom when H_{01} is true (as for the central and noncentral distributions of $T_0{}^2$ see Hotelling [7] and Ito [12, 13]). On the other hand, the critical region for the W test of 100 α% level of significance is given by

$$\{W: \quad W < W(\alpha)\}, \tag{$*5$}$$

where

$$W = |(N-k)\mathbf{S}_0| / |\mathbf{Q}_B + (N-k)\mathbf{S}_0|, \tag{$*6$}$$

(see, e.g., Anderson [1], p. 208). Under the assumption of normality of the parent populations (but without assuming homsty), James [16] proposed use of the T_v^2 test, which is a multivariate extension of Welch's v-test [28], and whose critical region of 100 α% level of significance is given by

$$\{T_v^2(k):\quad T_v^2(k) > T_{v\alpha}^2(k)\}, \tag{*7}$$

where

$$T_v^2(k) = \sum_{t=1}^{k} (\bar{\mathbf{x}}_t - \hat{\mathbf{x}})'\mathbf{W}_t(\bar{\mathbf{x}}_t - \hat{\mathbf{x}}), \tag{*8}$$

with

$$\mathbf{W}_t = (\mathbf{S}_t/N_t)^{-1}, \qquad \hat{\mathbf{x}} = \mathbf{W}^{-1}\sum_{t=1}^{k} \mathbf{W}_t\bar{\mathbf{x}}_t, \qquad \mathbf{W} = \sum_{t=1}^{k} \mathbf{W}_t.$$

Unfortunately, however, the exact distribution of $T_v^2(k)$ is not available at present.

In the following sections, we shall make a study of the effects of violation of the assumption of normality or of homsty or both upon these three tests together with a certain other test. Before going further, however, we shall consider a special case of one sample, i.e., $k = 1$. In this case the null hypothesis

$$H_{02}:\quad \boldsymbol{\mu} = \boldsymbol{\mu}_0 \tag{*9}$$

is tested in place of H_{01} of (*1), where $\boldsymbol{\mu}_0$ is a constant vector, and it is noted that the T_0^2 test, the W test, and the T_v^2 test become equivalent. The exact distributions of the test statistics are very difficult to obtain in the general case in which the distribution of $\mathbf{x}$ is not assumed to be normal, but Hsu [11] showed that the asymp distribution of T_0^2 when H_{02} is true is the χ^2 distribution with p degrees of freedom, valid for any arbitrary parent population. Hence, it may be said that for large values of N, a nominal 100 α% level of significance test:

$$\{T_0^2:\quad T_0^2 > \chi_\alpha^2(p)\}, \tag{*10}$$

is little affected by violation of the normality assumption of the parent population.

3. AN EXACT TEST IN THE NORMAL, HETSTIC CASE

In (2.6) let $k = 2$ and suppose that $\mathbf{x}_{1\alpha}$, $\alpha = 1, 2, \ldots, N_1$, and $\mathbf{x}_{2\beta}$, $\beta = 1, 2, \ldots, N_2$, where it is assumed that $N_1 \leq N_2$, represent two independent random samples from the p-variate normal populations $N(\boldsymbol{\mu}_1, \boldsymbol{\Sigma}_1)$ and

$N(\boldsymbol{\mu}_2, \boldsymbol{\Sigma}_2)$, respectively. It is, however, not assumed that $\boldsymbol{\Sigma}_1 = \theta\boldsymbol{\Sigma}_2$, where θ is a known scalar. Then the problem of testing the null hypothesis

$$H_{03}: \quad \boldsymbol{\mu}_1 = \boldsymbol{\mu}_2 \tag{3.1}$$

against any alternative

$$H_3: \quad \boldsymbol{\mu}_1 \neq \boldsymbol{\mu}_2 \tag{3.2}$$

will be called a multivariate Behrens-Fisher problem. We shall apply Scheffé's procedure in a general way to obtain a class D of exact tests for H_{03} against H_3 which makes use of the generalized Student T^2 statistic, and choose a most powerful test in D, which we shall call the T_s^2 test (Hotelling [5], Scheffé [22], Bennett [2], Anderson [1], pp. 118–122).

Consider a $p \times N$ matrix $\mathbf{Y} = (y_{i\gamma})$, $i = 1, 2, \ldots, p$; $\gamma = 1, 2, \ldots, N$, such that

$$\mathbf{Y}(p \times N) = \mathbf{X}_1(p \times N_1) \cdot \mathbf{A}(N_1 \times N) - \mathbf{X}_2(p \times N_2) \cdot \mathbf{B}(N_2 \times N), \tag{3.3}$$

where

$$\mathbf{X}_1 = [\mathbf{x}_{11}, \mathbf{x}_{12}, \ldots, \mathbf{x}_{1N_1}], \qquad \mathbf{X}_2 = [\mathbf{x}_{21}, \mathbf{x}_{22}, \ldots, \mathbf{x}_{2N_2}],$$

and $\mathbf{A} = (a_{\alpha\gamma})$ and $\mathbf{B} = (b_{\beta\gamma})$ and $N_1 \times N$ and $N_2 \times N$ matrices, respectively, whose elements and number of columns N are constants independent of population parameters and are to be determined subject to the following conditions:

$$E(\mathbf{y}_\gamma) \equiv \mathbf{v} = \boldsymbol{\mu}_1 - \boldsymbol{\mu}_2, \tag{3.4}$$

$$E(\mathbf{y}_\gamma - \mathbf{v})(\mathbf{y}_\varepsilon - \mathbf{v})' = \delta_{\gamma\varepsilon}\boldsymbol{\Sigma}, \tag{3.5}$$

where $\mathbf{y}_\gamma$ is the γth column vector of $\mathbf{Y}$, $\gamma = 1, 2, \ldots, N$, and $\delta_{\gamma\varepsilon} = 1$ if $\gamma = \varepsilon$ and $\delta_{\gamma\varepsilon} = 0$ if $\gamma \neq \varepsilon$ for $\gamma, \varepsilon = 1, 2, \ldots, N$, and $\boldsymbol{\Sigma} = (\sigma_{ij})$ is a $p \times p$ pds matrix. Then the null hypothesis H_{03} is equivalent to

$$H_{03}^*: \quad \mathbf{v} = \mathbf{0} \tag{3.6}$$

and can be tested against any alternative $H_3^*: \mathbf{v} \neq 0$ by means of the generalized Student T^2 statistic. That is, if we let

$$\bar{\mathbf{y}} = \sum_{\gamma=1}^{N} \mathbf{y}_\gamma / N \tag{3.7}$$

and

$$\mathbf{S}(p \times p) = \sum_{\gamma=1}^{N} (\mathbf{y}_\gamma - \bar{\mathbf{y}})(\mathbf{y}_\gamma - \bar{\mathbf{y}})'/n, \tag{3.8}$$

where $n = N - 1$, then a $100\,\alpha\%$ level of significance test for H_{03}^* against H_3^* consists of the critical region:

$$\{T_s^2: \quad T_s^2 > T_\alpha^2(n)\}, \tag{3.9}$$

where

$$T_s^2 = N\bar{\mathbf{y}}'\mathbf{S}^{-1}\bar{\mathbf{y}}. \tag{3.10}$$

When H_{03}^* is true, T_s^2 is distributed according to the generalized Student T^2 distribution with n degrees of freedom and when H_0^* is not true, it is distributed according to the noncentral generalized Student T^2 distribution with noncentrality parameter $\lambda = N\mathbf{v}'\mathbf{\Sigma}^{-1}\mathbf{v}$ and n degrees of freedom. Hence, the power of the test (3.9) is given by (Hsu [8]),

$$\begin{aligned} P\{T_s^2 > T_\alpha^2(n) \mid H_3^*\} &\equiv \beta(\alpha;\, p,\, n-p+1;\, \lambda) \\ &= 1 - e^{-\lambda/2} \sum_{i=0}^{\infty} \frac{(\lambda/2)^i}{i!}\, I_x(\tfrac{1}{2}p + i,\, \tfrac{1}{2}(n-p+1)), \end{aligned} \tag{3.11}$$

where $x = T_\alpha^2(n)/\{n + T_\alpha^2(n)\}$ and $I_x(a, b)$ is the incomplete beta-function ratio defined by

$$I_x(a, b) = \int_0^x x^{a-1}(1-x)^{b-1}\, dx \Big/ \int_0^1 x^{a-1}(1-x)^{b-1}\, dx.$$

Now, taking expectations, variances and covariances of the elements of both sides of Eq. (3.3), we see that conditions (3.4) and (3.5) are equivalent to

$$\mathbf{A}'\mathbf{e}(N_1) = \mathbf{e}(N), \qquad \mathbf{B}'\mathbf{e}(N_2) = \mathbf{e}(N), \tag{3.12}$$

$$\mathbf{A}'\mathbf{A} = c_1\mathbf{I}(N), \qquad \mathbf{B}'\mathbf{B} = c_2\,\mathbf{I}(N), \tag{3.13}$$

and

$$\mathbf{\Sigma} = c_1\mathbf{\Sigma}_1 + c_2\,\mathbf{\Sigma}_2, \tag{3.14}$$

where $\mathbf{e}(L)$ is a $L \times 1$ column vector whose elements are all unity, $\mathbf{I}(L)$ is an $L \times L$ unit matrix, and c_1, and c_2 are constants. Following arguments similar to Scheffé's it is easily shown that in order for $\mathbf{A}$ and $\mathbf{B}$ to satisfy (3.12) and (3.13), N, c_1, and c_2 must satisfy

$$N \leq N_1 \leq N_2 \tag{3.15}$$

and

$$c_1 \geq N/N_1, \qquad c_2 \geq N/N_2. \tag{3.16}$$

Hence, we have obtained a class D of exact tests of the type (3.9), each of which is given by a solution of (3.12) and (3.13) for $\mathbf{A}$ and $\mathbf{B}$ when N, c_1, and c_2, satisfying (3.15) and (3.16), respectively, are specified.

We note here that the power of a test in D against any specific alternative $H_3^* : \mathbf{v} = \boldsymbol{\mu}_1 - \boldsymbol{\mu}_2 \neq 0$ depends on the values of N, c_1, and c_2, and so our next problem is to choose N, c_1, and c_2 so as to obtain a most powerful test in D.

We shall first observe the following two properties of the power function given by (3.11):

(i) $\beta(\alpha; a, b; \lambda)$ is a nondecreasing function of b for fixed values of α, a, and λ. This is easily proved from Hsu's theorem (Hsu [10]) concerning the power function of the analysis of variance F test. As a matter of fact, tables of $\beta(\alpha; a, b; \lambda)$ (e.g., Tang [26]) indicate that it is actually a monotonically increasing function of b for fixed a and λ when α is a usual level of significance, i.e., $\alpha = 0.05$ or 0.01.

(ii) $\beta(\alpha; a, b; \lambda)$ is a monotonically increasing function of λ for fixed values of α, a, and b (see, e.g., Roy [21]).

We shall next show that the parameter λ in (3.11) is a monotonically decreasing function of c_1 and c_2. Let $\mathbf{\Sigma}_1 = \mathbf{M}\mathbf{D}_e\mathbf{M}'$ and $\mathbf{\Sigma}_2 = \mathbf{M}\mathbf{M}'$, where $\mathbf{M}$ is a $p \times p$ nonsingular matrix and $\mathbf{D}_e$ is a $p \times p$ diagonal matrix whose elements are the characteristic roots e_i, $i = 1, 2, \ldots, p$ (all positive) of $\mathbf{\Sigma}_1\mathbf{\Sigma}_2^{-1}$. Then

$$\lambda = N\mathbf{v}'\mathbf{\Sigma}^{-1}\mathbf{v} = N\sum_{i=1}^{p} \phi_i^2/(c_1 e_i + c_2), \tag{3.17}$$

where $\boldsymbol{\phi}'(1 \times p) = [\phi_1, \ldots, \phi_p] = \mathbf{v}'\mathbf{M}^{-1'}$. Since the e_i's and the ϕ_i's are independent of c_1 and c_2, our proposition follows. It is now clear that a most powerful test in D against any specific alternative is obtained when we ascribe to N its maximum value satisfying (3.15), i.e., N_1 and then to c_1 and c_2 their respective minimum values satisfying (3.16), i.e., 1 and N_1/N_2, respectively. Hence, a most powerful test in D is given by solving

$$\mathbf{A}'\mathbf{e}(N_1) = \mathbf{e}(N_1), \qquad \mathbf{B}'\mathbf{e}(N_2) = \mathbf{e}(N_1), \tag{3.18}$$

and

$$\mathbf{A}'\mathbf{A} = \mathbf{I}(N_1), \qquad \mathbf{B}'\mathbf{B} = (N_1/N_2)\mathbf{I}(N_1). \tag{3.19}$$

A simple particular solution of (3.18) and (3.19), given by Bennett [2], who adopted Scheffé's univariate expressions, is as follows:

$$\begin{aligned} a_{\alpha\gamma} &= \delta_{\alpha\gamma}, \qquad \alpha = 1, 2, \ldots, N_1, \\ b_{\beta\gamma} &= \begin{cases} \delta_{\beta\gamma}(N_1/N_2)^{1/2} - (N_1 N_2)^{-1/2} + N_2^{-1} & \text{for } \beta \le N_1, \\ N_2^{-1} & \text{for } N_1 < \beta \le N_2, \end{cases} \end{aligned} \tag{3.20}$$

where $\gamma = 1, 2, \ldots, N_1$. Substitution of (3.20) in (3.3) reduces the test statistic (3.10) to

$$T_s^2 = N_1(\bar{\mathbf{x}}_1 - \bar{\mathbf{x}}_2)'\,\mathbf{S}^{-1}(\bar{\mathbf{x}}_1 - \bar{\mathbf{x}}_2), \tag{3.21}$$

where

$$\bar{\mathbf{x}}_1 = \sum_{\alpha=1}^{N_1} \mathbf{x}_{1\alpha}/N_1, \qquad \bar{\mathbf{x}}_2 = \sum_{\beta=1}^{N_2} \mathbf{x}_{2\beta}/N_2 \tag{3.22}$$

and $\mathbf{S}$ of (3.8) is more conveniently expressed as

$$\mathbf{S} = \sum_{\gamma=1}^{N_1} (\mathbf{u}_\gamma - \bar{\mathbf{u}})(\mathbf{u}_\gamma - \bar{\mathbf{u}})'/n_1 , \tag{3.23}$$

with

$$\mathbf{u}_\gamma = \mathbf{x}_{1\gamma} - (N_1/N_2)^{1/2}\mathbf{x}_{2\gamma}, \qquad \gamma = 1, 2, \ldots, N_1,$$

and

$$\bar{\mathbf{u}} = \sum_{\gamma=1}^{N_1} \mathbf{u}_\gamma/N_1, \qquad n_1 = N_1 - 1.$$

Thus, we have proved that the critical region (3.9) with test statistic (3.21) is a most powerful test of significance level α for H_{03} against H_3 among all those obtainable under Scheffé's procedure.

We shall now compare the power of the test given by (3.9) with (3.21) with that of an optimum test for the case in which it is assumed that $\mathbf{\Sigma}_1 = \theta\mathbf{\Sigma}_2$.

The latter test is a special case of Hotelling's T_0^2 test (*3) where $k = 2$, and the test statistic is an ordinary generalized Student T^2 whose critical region of significance level α consists of

$$\{T_0^2\colon \quad T_0^2 > T_\alpha^2(N_1 + N_2 - 2)\}, \tag{3.24}$$

where

$$T_0^2 = N_1N_2(\bar{\mathbf{x}}_1 - \bar{\mathbf{x}}_2)'\mathbf{S}_0^{-1}(\bar{\mathbf{x}}_1 - \bar{\mathbf{x}}_2)/(N_1 + \theta N_2) \tag{3.25}$$

with

$$\mathbf{S}_0 = \left\{\theta^{-1} \sum_{\alpha=1}^{N_1} (\mathbf{x}_{1\alpha} - \bar{\mathbf{x}}_1)(\mathbf{x}_{1\alpha} - \bar{\mathbf{x}}_1)' + \sum_{\beta=1}^{N_2} (\mathbf{x}_{2\beta} - \bar{\mathbf{x}}_2)(\mathbf{x}_{2\beta} - \bar{\mathbf{x}}_2)'\right\}/(N_1 + N_2 - 2).$$

When H_{03} is true, the statistic T_0^2 follows the generalized Student T^2 distribution with $N_1 + N_2 - 2$ degrees of freedom.

The power of this test is given by

$$\Pr\{T_0^2 > T_\alpha^2(N_1 + N_2 - 2) \mid H_3\} = \beta(\alpha; p, N_1 + N_2 - p - 1; \lambda') \tag{3.26}$$

where $\beta(\alpha; a, b; \lambda)$ is the same as in (3.11) and $\lambda' = (\boldsymbol{\mu}_1 - \boldsymbol{\mu}_2)'\mathbf{\Sigma}_0^{-1}(\boldsymbol{\mu}_1 - \boldsymbol{\mu}_2)$ with $\mathbf{\Sigma}_0 = ((\theta/N_1) + N_2^{-1})\mathbf{\Sigma}_2$. The test (3.9) specified by (3.21) is a most powerful test in class D of tests for testing $H_{03} : \boldsymbol{\mu}_1 = \boldsymbol{\mu}_2$ when we do not assume that $\mathbf{\Sigma}_1 = \theta\mathbf{\Sigma}_2$, but since we deal with a less favorable situation where nothing is known of $\mathbf{\Sigma}_1$ and $\mathbf{\Sigma}_2$, this test cannot be expected to be as powerful as (3.24) if we know that $\mathbf{\Sigma}_1 = \theta\mathbf{\Sigma}_2$. It is easily seen that in the power functions (3.11) and (3.26), respectively, of the two tests, λ and λ' take on the same value for any specified alternative $H_3 : \boldsymbol{\mu}_1 \neq \boldsymbol{\mu}_2$. Hence, given λ and α, we may compare the two powers for various values of N_1 and N_2. Tables I–III give the ratios of the powers of the T_s^2 test to those of the T_0^2 for several values of λ, α, N_1, and N_2. They were calculated by means of Tang's tables [26].

The existence and construction of an "optimum" test for the multivariate Behrens-Fisher problem is a formidable affair, but it is of interest to know that the T_s^2 test provides an exact test and is a most powerful among all tests obtainable under Scheffé's procedure. Also Tables I–III indicate that the power of the test is fairly high compared with that of the optimum test (3.24) when it is known that $\mathbf{\Sigma}_1 = \theta\mathbf{\Sigma}_2$, provided that N_1 and N_2 are roughly equal. As is clear from the present status of the theory of multivariate analysis, an extension of the T_s^2 test to the case of k samples is not available, apart from the question of existence and construction of an optimum exact test.

TABLE I

Ratios of Powers of the T_s^2 Test to Those of the T_0^2 Test
$p = 2$, $\lambda = 3$ and $\alpha = 0.05$ (above), and $\alpha = 0.01$ (below)

N_1 \ N_2	6	10	15	20	∞
6	0.730 0.566	0.669 0.473	0.633 0.422	0.615 0.394	0.547 0.307
10		0.847 0.710	0.818 0.664	0.801 0.628	0.724 0.507
15			0.904 0.805	0.889 0.784	0.817 0.650
20				0.936 0.864	0.863 0.729
∞					1.000 1.000

TABLE II

Ratios of Powers of the T_s^2 Test to Those of the T_0^2 Test
$p = 3$, $\lambda = 4$ *for* $\alpha = 0.05$ (*above*), *and* $\alpha = 0.01$ (*below*)

$N_1 \backslash N_2$	7	10	15	20	∞
7	0.667 0.500	0.620 0.436	0.576 0.376	0.554 0.345	0.475 0.250
10		0.778 0.615	0.739 0.557	0.716 0.520	0.626 0.390
15			0.859 0.740	0.843 0.705	0.751 0.555
20				0.904 0.817	0.813 0.652
∞					1.000 1.000

TABLE III

Ratios of Powers of the T_s^2 Test to Those of the T_0^2 Test
$p = 4$, $\lambda = 5$ *and* $\alpha = 0.05$ (*above*), *and* $\alpha = 0.01$ (*below*)

$N_1 \backslash N_2$	8	10	15	20	∞
8	0.616 0.449	0.584 0.404	0.537 0.342	0.509 0.310	0.422 0.211
10		0.701 0.533	0.655 0.467	0.630 0.429	0.528 0.300
15			0.816 0.669	0.792 0.636	0.684 0.468
20				0.876 0.764	0.765 0.597
∞					1.000 1.000

4. TWO APPROXIMATE TESTS IN THE NORMAL, HETSTIC CASE

For the multivariate Behrens-Fisher problem treated in Section 3, James [16] proposed an approximate test which becomes exact asymp as the sample sizes become infinite. Suppose that the unbiased estimates $\mathbf{S}_1$ and $\mathbf{S}_2$ of $\boldsymbol{\Sigma}_1$ and Σ_2, respectively, are based on large numbers of degrees of freedom, then we have

$$\Pr\{T_v^2(2) \le 2\theta \mid H_{03}\} \doteqdot G_\rho(\theta) = 1 - \alpha, \tag{4.1}$$

where T_v^2 is obtained on substituting $k = 2$ in (*8) and equals to

$$(\bar{\mathbf{x}}_1 - \bar{\mathbf{x}}_2)'((\mathbf{S}_1/N_1) + (\mathbf{S}_2/N_2))^{-1}(\bar{\mathbf{x}}_1 - \bar{\mathbf{x}}_2) \tag{4.2}$$

and

$$2\theta = \chi_\alpha^2(p), \qquad \rho = p/2, \qquad G_\rho(\theta) = \{\Gamma(\rho)\}^{-1} \int_0^\theta t^{\rho-1} e^{-t}\, dt. \tag{4.3}$$

Since the exact distribution of $T_v^2(2)$ is difficult to obtain, James tried to find a function $h(\theta; \mathbf{S}_1, \mathbf{S}_2)$ on the basis of (4.1) such that

$$\Pr\{T_v^2(2) \le 2h(\theta; \mathbf{S}_1, \mathbf{S}_2) \mid H_{03}\} = G_\rho(\theta) = 1 - \alpha, \tag{4.4}$$

and expressed $h(\theta; \mathbf{S}_1, \mathbf{S}_2)$ as a series of terms of descending order of magnitude with θ as the first term.

Here, however, we shall make use of (4.1) to construct an approximate test that will be called the T_v^2 test and tests H_{03} against H_3 at a nominal 100 α% level of significance by means of the critical region:

$$\{T_v^2(2): \quad T_v^2(2) > 2\theta\}, \tag{4.5}$$

and consider the effect of $\boldsymbol{\Sigma}_1 \neq \boldsymbol{\Sigma}_2$ on its true level of significance and power. Let the noncentral cdf of the $T_v^2(2)$ statistic be denoted by $\Pr\{T_v^2(2) \le 2\theta \mid H_3\}$. Then

$$\Pr\{T_v^2(2) \le 2\theta \mid H_3\} = \boldsymbol{\Theta} \Pr\{\chi_v^2(2) \le 2\theta \mid H_3\}, \tag{4.6}$$

where $\boldsymbol{\Theta}$ is the asymp series with respect to n_1 and n_2 of the derivative operators given by (5.16) of James [16], i.e.,

$$\boldsymbol{\Theta} = 1 + \sum_t \sum_{ijlm} n_t^{-1} \sigma_{ij}^{(t)} \sigma_{lm}^{(t)} \partial_{jl}^{(t)} \partial_{mi}^{(t)} + O(n_t^{-2}), \tag{4.7}$$

with $\partial_{jl}^{(t)} = \frac{1}{2}(1 + \delta_{jl})\, \partial/\partial_{jl}^{(t)}$, etc., and $t = 1, 2$; $i, j, l, m = 1, 2, \ldots, p$; and the second expression on the right denotes the probability

$$\Pr\{\chi_v^2(2) \le 2\theta \mid H_3\} = G_\rho(\theta \mid \lambda) \tag{4.8}$$

where

$$G_\rho(\theta \mid \lambda) = e^{-\lambda/2} \sum_{i=0}^{\infty} (\lambda^i/2^i i!) G_{\rho+i}(\theta),$$

and $G_\rho(\theta \mid 0) = G_\rho(\theta)$ and $\lambda = \mathbf{v}'\mathbf{V}^{-1}\mathbf{v}$ with $\mathbf{v} = \boldsymbol{\mu}_1 - \boldsymbol{\mu}_2$ and $\mathbf{V} = (\boldsymbol{\Sigma}_1/N_1) + (\boldsymbol{\Sigma}_2/N_2)$, i.e., the noncentral cdf of a chi-square with p degrees of freedom and noncentrality parameter λ. Then, by means of the technique similar to the one used by James, an asymp expansion of the noncentral cdf of the $T_v{}^2(2)$ statistic is obtained in terms of the noncentral cdf of the χ^2 statistics as follows:

$$\begin{aligned}\Pr\{T_v{}^2(2) \le 2\theta \mid H_3\} = G_\rho(\theta \mid \lambda) - \sum_t n_t^{-1}[\tfrac{1}{4}\{[t \mid t] + [t]^2\}(E+1) \\ + \tfrac{1}{4}[t \mid t](E-1) + \tfrac{1}{2}\phi_{1t}(E-1)E + \phi_{2t}E^2 \\ + \tfrac{1}{4}\phi_{3t}(E-1)E^2](1-E)G_\rho(\theta \mid \lambda) + O(n_t^{-2}),\end{aligned} \tag{4.9}$$

where

$$\begin{aligned}
[t] &= \operatorname{tr} \mathbf{V}^{-1}(\boldsymbol{\Sigma}_t/N_t),\\
[t \mid s] &= \operatorname{tr} \mathbf{V}^{-1}(\boldsymbol{\Sigma}_t/N_t)\mathbf{V}^{-1}(\boldsymbol{\Sigma}_s/N_s),\\
\phi_{1t} &= \operatorname{tr} \mathbf{v}\mathbf{v}'\mathbf{V}^{-1}(\boldsymbol{\Sigma}_t/N_t)\mathbf{V}^{-1}(\boldsymbol{\Sigma}_t/N_t)\mathbf{V}^{-1},\\
\phi_{2t} &= \tfrac{1}{2}\{\phi_{1t} + \operatorname{tr} \mathbf{V}^{-1}(\boldsymbol{\Sigma}_t/N_t) \cdot \operatorname{tr} \mathbf{v}\mathbf{v}'\mathbf{V}^{-1}(\boldsymbol{\Sigma}_t/N_t)\mathbf{V}^{-1}\},\\
\phi_{3t} &= \operatorname{tr}\{\mathbf{v}\mathbf{v}'\mathbf{V}^{-1}(\boldsymbol{\Sigma}_t/N_t)\mathbf{V}^{-1}\}^2,
\end{aligned}$$

$t = 1, 2$, and $E^\alpha G_\rho(\theta \mid \lambda) = G_{\rho+\alpha}(\theta \mid \lambda)$, $\alpha = 0, \pm 1, \pm 2, \ldots$. When H_{03} is true, then $\mathbf{v} = \mathbf{0}$ and

$$\phi_{1t} = \phi_{2t} = \phi_{3t} = 0, \qquad t = 1, 2. \tag{4.10}$$

Hence, an asymp expansion of the central cdf of the $T_v{}^2(2)$ statistic is given by

$$\begin{aligned}\Pr\{T_v{}^2(2) \le 2\theta \mid H_{03}\} = G_\rho(\theta) - \tfrac{1}{4} \sum_t n_t^{-1}\{2[t \mid t]E + [t]^2(E+1)\} \\ \times (1-E)G_\rho(\theta) + O(n_t^{-2}).\end{aligned} \tag{4.11}$$

Therefore use is made of (4.11) and (4.9) to approximate the true level of significance and the true power, respectively of the test (4.5).

Extension of the test (4.5) to the case of k sample is obvious (James [16]). Suppose that each $\mathbf{x}_{t\alpha}$ of (2.6), $t = 1, 2, \ldots, k$; $\alpha = 1, 2, \ldots, N_t$, follows $N(\boldsymbol{\mu}_t, \boldsymbol{\Sigma}_t)$, where it is not assumed that the $\boldsymbol{\Sigma}_t$'s are equal. Then we may test H_{01} of (*1) against the alternative H_1 of (*2) at a nominal 100 $\alpha\%$ level of significance by means of the critical region:

$$\{T_v{}^2(k):\quad T_v{}^2(k) > \chi_\alpha{}^2(p(k-1))\} \tag{4.12}$$

where $T_v^2(k)$ is given by (*8), provided that the N_t's are large. The true level of significance of (4.12) is shown to have an asymp expansion similar to (4.11) for large values of the N_t's. That is,

$$\begin{aligned}\Pr\{T_v^2(k) > \chi_\alpha^2(p(k-1)) \mid H_{01}\} = 1 - G_{\rho'}(\theta') + \tfrac{1}{4}\sum_t n_t^{-1}\{2[t\,|\,t]E \\ + [t]^2(E+1)\} \\ \times (1-E)G_{\rho'}(\theta') + O(n_t^{-2}),\end{aligned} \tag{4.13}$$

where $\rho' = p(k-1)/2$, $2\theta' = \chi_\alpha^2(p(k-1))$, $[t] = \mathrm{tr}(\mathbf{I}(p) - \mathbf{\Lambda}^{-1}\mathbf{\Lambda}_t)$, $[t\,|\,t] = \mathrm{tr}(\mathbf{I}(p) - \mathbf{\Lambda}^{-1}\mathbf{\Lambda}_t)^2$, with $\mathbf{\Lambda}_t = (\mathbf{\Sigma}_t/N_t)^{-1}$ and $\mathbf{\Lambda} = \sum_t \mathbf{\Lambda}_t$ for $t = 1, 2, \ldots, k$.

TABLE IV

Approximate Values of the True Levels of Significance of the T_v^2 Test in the Case of Two Samples (Together with Those of the T_u^2 Test) when the Nominal Level is 0.05[a]

r	(N_1, N_2)	θ: 0	0.2	0.5	1	2	5	∞
		(a) Case $p = 1$, $c(\mathbf{\Sigma}_1 \mathbf{\Sigma}_2^{-1}) = \theta$						
1	(0) (10,10)	0.081	0.072	0.067	0.065	0.067	0.072	0.081
	(1) (150,150)	0.052	0.051	0.051	0.051	0.051	0.051	0.052
	(2) (300,300)	0.051	0.051	0.051	0.050	0.051	0.051	0.051
	(*) (∞,∞)	0.050	0.050	0.050	0.050	0.050	0.050	0.050
2	(1) (200,100)	0.053	0.052	0.052	0.051	0.051	0.051	0.051
	(2) (400,200)	0.051	0.051	0.051	0.051	0.051	0.050	0.051
	(*) (∞,∞)	0.166	0.118	0.080	0.050	0.028	0.014	0.006
5	(1) (250,50)	0.056	0.055	0.055	0.054	0.053	0.052	0.051
	(2) (500,100)	0.053	0.053	0.052	0.052	0.051	0.051	0.051
	(*) (∞,∞)	0.381	0.224	0.118	0.050	0.014	0.002	0.000
		(b) Case $p = 2$, $c(\mathbf{\Sigma}_1 \mathbf{\Sigma}_2^{-1}) = \theta, \theta$						
1	(0) (10,10)	0.116	0.098	0·087	0.083	0.087	0.098	0.116
	(1) (150,150)	0.054	0.053	0.052	0.052	0.052	0.053	0.054
	(2) (300,300)	0.052	0.051	0.051	0.051	0.051	0.051	0.052
	(*) (∞,∞)	0.050	0.050	0.050	0.050	0.050	0.050	0.050
2	(1) (200,100)	0.056	0.055	0.054	0.053	0.052	0.052	0.053
	(2) (400,200)	0.053	0.053	0.052	0.052	0.051	0.051	0.052
	(*) (∞,∞)	0.223	0.148	0.091	0.050	0.023	0.009	0.002
5	(1) (250,50)	0.062	0.061	0.060	0.059	0.056	0.054	0.052
	(2) (500,100)	0.056	0.056	0.055	0.054	0.053	0.052	0.051
	(*) (∞,∞)	0.549	0.316	0.148	0.050	0.009	0.000	0.000

TABLE IV—*continued*

r	(N_1, N_2)	θ_1: 0.40	0.60	0.85	1	1.35	3	∞
		θ_2: 0	0.30	0.65	1	0.90	0.80	0.75
		(c) Case $p = 2$, $c(\mathbf{\Sigma}_1 \mathbf{\Sigma}_2^{-1}) = \theta_1, \theta_2$						
1	(0) (10,10)	0.101	0.089	0.084	0.083	0.083	0.086	0.093
	(1) (150,150)	0.053	0.052	0.052	0.052	0.052	0.052	0.053
	(2) (300,300)	0.052	0.051	0.051	0.051	0.051	0.051	0.051
	(*) (∞,∞)	0.050	0.050	0.050	0.050	0.050	0.050	0.050
2	(1) (200,100)	0.055	0.054	0.053	0.053	0.053	0.053	0.052
	(2) (400,200)	0.053	0.052	0.052	0.052	0.051	0.051	0.051
	(*) (∞,∞)	0.167	0.102	0.066	0.050	0.045	0.037	0.029
5	(1) (250,50)	0.061	0.060	0.059	0.059	0.058	0.057	0.054
	(2) (500,100)	0.056	0.055	0.055	0.054	0.054	0.053	0.052
	(*) (∞,∞)	0.395	0.183	0.086	0.050	0.043	0.034	0.029
r	(N_1, N_2)	θ: 0	0.2	0.5	1	2	5	∞
		(d) Case $p = 3$, $c(\mathbf{\Sigma}_1 \mathbf{\Sigma}_2^{-1}) = \theta, \theta, \theta$						
1	(0) (10,10)	0.155	0.126	0.108	0.103	0.108	0.126	0.155
	(1) (150,150)	0.056	0.055	0.054	0.053	0.054	0.055	0.056
	(2) (300,300)	0.053	0.052	0.052	0.051	0.052	0.052	0.053
	(*) (∞,∞)	0.050	0.050	0.050	0.050	0.050	0.050	0.050
2	(1) (200,100)	0.060	0.058	0.056	0.055	0.054	0.053	0.055
	(2) (400,200)	0.055	0.054	0.053	0.052	0.052	0.052	0.052
	(*) (∞,∞)	0·272	0.174	0.100	0.050	0.021	0.007	0.001
5	(1) (250,50)	0.069	0.068	0.066	0.064	0.060	0.056	0.054
	(2) (500,100)	0.060	0.059	0.058	0.057	0.055	0.053	0.052
	(*) (∞,∞)	0.668	0.391	0.174	0.050	0.007	0.000	0.000
		(e) Case $p = 4$, $c(\mathbf{\Sigma}_1 \mathbf{\Sigma}_2^{-1}) = \theta, \theta, \theta, \theta$						
1	(0) (10,10)	0.197	0.156	0.132	0.123	0.132	0.156	0.197
	(1) (150,150)	0.059	0.056	0.055	0.054	0.055	0.056	0.059
	(2) (300,300)	0.054	0.053	0.052	0.052	0.052	0.053	0.054
	(*) (∞,∞)	0.050	0.050	0.050	0.050	0.050	0.050	0.050
2	(1) (200,100)	0.063	0.061	0.059	0.057	0.055	0.054	0.057
	(2) (400,200)	0.057	0.056	0.054	0.053	0.052	0.052	0.053
	(*) (∞,∞)	0.315	0.196	0.108	0.050	0.019	0.005	0.001
5	(1) (250,50)	0.077	0.075	0.072	0.069	0.064	0.058	0.055
	(2) (500,100)	0.063	0.062	0.061	0.059	0.057	0.054	0.053
	(*) (∞,∞)	0.755	0.456	0.196	0.050	0.005	0.000	0.000

[a] Figures in rows marked with (*) are for the T_u^2 test.

By means of (4.11) and (4.13) together with "Biometrika Tables for Statisticians" (Pearson and Hartley [19]), approximate values of $\Pr\{T_v^2(2) > \chi_\alpha^2(p) \mid H_{03}\}$ and $\Pr\{T_v^2(k) > \chi_\alpha^2(p(k-1)) \mid H_{01}\}$ are evaluated and given in Tables IV–VI when $\alpha = 0.05$; $p = 1, 2, 3, 4$; $k = 2, 3, 5$ for certain combinations of the $\boldsymbol{\Sigma}_t$'s and the N_t's. In Table IV, $c(\boldsymbol{\Sigma}_1 \boldsymbol{\Sigma}_2^{-1})$ are the characteristic roots of $\boldsymbol{\Sigma}_1 \boldsymbol{\Sigma}_2^{-1}$ and $r = N_1/N_2$, and the total sample size N equals 300 for row (1) and 600 for row (2), respectively, while row (0) is given for a total of $N = 20$ to compare the results with those given by Welch [28] although the present approximations are admittedly very crude for so small a value of N. In Table IV (a), (b), (d), and (e) all the characteristic roots of $\boldsymbol{\Sigma}_1 \boldsymbol{\Sigma}_2^{-1}$ are equal to 0, 0.2, 0.5, 1, 2, 5, and ∞, whereas some of the cases in which the characteristic roots are distinct are shown in (c) when $p = 2$ for $(\theta_1, \theta_2) = (0.40, 0)$, $(0.60, 0.30)$, $(0.85, 0.65)$, $(1, 1)$, $(1.35, 0.90)$, $(3, 0.80)$, and $(\infty, 0.75)$. Ito and Schull [15] made a study of the effect of hetsty upon the Hotelling's T_0^2 test which tests H_{01} at a nominal 100 α% level of significance as if the assumption of homsty were not violated by means of the critical region:

$$\{T_u^2(k):\quad T_u^2(k) > \chi_\alpha^2(p(k-1))\}, \tag{4.14}$$

where $T_u^2(k)$ is the same as T_0^2 in (*4). This test, which is a multivariate extension of Welch's u-test [28], will be called the T_u^2 test. Denote the true significance level of (4.14) by

$$\Pr\{T_u^2(k) > \chi_\alpha^2(p(k-1)) \mid H_{01}\}. \tag{4.15}$$

Since the exact distribution of $T_u^2(k)$ is difficult to obtain if the assumption of homsty is violated, Ito and Schull derived the asymp distribution of the statistic when the sample sizes become infinite simultaneously under the restriction that all r_t's are held fixed and N tends to infinity. By means of this they tabulated approximate values of (4.15) for $p = 1, 2, 3, 4$; $k = 2, 3, 5$; and certain combinations of the $\boldsymbol{\Sigma}_t$'s and the N_t's when $\alpha = 0.05$. For the sake of a comparison between the T_v^2 test and the T_u^2 test, some of their results are reproduced in the rows marked with an asterisk (*) of Tables IV–VI.

In Table IV, it is observed that for a fixed value of $r = N_1/N_2$, the true level of significance of the T_v^2 test is always greater than the nominal level 0.05 whatever the values of the θ's, the farther the values of θ are away from 1, the larger the discrepancy. This is contrary to the case of the T_u^2 test in which for large sample sizes the true level of significance is greater than the nominal level 0.05 when $\theta < 1$, and is less than 0.05 when $\theta > 1$ if $r \neq 1$. Hence, the T_v^2 test always tends to result in overestimation of significance, this tendency increasing with r and p. Unless $r = 1$, the smallest discrepancy of the true level of significance from 0.05 of the T_v^2 test does not take place when $\theta = 1$ while the true level of significance of the T_u^2 test is always asymp equal to 0.05 when $\theta = 1$. It is to be noted, however, that the discrepancy of the true level of significance from the nominal level is far less for the T_v^2 test than for the T_u^2 test whenever $\theta \neq 1$ or $t \neq 1$. Hence, it is concluded that if it is known that $\mathbf{\Sigma}_1 = \mathbf{\Sigma}_2$, then there can be no doubt that the T_u^2 test is better than the

TABLE V

Approximate Values of the True Levels of Significance of the T_v^2 Test in the Case of Three Samples (Together with Those of the T_u^2 Test) when the Nominal Level is 0.05[a]

$(\mathbf{\Sigma}_1, \mathbf{\Sigma}_2, \mathbf{\Sigma}_3)$ (r_1, r_2, r_3)	(N_1, N_2, N_3)	$p=1$	$p=2$	$p=3$	$p=4$
(a) $(\mathbf{\Sigma}_0, \mathbf{\Sigma}_0, \mathbf{\Sigma}_0)$	(1) (100,100,100)[b]	0.053	0.055	0.058	0.062
(r_1, r_2, r_3)	(2) (200,200,200)[b]	0.051	0.053	0.054	0.056
	(*) (∞,∞,∞)	0.050	0.050	0.050	0.050
(b) $(\mathbf{\Sigma}_0, 2\mathbf{\Sigma}_0, 3\mathbf{\Sigma}_0)$	(1) (100,100,100)	0.053	0.057	0.060	0.064
$(\frac{1}{3}, \frac{1}{3}, \frac{1}{3})$	(2) (200,200,200)	0.052	0.055	0.057	0.060
	(*) (∞,∞,∞)	0.054	0.055	0.055	0.056
(c) $(\mathbf{\Sigma}_0, 2\mathbf{\Sigma}_0, 3\mathbf{\Sigma}_0)$	(1) (60,180,60)	0.054	0.059	0.063	0.069
$(\frac{1}{5}, \frac{3}{5}, \frac{1}{5})$	(2) (120,360,120)	0.052	0.054	0.057	0.059
	(*) (∞,∞,∞)	0.058	0.059	0.060	0.060
(d) $(\mathbf{\Sigma}_0, 2\mathbf{\Sigma}_0, 3\mathbf{\Sigma}_0)$	(1) (140,100,60)	0.054	0.058	0.063	0.068
$(\frac{7}{15}, \frac{5}{15}, \frac{3}{15})$	(2) (280,200,120)	0.052	0.054	0.055	0.059
	(*) (∞,∞,∞)	0.092	0.108	0.121	0.132
(e) $(\mathbf{\Sigma}_0, 2\mathbf{\Sigma}_0, 3\mathbf{\Sigma}_0)$	(1) (60,100,140)	0.053	0.056	0.059	0.063
$(\frac{3}{15}, \frac{5}{15}, \frac{7}{15})$	(2) (120,200,280)	0.052	0.053	0.055	0.056
	(*) (∞,∞,∞)	0.031	0.026	0.022	0.020
(f) $(\mathbf{\Sigma}_0, \mathbf{\Sigma}_0, 3\mathbf{\Sigma}_0)$	(1) (100,100,100)	0.053	0.056	0.059	0.062
$(\frac{1}{3}, \frac{1}{3}, \frac{1}{3})$	(2) (200,200,200)	0.051	0.053	0.054	0.056
	(*) (∞,∞,∞)	0.058	0.060	0.060	0.060
(g) $(\mathbf{\Sigma}_0, \mathbf{\Sigma}_0, 3\mathbf{\Sigma}_0)$	(1) (140,100,60)	0.055	0.058	0.062	0.067
$(\frac{7}{15}, \frac{5}{15}, \frac{3}{15})$	(2) (280,200,120)	0.052	0.054	0.056	0.058
	(*) (∞,∞,∞)	0.107	0.130	0.147	0.163
(h) $(\mathbf{\Sigma}_0, \mathbf{\Sigma}_0, 3\mathbf{\Sigma}_0)$	(1) (180,100,20)	0.061	0.073	0.085	0.098
$(\frac{9}{15}, \frac{5}{15}, \frac{1}{15})$	(2) (360,200,40)	0.056	0.061	0.067	0.073
	(*) (∞,∞,∞)	0.178	0.241	0.292	0.337
(i) $(\mathbf{\Sigma}_0, \mathbf{\Sigma}_0, 3\mathbf{\Sigma}_0)$	(1) (20,100,180)	0.059	0.069	0.079	0.090
$(\frac{1}{15}, \frac{5}{15}, \frac{9}{15})$	(2) (40,200,360)	0.055	0.059	0.064	0.069
	(*) (∞,∞,∞)	0.011	0.006	0.004	0.003

[a] Figures in rows marked with (*) are for the T_u^2 test.
[b] In these two cases computation is done only for the case when $N_1 = N_2 = N_3$.

T_v^2 test, but if there exists the possibility that Σ_1 and Σ_2 differ, then the T_u^2 test may give very misleading results and it will be safer to use the T_v^2 test. The conclusion for the case of $p = 1$ tends to coincide with that given for Welch's u- and v-tests [28].

Perusal of Tables V and VI where $k = 3$ and 5, respectively, indicates that the T_v^2 test always tends to result in a slight overestimation of significance while the T_u^2 test results in a marked overestimation or underestimation of significance depending upon a combination of the Σ_t's and the N_t's. As for the T_v^2 test, the more variable populations the larger samples come from, the smaller the discrepancy in probability. Finally, all these effects upon the level of significance are found to increase with p.

TABLE VI

Approximate Values of the True Levels of Significance of the T_v^2 Test in the Case of Five Samples (Together with Those of the T_u^2 Test) when the Nominal Level is 0.05[a]

$(\mathbf{\Sigma}_1, \mathbf{\Sigma}_2, \mathbf{\Sigma}_3, \mathbf{\Sigma}_4, \mathbf{\Sigma}_5)$ $(r_1, r_2, r_3, r_4, r_5)$	$(N_1, N_2, N_3, N_4, N_5)$	$p=1$	$p=2$	$p=3$	$p=4$
(a) $(\mathbf{\Sigma}_0, \mathbf{\Sigma}_0, \mathbf{\Sigma}_0, \mathbf{\Sigma}_0, \mathbf{\Sigma}_0)$	(1) (60,60,60,60,60)[b]	0.058	0.064	0.072	0.080
$(r_1, r_2, r_3, r_4, r_5)$	(2) (120,120,120,120,120)[b]	0.054	0.057	0.061	0.065
	(*) $(\infty,\infty,\infty,\infty,\infty)$	0.050	0.050	0.050	0.050
(b) $(\mathbf{\Sigma}_0, \mathbf{\Sigma}_0, \mathbf{\Sigma}_0, \mathbf{\Sigma}_0, 3\mathbf{\Sigma}_0)$	(1) (60,60,60,60,60)	0.058	0.064	0.072	0.079
$(\frac{1}{5}, \frac{1}{5}, \frac{1}{5}, \frac{1}{5}, \frac{1}{5})$	(2) (120,120,120,120,120)	0.054	0.057	0.061	0.065
	(*) $(\infty,\infty,\infty,\infty,\infty)$	0.064	0.066	0.066	0.067
(c) $(\mathbf{\Sigma}_0, \mathbf{\Sigma}_0, \mathbf{\Sigma}_0, \mathbf{\Sigma}_0, 3\mathbf{\Sigma}_0)$	(1) (108,60,60,60,12)	0.067	0.083	0.100	0.118
$(\frac{9}{25}, \frac{5}{25}, \frac{5}{25}, \frac{5}{25}, \frac{1}{25})$	(2) (216,120,120,120,24)	0.058	0.059	0.074	0.083
	(*) $(\infty,\infty,\infty,\infty,\infty)$	0.157	0.204	0.242	0.276
(d) $(\mathbf{\Sigma}_0, \mathbf{\Sigma}_0, \mathbf{\Sigma}_0, \mathbf{\Sigma}_0, 3\mathbf{\Sigma}_0)$	(1) (12,60,60,60,108)	0.066	0.081	0.097	0.114
$(\frac{1}{25}, \frac{5}{25}, \frac{5}{25}, \frac{5}{25}, \frac{9}{25})$	(2) (24,120,120,120,216)	0.058	0.065	0.073	0.081
	(*) $(\infty,\infty,\infty,\infty,\infty)$	0.021	0.014	0.011	0.008

[a] Figures in rows marked with (*) are for the T_u^2 test.
[b] In these two cases computation is done only for the case when $N_1 = N_2 = N_3 = N_4 = N_5$.

5. THREE APPROXIMATE TESTS IN THE NONNORMAL CASE

In this section, instead of assuming normality of the parent populations, we shall suppose that each of the random vectors $\mathbf{x}_{t\alpha}$, $t = 1, 2, \ldots, k$; $\alpha = 1, 2, \ldots, N_t$, of (2.6) follows a p-variate distribution as specified in

Section 2. In testing the null hypotheses H_{01} against the alternative H_1, we shall consider the three tests, (i) $\hat{T}_u^2$ test, (ii) $\hat{T}_v^2$ test, and (iii) $\hat{T}_w^2$ test. As the small sample distributions of the test statistics are very difficult to obtain in the nonnormal case, we shall have to confine ourselves to the following three approximate tests of nominal 100 α% significance level. That is,

$$\hat{T}_u^2 \text{ test:} \quad \{\hat{T}_u^2(k): \quad \hat{T}_u^2(k) > \chi_\alpha^2(p(k-1))\}, \tag{5.1}$$

$$\hat{T}_v^2 \text{ test:} \quad \{\hat{T}_v^2(k): \quad \hat{T}_v^2(k) > \chi_\alpha^2(p(k-1))\}, \tag{5.2}$$

$$\hat{T}_w^2 \text{ test:} \quad \{\hat{T}_w^2(k): \quad \hat{T}_w^2(k) > \chi_\alpha^2(p(k-1))\}, \tag{5.3}$$

where $\hat{T}_u^2(k)$ is the same as $T_u^2(k)$ in (4.14) but (5.1) tests H_{01} as if the assumption of normality were not violated; $\hat{T}_v^2(k)$ is the same as $T_v^2(k)$ in (4.12) but (5.2) tests H_{01} as if the assumption of normality were not violated; and $\hat{T}_w^2(k) = -(N-k)\log W$, with W defined in (*6). Of course the central and noncentral distributions of test statistics $\hat{T}_u^2(k)$, $\hat{T}_v^2(k)$, and $\hat{T}_w^2(k)$ are different from those obtained under the assumption of normality, and we shall call these tests as $\hat{T}_u^2$ test, $\hat{T}_v^2$ test, and $\hat{T}_w^2$ test of nominal 100 α% significance level instead of T_0^2 test, T_v^2 test, and W-test under standard assumptions. In the following, an asymp study will be made of the effect of violation of the normality assumption on the level of significance and the power of these approximate tests when they are used as if the assumption were not violated.

(1) *The* $\hat{T}_v^2$ *test*

For large values of N such that the N_t's are large with the r_t's held fixed for all t, Hsu [11] showed that the limiting distribution of the $\hat{T}_v^2(k)$ statistic when H_{01} is true is the distribution of $\chi^2(p(k-1))$ for any nonnormal parent populations, and hence the true significance level of the $\hat{T}_v^2$ test (5.2) becomes asymp equal to α. In the following, however, we shall approximate the central and noncentral distributions of the $\hat{T}_v^2(k)$ under the two assumptions: (A) that the N_t's are so large that the elements of S_t's provide exact values of the elements of Σ_t's; (B) that the statistic obtained under assumption (A) is distributed like a constant multiple of a central chi-square. This procedure will facilitate a comparison of the $\hat{T}_v^2$ test with the $\hat{T}_u^2$ test and the $\hat{T}_w^2$ test. Under assumption (A), for large values of N, the critical region (5.2) may be approximated by the critical region:

$$\{\hat{\chi}_v^2(k): \quad \hat{\chi}_v^2(k) > \chi_\alpha^2(p(k-1))\}, \tag{5.4}$$

where the statistic $\hat{\chi}_v^2(k)$ is obtained on substituting Σ_t for S_t, $t = 1, 2, \ldots, k$, in (*8). We shall next approximate the actual distribution of $\hat{\chi}_v^2(k)$ by a constant multiple of a central chi-square by means of assumption (B), where the constant c and the degrees of freedom f are so adjusted as to give the correct first two moments. It is possible to derive the exact moments of $\hat{\chi}_v^2(k)$ by simple, if lengthy and laborious, algebra, using a technique similar to the one in Ito and Schull [15]. Let $\mathbf{x}_{t\alpha}$ of (2.6) be expressed as follows:

$$\mathbf{x}_{t\alpha} = \boldsymbol{\mu} + \boldsymbol{\mu}^{(t)} + \mathbf{y}_{t\alpha}, \tag{5.5}$$

where $t = 1, 2, \ldots, k$; $\alpha = 1, 2, \ldots, N_t$, $\boldsymbol{\mu}$, and $\boldsymbol{\mu}^{(t)}$ are $p \times 1$ constant vectors such that $\boldsymbol{\mu}_t = \boldsymbol{\mu} + \boldsymbol{\mu}^{(t)}$ and $\sum_{t=1}^{k} \boldsymbol{\Lambda}_t \boldsymbol{\mu}^{(t)} = \mathbf{0}$; $\mathbf{y}_{t\alpha}$ follows a p-variate distribution whose first four moments are given by

$$E(\mathbf{y}_{t\alpha}) = \mathbf{0}, \tag{5.6}$$

$$E(\mathbf{y}_{t\alpha}\mathbf{y}_{t\alpha}') = \boldsymbol{\Sigma}_t, \tag{5.7}$$

$$E(y_{it\alpha}\, y_{jt\alpha}\, y_{lt\alpha}) = \kappa_{ijl}^{(t)}, \tag{5.8}$$

$$E(y_{it\alpha}\, y_{jt\alpha}\, y_{lt\alpha}\, y_{mt\alpha}) = \kappa_{ijlm}^{(t)} + \sigma_{ij}^{(t)}\sigma_{lm}^{(t)} + \sigma_{il}^{(t)}\sigma_{jm}^{(t)} + \sigma_{im}^{(t)}\sigma_{jl}^{(t)}, \tag{5.9}$$

where $y_{it\alpha}$ is the ith element of $\mathbf{y}_{t\alpha}$, etc., and all other notations are the same as in (2.2)–(2.5). Then the null hypothesis H_{01} of (∗1) is equivalent to

$$H_{01}^{*}:\quad \boldsymbol{\mu}^{(1)} = \boldsymbol{\mu}^{(2)} = \cdots = \boldsymbol{\mu}^{(k)} = \mathbf{0}. \tag{5.10}$$

Let $\mathbf{F}_t$ be a $p \times p$ nonsingular matrix such that

$$\boldsymbol{\Lambda}_t(\equiv(\boldsymbol{\Sigma}_t/N_t)^{-1}) = \mathbf{F}_t\mathbf{F}_t' \tag{5.11}$$

and apply the following transformations to the $\hat{\chi}_v^{\,2}(k)$ statistic:

$$\mathbf{F}_t'\boldsymbol{\mu}^{(t)} = \boldsymbol{\zeta}_t, \qquad \mathbf{F}_t'\bar{\mathbf{y}}_t = \mathbf{z}_t, \tag{5.12}$$

where $\bar{\mathbf{y}}_t = \sum_{\alpha=1}^{N_t} \mathbf{y}_{t\alpha}/N_t$. Since $\hat{\bar{\mathbf{x}}}^* = \boldsymbol{\mu} + \hat{\bar{\mathbf{y}}}^*$, $\hat{\bar{\mathbf{y}}}^* = \boldsymbol{\Lambda}^{-1}\sum_{t=1}^{k} \boldsymbol{\Lambda}_t\bar{\mathbf{y}}_t$, $\hat{\chi}_v^{\,2}(k)$ becomes

$$\hat{\chi}_v^{\,2}(k) = \sum_{t=1}^{k} (\bar{\mathbf{x}}_t - \hat{\bar{\mathbf{x}}}^*)'\boldsymbol{\Lambda}_t(\bar{\mathbf{x}}_t - \hat{\bar{\mathbf{x}}}^*) = \sum_{t=1}^{k} (\boldsymbol{\zeta}_t + \mathbf{z}_t - \mathbf{u}_t)'(\boldsymbol{\zeta}_t + \mathbf{z}_t - \mathbf{u}_t) \tag{5.13}$$

where

$$\mathbf{u}_t = \mathbf{F}_t'\boldsymbol{\Lambda}^{-1}\sum_{s=1}^{k} \mathbf{F}_s\mathbf{z}_s.$$

Then, after some algebra, the first two moments of $\hat{\chi}_v^{\,2}(k)$ are found to be

$$E(\hat{\chi}_v^{\,2}(k)) = p(k-1) + \sum_{t=1}^{k} \boldsymbol{\zeta}_t'\boldsymbol{\zeta}_t \tag{5.14}$$

and

$$\begin{aligned} \sigma^2(\hat{\chi}_v^{\,2}(k)) = {} & 2p(k-1) + 4\sum_{t=1}^{k} \boldsymbol{\zeta}_t'\boldsymbol{\zeta}_t \\ & + 4\sum_{t=1}^{k}\sum_{i,j,l=1}^{p} N_t^{-2}\kappa_{ijl}^{(t)}(\boldsymbol{\zeta}_t'\mathbf{F}_t')_i\{(\mathbf{F}_t\mathbf{F}_t') - (\mathbf{F}_t\mathbf{F}_t'\boldsymbol{\Lambda}^{-1}\mathbf{F}_t\mathbf{F}_t')\}_{jl} \\ & + \sum_{t=1}^{k}\sum_{i,j,l,m=1}^{p} N_t^{-3}\kappa_{ijlm}^{(t)}\{(\mathbf{F}_t\mathbf{F}_t') - (\mathbf{F}_t\mathbf{F}_t'\boldsymbol{\Lambda}^{-1}\mathbf{F}_t\mathbf{F}_t')\}_{ij} \\ & \times\{(\mathbf{F}_t\mathbf{F}_t') - (\mathbf{F}_t\mathbf{F}_t'\boldsymbol{\Lambda}^{-1}\mathbf{F}_t\mathbf{F}_t')\}_{lm}, \end{aligned} \tag{5.15}$$

where $(\boldsymbol{\zeta}_t'\mathbf{F}_t')_i$ is the ith element of $1 \times p$ row vector $\boldsymbol{\zeta}_t'\mathbf{F}_t'$ and $\{(\mathbf{F}_t\mathbf{F}_t') - (\mathbf{F}_t\mathbf{F}_t'\Lambda^{-1}\mathbf{F}_t\mathbf{F}_t')\}_{ij}$ is the ith row, jth column element of $p \times p$ matrix $(\mathbf{F}_t\mathbf{F}_t') - (\mathbf{F}_t\mathbf{F}_t'\boldsymbol{\Lambda}^{-1}\mathbf{F}_t\mathbf{F}_t')$, etc. Application of transformations (5.12) to (5.14) and (5.15) yields

$$E(\hat{\chi}_v{}^2(k)) = p(k-1) + \operatorname{tr}\sum_{t=1}^{k} N_t \boldsymbol{\mu}^{(t)}\boldsymbol{\mu}^{(t)\prime}\boldsymbol{\Sigma}_t^{-1} \tag{5.16}$$

and

$$\begin{aligned}\sigma^2(\hat{\chi}_v{}^2(k)) &= 2p(k-1) + 4\operatorname{tr}\sum_{t=1}^{k} N_t \boldsymbol{\mu}^{(t)}\boldsymbol{\mu}^{(t)\prime}\boldsymbol{\Sigma}_t^{-1}\\ &\quad + 4\sum_{t=1}^{k}\sum_{i,j,l=1}^{p} \kappa_{ijl}^{(t)}(\boldsymbol{\mu}^{(t)\prime}\boldsymbol{\Sigma}_t^{-1})_i(\boldsymbol{\Sigma}_t^{-1} - N_t\boldsymbol{\Sigma}_t^{-1}\boldsymbol{\Lambda}^{-1}\boldsymbol{\Sigma}_t^{-1})_{jl}\\ &\quad + \sum_{t=1}^{k}\sum_{i,j,l,m=1}^{p} N_t^{-1}\kappa_{ijlm}^{(t)}(\boldsymbol{\Sigma}_t^{-1} - N_t\boldsymbol{\Sigma}_t^{-1}\boldsymbol{\Lambda}^{-1}\boldsymbol{\Sigma}_t^{-1})_{ij}\\ &\quad \times (\boldsymbol{\Sigma}_t^{-1} - N_t\boldsymbol{\Sigma}_t^{-1}\boldsymbol{\Lambda}^{-1}\boldsymbol{\Sigma}_t^{-1})_{lm},\end{aligned} \tag{5.17}$$

respectively, where $(\boldsymbol{\mu}^{(t)\prime}\boldsymbol{\Sigma}_t^{-1})_i$ is the ith element of $1 \times p$ row vector $\boldsymbol{\mu}^{(t)\prime}\boldsymbol{\Sigma}_t^{-1}$ and $(\boldsymbol{\Sigma}_t^{-1} - N_t\boldsymbol{\Sigma}_t^{-1}\boldsymbol{\Lambda}^{-1}\boldsymbol{\Sigma}_t^{-1})_{ij}$ is the ith row, jth column element of $p \times p$ matrix $(\boldsymbol{\Sigma}_t^{-1} - N_t\boldsymbol{\Sigma}_t^{-1}\boldsymbol{\Lambda}^{-1}\boldsymbol{\Sigma}_t^{-1})$, etc. Now let

$$\hat{\chi}_v{}^2(k) \doteqdot c\chi^2(f) \tag{5.18}$$

where c is a constant. We shall determine the values of c and f such that the first two moments of $\hat{\chi}_v{}^2(k)$ are equal to those of $c\chi^2(f)$, respectively (see, e.g., Welch [27]). Thus, c and f are obtained by solving simultaneously the equations

$$cf = E(\hat{\chi}_v{}^2(k)), \qquad 2c^2f = \sigma^2(\hat{\chi}_v{}^2(k)) \tag{5.19}$$

where $E(\hat{\chi}_v{}^2(k))$ and $\sigma^2(\hat{\chi}_v{}^2(k))$ are given by (5.16) and (5.17), respectively. These values of c and f specify the statistic $c\chi^2(f)$ which approximates the noncentral distribution of the $\hat{\chi}_v{}^2(k)$. When H_{01} is true, the central distribution of $\hat{\chi}_v{}^2(k)$ is approximated as $c\chi^2(f)$, where $c = 1 + O(N_t^{-1})$ and $f = p(k-1) + O(N_t^{-1})$. As a matter of fact, this last result is what would be expected, because as was noted already, the limiting distribution of $\hat{\chi}_v{}^2(k)$ is the distribution of $\chi^2(p(k-1))$ when H_{01} is true. By means of (5.18), the true level of significance and power of the test (5.2) may be approximated as follows:

$$\begin{aligned}\Pr\{\hat{T}_v{}^2(k) > \chi_\alpha{}^2(p(k-1)) \mid H_{01}\} &\doteqdot \Pr\{\chi^2(p(k-1)) > \chi_\alpha{}^2(p(k-1))\}\\ &= \alpha\end{aligned} \tag{5.20}$$

and

$$\Pr\{\hat{T}_v{}^2(k) > \chi_\alpha{}^2(p(k-1)) \mid H_1\} \doteqdot \Pr\{\chi^2(f) > \chi_\alpha{}^2(p(k-1))/c\}, \tag{5.21}$$

where c and f are given by (5.19). These results indicate that as long as the N_t's are very large, the $\hat{T}_v{}^2(k)$ statistic is not affected seriously by the existence of the third and higher cumulants of the parent populations when H_{01} is true, that is, it behaves as if the parent populations were normal and is asymp distributed as $\chi^2(p(k-1))$. When H_{01} is not true, and if $N_t^{1/2}\boldsymbol{\mu}^{(t)} = \mathbf{O}(1)$ for all t as the sample sizes N_t's become large with the r_t's held fixed and

$$\Psi(N) \equiv \operatorname{tr} \sum_{t=1}^{k} N_t \boldsymbol{\mu}^{(t)} \boldsymbol{\mu}^{(t)\prime} \boldsymbol{\Sigma}_t^{-1} \to \Psi_0$$

as $N \to \infty$, where Ψ_0 is a constant, then from (5.16) and (5.17), we have

$$E(\hat{\chi}_v{}^2(k)) = p(k-1) + \Psi_0 \tag{5.22}$$

and

$$\sigma^2(\hat{\chi}_v{}^2(k)) = 2p(k-1) + 4\Psi_0 + O(N^{-1/2}), \tag{5.23}$$

respectively. Therefore, we may say as in the case of H_{01} that as long as the N_t's are very large, the $\hat{T}_v{}^2(k)$ statistic is not affected seriously by the existence of the 3rd and higher cumulants of the parent populations and is asymp distributed as a noncentral chi-square with $p(k-1)$ degrees of freedom and noncentrality parameter Ψ_0.

(2) *The $\hat{T}_u{}^2$ test*

We shall next consider an approximate test of (5.1) which tests H_{01} at a nominal 100 α% level of significance, and make an asymp study of the effect of nonnormality upon its true significance level and power in a manner similar to the one used for the $\hat{T}_v{}^2$ test. Under assumption (A), the critical region (5.1) may be approximated, for large values of the N_t's such that the r_t's are held fixed for all t, by the critical region:

$$\{\hat{\chi}_u{}^2(k): \quad \hat{\chi}_u{}^2(k) > \chi_\alpha{}^2(p(k-1))\}, \tag{5.24}$$

where the statistic $\hat{\chi}_u{}^2(k)$ is defined by

$$\hat{\chi}_u{}^2(k) = \operatorname{tr} \mathbf{Q}_B \dot{\boldsymbol{\Sigma}}^{-1} \tag{5.25}$$

with $\dot{\boldsymbol{\Sigma}} = \sum_{t=1}^{k} (r_t \boldsymbol{\Sigma}_t)$. Slightly different from (5.5), let $\mathbf{x}_{t\alpha}$ be expressed as follows:

$$\mathbf{x}_{t\alpha} = \boldsymbol{\mu}_* + \boldsymbol{\mu}_*^{(t)} + \mathbf{y}_{t\alpha}, \tag{5.26}$$

where $t = 1, 2, \ldots, k$; $\alpha = 1, 2, \ldots, N_t$; $\boldsymbol{\mu}_*$ and $\boldsymbol{\mu}_*^{(t)}$ are such that $\boldsymbol{\mu}_t = \boldsymbol{\mu} + \boldsymbol{\mu}^{(t)} = \boldsymbol{\mu}_* + \boldsymbol{\mu}_*^{(t)}$ and $\sum_{t=1}^{k} N_t \boldsymbol{\mu}_*^{(t)} = \mathbf{0}$, and $\mathbf{y}_{t\alpha}$ follows the same distribution as that in (5.5). In this case the null hypothesis H_{01} is equivalent to

$$H_{01}^{**}: \quad \boldsymbol{\mu}_*^{(1)} = \boldsymbol{\mu}_*^{(2)} = \cdots = \boldsymbol{\mu}_*^{(k)} = \mathbf{0}. \tag{5.27}$$

Then, by means of the same transformations as used in Ito and Schull [15], the first two moments of the $\hat{\chi}_u{}^2(k)$ statistic are found to be

$$E(\hat{\chi}_u{}^2(k)) = \operatorname{tr}\sum_{t=1}^{k}\{(1 - r_t)\boldsymbol{\Sigma}_t\dot{\boldsymbol{\Sigma}}^{-1} + N_t\boldsymbol{\mu}_*^{(t)}\boldsymbol{\mu}_*^{(t)\prime}\dot{\boldsymbol{\Sigma}}^{-1}\} \tag{5.28}$$

and

$$\begin{aligned}\sigma^2(\hat{\chi}_u{}^2(k)) = 2\operatorname{tr}&\left\{\sum_{t=1}^{k}(1 - 2r_t)(\boldsymbol{\Sigma}_t\dot{\boldsymbol{\Sigma}}^{-1})^2 + \mathbf{I}(p)\right.\\ &\left.+ 2\sum_{t=1}^{k}N_t\boldsymbol{\mu}_*^{(t)}\boldsymbol{\mu}_*^{(t)\prime}\dot{\boldsymbol{\Sigma}}^{-1}\boldsymbol{\Sigma}_t\dot{\boldsymbol{\Sigma}}^{-1}\right\}\\ &+ 4\sum_{t=1}^{k}(1 - r_t)\sum_{i,j,l=1}^{p}\kappa_{ijl}^{(t)}(\boldsymbol{\mu}_*^{(t)\prime}\dot{\boldsymbol{\Sigma}}^{-1})_i(\dot{\boldsymbol{\Sigma}}^{-1})_{jl}\\ &+ \sum_{t=1}^{k}[(1 - r_t)^2/N_t]\left\{\sum_{i,j,l,m=1}^{p}\kappa_{ijlm}^{(t)}(\dot{\boldsymbol{\Sigma}}^{-1})_{ij}(\dot{\boldsymbol{\Sigma}}^{-1})_{lm}\right\},\end{aligned} \tag{5.29}$$

where $(\boldsymbol{\mu}_*^{(t)\prime}\dot{\boldsymbol{\Sigma}}^{-1})_i$ is the ith element of $1 \times p$ row vector $\boldsymbol{\mu}_*^{(t)\prime}\dot{\boldsymbol{\Sigma}}^{-1}$ and $(\dot{\boldsymbol{\Sigma}}^{-1})_{ij}$ is the ith row, jth column element of $\dot{\boldsymbol{\Sigma}}^{-1}$, etc. When all the $\kappa_{ijl}^{(t)}$ and $\kappa_{ijlm}^{(t)}$ are zero, then (5.28) and (5.29) coincide with the results given by Ito and Schull [15]. Now let

$$\hat{\chi}_u{}^2(k) \doteqdot c'\chi^2(f'), \tag{5.30}$$

where c' and f' are constants. As in the case of the $\hat{\chi}_v{}^2(k)$ statistic, c' and f' are so determined that the first two moments of $\hat{\chi}_u{}^2(k)$ are equal to those of $c'\chi^2(f')$, respectively. Thus, c' and f' are obtained by solving simultaneously the equations

$$c'f' = E(\hat{\chi}_u{}^2(k)), \qquad 2c'^2f' = \sigma^2(\hat{\chi}_u{}^2(k)) \tag{5.31}$$

where $E(\hat{\chi}_u{}^2(k))$ and $\sigma^2(\hat{\chi}_u{}^2(k))$ are given by (5.28) and (5.29), respectively. Then the true level of significance and power of the $\hat{T}_u{}^2$ test may be approximated by means of (5.30). When H_0 is true, then (5.28) and (5.29) are reduced to

$$E(\hat{\chi}_u{}^2(k)) = \operatorname{tr}\sum_{t=1}^{k}(1 - r_t)\boldsymbol{\Sigma}_t\dot{\boldsymbol{\Sigma}}^{-1} \tag{5.32}$$

and

$$\sigma^2(\hat{\chi}_u{}^2(k)) = 2\operatorname{tr}\left\{\sum_{t=1}^{k}(1 - 2r_t)(\boldsymbol{\Sigma}_t\dot{\boldsymbol{\Sigma}}^{-1})^2 + \mathbf{I}(p)\right\} + O(N^{-1}), \tag{5.33}$$

respectively, for large values of the N_t's. That is to say, as long as the N_t's are very large, the central distribution of $\hat{T}_u{}^2(k)$ is not very much different from that obtained by Ito and Schull [15] under the normality assumption. When H_{01} is not true, and if $N_t^{1/2}\boldsymbol{\mu}_*^{(t)} = \mathbf{O}(1)$ for all t, and if

$$\Psi_1(N) \equiv \operatorname{tr} \sum_{t=1}^{k} N_t \boldsymbol{\mu}_*^{(t)} \boldsymbol{\mu}_*^{(t)\prime} \dot{\boldsymbol{\Sigma}}^{-1} \to \Psi_{10},$$

$$\Psi_2(N) \equiv \operatorname{tr} \sum_{t=1}^{k} N_t \boldsymbol{\mu}_*^{(t)} \boldsymbol{\mu}_*^{(t)\prime} \dot{\boldsymbol{\Sigma}}^{-1} \boldsymbol{\Sigma}_t \dot{\boldsymbol{\Sigma}}^{-1} \to \Psi_{20}$$

as $N \to \infty$ where Ψ_{10} and Ψ_{20} are constants, then we have from (5.28) and (5.29)

$$E(\hat{\chi}_u^{\,2}(k)) = \operatorname{tr} \sum_{t=1}^{k} (1 - r_t) \boldsymbol{\Sigma}_t \dot{\boldsymbol{\Sigma}}^{-1} + \Psi_{10} \tag{5.34}$$

and

$$\sigma^2(\hat{\chi}_u^{\,2}(k)) = 2 \operatorname{tr}\left\{ \sum_{t=1}^{k} (1 - 2r_t)(\boldsymbol{\Sigma}_t \dot{\boldsymbol{\Sigma}}^{-1})^2 + \mathbf{I}(p) \right\} + 4\Psi_{20} + O(N^{-1/2}). \tag{5.35}$$

Therefore as long as the N_t's are very large, the asymp behavior of the $\hat{T}_u^{\,2}$ test when H_{01} is not true is not seriously affected by violation of the assumption of normality of the parent populations just as when H_{01} is true.

Now how is the $\hat{T}_v^{\,2}$ test related to the $\hat{T}_u^{\,2}$ test asymp? In view of the asymp properties of the two tests that we have found so far, the $\hat{T}_v^{\,2}$ test is asymp less affected than the $\hat{T}_u^{\,2}$ test by violation of the assumption of homsty as long as both approximate tests use the same $\chi_\alpha^{\,2}(p(k-1))$ to construct the critical regions (5.1) and (5.2). But violation of the assumption of normality affects both tests asymp in a similar way. When $k = 2$, it is easily shown that if either $N_1 = N_2$ or $\boldsymbol{\Sigma}_1 = \boldsymbol{\Sigma}_2$, not only the first two moments of the $\hat{\chi}_v^{\,2}(2)$ statistic and the $\hat{\chi}_u^{\,2}(2)$ statistic are equal but also the two statistics are identical. Hence, under either of the conditions (i) $N_1 = N_2$ and (ii) $\boldsymbol{\Sigma}_1 = \boldsymbol{\Sigma}_2$, the two tests are asymp equivalent. However, when k takes on general values greater than 2, the situation is a little different. When H_{01} is true and if the assumption of homsty holds, then

$$E(\hat{\chi}_v^{\,2}(k)) = E(\hat{\chi}_u^{\,2}(k)) = p(k-1) \tag{5.36}$$

and

$$\sigma^2(\hat{\chi}_v^{\,2}(k)) = \sigma^2(\hat{\chi}_u^{\,2}(k)) = 2p(k-1) + \sum_{t=1}^{k} [(1 - r_t)^2/N_t] \left\{ \sum_{i,j,l,m=1}^{p} \kappa_{ijlm}^{(t)} (\boldsymbol{\Sigma}_0^{-1})_{ij} (\boldsymbol{\Sigma}_0^{-1})_{lm} \right\}, \tag{5.37}$$

where $\boldsymbol{\Sigma}_0$ is a common var-covar matrix, which indicate that the significance levels of the two tests are asymp equal. However, when H_{01} is not true, even equality of only the first two moments of $\hat{\chi}_v{}^2(k)$ and $\hat{\chi}_u{}^2(k)$ requires the assumption of homsty together with the condition of equal sample sizes (under which the statistics themselves become identical).

(3) *The $\hat{T}_w{}^2$ test*

Under the assumptions of normality and homsty, Hsu [9] showed that the $T_0{}^2$ test of (*3) and the W-test of (*5) are asymp equivalent as the sample sizes become infinite. Now without assuming normality and homsty, it can be proved that the same holds true. For large values of N, the statistic $\hat{T}_w{}^2(k)$ tends in probability to a statistic,

$$\hat{\chi}_w{}^2(k) = -(N-k)\log|(N-k)\dot{\boldsymbol{\Sigma}}| / |\mathbf{Q}_B + (N-k)\dot{\boldsymbol{\Sigma}}| \tag{5.38}$$

under assumption (A). Now $\hat{\chi}_w{}^2(k)$ may be expanded in an asymp series as follows:

$$\begin{aligned}\hat{\chi}_w{}^2(k) &= (N-k)\log|\mathbf{I}(p) + \mathbf{Q}_B\dot{\boldsymbol{\Sigma}}^{-1}/(N-k)| \\ &= \operatorname{tr}\mathbf{Q}_B\dot{\boldsymbol{\Sigma}}^{-1} - \operatorname{tr}(\mathbf{Q}_B\dot{\boldsymbol{\Sigma}}^{-1})^2/2(N-k) + O(N^{-2}).\end{aligned} \tag{5.39}$$

Hence the $\hat{T}_u{}^2$ test of (5.1) and the $\hat{T}_w{}^2$ test of (5.3) are asymp equivalent for large values of the sample sizes even in the nonnormal general case. That is to say, the critical region (5.3) has the true level of significance and power which may be approximated by means of (5.30).

PART II. TESTING HYPOTHESES ABOUT VAR-COVAR MATRICES

In Part II consideration will be given to testing the null hypotheses:

$$H_{04}: \quad \boldsymbol{\Sigma} = \boldsymbol{\Sigma}_0 \tag{**1}$$

$$H_{05}: \quad \boldsymbol{\Sigma} = \sigma^2\mathbf{I}(p) \tag{**2}$$

$$H_{06}: \quad \boldsymbol{\Sigma}_{gh} = \mathbf{0}, \qquad g, h = 1, 2, \ldots, q \tag{**3}$$

in cases of one sample and

$$H_{07}: \quad \boldsymbol{\Sigma}_1 = \boldsymbol{\Sigma}_2 = \cdots = \boldsymbol{\Sigma}_k \tag{**4}$$

in a case of k samples, where $\boldsymbol{\Sigma}_0$ in (**1) is a given $p \times p$ pds matrix; σ^2 in (**2) is not specified, (testing (**2) is called the sphericity test); $\boldsymbol{\Sigma}_{gh}$ in (**3) is the $p_g \times p_h$ (g, h) minor of the $\mathbf{\Sigma}$ when it is partitioned into $q \times q$ minors as follows:

$$\mathbf{\Sigma}(p \times p) = \begin{bmatrix} \mathbf{\Sigma}_{11} & \mathbf{\Sigma}_{12} & \cdots & \mathbf{\Sigma}_{1q} \\ \mathbf{\Sigma}_{21} & \mathbf{\Sigma}_{22} & \cdots & \mathbf{\Sigma}_{2q} \\ & & & \vdots \\ \mathbf{\Sigma}_{q1} & \mathbf{\Sigma}_{q2} & \cdots & \mathbf{\Sigma}_{qq} \end{bmatrix} \begin{matrix} p_1 \\ p_2 \\ \vdots \\ p_q \end{matrix}$$
$$\qquad\qquad p_1 \quad p_2 \quad \cdots \quad p_q$$

and $\sum_{g=1}^{q} p_g = p$. Under the normality assumption for the distribution of the parent populations, the lrt's consist, respectively, of the critical regions of 100 α% significance level:

$$\text{for} \quad H_{04}, \quad \{\lambda_1\colon \ \lambda_1 < \lambda_1(\alpha)\}, \tag{**5}$$

where

$$\lambda_1 = |\mathbf{V\Sigma}_0^{-1}|^{N/2} \exp\{\tfrac{1}{2}N \operatorname{tr}(\mathbf{I}(p) - \mathbf{V\Sigma}_0^{-1})\}$$

with $\mathbf{V} = n\mathbf{S}/N$, S being defined in (*4) (see, e.g., Anderson [1], pp. 264–267);

$$\text{for} \quad H_{05}, \quad \{\lambda_2\colon \ \lambda_2 < \lambda_2(\alpha)\} \tag{**6}$$

where

$$\lambda_2 = |\mathbf{V}|^{N/2}/(\operatorname{tr} \mathbf{V}/p)^{pN/2},$$

with $\mathbf{V}$ the same as in (**5) (see, e.g., Anderson [1], pp. 259–263);

$$\text{for} \quad H_{06}, \quad \{\lambda_3\colon \ \lambda_3 < \lambda_3(\alpha)\} \tag{**7}$$

where

$$\lambda_3 = |\mathbf{V}|^{N/2} / \prod_{g=1}^{q} |\mathbf{V}_{gg}|^{N/2}$$

with $\mathbf{V}$ the same as in (**5) and $\mathbf{V}_{gg}$ the (g, g) minor of $\mathbf{V}$ when it is partitioned into $q \times q$ minors in the same way as $\mathbf{\Sigma}$ (see, e.g., Anderson [1], pp. 230–240); and

$$\text{for} \quad H_{07}, \quad \{\lambda_4\colon \ \lambda_4 < \lambda_4(\alpha)\} \tag{**8}$$

where

$$\lambda_4 = \prod_{t=1}^{k} |\mathbf{V}_t|^{N_t/2}/|\mathbf{V}|^{N/2},$$

with $\mathbf{V}_t = n_t \mathbf{S}_t/N_t$, $\mathbf{V} = \sum_{t=1}^{k}(r_t \mathbf{V}_t)$, $\mathbf{S}_t$ being given in (*4) (see, e.g., Anderson [1], pp. 247–259).

In the following section, we shall make an asymp study of the effect of violation of the normality assumption upon these four tests, on condition that the observations follow p-variate distributions as specified in Section 2.

6. FOUR APPROXIMATE TESTS IN THE NONNORMAL CASE

Following arguments for deriving the asymp distribution of a function of sample variances and covariances due to Hsu [11], Cramér [4], p. 366, and Siotani and Hayakawa [24], we shall reproduce here some of their results in a slightly different way. If $f(\mathbf{V}_1, \mathbf{V}_2, \ldots, \mathbf{V}_k)$ is a function of the elements of sample var-covar matrices $\mathbf{V}_1, \mathbf{V}_2, \ldots, \mathbf{V}_k$ having continuous derivatives of every kind of order up to and including three, then we have

$$\begin{aligned} f(\mathbf{V}_1, \mathbf{V}_2, \ldots, \mathbf{V}_k) &= f(\boldsymbol{\Sigma}_1, \boldsymbol{\Sigma}_2, \ldots, \boldsymbol{\Sigma}_k) + N^{-1/2} \sum_{t=1}^{k} r_t^{-1/2} \\ &\times \sum_{i,j=1}^{p} (\partial_{ij}^{(t)} f) Z_{ij}^{(t)} + N^{-1} \left\{ \sum_{t,s=1}^{k} (r_t r_s)^{-1/2} \right. \\ &\times \sum_{i,j,l,m=1}^{p} (\partial_{lm}^{(s)} \partial_{ij}^{(t)} f) Z_{ij}^{(t)} Z_{lm}^{(s)} - \sum_{t=1}^{k} r_t^{-1} \\ &\times \left. \sum_{i,j=1}^{p} (\partial_{ij}^{(t)} f) Z_i^{(t)} Z_j^{(t)} \right\} /2 + O(N^{-3/2}), \end{aligned} \tag{6.1}$$

where the derivative operator $\partial_{ij}^{(t)}$, etc., is as defined in (4.7), $f \equiv f(\boldsymbol{\Sigma}_1, \boldsymbol{\Sigma}_2, \ldots, \boldsymbol{\Sigma}_k)$, and as $N \to \infty$, the $Z_i^{(t)}$'s tend to be normal variates, independent of one another for different t, with zero means and the var-covar matrix whose ith row, jth column element is given by

$$\text{Asymp } E(Z_i^{(t)} Z_j^{(t)}) = E(x_{it} - \mu_{it})(x_{jt} - \mu_{jt}) = \sigma_{ij}^{(t)}, \tag{6.2}$$

and the $Z_{ij}^{(t)}$ $(=Z_{ji}^{(t)})$'s tend to be normal variates, independent of one another for different t, with zero means and the var-covar matrix whose typical element is given by

$$\begin{aligned} \text{Asymp } E(Z_{ij}^{(t)} Z_{lm}^{(t)}) &= E\{(x_{it} - \mu_{it})(x_{jt} - \mu_{jt}) - \sigma_{ij}^{(t)}\} \\ &\quad \times \{(x_{lt} - \mu_{lt})(x_{mt} - \mu_{mt}) - \sigma_{lm}^{(t)}\} \\ &= \kappa_{ijlm}^{(t)} + \sigma_{il}^{(t)} \sigma_{jm}^{(t)} + \sigma_{im}^{(t)} \sigma_{jl}^{(t)}, \\ t, s = 1, 2, \ldots, k; &\qquad i, j, l, m = 1, 2, \ldots, p. \end{aligned} \tag{6.3}$$

Now if $\partial_{ij}^{(t)} f \neq 0$ for some pair (i, j) in (6.1), then as $N \to \infty$, $\sqrt{N}\{f(\mathbf{V}_1, V_2, \ldots, \mathbf{V}_k) - f(\boldsymbol{\Sigma}_1, \boldsymbol{\Sigma}_2, \ldots, \boldsymbol{\Sigma}_k)\}$ tends to be normally distributed with zero mean and variance of $\sigma_f{}^2$, where

$$\sigma_f{}^2 = \text{Asymp}\, E\left\{\sum_{t=1}^{k} r_t^{-1/2} \sum_{i,j=1}^{p} (\partial_{ij}^{(t)} f) Z_{ij}^{(t)}\right\}^2$$

$$= \sum_{t=1}^{k} r_t^{-1} \sum_{i,j,l,m=1}^{p} (\partial_{ij}^{(t)} f)(\partial_{lm}^{(t)} f)(\kappa_{ijlm}^{(t)} + \sigma_{il}^{(t)}\sigma_{jm}^{(t)} + \sigma_{im}^{(t)}\sigma_{jl}^{(t)})$$

$$= \sum_{t=1}^{k} \left\{2\,\text{tr}(\mathbf{\Phi}_t \mathbf{\Sigma}_t)^2 + \sum_{i,j,l,m=1}^{p} \kappa_{ijlm}^{(t)} \times (\mathbf{\Phi}_t)_{ij}(\mathbf{\Phi}_t)_{lm}\right\}, \tag{6.4}$$

where $\mathbf{\Phi}_t = (\partial_{ij}^{(t)} f)$. If, however, $\partial_{ij}^{(t)} f = 0$ for all pairs (i, j), then (6.1) becomes

$$f(\mathbf{V}_1, \mathbf{V}_2, \ldots, \mathbf{V}_k) = f(\mathbf{\Sigma}_1, \mathbf{\Sigma}_2, \ldots, \mathbf{\Sigma}_k) + (2N)^{-1}$$
$$\times \left\{\sum_{t,s=1}^{k} (r_t r_s)^{-1/2} \sum_{i,j,l,m=1}^{p} (\partial_{lm}^{(s)} \partial_{ij}^{(t)} f) Z_{ij}^{(t)} Z_{lm}^{(s)}\right\} + O(N^{-3/2}), \tag{6.5}$$

and as $N \to \infty$ the statistic $N\{f(\mathbf{V}_1, \mathbf{V}_2, \ldots, \mathbf{V}_k) - f(\mathbf{\Sigma}_1, \mathbf{\Sigma}_2, \ldots, \mathbf{\Sigma}_k)\}$ tends to be distributed as a quadratic form

$$\frac{1}{2} \sum_{t,s=1}^{k} (r_t r_s)^{-1/2} \sum_{i,j,l,m=1}^{p} (\partial_{lm}^{(t)} \partial_{ij}^{(t)} f) Z_{ij}^{(t)} Z_{lm}^{(s)}, \tag{6.6}$$

where the asymp distribution of the $Z_{ij}^{(t)}$'s is given above. Now it is easily seen that (6.1) is precisely the expansion of $f(\mathbf{V}_1, \ldots, \mathbf{V}_k)$ that we shall obtain on making the direct substitution

$$v_{ij}^{(t)} = \sigma_{ij}^{(t)} + N_t^{-1/2} Z_{ij}^{(t)}, \qquad t = 1, 2, \ldots, k$$

and expanding the result into powers of $N^{-1/2}$.

(1) $H_{04} : \mathbf{\Sigma} = \mathbf{\Sigma}_0$

In a case of one sample, i.e., $k = 1$, let us suppose that the observations $\mathbf{x}_\alpha$, $\alpha = 1, 2, \ldots, N$, follow p-variate distributions as specified in Section 2 and study the limiting distribution of lrc λ_1 defined in (**5) as N tends to infinity. By an appropriate transformation the hypothesis H_{04} is shown to be equivalent to the hypothesis $H_{04}^* : \mathbf{\Sigma} = \mathbf{I}(p)$, for which λ_1 becomes

$$\lambda_1{}^* = |\mathbf{V}|^{N/2} \exp\{\tfrac{1}{2} N\, \text{tr}(\mathbf{I}(p) - \mathbf{V})\}. \tag{6.7}$$

Now let

$$f_1(\mathbf{V}) \equiv \lambda_1^{*2/N} = |\mathbf{V}| \exp\{\text{tr}(\mathbf{I}(p) - \mathbf{V})\}. \tag{6.8}$$

Then, by means of (6.1) we have

$$f_1(\mathbf{V}) = f_1(\mathbf{\Sigma}) + f_1(\mathbf{\Sigma}) N^{-1/2} \sum_{i,j=1}^{p} (\sigma^{ij} - \delta_{ij}) Z_{ij} + O(N^{-1}), \tag{6.9}$$

where $(\sigma^{ij} - \delta_{ij}) \neq 0$ for some pair (i, j) when H_{04}^* is not true. Hence, the noncentral limiting distribution of the statistic $\sqrt{N}\{f_1(\mathbf{V}) - f_1(\mathbf{\Sigma})\}$ is $N(0, \sigma_1{}^2)$, where

$$\sigma_1{}^2 = \{f_1(\mathbf{\Sigma})\}^2 \Big\{ 2 \operatorname{tr}(\mathbf{I}(p) - \mathbf{\Sigma})^2 + \sum_{i,j,l,m} \kappa_{ijlm} \times (\mathbf{\Sigma}^{-1} - \mathbf{I}(p))_{ij} (\mathbf{\Sigma}^{-1} - \mathbf{I}(p))_{lm} \Big\}. \tag{6.10}$$

Next, suppose that the hypothesis H_{04}^* is true, so that $x_1, x_2, \ldots, x_p$ have a unit variance and zero covariance. Making the substitution $v_{ii} = 1 + N^{-1/2} Z_{ii}$ and $v_{ij} = N^{-1/2} Z_{ij}$, $(i \neq j)$, in $f_1(\mathbf{V})$, we get

$$f_1(\mathbf{V}) = |\mathbf{I}(p) + N^{-1/2}\mathbf{Z}| \exp\{-N^{-1/2} \operatorname{tr} \mathbf{Z}\},$$

where $\mathbf{Z}$ is the $p \times p$ matrix obtained on replacing each v_{ij} by Z_{ij} in $\mathbf{V}$. The term $f_1(\mathbf{V})$ may be expanded in powers of $N^{-1/2}$ as follows:

$$\begin{aligned} f_1(\mathbf{V}) &= \{1 + N^{-1/2} \operatorname{tr} \mathbf{Z} + N^{-1} \operatorname{tr}_2 \mathbf{Z} + O(N^{-3/2})\} \\ &\quad \times \{1 - N^{-1/2} \operatorname{tr} \mathbf{Z} + (2N)^{-1} (\operatorname{tr} \mathbf{Z})^2 + O(N^{-3/2})\} \\ &= 1 - \{(\operatorname{tr} \mathbf{Z})^2/2 - \operatorname{tr}_2 \mathbf{Z}\}/N + O(N^{-3/2}) \\ &= 1 - \sum_{i,j=1}^{p} Z_{ij}^2/2N + O(N^{-3/2}), \end{aligned} \tag{6.11}$$

where $\operatorname{tr}_2\mathbf{Z}$ is the sum of all 2×2 minors found by the intersection of any 2 rows of $\mathbf{Z}$ with 2 columns bearing the same number. Hence, the limiting distribution of the statistic $N(1 - f_1(\mathbf{V}))$ when H_{04}^* is true is the limiting distribution of a quadratic form

$$\frac{1}{2} \sum_{i,j}^{p} Z_{ij}^2 \tag{6.12}$$

where it is shown that as $N \to \infty$ the Z_{ij}'s tend to be normal variates with zero means and asymp variances and covariances:

Asymp $E(Z_{ii}^2) = \kappa_{iiii} + 2$, Asymp $E(Z_{ii} Z_{jj}) = 0$ for $i \neq j$,
Asymp $E(Z_{ij}^2) = 1$ for $i \neq j$, Asymp $E(Z_{ij} Z_{lm}) = \kappa_{ijlm}$, $i \neq j \neq l \neq m$.

Thus, the limiting distribution of $N(1 - f_1(\mathbf{V}))$ depends on the fourth cumulants of $\mathbf{x}$, and becomes the χ^2 distribution under the condition that all the fourth cumulants of $\mathbf{x}$ are zero, whose degrees of freedom is equal to $\sum_{i,j=1}^{p} E(Z_{ij}^2)/2 = p(p+1)/2$. Under the normality assumption the statistic $-2 \log \lambda_1$ is shown to be distributed asymp as a χ^2 with $p(p+1)/2$ degrees of freedom (Anderson [1], p. 267), and it may be easily seen that the two statistics $N(1 - f_1(\mathbf{V}))$ and $-2 \log \lambda_1$ are equivalent if the absolute value of $|\mathbf{V}| \exp\{\operatorname{tr}(\mathbf{I}(p) - \mathbf{V})\}$ is less than unity.

Applying the above results about the limiting distribution of $f_1(\mathbf{V})$, we may test H_{04} by means of a critical region of nominal 100 α% significance level:

$$\{f_1(\mathbf{V}):\quad N(1-f_1(\mathbf{V})) > \chi_\alpha{}^2(p(p+1)/2)\}. \tag{6.13}$$

However, the true significance level of this test is seriously affected by the existence of the fourth cumulants of the parent population even for very large values of N. When H_{04} is not true, the power of the test (6.13) may be approximately evaluated by utilizing the fact that $\sqrt{N}\{f_1(\mathbf{V})-f_1(\mathbf{\Sigma})\}$ is asymp distributed as $N(0, \sigma_1{}^2)$, where $\sigma_1{}^2$ is given by (6.10), which is also affected by the existence of the fourth cumulants of the parent population.

(2) $H_{05}:\mathbf{\Sigma} = \sigma^2\mathbf{I}(p)$ (σ^2 *unknown*)

Let

$$f_2(\mathbf{V}) = \lambda_2^{2/pN} \equiv |\mathbf{V}|^{1/p}/(\mathrm{tr}\ \mathbf{V}/p). \tag{6.14}$$

Then, as in the case of H_{04}, it is shown by means of (6.1) that when H_{05} is not true, the limiting distribution of $\sqrt{N}\,\{f_2(\mathbf{V})-f_2(\mathbf{\Sigma})\}$ as $N\to\infty$ is $N(0, \sigma_2{}^2)$, where[1]

$$\begin{aligned}\sigma_2{}^2 = \{f_2(\mathbf{\Sigma})\}^2\Big[&2\{\mathrm{tr}\ \mathbf{\Sigma}^2/(\mathrm{tr}\ \mathbf{\Sigma})^2-(1/p)\}\\ &+\sum_{i,j,l,m}\kappa_{ijlm}(\mathbf{\Sigma}^{-1}/p-(\mathbf{I}(p)/\mathrm{tr}\ \mathbf{\Sigma}))_{ij}\\ &\times(\mathbf{\Sigma}^{-1}/p-(\mathbf{I}(p)/\mathrm{tr}\ \mathbf{\Sigma}))_{lm}\Big],\end{aligned} \tag{6.15}$$

and also that when H_{05} is true, $pN\times(1-f_2(\mathbf{V}))$ is distributed in the limit as $\chi^2((p+2)(p-1)/2)$ provided that all the fourth cumulants of the parent population vanish. Hence, an approximate test for H_{05}, whose critical region of nominal 100 α% significance level is given by

$$\{f_2(V):\quad pN(1-f_2(\mathbf{V})) > \chi_\alpha{}^2((p+2)(p-1)/2\} \tag{6.16}$$

has the effect of violation of the normality assumption upon both the significance level and the power even for very large values of N just as in the case of H_{04}.

(3) $H_{06}:\mathbf{\Sigma}_{gh}=0,\qquad g,h=1,2,\ldots,q$

Let

$$f_3(\mathbf{V}) \equiv \lambda_3^{2/N} = |V|/|V_1|, \tag{6.17}$$

[1] Hsu's result for $\sigma_2{}^2$ ($\sigma_6{}^2$ in his notation, Hsu [11], p. 376) seems to be slightly in error.

where $\mathbf{V}_1 = \prod_{g=1}^{q} |\mathbf{V}_{gg}|$. Then, application of (6.1) yields that when H_{06} is not true, the limiting distribution of $\sqrt{N}\{f_3(\mathbf{V}) - f_3(\boldsymbol{\Sigma})\}$ is $N(0, \sigma_3{}^2)$, where[2]

$$\sigma_3{}^2 = \{f_3(\boldsymbol{\Sigma})\}^2\Big\{2\,\mathrm{tr}(\mathbf{I}(p) - \boldsymbol{\Sigma}\boldsymbol{\Sigma}_1^{-1})^2 + \sum_{i,j,l,m} \kappa_{ijlm}(\boldsymbol{\Sigma}^{-1} - \boldsymbol{\Sigma}_1^{-1})_{ij}(\boldsymbol{\Sigma}^{-1} - \boldsymbol{\Sigma}_1^{-1})_{lm}\Big\}, \tag{6.18}$$

with

$$\Sigma_1 = \begin{bmatrix} \Sigma_{11} & & 0 \\ & \ddots & \\ 0 & & \Sigma_{qq} \end{bmatrix}$$

and that when H_{06} is true, the limiting distribution of $N(1 - f_3(\mathbf{V}))$ is the χ^2 distribution with degrees of freedom $f^* = \sum_{g<h} p_g p_h$ $(g, h = 1, 2, \ldots, q)$ for any parent population, i.e., the central distribution of $N(1 - f_3(V))$ in the limit is not affected by violation of the normality assumption. Therefore, an approximate test for H_{06} of nominal $100\,\alpha\%$ significance level:

$$\{f_3(\mathbf{V}):\quad N(1 - f_3(\mathbf{V})) > \chi^2(f^*)\} \tag{6.19}$$

has the true level of significance which tends to α as $N \to \infty$ even in case of a nonnormal population. However, the power of (6.19) is affected by violation of the normality assumption even for large values of N as is seen from (6.18).

(4) $H_{07} : \boldsymbol{\Sigma}_1 = \boldsymbol{\Sigma}_2 = \cdots = \boldsymbol{\Sigma}_k$

In this case let

$$f_4(\mathbf{V}_1, \mathbf{V}_2, \ldots, \mathbf{V}_k) \equiv \lambda_4^{2/N} = \prod_{t=1}^{k} |\mathbf{V}_t|^{r_t} \Big/ \Big|\sum_{t=1}^{k} r_t \mathbf{V}_t\Big|. \tag{6.20}$$

Then it is easily seen that

$$f_4(\mathbf{V}_1, \mathbf{V}_2, \ldots, \mathbf{V}_k) = f_4(\boldsymbol{\Sigma}_1, \boldsymbol{\Sigma}_2, \ldots, \boldsymbol{\Sigma}_k) + f_4(\boldsymbol{\Sigma}_1, \boldsymbol{\Sigma}_2, \ldots, \boldsymbol{\Sigma}_k) N^{-1/2} \sum_{t=1}^{k} r_t^{1/2}\,\mathrm{tr}(\boldsymbol{\Sigma}_t^{-1} - \dot{\boldsymbol{\Sigma}}^{-1})\mathbf{Z}_t + O(N^{-1}), \tag{6.21}$$

where $\mathbf{Z}_t$ is the $p \times p$ matrix obtained on replacing each $v_{ij}^{(t)}$ by $Z_{ij}^{(t)}$ in $\mathbf{V}_t$ and

[2] Hsu's result for $\sigma_3{}^2$ ($\sigma_5{}^2$ in his notation, Hsu [11], p. 374) seems to be slightly in error.

that when H_{07} is not true, the limiting distribution of $\sqrt{N}\{f(\mathbf{V}_1, \ldots, V_k) - f_4(\mathbf{\Sigma}_1, \ldots, \mathbf{\Sigma}_k)\}$ as $N \to \infty$ is $N(0, \sigma_4{}^2)$, where

$$\sigma_4{}^2 = \{f_4(\mathbf{\Sigma}_1, \ldots, \mathbf{\Sigma}_k)\}^2 \sum_{t=1}^{k} r_t \Big\{ 2 \operatorname{tr}(\mathbf{I}(p) - \mathbf{\Sigma}_t \dot{\mathbf{\Sigma}}^{-1})^2 + \sum_{i,j,l,m} \kappa_{ijlm}^{(t)} (\mathbf{\Sigma}_t^{-1} - \dot{\mathbf{\Sigma}}^{-1})_{ij} (\mathbf{\Sigma}_t^{-1} - \dot{\mathbf{\Sigma}}^{-1})_{lm} \Big\}. \quad (6.22)$$

When H_{07} is true, however, the expansion in powers of $N^{-1/2}$ of $f_4(\mathbf{V}_1, \mathbf{V}_2, \ldots, \mathbf{V}_k)$ becomes

$$f_4(\mathbf{V}_1, \ldots, \mathbf{V}_k) = 1 - (2N)^{-1} \Big\{ \sum_t \operatorname{tr}(\mathbf{Z}_t \mathbf{\Sigma}_0^{-1})^2 - \sum_{t,s} (r_t r_s)^{1/2} \times \operatorname{tr}(\mathbf{Z}_t \mathbf{\Sigma}_0^{-1} \mathbf{Z}_s \mathbf{\Sigma}_0^{-1}) \Big\} + O(N^{-3/2}), \quad (6.23)$$

and therefore, the limiting distribution of the statistic $N(1 - f_4(\mathbf{V}_1, \ldots, \mathbf{V}_k))$ is the limiting distribution of a quadratic form of the $Z_{ij}^{(t)}$'s:

$$\Big\{ \sum_t \operatorname{tr}(\mathbf{Z}_t \mathbf{\Sigma}_0^{-1})^2 - \sum_{t,s} (r_t r_s)^{1/2} \operatorname{tr}(\mathbf{Z}_t \mathbf{\Sigma}_0^{-1} \mathbf{Z}_s \mathbf{\Sigma}_0^{-1}) \Big\} / 2 \quad (6.24)$$

where, under the condition that H_{07} is true,

$$\text{Asymp } E(Z_{ij}^{(t)} Z_{lm}^{(t)}) = \kappa_{ijlm}^{(t)} + \sigma_{il}^{(0)} \sigma_{jm}^{(0)} + \sigma_{im}^{(0)} \sigma_{jl}^{(0)}$$

and

$$\text{Asymp } E(Z_{ij}^{(t)} Z_{lm}^{(s)}) = 0, \qquad t \neq s$$

with $\mathbf{\Sigma}_0 = (\sigma_{ij}^{(0)})$ a common var-covar matrix. Hence, Eq. (6.23) becomes $\chi^2(p(p+1)(k-1)/2)$ in the limit provided that all the fourth cumulants of the parent populations are zero. Thus, it is noted that an approximate test for H_{07} of nominal 100 α% level of significance:

$$\{f_4(\mathbf{V}_1, \ldots, \mathbf{V}_k): \quad N(1 - f_4(\mathbf{V}_1, \ldots, \mathbf{V}_k)) > \chi_\alpha{}^2(p(p+1)(k-1)/2)\} \quad (6.25)$$

has the effect of violation of the normality assumption upon both the significance level and the power even for very large values of N, as in the case of H_{04} and H_{05}.

Acknowledgments

Part of the work in Section 3 was carried out while the author was with the Institute of Statistics, University of North Carolina, Chapel Hill, North Carolina, sponsored by the Office of Naval Research (Contract NR042031) in 1954–1955. The author is grateful to Professor Harold Hotelling under whose kind supervision the work was done.

REFERENCES

1. ANDERSON, T. W. (1958). "An Introduction to Multivariate Statistical Analysis." Wiley, New York.
2. Bennett, B. M. (1951). Note on a solution of the generalized Behrens-Fisher problem. *Ann. Inst. Statist. Math.* **2** 87–90.
3. BOX, G. E. P. (1954). Some theorems on quadratic forms applied in the study of analysis of variance problems. I. Effects of inequality of variance in the one-way classification. *Ann. Math. Statist.* **25** 290–302.
4. CRAMÉR, H. (1951). "Mathematical Methods of Statistics." Princeton Univ. Press, Princeton, New Jersey.
5. HOTELLING, H. (1931). The generalization of Student's ratio. *Ann. Math. Statist.* **2** 360–378.
6. HOTELLING, H. (1947). Multivariate quality control illustrated by air testing of sample bomb sights. *In* "Selected Techniques of Statistical Analysis" (C. Eisenhart *et al.*, eds.), pp. 111–184. McGraw-Hill, New York.
7. HOTELLING, H. (1950). A generalized T-test and measure of multivariate dispersion. *Proc. Second Berkeley Symp. Math. Statist. Prob.* (J. Neyman, ed.), pp. 23–41. Univ. of California Press, Berkeley, California.
8. HSU, P. L. (1938). Notes on Hotelling's generalized T. *Ann. Math. Statist.* **9** 231–243.
9. HSU, P. L. (1940). On generalized analysis of variance. *Biometrika* **31** 221–237.
10. HSU, P. L. (1941). Analysis of variance from the power function point of view. *Biometrika* **32** 62–69.
11. HSU, P. L. (1949). The limiting distribution of functions of sample means and application to testing hypotheses. *Proc. First Berkeley Symp. Math. Statist. Prob.* (J. Neyman, ed.), pp. 359–402. Univ. of California Press, Berkeley, California.
12. ITO, K. (1956). Asymptotic formulae for the distribution of Hotelling's generalized T_0^2 statistic. *Ann. Math. Statist.* **27** 1091–1105.
13. ITO, K. (1960). Asymptotic formulae for the distribution of Hotelling's generalized T_0^2 statistic, II. *Ann. Math. Statist.* **31** 1148–1153.
14. ITO, K. (1966). On the heteroscedasticity in the linear normal regression model. "Research Papers in Statistics" (F. N. David, ed.), pp. 147–155. Wiley, New York.
15. ITO, K., and SCHULL, W. J. (1964). On the robustness of the T_0^2 test in multivariate analysis of variance when variance-covariance matrices are not equal. *Biometrika* **51** 71–82.
16. JAMES, G. S. (1954). Tests of linear hypotheses in univariate and multivariate analysis when the ratios of the population variances are unknown. *Biometrika* **41** 19–43.
17. KENDALL, M. G., and STUART, A. (1963). "The Advanced Theory of Statistics," Vol. I. Griffin, London.
18. LAWLEY, D. N. (1938). A generalization of Fisher's z test. *Biometrika* **30** 180–187.
19. PEARSON, E. S., and HARTLEY, H. O. (1954). "Biometrika Tables for Statisticians," Vol. I. Cambridge Univ. Press, London and New York.
20. PLACKETT, R. L. (1960). "Principles of Regression Analysis." Oxford Univ. Press, London and New York.
21. ROY, S. N. (1957). "Some Aspects of Multivariate Analysis." Wiley, New York.
22. SCHEFFÉ, H. (1943). On solutions of the Behrens-Fisher problem based on the t-distribution. *Ann. Math. Statist.* **14** 35–44.
23. SCHEFFÉ, H. (1959). "The Analysis of Variance." Wiley, New York.
24. SIOTANI, M., and HAYAKAWA, T. (1964). Asymptotic distributions of functions of Wishart Matrix (in Japanese). *Proc. Inst. Statist. Math.* **12** 191–198.

25. Srivastava, A. B. L. (1960). The distribution of regression coefficients in samples from bivariate nonnormal populations. *Biometrika* **47** 61–68.
26. Tang, P. C. (1938). The power function of the analysis of variance tests with tables and illustrations of their use. *Statist. Res. Mem.* **2** 126–157.
27. Welch, B. L. (1936). Specification of rules for rejecting too variable a product, with particular reference to an electric lamp problem. *J. Roy. Statist. Soc. Suppl.* **3** 29–48.
28. Welch, B. L. (1937). The significance of the difference between two means when the population variances are unequal. *Biometrika* **29** 350–362.
29. Wilks, S. S. (1932). Certain generalizations in the analysis of variance. *Biometrika* **24** 471–494.
30. Yao, Y. (1965). An approximate degrees of freedom solution to the multivariate Behrens-Fisher problem. *Biometrika* **52** 139–147.

Simultaneous Test Procedures under General MANOVA Models

P. R. KRISHNAIAH

AEROSPACE RESEARCH LABORATORIES
WRIGHT-PATTERSON AIR FORCE BASE, OHIO

1. INTRODUCTION

The tools of simultaneous test procedures under MANOVA models are of interest since, in many situations, the experimenter is interested in drawing inference on various component hypotheses when the overall hypothesis is rejected. In this volume, some of the known simultaneous test procedures under one-way MANOVA model are reviewed by Gabriel [6], and the optimum choices (in the sense of maximizing the power) of the critical values are considered by Srivastava [49] for some simultaneous test procedures. In this paper, we consider simultaneous test procedures under various MANOVA models which are especially useful in the analysis of data on growth curves. In Section 2, we briefly review the multivariate t, F, and χ^2 distributions since these distributions play an important role in computing the critical values associated with some of the simultaneous test procedures. In Section 3, various simultaneous test procedures are discussed under the Potthoff-Roy model [34]. Some relative merits of these procedures are also considered. In the case of the classical MANOVA model, some of these procedures are equivalent to the largest root test by S. N. Roy [41], the step-down procedure by J. Roy [39], finite intersection tests by Krishnaiah [22], the test based on correlated Hotelling T^2 statistics ($T^2_{\max}$ test) considered by Krishnaiah [21], Roy and Bose [40], and Siotani [45–47]. It is shown that, for testing component hypotheses, finite intersection tests are better, in a certain sense, than the step-down procedure whereas the $T^2_{\max}$ test is better than the largest root test. However, no investigation is made to compare the power functions of these procedures for testing the total hypothesis. But one would intuitively expect (Srivastava and Roy [48]) that none of these test procedures would be uniformly better than any of the others for testing the total hypothesis. In Section 4, we consider simultaneous test procedures under MANOVA models when the errors form a first order multivariate Markov process. To avoid very complicated distribution problems under the models in Section 4, we exploited the fact that the conditional distributions of the odd observations (or observation vectors), holding even observations (or observation vectors) fixed, are independently distributed. This fact was exploited earlier by various authors [9, 10, 17, 24, 26, 32] to solve some other problems. Finally, in Section 5, we consider the simultaneous test procedures under a model when the errors are correlated in the directions of the variates and observations, but the covariance matrix is known or an independent estimate of it is available.

2. NOTATION AND PRELIMINARIES

If G is a nonnegative definite square matrix, then $C_L(G)$ and $\text{tr}(G)$, respectively, denote the largest characteristic root and trace of G. If G is a positive definite square matrix, its inverse is denoted by G^{-1}. The transpose of a matrix Z is denoted by Z'; and I_p denotes a $p \times p$ identity matrix.

We will now discuss the multivariate t, F, and χ^2 distributions since they are needed in the sequel.

Let $\mathbf{z}' = (z_1, \ldots, z_q)$ be distributed as a q-variate normal distribution with mean vector $\boldsymbol{\mu}' = (\mu_1, \ldots, \mu_q)$ and covariance matrix $\sigma^2\ \Omega$ where $\Omega = (\rho_{ij})$ is the correlation matrix. Also, let s^2/σ^2 be distributed independently of $\mathbf{z}$ as chi-square distribution with n degrees of freedom. In addition, let $t_i = z_i\sqrt{n}/s$ for $i = 1, 2, \ldots, q$. Then, the joint distribution of $t_1, \ldots, t_q$ is known to be a central or noncentral multivariate t distribution according to whether $\boldsymbol{\mu} = 0$ or $\boldsymbol{\mu} \neq \mathbf{0}$; it is singular or nonsingular according to whether Ω is singular or nonsingular. The central nonsingular multivariate t distribution was derived independently by Dunnett and Sobel [4] and Cornish [3]; Kshirsagar [31] derived the noncentral, nonsingular multivariate t distribution. We will refer to the joint distribution of $t_1{}^2, \ldots, t_q{}^2$ as multivariate t^2 distribution; this distribution can be obtained easily starting from multivariate t. Extensive tables for the percentage points of the central, nonsingular and equicorrelated multivariate t and multivariate t^2 distributions were constructed by Krishnaiah and Armitage [28, 29]. Extensive tables of the cumulative distribution function of the central bivariate t and bivariate t^2 were constructed in the equicoordinate case by Krishnaiah *et al.* [30]. For a review of the literature on multivariate t, the reader is referred to Gupta [8]. We will now give the definition of multivariate χ^2 and F distributions.

Let $S = (s_{ij}) : q \times q$ be distributed as a Wishart distribution with m degrees of freedom, and let $E(S) = m\Sigma = m(\sigma_{ij})$. Then, the joint distribution of $s_{11}/\sigma_{11}, \ldots, s_{qq}/\sigma_{qq}$ is known to be a central or noncentral q-variate chi-square distribution with m degrees of freedom according to whether the distribution of S is central or noncentral. The frequency function of the central (nonsingular) multivariate chi-square distribution was derived by Krishnamoorthy and Parthasarathy [15]; some properties of this distribution were studied by Krishnaiah and Rao [16]. When $m = 1$, upper percentage points of this distribution were given by Krishnaiah and Armitage [27] in the equicorrelated case. If we now let $F_i = ns_{ii}\,\sigma_{00}/ms_{00}\,\sigma_{ii}$, $i = 1, 2, \ldots, q$, where s_{00} is distributed independently of s_{ii} as chi-square with n degrees of freedom, then the joint distribution of $F_1, \ldots, F_q$ is known to be a multivariate F distribution with (m, n) degrees of freedom and with Ω as the correlation matrix of the "accompanying" multivariate normal. The multivariate F distribution was proposed by Krishnaiah [19, 21, 22]. When $m = 1$, the multivariate F distribution reduces to multivariate t^2 distribution. When Ω is a diagonal matrix, the distribution of $\max(F_1, \ldots, F_q)$ reduces to the studentized largest chi-square distribution. Extensive tables of the percentage points of the studentized largest chi-square distribution were given by Armitage and Krishnaiah [2]. We need the following result in the sequel:

Lemma 2.1. *Let* $(\mathbf{y}_1', \ldots, \mathbf{y}_q')$ *be pq-dimensional normal variate with mean vector* $(\mathbf{0}', \ldots, \mathbf{0}')$ *and with covariance matrix* $\Omega^* = B \otimes \Sigma$ *(Kronecker product), where* $B : q \times q$ *and* $\Sigma : p \times p$ *are known, symmetric, positive definite matrices. Then the joint distribution of* $\chi_1^2, \ldots, \chi_q^2$*, where* $\chi_i^2 = \mathbf{y}_i'\Sigma^{-1}\mathbf{y}_i$ $(i = 1, 2, \ldots, q)$ *is a q-variate chi-square distribution with p degrees of freedom and with B as the covariance matrix of the accompanying q-variate normal.*

Proof. The joint distribution of $\mathbf{y}_1', \ldots, \mathbf{y}_q'$ is given by

$$f(\mathbf{y}_1', \ldots, \mathbf{y}_q') = [(2\pi)^{pq/2}|\Omega^*|^{1/2}]^{-1} \exp[-\tfrac{1}{2}\mathbf{Y}'\Omega^{*-1}\mathbf{Y}]$$

where $\mathbf{Y}' = (\mathbf{y}_1', \ldots, \mathbf{y}_q')$. Now, let $\mathbf{y}_i' = \mathbf{Z}_i'T'$ for $i = 1, 2, \ldots, q$ where $TT' = \Sigma$ and $Z_i' = (Z_{i1}, \ldots, Z_{ip})$. Then

$$f(\mathbf{Z}_1', \ldots, \mathbf{Z}_q') = [(2\pi)^{pq/2}|B|^{p/2}]^{-1} \exp[-\tfrac{1}{2}\mathbf{Z}'(B^{-1} \otimes I)\mathbf{Z}]$$

$$= [(2\pi)^{pq/2}|B|^{p/2}]^{-1} \prod_{j=1}^{p} \exp[-\tfrac{1}{2}\xi_j' B^{-1} \xi_j] \qquad (2.1)$$

where $Z' = (\mathbf{Z}_1', \ldots, \mathbf{Z}_q')$ and $\xi_j' = (Z_{1j}, \ldots, Z_{qj})$ for $j = 1, 2, \ldots, p$. But $\chi_i^2 = \mathbf{y}_i'\Sigma^{-1}\mathbf{y}_i = \mathbf{Z}_i'\mathbf{Z}_i$ for $i = 1, 2, \ldots, q$. Also, by (2.1) we know that $Z^* = (Z_{ij}) : q \times p$ is a matrix of p independent random vectors distributed as a q-variate normal with a common covariance matrix B. Hence, the joint distribution of $\chi_1^2, \ldots, \chi_q^2$ is a q-variate chi-square distribution with p degrees of freedom and with B as the covariance matrix of the accompanying q-variate normal.

When $q = 2$, the above theorem was proved by Siotani [45].

We now discuss the upper and lower bounds on the probability of several events occurring simultaneously. Let

$$P_0 = P(E_1 \cdots E_q)$$

$$S_r = 1 - \sum_{i=1}^{q} P(E_i^c) + \sum_{i_1 < i_2} P(E_{i_1}^c E_{i_2}^c) - \cdots + (-1)^r \sum_{i_1 < \cdots < i_r} P(E_{i_1}^c \cdots E_{i_r}^c)$$

where E_i^c denotes the complement of the event E_i. Using Poincare's formula, it is known that

$$P_0 = S_q. \tag{2.2}$$

Also, we know that

$$S_{2r+1} \leq P_0 \leq S_{2r+2}; \qquad r = 0, 1, 2, \cdots. \tag{2.3}$$

In *some* situations, we have

$$P(E_1 \cdots E_q) \geq \prod_{i=1}^{q} P(E_i).$$

In these situations, let $R_0 = P_0 - \prod_{i=1}^{q} P(E_i)$. In addition, let $R_1 = P_0 - S_1$ and $R_2 = S_2 - P_0$. Then

$$R_0 \gtrless R_2 \tag{2.4}$$

according to whether

$$P_0 \gtrless \left(S_2 + \prod_{i=1}^{q} P(E_i)\right)/2.$$

Also, we have

$$R_0 \leq R_1. \tag{2.5}$$

We can use (2.2)–(2.5) to obtain bounds or approximate values of the critical values associated with various simultaneous test procedures.

For illustration, if we let $E_i : t_i \leq c$ where t_i is defined earlier, we can compute S_1, S_2, and $\prod_{i=1}^{q} P(E_i)$ using the tables of bivariate t given by Krishnaiah *et al.* [30] and the tables of Student's t. We can construct similar bounds when $E_i : t_i^2 \leq c$.

For certain inequalities which are useful in the applications of simultaneous test procedures, the reader is referred to Khatri [14].

3. SIMULTANEOUS TESTS UNDER MODELS OF THE FORM $E(X) = A\mu B$

Consider the mode equation

$$E(X) = A\mu B \tag{3.1}$$

where the rows of $X : n \times p$ are independently distributed, and the elements in each row are jointly distributed as a multivariate normal with a common covariance matrix Σ and means given by (3.1). Here $A : n \times m$ and $B : r \times p$, $(m < n; r \leq p)$ are completely known and μ is unknown. Under the model (3.1), we are interested in testing the hypotheses $H_1, \ldots, H_q$ and H, simultaneously, against one-sided and two-sided alternatives where $H_l : \mathbf{c}_l'\mu = \mathbf{0}'$, $H = \bigcap_{l=1}^{q} H_l$, and $H : C\mu = 0$ where $C : u \times m$ is of rank u and $\mathbf{c}_1', \ldots, \mathbf{c}_q'$ are known. This model was considered by Potthoff and Roy [34]. They reduced the above model to

$$E(Y^*) = A\mu \tag{3.2}$$

where $Y^* = XG^{-1}B'(BG^{-1}B')^{-1}$, G is arbitrary and the rows of $Y^* : n \times r$ are independently distributed, and the elements in each row are jointly distributed as an r-variate normal with covariance matrix $\Sigma_0 = [B(G')^{-1}B']^{-1}B(G')^{-1}\,\Sigma G^{-1}B'(BG^{-1}B')^{-1}$. The reduced model is of the same form as the classical MANOVA model. Therefore, we can test the hypotheses of various forms by using known techniques. These test procedures are dependent upon the particular choice of G. Rao [38] and Khatri [13] have independently reduced the Potthoff-Roy model to a conditional model as follows: Let $F = (F_1 \vdots F_2)$ where $F_1 : p \times r$ and $F_2 : p \times (p - r)$ are such that $BF_2 = 0$ and $BF_1 = I$. Also, let $Y = XF_1$ and $Z = XF_2$. Then, the rows of $(Y \vdots Z)$ are independently distributed, and the elements in each row are jointly distributed as a multivariate normal with covariance matrix

$$W = \begin{pmatrix} W_{11} & W_{12} \\ W_{21} & W_{22} \end{pmatrix}$$

and means given by

$$E(Y \vdots Z) = (A\mu \vdots 0), \tag{3.3}$$

where $W_{ij} = F_i'\,\Sigma\,F_j$, $i, j = 1, 2$. When Z is held fixed, the elements in each row are jointly distributed as a multivariate normal with covariance matrix $\Sigma_0 = W_{11} - W_{12}\,W_{22}^{-1}\,W_{21}$ and means

$$E(Y/Z) = (A\ Z)\begin{pmatrix} \mu \\ \zeta \end{pmatrix} \tag{3.4}$$

where $\zeta' = W_{12}\,W_{22}^{-1}$. Khatri [13] considered the test based on the largest root for testing H and gave the confidence intervals associated with the test. The hypotheses $H_1, \ldots, H_q$ can be tested against $A_1^\circ, \ldots, A_q^\circ$, where A_l° : $\mathbf{c}_l'\,\mu \neq \mathbf{0}'$, by examining the confidence intervals on the parametric functions which measure departures from these hypotheses. This is equivalent to accepting or rejecting H_l according to whether

$$T_l^2 \lesseqgtr d_\alpha u$$

where

$$T_l^2 = (\mathbf{c}_l'\hat{\mu})S^{-1}(\mathbf{c}_l'\hat{\mu})'(n - m - p + r)/e_l,$$

and S is the error sums of squares and cross products matrix, $\hat{\mu}$ is the best linear unbiased estimate of μ under the model (3.4), and $e_l\,\Sigma_0$ is the covariance matrix of $\mathbf{c}_l'\hat{\mu}$. Also d_α is chosen such that

$$P[(n-m-p+r)C_L(S_H S^{-1}) \leq ud_\alpha \mid H] = (1-\alpha) \tag{3.5}$$

and S_H denotes the sums of squares and cross products matrix associated with H. It is known (see Kharti [13]) that

$$\hat{\mu} = (A'A)^{-1}A'XE^{-1}B'(BE^{-1}B')^{-1}, \qquad S_H = (C\hat{\mu})'R^{-1}(C\hat{\mu}),$$
$$S = (BE^{-1}B')^{-1},$$

where

$$R = (r_{ll'}) = C[(A'A)^{-1} + (A'A)^{-1}A'X\{E^{-1} - E^{-1}B'(BE^{-1}B')^{-1}BE^{-1}\}$$
$$X'A(A'A)^{-1}]C$$
$$E = X'[I_n - A(A'A)^{-1}A']X.$$

The critical values d_α can be obtained from the tables of Heck [11] and Pillai [33]. When $B = I_p$, S. N. Roy [41] proposed the largest root test for testing H, and the simultaneous confidence intervals associated with it are given by S. N. Roy and co-workers [40–43]. We will now consider test procedures based upon the maximum of correlated T^2 statistics. We will refer to these tests as $T^2_{\max}$ tests.

According to the $T^2_{\max}$ test, we accept or reject H_l, when Σ is unknown, according to whether

$$T_l^2 \lesseqgtr T_\alpha^2$$

where

$$P[T_l^2 \leq T_\alpha^2;\, l = 1, 2, \ldots, q \mid H] = (1-\alpha). \tag{3.6}$$

When $p = 1$, the joint distribution of $T_1^2, \ldots, T_q^2$ is a multivariate F distribution with $(1, n-m-p+r)$ degrees of freedom. For $p > 1$, the joint distribution of $T_1^2, \ldots, T_q^2$ involves nuisance parameters, and so the exact values of T_α^2 cannot be computed. For moderately large values of the error degrees of freedom, we can use Siotani's approximations [45, 46] to obtain approximate values of T_α^2. We can also obtain an upper bound on T_α^2 by applying a result of Khatri [14]. For an application of the $T^2_{\max}$ test, the reader is referred to Kaskey *et al.* [12]. We will now obtain the simultaneous confidence intervals associated with the $T^2_{\max}$ test.

Theorem 3.1. *For the $T^2_{\max}$ test, the confidence statements*

$$|\mathbf{c}_l'(\hat{\mu} - \mu)\mathbf{a}| \leq \{T_\alpha^2\mathbf{a}'S\mathbf{a}\; e_l(n-m-p+r)^{-1}\}^{1/2}, \qquad l = 1, 2, \ldots, q \tag{3.7}$$

hold simultaneously for all nonnull vectors $\mathbf{a}$ *with* $(1-\alpha)\%$ *confidence level.*

Proof. Let

$$T_l^{*2} = \mathbf{c}_l'(\hat{\mu} - \mu)S^{-1}(\hat{\mu} - \mu)'\mathbf{c}_l(n - m - p + r)/e_l,$$

for $l = 1, 2, \ldots, q$. Then

$$P\left[T_l^{*2} \le T_\alpha^{\ 2}; l = 1, 2, \ldots, q \mid \bigcup_{i=1}^{q} A_i^{\circ}\right] = P[T_l^2 \le T_\alpha^{\ 2}; l = 1, 2, \ldots, q \mid H]$$

$$= (1 - \alpha). \tag{3.8}$$

Also

$$T_l^{*2} \le T_\alpha^{\ 2}$$

is equivalent to

$$\bigcap_{\mathbf{a} \neq 0} \{|\mathbf{c}_l'(\hat{\mu} - \mu)\mathbf{a}|\} \le \{T_\alpha^{\ 2}\mathbf{a}'S\mathbf{a}e_l(n - m - p + r)^{-1}\}^{1/2} \tag{3.9}$$

Combining (3.8) and (3.9), we get the desired results.

The simultaneous confidence intervals (3.7) were obtained by S. N. Roy and Bose [40] and Siotani [45, 46] for some special cases under the classical one-way MANOVA model.

We will now discuss about step-down and finite intersection tests under the model (3.4). Let Σ_{0t} denote the top $t \times t$ left-hand corner of $\Sigma_0 = (\sigma_{0ij})$ and $\sigma_{0,t+1}^2 = |\Sigma_{0,t+1}|/|\Sigma_{0t}|$ for $t = 0, 1, \ldots, (r - 1)$ and $|\Sigma_{00}| = 1$. Also,

$$\boldsymbol{\beta}_t = \begin{pmatrix} \beta_{t1} \\ \vdots \\ \beta_{tt} \end{pmatrix} = \Sigma_{0t}^{-1}\begin{pmatrix} \sigma_{01,t+1} \\ \vdots \\ \sigma_{0t,t+1} \end{pmatrix}, \qquad \boldsymbol{\beta}_0 = 0.$$

In addition, let $Y_j = (\mathbf{y}_1, \ldots, \mathbf{y}_j)$, $\Phi_j = (\boldsymbol{\mu}_1, \ldots, \boldsymbol{\mu}_j)$, $U_j = (\boldsymbol{\zeta}_1, \ldots, \boldsymbol{\zeta}_j)$ for $j = 1, 2, \ldots, r$ where $\mathbf{y}_i$, $\boldsymbol{\mu}_i$ and $\boldsymbol{\zeta}_i$ are, respectively, the ith columns of Y, μ and ζ. When Y_j and Z are held fixed, the elements of $\mathbf{y}_{j+1}$ are distributed independently and normally with a common variance $\sigma_{0,j+1}^2$ and means given by

$$E(\mathbf{y}_{j+1}/Y_j, Z) = (A \,\vdots\, Z \,\vdots\, Y_j)\begin{pmatrix} \boldsymbol{\mu}_{j+1}^* \\ \cdots \\ \boldsymbol{\zeta}_{j+1}^* \\ \cdots \\ \boldsymbol{\beta}_j \end{pmatrix} \tag{3.10}$$

where $\boldsymbol{\mu}_{j+1}^* = \boldsymbol{\mu}_{j+1} - \Phi_j\boldsymbol{\beta}_j$ and $\boldsymbol{\zeta}_{j+1}^* = \boldsymbol{\zeta}_{j+1} - U_j\boldsymbol{\beta}_j$ for $j = 1, 2, \ldots, r - 1$. Also, when Z is held fixed, the elements of $\mathbf{y}_1$ are distributed independently and normally with variance σ_{01}^2 and means given by

$$E(\mathbf{y}_1) = (A \,\vdots\, Z)\begin{pmatrix} \boldsymbol{\mu}_1^* \\ \boldsymbol{\zeta}_1^* \end{pmatrix} \tag{3.10a}$$

where $\boldsymbol{\mu}_1{}^* = \boldsymbol{\mu}_1$ and $\boldsymbol{\zeta}_1{}^* = \boldsymbol{\zeta}_1$. For $j = 0, 1, \ldots, (r-1)$, let $\hat{\boldsymbol{\mu}}_{j+1}^*$ denote the least-square estimate of $\boldsymbol{\mu}_{j+1}^*$ and s_{j+1}^2 denote the error sum of squares under the model (3.10)–(3.10a). Also, let $V_j \sigma_{0j}^2$ be the covariance matrix of $C\hat{\boldsymbol{\mu}}_j{}^*$, $A_{lj}^\circ : \mathbf{c}_l{}'\boldsymbol{\mu}_j{}^* \neq 0$.

According to step-down procedure, we accept the total hypothesis H against $\bigcup_{j=1}^r [C\boldsymbol{\mu}_j{}^* \neq \mathbf{0}]$ if, and only if,

$$F_j \lessgtr F_{\alpha j} \quad \text{for} \quad j = 1, 2, \ldots, r$$

where

$$F_j = (C\hat{\boldsymbol{\mu}}_j{}^*)' V_j^{-1} (C\hat{\boldsymbol{\mu}}_j{}^*)(n - m - p + r - j + 1)/us_j{}^2,$$

and the critical values $F_{\alpha j}$ are chosen such that

$$P[F_j \leq F_{\alpha j}; j = 1, 2, \ldots, r \mid H] = \prod_{j=1}^{r} Q_j = (1 - \alpha) \tag{3.11}$$

where

$$Q_j = P[F_j \leq F_{\alpha j} \mid H].$$

We can impose the restriction that $Q_1 = \cdots = Q_r$ in choosing the critical values. When H is true, F_j is distributed as F distribution with $(u, n - m - p + r - j + 1)$ degrees of freedom. The simultaneous confidence intervals associated with the above test follow.

Theorem 3.2. *The* $(1 - \alpha)\%$ *simultaneous confidence intervals associated with the step-down procedure are given by*

$$|(C\hat{\boldsymbol{\mu}}_j{}^* - C\boldsymbol{\mu}_j{}^*)'\mathbf{a}| \leq \{F_{\alpha j} us_j{}^2 \mathbf{a}' V_j \mathbf{a}/(n - m - p + r - j + 1)\}^{1/2} \tag{3.12}$$

for all nonnull **a**.

The proof follows immediately by using

$$P\left[F_j{}^* \leq F_{\alpha j}; j = 1, 2, \ldots, r \mid \bigcup_{j=1}^{r} (C\boldsymbol{\mu}_j{}^* \neq 0)\right]$$
$$= P[F_j \leq F_{\alpha j}; j = 1, 2, \ldots, r \mid H]$$

where

$$F_j{}^* = (C\hat{\boldsymbol{\mu}}_j{}^* - C\boldsymbol{\mu}_j{}^*)' V_j^{-1} (C\hat{\boldsymbol{\mu}}_j{}^* - C\boldsymbol{\mu}_j{}^*)(n - m - p + r - j + 1)/us_j{}^2.$$

When $B = I_p$, the test procedure proposed above for testing H is equivalent to the procedure proposed by J. Roy [39]; but the lengths of the confidence intervals given by (3.12) for $B = I_p$ are shorter than those given by J. Roy [39]. If the total hypothesis H is rejected, the component hypotheses $H_1, \ldots, H_q$ can be tested by examining the confidence intervals given by (3.12), on the parametric functions which measure departures from these subhypotheses.

This is equivalent to accepting H_l $(l = 1, 2, \ldots, q)$ if, and only if,

$$F_{lj} \leq F_{\alpha j}\, u \qquad \text{for } j = 1, 2, \ldots, r$$

where $F_{lj} = (\mathbf{c}_l'\hat{\boldsymbol{\mu}}_j^*)^2(n - m - p + r - j + 1)/s_j^2 e_{lj}$ and $e_{lj}\sigma_{0j}^2$ is the variance of $\mathbf{c}_l'\hat{\boldsymbol{\mu}}_j^*$.

We will now consider finite intersection tests based on conditional distributions under the model (3.4). According to these tests, we accept H_l against $\bigcup_{j=1}^r A_{lj}^\circ$ if, and only if,

$$F_{lj} \leq F_{\alpha j}^*, \qquad j = 1, 2, \ldots, r$$

where

$$P[F_{lj} \leq F_{\alpha j}^*;\, l = 1, 2, \ldots, q;\, j = 1, 2, \ldots, r \mid H] = \prod_{j=1}^r Q_j^* = (1 - \alpha), \tag{3.13}$$

and

$$Q_j^* = P[F_{lj} \leq F_{\alpha j}^*;\, l = 1, 2, \ldots, q \mid H] = (1 - \alpha)^{1/r}.$$

The total hypothesis H is accepted if all the component hypotheses $H_1, \ldots, H_q$ are accepted. When H is true, the joint distribution of $F_{1j}, \ldots, F_{qj}$ is a multivariate F distribution with $(1, n - m - p + r - j + 1)$ degrees of freedom. We can easily prove the following result.

Theorem 3.3. *The $(1 - \alpha)\%$ simultaneous confidence intervals associated with the above test are given by*

$$|\mathbf{c}_l'\hat{\boldsymbol{\mu}}_j^* - \mathbf{c}_l'\boldsymbol{\mu}_j^*| \leq \{F_{\alpha j}^* s_j^2 e_{lj}/(n - m - p + r - j + 1)\}^{1/2} \tag{3.14}$$

for $l = 1, 2, \ldots, q$ and $j = 1, 2, \ldots, r$.

If we test the hypotheses H_l simultaneously against one-sided alternatives of the form $A_l^{\circ *}$ where $A_l^{\circ *} = \bigcup_{j=1}^r [\mathbf{c}_l'\boldsymbol{\mu}_j^* > 0]$, we accept H_l according to finite intersection tests, if, and only if,

$$t_{lj} \leq t_{\alpha j}; \qquad \text{for} \quad j = 1, 2, \ldots, r$$

where

$$P[t_{lj} \leq t_{\alpha j};\, l = 1, 2, \ldots, q;\, j = 1, 2, \ldots, r \mid H]$$

$$= \prod_{j=1}^r P[t_{lj} \leq t_{\alpha j};\, l = 1, 2, \ldots, q \mid H] = (1 - \alpha) \tag{3.15}$$

and

$$t_{lj} = (\mathbf{c}_l'\hat{\mu}_j^*)\{(n - m - p + r - j + 1)/s_j^2 e_{lj}\}^{1/2}.$$

When H is true, the joint distribution of $t_{1j}, \ldots, t_{qj}$ is a multivariate t distribution with $(1, n-m-p+r-j+1)$ degrees of freedom. The $(1-\alpha)\%$ simultaneous confidence intervals associated with the above test are

$$\mathbf{c}_l'\hat{\boldsymbol{\mu}}_j^* - t_{\alpha j}\{(n-m-p+r-j+1)/s_j^2 e_{lj}\}^{1/2} \leq \mathbf{c}_l'\boldsymbol{\mu}_j^* \tag{3.16}$$

for $l = 1, 2, \ldots, q$ and $j = 1, 2, \ldots, r$. Similarly, we can test the hypotheses H_l against alternatives of the form $\bigcup_{j=1}^{r} [\mathbf{c}_l'\boldsymbol{\mu}_j^* < 0]$.

When $B = I_p$ the finite intersection tests discussed above are equivalent to the tests proposed by Krishnaiah [22]. We will now consider finite intersection tests based on linear combinations of variates.

Let

$$H_{l\mathbf{a}_j}:\ \mathbf{c}_l'\mu\mathbf{a}_j = 0, \qquad H_l = \bigcap_{j=1}^{p^*} H_{l\mathbf{a}_j} \qquad \text{and} \qquad A_{l\mathbf{a}_j}^{\circ}:\ \mathbf{c}_l'\mu\mathbf{a}_j \neq 0$$

for $j = 1, 2, \ldots, p^*$, $l = 1, 2, \ldots, q$ and $\mathbf{a}_j$ are known. The elements of $\mathbf{a}_j$ can be treated as weights assigned to different variates. Now, let

$$t_{l\mathbf{a}_j} = (\mathbf{c}_l'\hat{\mu}\mathbf{a}_j)\{(n-m-p+r)/e_l(\mathbf{a}_j'S\mathbf{a}_j)\}^{1/2} \qquad \text{and} \qquad F_{l\mathbf{a}_j} = t_{l\mathbf{a}_j}^2.$$

Then, we accept or reject $H_{l\mathbf{a}_j}$ when tested against $A_{l\mathbf{a}_j}$, according to whether

$$F_{l\mathbf{a}_j} \lessgtr F_\alpha$$

where

$$P[F_{l\mathbf{a}_j} \leq F_\alpha;\quad l = 1, 2, \ldots, q, j = 1, 2, \ldots, p^* \mid H] = (1-\alpha). \tag{3.16a}$$

The hypothesis H_l is accepted if $H_{l\mathbf{a}_1}, \ldots, H_{l\mathbf{a}_{p^*}}$ are accepted. The joint distribution of the test statistics $F_{l\mathbf{a}_j}$ involve nuisance parameters and so the exact value of F_α cannot be computed. But an upper bound on F_α can be obtained by using Bonferroni's inequality. The $(1-\alpha)\%$ simultaneous confidence intervals associated with the above test are given by

$$|\mathbf{c}_l'\hat{\mu}\mathbf{a}_j - \mathbf{c}_l'\hat{\mu}\mathbf{a}_j| \leq \{F_\alpha e_l(\mathbf{a}_j'S\mathbf{a}_j)/(n-m-p+r)\}^{1/2} \tag{3.17}$$

for $l = 1, 2, \ldots, q$ and $j = 1, 2, \ldots, p^*$. If we test the hypotheses $H_{l\mathbf{a}_j}$ against alternatives of the form $\mathbf{c}_l'\mu\mathbf{a}_j > 0$, then we accept or reject $H_{l\mathbf{a}_j}$ according to whether

$$t_{l\mathbf{a}_j} \lessgtr t_\alpha$$

where

$$P[t_{l\mathbf{a}_j} \leq t_\alpha;\quad l = 1, 2, \ldots, q, j = 1, 2, \ldots, p^* | H] = (1-\alpha). \tag{3.18}$$

An upper bound on t_α can be obtained by using Bonferroni's inequality. The $(1-\alpha)\%$ simultaneous confidence intervals associated with the above test are given by

$$(\mathbf{c}_l'\hat{\mu}\mathbf{a}_j - \mathbf{c}_l'\mu\mathbf{a}_j) \leq t_\alpha\{e_l(\mathbf{a}_j'\,S\mathbf{a}_j)/(n-m-p+r)\}^{1/2} \tag{3.19}$$

for $l = 1, 2, \ldots, q$ and $j = 1, 2, \ldots, p^*$.

We will now compare the various simultaneous test procedures discussed in this section. We will first compare the $T_{\max}^2$ test with the largest root test.

Theorem 3.4. *The lengths of the confidence intervals associated with the $T_{\max}^2$ test are shorter than the lengths of the corresponding confidence intervals associated with the largest root test.*

Proof. By Theorem 3.1, the length of the confidence interval associated with the $T_{\max}^2$ test, on $\mathbf{c}_l'\mu\mathbf{a}$ is $2\{T_\alpha^2 e_l \mathbf{a}'S\mathbf{a}/(n-m-p+r)\}^{1/2}$ where T_α^2 is chosen satisfying (3.6). But the length of the corresponding confidence intervals associated with the largest root test is $2\{ud_\alpha e_l \mathbf{a}'S\mathbf{a}/(n-m-p+r)\}^{1/2}$ where d_α is chosen satisfying (3.5). But

$$\max(T_1^2, \ldots, T_q^2) \leq (n-m-p+r)C_L(S_H S^{-1}),$$

and hence

$$ud_\alpha \geq T_\alpha^2. \tag{3.20}$$

So, the desired result follows.

Theorem 3.5. *The $T_{\max}^2$ test is more powerful than the largest root test for testing the hypothesis H_l.*

Proof. The power of the $T_{\max}^2$ test, when used for testing the hypothesis H_l, is given by

$$P_1 = 1 - P[T_l^2 \leq T_\alpha^2 \mid A_l].$$

The power of the largest root test, when used for testing the hypothesis H_l, is given by

$$P_2 = 1 - [T_l^2 \leq ud_\alpha \mid A_l].$$

Using (3.20), we observe that $P_2 \leq P_1$, and hence the desired result follows.

Theorem 3.6. *The power of the $T_{\max}^2$ test for testing $H_1, \ldots, H_q$ simultaneously, becomes larger as q decreases. Also, the lengths of the confidence intervals associated with the $T_{\max}^2$ test becomes shorter as q decreases.*

Proof. The above theorem can easily be proved since

$$\max(T_1^2, \ldots, T_{q*}^2) \leq \max(T_1^2, \ldots, T_q^2)$$

when $q^* \leq q$.

We will now compare finite intersection tests based on conditional distributions with the step-down procedure.

Theorem 3.7. *The lengths of the confidence intervals associated with the finite intersection test based on conditional distributions are shorter than the lengths of the corresponding confidence intervals associated with the step-down procedure.*

Proof. By Theorem 3.3 the length of the confidence interval, associated with the finite intersection test, on $\mathbf{c}_l'\boldsymbol{\mu}_j^*$ is $2\{F_{\alpha j}^* s_j^2 e_{lj}/(n-m-p+r-j+1)\}^{1/2}$ where $F_{\alpha j}^*$ is chosen satisfying (3.13). The length of the corresponding confidence interval, associated with the step-down procedure, is $2\{uF_{\alpha j} s_j^2 e_{lj}/(n-m-p+r-j+1)\}^{1/2}$ by Theorem 3.2; here $F_{\alpha j}$ is chosen satisfying (3.11). But

$$\max(F_{1j}, \ldots, F_{qj}) \leq uF_j,$$

and hence

$$uF_{\alpha j} \geq F_{\alpha j}^*. \tag{3.21}$$

So, the desired result follows.

Theorem 3.8. *The finite intersection test based on conditional distributions is more powerful than the step-down procedure for testing the hypothesis* H_l for any given value of $l(l=1, 2, \ldots, q)$.

Proof. The power of the finite intersection test, when used for testing H_l, is given by

$$P_3 = 1 - \prod_{j=1}^{r} P\left[F_{lj} \leq F_{\alpha j}^* \mid \bigcup_{j=1}^{r} A_{lj}^{\circ}\right]$$

where $A_{lj}^{\circ} : \mathbf{c}_l'\boldsymbol{\mu}_j^* \neq 0$. The corresponding power associated with the step-down procedure is

$$P_4 = 1 - \prod_{j=1}^{r} P\left[F_{lj} \leq uF_{\alpha j} \mid \bigcup_{j=1}^{r} A_{lj}^{\circ}\right].$$

Now, using (3.21), the desired result follows.

Theorem 3.9. *For testing $H_1, \ldots, H_q$ simultaneously, the power of the finite intersection test based on conditional distribution becomes larger as q becomes smaller. Similarly, the lengths of the confidence intervals associated with the finite intersection test become shorter as q decreases.*

We will now compare the finite intersection test based on linear combinations of variates with the $T_{\max}^2$ test.

Theorem 3.10. *The lengths of the confidence intervals associated with the finite intersection tests based on linear combinations of variates are shorter than the lengths of the corresponding confidence intervals associated with the $T_{\max}^2$ test.*

Theorem 3.11. *For testing the hypotheses H_{la_j} ($l = 1, 2, \ldots, q$; $j = 1, 2, \ldots, p^*$) simultaneously, the power of the finite intersection test based on linear combinations of variates is greater than that of the $T^2_{\max}$ test.*

Theorems 3.10 and 3.11 can be proved by noting that

$$\max(F_{l\mathbf{a}_1}, \ldots, F_{l,\mathbf{a}_{p*}}) \leq T_l^2.$$

The confidence intervals are obtained by inversion of the power functions. Therefore, if the power of a test is greater than that of a rival test, then the confidence intervals associated with the former test are shorter in the Neyman sense than the confidence intervals associated with the latter test. So, for testing a given H_l, comparisons, in terms of the power functions of the rival tests, can be interpreted in terms of the probabilities of covering wrong values by the confidence intervals associated with these procedures.

These comparisons among the rival tests are based upon their performance for testing component hypotheses only but not the total hypothesis H. For testing the total hypothesis H, none of the tests is uniformly better than the other. It should be emphasized here that the comparisons are made on the basis of the exact critical values. When the exact critical values cannot be obtained, these comparisons are not useful unless the approximate critical values used are very close to the exact values.

When $p = 1$ and $H_1, \ldots, H_q$ are tested against two-sided alternatives, finite intersection tests and the step-down procedure are, respectively, equivalent to the $T^2_{\max}$ test and the largest root test.

For certain applications of the Potthoff-Roy model with unknown Σ_0, the readers are referred to Allen and Grizzle [1]. The unconditional likelihood-ratio test for the equality of the regressions coefficient vectors was considered by Gleser and Olkin [7] under a special case of the Potthoff-Roy model.

We will now discuss simultaneous test procedures under the model (3.1) with known Σ.

When Σ is known, we can make the transformation $Y^* = X\Sigma^{-1}B'(B\Sigma^{-1}B')^{-1}$ as suggested by Potthoff and Roy [34] to reduce the model (3.1) to the form

$$E(Y^*) = A\mu \tag{3.22}$$

where the rows of Y^* are independently distributed as r-variate normal with known covariance matrix $\Sigma_0 = (B\Sigma^{-1}B')^{-1}$. Now, let $\hat{\mu}$ be the best linear unbiased estimate of μ under the model (3.22) and $e_l\,\Sigma_0$ be the covariance matrix of $\mathbf{c}_l'\hat{\boldsymbol{\mu}}$. Then, according to the $\chi^2_{\max}$ test, we accept or reject H_l according to whether

$$\chi_l^2 \lessgtr \chi_\alpha^2$$

where

$$P[\chi^2 \leq \chi_\alpha^2;\quad l = 1, 2, \ldots, q \mid H] = (1 - \alpha)$$

and

$$\chi_l^2 = (\mathbf{c}_l'\hat{\mu})\Sigma_0^{-1}(\mathbf{c}_l'\hat{\mu})'/e_l.$$

When H is true, the joint distribution of $\chi_1^2, \ldots, \chi_q^2$ in the nonsingular case is a multivariate chi-square distribution with p degrees of freedom by Lemma 2.1.

Similarly, we can propose the largest root test, step-down procedure, and the finite intersection tests under the model (3.22) for testing $H_1, \ldots, H_q$, simultaneously. The details are omitted for the sake of brevity. Results analogous to Theorems 3.4–3.11 hold good for tests based on known Σ_0.

4. SIMULTANEOUS TEST PROCEDURES UNDER MANOVA MODELS WITH AUTOCORRELATED ERRORS

In this section, we shall consider the problem of testing various hypotheses simultaneously under MANOVA models when the errors follow a multivariate Markov process. To fix the ideas, we shall first consider the univariate model

$$E(\mathbf{X}) = A\boldsymbol{\mu} \tag{4.1}$$

where

$$\mathbf{X}' = (x_{11}, \ldots, x_{1n_1}, \ldots, x_{k1}, \ldots, x_{kn_k}), \qquad n = \sum_{i=1}^{k} n_i$$

$$A' = (\mathbf{A}_{11}, \ldots, \mathbf{A}_{1n_1}, \ldots, \mathbf{A}_{k1}, \ldots, \mathbf{A}_{kn_k}).$$

Here A is the design matrix which is known, and $\boldsymbol{\mu}$ is a $m \times 1$ vector of unknown parameters, and x_{it} denotes the observed value on the experimental unit from ith group at tth time point. Also

$$x_{it} = \mathbf{A}_{it}'\boldsymbol{\mu} + u_{it}$$

where

$$u_{it} = \rho_i u_{i,t-1} + \varepsilon_{it}$$

for $t = 1, 2, \ldots, n_i$ and ε_{it} are independently distributed normal variates with means zero and unknown variance σ^2. In addition, $\mathrm{Cov}(x_{it}, x_{i't'}) = 0$ for $i \neq i'$. In the above model, although the observations on any experimental unit are jointly distributed as a multivariate normal, the measurements are made on one variate only. Models of this type are sometimes referred to as quasimultivariate models. Under the model (4.1), it is of interest to test $H_1, \ldots, H_q$ simultaneously, where $H_l: \mathbf{c}_l'\boldsymbol{\mu} = 0$ and $\mathbf{c}_l'$ is known. We will assume that $n_i = 2a_i + 1$; if n_i is an even integer, we will delete the last observation.

It is known (e.g., see Hannan [9], Ogawara [32]) that the conditional distributions of $x_{i2}, \ldots, x_{i2a_i}$, holding $x_{i1}, \ldots, x_{i,2a_i+1}$ fixed, are distributed independently and normally with variance $\sigma_{ic}^2 = \sigma^2(1 - \rho_i^2)/(1 + \rho_i^2)$ and means given by

$$E_c(x_{i,2t}) = (\mathbf{A}'_{i,2t} \vdots \mathbf{A}^{*\prime}_{it} \vdots x^*_{it}) \begin{pmatrix} \boldsymbol{\mu} \\ \boldsymbol{\eta}_i \\ b_i \end{pmatrix} \tag{4.2}$$

where

$$\boldsymbol{\eta}_i = b_i \boldsymbol{\mu}, \qquad x^*_{it} = (x_{i,2t-1} + x_{i,2t+1})/2, \qquad b_i = 2\rho_i/(1 + \rho_i^2)$$

and

$$\mathbf{A}^{*\prime}_{it} = -(\mathbf{A}'_{i,2t-1} + \mathbf{A}'_{i,2t+1})/2.$$

If we ignore the relationships $\boldsymbol{\eta}_i = b_i \boldsymbol{\mu}$, we can estimate σ_{ic}^2 in the usual manner. Then the hypothesis $\sigma_{1c}^2 = \cdots = \sigma_{kc}^2$ can be tested by using known methods (e.g., see Krishnaiah [23]) for testing for the homogeneity of variances from normal populations. We will assume that $\rho_i = \rho$ and $\sigma_{ic}^2 = \sigma_c^2$, for all i, where ρ and σ_c^2 are unknown. Now, the conditional model (4.2) can be rewritten as follows:

$$E_c(\mathbf{X}_0) = (A_0 \vdots \mathbf{X}_0^*) \begin{pmatrix} \boldsymbol{\mu} \\ \boldsymbol{\eta} \\ \cdots \\ b \end{pmatrix} \tag{4.3}$$

where

$$\boldsymbol{\eta} = b\boldsymbol{\mu}, \mathbf{X}_0' = (x_{12}, \ldots, x_{1,2a_1}, \ldots, x_{k2}, \ldots, x_{k,2a_k})$$

$$\mathbf{X}_0^{*\prime} = (x^*_{11}, \ldots, x^*_{1a_1}, \ldots, x^*_{k1}, \ldots, x^*_{ka_k}),$$

$$A_0' = \begin{pmatrix} \mathbf{A}_{12} \cdots \mathbf{A}_{1,2a_1} & \cdots & \mathbf{A}_{k,2} \cdots \mathbf{A}_{k,2a_k} \\ \mathbf{A}^*_{11} \cdots \mathbf{A}^*_{1a_1} & \cdots & \mathbf{A}^*_{k1} \cdots \mathbf{A}^*_{ka_k} \end{pmatrix}. \tag{4.3a}$$

The parameters $\boldsymbol{\mu}$ can be estimated by ignoring the relations $\boldsymbol{\eta} = b\boldsymbol{\mu}$ and using the least-square method under the model (4.3). In one sample case, Hannan [9] showed that the estimates obtained by using the above method are, under certain conditions, asymptotically more efficient than the usual least-squares method; using those estimates, tests were also proposed by Hannan [9] for testing the hypotheses on regression coefficients *individually* against two-sided alternatives, under model (4.1) with $k = 1$. Now, let $\hat{\boldsymbol{\mu}}$ be the least-square estimate of $\boldsymbol{\mu}$ and s^2 be the error sum of squares under the model (4.3) ignoring the relation $\boldsymbol{\eta} = b\boldsymbol{\mu}$. Also, let

$$t_l = (\mathbf{c}_l'\hat{\boldsymbol{\mu}})(a - 2m - 1)^{1/2}/se_l^{1/2}, \qquad a = \sum_{i=1}^{k} a_i, \qquad F_l = t_l^2, \qquad A_l^\circ : \mathbf{c}_l'\boldsymbol{\mu} \neq 0$$

and $A_l^{\circ *}: \mathbf{c}_l'\boldsymbol{\mu} > 0$ where $e_l \sigma_c^2$ is the variance of $\mathbf{c}_l'\hat{\hat{\boldsymbol{\mu}}}$. Then we accept or reject H_l, when tested against A_l°, according to whether $F_l \lesseqgtr F_\alpha$ where

$$P[F_l \leq F_\alpha; \quad l = 1, 2, \ldots, q \mid H] = (1 - \alpha). \tag{4.4}$$

When H is true, the joint distribution of $F_1, \ldots, F_q$ is a multivariate F distribution with $(1, a - 2m - 1)$ degrees of freedom. If we test the hypotheses H_l against $A_l^{\circ *}$, we accept or reject H_l according as $t_l \lesseqgtr t_\alpha$ where

$$P[t_l \leq t_\alpha; \quad l = 1, 2, \ldots, q \mid H] = (1 - \alpha). \tag{4.5}$$

When H is true, the joint distribution of $t_1, \ldots, t_q$ is a multivariate t distribution with $(1, a - 2m - 1)$ degrees of freedom. Similarly, we can test the hypotheses H_l against alternatives of the form $\mathbf{c}_l'\boldsymbol{\mu} < 0$.

We will now consider the multivariate model

$$E(X) = A\mu, \tag{4.6}$$

where $X' = (\mathbf{x}_{11}, \ldots, \mathbf{x}_{1n}, \ldots, \mathbf{x}_{k1}, \ldots, \mathbf{x}_{kn_k}) : p \times n$, A is as defined earlier in this section, and μ is a $m \times p$ matrix of unknown parameters, and $\mathbf{x}_{it}$ denotes the vector of observed values on the experimental unit in ith group at tth time point. Let

$$\mathbf{x}_{it}' = \mathbf{A}_{it}'\mu + \mathbf{u}_{it}'$$

where

$$\mathbf{u}_{it} = R_i \mathbf{u}_{i,t-1} + \boldsymbol{\varepsilon}_{it}, \qquad t = 1, 2, \ldots, n_i,$$

and the roots of the unknown R_i are within the unit circle. Also, the vectors $\boldsymbol{\varepsilon}_{it}$ are independently and normally distributed with zero mean vector and covariance matrix Σ. In addition, the vectors $\mathbf{x}_{it}$ and $\mathbf{x}_{i't'}$ are independently distributed for $i \neq i'$. Under the model (4.6), we will consider testing the hypotheses $H_1, \ldots, H_q$ simultaneously, where $H_l : \mathbf{c}_l'\mu = \mathbf{0}'$.

It is known (see Hannan [10]) that the conditional distributions of $\mathbf{x}_{i2}, \ldots, \mathbf{x}_{i,2a_i}$, holding $\mathbf{x}_{i1}, \ldots, \mathbf{x}_{i,2a_i+1}$ fixed, are distributed independently and normally with covariance matrix $\Sigma_{ic} = \Sigma - M_i\,(R_i\Sigma \,\vdots\, \Sigma R_i')'$ where

$$M_i = (R_i\Sigma \,\vdots\, \Sigma R_i')\begin{pmatrix} \Sigma & \Sigma R_i'^2 \\ R_i^2\Sigma & \Sigma \end{pmatrix}^{-1} = (M_{i1} \,\vdots\, M_{i2})$$

and means are given by

$$E_c(\mathbf{x}_{i,2t}) = \mu'\mathbf{A}_{i,2t} + M_{i1}\mathbf{x}_{i,2t-1} + M_{i2}\,\mathbf{x}_{i,2t+1} + M_{i1}^*\,\mathbf{A}_{i,2t-1} + M_{i2}^*\mathbf{A}_{i,2t+1} \tag{4.7}$$

where

$$M_{ij}^* = -\,M_{ij}\,\mu', \qquad j = 1, 2. \tag{4.8}$$

If we ignore the relation (4.8), the unknown parameters μ', M_{i1}, M_{i2}, M_{i1}^*, M_{i2}^*, and Σ_{ic} can be estimated and tested by using the same methods as used in estimating and testing the parameters in the classical multivariate regression model. Then the hypothesis, that $\Sigma_{1c} = \cdots = \Sigma_{kc}$ against certain alternatives, can be tested by applying the methods proposed by Krishnaiah [25] for testing for the homogeneity of covariance matrices of multivariate normal populations. Now let us assume that

$$M_{i1} = M_{i2} = M'/2 \qquad \text{for} \quad i = 1, 2, \ldots, k, \tag{4.9}$$

and that M is unknown. Here we note that (4.9) holds good when $R_i' = R_i = R$ and Σ and R commute. Now, let $\Sigma_{ic} = \Sigma_c$. When (4.9) holds good, the model equation (4.7) can be rewritten as

$$E_c(X_0) = (A_0 \vdots X_0^*) \begin{pmatrix} \mu \\ \eta \\ \cdots \\ M \end{pmatrix} \tag{4.10}$$

where A_0 is defined by (4.3a), $\eta = \mu M$

$$X_0' = (\mathbf{x}_{12}, \ldots, \mathbf{x}_{1,2a_1}, \ldots, \mathbf{x}_{k2}, \ldots, \mathbf{x}_{k,2a_k})$$

and

$$X_0'^* = (\mathbf{x}_{11}^*, \ldots, \mathbf{x}_{1a_1}^*, \ldots, \mathbf{x}_{k1}^*, \ldots, \mathbf{x}_{ka_k}^*),$$
$$\mathbf{x}_{it}^* = (\mathbf{x}_{i,2t-1} + \mathbf{x}_{i,2t+1})/2.$$

In (4.10), the rows are independently distributed as multivariate normal with a common unknown covariance matrix Σ_c. So, if we ignore the relation $\eta = \mu M$, (4.10) is in the form of the classical MANOVA model, and hence the methods considered in the previous section can be used to test $H_1, \ldots, H_q$, simultaneously.

Let $\hat{\hat{\mu}}$ and S_0, respectively, denote the least-square estimate of μ and error SP matrix obtained under the model (4.10), ignoring the relations $\eta = \mu M$. Also, let

$$T_{l1}^2 = (\mathbf{c}_l'\hat{\hat{\mu}}) S_0^{-1} (\mathbf{c}_l'\hat{\hat{\mu}})'(a - 2m - p)/e_l^*$$

where $e_l^* \Sigma_c$ is the covariance matrix of $\mathbf{c}_l'\hat{\hat{\mu}}$. If we use the $T_{\max}^2$ test, we accept or reject H_l according to whether

$$T_{l1}^2 \lesseqgtr T_{\alpha 1}^2$$

where

$$P[T_{l1}^2 \leq T_{\alpha 1}^2;\, l = 1, 2, \ldots, q \mid H] = (1 - \alpha).$$

We can similarly propose a test procedure based on the largest root test. The efficiency of $\hat{\mu}$ relative to any alternative estimator of μ can be studied by using various criteria discussed below.

If $\hat{\boldsymbol{\theta}}_1$ and $\hat{\boldsymbol{\theta}}_2$ are two estimates of $\boldsymbol{\theta} : p \times 1$ and if $\Sigma_1{}^*$ and $\Sigma_2{}^*$ are respectively the covariance matrices of $\hat{\boldsymbol{\theta}}_1$ and $\hat{\boldsymbol{\theta}}_2$, then the efficiency of $\hat{\boldsymbol{\theta}}_1$ relative to $\hat{\boldsymbol{\theta}}_2$ can be defined by using any one of the criteria E_1, E_2, E_3, where $E_1 = \operatorname{tr} \Sigma_2{}^*/\operatorname{tr} \Sigma_1{}^*$, $E_2 = \{|\Sigma_2{}^*|/|\Sigma_1{}^*|\}^{1/p}$,

$$E_3 = \operatorname{tr}(\Sigma_2{}^*\Sigma_1^{*-1})/p.$$

In general, we can use $\psi(\lambda_1, \ldots, \lambda_p)$ as a criterion where $\lambda_1, \ldots, \lambda_p$ are characteristic roots of $\Sigma_2{}^* \Sigma_1^{*-1}$ and $\psi(\lambda_1, \ldots, \lambda_p)$ is a monotonic increasing function of $\lambda_1, \ldots, \lambda_p$; E_2 and E_3 are special cases of this criterion.

We shall now give details of the finite intersection tests based on conditional distributions under the model (4.10). Let Σ_{cb} denote the top $b \times b$ left-hand corner of $\Sigma_c = (\sigma_{cij})$ and $\sigma_{c,b+1}^2 = |\Sigma_{c,b+1}|/|\Sigma_{cb}|$ for $b = 0, 1, \ldots, (p-1)$ and $|\Sigma_{c0}| = 1$. For $b = 1, 2, \ldots, (p-1)$

$$\boldsymbol{\beta}_{cb} = \Sigma_{cb}^{-1}\begin{pmatrix} \sigma_{c1,b+1} \\ \vdots \\ \sigma_{cb,b+1} \end{pmatrix}, \qquad \text{and} \qquad \beta_{c0} = 0.$$

Also, let $s_1{}^2$ denote the top left-hand corner of S_0 and $\hat{\hat{\boldsymbol{\mu}}}_1{}^*$ be the first column of $\hat{\hat{\mu}}$.

In addition, let $X_{0j} = (\mathbf{x}_1, \ldots, \mathbf{x}_j)$, $\Phi_{0j} = (\boldsymbol{\mu}_1, \ldots, \boldsymbol{\mu}_j)$, $U_{0j} = (\boldsymbol{\eta}_1, \ldots, \boldsymbol{\eta}_j)$, $M_{0j} = (\mathbf{M}_1, \ldots, \mathbf{M}_j)$ for $j = 1, 2, \ldots, p$ where $\mathbf{x}_j$, $\boldsymbol{\mu}_j$, $\boldsymbol{\eta}_j$ and $\mathbf{M}_j$ are respectively jth columns of X_0, μ, η and M. When X_{0j} is held fixed, the elements of $\mathbf{x}_{j+1}$ are distributed independently and normally with a common variance $\sigma_{c,b+1}^2$ and means given by

$$E_c(\mathbf{x}_{j+1}/X_{0j}) = (A_0 \ \vdots\ X_0{}^* \ \vdots\ X_{0j})\begin{pmatrix} \boldsymbol{\mu}_{j+1}^* \\ \boldsymbol{\eta}_{j+1}^* \\ \cdots \\ \mathbf{M}_{j+1}^* \\ \cdots \\ \boldsymbol{\beta}_{cj} \end{pmatrix} \tag{4.11}$$

where

$$\boldsymbol{\mu}_{j+1}^* = \boldsymbol{\mu}_{j+1} - \Phi_{0j}\boldsymbol{\beta}_{cj}, \qquad \boldsymbol{\eta}_{j+1}^* = \boldsymbol{\eta}_{j+1} - U_{0j}\boldsymbol{\beta}_{cj},$$
$$\mathbf{M}_{j+1}^* = \mathbf{M}_{j+1} - M_{0j}\boldsymbol{\beta}_{cj}$$

for $j = 0, 1, \ldots, (p-1)$. Now, let $\hat{\hat{\boldsymbol{\mu}}}_{j+1}^*$ be the least-square estimate of $\boldsymbol{\mu}_{j+1}^*$, and s_{j+1}^2 denote the error sum of squares under the model (4.11) ignoring the relations among $\boldsymbol{\mu}_{j+1}^*$, $\boldsymbol{\eta}_{j+1}^*$, and $\mathbf{M}_{j+1}^*$. Also, let $F_{lj1} = t_{lj1}^2$ where $t_{lj1} = (c_l'\hat{\hat{\boldsymbol{\mu}}}_j{}^*)(a - 2m - p - j + 1)^{1/2}/\{s_j{}^2 e_{lj}^*\}^{1/2}$ and $e_{lj}^* \sigma_{cj}^2$ is the variance of $\mathbf{c}_l'\hat{\hat{\boldsymbol{\mu}}}_j{}^*$. Then we accept H_l against $\bigcup_{j=1}^{p} [\mathbf{c}_l'\boldsymbol{\mu}_j{}^* \neq 0]$ if, and only if,

$$F_{lj1} \leq F_{\alpha j1} \qquad \text{for} \quad j = 1, 2, \ldots, p$$

where

$$P[F_{lj1} \leq F_{\alpha j1};\, l = 1, 2, \ldots, q, j = 1, 2, \ldots, p \,|\, H]$$
$$= \prod_{j=1}^{p} P[F_{lj1} \leq F_{\alpha j1};\, l = 1, 2, \ldots, q \,|\, H] = (1 - \alpha).$$

For given j, the joint distribution of $F_{1j1}, \ldots, F_{qj1}$ is a multivariate F distribution with $(1, a - 2m - p - j + 1)$ degrees of freedom.

If we test the hypotheses H_l against alternatives of the form $\bigcup_{j=1}^{p}[\mathbf{c}_l'\boldsymbol{\mu}_j^* > 0]$, we accept H_l if, and only if,

$$t_{lj} \leq t_{\alpha j1} \qquad \text{for} \quad j = 1, 2, \ldots, p$$

where

$$P[t_{lj} \leq t_{\alpha j1};\, l = 1, 2, \ldots, q;\, j = 1, 2, \ldots, p \,|\, H]$$
$$= \prod_{j=1}^{p} P[t_{lj} \leq t_{\alpha j1};\, l = 1, 2, \ldots, p \,|\, H] = (1 - \alpha).$$

When H is true, the joint distribution of $t_{1j}, \ldots, t_{qj}$ is a multivariate t distribution with $(1, a - 2m - p - j + 1)$ degrees of freedom. The simultaneous confidence intervals associated with the above tests can be obtained easily. We can also easily propose a step-down procedure for testing the hypotheses H_l, simultaneously, against two-sided alternatives.

In this section, we have used conditional distributions of even observations holding odd observations fixed. We can also, in the same way, propose similar procedures by using conditional distributions of odd observations holding even observations fixed. In this case, we have to delete the first observation since its conditional variance is different from that of the other odd observations; for the same reason, we have to delete the last observation if the sample size is odd. One can pool the information obtained by using the conditional model of odd observations and the conditional model of even observations, but the distributions of the estimates obtained by this method involve nuisance parameters. Remarks similar to the above can be made for the multivariate case also.

5. SIMULTANEOUS TESTS UNDER MANOVA MODELS WITH A GENERAL CORRELATION PATTERN

Consider the model equation

$$E(X) = A\mu, \tag{5.1}$$

where $X = (\mathbf{x}_1, \ldots, \mathbf{x}_p) : n \times p$, and $A : n \times m$ is known and is of rank $m\,(<n)$ whereas $\mu : m \times p$ is unknown. Also, $(\mathbf{x}_1', \ldots, \mathbf{x}_p')$ is distributed as a

multivariate normal with covariance matrix Σ. Under the above model, we are interested in testing the hypotheses $H_1, \ldots, H_q$, simultaneously, where $H_l : \mathbf{c}_l'\mu = \mathbf{0}'$ and $\mathbf{c}_l'\mu$ is "estimable." First, we consider the test procedures when Σ is completely known. Now, let $\Sigma = TT'$ where $T : pn \times pn$ is a nonsingular triangular matrix. Also, let

$$(\mathbf{y}_1', \ldots, \mathbf{y}_p') = (\mathbf{x}_1', \ldots, \mathbf{x}_p')(T^{-1})' \qquad \text{and} \qquad \mu = (\boldsymbol{\mu}_1, \ldots, \boldsymbol{\mu}_p).$$

Then the elements of $(\mathbf{y}_1', \ldots, \mathbf{y}_p')$ are distributed independently as normal with unit variance and means given by

$$E(\mathbf{y}_1', \ldots, \mathbf{y}_p') = (\boldsymbol{\mu}_1'A', \ldots, \boldsymbol{\mu}_p'A')(T^{-1})'. \tag{5.2}$$

So, we can test the hypotheses H_l under the model (5.2) as follows. We accept H_l if

$$\chi_{lj}^2 \leq \chi_\alpha^2 \qquad \text{for} \quad j = 1, 2, \ldots, p$$

where χ_α^2 is chosen such that

$$P[\chi_{lj}^2 \leq \chi_\alpha^2; l = 1, 2, \ldots, q; j = 1, 2, \ldots, p \mid H] = (1 - \alpha), \chi_{lj}^2 = (\mathbf{c}_l' \hat{\boldsymbol{\mu}}_j)^2/v_{lj},$$

and $\hat{\boldsymbol{\mu}}_j$ is the least-square estimate of $\boldsymbol{\mu}_j$ under the model (5.2), and v_{lj} is the variance of $(\mathbf{c}_l'\hat{\boldsymbol{\mu}}_j)$. When H is true, the joint distribution of $\chi_{11}^2, \ldots, \chi_{qp}^2$ is a multivariate chi-square distribution with one degree of freedom. We can similarly propose procedures for testing the hypotheses H_l against one-sided alternatives.

We will now consider the problem of testing the hypotheses H_l simultaneously when Σ is unknown but an independent estimate of Σ is available. Let S/v be such an estimate and let S be distributed as Wishart distribution with v degrees of freedom. Let $z_{lj} = \mathbf{b}_l'\mathbf{x}_j$ where $\mathbf{b}_l'$ is such that $\mathbf{c}_l' = \mathbf{b}_l'A$.

Also, let $F_{lj} = z_{lj}^2/(\mathbf{b}_l'S_{jj}\mathbf{b}_l)$ where S_{jj}/v denotes the estimate of the covariance matrix of $\mathbf{x}_j$. Then, we accept H_l if

$$F_{lj} \leq F_\alpha^* \qquad \text{for} \quad j = 1, 2, \ldots, p$$

where

$$P[F_{lj} \leq F_\alpha^*; \quad l = 1, 2, \ldots, q \qquad j = 1, 2, \ldots, p \mid H] = (1 - \alpha).$$

We can obtain a bound on F_α^* using Bonferroni's inequality. We can obtain an alternative bound on F_α^* by using

$$(\mathbf{x}_1', \ldots, \mathbf{x}_p')S^{-1}\begin{pmatrix}\mathbf{x}_1\\ \vdots \\ \mathbf{x}_p\end{pmatrix} \leq F_\alpha^* \Rightarrow F_{lj} \leq F_\alpha^*; \quad l = 1, 2, \ldots, q; \quad j = 1, 2, \ldots, p.$$

When $p = 1$ and the estimate S/v of unknown Σ is available, Rao [35] considered the problem of testing the hypotheses H_l. His method is based upon using the information contained in certain concomitant variables; also, his tests are based on the overall F test. His method can be applied to the model (5.1) also with some minor modifications since the model (5.1) can be rewritten in the form of the model considered by Rao [35].

If the concomitant variables are highly correlated with the main variables, the efficiency of the estimates will be increased by using the information contained in the concomitant variables. If the correlation is very weak, there will be loss in the efficiency of the estimates by using concomitant variables. This point was discussed in detail by Rao [36–38].

Acknowledgment

The author wishes to thank Professor C. G. Khatri for going through the manuscript and making suggestions for its improvement.

REFERENCES

1. Allen, D. M., and Grizzle, J. E. (1968). Analysis of growth and response curves (abstract). *Biometrics* **24** 450.
2. Armitage, J. V., and Krishnaiah, P. R. (1964). Tables for the studentized largest chi-square distribution and their applications. ARL 64-188. Aerospace Res. Labs., Wright-Patterson Air Force Base, Ohio.
3. Cornish, E. A. (1954). The multivariate small t-distribution associated with a set of normal sample deviates. *Austral. J. Phys.* **7** 531–542.
4. Dunnett, C. W., and Sobel, M. (1954). A bivariate generalization of Student's t-distribution, with tables for certain cases. *Biometrika* **41** 153–169.
5. Feller, W. (1950). "Introduction to Probability Theory and Its Applications." Wiley, New York.
6. Gabriel, K. R. (1969). A comparison of some methods of simultaneous inference in MANOVA. *In* "Multivariate Analysis-II" (P. R. Krishnaiah, ed.). Academic Press, New York.
7. Gleser, L., and Olkin, I. (1966). A k-sample regression model with covariance. *In* "Multivariate Analysis" (P. R. Krishnaiah, ed.) pp. 59–72. Academic Press, New York.
8. Gupta, S. (1963). Probability integrals of multivariate normal and multivariate t. *Ann. Math. Statist.* **34** 792–828.
9. Hannan, E. J. (1955). Exact tests for serial correlation. *Biometrika* **42** 133–142.
10. Hannan, E. J. (1956). Exact tests for serial correlation in vector processes. *Proc. Cambridge Philos. Soc.* **52** 482–487.
11. Heck, D. L. (1960). Charts of some upper percentage points of the distribution of largest root. *Ann. Math. Statist.* **31** 625–642.
12. Kaskey, G., Krishnaiah, P. R., and Azzari, A. J. (1962). Cluster formation and diagnostic significance in psychiatric symptom evaluation. *Fall Joint Comput. Conf. Proc. Philadelphia, 1962*, pp. 285–302. Spartan Books, Washington, D.C.
13. Khatri, C. G. (1966). A note on a MANOVA model applied to problems in growth curves. *Ann. Inst. Statist. Math.* **18** 75–86.
14. Khatri, C. G. (1967). On certain inequalities for normal distribution and their applications to simultaneous confidence bounds. *Ann. Math. Statist.* **17** 175–183.

15. KRISHNAMOORTHY, A. S., and PARTHASARATHY, M. (1951). A multivariate gamma distribution. *Ann. Math. Statist.* **22** 549–557 [Erratum: *Ann. Math. Statist.* **31** 229 (1960)].
16. KRISHNAIAH, P. R., and RAO, M. M. (1961). Remarks on a multivariate gamma distribution. *Amer. Math. Monthly* **68** 342–346.
17. KRISHNAIAH, P. R., and MURTHY, V. K. (1966). Simultaneous tests for trend and serial correlations for Gaussian Markov residuals. *Econometrica* **34** 472–480 [Erratum: *Econometrica* **34**].
18. KRISHNAIAH, P. R. (1963). Simultaneous tests and the efficiency of generalized incomplete block designs. ARL 63-174. Aerospace Res. Labs., Wright-Patterson Air Force Base, Ohio.
19. KRISHNAIAH, P. R. (1965). On the simultaneous ANOVA and MANOVA tests. *Ann. Inst. Statist. Math.* **17** 35–53.
20. KRISHNAIAH, P. R. (1965). On a multivariate generalization of the simultaneous analysis of variance test. *Ann. Inst. Statist. Math.* **17** 167–173.
21. KRISHNAIAH, P. R. (1964). Multiple comparison tests in multivariate case. ARL 64-124. Aerospace Res. Labs., Wright-Patterson Air Force Base, Ohio.
22. KRISHNAIAH, P. R. (1965). Multiple comparison tests in multi-response experiments. *Sankhyā Ser. A* **27** 31–36.
23. KRISHNAIAH, P. R. (1965). Simultaneous tests for equality of variances against certain alternatives. *Austral. J. Statist.* **7** 105–109 [Erratum: *Austral. J. Statist.* **10** 43].
24. KRISHNAIAH, P. R. (1967). Simultaneous tests for multiple comparisons of growth curves. ARL 67-0199. Aerospace Res. Labs., Wright-Patterson Air Force Base, Ohio.
25. KRISHNAIAH, P. R. (1968). Simultaneous tests for the equality of covariance matrices against certain alternatives. *Ann. Math. Statist.* **39** 1303–1309.
26. KRISHNAIAH, P. R., and Jayachandran, K. (1968). Simultaneous tests and multiple decision procedures for multi-response growth curves (abstract). *Ann. Math. Statist.* **39**.
27. KRISHNAIAH, P. R., and ARMITAGE, J. V. (1965). Tables for the maximum of correlated chi-square variates with one degree of freedom. *Trabajos Estadist.* **16** 91–96.
28. KRISHNAIAH, P. R., and ARMITAGE, J. V. (1966). Tables for multivariate t distribution. *Sankhyā Ser. B* **28** 31–56.
29. KRISHNAIAH, P. R., and ARMITAGE, J. V. (1969). On a multivariate F distribution. *In* "Essays in Probability and Statistics" (R. C. Bose *et al.*, eds.). Univ. North Carolina Press, Chapel Hill, North Carolina.
30. KRISHNAIAH, P. R., ARMITAGE, J. V., and BREITER, M. C. (1967). Tables for the probability integrals of the bivariate t distribution. Unpublished work.
31. KSHIRSAGAR, A. M. (1961). Some extensions of the multivariate *t*-distribution and the multivariate generalization of the distribution of the regression coefficient. *Proc. Cambridge Philos. Soc.* **57** 80–85.
32. OGAWARA, M. (1953). A note on the test of serial correlation coefficients. *Ann. Math. Statist.* **22** 115–118.
33. PILLAI, K. C. S. (1960). "Statistical Tables for Tests of Multivariate Hypotheses." Univ. of the Philippines, Manila.
34. POTTHOFF, R. F., and ROY, S. N. (1964). A generalized multivariate analysis of variance model useful especially for growth curve problems. *Biometrika* **51** 313–326.
35. RAO, C. R. (1959). Some problems involving linear hypotheses in multivariate analysis. *Biometrika* **46** 49–58.
36. RAO, C. R. (1965). The theory of least squares when the parameters are stochastic and its application to the analysis of growth curves. *Biometrika* **52** 447–458.
37. RAO, C. R. (1966). Least square theory using an estimated dispersion matrix and its application to measurement of signals. *Proc. Fifth Berkeley Symp. Math. Statist.*

Prob. (L. LeCam and J. Neyman, eds.). Univ. of California Press, Berkeley, California.

38. Rao, C. R. (1966). Covariance adjustment and related problems in multivariate analysis. *In* "Multivariate Analysis" (P. R. Krishnaiah, ed.), pp. 87–103. Academic Press, New York.
39. Roy, J. (1958). Step-down procedure in multivariate analysis. *Ann. Math. Statist.* **29** 1177–1187.
40. Roy, S. N., and Bose, R. C. (1953). Simultaneous confidence interval estimation. *Ann. Math. Statist.* **24** 513–536.
41. Roy, S. N. (1957). "Some Aspects of Multivariate Analysis." Wiley, New York.
42. Roy, S. N., and Gnanadesikan, R. (1957). Further contributions to multivariate confidence bounds. *Biometrika* **45** 581.
43. Roy, S. N., and Gnanadesikan, R. (1958). A note on "Further contributions to multivariate confidence bounds." *Biometrika* **45** 581.
44. Scheffé, H. (1953). A method for judging all contrasts in the analysis of variance. *Biometrika* **40** 87–104.
45. Siotani, M. (1959). The extreme value of the generalized distances of the individual points in the multivariate normal sample. *Ann. Inst. Statist. Math.* **10** 183–203.
46. Siotani, M. (1960). Notes on multivariate confidence bounds. *Ann. Inst. Statist. Math.* **11** 167–182.
47. Siotani, M. (1961). The extreme value of the generalized distances and its applications. *Bull. Inst. Internat. Statist.* **38** 591–599.
48. Srivastava, J. N., and Roy, S. N. (1968). Inference on treatment effects in incomplete block designs. *Rev. Inst. Internat. Statist.* **36** 1–6.
49. Srivastava, J. N. (1969). Some studies on intersection tests in multivariate analysis of variance. *In* "Multivariate Analysis-II" (P. R. Krishnaiah, ed.). Academic Press, New York.

Some Studies on Intersection Tests in Multivariate Analysis of Variance[1]

J. N. SRIVASTAVA

DEPARTMENT OF MATHEMATICS AND STATISTICS
COLORADO STATE UNIVERSITY
FORT COLLINS, COLORADO

1. SUMMARY

This paper is concerned with certain problems concerning the power of tests of multivariate and univariate linear hypotheses when such tests are derived by decomposing the total hypothesis H_0 into smaller univariate subhypotheses H_{0j} and applying Roy's union-intersection principle. In particular, the problem of the optimal choice of the sizes of the acceptance regions (of F-tests) for the H_{0j}, which maximizes the power for the test for H_0 (for a given value of α, the error of the first kind) is considered. This is done when the H_{0j} are independent, quasi-independent, and (for a special case) dependent. The theory developed herein provides some further help to the methods for looking at multivariate problems in "univariate ways."

2. INTRODUCTION

Over the past decade and a half, a great deal of work has been done on the theory of union-intersection test procedures. Some of this will be found in the references. For further information, the interested reader may refer, for example, to the Bibliography of Krishnaiah (1965a).

Let H_0 be a linear hypothesis, such that $H_0 = \bigcap_i H_{0i}$, where the H_{0i} are simpler subhypotheses for which a test procedure (optimal in some sense) exists. Let D_i be an acceptance region for H_{0i}; then, broadly, Roy's union-intersection principle says that we can take $D = \bigcap_i D_i$, as the acceptance region for H_0. The general union-intersection principle does not specify how

[1] This research was done under Contract F 33615-67-C-1436, for the Aerospace Research Laboratories, Office of Aerospace Research, United States Air Force.

H_0 should be decomposed into the H_{0i}, how D_i should be formed corresponding to the H_{0i} after the decomposition is made, or what the sizes of the D_i should be, etc. The principle being so general and so broadly applicable; any such specification would obviously not be possible. Because of this vast generality, many different and large classes of procedures can be derived, for example, as is shown by Roy (1957), the likelihood ratio tests for any situation involving a simple hypothesis versus a composite alternative can be obtained in this manner. One beauty of the principle is that it lets us evolve tests "suited to the physical nature" of H_0 (and the alternative hypothesis), by allowing us to decompose H_0 in various physically meaningful ways. Thus, for example, in the context of linear models and hypotheses, four basically different decompositions of H_0 are possible, useful, and popular. Although, using Roy's union-intersection principle, tests for complex hypotheses can be constructed in many different kinds of situations, we shall restrict our discussion in this paper to the context of (multivariate and univariate) linear models and hypotheses. In this context, H_{0i} are usually (univariate) linear hypotheses under univariate linear models, and the D_i are usually regions corresponding to tests based on the F-distribution or t-distribution.

In this paper, the question of the sizes of the D_i is considered. In the next three sections, we will prove certain theorems (as mentioned in the summary) on the sizes of various kinds of intersecting F-test regions. In Section 6, we consider possible applications of this theory by showing how the various kinds of intersections arise through the different decompositions of multivariate (and univariate) linear hypotheses.

A few remarks here on the proofs of the theorems ahead are necessary. In many cases, we have treated random variables as if they had variance 1 (and not an unknown variance σ^2). However, as the reader can check, this is merely a canonical form and does not introduce any loss of generality. Also, we have often changed the orders of infinite sums and/or integrals and rearranged the terms in an infinite series, without proving the validity of the same. This, again, was done for brevity, and can be checked to hold.

3. CHOICES OF CONSTANTS IN SIMULTANEOUS BUT INDEPENDENT F-TESTS

Let $f(x; k, n; \delta^2)$ denote the density of a random variable X obeying the noncentral F-distribution with degrees of freedom k and n and noncentrality parameter δ^2. Thus

$$f(x; k, n; \delta^2) = \exp(-\delta^2/2) \sum_{r=0}^{\infty} \left(\frac{\delta^2}{2}\right)^r \frac{1}{r!} \left[\frac{1}{B((k/2)+r, n/2)} \frac{x^{r-1+(k/2)}}{(1+x)^{r+(k+n)/2}}\right]. \tag{3.1}$$

Also let $F(\mu; k, n; \delta^2)$ denote the corresponding distribution function, i.e.,

$$F(\mu; k, n; \delta^2) = \int_0^\mu f(x; k, n; \delta^2)\, dx. \tag{3.2}$$

Let X_i $(i = 1, 2)$ be independently distributed with the noncentral-F density, both having the same degrees of freedom k and n, but with different non-centrality parameters δ_i^2, where (without loss of generality) we assume that

$$\delta_1^2 \geq \delta_2^2 \geq 0. \tag{3.3}$$

Consider the null hypothesis $H_0 : \delta_1^2 = \delta_2^2 = 0$ decomposed into the two components

$$H_{01}:\ \delta_1^2 = 0, \qquad H_{02}:\ \delta_2^2 = 0, \qquad H_0 = H_{01} \cap H_{02}. \tag{3.4}$$

For H_{0i} $(i = 1, 2)$ consider a test with α_i as the first kind of error. Choose μ_i $(i = 1, 2)$ such that

$$F(\mu_i; k, n; 0) = 1 - \alpha_i, \tag{3.5}$$

so that H_{0i} is accepted if $X_i \leq \mu_i$, and is rejected otherwise. Suppose, using Roy's union-intersection principle, we take the acceptance region for H_0 to be: $X_1 \leq \mu_1$, $X_2 \leq \mu_2$. Then, α, the error of the first kind corresponding to H_0 is given by

$$1 - \alpha = (1 - \alpha_1)(1 - \alpha_2). \tag{3.6}$$

The following problem then arises. Given α, how should we choose α_1 (and hence α_2) so that the power of the above test for H_0 is maximized? Clearly, if we denote this expression for power by $p(k, n; \delta_1^2, \delta_2^2, \alpha, \alpha_1) = p$ (for short), then

$$p(k, n; \delta_1^2, \delta_2^2; \alpha, \alpha_1) = 1 - \mathrm{Prob}\{X_1 \leq \mu_1 \mid \delta_1^2\} \cdot \mathrm{Prob}\{X_2 \leq \mu_2 \mid \delta_2^2\}. \tag{3.7}$$

In the above, obviously, the alternative to H_0 is not-H_0, i.e., at least one of δ_1^2 and δ_2^2 is strictly positive. The problem is thus to choose α_1 and α_2, or in turn μ_1 and μ_2, so that p is maximized for a given α. In the sequel, we shall also write $p = p(\mu_1, \mu_2)$, where it is understood that the remaining parameters k, n, δ_1^2, δ_2^2, and α are fixed, and that μ_1, μ_2 are so chosen as to make the first kind of error equal to α. Also, for all permissible integers i, and all real μ, we shall frequently use the following abbreviations:

$$F(\mu; k, n; \delta_i^2) \equiv F(\mu, \delta_i^2) \equiv F_i(\mu); \qquad f(\mu; k, n; \delta_i^2) \equiv f(\mu, \delta_i^2) \equiv f_i(\mu)$$
$$F(\mu; k, n; 0) \equiv F(\mu, 0) \equiv F(\mu); \qquad f(\mu; k, n; 0) \equiv f(\mu, 0) \equiv f(\mu). \tag{3.8}$$

Lemma 1. *Suppose $\delta_1^2 > \delta_2^2 \geq 0$. Then there is a pair (μ_1, μ_2) with $\mu_1 < \mu_2$ such that $p(\mu_1, \mu_2) > p(\mu, \mu)$.*

Proof. The error of second kind is given by

$$1 - p(\mu_1, \mu_2) = F_1(\mu_1)F_2(\mu_2), \tag{3.9}$$

where

$$1 - \alpha = F(\mu_1)F(\mu_2). \tag{3.10}$$

Suppose $(\mu_1, \mu_2) = (\mu, \mu)$ satisfies (3.10). Consider the point $(\mu - d\mu_1, \mu + d\mu_2)$ where $d\mu_1$ and $d\mu_2$ are positive and arbitrarily small, such that (3.10) still holds. Now since $F(\mu)$ is a continuous function of μ, we have approximately

$$F(\mu - \mathrm{d}\mu_1) = F(\mu) - (\mathrm{d}\mu_1)f(\mu), \qquad F(\mu + \mathrm{d}\mu_2) = F(\mu) + (\mathrm{d}\mu_2)f(\mu). \tag{3.11}$$

Hence

$$\begin{aligned} 1 - \alpha = [F(\mu)]^2 &= [F(\mu - d\mu_1)][F(\mu + d\mu_2)] \\ &= [F(\mu)]^2 + f(\mu)F(\mu)[d\mu_2 - d\mu_1], \end{aligned} \tag{3.12}$$

the approximation being valid to order $(d\mu_1 \cdot d\mu_2)$. We shall assume that $d\mu_1$ is so small that this approximation could be ignored. Assuming, as we can, that $\mu > 0$, from (3.12), we get:

$$d\mu_2 = d\mu_1. \tag{3.13}$$

Again,

$$F_1(\mu - d\mu_1) = F_1(\mu) - (d\mu_1)f_1(\mu), \qquad F_2(\mu + d\mu_2) = F_2(\mu) + (d\mu_2)f_2(\mu).$$

Hence, ignoring terms of order $(d\mu_1)(d\mu_2)$, the error of second kind β is given by

$$\begin{aligned} \beta \equiv \beta(\mu - d\mu_1, \mu + d\mu_2) &= 1 - p(\mu - d\mu_1, \mu + d\mu_2) \\ &= [F_1(\mu)][F_2(\mu)] + [F_1(\mu) \cdot f_2(\mu)\, d\mu_2 - f_1(\mu)F_2(\mu)\, d\mu_1]. \end{aligned} \tag{3.14}$$

Hence, using (3.13), (3.9), and, (3.14), we get

$$\begin{aligned} &p(\mu - d\mu_1, \mu + d\mu_2) - p(\mu, \mu) \\ &\qquad = d\mu_1 f_2(\mu)F_2(\mu)\left[\frac{f_1(\mu)}{f_2(\mu)} - \frac{F_1(\mu)}{F_2(\mu)}\right]. \end{aligned} \tag{3.15}$$

Let the expression on the right-hand side of (3.15) in square brackets be denoted by $Q(\mu)$. We show that if α is small enough, i.e., if μ is large enough, then $Q(\mu) > 0$. Clearly, this will complete the proof of the lemma. Now, from the monotonicity property of the F-test, it follows that $F(\mu; k, n; \delta^2)$(which represents the second kind of error) is a monotonic decreasing function of

δ^2. Thus, since ${\delta_1}^2 > {\delta_2}^2$, we have $[F_1(\mu)/F_2(\mu)] < 1$, for all μ. Hence, clearly, it is enough to show that there exists $\mu_0 > 0$, such that for $\mu \geq \mu_0$, we have $[f_1(\mu)/f_2(\mu)] \geq 1$. Now, for $0 \leq x \leq \infty$,

$$f(x; k, n; \delta^2) = \exp(-\delta^2/2) \sum_{r=0}^{\infty} \frac{1}{r!} \left(\frac{\delta^2}{2}\right)^r \beta_2\left(x; \frac{k}{2} + r; \frac{n}{2}\right), \tag{3.16}$$

where β_2 denotes the β-distribution of the second kind, and is given by

$$\beta_2(x; v_1, v_2) = \frac{1}{B(v_1, v_2)} \cdot \frac{x^{v_1 - 1}}{(1 + x)^{v_1 + v_2}}; \qquad B(v_1, v_2) = \frac{\Gamma(v_1)\Gamma(v_2)}{\Gamma(v_1 + v_2)}. \tag{3.17}$$

Consider the equation

$$f_1(\mu) = f_2(\mu). \tag{3.18}$$

Put

$$\mu' = \mu/(1 + \mu). \tag{3.19}$$

Since $0 \leq \mu \leq \infty$, we have $0 \leq \mu' \leq 1$, and μ' is a strictly monotonically increasing function of μ. Then

$$\begin{aligned} f(\mu; k, n; \delta^2) &= \exp(-\delta^2/2) \sum_{r=0}^{\infty} \left(\frac{1}{r!}\right)\left(\frac{\delta^2}{2}\right)^r \cdot \frac{1}{B((k/2) + r, n/2)} \\ &\quad \frac{\mu^{(k/2)+r-1}}{(1 + \mu)^{(k/2)+r+(n/2)}} \\ &= \exp(-\delta^2/2) \sum_{r=0}^{\infty} \left(\frac{1}{r!}\right)\left(\frac{\delta^2}{2}\right)^r \cdot \left[B\left(\frac{k}{2} + r, \frac{n}{2}\right)\right]^{-1} \\ &\quad (\mu')^{(k/2)+r-1}(1 - \mu')^{(n/2)+1}. \end{aligned} \tag{3.20}$$

Hence, (for $\mu > 0$), Eq. (3.18) implies

$$\frac{\sum_{r=0}^{\infty} [(r!)B((k/2) + r, n/2)]^{-1} ({\delta_1}^2\mu'/2)^r}{\sum_{r=0}^{\infty} [(r!)B((k/2) + r, n/2)]^{-1} ({\delta_2}^2\mu'/2)^r} = \exp(\tfrac{1}{2}(\delta_1^2 - {\delta_2}^2)). \tag{3.21}$$

Both the numerator and the denominator of the ratio (say R) on the left-hand side of (3.21) consist of convergent series of positive terms. For $\mu' = 0$ (i.e., $\mu = 0$), $R = 1$. For $\mu' > 0$, since ${\delta_1}^2 > {\delta_2}^2$, the ratio $R > 1$. Also, as μ' increases, each term in the numerator of R increases faster than the corresponding term in the denominator. Thus R is a strictly monotonically increasing function of μ', and therefore of μ. Hence, there is at most one value of μ' such that $R = R(\mu')$ equals the right-hand side of (3.21). However, since

$f_1(\mu)$ and $f_2(\mu)$ are both densities, and the area under both in the range $0 \leq \mu \leq \infty$ equals 1, we cannot have $f_1(\mu) < f_2(\mu)$, for all μ. Thus, there exist values of μ, say $\mu^{(1)}$ and $\mu^{(2)}$, such that $f_1(\mu^{(1)}) < f_2(\mu^{(1)})$, $f_1(\mu^{(2)}) > f_2(\mu^{(2)})$. Since both $f_1(\mu)$ and $f_2(\mu)$ are continuous, the above facts imply that there exists exactly one value of μ' (say μ_0') satisfying (3.21). For all $\mu' > \mu_0'$, $R(\mu') > \exp(\frac{1}{2}(\delta_1^2 - \delta_2^2))$. Let $\mu_0' = \mu_0^*/(1 + \mu_0^*)$. Then it follows that for all $\mu > \mu_0^*$, we have either $f_1(\mu) > f_2(\mu)$ or $f_1(\mu)/f_2(\mu) > 1$. This completes the proof of the lemma.

It may be remarked that in actual practice the above result would hold for all $\mu \geq \mu_0$, where $\mu_0 < \mu_0^*$, the reason being the continuity of the functions $f_1(\mu)$ and $f_2(\mu)$.

Lemma 2. *Suppose, the pair* (μ_1, μ_2) *satisfies* (3.10), *i.e.*, $F(\mu_1)\ F(\mu_2) = 1 - \alpha$. *Then, if* α *is small enough and* $\mu_1 > \mu_2$, *we must have*

$$p(\mu_1, \mu_2) < p(\mu_2, \mu_1).$$

Proof. Let $\mu_1' = \mu_2$, $\mu_2' = \mu_1$. The pair (μ_1', μ_2') satisfies (3.10). Thus, we have to show

$$F_1(\mu_1)F_2(\mu_2) > F_1(\mu_2)F_2(\mu_1). \tag{3.22}$$

Now

$$\begin{aligned} \Delta &\equiv F_1(\mu_1)F_2(\mu_2) - F_1(\mu_2)F_2(\mu_1) \\ &= F_2(\mu_2)[F_1(\mu_2) + \Delta_1] - F_1(\mu_2)[F_2(\mu_2) + \Delta_2], \qquad \text{say} \\ &= (\Delta_1)F_2(\mu_2) - (\Delta_2)F_1(\mu_2), \end{aligned} \tag{3.23}$$

where

$$\Delta_1 = F_1(\mu_1) - F_1(\mu_2), \qquad \Delta_2 = F_2(\mu_1) - F_2(\mu_2). \tag{3.24}$$

Since $\mu_1 > \mu_2$, and F_1 and F_2 are distribution functions, clearly, Δ_1 and Δ_2 are both positive. Also, as before, because of the monotonicity property of the F-test, and since $\delta_1^2 > \delta_2^2$, we have $F_2(\mu_2) > F_1(\mu_2)$. Hence, to prove (3.22) (i.e., $\Delta > 0$), it is sufficient to prove that $\Delta_1 > \Delta_2$. Now, from the proof of the last lemma, it follows that if $\mu \geq \mu_0^*$, then $f_1(\mu) > f_2(\mu)$. Suppose temporarily that both μ_1 and μ_2 are $\geq \mu_0^*$. Then clearly,

$$\begin{aligned} \Delta_1 - \Delta_2 &= \int_{\mu=\mu_2}^{\mu_1} f_1(\mu)\, d\mu - \int_{\mu=\mu_2}^{\mu_1} f_2(\mu)\, d\mu \\ &= \int_{\mu=\mu_2}^{\mu_1} [f_1(\mu) - f_2(\mu)]\, d\mu > 0. \end{aligned} \tag{3.25}$$

This proves (3.22), when $\min(\mu_1, \mu_2) \geq \mu_0^*$. To complete the proof of the lemma, it is clearly sufficient to show that there exists a real number $\mu_0^{**} > 0$, such that when α is sufficiently small, then $\min(\mu_1, \mu_2) \geq \mu_0^{**}$. Recalling Eq. (3.10), which μ_1 and μ_2 must satisfy, we notice that as μ_1 increases, μ_2 decreases, and vice versa. Let

$$1 - \alpha = F(\mu_{00}) = F(\mu_0^{**})F(\infty). \tag{3.26}$$

This shows that both μ_1 and μ_2 are $\geq \mu_{00}$. This completes the proof.

The last two lemmas imply:

Theorem 3.1. *Let* $\delta_1^2 > \delta_2^2 \geq 0$, *and let* $\hat{\mu}_1$ *and* $\hat{\mu}_2$ *be the optimal values of* μ_1 *and* μ_2 *for which* $p(\mu_1, \mu_2)$ *is maximized subject to* (3.10). *Then* $\hat{\mu}_1 < \hat{\mu}_2$.

The above can be generalized to the case of m independent F-tests.

Theorem 3.2. *Let* $\delta_1^2 > \delta_2^2 > \cdots > \delta_g^2$. *Then using notations as at* (3.8) *the minimum of*

$$\beta = F(\mu_1, \delta_1^2)F(\mu_2, \delta_2^2) \cdots F(\mu_g, \delta_g^2) \tag{3.27}$$

subject to

$$1 - \alpha = F(\mu_1, 0)F(\mu_2, 0) \cdots F(\mu_g, 0), \tag{3.28}$$

is attained at a point $(\hat{\mu}_1, \hat{\mu}_2, \ldots, \hat{\mu}_g)$, *for which* $\hat{\mu}_1 < \hat{\mu}_2 < \cdots < \hat{\mu}_g$, *provided* α *is small enough.*

Proof. Suppose $(\hat{\mu}_1, \hat{\mu}_2, \ldots, \hat{\mu}_g)$ minimizes β. Consider the problem of minimization of $\beta = F(\mu_1, \delta_1^2)F(\mu_2, \delta_2^2)F(\hat{\mu}_3, \delta_3^2) \cdots F(\hat{\mu}_g, \delta_g^2)$ subject to $1 - \alpha = F(\mu_1, 0)F(\mu_2, 0)F(\hat{\mu}_3, 0) \cdots F(\hat{\mu}_g, 0)$, under the variation of μ_1 and μ_2. This is analogous to the problem of minimizing $F(\mu_1, \delta_1^2)F(\mu_2, \delta_2^2)$ subject to $1 - \alpha' = F(\mu_1, 0)F(\mu_2, 0)$, where $(1 - \alpha') = (1 - \alpha)[F(\hat{\mu}_3, 0) \ldots F(\hat{\mu}_g, 0)]^{-1}$. Thus $\alpha' \leq \alpha$. Hence, by Theorem 1, for α (hence α') small enough, the solution to this later problem is such that $\mu_1 < \mu_2$. Thus if $(\hat{\mu}_1, \hat{\mu}_2, \ldots, \hat{\mu}_g)$ minimizes β, then $\hat{\mu}_1 < \hat{\mu}_2$. Similarly $\hat{\mu}_i < \hat{\mu}_j$, if $i < j$, and the theorem is proved.

In closing this section, we remark that the actual calculation of $\hat{\mu}_1$ and $\hat{\mu}_2$ is not too difficult in practice, a good approximation usually being easily obtainable by trial and error.

For future reference, we call this Method I. We start with $\alpha_1 = \alpha_2 = 1-(1 - \alpha)^{1/2} = \alpha_0$, say. We first investigate for values of α_1 between α_0 and α, by considering values of α_1 of the form $\lambda\alpha_0 + (1 - \lambda)\alpha$, where $\lambda = 2^{-1}$, 2^{-2}, 2^{-3}, etc. For each α_1, using (3.6) and (3.5), we calculate (μ_1, μ_2) and, hence, $p(\mu_1, \mu_2)$. We go on increasing α_1 in this way until $p(\mu_1, \mu_2)$ is smaller than the previous α_1. If α_0^* is this value of α_1, and α_1^*, α_2^* are two previous values $(\alpha_2^* < \alpha_1^* < \alpha_0^*)$, then we now investigate between α_2^* and α_0^*, considering values of the form $\lambda\alpha_2^* + (1 - \lambda)\alpha_0^*$, $\lambda = 2^{-1}$, $2^{-2}, \ldots$; and, so on.

Another method would be to try to minimize (3.9) subject to (3.10), using Lagrange's multipliers. This gives the following two equations for the optimum $(\hat{\mu}_1, \hat{\mu}_2)$.

$$F(\hat{\mu}_1, 0)F(\hat{\mu}_2, 0) = 1 - \alpha \tag{3.29a}$$

$$[F(\hat{\mu}_1, 0)]^2 = (1 - \alpha) \cdot \frac{F(\hat{\mu}_1, \delta_1^2)}{F(\hat{\mu}_2, \delta_2^2)} \cdot \frac{f(\hat{\mu}_2, \delta_2^2)}{f(\hat{\mu}_1, \delta_1^2)} \cdot \frac{f(\hat{\mu}_1, 0)}{f(\hat{\mu}_2, 0)}. \tag{3.29b}$$

One iterative method of solving the above would be to start with a value of $\hat{\mu}_1(=\hat{\mu}_2)$ corresponding to $\alpha_1 = 1 - (1 - \alpha)^{1/2}$. We substitute this first pair of values of $(\hat{\mu}_1, \hat{\mu}_2)$ on the right-hand side of (3.29b), and obtain a new value of $\hat{\mu}_1$ by using the left-hand side of (3.29b). The new value of $\hat{\mu}_2$ is then obtained by using (3.29a). We use this new pair $(\hat{\mu}_1, \hat{\mu}_2)$ on the right-hand side of (3.29b) and proceed as before. The iteration is continued until the successive values of $\hat{\mu}_1$ are approximately equal.

It may be remarked that, by following the methods of the next section, one may prove the above results for all α, and not just for "α small enough." However, the present proof was included since as a technique it seemed a little different, and it might be useful elsewhere.

4. CHOICE OF CONSTANTS IN THE SIMULTANEOUS ANALYSIS OF VARIANCE TEST (QUASI-INDEPENDENT CASE)

Consider the usual univariate linear model

$$E(\mathbf{x}) = A\xi, \qquad \mathrm{Var}(\mathbf{x}) = \sigma^2 I_N, \tag{4.1}$$

where $\mathbf{x}$ $(N \times 1)$ is normally distributed, $A(N \times m)$ is the (known) design matrix, $\xi(m \times 1)$ the vector of unknown parameters, σ^2 is unknown, and I_N is the $(N \times N)$ identity matrix. Suppose that rank $(A) = r$. Let $A_1(N \times r)$ be a basis of the column space of A, and, without loss of generality, write

$$A = [A_1 \,\vdots\, A_2] \tag{4.2}$$

where A_2 is $N \times (m - r)$. Let

$$\xi' = [\xi_1' \,\vdots\, \xi_2'] \tag{4.3}$$

be the corresponding partition of ξ', so that ξ_1' is $(1 \times r)$. Consider the null hypothesis

$$H_{0i}\colon \quad C_{i1}\xi_1 + C_{i2}\xi_2 = \boldsymbol{\eta}_i \quad \text{(say)} \quad = 0; \quad i = 1, \ldots, g; \tag{4.4}$$

where $C_{i1}(s \times r)$, C_{i2} $(s \times \overline{m - r})$ are given matrices. Without loss of generality, we assume that $C_i = [C_{i1} \,\vdots\, C_{i2}]$ has rank s. The error mean square s_e^2

and the mean square s_{hi}^2 due to the hypothesis H_{0i} are well known to be given by

$$s_e^2 = n^{-1}\mathbf{x}'Q_e\mathbf{x}, \qquad \text{where} \quad Q_e = I_N - A_1(A_1'A_1)^{-1}A_1', \qquad n = N - r; \tag{4.5}$$

$$s_{hi}^2 = s^{-1}\mathbf{x}'Q_{hi}\mathbf{x}; \quad Q_{hi} = B_{i1}(B_{i1}'B_{i1})^{-1}B_{i1}'; \quad B_{i1} = A_1(A_1'A_1)^{-1}C_{i1}'. \tag{4.6}$$

We shall assume that the g null hypotheses H_{0i} are such that their mean squares s_{hi}^2 $(i = 1, \ldots, g)$ are independently distributed. However, for F-tests of the H_{0i} the same error mean square s_e^2 is to be used in each case. Thus the F-tests are in a sense quasi-independent. For this same reason, Roy (1957) called the H_{0i} themselves to be quasi-independent in this situation, and showed that a necessary and sufficient condition for the same is that for all permissible i and j, $i \neq j$, we have

$$B_{i1}'B_{j1} = C_{i1}(A_1'A_1)^{-1}C_{j1}' = 0. \tag{4.7}$$

Let $F_i = s_{hi}^2/s_e^2$. Under H_{0i}, F_i is distributed like the central F-distribution with s and n df. If H_{0i} is not true, then F_i follows the noncentral F-distribution, with (s, n) df, and some noncentrality parameter, say δ_i^2, where

$$\delta_i^2 = \sigma^{-2}\xi'C_i'[C_{i1}(A_1'A_1)^{-1}C_{i1}']C_i\xi. \tag{4.8}$$

Consider the case $g = 2$, and suppose that H_{01} and H_{02} are quasi-independent. Let $H_0 = H_{01} \cap H_{02}$, and consider the following test for H_0:
Acceptance region for

$$H_0\colon \; F_1 \leq \mu_1, \qquad F_2 \leq \mu_2; \tag{4.9}$$

where (μ_1, μ_2) are chosen such that the probability of accepting H_0 when it is true is $1 - \alpha$. Let the alternative be H: not-H_0, and under H, let δ_1^2, and δ_2^2 be respectively the noncentrality parameters for testing (individually) H_{01} and H_{02}. Then [see Rao (1965)] using (4.7), we can express (4.9) in the following canonical form:

$$F_1 = s_{h1}^2/s_e^2, \qquad F_2 = s_{h2}^2/s_e^2, \tag{4.10a}$$

where

$$s_e^2 = \sum_{i=1}^{n} z_i^2, \qquad s_{h1}^2 = \sum_{i=1}^{s} y_{1i}^2, \qquad s_{h2}^2 = \sum_{i=1}^{s} y_{2i}^2; \tag{4.10b}$$

where $z_1, \ldots, z_n; y_{11}, \ldots, y_{1s}; y_{21}, \ldots, y_{2s}$ are all independently and normally distributed with variance 1, and mean 0, except for y_{11} and y_{21} which have means δ_1 and δ_2, respectively.

The error of the second kind is then given by

$$\beta = \beta(\mu_1, \mu_2) = h_0 \int_D \exp[-\tfrac{1}{2}Q]\, dy\, dz, \tag{4.11}$$

where

$$h_0 = (2\pi)^{-(2s+n)/2}; \qquad Q = \sum_{i=1}^{2} \sum_{j=1}^{s} y_{ij}^2 + \sum_{1}^{n} z_j^2;$$

$$dy = \prod_{i=1}^{2} \prod_{j=1}^{s} dy_{ij}, \qquad dz = \prod_{j=1}^{n} dz_j \tag{4.12}$$

and D is the region given by

$$D = (y_{11} - \delta_1)^2 + \sum_{j=2}^{s} y_{1j}^2 \leq \mu_1 \sum_{1}^{n} z_j^2; \qquad (y_{21} - \delta_2)^2 + \sum_{j=2}^{s} y_{2j}^2 \leq \mu_2 \sum_{1}^{n} z_j^2. \tag{4.13}$$

The test region (4.9) or (4.13) is called "the simultaneous analysis of variance test (in the quasi-independent case)," and was proposed by Ghosh (1955). The monotonicity property of this test (wrt its noncentrality parameters) was established by Ramachandran (1956). Multivariate generalizations of the above test were considered by Krishnaiah (1965a,b). We now prove a new property of this test.

Theorem 4.1. *Suppose that* $\delta_1^2 > \delta_2^2 \geq 0$. *Then* $\beta(\mu_1, \mu_2)$ *attains a minimum (under variation of* μ_1 *and* μ_2*), subject to the restriction that the probability measure of the acceptance region is* $(1 - \alpha)$ *at a point* $(\hat{\mu}_1, \hat{\mu}_2)$ *for which* $\hat{\mu}_1 \leq \hat{\mu}_2$.

Proof. Clearly, the theorem is established if we prove the counterpart of Lemma 3.2. In other words, we must show that if $\delta_1^2 > \delta_2^2$, and $\mu_1 > \hat{\mu}_2$, then $\beta(\mu_1, \mu_2) > \beta(\mu_2, \mu_1)$. Let

$$w_1^2 = (y_{11} - \delta_1)^2 + \sum_{j=2}^{s} y_{ij}^2, \qquad w_2^2 = (y_{21} - \delta_2)^2 + \sum_{j=2}^{s} y_{2j}^2, \qquad z^2 = \sum_{1}^{n} z_j^2. \tag{4.14}$$

Then it is well known that w_1^2, w_2^2, and z^2 are independently distributed, respectively, as $\chi^2(w_1^2; s, \delta_1^2)$, $\chi^2(w_2^2; s, \delta_2^2)$, and $\chi^2(z^2; n, 0)$, where $\chi^2(u^2; m, \delta^2)$ denotes the density of a variable u^2 distributed according to the noncentral χ^2 distribution with m degrees of freedom and noncentrality parameter δ^2. Under this notation, we clearly have, for $i = 1, 2$,

$$\beta_i = \int_{D_i} \chi^2(z^2; n, 0)\chi^2(w_1^2; s, \delta_1^2)\chi^2(w_2^2, s, \delta_2^2)\, dw_1^2\, dw_2^2\, dz^2 = \int_{D_i} dW, \tag{4.15}$$

say, where dW denotes the entire integrand on the right-hand side of (4.15), and

$$\beta_1 = \beta(\mu_1, \mu_2), \qquad \beta_2 = \beta(\mu_2, \mu_1), \tag{4.16}$$

and D_1 and D_2 are regions of integration given by

$$D_1:\ w_1^2 \leq \mu_1 z^2, \qquad w_2^2 \leq \mu_2 z^2; \qquad D_2:\ w_1^2 \leq \mu_2 z^2, \qquad w_2^2 \leq \mu_1 z^2. \tag{4.17}$$

Now

$$\beta_1 = \beta_1^* + \beta_0, \qquad \beta_2 = \beta_2^* + \beta_0, \tag{4.18}$$

where

$$\beta_0 = \int_{D_0} dW, \qquad \beta_1^* = \int_{D_1^*} dW, \qquad \beta_2^* = \int_{D_2^*} dW, \tag{4.19}$$

and the regions D_0, D_1^*, and D_2^* are given by

$$D_0:\ w_1^2 \leq \mu_2 z^2, \qquad w_2^2 \leq \mu_2 z^2 \tag{4.20a}$$

$$D_1^*:\ \mu_2 z^2 \leq w_1^2 \leq \mu_1 z^2, \qquad w_2^2 \leq \mu_2 z^2;$$
$$D_2^*:\ w_1^2 \leq \mu_2 z^2, \qquad \mu_2 z^2 \leq w_2^2 \leq \mu_1 z^2. \tag{4.20b}$$

Clearly from the definitions of β_1, β_2, β_1^*, β_2^*, it is enough to show that $\beta_1^* > \beta_2^*$. But

$$\beta_1^* = \int_{z^2=0}^{\infty} \left[\chi^2(z^2; n, 0) \left\{ \int_{w_1^2=\mu_2 z^2}^{\mu_1 z^2} \chi^2(w_1^2; s, \delta_1^2) \right\} \right.$$
$$\left. \times \left\{ \int_{w_2^2=0}^{\mu_2 z^2} \chi^2(w_2^2; s, \delta_2^2)\, dw_2^2 \right\} \right] dz^2, \tag{4.21a}$$

and

$$\beta_2^* = \int_{z^2=0}^{\infty} \left[\chi^2(z^2; n, 0) \left\{ \int_{w_2^2=\mu_2 z^2}^{\mu_1 z^2} \chi^2(w_2^2; s, \delta_2^2)\, dw_2^2 \right\} \right.$$
$$\left. \times \left\{ \int_{w_1^2=0}^{\mu_2 z^2} \chi^2(w_1^2; s, \delta_1^2)\, dw_1^2 \right\} \right] dz^2. \tag{4.21b}$$

In (4.21a,b), make the transformation

$$w_1^2 = F_1 z^2, \qquad w_2^2 = F_2 z^2. \tag{4.22}$$

Also recall that [e.g., Rao (1965)],

$$\chi^2(w^2; s; \delta^2) = \exp(-\tfrac{1}{2}\delta^2) \sum_{r=0}^{\infty} \frac{1}{r!} \left(\frac{\delta^2}{2}\right)^r G\left(w^2; \frac{1}{2}, r + \frac{s}{2}\right), \tag{4.23}$$

where $G(x; \alpha, p)$ denotes the density of the gamma variable x, and is given by

$$G(x; \alpha, p) = [\alpha^p/\Gamma(p)]e^{-\alpha x}x^{p-1}, \qquad 0 \leq x \leq \infty. \tag{4.24}$$

Using (4.22)–(4.24), we get

$$\begin{aligned}\beta_1{}^* = \int_{z^2=0}^{\infty} & \left[\frac{1}{2^{n/2}\Gamma(n/2)} \exp(-\tfrac{1}{2}z^2)(z^2)^{(n/2)-1}\right] \\ & \times \left[\int_{F_1=\mu_2}^{\mu_1} \exp(-\tfrac{1}{2}\delta_1{}^2) \sum_{r=0}^{\infty} \frac{1}{r!} \left(\frac{\delta_1{}^2}{2}\right)^r \left(\frac{1}{2}\right)^{r+(s/2)} \right. \\ & \left. \times \frac{\exp(-\tfrac{1}{2}F_1 z^2)}{\Gamma(r+(s/2))} (F_1 z^2)^{r+(s/2)-1} z^2\right] \\ & \times \left[\int_{F_2=0}^{\mu_2} \exp(-\tfrac{1}{2}\delta_2{}^2) \sum_{t=0}^{\infty} \frac{1}{t!} \left(\frac{\delta_2{}^2}{2}\right)^t \left(\frac{1}{2}\right)^{t+(s/2)} \frac{1}{\Gamma(t+(s/2))} \right. \\ & \left. \times \exp(-\tfrac{1}{2}F_2 z^2)(F_2 z^2)^{t+(s/2)-1} z^2\right] dz^2. \end{aligned} \tag{4.25}$$

After some simplification, and interchange of various integration and summation signs (which can be easily checked to be valid), we get

$$\begin{aligned}\beta_1{}^* &= \int_{F_1=\mu_2}^{\mu_1} \int_{F_2=0}^{\mu_2} \exp(-\tfrac{1}{2}(\delta_1{}^2 + \delta_2{}^2)) \sum_{r=0}^{\infty} \sum_{t=0}^{\infty} \left(\frac{1}{2}\right)^{r+t+s+(n/2)} \\ & \quad \times \frac{(\delta_1{}^2/2)^r(\delta_2{}^2/2)^t F_1^{r+(s/2)-1} F_2^{t+(s/2)-1}}{\Gamma(n/2)\Gamma(r+(s/2))\Gamma(t+(s/2))r!t!} \\ & \quad \times \int_{z^2=0}^{\infty} (z^2)^{r+t+s+(n/2)-1} \exp(-\tfrac{1}{2}z^2(1+F_1+F_2))\, dz^2\, dw_2{}^2\, dw_1{}^2 \\ &= d_0 \sum_{r=0}^{\infty} \sum_{t=0}^{\infty} \int_{F_1=\mu_2}^{\mu_1} \int_{F_2=0}^{\mu_2} B\left(\frac{n}{2}, r+\frac{s}{2}, t+\frac{s}{2}\right) \frac{1}{r!} \frac{1}{t!} \left(\frac{\delta_1{}^2}{2}\right)^r \left(\frac{\delta_2{}^2}{2}\right)^t \\ & \quad \times [F_1^{r+(s/2)-1} F_2^{t+(s/2)-1}/(1+F_1+F_2)^{r+t+s+(n/2)-1}]\, dF_1\, dF_2 \end{aligned} \tag{4.26}$$

where

$$d_0 = \exp(-\tfrac{1}{2}(\delta_1{}^2 + \delta_2{}^2)), \qquad B\left(\frac{n}{2}, r+\frac{s}{2}, t+\frac{s}{2}\right) = \frac{\Gamma(r+t+s+(n/2))}{\Gamma(n/2)\Gamma(r+(s/2))\Gamma(t+(s/2))}. \tag{4.27}$$

Now make the transformation

$$\theta_1 = F_1/(1 + F_1 + F_2), \qquad \theta_2 = F_2/(1 + F_1 + F_2);$$
$$dF_1\, dF_2 = (1 - \theta_1 - \theta_2)^{-3}\, d\theta_1\, d\theta_2 . \quad (4.28)$$

Then, it can be checked that

$$\beta_1^* = \sum_{r=0}^{\infty} \sum_{t=0}^{\infty} \int_{D_0} d_0^*(\theta_1 \delta_1^2)^r (\theta_2 \delta_2^2)^t\, d\theta_1\, d\theta_2 , \quad (4.29)$$

where

$$d_0^* = \left(\frac{1}{2}\right)^{r+t} d_0\, B\left(\frac{n}{2}, r + \frac{s}{2}, t + \frac{s}{2}\right)[r!t!]^{-1} \theta_1^{(s/2)-1} \theta_2^{(s/2)-1} (1 - \theta_1 - \theta_2)^{(n/2)+1} \quad (4.30)$$

and where D_0 is a region in the (θ_1, θ_2) space satisfying $0 \le \theta_2(1 - \theta_1 - \theta_2)^{-1} \le \mu_2$, and $\mu_2 \le \theta_1(1 - \theta_1 - \theta_2)^{-1} \le \mu_1$. Indeed D_0 is the inside of a quadrilateral bounded by four lines:

$$D_0\colon \ \theta_2 = 0, \qquad \theta_2 \le (1 + \mu_2)^{-1}\mu_2(1 - \theta_1),$$
$$(1 + \mu_2)^{-1}\mu_2(1 - \theta_2) \le \theta_1 \le (1 + \mu_1)^{-1}\mu_1(1 - \theta_2). \quad (4.31)$$

Notice that in the region D_0, we have $\theta_1 > \theta_2$ (except for one point where $\theta_1 = \theta_2$). To see this, put $\mu_2/(1 + \mu_2) = \mu_2^*$. Then if $(\theta_1, \theta_2) \in D_0$, we have $\theta_2 \le \mu_2^*(1 - \theta_1)$, $\theta_1 \ge \mu_2^*(1 - \theta_2)$. Hence

$$\theta_1 \ge (1 - \theta_2)\theta_2(1 - \theta_1)^{-1}, \qquad \text{or} \qquad (\theta_1 - \theta_2)(1 - \theta_1 - \theta_2) \ge 0,$$

implying $\theta_1 > \theta_2$. Now, consider β_2^* in (4.21b). By a sequence of steps similar to the above, we can express β_2^* as

$$\beta_2^* = \sum_{r=0}^{\infty} \sum_{t=0}^{\infty} \int_{D_0} d_0^*(\theta_1 \delta_2^2)^r (\theta_2 \delta_1^2)^t\, d\theta_1\, d\theta_2 . \quad (4.32)$$

This is easily seen by noticing that the same range of integration is obtained in (4.21b) as in (4.21a), if in (4.21b), the dummy variables w_1^2 and w_2^2 are interchanged.

The sum of the (r, t) term and the (t, r) term in the integrand of β_1^* is

$$\Delta_3 \equiv d_0^*[(\theta_1\delta_1^2)^r(\theta_2\delta_2^2)^t + (\theta_1\delta_1^2)^t(\theta_2\delta_2^2)^r],$$

while its counterpart in β_2^* is

$$\Delta_4 \equiv d_0^*[(\theta_1\delta_2^2)^r(\theta_2\delta_1^2)^t + (\theta_1\delta_2^2)^t(\theta_2\delta_1^2)^r].$$

When r and t are equal, we have $\Delta_3 = \Delta_4$; otherwise, if $l = \theta_1 \mid \theta_2$, $k = \delta_1^2|\delta_2^2$,

$$\Delta_3 - \Delta_4 = d_0^*(\theta_2\delta_2^2)^{r+t}[(lk)^r + (lk)^t - l^r k^t - l^t k^r]$$
$$= d_0^*(\theta_2\delta_2^2)^{r+t}(l^r - l^t)(k^r - k^t). \quad (4.33)$$

Since $l > 1$ (a.e. in D_0) and $k > 1$ (given), it follows that $r > t$ implies $l^r > l^t$, $k^r > k^t$; and $r < t$ implies $l^r < l^t$, $k^r < k^t$. Thus in both cases, $\Delta_3 > \Delta_4$. Hence, (4.29) and (4.32) imply $\beta_1{}^* > \beta_2{}^*$. This completes the proof of the theorem.

The g-dimensional generalization of the above (which corresponds to $g = 2$) is given in

Theorem 4.2. *Let the hypotheses H_{0i} $(i = 1, \ldots, g)$ be defined as in the earlier part of this section, and assume that they are quasi-independent. In an obvious extension of the notation, let $\{F_i \le \mu_i, i = 1, \ldots, g\}$ be the acceptance region for testing $H_0 = \bigcap_{i=1}^{g} H_{0i}$, against not-$H_0$. Let $\beta(\mu_1, \mu_2, \ldots, \mu_g)$ be the corresponding error of the second kind. Let $\delta_1{}^2 > \delta_2{}^2 > \cdots > \delta_g{}^2$. Then if $\beta(\mu_1, \mu_2, \ldots, \mu_g)$ is minimized at the point $(\hat{\mu}_1, \hat{\mu}_2, \ldots, \hat{\mu}_g)$, we must have $\hat{\mu}_1 \le \mu_2 \le \cdots \le \hat{\mu}_g$.*

Proof. As in the proof of Theorem 3.2, it is sufficient to consider a fixed value of $\hat{\mu}_3, \ldots, \hat{\mu}_g$, and prove that β is minimized (under variation of μ_1 and μ_2) at a point $(\hat{\mu}_1, \hat{\mu}_2)$ such that $\hat{\mu}_1 \le \hat{\mu}_2$. (A similar proof then shows that $\hat{\mu}_i \le \hat{\mu}_j$, if $i < j$.) Now, by a development analogous to that for Theorem 4.1, it is easily seen that

$$\beta(\mu_1, \mu_2, \ldots, \mu_g) = \int_{z^2=0}^{\infty} \left[\chi^2(z^2; n, 0) \prod_{i=1}^{g} \left\{\int_{w_i{}^2=0}^{\mu_i z^2} \chi^2(w_i{}^2; s, \delta_i{}^2)\, dw_i{}^2\right\}\right] dz^2. \tag{4.34}$$

Now, keeping $\mu_3, \ldots, \mu_g$ fixed, define $\beta_1 = \beta(\mu_1, \mu_2, \mu_3, \ldots, \mu_g)$, $\beta_2 = \beta(\mu_2, \mu_1, \mu_3, \ldots, \mu_g)$, assuming $\mu_1 > \mu_2$. The result is obtained by making the transformation $F_i = w_i{}^2/z^2$ $(i = 1, \ldots, g)$, and proceeding step by step to the end as in the proof of the last theorem (including appropriate transformations which correspond to (4.28)).

We finally prove:

Theorem 4.3. *Under the conditions of Theorem* 4.2, *a stronger result holds; namely, that*

$$\hat{\mu}_1 < \hat{\mu}_2 < \cdots < \hat{\mu}_g.$$

Proof. For clarity and ease, we consider only the case $g = 2$; the generalization to $g > 2$ is straightforward. We compare $\beta_1 = \beta(\mu, \mu)$ with $\beta_2 = \beta(\mu - d\mu, \mu + d\mu)$, where $d\mu > 0$, μ is such that the error of the first kind is $1 - \alpha$ at the point (μ, μ), and $d\mu$ is arbitrarily small so that the error of the first kind at $(\mu - d\mu, \mu + d\mu)$ is also $(1 - \alpha)$ to order $(d\mu)^2$, which is assumed negligible compared to $(d\mu)$. Now, for $i = 1, 2$,

$$\beta_i = \int_{E+E_i} \chi^2(z^2; n, 0)\chi^2(w_1{}^2; s, \delta_1{}^2)\chi^2(w_2{}^2; s, \delta_2{}^2)\, dz^2\, dw_1{}^2\, dw_2{}^2, \tag{4.35}$$

where $E \cap E_i$ is the null set, and the regions E, E_1, E_2 are given by

$$E: \quad w_1^2 \le (\mu - d\mu)z^2, \qquad w_2^2 \le \mu z^2 \tag{4.36a}$$

$$E_1: \quad (\mu - d\mu)z^2 < w_1^2 \le \mu z^2, \qquad w_2^2 \le \mu z^2 \tag{4.36b}$$

$$E_2: \quad w_1^2 \le (\mu - d\mu)z^2, \qquad \mu z^2 < w_2^2 \le (\mu + d\mu)z^2. \tag{4.36c}$$

Clearly, it is enough to show that $\beta_2^* < \beta_1^*$, where β_i^* is obtained from the right-hand side of (4.35) by restricting the range of integration to E_i. Since $d\mu$ is small, we get

$$\beta_1^* = (d\mu) \int_{z^2=0}^{\infty} z^2\{\chi^2(z^2; n, 0)\chi^2(\mu z^2; s, \delta_1^2)\} \times \left\{\int_{w_2^2=0}^{\mu z^2} \chi^2(w_2^2; s, \delta_2^2)\, dw_2^2\right\} dz^2 \tag{4.37a}$$

$$\beta_2^* = (d\mu) \int_{z^2=0}^{\infty} z^2\{\chi^2(z^2; n, 0)\chi^2(\mu z^2; s, \delta_2^2)\} \times \left\{\int_{w_1^2=0}^{\mu z^2} \chi^2(w_1^2; s, \delta_1^2)\, dw_1^2\right\} dz^2. \tag{4.37b}$$

Compare now the expressions for β_1^* on the right-hand side of (4.37a) with that of β_1^* in Theorem 4.1, Eq. (4.21a). Apart from the factor $d\mu$, we find that the former is obtained from the latter by ignoring the integral sign wrt w_1^2, and replacing w_1^2, by μz^2, dw_1^2 by z^2 and μ_2 by μ. This amounts, in (4.25), to ignoring the integral sign wrt F_1, and replacing both F_1 and μ_2 by μ. Hence, (4.37a) is equivalent to

$$\beta_1^* = (d\mu)d_0 \sum_{r=0}^{\infty} \sum_{t=0}^{\infty} \int_{F=0}^{\mu} B\left(\frac{n}{2}, r + \frac{s}{2}, t + \frac{s}{2}\right)[r!t!]^{-1}\left(\frac{\delta_1^2}{2}\right)^r\left(\frac{\delta_2^2}{2}\right)^t \times \frac{u^{r+(s/2)-1}F^{t+(s/2)-1}\, dF}{(1 + \mu + F)^{r+t+s+(n/2)-1}}, \tag{4.38}$$

where, for simplicity, we have replaced the dummy variable F_2 by F. Make the transformation

$$F/(1 + \mu + F) = \theta, \qquad \mu/(1 + 2\mu) = \mu_0; \qquad d\theta = (1 + \mu)(1 + \mu + F)^{-2}\, dF \tag{4.39}$$

then

$$\beta_1^* = \sum_{r=0}^{\infty} \sum_{t=0}^{\infty} \int_{\theta=0}^{\mu_0} d_0^{**}(\theta\delta_2^2)^t[(1 - \theta)\,\delta_1^2]^r\, d\theta, \tag{4.40}$$

where

$$d_0^{**} = (d\mu)\, d_0\, B\left(\frac{n}{2}, r + \frac{s}{2}, t + \frac{s}{2}\right)[r!t!]^{-1}\left(\frac{1}{2}\right)^{r+t} \mu^{r+(s/2)-1}$$

$$\times (1+\mu)^{-[r+(s+n)/2-1]}\theta^{(s/2)-1}(1-\theta)^{(s+n)/2-2}. \quad (4.41a)$$

Looking at (4.37a,b), we find that $\beta_2{}^*$ is obtainable by interchanging $\delta_1{}^2$ and $\delta_2{}^2$ in the expression for $\beta_1{}^*$. Hence

$$\beta_2{}^* = \sum_{r=0}^{\infty} \sum_{t=0}^{\infty} \int_{\theta}^{\mu_0} d_0{}^*(\theta\delta_1{}^2)^t[(1-\theta)\,\delta_2{}^2]^r\, d\theta. \quad (4.41b)$$

Since, from (4.39), $\mu_0 < \frac{1}{2}$, we have $\theta < \frac{1}{2} < 1 - \theta$ for all θ in the range of integration in the expressions for both $\beta_1{}^*$ and $\beta_2{}^*$. But $(1-\theta) = l_1\theta$, $\delta_1{}^2 = k\delta_2{}^2$, so that $l_1 > 1$, $k > 1$. Let Δ denote the difference between the sum of the terms (r, t) and (t, r) in the expression for $\beta_1{}^*$ and the same sum in case of $\beta_2{}^*$. Then, unless $r = t$, we have

$$\Delta = d_0{}^*\theta^{r+t}\,\delta_2{}^{2(r+t)}(l^r - l^t)(k^r - k^t) > 0, \quad (4.42)$$

whereas for $r = t$, $\Delta = 0$. This completes the proof.

In passing, we remark that, given α, s, n, $\delta_1{}^2 > \cdots > \delta_g{}^2$, we do not have any special method to offer for the actual calculation of $\hat{\mu}_1, \ldots, \hat{\mu}_g$, except a possible analogue of Method I in the case of completely independent F's.

5. CHOICE OF CONSTANTS IN THE SIMULTANEOUS ANALYSIS OF VARIANCE TEST (DEPENDENT CASE)

In this section, we consider problems similar to those in Section 4, but we assume that the component hypotheses are not quasi-independent. As we shall see, this assumption leads to a wide variety of situations.

We continue using the notation of Section 4. Let E_j $(j = 1, \ldots, v)$ be $(s \times m)$ real matrices, and consider, under the model (4.1), the $(s \times 1)$ vectors ζ_j (all assumed to be distinct) given by

$$\zeta_j = E_j\,\xi = E_{j1}\,\xi_1 + E_{j2}\,\xi_2 \qquad \text{(say)}. \quad (5.1)$$

Let H_{0j}^* be the null hypothesis: $\zeta_j = \mathbf{0}$, and let $H_0{}^* = \bigcap_{j=1}^{v} H_{0j}^*$. Suppose that the H_{0j}^* are not quasi-independent, i.e., assume that there exist i and j $(i \neq j, 1 \leq i, j \leq v)$, such that

$$E_{i1}(A_1{}'A_1)^{-1}E_{j1}' \neq 0_{ss}. \quad (5.2)$$

This situation may arise in many ways. First, the ζ_j $(j = 1, \ldots, v)$ themselves may be linearly dependent. Second, they may all be linearly independent, but (5.2) may not be satisfied. Finally, the whole set of the v vectors ζ_j may be linearly dependent, and there may be subsets of this set which, though linearly independent, may not satisfy (5.2).

Again, even when a subset of (say) v' ($\leq v$) vectors ζ_j is linearly independent, the covariance matrices $V_{ij} = \text{Cov}(\hat{\zeta}_i, \hat{\zeta}_j)$ where ζ_i, ζ_j belong to this subset, and $\hat{\zeta}_j$ is the best linear unbiased estimate (BLUE) of ζ_j, may not all be the same, and may depend on i and j in various ways. In other words, there may be different correlation patterns between the estimates $\hat{\zeta}_j$.

To illustrate, recall the vectors $\boldsymbol{\eta}_i$ ($i = 1, \ldots, g$) of Section 4, and assume that the quasi-independence condition (4.7) is satisfied by them. Consider now the hypotheses $H_{0j}^{(k)}(k = 1, 2)$ given by

$$H_{0j}^{(1)}:\quad \zeta_j^{(1)} \equiv \boldsymbol{\eta}_j - \boldsymbol{\eta}_1 = 0_{s1}, \qquad j = 2, \ldots, g; \qquad H_0^{(1)} = \bigcap_2^g H_{0j}^{(1)} \tag{5.3}$$

$$H_{0j}^{(2)}:\quad \zeta_j^{(2)} \equiv \boldsymbol{\eta}_{j+1} - \boldsymbol{\eta}_j = 0_{s1}, \qquad j = 1, \ldots, g-1; \qquad H_0^{(2)} = \bigcap_1^{g-1} H_{0j}^{(2)}. \tag{5.4}$$

Then

$$\begin{aligned}(C_{i1} - C_{11})(A_1'A_1)^{-1}(C_{j1} - C_{11})' &= \text{Cov}(\hat{\zeta}_i^{(1)}, \hat{\zeta}_j^{(1)}) \\ &= C_{11}(A_1'A_1)^{-1}C_{11}' \neq 0_{ss},\end{aligned}$$

for $i \neq j$, $2 \leq i, j \leq g$. This shows that the hypotheses $H_{0j}^{(1)}$ are dependent though $\zeta_j^{(1)}$ are a set of v $(=g-1)$ linearly independent vectors. Similarly, the set $H_{0j}^{(2)}$ also is dependent since $H_{0i}^{(2)}$ and $H_{0j}^{(2)}$ are easily seen not to satisfy the quasi-independence condition when $i + 1 < j$. Also, though here, too, $v = g - 1$, the correlation pattern between the $H_{0j}^{(1)}$ is different from that between the $H_{0j}^{(2)}$. Notice that under $H_0^{(1)}$, we are comparing the different $\boldsymbol{\eta}_j$ with one "standard" vector $\boldsymbol{\eta}_1$ while for $H_0^{(2)}$, we have a cyclic sort of comparison.

To illustrate the case in which the ζ_j ($j = 1, \ldots, v$) are not linearly independent, consider the case (with $v = g(g-1)/2$) of $H_0^{(3)} \equiv \bigcap H_{0ij}^{(3)}$, where the intersection is over all i, j with $1 \leq i < j \leq g$, and where

$$H_{0ij}^{(3)} = \zeta_{ij}^{(3)} \equiv \boldsymbol{\eta}_i - \boldsymbol{\eta}_j = 0_{s1}. \tag{5.5}$$

This corresponds to the set of all pairwise comparisons of the $\boldsymbol{\eta}_i$ and $\boldsymbol{\eta}_j$. Notice that the null hypotheses $H_0^{(1)}$, $H_0^{(2)}$, and $H_0^{(3)}$ are identical (say $H_0^{(0)}$) where $H_0^{(0)}$ is: $\boldsymbol{\eta}_1 = \boldsymbol{\eta}_2 = \cdots = \boldsymbol{\eta}_g$, and that they differ only in their decomposition. Under the union-intersection principle, this decomposition, however, determines the test region, which is the intersection of the acceptance regions for the corresponding component hypotheses. For $H_0^{(1)}$ and $H_0^{(3)}$, these regions were proposed (under more special setups) by Dunnett (1955), and Tukey (1954). For $H_0^{(2)}$, one may see, for example, Roy and Srivastava (1968).

The above tests are examples of the simultaneous analysis of variance tests (dependent case). Some aspects of these were considered in Krishnaiah (1963, 1965a). The discussion in these works related to the case in which the sums of squares associated with various hypotheses are jointly distributed as a multivariate chi-square distribution. This case covers several important situations like the problem of testing contrasts simultaneously, investigating the heterogeneity of interactions in two-way layout when an independent estimate of the error is available, etc.

The above tests are most commonly used when $s = 1$. The setup is usually that of a block-treatment design. Thus let $\tau_1, \ldots, \tau_v$ denote the "true" treatment effects from a block-design, and $\hat{\tau}_1, \ldots, \hat{\tau}_v$ the corresponding estimates. Let $H_0 : \tau_1 = \cdots \tau_v$ be the null hypothesis. Then as above, we can consider decompositions like $H_0^{(1)}$ $(\tau_1 = \tau_2, \ldots, \tau_1 = \tau_v)$, etc.

Consider again the $H_{0j}^{(1)}$ in (5.3). For each $H_{0j}^{(1)}$, there is, of course, an associated noncentrality parameter say $\delta_{j(1)}^2$. Similarly corresponding to $H_{0j}^{(2)}$ and $H_{0ij}^{(3)}$, we have, say, $\delta_{j(2)}^2$ and $\delta_{ij(3)}^2$. Now the patterns in which the $\zeta_j^{(1)}$ are related to each other is different from that of $\zeta_j^{(2)}$ although there is some similarity between the two. The pattern for the $\zeta_{ij}^{(3)}$ is altogether different. This means we cannot arbitrarily prescribe inequalities among the $\delta_{j(1)}^2$, $\delta_{ij(3)}^2$, etc., in a manner analogous to the ones in the former sections (like $\delta_1{}^2 > \cdots > \delta_g{}^2$). For the above decompositions, the new inequalities must reflect the combinatorial patterns inherent therein.

These different varieties of patterns of dependence, with their appropriate properties, will be considered in a separate paper. Here we shall, however, consider the case $v = 2$, since in this situation, the question of different correlation patterns between the $\hat{\zeta}_j$ does not arise. Also, we restrict ourselves to the case $s = 1$, first, because of simplicity, and second, since (as will be seen in Section 6), this seems to arise most often.

Let (u_1, u_2) have a 2-variate normal distribution, with

$$E(u_i) = \delta_i \quad (i = 1, 2); \qquad \mathrm{Var}(u_i) = (a_0 + b_0)\sigma^2; \qquad \mathrm{Cov}(u_i, u_j) = b_0 \sigma^2, \tag{5.6}$$

where a_0 and b_0 are real numbers such that $A_0 = (a_0 I_2 + b_0 J_{22})$ is positive definite. Here I_2 is (2×2) identity matrix, and J_{22} (2×2) has 1 everywhere. Also let $\sigma^2 z^2$ be distributed independently of (u_1, u_2) according to a central χ^2-distribution with n df. Consider the null hypothesis

$$H_0\colon \quad \delta_1{}^2 = \delta_2{}^2 = 0, \tag{5.7}$$

with the acceptance region

$$D\colon \quad u_1{}^2 \le \mu_1 z^2, \qquad u_2{}^2 \le \mu_2 z^2. \tag{5.8}$$

It is seen from (5.3) and (5.4), that for $g = 3$ (or $v = 2$), both the Dunnett and the cyclic decompositions fall under this situation.

Then we prove

Theorem 5.1. *Let $\delta_1^2 > \delta_2^2$. Then the second kind of error β given by*

$$\beta \equiv \beta(\mu_1, \mu_2) = \text{Prob}(u_1^2 \leq \mu_1 z^2, u_2^2 \leq \mu_2 z^2) \tag{5.9}$$

is minimized wrt the variation of (μ_1, μ_2) under the restriction

$$1 - \alpha = \text{Prob}(u_1^2 \leq \mu_1 z^2, u_2^2 \leq \mu_2 z^2 \mid \delta_1^2 = \delta_2^2 = 0), \tag{5.10}$$

at a point $(\hat{\mu}_1, \hat{\mu}_2)$ such that $\hat{\mu}_1 < \hat{\mu}_2$.

Proof. Here, for brevity, we shall only prove $\mu_1 \leq \mu_2$; the proof for $\hat{\mu}_1 < \hat{\mu}_2$ can be obtained by appropriately combining the methods of the present proof and that of Theorem 4.3.

First, note that

$$A^{-1} = (a_0 I_2 + b_0 J_{22})^{-1} = aI_2 + bJ_{22}; \qquad a = a_0^{-1}, \quad b = (-b_0)/(a_0 + 2b_0). \tag{5.11}$$

Hence, the joint distribution of (u_1, u_2, z^2) is

$$\chi^2(z^2; n, 0) \cdot (2\pi)^{-1} |A_0|^{-1/2}$$
$$\times \exp\left[-1/2\left\{a \sum_1^2 (u_i - \delta_i)^2 + b\left[\sum_1^2 (u_i - \delta_i)\right]^2\right\}\right] du_1\, du_2\, dz^2 \equiv dW_1 \text{ say.} \tag{5.12}$$

As pointed out in the introduction, we are ignoring σ^2 in our calculations, as is clearly justifiable without loss of generality. Now, as in many earlier theorems, assume that $\mu_1 > \mu_2$; and let $\beta_1 = \beta(\mu_1, \mu_2)$ and $\beta_2 = \beta(\mu_2, \mu_1)$. Then we shall prove that $\beta_1 > \beta_2$. Now $\beta_1 > \beta_2$ is equivalent to $\beta_1{}^* > \beta_2{}^*$, where

$$\beta_1{}^* = \int_{D_0} dW_1, \qquad \beta_2{}^* = \int_{D_0} dW_2, \tag{5.13}$$

where the expression dW_2 is obtained from dW_1 by interchanging δ_1 and δ_2, and D_0 is the region

$$D_0\colon \quad \mu_2 z^2 \leq u_1^2 \leq \mu_1 z^2, \qquad u_2^2 \leq \mu_2 z^2. \tag{5.14}$$

Let

$$L_1{}^* \equiv a \sum_1^2 (u_i - \delta_i)^2 + b\left[\sum_1^2 (u_i - \delta_i)\right]^2 = R + (u_1 l_1 + u_2 l_2) \tag{5.15}$$

$$L_2{}^* \equiv a[(u_1 - \delta_2)^2 + (u_2 - \delta_1)^2] + b\left[\sum_1^2 (u_i - \delta_i)\right]^2 = R + (u_1 l_2 + u_2 l_1), \tag{5.16}$$

$$L_1 = L_1{}^* - R, \qquad L_2 = L_2{}^* - R, \tag{5.17}$$

where

$$R = (a + b)(u_1^2 + \delta_1^2 + u_2^2 + \delta_2^2) + 2b(u_1 u_2 + \delta_1 \delta_2) \tag{5.18}$$

$$l_1 = (a + b)(-2\delta_1) + 2b(-\delta_2), \qquad l_2 = (a + b)(-2\delta_2) + 2b(-\delta_1). \tag{5.19}$$

Then

$$\beta_k^* = \int_{D_0} U_0 \exp[-1/2L_k]\, du_1\, du_2\, dz^2; \qquad k = 1, 2; \tag{5.20}$$

where

$$U_0 = \chi^2(z^2; n, 0)|A_0|^{-1/2} \exp[-1/2R]. \tag{5.21}$$

Consider β_1^*, and add up the integrand in (5.20) (apart from U_0) over the two points (u_1, u_2) and $(-u_1, -u_2)$, both of which lie in D_0 if, and only if, at least one of them does. Notice that for both of these points U_0 has the same value. The sum so obtained is M_1 where

$$M_1 = \{\exp[-1/2(u_1 l_1 + u_2 l_2)]\} + \{\exp[\tfrac{1}{2}(u_1 l_1 + u_2 l_2)]\}$$

$$= \sum_{r=0}^{\infty} (1/(2r)!)(-\tfrac{1}{2})^{2r})(u_1 l_1 + u_2 l_2)^{2r}. \tag{5.22}$$

Similarly, if M_2 is obtained by forming the corresponding sum in the integrand for β_2, then

$$M_2 = \sum_{r=0}^{\infty} (1/(2r)!)(-\tfrac{1}{2})^{2r}(u_1 l_2 + u_2 l_1)^{2r}. \tag{5.23}$$

From (5.20), (5.22), and (5.23), it is clear that to prove $\beta_1^* > \beta_2^*$, it is sufficient to show that

$$(u_1 l_1 + u_2 l_2)^2 > (u_1 l_2 + u_2 l_1)^2, \tag{5.24}$$

which is equivalent to $(u_1^2 - u_2^2)(l_1^2 - l_2^2) > 0$. Since in D_0, $u_1^2 > u_2^2$, it is sufficient to show that $l_1^2 > l_2^2$, which (from (5.19)) is true if, and only if,

$$[(a + b)\delta_1 + b_0 \delta_2]^2 > [(a + b)\delta_2 + b\delta_1]^2. \tag{5.25}$$

This is equivalent to

$$[(a + b)^2 - b^2](\delta_1^2 - \delta_2^2) > 0. \tag{5.26}$$

Now, $\delta_1^2 > \delta_2^2$ is given, and $(a + b)^2 > b^2$ is implied by (5.11) and the positive definiteness of A_0. This completes the proof.

6. DISCUSSION

In this section, we show how various intersection tests considered in the previous sections arise through the decompositions of various linear hypotheses.

Consider the standard multivariate (SM) linear model:

$$E(\mathbf{y}_r) = A\xi_r; \qquad \text{Var}(\mathbf{y}_r) = \sigma_{rr} I_n; \qquad \text{Cov}(\mathbf{y}_r, \mathbf{y}_s) = \sigma_{rs} I_n;$$
$$r \neq s; \quad 1 \leq r, s \leq p. \quad (6.1)$$

Here we have p responses, (say $V_1, \ldots, V_p$), and $\mathbf{y}_r$ denotes the vector of n observations on response V_r. A $(n \times m)$ is a known design matrix, and $\xi_r(m \times 1)$ is a vector of unknown parameters corresponding to V_r. Also, the n observations correspond to n independent experimental units. The model is sometimes rewritten as

$$E(Y) = A\xi; \qquad Y = [\mathbf{y}_1, \ldots, \mathbf{y}_p]; \qquad \xi = [\xi_1, \ldots, \xi_p], \qquad (6.2)$$

where each row of Y $(n \times p)$ has dispersion matrix $\Sigma = ((\sigma_{rs}))$, and different rows of Y are independently normally distributed. The univariate model (4.1) corresponds to the above when $p = 1$.

More generally, consider a hierarchical multivariate (HM) linear model [for details, see Roy and Srivastava (1964), and Srivastava (1967)]. Here, we assume that the responses can be graded in a certain order of importance such that between any two of them, we can decide which needs to be measured on a larger number of units. For simplicity, let this ordering be $V_1, \ldots, V_p$. Let U_r be the set of units on which V_r is measured. Then, under the HM model we assume $U_1 \supset \cdots \supset U_p$. This implies that U_r can be broken up into disjoint (and independent) subsets $S_r, S_{r+1}, \ldots, S_p$, such that in S_j the responses $V_1, \ldots, V_j$ are measured and none else. We assume S_j has n_j independent experimental units. Let $Y_j(n_j \times j)$ be the matrix of observation on S_j. Then we assume that

$$E(Y_j) = A_j[\xi_1, \ldots, \xi_j], \qquad (6.3)$$

and that every row of Y_j has dispersion matrix Σ_j (which is the top left-hand $(j \times j)$ principal submatrix of Σ).

Consider now the null hypothesis $H_0 : C\xi = 0_{sp}$, where $C(s \times m)$ is a given matrix of rank s (without loss of generality). Four basically different kinds of decompositions of H_0 arise.

(I) Doubly (Responsewise and Contrastwise) Infinite Intersection Procedures

Here we let $H_0 = \bigcap H_{0,\mathbf{a},\mathbf{b}}$, where $H_{0,\mathbf{a},\mathbf{b}} : \mathbf{a}'C\xi\mathbf{b} = 0$, and the intersection is taken over all the infinitely many possible values of $\mathbf{a}$ and $\mathbf{b}$. One well-known test in this class is Roy's largest root criterion for H_0 under the SM model.

(II) Responsewise Infinite and Contrastwise Finite Intersection Procedures

First consider the univariate case $p = 1$. Then decompositions of H_0 of the type considered in (5.3)–(5.5) would belong to this class. These, of course, correspond to dependent F-tests. However, obviously, the quasi-independent case (Section 4) also falls under this category. For $p > 1$, generalizations of these criteria (which are responsewise infinite intersections) have also been considered [see, for example, Roy and Bose (1953), Siotani (1959a,b, 1960), Krishnaiah (1965a,c)]; the regions of this kind, however, do not fall under the theory of this paper, and will be considered elsewhere.

(III) Responsewise Finite and Contrastwise Infinite Intersection Procedures

Here, in $H_{0,\mathbf{a},\mathbf{b}}$, we let $\mathbf{a}$ vary over a finite set, and $\mathbf{b}$ take all possible values. The most important procedure in this class is the so-called step-down procedure [see Roy (1958), Roy and Srivastava (1964)]. We arrange the responses in a certain order, say $V_1, \ldots, V_p$. Observations on V_1 are first analyzed as usual ignoring the other responses. Next, the conditional distribution of the observations on V_2, given those on V_1 is considered. This leads to a (conditional) univariate model for V_2, and the analysis for V_2 is done under this model. Similarly, response V_j $(j = 2, \ldots, p)$ is analyzed conditionally given $V_1, \ldots, V_{j-1}$. The total procedure thus reduces to a set of p independent F-tests, and, therefore, falls under Section 3.

(IV) Doubly (Responsewise and Contrastwise) Finite Intersection Procedures

As the name suggests, this is a combination of (II) and (III). These tests were proposed by Krishnaiah (1965d). First, we consider a step-down procedure, as in (III), reducing the problem to p independent univariate cases. Then, at each of the p (univariate stages), we consider a contrastwise decomposition as, say, in (5.3)–(5.5). Thus, here, the acceptance region $D = \bigcap_{i=1}^{p} D_i$, where the D_i are all independent, and D_i is an intersection of ν (in the notation of Section 5) F-test acceptance regions (say D_{ij}), which may be independent, quasi-independent or dependent.

Thus, we find that under (III), (IV), and for $p = 1$ in (II), the problem under the SM model leads to intersection tests of the kind considered in this paper. Also, all the known methods so far for treating the general HM model, fall under (III) and (IV). Thus, by using the results in this paper, the power of the overall test for H_0 may be increased if we have some idea of the sizes of the noncentrality parameters. When the latter are not known, it might be fruitful to conduct a small pilot study.

The above provides motivation for many new test procedures as well. For example, in situations in which p is large, and it is expected that a few principal components of the responses would account for most of the variation, the power of the overall test may be considerably increased by first making such a transformation, and then using a step-down procedure with appropriate sizes of the various acceptance regions as indicated by the theory in the previous section. However, often the principal component may not be known to start with, and a two-stage procedure may be called for. These and similar problems would be considered elsewhere.

Acknowledgments

I am thankful to Mrs. La Vonne Helmling and L. L. McDonald for their help in respectively typing and proofreading the manuscript.

REFERENCES

1. Anderson, T. W. (1956). "Introduction to Multivariate Statistical Analysis." Wiley, New York.
2. Dunnett, C. W. (1955). A multiple comparison procedure for comparing several treatments with a control. *J. Amer. Statist. Assoc.* **50** 1091–1121.
3. Ghosh, M. N. (1955). Simultaneous tests of linear hypotheses. *Biometrika* **42** 441–449.
4. Krishnaiah, P. R. (1963). Simultaneous tests and the efficiency of generalized balanced incomplete block designs. ARL 63-174. Aerospace Res. Labs., Wright-Patterson Air Force Base, Ohio.
5. Krishnaiah, P. R. (1965a). On the simultaneous ANOVA and MANOVA tests. *Ann. Inst. Statist. Math.* **17** 35–53.
6. Krishnaiah, P. R. (1965b). On a multivariate generalization of the simultaneous analysis of variance test. *Ann. Inst. Statist. Math.* **17** 167–173.
7. Krishnaiah, P. R. (1965c). Multiple comparison tests in multivariate case. ARL 64–124. Aerospace Res. Labs., Wright-Patterson Air Force Base, Ohio.
8. Krishnaiah, P. R. (1965d). Multiple comparison tests in multiresponse experiments. *Sankhyā Ser. A* **27** 65–72.
9. Ramachandran, K. V. (1956). On the simultaneous analysis of variance test. *Ann. Math. Statist.* **27** 521–528.
10. Rao, C. R. (1965). "Linear Statistical Inference and its Applications." Wiley, New York.
11. Roy, J. (1958). Step-down procedure in multivariate analysis. *Ann. Math. Statist.* **29** 1177–1187.
12. Roy, S. N. (1953). On a heuristic method of test construction and its use in multivariate analysis. *Ann. Math. Statist.* **24** 220–238.
13. Roy, S. N. (1957). "Some Aspects of Multivariate Analysis." Wiley, New York.
14. Roy, S. N., and Bose, R. C. (1953). Simultaneous confidence interval estimation. *Ann. Math. Statist.* **24** 513–536.
15. Roy, S. N., and Srivastava, J. N. (1964). Hierarchical and p-block multiresponse designs and their analysis. *In* "Mahalanobis Dedicatory Volume." Statistical Publishing Society, Calcutta.

16. Roy, S. N., and Srivastava, J. N. (1968). Inference on treatment effects in incomplete block designs. *Rev. Inst. Internat. Statist.* **36** 1–6.
17. Siotani, M. (1959a). The extreme value of the generalized distances of the individual points in the multivariate normal sample. *Ann. Inst. Statist. Math.* **10** 183–203.
18. Siotani, M. (1959b). On the range in the multivariate case. *Proc. Inst. Statist. Math.* **6** 155–165.
19. Siotani, M. (1960). Notes on multivariate confidence bounds. *Ann. Inst. Statist. Math.* **11** 167–182.
20. Srivastava, J. N. (1966). Some generalizations of multivariate analysis of variance. *In* "Multivariate Analysis" (P. R. Krishnaiah, ed.). Academic Press, New York.
21. Srivastava, J. N. (1967). On the extension of Gauss-Markov theorem to complex multivariate linear models. *Ann. Inst. Statist. Math.* **19** 417–437.
22. Tukey, J. W. (1954). The problems of multiple comparisons. Dittoed notes. Princeton Univ., Princeton, New Jersey.

PART III

Distribution Theory

The Exact Distributions of Likelihood Criteria for Different Hypotheses

P. C. CONSUL

DEPARTMENT OF MATHEMATICS, STATISTICS, AND COMPUTER SCIENCES
UNIVERSITY OF CALGARY
CALGARY, ALBERTA, CANADA

1. INTRODUCTION

The exact theory of multivariate analysis is mostly concerned with normal variation and testing of various hypotheses. Wilks (1932, 1935, 1946) defined a number of Neyman-Pearson type likelihood ratio criteria for testing equality of means, equality of variances, equality of covariances, independence of sets of variates, and so forth. Such criteria were later on extended by many workers for testing many other hypotheses about regression coefficients, sphericity, compound symmetry of the respective matrices, and so forth. These criteria are being widely used for tests of significance in multivariate analysis of variance.

The exact distributions of these criteria are either unknown or are known for some particular cases only. The problem of finding the percentage points of these statistics has thus become rather difficult. In most cases, approximations to the exact distributions have been derived by Wald and Brookner (1941), Box (1949), Rao (1951), Roy (1951), and Consul (1965), either from the moments of the criteria or from the products of the roots of determinantal equations. The asymptotic expansion method of Box is quite general and is being widely used for large samples.

In most cases the hth moment of the criterion L $(0 \leq L \leq 1)$ for testing any particular hypothesis is of the form

$$E(L^h) = K \cdot T^h \cdot \prod_{j=1}^{p} \Gamma(v + b_j + ah) / \prod_{t=1}^{k} \Gamma(v + c_t + ah), \tag{1.1}$$

where K is some constant, T is another constant adjustable with the criterion L, v is of the order of sample size n, $p \leq k$, b_j is a constant dependent upon j and p, c_t is a constant dependent upon t and k but $c_t \geq b_j$ successively.

We shall first use the inversion theorem and then operational calculus to obtain the exact probability distribution function (pdf) of L from the above expression of the hth moment of the criterion.

In subsequent sections we shall discuss some of the Neyman-Pearson type likelihood criteria for testing different hypotheses and the manner in which our results can be ultilized to obtain the exact pdf's of these criteria.

2. EXACT PROBABILITY DISTRIBUTION FUNCTION OF *L*

By applying Mellin's inversion theorem on the expression (1.1) of hth moment of the criterion L, the exact pdf of L would be the complex integral

$$f(L) = K \cdot (2\pi i)^{-1} \int_{c'-i\infty}^{c'+i\infty} L^{-h-1} \cdot T^h \cdot \prod_{j=1}^{p} \Gamma(v + b_j + ah) \times \left[\prod_{t=1}^{k} \Gamma(v + c_t + ah)\right]^{-1} dh. \tag{2.1}$$

On putting the transformation $v + m + ah = -s$, and on further simplification, it takes the form

$$f(L) = K \cdot (aL)^{-1} (L/T)^{(m+v)/a} \cdot (2\pi i)^{-1} \int_{c-i\infty}^{c+i\infty} [(L/T)^{1/a}]^s \cdot \prod_{j=1}^{p} \Gamma(b_j - m - s) \left[\prod_{t=1}^{k} \Gamma(c_t - m - s)\right]^{-1} \cdot ds \tag{2.2}$$

where c is a constant different from c', dependent upon the transformation.

The above representation of the pdf as an inverse Mellin transform is interesting for two reasons. First, the distribution splits into a factor depending upon the sample size v and p or k and an integral depending upon the values of b_j and c_t only, and second, because the integral is a particular form of the Barnes type integrals by which Meijer's G-function is defined and which can be expressed as a sum of a finite number of generalized hypergeometric functions. So the integral can be easily expressed in the form of Meijer's G-function. Thus the exact pdf of the criterion L, for testing any particular hypothesis H, becomes of the form

$$f(L) = K \cdot (aL)^{-1} (L/T)^{(m+v)/a} \cdot G_{k,p}^{p,0}\left((L/T)^{1/a} \Big|_{b_1-m,\, b_2-m,\, \ldots,\, b_p-m}^{c_1-m,\, c_2-m,\, \ldots,\, c_k-m}\right). \tag{2.3}$$

If has been shown by Meijer (1946) that for special values of b_j, $j = 1, \ldots, p$ and c_t, $t = 1, 2, \ldots, k$ the G-function assumes the form of known functions like gamma function, beta function, Gauss hypergeometric function, Bessel function and so forth. Thus, we shall also show that the exact pdf of the different criteria for testing different hypotheses, obtained for some particular values of k and p, are special cases of the above form of the exact pdf of the criteria concerned.

3. TEST OF INDEPENDENCE OF TWO SETS OF VARIABLES

Consider a sample $(x_{1\xi}, x_{2\xi}, \ldots, x_{p\xi};\ \xi = 1, 2, \ldots, N)$ of size $N > p$ from the p-dimensional normal distribution with mean vectors μ_j and nonsingular covariance matrix $\|\sigma_{jt}\|$; $j, t = 1, 2, \ldots, p$. Let $\bar{x}_j$ and $\|u_{jt}\|$ be the corresponding mean and the internal scatter matrix of the sample, where

$$N\bar{x}_j = \sum_{\xi=1}^{N} x_{j\xi}, \qquad j = 1, 2, \ldots, p$$

and

$$u_{jt} = u_{tj} = \sum_{\xi=1}^{N} (x_{j\xi} - \bar{x}_j)(x_{t\xi} - \bar{x}_t), \qquad j, t = 1, 2, \ldots, p \tag{3.1}$$

and such that $\|u^{jt}\| = \|u_{jt}\|^{-1}$, that is $\|u_{jt}\|$ is a nonsingular sum of products matrix and the internal scatter $|u_{jt}|$ of the sample is minimum.

Now, if the p-component vector X, of the normal distribution, is partitioned into two subvectors with components s and $p - s$, the vector of means μ_j and the covariance matrix $\|\sigma_{jt}\|$ are also subdivided accordingly. We can partition each sample vector x_ξ and the corresponding mean vector and the internal scatter matrix $\|u_{jt}\|$ in the same manner. Let $\|u_1\|$ and $\|u_2\|$ denote the internal scatter matrices of the two partitions of the sample so that

$$\|u_1\| = \|u_{jt}\|, \qquad j, t = 1, 2, 3, \ldots, s$$

and

$$\|u_2\| = \|u_{jt}\|, \qquad j, t = s+1, s+2, \ldots, p.$$

Wilks (1932) has defined the likelihood ratio criterion L for testing the hypothesis that the two sets are mutually independent, i.e. whether each variable in one set is uncorrelated with each variable in the other set by

$$L = |u_{jt}|/(|u_1| \cdot |u_2|) \tag{3.2}$$

and obtained its hth moment in the form

$$E(L^h) = \prod_{j=1}^{s} \left\{ \frac{\Gamma[\frac{1}{2}(N-j)]}{\Gamma[\frac{1}{2}(N-p+s-j)]} \right\} \prod_{j=1}^{s} \left\{ \frac{\Gamma[\frac{1}{2}(N-p+s-j)+h]}{\Gamma[\frac{1}{2}(N-j)+h]} \right\} \tag{3.3}$$

which is of the same form as (1.1) and where the first product is K, $T = 1$, $t = j$, $a = 1$, $k = p = s$.

Wilks (1935) has shown that for $s = 1$, L has the beta distribution $B(\frac{1}{2}(N-p), \frac{1}{2}(p-1))$ and for $s = 2$, $\sqrt{L}$ has the beta distribution $B(N-p, p-2)$ and that for higher values of s the distribution was too complex to be determined.

Using the result (2.3) on the above expression of $E(L^h)$, the exact pdf of the criterion L, for testing the independence of two sets of variables, becomes

$$f(L) = \prod_{j=1}^{s} \left\{ \frac{\Gamma[\frac{1}{2}(N-j)]}{\Gamma[\frac{1}{2}(N-p+s-j)]} \right\} \cdot L^{(N-p-2)/2} \times G_{s,s}^{s,0}\left(L \Big|_{0, \frac{1}{2}, 1, \frac{3}{2}, \ldots, \frac{1}{2}(s-1)}^{\frac{1}{2}(p-s), \frac{1}{2}(p-s+1), \ldots, \frac{1}{2}(p-1)}\right). \tag{3.4}$$

It can be easily seen by the properties of G-functions (given in the Appendix) that for $s = 1$ and $s = 2$ the distribution (3.4) gets reduced to the beta distributions as obtained by Wilks (1935) and for $s = 3$ and 4 the distribution gets reduced to Gauss hypergeometric form, which can be changed to algebraic and trigonometrical expressions with the help of the formulas given by Consul (1966).

4. TESTING LINEAR HYPOTHESES ABOUT REGRESSION COEFFICIENTS

Let $X_1, \ldots, X_N$ be a set of N vector observations, X_α being drawn from a multivariate normal distribution given by $N(\beta Z_\alpha, \Sigma)$, where Z_α is a known q-component vector, but β is an unknown $p \times q$ matrix and Σ is the unknown $p \times p$ covariance matrix. The matrix β can be partitioned such that $\beta = (\beta_1 \beta_2)$ where β_1 has q_1 columns and β_2 has q_2 columns, $q_1 + q_2 = q$. For testing the hypothesis that the matrix β_1 is equal to some given matrix, the likelihood ratio criterion λ is defined by

$$\lambda = \{|S_1|/|S_2|\}^{N/2} \tag{4.1}$$

where the sum of product matrices S_1 and S_2 are the maximum likelihood estimates of $p \times p$ matrix Σ over the full range and over the restricted range under the hypothesis.

Wilks (1932) obtained the hth moment of the criterion $U = \lambda^{2/N}$ and also obtained its distribution in the form of a $(p-1)$ fold multiple integral, which he was able to evaluate for some specific values of p. Anderson (1958) has shown that the hth moment can be put in the form

$$E(U^h) = \prod_{j=1}^{p} \left\{ \frac{\Gamma[\frac{1}{2}(N+1-q_2-j)]\Gamma[\frac{1}{2}(N+1-q-j)+h]}{\Gamma[\frac{1}{2}(N+1-q_1-q_2-j)]\Gamma[\frac{1}{2}(N+1-q_2-j)+h]} \right\}. \tag{4.2}$$

Wilks (1935) and Anderson (1958) obtained the exact distributions of U for some particular values of p and q_1. Schatzoff (1964) determined exact distributions of U when either p or q_1 is an even integer. Consul (1966) found the exact and cumulative distributions of U for a wider range of values of p and q_1.

The expression (4.2) of moments of U is similar to (1.1) with the values of corresponding coefficients being $a = T = 1$, $t = j$, $k = p$, $b_j = -\frac{1}{2}j$, $c_j = \frac{1}{2}(q_1 - j)$, $m = -\frac{1}{2}p$, $v = \frac{1}{2}(N + 1 - q)$ and

$$K = \prod_{j=1}^{p} \left\{ \frac{\Gamma[\frac{1}{2}(N + 1 - q_2 - j)]}{\Gamma[\frac{1}{2}(N + 1 - q_1 - q_2 - j)]} \right\}. \tag{4.3}$$

Now, by applying the result (2.3), we obtain the exact pdf of the criterion U, for all values of p, q_1 and N, as

$$f(U) = K \cdot U^{(N-p-q-1)/2} \cdot G_{p,\,p}^{p,\,0}\left(U \,\middle|\, {}^{\frac{1}{2}q_1,\, \frac{1}{2}(q_1+1),\, \ldots,\, \frac{1}{2}(q_1+p-1)}_{0,\, \frac{1}{2},\, 1,\, \ldots,\, \frac{1}{2}(p-1)}\right) \tag{4.4}$$

where K is given by (4.3) and $0 \le U \le 1$.

It can be shown that for particular values of p and q_1, the above distribution will get reduced to simpler forms as obtained by other workers mentioned above.

5. TEST OF INDEPENDENCE OF MANY SETS OF VARIATES

Let p-component vectors $X_1, X_2, \ldots, X_N$ form a random sample from the multivariate normal distribution $N(\mu, \Sigma)$. Let each vector X be partitioned into q subvectors with components $p_1, p_2, \ldots, p_q$, respectively. The vector of means μ and the covariance matrix Σ and the maximum likelihood estimate matrix S of Σ can be partitioned similarly; i.e.,

$$X = \begin{pmatrix} X^{(1)} \\ X^{(2)} \\ \vdots \\ X^{(q)} \end{pmatrix}, \qquad \mu = \begin{pmatrix} \mu^{(1)} \\ \mu^{(2)} \\ \vdots \\ \mu^{(q)} \end{pmatrix} \tag{5.1}$$

and

$$\Sigma = \begin{pmatrix} \Sigma_{11} & \Sigma_{12} & \cdots & \Sigma_{1q} \\ \Sigma_{21} & \Sigma_{22} & \cdots & \Sigma_{2q} \\ \vdots & \vdots & & \vdots \\ \Sigma_{q1} & \Sigma_{q2} & \cdots & \Sigma_{qq} \end{pmatrix}, \qquad S = \begin{pmatrix} S_{11} & S_{12} & \cdots & S_{1q} \\ S_{21} & S_{22} & \cdots & S_{2q} \\ \vdots & \vdots & & \vdots \\ S_{q1} & S_{q2} & & S_{qq} \end{pmatrix} \tag{5.2}$$

To test the hypothesis that the q subsets are mutually independent of each other, Wilks (1935) defined the likelihood ratio criterion V by

$$V = \frac{|S|}{\prod_{j=1}^{q} |S_{jj}|}. \tag{5.3}$$

Daly (1940) and Narain (1950) have shown that the tests based on V are strictly unbiased. Anderson (1958) has shown that the criterion V is invariant with respect to linear transformations within each subset and that it can be expressed in terms of sample correlation coefficients.

The hth moment of the criterion V is given by Anderson (1958), and it can be easily changed to the form

$$E(V^h) = K(N) \frac{\prod_{j=1}^{p-p_q} \{\Gamma[\frac{1}{2}(N-p_q-j)+h]\}}{\prod_{i=1}^{q-1}\{\prod_{j=1}^{p_i} \Gamma[\frac{1}{2}(N-j)+h]\}} \tag{5.4}$$

where

$$K(N) = \frac{\prod_{i=1}^{q-1} \{\prod_{j=1}^{p_i} \Gamma[\frac{1}{2}(N-j)]\}}{\prod_{j=1}^{p-p_q} \Gamma[\frac{1}{2}(N-p_q-j)]}. \tag{5.5}$$

Wilks (1935) obtained the distributions of V in some special cases by the method of integrals of joint densities of independent variables. Consul (1967b) used inversion theorem and operational calculus to obtain the exact distributions of V for a large number of more general cases.

The expression for $E(V^h)$ is slightly more complicated than (1.1), but the result (2.3) can still be applied. One can easily see that $a = T = 1$, $v = \frac{1}{2}(N-p)$, $b_j = \frac{1}{2}(p-p_q-j)$, $c_j = \frac{1}{2}(p-j)$ and $p = k = (p-p_q)$. Thus the exact pdf of the criterion V, for testing the independence of q sets of variables, is given by

$$f(V) = K(N) \cdot V^{(N-p-2)/2} G_{p-p_q,\, p-p_q}^{p-p_q,\, 0}\left(V\middle|_{b_s}^{a_r}\right) \tag{5.6}$$

where b_s stands for $0, \frac{1}{2}, 1, \ldots, \frac{1}{2}(p-p_q-1)$ and a_r stands for $\frac{1}{2}(p-p_i)$, $\frac{1}{2}(p-p_i+1), \ldots, \frac{1}{2}(p-1)$; $i = 1, 2, \ldots, q-1$; and where $K(N)$ is given by (5.5).

For $q = 2$ and $q = 3$ the expression (5.6) becomes the same as obtained by Consul (1967b).

6. TESTING SPHERICITY AND SYMMETRY

Consider a random sample $X_1, X_2, \ldots, X_N$ of p-component vectors drawn from the multivariate normal distribution $N(\mu, \Sigma)$. Let S be the internal matrix of the sample. The hypothesis H that $\Sigma = \sigma^2 I$, where $\sigma^2 > 0$ is not specified, can be put in the form that the arithmetic mean of the roots of $\phi_1, \phi_2, \ldots, \phi_p$ of $|\Sigma - \phi I| = 0$ is equal to the geometric mean. i.e.

$$\prod \phi_i^{1/p}/\{(\Sigma\phi_i)/p\} = |\Sigma|^{1/p}/\{(\text{tr } \Sigma)/p\} = 1.$$

As the squares of the lengths of principal axes of ellipsoids of constant density are proportional to the roots ϕ_i, which are now equal, the ellipsoids become spheres under the hypothesis H. The criterion W for testing this sphericity in a p-variate normal distribution was defined by Mauchly (1940a, b) as

$$W = |S|/\{(\text{tr } S)/p\}^p. \tag{6.1}$$

Mauchly obtained the moments of the sphericity criterion W in the form

$$E(W^h) = (p^p)^h \cdot \frac{\Gamma[\frac{1}{2}p(N-1)]}{\Gamma[\frac{1}{2}p(N-1)+ph]} \cdot \prod_{j=1}^{p} \frac{\Gamma[\frac{1}{2}(N-j)+h]}{\Gamma[\frac{1}{2}(N-j)]} \tag{6.2}$$

and proved that for $p = 2$, $\sqrt{W}$ has the beta distribution $B(N-2, 1)$. Girshik (1941) and Hickman (1953) did further work on the subject. Consul (1967a) obtained the exact and cumulative distribution functions of W for $p = 2$, 3, 4, and 6 by another method. Gleser (1966) has shown that the sphericity test is unbiassed.

Though the expression for $E(W^h)$ is not exactly like (1.1), but by using the Gauss and Legendre multiplication theorem

$$\prod_{r=1}^{n} \Gamma(z + (r-1)/n) = (2\pi)^{\frac{1}{2}(n-1)} \cdot n^{\frac{1}{2}-nz}\Gamma(nz) \tag{6.3}$$

on $\Gamma[\frac{1}{2}p(N-1)+ph]$ in (6.2) and on simplification, we get

$$E(W^h) = K(N) \cdot \prod_{j=1}^{p} \frac{\Gamma[\frac{1}{2}(N-j)+h]}{\Gamma[\frac{1}{2}(N-1)+(j-1)/p+h]} \tag{6.4}$$

where

$$K(N) = (2\pi)^{\frac{1}{2}(p-1)} \cdot p^{\frac{1}{2}-\frac{1}{2}p(N-1)}\Gamma[\tfrac{1}{2}p(N-1)]/\prod_{j=1}^{p}\Gamma[\tfrac{1}{2}(N-j)]. \tag{6.5}$$

The expression of moments, given by (6.4) and (6.5), resembles our expression (1.1), for which the exact pdf was obtained in (2.3). Thus the exact pdf for the criterion W becomes

$$f(W) = K(N) \cdot W^{(N-p-2)/2} \cdot G_{p,p}^{p,0}\left(W\,\middle|\,{}^{\frac{1}{2}(p-1)+(p-1)/p,\ \ldots,\ \frac{1}{2}(p-1)+1/p,\ \frac{1}{2}(p-1)}_{0,\ \frac{1}{2},\ 1,\ \ldots,\ \frac{1}{2}(p-1)}\right), \tag{6.6}$$

where $K(N)$ is given by (6.5) and $0 \leq W \leq 1$.

For $p = 2, 3, 4, 6$ the expression $f(W)$ becomes the same as obtained earlier by Consul (1967a).

When

$$S_{aa} = p^{-1}(\text{tr } S) \qquad \text{and} \qquad S_{aa'} = (p^2 - p)^{-1} \sum_{j \neq j'} S_{jj'},$$

the likelihood criterion for testing the statistical hypothesis, that the p-dimensional distribution is symmetric in the variables, is given by

$$W^* = |S|/\{(S_{aa} + (p-1)S_{aa'})(S_{aa} - S_{aa'})^{p-1}\} \tag{6.7}$$

for which the hth moment is given by

$$E(W^*)^h = (p-1)^{h(p-1)} \cdot \frac{\Gamma[\frac{1}{2}(N-1)(p-1)]}{\Gamma[\frac{1}{2}(N-1)(p-1) + h(p-1)]} \cdot \prod_{j=1}^{p-1} \frac{\Gamma[\frac{1}{2}(N-1-j)+h]}{\Gamma[\frac{1}{2}(N-1-j)]} \tag{6.8}$$

which is similar to the expression (6.2), the only difference being $(p-1)$ in place of p. Thus the exact pdf of the criterion W^* can be written from (6.6) by replacement of p with $p-1$ and by replacing N with $N-1$ in denominator of the value of $K(N)$.

7. TESTING COMPOUND SYMMETRY

Consider a random sample $X_1, X_2, \ldots, X_N$ of $(p+q)$ component vectors drawn from a $(p+q)$ variate normal distribution $N(\mu, \Sigma)$. Let $S = \|s_{jj'}\|$ be the internal scatter matrix (SP) of the sample. Also

$$S_{aa} = p^{-1}\sum_{j=1}^{p} s_{jj} \qquad S_{aa'} = 2(p^2-p)^{-1}\sum_{j>j'=1}^{p} s_{jj'}$$

$$S_{bb} = q^{-1}\sum_{j=p+1}^{p+q} s_{jj} \qquad S_{bb'} = 2(q^2-q)^{-1}\sum_{j>j'=p+1}^{p+q} s_{jj'}$$

$$S_{ab} = (pq)^{-1}\sum_{j=1}^{p}\sum_{j'=p+1}^{p+q} s_{jj'} \tag{7.1}$$

If the covariance matrix Σ is partitioned into four matrices, then to test the hypothesis H that Σ is of the bipolar form

$$\begin{bmatrix} \Sigma_1 & \Sigma_2 \\ \Sigma_2 & \Sigma_3 \end{bmatrix} \tag{7.2}$$

where Σ_1 is a $p \times p$ matrix with all diagonal elements σ_{aa} and other elements $\sigma_{aa'}$, Σ_2 is a $p \times q$ matrix with all elements σ_{ab} and Σ_3 is a $q \times q$ matrix with all diagonal elements σ_{bb} and other elements $\sigma_{bb'}$, the likelihood ratio criterion L^* was defined by Votaw (1948) as

$$L^* = |S|/[\{(S_{aa} + (p-1)S_{aa'})(S_{bb} + (q-1)S_{bb'}) - pqS_{ab}^2\} \times (S_{aa} - S_{aa'})^{p-1}(S_{bb} - S_{bb'})^{q-1}]. \tag{7.3}$$

Votaw (1948) also derived the hth moment $E(L^*)^h$ of the criterion when H is true. Later on Roy (1951) proved that $E(L^*)^h$ could be put in the form

$$E(L^*)^h = \{(p-1)^{p-1}(q-1)^{q-1}\}^h \cdot \frac{\Gamma[\frac{1}{2}(p-1)(N-1)]\Gamma[\frac{1}{2}(q-1)(N-1)]}{\Gamma[(p-1)(h+\frac{1}{2}(N-1))]\Gamma[(q-1)(h+\frac{1}{2}(N-1))]} \times \prod_{j=1}^{p+q-2} \frac{\Gamma[h+\frac{1}{2}(N-2)-\frac{1}{2}j]}{\Gamma[\frac{1}{2}(N-2)-\frac{1}{2}j]} \tag{7.4}$$

and obtained the distribution of L^* as an asymptotic series.

By use of the Gauss and Legendre multiplication theorem, expression (7.4) can be transformed into

$$E(L^*)^h = K_1(N) \cdot \frac{\prod_{j=1}^{p+q-2} \Gamma[h+\frac{1}{2}(N-2)-\frac{1}{2}j]}{\prod_{j=1}^{p-1} \Gamma\left[h+\frac{1}{2}(N-1)+\frac{j-1}{p-1}\right] \prod_{j=1}^{q-1} \Gamma\left[h+\frac{1}{2}(N-1)+\frac{j-1}{q-1}\right]} \tag{7.5}$$

where

$$K_1(N) = \frac{\prod_{j=1}^{p-1} \Gamma\left[\frac{1}{2}(N-1)+\frac{j-1}{p-1}\right] \prod_{j=1}^{q-1} \Gamma\left[\frac{1}{2}(N-1)+\frac{j-1}{q-1}\right]}{\prod_{j=1}^{p+q-2} \Gamma[\frac{1}{2}(N-2)-\frac{1}{2}j]} \tag{7.6}$$

The expression (7.5) is similar to the form (1.1). So the exact pdf of the criterion L^* can be obtained by proper substitutions in (2.3). Putting

$$v = \tfrac{1}{2}(N-p-q), \qquad a = T = 1, \qquad k = p = p+q-2,$$
$$b_j = \tfrac{1}{2}(p+q-2-j),$$
$$c_j = \tfrac{1}{2}(p+q-1) + (j-1)/(p-1) \quad \text{or} \quad (j-1)/(q-1),$$

we have

$$f(L^*) = K_1(N) \cdot (L^*)^{\frac{1}{2}(N-p-q-2)} \cdot G_{\lambda,\lambda}^{\lambda,0}\left(^{a_r,\, a_s}_{0,\, \frac{1}{2},\, 1,\, \ldots,\, \frac{1}{2}(p+q-3)}\right) \tag{7.7}$$

where

$$\lambda = p+q-2;$$
$$a_r = \tfrac{1}{2}(p+q-1), \tfrac{1}{2}(p+q-1)+1/(p-1), \ldots, \tfrac{1}{2}(p+q-1)+(p-2)/(p-1);$$
$$a_s = \tfrac{1}{2}(p+q-1), \tfrac{1}{2}(p+q-1)+1/(q-1), \ldots, \tfrac{1}{2}(p+q-1)+(q-2)/(q-1)$$

and $K_1(N)$ is given by (7.6).

It can be easily seen by the identities (given in Appendix) that for $p = q = 2$; $p = q = 3$; $p = 3, q = 2$; $p = 5, q = 2$ and $p = 5, q = 3$ the exact pdf's obtained from (7.7) as particular cases are the same as obtained by Consul (1969).

APPENDIX

MEIJER'S FUNCTION AND SOME IDENTITIES

Meijer (1946) defined G-function by

$$G^{m,n}_{p,q}\left(x\middle|{}^{a_1,\,\dots,\,a_p}_{b_1,\,\dots,\,b_q}\right) = (2\pi i)^{-1} \int_c \frac{\prod_{j=1}^{m} \Gamma(b_j - s) \prod_{j=1}^{n} \Gamma(1 - a_j + s)}{\prod_{j=m+1}^{q} \Gamma(1 - b_j + s) \prod_{j=n+1}^{p} \Gamma(a_j - s)}\, x^s \cdot ds \tag{1}$$

where c is a curve separating the singularities of $\prod_{j=1}^{m} \Gamma(b_j - s)$ from the singularities of $\prod_{j=1}^{n} \Gamma(1 - a_j + s)$. The values of G-function are given in a number of ways.

The following identities between G-functions can be easily verified.

$$x^{\sigma} G^{m,n}_{p,q}\left(x\middle|{}^{a_r}_{b_s}\right) = G^{m,n}_{p,q}\left(x\middle|{}^{a_r+\sigma}_{b_s+\sigma}\right) \tag{2}$$

$$G^{1,0}_{1,1}\left(x\middle|{}^{a}_{b}\right) = x^b(1-x)^{a-b-1}/\Gamma(a-b), \qquad 0 < x < 1 \tag{3}$$

$$G^{2,0}_{2,2}\left(x\middle|{}^{a_1,\,a_2}_{b_1,\,b_2}\right) = \frac{x^{b_1}(1-x)^{a_1+a_2-b_1-b_2-1}}{\Gamma(a_1 + a_2 - b_1 - b_2)} \cdot {}_2F_1(a_2 - b_2, a_1 - b_2; a_1 + a_2 - b_1 - b_2; 1 - x) \tag{4}$$

for $0 < x < 1$.

When p is an even number $2m$, the use of Legendre's duplication formula gives

$$G^{2m,0}_{2m,2m}\left(x\middle|{}^{\frac{1}{2}a_r,\quad \frac{1}{2}a_r+\frac{1}{2}}_{\frac{1}{2}b_r,\quad \frac{1}{2}b_r+\frac{1}{2}}\right) = 2^{\Sigma(a_r-b_r)-1} \cdot G^{m,0}_{m,n}\left(x\middle|{}^{a_r}_{b_r}\right) \tag{5}$$

REFERENCES

ANDERSON, T. W. (1958). "An Introduction to Multivariate Statistical Analysis." Wiley, New York.

BOX, G. E. P. (1949). A general distribution theory for a class of likelihood criteria. *Biometrika* **36** 317–346.

CONSUL, P. C. (1965). The exact distributions of certain likelihood criteria useful in multivariate analysis. *Bull. Cl. Sci. Acad. Roy. Belg.* **51** 683–691.

CONSUL, P. C. (1966). On the exact distribution of likelihood ratio criteria for testing linear hypotheses about regression coefficients. *Ann. Math. Statist.* **37** 1319–1330.

CONSUL, P. C. (1967a). On the exact distributions of the criterion W for testing sphericity in a p-variate normal distribution. *Ann. Math. Statist.* **38** 1170–1174.

CONSUL, P. C. (1967b). On the exact distributions of likelihood ratio criteria for testing independence of sets of variates under null hypothesis. *Ann. Math. Statist.* **38** 1160–1169.

CONSUL, P. C. (1969). On the exact distributions of Votaw's criteria for testing compound symmetry of a covariance matrix. *Ann. Math. Statist.* **40** (in press).

DALY, J. F. (1940). On the unbiased character of likelihood ratio tests for independence in normal systems. *Ann. Math. Statist.* **11** 1–32.

GIRSHIK, M. A. (1941). The distribution of the ellipticity statistic L_e when the hypothesis is false. *Terrestial Magnetism & Atmospheric Electricity* **46** 455–457.

GLESER, L. J. (1966). A note on the sphericity test. *Ann. Math. Statist.* **37** 464.

HICKMAN, W. B. (1953). "The Volume of Corporate Bond Financing since 1900." Princeton Univ. Press, Princeton, New Jersey.

KENDALL, M. G., and STUART, A. (1966). "The Advanced Theory of Statistics." Vol. 3. Griffen, London.

MAUCHLY, J. W. (1940a). A significance test for ellipticity in the harmonic dial. *Terrestial Magnetism & Atmospheric Electricity* **45** 145–148.

MAUCHLY, J. W. (1940b). Significance test for sphericity of a normal n-variate distribution. *Ann. Math. Statist.* **11** 204–209.

MEIJER, C. S. (1946). *Nederl. Akad. Wetensch. Proc.* **49** 344–456, 457–469, 632–641, 765–772, 936–943, 1063–1072, 1165–1175.

NARAIN, R. D. (1950). On the completely unbiased character of tests of independence in multivariate normal systems. *Ann. Math. Statist.* **21** 293–298.

RAO, C. R. (1951). An asymptotic expansion of the distribution of Wilks' Λ-criteria. *Bull. Inst. Internat. Statist.* **33** 177–180.

ROY, J. (1951). Distribution of certain likelihood criteria useful in multivariate analysis. *Bull. Inst. Internat. Stat.* **33** Pt. II 219–230.

SCHATZOFF, M. (1964). Exact distributions of Wilks' likelihood ratio criterion and comparisons with competitive tests. Ph.D. Thesis, Harvard Univ., Cambridge, Massachusetts; Abstract. *Ann. Math. Statist.* **35** 1397.

VOTAW, D. F. (1948). Testing compound symmetry in a normal multivariate distribution. *Ann. Math. Statist.* **19** 447–473.

WALD, A., and BROOKNER, R. J. (1941). On the distribution of Wilks' statistic for testing independence of several groups of variables. *Ann. Math. Statist.* **12** 137–152.

WILKS, S. S. (1932). Certain generalizations in the analysis of variance. *Biometrika* **24** 471–494.

WILKS, S. S. (1935). On the independence of k sets of normally distributed statistical variables. *Econometrica* **3** 309–326.

WILKS, S. S. (1946). Sample criteria for testing equality of means, equality of variances and equality of covariances in a normal multivariate distribution. *Ann. Math. Statist.* **17** 257–281.

WILKS, S. S. (1963). "Mathematical Statistics." Wiley, New York.

What Is the Use of a Distribution?

I. J. GOOD

STATISTICS DEPARTMENT
VIRGINIA POLYTECHNIC INSTITUTE
BLACKSBURG, VIRGINIA

SUMMARY

Let $U(G \mid F)$ denote the utility of asserting that a distribution is G when, in fact, it is F. Some specific forms for U are suggested, denoted by $U_\alpha^\gamma(G \mid F)$ $(0 \leq \alpha \leq \infty, 0 \leq \gamma \leq \infty)$. (The superscript γ does not denote a power.) These depend on $v(\mathbf{x}, \mathbf{y})$, which is defined as the utility of asserting that the value of the variable on some occasion is $\mathbf{y}$ when it is really $\mathbf{x}$. (Here $\mathbf{x}$ and $\mathbf{y}$ are n-dimensional vectors.) Of the various measures suggested perhaps the most interesting is U_∞^γ which, when G has the density function g, turns out to be mathematically independent of γ and to have the form

$$U_\infty(G|F) = \int \log\{g(\mathbf{x})\,|\Delta(\mathbf{x})|^{-1/2}\}\, dF(\mathbf{x})$$

where $|\Delta(\mathbf{x})|$ is $(-)^n$ times the Hessian of $v(\mathbf{x}, \mathbf{y})$ with respect to $\mathbf{y}$, at $\mathbf{y} = \mathbf{x}$. For a given F, the optimal G is then F, but this is not necessarily so when the measure used is $U_\alpha^\gamma(G \mid F)$ for finite α. For search problems, and for problems where the application of the assertion of G is entirely open-ended, it is right to take $\alpha = \infty$ and $\gamma = 0$, but for other problems finite values of α might well be better. Further conditions for the applicability of the work are given.

Applications would be both to the design of experiments and to the summarization of their results, including the selection of a confidence region when it is thought that later this will be loosely interpreted as a probability distribution.

If $\mathbf{x}$ is a parameter in the distribution law $T(\mathbf{z} \mid \mathbf{x})$ of another random variable $\mathbf{z}$, then $v(\mathbf{x}, \mathbf{y}) = U(T(\mathbf{z} \mid \mathbf{y}) \,|\, T(\mathbf{z} \mid \mathbf{x}))$. If we take U as U_∞, we deduce that

$$v(\mathbf{x}, \mathbf{x}) - v(\mathbf{x}, \mathbf{y}) = \int \log \frac{dT(\mathbf{z} \mid \mathbf{x})}{dT(\mathbf{z} \mid \mathbf{y})}\, dT(\mathbf{z} \mid \mathbf{x})$$

and that $\Delta(\mathbf{x})$ is Fisher's information matrix.

The "least favorable" initial distribution, if it exists, with respect to the utility $U_\infty(F|F)$, has density proportional to $|\mathbf{\Delta}(\mathbf{x})|^{1/2}$ and is an invariant initial distribution. It generalizes (i) the Jeffreys-Perks invariance theory; (ii) a principle of minimum discriminability for determining a distribution (Kullback, 1959); and (iii) the similar principle of maximum entropy for initial distributions (Jaynes, 1957).

INTRODUCTION

The topic of this paper is one that the author discussed very briefly following a paper concerning confidence regions presented by E. M. L. Beale in 1959 (Good, 1960). The questions raised in this discussion were: (i) How are confidence regions used in practice? and (ii) What is the utility of an asserted probability distribution?

It was suggested that the first question would justify some operational research, but apparently this research has not yet been carried out. The question arises mainly when the statistician's client is not a regular customer. It is not enough, from the point of view of the rare client, for the statistician to be right, say, 95% of the time in the long run. The rare client is more interested in the probability that an assertion will be right on a given occasion than he is in the long-run reputation of the statistician. Moreover, it is unethical for a statistician to be concerned only with his own reputation or even with the reputation of the entire statistical profession.

The use of a confidence region would, of course, vary from one application to another, but I believe that the client would often interpret the region as in same sense representing a posterior, i.e., final distribution. Suppose, for example, the region were obtained by the process of direction finding of the position of a submarine. The client might decide to search this region giving equal attention to all its parts: This would be equivalent to interpreting the region as one of uniform probability density. Or more weight might well be given to its center, and some small weight to points outside the region. This could be done, for example (Good, 1960), by replacing the region by a multivariate normal distribution with mean at the center of gravity of the confidence region and with second-order moments proportional to the moments of inertia of the region. The constant of proportionality might be chosen so that the total probability enclosed in the region is equal to the confidence coefficient. Of course, it might be better to use a more Bayesian approach from the start, but what was just described was intended to be a plausible formalization of how the confidence region is, in fact, often interpreted by the client. The client often wants a probability distribution, so perhaps that is what the statistician should aim to give him; but since it is fashionable to specify confidence regions, and since these are often interpreted in practice as if they were probability distributions, it is of practical interest to evaluate the utility of distributions that are not "correct." It is also of interest when the asserted distribution does not arise by the misinterpretation of a confidence region.

Whether a "correct" distribution always exists is a controversial matter related on the one hand to the distinction between physical, logical, and subjective probabilities, and on the other to the notion that subjective probabilities are only partially ordered. But it is at least often convenient to suppose that a correct logical or subjective distribution, on the evidence available, does exist, and this will be assumed throughout the present paper. It will usually be possible also to interpret the "correct" distribution as physical.

The value of asserting a distribution, whether or not it is correctly asserted, will clearly depend on the purpose of the investigation. For example, if the distribution deals with the output of a chemical process, and if the utility of each possible output can be estimated, then the distribution leads to an estimate of the expected utility of the process, and helps the chemist to decide whether the process is economically viable. On the other hand, if the distribution is concerned with the location of a submarine, then it leads to an estimate of the cost of a search before the submarine is found. In such a search problem, the expected cost might be roughly proportional to the expected n-dimensional volume of the "ellipsoid" of constant density, which just includes the submarine or other object looked for. In other situations, a distribution gives an indication of how to collect further information, and an estimate of its utility depends on the utilities of the distributions that might later be attained. Hence, an exact solution must then depend on dynamic "programming" or rather dynamic "planning." This happens, for example, in the problem of the two-armed bandit. [See for example, Thompson (1933, 1935), Robbins (1952, 1956), Bellman (1956), Good (1968b).] It would certainly be convenient if a formula could be found for the expected utility of an asserted distribution which could be used when the purpose of the investigation is vague, as in problems of inference in pure science and also in applied problems involving search trees, such as medical diagnosis, before we have reached the terminal nodes of the tree.

No attempt will be made here to give a complete account of the history of rules for assigning a utility to an asserted probability distribution. Much of the history can be traced through the following papers: Bartlett (1950), Good (1950b, 1952, 1956a, 1960, 1966), Cronbach (1953), Schützenberger (1954), Lindley (1956), McCarthy (1956), Marschak (1959), Mallows (1959), Kerridge (1961), Rényi (1961, 1965), DeGroot (1962), Hartigan (1964). The main application would be to the calculation of the expected utility of experiments in order to rationalize their design, including the design of search strategies.

Previous attempts to do this have usually depended exclusively on probabilities and have thus been associated with measures of (expected) information, (Fisher, 1925; Shannon and Weaver, 1949), (expected) weight of evidence (Jeffreys, 1948; Turing and Good, see Good, 1950a), entropy and uncertainty (Shannon and Weaver, 1949), and cross-entropy (Good, 1950b, 1952, 1954; Kerridge, 1961). Exceptions are Good (1960) and DeGroot (1962). (DeGroot refers to an "uncertainty" function but uses a utility function in some of his examples. He is concerned, as in most of the literature, with the value of a correct probability distribution, correct, that is, on the available evidence.)

What we should like to do is to constrain the form of the utility irrespective of the application. (We shall not fully succeed in this aim.) Our approach, like that of Good (1960), is based on the function $v(\mathbf{x}, \mathbf{y})$ which is defined as the utility of saying that a random variable has the value $\mathbf{y}$ when the true value is $\mathbf{x}$, where the random variable might be a scalar or a vector.

1. A PROPOSED UTILITY MEASURE

Denote by $U(G \mid F)$ the utility of asserting that the distribution is G when in fact it is F. In particular, suppose that F is $H_{\boldsymbol{\xi}}$, the multivariate Heaviside function defined by

$$H_{\boldsymbol{\xi}}(\mathbf{x}) = \begin{cases} 1 & (\mathbf{x} \geq \boldsymbol{\xi}) \\ 0 & \text{otherwise.} \end{cases}$$

where $\mathbf{x} \geq \boldsymbol{\xi}$ means that $x_1 \geq \xi_1$, $x_2 \geq \xi_2$ etc. Then $U(G \mid H_{\boldsymbol{\xi}})$ denotes the utility of asserting the distribution G when the random variable has the value $\boldsymbol{\xi}$. If we write $\mathbf{x} \sim F$ to denote that $\mathbf{x}$ has the distribution F, then a natural desideratum in search problems is

$$U(G \mid \mathbf{x} \sim F) = U(G \mid F) = \int U(G \mid H_{\boldsymbol{\xi}})\, dF(\boldsymbol{\xi}) = \mathscr{E}_{\boldsymbol{\xi}}\{U(G \mid H_{\boldsymbol{\xi}}) \mid \boldsymbol{\xi} \sim F\} \tag{1}$$

A more general assumption is given in Eq. (50).

Since, by the definition of v, we have

$$U(H_{\boldsymbol{\eta}} \mid H_{\boldsymbol{\xi}}) = v(\boldsymbol{\xi}, \boldsymbol{\eta}), \tag{2}$$

it follows from (1) that

$$U(H_{\boldsymbol{\eta}} \mid \mathbf{x} \sim F) = \int v(\mathbf{x}, \boldsymbol{\eta})\, dF(\mathbf{x}) = \mathscr{E}_{\mathbf{x}}\{v(\mathbf{x}, \boldsymbol{\eta}) \mid \mathbf{x} \sim F\}. \tag{3}$$

A simple assumption, but *not* a clear desideratum, would now be that U is U_0 where

$$U_0(G \mid F) = \int dF(\mathbf{x}) \int v(\mathbf{x}, \mathbf{y})\, dG(\mathbf{y}) = \mathscr{E}_{\mathbf{x},\mathbf{y}}\{v(\mathbf{x}, \mathbf{y}) \mid \mathbf{x} \sim F, \mathbf{y} \sim G\}. \tag{4}$$

This is not a clear desideratum even in the special case

$$U_0(G \mid H_\xi) = \int v(\xi, \mathbf{y})\, dG(\mathbf{y}) = \mathscr{E}_\mathbf{y}\{v(\xi, \mathbf{y}) \mid \mathbf{y} \sim G\}. \tag{5}$$

This would be sensible only if we selected a value to act on, the selected value having the distribution G. This is not a usual method for making use of a distribution. When a distribution is used for the selection of a single value, the mode would often be selected, at least in terminal decisions. In the problem of the two-armed bandit, the optimal strategy presumably lies somewhere between the selection of the mode (the "arm" with the larger probability of being the "better") and the selection of each arm with a probability equal to the probability that it is the "better" arm.

When a retailer decides to lay in a stock of some commodity such as shoes, he might regard it as sensible to lay in stocks in proportions provided by the asserted distribution. Actually, if allowance is made both for the expected costs of over-stocking and for the disutility of turning away unsatisfied customers, this naive use of the distribution is not optimal.

Instead of assuming that U is U_0, that is, of taking the expectation of v with respect to $\mathbf{y}$, we shall use a generalized expectation, that is,

$$U(G \mid H_\xi) = \phi^{-1} \int \phi(v(\xi, \mathbf{y}))\, dG(\mathbf{y}), \tag{6}$$

where ϕ is a continuous function. We now ask for what functions ϕ this formula has the additive property of utilities when two entirely independent random variables are considered,

$$U(GG^* \mid H_\xi H_{\xi^*}) = U(G \mid H_\xi) + U(G^* \mid H_{\xi^*}), \tag{7}$$

that is,

$$\phi^{-1} \iint \{\phi(v(\xi, \mathbf{y}) + v^*(\xi^*, \boldsymbol{\eta}))\}\, dG(\mathbf{y})\, dG^*(\boldsymbol{\eta})$$

$$= \phi^{-1} \int \phi(v(\xi, \mathbf{y}))\, dG(\mathbf{y}) + \phi^{-1} \int \phi(v^*(\xi^*, \mathbf{y}))\, dG^*(\mathbf{y}). \tag{8}$$

[DeGroot (1962, p. 407) mentions that an additive property different from (7) is valid under much weaker conditions: In fact, it leads to no constraint on the utility function.]

Presumably all continuous solutions for ϕ are of the form $\phi(z) = e^{\alpha z}$, where α is real. Now we can nearly always assume that

$$v(\mathbf{x}, \mathbf{y}) \leq v(\mathbf{x}, \mathbf{x}) \tag{9}$$

so our integral will converge if $\alpha > 0$, but it will not converge for all G if $\alpha < 0$. We therefore define

$$U_\alpha(G \mid H_\xi) = \alpha^{-1} \log \int e^{\alpha v(\xi, \mathbf{y})}\, dG(\mathbf{y}) \qquad (\alpha > 0) \tag{10}$$

and this satisfies all our desiderata so far. Note that when α is very large, $U_\alpha(G \mid H_\xi)$ depends almost entirely on the density or jump of G at ξ, and also that

$$\lim_{\alpha \to +0} U_\alpha(G \mid H_\xi) = \int v(\xi, \mathbf{y})\, dG(\mathbf{y}) = U_0(G \mid H_\xi). \tag{11}$$

This "justifies" the notation U_0 when $F = H_\xi$.

An even more general formula with the additive property (7), when G has a density function g, is

$$U_{\alpha,\beta}(G \mid H_\xi) = \alpha^{-1} \log\left[\int e^{\alpha v(\xi, \mathbf{y})} \{g(\mathbf{y})\}^\beta\, d\mathbf{y} \Big/ \int \{g(\mathbf{y})\}^\beta\, d\mathbf{y}\right]. \tag{12}$$

But this formula is not invariant under transformations of $\mathbf{y}$ unless $\beta = 1$. A different generalization, given in the discussion at the end of the paper, might be useful for coping with the "retailer" problem mentioned above. We shall continue to assume that $\beta = 1$.

By means of the desideratum (1), we see that

$$U_\alpha(G \mid F) = \alpha^{-1} \int dF(\mathbf{x}) \log \int e^{\alpha v(\mathbf{x}, \mathbf{y})}\, dG(\mathbf{y}), \tag{13}$$

as proposed by Good (1960) without published supporting arguments. Note that $U_\alpha(G \mid F)$ is invariant under any nonsingular transformation of the independent variable, say $\mathbf{x} = \psi(\mathbf{x}')$, $\mathbf{y} = \psi(\mathbf{y}')$ since the distribution functions of $\mathbf{x}'$ and $\mathbf{y}'$ are $F(\psi(\mathbf{x}'))$ and $G(\psi(\mathbf{y}'))$, and the utility of asserting $\mathbf{y}'$ when $\mathbf{x}'$ is true must be $v(\psi(\mathbf{x}'), \psi(\mathbf{y}'))$. Likewise, the formula (6) is invariant under the transformation $\xi = \psi(\xi')$, $\mathbf{y} = \psi(\mathbf{y}')$.

Again

$$\lim_{\alpha \to +0} U_\alpha(G \mid F) = U_0(G \mid F), \tag{14}$$

and also $U_\alpha(G \mid F)$ is additive when two entirely independent random variables are considered,

$$U_\alpha(GG^* \mid FF^*) = U_\alpha(G \mid F) + U_\alpha(G^* \mid F^*) \tag{15}$$

Note that if we add a constant to $v(\mathbf{x}, \mathbf{y})$, we add the same constant to $U_\alpha(G \mid F)$. This could have been taken as a desideratum.

Since $v(\mathbf{x}, \mathbf{y}) \le v(\mathbf{x}, \mathbf{x})$, we have

$$U_\alpha(G \mid H_\xi) \le \alpha^{-1} \log \int e^{\alpha v(\xi, \xi)} dG(\mathbf{y}) = v(\xi, \xi) \tag{16}$$

as would be expected

2. INFINITE α

Next consider what happens to $U_\alpha(G \mid F)$ when α is very large. For simplicity we suppose, for the present, that the distributions are discrete, with F and G corresponding to two probability vectors $\mathbf{p} = (p_1, p_2, \ldots,)$ and $\mathbf{q} = (q_1, q_2, \ldots,)$. Strictly, the distributions would correspond to cumulative sums of the components of these vectors, but our nonrigorous notation is easy to understand. We also use the notation $U_\alpha(\mathbf{q} \mid \mathbf{p})$ in place of $U_\alpha(G \mid F)$, so that

$$U_\alpha(\mathbf{q} \mid \mathbf{p}) = \alpha^{-1} \sum_i p_i \log \sum_j q_j e^{\alpha v(i,j)}. \tag{17}$$

If $\mathbf{p}$ is fixed what vector $\mathbf{q}$ maximizes $U_\alpha(\mathbf{q} \mid \mathbf{p})$? Leaving aside for the present a proof that minus the Hessian matrix is positive definite, let us assume that Lagrange's method of undetermined multipliers is applicable. We obtain

$$\sum_i p_i \frac{e^{\alpha v(i,j)}}{\sum_k q_k e^{\alpha v(i,k)}} = c, \tag{18}$$

where c is independent of j. Let us now make the assumption that

$$v(i,j) \leq v(j,j) \tag{19}$$

which is not unreasonable although it is not as compelling as (9). Equation (19) follows from (9) when $v(i,j)$ is a symmetric function of i and j as it is, for example, when quadratic loss is assumed. It means that to "assert" a value for j is more useful when j is correct than when any other value of the random variable is correct. Then, for large α, the left side of (18) is approximately

$$\frac{p_j e^{\alpha v(j,j)}}{q_j e^{\alpha v(j,j)}} = \frac{p_j}{q_j},$$

so that $\mathbf{q} \simeq \mathbf{p}$ gives a stationary value of $U_\alpha(\mathbf{q} \mid \mathbf{p})$ when α is large. In order to prove that it is a maximum, we now consider minus the Hessian matrix of second derivatives,

$$-\frac{\partial^2 U_\alpha(\mathbf{q} \mid \mathbf{p})}{\partial q_j \, \partial q_{j'}} = \alpha^{-1} \sum_i p_i \frac{e^{\alpha[v(i,j)+v(i,j')]}}{[\sum_k q_k e^{\alpha v(i,k)}]^2}.$$

Since the sum of positive semidefinite matrices is itself positive semidefinite, it is now sufficient to prove that the matrix

$$\mathbf{M}_i = \left\{ \frac{p_i e^{\alpha[v(i,j)+v(i,j')]}}{[\sum_k q_k e^{\alpha v(i,k)}]^2} \right\}$$

is positive semidefinite, where j and j' index the rows and columns of $\mathbf{M}_i$. To prove this, let

$$p_i \left[\sum_k q_k e^{\alpha v(i,k)} \right]^{-2} = a, \qquad e^{\alpha v(i,j)} = b_j$$

where a and b_j depend also on i. Then $\mathbf{M}_i = a\{b_j b_{j'}\}$, so $\mathbf{M}_i$ is a matrix of rank 1 with one nonzero eigenvalue, namely $a \sum b_j^2$ and it is, therefore, positive semidefinite as required.

We have therefore proved, under assumption (19), that when α is very large, the optimal G for a given F is close to F itself when the distributions are discrete, that is, $U_\alpha(G \mid F)$ is maximized when $G \simeq F$. It is natural to conjecture with some confidence that the same is true for arbitrary distributions.

It is, in any case, of interest to consider the behavior of $U_\alpha(G \mid F)$ when F and G are continuous and n-dimensional, and α is large. We shall assume that G has a density function g which never vanishes, that $v(\mathbf{x}, \mathbf{x}) > v(\mathbf{x}, \mathbf{y})(\mathbf{x} \neq \mathbf{y})$, and that, for all $\mathbf{x}$,

$$\frac{\partial^2 v(\mathbf{x}, \mathbf{y})}{\partial y_j \, \partial y_k} \qquad (j, k = 1, 2, \ldots, n)$$

is continuous when $\mathbf{y}$ is in the neighborhood of $\mathbf{x}$. Then

$$\int e^{\alpha v(\mathbf{x}, \mathbf{y})} \, dG(\mathbf{y}) \simeq g(\mathbf{x})(2\pi/\alpha)^{n/2} |\Delta(\mathbf{x})|^{-1/2}$$

where

$$\Delta(\mathbf{x}) = \left\{ - \left. \frac{\partial^2 v(\mathbf{x}, \mathbf{y})}{\partial y_j \, \partial y_k} \right|_{\mathbf{y}=\mathbf{x}} \right\}$$

Thus, for large α,

$$U_\alpha(G \mid F) \simeq (n/2\alpha) \log(2\pi/\alpha) + (1/\alpha) \int \log\{g(\mathbf{x}) |\Delta(\mathbf{x})|^{-1/2}\} \, dF(\mathbf{x})$$

and, "up to a linear transformation,"

$$U_\infty(G \mid F) = \int \log\{g(\mathbf{x}) |\Delta(\mathbf{x})|^{-1/2}\} \, dF(\mathbf{x}) \tag{20}$$

which is an "invariantized" cross negentropy (see the discussion of terminology later in this paper). A direct proof of invariance can be given, but it is simpler to infer it from the invariance of U_α for each α. If F has a density function f, then U_∞ is maximized when $g = f$ and is

$$U_\infty(F \mid F) = \int f(\mathbf{x}) \log\{f(\mathbf{x}) |\Delta(\mathbf{x})|^{-1/2}\} \, d\mathbf{x}, \tag{21}$$

an invariantized negentropy. If we can define an artificial initial density $f_0(\mathbf{x})$ proportional to $|\Delta(\mathbf{x})|^{1/2}$, then, apart from a constant, Eq. (20) is a "trientropy," and Eq. (21) a "dientropy."

A recommendation that follows from the use of the utility function $U_\infty(F \mid F)$ is that an experiment of a given expected cost should be designed so as to maximize the expected weight of evidence per observation when discriminating between the final distribution and the artificial distribution of density $f_0(\mathbf{x})$.

On the other hand, the increase of utility in changing from the assertion of G to that of F, when F is true, and when $\alpha = \infty$, is given by the difference of (21) and (20) and is

$$U_\infty(F \mid F) - U_\infty(G \mid F) = \int f(\mathbf{x}) \log\{f(\mathbf{x})/g(\mathbf{x})\}\, d\mathbf{x} \tag{22}$$

in which $\boldsymbol{\Delta}(\mathbf{x})$ has dropped out of the formula. This again is a "dientropy" or "expected weight of evidence." This is nonnegative (Good, 1950a, p. 72), so that in terms of the utility measure U_∞, it is best to assert the truth.

3. APPLICATION TO THE DISTRIBUTION OF PARAMETERS

Let us now apply our theory, with $\alpha = \infty$, to the problem of estimating a parameter; more precisely to that of determining the distribution of a parameter $\mathbf{x}$ in a distribution law $T(\mathbf{z} \mid \mathbf{x})$ of *another* random variable $\mathbf{z}$, where we shall assume that T has a density t. The dimensionalities of $\mathbf{x}$ and $\mathbf{z}$, are, of course, not usually equal. To assert a *value* for $\mathbf{x}$ is to assert a *distribution* for $\mathbf{z}$ so that we can obtain a formula for $v(\mathbf{x}, \mathbf{y})$ from Eq. (20) by replacing $\mathbf{x}$ in that equation by $\mathbf{z}$, $dF(\mathbf{x})$ by $t(\mathbf{z} \mid \mathbf{x})\, d\mathbf{z}$, and $g(x)$ by $t(\mathbf{z} \mid \mathbf{y})$. From this formula for $v(\mathbf{x}, \mathbf{y})$, we obtain at once a formula for $v(\mathbf{x}, \mathbf{x}) - v(\mathbf{x}, \mathbf{y})$ in which $\boldsymbol{\Delta}(\mathbf{z})$ drops out:

$$v(\mathbf{x}, \mathbf{x}) - v(\mathbf{x}, \mathbf{y}) = \int t(\mathbf{z} \mid \mathbf{x}) \log \frac{t(\mathbf{z} \mid \mathbf{x})}{t(\mathbf{z} \mid \mathbf{y})}\, d\mathbf{z}. \tag{23}$$

This difference between values of v is all that is required for the calculation of $\boldsymbol{\Delta}(\mathbf{x})$. [This matrix should not be confused with $\boldsymbol{\Delta}(\mathbf{z})$: It will often not even be of the same order, and it will often exist when $\boldsymbol{\Delta}(\mathbf{z})$ does not. Similarly, of course, $v(\mathbf{x}, \mathbf{y})$ now refers to the parameters, not to $\mathbf{z}$. We have temporarily overburdened the notations v and $\boldsymbol{\Delta}$, but because of this warning, little confusion should arise.] We infer that, irrespective of what the v function for $\mathbf{z}$ happens to be (provided that it satisfies some weak conditions), $\boldsymbol{\Delta}(\mathbf{x})$ *is the Hessian matrix with respect to* $\mathbf{y}$, *at* $\mathbf{x}$, *of the cross entropy*

$$-\int t(\mathbf{z} \mid \mathbf{x}) \log t(\mathbf{z} \mid \mathbf{y})\, d\mathbf{z}.$$

Therefore, if the order of the integrations and differentiations can be inverted, $\boldsymbol{\Delta}(\mathbf{x})$ *is Fisher's information matrix*,

$$\boldsymbol{\Delta}(\mathbf{x}) = \left\{ -\int t(\mathbf{z} \mid \mathbf{x}) \frac{\partial^2 \log t(\mathbf{z} \mid \mathbf{x})}{\partial x_j\, \partial x_k}\, d\mathbf{z} \right\}, \qquad j, k = 1, 2, \ldots. \tag{23a}$$

The utilities of making assertions concerning the distributions of the parameters can now be written down by means of formulas (23a) and (20) or (21). The expected utilities of experiments could then be derived along Bayesian lines.

4. MINIMAX UTILITY AND INVARIANT INITIAL DISTRIBUTIONS

Without philosophical commitment, let us consider the minimax procedure applied to $U_\infty(G \mid F)$ where G and F might be constrained to belong to some specified class of distributions: We shall suppose at least that they have density functions. We maximize $U_\infty(G \mid F)$, for fixed F, by taking $G = F$ (since $\alpha = \infty$), and then we minimize $U_\infty(F \mid F)$. Thus the minimax distribution is the *least favorable initial distribution* in the sense that it minimizes $U_\infty(F \mid F)$. A minimax solution is also the least favorable distribution in Wald's theory (Wald, 1950, p. 91), although I have not checked whether all his assumptions are applicable here. (The theorem would not, I think, be applicable if α were finite.) The choice of F to minimize a functional $U(F \mid F)$ will be called the *principle of least utility* whatever constraints are put on F. For differentiable F this "principle" is seen from (21) to imply a *principle of maximum invariantized entropy*.

If $\mathbf{x}$ undergoes a nonsingular transformation, $\mathbf{x} = \boldsymbol{\psi}(\mathbf{x}')$, then the least favorable initial distribution, if unique, must be invariant in the sense that it will transform into the least favorable initial distribution in the new coordinate system. Of course, $v(\mathbf{x}, \mathbf{y})$ must transform to $v(\psi(\mathbf{x}'), \psi(\mathbf{y}'))$ for consistency.

The constraints on F should be those implied by our model, assumptions, or state of knowledge. In particular, if we have already assumed an initial distribution, it is trivially the least favorable one.

If the only contraint on F is that it has a density function, then the minimax theory applied to U_∞ gives the initial density f_0 proportional to $|\boldsymbol{\Delta}(\mathbf{x})|^{1/2}$. In particular, if we apply the minimax method to the distribution of a parameter $\mathbf{x}$ in a distribution $T(\mathbf{z} \mid \mathbf{x})$, then the initial distribution of "least utility" has density proportional to the square root of the determinant of Fisher's information matrix (23a). The invariance of this distribution follows at once from the above discussion: This invariance was first proved by Jeffreys (1946) by an entirely different method. The univariate case of Jeffreys's theory was given independently by Perks (1947).

We thus see that the Jeffreys-Perks invariant distributions can be derived from the minimax procedure when utilities are measured by the functional U_∞. This functional is used twice in the derivation: first for $\mathbf{z}$ to obtain $v(\mathbf{x}, \mathbf{y})$, and then for $\mathbf{x}$. We could obtain a two-parameter family of invariant initial distributions by using U_α with two values for α; or even a four-parameter family by allowing for γ, as introduced at the end of this paper. When α is finite, the principle of least utility would presumably not agree with the minimax method.

A logical objection to the Jeffrey-Perks invariance theory, pointed out by Savage (1955), is that the initial distribution of $\mathbf{x}$ ought not to depend on the application that the statistician has in mind. Thus, if $\mathbf{x}$ could appear as a parameter in two different distributions, which would be possible if $\mathbf{x}$ has a physical interpretation, then the invariance theory would lead to a contradiction. We now see that this objection is a special case of the objection to minimax methods, in general, when they are used for the selection of initial distributions: The least favorable initial distribution can change when our objectives change. This is a more serious objection within those Bayesian theories for which subjective probabilities are supposed to be "sharp" than in those in which they are only partially ordered.

Of course, most of our work does not depend on the minimax interpretation since, for example, formulas (21) and (23a) can be used without introducing f_0.

5. FINITE α

If it is desired to have a procedure that depends on values of $v(\mathbf{x}, \mathbf{y})$ where $\mathbf{x}$ and $\mathbf{y}$ are not close together, then it is necessary to use a finite value of α (when G has a density function) although the optimal G will then not necessarily be the true distribution.

It could be argued that any sensible utility function $U(G \mid F)$ should be maximized by taking $G = F$ when F is fixed. But this is true only if the asserted distribution is used optimally. It may be noted, too, that in some search problems other distributions can be as good as the correct one since probabilities below a certain level can be entirely ignored (Koopman, 1957). (For ordinary betting purposes, however, we must never equate a positive probability to zero and in this case $v(\mathbf{x}, \mathbf{y}) \simeq -\infty$ when $\mathbf{y} \neq \mathbf{x}$.) If allowance is made for the cost of calculation and other thought processes, the correct distribution is not necessarily even "best equal." This can be appreciated by means of an example: In a communication system, square pulses usually degenerate in shape and it is often profitable to regenerate them or "square them up" from time to time. In other words, it is often profitable to throw information away in order to economize in later information processing. A similar phenomenon occurs whenever a statistician makes use of "insufficient" statistics in order to obtain the advantage of reduction of the data, and whenever "over"-simplifications are made when teaching. The author has argued (Good, 1962) that it is necessary to distinguish between rationality of Type I, for which the cost of theorizing is ignored, and that of Type II, where the cost is allowed for; and he believes that this second type of rationality is by far the more important of the two, and that the distinction leads to a resolution of most statistical controversy at a philosophical level. The fact that the cost of thought cannot be ignored is especially clear in a game such as chess in which it is usually virtually impossible to carry out an exhaustive analysis [compare Good (1968a)]. It might also be true in other dendroidal (tree-type) searches such as chemical analysis, information retrieval, and especially in the search for the proof of a mathematical theorem. In short, the assertion of an incorrect probability distribution might be better than that of a correct one when the expense of exhaustive dynamic planning is too great. Again, suppose that a univariate distribution is known to be contained in the interval $(\mu - c, \mu + c)$, and suppose that (i) a terminal decision is to be based on values of x near the mode, (ii) it is important not to make errors greater than c, (iii) the client is known to pay more attention to probabilities than to utilities. Then it will be wise for the statistician to push the true distribution towards μ whether or not the client is intending to gather further information. More generally, if the interpretation that is to be made for a probability distribution is to pay more attention to values of $\mathbf{x}$ where the probability density is the greater, then it might be wise for the statistician to make some allowance for his understanding of the utilities when he asserts the distribution. This has usually been the implicit attitude of those who have provided confidence regions, even when they were not quite conscious of it; for otherwise there would have been no rationale for trying to supply small confidence regions rather than large ones, having an assigned confidence coefficient.

Our example of the stocking of goods again exemplifies the point: If the statistician knows that the stock will be naively geared to the asserted distribution, he will serve his client's interests by giving greater weight to the higher densities or, for unimodal distributions, heaping the distribution toward its mode. The extent to which this should be done depends on circumstances which are often extremely complicated so that it will usually be necessary to make an informed guess.

On the other hand under rationality of Type I, it is best to assert the correct distribution and so, apparently, to let $\alpha \to \infty$.

6. MULTINORMAL EXAMPLE

Let us now consider a multivariate normal example, with F and G corresponding to density functions f and g given by

$$f(\mathbf{x}) = [(2\pi)^{n/2}|\mathbf{A}|^{1/2}]^{-1} \exp\{-\tfrac{1}{2}(\mathbf{x} - \boldsymbol{\mu})'\mathbf{A}^{-1}(\mathbf{x} - \boldsymbol{\mu})\} \tag{24}$$

$$g(\mathbf{y}) = [(2\pi)^{n/2}|\mathbf{B}|^{1/2}]^{-1} \exp\{-\tfrac{1}{2}(\mathbf{y} - \boldsymbol{\nu})'\mathbf{B}^{-1}(\mathbf{y} - \boldsymbol{\nu})\} \tag{25}$$

and that the utility is quadratic, that is,

$$v(\mathbf{x}, \mathbf{y}) = -\tfrac{1}{2}(\mathbf{x}-\mathbf{y})'\mathbf{D}^{-1}(\mathbf{x}-\mathbf{y}), \tag{26}$$

where $\mathbf{D}$ is positive definite. It should be noted that the assumption of a constant quadratic loss function in the neighborhood of each point $\mathbf{x}$ is not invariant under a transformation $\mathbf{x} = \boldsymbol{\psi}(\mathbf{x}')$, $\mathbf{y} = \boldsymbol{\psi}(\mathbf{y}')$. Hence, this assumption suffers from the same kind of familiar disadvantage as the "Bayes postulate" for initial probability distributions. A quadratic loss function in the immediate neighborhood of each $\mathbf{x}$, depending on $\mathbf{x}$, that is, for which $\mathbf{D}$ is replaced by $\mathbf{D}(\mathbf{x})$, a positive definite matrix function of $\mathbf{x}$, would be very reasonable for most continuous models. (It is the inverse of $\boldsymbol{\Delta}(\mathbf{x})$, as defined before.) The *property* of having a local quadratic loss, varying from one locality to another, is invariant under transformations in which $\boldsymbol{\psi}$ has continuous second derivatives. But the familiar assumption of a constant $\mathbf{D}$ will serve as an example. Then

$$\int g(\mathbf{y})e^{\alpha v(\mathbf{x},\mathbf{y})}\,d\mathbf{y} = (2\pi)^{n/2}\,|\alpha^{-1}\mathbf{D}|^{1/2}$$

times the density at $\mathbf{x}$ of the sum of two random vectors whose means are $\mathbf{v}$ and $\mathbf{0}$ and whose covariance matrices are $\mathbf{B}$ and $\alpha^{-1}\mathbf{D}$,

$$= \frac{|\alpha^{-1}\mathbf{D}|^{1/2}}{|\mathbf{B}+\alpha^{-1}\mathbf{D}|^{1/2}}\exp\{-\tfrac{1}{2}(\mathbf{x}-\mathbf{v})'(\mathbf{B}+\alpha^{-1}\mathbf{D})^{-1}(\mathbf{x}-\mathbf{v})\}.$$

Therefore, we have (writing N for "normal distribution")

$$U_\alpha(N(\mathbf{v},\mathbf{B})\,|\,H_{\mathbf{x}}) = -\frac{1}{2\alpha}\log|\mathbf{I}+\alpha\mathbf{B}\mathbf{D}^{-1}| - \frac{1}{2\alpha}(\mathbf{x}-\mathbf{v})'\left(\mathbf{B}+\frac{1}{\alpha}\mathbf{D}\right)^{-1}(\mathbf{x}-\mathbf{v}) \tag{27}$$

and

$$U_\alpha(N(\mathbf{v},\mathbf{B})\,|\,N(\boldsymbol{\mu},\mathbf{A})) = -\frac{1}{2\alpha}\log|\mathbf{I}+\alpha\mathbf{B}\mathbf{D}^{-1}| - \frac{1}{2\alpha}\operatorname{tr}\{\mathbf{A}(\mathbf{B}+\alpha^{-1}\mathbf{D})^{-1}\}$$
$$-\frac{1}{2\alpha}(\boldsymbol{\mu}-\mathbf{v})'(\mathbf{B}+\alpha^{-1}\mathbf{D})^{-1}(\boldsymbol{\mu}-\mathbf{v}). \tag{28}$$

(See also the comments concerning Eqs. (46) and (47).) If $\boldsymbol{\mu}$ and $\mathbf{A}$ are fixed, the optimal value of $\mathbf{v}$ is $\boldsymbol{\mu}$, but the optimal $\mathbf{B}$ is not necessarily equal to $\mathbf{A}$. It must be approximately $\mathbf{A}$ if $\alpha^{-1}\mathbf{D}$ is small, that is, if α is large or if e^v is closely proportional to a multivariate Dirac function. When $\alpha = 0$, the optimal value of $\mathbf{B}$ is $\mathbf{0}$ since $U_0 = -\frac{1}{2}\operatorname{tr}(\mathbf{A}\mathbf{D}^{-1}) - \frac{1}{2}\operatorname{tr}(\mathbf{B}\mathbf{D}^{-1})$ when $\boldsymbol{\mu} = \mathbf{v}$.

Some special cases are:

$$U_0(N(\mathbf{v}, \mathbf{B}) \mid N(\boldsymbol{\mu}, \mathbf{A})) = -\tfrac{1}{2}\{\mathrm{tr}((\mathbf{A}+\mathbf{B})\mathbf{D}^{-1}) + (\boldsymbol{\mu}-\mathbf{v})'\mathbf{D}^{-1}(\boldsymbol{\mu}-\mathbf{v})\} \tag{29}$$

$$U_\infty(N(\mathbf{v}, \mathbf{B}) \mid N(\boldsymbol{\mu}, \mathbf{A})) = \log|\mathbf{D}\mathbf{B}^{-1}| - \mathrm{tr}(\mathbf{A}\mathbf{B}^{-1}) - (\boldsymbol{\mu}-\mathbf{v})'\mathbf{B}^{-1}(\boldsymbol{\mu}-\mathbf{v}) \tag{30}$$

apart from a linear transformation (this agrees with (21)):

$$U_\alpha(N(\boldsymbol{\mu}, \mathbf{A}) \mid N(\boldsymbol{\mu}, \mathbf{A})) = -\frac{1}{2\alpha}\log|\mathbf{I} + \alpha\mathbf{A}\mathbf{D}^{-1}| - \frac{1}{2\alpha}\mathrm{tr}(\mathbf{I} + \alpha^{-1}\mathbf{D}\mathbf{A}^{-1})^{-1} \tag{31}$$

and

$$U_0(N(\boldsymbol{\mu}, \mathbf{A}) \mid N(\boldsymbol{\mu}, \mathbf{A})) = -\mathrm{tr}(\mathbf{A}\mathbf{D}^{-1}). \tag{32}$$

In the univariate case, if $v(x, y) = -\lambda(x-y)^2$, we have

$$U_\alpha\{N(\nu, \tau^2) \mid N(\mu, \sigma^2)\}$$

$$= -\frac{1}{2\alpha}\left\{\log(1 + 2\alpha\lambda\tau^2) + [\sigma^2 + (\mu-\nu)^2]\left(\tau^2 + \frac{1}{2\alpha\lambda}\right)^{-1}\right\} \tag{33}$$

$$U_0\{N(\nu, \tau^2) \mid N(\mu, \sigma^2)\} = -(\tau^2 + \sigma^2 + (\mu-\nu)^2)/4\lambda \tag{34}$$

$$U_\infty\{N(\nu, \tau^2) \mid N(\mu, \sigma^2)\} = -(\sigma^2 + (\mu-\nu)^2)/(\tau^2) - \log(\lambda\tau^2) \tag{35}$$

apart from a linear transformation.

For the univariate case (33) confirms that the optimal value of μ is ν, as we would expect, but the optimal value of τ is not σ, when quadratic loss is assumed, except when $\alpha = \infty$. In fact the optimal value of τ, after taking $\mu = \nu$, is

$$\begin{cases} (\sigma^2 - 1/2\alpha\lambda)^{1/2} & (\sigma^2 > 1/2\alpha\lambda) \\ 0 & (\sigma^2 < 1/2\alpha\lambda) \end{cases} \tag{36}$$

and, in particular, if $\alpha = 0$ the optimal value of τ is always 0. If λ is large, then $\tau = \sigma$ is nearly optimal. This confirms what we said for the multivariate case when $\alpha^{-1}\mathbf{D}$ is small.

When F is $N(\mu, \sigma^2)$ the optimal G is not necessarily normal, and it would be interesting to know what it is.

Light can be shed on the value of α appropriate to any given situation by the following argument. It will be convenient to consider the discrete case. Let the asserted probabilities of various hypotheses be $q_1, q_2, \ldots$, and denote the utility of this assertion by $U_\alpha(\mathbf{q} \mid i)$, when the ith hypothesis is true. We have

$$U_\alpha(\mathbf{q} \mid i) = \alpha^{-1}\log\sum_j q_j e^{\alpha v(i,j)}. \tag{37}$$

Suppose that $v(i, i) = a$, $v(i, j) = b\,(i \neq j)$. This corresponds to a situation where all incorrect predictions are equally bad. Then

$$U_\alpha(\mathbf{q} \mid i) = a + \alpha^{-1}\log\{q_i + (1-q_i)e^{-\alpha(a-b)}\}. \tag{38}$$

If $\alpha(a - b)$ is at all large, this is approximately $a + \alpha^{-1} \log q_i$, and, since linear transformations of utilities are irrelevant, this is equivalent to $\log q_i$. Thus, taking $\alpha(a - b)$ large is equivalent to treating information, in the sense of communication theory, as a utility. This can be achieved by making $a - b$ large irrespective of the value of α, provided that $\alpha \neq 0$. When $\alpha = 0$, we have $U_0(\mathbf{q} \mid i) = q_i a + (1 - q_i)b$ which, as we said before, is often an unreasonable utility function.

If the value of asserting that the probability of i is q_i is assumed to be some other function of q_i, then we can select α to make $\log[q_i + (1 - q_i) e^{-\alpha(a-b)}]$ as close a fit to a multiple of this function as we can.

Similarly, for the multinormal model, we can try to choose α to satisfy our judgments of the utility losses (or rather inequalities between them) in a few imagined circumstances. *If we are totally unable to do this, then it is not easy to see why we should be interested in obtaining a probability distribution at all.*

7. ENTROPY, DIENTROPY, AND TRIENTROPY

We return now to the consideration of the discrete model with large α. Under the weak condition

$$v(i, i) > v(i, j) \qquad (i \neq j) \tag{39}$$

we have

$$U_\alpha(\mathbf{q} \mid i) \simeq \alpha^{-1} \log q_i e^{-\alpha v(i,i)} = v(i, i) + \alpha^{-1} \log q_i. \tag{40}$$

We have no "control" over the first term, $v(i, i)$, by our assertion of $\mathbf{q}$, and the "regret" or "loss" is $-\alpha^{-1} \log q_i$ [see Savage (1954), p. 163]. This can be interpreted as the "cost of locating i" when its asserted probability is q_i. Similarly,

$$U_\alpha(\mathbf{q}|\mathbf{p}) \simeq \sum p_i v(i,i) + \alpha^{-1} \sum p_i \log q_i \tag{41}$$

and the corresponding (expected) regret is approximately proportional to

$$-\sum p_i \log q_i \tag{42}$$

which agrees with the measure of "inaccuracy" of the assertion of $\mathbf{q}$ when $\mathbf{p}$ is true given by Kerridge (1961) [see also Good (1952, 1954)]. In the terminology of Good (1950b), it is minus the crossentropy of $\mathbf{p}$ and $\mathbf{q}$. If $\mathbf{p}$ is true (and fixed), then the distribution to assert, of least expected regret, and of maximum expected utility (for large α) is $\mathbf{p}$ itself.

When we assert $\mathbf{q} = \mathbf{p}$, our expected utility is

$$U_\alpha(\mathbf{p} \mid \mathbf{p}) \simeq \sum p_i v(i, i) + \alpha^{-1} \sum p_i \log p_i. \tag{43}$$

If we were playing an intelligent and antagonistic opponent who could select $\mathbf{p}$, he would choose it so that this expected utility is minimized. In the special case in which $v(i, i)$ is mathematically independent of i, this comes to the same thing as maximizing our expected regret. This shows how the principle of maximum entropy for the selection of initial distributions (Jaynes, 1957) can be regarded as an example of the minimax procedure. Note that for continuous models the constancy of $v(i, i)$ is replaced by that of $|\boldsymbol{\Delta}(\mathbf{x})|$ [see Eq. (21)], and the minimization of (43) corresponds to the maximization of *invariantized* entropy. Criticisms of the minimax procedure are less relevant when the suggested initial distributions are interpreted only as hypotheses as by Good (1963).

The value or utility of moving from one asserted "distribution" π to another one $\mathbf{q}$ is (writing $V(\mathbf{q} \mid \mathbf{p})$ for the cross-entropy of $\mathbf{p}$ and $\mathbf{q}$)

$$V(\boldsymbol{\pi} \quad \text{to} \quad \mathbf{q} \mid \mathbf{p}) = V(\mathbf{q} \mid \mathbf{p}) - V(\boldsymbol{\pi} \mid \mathbf{p}) = \sum p_i \log(q_i/\pi_i). \tag{44}$$

Assuming this formula, the optimal asserted distribution $\mathbf{q}$ is $\mathbf{p}$ and

$$V(\boldsymbol{\pi} \quad \text{to} \quad \mathbf{p} \mid \mathbf{p}) = V(\mathbf{p} \mid \mathbf{p}) - V(\boldsymbol{\pi} \mid \mathbf{p}) = \sum p_i \log(p_i/\pi_i) \tag{45}$$

which could be called "minus the dientropy" or the "dinegentropy," or expected weight of evidence per observation when discriminating between two multinomial distributions.

Suppose that $\boldsymbol{\pi}$ is a distribution assumed in the course of an argument but that later we wish to modify this distribution in order to take some constraints into account, then (22) and (45) show that the principle of least utility implies the principle of minimum discriminability (Kullback, 1959) when $\alpha = \infty$.

The sum in (44) could be called a "trientropy." The generalization of entropy and cross-entropy to continuous distributions is artificial but that of dientropy and trientropy is obvious and natural. Dientropy seems to be a more natural and useful concept than ("uninvariantized") entropy in all applications including the coding theorems of information theory (Good and Toulmin, 1968), statistical mechanics where its relevance was conjectured by Good (1950b) and established by Koopman (1968), and probability estimation (Good, 1966, 1969; Ireland and Kullback, 1968).

The dientropy in proceeding from an incorrect multigaussian hypothesis to a correct one is given by

$$V(N(\nu, \mathbf{B}) \quad \text{to} \quad N(\boldsymbol{\mu}, \mathbf{A}) \mid N(\boldsymbol{\mu}, \mathbf{A})) = \int f(\mathbf{x}) \log \frac{f(\mathbf{x})}{g(\mathbf{x})}\, d\mathbf{x}$$

$$= \tfrac{1}{2} \operatorname{tr}(\mathbf{AB}^{-1}) - \tfrac{1}{2} n - \tfrac{1}{2} \log |\mathbf{AB}^{-1}| + \tfrac{1}{2}(\boldsymbol{\mu} - \boldsymbol{\nu})' \mathbf{B}^{-1}(\boldsymbol{\mu} - \boldsymbol{\nu}). \tag{46}$$

[As a check this can be shown directly to be nonnegative. Note first, as Dr. D. R. Jensen kindly commented, that $\mathbf{AB}^{-1}$ may be replaced by $\mathbf{B}^{-1/2}\mathbf{AB}^{-1/2}$ without effect, and that this matrix is nonnegative definite. The rest of the proof is straightforward in terms of eigenvalues.] Of course, the so-called incorrect hypothesis might be correct on previous evidence and the formula then measures the gain in dientropy from the new evidence. In particular, the formula suggests the relative importance of getting the mean right as compared with the covariance matrix. In the design of experiments, the merit of a particular design can be measured by the expected value of the above expression when information or evidence is regarded as the only utility [compare Good (1950a, p. 75; 1956a; 1960), Cronbach (1953), Lindley (1956), Mallows (1959)].

If instead we use the utility measure U_α, we have, by (28),

$$\begin{aligned} &U_\alpha(N(\mathbf{v}, \mathbf{B}) \quad \text{to} \quad N(\boldsymbol{\mu}, \mathbf{A}) \mid N(\boldsymbol{\mu}, \mathbf{A})) \\ &\quad = U_\alpha(N(\boldsymbol{\mu}, \mathbf{A}) \mid N(\boldsymbol{\mu}, \mathbf{A})) - U_\alpha(N(\mathbf{v}, \mathbf{B}) \mid N(\boldsymbol{\mu}, \mathbf{A})) \\ &\quad = (1/2\alpha)\Big\{\mathrm{tr}[\mathbf{A}(\mathbf{B} + \alpha^{-1}\mathbf{D})^{-1} - (\mathbf{I} + \alpha^{-1}\mathbf{D}\mathbf{A}^{-1})^{-1}] \\ &\qquad + \log \frac{|\mathbf{D} + \alpha\mathbf{B}|}{|\mathbf{D} + \alpha\mathbf{A}|} + (\boldsymbol{\mu} - \mathbf{v})'(\mathbf{B} + \alpha^{-1}\mathbf{D})^{-1}(\boldsymbol{\mu} - \mathbf{v})\Big\}. \end{aligned} \tag{47}$$

If all the elements of the matrix **D** are very small this expression tends to α^{-1} times the right side of (46). Thus, for this problem, if e^v is proportional to a Dirac function, the maximization of the expectation of (47) comes to the same as that of dientropy or expected weight of evidence, irrespective of the value of α. The same is true when $\alpha \to \infty$ whatever **D** may be.

There is some analogy of formula (10) with the generalized surprise index (Good, 1954, 1956b) where the expression

$$\alpha^{-1} \log \sum p_i^{\alpha+1} \tag{48}$$

occurs as a generalization of negentropy, and with the further extension by Rényi (1961) where

$$\alpha^{-1} \log \sum_i q_i^{\alpha+1}/p_i^{\alpha} \tag{49}$$

occurs as a generalization of dinegentropy. But the analogy arises only because of the additivity for entirely independent circumstances and these expressions cannot be examples or limiting cases of U_α.

8. DISCUSSION AND GENERALIZATION

When we are not dealing with search problems, the above work is open to the following logical objection: (i) It might be intended to make optimal use, in the sense of Type I rationality, of the asserted distribution G, in which case the best G to assert is the true one F; (ii) At the same time, values of $v(\mathbf{x}, \mathbf{y})$ might be relevant where $\mathbf{y}$ is not close to $\mathbf{x}$. Condition (i) seems to imply that α is infinite, whereas condition (ii) implies that it is finite when G is absolutely continuous (and g therefore exists). This objection applies also to much of the previous relevant literature, which is a special case of our work with infinite α. In addition, it applies to Fisherian information [which incidentally is not invariant: Mallows agrees he made a slip on this point (see Mallows (1959), p. 68, footnote added in proof). It can be regarded as an absolute covariant tensor or rank 2, as follows from Jeffreys (1946). Schützenberger (1954, p. 53), also makes a slip when he says that the information matrix is multiplied by the Hessian of the transformation].

For search problems this objection does not apply: For such problems it is only natural that $U(G \mid F)$ should not depend on the values of $v(\mathbf{x}, \mathbf{y})$ when $\mathbf{y}$ is far from $\mathbf{x}$ since a clear miss is as bad as a nautical mile. Before discussing the objection further, we consider a generalization of Desideratum (1).

Desideratum (1) is unclear for applications other than search problems, and is certainly wrong for the "retailer" and similar problems, such as the problem of mass production of shoes, when G is *interpreted* as providing the proportions of the various sizes of shoes that should be stocked or produced. It is therefore natural to consider a generalization of (1) along the same lines as that made for (5). Then (1) would be replaced by

$$U^{\gamma}(G \mid F) = \gamma^{-1} \log \int e^{\gamma U(G \mid H_{\xi})}\, dF(\xi) \qquad (\gamma > 0) \tag{50}$$

and (13) would be replaced by

$$U_{\alpha}^{\gamma}(G \mid F) = \gamma^{-1} \log \int dF(\mathbf{x}) \left[\int e^{\alpha v(\mathbf{x}, \mathbf{y})}\, dG(\mathbf{y}) \right]^{\gamma/\alpha}. \tag{51}$$

This is invariant under all transformations of the form $\mathbf{x} = \psi(\mathbf{x}')$, $\mathbf{y} = \psi(\mathbf{y}')$, and it has the properties defined by Eqs. (15) and (16) and by the remark following Eq. (15). Further connections with U_{α} are given by the following two limiting relationships:

$$\lim_{\gamma \to 0} U_{\alpha}^{\gamma}(G \mid F) = U_{\alpha}(G \mid F). \tag{52}$$

Again, up to a linear transformation, if G has a density function g, $U_{\infty}^{\gamma}(G \mid F)$ is mathematically independent of γ and is the same as $U_{\infty}(G \mid F)$, as in Eq. (20). Thus, for "continuous" search problems, for which it is appropriate to take $\alpha = \infty$, we do not lose uniqueness by our generalization of Desideratum (1), which was compelling anyway for such problems. But for other applications we are at present saddled with the flexibility of two parameters α and γ: Flexibility is always double-edged. (For the discrete model, U_{∞}^{γ} can be seen to be mathematically independent of γ only when $v(i, i)$ is independent of i.)

The term U_α^γ could be explicitly calculated for the multinormal model with quadratic loss defined by equations (24), (25), and (26). For the univariate normal model discussed previously, I find that the optimal (ν, τ), for given (μ, σ), is $\nu = \mu$ and

$$\tau^2 = \max\{0, \sigma^2(1 - \gamma/\alpha) - (1/2\alpha\lambda)\} \tag{53}$$

which generalizes (36).

Thus, even when (1) is generalized to (50), and when the utility of asserting G is assumed to depend on values of $v(\mathbf{x}, \mathbf{y})$ where $\mathbf{y}$ is not close to $\mathbf{x}$ (in which case α must be finite), our assumptions lead to the conclusion that the "truth" $(G = F)$ is not necessarily nearly optimal unless $v(\mathbf{x}, \mathbf{y}) \simeq -\infty$ when $\mathbf{y}$ is not close to $\mathbf{x}$. (Perhaps it is sufficient to interpret $v \simeq -\infty$ to mean that v is negative and not absolutely small.) This result is not as paradoxical as it seems. For let us consider the special case in which a variable is said to have the value $\mathbf{y}$ when its correct value is $\mathbf{x}$, and suppose that this assertion is accepted as precisely true and is to be used in accordance with the principle of rationality, where the possible uses of the assertion are left open. One of the permitted acts will then be to place a bet, at arbitrarily large odds, that the value is $\mathbf{y}$. The expected utility of the assertion will therefore be very large and negative. Therefore, when the uses of the assertion are unspecified, we must assume that $v(\mathbf{x}, \mathbf{y}) \simeq -\infty$ when $\mathbf{y}$ is not close to $\mathbf{x}$. In practice if a point estimate $\mathbf{y}$ is made, it is *not* usually assumed to be precisely true; in other words, it is not interpreted as a Dirac distribution: This is why the assumption of a "finite" loss function is often reasonable.

In conclusion, we can categorize the possible applications of our work into four categories, depending on the use that is to be made of the assertion of G:

(i) *when the use is to be optimal but the nature of the use is unspecified; and*

(ii) *when G is to be used for a search.* Then $v(\mathbf{x}, \mathbf{y}) \simeq -\infty$ when $\mathbf{y}$ is not close to $\mathbf{x}$ and we can apply our work with $\alpha = \infty$ or large. For search problems we should take $\gamma = 0$.

(iii) *When the use is to be optimal and the nature of the use is specified.* Then our Desiderata (1) and (50) might well be invalid, but this will not matter since the problem is to be treated on its own merits.

(iv) *When the use is to be nonoptimal* (for example, when G is interpreted "naively" in the problem of stocking or producing shoes). In this case, there is no paradox in the fact that the optimal G is not F. Here it seems reasonable to take α finite and to judge the values of α and γ by the method suggested for judging α before γ was introduced. The condition for the applicability of our methods, both here and under (iii) is that α and γ can be found to match our judgments concerning several real or imaginary pairs (F, G). (There seem to be psychological reasons for forgetting to allow for imaginary situations in the making of judgments. They are often more important, because of their inexhaustible supply, than the real situations.)

When G arises by misinterpreting a confidence region we should usually be in category (iv), since G will then probably be misinterpreted in its turn!

REFERENCES

BARTLETT, M. S. (1950). The statistical approach to the analysis of time series. *Symp. Information Theory, London, 1950*, pp. 81–101. Ministry of Supply, London [reprinted in *IRE Trans. Information Theory* **PGIT–1** (1953)].

BELLMAN, R. E. (1956). A problem in the sequential design of experiments. *Sankhyā* **16** 221–229.

CRONBACH, L. J. (1953). A consideration of information theory and utility theory as tools for psychometric problems. Tech. Rept. No. 1, Contract N6ori–07146. College of Education, Univ. of Illinois, Urbana, Illinois [mentioned by Lindley (1956)].

DEGROOT, M. H. (1962). Uncertainty, information, and sequential experiments. *Ann. Math. Statist.* **33** 404–419.

FISHER, R. A. (1925). Theory of statistical estimation. *Proc. Cambridge Philos. Soc.* **22** 700–725 [reprinted in "Contributions to Mathematical Statistics," Paper no. 11. Wiley, New York].

GOOD, I. J. (1950a). "Probability and the Weighing of Evidence." Griffin, London and Hafner Publ., New York.

GOOD, I. J. (1950b). Contribution to the discussion of a paper by M. S. Bartlett. *Symp. Information Theory, London, 1950*, pp. 180–181. Ministry of Supply, London [reprinted in *IRE Trans. Information Theory* **PGIT–1**, (1953)].

GOOD, I. J. (1952). Rational decisions. *J. Roy. Statist. Soc. Ser. B* **14** 107–114.

GOOD, I. J. (1954). The appropriate mathematical tools for describing and measuring uncertainty. *In* "Uncertainty and Business Decisions" (C. F. Carter, G. P. Meredith, and G. L. S. Shackle, eds.), pp. 20–36. Univ. Press, Liverpool.

GOOD, I. J. (1956a). Some terminology and notation of information theory. *Proc. Inst. Elec. Engrs. C*, **103** 200–204 [or Monograph No. 155R (1955)].

GOOD, I. J. (1956). The surprise index for the multivariate normal distribution. *Ann. Math. Statist.* **27** 1130–1135 [Erratum: **28** (1957).]

GOOD, I. J. (1960). Discussion of a paper by E. M. L. Beale. *J. Roy. Statist. Soc. Ser. B* **22** 79–82.

GOOD, I. J. (1962). How rational should a manager be? *Management Sci.* **8** 383–393 [reprinted with corrections. *In* "Executive Readings in Management Science" (M. K. Starr, ed.), pp. 88–98. Macmillan, New York, 1965].

GOOD, I. J. (1963). Maximum entropy for hypothesis formulation, especially for multidimensional contingency tables. *Ann. Math. Statist.* **34** 911–934.

GOOD, I. J. (1966). On the principle of total evidence. *British J. Philos. Sci.* **17** 319–322.

GOOD, I. J. (1968a). A five-year plan for automatic chess. *In* "Machine Intelligence II" (E. Dale, and D. Michie, eds.), pp. 89–118. Oliver & Boyd, Edinburgh and London.

GOOD, I. J. (1968b). Some statistical methods in machine intelligence research. *Virginia J. Sci.* **19** 101–110.

GOOD, I. J. (1969). Review of Ireland and Kullback (1968). *Math. Rev.* **37**.

GOOD, I. J., and TOULMIN, G. H. (1968). Coding theorems and weight of evidence. *J. Inst. Math. Appl.* **4** 94–105.

HARTIGAN, J. (1964). Invariant prior distributions. *Ann. Math. Statist.* **35** 836–845.
IRELAND, C. T., and KULLBACK, S. (1968). Contingency table with given marginals. *Biometrika* **55** 179–188.
JAYNES, E. T. (1957). Information theory and statistical mechanics. *Phys. Rev.* **106** 620–630.
JEFFREYS, H. (1946). An invariant form for the prior probability in estimation problems. *Proc. Roy. Soc. A* **186** 453–461.
JEFFREYS, H. (1948). "Theory of Probability," 2nd ed. Oxford Univ. Press (Clarendon), London and New York.
KERRIDGE, D. F. (1961). Inaccuracy and inference. *J. Roy. Statist. Soc. Ser. B* **23** 184–194.
KOOPMAN, B. O. (1957). The theory of search, III. The optimum distribution of searching effort. *Operations Res.* **5** 613–626.
KOOPMAN, B. O. (1968). Relaxed motion in irreversible molecular statistics. *Advan. Chem. Phys.* To be published.
KULLBACK, S. (1959). "Information Theory and Statistics." Wiley, New York.
LINDLEY, D. V. (1956). On the measure of the information provided by an experiment. *Ann. Math. Statist.* **27** 986–1005.
MALLOWS, C. L. (1959). The information in an experiment. *J. Roy. Statist. Soc. Ser. B* **21** 67–72.
MARSCHAK, J. (1959). Remarks on the economics of information. *In* "Contributions to Scientific Research in Management," pp. 79–98. Univ. of California Press, Berkeley, California.
MCCARTHY, J. (1956). Measures of the value of information. *Proc. Nat. Acad. Sci. U.S.A.* **42** 654–655.
PERKS, W. (1947). Some observations on inverse probability including a new indifference rule. *J. Inst. Actuar. Students' Soc.* **73** 285–334 (with discussion).
RÉNYI, A. (1961). On measures of entropy and information. *Proc. Fourth Berkeley Symp. Math. Statist. Prob.* (J. Neyman, ed.), pp. 547–561. Univ. of California Press, Berkeley, California.
RÉNYI, A. (1965). On the foundations of information theory. *Rev. Inst. Internat. Statist.* **33** 1–14.
ROBBINS, H. E. (1952). Some aspects of the sequential design of experiments. *Bull. Amer. Math. Soc.* **58** 529–532.
ROBBINS, H. E. (1956). A sequential decision problem with a finite memory. *Proc. Nat. Acad. Sci. U. S. A.* **42** 920–923.
SAVAGE, L. J. (1954). "The Foundations of Statistics." Wiley, New York.
SAVAGE, L. J. (1955). Private communication.
SCHÜTZENBERGER, M. P. (1954). Contribution aux applications statistiques de la thèorie de l'information. *Publ. Inst. Statist. Univ. Paris* **3** no. 1–2, 3–117.
SHANNON, C. E., and WEAVER, W. (1949). "The Mathematical Theory of Communication." Univ. of Illinois Press, Urbana, Illinois.
THOMPSON, W. R. (1933). On the likelihood that one unknown probability exceeds another in view of the evidence of two samples. *Biometrika* **25** 285–294.
THOMPSON, W. R. (1935). On the theory of apportionment. *Amer. J. Math.* **57** 450–456.
WALD, A. (1950). "Statistical Decision Functions." Wiley, New York.

Tests of Equality of Latent Roots of the Covariance Matrix

A. T. JAMES

DEPARTMENT OF STATISTICS
UNIVERSITY OF ADELAIDE
ADELAIDE, SOUTH AUSTRALIA

1. SUMMARY

A study is made of the Bartlett-Lawley tests of equality of the smaller latent roots of the covariance matrix using a conditional distribution of the smaller sample roots given the larger sample roots, obtained from a gamma type asymptotic approximation to the roots distribution with linkage factors between sample roots corresponding to larger and smaller population roots.

2. INTRODUCTION

In principal component analysis, tests are needed for equality of latent roots of the covariance matrix because if a subset of the roots of the population covariance matrix are all equal, the corresponding vectors are arbitrary to the extent that they can be replaced by a rotated set within the subspace that they span.

Mauchley (1940) obtained the likelihood ratio test for equality of all the roots of covariance matrix, and Bartlett (1954) obtained an approximation to its asymptotic distribution by use of χ^2 with an appropriate multiplying factor. Bartlett suggested further that a similar test could be used for equality of a subset of the roots, ignoring the other roots, provided that the number of degrees of freedom of the covariance matrix was reduced by one for every one of the larger roots ignored. Anderson (1958), by use of the methods of Box (1949), gives an asymptotic series in χ^2 probabilities, for the test of equality of all roots which begins with Bartlett's approximation.

In testing equality of the smaller roots, the larger population roots are nuisance parameters. Lawley (1956) investigated the influence of the larger roots on the test statistic by an asymptotic approximation to its mean and variance though calculations for the latter are omitted from his paper because they become so heavy. He found minor corrections to Bartlett's multiplying factor which depend on the population roots. As the population roots will usually be unknown, he suggested that sample roots be substituted for them.

The present paper is devoted to an investigation of the Bartlett-Lawley tests from a different inferential standpoint using different mathematical techniques. It confirms the Lawley tests but provides more information on the accuracy of the approximations. The inferential approach is to test equality of the smaller roots using the distribution of them conditional on the larger sample roots. By some modification of the mathematical methods used by Anderson (1965), an asymptotic distribution of the roots is obtained in the case in which the smallest q population roots are equal, and the largest k population roots are greater than they. The largest k sample roots turn out to be asymptotically sufficient statistics for the largest k population roots, and hence the asymptotic distribution of the smallest q sample roots conditional on the k largest sample roots does not depend upon the unknown parameters.

Anderson (1963) made a thorough study of the asymptotic theory of roots and vectors which revealed much of the structure. However, in his more highly asymptotic normal approximation, the distribution of the smaller roots becomes independent of the larger ones, but our distribution is presumably subasymptotic to his because it has a linkage factor, which is a function of the larger and smaller sample roots. From the linkage factor, the Lawley correction to Bartlett's test is obtained.

Besides preserving linkage factors between sample roots corresponding to population roots of different magnitudes, our asymptotic distributions are of gamma rather than normal type. Of course, a gamma distribution eventually tends to a normal distribution as the parameter increases.

The case of 3 roots, one large and two smaller ones to be tested for equality, is closely examined because linkage is strongest between adjacent roots.

In the chapter by James (1966), there is a combined asymptotic and power series approximation to the distribution of the latent roots of the covariance matrix.

3. ASYMPTOTIC APPROXIMATION TO THE ROOTS DISTRIBUTION

Let $L = \mathrm{diag}(l_i)$ where the l_i are the latent roots in descending order of a sample covariance matrix S with n degrees of freedom calculated from a sample from a normal population with covariance matrix Σ. We suppose that the q smallest latent roots of Σ are all equal to say α^{-1}, and let $\alpha_1, \ldots, \alpha_k$, $\alpha, \ldots, \alpha$, where $k = m - q$, be the latent roots of Σ^{-1} in ascending order. Then the joint distribution of $l_1, \ldots, l_m$ is

$$k_1 \prod_{i=1}^{k} \alpha_i^{n/2} \alpha^{qn/2} \int_{O(m)} \operatorname{etr}(-\tfrac{1}{2} nAHLH') k_2 \, (dH)$$

$$\prod_{i=1}^{m} l_i^{(n-m-1)/2} \prod_{i<j}^{m} (l_i - l_j) \bigwedge_{i=1}^{m} dl_i \tag{3.1}$$

where

$$k_1 = n^{mn/2}/(2^{mn/2}\Gamma_m(\tfrac{1}{2}n)), \qquad k_2 = \pi^{m^2/2}/\Gamma_m(\tfrac{1}{2}m),$$

The diagonal matrix of latent roots of Σ^{-1} is A, and (dH) is the invariant measure on the group, $O(m)$, of orthogonal matrices, H, normalized so that $\int_{O(m)}(dH) = 1$. The function "etr" of a matrix is defined to be the exponential function of the trace of the matrix. The multivariate gamma function $\Gamma_m(a)$ is defined by James (1964).

If we partition the matrix H into the submatrices H_1 and H_2 consisting of its first k and q rows, respectively, we see that the integrand in Eq. (3.1) does not depend upon H_2. Hence, we integrate over H_2 for fixed H_1 by the formula

$$\int_{H_2} k_2(dH) = k_2(dH_1) \tag{3.2}$$

and the symbol (dH_1) stands for the invariant volume element on the Steifel manifold of orthonormal k-frames in m-space.

A parameterization of H_1 may be obtained by writing [cf. Anderson (1965) p. 1158, Eq. (2.2)],

$$H = \begin{bmatrix} H_1 \\ \text{- - -} \\ H_3 \end{bmatrix} = \exp\left(\begin{bmatrix} S_{11} & S_{12} \\ -S'_{12} & 0 \end{bmatrix}\right) \tag{3.3}$$

where S_{11} is a $k \times k$ skew symmetric matrix and S_{12} is a $k \times q$ rectangular matrix. Now

$$\begin{aligned} \operatorname{tr}(AHLH') &= \sum_{i=1}^{k} \sum_{j=1}^{m} \alpha_i l_j h_{ij}^2 + \alpha \sum_{j=1}^{m} l_j \sum_{i=k+1}^{m} h_{ij}^2 \\ &= \alpha \sum_{j=1}^{m} l_j + \sum_{i=1}^{k} \sum_{j=1}^{m} (\alpha_i - \alpha) l_j h_{ij}^2 \end{aligned} \tag{3.4}$$

since

$$\sum_{i=k+1}^{m} h_{ij}^2 = 1 - \sum_{i=1}^{k} h_{ij}^2 \qquad \text{for} \quad j = 1, \ldots, m$$

because the matrix H is orthogonal.

For n large and $\alpha_1, \ldots, \alpha_k$ and $l_1, \ldots, l_k$ well spaced, most of the integral in (3.1) will be obtained from small values of the elements of S_{11} and S_{12}.

We have, by analogy with Anderson [(1965), p. 1159, Eq. (2.3)],

$$k_2(dH_1) = k_3(dS_{11})(dS_{12})(1 + O\ (\text{squares of } s_{ij}\text{'s})) \tag{3.5}$$

where the symbols (dS_{11}) and (dS_{12}) stand for

$$\bigwedge_{i<j}^{k} ds_{ij} \qquad \text{and} \qquad \bigwedge_{i=1}^{k} \bigwedge_{j=k+1}^{m} ds_{ij},$$

respectively, and

$$k_3 = \pi^{q^2/2}/\Gamma_q(\tfrac{1}{2}q) \qquad \text{where} \quad q = m - k.$$

From Eq. (3.3), we have

$$h_{ii} = 1 - \tfrac{1}{2}\sum_{j=1}^{m} s_{ij}^2 + \text{higher order terms}, \qquad i \leq k. \tag{3.6}$$

$$h_{ij} = s_{ij} + \text{higher order terms} \qquad (i \neq j), \qquad s_{ij} = -s_{ji}. \tag{3.7}$$

Hence, from (3.4), remembering that the matrix S_{11} is skew symmetric, we have

$$\begin{aligned}
\operatorname{tr}(AHLH') \\
&= \alpha \sum_{i=1}^{m} l_i + \sum_{i=1}^{k} (\alpha_i - \alpha) l_i - \sum_{i=1}^{k} (\alpha_i - \alpha) l_i \sum_{j=1}^{m} s_{ij}^2 \\
&\quad + \sum_{i=1}^{k} \sum_{j=1}^{m} (\alpha_i - \alpha) l_j s_{ij}^2 \\
&\quad + \text{higher order terms in the } s_{ij}\text{'s} \\
&= \alpha \sum_{i=k+1}^{m} l_i + \sum_{i=1}^{k} \alpha_i l_i + \sum_{i<j}^{k} (\alpha_j - \alpha_i)(l_i - l_j) s_{ij}^2 \\
&\quad + \sum_{i=1}^{k} \sum_{j=k+1}^{m} (\alpha - \alpha_i)(l_i - l_j) s_{ij}^2 \\
&\quad + \text{higher order terms in the } s_{ij}\text{'s}.
\end{aligned} \tag{3.8}$$

When we substitute from Eq. (3.8) in the integral in (3.1), we see that the integrand tends to zero as each s_{ij} tends to ∞, and in fact, for large n, the integrand will be very small for all but small values of the s_{ij}. Hence, to obtain an asymptotic series, we can replace the finite range of the s_{ij}, corresponding to the range of H_1, by the range of all real values of s_{ij}.

We then have, in an asymptotic sense,

$$\int_{O(m)} \operatorname{etr}(-\tfrac{1}{2}nAHLH')(dH)$$

$$= k_2^{-1}k_3 \exp\left(-\tfrac{1}{2}n\sum_{i=1}^{k}\alpha_i l_i\right)\exp\left(-\tfrac{1}{2}\alpha n\sum_{j=k+1}^{m} l_i\right)$$

$$\times \iint_{s_{11}s_{12}} \prod_{i<j}^{k} \exp(-\tfrac{1}{2}n(\alpha_j-\alpha_i)(l_i-l_j)s_{ij}^2)$$

$$\times \prod_{i=1}^{k}\prod_{j=k+1}^{m} \exp(-\tfrac{1}{2}n(\alpha-\alpha_i)(l_i-l_j)s_{ij}^2)\,ds_{ij}$$

$$= k_2^{-1}k_3 \exp\left(-\tfrac{1}{2}n\sum_{i=1}^{k}\alpha_i l_i\right)\exp\left(-\tfrac{1}{2}\alpha n\sum_{j=k+1}^{m} l_i\right)$$

$$\times \prod_{i<j}^{k}\int_{-\infty}^{\infty} \exp(-\tfrac{1}{2}n(\alpha_j-\alpha_i)(l_i-l_j)s_{ij}^2)\,ds_{ij}$$

$$\times \prod_{i=1}^{k}\prod_{j=k+1}^{m}\int_{-\infty}^{\infty} \exp(-\tfrac{1}{2}n(\alpha-\alpha_i)(l_i-l_j)s_{ij}^2)\,ds_{ij}\{1+O(1/n)\}$$

$$= \frac{k_4\exp(-\tfrac{1}{2}n\sum_{i=1}^{k}\alpha_i l_i)\exp(-\tfrac{1}{2}\alpha n\sum_{j=k+1}^{m} l_i)}{\prod_{i<j}^{k}[n(\alpha_j-\alpha_i)(l_i-l_j)]^{1/2}\prod_{i=1}^{k}\prod_{j=k+1}^{m}[n(\alpha-\alpha_i)(l_i-l_j)]^{1/2}}$$

$$\times\{1+O(1/n)\} \tag{3.9}$$

where

$$k_4 = \Gamma_k(\tfrac{1}{2}m)\,2^{k(2m-k-1)/4}/\pi^{k(k+1)/4}. \tag{3.10}$$

Substituting in (3.1), we have the:

Theorem. *The asymptotic distribution of the roots $l_1 \cdots l_k, l_{k+1}, \ldots, l_m$, in descending order, of the sample covariance matrix S for large degrees of freedom n, when the $m = k + q$ roots of the information matrix Σ^{-1} in ascending order are $\alpha_1, \ldots, \alpha_k, \alpha, \ldots, \alpha$, is*

$$k_5\left(\prod_{i=1}^{k}\alpha_i^{n/2}\right)\exp\left(-\tfrac{1}{2}n\sum_{i=1}^{k}(\alpha_i l_i)\right)\prod_{i=1}^{k} l_i^{(n-m-1)/2}\prod_{i<j}^{k}\left(\frac{l_i-l_j}{\alpha_j-\alpha_i}\right)^{1/2}\bigwedge_{i=1}^{k} dl_i$$

$$\times\prod_{i=1}^{k}\prod_{j=k+1}^{m}\left(\frac{l_i-l_j}{\alpha-\alpha_i}\right)^{1/2}$$

$$\times\,\alpha^{qn/2}\exp\left(-\tfrac{1}{2}n\alpha\sum_{i=k+1}^{m} l_i\right)\prod_{i=k+1}^{m} l_i^{(n-k-q-1)/2}\prod_{\substack{k+1\\ i<j}}^{m}(l_i-l_j)\bigwedge_{i=k+1}^{m} dl_i \tag{3.11}$$

where

$$k_5 = \{\pi^{q^2/2}(\tfrac{1}{2}n)^{mn/2}/\Gamma_q(\tfrac{1}{2}q)\Gamma_m(\tfrac{1}{2}n))\}\{1 + O(n^{-1})\}. \tag{3.12}$$

Corollary 1. *The first k sample roots $l_1, \ldots, l_k$ are asymptotically sufficient for the population roots $\alpha_1^{-1}, \ldots, \alpha_k^{-1}$.*

Corollary 2. *The asymptotic conditional distribution of the last roots $l_{k+1}, \ldots, l_m$ given the first is*

$$P(l_{k+1}, \ldots, l_m \mid l_1, \ldots, l_k)$$
$$= \text{const} \prod_{i=1}^{k} \prod_{j=k+1}^{m} (l_i - l_j)^{1/2} \alpha^{qn/2} \exp\left(-\tfrac{1}{2}n\alpha \sum_{i=k+1}^{m} l_i\right)$$
$$\times \prod_{i=k+1}^{m} l_i^{(n-k-q-1)/2} \prod_{\substack{k+1 \\ i<j}}^{m} (l_i - l_j) \bigwedge_{i=k+1}^{m} dl_i \tag{3.13}$$

which does not depend on the population parameters $\alpha_1, \ldots, \alpha_k$.

4. TEST OF EQUALITY OF THE LAST q ROOTS

In the asymptotic conditional distribution, the statistic $\bar{l}$ given by

$$\bar{l} = q^{-1} \sum_{i=k+1}^{m} l_i \tag{4.1}$$

is a sufficient estimate of the parameter α^{-1} and if we put

$$u_i = l_i/\bar{l}, \qquad i = k+1, \ldots, m$$

then the joint distribution of $u_{k+1}, \ldots, u_{m-1}$ conditional on $l_1, \ldots, l_k, \bar{l}$, clearly follows from formula (3.13) as

$$P(u_{k+1}, \ldots, u_{m-1} \mid l_1, \ldots, l_k, \bar{l}) = \text{const} \prod_{i=1}^{k} \prod_{j=k+1}^{m} (r_i - u_j)^{1/2}$$
$$\times \prod_{j=k+1}^{m} u_j^{(n-k-q-1)/2} \prod_{\substack{k+1 \\ i<j}}^{m} (u_i - u_j) \bigwedge_{j=k+1}^{m-1} du_j, \tag{4.2}$$

where $r_i = l_i/\bar{l}$ for $i = 1, \ldots, k$.

Although the expressions (3.13), and hence (4.2), have an error term of magnitude $O(n^{-1})$, the error term will vary by an amount of only $O(n^{-1/2})$ of its magnitude as the l_i vary within ranges of length $O(n^{-1/2})$, which they do with probability arbitrarily near one. Hence (3.13) and (4.2) will be accurate to $O(n^{-3/2})$.

The test of equality of roots can be made from the distribution (4.2).

If k were equal to zero, i.e. if we were simply concerned with the equality of q roots, then the distribution of the likelihood ratio statistic

$$\prod_{i=k+1}^{m} (l_i/\bar{l}) = \prod_{i=k+1}^{m} u_i$$

would be derived from the formula in the second line of the distribution. Bartlett (1954) [see Anderson (1958)], has given an approximation as

$$\chi_d^{\,2} = (n - (2q^2 + q + 2)/6q) \log \prod_{i=1}^{q} l_i/\bar{l} \tag{4.3}$$

where the number d of degrees of freedom is given by

$$d = \tfrac{1}{2}(q - 1)(q + 2). \tag{4.4}$$

In testing the last q roots when $k \neq 0$, one could, as a first approximation, ignore the factor involving the r_i if these were large and one would have the usual distribution with n replaced by $n - k$, i.e., with the loss of one degree of freedom for each variable eliminated. Hence

$$\chi_d^{\,2} = (n - k - (2q^2 + q + 2)/6q) \log \prod_{i=1}^{q} (l_i/\bar{l}). \tag{4.5}$$

This is the approximation suggested by Bartlett (1954). By an asymptotic approximation to the factor involving the u_i, we can obtain the refinement suggested by Lawley (1956).

Since

$$(1 - u_j) = O(n^{-1/2}), \tag{4.6}$$

we can make the expansion,

$$(r_i - u_j)^{1/2} = (r_i - 1)^{1/2}\left(1 + \frac{1 - u_j}{r_i - 1}\right)^{1/2}$$

$$= (r_i - 1)^{1/2}\left(1 + \frac{1 - u_j}{2(r_i - 1)} - \frac{(1 - u_j)^2}{8(r_i - 1)^2} + O(n^{-3/2})\right).$$

Hence, remembering that $\Sigma(1 - u_j) = 0$, we have

$$\prod_{i=1}^{k} \prod_{j=k+1}^{m} (r_i - u_j)^{1/2}$$

$$= \prod_i \left\{(r_i - 1)^{q/2}\left(1 + \frac{1}{2(r_i - 1)^2} \sum_{j<p} (1 - u_j)(1 - u_p)\right\} + O(n^{-3/2})\right)$$

$$= \left(\prod_i (r_i - 1)^{q/2}\right)\left[1 + \tfrac{1}{2}L\left(a_2 - \binom{q}{2}\right) + O(n^{-3/2})\right] \tag{4.7}$$

where L is the Lawley term given by

$$L = \sum_{i=1}^{k} 1/(r_i - 1)^2 \tag{4.8}$$

and

$$a_2 = \sum_{\substack{k+1 \\ i<j}}^{m} u_i u_j . \tag{4.9}$$

Hence, the distribution (4.2) may be approximated as

$$\text{const}\left(1 + \tfrac{1}{2}L\left(a_2 - \binom{q}{2}\right) + O(n^{-3/2})\right) \underset{\text{distribution}}{\text{null}} \tag{4.10}$$

where the null distribution is given by

$$\text{const} \prod_{j=k+1}^{m} u_j^{(n-k-q-1)/2} \prod_{k+1}^{m} (u_i - u_j) \bigwedge_{j=k+1}^{m-1} du_j . \tag{4.11}$$

The distribution (4.2) and its approximation (4.10) will be called the modified distribution.

The multiplier of χ^2 can be obtained from the first moment of our statistic

$$-\log \prod_{j=k+1}^{q} u_j .$$

To obtain this, we find the tth moment of $\prod u_j$.

From the Wishart distribution, one can derive the:

Lemma.

$$\underset{\substack{\text{null} \\ \text{distribution}}}{E} [a_2 \prod u_j^t] = \binom{q}{2} \frac{\frac{1}{2}n - k - \frac{1}{2} + t}{\frac{1}{2}n - k + q^{-1} + t} E_0(t) \tag{4.12}$$

where

$$E_0(t) = \underset{\substack{\text{null} \\ \text{distribution}}}{E} [\prod u_j^t]. \tag{4.13}$$

Proof. Clearly, we have

$$\left(\sum_{\substack{k+1 \\ i<j}}^{k+q} l_i l_j\right) \prod_{k+1}^{k+q} l_i^t = \bar{l}^{qt+2} a_2 \prod_{k+1}^{k+q} u_i^t .$$

The null distribution of $l_{k+1}, \ldots, l_m$ is the same as the distribution of the latent roots of a $q \times q$ covariance matrix S distributed in a Wishart distribution with $n' = n - k$ degrees of freedom and $\sum = \alpha^{-1} I_q$. Hence, let us regard $l_{k+1}, \ldots, l_n$ as the latent roots of S. Furthermore, since the expectation of $a_2 u_i^t$ clearly does not depend upon α, we may take $\alpha = 1$. Since

$$\bar{l} = q^{-1} \operatorname{tr} S$$

we have

$$\underset{\text{null}}{E}\,[\bar{l}^{qt+2}] = (\tfrac{1}{2}qn')_{qt+2}(\tfrac{1}{2}qn')^{-(qt+2)}$$

where $(b)_s = \Gamma(b+s)/\Gamma(b)$. Also, we have

$$\prod l_i^t = \det S^t$$

and the term $\sum l_i l_j$ = sum of second order principal minors of S. Since the principal minors all yield the same expectation, we find the expectation including only the first one, Δ, and then multiply by the number, $\binom{q}{2}$, of them.

On substituting $S = T'T$ in the Wishart distribution, where T is an upper triangular matrix, and noting that $\Delta = t_{11}^2 t_{22}^2$, and the volume element is given by $(dS) = 2^q t_{11}^q t_{22}^{q-1} \cdots t_{qq}\, dt_{11} \cdots dt_{qq}$, one can calculate that

$$E[\Delta \det S^t] = (\tfrac{1}{2}n')^{-(qt+2)}(\tfrac{1}{2}n')_{t+1}(\tfrac{1}{2}(n'-1))_{t+1}(\tfrac{1}{2}(n'-2))_t \cdots (\tfrac{1}{2}(n'-q+1))_t$$

and

$$E[\det S^t] = (\tfrac{1}{2}n')^{-qt}(\tfrac{1}{2}n')_t(\tfrac{1}{2}(n'-1))_t(\tfrac{1}{2}(n'-2))_t \cdots (\tfrac{1}{2}(n'-q+1))_t.$$

Since, relative to the distribution of S, i.e., the null distribution, $\bar{l}$ is clearly statistically independent of $u_{k+1}, \ldots, u_{n-1}$, we have

$$\underset{\text{null}}{E}\,[a_2 \prod u_1{}^t] = \underset{\text{null}}{E}\,[(\textstyle\sum l_i l_j) \prod l_i^t] / \underset{\text{null}}{E}\,[\bar{l}^{qt+2}].$$

Hence

$$\begin{aligned} &E[a_2 \textstyle\prod u_j^t]/E[\prod u_j^t] \\ &= \binom{q}{2} \frac{E[\Delta \det S^t]}{E[\det S^t]} \frac{E[\bar{l}^{qt}]}{E[\bar{l}^{qt+2}]} \\ &= \binom{q}{2} \frac{(\frac{1}{2}n'+t)(\frac{1}{2}n'-\frac{1}{2}+t)}{(\frac{1}{2}n')^2} \frac{(\frac{1}{2}qn')^2}{(\frac{1}{2}qn'+1+qt)(\frac{1}{2}qn'+qt)} \\ &= \binom{q}{2} \frac{\frac{1}{2}n-k-\frac{1}{2}+t}{\frac{1}{2}n-k+q^{-1}+t} \end{aligned}$$

as stated in the lemma. Hence

$$\underset{\substack{\text{modified}\\ \text{distribution}}}{E}\,[\textstyle\prod u_j^t] = \varphi(t)/\varphi(0) \tag{4.14}$$

where

$$\varphi(t) = E_0(t) f(t) \tag{4.15}$$

and

$$f(t) = 1 + \tfrac{1}{2}L\left(\frac{\frac{1}{2}n-k-\frac{1}{2}+t}{\frac{1}{2}n-k+q^{-1}+t} - 1\right)\binom{q}{2}. \tag{4.16}$$

Now, we have

$$\underset{\substack{\text{modified}\\ \text{distribution}}}{E}[-\log \textstyle\prod u_j] = -\frac{d}{dt}\left[\frac{\varphi(t)}{\varphi(0)}\right]_{t=0}$$

$$= -E_0'(0) - \frac{f'(0)}{f(0)} = -E_0'(0) - \frac{Ld}{n^2} + O(n^{-5/2}) \tag{4.17}$$

when L and d are given by Eqs. (4.8) and (4.4), respectively.

Now $-E_0'(0)$ is the expectation of the statistic $-\log \prod u_j$ under the null distribution. Since, in the case of the null distribution,

$$(n-c)\left(-\log \prod_j u_j\right)$$

is approximately χ^2 on d degrees of freedom, where

$$c = k + (2q^2 + q + 2)/6q \tag{4.18}$$

we have

$$-E_0'(0) = E[\chi^2]/(n-c) = d/(n-c).$$

Hence, we have

$$\underset{\substack{\text{modified}\\ \text{distribution}}}{E}[-\log \textstyle\prod u_j] = \frac{d}{n-c} - \frac{Ld}{n^2} + O(n^{-5/2}) = \frac{d}{n-c+L+O(n^{-1})}, \tag{4.19}$$

and the multiplier of χ^2 is thus

$$n - c + L.$$

To sum up, we have the:

Theorem (Lawley, 1956). *The statistic*

$$\left(n - k - (2q^2 + q + 2)/6q + \sum_{i=1}^{k}(r_i - 1)^{-2}\right)\left(q \log \bar{l} - \sum_{j=k+1}^{m} \log l_j\right) \tag{4.20}$$

is approximately distributed as χ^2 on degrees of freedom given by

$$d = \tfrac{1}{2}(q-1)(q+2). \tag{4.21}$$

5. TEST OF EQUALITY OF TWO LATENT ROOTS IN THE TRIVARIATE CASE

The test of equality of the last two roots conditional on the first, uses the statistic

$$x = (u_2 u_3)^{1/2} = 2(l_2 l_3)^{1/2}/(l_2 + l_3) = u_2^{1/2}(2 - u_2)^{1/2}. \tag{5.1}$$

Putting $k = 1$, $q = 2$ in formula (4.4) and remembering that $u_2 + u_3 = 2$, we have the distribution of u_2 conditional on l_1 as

$$\begin{aligned} &\text{const}((r - u_2)(r - u_3))^{1/2}(u_2(2 - u_2))^{\frac{1}{4}(n-4)}(u_2 - 1)\,du_2 \\ &\quad = \text{const}(r^2 - 2r + x^2)^{1/2}x^{n-3}\,dx \end{aligned} \tag{5.2}$$

where

$$r = r_1 = l_1/\bar{l} \qquad \text{and} \qquad \bar{l} = \tfrac{1}{2}(l_2 + l_3).$$

When $r \geq 2$, the range of x is $0 \leq x \leq 1$. When $1 \leq r \leq 2$, the range of x is

$$r^{1/2}(2 - r)^{1/2} \leq x \leq 1. \tag{5.3}$$

The lower bound for x follows from the inequality

$$(l_1 - l_2)(l_1 - l_3) \geq 0, \tag{5.4}$$

i.e.,

$$l_2 l_3 \geq l_1(l_2 + l_3 - l_1),$$

i.e.,

$$\frac{4l_2 l_3}{(l_2 + l_3)^2} \geq \frac{2l_1}{l_2 + l_3}\left(2 - \frac{2l_1}{l_2 + l_3}\right).$$

Hence, we have

$$x^2 \geq r(2 - r). \tag{5.5}$$

Put

$$\Phi(x) = \int_0^x (v + \xi^2)^{1/2}\xi^{n-3}\,d\xi, \tag{5.6}$$

where $v = r(r - 2)$, and substitute $\xi^2 = x^2 t$. Then for $v > 0$,

$$\begin{aligned} \Phi(x) &= \tfrac{1}{2}v^{1/2}x^{n-2}\int_0^1 \left(1 + \frac{x^2}{v}t\right)^{1/2} t^{(n-4)/2}\,dt \\ &= d^{1/2}(n-2)^{-1}x^{n-2}\,{}_2F_1(-\tfrac{1}{2}, \tfrac{1}{2}n - 1; \tfrac{1}{2}n; -x^2/v), \end{aligned} \tag{5.7}$$

from Erdelyi *et al.* [(1953), Vol. 1, p. 59 Eq. (10)]. For $v < 0$

$$\begin{aligned} \Phi(x) &= \tfrac{1}{2}(-v)^{1/2}x^{n-2}\int_0^1 \left(1 - \frac{x^2}{v}t\right)^{1/2} t^{(n-4)/2}\,dt \\ &= (-d)^{1/2}(n-2)^{-1}x^{n-2}\,{}_2F_1(-\tfrac{1}{2}, \tfrac{1}{2}n - 1; \tfrac{1}{2}n; x^2/v). \end{aligned}$$

Hence, the distribution function $F(x)$ of x is

$$F(x) = x^{n-2}\,\frac{{}_2F_1(-\tfrac{1}{2}, \tfrac{1}{2}n - 1; \tfrac{1}{2}n; -x^2/(r(r-2)))}{{}_2F_1(-\tfrac{1}{2}, \tfrac{1}{2}n - 1; \tfrac{1}{2}n; -1/(r(r-2)))} \tag{5.8}$$

for $r > 2$

$$F(x) = x^{n-1} \qquad \text{for } r = 2 \tag{5.9}$$

$$F(x) = x^{n-2}\,\frac{{}_2F_1(-\tfrac{1}{2}, \tfrac{1}{2}n - 1; \tfrac{1}{2}n; x^2/(r(2-r))) - {}_2F_1(-\tfrac{1}{2}, \tfrac{1}{2}n - 1; \tfrac{1}{2}n; 1)}{{}_2F_1(-\tfrac{1}{2}, \tfrac{1}{2}n - 1; \tfrac{1}{2}n; 1/(r(2-r))) - {}_2F_1(-\tfrac{1}{2}, \tfrac{1}{2}n - 1; \tfrac{1}{2}n; 1)}$$

$$\text{for} \quad r < 2. \tag{5.10}$$

Note that from Erdelyi *et al.* [(1953), p. 104, Eq. (46)], we have

$${}_2F_1(-\tfrac{1}{2}, \tfrac{1}{2}n - 1; \tfrac{1}{2}n; 1) = \frac{\pi^{1/2}\Gamma(\tfrac{1}{2}n)}{2\Gamma(\tfrac{1}{2}n + \tfrac{1}{2})} = (\pi/(2n))^{1/2} + O(1/n). \tag{5.11}$$

An asymptotic series in inverse powers of n can be found for the case in which $v \geq 0$, i.e., $r \geq 2$ as follows from the integral (5.6):

$$\Phi(x) = \tfrac{1}{2}x^{n-2}(x^2 + v)^{1/2} \int_0^1 \left(1 - \frac{x^2}{x^2 + v}(1 - t)\right)^{1/2} t^{(n-2)/2}\,dt. \tag{5.12}$$

On expanding the square root under the integral sign in the binomial series and integrating term by term, we obtain

$$\Phi(x) = (n-2)^{-1}x^{n-2}(v + x^2)^{1/2}\left(1 - \frac{x^2}{v + x^2}\frac{1}{n} + O(n^{-2})\right). \tag{5.13}$$

Hence

$$F(x) = \frac{\Phi(x)}{\Phi(1)} = x^{n-2}\,\frac{(x^2 + r(r-2))^{1/2}}{r - 1}$$

$$\times \left(1 + \frac{r(r-2)}{(r-1)^2}\frac{(1 - x^2)}{(x^2 + r(r-2))}\frac{1}{n} + O(n^{-2})\right). \tag{5.14}$$

For x close to one, the first term approximates to

$$F(x) = x^{n-2+1/(r-1)^2} \tag{5.15}$$

which agrees with Lawley's approximation.

For the case $v < 0$, i.e., $r < 2$, let us transform x to a new variate y on a (0, 1) range by putting

$$y = \frac{x^2 - r(2-r)}{1 - r(2-r)}, \qquad 0 < y < 1. \tag{5.16}$$

The distribution (5.2) then becomes

$$\text{const}\; y^{1/2}\left(\frac{r(2-r)}{(r-1)^2} + y\right)^{(n-4)/2} dy. \tag{5.17}$$

Significantly low values of y would lead to rejection of the null hypothesis of equality of the last two roots.

For low values of y, the asymptotic approximation (3.12) on which the formula for the distribution is based may break down. But there is reason to believe that the test is conservative because if the first population root were equal to the last two, then the *square root* of the factor

$$(l_1 - l_2)(l_1 - l_3) \tag{5.18}$$

which appears in $P(l_2, l_3 \mid l_1)$ would be replaced by the factor itself, and hence in the distribution (5.17), the factor $y^{1/2}$ would be replaced by y. This would lead to higher significance levels and hence the test is conservative.

There is similar reason to believe that Lawley's corrections to Bartlett's test may be, if anything, a little conservative because the distribution when some of the first k roots of the population are equal to the last q will have factors

$$\prod_{j=k+1}^{q} (l_i - l_j), \qquad i \leq k \tag{5.19}$$

instead of their square roots which appear in the asymptotic distribution. This would replace the Lawley corrections of $(r_i - 1)^{-2}$ by double the value.

The theory indicates that the test may be used to test equality of any set of adjacent roots. Asymptotically, the effect of the smaller roots is negligible and they can be ignored. In practice, there will often be several components of "error" within an m-variate distribution, and a test of equality of the smallest roots, being only concerned with the significance of the difference of such components of error, will be of little interest compared with tests of equality of groups of larger roots.

REFERENCES

ANDERSON, G. A. (1965). An asymptotic expansion for the distribution of the latent roots of the estimated covariance matrix. *Ann. Math. Statist.* **36** 1153–1173.

ANDERSON, T. W. (1963). Asymptotic theory for principal component analysis. *Ann. Math. Statist.* **34** 122–148.

ANDERSON, T. W. (1958). "An Introduction to Multivariate Statistical Analysis." Wiley, New York.

BARTLETT, M. S. (1954). A note on multiplying factors for various χ^2 approximations. *J. Roy. Statist. Soc. Ser. B* **16** 296–298.

BOX, G. E. P. (1949). A general distribution theory for a class of likelihood ratio criteria. *Biometrika* **36** 317–346.

ERDELYI, A., MAGNUS, W., OBERHETTINGER, F., and TRICOMI, F. G. (1953). "Higher Transcendental Functions." McGraw-Hill, New York.

JAMES, A. T. (1964). Distribution of matrix variates and latent roots derived from normal samples. *Ann. Math. Statist.* **35** 475–501.

JAMES, A. T. (1966). Inference on latent roots by calculation of hypergeometric functions of matrix argument. *In* "Multivariate Analysis" (P. R. Krishnaiah, ed.). Academic Press, New York.

LAWLEY, D. N. (1956). Tests of significance of the latent roots of covariance and correlation matrices. *Biometrika* **43** 128–136.

MAUCHLEY, J. W. (1940). Significance test for sphericity of a normal *n*-variate distribution. *Ann. Math. Statist.* **11** 204–209.

Distributions of Vectors Corresponding to the Largest Roots of Three Matrices[1]

C. G. KHATRI[2]

INDIAN STATISTICAL INSTITUTE
CALCUTTA, INDIA

DEPARTMENT OF STATISTICS
PURDUE UNIVERSITY
LAFAYETTE, INDIANA

K. C. S. PILLAI

DEPARTMENT OF STATISTICS
PURDUE UNIVERSITY
LAFAYETTE, INDIANA

1. INTRODUCTION AND SUMMARY

The distributions of the characteristic vectors corresponding to the largest roots (CVCLR) of matrices are studied in this paper (1) in the single-sample case and (2) in the two-sample case, in which the samples are drawn from p-variate normal populations. For $N(\boldsymbol{\mu}, \boldsymbol{\Sigma})$, the distributions of CVCLR considered in (1) are for the special cases in which (i) $\boldsymbol{\mu} = \mathbf{0}$, (ii) $\boldsymbol{\Sigma} = \mathbf{I}$, and (iii) the rank of $\boldsymbol{\mu}$ is one and $\boldsymbol{\mu}$ can be random, as well. The case $\boldsymbol{\mu} = \mathbf{0}$ was studied earlier by Sugiyama [11]. In the two-sample case, for $N(\boldsymbol{\mu}, \boldsymbol{\Sigma}_1)$ and $N(\mathbf{0}, \boldsymbol{\Sigma}_2)$, the cases discussed are the same as above except that (ii) should be replaced by $\boldsymbol{\Sigma}_1 = \boldsymbol{\Sigma}_2 = \boldsymbol{\Sigma}$. It may be noted that the two-sample case in which $\boldsymbol{\mu}$ is fixed and $\boldsymbol{\Sigma}_1 = \boldsymbol{\Sigma}_2$ corresponds to the MANOVA model; and when $\boldsymbol{\mu}$ is random and $\boldsymbol{\Sigma}_1 = \boldsymbol{\Sigma}_2$, it corresponds to the canonical correlation situation. Case (ii) with $\boldsymbol{\mu} = \mathbf{0}$ in the two-sample case deals with the testing of the equality of two covariance matrices. In addition, a section is devoted to the testing of hypothetical vectors of $\boldsymbol{\Sigma}_1$ in the fields of $\boldsymbol{\Sigma}_2$ suggesting relevant criteria and deriving their distributions. In the single-sample case, tests of hypothetical principal components were developed earlier [7, 8].

[1] This research was supported by the National Science Foundation, Grant No. GP-7663.

[2] Present address: Department of Statistics, Gujarat University, Ahmedabad, India.

2. NOTATIONS AND SOME USEFUL RESULTS

Let $\mathbf{\Gamma} : n \times n$ be an orthogonal matrix such that first p $(\leq n)$ columns have random elements and the other $(n - p)$ columns depend on these random elements. We shall write $d\mathbf{\Gamma}^{(n,p)}$, a normalized measure over this space, i.e.,

$$\int_{O(n)} d\mathbf{\Gamma}^{(n,p)} = 1.$$

In terms of Roy's notations [10] let

$$J(\mathbf{\Gamma}) = 2^n \Big/ \left| \frac{\partial(\mathbf{LL}')}{\partial(\mathbf{L}_D)} \right|_{\mathbf{L}_I}$$

equal a function of random elements. Then we shall write

$$d\mathbf{\Gamma}^{(n,p)} = \Gamma_p(\tfrac{1}{2}n) J(\mathbf{\Gamma}) / \Pi^{\frac{1}{2}pn}.$$

The following lemma has been established by Khatri [5].

Lemma 1. *Let* $\mathbf{U} : p \times n = \mathbf{L}\begin{pmatrix} \alpha & 0 \\ 0 & \mathbf{V} \end{pmatrix} M'$ *be a transformation such that first column vectors of* $\mathbf{L} : p \times p$ *and* $\mathbf{M} : n \times n$ *contain random elements,* $\alpha \neq 0$, α^2 *is the maximum characteristic* (max ch) *root of* $\mathbf{UU}'$, *and* $\mathbf{V} : (p-1) \times (n-1)$ *is a random matrix. Then, the Jacobian of the transformation is given by*

$$J(\mathbf{U}; \mathbf{L}, \alpha, \mathbf{V}, \mathbf{M}) = |\alpha|^{n-p} |\alpha^2 \mathbf{I}_{p-1} - \mathbf{VV}'|$$
$$\times\ \Pi^{\frac{1}{2}(p+n)} \{\Gamma(\tfrac{1}{2}n)\Gamma(\tfrac{1}{2}p)\}^{-1}\, d\mathbf{\Gamma}^{(p,1)}\, d\mathbf{M}^{(n,1)}.$$

Lemma 2. *Let* $\mathbf{Y} : m \times q$ *be a random matrix and* $\mathbf{A} : m \times m$ *be a symmetric matrix. Then*

$$\int_{\mathscr{D}} |\mathbf{I}_m - \mathbf{YY}'|^{\alpha} C_{\mathscr{K}}(\mathbf{AYY}')\, d\mathbf{Y}$$

$$= \frac{C_{\mathscr{K}}(\mathbf{A}) \Pi^{\frac{1}{2}mq} (\frac{1}{2}q)_{\mathscr{K}}\, \Gamma_q(\alpha + \frac{1}{2}(q+1))}{\Gamma_q(\alpha + \frac{1}{2}(m+q+1))(\alpha + \frac{1}{2}(m+q+1))_{\mathscr{K}}} \qquad \textit{if}\ \ m \geq q,\ \ k_{q+1} = 0;$$

$$= 0 \qquad \textit{if}\ \ m \geq q\ \ \textit{and}\ \ k_{q+1} \neq 0;$$

$$= \frac{C_{\mathscr{K}}(\mathbf{A}) \Pi^{\frac{1}{2}mq} (\frac{1}{2}q)_{\mathscr{K}}\, \Gamma_m(\alpha + \frac{1}{2}(q+1))}{\Gamma_m(\alpha + \frac{1}{2}(m+q+1))(\alpha + \frac{1}{2}(m+q+1))_{\mathscr{K}}} \qquad \textit{if}\ \ m \leq q;$$

where $\mathscr{D} = \mathscr{D}\{\mathbf{Y}$ *such that* $\mathbf{I}_m - \mathbf{YY}'$ *is positive definite*$\}$, $\mathscr{K} = \{k_1, \ldots, k_m\}$,

$$\Gamma_m(x) = \Pi^{\frac{1}{4}m(m-1)} \prod_{i=1}^{m} \Gamma(x - \tfrac{1}{2}(i-1)), \qquad (x)_{\mathscr{K}} = \Gamma_m(x, \mathscr{K}) / \Gamma_m(x)$$

and

$$\Gamma_m(x, \mathscr{K}) = \Pi^{\frac{1}{4}m(m-1)} \prod_{i=1}^{m} \Gamma(x + k_i - \tfrac{1}{2}(i-1)).$$

Proof. Let us write

$$g = \int_{\mathscr{D}} |\mathbf{I}_m - \mathbf{YY}'|^\alpha C_{\mathscr{K}}(\mathbf{AYY}')\, d\mathbf{Y} \int_{O(m)} d\mathbf{H},$$

i.e.,

$$g = \int_{\mathscr{D}} |\mathbf{I}_m - \mathbf{YY}'|^\alpha \int_{O(m)} C_{\mathscr{K}}(\mathbf{AHYY}'\mathbf{H}') d\mathbf{H}\, d\mathbf{Y}, \tag{2.1}$$

using $\mathbf{Y} \to \mathbf{HY}$. James [3] has proved the following important result

$$\int_{O(m)} C_{\mathscr{K}}(\mathbf{AHBH}')\, d\mathbf{H} = C_{\mathscr{K}}(\mathbf{A}) C_{\mathscr{K}}(\mathbf{B})/k!\, C_{\mathscr{K}}(\mathbf{I}_m), \tag{2.2}$$

where $\mathbf{A}$ and $\mathbf{B}$ are symmetric matrices, and $C_{\mathscr{K}}(\mathbf{Z})$ is a zonal polynomial corresponding to the partition $\mathscr{K} = \{k_1, k_2, \ldots, k_m\}$, $k_1 \geq k_2 \geq \cdots \geq k_m \geq 0$, and $k = \sum_{i=1}^m k_i$. Moreover, we may note that

$$\begin{aligned} C_{\mathscr{K}}(\mathbf{YY}') &= C_{\mathscr{K}}(\mathbf{Y}'\mathbf{Y}) \qquad \text{if} \quad m \geq q, \quad k_{q+1} = 0; \\ &= 0 \qquad \text{otherwise for} \quad m \geq q. \end{aligned} \tag{2.3}$$

Let $m \geq q$. Then using (2.2) and (2.3) in (2.1), we get

$$\begin{aligned} g &= C_{\mathscr{K}}(\mathbf{A}) \{C_{\mathscr{K}}(\mathbf{I}_m)\}^{-1} \int_{\mathscr{D}} |\mathbf{I}_m - \mathbf{YY}'|^\alpha C_{\mathscr{K}}(\mathbf{Y}'\mathbf{Y})\, d\mathbf{Y} \qquad \text{if} \quad k_{q+1} = 0; \\ &= 0, \qquad \text{otherwise.} \end{aligned} \tag{2.4}$$

Now, integrating $\mathbf{Y}$ such that $\mathbf{Y}'\mathbf{Y} = \mathbf{S}$, we get

$$\int_{\mathscr{D}} |\mathbf{I}_m - \mathbf{YY}'|^\alpha C_{\mathscr{K}}(\mathbf{Y}'\mathbf{Y})\, d\mathbf{Y} = \Pi^{\frac{1}{2}mq} \int_{\mathbf{S}>0} |\mathbf{I}_q - \mathbf{S}|^\alpha |\mathbf{S}|^{\frac{1}{2}(m-q-1)} C_{\mathscr{K}}(\mathbf{S})\, d\mathbf{S}/\Gamma_q(\tfrac{1}{2}m),$$

and using Constantine's result [1], we get

$$\int_{\mathscr{D}} |\mathbf{I}_m - \mathbf{YY}'|^\alpha C_{\mathscr{K}}(\mathbf{Y}'\mathbf{Y})\, d\mathbf{Y} = \frac{\Pi^{\frac{1}{2}mq} \Gamma_q(\frac{1}{2}m, \mathscr{K}) \Gamma_q(\alpha + \frac{1}{2}q + \frac{1}{2}) C_{\mathscr{K}}(\mathbf{I}_q)}{\Gamma_q(\frac{1}{2}m) \Gamma_q(\alpha + \frac{1}{2}(m + q + 1), \mathscr{K})}. \tag{2.5}$$

Using (2.5) in (2.4) and noting that $C_{\mathscr{K}}(\mathbf{I}_q)/C_{\mathscr{K}}(\mathbf{I}_m) = (\frac{1}{2}q)_{\mathscr{K}}/(\frac{1}{2}m)_{\mathscr{K}}$, we get the first part of Lemma 2 for $m \geq q$. Similarly, the second part of Lemma 2 can be proved. Thus, Lemma 2 is established.

Lemma 3. *Let $\mathbf{Y} : m \times q$ be a random matrix and $\mathbf{A} : m \times m$ be a positive definite matrix. Then*

$$\begin{aligned} &\int_{\mathscr{D}} |\mathbf{I}_m - \mathbf{YY}'|^\alpha C_{\mathscr{K}}(\mathbf{AYY}') \exp(-\operatorname{tr} \mathbf{AYY}')\, d\mathbf{Y} \\ &\quad = \sum_{j=k}^{\infty} \sum_{J} (-1)^{j+k} k!\, a_{J,\mathscr{K}} (j!)^{-1} \int_{\mathscr{D}} |\mathbf{I}_m - \mathbf{YY}'|^\alpha C_J(\mathbf{AYY}')\, d\mathbf{Y}; \end{aligned} \tag{2.6}$$

where

$$C_J(\mathbf{I}_m - \mathbf{Z})/C_J(\mathbf{I}_m) = \sum_{t=0}^{j} \sum_{\tau} (-1)^t a_{J,\tau} C_\tau(\mathbf{Z})/C_\tau(\mathbf{I}_m),$$

[2, 9], *and* $\mathscr{D} = \mathscr{D}\{\mathbf{Y}$ *such that* $\mathbf{I} - \mathbf{YY}'$ *is positive definite*$\}$.

Proof. Let the left-hand side of (2.6) be denoted as $g_{\mathscr{K}}(\mathbf{A})$. Then

$$G = \sum_{k=0}^{\infty} \sum_{\mathscr{K}} g_{\mathscr{K}}(\mathbf{A}) C_{\mathscr{K}}(\mathbf{Z}) / k!\, C_{\mathscr{K}}(\mathbf{I}_m)$$

$$= \int_{O(m)} \int_{\mathscr{D}} |\mathbf{I}_m - \mathbf{YY}'|^{\alpha} \exp[\operatorname{tr} \mathbf{A}^{1/2}(\mathbf{H}'\mathbf{ZH} - \mathbf{I})\mathbf{A}^{1/2}\mathbf{YY}']\, d\mathbf{Y}\, d\mathbf{H}$$

$$= \sum_{j=0}^{\infty} \sum_{J} (j!)^{-1} \int_{\mathscr{D}} |\mathbf{I}_m - \mathbf{YY}'|^{\alpha} \int_{O(m)} C_J[\mathbf{H}'(\mathbf{Z} - \mathbf{I})\mathbf{HA}^{1/2}\mathbf{YY}'\mathbf{A}^{1/2}]\, d\mathbf{Y}\, d\mathbf{H}$$

$$= \sum_{j=0}^{\infty} \sum_{J} \frac{C_J(\mathbf{Z} - \mathbf{I}_m)}{j!\, C_J(\mathbf{I}_m)} \int_{\mathscr{D}} |\mathbf{I}_m - \mathbf{YY}'|^{\alpha} C_J(\mathbf{AYY}')\, d\mathbf{Y}.$$

This proves Lemma 3.

3. DISTRIBUTION OF CVCLR IN THE SINGLE SAMPLE CASE

Here, we shall consider the density function of $\mathbf{X} : p \times n$ given by

$$(2\Pi)^{-\frac{1}{2}pn} |\mathbf{\Sigma}|^{-\frac{1}{2}n} \exp[-\tfrac{1}{2} \operatorname{tr} \mathbf{\Sigma}^{-1} \boldsymbol{\mu\mu}' + \operatorname{tr} \mathbf{\Sigma}^{-1}\mathbf{X}\boldsymbol{\mu}' - \tfrac{1}{2} \operatorname{tr} \mathbf{\Sigma}^{-1}\mathbf{XX}'], \quad (3.1)$$

and we are interested in obtaining the density function of the first column of $\mathbf{L}$ or $\mathbf{M}$ given by the following transformation

$$\mathbf{X} = \mathbf{L}\begin{pmatrix} \alpha & \mathbf{0} \\ \mathbf{0} & \mathbf{Y} \end{pmatrix}\mathbf{M}', \qquad \mathbf{L}:\ p \times p, \qquad \mathbf{M}:\ n \times n \qquad \text{and} \qquad \mathbf{Y}:\ (p-1) \times (n-1).$$

Using Lemma 1, the joint density function of $\mathbf{L}$, $\mathbf{M}$, $\mathbf{Y}$, and α is given by

$$c\, |\alpha|^{n-p} |\alpha^2 \mathbf{I}_{p-1} - \mathbf{YY}'|\, |\mathbf{\Sigma}|^{-\frac{1}{2}n} \exp\left[-\tfrac{1}{2} \operatorname{tr} \mathbf{\Sigma}^{-1}\boldsymbol{\mu\mu}' + \operatorname{tr} \mathbf{\Sigma}^{-1}\mathbf{L}\begin{pmatrix} \alpha & 0 \\ 0 & \mathbf{Y} \end{pmatrix}\mathbf{M}'\boldsymbol{\mu}' \right.$$

$$\left. -\tfrac{1}{2} \operatorname{tr} \mathbf{\Sigma}^{-1}\mathbf{L}\begin{pmatrix} \alpha^2 & \mathbf{0} \\ \mathbf{0} & \mathbf{YY}' \end{pmatrix}\mathbf{L}'\right] d\mathbf{L}^{(p,1)}\, d\mathbf{M}^{(n,1)}, \quad (3.2)$$

where $c^{-1} = (2\Pi)^{\frac{1}{2}pn}\Gamma(\frac{1}{2}n)\Gamma(\frac{1}{2}p)/\,\Pi^{\frac{1}{2}(p+n)}$. In order to integrate α, $\mathbf{Y}$, $\mathbf{M}$, or $\mathbf{L}$, we consider the following particular cases because the general problem is extremely difficult.

Case 1. Let $\boldsymbol{\mu} = \mathbf{0}$. In this case, $\mathbf{M}$ and $(\lambda = \alpha^2, \mathbf{Y}, \mathbf{L})$ are independently distributed and their respective densities are given by

$$d\mathbf{M}^{(n,1)} \quad (3.3)$$

and

$$c\lambda^{\frac{1}{2}(n-p-1)} |\lambda\mathbf{I} - \mathbf{YY}'|\, |\mathbf{\Sigma}|^{-\frac{1}{2}n} \exp\left[-\tfrac{1}{2} \operatorname{tr} \mathbf{\Sigma}^{-1}\mathbf{L}\begin{pmatrix} \lambda & \mathbf{0} \\ \mathbf{0} & \mathbf{YY}' \end{pmatrix}\mathbf{L}'\right] d\mathbf{L}^{(p,1)}. \quad (3.4)$$

Integrating over λ and $\mathbf{Y}$, we get the same density of $\mathbf{L}$ as given by Sugiyama [11] when $n \geq p$, and using Lemma 2, it can be written as[3]

$$c_1 |\boldsymbol{\Sigma}|^{-\frac{1}{2}n} \sum_{j=0}^{\infty} (-1)^j (l'\boldsymbol{\Sigma}^{-1}l)^{-j-\frac{1}{2}pn} \binom{\frac{1}{2}pn+j-1}{j} \times \sum_J \tfrac{1}{2}(n-1)_J \{\tfrac{1}{2}(n+p+1)_J\}^{-1} C_J(\mathbf{L}_1'\boldsymbol{\Sigma}^{-1}\mathbf{L}_1)\, d\mathbf{L}^{(p,1)}, \quad (3.5)$$

when $n \geq p$ and $J = \{j_1, \ldots, j_{p-1}\}$; and while $n \leq p$ and $J = \{j_1, \ldots, j_{n-1}\}$,

$$c_2 |\Sigma|^{-\frac{1}{2}n} \sum_{j=0}^{\infty} (-1)^j (l'\Sigma^{-1}l)^{-\frac{1}{2}pn-j} \binom{\frac{1}{2}pn+j-1}{j} \times \sum_J \tfrac{1}{2}(p-1)_J \{\tfrac{1}{2}(n+p+1)_J\}^{-1} C_J(\mathbf{L}_1'\boldsymbol{\Sigma}^{-1}\mathbf{L}_1)\, d\mathbf{L}^{(p,1)}, \quad (3.6)$$

where

$$c_1 = \pi^{1/2}\Gamma(\tfrac{1}{2}pn)\Gamma_{p-1}\tfrac{1}{2}(p+2)/\{\Gamma_{p-1}\tfrac{1}{2}(n+p+1)\Gamma(\tfrac{1}{2}p)\Gamma(\tfrac{1}{2}n)\}, \qquad \mathbf{L} = (\mathbf{l}, \mathbf{L}_1)$$

and

$$c_2 = \Pi^{1/2}\Gamma(\tfrac{1}{2}pn)\Gamma_{n-1}\tfrac{1}{2}(n+2)/\{\Gamma_{n-1}\tfrac{1}{2}(n+p+1)\Gamma(\tfrac{1}{2}p)\Gamma(\tfrac{1}{2}n)\}.$$

We may note that (3.5) can be rewritten in the following form in view of the fact that the exponential term in (3.4) can be expressed as $-\frac{1}{2}\lambda \operatorname{tr} \boldsymbol{\Sigma}^{-1} + \frac{1}{2}\operatorname{tr}(\mathbf{L}_1'\boldsymbol{\Sigma}^{-1}\mathbf{L}_1)(\lambda\mathbf{I} - \mathbf{YY}')$ and expanded in terms of zonal polynomials, and since $n \geq p$, the density of $(\lambda\mathbf{I} - \mathbf{YY}')$ in beta-type with conditions mentioned above.

$$c_1 |\boldsymbol{\Sigma}|^{-\frac{1}{2}n} \sum_{j=0}^{\infty} \binom{\frac{1}{2}pn+j-1}{j} (\operatorname{tr} \boldsymbol{\Sigma}^{-1})^{-\frac{1}{2}pn-j} \times \sum_J \tfrac{1}{2}(p+2)_J \{\tfrac{1}{2}(n+p+1)_J\}^{-1} C_J(\mathbf{L}_1'\boldsymbol{\Sigma}^{-1}\mathbf{L}_1)\, d\mathbf{L}^{(p,1)}. \quad (3.5')$$

Case 2. Let $\boldsymbol{\Sigma} = \mathbf{I}$. Then (3.2) can be rewritten as

$$c\,|\alpha|^{n-p}|\alpha^2\mathbf{I}_{p-1} - \mathbf{YY}'| \exp\left[-\tfrac{1}{2}\operatorname{tr} \boldsymbol{\mu\mu}' - \tfrac{1}{2}\alpha^2 - \tfrac{1}{2}\operatorname{tr} \mathbf{YY}' + \operatorname{tr}\begin{pmatrix}\alpha & \mathbf{0}\\ \mathbf{0} & \mathbf{Y}\end{pmatrix}\mathbf{M}'\boldsymbol{\mu}'\mathbf{L}\right] d\mathbf{L}^{(p,1)}\, d\mathbf{M}^{(n,1)}. \quad (3.2')$$

Here, we shall obtain the joint density function of $\mathbf{M}$ and $\mathbf{L}$. Let $M = (\mathbf{m}, \mathbf{M}_1)$ and $\mathbf{L} = (\mathbf{l}, \mathbf{L}_1)$. Then

$$\operatorname{tr}\begin{pmatrix}\alpha & \mathbf{0}\\ \mathbf{0} & \mathbf{Y}\end{pmatrix}\mathbf{M}'\boldsymbol{\mu}'\mathbf{L} = \alpha\mathbf{m}'\boldsymbol{\mu}'\mathbf{l} + \operatorname{tr} \mathbf{YM}_1'\boldsymbol{\mu}'\mathbf{L}_1.$$

[3] Throughout this paper $\Gamma_m\frac{1}{2}(x)$, $\frac{1}{2}(x)_J$, and $\frac{1}{2}(x)_{\mathscr{K}}$ mean the same as $\Gamma_m(x/2)$, $(x/2)_J$, and $(x/2)_{\mathscr{K}}$, respectively.

We consider the following integration:

$$\int_{\mathbf{Y}} |\alpha^2 \mathbf{I}_{p-1} - \mathbf{YY}'| \exp[-\tfrac{1}{2} \operatorname{tr} \mathbf{YY}' + \operatorname{tr} \mathbf{YM}_1'\boldsymbol{\mu}'\mathbf{L}_1]\, d\mathbf{Y}$$

$$= \sum_{k=0}^{\infty} \sum_{\mathscr{K}} \frac{C_{\mathscr{K}}(\frac{1}{2}\mathbf{M}_1'\boldsymbol{\mu}'\mathbf{L}_1\mathbf{L}_1'\boldsymbol{\mu}\mathbf{M}_1)}{k!\,\frac{1}{2}(n-1)_{\mathscr{K}}\, C_{\mathscr{K}}(\mathbf{I}_{p-1})} \int_{\mathbf{Y}} |\alpha^2 \mathbf{I}_{p-1} - \mathbf{YY}'|\, C_{\mathscr{K}}(\tfrac{1}{2}\mathbf{YY}') e^{-\frac{1}{2}\operatorname{tr}\mathbf{YY}'}\, d\mathbf{Y}, \tag{3.7}$$

and, using Lemma 3

$$\int_{\mathbf{Y}} |\alpha^2 \mathbf{I}_{p-1} - \mathbf{YY}'|\, C_{\mathscr{K}}(\tfrac{1}{2}\mathbf{YY}') \exp(-\tfrac{1}{2} \operatorname{tr} \mathbf{YY}')\quad \mathbf{Y}$$

$$= \sum_{j=k} \sum_{J} (-1)^{j+k} k!\, a_{J,\mathscr{K}} (j!)^{-1} \int_{\mathbf{Y}} |\alpha^2 \mathbf{I}_{p-1} - \mathbf{YY}'|\, C_J(\tfrac{1}{2}\mathbf{YY}')\, d\mathbf{Y}. \tag{3.8}$$

Using (3.8) and Lemma 2 in (3.7) and then (3.7) in (3.2′) and integrating over α, we get the joint density function of $\mathbf{L}$ and $\mathbf{M}$ as

$$c_3 \sum_{i=0}^{\infty} \sum_{k=0}^{\infty} \sum_{\mathscr{K}} \sum_{j=k}^{\infty} \sum_{J} \frac{2^i \Gamma(\frac{1}{2}pn + i + j)}{(2i)!\,\frac{1}{2}(n-1)_{\mathscr{K}}} \frac{(-1)^{j+k} \frac{1}{2}(n-1)_J (\mathbf{m}'\boldsymbol{\mu}'\boldsymbol{l})^{2i}}{j!\,\frac{1}{2}(n+p+1)_J} a_{\mathscr{K},J}$$
$$\times\, C_{\mathscr{K}}(\tfrac{1}{2}\mathbf{M}_1'\boldsymbol{\mu}'\mathbf{L}_1\mathbf{L}_1'\boldsymbol{\mu}\mathbf{M}_1)\, d\mathbf{L}^{(p,1)}\, d\mathbf{M}^{(n,1)} \tag{3.9}$$

for $n \geq p$, while for $n \leq p$

$$c_4 \sum_{i=0}^{\infty} \sum_{k=0}^{\infty} \sum_{j=k}^{\infty} \sum_{\mathscr{K}} \sum_{J} \frac{2^i \Gamma(\frac{1}{2}pn + i + j)(-1)^{j+k} \frac{1}{2}(p-1)_J}{(2i)!\,\frac{1}{2}(p-1)_{\mathscr{K}}\, j!\,\frac{1}{2}(n+p+1)_J} (\mathbf{m}'\boldsymbol{\mu}'l)^{2i} a_{\mathscr{K},J}$$
$$\times\, C_{\mathscr{K}}(\tfrac{1}{2}\boldsymbol{\mu}'\mathbf{L}_1\mathbf{L}_1'\boldsymbol{\mu}\mathbf{M}_1\mathbf{M}_1')\, d\mathbf{L}^{(p,1)}\, d\mathbf{M}^{(n,1)} \tag{3.10}$$

where $c_3 = c_1/\Gamma(\frac{1}{2}pn)$ and $c_4 = c_2/\Gamma(\frac{1}{2}pn)$ and $a_{\mathscr{K},J}$ is defined in Lemma 3. (Note that in (3.9), $\mathscr{K} = \{k_1, \ldots, k_{p-1}\}$ and $J = \{j_1, \ldots, j_{p-1}\}$ while in (3.10), $\mathscr{K} = \{k_1, \ldots, k_{n-1}\}$ and $J = \{j_1, \ldots, j_{n-1}\}$.)

Case 3. Let the rank of $\boldsymbol{\mu} : p \times n$ be one, and we try to obtain the density function of $\mathbf{L}$. The density function of $\mathbf{M}$ requires the integration

$$\int_{O(p)} \exp[\operatorname{tr} \mathbf{CHAH}' + \operatorname{tr} \mathbf{HB}]\, d\mathbf{H}$$

where $\mathbf{C}$ and $\mathbf{A}$ are symmetric matrices of order $p \times p$, and $\mathbf{B} : p \times p$ is a square matrix of rank equal to that of $\boldsymbol{\mu}$. The result for the above integral is unknown, and hence we omit this problem at present.

From (3.2), integrating $\mathbf{M}$ and $\mathbf{Y}$, the joint density function of α and $\mathbf{L}$ can be written as

$$c\, |\alpha|^{n-p} |\boldsymbol{\Sigma}|^{-\frac{1}{2}n} \exp[-\tfrac{1}{2} \operatorname{tr} \boldsymbol{\Sigma}^{-1}\boldsymbol{\mu}\boldsymbol{\mu}'] \sum_{k=0}^{\infty} \{k!(\tfrac{1}{2}n)_k\}^{-1}\, d\mathbf{L}^{(p,1)} f_k(\alpha, \mathbf{L}), \tag{3.11}$$

where

$$f_k(\alpha, \mathbf{L}) = \int_{\mathbf{Y}} |\alpha^2 \mathbf{I}_{p-1} - \mathbf{YY}'| \left\{ \mathrm{tr}\left[\tfrac{1}{4}\boldsymbol{\Sigma}^{-1}\mathbf{L}\begin{pmatrix} \alpha^2 & \mathbf{0} \\ \mathbf{0} & \mathbf{YY}' \end{pmatrix}\mathbf{L}'\boldsymbol{\Sigma}^{-1}\boldsymbol{\mu}\boldsymbol{\mu}' \right] \right\}^k$$

$$\times \exp\left[-\tfrac{1}{2}\,\mathrm{tr}\,\boldsymbol{\Sigma}^{-1}\mathbf{L}\begin{pmatrix} \alpha^2 & \mathbf{0} \\ \mathbf{0} & \mathbf{YY}' \end{pmatrix}\mathbf{L}' \right] d\mathbf{Y} \tag{3.12}$$

or

$$\begin{aligned} f(\theta, \alpha, \mathbf{L}) &= \sum_{k=0}^{\infty} (\theta^k/k!) f_k(\alpha, \mathbf{L}) \\ &= \int_{\mathbf{Y}} |\alpha^2 \mathbf{I}_{p-1} - \mathbf{YY}'| \\ &\quad \times \exp\left[-\tfrac{1}{2}\,\mathrm{tr}\,\boldsymbol{\Sigma}^{-1}\mathbf{L}\begin{pmatrix} \alpha^2 & \mathbf{0} \\ \mathbf{0} & \mathbf{YY}' \end{pmatrix}\mathbf{L}'(\mathbf{I} - \tfrac{1}{2}\theta\boldsymbol{\Sigma}^{-1}\boldsymbol{\mu}\boldsymbol{\mu}') \right] d\mathbf{Y} \\ &= \exp(-\tfrac{1}{2}\alpha^2 \mathbf{l}'(\boldsymbol{\Sigma}^{-1} - \tfrac{1}{2}\theta\boldsymbol{\Sigma}^{-1}\boldsymbol{\mu}\boldsymbol{\mu}'\boldsymbol{\Sigma}^{-1})\mathbf{l}) \\ &\quad \times \sum_{k=0}^{\infty} \sum_{\mathscr{K}} \frac{(-1)^k C_{\mathscr{K}}[\tfrac{1}{2}\mathbf{L}_1{}'(\boldsymbol{\Sigma}^{-1} - \tfrac{1}{2}\theta\boldsymbol{\Sigma}^{-1}\boldsymbol{\mu}\boldsymbol{\mu}'\boldsymbol{\Sigma}^{-1})\mathbf{L}_1]}{k!\, C_{\mathscr{K}}(\mathbf{I}_{p-1})} g_{\mathscr{K}}(\alpha), \end{aligned} \tag{3.13}$$

where

$$\begin{aligned} g_{\mathscr{K}}(\alpha) &= \int_{\mathbf{Y}} |\alpha^2 \mathbf{I}_{p-1} - \mathbf{YY}'|\, C_{\mathscr{K}}(\mathbf{YY}')\, d\mathbf{Y} \\ &= |\alpha|^{np-n+p-1+2k} \Pi^{\frac{1}{2}(p-1)(n-1)} \tfrac{1}{2}(n-1)_{\mathscr{K}} \frac{\Gamma_{p-1}\tfrac{1}{2}(p+2) C_{\mathscr{K}}(\mathbf{I}_{p-1})}{\Gamma_{p-1}\{\tfrac{1}{2}(n+p+1), \mathscr{K}\}} \\ &\qquad\qquad \text{if} \quad n \geq p; \\ &= |\alpha|^{np-n+p-1+2k} \Pi^{\frac{1}{2}(p-1)(n-1)} \tfrac{1}{2}(p-1)_{\mathscr{K}} \frac{\Gamma_{n-1}\tfrac{1}{2}(n+2) C_{\mathscr{K}}(\mathbf{I}_{n-1})}{\Gamma_{n-1}\{\tfrac{1}{2}(n+p+1), \mathscr{K}\}} \\ &\qquad\qquad \text{if} \quad n \leq p. \end{aligned} \tag{3.14}$$

Substituting (3.14) in (3.13), we get $f(\theta, \alpha, \mathbf{L})$ and the coefficient of $\theta^k/k!$ from $f(\theta, \alpha, \mathbf{L})$ gives $f_k(\alpha, \mathbf{L})$. Then using this value in (3.11), we get the joint density function of $\mathbf{L}$ and α. Integrating α, we get the density function of $\mathbf{L}$ as

$$|\boldsymbol{\Sigma}|^{-\frac{1}{2}n} \exp[-\tfrac{1}{2}\,\mathrm{tr}\,\boldsymbol{\Sigma}^{-1}\boldsymbol{\mu}\boldsymbol{\mu}'] \sum_{k=0}^{\infty} \{k!(\tfrac{1}{2}n)_k\}^{-1}\, d\mathbf{L}^{(p,1)} f_k(\mathbf{L}) \tag{3.15}$$

where

$$f(\theta, \mathbf{L}) = \sum_{k=0}^{\infty} \theta^k f_k(\mathbf{L})/k!$$

$$= c_1 \sum_{k=0}^{\infty} (-1)^k \binom{\frac{1}{2}pn + k - 1}{k} \{\mathbf{l}'(\boldsymbol{\Sigma}^{-1} - \tfrac{1}{2}\theta\boldsymbol{\Sigma}^{-1}\boldsymbol{\mu}\boldsymbol{\mu}'\boldsymbol{\Sigma}^{-1})\mathbf{l}\}^{-\frac{1}{2}pn-k}$$

$$\times \sum_{\mathscr{K}} \tfrac{1}{2}(n-1)_{\mathscr{K}}\{\tfrac{1}{2}(n+p+1)_{\mathscr{K}}\}^{-1} C_{\mathscr{K}}[\mathbf{L}_1'(\boldsymbol{\Sigma}^{-1} - \tfrac{1}{2}\theta\boldsymbol{\Sigma}^{-1}\boldsymbol{\mu}\boldsymbol{\mu}'\boldsymbol{\Sigma}^{-1})\mathbf{L}_1]$$

$$\text{if} \quad n \geq p;$$

$$= c_2 \sum_{k=0}^{\infty} (-1)^k \binom{\frac{1}{2}pn + k - 1}{k} \{\mathbf{l}'(\boldsymbol{\Sigma}^{-1} - \tfrac{1}{2}\theta\boldsymbol{\Sigma}^{-1}\boldsymbol{\mu}\boldsymbol{\mu}'\boldsymbol{\Sigma}^{-1})\mathbf{l}\}^{-\frac{1}{2}pn-k}$$

$$\times \sum_{\mathscr{K}} \tfrac{1}{2}(n-1)_{\mathscr{K}}\{\tfrac{1}{2}(n+p+1)_{\mathscr{K}}\}^{-1} C_{\mathscr{K}}[\mathbf{L}_1'(\boldsymbol{\Sigma}^{-1} - \tfrac{1}{2}\theta\boldsymbol{\Sigma}^{-1}\boldsymbol{\mu}\boldsymbol{\mu}'\boldsymbol{\Sigma}^{-1})\mathbf{L}_1]$$

$$\text{if} \quad n \leq p; \qquad (3.16)$$

where c_1 and c_2 are defined in (3.5) and (3.6). Note that for $n \leq p$, $\mathscr{K} = \{k_1, \ldots, k_{n-1}\}$, while for $n \geq p$, $\mathscr{K} = \{k_1, \ldots, k_{p-1}\}$. For $n \geq p$, (3.16) can be written as

$$f(\theta, \mathbf{L}) = c_1 \sum_{k=0}^{\infty} \binom{\frac{1}{2}pn + k - 1}{k} \{\operatorname{tr} \boldsymbol{\Sigma}^{-1} - \tfrac{1}{2}\theta \operatorname{tr} \boldsymbol{\Sigma}^{-1}\boldsymbol{\mu}\boldsymbol{\mu}'\boldsymbol{\Sigma}^{-1}\}^{-\frac{1}{2}pn-k}$$

$$\times \sum_{\mathscr{K}} \tfrac{1}{2}(p+2)_{\mathscr{K}}\{\tfrac{1}{2}(n+p+1)_{\mathscr{K}}\}^{-1}$$

$$\times C_{\mathscr{K}}[\mathbf{L}_1'(\boldsymbol{\Sigma}^{-1} - \tfrac{1}{2}\theta\boldsymbol{\Sigma}^{-1}\boldsymbol{\mu}\boldsymbol{\mu}'\boldsymbol{\Sigma}^{-1})\mathbf{L}_1]. \qquad (3.16')$$

Note that explicit expression will be obtained by evaluating the coefficient of $\theta^k/k!$ from $f(\theta, \mathbf{L})$. When $\boldsymbol{\mu} = \mathbf{0}$, we get the results mentioned in (3.5) and (3.6).

Case 4. In Case 3, we have assumed that $\boldsymbol{\mu}$ is fixed. Now, suppose that $\boldsymbol{\mu} = \boldsymbol{\beta}\mathbf{V}$, $\boldsymbol{\beta} : p \times q$ is fixed having its rank equal to one, and the density function of $\mathbf{V}\mathbf{V}' : q \times q$ is given by

$$\{2^{\frac{1}{2}qn_1}\Gamma_q(\tfrac{1}{2}n_1)\,|\boldsymbol{\Sigma}_3|^{\frac{1}{2}n_1}\}^{-1}\,|(\mathbf{V}\mathbf{V}')|^{\frac{1}{2}(n_1-q-1)} \exp[-\tfrac{1}{2}\operatorname{tr}\boldsymbol{\Sigma}_3^{-1}\mathbf{V}\mathbf{V}']\, d(\mathbf{V}\mathbf{V}'). \quad (3.17)$$

Now, using the integral

$$\int_{\mathbf{V}\mathbf{V}'>0} |(\mathbf{V}\mathbf{V}')|^{\frac{1}{2}(n_1-q-1)}(\operatorname{tr}\tfrac{1}{2}\mathbf{Q}\mathbf{V}\mathbf{V}')^k \exp[-\tfrac{1}{2}\operatorname{tr}\boldsymbol{\Sigma}_4^{-1}(\mathbf{V}\mathbf{V}')]\, d(\mathbf{V}\mathbf{V}')$$

$$= \{2^{\frac{1}{2}qn_1}\Gamma_q(\tfrac{1}{2}n_1)\,|\boldsymbol{\Sigma}_4|^{\frac{1}{2}n_1}\}(\tfrac{1}{2}n_1)_k(\operatorname{tr}\mathbf{Q}\boldsymbol{\Sigma}_4)^k \qquad \text{if rank of} \quad \mathbf{Q} = 1, \quad (3.18)$$

in (3.11), we get the joint density function of α and $\mathbf{L}$ as

$$c\,|\mathbf{I} + \boldsymbol{\Sigma}^{-1}\boldsymbol{\beta}\boldsymbol{\Sigma}_3\boldsymbol{\beta}'|^{-\frac{1}{2}n_1}\,|\boldsymbol{\Sigma}|^{-\frac{1}{2}n}\,|\alpha|^{n-p} \sum_{k=0}^{\infty} (\tfrac{1}{2}n_1)_k\{k!(\tfrac{1}{2}n)_k\}^{-1}\, d\mathbf{L}^{(p,1)} g_k(\alpha, \mathbf{L})$$

$$(3.19)$$

where $g_k(\alpha, \mathbf{L})$ is the same as $f_k(\alpha, \mathbf{L})$ in (3.12) and (3.13) after replacing $\frac{1}{2}\boldsymbol{\Sigma}^{-1}\boldsymbol{\mu}\boldsymbol{\mu}'$ by $\boldsymbol{\Sigma}^{-1}\boldsymbol{\beta}(\boldsymbol{\Sigma}_3^{-1} + \boldsymbol{\beta}'\boldsymbol{\Sigma}^{-1}\boldsymbol{\beta})^{-1}\boldsymbol{\beta}'$. Hence proceeding in the same manner as in Case 3, we get the density function of $\mathbf{L}$ as

$$|\boldsymbol{\Sigma}|^{-\frac{1}{2}n}|\mathbf{I} + \boldsymbol{\Sigma}^{-1}\boldsymbol{\beta}\boldsymbol{\Sigma}_3\boldsymbol{\beta}'|^{-\frac{1}{2}n_1}\sum_{k=0}^{\infty}(\tfrac{1}{2}n_1)_k\{k!(\tfrac{1}{2}n)_k\}^{-1}g_k(\mathbf{L})\,d\mathbf{L}^{(p,1)} \tag{3.20}$$

where

$$g(\theta, \mathbf{L}) = \sum_{k=0}^{\infty}\theta^k g_k(\mathbf{L})/k! \tag{3.21}$$

is the same as that of (3.16) after replacing $(\frac{1}{2}\boldsymbol{\Sigma}^{-1}\boldsymbol{\mu}\boldsymbol{\mu}'\boldsymbol{\Sigma}^{-1})$ by $[\boldsymbol{\Sigma}^{-1}\boldsymbol{\beta}(\boldsymbol{\Sigma}_3^{-1} + \boldsymbol{\beta}'\boldsymbol{\Sigma}^{-1}\boldsymbol{\beta})^{-1}\boldsymbol{\beta}'\boldsymbol{\Sigma}^{-1}]$.

4. DISTRIBUTIONS OF CVCLR'S IN THE TWO SAMPLE CASE

Let us consider the joint density function of $\mathbf{S}: p \times p$ and $\mathbf{X}: p \times n$ as given by

$$\{2^{\frac{1}{2}p(m+n)}\Pi^{\frac{1}{2}pn}\Gamma_p(\tfrac{1}{2}m)\,|\boldsymbol{\Sigma}_2|^{\frac{1}{2}m}|\boldsymbol{\Sigma}_1|^{\frac{1}{2}n}\}^{-1}|\mathbf{S}|^{\frac{1}{2}(m-p-1)}$$
$$\times \exp[-\tfrac{1}{2}\operatorname{tr}\boldsymbol{\Sigma}_2^{-1}\mathbf{S} - \tfrac{1}{2}\operatorname{tr}\boldsymbol{\Sigma}_1^{-1}(\mathbf{X}-\boldsymbol{\mu})(\mathbf{X}-\boldsymbol{\mu})'], \tag{4.1}$$

where $\boldsymbol{\mu}: p \times n$ is a matrix having fixed or random elements. The joint distribution of the random elements of $\boldsymbol{\mu}$ will have measure $d\boldsymbol{\mu}$, say. First, we shall consider the case in which $\boldsymbol{\mu}$ is fixed.

Let us use the tranformations

$$\mathbf{S} = \mathbf{H}\mathbf{D}_\lambda\mathbf{H}', \qquad \mathbf{D}_\lambda^{-1/2}\mathbf{H}'\mathbf{X} = \boldsymbol{\Gamma}\begin{pmatrix}\alpha & \mathbf{0}\\ \mathbf{0} & \mathbf{Y}\end{pmatrix}\boldsymbol{\Delta}' \tag{4.2}$$

where $\mathbf{H}: p \times p$ is a random orthogonal matrix, $\mathbf{D}_\lambda = \operatorname{diag}(\lambda_1, \ldots, \lambda_p)$, the first column vectors of orthogonal matrices $\boldsymbol{\Gamma}: p \times p$ and $\boldsymbol{\Delta}: n \times n$ have random elements, $\alpha \neq 0$, α^2 = maximum ch root of $\mathbf{X}\mathbf{X}'\mathbf{S}^{-1}$ and $\mathbf{Y}: (p-1) \times (n-1)$ is a random matrix.

Note that the first column vector of $\boldsymbol{\Delta}$ is the ch vector of the matrix $\mathbf{X}'\mathbf{S}^{-1}\mathbf{X}$ corresponding to α^2, while the first column vector of $(\mathbf{H}\,\mathbf{D}^{1/2}\,\boldsymbol{\Gamma})$ is the ch vector of the matrix $(\mathbf{X}\mathbf{X}'\mathbf{S}^{-1})$ corresponding to α^2.

With the help of Lemma 1, the Jacobian of the transformation given in (4.2) can be obtained as

$$J(\mathbf{S}, \mathbf{X}; \mathbf{H}, \mathbf{D}_\lambda, \mathbf{Y}, \alpha, \boldsymbol{\Gamma}, \boldsymbol{\Delta}) = \Pi^{\frac{1}{2}(p^2+p+n)}\{\Gamma_p(\tfrac{1}{2}p)\Gamma(\tfrac{1}{2}n)\Gamma(\tfrac{1}{2}p)\}^{-1}\,|\alpha|^{n-p}\,|\mathbf{D}_\lambda|^{\frac{1}{2}n}$$
$$\times |\alpha^2\mathbf{I}_{p-1} - \mathbf{Y}\mathbf{Y}'|$$
$$\times \left\{\prod_{i<j=1}^{p}(\lambda_i - \lambda_j)\right\} d\mathbf{H}^{(p,p)}\,d\boldsymbol{\Gamma}^{(p,1)}\,d\boldsymbol{\Delta}^{(n,1)}. \tag{4.3}$$

Using (4.3) and (4.2) in (4.1), we get the joint density function of $\mathbf{Y}$, $\mathbf{H}$, $\mathbf{D}_\lambda$, α, $\mathbf{\Gamma}$, and $\mathbf{\Delta}$ when $\boldsymbol{\mu}$ is fixed. Now, for the joint density of the required joint ch vectors, we use the following transformations:

First, we consider the transformations when $n \leq p$. Let $\mathbf{Y} = \mathbf{\Gamma}_1\binom{\mathbf{D}_\alpha}{\mathbf{0}}\mathbf{\Delta}_1'$ where $\mathbf{D}_\alpha = \operatorname{diag}(\alpha_2, \ldots, \alpha_n)$, $\alpha_i \neq 0$, $\mathbf{\Delta}_1 : (n-1) \times (n-1)$ is a random orthogonal matrix and the first $(n-1)$ column vectors of an orthogonal matrix $\mathbf{\Gamma}_1 : (p-1) \times (p-1)$ have random elements. Let us introduce a random orthogonal matrix $\mathbf{\Gamma}_2 : (p-n) \times (p-n)$ with measure $d\mathbf{\Gamma}^{(p-n,\,p-n)}$ and be independent of $\mathbf{Y}$, $\mathbf{H}$, $\mathbf{D}_\lambda$, $\boldsymbol{\alpha}$, $\mathbf{\Gamma}$ and $\mathbf{\Delta}$. Then, use the transformations

$$\mathbf{Y} = \mathbf{\Gamma}_1\begin{pmatrix}\mathbf{D}_\alpha\\ \mathbf{0}\end{pmatrix}\mathbf{\Delta}_1', \qquad \mathbf{A} = \mathbf{H}\mathbf{D}_\lambda^{1/2}\mathbf{\Gamma}\begin{pmatrix}1 & \mathbf{0}\\ \mathbf{0} & \mathbf{\Gamma}_1\end{pmatrix}\begin{pmatrix}\mathbf{I}_n & \mathbf{0}\\ \mathbf{0} & \mathbf{\Gamma}_2\end{pmatrix}. \tag{4.4}$$

(Note that the first column vector of $\mathbf{A}$ is the required vector as defined above. If $\mathbf{A} = (\mathbf{A}_1, \mathbf{A}_2)$, $\mathbf{A}_1 : p \times n$ and $\mathbf{A}_2 : p \times (p-n)$, then $\mathbf{A}_2$ depends on random measure $d\mathbf{\Gamma}_2$ and hence we shall integrate $\mathbf{A}_2$). The Jacobian of the transformations is

$$J(\mathbf{Y}, \mathbf{\Gamma}, \mathbf{\Gamma}_2, \mathbf{D}_\lambda, \mathbf{H}; \mathbf{A}, \mathbf{D}_\alpha, \mathbf{\Delta}_1) = J(\mathbf{Y}; \mathbf{\Gamma}_1, \mathbf{D}_\alpha, \mathbf{\Delta}_1)J(\mathbf{\Gamma}_1, \mathbf{\Gamma}, \mathbf{\Gamma}_2, \mathbf{D}_\lambda, \mathbf{H}; \mathbf{A})$$

$$= \frac{\Pi^{\frac{1}{2}(n-1)(p+n-2)}\left(\prod_{i=2}^{n}|\alpha_i|\right)^{p-n}\prod_{i<j=2}^{n}(\alpha_i^2-\alpha_j^2)\left(\prod_{i=1}^{p}\lambda_i\right)^{\frac{1}{2}}\{\Gamma_p(\tfrac{1}{2}p)\}^2\,d\mathbf{\Delta}_1^{(n-1,\,n-1)}}{\Pi^{p^2}\Gamma_{n-1}\tfrac{1}{2}(p-1)\Gamma_{n-1}\tfrac{1}{2}(n-1)\prod_{i<j=1}^{p}(\lambda_i-\lambda_j)\,d\mathbf{\Gamma}^{(p,\,1)}\,d\mathbf{\Gamma}_2^{(p-n,\,p-n)}\,d\mathbf{H}^{(p,\,p)}}. \tag{4.5}$$

Using this in the joint density function of $\mathbf{\Gamma}_2$, $\mathbf{\Gamma}$, $\mathbf{D}_\lambda$, $\mathbf{H}$, $\mathbf{\Delta}$ and $\mathbf{Y}$, we get the joint density function of $\mathbf{A}$, $\mathbf{\Delta}_1$, $\mathbf{\Delta}$ and $\mathbf{D}_\alpha = \operatorname{diag}(\alpha_1, \alpha_2, \ldots, \alpha_n)$ (where $\alpha = \alpha_1$) as

$$c_5\,|\mathbf{A}'\mathbf{A}|^{\frac{1}{2}(m+n-p)}\left(\prod_{i=1}^{n}|\alpha_i|\right)^{p-n}\left(\prod_{i<j=1}^{n}(\alpha_i^2-\alpha_j^2)\right)$$
$$\times \exp\left[-\tfrac{1}{2}\operatorname{tr}\mathbf{\Sigma}_2^{-1}\mathbf{A}\mathbf{A}' - \tfrac{1}{2}\operatorname{tr}\mathbf{\Sigma}_1^{-1}\mathbf{A}\begin{pmatrix}\mathbf{D}_\alpha^2 & \mathbf{0}\\ \mathbf{0} & \mathbf{0}\end{pmatrix}\mathbf{A}'\right]$$
$$\times \exp\left[\operatorname{tr}\mathbf{\Sigma}_1^{-1}\mathbf{A}\begin{pmatrix}\mathbf{D}_\alpha\\ \mathbf{0}\end{pmatrix}\begin{pmatrix}1 & \mathbf{0}\\ \mathbf{0} & \mathbf{\Delta}_1'\end{pmatrix}\mathbf{\Delta}'\boldsymbol{\mu}' - \tfrac{1}{2}\operatorname{tr}\mathbf{\Sigma}_1^{-1}\boldsymbol{\mu}\boldsymbol{\mu}'\right]d\mathbf{\Delta}_1^{(n-1,\,n-1)}\,d\mathbf{\Delta}^{(n,\,1)}, \tag{4.6}$$

where

$$c_5^{-1} = \{2^{\frac{1}{2}p(m+n)}\Gamma_p(\tfrac{1}{2}m)\Gamma_n(\tfrac{1}{2}n)\Gamma_n(\tfrac{1}{2}p)\,\Pi^{\frac{1}{2}p^2}\}\{\Pi^{\frac{1}{2}n^2}\Gamma_p(\tfrac{1}{2}p)\}^{-1}$$
$$\times\{|\mathbf{\Sigma}_2|^{\frac{1}{2}m}|\mathbf{\Sigma}_1|^{\frac{1}{2}n}\}.$$

Now, $\mathbf{A} = (\mathbf{A}_1, \mathbf{A}_2)$, $\mathbf{A}_1 : p \times n$. We integrate $\mathbf{A}_2$ from (4.6). This requires the value of the following integral,

$$\int_{\mathbf{A}_2}|\mathbf{A}_2'(\mathbf{I} - \mathbf{A}_1(\mathbf{A}_1'\mathbf{A}_1)^{-1}\mathbf{A}_1')\mathbf{A}_2|^{\frac{1}{2}(m+n-p)}\exp[-\tfrac{1}{2}\operatorname{tr}\mathbf{\Sigma}_2^{-1}\mathbf{A}_2\mathbf{A}_2']\,d\mathbf{A}_2. \tag{4.7}$$

Let us write $\mathbf{T}_1 = \mathbf{A}_1(\mathbf{A}_1'\mathbf{A}_1)^{-1/2}$ and $\mathbf{T}_2\mathbf{T}_2' = \mathbf{I}_n - \mathbf{T}_1\mathbf{T}_1'$ such that $\mathbf{T} = (\mathbf{T}_1, \mathbf{T}_2)$ is an orthogonal matrix. Let $\mathbf{Q}_1 = \mathbf{T}_1'\mathbf{\Sigma}_2^{-1}\mathbf{T}_1$, $\mathbf{Q}_2 = \mathbf{T}_1'\mathbf{\Sigma}_2^{-1}\mathbf{T}_2$, and $\mathbf{Q}_3 = \mathbf{T}_2'\mathbf{\Sigma}_2^{-1}\mathbf{T}_2$. Then using the transformation $\mathbf{T}'\mathbf{A}_2 = \begin{pmatrix}\mathbf{A}_{21}\\ \mathbf{A}_{22}\end{pmatrix}$, (4.7) becomes

$$\begin{aligned}
&\int_{\mathbf{A}_{22}}\int_{\mathbf{A}_{21}} |\mathbf{A}_{22}'\mathbf{A}_{22}|^{\frac{1}{2}(m+n-p)} \\
&\quad \times \exp[-\tfrac{1}{2}\operatorname{tr}\mathbf{Q}_1\mathbf{A}_{21}\mathbf{A}_{21}' - \operatorname{tr}\mathbf{Q}_2\mathbf{A}_{22}\mathbf{A}_{21}' - \tfrac{1}{2}\operatorname{tr}\mathbf{Q}_3\mathbf{A}_{22}\mathbf{A}_{22}']\, d\mathbf{A}_{21}\, d\mathbf{A}_{22} \\
&\quad = (2\Pi)^{\frac{1}{2}n(p-n)}|\mathbf{Q}_1|^{-\frac{1}{2}(p-n)}\Pi^{\frac{1}{2}(p-n)^2}\{\Gamma_{p-n}\tfrac{1}{2}(p-n)\}^{-1} \\
&\quad \times \int_{\mathbf{S}>0} |\mathbf{S}|^{\frac{1}{2}(m+n-p-1)} \exp[-\tfrac{1}{2}\operatorname{tr}(\mathbf{Q}_3 - \mathbf{Q}_2'\mathbf{Q}_1^{-1}\mathbf{Q}_2)\mathbf{S}]\, d\mathbf{S} \\
&\quad = 2^{\frac{1}{2}n(p-n)+\frac{1}{2}(p-n)(m)}\Pi^{\frac{1}{2}n(p-n)+\frac{1}{2}(p-n)^2} \\
&\quad \times |\mathbf{Q}_1|^{-\frac{1}{2}(p-n)}|\mathbf{Q}_3 - \mathbf{Q}_2'\mathbf{Q}_1^{-1}\mathbf{Q}_2|^{-\frac{1}{2}m}\Gamma_{p-n}(\tfrac{1}{2}m)\{\Gamma_{p-n}\tfrac{1}{2}(p-n)\}^{-1} \\
&\quad = 2^{\frac{1}{2}(p-n)(m+n)}\Pi^{\frac{1}{2}p(p-n)}|\mathbf{\Sigma}_2|^{\frac{1}{2}m}|\mathbf{A}_1'\mathbf{\Sigma}_2^{-1}\mathbf{A}_1|^{\frac{1}{2}(m+n-p)} \\
&\quad \times |\mathbf{A}_1'\mathbf{A}_1|^{-\frac{1}{2}(m+n-p)}\Gamma_{p-n}(\tfrac{1}{2}m)\{\Gamma_{p-n}\tfrac{1}{2}(p-n)\}^{-1}. \qquad (4.8)
\end{aligned}$$

Hence, we get the joint density function of $\mathbf{A}_1$, $\mathbf{D}_\alpha$, $\mathbf{\Delta}_1$ and $\mathbf{\Delta}$ as

$$\begin{aligned}
&c_6\,|\mathbf{A}_1'\mathbf{\Sigma}_2^{-1}\mathbf{A}_1|^{\frac{1}{2}(m+n-p)}\left(\prod_{i=1}^{n}|\alpha_i|\right)^{p-n}\left(\prod_{i<j=1}^{n}(\alpha_i^2-\alpha_j^2)\right) \\
&\quad \times \exp[-\tfrac{1}{2}\operatorname{tr}\mathbf{\Sigma}_2^{-1}\mathbf{A}_1\mathbf{A}_1' - \tfrac{1}{2}\operatorname{tr}\mathbf{\Sigma}_1^{-1}\mathbf{A}_1\mathbf{D}_\alpha^2\mathbf{A}_1'] \\
&\quad \times \exp\left[\operatorname{tr}\mathbf{\Sigma}_1^{-1}\mathbf{A}_1\mathbf{D}_\alpha\begin{pmatrix}1 & \mathbf{0}\\ \mathbf{0} & \mathbf{\Delta}_1'\end{pmatrix}\mathbf{\Delta}'\boldsymbol{\mu}' - \tfrac{1}{2}\operatorname{tr}\mathbf{\Sigma}_1^{-1}\boldsymbol{\mu}\boldsymbol{\mu}'\right] \\
&\quad \times d\mathbf{\Delta}_1^{(n-1,n-1)}\, d\mathbf{\Delta}^{(n,1)} \qquad \text{for} \quad n \le p \qquad (4.9)
\end{aligned}$$

and

$$c_6^{-1} = \{2^{\frac{1}{2}n(n+m)}\Gamma_n\tfrac{1}{2}(m+n-p)\Gamma_n(\tfrac{1}{2}n)\Pi^{\frac{1}{2}pn-\frac{1}{2}n^2}\}\,|\mathbf{\Sigma}_1|^{\frac{1}{2}n}.$$

Similarly, for $n \ge p$, it is easy to obtain the joint density function of $\mathbf{A}: p \times p$, $\mathbf{\Delta}_1 : (n-1)\times(n-1)$ having random elements in first $(p-1)$ columns, $\mathbf{\Delta}$ and $\mathbf{D}_\alpha = \operatorname{diag}(\alpha_1, \ldots, \alpha_p)$ as

$$\begin{aligned}
&c_7\,|\mathbf{A}'\mathbf{A}|^{\frac{1}{2}(m+n-p)}\left(\prod_{i=1}^{p}|\alpha_i|\right)^{n-p}\left(\prod_{i<j=1}^{p}(\alpha_i^2-\alpha_j^2)\right) \\
&\quad \times \exp[-\tfrac{1}{2}\operatorname{tr}\mathbf{\Sigma}_2^{-1}\mathbf{A}\mathbf{A}' - \tfrac{1}{2}\operatorname{tr}\mathbf{\Sigma}_1^{-1}\mathbf{A}\mathbf{D}_\alpha^2\mathbf{A}'] \\
&\quad \times \exp\left(\operatorname{tr}\mathbf{\Sigma}_1^{-1}\mathbf{A}(\mathbf{D}_\alpha\mathbf{0})\begin{pmatrix}1 & \mathbf{0}\\ \mathbf{0} & \mathbf{\Delta}_1'\end{pmatrix}\mathbf{\Delta}'\boldsymbol{\mu}' - \tfrac{1}{2}\operatorname{tr}\mathbf{\Sigma}_1^{-1}\boldsymbol{\mu}\boldsymbol{\mu}'\right) \\
&\quad \times d\mathbf{\Delta}_1^{(n-1,p-1)}\, d\mathbf{\Delta}^{(n,1)} \qquad \text{for} \quad n \ge p \qquad (4.10)
\end{aligned}$$

and

$$c_7^{-1} = \{2^{\frac{1}{2}p(m+n)}\Gamma_p(\tfrac{1}{2}m)\,\Gamma_p(\tfrac{1}{2}n)\}\{|\mathbf{\Sigma}_2|^{\frac{1}{2}m}|\mathbf{\Sigma}_1|^{\frac{1}{2}n}\}.$$

Now, the problem is to obtain the density function of the first column vector of $\mathbf{A}$ (or $\mathbf{A}_1$) and/or $\mathbf{\Delta}$. The general problem is extremely difficult and hence we consider below some particular cases.

Case 1. Let $\boldsymbol{\mu} = \mathbf{0}$. Then $\mathbf{\Delta}$, $\mathbf{\Delta}_1$ and ($\mathbf{A}$ or $\mathbf{A}_1$, $\mathbf{D}_\alpha^{\;2}$) are independently distributed, and their density functions are respectively given by

$$d\mathbf{\Delta}^{(n,1)}, \qquad d\mathbf{\Delta}_1^{(n-1,p-1)} \quad \text{if} \quad n \geq p \qquad \text{or} \qquad d\mathbf{\Delta}_1^{(n-1,n-1)} \quad \text{if} \quad n \leq p$$

and if $\alpha_i^{\;2} = \lambda_i$, $i = 1, 2, \ldots, p$ or n,

$$c_6\,|\mathbf{A}_1{}'\mathbf{\Sigma}_2^{-1}\mathbf{A}_1|^{\frac{1}{2}(m+n-p)}\left(\prod_{i=1}^{n}\lambda_i\right)^{\frac{1}{2}(p-n-1)}\left(\prod_{i<j=1}^{n}(\lambda_i-\lambda_j)\right)$$
$$\times \exp[-\tfrac{1}{2}\operatorname{tr}\mathbf{\Sigma}_2^{-1}\mathbf{A}_1\mathbf{A}_1{}' - \tfrac{1}{2}\operatorname{tr}\mathbf{\Sigma}_1^{-1}\mathbf{A}_1\mathbf{D}_\lambda\mathbf{A}_1{}'] \tag{4.9$'$}$$

for $n \leq p$, $A_1 : p \times n$ and $D_\lambda = \operatorname{diag}(\lambda_1, \ldots, \lambda_n)$, and

$$c_7\,|\mathbf{A}'\mathbf{A}|^{\frac{1}{2}(m+n-p)}\left(\prod_{i=1}^{p}\lambda_i\right)^{\frac{1}{2}(n-p-1)}\left(\prod_{i<j=1}^{p}(\lambda_i-\lambda_j)\right)$$
$$\times \exp[-\tfrac{1}{2}\operatorname{tr}\mathbf{\Sigma}_2^{-1}\mathbf{A}\mathbf{A}' - \tfrac{1}{2}\operatorname{tr}\mathbf{\Sigma}_1^{-1}\mathbf{A}\mathbf{D}_\lambda\mathbf{A}'] \tag{4.10$'$}$$

for $n \geq p$, $\mathbf{A} : p \times p$ and $\mathbf{D}_\lambda = \operatorname{diag}(\lambda_1, \ldots, \lambda_p)$.

From (4.9′), we shall try to obtain the density function of the first column vector of $\mathbf{A}_1$. Let $\mathbf{A}_1 = (\mathbf{a}, \mathbf{A}_3)$, $\mathbf{\Sigma}_2 = (\mathbf{\Sigma}_2^{1/2})^2$, $\mathbf{Z} = \mathbf{\Sigma}_2^{1/2}\mathbf{\Sigma}_1^{-1}\mathbf{\Sigma}_2^{1/2}$, and $\mathbf{b} = \mathbf{\Sigma}_2^{-1/2}a$. Let us transform $\mathbf{B} = \mathbf{\Sigma}_2^{-1/2}\mathbf{A}_3$. Then the joint density function of $\mathbf{B} : p \times (n-1)$, $\mathbf{a}$ and $\mathbf{D}_\lambda$ is given by

$$c_6\,|\mathbf{\Sigma}_2|^{\frac{1}{2}(n-1)}(\mathbf{b}'\mathbf{b})^{\frac{1}{2}(m+n-p)}\left|\mathbf{B}'\left(\frac{\mathbf{I}_p - \mathbf{b}\mathbf{b}'}{(\mathbf{b}'\mathbf{b})}\right)\mathbf{B}\right|^{\frac{1}{2}(m+n-p)}\left(\prod_{i=1}^{n}\lambda_i\right)^{\frac{1}{2}(p-n-1)}$$
$$\times\left(\prod_{i<j=1}^{n}(\lambda_i-\lambda_j)\right)\exp[-\tfrac{1}{2}\mathbf{b}'\mathbf{b} - \tfrac{1}{2}\lambda_1\mathbf{b}'\mathbf{Z}\mathbf{b} - \tfrac{1}{2}\operatorname{tr}\mathbf{B}'\mathbf{B} - \tfrac{1}{2}\operatorname{tr}\mathbf{B}'\mathbf{Z}\mathbf{B}\mathbf{D}_1], \tag{4.11}$$

where $\mathbf{D}_1 = \operatorname{diag}(\lambda_2, \lambda_3, \ldots, \lambda_n)$.

For integration over $\mathbf{B} : p \times (n-1)$, we require the following integral

$$h(\mathbf{b}, \mathbf{D}_1) = \int_B \left|\mathbf{B}'\left(\frac{\mathbf{I}_p - \mathbf{b}\mathbf{b}'}{(\mathbf{b}'\mathbf{b})}\right)\mathbf{B}\right|^{\frac{1}{2}(m+n-p)} \exp[-\tfrac{1}{2}\operatorname{tr}\mathbf{B}'\mathbf{B} - \tfrac{1}{2}\operatorname{tr}\mathbf{B}'\mathbf{Z}\mathbf{B}\mathbf{D}_1]\,d\mathbf{B}. \tag{4.12}$$

Introduce a random orthogonal matrix $\mathbf{H} : (n-1) \times (n-1)$ with measure $d\mathbf{H}^{(n-1,n-1)}$, use the transformation $\mathbf{B} \to \mathbf{B}\mathbf{H}$ and then integrate over $\mathbf{H}$. This reduces (4.12) to

$$h(\mathbf{b}, \mathbf{D}_1) = \sum_{k=0}^{\infty}\sum_{\mathscr{K}} \frac{C_{\mathscr{K}}(-\tfrac{1}{2}\mathbf{D}_1)}{k!\,C_{\mathscr{K}}(\mathbf{I}_{n-1})}\int_B \left|\mathbf{B}'\left(\frac{\mathbf{I}_p - \mathbf{b}\mathbf{b}'}{(\mathbf{b}'\mathbf{b})}\right)\mathbf{B}\right|^{\frac{1}{2}(m+n-p)}$$
$$\times C_{\mathscr{K}}(\mathbf{B}'\mathbf{Z}\mathbf{B})e^{-\frac{1}{2}\operatorname{tr}\mathbf{B}'\mathbf{B}}\,d\mathbf{B}. \tag{4.13}$$

Let us make the transformation $\mathbf{B} = \mathbf{L}_1\mathbf{D}_\delta\mathbf{M}$ where $\mathbf{M} : (n-1) \times (n-1)$ is a random orthogonal matrix, $\delta_i \neq 0$, $\mathbf{D}_\delta = \text{diag}(\delta_1, \ldots, \delta_{n-1})$, and $\mathbf{L}_1 : p \times (n-1)$ has random elements such that $\mathbf{L}_1'\mathbf{L}_1 = \mathbf{I}_{n-1}$. Let $\mathbf{L} : p \times p$ be a complete orthogonal matrix due to $\mathbf{L}_1$. Then the Jacobian of the transformation is

$$J(\mathbf{B}; \mathbf{L}, \mathbf{D}_\delta, \mathbf{M}) = \frac{\Pi^{\frac{1}{2}(n-1)(p+n-1)}}{\Gamma_{n-1}(\frac{1}{2}p)\Gamma_{n-1}\frac{1}{2}(n-1)} \, d\mathbf{L}^{(p,n-1)} \, d\mathbf{M}^{(n-1,n-1)} \times \left(\prod_{i=1}^{n-1} |\delta_i|\right)^{p-n+1} \left(\prod_{i<j=1}^{n-1} (\delta_i^2 - \delta_j^2)\right).$$

Use the transformation $\delta_i^2 = \omega_i$, $i = 1, 2, \ldots, n-1$ and $\mathbf{D}_\omega = \text{diag}(\omega_1, \ldots, \omega_{n-1})$. Using this in (4.13), we get

$$h(\mathbf{b}, \mathbf{D}_1) = \frac{\Pi^{\frac{1}{2}(n-1)(p+n-1)}}{\Gamma_{n-1}(\frac{1}{2}p)\Gamma_{n-1}\frac{1}{2}(n-1)} \sum_{k=0}^{\infty} \sum_{\mathscr{K}} \frac{C_{\mathscr{K}}(-\frac{1}{2}\mathbf{D}_1)}{k!\,C_{\mathscr{K}}(\mathbf{I}_{n-1})} \times \int_{\mathbf{D}_\omega} \int_{\mathbf{L}} |\mathbf{D}_\omega|^{\frac{1}{2}m} \left[\frac{1 - \mathbf{b}'\mathbf{L}_1\mathbf{L}_1'\mathbf{b}}{\mathbf{b}'\mathbf{b}}\right]^{\frac{1}{2}(m+n-p)} \left(\prod_{i<j=1}^{n-1} (\omega_i - \omega_j)\right) \times C_{\mathscr{K}}(\mathbf{L}_1'\mathbf{Z}\mathbf{L}_1\mathbf{D}_\omega)\exp(-\tfrac{1}{2}\operatorname{tr}\mathbf{D}_\omega)\, d\mathbf{L}^{(p,n-1)}\, d\mathbf{D}_\omega. \tag{4.14}$$

For the integration over $\mathbf{D}_\omega$, we introduce a random orthogonal matrix $\mathbf{H} : (n-1) \times (n-1)$ with normalized measure $d\mathbf{H}^{(n-1,n-1)}$. Let us transform $\mathbf{L}$ by

$$\mathbf{L} \to \mathbf{L}\begin{pmatrix} \mathbf{H} & \mathbf{0} \\ \mathbf{0} & \mathbf{I}_{p-n+1} \end{pmatrix}$$

and then integrating over $\mathbf{H}$ and then $\mathbf{D}_\omega$, we can write (4.14) as

$$h(\mathbf{b}, \mathbf{D}_1) = \frac{2^{\frac{1}{2}(n-1)(m+n)}\Pi^{\frac{1}{2}(n-1)p}}{\Gamma_{n-1}(\frac{1}{2}p)} \sum_{k=0}^{\infty} \sum_{\mathscr{K}} \frac{\Gamma_{n-1}(\frac{1}{2}(m+n), \mathscr{K})C_{\mathscr{K}}(-\mathbf{D}_1)}{k!\,C_{\mathscr{K}}(\mathbf{I}_{n-1})} \times \int_{\mathbf{L}} \left[\frac{1 - \mathbf{b}'\mathbf{L}_1\mathbf{L}_1'\mathbf{b}}{(\mathbf{b}'\mathbf{b})}\right]^{\frac{1}{2}(m+n-p)} C_{\mathscr{K}}(\mathbf{L}_1'\mathbf{Z}\mathbf{L}_1)\, d\mathbf{L}^{(p,n-1)}. \tag{4.15}$$

Let us write

$$h_1(\mathbf{b}, \mathscr{K}) = \int_{O(p)} [\mathbf{b}'(\mathbf{I} - \mathbf{L}_1\mathbf{L}_1')\mathbf{b}]^{\frac{1}{2}(m+n-p)} C_{\mathscr{K}}(\mathbf{L}_1'\mathbf{Z}\mathbf{L}_1)\, d\mathbf{L}^{(p,n-1)}. \tag{4.16}$$

Transform $\lambda_i/\lambda_1 = y_{i-1}$, $i = 2, 3, \ldots, n$ in (4.11), and then integrate over λ_1 and $y_1, \ldots, y_{n-1}$. This gives us the density function of $\mathbf{a}$ for $n \leq p$ as

$$c_8 \sum_{k=0}^{\infty} (-1)^k \binom{\frac{1}{2}pn + k - 1}{k} \left(\frac{2}{b'\mathbf{Z}b}\right)^{\frac{1}{2}pn+k} \times e^{-\frac{1}{2}\mathbf{b}'\mathbf{b}} \sum_{\mathscr{K}} \frac{\frac{1}{2}(m+n)_{\mathscr{K}}\,\frac{1}{2}(p-1)_{\mathscr{K}}}{\frac{1}{2}(n+p+1)_{\mathscr{K}}} h_1(\mathbf{b}, \mathscr{K}), \tag{4.17}$$

where

$$c_8 = \Gamma(\tfrac{1}{2}pn)\Gamma_{n-1}\tfrac{1}{2}(n+2)\Gamma_{n-1}\tfrac{1}{2}(m+n)\{2^{\frac{1}{2}(m+n)}\Pi^{\frac{1}{2}(p-1)}\Gamma\tfrac{1}{2}(m-p)\Gamma(\tfrac{1}{2}n) \times \Gamma_{n-1}\tfrac{1}{2}(n+p+1)\Gamma_{n-1}\tfrac{1}{2}(m+n-p)\}^{-1}|\mathbf{Z}|^{\frac{1}{2}n}|\mathbf{\Sigma}_2|^{-1/2}$$

and $h_1(\mathbf{b}, \mathscr{K})$ is defined in (4.16).

Similarly, the density function of $\mathbf{a}$ for $n \geq p$ can be given by

$$c_9 \sum_{k=0}^{\infty} (-1)^k \binom{\frac{1}{2}pn + k - 1}{k} \left(\frac{2}{b'\mathbf{Z}b}\right)^{\frac{1}{2}pn+k} \times e^{-\frac{1}{2}\mathbf{b}'\mathbf{b}} \sum_{\mathscr{K}} \frac{\frac{1}{2}(m+n)_{\mathscr{K}}\frac{1}{2}(n-1)_{\mathscr{K}}}{\frac{1}{2}(n+p+1)_{\mathscr{K}}} h_2(\mathbf{b}, \mathscr{K}), \tag{4.18}$$

where

$$c_9 = \Gamma(\tfrac{1}{2}pn)\Gamma_{p-1}\tfrac{1}{2}(m+n)\Gamma_{p-1}\tfrac{1}{2}(p+2) \times \{2^{\frac{1}{2}(m+n)}\Gamma_p(\tfrac{1}{2}m)\Gamma_{p-1}\tfrac{1}{2}(n+p+1)\Gamma(\tfrac{1}{2}n)\Gamma_{p-1}(\tfrac{1}{2}p)\}^{-1}|\mathbf{Z}|^{\frac{1}{2}n}|\mathbf{\Sigma}_2|^{-1/2}$$

and

$$h_2(\mathbf{b}, \mathscr{K}) = \int_{O(p)} [\mathbf{b}'(\mathbf{I} - \mathbf{L}_1\mathbf{L}_1')\mathbf{b}]^{\frac{1}{2}(m+n-p)} C_{\mathscr{K}}(\mathbf{L}_1'\mathbf{Z}\mathbf{L}_1)\, d\mathbf{L}^{(p,\,p-1)}, \quad \mathbf{L}_1:\ p \times (p-1) \tag{4.19}$$

and $\mathscr{K} = \{k_1, \ldots, k_{p-1}\}$.

Case 2. Let $\boldsymbol{\mu} \neq \mathbf{0}$ and the rank of $\boldsymbol{\mu}$ be one. The density function of $\mathbf{\Delta}$ is extremely difficult and hence we try to obtain the density function of $\mathbf{a}$. For this purpose, we integrate from (4.9) and (4.10) $\mathbf{\Delta}_1$ and $\mathbf{\Delta}$ and transform $\alpha_i^2 = \lambda_i$ $i = 1, 2, \ldots, p$ or n. Then, the joint density function of $\mathbf{A}_1 : p \times n$ and $\mathbf{D}_\lambda = \operatorname{diag}(\lambda_1, \ldots, \lambda_n)$ for $n \leq p$ is given by

$$c_6\, |\mathbf{A}_1'\mathbf{\Sigma}_2^{-1}\mathbf{A}_1|^{\frac{1}{2}(m+n-p)}\, |\mathbf{D}_\lambda|^{\frac{1}{2}(p-n-1)} \left(\prod_{i<j=1}^{n} (\lambda_i - \lambda_j)\right) \times \exp[-\tfrac{1}{2}\operatorname{tr}\mathbf{\Sigma}_2^{-1}\mathbf{A}_1\mathbf{A}_1' - \tfrac{1}{2}\operatorname{tr}\mathbf{\Sigma}_1^{-1}\mathbf{A}_1\mathbf{D}_\lambda\mathbf{A}_1' - \tfrac{1}{2}\operatorname{tr}\mathbf{\Sigma}_1^{-1}\boldsymbol{\mu}\boldsymbol{\mu}'] \times \sum_{k=0}^{\infty} \{k!(\tfrac{1}{2}n)_k\}^{-1}\{\tfrac{1}{4}\operatorname{tr}\boldsymbol{\mu}'\mathbf{\Sigma}_1^{-1}\mathbf{A}_1\mathbf{D}_\lambda\mathbf{A}_1'\mathbf{\Sigma}_1^{-1}\boldsymbol{\mu}\}^k \tag{4.20}$$

and the joint density function of $\mathbf{A} : p \times p$ and $\mathbf{D}_\lambda = \operatorname{diag}(\lambda_1, \ldots, \lambda_p)$ for $n \geq p$ is given by

$$c_7\, |\mathbf{A}'\mathbf{A}|^{\frac{1}{2}(m+n-p)}\, |\mathbf{D}_\lambda|^{\frac{1}{2}(n-p-1)} \left(\prod_{i<j=1}^{p} (\lambda_i - \lambda_j)\right) \times \exp[-\tfrac{1}{2}\mathbf{\Sigma}_2^{-1}\mathbf{A}\mathbf{A}' - \tfrac{1}{2}\operatorname{tr}\mathbf{\Sigma}_1^{-1}\mathbf{A}\mathbf{D}_\lambda\mathbf{A}' - \tfrac{1}{2}\operatorname{tr}\mathbf{\Sigma}_1^{-1}\boldsymbol{\mu}\boldsymbol{\mu}'] \sum_{k=0}^{\infty} \{k!(\tfrac{1}{2}n)_k\}^{-1} \times [\operatorname{tr}(\tfrac{1}{4}\mathbf{\Sigma}_1^{-1}\mathbf{A}\mathbf{D}_\lambda\mathbf{A}'\mathbf{\Sigma}_1^{-1}\boldsymbol{\mu}\boldsymbol{\mu}')]^k. \tag{4.21}$$

Case (i). Let us write $\mathbf{Z}_1 = \mathbf{\Sigma}_2^{1/2}\mathbf{\Sigma}_1^{-1/2}$ and $\mathbf{\Sigma}_1^{-1/2}\boldsymbol{\mu}\boldsymbol{\mu}'\mathbf{\Sigma}_1^{-1/2} = \mathbf{x}\mathbf{x}'$, where $\mathbf{x} : p \times 1$ is a vector. Note that $\mathbf{Z} = \mathbf{Z}_1\mathbf{Z}_1'$. First of all, we consider $n \leq p$. Let us write $\mathbf{A}_1 = (\mathbf{a},\mathbf{A}_3)$, $\mathbf{b} = \mathbf{\Sigma}_2^{-1/2}\mathbf{a}$. Using the transformation $\mathbf{B} = \mathbf{\Sigma}_2^{-1/2}\mathbf{A}_3$, and then integrating over $\mathbf{B}$, we get the joint density function of $\mathbf{a}$ and $\mathbf{D}_\lambda = \operatorname{diag}(\lambda_1, \mathbf{D}_1)$, $\mathbf{D}_1 = \operatorname{diag}(\lambda_2, \ldots, \lambda_n)$ as

$$c_6 |\mathbf{\Sigma}_2|^{\frac{1}{2}(n-1)} |\mathbf{D}_\lambda|^{\frac{1}{2}(p-n-1)} \left(\prod_{i<j=1}^{n} (\lambda_i - \lambda_j) \right) \times \exp[-\tfrac{1}{2}(\mathbf{x}'\mathbf{x} + \mathbf{b}'\mathbf{b})] \sum_{k=0}^{\infty} \{(\tfrac{1}{2}n)_k\}^{-1} h(\mathbf{b}, \mathbf{D}_\lambda, k) \quad \text{for} \quad n \leq p, \tag{4.22}$$

where

$$h(\mathbf{b}, \mathbf{D}_\lambda, k) = (k!)^{-1} \int_{\mathbf{B}} \left| \begin{pmatrix} \mathbf{b}' \\ \mathbf{B}' \end{pmatrix} (\mathbf{b} \quad \mathbf{B}) \right|^{\frac{1}{2}(m+n-p)} \left[\tfrac{1}{4}\mathbf{x}'\mathbf{Z}_1'(\mathbf{b} \quad \mathbf{B})\mathbf{D}_\lambda \begin{pmatrix} \mathbf{b}' \\ \mathbf{B}' \end{pmatrix} \mathbf{Z}_1\mathbf{x} \right]^k \times \exp\left[-\tfrac{1}{2} \operatorname{tr} \mathbf{B}\mathbf{B}' - \tfrac{1}{2} \operatorname{tr} \mathbf{Z}_1'(\mathbf{b} \quad \mathbf{B})\mathbf{D}_\lambda \begin{pmatrix} \mathbf{b}' \\ \mathbf{B}' \end{pmatrix} \mathbf{Z}_1 \right] d\mathbf{B}. \tag{4.23}$$

Hence

$$h_\theta(b, \mathbf{D}_\lambda) = \sum_{k=0}^{\infty} \theta^k h(\mathbf{b}, \mathbf{D}_\lambda, k) = \int_{\mathbf{B}} \left| \begin{pmatrix} \mathbf{b}' \\ \mathbf{B}' \end{pmatrix} (\mathbf{b} \quad \mathbf{B}) \right|^{\frac{1}{2}(m+n-p)} \times \exp[-\tfrac{1}{2} \operatorname{tr} \mathbf{B}\mathbf{B}' - \tfrac{1}{2} \operatorname{tr} Q(\theta)\mathbf{B}\mathbf{D}_1\mathbf{B}'] \, d\mathbf{B} \exp[-\tfrac{1}{2}\lambda_1 \mathbf{b}'Q(\theta)\mathbf{b}] \tag{4.24}$$

where $Q(\theta) = \mathbf{Z}_1(\mathbf{I}_p - \frac{1}{2}\theta\mathbf{x}\mathbf{x}')\mathbf{Z}_1'$. Employing the technique used in Case 1 of this section and integrating over $\mathbf{D}_\lambda$, we get the density function of $\mathbf{a}$ as

$$\exp[-\tfrac{1}{2} \operatorname{tr} \Sigma_1^{-1}\mu\mu' - \tfrac{1}{2}b'b] \sum_{k=0}^{\infty} \{(\tfrac{1}{2}n)_k\}^{-1} g_1(k, \mathbf{b}) \quad \text{for} \quad n \leq p, \tag{4.25}$$

where $g_1(k, b)$ is the coefficient of θ^k in the expansion of

$$g_1(\theta, b) = c_8 \sum_{j=0}^{\infty} (-1)^j \binom{\frac{1}{2}pn + j - 1}{j} \left(\frac{2}{\mathbf{b}'Q(\theta)\mathbf{b}} \right)^{\frac{1}{2}pn+j} \times \sum_{J} \frac{\frac{1}{2}(m+n)_J \frac{1}{2}(p-1)_J}{\frac{1}{2}(n+p+1)_J} h_1(\mathbf{b}, \mathscr{K}, \theta). \tag{4.26}$$

$$h_1(\mathbf{b}, \mathscr{K}, \theta) = \int_{O(p)} [\mathbf{b}'(\mathbf{I} - \mathbf{L}_1\mathbf{L}_1')\mathbf{b}]^{\frac{1}{2}(m+n-p)} \times C_{\mathscr{K}}(\mathbf{L}_1'Q(\theta)\mathbf{L}_1) \, d\mathbf{L}^{(p,n-1)}, \qquad \mathbf{L}_1: \; p \times (n-1) \tag{4.27}$$

and $Q(\theta) = \mathbf{Z}_1[\mathbf{I} - \frac{1}{2}\theta\mathbf{x}\mathbf{x}']\mathbf{Z}_1'$.

Similarly, the density function of $\mathbf{a}$ for $n \geq p$ is given by

$$\exp(-\tfrac{1}{2}\operatorname{tr}\boldsymbol{\Sigma}_1^{-1}\boldsymbol{\mu}\boldsymbol{\mu}' - \tfrac{1}{2}\mathbf{b}\mathbf{b}')\sum_{k=0}^{\infty}\{(\tfrac{1}{2}n)_k\}^{-1}g_2(\mathbf{k}, \mathbf{b}), \tag{4.28}$$

where $g_2(k, \mathbf{b})$ is the coefficient of θ^k in the expansion of

$$g_2(\theta, b) = c_9\sum_{j=0}^{\infty}(-1)^j\binom{\frac{1}{2}pn + j - 1}{j}\left(\frac{2}{\mathbf{b}'Q(\theta)\mathbf{b}}\right)^{\frac{1}{2}pn+j}$$
$$\times\sum_J\frac{\frac{1}{2}(m+n)_J\,\frac{1}{2}(n-1)_J}{\frac{1}{2}(n+p+1)_J}h_2(\mathbf{b}, x, \theta), \tag{4.29}$$

$$h_2(b, x, \theta) = \int_{O(p)}[\mathbf{b}'(\mathbf{I} - \mathbf{L}_1\mathbf{L}_1{}')\mathbf{b}]^{\frac{1}{2}(m+n-p)}C_{\mathscr{K}}(\mathbf{L}_1{}'Q(\theta)\mathbf{L}_1)\,d\mathbf{L}^{(p,\,p-1)},$$
$$\times\,\mathbf{L}_1\colon\ p\times(p-1)\quad\text{and}\quad Q(\theta) = \mathbf{Z}_1[\mathbf{I}_p - \tfrac{1}{2}\theta\mathbf{x}\mathbf{x}']\mathbf{Z}_1{}'. \tag{4.30}$$

Case (ii). In the above case, we have assumed that $\boldsymbol{\mu}$ is fixed. Now suppose that $\boldsymbol{\mu} = \boldsymbol{\beta}\mathbf{Y}$, $\boldsymbol{\beta} : p \times q$ is fixed having its rank equal to one, and the density function of $\mathbf{YY}' : q \times q$ is given by

$$\{2^{\frac{1}{2}qn_1}\Gamma_q(\tfrac{1}{2}n_1)\,|\boldsymbol{\Sigma}_3|^{\frac{1}{2}n_1}\}^{-1}\,|(\mathbf{YY}')|^{\frac{1}{2}(n_1-q-1)}\exp[-\tfrac{1}{2}\operatorname{tr}\boldsymbol{\Sigma}_3^{-1}(\mathbf{YY}')]\,d(\mathbf{YY}'). \tag{4.31}$$

Then for $n \leq p$, the joint density function of $\mathbf{A}_1$ and $\mathbf{D}_\lambda$ is obtained from (4.20) by integrating over $\mathbf{YY}'$. This gives us the density function of $\mathbf{A}_1$ and $\mathbf{D}_\lambda$ as

$$c_6\,|\mathbf{I}_q + \boldsymbol{\Sigma}_3\boldsymbol{\beta}'\boldsymbol{\Sigma}_1^{-1}\boldsymbol{\beta}|^{-\frac{1}{2}n_1}\,|\mathbf{A}_1{}'\boldsymbol{\Sigma}_2^{-1}\mathbf{A}_1|^{\frac{1}{2}(m+n-p)}\,|\mathbf{D}_\lambda|^{\frac{1}{2}(p-n-1)}\left(\prod_{i<j=1}^{n}(\lambda_i - \lambda_j)\right)$$
$$\times\exp[-\tfrac{1}{2}\operatorname{tr}\boldsymbol{\Sigma}_2^{-1}\mathbf{A}_1\mathbf{A}_1{}']\exp(-\tfrac{1}{2}\operatorname{tr}\boldsymbol{\Sigma}_1^{-1}\mathbf{A}_1\mathbf{D}_\lambda\mathbf{A}_1{}')$$
$$\times\sum_{k=0}^{\infty}\left(\frac{n_1}{2}\right)_k\{k!(n/2)_k\}^{-1}\{\tfrac{1}{2}\operatorname{tr}\boldsymbol{\Sigma}_1^{-1/2}\mathbf{A}_1\mathbf{D}_\lambda\mathbf{A}_1{}'\boldsymbol{\Sigma}_1^{-1/2}\mathbf{y}\mathbf{y}'\}^k \tag{4.32}$$

where $\mathbf{y}\mathbf{y}' = \boldsymbol{\Sigma}_1^{-1/2}\boldsymbol{\beta}(\boldsymbol{\Sigma}_3^{-1} + \boldsymbol{\beta}'\boldsymbol{\Sigma}_1^{-1}\boldsymbol{\beta})^{-1}\boldsymbol{\beta}'\boldsymbol{\Sigma}_1^{-1/2}$, because $\boldsymbol{\beta}$ is of rank one. Similarly for $n \geq p$, the joint density function of $\mathbf{A}$ and $\mathbf{D}_\lambda$ is given by

$$c_7\,|\mathbf{I}_q + \boldsymbol{\Sigma}_3\boldsymbol{\beta}'\boldsymbol{\Sigma}_1^{-1}\boldsymbol{\beta}|^{-\frac{1}{2}n_1}\,|\mathbf{A}'\mathbf{A}|^{\frac{1}{2}(m+n-p)}\,|\mathbf{D}_\lambda|^{\frac{1}{2}(n-p-1)}\left(\prod_{i<j=1}^{p}(\lambda_i - \lambda_j)\right)$$
$$\times\exp[-\tfrac{1}{2}\operatorname{tr}\boldsymbol{\Sigma}_2^{-1}\mathbf{A}\mathbf{A}']\exp[-\tfrac{1}{2}\operatorname{tr}\boldsymbol{\Sigma}_1^{-1}\mathbf{A}\mathbf{D}_\lambda\mathbf{A}']$$
$$\times\sum_{k=0}^{\infty}(\tfrac{1}{2}n_1)_k\{k!(\tfrac{1}{2}n)_k\}^{-1}\{\tfrac{1}{2}\operatorname{tr}\boldsymbol{\Sigma}_1^{-1}\mathbf{A}\mathbf{D}_\lambda\mathbf{A}'\boldsymbol{\Sigma}_1^{-1/2}\mathbf{y}\mathbf{y}'\}^k \tag{4.33}$$

where $\mathbf{y}\mathbf{y}' = \boldsymbol{\Sigma}_1^{-1/2}\boldsymbol{\beta}(\boldsymbol{\Sigma}_3^{-1} + \boldsymbol{\beta}'\boldsymbol{\Sigma}_1^{-1}\boldsymbol{\beta})^{-1}\boldsymbol{\beta}'\boldsymbol{\Sigma}_1^{-1/2}$.

Note that the method for obtaining the density function of **a** is the same as that of case (i). Hence, we write down the density function of **a** as

$$(1-\mathbf{yy}')^{-\frac{1}{2}n_1}\exp(-\tfrac{1}{2}\mathbf{b}'\mathbf{b})\sum_{k=0}^{\infty}\{(\tfrac{1}{2}n_1)_k\}\{(\tfrac{1}{2}n)_k\}^{-1}g_3(k,\mathbf{b}) \qquad \text{for} \quad n\le p \tag{4.34}$$

where $g_3(k, \mathbf{b})$ is the coefficient of θ^k in the expansion of $g_3(\theta, \mathbf{b})$ which is the same as $g_1(\theta, \mathbf{b})$ after replacing $Q(\theta)$ by $\mathbf{Z}_1(\mathbf{I}_p-\theta\mathbf{yy}')\mathbf{Z}_1'$ and $\mathbf{b}=\mathbf{\Sigma}_2^{-1/2}\mathbf{a}$, while for $n\ge p$

$$(1-\mathbf{y}'\mathbf{y})^{-\frac{1}{2}n_1}\exp(-\tfrac{1}{2}\mathbf{b}'\mathbf{b})\sum_{k=0}^{\infty}(\tfrac{1}{2}n_1)_k\{(\tfrac{1}{2}n)_k\}^{-1}g_4(k,\mathbf{b}),\ \mathbf{b}=\mathbf{\Sigma}_2^{-1/2}\mathbf{a}, \tag{4.35}$$

where $g_4(k, \mathbf{b})$ is the coefficient of θ^k in the expansion of $g_4(\theta, \mathbf{b})$ which is the same as $g_2(\theta, \mathbf{b})$ after replacing $Q(\theta)$ by $\mathbf{Z}_1(\mathbf{I}_p-\theta\mathbf{yy}')\mathbf{Z}_1'$.

Case 3. Let $\mathbf{\Sigma}_1=\mathbf{\Sigma}_2=\mathbf{\Sigma}$, (say) and $\boldsymbol{\mu}$ is fixed and of rank one.

Here, we shall try to obtain the density function of $\mathbf{\Delta}$ from (4.9) and (4.10).

Let $n\le p$. Using the transformation $\alpha_i^2=\lambda_i$, $i=1,2,\ldots,n$, $\mathbf{\Sigma}^{-1/2}\mathbf{A}_1(\mathbf{I}+\mathbf{D}_\alpha^{\ 2})^{1/2}\to\mathbf{A}_1$ and then integrating over A_1, we get the joint density function of $\mathbf{D}_\lambda$, $\mathbf{\Delta}_1:(n-1)\times(n-1)$ and $\mathbf{\Delta}:n\times n$ as

$$\begin{aligned} &c_{10}\,|\mathbf{D}_\lambda|^{\frac{1}{2}(p-n-1)}\,|\mathbf{I}+\mathbf{D}_\lambda|^{-\frac{1}{2}(m+n)}\left(\prod_{i<j=1}^{n}(\lambda_i-\lambda_j)\right)\\ &\times\exp(-\tfrac{1}{2}\operatorname{tr}\mathbf{\Sigma}^{-1}\boldsymbol{\mu}\boldsymbol{\mu}')\sum_{k=0}^{\infty}\{k!(p/2)_k\}^{-1}\tfrac{1}{2}(m+n)_k\\ &\times\left\{\operatorname{tr}\tfrac{1}{2}\left[\mathbf{D}_\lambda(\mathbf{I}+\mathbf{D}_\lambda)^{-1}\begin{pmatrix}1&\mathbf{0}\\0&\mathbf{\Delta}_1'\end{pmatrix}\mathbf{\Delta}'\boldsymbol{\mu}'\mathbf{\Sigma}^{-1}\boldsymbol{\mu}\mathbf{\Delta}\begin{pmatrix}1&\mathbf{0}\\\mathbf{0}&\mathbf{\Delta}_1\end{pmatrix}\right]\right\}^k\\ &\times d\mathbf{\Delta}_1^{(n-1,n-1)}\,d\mathbf{\Delta}^{(n,1)} \end{aligned} \tag{4.36}$$

where

$$c_{10}=\Pi^{\frac{1}{2}n^2}\Gamma_n\tfrac{1}{2}(m+n)/\{\Gamma_n(\tfrac{1}{2}p)\Gamma_n(\tfrac{1}{2}n)\Gamma_n\tfrac{1}{2}(m+n-p)\}.$$

Integrating with respect to $\mathbf{D}_\lambda$ and $\mathbf{\Delta}_1$, we get the density function of $\mathbf{\Delta}$ as

$$\exp(-\tfrac{1}{2}\operatorname{tr}\mathbf{\Sigma}^{-1}\boldsymbol{\mu}\boldsymbol{\mu}')\sum_{k=0}^{\infty}\{(\tfrac{1}{2}p)_k\}^{-1}\tfrac{1}{2}(m+n)_k\,g_5(k,\mathbf{\Delta})\,d\mathbf{\Delta}^{(n,1)}, \tag{4.37}$$

where $g_5(k, \Delta)$ is the coefficient of θ^k in the expansion of

$$\begin{aligned} g_5(\theta,\mathbf{\Delta})&=c_{10}\\ &\times\int_{\mathbf{D}_\lambda}\int_{\mathbf{\Delta}_1}\frac{|\mathbf{D}_\lambda|^{\frac{1}{2}(p-n-1)}\exp\left[\operatorname{tr}\tfrac{1}{2}\theta(\mathbf{I}_n+\mathbf{D}_\lambda^{-1})^{-1}\begin{pmatrix}1&\mathbf{0}\\\mathbf{0}&\mathbf{\Delta}_1'\end{pmatrix}\mathbf{\Delta}'\boldsymbol{\mu}'\mathbf{\Sigma}^{-1}\boldsymbol{\mu}\mathbf{\Delta}\begin{pmatrix}1&0\\0&\mathbf{\Delta}_1\end{pmatrix}\right]}{|\mathbf{I}_n+\mathbf{D}_\lambda|^{\frac{1}{2}(m+n)}\left\{\prod_{i<j}(\lambda_i-\lambda_j)\right\}^{-1}}\\ &\times d\mathbf{\Delta}_1^{(n-1,n-1)}\,d\mathbf{D}_\lambda. \end{aligned} \tag{4.38}$$

Let us write $(\mathbf{I}_n + \mathbf{D}_\lambda^{-1})^{-1} = \mathbf{W} = \operatorname{diag}(\omega_1, \ldots, \omega_n)$, and if $\boldsymbol{\Delta} = (\boldsymbol{\delta}_1, \boldsymbol{\Delta}_2)$, then

$$\tfrac{1}{2}\operatorname{tr}(\mathbf{I}_n + \mathbf{D}_\lambda^{-1})^{-1}\begin{pmatrix}1 & \mathbf{0}\\ \mathbf{0} & \boldsymbol{\Delta}_1{}'\end{pmatrix}\boldsymbol{\Delta}'\boldsymbol{\mu}'\boldsymbol{\Sigma}^{-1}\boldsymbol{\mu}\boldsymbol{\Delta}\begin{pmatrix}1 & 0\\ 0 & \boldsymbol{\Delta}_2\end{pmatrix} = \omega_1\emptyset + \operatorname{tr}\mathbf{W}_1\,\boldsymbol{\Delta}_1{}'\mathbf{R}\,\boldsymbol{\Delta}_1,$$

where

$$\emptyset = \tfrac{1}{2}(\boldsymbol{\delta}_1{}'\boldsymbol{\mu}'\boldsymbol{\Sigma}^{-1}\boldsymbol{\mu}\boldsymbol{\delta}_1), \qquad \mathbf{R} = \tfrac{1}{2}\,\boldsymbol{\Delta}_2{}'\boldsymbol{\mu}'\boldsymbol{\Sigma}^{-1}\,\boldsymbol{\mu}\,\boldsymbol{\Delta}_2$$

and

$$\mathbf{W}_1 = \operatorname{diag}(\omega_2, \ldots, \omega_n).$$

Then (4.38) can be written as

$$\begin{aligned}
g_5(\theta, \boldsymbol{\Delta}) &= c_{10}\int_{\mathbf{W}}\int_{\boldsymbol{\Delta}_1}|\mathbf{W}|^{\frac{1}{2}(p-n-1)}|\mathbf{I}_n - \mathbf{W}|^{\frac{1}{2}(m-p-1)}\left(\prod_{i<j=1}^{n}(\omega_i - \omega_j)\right)\\
&\quad\times \exp[\theta\omega_1\emptyset + \theta\operatorname{tr}\mathbf{W}_1\,\boldsymbol{\Delta}_1{}'\mathbf{R}\,\boldsymbol{\Delta}_1]\,d\boldsymbol{\Delta}_1^{(n-1,n-1)}\,d\mathbf{W}\\
&= c_{10}\sum_{k=0}^{\infty}\sum_{\mathscr{K}} C_{\mathscr{K}}(\theta\mathbf{R})\{k!\,C_{\mathscr{K}}(\mathbf{I}_{n-1})\}^{-1}\int_{\mathbf{W}}|\mathbf{W}|^{\frac{1}{2}(p-n-1)}|\mathbf{I} - \mathbf{W}|^{\frac{1}{2}(m-p-1)}\\
&\quad\times\left(\prod_{i<j=1}^{n}(\omega_i - \omega_j)\right)C_{\mathscr{K}}(\mathbf{W}_1)\exp(\theta\omega_1\emptyset)\,d\mathbf{W}. \qquad (4.39)
\end{aligned}$$

Making the transformation $\omega_i/\omega_1 = y_{i-1}$ for $i = 1, 2, \ldots, n-1$ and letting $\mathbf{Y} = \operatorname{diag}(y_1, \ldots, y_{n-1})$, we get (4.39) as

$$\begin{aligned}
g_5(\theta, \boldsymbol{\Delta}) &= c_{10}\sum_{k=0}^{\infty}\sum_{\mathscr{K}}\sum_{j=0}^{\infty}\sum_{J}\sum_{i=0}^{\infty}\theta^{k+i}C_{\mathscr{K}}(\mathbf{R})\emptyset^i\{i!\,k!\,j!\,C_{\mathscr{K}}(\mathbf{I}_{n-1})\}^{-1}(-1)^j\\
&\quad\times\frac{\Gamma(\frac{1}{2}pn + i + k + j)\Gamma\frac{1}{2}(m - p + 1)}{\Gamma\{\frac{1}{2}(m + pn - p + 1) + i + k + j\}}\sum_{\eta} b^{\eta}_{\mathscr{K},J}\\
&\quad\times\frac{\Gamma_{n-1}\frac{1}{2}(n-1)\Gamma_{n-1}\{\frac{1}{2}(p-1), \mathscr{K}\}\Gamma_{n-1}\frac{1}{2}(n+2)}{\Pi^{\frac{1}{2}(n-1)^2}\Gamma_{n-1}\{\frac{1}{2}(n+p+1), \mathscr{K}\}}\,C_{\eta}(\mathbf{I}_{n-1}), \qquad (4.40)
\end{aligned}$$

where $\Sigma_\eta b^{\eta}_{\mathscr{K},J}\,C_\eta(\mathbf{X}) = C_{\mathscr{K}}(\mathbf{X})C_J(\mathbf{X})$, [6]. Similarly when $n \geq p$, the density function of $\boldsymbol{\Delta}$ can be given in the same way, but we are not giving this explicitly here.

5. TESTING OF HYPOTHETICAL PRINCIPAL VECTORS OF Σ_1 IN THE FIELD OF Σ_2

Let us suppose that $b_1, \ldots, b_r$ are hypothetical principal vectors of $\boldsymbol{\Sigma}_1$ in the field of $\boldsymbol{\Sigma}_2$, i.e.,

$$\boldsymbol{\Sigma}_1\mathbf{b}_i = \lambda_i\boldsymbol{\Sigma}_2\,\mathbf{b}_i \qquad \text{for} \quad i = 1, 2, \ldots, r,$$

where λ_i's are r of the characteristic roots of $\mathbf{\Sigma}_1\mathbf{\Sigma}_2^{-1}$. Let $\mathbf{B}_1 = (\mathbf{b}_1, \ldots, \mathbf{b}_r) : p \times r\ (r \leq p)$ be of rank r, and $\mathbf{B}_2 : p \times (p-r)$ be a completion of $\mathbf{B}_1$ such that $\mathbf{B} = (\mathbf{B}_1, \mathbf{B}_2) : p \times p$ is nonsingular and $\mathbf{B}_1'\mathbf{B}_2 = \mathbf{0}$. Then, we can write

$$\mathbf{B}'\mathbf{\Sigma}_1\mathbf{B} = \begin{pmatrix} \mathbf{D}_\omega & \mathbf{D}_\lambda \mathbf{A}_3 \\ \mathbf{A}_3'\mathbf{D}_\lambda & \mathbf{A}_1 \end{pmatrix}, \qquad \mathbf{B}'\mathbf{\Sigma}_2\mathbf{B} = \begin{pmatrix} \mathbf{D}_\eta & \mathbf{A}_3 \\ \mathbf{A}_3' & \mathbf{A}_2 \end{pmatrix} \tag{5.1}$$

if λ_i are all distinct, where $\mathbf{D}_\lambda : r \times r$, $\mathbf{D}_\omega : r \times r$, and $\mathbf{D}_\eta : r \times r$ are diagonal matrices with positive diagonal elements such that $\omega_i/\eta_i = \lambda_i$, $i = 1, 2, \ldots, r$, $\mathbf{A}_j : (p-r) \times (p-r)$ for $j = 1, 2$ are symmetric positive definite matrices and $\mathbf{A}_3 : r \times (p-r)$.

Now, let us consider the joint density function of $\mathbf{S}_1 : p \times p$ and $\mathbf{S}_2 : p \times p$ given by

$$\begin{aligned} &\{|2\mathbf{\Sigma}_1|^{\frac{1}{2}\nu_1}|2\mathbf{\Sigma}_2|^{\frac{1}{2}\nu_2}\Gamma_p(\tfrac{1}{2}\nu_1)\Gamma_p(\tfrac{1}{2}\nu_2)\}^{-1} \\ &\qquad \times |\mathbf{S}_1|^{\frac{1}{2}(\nu_1-p-1)}|\mathbf{S}_2|^{\frac{1}{2}(\nu_2-p-1)}\operatorname{etr}(-\tfrac{1}{2}\mathbf{\Sigma}_1^{-1}\mathbf{S}_1 - \tfrac{1}{2}\mathbf{\Sigma}_2^{-1}\mathbf{S}_2). \end{aligned} \tag{5.2}$$

We note that $H_0(\mathbf{\Sigma}_1 = \mathbf{\Sigma}_2)$ against $H_1(\mathbf{\Sigma}_1 \neq \mathbf{\Sigma}_2)$ can be tested by the statistic

$$\Lambda = |\mathbf{S}_2|/|\mathbf{S}_1 + \mathbf{S}_2|. \tag{5.3}$$

Suppose the structure of $\mathbf{\Sigma}_1$ and $\mathbf{\Sigma}_2$ is given by (5.1). Under this structure, the joint density function of

$$\mathbf{V} = \mathbf{B}'\mathbf{S}_1\mathbf{B} = \begin{pmatrix} \mathbf{V}_{11} & \mathbf{V}_{12} \\ \mathbf{V}_{12}' & \mathbf{V}_{22} \end{pmatrix}\begin{matrix} r \\ p-r \end{matrix} \quad \text{and} \quad \mathbf{W} = \mathbf{B}'\mathbf{S}_2\mathbf{B} = \begin{pmatrix} \mathbf{W}_{11} & \mathbf{W}_{12} \\ \mathbf{W}_{12}' & \mathbf{W}_{22} \end{pmatrix}\begin{matrix} r \\ p-r \end{matrix}$$
$$\qquad\quad r \quad p-r \qquad\qquad\qquad\qquad\qquad\qquad r \quad p-r$$

is given by

$$\begin{aligned} &\{|2\mathbf{D}_\omega|^{\frac{1}{2}\nu_1}|2(\mathbf{A}_2 - \mathbf{A}_3'\mathbf{D}_\eta^{-1}\mathbf{A}_3)|^{\frac{1}{2}\nu_2}|2\mathbf{D}_\eta|^{\frac{1}{2}\nu_2} \\ &\quad \times |2(\mathbf{A}_1 - \mathbf{A}_3'\mathbf{D}_\lambda\mathbf{D}_\omega^{-1}\mathbf{D}_\lambda\mathbf{A}_3)|^{\frac{1}{2}\nu_1}\Gamma_p(\tfrac{1}{2}\nu_1)\Gamma_p(\tfrac{1}{2}\nu_2)\}^{-1} \\ &\quad \times |\mathbf{V}|^{\frac{1}{2}(\nu_1-p-1)}|\mathbf{W}|^{\frac{1}{2}(\nu_2-p-1)} \\ &\quad \times \operatorname{etr}\left[-\frac{1}{2}\begin{pmatrix} \mathbf{D}_\omega & \mathbf{D}_\lambda\mathbf{A}_3 \\ \mathbf{A}_3'\mathbf{D}_\lambda & \mathbf{A}_1 \end{pmatrix}^{-1}\mathbf{V} - \frac{1}{2}\begin{pmatrix} \mathbf{D}_\eta & \mathbf{A}_3 \\ \mathbf{A}_3' & \mathbf{A}_2 \end{pmatrix}^{-1}\mathbf{W}\right]. \end{aligned} \tag{5.4}$$

Noting the distributions of (5.2) and (5.4), $H_0' = H_{0,1}(\mathbf{A}_3 = \mathbf{0}) \bigcap H_{0,2}(\mathbf{A}_1 = \mathbf{A}_2)$ against $H_1' \neq H_0'$ can be tested by the statistic

$$\Lambda_2 = \frac{|\mathbf{W}_{22}|}{|\mathbf{V}_{22} + \mathbf{W}_{22}|} \tag{5.5}$$

in the same way as (5.3) is defined. Suppose that the hypothetical vector $\mathbf{b}_i$'s are given, i.e., $\mathbf{B}_1$ is given. Then, we shall write Λ_2 in terms of $\mathbf{B}_1$ as under

$$\Lambda_2 = \frac{|\mathbf{S}_2|}{|\mathbf{S}_1 + \mathbf{S}_2|}\,\frac{|(\mathbf{B}_1'\mathbf{S}_2^{-1}\mathbf{B}_1)|}{|\mathbf{B}_1'(\mathbf{S}_1 + \mathbf{S}_2)^{-1}\mathbf{B}_1|} \tag{5.6}$$

because

$$\begin{aligned}\Lambda_2^{-1} &= |\mathbf{I}_{p-r} + \mathbf{W}_{22}^{-1}\mathbf{V}_{22}| = |\mathbf{I}_p + \mathbf{B}_2(\mathbf{B}_2'\mathbf{S}_2\ \mathbf{B}_2)^{-1}\mathbf{B}_2'\mathbf{S}_1| \\ &= |\mathbf{I}_p + \{\mathbf{S}_2^{-1} - \mathbf{S}_2^{-1}\mathbf{B}_1(\mathbf{B}_1'\mathbf{S}_2^{-1}\mathbf{B}_1)^{-1}\mathbf{B}_1'\mathbf{S}_2^{-1}\}\mathbf{S}_1| \\ &= |\mathbf{S}_2|^{-1}\,|\mathbf{S}_2 + \mathbf{S}_1|\,|\mathbf{I}_p - (\mathbf{S}_1 + \mathbf{S}_2)^{-1}\mathbf{B}_1(\mathbf{B}_1'\mathbf{S}_2^{-1}\mathbf{B}_1)^{-1}\mathbf{B}_1'\mathbf{S}_2^{-1}\mathbf{S}_1 \\ &= \Lambda^{-1}\,|\mathbf{I}_p - \mathbf{B}_1'\mathbf{S}_2^{-1}\mathbf{S}_1(\mathbf{S}_1 + \mathbf{S}_2)^{-1}\mathbf{B}_1(\mathbf{B}_1'\mathbf{S}_2^{-1}\mathbf{B}_1)^{-1}| \\ &= \Lambda^{-1}\,|(\mathbf{B}_1'\mathbf{S}_2^{-1}\mathbf{B}_1)|^{-1}\,|\mathbf{B}_1'\{\mathbf{S}_2^{-1} - \mathbf{S}_2^{-1}\mathbf{S}_1(\mathbf{S}_1 + \mathbf{S}_2)^{-1}\}\mathbf{B}_1| \\ &= \Lambda^{-1}\,|(\mathbf{B}_1'\mathbf{S}_2^{-1}\mathbf{B}_1)|^{-1}\,|\mathbf{B}_1'(\mathbf{S}_1 + \mathbf{S}_2)^{-1}\mathbf{B}_1|.\end{aligned}$$

In the above proof, we have used the following results:

$$|\mathbf{I} + \mathbf{XY}| = |\mathbf{I} + \mathbf{YX}| \tag{5.7}$$

and

$$\mathbf{B}_2(\mathbf{B}_2'\mathbf{S}_2\mathbf{B}_2)^{-1}\mathbf{B}_2' = \mathbf{S}_2^{-1} - \mathbf{S}_2^{-1}\mathbf{B}_1(\mathbf{B}_1'\mathbf{S}_2^{-1}\mathbf{B}_1)^{-1}\mathbf{B}_1'\mathbf{S}_2^{-1} \qquad \text{if} \quad \mathbf{B}_1'\mathbf{B}_2 = \mathbf{0}. \tag{5.8}$$

The result (5.8) is proved by Khatri [4] while (5.7) is well known. Hence, noting (5.6) and (5.3), we get

$$\Lambda = \Lambda_1\Lambda_2, \tag{5.9}$$

where

$$\begin{aligned}\Lambda_1 &= \frac{|\mathbf{B}_1'(\mathbf{S}_1 + \mathbf{S}_2)^{-1}\mathbf{B}_1|}{|(\mathbf{B}_1'\mathbf{S}_2^{-1}\mathbf{B}_1)|} \\ &= \frac{|(\mathbf{W}_{11} - \mathbf{W}_{12}\mathbf{W}_{22}^{-1}\mathbf{W}_{12}')|}{|\mathbf{W}_{11} + \mathbf{V}_{11} - (\mathbf{W}_{12} + \mathbf{V}_{12})(\mathbf{W}_{22} + \mathbf{V}_{22})^{-1}(\mathbf{W}_{12} + \mathbf{V}_{12})'|}.\end{aligned} \tag{5.10}$$

We may note that Λ_1 can be used for testing $H_0''(\lambda_i = 1, i = 1, 2, \ldots, r)$ (i.e., ch roots λ_i corresponding to hypothetical vector $\mathbf{b}_i$ in $\Sigma_2^{-1}\Sigma_1 = 1$ for $i = 1, 2, \ldots, r$) against H_1'' (at least one $\lambda_i \neq 1$) when $H_{01}(\mathbf{A}_3 = \mathbf{0})$ is given. It can be shown that under $H_{01}(\mathbf{A}_3 = \mathbf{0})$ and $H_0''(\lambda_i = 1, i = 1, 2, \ldots, r)$, Λ_1 and Λ_2 are independently distributed and the distribution of Λ_1 is similar to that of Λ, under H_0 (or Λ_2 under H_0').

For the proof of the above result, let us put $\mathbf{D}_\omega = \mathbf{D}_\eta = \mathbf{D}$ (say) in (5.4), and let us use the transformation:

$$\mathbf{V} + \mathbf{W} = \mathbf{R} = \begin{pmatrix}\mathbf{R}_{11} & \mathbf{R}_{12} \\ \mathbf{R}_{12}' & \mathbf{R}_{22}\end{pmatrix}, \qquad \mathbf{H} = \begin{pmatrix}\mathbf{H}_{11} & \mathbf{H}_{12} \\ \mathbf{H}_{12}' & \mathbf{H}_{22}\end{pmatrix} = \mathbf{T}'^{-1}\mathbf{W}\mathbf{T}^{-1}$$

where $\mathbf{T}'\mathbf{T} = \mathbf{R}$ and

$$\mathbf{T} = \begin{pmatrix}\mathbf{T}_{11} & \mathbf{0} \\ \mathbf{T}_{21} & \mathbf{T}_{22}\end{pmatrix}$$

is a lower triangular matrix. Then $\mathbf{W}_{22} = \mathbf{T}'_{22}\mathbf{H}_{22}\mathbf{T}_{22}$, $\mathbf{T}'_{22}\mathbf{T}_{22} = \mathbf{V}_{22} + \mathbf{W}_{22}$, and if $\mathbf{H}_{11} - \mathbf{H}_{12}\mathbf{H}_{22}^{-1}\mathbf{H}'_{12} = \mathbf{H}_{11}^{(1)}$, then $|\mathbf{H}_{11}^{(1)}| = \Lambda_1$. Using the Jacobian of the transformation $|R|^{\frac{1}{2}(p+1)}$ in (5.4), we get the joint density function of $\mathbf{R}$ and $\mathbf{H}$ under H_0'' as

$$c\,|\mathbf{R}|^{\frac{1}{2}(\nu_1+\nu_2-p-1)}|\mathbf{H}|^{\frac{1}{2}(\nu_2-p-1)}|\mathbf{I}-\mathbf{H}|^{\frac{1}{2}(\nu_1-p-1)}\operatorname{etr}(-\tfrac{1}{2}\mathbf{D}^{-1}\mathbf{R}_{11})$$
$$\times \operatorname{etr}(-\tfrac{1}{2}\mathbf{A}_1^{-1}\mathbf{R}_{22} - \tfrac{1}{2}(\mathbf{A}_2^{-1} - \mathbf{A}_1^{-1})\mathbf{T}'_{22}\mathbf{H}_{22}\mathbf{T}_{22}) \tag{5.11}$$

where c is the constant term of the density given in (5.4).

Now, we note that

$$|\mathbf{H}| = |\mathbf{H}_{22}|\,|\mathbf{H}_{11}^{(1)}| \qquad \text{and} \qquad |\mathbf{I}_p - \mathbf{H}| = |\mathbf{I}_{p-r} - \mathbf{H}_{22}|\,|\mathbf{I}_r - \mathbf{H}_{11}^{(1)}|\,|\mathbf{I}_r - \mathbf{G}\mathbf{G}'|,$$

where $\mathbf{H}_{11}^{(1)} = \mathbf{H}_{11} - \mathbf{H}_{12}\mathbf{H}_{22}^{-1}\mathbf{H}'_{12}$ and $\mathbf{G} = (\mathbf{I} - \mathbf{H}_{11}^{(1)})^{1/2}\mathbf{H}_{12}\{\mathbf{H}_{22}^{-1} + (\mathbf{I} - \mathbf{H}_{22})^{-1}\}^{1/2}$. Using the above transformations and their Jacobian in (5.11), we see that $\mathbf{H}_{11}^{(1)}$, $\mathbf{G}$, and $(\mathbf{H}_{22}, \mathbf{R})$ are independently distributed. Note that $|\mathbf{H}_{11}^{(1)}| = \Lambda_1$ and $|\mathbf{H}_{22}| = \Lambda_2$, and hence Λ_1 and Λ_2 are independently distributed. The density function of $\mathbf{H}_{11}^{(1)}$ is given by

$$\left\{\Pi^{-r(r-1)/4}\prod_{i=1}^{r}\frac{\Gamma\frac{1}{2}(\nu_1+\nu_2-p+r-i+1)}{\Gamma\frac{1}{2}(\nu_1-p+r-i+1)\Gamma\frac{1}{2}(\nu_2-i+1)}\right\}$$
$$|\mathbf{H}_{11}^{(1)}|^{\frac{1}{2}(\nu_2-r-1)}|\mathbf{I}_r - \mathbf{H}_{11}^{(1)}|^{\frac{1}{2}(\nu_1-p+r-r-1)}. \tag{5.12}$$

Hence, the distribution of Λ_1 under H_0'' is the same as that of Λ under H_0 by changing the parameter p, ν_1, and ν_2 to r, $\nu_1 - p + r$ and ν_2, respectively.

We note that the hypothesis H_0' is the intersection of the three hypotheses, namely, H_{03}: $(b_1, b_2, \ldots, b_r)$ are the true principal vectors of Σ_1 in the field of Σ_2, H_{01}: all the orthogonal vectors to the vector space generated by $(\mathbf{b}_1, \ldots, \mathbf{b}_r)$ lie in the vector space generated by the ch vectors (due to ch roots other than λ_i, $i = 1, 2, \ldots, r$) and $\mathbf{H}_{02}$ (the ch roots of $\Sigma_2\Sigma_1^{-1}$, other than λ_i, $i = 1, 2, \ldots, r$, are equal to unity). Thus, Λ_2 is an appropriate overall test for H_{01}, H_{02}, and H_{03}.

6. REMARKS

In respect to the transformation (4.2), we may further consider the following types of CVCLR.

Let $\mathbf{\Gamma} = (\mathbf{r}, \mathbf{\Gamma}_1)$ in (4.2). Then,

(I) The vector $\mathbf{H}\mathbf{D}_\lambda^{1/2}\mathbf{r}\,(1+\alpha^2)^{1/2}$ is the ch vector of the matrix $\mathbf{XX}'(\mathbf{S} + \mathbf{XX}')^{-1}$ corresponding to the ch root $\alpha^2/(1+\alpha^2)$,

(II) The vector $\mathbf{H}\mathbf{D}_\lambda^{-1/2}\mathbf{r}$ is the ch vector of the matrix $\mathbf{S}^{-1}\mathbf{XX}'$ corresponding to the ch root α^2, and

(III) The vector $\mathbf{HD}_\lambda^{-1/2}\mathbf{r}\ (1+\alpha^2)^{-1/2}$ is the ch vector of the matrix $(\mathbf{S}+\mathbf{XX}')^{-1}\mathbf{XX}'$ corresponding to the ch root $\alpha^2/(1+\alpha^2)$.

In the case of (I), it may be noted that we may obtain the results with necessary changes in (4.9) and (4.10). As for example, when $\mathbf{\Sigma}_1 = \mathbf{\Sigma}_2 = \mathbf{\Sigma}$ and $\boldsymbol{\mu} = \mathbf{0}$ in (4.9′) and (4.10′), it is easy to see that the density function of the ch vector $\mathbf{HD}_\lambda^{1/2}\mathbf{r}(1+\alpha^2)^{1/2} = \mathbf{t}$ is given by

$$\text{const}(\mathbf{t}'\mathbf{\Sigma}^{-1}\mathbf{t})^{\frac{1}{2}(m+n-p)} \exp(-\tfrac{1}{2}\mathbf{t}'\mathbf{\Sigma}^{-1}\mathbf{t}).$$

The distribution of $\mathbf{t}$ is independent of the ch root α^2 while this is not so for the ch vector $\mathbf{a}$ obtainable from (4.9′) and (4.10′) under the same assumptions. The results for (II) and (III) are under consideration.

(IV) The first column vector of $\mathbf{\Delta}$ in the transformation (4.2) is the ch vector of $\mathbf{X}'(\mathbf{S}+\mathbf{XX}')^{-1}\mathbf{X}$ corresponding to the ch root $\alpha^2/(1+\alpha^2)$. This part has already been considered.

REFERENCES

1. Constantine, A. G. (1963). Some non-central distribution problems in multivariate analysis. *Ann. Math. Statist.* **34** 1270–1285.
2. Constantine, A. G. (1966). The distribution of Hotelling's generalized T_0^2. *Ann. Math. Statist.* **35** 215–225.
3. James, A. T. (1964). Distributions of matrix variates and latent roots derived from normal samples. *Ann. Math. Statist.* **35** 475–501.
4. Khatri, C. G. (1966). A note on a MANOVA model applied to problems in growth curve. *Ann. Inst. Statist. Math.* **18** 75–86.
5. Khatri, C. G. (1968). Some Jacobian transformations and their applications in multivariate distribution theory. Unpublished work.
6. Khatri, C. G., and Pillai, K. C. S. (1968). On the non-central distributions of two test criteria in multivariate analysis of variance. *Ann. Math. Statist.* **39** 215–226.
7. Kshirsagar, A. M. (1960). The goodness of fit of a single (nonisotropic) hypothetical principal component. *Biometrika* **48** 397–407.
8. Kshirsagar, A. M., and Gupta, R. P. (1965). The goodness of fit of two (or more) hypothetical principal components. *Ann. Inst. Statist. Math.* **17** 347–356.
9. Pillai, K. C. S., and Jouris, G. M. (1969). On the moments of elementary symmetric functions of the roots of two matrices. *Ann. Inst. Statist. Math.* (in press).
10. Roy, S. N. (1958). "Some Aspects of Multivariate Analysis." Wiley, New York.
11. Sugiyama, T. (1966). On the distribution of the largest latent root and the corresponding latent vector for principal component analysis. *Ann. Math. Statist.* **37** 995–1001.

Some Identities and Approximations Concerning Positive and Negative Multinomial Distributions

C. G. KHATRI[1]

INDIAN STATISTICAL INSTITUTE
CALCUTTA, INDIA

DEPARTMENT OF STATISTICS
PURDUE UNIVERSITY
LAFAYETTE, INDIANA

SUJIT KUMAR MITRA

INDIAN STATISTICAL INSTITUTE
CALCUTTA, INDIA

SUMMARY

Some results, well known for positive and negative binomial distributions, are generalized. Identities are obtained which connect incomplete sums of multinomial probabilities with incomplete probability integrals of Dirichlet distributions of the first and second kind. For approximations to the multinomial distribution by normal distribution and product of normal and Poisson distributions, correction terms are obtained up to order $O(1/n)$, while correction terms for the Poisson approximation are given up to order $O(1/n^4)$. The final section deals with approximations to the cdf of compound multinomial distributions.

1. INTRODUCTION

Though in statistical literature, there is no dearth of studies on the positive and negative binomial distributions, relatively scant attention seems to have been paid to the multinomial (positive or negative), excluding, of course, the results regarding large sample tests on positive multinomial models including

[1] Present address: Department of Statistics, Gujarat University, Ahmedabad 9, India.

estimation of specifying parameters [see, e.g., Rao (1965), Roy and Mitra (1958)]. Thus, no table of cumulative multinomial probabilities is available, and though it is known that individual multinomial terms could be computed from a table of individual terms of the binomial or the Poisson distribution, no one seems to have inquired whether or not the existing tabulations of these univariate distributions are adequate for the purpose. That, as limiting cases, the multivariate normal or Poisson distribution obtains, is of little value from practical considerations unless one is able to estimate the extent of error that is committed when these limiting forms are used as approximation. The authors of the present paper obtain equations connecting the cumulative multinomial probabilities with the incomplete multivariate beta integral (Dirichlet's distribution) and derive leading correction terms for approximations by Poisson, normal, and product of Poisson and normal distributions. The final section on approximations to cumulative compound multinomial probabilities contains a multivariate generalization of a recent result due to Mitra and Subramannya (1967). Relations between incomplete sums of multinomial terms cumulated from below (or from above) and incomplete Dirichlet integrals were obtained earlier by Olkin and Sobel (1966) by a more direct approach. These authors also developed several recursion formulas for evaluating Dirichlet integrals.

The frequency functions of the positive and negative multinomial distributions are given by

$$m(v_1, v_2, \ldots, v_k \mid n, \pi_1, \pi_2, \ldots, \pi_k) = m(\mathbf{v} \mid n, \boldsymbol{\pi})$$
$$= \frac{(n)^{[T]}}{\prod v_i\,!} \prod \pi_i^{v_i} \left(1 - \sum_{j=1}^{k} \pi_j\right)^{n-T},$$
$$v_i = O(1)n, \qquad \sum_j v_j = T \le n, \qquad 0 < \pi_i < 1, \qquad \sum \pi_i < 1 \quad (1.1)$$

and

$$nm(v_1, v_2, \ldots, v_k \mid \kappa, \rho_1, \rho_2, \ldots, \rho_k) = nm(\mathbf{v} \mid \kappa, \boldsymbol{\rho})$$
$$= \frac{(-\kappa)^{[T]}}{\prod v_i\,!} \prod (-\rho_i)^{v_i} \left(1 + \sum_{j=1}^{k} \rho_j\right)^{-\kappa-T},$$
$$v_i = O(1)\infty, \qquad \sum_j v_j = T, \qquad (\rho_i, \kappa) > 0 \qquad (1.2)$$

(Bates and Neyman, 1952; Khatri, 1959), respectively, where $(a)^{[T]} = a(a-1)\cdots(a-T+1)$. The two forms are thus almost identical except that in the negative multinomial, $-\kappa$ and $-\rho_i$ replaces n and π_i of the positive multinomial. The resemblance is, indeed, carried deeper into their respective characteristic functions

$$[1 + \sum \pi_i(\exp(\sqrt{-1}\,t_i) - 1)]^n \quad \text{and} \quad [1 - \sum \rho_i(\exp(\sqrt{-1}\,t_i) - 1)]^{-\kappa},$$

and naturally into their respective generating functions for individual terms and cumulative probabilities. In their present treatment of these distributions, if the authors have shown any undue preference towards the positive multinomial, it is only because the results for the negative multinomial run parallel and are obtainable through the substitution indicated above.

2. RELATION BETWEEN MULTINOMIAL AND MULTIVARIATE BETA DISTRIBUTIONS

Consider n independent observations from a uniform distribution over (0, 1) and denote the ordered observations by $y_{(1)} \le y_{(2)} \le \cdots \le y_{(n)}$. Let $s_1, s_2, \ldots, s_k$ be a set of nonnegative integers such that $s_1 + s_2 + \cdots + s_k + (k-2) < n$. For notational convenience write $z_1 = 0, z_{i+1} = y_{(s_1+s_2+\cdots+s_i+i)}$ for $i = 1, 2, \ldots, (k-2)$, $z_k = 1 - \pi_k$ and consider intervals $I_i = (z_i, z_i + \pi_i)$, $i = 1, 2, \ldots, k$ where $0 < \pi_i < 1$ for each i, $\sum_1^k \pi_i < 1$. Let the frequency of observations in I_i be denoted by v_i. In the sample space of the v_i's, let R denote the subset of sample points satisfying $v_i \le s_i$ $(i = 1, 2, \ldots, k)$. The term R^+ will represent the subset satisfying $v_i \le s_i$ $(i = 2, 3, \ldots, k)$. We shall prove:

Theorem 2.1.

$$\text{Prob}\{R\} = \sum_R m(\mathbf{v} \mid n, \boldsymbol{\pi}) \qquad \textit{if} \quad n > \sum_{i=1}^k s_i + k - 2.$$

Proof. For $k = 1$ and 2 the theorem is obvious. The theorem in the general case is proved by induction. For this, assume that the result is true for some $(k-1) \ge 0$. Consider z_2. It is clear that in order for the event R to happen, z_2 has to lie in the interval $(\pi_1, 1 - \sum_2^k \pi_i)$. In order to satisfy

$$v_i \le s_i \qquad (i = 1, 2, \ldots, k-1),$$

it will be necessary for z_{i+1} to be greater than or equal to $z_i + \pi_i$ for $i = 1, 2, \ldots, (k-2)$, and for $y_{(s_1+s_2+\cdots+s_{k-1}+k-1)}$ to be greater than or equal to $z_{k-1} + \pi_{k-1}$. Hence, if z_2 exceeds $1 - \sum_2^k \pi_i$, $y_{(s_1+\cdots+s_{k-1}+k-1)}$ will belong to I_k. This in turn would imply that I_k contains at least

$$n - (s_1 + s_2 + \cdots + s_{k-1} + k - 1) + 1 > s_k$$

observations contradicting $v_k \le s_k$. Given $z_2 = z$, a value in the interval $(\pi_1, 1 - \sum_2^k \pi_i)$, for any integer $m \le s_1$, the conditional probability of $v_1 = m$ and $v_i \le s_i$ $(i = 2, 3, \ldots, k)$ is

$$\binom{s_1}{m}\left(\frac{\pi_1}{z}\right)^m\left(1-\frac{\pi_1}{z}\right)^{s_1-m}$$
$$\times \sum_{R^+} m\left(v_2, v_3, \ldots, v_k \mid n - s_1 - 1, \frac{\pi_2}{1-z}, \frac{\pi_3}{1-z}, \ldots, \frac{\pi_k}{1-z}\right).$$

This is because, given $z_2 = z$, conditionally, the s_1 observations below z and the $n - s_1 - 1$ above z could be regarded as independent observations from uniform distributions over the intervals (0, z) and (z, 1), respectively [see, e.g., Anderson (1966)]. Note that simple linear transformations of observations involving translation and scale changes would reduce each of these intervals to (0, 1), and that such transformations keep the order of observations invariant in each group and, hence, make the frequencies $v_2, v_3, \ldots, v_k$ conditionally amenable to the application of Theorem 2.1 which is assumed to be true for $(k-1)$ frequencies. The marginal density of z_2 at z being $[B(s_1+1, n-s_1)]^{-1} z^{s_1}(1-z)^{n-s_1-1}$, the unconditional probability of $v_1 = m$, $v_i \leq s_i$ $(i = 2, 3, \ldots, k)$ is obtained by integration as follows:

$$\int_{\pi_1}^{1-\sum_2^k \pi_i} \frac{n!}{s_1!(n-s_1-1)!} z^{s_1}(1-z)^{n-s_1-1} \frac{s_1!}{m!(s_1-m)!} \frac{\pi_1{}^m (z-\pi_1)^{s_1-m}}{z^{s_1}}$$
$$\times \sum_{R^+} m(v_2, \ldots, v_k \mid n - s_1 - 1, \pi_2/(1-z), \ldots, \pi_k/(1-z))\, dz$$

$$= \frac{\pi_1{}^m}{m!} \sum_{R^+} \frac{n!}{\prod_2^k v_i!} \prod_2^k \pi_i^{v_i} \int_{\pi_1}^{1-\sum_2^k \pi_i}$$
$$\times \frac{(z-\pi_1)^{s_1-m}(1-\sum_2^k \pi_i - z)^{n-s_1-1-\sum_2^k v_i}}{(s_1-m)!(n-s_1-1-\sum_2^k v_i)!}\, dz.$$

This expression summed over $m = 0, 1, \ldots, s_1$ establishes Theorem 2.1.

Theorem 2.2.

$$\operatorname{Prob}\{R\} = \underset{\substack{x_i \geq \pi_i \\ i=1(1)k \\ \sum x_i < 1}}{\iint\cdots\int} \beta_k\left(s_1, s_2, \ldots, s_k; n - \sum_{i=1}^k s_i - k; \mathbf{x}\right) \prod_{i=1}^k dx_i$$

if $n \geq \sum s_i + k$

$$= \int_{\pi_1}^{1-\sum_{i=2}^k \pi_i} \int_{\pi_2}^{1-x_1-\sum_{i=3}^k \pi_i} \cdots \int_{\pi_k}^{1-\sum_{i=1}^{k-1} x_i}$$
$$\times \beta_k\left(s_1, s_2, \ldots, s_k; n - \sum_{i=1}^k s_i - k; \mathbf{x}\right) \prod_{i=1}^k dx_i,$$

$$= \underset{\substack{x_i \geq \pi_i \\ i=1(1)k-1 \\ \sum x_i \leq 1-\pi_k}}{\iint\cdots\int} \beta_{k-1}(s_1, s_2, \ldots, s_{k-1}; s_k; \mathbf{x}) \prod_{i=1}^{k-1} dx_i$$

if $n = \sum s_i + (k-1)$

$$= \int_{\pi_1}^{1-\sum_{i=2}^{k}\pi_i} \int_{\pi_2}^{1-x_1-\sum_{i=3}^{k}\pi_i} \cdots \int_{\pi_{k-1}}^{1-\sum_{i=1}^{k-1}x_i-\pi_k} \times \beta_{k-1}(s_1, \ldots, s_{k-1}; s_k; \mathbf{x}) \prod_{i=1}^{k-1} dx_i,$$

where,

$$\beta_s(a_1, a_2, \ldots, a_s; b; \mathbf{x}) = \frac{\Gamma(\sum_{i=1}^{s} a_i + b + s + 1)}{\{\prod_{i=1}^{s}\Gamma(a_i+1)\}\Gamma(b+1)} x_1^{a_1}x_2^{a_2}\cdots x_s^{a_s}\left(1-\sum_{i=1}^{s}x_i\right)^b$$

for $0 < x_i \le 1$, $\sum_{i=1}^{s} x_i < 1$, *and* $a_i > -1$, $b > -1$, $i = 1, 2, \ldots, s$.

Proof. $n > \sum s_i + (k-1)$: Note that

$R \Leftrightarrow z_2 \ge \pi_1, (z_3 - z_2) \ge \pi_2, \ldots, (z_{k-1} - z_{k-2}) \ge \pi_{k-2}, (z_k^* - z_{k-1}) \ge \pi_{k-1}$,

and $z_{k+1}^* \le 1 - \pi_k$ where $z_k^* = y_{(s_1+s_2+\cdots+s_{k-1}+k-1)}$ and $z_{k+1}^* = y_{(n-s_k)}$. The joint distribution of the k selected order statistics has the density function

$$\frac{n!}{(n - \sum s_i - k)! \prod s_i!} z_2^{s_1} \times \prod_{i=2}^{k-2}(z_{i+1} - z_i)^{s_i}(z_k^* - z_{k-1})^{s_{k-1}}(z_{k+1}^* - z_k^*)^{n-\sum s_i - k}(1 - z_{k+1}^*)^{s_k}.$$

A simple change of variables will establish the first of these relations.

Proof. $n = \sum s_i + (k-1)$: Here $z_{k+1}^* = z_k^*$. The joint distribution of the $(k-1)$ selected order statistics has the density function

$$\frac{n!}{\prod s_i!} z_2^{s_1} \prod_{i=2}^{k-2}(z_{i+1} - z_i)^{s_i}(z_k^* - z_{k-1})^{s_{k-1}}(1 - z_k^*)^{s_k}$$

which has to be integrated over the region $z_2 \ge \pi_1$, $(z_{i+1} - z_i) \ge \pi_i$, $i = 2, \ldots, k-2$, $z_{k-1} + \pi_{k-1} \le z_k^* \le 1 - \pi_k$. The change of variables required to establish the second of the two relations is almost obvious.

For cases $n < \sum s_i + (k-1)$, see the note following Theorem 2.4. With the same setup as before, let S denote the subset of sample points satisfying $v_i \ge s_i + 1$ $(i = 1, 2, \ldots, k)$ and S^+ the subset satisfying $v_i \ge s_i + 1$ $(i = 2, 3, \ldots, k)$. We shall prove:

Theorem 2.3. *If* $n > \sum_{i=1}^{k} s_i + k$,

$$\text{Prob}\{S\} = \sum_S m(\mathbf{v} \mid n, \boldsymbol{\pi}) = \int_0^{\pi_1}\int_0^{\pi_2}\cdots\int_0^{\pi_k} \beta_k\left(s_1, s_2, \ldots, s_k; n - \sum_{i=1}^{k} s_i - k; \mathbf{x}\right)\prod dx_i$$

and if $n = \sum_{i=1}^k s_i + k$, *then*

$$\operatorname{Prob}\{S\} = n! \prod_{i=1}^{k} [\pi_i^{s_i+1}/(s_i+1)!].$$

Proof. The first of these equations is obvious if $k = 1, 2$. The proof in the general case is obtained by induction. Assume the result to be true for some $(k-1) \geq 1$. Given $z_2 = z$, the conditional probability of S^+ is, by this assumption, expressible as

$$\sum_{S^+} m(v_2, \ldots, v_k \mid n - s_1 - 1, \pi_2/(1-z), \ldots, \pi_k/(1-z)).$$

Multiplying this by the density function of z_2 at z and integrating over $0 \leq z < \pi_1$ so that $v_1 \geq s_1 + 1$ is also satisfied, we have the unconditional probability of S as

$$\sum_{S^+} \frac{n!}{\prod_2^k v_i!} \prod_2^k \pi_i^{v_i} \int_0^{\pi_1} \frac{z^{s_1}(1 - z - \sum_2^k \pi_i)^{n - s_1 - \sum_2^k v_i}}{s_1!(n - s_1 - 1 - \sum_2^k v_i)!}\, dz.$$

The first equation is established for k when the integral is computed through integration by parts.

The proof of the second equation is obtained as in the proof of Theorem 2.2. For cases $n < \sum s_i + k$, see note below Theorem 2.4. With the same setup as before, let T denote the subset of sample points satisfying $v_i \geq s_i + 1$ $(i = 1, 2, \ldots, j < k)$ and $v_i \leq s_i$ $(i = j+1, \ldots, k)$. The following result can be proved in the same manner.

Theorem 2.4. *If* $n \geq \sum_1^k s_i + k$,

$$\begin{aligned}\operatorname{Prob}\{T\} &= \sum_T m(\mathbf{v} \mid n, \boldsymbol{\pi}) \\ &= \underset{\substack{0 \leq x_i \leq \pi_i \\ i = 1, 2, \ldots, j \\ \pi_i \leq x_i \\ i = j+1, j+2, \ldots, k \\ \sum x_i \leq 1}}{\iint \cdots \int} \beta_k\left(s_1, \ldots, s_k; n - \sum_{i=1}^k s_i - k, \mathbf{x}\right) \prod_{i=1}^k dx_i.\end{aligned}$$

Note. If $n = \sum s_i + (k-2)$ and $s_1 \geq 1$,

$$\begin{aligned}&\sum_R m(\mathbf{v} \mid n, \boldsymbol{\pi}) \\ &= \binom{n}{s_1} \pi_1^{s_1} (1 - \pi_1)^{n - s_1} \underset{\substack{x_i \geq \pi_i/(1-\pi_1) \\ i = 2(1)k-1 \\ \sum_{i=2}^{k-1} x_i < 1 - \pi_k/(1-\pi_1)}}{\iint \cdots \int} \beta_{k-2}(s_2, \ldots, s_{k-1}; s_k; \mathbf{x}) \prod_{i=2}^{k-1} dx_i \\ &\quad + \underset{\substack{x_i \geq \pi_i \\ i = 1(1)k-1 \\ \sum_{i=1}^{k} x_i \leq 1 - \pi_k}}{\iint \cdots \int} \beta_{k-1}(s_1 - 1, s_2, \ldots, s_{k-1}; s_k; \mathbf{x}) \prod_{i=1}^{k-1} dx_i.\end{aligned}$$

The proof consists in reducing the problem to the second case covered under Theorem 2.2 by noting that the event R is expressible as the union of two mutually exclusive events R_1 and R_2

$$R_1 = R^+\{v_1 = s_1\}, \qquad R_2 = R^+\{v_1 \le s_1 - 1\}.$$

Note that the probability of each of R_1 and R_2 can be computed by the second formula of Theorem 2.2. If $n = \sum s_i + (k-1)$ and $s_1 \ge 1$, we have similarly

$$\sum_S m(\mathbf{v} \mid n, \boldsymbol{\pi}) = -\binom{n}{s_1 - 1} \pi_1^{s_1 - 1}(1-\pi_1)^{n - s_1 + 1}$$
$$\times \int_0^{\pi_2/(1-\pi_1)} \cdots \int_0^{\pi_k/(1-\pi_1)} \beta_{k-1}(s_2, \ldots, s_k ; 0; \mathbf{x}) \prod_{i=2}^{k} dx_i$$
$$+ \int_0^{\pi_1} \cdots \int_0^{\pi_k} \beta_k(s_1, s_2, \ldots, s_k ; 0; \mathbf{x}) \prod_{i=1}^{k} dx_i$$
$$= \frac{n!\, \pi_1^{s_1 - 1} \prod_{i=2}^k \pi_i^{s_i + 1}}{\prod_{i=2}^k (s_i + 1)!\, s_1!(\sum_{i=2}^k s_i + k)} \{(n+1)\pi_1 - s_1\}.$$

The manner in which the marginal cases are to be treated is clear enough, and we do not propose to give any general formula here. This applies to Theorem 2.4 as well.

Theorem 2.5.

$$\sum_{\substack{v_i \le s_i \\ i = 1, 2, \ldots, j \\ v_i \ge s_i + 1 \\ i = j+1, \ldots, k}} nm(\mathbf{v} \mid \kappa, \boldsymbol{\rho})$$
$$= \int_{\substack{y_i = \rho_i \\ i = 1, 2, \ldots, j}}^{\infty} \int_{\substack{y_i = 0 \\ i = j+1, \ldots, k}}^{\rho_i} \beta_k^{(2)}(s_1, \ldots, s_k ; \kappa - 1; \mathbf{y}) \prod_{i=1}^{k} dy_i .$$

where

$$\beta_k^{(2)}(s_1, \ldots, s_k ; \kappa - 1; \mathbf{y}) = \frac{\Gamma(\kappa + \sum_{i=1}^k s_i + k)}{\Gamma(\kappa) \prod_{i=1}^k \Gamma(s_i + 1)} \frac{\prod_{i=1}^k y_i^{s_i}}{(1 + \sum_{i=1}^k y_i)^{\kappa + \sum s_i + k}} .$$

Proof. For the general case, consider the negative multinomial distribution as product of independent Poisson s with parameters $\rho_i \lambda$ compounded over a gamma distribution for λ with density $\{\Gamma(\kappa)\}^{-1} \lambda^{\kappa + 1} \exp(-\lambda)$ (Bates and Neyman, 1952). Then using well-known relations between cumulative sum of Poisson terms and incomplete gamma integral, we obtain, for $s_i \ge 0$, $i = 1, 2, \ldots, k$,

$$\sum_{\substack{v_i \leq s_i \\ i=1,2,\ldots,j \\ v_i \geq s_i+1 \\ i=(j+1),\ldots,k}} nm(\mathbf{v} \mid \kappa, \boldsymbol{\rho})$$

$$= \int_{\lambda=0}^{\infty} \int_{\substack{x_i=\lambda\rho_i \\ i=1,\ldots,j}}^{\infty} \int_{\substack{x_i=0 \\ i=j+1,\ldots,k}}^{\lambda\rho_i} \frac{\prod_{i=1}^{k} x_i^{s_i}}{\prod_{i=1}^{k} s_i\,!} \exp(-\textstyle\sum x_i - \lambda) \frac{\lambda^{\kappa-1}}{\Gamma(\kappa)} \prod_{i=1}^{k} dx_i\, d\lambda$$

$$= \int_{\substack{y_i=\rho_i \\ i=1,\ldots,j}}^{\infty} \int_{\substack{y_i=0 \\ i=j+1,\ldots,k}}^{\rho_i} \beta_k^{(2)}(s_1, \ldots, s_k\,; \kappa - 1; \mathbf{y}) \prod_{i=1}^{k} dy_i .$$

Note that if for some i, $j+1 \leq i \leq k$, $s_i = -1$, then $v_i \geq 0$ ceases to be a restriction on v_i, and that the required event can be described in terms of negative multinomial of one dimension less, obtained by omitting the variable v_i.

3. USEFUL APPROXIMATIONS TO THE MULTINOMIAL DISTRIBUTIONS

3.1.a. Product of Independent Poisson Terms for Positive Multinomial

Write $\lambda_i = n\pi_i$ $(i = 1, 2, \ldots, k)$, $T = \sum_1^k v_i$, $\tau = \sum_1^k \lambda_i = E(T)$.

$$R^{[r]} \quad (\text{or}(T)^{[r]} = T(T-1)\cdots(T-r+1)),$$

$$[T-\tau]^{[r]} = T^{[r]} - \binom{r}{1}\tau T^{[r-1]} + \binom{r}{2}\tau^2 T^{[r-2]} - \cdots + (-1)^r \tau^r.$$

Then

$$m(\mathbf{v} \mid n, \boldsymbol{\pi}) = \prod_{i=1}^{k} \frac{e^{-\lambda_i}\lambda_i^{v_i}}{v_i\,!} A \tag{3.1.1}$$

where

$$A = e^{\tau}\left(1 - \frac{\tau}{n}\right)^{n-T}\left(1 - \frac{1}{n}\right)\left(1 - \frac{2}{n}\right)\cdots\left(1 - \frac{T-1}{n}\right)$$

which to order $O(1/n^4)$ is equal to

$$\begin{aligned} 1 &- (1/2n)[T-\tau]^{[2]} + (1/n^2)\{\tfrac{1}{3}[T-\tau]^{[3]} + \tfrac{1}{8}[T-\tau]^{[4]}\} \\ &-(1/n^3)\{\tfrac{1}{4}[T-\tau]^{[4]} + \tfrac{1}{6}[T-\tau]^{[5]} + (1/48)[T-\tau]^{[6]}\} \\ &+(1/n^4)\{\tfrac{1}{5}[T-\tau]^{[5]} + (13/72)[T-\tau]^{[6]} + (1/24)[T-\tau]^{[7]} \\ &+(1/384)[T-\tau]^{[8]}\} + O(1/n^5). \end{aligned} \tag{3.1.2}$$

One may verify that the coefficients in this expansion are precisely the same as they appear in the expansion of $(1 + (x/n))^n$. To establish (3.1.1), one has merely to consider the probability generating function of the multinomial distribution, express it in terms of the λ's, expand it and collect terms in various order of $1/n$, or alternatively the exact expression follows from the well-known result that the conditional distribution of a finite number of independent Poisson variables, given their total, is multinomial. The special case of $k = 1$, which gives the correction terms for the Poisson approximation to the binomial is interesting. If $p_\lambda(v) = (e^{-\lambda}\lambda^v/v!)$,

$$\binom{n}{v}\pi^v(1-\pi)^{n-v} = p_\lambda(v) - (\lambda^2/2n)\,\Delta^2 p_\lambda(v-2)$$
$$+ (1/n^2)[-(\lambda^3/3)\,\Delta^3 p_\lambda(v-3) + (\lambda^4/8)\,\Delta^4 p_\lambda(v-4)] + \cdots. \quad (3.1.3)$$

where $\lambda = n\pi$ and Δ, Δ^2, etc., denote differences of successive order taken with respect to v. Thus, not only does an individual term of a Poisson distribution approximate the binomial term $\binom{n}{v}\pi^v(1-\pi)^{n-v}$ for small π and large n, the correction terms also, apart from certain coefficients depending on n and the Poisson mean λ, involve only the finite differences of the Poisson terms. Equation (3.1.3) is the well-known Gram Charlier Type B expansion for the frequency function of the binomial distribution. The cumulative sum

$$\sum_{\substack{v_i \le s_i \\ i=1(1)k}} m(\mathbf{v} \mid n, \boldsymbol{\pi})$$

can be evaluated from (3.1.1) and (3.1.2) noting that

$$\sum_{\substack{v_i \le s_i \\ i=1(1)k}} (T-\tau)^{[r]} \prod_{i=1}^{k} \frac{e^{-\lambda_i}\lambda_i^{v_i}}{v_i!}$$
$$= \sum_{\sum e_i = r} \frac{r!}{\prod_{i=1}^k e_i!} \prod_{i=1}^{k} \lambda_i^{e_i}\,\Delta_i^{e_i} Q_i(s_i - e_i) \quad (3.1.4)$$

where

$$Q_i(s_i) = \sum_{v \le s_i} \frac{e^{-\lambda_i}\lambda_i^{v}}{v!},$$

and Δ_i, Δ_i^2, ..., etc. represent differences of successive order taken with respect to s_i. If E_i indicates the operation of raising s_i by 1, one can symbolically represent the right-hand side of (3.1.4) as

$$(\sum \lambda_i\,\Delta_i E_i^{-1})^r \prod_{i=1}^{k} Q_i(s_i). \quad (3.1.5)$$

Hence, we have

$$\begin{aligned}\sum_{\substack{v_i \le s_i \\ i=1(1)k}} m(\mathbf{v} \mid n, \boldsymbol{\pi}) \\ &= [1 - (1/2n)(\sum \lambda_i \Delta_i E_i^{-1})^2 + (1/n^2)\{\tfrac{1}{3}(\sum \lambda_i \Delta_i E_i^{-1})^3 \\ &\quad + \tfrac{1}{8}(\sum \lambda_i \Delta_i E_i^{-1})^4\} - (1/n^3)\{\tfrac{1}{4}(\sum \lambda_i \Delta_i E_i^{-1})^4 + \tfrac{1}{6}(\sum \lambda_i \Delta_i E_i^{-1})^5 \\ &\quad + (1/48)(\sum \lambda_i \Delta_i E_i^{-1})^6\} + (1/n^4)\{\tfrac{1}{5}(\sum \lambda_i \Delta_i E_i^{-1})^5 \\ &\quad + (13/72)(\sum \lambda_i \Delta_i E_i^{-1})^6 + (1/24)(\sum \lambda_i \Delta_i E_i^{-1})^7 \\ &\quad + (1/384)(\sum \lambda_i \Delta_i E_i^{-1})^8\} + \cdots] \prod_{i=1}^{k} Q_i(s_i). \qquad (3.1.6)\end{aligned}$$

Numerical Example

To compute

$$\sum_{v_1=0}^{16} \sum_{v_2=0}^{24} \frac{100!}{v_1!\, v_2!\,(100 - v_1 - v_2)!} (0.20)^{v_1}(0.20)^{v_2}(0.60)^{100 - v_1 - v_2}.$$

Note that here $\lambda_1 = \lambda_2 = 20$. The following values of cumulative Poisson probabilities and their differences are obtained from "Biometrika Tables for Statisticians," Vol. I (Table 7).

$$\begin{aligned}&Q_1(16) = 0.22107, \quad &&\Delta_1 Q_1(15) = 0.06456, \quad &&\Delta_1^2 Q_1(14) = 0.01291. \\ & &&\Delta_1^3 Q_1(13) = -0.00001, &&\Delta_1^4 Q_1(12) = -0.00132 \\ &Q_2(24) = 0.84323, &&\Delta_2 Q_2(23) = 0.05574, &&\Delta_2^2 Q_2(22) = -0.01114 \\ & &&\Delta_2^3 Q_2(21) = -0.00111, &&\Delta_2^4 Q_2(20) = 0.00122.\end{aligned}$$

Hence $Q_1(16)Q_2(24) = 0.18641$ (first approximation).

$$\begin{aligned}(\textstyle\sum \lambda_i \Delta_i E_i^{-1})^2 Q_1(16)Q_2(24) &= 6.2502 \\ (\textstyle\sum \lambda_i \Delta_i E_i^{-1})^3 Q_1(16)Q_2(24) &= 2.0208 \\ (\textstyle\sum \lambda_i \Delta_i E_i^{-1})^4 Q_1(16)Q_2(24) &= -319.2160\end{aligned}$$

leading to

$$0.18641 - \frac{1}{2(100)} 6.2502 = 0.15516 \text{ (second approximation)},$$

and

$$0.15516 + \frac{1}{(100)^2} \{\tfrac{1}{3}(2.0208) + \tfrac{1}{8}(-319.2160)\}$$

$$= 0.15124 \text{ (third approximation)}.$$

The exact value to six decimal places is 0.150477.

3.1.b. Product of Independent Poisson Terms for Negative Multinomial

The result for this is obtainable from (3.1.1) by changing n to $-\kappa$. The result can be mentioned as below:

$$nm(\mathbf{v} \mid \kappa, \rho) = \prod_{i=1}^{k} (e^{-\lambda_i}(\lambda_i^{v_i}/v_i!))A \tag{3.1.1$'$}$$

where $\lambda_i = \rho_i \kappa$, $\tau = \sum \lambda_i$, $T = \sum v_i$, and

$$A = e^{\tau}\left(1 + \frac{\tau}{\kappa}\right)^{-\kappa - T}\left(1 + \frac{1}{\kappa}\right) \cdots \left(1 + \frac{\tau - 1}{\kappa}\right)$$

To evaluate the cumulative sum of negative multinomial probabilities (cumulated from below), one can similarly use (3.1.6), replacing n by $-\kappa$ throughout this expression.

3.2.a. Multivariate Chebyshev Hermite Polynomials and Normal Approximation for Positive Multinomial

Consider a k-variate normal distribution with mean values all equal to zero, variances all equal to unity, and correlation matrix $\{\rho_{\alpha\beta}\}$. The density of this distribution at $x_1, x_2, \ldots, x_k$ will be indicated by

$$N_k(x_1, x_2, \ldots, x_k \mid \rho_{\alpha\beta}) = N_k(\mathbf{x} \mid \rho_{\alpha\beta})$$

and the incomplete probability integral

$$\int_{-\infty}^{t_1} \int_{-\infty}^{t_2} \cdots \int_{-\infty}^{t_k} N_k(\mathbf{x} \mid \rho_{\alpha\beta}) \prod_{1}^{k} dx_i \tag{3.2.1}$$

will be denoted by $P_k(t_1, t_2, \ldots, t_k \mid \rho_{\alpha\beta}) = P_k(\mathbf{t} \mid \rho_{\alpha\beta})$. It is well-known that a subset containing s out of these k variables also obeys an s-variate normal distribution with the same correlations $\rho_{\alpha\beta}$, with α, β, running over the subset. Thus without risking any confusion, we shall write $N_s(x_{i_1}, x_{i_2}, \ldots, x_{i_s} \mid \rho_{\alpha\beta})$ to indicate the density function of the distribution of the i_1th, i_2th , $\ldots$, i_sth variables. If $i_1, i_2, \ldots, i_k$ is a permutation of integers $1, 2, \ldots, k$, $I^{(k)}_{i_1, i_2, \ldots, i_s}(\mathbf{t})$ is defined as follows:

$$I^{(k)}_{i_1, i_2, \ldots, i_s}(\mathbf{t}) = \frac{\partial^s}{\partial t_{i_1}\, \partial t_{i_2} \cdots \partial t_{i_s}} P_k(\mathbf{t} \mid \rho_{\alpha\beta}) \tag{3.2.2}$$

which is easily seen to be equal to

$$N_s(t_{i_1}, t_{i_2}, \ldots, t_{i_s} \mid \rho_{\alpha\beta}) P_{k-s}(t_{i_{s+1}}^{(i_1, \ldots, i_s)}, \ldots, t_{i_k}^{(i_1, \ldots, i_s)} \mid \rho_{\alpha\beta \cdot i_1, i_2, \ldots, i_s}) \tag{3.2.3}$$

where $\rho_{\alpha\beta \cdot i_1, i_2, \ldots, i_s}$ indicates the partial correlation coefficient with the usual meaning and $t^{(i_1, \ldots, i_s)}$ is the standardized residual of the αth variable eliminating i_1th, i_2th $\cdots$ i_sth variable computed at $x_i = t_i$ $(i = 1, 2, \ldots, k)$.

Let $j_1, j_2, \ldots, j_s$ be s integers not necessarily all different such that $1 \le j_i \le k$ $(i = 1, 2, \ldots, s)$. Consider the sth degree polynomial $H_{j_1, j_2, \ldots, j_s}(\mathbf{x})$ defined by

$$H_{j_1, j_2, \ldots, j_s}(\mathbf{x}) N_k(\mathbf{x} \mid \rho_{\alpha\beta}) = (-1)^s \frac{\partial^s}{\partial x_{j_1} \, \partial x_{j_2} \cdots \partial x_{j_s}} N_k(\mathbf{x} \mid \rho_{\alpha\beta}). \quad (3.2.4)$$

These polynomials, first studied by Hermite (1864)[1], depend on the x's only through $u_1, u_2, \ldots, u_k$ where $u_i = \sum_j x_j \rho^{ij}$. The first few polynomials are given in Table I. The generating function of these polynomials is given by

$$G(\boldsymbol{\theta}) = \exp\{\sum u_i \theta_i - \sum \theta_i \theta_j \rho^{ij}\}.$$

Thus $H_{1,1,2}(\mathbf{x})$ is the coefficient of $\theta_1{}^2 \theta_2 / 2!1!$ in the expansion of $G(\boldsymbol{\theta})$.

TABLE I

Degree	Symbol	Expression
1	$H_i(\mathbf{x})$	u_i
2	$H_{i,j}(\mathbf{x})$	$u_i u_j - \rho^{ij}$
3	$H_{i,j,m}(\mathbf{x})$	$u_i u_j u_m - (\rho^{ij} u_m + \rho^{im} u_j + \rho^{jm} u_i)$
4	$H_{i,j,m,p}(\mathbf{x})$	$u_i u_j u_m u_p - (\rho^{ij} u_m u_p + \rho^{im} u_j u_p$ $+ \rho^{ip} u_j u_m + \rho^{jm} u_i u_p + \rho^{jp} u_i u_m + \rho^{mp} u_i u_j)$ $+ (\rho^{ij} \rho^{mp} + p^{im} p^{jp} + p^{ip} p^{jm})$, etc.

One may verify that here polynomials of unlike degree are mutually orthogonal with respect to the k-variate normal distribution with density $N_k(\mathbf{x} \mid \rho_{\alpha\beta})$, whereas two polynomials of like degree are not so. In fact,

$$\int_{-\infty}^{\infty} \cdots \int_{-\infty}^{\infty} H_{\alpha_1, \alpha_2, \ldots, \alpha_s}(\mathbf{x}) H_{j_1, j_2, \ldots, j_s}(\mathbf{x}) N_k(\mathbf{x} \mid \rho_{\alpha\beta}) \prod_1^k dx_i$$

$$= \frac{\partial^s}{\partial x_{\alpha_1} \, \partial x_{\alpha_2} \cdots \partial x_{\alpha_s}} u_{j_1} u_{j_2} \cdots u_{j_s}.$$

Also check that

$$\int_{-\infty}^{\infty} \cdots \int_{-\infty}^{\infty} \exp(\sqrt{-1} \sum \theta_j x_j) H_{j_1, j_2, \ldots, j_s}(\mathbf{x}) N_k(\mathbf{x} \mid \rho_{\alpha\beta}) \prod_1^k dx_i$$

$$= (-1)^{s/2} \theta_{j_1} \theta_{j_2} \cdots \theta_{j_s} \exp(-\tfrac{1}{2} \sum \theta_i \theta_j \rho_{ij}).$$

[1] See also Appel and Kampe de Feriet (1926).

Consider now the multinomial frequencies $v_1, v_2, \ldots, v_k$ ignoring $n - \sum_1^k v_i$ and standardize these frequencies to obtain $x_i = (v_i - n\pi_i)/(n\pi_i(1-\pi_i))^{1/2}$. Write $\rho_{\alpha\alpha} = 1$, $\rho_{\alpha\beta} = -(\pi_\alpha\pi_\beta)^{1/2}/\{(1-\pi_\alpha)(1-\pi_\beta)\}^{1/2}$ for $\alpha \neq \beta$. The characteristic function of $x_1, x_2, \ldots, x_k$ to terms of order $O(1/n)$ can be written as

$$\exp\left(-\tfrac{1}{2}\sum \theta_\alpha\theta_\beta\rho_{\alpha\beta}\right)\left[1 + ((-1)^{3/2}/\sqrt{n})\,A_k(\boldsymbol{\theta}) + (1/n)B_k(\boldsymbol{\theta}) + O\left(1/n\sqrt{n}\right)\right] \tag{3.2.5}$$

where

$$A_k(\boldsymbol{\theta}) = \sum{}' a_i^{(3)}\theta_i^3 + \sum{}' a_{ij}^{(21)}\theta_i^2\theta_j + \sum{}' a_{ijm}^{(111)}\theta_i\theta_j\theta_m,$$

$$\begin{aligned}
B_k(\boldsymbol{\theta}) = {} & \sum{}' b_i^{(4)}\theta_1^4 + \sum{}' b_{ij}^{(31)}\theta_i^3\theta_j + \sum{}' b_{ij}^{(22)}\theta_i^2\theta_j^2 \\
& + \sum{}' b_{ijm}^{(211)}\theta_i^2\theta_j\theta_m + \sum{}' b_{ijmp}^{(1111)}\theta_i\theta_j\theta_m\theta_p + \sum{}' b_i^{(6)}\theta_i^6 \\
& + \sum{}' b_{ij}^{(51)}\theta_i^5\theta_j + \sum{}' b_{ij}^{(42)}\theta_i^4\theta_j^2 + \sum{}' b_{ij}^{(33)}\theta_i^3\theta_j^3 + \sum{}' b_{ijm}^{(411)}\theta_i^4\theta_j\theta_m \\
& + \sum{}' b_{ijm}^{(321)}\theta_i^3\theta_j^2\theta_m + \sum{}' b_{ijm}^{(222)}\theta_i^2\theta_j^2\theta_m^2 + \sum{}' b_{ijmp}^{(3111)}\theta_i^3\theta_j\theta_m\theta_p \\
& + \sum{}' b_{ijmp}^{(2211)}\theta_i^2\theta_j^2\theta_m\theta_p + \sum{}' b_{ijmpq}^{(21111)}\theta_i^2\theta_j\theta_m\theta_p\theta_q \\
& + \sum{}' b_{ijmpqr}^{(111111)}\ \theta_i\theta_j\theta_m\theta_p\theta_q\theta_r.
\end{aligned}$$

The $\sum'$ indicates summation taking place over unequal values of the suffices, each suffix otherwise ranging over 1 to k,

$$a_i^{(3)} = \frac{(1-2\pi_i)}{6[\pi_i(1-\pi_i)]^{1/2}}, \qquad a_{ij}^{(21)} = \frac{\pi_j^{1/2}(-1+2\pi_i)}{2(1-\pi_i)[(1-\pi_j)]^{1/2}},$$

$$a_{ijm}^{(111)} = \frac{(\pi_i\pi_j\pi_m)^{1/2}}{3[(1-\pi_i)(1-\pi_j)(1-\pi_m)]^{1/2}},$$

$$b_i^{(4)} = \frac{(1-6\pi_i+6\pi_i^2)}{24\pi_i(1-\pi_i)}, \qquad b_{ij}^{(31)} = -\frac{(1-6\pi_i+6\pi_i^2)\pi_j^{1/2}}{6(1-\pi_i)[\pi_i(1-\pi_i)(1-\pi_j)]^{1/2}}$$

$$b_{ij}^{(22)} = -\frac{1-2\pi_i-2\pi_j+6\pi_i\pi_j}{8(1-\pi_i)(1-\pi_j)},$$

$$b_{ijm}^{(211)} = \frac{(1-3\pi_i)(\pi_j\pi_m)^{1/2}}{2(1-\pi_i)[(1-\pi_j)(1-\pi_m)]^{1/2}}$$

$$b_{ijmp}^{(1111)} = -\frac{(\pi_i\pi_j\pi_m\pi_p)^{1/2}}{4[(1-\pi_i)(1-\pi_j)(1-\pi_m)(1-\pi_p)]^{1/2}},$$

$$b_i^{(6)} = -\frac{(1-2\pi_i)^2}{72\pi_i(1-\pi_i)},$$

$$b_{ij}^{(51)} = \frac{(1-2\pi_i)^2\pi_j^{1/2}}{12(1-\pi_i)[\pi_i(1-\pi_i)(1-\pi_j)]^{1/2}},$$

$$b_{ij}^{(42)} = \frac{(1-2\pi_i)[2(1-\pi_i) - \pi_j(7-10\pi_i)]}{24(1-\pi_i)^2(1-\pi_j)}$$

$$b_{ij}^{(33)} = -\frac{(1-2\pi_i)(1-2\pi_j)[1-\pi_i-\pi_j+10\pi_i\pi_j]}{72(1-\pi_i)(1-\pi_j)[\pi_i\pi_j(1-\pi_i)(1-\pi_j)]^{1/2}},$$

$$b_{ijm}^{(411)} = -\frac{(1-2\pi_i)(7-10\pi_i)(\pi_j\pi_m)^{1/2}}{24(1-\pi_i)^2[(1-\pi_j)(1-\pi_m)]^{1/2}},$$

$$b_{ijm}^{(321)} = \frac{(1-2\pi_i)\pi_m^{1/2}[1-4\pi_i-2\pi_j+20\pi_i\pi_j]}{12(1-\pi_i)(1-\pi_j)[\pi_i(1-\pi_i)(1-\pi_m)]^{1/2}},$$

$$b_{ijm}^{(222)} = -\frac{[\pi_i+\pi_j+\pi_m-4(\pi_i\pi_j+\pi_i\pi_m+\pi_j\pi_m)+20\pi_i\pi_j\pi_m]}{24(1-\pi_i)(1-\pi_j)(1-\pi_m)}$$

$$b_{ijmp}^{(3111)} = -\frac{(1-2\pi_i)(1-10\pi_i)(\pi_j\pi_m\pi_p)^{1/2}}{18(1-\pi_i)[\pi_i(1-\pi_i)(1-\pi_j)(1-\pi_m)(1-\pi_p)]^{1/2}}$$

$$b_{ijmp}^{(2211)} = -\frac{[1-4(\pi_i+\pi_j)+20\pi_i\pi_j](\pi_m\pi_p)^{1/2}}{8(1-\pi_i)(1-\pi_j)[(1-\pi_m)(1-\pi_p)]^{1/2}}$$

$$b_{ijmpq}^{(21111)} = \frac{(1-5\pi_i)(\pi_j\pi_m\pi_p\pi_q)^{1/2}}{6(1-\pi_i)[(1-\pi_j)(1-\pi_m)(1-\pi_p)(1-\pi_q)]^{1/2}}$$

$$b_{ijmpqr}^{(111111)} = -\frac{(\pi_i\pi_j\pi_m\pi_p\pi_q\pi_r)^{1/2}}{18[(1-\pi_i)(1-\pi_j)(1-\pi_m)(1-\pi_p)(1-\pi_q)(1-\pi_r)]^{1/2}}$$

Hence applying inversion formula, we have

$$\begin{aligned}
&\operatorname{Prob}\{v_i \le n\pi_i + t_i[n\pi_i(1-\pi_i)]^{1/2},\ i = 1(1)k\} \\
&= \int_{-\infty}^{t_1}\int_{-\infty}^{t_2}\cdots\int_{-\infty}^{t_k} N_k(\mathbf{x}\mid\rho_{\alpha\beta}) \\
&\times\Bigg[1 + (1/\sqrt{n})\sum_{(3)}\sum{}' a_{j_1j_2\cdots j_s}^{(i_1i_2\cdots i_s)} H_{j_1j_2\cdots j_s}^{(i_1i_2\cdots i_s)}(\mathbf{x}) \\
&+ (1/n)\Bigg\{\sum_{(4)}\sum{}' b_{j_1j_2\cdots j_s}^{(i_1i_2\cdots i_s)} H_{j_1j_2\cdots j_s}^{(i_1i_2\cdots i_s)}(\mathbf{x}) \\
&- \sum_{(6)}\sum{}' b_{j_1j_2\cdots j_s}^{(i_1i_2\cdots i_s)} H_{j_1j_2\cdots j_s}^{(i_1i_2\cdots i_s)}(\mathbf{x})\Bigg\}\Bigg] \prod_1^k dx_i + O(1/n\sqrt{n})
\end{aligned} \tag{3.2.6}$$

where

$$H_{j_1j_2\cdots j_s}^{(i_1i_2\cdots i_s)}(\mathbf{x})$$

is just an abbreviated notation for

$$H_{\underbrace{j_1,j_1,\ldots,j_1}_{i_1\text{ times}},\ \underbrace{j_2,j_2,\ldots,j_2}_{i_2\text{ times}},\ \ldots,\ \underbrace{j_s,j_s,\ldots,j_s}_{i_s\text{ times}}}(\mathbf{x})$$

and $\sum_{(u)}$ indicates a summation over all possible choices of the integer $s(\leq u)$ and of superfixes $i_1, i_2, \ldots, i_s$, as nonincreasing positive integers

$$i_1 \geq i_2 \geq \cdots \geq i_s,$$

adding up to u. For $u = 3, 4, 6$, there are 3, 5, 11 such terms, respectively, as listed in (3.2.5).

Let the operator D_i stand for the computation of partial derivative with respect to t_i, then the expression (3.2.6) simplifies to

$$P_k(\mathbf{t} \mid \rho_{\alpha\beta}) - \frac{C_{k1}(\mathbf{t})}{\sqrt{n}} - \frac{C_{k2}(\mathbf{t})}{n} + O\left(\frac{1}{n\sqrt{n}}\right) \tag{3.2.7}$$

where

$$C_{k1}(\mathbf{t}) = \sum_{(3)} \sum{}' \, a_{j_1 j_2 \cdots j_s}^{(i_1 i_2 \cdots i_s)} p_{j_1 j_2 \cdots j_s}^{(i_1 i_2 \cdots i_s)}(\mathbf{t})$$

$$C_{k2}(\mathbf{t}) = -\sum_{(4)} \sum{}' \, b_{j_1 j_2 \cdots j_s}^{(i_1 i_2 \cdots i_s)} p_{j_1 j_2 \cdots j_s}^{(i_1 i_2 \cdots i_s)}(\mathbf{t})$$

$$+ \sum_{(6)} \sum{}' \, b_{j_1 j_2 \cdots j_s}^{(i_1 i_2 \cdots i_s)} p_{j_1 j_2 \cdots j_s}^{(i_1 i_2 \cdots i_s)}(\mathbf{t})$$

$$p_{j_1 j_2 \cdots j_s}^{(i_1 i_2 \cdots i_s)}(\mathbf{t}) = (-1)^s \int_{-\infty}^{t_1} \int_{-\infty}^{t_2} \cdots \int_{-\infty}^{t_k} H_{j_1 j_2 \cdots j_s}^{(i_1 i_2 \cdots i_s)}(x) N_k(\mathbf{x} \mid \rho_{\alpha\beta}) \prod_1^k dx_i$$

$$= D_{j_1}^{i_1} D_{j_2}^{i_2} \cdots D_{j_s}^{i_s} P_k(\mathbf{t} \mid \rho_{\alpha\beta})$$

$$= D_{j_1}^{i_1 - 1} D_{j_2}^{i_2 - 1} \cdots D_{j_s}^{i_s - 1} I_{j_1, j_2, \ldots, j_s}^{(k)}(\mathbf{t})$$

in terms of the I functions introduced in (3.2.2). Thus

$$p_{ijm}^{(111)}(\mathbf{t}) = I_{i,j,m}^{(k)}(\mathbf{t}) \qquad \text{for} \quad i \neq j \neq m$$

$$p_{ij}^{(21)}(\mathbf{t}) = D_i I_{ij}^{(k)}(\mathbf{t}) \qquad \text{for} \quad i \neq j$$

$$= -\frac{t_i - \rho_{ij} t_j}{1 - \rho_{ij}^2} I_{i,j}^{(k)}(\mathbf{t}) - \sum_{\substack{\alpha=1 \\ \alpha \neq i \neq j}}^{k} \left(\frac{\rho_{\alpha i} - \rho_{ij}\rho_{\alpha j}}{1 - \rho_{ij}^2}\right) I_{\alpha,i,j}^{(k)}(\mathbf{t})$$

$$p_i^{(3)}(\mathbf{t}) = D_i^2 I_i^{(k)}(\mathbf{t}) = (t_i^2 - 1) I_i^{(k)}(\mathbf{t})$$

$$+ \sum_{\substack{\alpha=1 \\ \alpha \neq i}}^{k} \rho_{\alpha i}\left[t_i + \frac{t_i - \rho_{\alpha i} t_\alpha}{1 - \rho_{\alpha i}^2}\right] I_{\alpha,i}^{(k)}(\mathbf{t})$$

$$+ \sum_{\substack{\alpha,\beta=1 \\ \alpha \neq \beta \neq i}}^{k} \rho_{\alpha i}\left[\frac{\rho_{\beta i} - \rho_{\alpha i}\rho_{\alpha\beta}}{1 - \rho_{\alpha i}^2}\right] I_{\alpha,\beta,i}^{(k)}(\mathbf{t}), \text{ etc.}$$

Thus after simplification, we have

$$C_{k1}(\mathbf{t}) = \tfrac{1}{6}\sum \frac{1-2\pi_i}{[\pi_i(1-\pi_i)]^{1/2}}(t_i{}^2-1)I_i^{(k)}(\mathbf{t})$$
$$-\tfrac{1}{6}\sum{}' \frac{t_i}{(1-\pi_i)}\left(\frac{\pi_j}{1-\pi_j}\right)^{1/2} I_{ij}^{(k)}(\mathbf{t}). \qquad (3.2.8)$$

The expression for $C_{k2}(\mathbf{t})$ can be simplified in a like manner. In the special cases of $k = 1, 2$, we have

$$C_{11}(\mathbf{t}) = \frac{1-2\pi_1}{6[\pi_1(1-\pi_1)]^{1/2}}(t_1{}^2-1)N_1(t_1)$$

$$C_{21}(\mathbf{t}) = \frac{1-2\pi_1}{6[\pi_1(1-\pi_1)]^{1/2}}(t_1{}^2-1)N_1(t_1)P_1(t_2^{(1)})$$
$$+\frac{1-2\pi_2}{6[\pi_2(1-\pi_2)]^{1/2}}(t_2{}^2-1)N_1(t_2)P_1(t_1^{(2)})$$
$$-\tfrac{1}{6}N_2(\mathbf{t}\,|\,\rho_{12})\left[\frac{t_1}{1-\pi_1}\left(\frac{\pi_2}{1-\pi_2}\right)^{1/2}+\frac{t_2}{1-\pi_2}\left(\frac{\pi_1}{1-\pi_1}\right)^{1/2}\right]. \qquad (3.2.9)$$

3.2.b. Normal Approximation for Negative Multinomial

Here the final result corresponding to (3.2.7) is obtained as

$$\operatorname{Prob}[v_i \le \kappa\rho_i + t_i[\kappa\rho_i(1+\rho_i)]^{1/2},\ i = 1(1)k]$$
$$= P_k(\mathbf{t}\,|\,\rho_{\alpha\beta}) + \frac{C_{k1}(t)}{\sqrt{\kappa}} + O\left(\frac{1}{\kappa}\right) \qquad (3.2.7')$$

where

$$C_{k1}(\mathbf{t}) = \frac{1}{6}\sum_{i=1}^{k} p_i^{(3)}(\mathbf{t})\frac{1+2\rho_i}{[\rho_i(1+\rho_i)]^{1/2}}$$
$$-\frac{1}{2}\sum_{i\neq j=1}^{k} p_{ij}^{(21)}(\mathbf{t})\frac{1+2\rho_i}{1+\rho_i}\left(\frac{\rho_j}{1+\rho_j}\right)^{1/2}$$
$$+\frac{1}{3}\sum_{i\neq j\neq m=1}^{k} p_{ijm}^{(111)}(\mathbf{t})\left[\frac{\rho_i\rho_j\rho_m}{(1+\rho_i)(1+\rho_j)(1+\rho_m)}\right]^{1/2}$$

with

$$p_i^{(3)}(\mathbf{t}) = D_i{}^3 P_k(\mathbf{t}\,|\,\rho_{\alpha\beta}), \qquad p_{ij}^{(21)}(\mathbf{t}) = D_i{}^2 D_j P_k(\mathbf{t}\,|\,\rho_{\alpha\beta})$$

and

$$p_{ijm}^{(111)}(t) = D_i D_j D_m P_k(\mathbf{t}\,|\,\rho_{\alpha\beta})$$

noting that

$$\rho_{\alpha\beta} = \{\rho_\alpha\rho_\beta/(1+\rho_\alpha)(1+\rho_\beta)\}^{1/2} \qquad \text{for} \quad \alpha\neq\beta$$

and

$$\rho_{\alpha\beta} = 1 \qquad \text{for} \quad \alpha=\beta.$$

3.3.a. Approximation to Positive Multinomial by Product of Poisson and Normal Distributions

Consider now a situation in which some of the $n\pi_i$'s (say for $i = s+1, s+2, \ldots, k$) are small and others are large, thus indicating a Poisson approximation for some frequencies, and normal for the rest. The characteristic function of $x_1, x_2, \ldots, x_s, v_{s+1}, \ldots, v_k$ where $x_i = (v_i - n\pi_i)/[n\pi_i(1-\pi_i)]^{1/2}$, $i = 1(1)s$ is given by

$$\left[\exp\left\{-\frac{1}{2}\sum_{\alpha,\beta=1}^{s}\theta_\alpha\theta_\beta\theta_{\alpha\beta} + \sum_{\alpha=s+1}^{k}\lambda_\alpha(\exp(\sqrt{-1}\,\theta_\alpha) - 1)\right\}\right]$$
$$\times\left[1 + \frac{(-1)^{3/2}}{\sqrt{n}}\{A_s(\boldsymbol{\theta}) + A^*(\boldsymbol{\theta})\} + \frac{1}{n}\{B_s(\boldsymbol{\theta}) + B^*(\boldsymbol{\theta})\}\right.$$
$$\left. + O(1/n\sqrt{n})\right] \tag{3.3.1}$$

where $A_s(\boldsymbol{\theta})$ and $B_s(\boldsymbol{\theta})$ are as defined in (3.2.5),

$$A^*(\boldsymbol{\theta}) = \left[\sum_{\alpha=s+1}^{k}\lambda_\alpha(\exp(\sqrt{-1}\,\theta_\alpha) - 1)\right]\left[\sum_{\alpha=1}^{s}\theta_\alpha\left(\frac{\pi_\alpha}{1-\pi_\alpha}\right)^{1/2}\right.$$

$$B^*(\theta) = \left[\sum_{\alpha=s+1}^{k}\lambda_\alpha(\exp(\sqrt{-1}\,\theta_\alpha) - 1)\right]\left[\sum_{\alpha=1}^{s}\frac{\theta_\alpha^{\,2}}{1-\pi_\alpha} - \left[\sum_{\alpha=1}^{s}\theta_\alpha\left(\frac{\pi_\alpha}{1-\pi_\alpha}\right)^{1/2}\right]^2\right.$$
$$\left. - \frac{1}{2}\sum_{\alpha=s+1}^{k}\lambda_\alpha(\exp(\sqrt{-1}\,\theta_\alpha) - 1)\right].$$

Hence, the inversion formula gives

$$\text{Prob}\{v_\alpha \le n\pi_\alpha + t_\alpha[n\pi_\alpha(1-\pi_\alpha)]^{1/2}, \alpha = 1(1)s;\ v_\alpha = a_\alpha, \alpha = (s+1)(1)k\}$$
$$= \prod_{\alpha=s+1}^{k}\exp(-\lambda_\alpha)\frac{\lambda_\alpha^{a_\alpha}}{a_\alpha\,!}\left[P_s(\mathbf{t}\,|\,\rho_{\alpha\beta}) - \frac{1}{\sqrt{n}}C_{s1}(\mathbf{t})\right.$$
$$+ \frac{1}{\sqrt{n}}\left\{\sum_{\alpha=s+1}^{k}(a_\alpha - \lambda_\alpha)\right\}\left\{\sum_{\alpha=1}^{s}\left(\frac{\pi_\alpha}{1-\pi_\alpha}\right)^{1/2} I_\alpha^{(s)}(\mathbf{t})\right\}$$
$$- \frac{C_{s2}(\mathbf{t})}{n} + \frac{1}{n}\left\{\sum_{\alpha=s+1}^{k}(a_\alpha - \lambda_\alpha)\right\}\left\{\sum_{\alpha=1}^{s}D_\alpha I_\alpha^{(s)}(\mathbf{t})\right.$$
$$\left.\left. - \sum_{\alpha,\beta=1}^{s}\rho_{\alpha\beta}I_{\alpha,\beta}^{(s)}(\mathbf{t})\right\} - \frac{1}{2n}\sum_{\alpha=s+1}^{k}\{(a_\alpha - \lambda_\alpha)^2 - a_\alpha\}\right]$$
$$+ O(1/n\sqrt{n}) \tag{3.3.2}$$

where $P_s(\mathbf{t}\,|\,\rho_{\alpha\beta})$ is as defined in (3.2.1), $I_\alpha^{(s)}(\mathbf{t})$ and $I_{\alpha,\beta}^{(s)}(\mathbf{t})$ are as defined in (3.2.2), $C_{s1}(\mathbf{t})$ and $C_{s2}(\mathbf{t})$ are as defined in (3.2.7).

3.3.b. Approximation to Negative Multinomial by Product of Poisson and Normal Distributions

We get the result corresponding to (3.3.2) if we make the substitutions $\lambda_\alpha = \kappa\rho_\alpha$ and $\rho_{\alpha\beta} = \{\rho_\alpha \rho_\beta/(1+\rho_\alpha)(1+\rho_\beta)\}^{1/2}$ and replace π_i by $-\rho_i$, n by $-\kappa$.

4. APPROXIMATIONS TO THE CDF OF A COMPOUND MULTINOMIAL

Let us consider nonnegative integer valued variables $X_1, X_2, \ldots, X_k$ which for a fixed set of values $\pi_1, \pi_2, \ldots, \pi_k \left(\sum \pi_i < 1\right)$ follows a positive multinomial distribution with frequency function $m(\mathbf{v} \mid n, \boldsymbol{\pi})$. Consider a situation in which the π's are random variables with distribution function $F(\boldsymbol{\pi})$. The joint distribution of $X_1, X_2, \ldots, X_k$ in this case is called a compound multinomial. Let us write

$$L(\mathbf{c} \mid n, \boldsymbol{\pi}) = \sum_{\substack{v_i \le c_i \\ i=1,2,\ldots,k}} m(\mathbf{v} \mid n, \boldsymbol{\pi}).$$

Then, the cdf of the compound multinomial is obtained as

$$\underset{\pi}{E}\, L(\mathbf{c} \mid n, \boldsymbol{\pi}) = G(\mathbf{c} \mid n).$$

We shall prove:

Theorem 4.1. *If $F(\boldsymbol{\pi}) = F(\pi_1, \pi_2, \ldots, \pi_k)$ has continuous first and second order partial derivatives*

$$\frac{\partial F}{\partial \pi_i} \quad \text{and} \quad \frac{\partial^2 F}{\partial \pi_i\, \partial \pi_j}, \quad \text{and} \quad \left|\frac{\partial^2 F}{\partial \pi_i\, \partial \pi_j}\right| \le M_{ij},$$

then for $n > \sum_{i=1}^k c_i + k - 2$

$$G(\mathbf{c} \mid n) = F\left(\frac{c_1+1}{n+1}, \frac{c_2+1}{n+1}, \ldots, \frac{c_k+1}{n+1}\right) + R$$

and

$$|R| \le \sum_{ij} M_{ij} \frac{[(c_i+1)(c_j+1)(n-c_i)(n-c_j)]^{1/2}}{2(n+1)^2(n+2)} \le \frac{\sum M_{ij}}{8(n+2)}.$$

Theorem 4.2. *If the first partial derivatives of $F(\boldsymbol{\pi})$ are continuous and $|\partial F/\partial \pi_i| < M_i^*$, $i = 1, 2, \ldots, k$, then for $n > \sum c_i + k - 2$,*

$$G(\mathbf{c} \mid n) = F\left(\frac{c_1+1}{n+1}, \frac{c_2+1}{n+1}, \ldots, \frac{c_k+1}{n+1}\right) + R$$

where

$$|R| \leq \frac{1}{2} \sum_i M_i^* \{(c_i + 1)(n - c_i)/(n + 1)^2(n + 2)\}^{1/2} \leq \sum_i M_i^*/4(n + 2)^{1/2}.$$

Proof of Theorems 4.1 *and* 4.2. Let $b_1, b_2, \ldots, b_k$ denote random variables with joint probability density function $\beta_k(c_1, c_2, \ldots, c_k; n - \sum c_i - k; \mathbf{b})$. Then it is easy to check that

$$G(\mathbf{c} \mid n) = E_b F(\mathbf{b}).$$

The proof of Theorems 4.1 and 4.2 can then be completed on the same lines as in Theorems 2.1 and 2.2 of Mitra and Subramannya (1967).

Similarly, if the parameters $\rho_1, \rho_2 \cdots \rho_k$ of a negative multinomial $nm(\mathbf{v} \mid \kappa, \boldsymbol{\rho})$ are random variables with cdf $F_1(\rho)$, one can obtain the cdf of the compound negative multinomial, and corresponding to Theorems 4.1 and 4.2, we have here:

Theorem 4.3. *If $F_1(\boldsymbol{\rho})$ has continuous first and second order partial derivatives $\partial F_1/\partial \rho_i$ and $\partial^2 F_1/\partial \rho_i \, \partial \rho_j$, and $|\partial^2 F_1/\partial \rho_i \, \partial \rho_j| \leq M_{ij}$, then*

$$G_1(\mathbf{c} \mid \kappa) = F_1\left(\frac{c_1 + 1}{\kappa - 1}, \ldots, \frac{c_k + 1}{\kappa - 1}\right) + R$$

where

$$|R| \leq \sum_{i,j} M_{ij} \{(c_i + 1)(c_j + 1)(\kappa + c_i)(\kappa + c_j)\}^{1/2}/(\kappa - 1)^2(\kappa - 2),$$

and

Theorem 4.4. *If the first partial derivatives of $F_1(\boldsymbol{\rho})$ are continuous and $|\partial F_1/\partial \rho_i| \leq M_i^*$, $i = 1, 2, \ldots, k$, then*

$$G_1(\mathbf{c} \mid \kappa) = F_1\left(\frac{c_1 + 1}{\kappa - 1}, \ldots, \frac{c_k + 1}{\kappa - 1}\right) + R$$

where $|R| \leq \sum_{i=1}^k M_i^* E\,|b_i - E(b_i)|$, and $b_1, \ldots, b_k$ have the joint density function $\beta_k^{(2)}(c_1, \ldots, c_k; \kappa - 1; \mathbf{b})$.

Remark: Let $b_i = g_i(h_1, h_2, \ldots, h_k) = g_i(\mathbf{h})$, $i = 1, 2, \ldots, k$ define a one to one differentiable and measurable transformation of $b_1, b_2, \ldots, b_k$ to $h_1, \ldots, h_k$ such that $E(h_i) = \mu_i$ exists for $i = 1, 2, \ldots, k$. Then it is easy to check in the same manner as in Theorem 4.2 that

$$G(\mathbf{c} \mid n) = F(g_1(\boldsymbol{\mu}), g_2(\boldsymbol{\mu}), \ldots, g_k(\boldsymbol{\mu})) + O(1/\sqrt{n}),$$

and in Theorem 4.4,

$$G_1(\mathbf{c} \mid \kappa) = F_1(g_1(\boldsymbol{\mu}), g_2(\boldsymbol{\mu}), \ldots, g_k(\boldsymbol{\mu})) + O(1/\sqrt{\kappa}).$$

It is easily seen that the approximations

$$F\left(\frac{c_1+1}{n+1}, \frac{c_2+1}{n+1}, \ldots, \frac{c_k+1}{n+1}\right)$$

and $F(g_1(\boldsymbol{\mu}), g_2(\boldsymbol{\mu}), \ldots, g_k(\boldsymbol{\mu}))$ are equivalent in large samples, but that they might differ for moderate sample sizes. The same would be true for approximations to cdf of compound negative multinomial distributions. The question of choosing optimum transformations of $b_1, b_2, \ldots, b_k$ is yet to be settled.

ACKNOWLEDGMENT

The authors wish to thank the referee for his valuable comments.

REFERENCES

ANDERSON, T. W. (1966). Some nonparametric multivariate procedures based on statistically equivalent blocks. *In* " Multivariate Analysis " (P. R. Krishnaiah, ed.), pp. 5–27. Academic Press, New York.

APPEL, P., and KAMPE DE FERIET, J. (1926). " Functions Hypergeometriques et Hyperspheriques." Gauthier-Villars, Paris.

BATES, G. E., and NEYMAN, J. (1952). Contributions to the theory of accident proneness, I—an optimistic model of the correlation between light and severe accidents. *Univ. California Publ. Statist.* **1** 215–253.

HERMITE, C. (1864). Sur un nouveau development en sierie des fonctions. *C.R. Acad. Sci. Paris* **58** 93–100, 266–273.

KHATRI, C. G. (1959). On certain properties of power series distributions. *Biometrika* **46** 486–496.

MITRA, S. K., and SUBRAMANNYA, M. T. (1967). A robust property of the OC of binomial and Poisson sampling inspection plans. Tech. Rept. No. 36/67. Indian Statist. Inst., Calcutta, India.

OLKIN, I., and SOBEL, M. (1966). Integral expressions for tail probabilities of the multinomial and negative multinomial distributions. *Biometrika* **52** 167–179.

OWEN, D. B. (1956). Tables for computing bivariate normal distribution. *Ann. Math. Statist.* **27** 1075–1090.

RAO, C. R. (1965). " Linear Statistical Inference and Its Applications." Wiley, New York.

ROY, S. N., and MITRA, S. K. (1956). An introduction to some nonparametric generalizations of analysis of variance and multivariate analysis. *Biometrika* **43** 361–376.

Approximate Confidence Regions for Constraint Parameters[1]

ALBERT MADANSKY

DATAPLAN, INC.
NEW YORK, NEW YORK

INGRAM OLKIN

DEPARTMENT OF STATISTICS
STANFORD UNIVERSITY
STANFORD, CALIFORNIA

1. INTRODUCTION

Suppose we have a probability distribution $p_\theta(x)$, where the natural parameter θ may be vector-valued, and we wish to find a confidence region for some vector-valued function, $h(\theta) = (h_1(\theta), \ldots, h_q(\theta))$, of θ. For reasons which will be clear later, we will call $h(\theta)$ a "constraint parameter." If $h(\theta)$ is complicated, it may be difficult to obtain exact confidence regions. However, asymptotic confidence regions frequently are available by using "linearization," i.e., if $h(\hat{\theta})$ is an estimate of $h(\theta)$, and the appropriate regularity conditions are satisfied, $[h(\hat{\theta}) - h(\theta)]V_n^{-1}(\hat{\theta})[h(\hat{\theta}) - h(\theta)]'$ is approximately $\chi_q^{\,2}$, where $V_n(\hat{\theta})$ is an appropriately normalized estimate of the asymptotic covariance matrix of $h(\hat{\theta})$ based on a sample of size n. For $q = 1$, we obtain the usual normal approximation, namely, $[h(\hat{\theta}) - h(\theta)]/(v_n(\hat{\theta}))^{1/2}$ is approximately $N(0, 1)$, where $v_n(\hat{\theta})$ is the normalized estimate of the asymptotic variance of $h(\hat{\theta})$.

The purpose of this paper is to present an alternative method for obtaining confidence regions. The method is also asymptotic and is based on the asymptotic distribution of the likelihood ratio statistic (LRS). The particular novelty of the procedure rests in the fact that the LRS is not determined explicitly as a function of $\hat{\theta}$, the maximum likelihood estimator (MLE) of θ under the null hypothesis, but instead, as a function of certain Lagrangian multipliers. If, then, $h(\hat{\theta})$ as a function of the Lagrangian multipliers possesses appropriate

[1] This work was sponsored in part by the RAND Corporation, Center for Advanced Study in the Behavioral Sciences, and the National Science Foundation Contract GP–6681, Stanford University.

monotonicity properties, then the LRS also possesses certain monotonicity or convexity properties, which permits the determination of a confidence region for $h(\theta)$ in a simple way.

Lagrangian multipliers arise naturally in the problem of finding the constrained MLE $\hat{\theta}$ of θ when $h(\theta)$ is specified to be a particular vector, ρ. Since the Lagrangian multipliers, as functions of $\hat{\theta}$, should equal zero when $h(\theta) = \rho$, Aitchison and Silvey (1958) suggest that one test the hypothesis that $h(\theta) = \rho$ by testing the equivalent hypothesis that the Lagrangian multipliers equal zero. To this end, Silvey (1959) obtains the asymptotic distribution of the Lagrangian multipliers as a function of the constrained MLE $\hat{\theta}$.

Approximate confidence regions for the Lagrangian multipliers may be obtained using either Silvey's result or by using the approximate distribution of the LRS as a function of the multipliers. The essence of this paper is that it presents a method for converting a confidence region for the multipliers into a confidence region for $h(\theta)$.

The general procedure and relevant preliminaries are presented in Sections 2 and 3. Section 4 is concerned with one sample problems for the Wishart distribution. There confidence bounds for $\operatorname{tr} \Sigma A$, $\operatorname{tr} \Sigma^{-1} A$, $|\Sigma|$, and the characteristic roots of Σ are obtained. Two sample problems are in Section 5 and include confidence bounds for $\operatorname{tr}(A_1\Sigma_1 + A_2\Sigma_2)$, $\operatorname{tr}(A_1\Sigma_1^{-1} + A_2\Sigma_2^{-1})$, $|\Sigma_1|^{a_1}|\Sigma_2|^{a_2}$, $a_1|\Lambda_1| + a_2|\Lambda_2|$, and $\operatorname{tr} \Sigma_1^{-1}\Sigma_2$. Section 6 deals with confidence bounds for $\mu\Sigma^{-1}\mu'$, and Section 7 with the Behrens-Fisher problem.

2. A METHOD FOR OBTAINING APPROXIMATE CONFIDENCE REGIONS

Let X be a random variable (possibly vector valued) with distribution function $F(x; \theta)$, where $\theta = (\theta_1, \ldots, \theta_m)$ is a vector of real parameters of the distribution, and assume that $F(x; \theta)$ has a density $f(x; \theta)$. Given n independent observations $X_1, \ldots, X_n$ on X, define

$$L_n(x; \theta) = \prod_{i=1}^{n} f(x_i; \theta).$$

Let the parameter space Ω be a subset of Euclidean m-space, and ω be an $(m-q)$-dimensional subset of Ω defined by the constraints $h_i(\theta) = \rho_i$, $i = 1, \ldots, q$, where the ρ_i are real numbers. Let λ be the likelihood ratio statistic (LRS) for testing the hypothesis $\theta \in \omega = \{\theta : h_i(\theta) = \rho_i, i = 1, \ldots, q\}$, and suppose that $-2 \log \lambda$ is asymptotically distributed as a chi-square variable with q degrees of freedom.

An approximate confidence region, with confidence coefficient γ, for the vector of parameters $\rho = (\rho_1, \ldots, \rho_q)$ is then given by $\{\rho : -2 \log \lambda \leq \chi_\alpha^2(q)\}$, where the level of significance is $\alpha = 1 - \gamma$, and $\chi_\alpha^2(q)$ is the upper $100\alpha\%$

point of the chi-square distribution with q degrees of freedom. In the expression

$$\lambda = \frac{\sup_{\theta \in \omega} L_n(x; \theta)}{\sup_{\theta \in \Omega} L_n(x; \theta)},$$

it is usually a simple task to determine the denominator of λ. To determine the numerator, we must find the maximum likelihood estimator (MLE) of $\theta \in \omega$, i.e., that value $\hat{\theta} \in \omega$ which satisfies

$$\log L_n(x; \hat{\theta}) = \sup_{\theta \in \omega} \log L_n(x; \theta).$$

Consider the Lagrangian expression

$$M_n(x; \theta) = \log L_n(x; \theta) - \sum_{i=1}^{q} \xi_i [h_i(\theta) - \rho_i].$$

(For simplicity of notation, the subscript n in $M_n(x; \theta)$ and $L_n(x; \theta)$ is omitted whenever the context is clear.)

Let $\hat{\theta}(\xi) = (\hat{\theta}_1(\xi), \ldots, \hat{\theta}_m(\xi))$, where $\xi = (\xi_1, \ldots, \xi_q)$, denote a generic member of the family of vectors in ω which satisfy the equations

$$\frac{\partial M(x; \theta)}{\partial \theta_\alpha} = (L(x; \theta))^{-1} \frac{\partial L(x; \theta)}{\partial \theta_\alpha} - \sum_{i=1}^{q} \xi_i \frac{\partial h_i(\theta)}{\partial \theta_\alpha} = 0, \qquad \alpha = 1, \ldots, m. \tag{2.1}$$

The usual procedure at this point is to find the vector ξ_0 which satisfies the constraint equations

$$h_i(\hat{\theta}(\xi)) = \rho_i, \qquad i = 1, \ldots, q.$$

Then the MLE of $\theta \in \omega$ is a solution, $\hat{\theta}(\xi_0)$, of (2.1).

In many cases it is difficult or cumbersome to explicitly express the solution ξ_0 of the constraint equations as a function of the ρ_i. However, suppose there exists a transformation taking θ into $h^*(\theta) = (h_1(\theta), \ldots, h_q(\theta), h_{q+1}(\theta), \ldots, h_m(\theta))$, where $h_{q+1}\theta, \ldots, h_m(\theta)$ are so defined that the transformation $\theta \to h^*(\theta)$ is a one-to-one and continuously invertible transformation of Ω into itself. Suppose further that there exists a transformation taking $h^*(\theta)$ into $\xi^* = (\xi_1, \ldots, \xi_q, h_{q+1}(\theta), \ldots, h_m(\theta))$, where the transformation $h^*(\theta) \to \xi^*$ is a one-to-one and continuously invertible transformation of Ω into itself. Then we can successively reparameterize our distribution from θ through $h^*(\theta)$ to ξ^*. Given a confidence region for $\xi = (\xi_1, \ldots, \xi_m)$, the image region for $h(\hat{\theta}(\xi)) = (h_1(\hat{\theta}(\xi)), \ldots, h_m(\hat{\theta}(\xi)))$ induced by the transformation $\xi \to h(\hat{\theta}(\xi))$ is a confidence region for $\rho = (\rho_1, \ldots, \rho_m)$.

The following conditions are necessary to carry out this procedure:

(a) The MLE of $\theta \in \Omega$ is obtained as the solution of the equation

$$\left. \frac{\partial \log L_n(x; \theta)}{\partial \theta} \right|_{\theta = \hat{\theta}} = 0;$$

(b) The MLE of $\theta \in \omega$ is obtained as the solution of the equations

$$\left.\frac{\partial M_n(x;\theta)}{\partial \theta}\right|_{\theta=\hat{\theta}} = 0, \qquad h(\theta(\xi)) = \rho;$$

(c) The statistic $-2 \log \lambda$ is asymptotically distributed as a chi-square variable with q degrees of freedom when $\theta = \theta_0$.

Various sufficient conditions and specific examples for (a)–(c) are given in the literature (cf. Aitchison and Silvey (1960), Wald (1943)). However, the hypotheses are sufficiently restrictive so that one cannot apply them to the applications we shall deal with, namely the normal and Wishart families. Instead, we show that (a) and (b) hold; it is relatively straightforward to show that (c) holds using standard asymptotic results.

2.1. The Simple Constraint Case

In general, it may be hard to characterize this region, even when the region for ξ is simple. However, in the important special case when $q = 1$ and $h(\hat{\theta}(\xi))$ is a continuous monotonic function of ξ, the characterization is simple since intervals are carried into intervals. The following lemma points out that this monotonicity is equivalent to a very convenient property of the likelihood ratio as a function of ξ.

Lemma 2.1. *When there is only one constraint, i.e., when $q = 1$, the derivative of $g(\xi) \equiv -2 \log \lambda$, with respect to ξ, changes sign only once, when $\xi = 0$, if and only if $h(\hat{\theta}(\xi))$ is a monotonic function of ξ.*

Proof. Differentiating $g(\xi)$ with respect to ξ, and using (2.1), we obtain

$$\frac{\partial g(\xi)}{\partial \xi} = -\frac{2}{L(x;\hat{\theta}(\xi))} \sum_{\alpha=1}^{m} \frac{\partial L(x;\hat{\theta}(\xi))}{\partial \hat{\theta}_\alpha(\xi)} \frac{\partial \hat{\theta}_\alpha(\xi)}{\partial \xi} = -2\xi \frac{\partial h(\hat{\theta}(\xi))}{\partial \xi}, \tag{2.2}$$

from which the result follows. ||

An approximate confidence region for ξ is the set

$$C(\xi) = \{\xi : g(\xi) \leq \chi_\alpha^2(q)\}.$$

When $h(\hat{\theta}(\xi))$ is a monotonic function of ξ, the equation $g(\xi) = \chi_\alpha^2(q)$ will, by Lemma 2.1, typically have two solutions, so that $C(\xi)$ will either be a bounded interval or its complement. By the monotonicity of $g(\xi) = -2 \log \lambda$ for $\xi > 0$ and for $\xi < 0$ separately, one can easily compute the solution of $g(\xi) = \chi_\alpha^2(q)$. Since $h(\hat{\theta}(\xi))$ carries intervals into intervals, this region can be converted directly into a confidence region for ρ. (The cases in which $g(\xi) = \chi_\alpha^2(q)$ has either no solution or one solution can be handled similarly.)

An alternative procedure, which exploits the monotonicity of $h(\hat{\theta}(\xi))$ as a function of ξ, but not the "butterfly" property of $g(\xi)$, is to use Silvey's result to obtain a confidence region for ξ and convert this region into a confidence region for ρ. The confidence region for ξ based on Silvey's work is

$$\left\{\xi: \frac{n(\hat{\xi} - \xi)^2}{r(\hat{\xi})} \leq \chi_\alpha^2(1)\right\},$$

where $\hat{\xi}$ satisfies

$$\left.\frac{\partial \log L_n(x;\theta)}{\partial \theta}\right|_{\theta=\hat{\theta}(\hat{\xi})} = \hat{\xi} \left.\frac{\partial h(\theta)}{\partial \theta}\right|_{\theta=\hat{\theta}(\hat{\xi})},$$

$h(\hat{\theta}(\hat{\xi})) = \rho$, and

$$r(\hat{\xi}) = \left.\frac{(\partial^2/\partial\theta^2)E \log f(x;\theta) + \xi(\partial^2/\partial\theta^2)h(\theta)}{(\partial h(\theta)/\partial\theta)^2}\right|_{\xi=\hat{\xi},\, \theta=\hat{\theta}(\hat{\xi})}.$$

Our method has the advantage that we need never compute $\hat{\xi}$ in order to determine a confidence interval for ξ.

Ascertaining that $-2 \log \lambda$ is a convex function of ξ may be useful for computational purposes, for then the confidence region $C(\xi)$ is a convex set. One can then solve the equation $g(\xi) = \chi_\alpha^2(q)$ numerically, e.g., by using the efficient algorithm of Gross and Johnson (1959), and thereby determine the boundary of this set. Similarly, if $-2 \log \lambda$ is a concave function of ξ, $C(\xi)$ is the complement in the subspace of ξ's of a convex set. When $q = 1$, the following lemma gives a necessary and sufficient condition for the concavity or convexity of $g(\xi)$.

Lemma 2.2. *For $q = 1$, $g(\xi)$ is concave in ξ if and only if*

$$\frac{\partial h(\hat{\theta}(\xi))}{\partial \xi} + \xi \frac{\partial^2 h(\hat{\theta}(\xi))}{\partial \xi^2} > 0.$$

Proof. The result follows immediately upon differentiation of (2.2). ||

Remark. A sufficient condition for concavity is that $h(\hat{\theta}(\xi))$ be an increasing function of ξ and $\xi\, \partial^2 h(\hat{\theta}(\xi))/\partial \xi^2 > 0$.

When $h(\theta)$ is linear in θ, we have the following lemma.

Lemma 2.3. *If $L(x;\theta)$ is log concave in θ and $h(\theta) = \sum_1^m a_i \theta_i$, then $h(\hat{\theta}(\xi))$ is monotone decreasing in ξ.*

Proof. In (2.1) let $S_i(\theta) = \partial \log L(x;\theta)/\partial\theta_i$, so that the equations $S_i(\theta) - \xi a_i = 0$, $i = 1, \ldots, m$, define the $\hat{\theta}_i(\xi)$. Then

$$\frac{\partial S_i(\hat{\theta}(\xi))}{\partial \xi} = \sum_{j=1}^{m} \frac{\partial S_i(\hat{\theta}(\xi))}{\partial \hat{\theta}_j(\xi)} \frac{\partial \hat{\theta}_j(\xi)}{\partial \xi} = a_i, \qquad i = 1, \ldots, m.$$

But

$$\frac{\partial S_i(\hat{\theta}(\xi))}{\partial \hat{\theta}_j(\xi)} = \frac{\partial^2 \log L(x;\theta)}{\partial \theta_i \, \partial \theta_j}\bigg|_{\theta=\hat{\theta}(\xi)} \equiv d_{ij}.$$

Let

$$a = (a_1, \ldots, a_m), \qquad \frac{\partial \hat{\theta}(\xi)}{\partial \xi} = \left(\frac{\partial \hat{\theta}_1(\xi)}{\partial \xi}, \ldots, \frac{\partial \hat{\theta}_m(\xi)}{\partial \xi}\right)$$

and $D = (d_{ij})$, so that $a = (\partial\hat{\theta}(\xi)/\partial\xi)D$. Then

$$\frac{\partial h(\hat{\theta}(\xi))}{\partial \xi} = \left(\frac{\partial \hat{\theta}(\xi)}{\partial \xi}\right) a' = aD^{-1}a'.$$

By hypothesis D is negative definite so that $aD^{-1}a' < 0$. ||

2.2. The Multiconstraint Case

Lemmas 2.1 and 2.2 do not generalize readily, as the region $\{\xi : \xi > 0\}$ when $q = 1$ must be translated to an orthant of Euclidean q-space, and the appropriate orthant in this case would depend on the magnitudes of the components of the vectors of partial derivatives of $h_i(\hat{\theta}(\xi))$ with respect to the ξ's, and not just their signs. However, we may be able to find conditions for the convexity of

$$g(\xi_1, \ldots, \xi_q) = -2 \log \sup_{\omega} L(x;\theta) + 2 \log \sup_{\Omega} L(x;\theta).$$

Since the second term is independent of ξ, we need only show that $-2 \log \sup_\omega L(x;\theta)$ is convex in the vector ξ. As $-\log$ is a monotone decreasing and convex function, if we could show that sup $L(x;\theta)$ is concave in ξ, then $g(\xi)$ will be convex. But sup is a convex function, so that we cannot expect simple conditions on $L(x;\theta)$ to guarantee the convexity of $g(\xi)$. The following discussion leads to a sufficient condition for the convexity of $g(\xi)$.

First note that

$$\begin{aligned}
\frac{\partial^2 g(\xi)}{\partial \xi_i \, \partial \xi_j} &= -2 \frac{\partial^2 \log L(x;\hat{\theta}(\xi))}{\partial \xi_i \, \partial \xi_j} \\
&= \frac{2}{[L(x;\hat{\theta}(\xi))]^2} \frac{\partial L(x;\hat{\theta}(\xi))}{\partial \xi_i} \frac{\partial L(x;\hat{\theta}(\xi))}{\partial \xi_j} \\
&\quad - \frac{2}{L(x;\hat{\theta}(\xi))} \sum_{\alpha=1}^{m} \frac{\partial L(x;\hat{\theta}(\xi))}{\partial \hat{\theta}_\alpha(\xi)} \frac{\partial^2 \hat{\theta}_\alpha(\xi)}{\partial \xi_i \, \partial \xi_j} \\
&\quad - \frac{2}{L(x;\hat{\theta}(\xi))} \sum_{\alpha=1}^{m} \sum_{\beta=1}^{m} \frac{\partial^2 L(x;\hat{\theta}(\xi))}{\partial \hat{\theta}_\alpha(\xi) \, \partial \hat{\theta}_\beta(\xi)} \frac{\partial \hat{\theta}_\alpha(\xi)}{\partial \xi_i} \frac{\partial \hat{\theta}_\beta(\xi)}{\partial \xi_j},
\end{aligned} \tag{2.3}$$

and hence the quadratic form of second derivatives can be written as

$$\sum_{i=1}^{m}\sum_{j=1}^{m} u_i u_j \frac{\partial^2 g(\xi)}{\partial \xi_i\, \partial \xi_j}$$

$$= \frac{2}{[L(x;\hat{\theta}(\xi))]^2}\left[\sum_{i=1}^{q} u_i \frac{\partial L(x;\hat{\theta}(\xi))}{\partial \xi_i}\right]^2$$

$$- \frac{2}{L(x;\hat{\theta}(\xi))}\sum_{\alpha=1}^{m} \frac{\partial L(x;\hat{\theta}(\xi))}{\partial \hat{\theta}_\alpha(\xi)} \sum_{i=1}^{q}\sum_{j=1}^{q} u_i u_j \frac{\partial^2 \hat{\theta}_\alpha(\xi)}{\partial \xi_i\, \partial \xi_j}$$

$$- \frac{2}{L(x;\hat{\theta}(\xi))}\sum_{\alpha=1}^{m}\sum_{\beta=1}^{m} \frac{\partial^2 L(x;\hat{\theta}(\xi))}{\partial \hat{\theta}_\alpha(\xi)\, \partial \hat{\theta}_\beta(\xi)} \left[\sum_{i=1}^{q} u_i \frac{\partial \hat{\theta}_\alpha(\xi)}{\partial \xi_i}\right]\left[\sum_{j=1}^{q} u_j \frac{\partial \hat{\theta}_\beta(\xi)}{\partial \xi_j}\right].$$

If we let

$$y_\alpha = \sum_{i=1}^{q} u_i \frac{\partial \hat{\theta}_\alpha(\xi)}{\partial \xi_i},$$

then the sum of the first and last terms is

$$\frac{2}{[L(x;\hat{\theta}(\xi))]^2}\sum_{\alpha=1}^{m}\sum_{\beta=1}^{m} y_\alpha y_\beta \left[\frac{\partial^2 L(x;\hat{\theta}(\xi))}{\partial \hat{\theta}_\alpha(\xi)\, \partial \hat{\theta}_\beta(\xi)} - \frac{\partial L(x;\hat{\theta}(\xi))}{\partial \hat{\theta}_\alpha(\xi)} \frac{\partial L(x;\hat{\theta}(\xi))}{\partial \hat{\theta}_\beta(\xi)}\right]$$

$$= -2\sum_{\alpha=1}^{m}\sum_{\beta=1}^{m} y_\alpha y_\beta \frac{\partial^2 \log L(x;\hat{\theta}(\xi))}{\partial \hat{\theta}_\alpha(\xi)\, \partial \hat{\theta}_\beta(\xi)},$$

and hence

$$\sum_{i=1}^{q}\sum_{j=1}^{q} u_i u_j \frac{\partial^2 g(\xi)}{\partial \xi_i\, \partial \xi_j} = -2\sum_{\alpha=1}^{m}\sum_{\beta=1}^{m} y_\alpha y_\beta \frac{\partial^2 \log L(x;(\xi))}{\partial \hat{\theta}_\alpha(\xi)\, \partial \hat{\theta}_\beta(\xi)}$$

$$- \frac{2}{L(x;\hat{\theta}(\xi))}\sum_{\alpha=1}^{m} \frac{\partial L(x;\hat{\theta}(\xi))}{\partial \hat{\theta}_\alpha(\xi)} \sum_{i=1}^{q}\sum_{j=1}^{q} u_i u_j \frac{\partial^2 \hat{\theta}_\alpha(\xi)}{\partial \xi_i\, \partial \xi_j}. \quad (2.4)$$

Thus, conditions for which (2.4) is of one sign will yield convexity or concavity of $g(\xi)$. One such condition is given in the following lemma.

Lemma 2.4. *Define*

$R_i = \{\theta_i : \theta_i \in \omega,\ L(x;\theta)$ *is nondecreasing in* $\theta_i\}$,

$S_i = \{\theta_i : \theta_i \in \omega,\ L(x;\theta)$ *is nonincreasing in* $\theta_i\}$, $\quad i = 1, \ldots, m.$

If $\log L(x;\theta)$ *is concave in* θ, *and for* $i = 1, \ldots, m$, $\hat{\theta}_i(\xi)$ *is concave in* ξ *for* $\hat{\theta}_i(\xi) \in R_i$, *and convex for* $\hat{\theta}_i(\xi) \in S_i$, *then* $g(\xi)$ *is convex.*

3. PRELIMINARIES AND NOTATION

As certain distributions appear throughout this paper, we establish some notation and properties needed later. By $\mathscr{L}(X)$, we mean the law of the random variable (vector) X. In particular, $\mathscr{L}(X) = N(\mu, \Sigma)$ means that the random vector X has a normal distribution with mean vector μ and covariance matrix Σ, with density function

$$p(x; \mu, \Sigma) = c_0 |\Sigma|^{-1/2} \exp[-\tfrac{1}{2}(x - \mu)\Sigma^{-1}(x - \mu)'], \tag{3.1}$$

$-\infty < x_i < \infty$, $i = 1, \ldots, k$, $c_0 = (2\pi)^{-k/2} N^{kN/2}$.

By $\mathscr{L}(S) = W(\Sigma; k, n)$, we mean that the random $k \times k$ matrix S has a Wishart distribution with parameter Σ and n degrees of freedom, with density function

$$p(S; \Sigma) = c(k, n) |\Sigma|^{-n/2} |S|^{\frac{1}{2}(n-k-1)} \exp[-\tfrac{1}{2} \operatorname{tr} \Sigma^{-1} S], \qquad S > 0, \quad \Sigma > 0,^2 \tag{3.2}$$

where

$$c(k, n) = \left[2^{nk/2} \pi^{\frac{1}{4}k(k-1)} \prod_1^k \Gamma(\tfrac{1}{2}(n - i + 1))\right]^{-1}.$$

We note immediately that $p(x; \mu, \Sigma)$ is log concave in μ (but not concave). Neither $p(x; \mu, \Sigma)$ nor $p(S; \Sigma)$ is convex, concave, log convex, or log concave in Σ. However, both $p(x; \mu, \Sigma)$ and $p(S; \Sigma)$ are log concave in $\Lambda \equiv \Sigma^{-1}$. This follows from the fact that $|\Lambda|$ is log concave in Λ (e.g., see Beckenbach and Bellman (1961)).

Other common distributions whose densities are log concave are the multinomial and Poisson with the usual parameterization. A general class of (univariate) densities with this property is the class of Pólya frequency functions of order 2, i.e., densities of the form $p(x - \theta)$ which are totally positive of order 2. One can then use the above method to construct approximate confidence regions for appropriate parameters from these distributions. An application to the binomial distribution is given by Madansky (1965).

If we observe N independent observations $x_\alpha = (x_{1\alpha}, \ldots, x_{k\alpha})$, $\alpha = 1, \ldots, N$, from a k-variate normal population, we need only consider the joint distribution of the sample mean vector $\bar{x} = \sum_{\alpha=1}^n x_\alpha / N$, and the $k \times k$ sample covariance matrix

$$V = (v_{ij}), \qquad v_{ij} = \sum_{\alpha=1}^N (x_{i\alpha} - \bar{x}_i)(x_{j\alpha} - \bar{x}_j)/n, \qquad n = N - 1.$$

Since $\bar{x}$ and $S \equiv nV$ are independently distributed, with $\mathscr{L}(\bar{x}) = N(\mu, \Sigma/N)$, $\mathscr{L}(S) = W(\Sigma; k, n)$, only the marginal densities are needed, and this will generally be our starting point.

The extremal problems encountered in verifying that the maximizers under Ω and ω satisfy the standard first order conditions given earlier generally fall into two categories. The simplest is where we require the maximum of a concave function $l(\theta)$ (the logarithm of the density function) subject to a concave

[2] If A and B are symmetric matrices, the inequality $A > B$ means that $A - B$ is positive definite.

constraint $h(\theta) = 0$. In this instance, the maximizer of $l(\theta)$ in ω is an interior point; it is obtained from $\partial M(\theta)/\partial\theta = 0$, $h(\theta) = 0$ (e.g., Kuhn and Tucker (1951)).

When $l(\theta)$ is concave, but $h(\theta)$ is not, the maximum occurs either at a unique interior point or on the boundary. Thus we need only check whether it occurs on the boundary. Usually $l(\theta) \to -\infty$ as θ approaches a boundary point.

When neither $l(\theta)$ nor $h(\theta)$ is concave, there may be many local maxima or there may be a maximum at a boundary point. Then all the local maxima must be compared to determine the global maximum, and must be compared to boundary points.

The two results needed later are the following. If

$$M(\Lambda) = n \log |\Lambda| - \xi \operatorname{tr} \Lambda S,$$

$\Lambda > 0$, and $S > 0$ is a fixed matrix, then $M(\Lambda) \to -\infty$ as Λ approaches a singular matrix (or equivalently, the smallest characteristic root approaches 0), or as the largest characteristic root approaches ∞.

If

$$M(\Lambda, \mu) = n \log |\Lambda| - \operatorname{tr} \Lambda S - \xi(t - \mu)\Lambda(t - \mu)',$$

$-\infty < \mu_i < \infty$, $\Lambda > 0$, and S and t are fixed with $S > 0$, $-\infty < t_i < \infty$, then $M(\Lambda, \mu) \to -\infty$ as Λ approaches a singular matrix or as the largest characteristic root of Λ approaches ∞.

4. ONE SAMPLE PROBLEM FOR THE WISHART DISTRIBUTION

Let $S \equiv nV$ be a $k \times k$ random symmetric matrix having a Wishart distribution $W(\Sigma; k, n)$ with density function given by (3.2), let $\Lambda = \Sigma^{-1}$, and let A be an arbitrary symmetric matrix. We obtain approximate confidence intervals for $\operatorname{tr} \Lambda A$ (Section 4.2), $\operatorname{tr} \Sigma A$ (Section 4.3), $|\Sigma|$ (Section 4.3), and all the characteristic roots of Σ (Section 4.4), using the method proposed in Section 2, as well as by the method of linearization (Section 4.1). Finally, we present an example of each of these intervals.

4.1. Linearization

The method of linearization for functions of Σ is based on the approximation

$$h(V) \simeq h(\Sigma) + \sum_{i,j=1}^{k} \frac{\partial h(\Sigma)}{\partial \sigma_{ij}} (v_{ij} - \sigma_{ij}), \tag{4.1}$$

$$\operatorname{Var} h(\mathrm{V}) \simeq (2/n) \operatorname{tr} \Sigma H(\Sigma) \Sigma H(\Sigma), \tag{4.2}$$

where $H(\Sigma) = \partial h(\Sigma)/\partial\sigma_{ij}$. Since $h(V)$ is a function of moments, and

$$p \lim_{n\to\infty} v_{ij} = \sigma_{ij},$$

it follows that

$$\mathscr{L}\left[\frac{h(V) - h(\Sigma)}{(2n^{-1} \operatorname{tr}[VH(V)]^2)^{1/2}}\right] \to N(0, 1).$$

Thus, an equal tailed approximate $100\gamma\%$ confidence interval for $h(\Sigma)$ is given by

$$h(V) \pm z_\gamma(2n^{-1} \operatorname{tr}[VH(V)]^2)^{1/2},$$

where z_γ is the $100(1+\gamma)/2\%$ point of the standard normal distribution.

To apply this, we need the derivatives $\partial H(\Sigma)/\partial\sigma_{ij}$ for the functions $\operatorname{tr}\Sigma^{-1}A$, $\operatorname{tr}\Sigma A$, and $|\Sigma|$ playing the role of $h(\Sigma)$. These derivatives and the corresponding expressions for $\operatorname{tr}(\Sigma H(\Sigma))^2$ are given by

$$\frac{\partial \operatorname{tr}\Lambda A}{\partial\sigma_{ij}} = -(\Lambda A\Lambda)_{ij}, \qquad \operatorname{tr}(\Sigma H(\Sigma))^2 = \operatorname{tr}(\Lambda A)^2, \tag{4.3}$$

$$\frac{\partial \operatorname{tr}\Sigma A}{\partial\sigma_{ij}} = a_{ij}, \qquad \operatorname{tr}(\Sigma H(\Sigma))^2 = \operatorname{tr}(\Sigma A)^2, \tag{4.4}$$

$$\frac{\partial|\Sigma|}{\partial\sigma_{ij}} = |\Sigma|\,\lambda_{ij}, \qquad \operatorname{tr}(\Sigma H(\Sigma))^2 = k|\Sigma|^2. \tag{4.5}$$

Consequently,

$$\mathscr{L}\left[\frac{\sqrt{n}(\operatorname{tr}V^{-1}A - \operatorname{tr}\Sigma^{-1}A)}{(2\operatorname{tr}(V^{-1}A)^2)^{1/2}}\right] \to N(0, 1), \tag{4.6}$$

$$\mathscr{L}\left[\frac{\sqrt{n}(\operatorname{tr}VA - \operatorname{tr}\Sigma A)}{(2\operatorname{tr}(VA)^2)^{1/2}}\right] \to N(0, 1), \tag{4.7}$$

$$\mathscr{L}\left(\frac{\sqrt{n}}{\sqrt{2k}}\left[\frac{|V|}{|\Sigma|} - 1\right]\right) \to N(0, 1), \tag{4.8}$$

from which we can easily obtain confidence intervals for the constraint parameters.

4.2. Confidence Interval for tr ΛA

From (3.2) with $\Omega = \{\Sigma : \Sigma > 0\}$, we have $\hat{\Sigma} = V = S/n$, and

$$\sup_{\Omega} p(S; \Sigma) = c(k, n)\,|S|^{-(k+1)/2}\, n^{kn/2} e^{-kn/2}. \tag{4.9}$$

To find $\sup_\omega p(S;\Sigma)$, where $\omega = \{\Lambda : \Lambda > 0, \operatorname{tr} \Lambda A = \rho\}$, we form the Lagrangian

$$M(\Lambda) = n \log |\Lambda| - \operatorname{tr} \Lambda S - \xi(\operatorname{tr} \Lambda A - \rho),$$

and note that $p(S;\Sigma)$ and $\operatorname{tr} \Lambda A$ are concave functions of Λ. Setting the derivatives of $M(\Lambda)$ with respect to λ_{ij} equal to zero yields the matrix equation

$$n\Sigma - S - A = 0,$$

so that

$$\hat{\Lambda}(\xi) = n(S + \xi A)^{-1},$$

where ξ is such that $\hat{\Lambda}(\xi) > 0$. Consequently,

$$\sup_\omega p(S;\Sigma) = c(k,n)\,|S|^{(n-k-1)/2}\, n^{kn/2}\, |S + \xi A|^{-n/2} \exp[-\tfrac{1}{2}n \operatorname{tr} S(S + \xi A)^{-1}],$$

and

$$g(\xi) = n \operatorname{tr} S(S + \xi A)^{-1} - n \log |S(S + \xi A)^{-1}| - kn.$$

Since $p(S;\Sigma)$ is log concave in Λ and $h(\Lambda) = \operatorname{tr} \Lambda A$ is linear in Λ, by Lemma 2.3, $h(\hat{\Lambda}(\xi))$ is a monotonically decreasing function of ξ. Hence, from Lemma 2.1, $g(\xi)$ is monotone increasing for $\xi > 0$ and decreasing for $\xi < 0$.

4.3. Confidence Interval for tr ΣA

The region $\Omega = \{\Lambda : \Lambda > 0\}$, so that $\sup_\Omega p(S;\Sigma)$ is given by (4.9). Now $\omega = \{\Lambda : \Lambda > 0, \operatorname{tr} \Lambda^{-1} A = \rho, A \geq 0\}$ and we form the Lagrangian

$$M(\Lambda) = n \log |\Lambda| - \operatorname{tr} \Lambda S - \xi(\operatorname{tr} \Lambda^{-1} A - \rho).$$

Recalling that at the boundary of Ω, $n \log |\Lambda| - \operatorname{tr} \Lambda S$ approaches infinity, we see that the interior saddlepoint is a maximizer. Setting the derivatives of $M(\Lambda)$, with respect to the λ_{ij}, equal to zero yields the matrix equation

$$n\Sigma - S - \xi\Lambda^{-1} A \Lambda^{-1} = 0, \tag{4.10}$$

or equivalently, after pre- and post-multiplying (4.10) by $S^{1/2}\Lambda$,

$$(S^{1/2}\Lambda S^{1/2})^2 - n(S^{1/2}\Lambda S^{1/2}) - \xi S^{1/2} A S^{1/2} = 0. \tag{4.11}$$

Letting $\psi = S^{1/2}\Lambda S^{1/2}$ and completing the square in (4.11) yields

$$(\psi - \tfrac{1}{2}nI)^2 = \tfrac{1}{4}n^2 I + \xi S^{1/2} A S^{1/2} \equiv B,$$

where ξ is such that $B > 0$. Hence

$$\psi = \tfrac{1}{2}nI + B^{1/2},$$

where $B^{1/2}$ is any symmetric square root of B.

From

$$n \log |\Lambda| - \operatorname{tr} \Lambda S = n \log |\psi| - \operatorname{tr} \psi - n \log |S|,$$

we require that square root $B^{1/2}$ which maximizes

$$s(B^{1/2}) \equiv n \log |\tfrac{1}{2}nI + B^{1/2}| - \operatorname{tr} B^{1/2}.$$

But $s(B^{1/2})$ is a function of the eigenvalues of $B^{1/2}$, and the eigenvalues of any square root $B^{1/2}$ differ only in sign, i.e.,

$$\lambda(B^{1/2}) = \pm[\lambda(B^2)]^{1/2}.$$

Consequently, the problem reduces to the following. If $\theta_1, \ldots, \theta_k$ are the positive eigenvalues of B, we must determine the set of signs $\varepsilon_i = \pm 1$, $i = 1, \ldots, k$ which maximizes

$$n \log \prod (\tfrac{1}{2}n + \varepsilon_i \theta_i) - \Sigma \varepsilon_i \theta_i.$$

We assert that $\varepsilon_1 = \cdots = \varepsilon_k = 1$ is the maximizer, i.e.,

$$n\Sigma \log(\tfrac{1}{2}n + \varepsilon_i \theta_i) - \Sigma\varepsilon_i\theta_i \le n\Sigma \log(\tfrac{1}{2}n + \theta_i) - \Sigma\theta_i.$$

For any single term for which $\varepsilon_i = -1$, we have

$$n \log(\tfrac{1}{2}n - \theta) + \theta \le \log(\tfrac{1}{2}n + \theta) - \theta,$$

which holds if and only if

$$x \le \frac{\log(1+x)}{\log(1-x)}, \qquad 0 < x < 1.$$

But $t(x) = e^{-x}(1+x)/(1-x)$ is a monotone increasing function with $t(0) = 1$, from which the result follows.

Hence, we obtain

$$\sup_{\omega} p(S; \Sigma) = c(k, n)\,|S|^{-(k+1)/2}\,(\tfrac{1}{2}n)^{kn/2}\,|I + (I + \xi C)^{1/2}|^{n/2}$$
$$\times \exp -\tfrac{1}{2}n[k + \operatorname{tr}(I + \xi C)^{1/2}],$$

where $C = 4S^{1/2}AS^{1/2}/n^2$, so that

$$g(\xi) = kn \log 2 - n \log |I + (I + \xi C)^{1/2}| + \tfrac{1}{2}n[-k + \operatorname{tr}(I + \xi C)^{1/2}]. \quad (4.12)$$

Also,

$$h(\hat{\Lambda}(\xi)) = \operatorname{tr} \hat{\Sigma} A = (2/n) \operatorname{tr} C[I + (I + \xi C)^{1/2}]^{-1} = (2/n) \sum_1^k \frac{c_j}{1 + (1 + \xi c_j)^{1/2}},$$

where $c_1, \ldots, c_k$ are the characteristic roots of C. Thus $h(\hat{\Lambda}(\xi))$ is a monotone function of ξ.

4.4. Confidence Interval for $|\Sigma|$

The region Ω is as in Section 4.2, so that $\sup_\Omega p(S; \Sigma)$ is given by (4.9). Now $\omega = \{\Lambda : \Lambda > 0, \log |\Lambda| = \rho\}$, and we form the Lagrangian

$$M(\Lambda) = n \log |\Lambda| - \operatorname{tr} \Lambda S - \xi(\log |\Lambda| - \rho),$$

and note that $\log|\Lambda|$ is a concave function of Λ. Equating the derivatives of $M(\Lambda)$ with respect to the λ_{ij} to zero yields the matrix equation

$$n\Sigma - S - \xi\Sigma = 0,$$

so that $\hat{\Sigma} = S/(n - \xi)$, $\xi < n$. However, in this case we can easily solve for ξ in terms of ρ, namely,

$$n - \xi(|S|\,e^{\rho})^{1/k} \equiv [\eta(S, \rho]^{1/k}.$$

Hence

$$g(\eta) = -n \log \eta(S, \rho) + k[\eta(S, \rho)]^{1/k} + kn \log n - kn. \qquad (4.13)$$

Since $g(\eta)$ is convex in η, the interval $[\eta_1, \eta_2]$ is a confidence interval for η, with confidence coefficient $1 - \alpha$, where η_1 and η_2 are the roots of $g(\eta) = \chi_\alpha^{\ 2}(1)$. Clearly, for any S, we can convert to a confidence interval $[\exp(-\rho_1), \exp(-\rho_2)]$ for $|\Sigma|$, where $\exp(-\rho_j) = |S|/\eta_j$, $j = 1, 2$.

To make a comparison between linearization and likelihood ratio inversion confidence limits for $|\Sigma|$, we recall from (4.8) that the linearization confidence limits are given by

$$P\{a_1\,|V| \le |\Sigma| \le a_2\,|V|\} = \gamma,$$

TABLE I

Factor for Confidence Limit for Determinant of Covariance Matrix

	$n = 10$		$n = 20$		$n = 30$		$n = 40$	
k	lower	upper	lower	upper	lower	upper	lower	upper
2	0.251	3.076	0.389	2.263	0.467	1.965	0.520	1.803
4	0.151	5.123	0.271	3.250	0.348	2.641	0.403	2.329
6	0.102	7.585	0.205	4.292	0.277	3.314	0.331	2.836
8	0.073	10.563	0.162	5.426	0.229	4.014	0.280	3.348
10	0.055	14.144	0.132	6.672	0.193	4.752	0.242	3.875
12			0.109	8.043	0.166	5.536	0.212	4.423
14			0.092	9.551	0.144	6.370	0.188	4.994
16			0.078	11.208	0.126	7.260	0.168	5.593
18			0.068	13.026	0.112	8.208	0.151	6.220
20			0.059	15.015	0.100	9.218	0.136	6.878
22					0.089	10.294	0.124	7.568
24					0.080	11.440	0.113	8.293
26					0.073	12.658	0.104	9.052
28					0.066	13.952	0.095	9.849
30					0.060	15.327	0.088	10.683
32							0.081	11.559
34							0.075	12.475
36							0.070	13.434
38							0.065	14.438
40							0.061	15.487

where

$$a_1 = \{1 + (2k/n)^{1/2} z_\gamma\}^{-1}, \qquad a_2 = \{\max(0, 1 - (2k/n)^{1/2} z/\gamma\}^{-1}.$$

The limits based on inverting the LRT are given by

$$P\{b_1|V| \leq |\Sigma| \leq b_2|V|\} = \gamma, \tag{4.14}$$

where $b_i = n^k/\eta_i$, $i = 1, 2$, and (η_1, η_2) are the roots of $g(\eta) = \chi^2_{1-\gamma}(1)$.

Values of b_i to $3D$ are given in Table I for $n = 10(10)40$, $k = 2(2)n$, $\gamma = 0.95$. We have computed, though not tabled, a_i as well, and note that $a_1 \leq b_1$, $a_2 \leq b_2$, and a_2 is typically infinite for the tabled values. Though as n gets large, a_i and b_i should converge to the same value, the convergence is slow even for small values of k; for lower one-sided intervals, linearization yields a larger lower limit, but for two-sided intervals, likelihood ratio inversion yields a finite band which is quite usable.

4.5. Confidence Intervals for the Characteristic Roots of Σ

Consider in detail the development of Section 4.2 when $A = u'u$, $u = (u_1, \ldots, u_k)$, $uu' = 1$. Noting that

$$|S + \xi u'u| = |S|(1 + \xi u S^{-1} u'),$$

and

$$(S + \xi u'u)^{-1} = S^{-1} - \xi(S^{-1}u'uS^{-1})(1 + \xi u S^{-1} u')^{-1},$$

we see that $g(\xi)$ can be expressed as a function $t(x)$ of $x = \xi u S^{-1} u'$, namely

$$t(x) = n \log(1 + x) - nx/(1 + x).$$

Solving $t(x) = \chi^2_{1-\gamma}(1)$ for the two roots x_1 and x_2, $x_1 > x_2$, we have

$$P\left\{\frac{nuS^{-1}u'}{1 + x_1} \leq u\Lambda u' \leq \frac{nuS^{-1}u'}{1 + x_2}\right\} = \gamma.$$

Hence

$$P\left\{\frac{\lambda_1(V^{-1})}{1 + x_1} \leq u\Lambda u' \leq \frac{\lambda_k(V^{-1})}{1 + x_2}\right\} \geq \gamma, \tag{4.15}$$

where $\lambda_1(V^{-1})$ and $\lambda_k(V^{-1})$ are the smallest and largest characteristic roots of $V^{-1} = nS^{-1}$, respectively. To obtain confidence bounds for the characteristic roots of Σ, we take reciprocals in (4.15).

When $A = u'u$, the asymptotic variance of $uV^{-1}u'$ is $(2/n)(u\Lambda u')^2$, and need not be estimated, so that (4.6) becomes

$$\mathscr{L}\left(\sqrt{n}\,\frac{(uV^{-1}u' - u\Lambda u')}{\sqrt{2}\,u\Lambda u'}\right) \to N(0, 1),$$

from which

$$P\{a_1 uV^{-1}u' < u\Lambda u' < a_2 uV^{-1}u'\} = \gamma, \tag{4.16}$$

where $a_1 = [1 + z_\gamma(2/n)^{1/2}]^{-1}$ and $a_2 = [\max(0, 1 - z_\gamma(2/n)^{1/2})]^{-1}$.

Table II permits comparison of the two procedures by presenting values of the a_i and $b_i = (1 + x_i)^{-1}$, $i = 1, 2$, for $n = 2(2)50$, $\gamma = 0.95$. Another procedure for obtaining confidence bounds for the characteristic roots is given by Roy and Bose (1953).

TABLE II
Factors for Confidence Limits for Characteristic Roots of a Covariance Matrix

	$-2 \log \lambda$		linearization	
n	lower	upper	lower	upper
2	0.0570	4.4027	0.3378	
4	0.1663	3.0876	0.4191	
6	0.2487	2.5929	0.4691	
8	0.3104	2.322	0.5050	50.0000
10	0.3586	2.149	0.5328	8.0997
12	0.3974	2.026	0.5555	5.0041
14	0.4297	1.933	0.5744	3.8581
16	0.4570	1.861	0.5906	3.2569
18	0.4805	1.802	0.6048	2.8846
20	0.5011	1.753	0.6173	2.6302
22	0.5192	1.712	0.6285	2.4447
24	0.5355	1.677	0.6386	2.3031
26	0.5501	1.646	0.6478	2.1910
28	0.5633	1.618	0.6562	2.1000
30	0.5754	1.594	0.6639	2.0245
32	0.5865	1.573	0.6711	1.9607
34	0.5968	1.553	0.6777	1.9061
36	0.6062	1.535	0.6840	1.8586
38	0.6150	1.519	0.6898	1.8170
40	0.6233	1.504	0.6952	1.7802
42	0.6309	1.490	0.7004	1.7473
44	0.6382	1.477	0.7052	1.7178
46	0.6450	1.466	0.7098	1.6911
48	0.6514	1.455	0.7142	1.6668
50	0.6574	1.444	0.7183	1.6447

4.6. An Example

As an example of the use of our method of obtaining confidence limits for the various functions of the covariance matrix of a multivariate normal distribution treated in Sections 4.2–4.5, we consider the data from Barnard's study of Egyptian skulls (see Anderson (1958), p. 214) in which there are four populations: Late Predynastic, Sixth to Twelfth, Twelfth to Thirteenth, and Ptolemaic Dynasties, each being a 4-variate (maximum breadth, basialveolar length, nasal height, basibregmatic height) normal population with common covariance matrix. The sample matrix of cross products, S, distributed as $W(\Sigma, 4, 394)$, is

$$S = \begin{pmatrix} 9661.997 & 445.573 & 1130.624 & 2148.584 \\ & 9073.115 & 1239.212 & 2255.813 \\ & & 3938.320 & 1271.055 \\ & & & 8741.509 \end{pmatrix}.$$

We record that the characteristic roots of $V = S/394$ are 32.828, 22.689, 15.483, 8.732, so that

$$\operatorname{tr} V = 79.732, \quad \operatorname{tr} V^{-1} = 0.2536, \quad |V| = 1.007 \times 10^5.$$

In determining 95% confidence limits for tr Λ, we first find the two solutions of the equation $g(\xi) = \chi^2_{0.95}(1) = 3.841$, where $g(\xi)$ is given by (4.10). These are $\xi_1 = 412.264$ and $\xi_2 = -364.683$, so that

$$(\operatorname{tr} \hat{\Lambda}(\xi_1), \operatorname{tr} \hat{\Lambda}(\xi_2)) = (0.2344, 0.2741)$$

is a 95% confidence interval for tr Λ.

In determining 95% confidence limits for tr Σ, we find that the two solutions of $g(\xi) = 3.841$, where $g(\xi)$ is given by (4.12), are $\xi_1 = -1.118$ and $\xi_2 = 1.408$, so that a 95% confidence interval for tr Σ is

$$(\operatorname{tr} \hat{\Sigma}(\xi_1), \operatorname{tr} \hat{\Sigma}(\xi_2)) = (73.964, 86.206).$$

To determine a confidence interval for $|\Sigma|$, we need multiplicative factors akin to those of Table I for $n = 394$, $k = 4$, which we apply to $|V|$ or $|S|$ as in (4.14). These factors are 0.75386 and 1.31792, so that a 95% confidence interval for $|\Sigma|$ is

$$1.007 \times 10^{-5}(0.75386, 1.31792) = (0.759, 1.327) \times 10^{-5}.$$

To determine a confidence interval for all the characteristic roots of Σ, we need multiplicative factors akin to those of Table II for $n = 394$, which we apply to the minimum and maximum characteristic roots of V^{-1} as per (4.15). These factors are 0.86679 and 1.14621, so that the 95% confidence interval for all the characteristic roots of Σ are

$$(8.732/1.14621, \quad 32.828/0.86679) = (7.618, 37.873).$$

5. TWO SAMPLE PROBLEMS FOR THE WISHART DISTRIBUTION

Let S_1 and S_2 be independent $k \times k$ random symmetric matrices having Wishart distributions $W(\Sigma_1; k, n_1)$ and $W(\Sigma_2; k, n_2)$, respectively, and let $\Lambda_1 = \Sigma_1^{-1}$, $\Lambda_2 = \Sigma_2^{-1}$. Using the method of Section 2, we obtain approximate confidence regions for various functions of Σ_1 and Σ_2 : $\operatorname{tr}(A_1\Lambda_1 + A_2\Lambda_2)$ and $\operatorname{tr}(A_1\Sigma_1 + A_2\Sigma_2)$, where A_1 and A_2 are $k \times k$ symmetric matrices (Section 5.2), $|\Sigma_1|^{a_1}|\Sigma_2|^{a_2}$ (Section 5.3), $a_1|\Lambda_1| + a_2|\Lambda_2|$ (Section 5.4), and $\operatorname{tr}\Sigma_1^{-1}\Sigma_2$ (Section 5.5). For example, $\operatorname{tr}(\Sigma_1 - \Sigma_2)$, $|\Sigma_1|/|\Sigma_2|$ and $|\Lambda_1| - |\Lambda_2|$, which are of particular interest, are included as special cases. In addition, approximate confidence regions for these functions by the method of linearization are also obtained in Section 5.1.

The results of Section 5.2 reduce in the case in which $k = 1$ (the univariate normal case) to confidence limits for a linear combination of variances or reciprocals of variances of two (or more) normal distributions. The results of the other sections specialize similarly when $k = 1$.

We note that as in Section 4, for each problem the logarithm of the joint density function is a concave function of (Λ_1, Λ_2).

5.1. Linearization

The development is similar to that of Section 4.1, and we have

$$h(V_1, V_2) \simeq h(\Sigma_1, \Sigma_2) + \sum_{\alpha=1}^{2} \sum_{i,j=1}^{k} \frac{\partial h(\Sigma_1, \Sigma_2)}{\partial \sigma_{ij}^{(\alpha)}} (v_{ij}^{(\alpha)} - \sigma_{ij}^{(\alpha)}), \tag{5.1}$$

where

$$V_\alpha = (v_{ij}^{(\alpha)}), \qquad \Sigma_\alpha = (\sigma_{ij}^{(\alpha)}), \qquad \text{and} \qquad V_\alpha = S_\alpha/n_\alpha, \qquad \alpha = 1, 2.$$

Then

$$\operatorname{Var} h(V_1, V_2) \simeq 2\{n_1^{-1} \operatorname{tr}[\Sigma_1 H_1(\Sigma_1, \Sigma_2)]^2 + n_2^{-1} \operatorname{tr}[\Sigma_2 H_2(\Sigma_1, \Sigma_2)]^2\}, \tag{5.2}$$

where $H_\alpha \equiv H_\alpha(\Sigma_1, \Sigma_2) = [\partial h(\Sigma_1, \Sigma_2)/\partial\sigma_{ij}^{(\alpha)}]$, $\alpha = 1, 2$. The additional necessary derivatives for the functions $h(\Sigma_1, \Sigma_2)$ to be considered in this section are: Combinations of traces

$$\frac{\partial \operatorname{tr}(A_1\Lambda_1 + A_2\Lambda_2)}{\partial\sigma_{ij}^{(\alpha)}} = -(\Lambda_\alpha A_\alpha \Lambda_\alpha)_{ij}, \qquad \operatorname{tr}(\Sigma_\alpha H_\alpha)^2 = \operatorname{tr}(A_\alpha\Lambda_\alpha)^2, \tag{5.3}$$

$$\frac{\partial \operatorname{tr}(A_1\Sigma_1 + A_2\Sigma_2)}{\partial\sigma_{ij}^{(\alpha)}} = a_{ij}^{(\alpha)}, \qquad \operatorname{tr}(\Sigma_\alpha H_\alpha)^2 = \operatorname{tr}(\Sigma_\alpha A_\alpha)^2; \tag{5.4}$$

combinations of determinants

$$\frac{\partial(|\Sigma_1|^{a_1}|\Sigma_2|^{a_2})}{\partial\sigma_{ij}^{(\alpha)}} = a_\alpha|\Sigma_1|^{a_1}|\Sigma_2|^{a_2}\lambda_{ij}^{(\alpha)},$$
$$\operatorname{tr}(\Sigma_\alpha H_\alpha)^2 = k{a_\alpha}^2|\Sigma_1|^{2a_1}|\Sigma_2|^{2a_2} \tag{5.5}$$

$$\frac{\partial(a_1|\Sigma_1|^{-1} + a_2|\Sigma_2|^{-1}}{\partial\sigma_{ij}^{(\alpha)}} = a_\alpha\frac{\lambda_{ij}^{(\alpha)}}{|\Sigma_\alpha|}, \qquad \operatorname{tr}(\Sigma_\alpha H_\alpha)^2 = \frac{k{a_\alpha}^2}{|\Sigma_\alpha|^2}; \tag{5.6}$$

a mixed case

$$\frac{\partial \operatorname{tr}(\Lambda_1\Sigma_2)}{\partial \sigma_{ij}^{(1)}} = -(\Lambda_1\Sigma_2\Lambda_1)_{ij}, \qquad \operatorname{tr}(\Sigma_1 H_1)^2 = \operatorname{tr}(\Lambda_1\Sigma_2)^2, \tag{5.7}$$

$$\frac{\partial \operatorname{tr}(\Lambda_1\Sigma_2)}{\partial \sigma_{ij}^{(2)}} = (\Lambda_1)_{ij}, \qquad \operatorname{tr}(\Sigma_2 H_2)^2 = \operatorname{tr}(\Lambda_1\Sigma_2)^2. \tag{5.8}$$

It then follows that

$$\mathscr{L}\left\{\frac{\operatorname{tr}(A_1 V_1^{-1} + A_2 V_2^{-1}) - \operatorname{tr}(A_1\Sigma_1^{-1} + A_2\Sigma_2^{-1})}{(2[n_1^{-1}\operatorname{tr}(A_1V_1^{-1})^2 + n_2^{-1}\operatorname{tr}(A_2V_2^{-1})^2])^{1/2}}\right\} \to N(0, 1), \tag{5.9}$$

$$\mathscr{L}\left\{\frac{\operatorname{tr}(A_1S_1 + A_2S_2) - \operatorname{tr}(A_1\Sigma_1 + A_2\Sigma_2)}{(2[n_1^{-1}\operatorname{tr}(A_1V_1)^2 + n_2^{-1}\operatorname{tr}(A_2V_2)^2])^{1/2}}\right\} \to N(0, 1), \tag{5.10}$$

$$\mathscr{L}\left\{\frac{|V_1|^{a_1}|V_2|^{a_2} - |\Sigma_1|^{a_1}|\Sigma_2|^{a_2}}{|\Sigma_1|^{a_1}|\Sigma_2|^{a_2}(2k[(a_1{}^2/n_1) + (a_2{}^2/n_2)])^{1/2}}\right\} \to N(0, 1), \tag{5.11}$$

$$\mathscr{L}\left\{\frac{(a_1|S_1^{-1}| + a_2|S_2^{-1}|) - (a_1|\Sigma_1^{-1}| + a_2|\Sigma_2^{-1}|)}{(2k[(a_1{}^2/n_1|V_1|^2) + (a_2{}^2/n_2|V_2|^2)])^{1/2}}\right\} \to N(0, 1), \tag{5.12}$$

$$\mathscr{L}\left\{\frac{\operatorname{tr} V_1^{-1}V_2 - \operatorname{tr}\Sigma_1^{-1}\Sigma_2}{(2(n_1^{-1} + n_2^{-1})\operatorname{tr}(V_1^{-1}V_2)^2)^{1/2}}\right\} \to N(0, 1). \tag{5.13}$$

Approximate confidence regions for the various functions $h(\Sigma_1, \Sigma_2)$ may be obtained by using these results as outlined in Section 4.1.

5.2. Confidence Intervals for $\operatorname{tr}(A_1\Lambda_1 + A_2\Lambda_2)$ and $\operatorname{tr}(A_1\Sigma_1 + A_2\Sigma_2)$

By a straightforward analog of Sections 4.2 and 4.3, we obtain the following results.

The interval

$$\left[\sum_1^2 n_j \operatorname{tr} A_j(S_j + \xi_1 A_j)^{-1},\quad \sum_1^2 n_j \operatorname{tr} A_j(S_j + \xi_2 A_j)^{-1}\right]$$

is a confidence interval for $\operatorname{tr}(A_1\Lambda_1 + A_2\Lambda_2)$ with confidence coefficient $1 - \alpha$, where ξ_1 and ξ_2 are the two roots of

$$g(\xi) = \sum_1^2 \{n_j \log|I + \xi S_j^{-1}A_j| + n_j \operatorname{tr}(I + \xi S_j^{-1}A_j)^{-1} - kn_j\} = \chi_\alpha{}^2(1).$$

The interval

$$\left[\sum_1^2 \tfrac{1}{2}n_j \operatorname{tr} C_j[I + (I - \xi_1 C_j)^{1/2}], \sum_1^2 \tfrac{1}{2}n_j \operatorname{tr} C_j[I + (I - \xi_2 C_j)^{1/2}]^{-1}\right],$$

where $C_j = 4S_j^{1/2}A_j S_j^{1/2}/n_j^2$, is a confidence interval for $\operatorname{tr}(A_1\Sigma_1 + A_2\Sigma_2)$ with confidence coefficient $1 - \alpha$, where ξ_1 and ξ_2 are the two roots of

$$g(\xi) = \sum_1^2 \{kn_j(\log 2 - \tfrac{1}{2}) - n_j \log|I + (1 - \xi C_j)^{1/2}| + \tfrac{1}{2}n_j \operatorname{tr}(I - \xi C_j)^{1/2}\}$$
$$= \chi_\alpha^2(1).$$

5.3. Confidence Interval for $|\Sigma_1|^{a_1}|\Sigma_2|^{a_2}$

Since we can obtain a confidence interval for $|\Sigma_1|^{a_1}\,|\Sigma_2|^{a_2}$ from a confidence interval for $a_1 \log|\Lambda_1| + a_2 \log|\Lambda_2|$ by exponentiation, we consider as in Section 3.2, $\omega = \{\Lambda_1, \Lambda_2 : \Lambda_1 > 0, \Lambda_2 > 0, a_1 \log|\Lambda_1| + a_2 \log|\Lambda_2| = \rho\}$ and obtain $\sup_\omega p(S_1, S_2; \Sigma_1, \Sigma_2)$. The appropriate Lagrangian is

$$M(\Lambda_1, \Lambda_2) = \sum_{\alpha=1}^2 (n_\alpha \log|\Lambda_\alpha| - \operatorname{tr}\Lambda_\alpha S_\alpha) - \xi(a_1 \log|\Lambda_1| + a_2 \log|\Lambda_2| - \rho).$$

As in Section 4.4, the MLE for Λ_α in ω is

$$\hat{\Lambda}_\alpha = (n_\alpha - a_\alpha \xi)S_\alpha^{-1},$$

where ξ is such that $n_\alpha - \alpha_\alpha \xi > 0$ for $\alpha = 1, 2$. In contrast to the case of one covariance matrix, we cannot in general solve the constraint equation for ξ in terms of ρ. It is easily verified that

$$g(\xi) = -\sum_{\alpha=1}^2 ka_\alpha \xi + kn_\alpha \log[(n_\alpha - \xi a_\alpha)/n_\alpha],$$

and

$$h(\hat{\Sigma}_1(\xi), \hat{\Sigma}_2(\xi)) = \sum_{\alpha=1}^2 a_\alpha \log|S_\alpha^{-1}(n_\alpha - a_\alpha \xi)|.$$

Since $h(\hat{\Sigma}_1(\xi), \hat{\Sigma}_2(\xi))$ is a monotonically decreasing function of ξ, it follows from Lemma 2.1, that $g(\xi)$ is monotone increasing for $\xi > 0$ and monotone decreasing for $\xi < 0$.

5.4. Confidence Interval for $a_1|\Lambda_1| + a_2|\Lambda_2|$

To find $\sup_\omega p(S_1, S_2; \Lambda_1, \Lambda_2)$, where $\omega = \{\Lambda_1, \Lambda_2 : a_1|\Lambda_1| + a_2|\Lambda_2| = \rho\}$, we use the Lagrangian

$$M(\Delta_1, \Delta_2) = \sum_{j=1}^2 (n_j \log|\Lambda_j| - \operatorname{tr} S_j\Lambda_j) - \xi(a_1|\Lambda_1| + a_2|\Lambda_2| - \rho).$$

Setting the derivatives of $M(\Lambda_1, \Lambda_2)$ with respect to the elements of Λ_1 and Λ_2 equal to zero yields the matrix equations

$$n_j\Sigma_j - S_j - \xi a_j|\Lambda_j|\Sigma_j = 0, \qquad j = 1, 2.$$

Thus

$$(n_j - \xi a_j |\Lambda_j|)I = \Lambda_j S_j,$$

so that

$$(\text{tr } \Lambda_j S_j)/k = n_j - \xi a_j |\Lambda_j|,$$

and

$$|\Lambda_j S_j|^{1/k} = n_j - \xi a_j |\Lambda_j|, \qquad j = 1, 2.$$

But tr $\Lambda_j S_j/k$ is the arithmetic mean and $|\Lambda_j S_j|^{1/k}$ is the geometric mean of the characteristic roots of $\Lambda_j^{1/2} S_j \Lambda_j^{1/2}$. These two means are equal if and only if all the characteristic roots are equal to a constant, say c_j. Thus

$$\Delta_j^{1/2} S_j \Lambda_j^{1/2} = c_j I,$$

so that $\hat{\Lambda}_j = c_j S_j^{-1}, j = 1, 2$. Since

$$|\hat{\Lambda}_j S_j| = c_j^k = (n_j - \xi a_j |\hat{\Lambda}_j|)^k = (n_j - \xi a_j c_j^k |S_j^{-1}|)^k,$$

we see that c_j must be a positive root of the equation

$$\xi a_j |S_j^{-1}| x^k + x - n_j = 0, \qquad j = 1, 2,$$

or alternatively, $d_j = c_j^{-1}$ must be a positive root of the equation

$$\varphi_j(y) = n_j y^k - y^{k-1} - \xi b_j = 0, \qquad j = 1, 2,$$

where $b_j = a_j |S_j^{-1}|$.

We next show that when there are multiple positive roots, the smallest root (c_j) is the maximizer of $M(\hat{\Lambda}_1, \hat{\Lambda}_2)$.

When $\xi b_j > 0$, there is exactly one positive root of $\varphi_j(y) = 0$. To see this note that $\varphi_j(0) = -\xi b_j < 0$ and $\lim_{y \to \infty} \varphi_j(y) = \infty$ guarantees the existence of at least one positive root, and by Descartes rule of signs there is at most one positive root. Also, from $\varphi_j(x^{-1}) = 0$, we see that $c_j < n_j$, a fact which will be needed later.

When $\xi b_j < 0$, by Descartes rule of signs there exist at most two positive roots of $\varphi_j(y) = 0$. When k is even, there must be at least one positive root, for if $y < 0$, $n_j y^k - y^{k-1} - \xi b_j > 0$. However, when k is odd, it may happen that there are no positive roots of $\varphi_j(y) = 0$ (e.g., if $k = 1$, $\varphi_j(y) = n_j y - 1 - \xi b_j = 0$, implies that $y = (1 + \xi b_j)/n$, which may be negative for arbitrary ξ). This imposes a constraint on ξ, namely that in case k is odd and $\xi b_j < 0$, ξ must be such that there exists at least one positive root of $\varphi_j(y) = 0$. This constraint is equivalent to

$$\xi b_j \geq -k^{-1}[(k-1)/nk]^{k-1}.$$

To see this note that $\varphi_j'(y) = 0$ at $y = (k-1)/nk$, and we require that $\varphi_j[(k-1)/nk] \leq 0$. Thus when $\xi b_j < 0$, there is at least one, and at most two, positive roots of $\varphi_j(y) = 0$.

In the event there are two positive roots, we show that the larger root is the maximizer of

$$\psi_j(y) = n_j \log|\Lambda_j| - \operatorname{tr} S_j \hat{\Lambda}_j = -n_j \log|S_j| - kn_j \log y - k/y.$$

Then

$$\psi_j'(y) = (-n_j k/y) + (k/y^2),$$

which is positive if and only if $y < n_j^{-1}$. But $\varphi_j(n_j^{-1}) = -\xi b_j > 0$, $\varphi_j'(n_j^{-1}) = n_j^{-k-1} > 0$, so that all positive roots of $\varphi_j(y)$ are smaller than n_j^{-1}. Consequently, $\psi_j'(y) > 0$ and the larger of the two positive roots of $\varphi_j(y)$ is to be used as d_j, or equivalently, c_j is the smallest positive root of $\varphi_j(x^{-1}) = 0$. Further, note that since d_j is the largest root of $\varphi_j(y)$, and $\lim_{y\to\infty} \varphi_j(y) = \infty$, $\varphi_j'(d_j) = [n_j k d_j - (k-1)]d_j^{k-2} > 0$, so that $c_j = d_j^{-1} < n_j k/(k-1)$.

We now return to a consideration of the function

$$g(\xi) = k\sum_1^2 (n_j \log n_j - n_j) - k\sum_1^2 (n_j \log c_j - c_j).$$

Then

$$\frac{dg}{d\xi} = k\sum_1^2 \left(\frac{n_j - c_j}{c_j}\right)\frac{\partial c_j}{\partial \xi} = k\sum_1^2 (\xi b_j c_j^{k-1})\left(\frac{b_j c_j^k}{1 + \xi b_j k c_j^{k-1}}\right)$$

$$= k\xi \sum_1^2 \frac{b_j^2 c_j^{2k-1}}{(1 + \xi b_j k c_j^{k-1})} = k\xi \sum_1^2 \frac{b_j^2 c_j^{2k}}{[kn - c(k-1)]}.$$

Recalling that $c_j < n_j$ when $\xi b_j > 0$ and $c_j < kn_j/(k-1)$ when $\xi b_j < 0$, it is immediate that $g(\xi)$ is increasing when $\xi > 0$ and decreasing when $\xi < 0$.

5.5. Confidence Region for $\operatorname{tr}\Sigma_1^{-1}\Sigma_2$

For this problem, $\omega = \{\Lambda_1, \Lambda_2 : \Lambda_1 > 0, \Lambda_2 > 0, \operatorname{tr}\Lambda_1\Lambda_2^{-1} = \rho\}$, and we use the Lagrangian

$$M(\Lambda_1, \Lambda_2) = n \log|\Lambda_1| + m \log|\Lambda_2| - \operatorname{tr}\Lambda_1 S_1 - \operatorname{tr}\Lambda_2 S_2 - \xi(\operatorname{tr}\Lambda_1\Lambda_2^{-1} - \rho).$$

Differentiating with respect to the elements of Λ_1 and Λ_2, and setting the derivatives equal to zero yields the equations

$$n\Sigma_1 - S_1 - \xi\Sigma_2 = 0, \tag{5.14}$$

$$m\Sigma_2 - S_2 + \xi\Sigma_2\Lambda_1\Sigma_2 = 0. \tag{5.15}$$

Pre- and postmultiplying (5.14) by $\Lambda_1^{1/2}$, (5.15) by $\Lambda_2^{1/2}$, taking traces and adding yields,

$$(n+m)k = \operatorname{tr}(\Lambda_1 S_1 + \Lambda_2 S_2).$$

From (5.14), we have $\hat{\Sigma}_2(\xi) = (n\hat{\Sigma}_1(\xi) - S_1)/\xi$, which together with (5.15) yields

$$S_1\Lambda_1 S_1 + n(m+n)\Sigma_1 - (m+2n)S_1 - \xi S_2 = 0,$$

or equivalently,

$$\frac{S_1^{1/2}\Lambda_1 S_1^{1/2}}{(n(m+n))^{1/2}} + (n(m+n))^{1/2} S_1^{-1/2}\Sigma_1 S_1^{-1/2} - \frac{(m+2n)I + \xi S_1^{-1/2} S_2 S_1^{-1/2}}{(n(m+n))^{1/2}} = 0. \quad (5.16)$$

Letting

$$\psi = \frac{S_1^{1/2}\Lambda_1 S_1^{1/2}}{(n(m+n))^{1/2}}, \qquad T = \frac{(m+2n)I + \xi S_1^{-1/2} S_2 S_1^{-1/2}}{2(n(m+n))^{1/2}}, \quad (5.17)$$

(5.16) becomes

$$\psi + \psi^{-1} = 2T, \quad (5.18)$$

where ξ is such that $T > I$. Because $\psi + \psi^{-1}$ commutes with ψ, T must commute with ψ, so that $\psi^2 - 2T\psi + I = 0$. Hence

$$(\psi - T)^2 = T^2 - I > 0,$$

and

$$\psi = T + (T^2 - I)^{1/2}, \quad (5.19)$$

where $(T^2 - I)^{1/2}$ is any symmetric square root of $T^2 - I$.

We now determine which square root is the maximizer of

$$M^*(\hat{\Lambda}_1, \hat{\Lambda}_2) = n \log|\hat{\Lambda}_1| + m \log|\hat{\Lambda}_2| - \operatorname{tr} \hat{\Lambda}_1 S_1 - \operatorname{tr} \hat{\Lambda}_2 S_2 .$$

Because of (5.16), and the fact that

$$|\hat{\Sigma}_2| = |S_1|\,|\psi^{-1}|\,|\{(n/(n+m))^{1/2} I - \psi\}/\xi|,$$

$$M^*(\hat{\Lambda}_1, \hat{\Lambda}_2) = (n+m)\log|\psi| - m \log|\{(n/(n+m))^{1/2} I - \psi\}/\xi| - k(n+m) + (kn/2)\log n(n+m) - (n+m)\log|S_1|.$$

Consequently, $M^*(\hat{\Lambda}_1, \hat{\Lambda}_2)$ is a function of the characteristic roots of ψ. If $t_1, \ldots, t_k$ denote the roots of T, then $\varepsilon_j(t_j^2 - 1)$ are the roots of any symmetric square root, $(T^2 - I)^{1/2}$, where $\varepsilon_j = \pm 1, j = 1, \ldots, k$. Hence the roots of $\psi = T + (T^2 - I)^{1/2}$ are $t_j + \varepsilon_j(t_j^2 - 1)^{1/2}$. The determination of which of the 2^k square roots is the maximizer of $M^*(\hat{\Lambda}_1, \hat{\Lambda}_2)$ depends on the maximization of $M^*(\hat{\Lambda}_1, \hat{\Lambda}_2)$ with respect to ε_j, i.e., of

$$(m+n)\sum_1^k \log(t_j + \varepsilon_j(t_j^2 - 1)^{1/2}) - m \sum_1^k \log\{[n/(n+m)]^{1/2} - t_j - \varepsilon_j(t_j^2 - 1)^{1/2}\}.$$

We now show that the maximizer is achieved for $\varepsilon_1 = \cdots = \varepsilon_k = 1$. Let $\alpha = n/(n+m)$, $\bar{\alpha} = 1 - \alpha$, and note that $\sqrt{\alpha} > t + \varepsilon(t^2 - 1)^{1/2} > 0$. Consider the function

$$\begin{aligned} s(t) &= s_+(t) - s_-(t) \\ &= \{\log[t + (t^2 - 1)^{1/2}] - \bar{\alpha}\log[\sqrt{\alpha} - t - (t^2 - 1)^{1/2}]\} \\ &\quad - \{\log[t - (t^2 - 1)^{1/2}] - \bar{\alpha}\log[\sqrt{\alpha} - t + (t^2 - 1)^{1/2}]\}; \end{aligned}$$

then $s(1) = 0$. A direct computation shows that $ds/dt > 0$ for $0 < t \pm (t^2 - 1)^{1/2} < \sqrt{\alpha}$, from which the result follows.

From (5.14), (5.15), and (5.17), note that $|\Lambda_2 S_2| = |(n+m)I - \Lambda_1 S_1| = |(n+m)I - (n(m+n))^{1/2}\psi|$, so that

$$\begin{aligned} g(\xi) = &-n\log|\psi| - m\log|I - \psi(n/(n+m))^{1/2}| \\ &+ (nk/2)\log[n/(n+m)] + mk\log[m/(m+n)]. \end{aligned}$$

Recall that the roots of ψ are $\psi_j = t_j + (t_j^2 - 1)^{1/2}, j = 1, \ldots, p$. Then

$$\frac{\partial g}{\partial \xi} = \sum_j \frac{\partial g}{\partial \psi_j}\frac{\partial \psi_j}{\partial \xi} = -\sum_j \left(\frac{n}{\psi_j} - \frac{mn}{(n+m)^{1/2} - n\psi_j}\right)\frac{\partial \psi_j}{\partial \xi}.$$

But $\partial\psi_j/\partial\xi = \psi_j/(t_j^2 - 1)^{1/2} > 0$, and hence $g(\xi)$ is a decreasing function.

6. CONFIDENCE INTERVAL FOR $\mu\Sigma^{-1}\mu'$

Let x be a k-dimensional random vector having a multivariate normal distribution, $N(\mu, \Sigma/N)$, and let $S \equiv Vn$ be an independent $k \times k$ random symmetric matrix having a Wishart distribution $W(\Sigma, k, N-1)$. Although $xS^{-1}x'$ (except for a constant) has a noncentral F-distribution with noncentrality parameter $(\mu\Sigma^{-1}\mu')^{1/2}$, it is not simple to use this exact result to obtain a confidence interval for $\mu\Sigma^{-1}\mu'$.

The method of linearization is based on

$$\mathscr{L}\left\{\frac{xV^{-1}x' - \mu\Sigma^{-1}\mu'}{((2/n)[(xV^{-1}x')^2 + (xV^{-1}x')])^{1/2}}\right\} \to N(0, 1),$$

and yields an approximate confidence interval for $\mu\Sigma^{-1}\mu'$.

We now obtain an approximate confidence interval for $\mu\Sigma^{-1}\mu'$ using the method of Section 2. From the joint distribution of x and S given by (3.1) and (3.2) and $\Omega = \{\mu, \Sigma : \Sigma > 0, -\infty < \mu_i < \infty, i = 1, \ldots, k\}$, we obtain $\hat{\Sigma} = S/N$, $\hat{\mu} = x$, so that

$$\sup_{\Omega} p(x, s; \mu, \Sigma) = Cc(k, N-1)|S|^{-(k+2)/2}N^{kN/2}e^{-kN/2}.$$

To find $\sup_\omega p(x, S; \mu, \Sigma)$, where $\omega = \{\mu, \Sigma\colon \Sigma > 0, \mu\Sigma^{-1}\mu' = \rho\}$, we use the Lagrangian

$$M(\mu, \Lambda) = N \log|\Lambda| - \operatorname{tr} \Lambda S - N(x-\mu)\Lambda(x-\mu)' - \xi(\mu\Lambda\mu' - \rho),$$

where $\Lambda = \Sigma^{-1}$. Differentiating $M(\mu, \Lambda)$ with respect to the μ_i and λ_{ij} and setting the derivatives equal to zero yields the equations

$$N(x-\mu)\Lambda - \xi\mu\Lambda = 0, \qquad N\Sigma - S - N(x-\mu)'(x-\mu) - \xi\mu'\mu = 0,$$

so that

$$\hat{\mu}(\xi) = \frac{N}{N+\xi}\, x, \tag{6.1}$$

$$\hat{\Sigma}(\xi) = N^{-1}\left(S + \frac{N\xi}{N+\xi}\, x'x\right). \tag{6.2}$$

Consequently,

$$\sup_\omega p(x, S; \mu, \Sigma) = Cc(k, n)\,|S|^{-(k+2)/2} N^{kN/2} e^{-kN/2}$$
$$\times \left(1 + \frac{N\xi}{N+\xi}\, xS^{-1}x'\right)^{-N/2} \exp\left[\frac{N^3\xi xS^{-1}x'}{2(N+\xi)(N+\xi+N\xi xS^{-1}x')}\right].$$

Thus

$$g(\xi) = -2\log\frac{p_\omega}{p_\Omega}$$
$$= N\log\left(1 + \frac{N\xi}{N+\xi}\, xS^{-1}x'\right) - \frac{N^3\xi xS^{-1}x'}{(N+\xi)(N+\xi+N\xi xS^{-1}x')}.$$

The function $g(\xi)$ is monotone increasing in $(-\infty, -1)$ with $g(-\infty) = N\log(1 + NxS^{-1}x')$ and $g(-1) = \infty$; $g(\xi)$ is undefined on $[1, -(1+q)^{-1}]$; and $g(\xi)$ is bowl-shaped in $(-(1+q)^{-1}, \infty)$—monotone decreasing in $(-(1+q)^{-1}, 0)$ and increasing in $(0, \infty)$—with $g(-(1+q)^{-1}) = \infty$, $g(0) = 0$, $g(\infty) = N\log(1 + NxS^{-1}x')$.

Consequently, the equation $g(\xi) =$ constant has two solutions. If $\chi_\alpha^2(1) < N\log(1 + NxS^{-1}x')$, we obtain an interval about zero, and if $\chi_\alpha^2(1) > N\log(1 + NxS^{-1}x')$, we obtain two semi-infinite intervals.

7. BEHRENS-FISHER MODEL

Here we study the multivariate Behrens-Fisher problem, which in its canonical form may be expressed as follows. Let x and y be random vectors having k-variate normal distributions with $\mathscr{L}(x) = N(\mu_1, \Sigma_1)$, $\mathscr{L}(y) = N(\mu_2, \Sigma_2)$; let S_1 and S_2 be random $k \times k$ matrices having Wishart distributions $\mathscr{L}(S_1) = W(\Sigma_1; k, n)$, $\mathscr{L}(S_2) = W(\Sigma_2; k, m)$, where x, y, S_1, S_2 are independent. The joint density is given by

$$p(x, y, S_1, S_2; \mu, \nu, \Lambda_1, \Lambda_2) = C\,|\Lambda_1|^{N/2}\,|\Lambda_2|^{M/2}$$
$$\times \exp -\tfrac{1}{2}[(x-\mu)\Lambda_1(x-\mu)' + (y-\nu)\Lambda_2(y-\nu)' + \operatorname{tr}\Lambda_1 S_1 + \operatorname{tr}\Lambda_2 S_2],$$

where $\Lambda_1 = \Sigma_1^{-1}$, $\Lambda_2 = \Sigma_2^{-1}$, $N = n+1$, $M = m+1$. The problem is to find a confidence region for $\mu - \nu = (\mu_1 - \nu_1, \ldots, \mu_k - \nu_k)$.

For $\Omega = \{\mu, \nu, \Lambda_1, \Lambda_2 : -\infty < \mu_i < \infty, -\infty < \nu_i < \infty, i = 1, \ldots, k, \Lambda_1 > 0, \Lambda_2 > 0\}$, a straightforward calculation yields

$$\sup_{\Omega} p(x, y, S_1, S_2; \mu, \nu, \Lambda_1, \Lambda_2\}$$
$$= C\,|S_1/N|^{-N/2}\,|S_2/M|^{-M/2} \exp[-\tfrac{1}{2}k(N+M)].$$

In $\omega = \{\mu, \nu, \Lambda_1, \Lambda_2 : \mu - \nu = \rho, \Lambda_1 > 0, \Lambda_2 > 0\}$, we consider the Lagrangian

$$\begin{aligned} M(\mu, \nu, \Lambda_1, \Lambda_2) = N\log|\Lambda_1| &+ M\log|\Lambda_2| - (x-\mu)\Lambda_1(x-\mu)' \\ &- (y-\mu)\Lambda_2(y-\nu)' - \operatorname{tr}\Lambda_1 S_1 - \operatorname{tr}\Lambda_2 S_2 \\ &- 2\xi[(\mu-\nu)-\rho]', \end{aligned} \tag{7.1}$$

where now $\xi = (\xi_1, \ldots, \xi_k)$. Equating to zero the derivatives of (7.1) with respect to the elements of μ, ν, Λ_1, Λ_2 yields the equations

$$(x-\mu)\Lambda_1 = \xi, \tag{7.2}$$
$$(y-\nu)\Lambda_2 = -\,\xi, \tag{7.3}$$
$$N\Sigma_1 = S_1 + (x-\mu)'(x-\mu), \tag{7.4}$$
$$M\Sigma_2 = S_2 + (y-\nu)'(y-\nu). \tag{7.5}$$

These equations need not be solved explicitly since we only need the quantities $|\hat{\Lambda}_1(\xi)|$, $|\hat{\Lambda}_2(\xi)|$, $\operatorname{tr}\hat{\Lambda}_1(\xi)[S_1 + (x - \hat{\mu}(\xi))'(x - \hat{\mu}(\xi))]$, and $\operatorname{tr}\hat{\Lambda}_2(\xi) \times [S_2 + (y - \hat{\nu}(\xi))'(y - \hat{\nu}(\xi))]$, in order to compute $\sup_\omega \log p(x, y, S_1, S_2; \mu, \nu, \Lambda_1, \Lambda_2)$ as a function of ξ.

Premultiplication of (7.4) and (7.5) by Λ_1 and Λ_2, respectively, and taking the trace of both sides yields

$$k(N+M) = \operatorname{tr}\{\hat{\Lambda}_1[S_1 + (x-\hat{\mu})'(x-\hat{\mu})] + \hat{\Lambda}_2[S_2 + (y-\hat{\nu})'(y-\hat{\nu})]\},$$

where the dependence on ξ is omitted. From (7.4),

$$|\hat{\Sigma}_1|\,N^k = |S_1|\,[1 + (x-\hat{\mu})S_1^{-1}(x-\hat{\mu})'],$$

$$N^{-1}(x-\hat{\mu})\hat{\Lambda}_1(x-\hat{\mu})' = \frac{(x-\hat{\mu})S^{-1}(x-\hat{\mu})'}{1 + (x-\hat{\mu})S^{-1}(x-\hat{\mu})'},$$

and from (7.2)

$$(x-\hat{\mu})\hat{\Lambda}_1(x-\hat{\mu})' = \xi(x-\hat{\mu})'.$$

Multiplication of the left-hand and right-hand sides of (7.2) and (7.4), respectively, yields

$$N(x - \hat{\mu}) = \xi S_1 + \xi(x - \hat{\mu})'(x - \hat{\mu});$$

post-multiplication by ξ yields a quadratic in $\xi(x - \hat{\mu})'$ the solution of which is

$$\xi(x - \hat{\mu})' = \tfrac{1}{2}[N \pm (N^2 - 4\xi S_1 \xi')^{1/2}],$$

so that

$$[1 + (x - \hat{\mu})S^{-1}(x - \hat{\mu})']^{-1} = [N \mp (N^2 - 4\xi S_1 \xi')^{1/2}]/2N.$$

A simple direct calculation shows that the positive sign is the maximizer, so that

$$\sup_{\omega} p(x, y, S_1, S_2; \mu, \nu, \Lambda_1, \Lambda_2) = C\,|S_1/N|^{-N/2}\,|S_2/M|^{-M/2}\,e^{-k(N+M)/2}$$
$$\times \frac{[N + (N^2 - 4\xi S_1 \xi')^{1/2}]^{N/2}}{(2N)^{N/2}} \frac{[M + (M^2 - 4\xi S_2 \xi')^{1/2}]^{M/2}}{(2M)^{M/2}}.$$

Consequently,

$$g(\xi_1, \ldots, \xi_k) = -2\log(p_\omega/p_\Omega) = N\log 2N + M\log 2M$$
$$- N\log[N + (N^2 - 4\xi S_1 \xi')^{1/2}] - M\log[M + (M^2 - 4\xi S_2 \xi')^{1/2}].$$

Finally, we note that $\xi S_j \xi'$ is a convex function of ξ for $j = 1, 2$, and as both the square root and logarithm are monotone increasing and concave, it follows that $-g(\xi)$ is concave, so that $g(\xi)$ is a convex function of ξ.

REFERENCES

AITCHISON, J., and SILVEY, S. D. (1958). Maximum likelihood estimation of parameters subject to restraints. *Ann. Math. Statist.* **29** 813–825.

AITCHISON, J., and SILVEY, S. D. (1960). Maximum likelihood estimation procedures and associated tests of significance. *J. Roy. Statist. Soc. Ser. B* **22** 154–171.

ANDERSON, T. W. (1958). "An Introduction to Multivariate Statistical Analysis." Wiley, New York.

BECKENBACH, E. F., and BELLMAN, R. (1961). "Inequalities." Springer-Verlag, Berlin.

GROSS, O. A., and JOHNSON, S. M. (1959). Sequential minimax search for a zero of a convex function. *Math. Tables Aids Comput.* **13** 44–51.

KUHN, H. W., and TUCKER, A. W. (1951). Nonlinear programming. *Proc. Second Berkeley Symp. Math. Statist. Prob.* (J. Neyman, ed.), 481–492. Univ. of California Press, Berkeley, California.

MADANSKY, A. (1965). Approximate confidence limits for the reliability of series and parallel systems. *Technometrics* **7** 495–503.

ROY, S. N., and BOSE, R. C. (1953). Simultaneous confidence interval estimation. *Ann. Math. Statist.* **24** 513–536.

SILVEY, S. D. (1959). The Lagrangian multiplier test. *Ann. Math. Statist.* **30** 389–407.

WALD, A. (1943). Tests of statistical hypotheses concerning several parameters when the number of observations is large. *Trans. Amer. Math. Soc.* **54** 426–482.

PART IV

Characteristic Functions and Characterization Problems

Characteristic Functions of Random Variables Connected with Brownian Motion and of the von Mises Multidimensional ω_n^2

DANIEL DUGUE

UNIVERSITY OF PARIS
PARIS, FRANCE

1. MULTIVARIATE CHARACTERISTIC FUNCTIONS

Dugue [3] has proved the following results.

Let us call B_s a symmetrical $s \times s$ matrix where $b_{ij} = \min(s - i + 1, s - j + 1)$, and M_s the matrix in which all the terms are equal to 1. The latent roots of B_s are the reciprocals of z_k with

$$z_k = 4 \sin^2 \left[\frac{(2k-1)\pi}{2(2s+1)}\right] \qquad (k = 1, \ldots, s).$$

If S_s is a matrix such that $S_s B_s S_s^{-1} = D_s$ is diagonal, the diagonal terms of the matrix $N_s = S_s M_s S_s^{-1}$ (obviously of rank 1) are

$$n_k = \{(2s+1)\tan^2[(2k-1)\pi/2(2s+1)]\}^{-1} = (2s+1)^{-1}[(4/z_k) - 1],$$

where $k = 1, \ldots, s$ and $\sum_{i=1}^{s} n_i = s$. Dugue [2] also proved the following result: $x(u_1, u_2, \ldots, u_p)$ being a Gaussian random process with $0 \le u_i \le 1$, $0 \le v_i \le 1$, $E(x(u_1, \ldots, u_p)) = 0$ and the covariance function being $\prod_{i=1}^{p} \min (u_i, v_i)$, the characteristic function $\phi_{(p)}(t)$ of the integral

$$\int_0^1 \cdots \int_0^1 x^2(u_1, u_2, \ldots, u_p)\, du_1\, du_2 \cdots du_p$$

is given by the recurrence relation

$$\phi_{(p)}(t) = \prod_{n=1}^{\infty} \phi_{(p-1)}[t/(n - \tfrac{1}{2})^2\pi^2] \qquad \text{with} \quad \phi_{(1)}(t) = [\cos(2it)^{1/2}]^{-1/2}.$$

Using these results, two theorems will be obtained in this paper. The first one is to obtain the joint characteristic function of a pair of functionals of the Brownian motion processes, and the next result is to obtain the characteristic functions of the asymptotic distribution of the multidimensional analog of the von Mises ω_n^2 statistic. We shall prove in this section the following:

Theorem 1. *The function* $x(u)$ $(0 \le u \le 1)$ *being a Gaussian random function with* $E(x(u)) = 0$ *and covariance function equal to* $\min(u, v)$, *the characteristic function of* $X = x(1)$ *and* $Y = \int_0^1 x^2(u)\,du$ *is*

$$E(e^{iuX+ivY}) = [(\cos(2iv)^{1/2}]^{-1/2} \exp[-u^2 \tan(2iv)^{1/2}/2(2iv)^{1/2}]$$

and also

$$E(e^{iuX^2+ivY}) = [\cos(2iv)^{1/2} - 2iu(\sin(2iv)^{1/2}/(2iv)^{1/2})]^{-1/2},$$

and X^2/Y *is obviously nonparametric.*

Since s is an integer, let us put $x(k/s) - x((k-1)/s) = y_k$ $(k = 1, \ldots, s)$. We have $X = y_1 + \cdots + y_s$ and $Y = \lim_{s\to\infty} s^{-1}[y_1{}^2 + (y_1 + y_2)^2 \cdots + (y_1 + \cdots + y_s)^2]$. The $y_1, y_2, \ldots, y_s$ are independent in the whole, their variance being s^{-1}. Let Z_s denote an $n \times 1$ matrix in which the term in the ith line is y_i and T_s an $n \times 1$ matrix whose terms are all equal to 1. We have

$$\begin{aligned} E[e^{iuX+ivY}] &= \lim_{s\to\infty} E[\exp(iu\,{}^tZ_s T_s + i(v/s)\,{}^tZ_s B_s Z_s] \\ &= [(2\pi)^{s/2}(\det C_s)^{1/2}]^{-1} \int \exp[iu\,{}^tZ_s T_s + i(v/s)\, Z_s B_s Z_s \\ &\quad - ({}^tZ_s C_s^{-1} Z_s/2)]\, dZ_s \end{aligned}$$

with $C_s = s^{-1}I_s$ (I_s being the unit $s \times s$ matrix and ${}^tT$ being the transpose of a matrix T) which gives

$$\begin{aligned} &E[\exp(iu\,{}^tZ_s T_s + i(v/s)\,{}^tZ_s B_s Z_s)] \\ &\quad = (\det C_s)^{-1/2}[\det(C_s^{-1} - (2iv/s)B_s)]^{-1/2} \\ &\qquad \times (2\pi)^{-s/2}[\det(C_s^{-1} - (2iv/s)B_s)]^{1/2} \\ &\qquad \times \int \exp(iu\,{}^tZ_s T_s) \exp\{-\tfrac{1}{2}{}^tZ_s[C_s^{-1} - (2iv/s)B_s]Z_s\}\, dZ_s. \end{aligned}$$

The well-known properties of the characteristic function of an n-dimensional Gaussian law show us that the product of the two last lines is equal to

$$\exp\{-(u^2/2)\,{}^tT_s[C_s^{-1} - (2iv/s)B_s]^{-1}T_s\}.$$

So we have

$$\begin{aligned} E[\exp(iu\,{}^tZ_s T_s + i(v/s)\,{}^tZ_s B_s Z_s)] &= \det[I_s - (2iv/s^2)B_s]^{-1/2} \\ &\quad \times \exp\{-(u^2/2)\,{}^tT_s[C_s^{-1} - (2iv/s)B_s]^{-1}T_s\} \end{aligned}$$

It is a known result (due to Cameron and Martin [1]) recalled by Dugue [2] that

$$\lim_{s\to\infty} [\det(I_s - (2iv/s^2)B_s)]^{-1/2} = [\cos(2iv)^{1/2}]^{-1/2}$$

Let us find the limit of

$${}^tT_s[C_s^{-1} - (2iv/s)B_s]^{-1}T_s = s^{-1}\,{}^tT_s[I_s - (2iv/s^2)B_s]^{-1}T_s.$$

We have

$$[I_s - (2iv/s^2)B_s]^{-1} = \sum_{n=0}^{\infty} (2iv/s^2)^n B_s^{\,n}.$$

Also, we have ${}^tT_s B_s^{\,n} T_s = \mathrm{tr}\ B_s^{\,n} T_s\,{}^tT_s = \mathrm{tr}\ B_s^{\,n} M_s$. If S_s diagonalizes B_s with $S_s B_s S_s^{-1} = D_s$ and $S_s M_s S_s^{-1} = N_s$, we have $\mathrm{tr}\ B_s^{\,n} M_s = \mathrm{tr}\ D_s^{\,n} N_s$, and so

$$s^{-1}\,{}^tT_s[I_s - (2iv/s^2)B_s]^{-1}T_s = \sum_{n=0}^{+\infty} (2iv)^n/(s^{2n+1})\ \mathrm{tr}\ D_s^{\,n} N_s.$$

According to what is recalled at the beginning of this paper, we have

$$\mathrm{tr}\ D_s^{\,n} N_s = \sum_{k=1}^{s} \left[4\sin^2\left(\frac{2k-1}{2s+1}\frac{\pi}{2}\right)\right]^{-n}\left[(2s+1)\tan^2\left(\frac{2k-1}{2s+1}\frac{\pi}{2}\right)\right]^{-1}$$

The coefficient of $(2iv)^n$ in the expansion is

$$[s^{2n+1}(2s+1)2^{2n}]^{-1}\left\{\sum_{k=1}^{s}\left[\sin^{2n+2}\left(\frac{2k-1}{2s+1}\frac{\pi}{2}\right)\right]^{-1} - \sum_{k=1}^{s}\left[\sin^{2n}\left(\frac{2k-1}{2s+1}\frac{\pi}{2}\right)\right]^{-1}\right\} = \alpha_{n,s}.$$

Let us show that S independent of $n > 0$ exists such that $s > S$ implies

$$\left|\sum_{k=1}^{s}\left[(2s)^{2n}\sin^{2n}\left(\frac{2k-1}{2s+1}\frac{\pi}{2}\right)\right]^{-1} - \sum_{k=1}^{\infty}\left[(2k-1)\frac{\pi}{2}\right]^{-2n}\right| < \varepsilon + nA\varepsilon(1+\varepsilon)^{2n} \tag{A}$$

whatever ε may be, A being independent on n. Let us take $0 < x_0 < \pi/2$ and put $(\sin x_0)/x_0 = \alpha$. For given s, if

$$\frac{2k-1}{2s+1}\frac{\pi}{2} > x_0,$$

we have

$$(2s)^{2n}\sin^{2n}\left(\frac{2k-1}{2s+1}\frac{\pi}{2}\right) > (2s)^{2n}(\sin x_0)^{2n}$$

and if

$$\frac{2k-1}{2s+1}\frac{\pi}{2} < x_0, \qquad \sin\left(\frac{2k-1}{2s+1}\frac{\pi}{2}\right) \Big/ \left(\frac{2k-1}{2s+1}\frac{\pi}{2}\right) > \alpha$$

and consequently

$$(2s)^{2n}\sin^{2n}\left(\frac{2k-1}{2s+1}\frac{\pi}{2}\right) > (\alpha 2s)^{2n}\left(\frac{2k-1}{2s+1}\frac{\pi}{2}\right)^{2n}.$$

So, whatever k may be

$$\left[(2s)^{2n}\sin^{2n}\left(\frac{2k-1}{2s+1}\frac{\pi}{2}\right)\right]^{-1} < [(2s)^{2n}\sin^{2n}x_0]^{-1} + \left[(\alpha 2s)^{2n}\left(\frac{2k-1}{2s+1}\frac{\pi}{2}\right)^{2n}\right]^{-1}.$$

Let us choose K such that $\sum_{k=K}^{\infty}(2k-1)^{-2} < \varepsilon'$. Whatever n may be, we have for $s > K$ as $2/\pi\alpha < 1$

$$\sum_{k=K}^{s}\left[(2s)^{2n}\sin^{2n}\left(\frac{2k-1}{2s+1}\frac{\pi}{2}\right)\right]^{-1} < [(2s)^{2n}\sin^{2n}x_0]^{-1}s + \left(\frac{2s+1}{2s}\right)^{2n}\varepsilon'.$$

And so for $s > S_1 > K$ (S_1 independent of n)

$$\sum_{k=K}^{s}\left[(2s)^{2n}\sin^{2n}\left(\frac{2k-1}{2s+1}\frac{\pi}{2}\right)\right]^{-1} < \varepsilon' + \varepsilon'(1+\varepsilon')^{2n},$$

and

$$\left|\sum_{k=1}^{s}\left[(2s)^{2n}\sin^{2n}\left(\frac{2k-1}{2s+1}\frac{\pi}{2}\right)\right]^{-1} - \sum_{k=1}^{\infty}\left[(2k-1)\frac{\pi}{2}\right]^{-2n}\right|$$

$$< \left|\sum_{k=1}^{K}\left[(2s)^{2n}\sin^{2n}\left(\frac{2k-1}{2s+1}\frac{\pi}{2}\right)\right]^{-1} - \sum_{k=1}^{K}\left[(2k-1)\frac{\pi}{2}\right]^{-2n}\right| + 2\varepsilon' + \varepsilon'(1+\varepsilon')^{2n}. \tag{1}$$

Let us have $S_2 > S_1$ such that $k < K$ and $s > S_2$ implies

$$(1+\varepsilon')^{-1} < 2s\sin\left(\frac{2k-1}{2s+1}\frac{\pi}{2}\right)\left[(2k-1)\frac{\pi}{2}\right]^{-1} < 1.$$

We have

$$\sum_{k=1}^{K}\left[(2s)^{2n}\sin^{2n}\left(\frac{2k-1}{2s+1}\frac{\pi}{2}\right)\right]^{-1} - \sum_{k=1}^{K}\left[(2k-1)\frac{\pi}{2}\right]^{-2n}$$

$$< [(1+\varepsilon')^{2n}-1]\sum_{k=1}^{K}\left[(2k-1)\frac{\pi}{2}\right]^{-2n}$$

and consequently

$$\sum_{k=1}^{K}\left[(2s)^{2n}\sin^{2n}\left(\frac{2k-1}{2s+1}\frac{\pi}{2}\right)\right]^{-1} - \sum_{k=1}^{K}\left[(2k-1)\frac{\pi}{2}\right]^{-2n} < Bn\varepsilon'(1+\varepsilon')^{2n-1}. \tag{2}$$

Taking ε' conveniently we get the formula (A) from the inequalities (1) and (2). From (A), it results that for $s > S$ independent of n we have

$$\left| \alpha_{n,s} - 2\sum_{k=1}^{\infty} [(2k-1)(\pi/2)]^{-(2n+2)} \right| < \varepsilon + n B\varepsilon(1+\varepsilon)^n \quad (B \text{ independent of } n).$$

Consequently for $|v| < 1$, the limit of $s^{-1}\,{}^tT_s[I_s - (2iv/s^2)B_s]^{-1}T_s$ is

$$\sum_{n=0}^{+\infty} (2iv)^n \left[2\sum_{k=1}^{\infty} [(2k-1)(\pi/2)]^{-(2n+2)} \right].$$

According to the analytic properties of the characteristic functions this limit is attained for any real v. So

$$2\sum_{k=1}^{\infty} [(2k-1)(\pi/2)]^{-(2n+2)} = \sum_{k=\infty}^{+\infty} [(2k-1)(\pi/2)]^{-(2n+2)}.$$

We know that

$$\sum_{n=-\infty}^{\infty} (n+z)^{-2} = \pi^2(\sin^2 \pi z)^{-1};$$

$$\frac{d^{2p}}{dz^{2p}} \sum_{n=-\infty}^{+\infty} (n+z)^{-2} = (2p+1)! \sum_{n=-\infty}^{+\infty} (n+z)^{-2p-2}.$$

and

$$\sum_{n=-\infty}^{+\infty} (n - \tfrac{1}{2})^{-(2p+2)} = [(2p+1)!]^{-1} \left[\frac{d^{2p}}{dz^{2p}} \left(\frac{\pi^2}{\sin^2 \pi z} \right) \right]_{z=-1/2}$$

$$= \frac{\pi^{2p}}{(2p+1)!} \left[\frac{d^{2p}}{d\pi z^{2p}} \left(\frac{\pi^2}{\sin^2 \pi z} \right) \right]_{\pi z = -\pi/2}.$$

So

$$\sum_{-\infty}^{+\infty} [(n - \tfrac{1}{2})^{2p+2} \pi^{2p+2}]^{-1} = [(2p+1)!]^{-1} \left[\frac{d^{2p}}{du^{2p}} \frac{1}{\sin^2 u} \right]_{u=-\pi/2}.$$

And then

$$\lim_{s\to\infty} s^{-1}\,{}^tT_s[I_s - (2iv/s^2)B_s]^{-1}\, T_s = \sum_{p=0}^{+\infty} \frac{(2iv)^p}{(2p+1)!} \left[\frac{d^{2p}}{dv^{2p}} \frac{1}{\sin^2 v} \right]_{v=-\pi/2}$$

$$= \sum_{p=0}^{+\infty} \frac{(2iv)^p}{(2p+1)!} \left[\frac{d^{2p}}{dv^{2p}} \frac{1}{\cos^2 v} \right]_{v=0}$$

$$= \sum_{p=0}^{+\infty} \frac{(2iv)^p}{(2p+1)!} \left[\frac{d^{2p+1}}{dv^{2p+1}} \tan v \right]_{v=0}$$

$$= \frac{\tan(2iv)^{1/2}}{(2iv)^{1/2}}.$$

The characteristic function we are looking for is, therefore,

$$[\cos(2iv)^{1/2}]^{-1/2} \exp\left(-\frac{u^2}{2}\frac{\tan(2iv)^{1/2}}{(2iv)^{1/2}}\right).$$

Each of the marginal laws, the characteristic functions of which are $[\cos(2iv)^{1/2}]^{-1/2}$ and $\exp(-u^2/2)$ are infinitely divisible. It is a problem whether the law of both variables is infinitely divisible. There is an argument against this assumption. It is easy to show that the law is the sum of a series of independent laws each one being indecomposable. For we have

$$[\cos(2iv)^{1/2}]^{-1/2} \exp\left(-\frac{u^2}{2}\frac{\tan(2iv)^{1/2}}{(2iv)^{1/2}}\right)$$

$$= \prod_{n=1}^{\infty} \exp\{-u^2/[(n-\tfrac{1}{2})^2\pi^2 - 2iv]\}\{[1-(2iv/(n-\tfrac{1}{2})^2\pi^2)]^{1/2}\}^{-1}.$$

The general term of this infinite product is the characteristic function of two variables $\sqrt{2}\,X$ and X^2, X being a Gaussian random variable of zero mean and standard deviation $1/(n-\frac{1}{2})\pi$. The support of the probability of this pair is in R^2 the curve $y = x^2/2$, which cannot be the closure of the vectorial sum of two sets. This is sufficient to show that the pair is indecomposable even if the two margins are infinitely divisible. Now we shall find the characteristic function of X^2 and Y. We have

$$E[\exp(iuX^2 + ivY)] = \lim_{s\to\infty} E[\exp(iu\,{}^tZ_s M_s Z_s + i(v/s)^t Z_s B_s Z_s)]$$

$$= \lim_{s\to\infty} [(2\pi)^{s/2}(\det C_s)^{1/2}]^{-1} \int \text{ex}\{-\tfrac{1}{2}\,{}^tZ_s[C_s^{-1} - 2iuM_s - (2iv/s)B_s]Z_s\}\, dZ_s$$

$$= \lim_{s\to\infty}[\det(I_s - (2iu/s)M_s - (2iv/s^2)B_s)]^{-1/2}.$$

The diagonalization of B_s by S_s gives

$$E[\exp(iuX^2 + ivY)] = \lim[\det(I_s - (2iu/s)N_s - (2iv/s^2)D_s)]^{-1/2}.$$

The expansion of the determinant by the method of polynomial columns, N_s being of rank 1, gives

$$\det\left[I_s - \frac{2iu}{s}N_s - \frac{2iv}{s^2}D_s\right] = \prod_{k=1}^{s}\left[1 - \frac{2iv}{s^2 z_k}\right]\left[1 - \sum_{k=1}^{s}\frac{\frac{2iu}{s}n_k}{1-\frac{2iv}{s^2 z_k}}\right].$$

After Cameron and Martin [1],

$$\lim_{s\to\infty}\prod_{k=1}^{s}\left(1-\frac{2iv}{s^2 z_k}\right) = \cos(2iv)^{1/2},$$

and we have

$$\sum_{k=1}^{s} \frac{\dfrac{2iu}{s} n_k}{1 - \dfrac{2iv}{s^2 z_k}} = \sum_{k=1}^{s} \frac{\dfrac{2iu}{s} \dfrac{1}{2s+1} \left[\dfrac{4}{z_k} - 1\right]}{1 - \dfrac{2iv}{s^2 z_k}},$$

with s increasing indefinitely and k being fixed, $s^2 z_k$ tends toward $(2k-1)^2(\pi^2/4) = u_k$. Let us consider in the complex plane the domain interior to a circle of center 0 and radius R, and exterior to all the circles of centers u_k having an arbitrarily small radius. It is clear that if $2iv$ is in this domain, s being sufficiently large,

$$\left| \frac{s^2 z_k}{s^2 z_k - 2iv} \right| < M \qquad \text{and so} \qquad [s(2s+1)]^{-1} \sum_{k=1}^{s} \left(1 - \frac{2iv}{s^2 z_k}\right)^{-1}$$

tends toward 0. We have

$$\sum_{k=1}^{s} \frac{\dfrac{2iu}{s(2s+1)} \dfrac{4}{z_k}}{1 - \dfrac{2iv}{s^2 z_k}} = - \frac{4s^2}{s(2s+1)} \sum_{k=1}^{s} \frac{-\dfrac{2iu}{s^2 z_k}}{1 - \dfrac{2iv}{s^2 z_k}}$$

$$= - \frac{4s^2}{s(2s+1)} u \frac{d}{dv} \log \prod_{k=1}^{s} \left(1 - \frac{2iv}{s^2 z_k}\right),$$

and

$$\lim_{s \to \infty} \sum_{k=1}^{s} \frac{\dfrac{2iu}{s(2s+1)} \dfrac{4}{z_k}}{1 - \dfrac{2iv}{s^2 z_k}} = 2iu \frac{\tan(2iv)^{1/2}}{(2iv)^{1/2}}.$$

So

$$E[\exp(iuX^2 + ivY)] = [\cos(2iv)^{1/2}]^{-1/2} \left\{1 - 2iu \frac{\tan(2iv)^{1/2}}{(2iv)^{1/2}}\right\}^{-1/2}$$

It is clear that the law of X^2/Y is nonparametric.

2. MULTIDIMENSIONAL VON MISES ω_n^2

Let us call $I_n(x_1, \ldots, x_p)$ the histogram of frequency in R^p of n results, each of the components $x_1, \ldots, x_p$ having a continuous cumulative distribution function $F_i(x_i)$, the p components being mutually independent. Let us consider

$$Y_n = n \int_{-\infty}^{+\infty} \cdots \int_{-\infty}^{+\infty} [I_n(x_1, \ldots, x_p) - F_1(x_1) \cdots F_p(x_p)]^2 \, dF_1(x_1) \cdots dF_p(x_p).$$

The limit law of Y_n is a generalization of the von Mises $\omega_n{}^2$ in R^p. It is easy to show that whatever may be the continuous $F_1, \ldots, F_p$, the law of Y_n is the same as that of

$$X_n = n \int_0^1 \cdots \int_0^1 [H_n(x_1, \ldots, x_p) - x_1 \ldots x_p]^2 \, dx_1 \cdots dx_p,$$

and H_n being the histogram of frequency in the p-cube C of sides 0, 1 of n variables with each component being equidistributed, all the components are mutually independent. Let us divide, in s equal parts, the sides of the p-cube C which gives s^p elementary subcubes, and call $C_{x_1, \ldots, x_p}$ the elementary p cube whose sides are

$$\left(\frac{x_1 - 1}{s}, \frac{x_1}{s}\right), \ldots, \left(\frac{x_p - 1}{s}, \frac{x_p}{s}\right) \qquad \text{with} \quad x_1, \ldots, x_p = 1, \ldots, s,$$

The number of results in $C_{x_1, \ldots, x_p}$ will be $n_{x_1, \ldots, x_p}$. The random variable with s^p components

$$z_{x_1, \ldots, x_p} = \sqrt{n}\left[\frac{n_{x_1, \ldots, x_p}}{n} - \frac{1}{s^p}\right]$$

legally converges in law, when n increases indefinitely, towards the s-dimensional Gaussian variable whose mean is zero and whose covariance matrix $(s^{-p} I_s^{\otimes p} - s^{-2p} M_s^{\otimes p})$ where $I^{\otimes p}$ is the pth tensorial power of I_s and $M_s^{\otimes p}$ the same for M_s. Here $M_s^{\otimes p}$ is of rank 1, and $(s^{-p} I_s^{\otimes p} - s^{-2p} M_s^{\otimes p})$ is of rank $s^p - 1$. Now put Z, a vector, in R^{s^p} whose coordonates are $z_{x_1, \ldots, x_p}$ ranked in the same increasing order as the numbers $x_p x_{p-1} \cdots x_1$ written in the system of base $s + 1$. As shown by Dugue [2], X_n will be the limit of the quadratic form $s^{-p}\, {}^t Z B_s^{\otimes p} Z$. Under these conditions the characteristic function of the limit of X_n will be the limit of

$$\{\det[I_s^{\otimes p} - (2iu/s^p) B_s^{\otimes p}(s^{-p} I_s^{\otimes p} - s^{-2p} M_s^{\otimes p})]\}^{-1/2},$$

as shown by ordinary calculus. If we diagonalize B_s using S_s, we get for the determinant

$$\det[I_s^{\otimes p} - (2iu/s^{2p}) D_s^{\otimes p}(I_s^{\otimes p} - s^{-p} N_s{}^{\otimes p})],$$

and $N_s^{\otimes p}$ has a rank equal to 1, like N_s and M_s. $D_s^{\otimes p}$ is diagonal and its diagonal elements are the s^p products $(z_{i_1} z_{i_2} \cdots z_{i_p})^{-1}$ $(i_1, i_2, \ldots, i_p = 1, 2, \ldots, s)$, the diagonal elements of $N_s^{\otimes p}$ being $n_{i_1} n_{i_2} \cdots n_{i_p}$. Expanding the determinant by the method of polynomials columns, we find

$$\det[I_s^{\otimes p} - (2iu/s^{2p})\, D_s^{\otimes p}(I_s^{\otimes p} - s^{-p}\, N_s^{\otimes p})]$$

$$= \prod_{i_1, \ldots, i_p = 1, \ldots s} \left(1 - \frac{2iu}{s^{2p} z_{i_1} \cdots z_{i_p}}\right)$$

$$\times \left[1 + \sum_{i_1, \ldots, i_p = 1, \ldots, s} \left(\frac{2iu}{s^{3p}} \frac{n_{i_1} \cdots n_{i_p}}{z_{i_1} \cdots z_{i_p}}\right)\left(1 - \frac{2iu}{s^{2p} z_{i_1} \cdots z_{i_p}}\right)^{-1}\right].$$

Let us replace 1 by $[\sum_{i=1}^{s} n_i/s]^p$ in the last set of brackets. This expression will be equal to

$$\sum_{i_1,\ldots,i_p=1,\ldots,s} \left(\frac{n_{i_1}}{s} \cdots \frac{n_{i_p}}{s}\right)\left(1 - \frac{2iu}{s^{2p} z_{i_1} \cdots z_{i_p}}\right)^{-1}.$$

We have

$$(n_{i_1}/s) \cdots (n_{i_p}/s) = [s(2s+1)]^{-p} [(4/z_{i_1}) - 1] \cdots [(4/z_{i_p}) - 1].$$

So

$$\sum_{i_1,\ldots,i_p=1,\ldots,s} \left(\frac{n_{i_1}}{s} \cdots \frac{n_{i_p}}{s}\right)\left(1 - \frac{2iu}{s^{2p} z_{i_1} \cdots z_{i_p}}\right)^{-1}$$

will be the sum of 2^p sums of the form

$$\frac{(-1)^{p-k} 4^k}{[s(2s+1)]^p} \sum_{i_1,\ldots,i_p=1,\ldots,s} \frac{s^{2p} z_{i_1} \cdots z_{i_p}}{s^{2p} z_{i_1} \cdots z_{i_p} - 2iu} \frac{1}{z_{i_1}} \cdots \frac{1}{z_{ik}}.$$

Since $2iu$ is interior to a circle of center 0 and radius R, and exterior to circles of centers $(2k_1 - 1)^2(\pi/2)^2 \cdots (2k_p - 1)^2(\pi/2)^2$ and of radius arbitrarily small we have

$$\left| \frac{s^{2p} z_{i_1} \cdots z_{i_p}}{s^{2p} z_{i_1} \cdots z_{i_p} - 2iu} \right| < M,$$

and as $\sum_{i=1}^{s} z_i^{-1} = s(s+1)/2$ and naturally $\sum_{i=1}^{s} 1_i = s$

$$\left| \frac{4^k}{[s(2s+1)]^p} \sum_{i_1 \ldots i_p=1,\ldots,s} \frac{s^{2p} z_{i_1} \cdots z_{i_p}}{s^{2p} z_{i_1} \cdots z_{i_p} - 2iu} \frac{1}{z_{i_1}} \cdots \frac{1}{z_{i_p}} \right|$$
$$< \frac{4^k M s^{p-k}}{(s(2s+1))^p} \left[\frac{s(s+1)}{2}\right]^k.$$

This sum tends toward 0 with s^{-1} for $k = 0, 1, \ldots, p-1$. And so

$$\lim_{s\to\infty} 1 + \sum_{i_1,\ldots,i_p=1,\ldots,s} \left(\frac{2iu}{s^{3p}} \frac{n_{i_1}}{z_{i_1}} \cdots \frac{n_{i_p}}{z_{i_p}}\right)\left(1 - \frac{2iu}{s^{2p} z_{i_1} \cdots z_{i_p}}\right)^{-1}$$
$$= \lim_{s\to\infty} \frac{4^p s^{2p}}{[s(2s+1)]^p} \sum_{i_1,\ldots,i_p=1,\ldots,s} (s^{2p} z_{i_1} \cdots z_{i_p})^{-1} \left(1 - \frac{2iu}{s^{2p} z_{i_1} \cdots z_{i_p}}\right)^{-1}$$
$$= -2^p \frac{d}{d2iu} \lim_{s\to\infty} \log \prod_{i_1,\ldots,i_p=1,\ldots,s} \left(1 - \frac{2iu}{s^{2p} z_{i_1}, \ldots, z_{i_p}}\right).$$

So

$$\lim_{s\to\infty} \det\left[I_s^{\otimes p} - \frac{2iu}{s^{2p}} D_s^{\otimes p}[I_s^{\otimes p} - s^{-p} N_s^{\otimes p}]\right]$$
$$= i2^{p-1} \frac{d}{du} \lim \prod_{i_1,\ldots,i_p=1,\ldots,s} \left(1 - \frac{2iu}{s^{2p} z_{i_1}, \ldots, z_{i_p}}\right).$$

Going back to the notations of the beginning of paragraph 2 and putting $\phi_{(p)}(t) = (C_{(p)}(t))^{-1/2}$, we have

$$\lim_{s\to\infty} E(e^{iuY_n}) = [i2^{p-1}\, d/du\, C_{(p)}(u)]^{-1/2}.$$

In the case of $p = 1$, $C_{(p)}(u) = \cos(2iu)^{1/2}$, and we find the von Mises-Smirnov formula $\lim_{s\to\infty} E(e^{iuY_n}) = [i(d/du)\cos(2iu)^{1/2}]^{-1/2} = [(2iu)^{1/2}/\sin(2iu)^{1/2}]^{1/2}$. We have a Laguerrian type theorem about $d/du C_{(p)}(u)$.

Theorem 2. *All the zeros of $C_{(p)}(u)$ are on the half straight line $Ru = 0$, $Iu \le 0$.*

It is an immediate consequence of:

Lemma 1. *If B and A are two Hermitian, definite positive matrices, B^{-1} existing, BA has all its eigenvalues real and positive.*

Thus if X is an eigenvector of BA, we have $BAX = \lambda X$ and so $AX = \lambda B^{-1}X$ and ${}^tXAX = \lambda{}^tXB^{-1}X$, which proves Lemma 1, since B^{-1} is Hermitian and positive definite. Theorem 2 is a consequence since the zeros of $(d/du)C_{(p)}(u)$ are the limits of $s^{2p}/2i\lambda$, λ being an eigenvalue of

$$B_s^{\otimes p}[I_s^{\otimes p} - s^{-p}M_s^{\otimes p}].$$

From this the theorem is established. A consequence is the infinite divisibility of the law of Y_n because (a) The term $C_{(p)}$ is an integral function of order less than one which has as a consequence that $(d/du)C_{(p)}(u)$ is an integral function of order less than one. (b) The zeros of $(d/du)C_{(p)}(u)$ are on the pure imaginary axis.

3. TWO VARIABLES IN UNIDIMENSIONAL BROWNIAN MOTION

Let us now consider a histogram of n results of variables of an equi-distribution between 0 and 1 sample, H_n.

Put

$$X_n = n\int_0^{1/2} [H_n(x) - x]^2\, dx \qquad \text{and} \qquad Y_n = n\int_{1/2}^{1} [H_n(x) - x]^2\, dx$$

and get $\lim_{n\to\infty} E[e^{iuX_n + ivY_n}]$. Divide the side (0, 1) in $2s$ equal parts and put

$$x_k = \sqrt{n}[H_n(k/2s) - H_n((k-1)/2s) - (1/2s)], \qquad k = 1, \ldots, 2s \qquad \text{and}$$
$$X = (x_1, \ldots, x_s, x_{2s}, x_{2s-1}, \ldots, x_{s+1}).$$

It is easily seen that when n increases indefinitely, the vector X tends in law toward a Gaussian vector of mean zero and of covariance matrix

$$((2s)^{-1}I_{2s} - (4s^2)^{-1}M_{2s}) = ((2s)^{-1}I_s \otimes I_2 - (4s^2)^{-1}M_s \otimes M_2).$$

We have

$$X_n = \lim_{s\to\infty} (2s)^{-1}[x_1{}^2 + (x_1 + x_2)^2 + \cdots + (x_1 + \cdots + x_s)^2],$$

and

$$Y_n = \lim_{s\to\infty} (2s)^{-1}[x_{2s}^2 + (x_{2s} + x_{2s-1})^2 + \cdots + (x_{2s} + \cdots + x_{s+1})^2].$$

Call α the matrix $\begin{pmatrix}1 & 0\\ 0 & 0\end{pmatrix}$ and β the matrix $\begin{pmatrix}0 & 0\\ 0 & 1\end{pmatrix}$. We have

$$X_n = \lim_{s\to\infty} (2s)^{-1}\,{}^tXB_s \otimes \alpha X \qquad \text{and} \qquad Y_n = \lim_{s\to\infty} (2s)^{-1}\,{}^tXB_s \otimes \beta X.$$

So we have to look for

$$\lim_{s\to\infty} E\left[\exp\left(i\frac{u}{2s}\,{}^tXB_s \otimes \alpha X + i\frac{v}{2s}\,{}^tXB_s \otimes \beta X\right)\right],$$

with X being Gaussian and having the covariance matrix

$$((2s)^{-1}I_s \otimes I_2 - (4s)^{-1}M_s \otimes M_2).$$

This characteristic function is

$$\lim_{s\to\infty} \{\det[I_s \otimes I_2] - (2iu/4s^2)[B_s \otimes \alpha][I_s \otimes I_2 - (2s)^{-1}M_s \otimes M_2]$$
$$- (2iv/4s^2)[B_s \otimes \beta][I_s \otimes I_2 - (2s)^{-1}M_s \otimes M_2]\}^{-1/2}.$$

Diagonalize B_s by the mean of S_s, we have with the preceeding notations multiplying on the right by $S_s^{-1} \otimes I_2$, and on the left by $S_s \otimes I_2$.

$$\lim_{s\to\infty} E[\exp(iuX_n + ivY_n)]$$
$$= \lim_{s\to\infty} \{\det[I_s \otimes I_2] - (2iu/4s^2)[D_s \otimes \alpha - (2s)^{-1}D_sN_s \otimes \alpha M_2]$$
$$- (2iv/4s^2)[D_s \otimes \beta - (2s)^{-1}D_sN_s \otimes \beta M_2]\}^{-1/2}.$$

Put

$$\gamma = \alpha M_2 = \begin{pmatrix}1 & 1\\ 0 & 0\end{pmatrix} \qquad \text{and} \qquad \delta = \beta M_2 = \begin{pmatrix}0 & 0\\ 1 & 1\end{pmatrix}.$$

The matrix $D_s \otimes \alpha$ will be a diagonal $2s \times 2s$ matrix in which the s first diagonal elements are those of D_s, the other diagonal elements being 0. The matrices $D_sN_s \otimes \gamma$ and $D_sN_s \otimes \delta$ will be of rank 1. The matrix $D_sN_s \otimes \gamma$ will be a $2s \times 2s$ matrix such that in the upper left corner, we find D_sN_s, in the upper right corner the same matrix; and in the other two corners, we have the null matrix. We have an analogous form for $D_s N_s \otimes \delta$. Again using the polynomial column method, we first find

$$\prod_{i=1}^{s}\left(1-\frac{2iu}{4s^2 z_i}\right)\prod_{i=1}^{s}\left(1-\frac{2iv}{4s^2 z_i}\right),$$

and taking each column of $D_s N_s \otimes \gamma$ and $D_s N_s \otimes \delta$, we have a sum of terms of the form

$$\prod_{i=1}^{s}\left(1-\frac{2iu}{4s^2 z_i}\right)\prod_{i=1}^{s}\left(1-\frac{2iv}{4s^2 z_i}\right)\frac{\dfrac{2iun_j}{8s^3 z_j}}{1-\dfrac{2iu}{4s^2 z_j}}$$

and analogous terms in v. Finally, the determinant is equal to

$$\prod_{i=1}^{s}\left(1-\frac{2iu}{4s^3 z_i}\right)\prod_{i=1}^{s}\left(1-\frac{2iv}{4s^3 z_i}\right)\left[1+\sum_{j=1}^{s}\frac{\dfrac{2iun_j}{8s^3 z_j}}{1-\dfrac{2iu}{4s^2 z_i}}+\sum_{j=1}^{s}\frac{\dfrac{2ivn_j}{8s^3 z_j}}{1-\dfrac{2iv}{4s^2 z_j}}\right].$$

As $(n_1+\cdots+n_s)/s=1$, you can write it as

$$\prod_{i=1}^{s}\left(1-\frac{2iu}{4s^2 z}\right)\prod_{i=1}^{s}\left(1-\frac{2iv}{4s^2 z_i}\right)\left[\sum_{j=1}^{s}\frac{\dfrac{n_j}{2s}}{1-\dfrac{2iu}{4s^2 z_j}}+\sum_{j=1}^{s}\frac{\dfrac{n_j}{2s}}{1-\dfrac{2iv}{4s^2 z_j}}\right];$$

and $\prod_{i=1}^{s}(1-2iu/s^2 z)$ tends toward $\cos(2iu)^{1/2}$, with s increasing indefinitely. As we saw at the end of paragraph 1

$$\sum_{k=1}^{s}\frac{\dfrac{2iu}{s}n_k}{1-\dfrac{2iv}{s^2 z_k}}$$

tends in the same conditions toward $2iu[\tan(2iv)^{1/2}]/(2iv)^{1/2}$. So we have

$$\lim_{n\to\infty} E[\exp(iuX_n+ivY_n)]$$

$$=\left\{\cos(\tfrac{1}{2}iu)^{1/2}\cos(\tfrac{1}{2}iv)^{1/2}\left(\frac{\tan(\frac{1}{2}iu)^{1/2}}{2(\frac{1}{2}iu)^{1/2}}+\frac{\tan(\frac{1}{2}iv)^{1/2}}{2(\frac{1}{2}iv)^{1/2}}\right)\right\}^{-1/2}.$$

The characteristic function of X_n+Y_n tends toward $[(2it)^{1/2}/\sin(2it)^{1/2}]^{1/2}$.

That is the Smirnov result. This law is infinitely divisible. So are the margin laws whose characteristic functions are

$$[\tfrac{1}{2}(\cos(\tfrac{1}{2}it)^{1/2} + \sin(\tfrac{1}{2}it)^{1/2}/(\tfrac{1}{2}it)^{1/2})]^{-1/2}.$$

In this second case, we can wonder whether the joint law is indefinitely divisible. This time it seems to me a likely result.

REFERENCES

1. Cameron, R. H., and Martin, W. T. (1944). The Wiener's measure of Hilbert neighborhood in the space of real continuous functions. *J. Massachusetts Inst. Technol.* **23** 195–209.
2. Dugue, D. (1967). Fonctions caracteristique d'integrales Browniennes. *Revue Roumaine Math. Pures Appl.* **12** 1207–1215.
3. Dugue, D. (1968). Valeurs propres de matrices jouant un role important dans l'etude d'integrales Browniennes. *Rev. Inst. Internat. Statist.* To be published.

Some Recent Developments in the Theory of Multivariate Characteristic Functions

EUGENE LUKACS[1]

STATISTICAL LABORATORY
THE CATHOLIC UNIVERSITY OF AMERICA
WASHINGTON, D.C.

1. INTRODUCTION

In his famous treatise, Laplace introduced the concept of generating functions and employed these functions as an extremely useful tool in his investigations. His idea was adopted by subsequent mathematicians; the term characteristic function was apparently coined by Poincaré and originally denoted the expectation $\mathscr{E}(e^{tX})$. The method was still subject to a severe limitation since the expectation $\mathscr{E}(e^{tX})$ does not exist for all random variables X. Paul Lévy removed this limitation by modifying the definition and using $\mathscr{E}(e^{itX})$ as the characteristic function of the random variable X. Since e^{itX} is always bounded, the characteristic function exists for all random variables and is, therefore, a universally applicable tool. Characteristic functions were first employed to study the limit theorems of probability theory but later were also used in connection with other problems. Moreover, it soon became clear that the theory of characteristic functions has an independent mathematical interest and leads to many remarkable problems requiring attractive methods for their solution. The interest presented by this branch of probability theory is evidenced by the number of books [26, 27, 24, 41] that were published on this subject during the last few years.

These books, as well as most of the papers on the subject, deal with characteristic functions of one variable. While some of the basic concepts and theorems were derived at an early date for the univariate as well as for the multivariate case, the later developments were restricted to univariate problems. This is particularly true for the arithmetic of distribution functions. Only recently did one succeed in deriving the theory of multivariate analytic

[1] Research supported by the Air Force Office of Scientific Research, Office of Aerospace Research, United States Air Force under AFOSR grant AF-AFOSR-437-65.

characteristic functions. This theory could then be used to extend the arithmetic of distribution functions to the multivariate case.

In this paper, we survey these developments: in Section 2, we briefly discuss some classical results; Section 3 deals with multivariate analytic characteristic functions; Section 4 is devoted to certain results in the arithmetic of distribution functions. Section 5 treats a generalization of the decomposition theorems of Section 4 while a variety of problems (boundary characteristic functions, special multivariate distributions, and characterization problems) are discussed in Section 6.

2. SOME CLASSICAL RESULTS ON MULTIVARIATE CHARACTERISTIC FUNCTIONS

In this paper, we study Fourier transforms of probability measures in n-dimensional space and shall use the following notations. We write R_n for the real and C_n for the complex n-dimensional space. Let $\mathbf{x} = (x_1, x_2, \ldots, x_n)$ and $\mathbf{y} = (y_1, y_2, \ldots, y_n)$ be points (vectors) of R_n; we denote by $\mathbf{xy} = \sum_{j=1}^{n} x_j y_j$ the inner (scalar) product of $\mathbf{x}$ and $\mathbf{y}$. If $\mathbf{x} \in C_n$, we write $\operatorname{Re} \mathbf{x} = (\operatorname{Re} x_1, \operatorname{Re} x_2, \ldots, \operatorname{Re} x_n)$, and $\operatorname{Im} \mathbf{x} = (\operatorname{Im} x_1, \operatorname{Im} x_2, \ldots, \operatorname{Im} x_n)$; here, $\operatorname{Re} x_j$ (resp. $\operatorname{Im} x_j$) mean the real (resp. imaginary) part of the complex number x_j. We also introduce the following symbols:

$$|\mathbf{x}| = (\mathbf{xx})^{1/2} \quad \text{if} \quad x \in R_n \quad \text{and} \quad |\mathbf{x}| = (|\operatorname{Re} \mathbf{x}|^2 + |\operatorname{Im} \mathbf{x}|^2)^{1/2} \quad \text{if} \quad \mathbf{x} \in C_n.$$

We consider the family $\mathfrak{B}_n$ of Borel sets of R_n and probability measures[2] P defined on $\mathfrak{B}_n$. The characteristic function of a probability measure P is defined by

$$f(\mathbf{t}) = f(t_1, t_2, \ldots, t_n) = \int_{R_n} e^{i\mathbf{tx}} \, dP \qquad (\mathbf{t} \in R_n). \tag{2.1}$$

In the following, we denote probability measures by italic capital letters P, Q, R, and their characteristic functions by lower case italic letters f, g, h. If a subscript is used on the symbol for a probability measure, then the same subscript is attached to its characteristic function.

Many of the results concerning univariate distributions and characteristic functions can be carried over to the multivariate case. Thus $f(\mathbf{t})$ is a complex valued function of the real variables $t_1, t_2, \ldots, t_n$ which is uniformly continuous and which satisfies the conditions

$$|f(\mathbf{t})| \le f(\mathbf{0}) = 1, \qquad f(-\mathbf{t}) = \overline{f(\mathbf{t})}.$$

Here, we write $\mathbf{0} = (0, 0, \ldots, 0)$ for the origin of R_n and use the horizontal bar to denote the complex conjugate. Bochner's theorem, which states that a

[2] A nonnegative, countably additive set function P defined on $\mathfrak{B}_n$ is said to be a probability measure if $P(R_n) = 1$.

function $f(\mathbf{t})$ is a characteristic function if, and only if, it is positive definite, continuous at $\mathbf{0}$, and if $f(\mathbf{0}) = 1$ is also valid for characteristic functions defined on R_n.

Next, we list some important theorems on characteristic functions which can be extended to the multivariate case.

Theorem 2.1 (Uniqueness theorem). *Two characteristic functions* $f_1(\mathbf{t})$ *and* $f_2(\mathbf{t})$ *are identical if, and only if, the corresponding probability measures* P_1 *and* P_2 *are identical.*

We also note that an inversion formula holds which determines a probability measure in terms of its characteristic function.

Theorem 2.2 (Convolution theorem). *A probability measure* P *is the convolution of two probability measures* P_1 *and* P_2, *that is*

$$P(A) = \int_{R_n} P_1(A - \mathbf{x})\, dP_2 = \int_{R_n} P_2(A - \mathbf{x})\, dP_1 = P_2 {}^* P_1$$

if, and only if, the relation

$$f(\mathbf{t}) = f_1(\mathbf{t}) f_2(\mathbf{t})$$

holds for the corresponding characteristic functions. Here, $A - \mathbf{x}$ *is the set of all points*[3] $\mathbf{a} - \mathbf{x}$ *where* $\mathbf{a} \in A$.

Theorem 2.3 (Continuity theorem). *Let* $\{P_k\}$ *be a sequence of probability measures and* $[f_k]$ *be the corresponding sequence of characteristic functions. The sequence* P_k *converges weakly*[4] *to a probability measure* P *if, and only if, the sequence* f_k *converges to a function* f *which is continuous at the origin. The function* f *is then the characteristic function of the probability measure* P.

The connection between the existence of the moments and the differentiability of characteristic functions is similar in the univariate and in the multivariate case. It is possible to express the moments of an n-dimensional probability measure in terms of the derivatives of its characteristic function at the origin.

Next, we mention an important theorem which makes it possible to derive certain multivariate theorems from the corresponding univariate statements.

[3] If

$$\mathbf{a} = (a_1, a_2, \ldots, a_n) \text{ and } \mathbf{x} = (x_1, x_2, \ldots, x_n),$$

then

$$\mathbf{a} - \mathbf{x} = (a_1 - x_1, a_2 - x_2, \ldots, a_n - x_n).$$

[4] A sequence P_k is said to converge weakly to a probability measure P if it converges on all continuity sets of P. A set A is said to be a continuity set of the measure P if the P-measure of its interior equals the P-measure of its closure.

Let P be a probability measure and $\mathbf{t} \in R_n$, and suppose that $\mathbf{t} \neq \mathbf{0}$ is a fixed point. The set of all points $\mathbf{x} \in R_n$ which satisfy the inequality

$$\mathbf{xt} \leq u$$

forms a half-space $A_{\mathbf{t},u}$. It is easily seen that

$$G_{\mathbf{t}}(u) = P(A_{\mathbf{t},u})$$

is a distribution function.

The (univariate) probability measure determined by $G_{\mathbf{t}}(u)$ is called the projection of the multivariate distribution P on the vector $\mathbf{t}$. It is a univariate distribution function. The characteristic function of $G_{\mathbf{t}}(u)$ is

$$g_{\mathbf{t}}(v) = \int_{-\infty}^{\infty} e^{iuv}\, dG_{\mathbf{t}}(u) = \int_{R_n} \exp(iv\mathbf{xt})\, dP.$$

Theorem 2.4. *Suppose that two probability measures P_1 and P_2 have the same projections on every vector $\mathbf{t} \neq \mathbf{0}$, then P_1 and P_2 are identical.*

Proofs of Theorems 2.1–2.4 may be found in the work of Cramér [2 or 3].

Limit theorems for random vectors were also studied at an early date and led to the introduction of the concept of infinitely divisible characteristic functions. A characteristic function $f(\mathbf{t})$ is said to be infinitely divisible, if for every positive integer n, there exists a characteristic function $f_n(\mathbf{t})$ such that

$$f(\mathbf{t}) = [f_n(\mathbf{t})]^n.$$

Infinitely divisible characteristic functions admit, as in the univariate case, canonical representations. Lévy ([20], pp. 214–221) showed that every infinitely divisible multivariate characteristic function can be written in the form

$$f(\mathbf{t}) = \exp\left\{iP_1(\mathbf{t}) - P_2(\mathbf{t}) + \rlap{\,-}\int_{R_n} [\exp(i\mathbf{tu}) - 1 - (i\mathbf{tu})/(1 + |\mathbf{u}|^2)]\, dm\right\}. \quad (2.2)$$

Here, $P_1(\mathbf{t})$ is a homogeneous linear form with real coefficients, and $P_2(\mathbf{t})$ is a homogeneous nonnegative quadratic form in $t_1, \ldots, t_n$ while m is a measure defined on the Borel sets of R_n such that

$$\rlap{\,-}\int_{R_n} |\mathbf{u}|^2/(1 + |\mathbf{u}|^2)\, dm < \infty. \quad (2.3)$$

The bar across the integral sign means that the origin is omitted from the range of integration.

It is also known that the representation (2.2) is unique. Multivariate infinitely divisible characteristic functions have many of the properties of univariate infinitely divisible characteristic functions, for instance

(i) An infinitely divisible characteristic function does not vanish for $\mathbf{t} \in R_n$;

(ii) The product of a finite number of infinitely divisible characteristic functions is infinitely divisible;

(iii) If $f(\mathbf{t})$ is infinitely divisible, then $[f(\mathbf{t})]^\alpha$ is a characteristic function for any $\alpha > 0$.

Some multivariate distributions can be considered as generalizations of univariate distributions to the n-dimensional case. We mention two important examples.

(A). *The multivariate normal distribution* is defined by its characteristic function

$$f(\mathbf{t}) = \exp\{iP_1(\mathbf{t}) - P_2(\mathbf{t})\} \qquad (\mathbf{t} \in R_n) \tag{2.4}$$

where $P_1(\mathbf{t}) = \mathbf{at}$ is a linear form with real coefficients while $P_2(\mathbf{t})$ is a homogeneous, nonnegative quadratic form in $t_1, t_2, \ldots, t_n$.

(B). *The multivariate Poisson distribution* was defined by Teicher [45] in terms of its characteristic function. Let $\boldsymbol{\varepsilon} = (\varepsilon_1, \varepsilon_2, \ldots, \varepsilon_n)$ be a vector whose components assume only the values 0 to 1 so that there are exactly 2^n such vectors. The function

$$f(\mathbf{t}) = \exp\left\{i\boldsymbol{\beta}\mathbf{t} + \sum_{\boldsymbol{\varepsilon} \neq \mathbf{0}} \lambda_{\varepsilon_1, \ldots, \varepsilon_n}(e^{i\mathbf{t}\boldsymbol{\varepsilon}} - 1)\right\} \qquad (\mathbf{t} \in R_n) \tag{2.5}$$

is called the characteristic function of the multivariate Poisson distribution. Here $\boldsymbol{\beta}$ is a given constant vector. The summation in (2.5) runs over all $\boldsymbol{\varepsilon} \neq \mathbf{0}$.

We remark that one cannot expect that the multivariate generalization of a univariate distribution has all the desirable properties of the corresponding univariate distribution. Therefore, it is rarely possible to find a unique generalization for a given univariate distribution. Thus, Lévy [22] proposed a different multivariate Poisson distribution which is, however, a particular case of (2.5). To illustrate the difficulty of defining suitable extensions of univariate distributions, we note that attempts to give a satisfactory definition for the multivariate gamma distribution were not yet fully successful (see Lukacs and Laha [27]); these difficulties also become apparent by examples where the marginal distributions show a peculiar behavior (see Lévy [21]).

Let $f(\mathbf{t})$ be an infinitely divisible distribution having the representation (2.2). We call $\exp[-P_2(\mathbf{t})]$ the normal (or Gaussian) component of $f(\mathbf{t})$ and refer to the measure m as the spectral measure of $f(\mathbf{t})$. The support of the spectral measure is called the Poisson spectrum of $f(\mathbf{t})$. If the Poisson spectrum of $f(\mathbf{t})$ is a bounded set, then the canonical representation of $f(\mathbf{t})$ reduces to

$$f(\mathbf{t}) = \exp\left\{iP_1(\mathbf{t}) - P_2(\mathbf{t}) + \int_{R_n} [\exp(i\mathbf{tu}) - 1]\, dm\right\}. \tag{2.6}$$

The concept of stable distributions can also be extended to the multivariate case (see Lévy [20]), the stable distributions form a subset of the family of infinitely divisible distributions. Domains of attraction of stable laws were studied by Rvaceva [44]. Most of the more recent investigations concerning univariate stable frequency functions were not yet extended to the multivariate case, the problem of stable distributions in the wide sense, raised by Rvaceva [44] also remains unsolved.

We see from the convolution theorem that the product of two characteristic functions is always a characteristic function. This fact suggests the problem of whether it is possible to write a given characteristic function as the product of two characteristic functions. This problem is the subject of the so-called arithmetic of distribution functions. Since every characteristic function $f(\mathbf{t})$ can be written as a product

$$f(\mathbf{t}) = f_1(\mathbf{t}) f_2(\mathbf{t}) \tag{2.7}$$

where one factor is degenerate[5], one has to study only nontrivial factorizations, that is, decompositions (2.7) where both factors $f_1(\mathbf{t})$ and $f_2(\mathbf{t})$ belong to nondegenerate distributions. A characteristic function $f(\mathbf{t})$ is said to be indecomposable if it admits only trivial factorizations.

Next, we mention two important results which are generalizations of classical univariate theorems due to Khinchine (see Lukacs [26], Theorem 6.2.1, and 6.2.2).

Theorem 2.5. *A characteristic function which has no indecomposable factor is infinitely divisible.*

Theorem 2.6. *Every characteristic function $f(\mathbf{t})$ can be represented as a product of, at most, two factors which have the following properties: One does not have any indecomposable factors while the other is the product of an at most denumerable sequence of indecomposable factors.*

Theorems 2.5 and 2.6 are particular cases of a theorem which was proven in a more general context (namely for locally compact Abelian groups) by Parthasaraty *et al.* [39].

We note that the converse of Theorem 2.5 is not true since examples of infinitely divisible characteristic functions which have indecomposable factors can easily be constructed. However, the next two theorems show that there exist infinitely divisible characteristic functions which have no indecomposable factors.

[5] A probability measure $\varepsilon_{\mathbf{c}}(A)$ is said to be degenerate if

$$\varepsilon_{\mathbf{c}}(A) = \begin{cases} 1 & \text{if} \quad \mathbf{c} \in A \\ 0 & \text{if} \quad \mathbf{c} \in \bar{A} \end{cases}$$

for every $A \in \mathfrak{B}_n$. The characteristic function of a degenerate probability measure is called a degenerate characteristic function; it has the form $\exp(i\mathbf{tc})$.

Theorem 2.7. *All factors of multivariate normal characteristic functions are multivariate normal characteristic functions.*

This theorem is due to H. Cramér, a proof may be found in his work [2].

Theorem 2.8. *All factors of a multivariate Poisson distribution are multivariate Poisson distributions.*

The result was obtained by Teicher [45].

The last four theorems suggest the investigation of the class of infinitely divisible characteristic functions which have no indecomposable factors. The theory of analytic characteristic functions is not only an important tool for these studies but also has independent interest.

3. MULTIVARIATE ANALYTIC CHARACTERISTIC FUNCTIONS

Characteristic functions were originally introduced as complex valued functions of a real vector. The reason is that the integral (2.1), defining the characteristic function is, in general, convergent only for $\mathbf{t} \in R_n$. However, it can happen that a characteristic function can be continued into some region of the complex space C_n; this fact justifies the introduction of the following definition.

A characteristic function $f(\mathbf{t}) = f(t_1, t_2, \ldots, t_n)$ is said to be an analytic characteristic function if there exists a function $A(\mathbf{z}) = A(z_1, z_2, \ldots, z_n)$ of the complex vector $\mathbf{z} = (z_1, z_2, \ldots, z_n) \in C_n$ and a real number $\Delta > 0$ such that $A(\mathbf{z})$ is regular at the origin and $f(\mathbf{t}) = A(\mathbf{t})$ for $\mathbf{t} = (t_1, t_2, \ldots, t_n) \in R_n$ and $|t_i| < \Delta$ $(i = 1, 2, \ldots, n)$.

For the statement of the basic properties of analytic characteristic functions, we have to introduce a suitable terminology.

A set $T \subset C_n$ is said to be a convex tube if $T = \{\mathbf{z} : \mathbf{z} \in C_n, \operatorname{Im} \mathbf{z} \in B\}$ where B is a convex set of R_n which is called the basis of T.

A convex tube T of C_n can be written as a product set, $T = R_n \times iB$, that is, the set of all points $\mathbf{z} = \mathbf{t} + i\mathbf{y}$ of C_n where $\mathbf{t} \in R_n$ while $\mathbf{y} \in B$.

The most important property of analytic characteristic functions is stated in the following theorem.

Theorem 3.1. *An analytic characteristic function $f(\mathbf{t}) = \int_{R_n} e^{i\mathbf{tx}}\, dP$ is regular in a convex tube $T = R_n + iB$ where the basis B is the interior of the domain of convergence of the integral $\int_{R_n} \exp[-\mathbf{yx}]\, dP$. The Fourier integral $\int_{R_n} \exp(i\mathbf{zx})\, dP$ is then convergent and analytic in T, and we write $f(\mathbf{z}) = \int_{R_n} \exp(i\mathbf{zx})\, dP$ with $\mathbf{z} = \mathbf{t} + i\mathbf{y} \in T$.*

Theorem 3.1 was derived almost simultaneously and independently by two authors: Ostrovskii [36, 37] and Cuppens [5]. Theorem 3.1 is proved by

Cuppens [8] along the lines of the univariate proof while Ostrovskii uses [36] the method of Cramér and Wold (Theorem 2.4).

Multivariate analytic characteristic functions share a number of properties with univariate characteristic functions, we now list some of these.

Corollary 1 to Theorem 3.1. *Every boundary point of the basis B of the tube of regularity T of a multivariate analytic characteristic function $f(\mathbf{z})$ is a singular point of $f(\mathbf{z})$.*

Corollary 2 to Theorem 3.1. *Multivariate analytic characteristic functions have the "ridge property," that is, $|f(\mathbf{t} + i\mathbf{y})| \leq f(i\mathbf{y})$ where $\mathbf{t} \in R_n$ and $\mathbf{y} \in B$. Here, B is the basis of the tube of regularity of $f(\mathbf{z})$.*

It can be shown that the derivatives of even order of a multivariate analytic characteristic function also have the ridge property.

Multivariate analytic characteristic functions can often be continued beyond their tube of regularity. It is very likely that one should be able to construct multivariate analytic characteristic functions which have a preassigned natural domain and can not be continued beyond this domain. This domain must, of course, include the tube of regularity in its interior and satisfy certain, rather obvious, conditions. At the present moment, one has not yet succeeded in carrying out this construction although the problem of a natural boundary for analytic characteristic functions is solved in the univariate case.

The next theorem is an extension of a useful univariate result due to Dugué [11].

Theorem 3.2. *Let $f(\mathbf{z})$ be an analytic characteristic function whose tube of regularity is $T = R_n \times i\, B$ and let $\boldsymbol{\eta} \in B$, then the function*

$$g(\mathbf{z}) = f(\mathbf{z} + i\boldsymbol{\eta})/f(i\boldsymbol{\eta})$$

is an analytic characteristic function which is regular in a tube $T' = R_n + iB'$ where $B' = B - \boldsymbol{\eta} = \{\mathbf{y}' : \mathbf{y}' = \mathbf{y} - \boldsymbol{\eta}, \mathbf{y} \in B\}$.

It is rather natural to ask whether there is a connection between the analyticity of the characteristic function of a random vector and the corresponding property of its components. The following result answers this question.

Theorem 3.3. *Let $f(\mathbf{z}) = f(z_1, z_2, \ldots, z_n)$ be an analytic characteristic function and suppose that the characteristic functions $f_j(z_j) = f(0, \ldots, 0, z_j, 0, \ldots, 0)$ of the n-univariate marginal distributions are regular in the strips $|\text{Im}\, z_j| < R$ $(j = 1, 2, \ldots, n)$, then $f(\mathbf{z})$ is an analytic characteristic function and is regular in the region $|\text{Im}\, z_j| < R/n$ $(j = 1, \ldots, n)$.*

Problems of factorizing analytic characteristic functions are of great interest also in the multivariate case. One of the most important results is a generalization of a classical theorem of Raikov [40].

Theorem 3.4. *Let $f(\mathbf{z})$ be an analytic characteristic function whose tube of regularity is $T = R_n \times iB$ and suppose that $f_1(\mathbf{t})$ and $f_2(\mathbf{t})$ are two characteristic functions such that the relation*

$$f(\mathbf{t}) = f_1(\mathbf{t}) f_2(\mathbf{t}) \qquad (\mathbf{t} \in R_n) \tag{3.1}$$

holds in some real neighborhood of the origin. The factors $f_j(\mathbf{t})$, $j = 1, 2$ are analytic characteristic functions regular at least in T, and the relation (3.1) *holds throughout T.*

It is also possible to consider entire characteristic functions, i.e., characteristic functions whose tube of regularity consists of the entire space C_n. It follows from Theorem 3.4 that factors of entire characteristic functions are also entire characteristic functions. Using a suitable norm, a maximum modulus, also the order and type of multivariate entire functions can be defined. It can be shown (see Fuks [14], p. 338 ff) that the order is independent of the choice of the norm[6] while the type depends on the norm. In discussing statements concerning the type, one must therefore specify the norm, we say that an entire function has the σ-type τ if the modulus and the type are defined using a norm σ. The properties of the order and σ-type of entire characteristic functions are analogous to those known in the univariate case. We mention an example: Let $f(\mathbf{t})$ be an entire characteristic function of order ρ then the order of factors of $f(\mathbf{t})$ can not exceed ρ.

Finally, it is worthwhile to remark that the canonical representation (2.2) is valid for an infinitely divisible analytic multivariate characteristic function in its entire tube of regularity.

4. FACTORIZATION PROBLEMS—THE CLASS I_0

Theorems 2.5 and 2.6 indicate the importance of infinitely divisible characteristic functions which have no indecomposable factors. This class of infinitely divisible characteristic functions is usually called[7] the class I_0. The question of the structure of I_0 and of the properties of its elements are probably the most important problem in the arithmetic of distribution functions, and the greatest activity is now concentrated in this area. The content of Theorems 2.7 and 2.8 can be reformulated by stating that the multivariate normal and the multivariate Poisson distribution belong to I_0.

A few univariate results were obtained by Raikov [40] at an early date (see

[6] The norm σ must satisfy the condition $\sigma(\mathbf{z}) = \sigma(\bar{\mathbf{z}})$.

[7] We say then that the corresponding probability measure also belongs to I_0.

also Lukacs [26], Theorems 8.2.5 and 8.2.6) which indicate that certain convolutions of Poisson type distributions belong to I_0. The next result, again univariate, is due to Linnik [23, 24] who showed that the characteristic function of the convolution of a Normal and a Poisson distribution belongs to I_0. Linnik's proof was later simplified by Ostrovskii [34] and Linnik's theorem, mentioned above, became the starting point for the univariate as well as the multivariate investigations concerning the class I_0. Next, we state the multivariate generalization of Linnik's theorem; its proof was given simultaneously and independently by Ostrovskii [33] and Cuppens [4].

Theorem 4.1. *Let $f(\mathbf{z})$ be the characteristic function of the convolution of an n-dimensional Normal and an n-dimensional Poisson distribution. Then $f(\mathbf{z})$ has only factors which belong to convolutions of Normal and Poisson distributions.*

The methods used in the proof of Theorem 4.1 suggested the study of conditions for membership in I_0. Necessary and sufficient conditions are not available at present but Linnik derived a number of univariate theorems, some of these give necessary conditions, others give sufficient conditions for membership in I_0 (see Linnik [24] for a detailed presentation). In the necessary conditions, the presence of a Normal component is essential while this need not be assumed in deriving Linnik's sufficient conditions. Ostrovskii [35] simplified the proof and also obtained a number of interesting results concerning membership in I_0 and also about the factors of certain infinitely divisible characteristic functions.

Many of these results could be extended to the multivariate case; a few examples follow.

Theorem 4.2. *Let $f(\mathbf{t})$ be the characteristic function of an infinitely divisible distribution whose Poisson spectrum consists of a finite number of points $\mathbf{a_j} = (a_{j1}, \ldots, a_{jn}) \in R_n$, $j = 1, \ldots, p$. Suppose that the quotients a_{jq}/a_{kq} are integers greater than 1 for every $j > k$ provided that a_{jq} and a_{kq} have the same sign. Then $f(\mathbf{t}) \in I_0$.*

Theorem 4.2 was announced by Cuppens [6]; and he has given a proof [8]. Cuppens [18] also gave an extension of Theorem 4.2 to the case in which $f(\mathbf{t})$ has a denumerable Poisson spectrum.

The Poisson spectrum of the characteristic function $f(\mathbf{t})$ of Theorem 4.2 is a bounded and finite set. We now give two results on infinitely divisible characteristic functions which have no normal component[8] and whose Poisson spectrum is a bounded (but not necessarily finite or discrete) set of R_n. For the formulation of these results, we need the following notation.

Let A and B be two sets of R_n, we define the vectorial sum $A(+)B$ of the sets A and B as the set of all points $\mathbf{x} = (x_1, x_2, \ldots, x_n)$ which can be written

[8] This means that the polynomial $P_2(t) \equiv 0$ in the canonical representation (2.2).

in at least one way in the form $\mathbf{x} = (a_1 + b_1, a_2 + b_2, \ldots, a_n + b_n)$ where $\mathbf{a} = (a_1, a_2, \ldots, a_n) \in A$ and $\mathbf{b} = (b_1, b_2, \ldots, b_n) \in B$. It is easily seen that the vectorial sum of two closed and bounded sets is closed. We define the symbol $(n)A$ by putting $(1)A = A$ and $(n)A = (n-1)A\,(+)\,A$ for $n = 2, 3, \ldots$, and also write $(\infty)A = \bigcup_{n=1}^{\infty} (n)A$.

Theorem 4.3. *Let $f(\mathbf{t})$ be the characteristic function of an infinitely divisible law without normal component whose Poisson spectrum $A \subset R_n$ is a bounded, positive, convex set such that $A \cap (2)A = \emptyset$. Then $f(t)$ belongs to I_0.*

Theorem 4.3 has some remarkable consequences.

Corollary 1 to Theorem 4.3. *Every infinitely divisible characteristic function can be written as a product of an at most denumerable sequence of characteristic functions belonging to I_0.*

Corollary 2 to Theorem 4.3. *There exist n-variate probability measures* $(n > 1)$ *which belong to I_0 and which have the property that its projections on the basis vectors of R_n, with the exception of two vectors, do not belong to I_0.*

This is particularly interesting if we compare it with Lévy's observation [21] that there exist multivariate indecomposable distributions whose projections belong to I_0.

Theorem 4.4. *Let $f(\mathbf{t})$ be an infinitely divisible characteristic function and suppose that* (i) *$f(\mathbf{t})$ has no normal component,* (ii) *the Poisson spectrum of $f(\mathbf{t})$ is a closed bounded set A contained in the positive octant,* (iii) *every finite set of points from A is rationally independent. Then $f(\mathbf{t})$ belongs to I_0.*

The univariate case of Theorems 4.3 and 4.4 was proved by Ostrovskii [35] who also announced the multivariate result in his Doklady note [36]; proofs of these theorems were given by Ostrovskii [38] and by Cuppens [8]. Particular cases of Theorems 4.3 and 4.4 were given by Raikov [40]; these are the results of Raikov to which we referred earlier.

Ostrovskii [32] derived a sufficient condition which assures that a (univariate) lattice distribution belongs to I_0. It is possible to introduce the concept of multivariate lattice distributions. A probability measure P, defined on R_n, is said to be a lattice probability measure P with span $\xi = (\xi_1, \xi_2, \ldots, \xi_n)$ if P is concentrated on the point set $(a_1 + k_1\xi_1, \ldots, a_n + k_n\xi_n)$ where $\mathbf{a} = (a_1, a_2, \ldots, a_n)$ is a fixed point while $\mathbf{k} = (k_1, k_2, \ldots, k_n)$ runs through all points with integer coordinates. Cuppens [8] gave a multivariate extension of Ostrovskii's result mentioned above. The investigation of finite products of Poisson distributions is interesting also in the multivariate case, some results indicating the different behavior of products of multivariate

Poisson distributions were announced by Cuppens [9]. He also stated in a second note [10] some sufficient conditions for membership in I_0 which are generalizations of earlier results of Ostrovskii.

5. THE α-DECOMPOSITIONS

In this section, we extend the concept of factorizations of characteristic functions. In contrast to the statements of the preceding section, it is not possible to give a probabilistic interpretation to α-decompositions. The α-decomposition theorems are essentially of an analytical nature but are closely related to the arithmetic of distribution functions.

We say that a multivariate characteristic function $f(\mathbf{t})$ admits a finite α-decomposition if there exist s characteristic functions $f_1(\mathbf{t}), \ldots, f_s(\mathbf{t})$ and s positive numbers $\alpha_1, \ldots, \alpha_s$ such that the relation

$$f(\mathbf{t}) = \prod_{j=1}^{s} [f_j(\mathbf{t})]^{\alpha_j} \qquad (\mathbf{t} \in R_n) \tag{5.1}$$

holds in a certain neighborhood of the origin. The powers of the characteristic functions $f_j(\mathbf{t})$ are defined by $[f_j(\mathbf{t})]^{\alpha_j} = \exp[\alpha_j \log f_j(\mathbf{t})]$ where we take for $\log f_j(\mathbf{t})$ the branch of the logarithms for which $\log f_j(0) = 0$ and which is continuous. Denumerable α-decompositions are defined in a similar way. One must then consider sequences of positive numbers $\{\alpha_j\}$ and sequences of characteristic functions $\{f_j(\mathbf{t})\}$ and replace (5.1) by

$$f(\mathbf{t}) = \prod_{j=1}^{\infty} [f_j(\mathbf{t})]^{\alpha_j}, \tag{5.1a}$$

valid again in a neighborhood of the origin. In α-decomposition theorems it is assumed that a characteristic function admits a decomposition (5.1) [resp. (5.1a)] and has certain properties. An α-decomposition theorem asserts that the functions $f_j(\mathbf{t})$ also have these properties.

We give two examples.

Theorem 5.1. *Let $f(\mathbf{z})$ be an analytic characteristic function whose tube of regularity is $T = R_n + iB$ where B is the basis of T, and let $f_1(\mathbf{t}), f_2(\mathbf{t}), \ldots, f_s(\mathbf{t})$ be s characteristic functions and $\alpha_1, \alpha_2, \ldots, \alpha_s$ be s positive numbers. Let δ be a positive number, and suppose that the relation*

$$\prod_{j=1}^{s} [f_j(\mathbf{t})]^{\alpha_j} = f(\mathbf{t}) \tag{5.2}$$

holds for $|\mathbf{t}| < \delta$, $\mathbf{t} \in R_n$. Then the functions $f_j(\mathbf{t})$ are analytic characteristic functions and are regular at least in T, and the relation (5.2) *is valid in every point of iB. Moreover, if $f(\mathbf{t})$ has no zeros in T, then* (5.2) *holds in the interior of T.*

Theorem 5.2. *Let $f(\mathbf{z})$ be an analytic characteristic function whose tube of regularity is $T = R_n + iB$ where B is the basis of T, and let $\{f_j(\mathbf{t})\}$ be a sequence of characteristic functions and $\{\alpha_j\}$ be a sequence of positive numbers and suppose that there exists an ε_0 such that $\alpha_j \geq \varepsilon_0 > 0$ ($j = 1, 2, \ldots$ ad inf.). Assume further that for some $\delta > 0$, the relation*

$$\prod_{j=1}^{\infty} [f_j(\mathbf{t})]^{\alpha_j} = f(\mathbf{t}) \qquad (\mathbf{t} \in R_n, |\mathbf{t}| < \delta) \tag{5.3}$$

holds. Then the $f_j(\mathbf{t})$ are analytic characteristic functions and are regular at least in T. Moreover (5.3) *holds in iB and even in T when $f(\mathbf{z})$ has no zeros in T.*

It is also possible to obtain α-decomposition theorems by assuming that the relations (5.2)–(5.3) respectively, are satisfied only in certain sequences of points which converge to the origin.

A detailed discussion of α-decomposition theorems may be found for the univariate case in the work of Linnik [24] or Ramachandran [41]. Proofs of the multivariate α-decomposition theorems mentioned in this section are given by Cuppens [8].

6. CONCLUDING REMARKS

In this section, we briefly mention a variety of studies concerning multivariate characteristic functions and also indicate their connection with the corresponding univariate problems.

Characteristic functions which are boundary values of analytic functions (the so-called boundary characteristic functions) were introduced in the univariate case by Marcinkiewicz [28] but received little attention until Esseen [12] used properties of this class of characteristic functions systematically. The definition can easily be extended to the multivariate case; multivariate boundary characteristic functions also have a tube of regularity which contains the real space R_n (on which the characteristic functions are originally defined) as part of its boundary. Boundary characteristic functions have an important property in common with analytic characteristic functions: The representation of a boundary characteristic function by a Fourier integral is still valid in its tube of regularity. This fact permits the extension of a number of theorems on analytic characteristic functions to boundary characteristic functions. We mention a few examples: (i) The factors of boundary characteristic functions are either boundary characteristic functions or analytic characteristic functions. (ii) If a probability measure P is bounded in a particular direction $\boldsymbol{\theta}$ of R_n, then one can express the extremity $\text{ext}_{\boldsymbol{\theta}} P$ of the probability measure P in the direction $\boldsymbol{\theta}$ in terms of the characteristic function

f of P in a similar manner as in the univariate case. One obtains $\text{ext}_{\boldsymbol{\theta}}(P) = \lim_{\lambda \to 0}[\log f(-i\lambda\boldsymbol{\theta})]/\lambda$. (iii) The canonical representation of infinitely divisible boundary characteristic functions is also valid in its tube of regularity. For further details and proofs, we refer to Cuppens [7, 8].

Comparatively little work was done on special nonnormal, multivariate distributions. The reason is the impossibility to give a criterion which a multivariate distribution must satisfy in order to justify the claim that it is the extension of a familiar univariate distribution. It seems to be a natural requirement that the univariate marginal distributions should be the univariate distribution which one wishes to generalize. However, it is known (see Fréchet [13]) that a rather large family of multivariate distributions can have the same marginals. It is, therefore, not surprising that it is difficult to reach agreement concerning the multivariate extensions of univariate distributions.[9] We give a few references to work dealing with special multivariate distributions. Some nonnormal multivariate distributions are discussed by Lukacs and Laha [27]. A number of authors (see, for instance, Kibble [16], Krishnamoorthy and Parthasarathy [18], Krishnaiah and Rao [17]) investigated multivariate extensions of the gamma distribution in some detail. The problem of the infinite divisibility of these distributions is solved only for the bivariate case (Vere-Jones [46]), at present. A multivariate negative binomial distribution was used by Bates and Neyman [1] in studying the theory of accident proneness. A bivariate exponential distribution is the topic of a paper by Marshall and Olkin [29]; Olkin and Rubin [31] also discussed multivariate generalizations of the beta distribution.

Characterization problems involving multivariate distributions also received some attention. Most of the work again deals with the multivariate Normal distribution. The characterization of the Normal distribution by the independence of the sample mean and the sample variance can easily be extended to the multivariate case. Lukacs [25] proved that the multivariate Normal distribution is characterized by the property that the joint distribution of the sample means is independent of the joint distribution of the sample variances and sample covariances. Other characterizations of the normal distribution may be found in the work of Lukacs and Laha [27] (Theorem 6.2.9), Laha [19] (using a regression property) and Rao [43] (who gives a univariate characterization theorem but only a necessary condition for normality in the multivariate case). Rao's study [42] of linear structural relations also lead to a characterization of the multivariate Normal distribution. Ghurye and Olkin [15] considered two linear forms in independent random vectors. The coefficients of these forms were assumed to be nonsingular (nonrandom) matrices. Ghurye and Olkin then obtained a charac-

[9] We noted in the remarks following formula (2.4) that complete agreement does not exist concerning the multivariate extension of the Poisson distribution.

terization of the multivariate Normal distribution which is a generalization of the well-known Darmois-Skitovic theorem. Olkin and Rubin [30, 31] also derived interesting characterization theorems for the Wishart distribution.

REFERENCES

1. Bates, G. A., and Neyman, J. (1952). Contributions to the theory of accident proneness I, II. *Univ. California Publ. Statist.* pp. 213–253, 255–275.
2. Cramér, H. (1937). "Random Variables and Probability Distributions." Cambridge Univ. Press, London and New York.
3. Cramér, H. (1946). "Mathematical Methods of Statistics." Princeton Univ. Press, Princeton, New Jersey.
4. Cuppens, R. (1966). Sur la décomposition de la composition d'une loi normale et d'une loi de Poisson. *C. R. Acad. Sci. Paris* **262** 1113–1116.
5. Cuppens, R. (1966). Sur les fonctions caractéristiques analytiques. *C. R. Acad. Sci. Paris* **263** 86–88.
6. Cuppens, R. (1966). Décomposition des fonctions caractéristiques indéfiniment divisibles. *C. R. Acad. Sci. Paris* **263** 616–619.
7. Cuppens, R. (1966). Extensions de la notion de fonction caractéristique analytique. *C. R. Acad. Sci. Paris* **263** 682–684.
8. Cuppens, R. (1968). Décomposition des fonctions caractéristiques des vecteurs aléatoires. *Publ. Inst. Statist. Univ. Paris* **16** 61–153.
9. Cuppens, R. (1968). Sur les produits finis des lois de Poisson. *C. R. Acad. Sci. Paris* **266** 726–728.
10. Cuppens, R. (1968). Décomposition des fonctions caractéristiques indéfiniment divisibles à spectre de Poisson positif. *C. R. Acad. Sci. Paris* **266** 877–879.
11. Dugué, D. (1957). Sur le théorème de Lévy-Cramér. *Publ. Inst. Statist. Univ. Paris* **6** 213–225.
12. Esseen C. G. (1965). On infinitely divisible one-sided distributions. *Math. Scand.* **17** 65–76.
13. Fréchet, M. (1951). Sur les tableaux de corrélation dont les marges sont données. *Ann. Univ. Lyon Sect. A, Ser.* 3, No. 14 53–77.
14. Fuks, B. A. (1963). Introduction to the theory of analytic functions of several complex variables [translated from the Russian ed. of 1962]. "Translations of Mathematical Monographs," vol. 8. Amer. Math. Soc., Providence, Rhode Island.
15. Ghurye, S. G., and Olkin, I. (1962). A characterization of the multivariate normal distribution. *Ann. Math. Statist.* **33** 533–541.
16. Kibble, W. F. (1941). A two-variate Gamma type distribution. *Sankhyā* **5** 137–150.
17. Krishnaiah, P. R., and Rao, M. M. (1961). Remarks on a multivariate Gamma distribution. *Amer. Math. Monthly* **68** 342–346.
18. Krishnamoorthy, A. S., and Parthasarathy, M. (1951). A multi-variate Gamma type distribution. *Ann. Math. Statist.* **22** 549–557 [Erratum. *Ann. Math. Statist.* **31** 229 (1960)].
19. Laha, R. G. (1955). On a characterization of the multivariate normal distribution. *Sankhyā* **14** 367–368.
20. Lévy, P. (1937)."Théorie de l'Addition des Variables Aléatoires." Gauthier Villars, Paris (2nd ed., 1954).
21. Lévy, P. (1948). The arithmetic character of the Wishart distribution. *Proc. Cambridge Philos. Soc.* **44** 295–297.

22. LÉVY, P. (1968). Observations sur la note précédente. *C. R. Acad. Sci. Paris* **266** 728–729.
23. LINNIK, YU. V. (1957). On factorizing the composition of a Gaussian and Poissonian law. *Teor. Veroyatnost. i Primenen.* **2** 34–59 [English transl. (1957). *Theory Probability Appl.* **2** 31–57].
24. LINNIK, YU. V. (1964). "Decomposition of Probability Distributions." Oliver & Boyd, Edinburgh and London [translated from the Russian original, published in Leningrad, 1960].
25. LUKACS, E. (1942). A characterization of the Normal distribution. *Ann. Math. Statist.* **13** 91–93.
26. LUKACS, E. (1960). "Characteristic Functions." Charles Griffin, London, 1960.
27. LUKACS, E., and LAHA, R. G. (1964). "Applications of Characteristic Functions." Charles Griffin, London.
28. MARCINKIEWICZ, J. (1938). Sur les fonctions indépendentes III. *Fund. Math.* **31** 86–102 [also reprinted in "Collected Papers of J. Marcinkiewicz," pp. 397–412. Polskie Akad. Nauk, Warszawa, 1964].
29. MARSHALL, A. W., and OLKIN, I. (1967). A generalized bivariate exponential distribution. *J. Appl. Probability* **4** 291–302.
30. OLKIN, I., and RUBIN, H. (1962). A characterization of the Wishart distribution. *Ann. Math. Statist.* **33** 1272–1280.
31. OLKIN, I., and RUBIN, H. (1964). Multivariate beta distributions and independence properties of the Wishart distribution. *Ann. Math. Statist.* **35** 261–269.
32. OSTROVSKII, I. V. (1964). On the decomposition of infinitely divisible lattice laws (in Russian). *Vestnik Leningrad. Univ.* **19** 51–60.
33. OSTROVSKII, I. V. (1965). A multidimensional analog of Yu. V. Linnik's theorem on decompositions of a composition of a Gaussian and a Poissonian law. *Teor. Veroyatnost. i Primenen.* **10** 742–745 [English transl. (1965). *Theory Probability Appl.* **10** 673–677].
34. OSTROVSKII, I. V. (1965). On factorizing the composition of a Gauss and a Poisson distribution. *Uspehi Mat. Nauk* **20**, No. 4 (124), 166–171.
35. OSTROVSKII, I. V. (1965). Some theorems on decompositions of probability laws. *Trudi Mat. Inst. Steklov* **79** 198–235 [English transl. (1965). *Proc. Steklov Inst. Math.* **79** 221–259].
36. OSTROVSKII, I. V. (1966). Decomposition of multidimensional probability laws. *Dokl. Akad. Nauk SSSR* **169** 1017–1019 [English transl. (1966). *Soviet Math. Dokl.* **7** 1052–1055].
37. OSTROVSKII, I. V. (1966). Some properties of holomorphic characteristic functions of multidimensional probability laws (in Russian). *Teor. Funkcii. Funkcional Anal. i Priložen* **1** 169–177.
38. OSTROVSKII, I. V. (1966). On the decomposition of multidimensional infinitely divisible laws without Gaussian component (in Russian). *Vesntik Har'kov. Gos. Univ.* **32** 51–72.
39. PARTHASARATHY, K. R., RAO, R. R., and VARADHAN, S. R. S. (1963). Probability distributions on locally compact abelian groups. *Ill. J. Math.* **7** 337–369.
40. RAIKOV, D. A. (1938). On the decomposition of Gauss and Poisson laws. *Izv. Akad. Nauk SSSR Ser. Mat.* **2** 91–124.
41. RAMACHANDRAN, B. (1967). "Advanced Theory of Characteristic Functions." Statist. Publ. Soc., Calcutta.
42. RAO, C. R. (1966). Characterization of the distribution of random variables in linear structural relations. *Sankhyā Ser A* **28** 251–260.
43. RAO, J. N. K. (1958). A characterization of the normal distribution. *Ann. Math. Statist.* **29** 914–919.

44. RVACEVA, E. L. (1954). Domains of attraction of multidimensional distributions. *Lvov Gosud. Univ. Ucen. Zap. Ser. Meh.-Mat.* **29** 5–44 [English transl. (1962). *Selected Translations. Math. Statist. Probability* **2** 183–206. Amer. Math. Soc.].
45. TEICHER, H. (1954). On the multivariate Poisson distribution. *Skand. Aktuarietidskr.* **37** 1–9.
46. VERE-JONES, D. (1967). The infinite divisibility of a bivariate gamma distribution. *Sankhyā Ser A* **29** 421–422.

Some Characterizations of the Multivariate Normal Distribution

C. RADHAKRISHNA RAO

INDIAN STATISTICAL INSTITUTE
CALCUTTA, INDIA

SUMMARY

The paper describes two recent lines of development in the characterization of the multivariate normal distribution.

Let $\mathbf{X}_1, \ldots, \mathbf{X}_n$ be n independent vector variables and $\mathbf{Y}_i = \mathbf{A}_{i1}\mathbf{X}_1 + \cdots + \mathbf{A}_{in}\mathbf{X}_n$, $i = 1, \ldots, n$ be n linear functions with matrix coefficients $\mathbf{A}_{ij}$. The conditions under which $E(\mathbf{Y}_1 \mid \mathbf{Y}_2, \ldots, \mathbf{Y}_n) = 0$ implies multivariate normality of $\mathbf{X}_i$ have been investigated when $n \geq 3$ and when $n = 2$. The general problem of investigating the conditions under which $E(\mathbf{Y}_i \mid \mathbf{Y}_j, \ldots, \mathbf{Y}_n) = \mathbf{0}$, $i = 1, \ldots, p$, imply multivariate normality of $\mathbf{X}_i$ has been stated.

It is well known that if $\mathbf{X}$ is a multivariate normal variable, then it can be represented as $\mathbf{AY}$, where $\mathbf{A}$ is a matrix and $\mathbf{Y}$ is a vector of independent $N(0, 1)$ variables. However, neither $\mathbf{A}$ nor the number of components of $\mathbf{Y}$ is unique. In fact, $\mathbf{X} = \mathbf{BZ}$ will be an alternative representation provided that only $\mathbf{BB}' = \mathbf{AA}'$, admitting the possibility of the numbers of columns $\mathbf{A}$ and $\mathbf{B}$ being different. We consider the converse problem, and investigate the nature of nonuniqueness of linear structure of a vector variable, which restricts it to having a multivariate normal distribution. A general decomposition theorem of a random variable with a linear structure has been stated.

1. INTRODUCTION

The paper deals with two recent lines of development in characterizing the multivariate normal distribution, one based on constant regression of a linear function of independent vector random variables given another such linear function, and the other on structural representations of a vector random variable.

The former line of development arose in attempts to generalize some recent results in the characterization of a univariate normal distribution. Let $x_1, \ldots, x_n$ be n independent one-dimensional random variables and

$$y_i = a_{i1}x_1 + \cdots + a_{in}x_n, \qquad i = 1, \ldots, n \tag{1.1}$$

be n linear functions, where a_{ij} are scalars. Following a special theorem by Kagan *et al.* (1965), the author (Rao, 1967a) started a new line of investigation by asking for minimum assumptions on the variables and coefficients under which the conditions

$$E(y_i \mid y_j, y_{j+1}, \ldots, y_n) = 0, \qquad i = 1, \ldots, p; \qquad j = p + s \qquad (s > 0) \tag{1.2}$$

imply the normality of x_i, and also to determine the class of distributions for which (1.2) holds for a given set of coefficients. The problem has not been completely solved although a wide variety of cases have been covered in a number of papers, (Rao, 1967a; Khatri and Rao, 1968a,b; Pathak and Pillai, 1968; Pillai, 1968; and especially Ramachandran and Rao, 1968 who introduced the class of generalized stable laws.)

There are two ways of generalizing the results to the multivariate case. One way is to consider vector variables $\mathbf{X}_i$ instead of x_i, linear functions $\mathbf{Y}_i$,

$$\mathbf{Y}_i = a_{i1}\mathbf{X}_1 + \cdots + a_{in}\mathbf{X}_n, \qquad i = 1, \ldots, n \tag{1.3}$$

where a_{ij} are scalars, and the conditions

$$E(\mathbf{Y}_i \mid \mathbf{Y}_j, \ldots, \mathbf{Y}_n) = 0, \qquad i = 1, \ldots, p. \tag{1.4}$$

Such a problem can always be reduced to the univariate case by considering the variables

$$\mathbf{L}'\mathbf{Y}_i = a_{i1}\mathbf{L}'\mathbf{X}_1 + \cdots + a_{in}\mathbf{L}'\mathbf{X}_n, \qquad i = 1, \ldots, n \tag{1.5}$$

where $\mathbf{L}$ is an arbitrary vector. Equations (1.5) imply

$$E(\mathbf{L}'\mathbf{Y}_i \mid \mathbf{L}'\mathbf{Y}_j, \ldots, \mathbf{L}'\mathbf{Y}_n) = 0, \tag{1.6}$$

and the conditions on the coefficients a_{ij} under which univariate normality of $\mathbf{L}'\mathbf{Y}_i$ can be asserted are then the same for asserting multivariate normality of $\mathbf{Y}_i$ (see Rao, 1965, Chapter 8).

Another way of generalizing is to consider matrix coefficients $\mathbf{A}_{ij}$ instead of scalars a_{ij} in (1.3),

$$\mathbf{Y}_i = \mathbf{A}_{i1}\mathbf{X}_1 + \cdots + \mathbf{A}_{in}\mathbf{X}_n, \qquad i = 1, \ldots, n \tag{1.7}$$

and investigate the conditions on the matrix coefficients under which

$$E(\mathbf{Y}_i \mid \mathbf{Y}_j, \ldots, \mathbf{Y}_n) = \mathbf{0}, \qquad i = 1, \ldots, p \tag{1.8}$$

imply multivariate normality of $\mathbf{X}_i$. Such a problem cannot be reduced to the univariate case, and essentially new techniques seem to be necessary. In this paper, we consider only two particular cases of the general problem. Other cases are currently under investigation.

Another line of development is concerned with vector variables which have a linear structure, a problem which received some attention in the past (Reiersol, 1960), and for which a satisfactory solution has recently been given by the author (Rao, 1966, 1967b,c).

Consider a vector variable **X**, with components x_1, x_2, such that

$$x_1 = 2y_1, \qquad x_2 = 5y_1 + \sqrt{5}\,y_2 \tag{1.9}$$

where y_1, y_2 (called structural variables) are independent $N(0, 1)$ variables. Then **X** has bivariate normal distribution $N_2(\mathbf{0}, \mathbf{\Sigma})$ where the dispersion matrix $\mathbf{\Sigma}$ is

$$\begin{pmatrix} 4 & 10 \\ 10 & 30 \end{pmatrix}. \tag{1.10}$$

It may be seen that the alternative representation

$$x_1 = \sqrt{2}\,u_1 + \sqrt{2}\,u_2,$$

$$x_2 = \{(5/\sqrt{2}) + (\sqrt{5}/\sqrt{2})\}u_1 + \{(5/\sqrt{2}) - (\sqrt{5}/\sqrt{2})\}u_2 \tag{1.11}$$

where u_1, u_2 are independent $N(0, 1)$ variables also leads to the same bivariate normal distribution. Thus the coefficients in the structural representation of **X** are not unique. In fact, even the number of structural variables need not be unique. For example, the representation

$$X_1 = w_1 + w_2 + w_3 + w_4, \qquad X_2 = w_1 + 2w_2 + 3w_3 + 4w_4 \tag{1.12}$$

where w_1, w_2, w_3, w_4 are independent $N(0, 1)$ variables also leads to the same bivariate distribution for **X**. The examples considered raise the question whether a nonunique linear structure is a characteristic property of multivariate normal variables. A complete answer to this question is provided in Section 4. The nature of the nonuniqueness of the linear structure which implies normality is given, and a complete characterization of a vector variable with a linear structure is provided.

2. MULTIVARIATE EXTENSION OF KAGAN-LINNIK-RAO THEOREM

In this section, we give a sufficient condition for multivariate normality of $\mathbf{X}_i$ when

$$E(\mathbf{Y}_1 \mid \mathbf{Y}_2, \ldots, \mathbf{Y}_n) = 0 \tag{2.1}$$

where $\mathbf{Y}_i = \mathbf{A}_{i1}\mathbf{X}_1 + \cdots + \mathbf{A}_{in}\mathbf{X}_n$, $\mathbf{X}_i$ are independent (not necessarily identically distributed) vector variables and $\mathbf{A}_{ij}$ are matrices.

Theorem 1. *Let $n \geq 3$ and $\mathbf{A}_{11}, \ldots, \mathbf{A}_{1n}$ be nonsingular matrices. Furthermore, let it be possible by sweep out to reduce $\mathbf{Y}_2, \ldots, \mathbf{Y}_n$ to the canonical form*

$$\mathbf{Z}_2 = \mathbf{B}_{21}\mathbf{X}_1 + \mathbf{X}_2$$
$$\vdots$$
$$\mathbf{Z}_n = \mathbf{B}_{n1}\mathbf{X}_1 + \mathbf{X}_n$$

where $\mathbf{B}_{i1}$ are all nonsingular matrices. Then the condition (2.1) *implies that each $\mathbf{X}_i$ is multivariate normal.*

Let $\psi_i(\mathbf{t})$, where $\mathbf{t}$ is a vector, be the characteristic function of $\mathbf{X}_i$ and $\phi_i(\mathbf{t})$ be a vector function such that its jth component is

$$(\partial\psi_i(\mathbf{t})/\partial t_j) \div \psi_i(\mathbf{t}) \tag{2.2}$$

where t_j is the jth component of $\mathbf{t}$.

It is easily seen that

$$E(\mathbf{Y}_1 \mid \mathbf{Y}_2, \ldots, \mathbf{Y}_n) = E(\mathbf{Y}_1 \mid \mathbf{Z}_2, \ldots, \mathbf{Z}_n) = \mathbf{0} \tag{2.3}$$

which implies that

$$E\{\mathbf{Y}_1 \exp[i(\mathbf{t}_2'\mathbf{Z}_2 + \cdots + \mathbf{t}_n'\mathbf{Z}_n)]\} = \mathbf{0} \tag{2.4}$$

where $\mathbf{t}_2, \ldots, \mathbf{t}_n$ are vectors and $i = \sqrt{-1}$. From (2.4), we have the equation

$$\mathbf{A}_{11}\phi_1(\mathbf{B}_{21}'\mathbf{t}_2 + \cdots + \mathbf{B}_{n1}'\mathbf{t}_n) + \mathbf{A}_{12}\phi_2(\mathbf{t}_2) + \cdots + \mathbf{A}_{1n}\phi_n(\mathbf{t}_n) = \mathbf{0} \tag{2.5}$$

valid for $\mathbf{t}_2, \ldots, \mathbf{t}_n$ in a small neighborhood around the origin. Putting $\mathbf{t}_4 = \cdots = \mathbf{t}_n = \mathbf{0}$,

$$\mathbf{A}_{11}\phi_1(\mathbf{B}_{21}'\mathbf{t}_2 + \mathbf{B}_{31}'\mathbf{t}_3) + \mathbf{A}_{12}\phi_2(\mathbf{t}_2) + \mathbf{A}_{13}\phi_3(\mathbf{t}_3) = \mathbf{0}. \tag{2.6}$$

Applying Linnik's lemma as extended by Ghurye and Olkin (1962) to the multivariable case, we find that ϕ_1, ϕ_2, ϕ_3 are all linear functions of the vector argument. If $\phi_i(\mathbf{t})$ is linear, then $\log \psi_i(\mathbf{t})$ is quadratic in $\mathbf{t}$, and hence $\mathbf{X}_i$ has a multivariate normal distribution. Thus $\mathbf{X}_1$, $\mathbf{X}_2$, $\mathbf{X}_3$ are multivariate normal and so also are the other variables.

Note. Obviously, the conditions of Theorem 1 are not necessary for $\mathbf{X}_i$ to be normal, but it is easy to construct examples in which $\mathbf{X}_i$ need not be normal if some of the conditions are not satisfied.

3. THE SPECIAL CASE OF $n = 2$

The case of $n = 2$ is of special interest since the proof of Theorem 1 does not hold good as in the univariate case (see Rao, 1967a). We prove the following theorem.

Theorem 2. *Let* $\mathbf{X}_1$, $\mathbf{X}_2$ *be two identically distributed vector random variables. Consider two linear functions*

$$\mathbf{X}_1 - \mathbf{A}\mathbf{X}_2 \quad \text{and} \quad \mathbf{X}_1 + \mathbf{B}'\mathbf{X}_2$$

where $\mathbf{B}$ *is a symmetric matrix, i.e., of the form* $\mathbf{P}'\,\mathbf{\Delta}\mathbf{P}$, $\mathbf{P}'\mathbf{P} = \mathbf{I}$, $\mathbf{\Delta}$ *being a diagonal matrix. If there exists a nonsingular matrix* $\mathbf{\Sigma}$ *such that* $\mathbf{A}\mathbf{\Sigma}\mathbf{B} = \mathbf{\Sigma}$ *and the diagonal entries of* $\mathbf{\Delta}$ *are all different from* ± 1, *then* $E(\mathbf{X}_1 - \mathbf{A}\mathbf{X}_2 \,|\, \mathbf{X}_2 + \mathbf{B}'\mathbf{X}_2) = \mathbf{0}$ *implies that* $\mathbf{X}_1$ *has a multivariate normal distribution.*

We assume without loss of generality that $\mathbf{\Sigma} = \mathbf{I}$ since we can consider the variable $\mathbf{\Sigma}^{-1/2}\mathbf{X}$ instead of $\mathbf{X}$. In such a case, the condition $\mathbf{A}\mathbf{\Sigma}\mathbf{B} = \mathbf{\Sigma}$ reduces to $\mathbf{A} = \mathbf{B}^{-1}$. Let ψ and ϕ be as defined in Theorem 1. Then

$$E(\mathbf{X}_1 - \mathbf{A}\mathbf{X}_2 \,|\, \mathbf{X}_1 + \mathbf{B}'\mathbf{X}_2) = \mathbf{0}$$

implies

$$\phi(\mathbf{t}) = \mathbf{A}\phi(\mathbf{B}\mathbf{t}). \tag{3.1}$$

Writing $\mathbf{B} = \mathbf{P}'\,\mathbf{\Delta}\mathbf{P}$, $\mathbf{A} = \mathbf{P}'\,\mathbf{\Delta}^{-1}\mathbf{P}$, $\mathbf{P}'\boldsymbol{\tau} = \mathbf{t}$ in (3.1) and rearranging terms, we obtain

$$\mathbf{P}\phi(\mathbf{P}'\boldsymbol{\tau}) = \mathbf{\Delta}^{-1}\mathbf{P}\phi(\mathbf{P}'\,\mathbf{\Delta}\boldsymbol{\tau}). \tag{3.2}$$

Denoting $\mathbf{P}\phi(\mathbf{P}'\boldsymbol{\tau}) = \omega(\boldsymbol{\tau})$ in (3.2),

$$\omega(\boldsymbol{\tau}) = \mathbf{\Delta}^{-1}\omega(\mathbf{\Delta}\boldsymbol{\tau}) \tag{3.3}$$

where, it may be observed, ω is the vector derivative of the log characteristic function of the variable $\mathbf{Z} = \mathbf{P}\mathbf{X}$. Considering the first components of the vector functions on either side of (3.3), we have

$$\omega_1(\boldsymbol{\tau}) = \delta_1^{-1}\omega_1(\mathbf{\Delta}\boldsymbol{\tau}) \tag{3.4}$$

with the obvious notation. Substituting the value zero for all the components of $\boldsymbol{\tau}$ except the first in (3.4) and writing $\omega_1(\tau_1, 0, 0, \ldots,)$ as $w_1(\tau_1)$,

$$w_1(\tau_1) = \delta_i^{-1} w_1(\delta_1 \tau_1) \tag{3.5}$$

which is the equation considered by Rao (1967a). It may be observed that in the Eq. (3.5), the function w_1 is the derivative of the log-characteristic function of the variable Z_1, the first component of $\mathbf{Z}$. Since $\delta_1 \neq \pm 1$, it follows from previous results (Rao, 1967a; Ramachandran and Rao, 1968; Pathak and Pillai, 1968) that Z_1 has univariate normal distribution. Similarly, the marginal distributions of all the components of $\mathbf{Z}$ are normal, and hence all the joint cumulants of the components of $\mathbf{Z}$ are finite. This implies that the functions

$$\omega_i(\boldsymbol{\tau}) = \delta_i^{-1}\omega_i(\mathbf{\Delta}\boldsymbol{\tau}) \tag{3.6}$$

are infinitely differentiable. To determine a cumulant of the type $K_{r_1 r_2 \cdots}$, we can differentiate $\omega_i(\boldsymbol{\tau})$, r_1 times with respect to $\tau_1, \ldots, (r_i - 1)$ times with respect to τ_i, r_{i+1} times with respect to τ_{i+1}, etc. Carrying out these differentiations on both sides of (3.6) and putting $\boldsymbol{\tau} = 0$, we obtain

$$K_{r_1 r_2 \ldots}(1 - \delta_1^{r_1} \cdots \delta_i^{r_i - 2} \delta_{i+1}^{r_{i+1}} \cdots) = 0, \qquad i = 1, 2, \ldots. \tag{3.7}$$

Since $\delta_i \neq \pm 1$, Eq. (3.7) implies that $K_{r_1 r_2 \ldots} = 0$. Thus cumulants of all orders except possibly the second are all zero. Hence, **Z** has a multivariate normal distribution, which shows that **X** has a multivariate normal distribution.

Note. It may be seen that Theorem 2 is proved under the severe condition that the matrix **B** is a nonsingular symmetric matrix. It is not known to what extent this can be relaxed without making further conditions on random variables. For instance, existence of the dispersion matrix of **X** and the modulus of maximum eigenvalue of **B** being less than unity constitute a set of sufficient conditions. Some results on other sets of conditions seem to have been obtained by Pathak. Part of the argument used in Theorem 2 was obtained during a discussion with Pathak.

4. THEOREMS ON VARIABLES WITH A LINEAR STRUCTURE

Definition 1. *A vector variable* **X** *is said to have a linear structure if it can be expressed as*

$$\mathbf{X} = \boldsymbol{\mu} + \mathbf{AY} \tag{4.1}$$

where $\boldsymbol{\mu}$ *is a constant vector,* **Y** *is a vector of nondegenerate independent one-dimensional variables (called structural variables), and* **A** *is a matrix such that, without loss of generality, there are no two columns of which one is a multiple of the other.*

Definition 2. *Two structural representations*

$$\mathbf{X} = \boldsymbol{\mu}_1 + \mathbf{AY}, \qquad \mathbf{X} = \boldsymbol{\mu}_2 + \mathbf{BZ} \tag{4.2}$$

are said to be equivalent if every column of **A** *is a multiple of some column of* **B** *and vice versa. Otherwise, they are nonequivalent.*

It can be shown that if $\mathbf{X} = \boldsymbol{\mu}_1 + \mathbf{AY}$ and $\mathbf{X} = \boldsymbol{\mu}_2 + \mathbf{BZ}$ are two structural representations, the linear manifolds generated by the columns of **A** and **B** are the same, and that $\boldsymbol{\mu}_1 - \boldsymbol{\mu}_2$ belongs to this common linear manifold. In view of this result, by subtracting a suitable constant vector from **X**, we can represent a structural representation simply as **AY**.

We quote an important theorem from a previous paper of the author (Rao, 1966), which plays a key role in the proofs of theorems considered in this paper.

Theorem 3. *Let* $\mathbf{X} = \mathbf{AY}$ *and* $\mathbf{X} = \mathbf{BZ}$ *be two representations of a vector variable* $\mathbf{X}$, *where* $\mathbf{A}$ *and* $\mathbf{B}$ *are fixed matrices with possibly different numbers of columns,* $\mathbf{Y}$ *and* $\mathbf{Z}$ *are vectors of independent nondegenerate random variables. Furthermore, let* $Y_1, Y_2, \ldots$ *be the components of* $\mathbf{Y}$ *and* $Z_1, Z_2, \ldots$ *be those of* $\mathbf{Z}$. *If the ith column of* $\mathbf{A}$ *is not a multiple of any column of* $\mathbf{B}$, *then* Y_i *has a univariate normal distribution.*

We state the following theorems which are consequences of Theorem 3.

Theorem 4. *Let* $\mathbf{X} = \mathbf{AY}$ *and* $\mathbf{X} = \mathbf{BZ}$ *be two representations of* $\mathbf{X}$. *If no column of* $\mathbf{A}$ *is a multiple of any column of* $\mathbf{B}$, *then* $\mathbf{X}$ *has a multivariate normal distribution.*

The result follows since by Theorem 3 every component of Y is univariate normal. Theorem 4 provides a characterization of the multivariate normal distribution through complete nonuniqueness of the linear structure.

Theorem 5. *Consider a structural representation* $\mathbf{X} = \mathbf{AY}$ *of a vector random variable* $\mathbf{X}$. *Let* $\mathbf{Y}_1, \mathbf{Y}_2$ *be two subsets of* $\mathbf{Y}$ *such that the components of* $\mathbf{Y}_1$ *are nonnormal and those of* $\mathbf{Y}_2$ *are normal variables. Furthermore, let* $\mathbf{A}_1, \mathbf{A}_2$ *be the corresponding partitions of* $\mathbf{A}$ *so that*

$$\mathbf{X} = \mathbf{A}_1\mathbf{Y}_1 + \mathbf{A}_2\mathbf{Y}_2. \tag{4.3}$$

Then any other structure of $\mathbf{X}$ *is of the form*

$$\mathbf{X} = \mathbf{A}_1\mathbf{U}_1 + \mathbf{B}_2\mathbf{U}_2 \tag{4.4}$$

where, after suitable scaling, the elements of $\mathbf{U}_1$ *are nonnormal with the same structural matrix* $\mathbf{A}_1$ *as for* $\mathbf{Y}_1$, *and those of* $\mathbf{U}_2$ *are normal with a structural matrix* $\mathbf{B}_2$ *which is not necessarily equivalent to* $\mathbf{A}_2$.

The result follows from Theorem 3 and the nonuniqueness of the structure for a multivariate normal variable. As a consequence of Theorem 5, we have the following theorem.

Theorem 6. *Let* $\mathbf{X} = \mathbf{AY}$ *be a structural representation of* $\mathbf{X}$ *and let the components of* $\mathbf{Y}$ *be all nonnormal variables. Then there does not exist a non-equivalent structure involving the same number or a smaller number of structural variables than that of* $\mathbf{Y}$.

However, Theorem 6 does not say that the structure $\mathbf{X} = \mathbf{AY}$ is unique when the components of $\mathbf{Y}$ are nonnormal. There is a possibility of a representation such as $\mathbf{X} = \mathbf{AZ} + \mathbf{BU}$, with an expanded structure. We quote a theorem providing a complete characterization of a vector variable with a linear structure.

Theorem 7. *Let* $\mathbf{X}$ *be a vector random variable with a linear structure* $\mathbf{X} = \mathbf{AY}$. *Then* $\mathbf{X}$ *admits the decomposition*

$$\mathbf{X} = \mathbf{X}_1 + \mathbf{X}_2 \tag{4.5}$$

where $\mathbf{X}_1$ *and* $\mathbf{X}_2$ *are independent,* $\mathbf{X}_1$ *has an essentially unique linear structure and* $\mathbf{X}_2$ *is multivariate normal (with a nonunique linear structure). It is possible that* $\mathbf{X}_1$ *or* $\mathbf{X}_2$ *is a null vector.*

A detailed proof of this theorem, which is somewhat involved, is given in (Rao, 1967c) which will be published elsewhere.

REFERENCES

1. GHURYE, S. G., and OLKIN, I. (1962). A characterization of the multivariate normal distribution. *Ann. Math. Statist.* **33** 533–541.
2. KAGAN, A. M., LINNIK, YU., and RAO, C. R. (1965). On a characterization of the normal law based on a property of the sample average. *Sankhyā Ser. A* **27** 405–406.
3. KHATRI, C. G., and RAO, C. R. (1968a). Some characterizations of the Gamma distribution. *Sankhyā Ser. A* **30** 157–166.
4. KHATRI, C. G., and RAO, C. RADHAKRISHNA (1968b). Solutions to some functional equations and their applications to characterization of probability distributions. *Sankhyā Ser A.* **30** 167–180.
5. PATHAK, P. K., and PILLAI, R. N. (1968). On a characterization of the normal law. *Sankhyā Ser. A* **30** 141–144.
6. PILLAI, R. N. (1968). On some characterizations of the normal law. *Sankhyā Ser. A* **30** 145–146.
7. RAMACHANDRAN, B., and RAO, C. Radhakrishna (1968). Some results on characteristic functions and characterizations of the normal and generalized stable laws. *Sankhyā Ser. A* **30** 125–140.
8. RAO, C. RADHAKRISHNA (1965). "Linear Statistical Inference and Its Applications." Wiley, New York.
9. RAO, C. RADHAKRISHNA (1966). Characterization of the distribution of random variables in linear structural relations. *Sankhyā Ser. A* **28** 252–260.
10. RAO, C. RADHAKRISHNA (1967a). On some characterizations of the normal law. *Sankhyā Ser. A* **29** 1–14.
11. RAO, C. RADHAKRISHNA (1967b). On a vector variable with a linear structure and a characterization of the multivariate normal distribution. *Proc. Session Internat. Statist. Inst.*, 36*th*, Sydney, 1967.
12. RAO, C. RADHAKRISHNA (1967c). A decomposition theorem for vector variables with a linear structure. Tech. Rept. No. 16/67. Res. and Training School, Indian Statist. Inst., Calcutta.
13. REIERSOL, O. (1960). Identifiability of a linear relation between variables which are subject to error. *Econometrica* **18** 375–389.

PART V

Time Series and Stochastic Processes

The Canonical Analysis of Stationary Time Series[1]

DAVID R. BRILLINGER

DEPARTMENT OF STATISTICS[2]
THE LONDON SCHOOL OF ECONOMICS AND POLITICAL SCIENCE
ALDWYCH, LONDON

DEPARTMENT OF STATISTICS
THE UNIVERSITY OF CALIFORNIA
BERKELEY, CALIFORNIA

1. SUMMARY

Given a vector-valued stationary series with finite second-order moments, this article considers a class of problems leading to the calculation of the latent values and vectors of matrices based on the spectral density matrix of the series. Certain statistical properties of these characteristics are considered for the case in which they are based on an estimated spectral density matrix. Calculations,[3] of the type discussed in this article, are carried out for a series consisting of the mean monthly temperatures recorded at fourteen European cities over a 170 year period.

2. INTRODUCTION AND NOTATION

Throughout the article, matrices will be denoted by boldface letters, $\mathbf{A}$, $\mathbf{a}$, for example. The term $\mathbf{I}$ will denote the identity matrix and $\mathbf{0}$ the matrix with all entries 0. The term $\mathbf{A}^\tau$ will denote the transpose of $\mathbf{A}$, and $\overline{\mathbf{A}}$ will denote the matrix whose entries are the complex conjugates of those of $\mathbf{A}$. The term A_{jk} will denote the entry in the jth row and kth column of $\mathbf{A}$, and we will write

[1] This research was partially supported by the National Science Foundation Grant NSF-7454.

[2] Present address. The author was on leave of absence from The London School of Economics when this paper was written.

[3] These calculations were carried out at the Bell Telephone Laboratories, Murray Hill, New Jersey, on their GE 645 computer while the author was a summer visitor in 1967. The original data was provided by J. M. Craddock of the Meteorological Office, England.

$\mathbf{A} = [A_{jk}]$. If $\mathbf{A} = [A_{jk}]$, $|\mathbf{A}|$ will denote $[|A_{jk}|]$. The trace of $\mathbf{A}$ will be denoted by tr $\mathbf{A}$. If the Hermitian matrix $\mathbf{A}$ is nonnegative definite, we will write $\mathbf{A} \geq \mathbf{0}$. The latent values $\mu_1, \mu_2, \ldots,$ of a Hermitian $\mathbf{A}$ will be ordered so that $\mu_1 \geq \mu_2 \geq, \ldots$. If $\mathbf{a}(t) = [a_{jk}(t)]$, $t = 0, \pm 1, \ldots$ is an $s \times q$ matrix-valued function and $\mathbf{b}(t) = [b_{jk}(t)]$ is a $q \times r$ matrix-valued function satisfying

$$\sum_{t=-\infty}^{\infty} |a_{jk}(t)| < \infty \tag{2.1}$$

$$\sum_{t=-\infty}^{\infty} |b_{jk}(t)| < \infty, \tag{2.2}$$

we will write $\mathbf{a} * \mathbf{b}(t)$ for the convolution

$$\sum_{u=-\infty}^{\infty} \mathbf{a}(t-u)\mathbf{b}(u). \tag{2.3}$$

If $\mathbf{Z} = [Z_j]$ is an r vector-valued random variable, and $E|Z_j|^r < \infty$, $j = 1, \ldots, r$, we denote its joint cumulant of order r by

$$\text{cum}[Z_1, \ldots, Z_r]. \tag{2.4}$$

Let $\mathbf{W}(t)$, $t = 0, \pm 1, \ldots$ be an m vector-valued time series with real-valued components. Suppose the second order moments of $\mathbf{W}(t)$ are finite, and

$$E\mathbf{W}(t) = \mathbf{c}_W, \qquad E\{\mathbf{W}(t+u) - \mathbf{c}_W\}\{\mathbf{W}(t) - \mathbf{c}_W\}^\tau = \mathbf{c}_{WW}(u) \tag{2.5}$$

for $t, u = 0, \pm 1, \ldots$.

Definition 2.1. *$H_W{}^n$ is the closure, in the norm, $E\{\text{tr } \mathbf{ff}^\tau\}$, of the space of n vector-valued linear combinations, $\mathbf{f}$, of the form*

$$\mathbf{f} = \sum_t \mathbf{a}(t)\{\mathbf{W}(t) - \mathbf{c}_W\} \tag{2.6}$$

where $\mathbf{a}(t)$ is $n \times m$ matrix-valued and such that only a finite number of the $\mathbf{a}(t)$ are nonzero.

The space $H_W{}^n$ is the space of n vector-values of the series $\mathbf{W}(t)$. An $n \times n$ matrix valued inner product, $\langle \mathbf{f}, \mathbf{g} \rangle$ may be introduced in $H_W{}^n$ by

$$\langle \mathbf{f}, \mathbf{g} \rangle = E\mathbf{fg}^\tau \tag{2.7}$$

and, $\mathbf{f}, \mathbf{g} \in H_W{}^n$. Now $H_W{}^n$ becomes an LVH space in the terminology of Loynes [13]. Related spaces are considered by Masani [15] and Rozanov [23].

Let

$$\mathbf{W}(t) - \mathbf{c}_W = \int_{-\pi}^{\pi} \exp\{i\lambda t\}\, d\mathbf{Z}_W(\lambda) \tag{2.8}$$

be the Cramér representation of $\mathbf{W}(t)$, and

$$\mathbf{c}_{WW}(u) = \int_{-\pi}^{\pi} \exp\{i\lambda u\}\, d\mathbf{F}_{WW}(\lambda) \tag{2.9}$$

be the Bochner representation of $\mathbf{c}_{WW}(u)$. (See Rozanov [23] for a discussion of these representations.) In (2.8), $\mathbf{Z}_W(\lambda)$ is an m vector-valued process with orthogonal increments. In (2.9), $\mathbf{F}_{WW}(\lambda)$ is an $m \times m$ matrix-valued, bounded, Hermitian, nondecreasing function.

Definition 2.2. *$L_2^{n\times m}(\mathbf{F}_{WW})$ is the space of $n \times m$ matrix-valued functions $\mathbf{A}(\lambda)$ (with complex-valued entries), such that*

$$\int_{-\pi}^{\pi} \operatorname{tr}\{\mathbf{A}(\lambda)\, d\mathbf{F}_{WW}(\lambda)\overline{\mathbf{A}(\lambda)^{\tau}}\} < \infty. \tag{2.10}$$

See Rosenberg [22] for the specific meaning of (2.10). We have:

Theorem 2.1. *If $\mathbf{f} \in H_W{}^m$, then there exists $\mathbf{A}(\lambda) \in L_2^{n\times m}(\mathbf{F}_{WW})$ such that*

$$\mathbf{f} = \int_{-\pi}^{\pi} \mathbf{A}(\lambda)\, d\mathbf{Z}_W(\lambda). \tag{2.11}$$

This result is proved by Rosenberg [22].

Suppose now that $\mathbf{W}(t)$ has the form,

$$\mathbf{W}(t) = \begin{bmatrix} \mathbf{X}(t) \\ \mathbf{Y}(t) \end{bmatrix} \tag{2.12}$$

with $\mathbf{X}(t)$ r vector-valued, $\mathbf{Y}(t)$ s vector-valued. In obvious notation, we write

$$\mathbf{c}_W = \begin{bmatrix} \mathbf{c}_X \\ \mathbf{c}_Y \end{bmatrix} \tag{2.13}$$

$$\mathbf{c}_{WW}(u) = \begin{bmatrix} \mathbf{c}_{XX}(u) & \mathbf{c}_{XY}(u) \\ \mathbf{c}_{YX}(u) & \mathbf{c}_{YY}(u) \end{bmatrix} \tag{2.14}$$

$$\mathbf{F}_{WW}(\lambda) = \begin{bmatrix} \mathbf{F}_{XX}(\lambda) & \mathbf{F}_{XY}(\lambda) \\ \mathbf{F}_{YX}(\lambda) & \mathbf{F}_{YY}(\lambda) \end{bmatrix} \tag{2.15}$$

$$\mathbf{Z}_W(\lambda) = \begin{bmatrix} \mathbf{Z}_X(\lambda) \\ \mathbf{Z}_Y(\lambda) \end{bmatrix}. \tag{2.16}$$

Consider $H_W{}^s$. We note that $\mathbf{Y}(t) - \mathbf{c}_Y \in H_W{}^s$. We also note that

$$\sum_t \mathbf{d} * \mathbf{b}(t)\{\mathbf{X}(t) - \mathbf{c}_X\} \tag{2.17}$$

is in $H_W{}^s$ if $\mathbf{d}(t)$ is $s \times q$ matrix-valued, $\mathbf{b}(t)$ is $q \times r$ matrix valued, $q \le s, r$, and only a finite number of the coefficients are nonzero.

Definition 2.3. *$J_X{}^q$ is the closure in $H_W{}^s$ of the set of s vectors of the form* (2.17).

Theorem 2.2. *If* $\mathbf{f} \in J_X{}^q$, *then*

$$\mathbf{f} = \int_{-\pi}^{\pi} \mathbf{A}(\lambda)\, d\mathbf{Z}_X(\lambda) \tag{2.18}$$

where $\mathbf{A}(\lambda) \in L_2^{s \times r}\,(\mathbf{F}_{XX})$ *has rank* $\leq q$ *for almost all* λ.[4]

Intuitively, $J_X{}^q$ may be thought of as containing s vectors derived from $\mathbf{X}(t)$ by first filtering $\mathbf{X}(t)$ to have dimension q and then filtering this result to have dimension s.

We note that $\mathbf{A}(\lambda)$, of the theorem, may be written $\mathbf{D}(\lambda)\mathbf{B}(\lambda)$ where $\mathbf{D}(\lambda)$ is $s \times q$ and $\mathbf{B}(\lambda)$ is $q \times r$ matrix-valued.

3. CANONICAL VARIATES FOR TIME SERIES

Suppose that $\mathbf{X}(t)$ is an r vector-valued series related to the s vector-valued series $\mathbf{Y}(t)$. Suppose that $q \leq r$ channels are available for the transmission of values derived from the $\mathbf{X}(t)$ series and that on receipt of these values one desires to form a series near $\mathbf{Y}(t)$. One can imagine forming the series

$$\boldsymbol{\zeta}(t) = \sum_u \mathbf{b}(t-u)\{\mathbf{X}(u) - \mathbf{c}_X\}, \tag{3.1}$$

with $\mathbf{b}(u)$ $q \times r$ matrix-valued, and transmitting this series over the q available channels. On receipt one can form

$$\mathbf{m} + \sum_u \mathbf{d}(t-u)\boldsymbol{\zeta}(u) \tag{3.2}$$

where $\mathbf{d}(u)$ is $s \times q$ matrix-valued and $\mathbf{m}$ an s vector. Consider the problem of choosing $\mathbf{m}$, $\mathbf{b}(u)$, $\mathbf{d}(u)$ so that the value of (3.2) is near that of $\mathbf{Y}(t)$. From the form of (3.2), we can consider the problem of finding $\mathbf{m} + \hat{\mathbf{Y}}(t)$, $\hat{\mathbf{Y}}(t) \in J_X{}^q$, with a value that is near $\mathbf{Y}(t)$. We have:

Theorem 3.1. *Let* $\mathbf{W}(t)$ $t = 0, \pm 1, \ldots$ *be an* $(r + s)$ *vector-valued time series of the form* (2.2). *Suppose*

$$d\mathbf{F}_{WW}(\lambda) = \begin{bmatrix} \mathbf{f}_{XX}(\lambda) & \mathbf{f}_{XY}(\lambda) \\ \mathbf{f}_{YX}(\lambda) & \mathbf{f}_{YY}(\lambda) \end{bmatrix} d\Phi(\lambda) \tag{3.3}$$

for some[5] *nonnegative measure* $\Phi(\lambda)$. *Suppose* $\mathbf{f}_{XX}(\lambda)$ *is nonsingular for almost all* λ, *then*

$$E\{\mathbf{Y}(t) - \mathbf{m} - \hat{\mathbf{Y}}(t)\}^\tau\{\mathbf{Y}(t) - \mathbf{m} - \hat{\mathbf{Y}}(t)\} \tag{3.4}$$

[4] The proof of this, and other theorems, may be found in Section 7.

[5] Such a measure always exists. Take $\Phi(\lambda)$ proportional to tr $\mathbf{F}_{WW}(\lambda)$, for example.

is minimized, for $\hat{\mathbf{Y}}(t) \in J_X{}^q$, *by*

$$\mathbf{m} = \mathbf{c}_Y \tag{3.5}$$

$$\hat{\mathbf{Y}}(t) = \int_{-\pi}^{\pi} \exp\{i\lambda t\}\mathbf{A}(\lambda)\, d\mathbf{Z}_X(\lambda) \tag{3.6}$$

where

$$\mathbf{A}(\lambda) = \sum_{j=1}^{q} \mathbf{V}_j(\lambda)\overline{\mathbf{V}_j(\lambda)}^{\tau}\mathbf{f}_{YX}(\lambda)\mathbf{f}_{XX}(\lambda)^{-1}. \tag{3.7}$$

Here, $\mathbf{V}_j(\lambda)$ *is the jth latent vector of* $\mathbf{f}_{YX}(\lambda)\mathbf{f}_{XX}(\lambda)^{-1}\mathbf{f}_{XY}(\lambda)$. *Letting* $\mu_j(\lambda)$ *denote the corresponding latent root, the minimum achieved in* (3.4) *is*

$$\int_{-\pi}^{\pi} \operatorname{tr}\{\mathbf{f}_{YY}(\lambda) - \mathbf{f}_{YX}(\lambda)\mathbf{f}_{XX}(\lambda)^{-1}\mathbf{f}_{XY}(\lambda)\}\, d\Phi(\lambda)$$
$$+ \int_{-\pi}^{\pi} \{\mu_{q+1}(\lambda) + \cdots + \mu_Q(\lambda)\}\, d\Phi(\lambda) \tag{3.8}$$

with $Q = \min(r, s)$. *The spectral density matrix of the residuals* $\mathbf{Y}(t) - \mathbf{c}_W - \hat{\mathbf{Y}}(t)$ *is*

$$\mathbf{f}_{YY}(\lambda) - \mathbf{f}_{YX}(\lambda)\mathbf{f}_{XX}(\lambda)^{-1}\mathbf{f}_{XY}(\lambda) + \sum_{j=q+1}^{Q} \mu_j(\lambda)V_j(\lambda)\overline{V_j(\lambda)}^{\tau} \tag{3.9}$$

with respect to the measure $\Phi(\lambda)$.

This theorem was presented by Brillinger [1]. For the case of vector-valued random variables see Rao [20, 21] (see also Kramer and Matthews [12]).

Corollary 3.1.1. *Under the conditions of the theorem, if* $q = r$,

$$\mathbf{A}(\lambda) = \mathbf{f}_{YX}(\lambda)\mathbf{f}_{XX}(\lambda)^{-1}. \tag{3.10}$$

The spectral density matrix of the residuals is

$$\mathbf{f}_{YY}(\lambda) - \mathbf{f}_{YX}(\lambda)\mathbf{f}_{XX}(\lambda)^{-1}\mathbf{f}_{XY}(\lambda) \tag{3.11}$$

with respect to the measure $\Phi(\lambda)$.

In the case $s = 1$, this corollary provides the result of the usual multiple linear time invariant regression of time series (see Koopmans [11], Rozanov [23], Masani [15], Parzen [17]).

Corollary 3.1.2. *Let* $\mathbf{X}(t)$ $t = 0, \pm 1, \ldots$ *be an r vector-valued time series having spectral density matrix* $\mathbf{f}_{XX}(\lambda)$ *with respect to the nonnegative measure* $\Phi(\lambda)$. *For* $\hat{\mathbf{X}}(t) \in J_X{}^q$,

$$E\{\mathbf{X}(t) - \mathbf{m} - \hat{\mathbf{X}}(t)\}^{\tau}\{\mathbf{X}(t) - \mathbf{m} - \hat{\mathbf{X}}(t)\} \tag{3.12}$$

is minimized by

$$\mathbf{m} = \mathbf{c}_X \tag{3.13}$$

$$\mathbf{X}(t) = \int_{-\pi}^{\pi} \exp\{i\lambda t\}\mathbf{A}(\lambda)\, d\mathbf{Z}_X(\lambda) \tag{3.14}$$

where

$$\mathbf{A}(\lambda) = \sum_{j=1}^{q} \mathbf{V}_j(\lambda)\overline{\mathbf{V}_j(\lambda)}^{\tau}. \tag{3.15}$$

Here, $\mathbf{V}_j(\lambda)$ *is the jth latent vector of* $\mathbf{f}_{XX}(\lambda)$, *and* $\mu_j(\lambda)$ *the corresponding latent root. If* $\mathbf{V}(\lambda) = [\mathbf{V}_1(\lambda), \ldots, \mathbf{V}_r(\lambda)]$, *the spectral density matrix of* $\int_{-\pi}^{\pi} \exp\{i\lambda t\}$ $\overline{\mathbf{V}(\lambda)}^{\tau}\, d\mathbf{Z}_X(\lambda)$ *is* $\text{diag}\{\mu_1(\lambda), \ldots, \mu_r(\lambda)\}$ *with respect to* $\Phi(\lambda)$.

In Section 5, we provide a worked example of this corollary. The latent roots and vectors of spectral density matrices appear in the work of Wiener [26], Whittle [25], and Pinsker [18].

Notice that the criterion (3.4) is not invariant with respect to linear time invariant transformations (filterings) of $\mathbf{Y}(t)$. For this reason, we may sometimes take, for an $s \times s$ positive definite $\mathbf{\Gamma}(\lambda)$,

$$\mathbf{A}(\lambda) = \mathbf{\Gamma}(\lambda)^{-1/2}\left\{\sum_{j=1}^{q} \mathbf{U}_j(\lambda)\overline{\mathbf{U}_j(\lambda)}^{\tau}\right\}\mathbf{\Gamma}(\lambda)^{1/2}\mathbf{f}_{YX}(\lambda)\mathbf{f}_{XX}(\lambda)^{-1} \tag{3.16}$$

where $\mathbf{U}_j(\lambda)$ is the jth latent vector of $\mathbf{\Gamma}(\lambda)^{1/2}\mathbf{f}_{YX}(\lambda)\mathbf{f}_{XX}(\lambda)^{-1}\mathbf{f}_{XY}(\lambda)\mathbf{\Gamma}(\lambda)^{1/2}$. The choice $\mathbf{\Gamma}(\lambda) = \mathbf{f}_{YY}(\lambda)^{-1}$ gives an invariant procedure that is a generalization of Hotelling's canonical correlation analysis.

In certain cases one can obtain expressions for $\hat{\mathbf{Y}}(t)$ of (3.6) in terms of $\ldots, \mathbf{X}(-1) - \mathbf{c}_X, \mathbf{X}(0) - c_X, \mathbf{X}(1) - \mathbf{c}_X, \ldots$. Suppose that $\Phi(\lambda)$ of Theorem 3.1 is Lebesgue measure on $(-\pi, \pi)$ and that the entries of $\mathbf{f}_{XX}(\lambda)$ are bounded. In this case, if $\mathbf{A}(\lambda) \in L_2^{s\times r}(\mathbf{F}_{XX})$, it results that

$$\int_{-\pi}^{\pi} \text{tr}\{\mathbf{A}(\lambda)\overline{\mathbf{A}(\lambda)}^{\tau}\}\, d\lambda < \infty \tag{3.17}$$

and so for $\mathbf{a}(u)$ given by

$$(2\pi)^{-1} \int_{-\pi}^{\pi} \exp\{i\lambda u\}\mathbf{A}(\lambda)\, d\lambda, \tag{3.18}$$

one has

$$\sum_{u=-\infty}^{\infty} \text{tr}\{\mathbf{a}(u)\mathbf{a}(u)^{\tau}\} < \infty. \tag{3.19}$$

We therefore have:

Theorem 3.2. *Under the conditions of Theorem* 3.1, *with* $\Phi(\lambda)$ *Lebesgue measure and the entries of* $\mathbf{f}_{XX}(\lambda)$ *bounded,*

$$\hat{Y}(t) = \sum_{u=-\infty}^{\infty} \mathbf{a}(t-u)\{\mathbf{X}(u) - \mathbf{c}_X\} \tag{3.20}$$

where $\mathbf{a}(u)$ *is given by* (3.18) *and satisfies* (3.19).

Unfortunately the convolution form of $\mathbf{a}(u)$, suggested by (3.1) and (3.2), is apparently not deducible under the conditions of the theorem. It does follow under alternate assumptions. Let $\alpha(u)$ be a positive function defined for $u = 0, \pm 1, \ldots,$ and such that

$$\alpha(u+v) \leq K\alpha(u)\alpha(v) \tag{3.21}$$

for some K, and $u, v = 0, \pm 1, \ldots$. (An example of such a function is $\alpha(u) = 1 + |u|^l$, $l \geq 0$.) We have:

Theorem 3.3. *Suppose the conditions of Theorem* 3.2 *are satisfied. Suppose also that the entries of* $\sum_{u=-\infty}^{\infty} \alpha(u)\,|\mathbf{c}_{WW}(u)|$ *are bounded and that the latent roots of* $\mathbf{f}_{YX}(\lambda)\mathbf{f}_{XX}(\lambda)^{-1}\mathbf{f}_{XY}(\lambda)$ *are simple for all* λ. *Then*

$$\hat{\mathbf{Y}}(t) = \sum_{u=-\infty}^{\infty} \mathbf{d} * \mathbf{b}(t-u)\{\mathbf{X}(u) - \mathbf{c}_X\} \tag{3.22}$$

with $\mathbf{d}(u)$ $s \times q$, $\mathbf{b}(u)$ $q \times r$ *and*

$$\sum_{u=-\infty}^{\infty} \alpha(u)\,|\mathbf{d}(u)| \tag{3.23}$$

$$\sum_{u=-\infty}^{\infty} \alpha(u)\,|\mathbf{b}(u)| \tag{3.24}$$

both being finite.

We see that the manner in which $\mathbf{d}(u)$ and $\mathbf{b}(u)$ fall off as $|u| \to \infty$ is directly related to the falloff of $\mathbf{c}_{WW}(u)$. In fact if $\mathbf{W}(t)$ is an m dependent process, we see that $\mathbf{d}(u), \mathbf{b}(u) = \mathbf{0}$ for $|u| > m$.

Other examples of canonical variates, for time series, appear in the work of Hannan [9] and Yaglom [28]. Further results of the type in this section are given by Brillinger [2]. Principal component analyses, in the time domain, occur in the work of Stone [24] and Craddock [5].

4. STATISTICAL PROPERTIES

Suppose one has available a stretch, $\mathbf{X}(t)$, $t = 0, \ldots, T-1$ of the r vector-valued stationary series $\mathbf{X}(t)$, and one wishes to construct estimates of the $\mu_j(\lambda)$, $\mathbf{V}_j(\lambda)$, $j = 1, \ldots, r$, and $\mathbf{A}(\lambda)$, for a particular q, of Corollary 3.1.2. One means of doing this is to construct an estimate, $\mathbf{f}_{XX}^{(T)}(\lambda)$, of $\mathbf{f}_{XX}(\lambda)$, and then to determine the latent values, $\mu_j^{(T)}(\lambda)$ and latent vectors, $\mathbf{V}_j^{(T)}(\lambda)$, of this matrix. We turn to a variety of statistical properties of a class of such estimates:

Let

$$\mathbf{d}_X^{(T)}(\lambda) = \sum_{t=0}^{T-1} \exp\{-i\lambda t\}\mathbf{X}(t) \tag{4.1}$$

$$\mathbf{I}_{XX}^{(T)}(\lambda) = (2\pi T)^{-1}\, \mathbf{d}_X^{(T)}(\lambda)\, \overline{\mathbf{d}_X^{(T)}(\lambda)}^{\tau} \tag{4.2}$$

$$\mathbf{f}_{XX}^{(T)}(\lambda) = 2\pi T^{-1} \sum_{s=1}^{T-1} H^{(T)}[\lambda - (2\pi s/T)]\mathbf{I}_{XX}^{(T)}(2\pi s/T) \tag{4.3}$$

$-\infty < \lambda < \infty$. In (4.3), $H^{(T)}(\alpha)$ is determined as follows: There is an $H(\alpha)$ satisfying:

Assumption 4.1. *$H(\alpha)$, $-\infty < \alpha < \infty$, is real-valued, continuously differentiable, $H(\alpha) = H(-\alpha)$, $\int_{-\infty}^{\infty} H(\alpha)\, d\alpha = 1$, and there exist finite K, $\varepsilon > 0$ such that*

$$|\alpha H(\alpha)|, \qquad \left|\frac{dH(\alpha)}{d\alpha}\right| \le K(|+|\alpha|)^{-1-\varepsilon}. \tag{4.4}$$

For $B_T > 0$, one then sets

$$H^{(T)}(\alpha) = B_T^{-1} \sum_{j=-\infty}^{\infty} H(B_T^{-1}[\alpha + 2\pi j]). \tag{4.5}$$

Omitting the term with $s = 0$, from (4.3), has the effect of removing the sample mean from the data. Before turning to asymptotic properties of the latent roots and vectors of $\mathbf{f}_{XX}^{(T)}(\lambda)$, we set down:

Assumption 4.2. $\mathbf{X}(t) = [X_j(t)]$, $t = 0, \pm 1, \ldots,$ *is a strictly stationary, r vector-valued series, all of whose moments exist and with*

$$c_{a_1,\ldots,a_k}(u_1, \ldots, u_{k-1}) = \operatorname{cum}\{X_{a_1}(t + u_1), \ldots X_{a_{k-1}}(t + u_{k-1}), X_{a_k}(t)\} \tag{4.6}$$

$$\sum_{u_1,\ldots,u_{k-1}=-\infty}^{\infty} |c_{a_1,\ldots,a_k}(u_1, \ldots, u_{k-1})| < \infty \tag{4.7}$$

for $a_1, \ldots, a_k = 1, \ldots, r$, and $k = 2, 3, \ldots$.

This kind of assumption is made by Brillinger and Rosenblatt [3].

We will sometimes require:

Assumption 4.3 (P). $\mathbf{X}(t)$ *satisfies Assumption* 4.2 *and for $P > 0$*

$$\sum_{u=-\infty}^{\infty} |u|^P\, |c_{a_1,a_2}(u)| < \infty \tag{4.8}$$

$a_1, a_2 = 1, \ldots, r.$

Denoting the latent roots and vectors of

$$\int_0^{2\pi} H^{(T)}(\lambda - \alpha)\mathbf{f}_{XX}(\alpha)\, d\alpha \tag{4.9}$$

by $\nu_j^{(T)}(\lambda)$, $\mathbf{W}_j^{(T)}(\lambda)$, $j = 1, \ldots, r$, we have:

Theorem 4.1. *Let* $\mathbf{X}(t)$ *be an r vector-valued series satisfying Assumption* 4.3(1). *Let* $\mu_j^{(T)}(\lambda)$, $\mathbf{V}_j^{(T)}(\lambda)$, $j = 1, \ldots, r$ *be the latent roots and vectors of* $\mathbf{f}_{XX}^{(T)}(\lambda)$ *where* $\mathbf{f}_{XX}^{(T)}(\lambda)$ *has been constructed in the manner of* (4.3) *with* $H(\alpha)$ *satisfying Assumption* 4.1. *If* $B_T \to 0$, $B_T T \to \infty$ *as* $T \to \infty$, *then*

$$E\mu_j^{(T)}(\lambda) = \nu_j^{(T)}(\lambda) + O(B_T T)^{-1/2}. \tag{4.10}$$

If the latent roots of $\mathbf{f}_{XX}(\lambda)$ *are simple, then*

$$\overrightarrow{\text{ave}}\; \mu_j^{(T)}(\lambda) = \nu_j^{(T)}(\lambda) + O(B_T T)^{-1} \tag{4.11}$$

$$\overrightarrow{\text{ave}}\; \mathbf{V}_j^{(T)}(\lambda) = \mathbf{W}_j^{(T)}(\lambda) + O(B_T T)^{-1}. \tag{4.12}$$

(In this theorem, $\overrightarrow{\text{ave}}$ has a technical definition allowing the use of the Δ-method. See Brillinger and Tukey [4].)

We have:

Corollary 4.1.1. *Under the conditions of the theorem,*

$$E\mu_j^{(T)}(\lambda), \overrightarrow{\text{ave}}\; \mu_j^{(T)}(\lambda) \to \mu_j(\lambda) \qquad \text{and} \qquad \overrightarrow{\text{ave}}\; \mathbf{V}_j^{(T)}(\lambda) \to \mathbf{V}_j(\lambda).$$

In connection with $\nu_j^{(T)}(\lambda)$, $\mathbf{W}_j^{(T)}(\lambda)$, we have:

Theorem 4.2. *Let* $H(\alpha)$ *satisfy Assumption* 4.1 *and suppose* $H(\alpha) \geq 0$, *then*

$$0 \leq \nu_j^{(T)}(\lambda) \leq \int_0^{2\pi} H^{(T)}(\lambda - \alpha)\mu_j(\alpha)\, d\alpha. \tag{4.13}$$

Let $H(\alpha)$ *satisfy Assumption* 4.1, *and let*

$$H_2 = \int_{-\infty}^{\infty} \alpha^2 H(\alpha)\, d\alpha \tag{4.14}$$

with $\int_{-\infty}^{\infty} |\alpha|^3 H(\alpha)\, d\alpha < \infty$. *Let* (4.8) *be satisfied with* $P = 3$. *Suppose the* $\mu_j(\lambda)$, $j = 1, \ldots, r$ *are distinct, then if* $B_T \to 0$ *as* $T \to \infty$,

$$\nu_j^{(T)}(\lambda) = \mu_j(\lambda) + \tfrac{1}{2}B_T^{\,2} H_2 \overline{\mathbf{V}_j(\lambda)}^{\tau} \frac{d^2\, \mathbf{f}_{XX}(\lambda)}{d\lambda^2} \mathbf{V}_j(\lambda) + O(B_T^{\,3}) \tag{4.15}$$

and

$$\mathbf{W}_j^{(T)}(\lambda) = \mathbf{V}_j(\lambda) + \tfrac{1}{2}B_T^{\,2} H_2 \sum_{k \neq j} \{\overline{\mathbf{V}_k(\lambda)}^{\tau} \frac{d^2 \mathbf{f}_{XX}(\lambda)}{d\lambda^2} \mathbf{V}_j(\lambda)\} \mathbf{V}_k(\lambda) / \{\mu_j(\lambda) - \mu_k(\lambda)\} + O(B_T^{\,3}). \tag{4.16}$$

This theorem, together with Theorem 4.1, indicates that the asymptotic biases of the $\mu_j^{(T)}(\lambda)$, $\mathbf{V}_j^{(T)}(\lambda)$ depend directly on the bandwidth, B_T, employed and the smoothness, with respect to λ, of the entries of $\mathbf{f}_{XX}(\lambda)$. The importance of prefiltering is apparent. Continuing we have:

Theorem 4.3. *Let* $\mathbf{X}(t)$ *be* r *vector-valued, satisfying Assumption* 4.2, *and such that the latent roots of* $\mathbf{f}_{XX}(\lambda)$ *are simple for* $\lambda = \lambda_1, \lambda_2$. *Let* $\mathbf{f}_{XX}^{(T)}(\lambda)$ *be constructed in the manner of* (4.3) *with* $H(\alpha)$ *satisfying Assumption* 4.1. *If* $B_T \to 0$, $B_T T \to \infty$ *as* $T \to \infty$, *then the variate*

$$\{\mu_j^{(T)}(\lambda_1), \mathbf{V}_j^{(T)}(\lambda_1), \mu_j^{(T)}(\lambda_2), \mathbf{V}_j^{(T)}(\lambda_2);\quad j = 1, \ldots, r\}$$

is asymptotically Gaussian with

$$\{\mu_j^{(T)}(\lambda_1), \mu_j^{(T)}(\lambda_2);\quad j = 1, \ldots, r\}$$

asymptotically independent of

$$\{\mathbf{V}_j^{(T)}(\lambda_1), \mathbf{V}_j^{(T)}(\lambda_2);\quad j = 1, \ldots, r\}.$$

The asymptotic covariance structure is given by

$$\lim_{T\to\infty} B_T T \overrightarrow{\text{cov}}\, \{\mu_j^{(T)}(\lambda_1), \mu_k^{(T)}(\lambda_2)\}$$
$$= \delta_{jk} 2\pi \left[\int H^2(\alpha)\, d\alpha\right] [\eta\{\lambda_1 - \lambda_2\} + \eta\{\lambda_1 + \lambda_2\}][\mu_j(\lambda_1)]^2 \tag{4.17}$$

$$\lim_{T\to\infty} B_T T \overrightarrow{\text{cov}}\, \{V_{pj}^{(T)}(\lambda_1), V_{qk}^{(T)}(\lambda_2)\}$$
$$= 2\pi \left[\int H^2(\alpha)\, d\alpha\right] \Bigg[\eta\{\lambda_1 - \lambda_2\}\delta_{jk}\mu_j(\lambda_1)$$
$$\cdot \left\{\sum_{l \neq j} \mu_l(\lambda_1)(\mu_j(\lambda_1) - \mu_l(\lambda_1))^{-2}\overline{V}_{pl}(\lambda_1)V_{ql}(\lambda_1)\right\} + \eta\{\lambda_1 - \lambda_2\}$$
$$\cdot \{1 - \delta_{jk}\}\mu_k(\lambda_1)\mu_j(\lambda_1)(\mu_j(\lambda_1) - \mu_k(\lambda_1))^{-2}\overline{V}_{pj}(\lambda_1)V_{qk}(\lambda_1)\Bigg]. \tag{4.18}$$

(In (4.17), (4.18); $\delta_{jk} = 1$ if $j = k$ and $=0$ otherwise, $\eta\{\lambda\} = 1$ if $\lambda \equiv 0$ (mod 2π) and $=0$ otherwise, the covariance of complex-valued random variables X_1, X_2 is taken to be $E\{X_1 - EX_1\}\overline{\{X_2 - EX_2\}}$.)

We see that (4.17) implies

$$\lim_{T\to\infty} B_T T \overrightarrow{\text{var}} \log \mu_j^{(T)}(\lambda) = [1 + \eta\{2\lambda\}]2\pi \int H^2(\alpha)\, d\alpha. \tag{4.19}$$

This is the same result as that obtained for the asymptotic variance of a power spectral estimate (see Parzen [16], for example).

On occasion, an alternate form of asymptotic distribution may prove relevant. Suppose we estimate $\mathbf{f}_{XX}(\lambda)$ by a simple average of periodograms. For example, with $s(T)$, m integers and $2\pi s(T)/T$ near λ, consider

$$(2m + 1)^{-1} \sum_{s=-m}^{m} \mathbf{I}_{XX}^{(T)}(2\pi[s(T) + s]/T) \tag{4.20}$$

if $\lambda \not\equiv 0 \pmod{\pi}$. Consider

$$(2m+2)^{-1}\left[\mathbf{I}_{XX}^{(T)}(\pi) + \sum_{s=-m}^{m} \mathbf{I}_{XX}^{(T)}(\pi + 2\pi s/T)\right] \tag{4.21}$$

if $\lambda = \pm\pi, \pm 3\pi, \ldots$, and consider

$$(2m)^{-1}\left\{\sum_{s=-m}^{-1} + \sum_{s=1}^{m}\right\}\mathbf{I}_{XX}^{(T)}(2\pi s/T) \tag{4.22}$$

if $\lambda \equiv 0 \pmod{2\pi}$. We have:

Theorem 4.4. *Let* $\mathbf{X}(t)$ *be an* r *vector-valued series satisfying Assumption* 4.2. *Let* m *be fixed and* $2\pi s(T)/T \to \lambda$ *as* $T \to \infty$. *If* $\lambda \not\equiv 0 \pmod{\pi}$, (4.20) *tends, in distribution, to* $(2m+1)^{-1} W_r^C(2m+1, \mathbf{f}_{XX}(\lambda))$. *If* $\lambda = \pm\pi, \pm 3\pi, \ldots$, (4.21) *tends to* $(2m+1)^{-1} W_r(2m+1, \mathbf{f}_{XX}(\lambda))$. *If* $\lambda = 0, \pm 2\pi, \pm 4\pi, \ldots$, (4.22) *tends to* $(2m)^{-1} W_r(2m, \mathbf{f}_{XX}(\lambda))$.

(In this theorem $W_r(\nu, \mathbf{\Sigma})$ denotes a real Wishart variable of dimension r, degrees of freedom ν and var-covar matrix $\mathbf{\Sigma}$. See Rao [20]. Whereas $W_r^C(\nu, \mathbf{\Sigma})$ denotes a complex Wishart variable of dimension r, degrees of freedom ν and var-covar matrix $\mathbf{\Sigma}$. See Goodman [8].)

Corollary 4.4.1. *Under the conditions of the theorem, the latent roots and vectors of* (4.20)–(4.22) *tend, in distribution, to the latent roots and vectors of the limiting Wishart distributions of the theorem.*

The distributions of the latent roots of matrices, with real and complex Wishart distributions, are given by James [10].

The estimates (4.20) and (4.21) correspond, approximately, to taking $H(\alpha) = (2\pi)^{-1}$ for $|\alpha| \le \pi$ and 0 otherwise in (4.3), implying $m \doteq B_T T/2$. This leads us to approximate the distribution of $\mathbf{f}_{XX}^{(T)}(\lambda)$, constructed in the manner of (4.3) with general $H(\alpha)$, by a $\nu^{-1} W_r^C(\nu, \mathbf{f}_{XX}(\lambda))$ or $\nu^{-1} W_r(\nu, \mathbf{f}_{XX}(\lambda))$ variate having

$$\nu = B_T T \Big/ \left\{2\pi \int H^2(\alpha)\, d\alpha\right\}. \tag{4.23}$$

This was suggested by Goodman [8]. One can then approximate the distributions of the $\mu_j^{(T)}(\lambda)$, $\mathbf{V}_j^{(T)}(\lambda)$ by the distributions of corresponding variates based on a Wishart distribution. Notice that as $m \to \infty$, one is led back to the approximation of Theorem 4.3.

If one takes $m = T$ in (4.22), that is, one is smoothing the matrix of periodograms across the whole frequency domain, then (4.22) becomes $(2\pi)^{-1}\mathbf{c}_{XX}^{(T)}(0)$. The suggested analysis is seen to reduce to a standard principal component analysis of the estimated variance-covariance matrix of the variate $\mathbf{X}(t)$.

Analogs of Theorems 4.1 to 4.4 exist for the variates of Theorem 3.1. These are given by Brillinger [2]. There are also direct extensions to the case of a continuous time parameter.

5. A WORKED EXAMPLE

In this section, we provide a preliminary report of the empirical analysis of a vector-valued series along the lines suggested by Corollary 3.1.2 and Section 4. The components of the series analyzed are the monthly mean temperatures, in °C, recorded at fourteen European stations over a period of approximately 170 years. The stations and the periods of available data are listed in Table I.

TABLE I

City	Period available	City	Period available
Basle	1755–1957	Greenwich	1763–1962
Berlin	1769–1950	New Haven	1780–1950
Breslau	1792–1950	Prague	1775–1939
Budapest	1780–1947	Stockholm	1756–1960
Copenhagen	1798–1950	Trondheim	1761–1946
De Bilt	1711–1960	Vienna	1775–1950
Edinburgh	1764–1959	Vilna	1781–1938

In the analysis, the series were first seasonally adjusted, then $\mathbf{d}^{(T)}(\lambda)$ of (4.1) was calculated for $\lambda = 2\pi k/2048$, $k = 0, \ldots, 2047$ using a fast Fourier transform algorithm. These values were then used to estimate $\mathbf{f}_{XX}(\lambda)$, $\lambda = \pi k/64$, $k = 0, \ldots, 64$ in the manner of (4.20) and (4.21) with $m = 57$. The logarithms (base 10) of the resulting power spectral estimates are given in Fig. 1 for the various components. The bandwidth of these estimates $\doteq 0.11\pi$ and the asymptotic standard error $\doteq 0.09$ if $\lambda \neq 0, \pi$. At these last points it is 0.18.

Next the latent values, $\mu_j^{(T)}(\lambda)$, and latent vectors, $\mathbf{V}_j^{(T)}(\lambda)$, of the estimated spectral density matrix, $\mathbf{f}_{XX}^{(T)}(\lambda)$, were calculated for $\lambda = \pi k/64$, $k = 0, \ldots, 64$, and $j = 1, \ldots, 14$. This was done by associating a real matrix with $\mathbf{f}_{XX}^{(T)}(\lambda)$ in the manner of Wilkinson [27, p. 174]. $\text{Log}_{10}\, \mu_j^{(T)}(\lambda)$ is plotted in Fig. 2 for $j = 1, \ldots, 14$. The asymptotic standard error of these estimates, following (4.19), is approximately 0.09 if $\lambda \neq 0, \pi$. At these last points it is 0.18.

A comparison of Figs. 1 and 2 indicates that adjacent estimates of the latent roots are apparently less correlated than are the corresponding power spectral estimates. This and (4.19) suggest that one smooth the plots of the logarithms.

Plots of the latent vectors are given by Brillinger [2]. A preliminary examination of the first latent vector suggests that it corresponds, in large part, with a simple average of the fourteen series.

6. OPEN QUESTIONS

A number of interesting problems remain. How are the results of this article affected if one requires that the filters employed be realizable? In this case $J_X{}^q$ of Section 2 would be replaced by $J_X{}^q(t)$, the closure of s vectors of the form

$$\sum_{u \leq t} \mathbf{d} * \mathbf{b}(u)\{\mathbf{X}(u) - \mathbf{c}_X\}, \tag{6.1}$$

and one would seek $\hat{\mathbf{Y}}(t)$ in this space. If one wishes a realtime procedure, as in the construction of a vocoder, or if one is interested in prediction, these results are important.

No one appears to have derived the exact distribution of the latent vectors of a real or complex Wishart matrix. James [10] has derived the distribution of the latent roots.

Finally, the discovery of techniques of rotating the factor series,

$$\int_{-\pi}^{\pi} \exp\{i\lambda t\}\overline{\mathbf{V}_j(\lambda)}^{\tau}\, d\mathbf{Z}_X(\lambda), \qquad j = 1, \ldots, q$$

of Corollary 3.1.2, to ease their interpretation, seems especially important. The difficulty of direct interpretation is augmented by the fact that if $\mathbf{V}_j(\lambda)$ is a latent vector of $\mathbf{f}_{XX}(\lambda)$, then so is $\pm i\mathbf{V}_j(\lambda)$.

7. PROOFS

Generally the proofs are only sketched. More extensive results are given by Brillinger [2].

Theorem 2.2. Equation (2.15) has the form (2.16) with $\mathbf{A}(\lambda) = \mathbf{D}(\lambda)\mathbf{B}(\lambda)$, $\mathbf{D}(\lambda)$, $\mathbf{B}(\lambda)$ being the Fourier transforms of $\mathbf{d}(u)$, $\mathbf{b}(u)$. This $\mathbf{A}(\lambda)$ has rank $\leq q$ and so $\mathbf{A}(\lambda)\overline{\mathbf{A}(\lambda)}^{\tau}$ has at most q nonzero latent roots. Consider a convergent sequence of $\mathbf{A}(\lambda)$'s in $L_2^{s \times r}(F_{XX})$. (Rosenberg [22] proved that this space is complete.) The latent roots are continuous functions of the entries of a matrix and so the limit of the sequence of $\mathbf{A}(\lambda)$'s can have at most q nonzero latent roots. The result follows.

Theorem 3.1.

$$E\{\mathbf{Y}(t) - \mathbf{m} - \hat{\mathbf{Y}}(t)\}^{\tau}\{\mathbf{Y}(t) - \mathbf{m} - \hat{\mathbf{Y}}(t)\}$$
$$= E\{\mathbf{Y}(t) - \mathbf{c}_Y - \hat{\mathbf{Y}}(t)\}^{\tau}\{\mathbf{Y}(t) - \mathbf{c}_Y - \hat{\mathbf{Y}}(t)\} + E\{\mathbf{c}_Y - \mathbf{m}\}^{\tau}\{\mathbf{c}_Y - \mathbf{m}\}$$

and (3.5) follows. Now

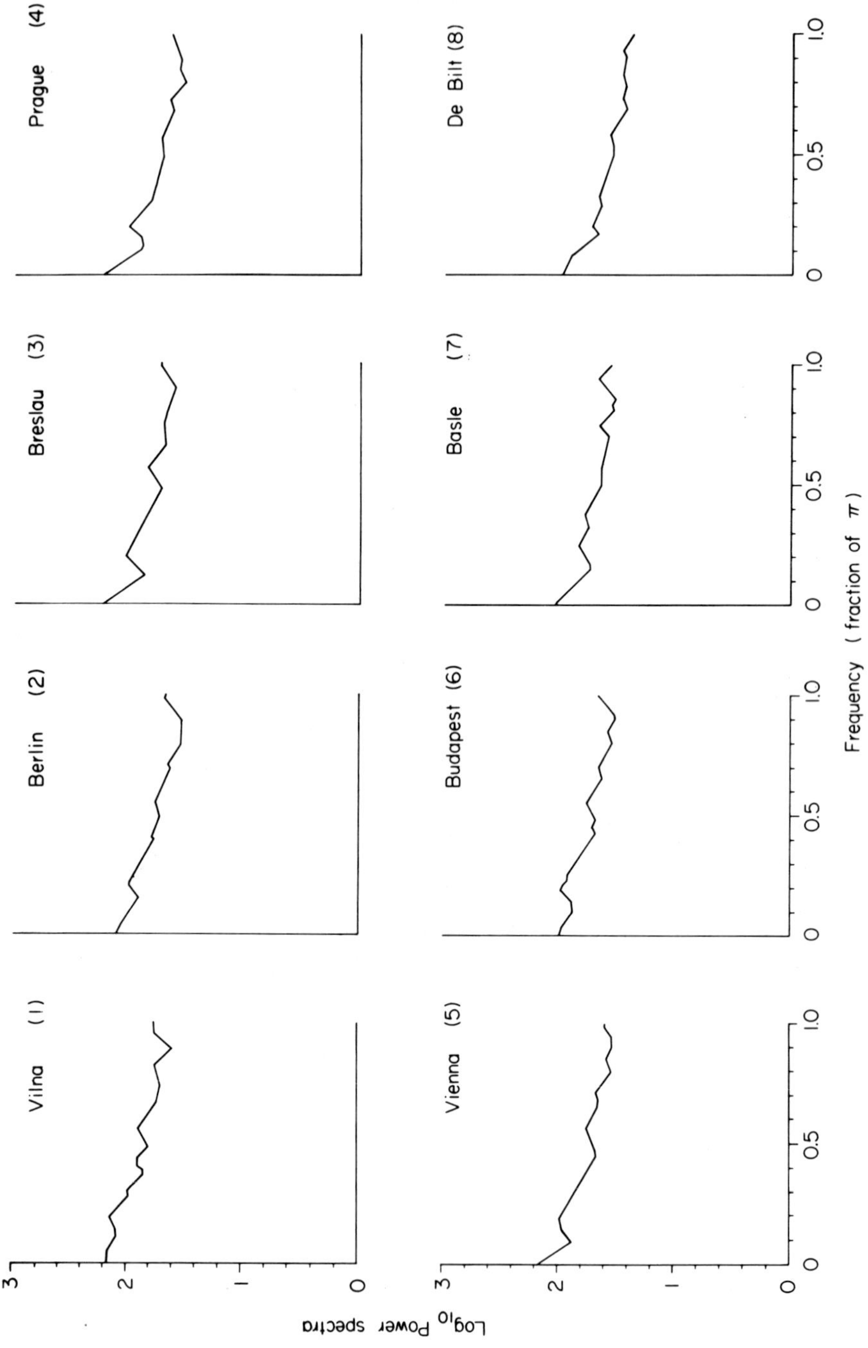

Vilna (1)
Berlin (2)
Breslau (3)
Prague (4)
Vienna (5)
Budapest (6)
Basle (7)
De Bilt (8)
Log10 Power spectra
0
1
2
3
0
0.5
1.0
Frequency (fraction of π)

Fig. 1.

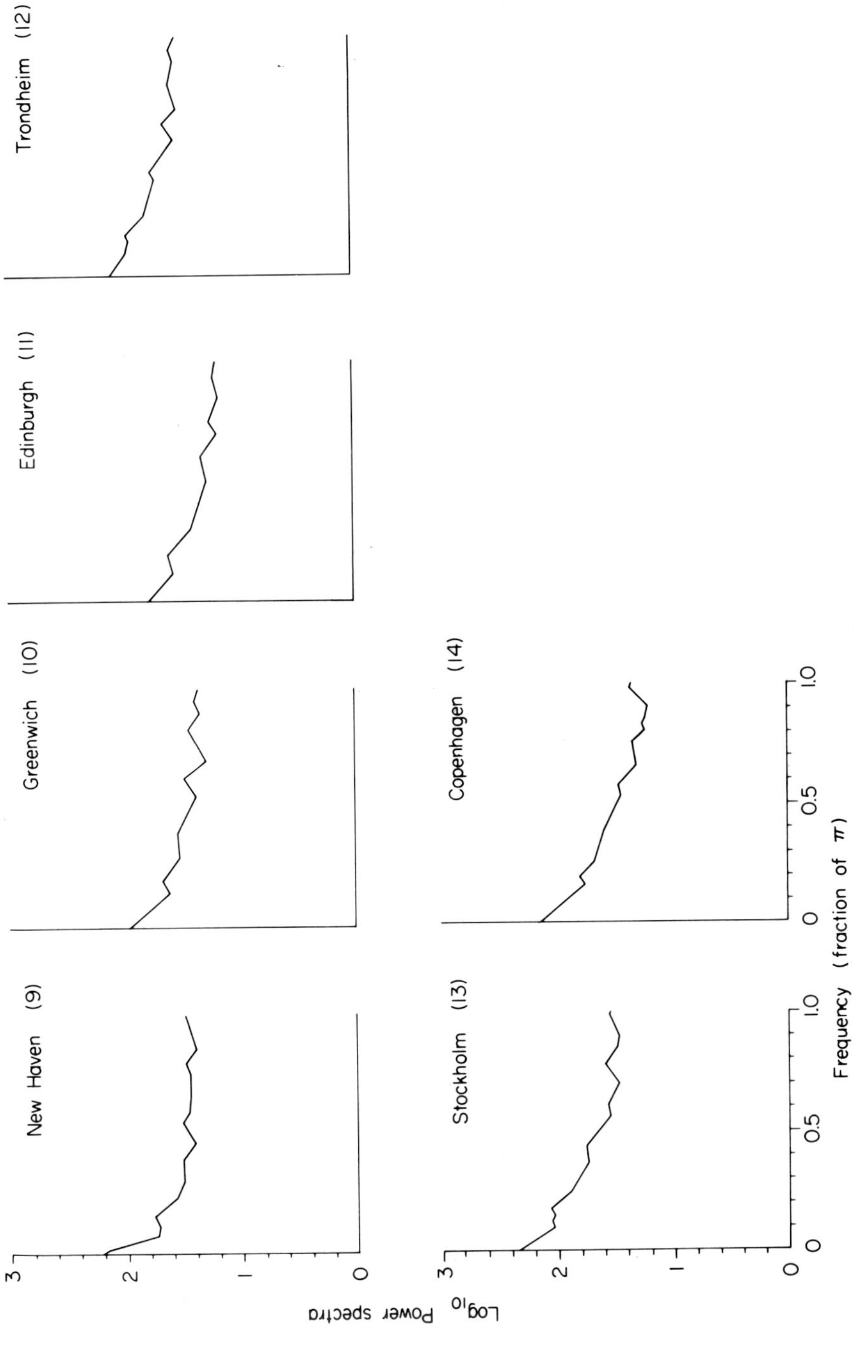

Fig. 1 (continued).

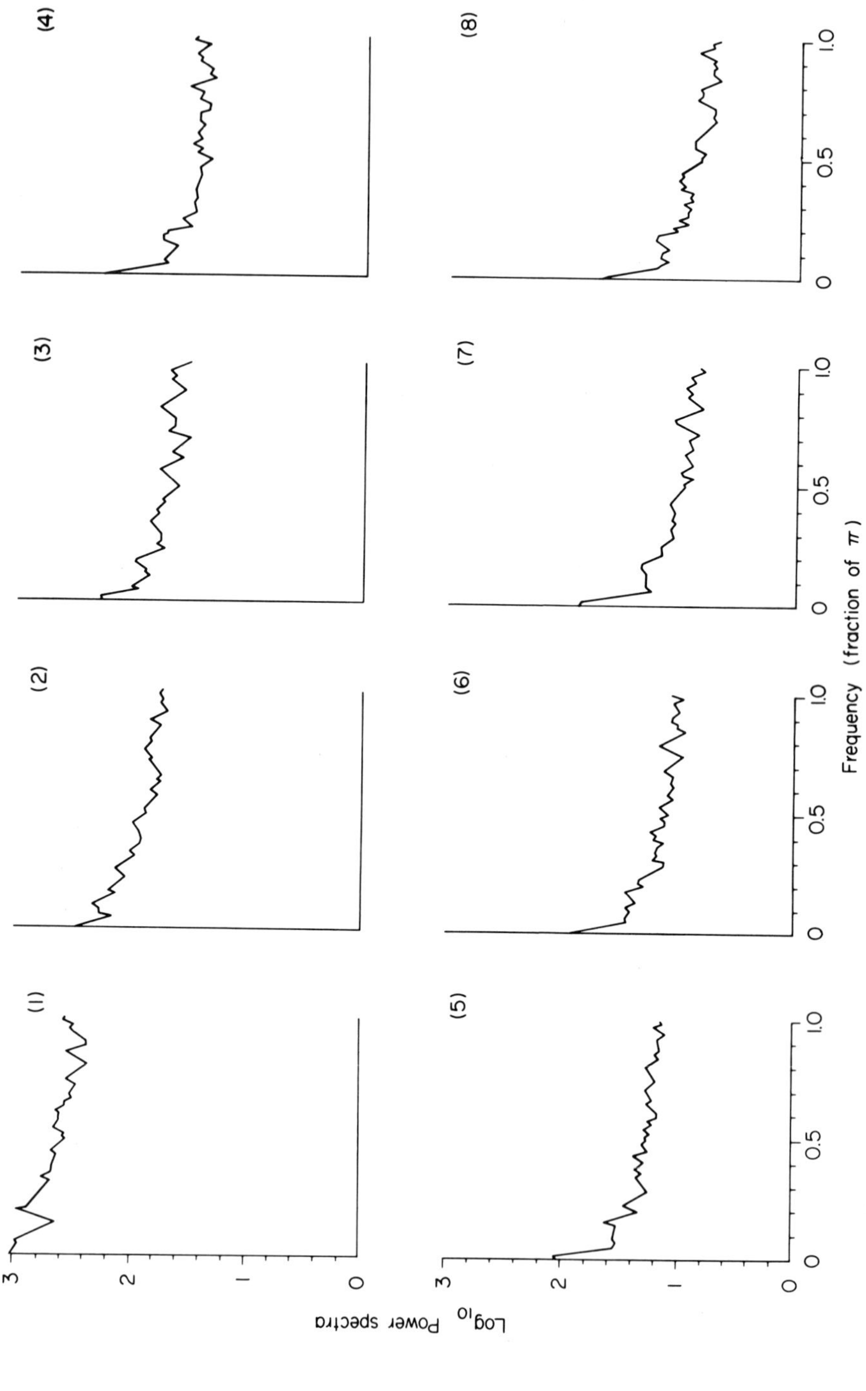
(1)
(2)
(3)
(4)
(5)
(6)
(7)
(8)
Log10 Power spectra
3
2
1
0
0
0.5
1.0
Frequency (fraction of π)

Fig. 2.

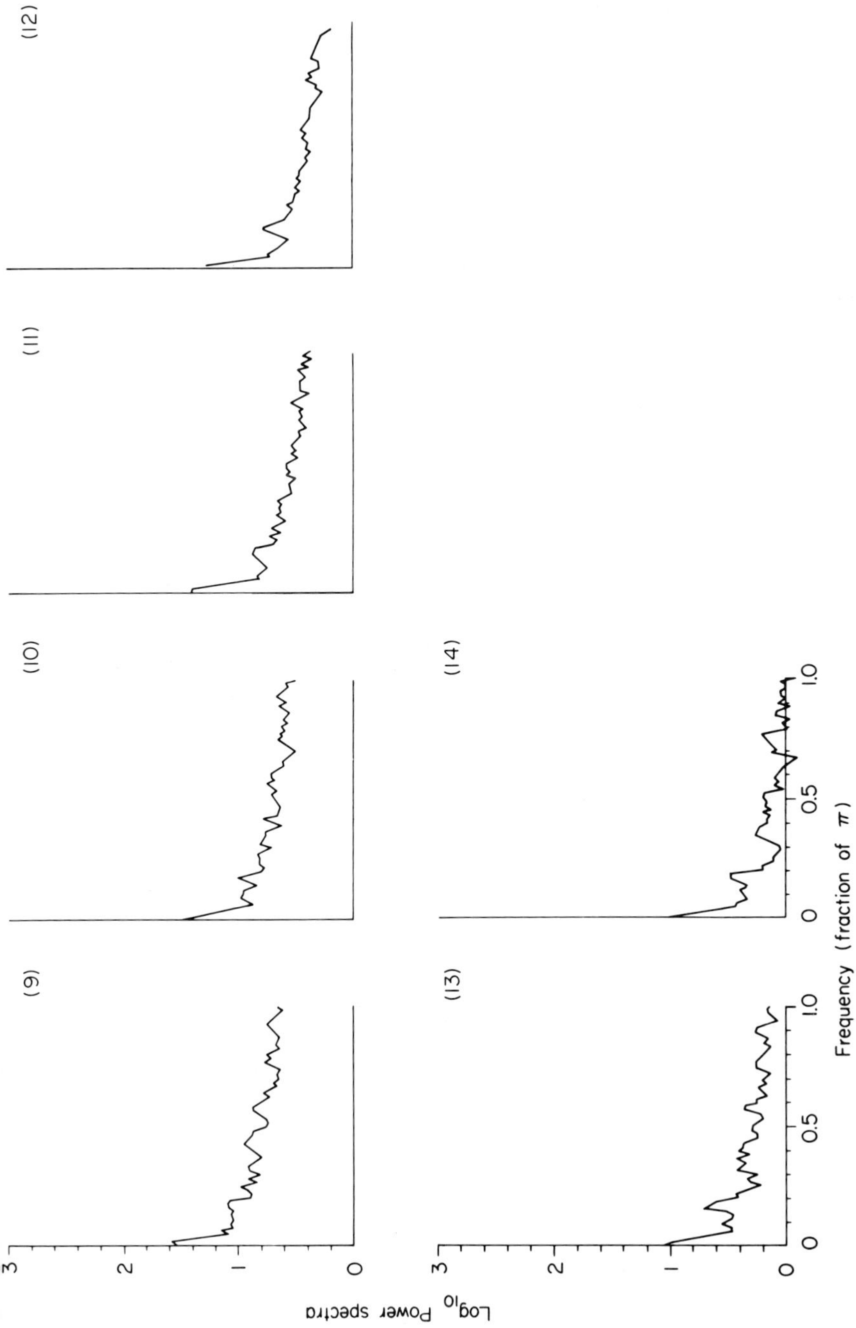

Fig. 2 (continued).

$$E\{\mathbf{Y}(t)-\mathbf{c}_Y-\hat{\mathbf{Y}}(t)\}^\tau\{\mathbf{Y}(t)-\mathbf{c}_Y-\hat{\mathbf{Y}}(t)\}$$
$$=\int_{-\pi}^{\pi}\operatorname{tr}\{\mathbf{f}_{YY}(\lambda)-\mathbf{f}_{YX}(\lambda)\mathbf{f}_{XX}(\lambda)^{-1}\mathbf{f}_{XY}(\lambda)\}\,d\Phi(\lambda)$$
$$+\int_{-\pi}^{\pi}\operatorname{tr}\{\mathbf{A}(\lambda)-\mathbf{f}_{YX}(\lambda)\mathbf{f}_{XX}(\lambda)^{-1}\}$$
$$\times\,\mathbf{f}_{XX}(\lambda)\overline{\{\mathbf{A}(\lambda)-f_{YX}(\lambda)\mathbf{f}_{XX}(\lambda)^{-1}\}}^\tau\,d\Phi(\lambda).$$

As $\mathbf{A}(\lambda)$ has rank $\leq q$, the question becomes one of approximating one matrix by another of smaller rank. The indicated result follows from a complex generalization of a theorem of Eckart and Young [6]. Related real variate results may be found in Rao [20, 21].

Theorem 3.3. We begin by noting that the latent vectors of a matrix with simple latent roots are real-analytic functions of the entries. (This follows from Portman [19].) Next we take

$$\mathbf{D}(\lambda)=[\mathbf{V}_1(\lambda),\ldots,\mathbf{V}_q(\lambda)],\qquad \mathbf{B}(\lambda)=\overline{\mathbf{D}(\lambda)}^\tau\mathbf{f}_{YX}(\lambda)\mathbf{f}_{XX}(\lambda)^{-1}.$$

Both of these are real-analytic functions of the elements of $\mathbf{f}_{WW}(\lambda)$. The theorem now follows from the Wiener-Levy Theorem on functions that operate on Fourier transforms (see Gelfand *et al.* [7]).

Theorem 4.1. From the Wielandt-Hoffman theorem (see Wilkinson [27]),

$$\sum_{j=1}^{r}\{\mu_j^{(T)}(\lambda)-\nu_j^{(T)}(\lambda)\}^2\leq\sum_{j,k=1}^{r}\left|f_{jk}^{(T)}(\lambda)-\int_0^{2\pi}H^{(T)}(\lambda-\alpha)f_{jk}(\alpha)\,d\alpha\right|^2.$$

Now

$$E\left|f_{jk}^{(T)}(\lambda)-\int_0^{2\pi}H^{(T)}(\lambda-\alpha)f_{jk}(\alpha)\,d\alpha\right|^2=O(B_TT)^{-1}$$

under the stated conditions (see Brillinger and Rosenblatt [3]) giving (4.10).

Following Wilkinson [27, p. 68], we have the following Taylor series expansions:

$$\mu_j^{(T)}(\lambda)=\nu_j^{(T)}(\lambda)+\overline{\mathbf{W}_j^{(T)}(\lambda)}^\tau\left\{\mathbf{f}_{XX}^{(T)}(\lambda)-\int_0^{2\pi}H^{(T)}(\lambda-\alpha)\right.$$
$$\left.\cdot\,\mathbf{f}_{XX}(\alpha)\,d\alpha\right\}\mathbf{W}_j^{(T)}(\lambda)+\text{higher order terms}.$$

and

$$\mathbf{V}_j^{(T)}(\lambda)=\mathbf{W}_j^{(T)}(\lambda)+\sum_{k\neq j}\left[\overline{\mathbf{W}_k(\lambda)}^\tau\left\{\mathbf{f}_{XX}^{(T)}(\lambda)-\int_0^{2\pi}H^{(T)}(\lambda-\alpha)\right.\right.$$
$$\left.\left.\cdot\,\mathbf{f}_{XX}(\alpha)d\alpha\right\}\mathbf{W}_j(\lambda)\right]\mathbf{W}_k(\lambda)/\{\nu_j^{(T)}(\lambda)-\nu_k^{(T)}(\lambda)\}+\text{higher order terms}.$$

Under the stated conditions, Eqs. (4.11) and (4.12) follow by taking expected values in these expressions (see Brillinger and Tukey [4]).

Theorem 4.2. Equations (4.15) and (4.16) follow from perturbation expansions of the type used in Theorem 4.1. Equation (4.16) follows from Weyl's characterization of latent values.

Theorem 4.3. It follows from the results of Brillinger and Rosenblatt [3] that the entries of $\mathbf{f}_{XX}^{(T)}(\lambda_1)$, $\mathbf{f}_{XX}^{(T)}(\lambda_2)$ are asymptotically jointly normal with covariance structure given by

$$\lim_{T\to\infty} B_T\, T \operatorname{cov}\{f_{a_1a_2}^{(T)}(\lambda_1), f_{b_1b_2}^{(T)}(\lambda_2)\}$$
$$= 2\pi \int H(\alpha)^2\, d\alpha[\eta\{\lambda_1 - \lambda_2\} f_{a_1b_1}(\lambda_1) f_{a_2b_2}(-\lambda_1) + \eta\{\lambda_1 + \lambda_2\}$$
$$\cdot f_{a_1b_2}(\lambda_1) f_{a_2b_1}(-\lambda_1)],$$

for

$$a_1, a_2, b_1, b_2 = 1, \ldots, r.$$

The result of the theorem now follows from the perturbation exapansions of Theorem 4.1 and a theorem of Mann and Wald [14].

Theorem 4.4. This is proved by Brillinger [2]. The corollary follows from a theorem of Mann and Wald [14].

REFERENCES

1. Brillinger, D. R. (1964). The generalization of the techniques of factor analysis, canonical correlation and principal components to stationary time series. *Roy. Statist. Soc. Conf. Cardiff, Wales*, 1964.
2. Brillinger, D. R. (1970). "An Introduction to the Frequency Analysis of Vector-Valued Time Series." Holt, New York. To be published.
3. Brillinger, D. R., and Rosenblatt, M. (1967). Asymptotic theory of kth order spectra. *In* "Spectral Analysis of Time Series" (B. Harris, ed.), pp. 153–188. Wiley, New York.
4. Brillinger, D. R., and Tukey, J. W. (1964). "Asymptotic Variances, Moments, Cumulants and Other Average Values." Unpublished manuscript.
5. Craddock, J. M. (1965). The analysis of meteorological time series for use in forecasting. *Statistician* **15** 167–190.
6. Eckhart, C., and Young, G. (1936). On the approximation of one matrix by another of lower rank. *Psychometrika* **1** 211–218.
7. Gelfand, I., Raikov, D., and Shilov, G. (1964). "Commutative Normed Rings." Chelsea, New York.
8. Goodman, N. R. (1963). Statistical analysis based upon a certain multivariate complex Gaussian distribution (an introduction). *Ann. Math. Statist.* **34** 152–177.
9. Hannan, E. J. (1961). The general theory of canonical correlation and its relation to functional analysis. *J. Austral. Math. Soc.* **2** 229–242.

10. James, A. T. (1964). Distributions of matrix variates and latent roots derived from normal samples. *Ann. Math. Statist.* **35** 475–501.
11. Koopmans, L. H. (1964). On the multivariate analysis of weakly stationary stochastic processes. *Ann. Math. Statist.* **35** 1765–1780.
12. Kramer, H. P., and Matthews, M. V. (1956). A linear coding for transmitting a set of correlated signals. *IRE Trans. Information Theory* **2** 41–46.
13. Loynes, R. M. (1965). On a generalization of second order stationarity. *Proc. London Math. Soc.* **15** 385–398.
14. Mann, H. B., and Wald, A. (1943). On stochastic limit and order relationships. *Ann. Math. Statist.* **14** 217–226
15. Masani, P. (1966). Recent trends in multivariate prediction theory. *In* "Multivariate Analysis" (P. R. Krishnaiah, ed.), pp. 351–382. Academic Press, New York.
16. Parzen, E. (1957). On consistent estimates of the spectrum of a stationary time series. *Ann. Math. Statist.* **28** 329–348.
17. Parzen, E. (1966). On empirical multiple time series analysis. *Proc. Fifth Berkeley Symp. Math. Statist. Prob.* (L. LeCam and J. Neyman, eds.), pp. 305–340. Univ. of California Press, Berkeley, California.
18. Pinsker, M. S. (1964). "Information and Information Stability of Random Variables and Processes." Holden-Day, San Francisco, California.
19. Portman, W. O. (1960). Hausdorff-analytic functions of matrices. *Proc. Amer. Math. Soc.* **11** 97–101.
20. Rao, C. R. (1965). "Linear Statistical Inference and its Applications." Wiley, New York.
21. Rao, C. R. (1965). The use and interpretation of principal component analysis in applied research. *Sankhyā Ser. A* **26** 329–358.
22. Rosenberg, M. (1964). The square-integrability of matrix-valued functions with respect to nonnegative hermitian measure. *Duke Math. J.* **31** 291–298.
23. Rozanov, Yu. A. (1967). "Stationary Random Processes." Holden-Day, San Francisco, California.
24. Stone, R. (1947). On the interdependence of blocks of transactions. *J. Roy. Statist. Soc. Ser. B* **9** 1–32.
25. Whittle, P. (1953). The analysis of multiple stationary time series. *J. Roy. Statist. Soc. Ser. B* **15** 125–139.
26. Wiener, N. (1930). Generalized harmonic analysis. *Acta Math.* **55** 117–258.
27. Wilkinson, J. H. (1965). "The Algebraic Eigenvalue Problem." Oxford Univ. Press (Clarendon), London and New York.
28. Yaglom, A. M. (1965). Stationary Gaussian processes satisfying the strong mixing condition and best predictable functionals. *In* "Bernoulli, Bayes, Laplace" (J. Neyman and L. M. LeCam, eds.), pp. 241–252. Springer, New York.

Theory of Time-Varying Spectral Analysis and Complex Wishart Matrix Processes[1,2]

N. R. GOODMAN

INDEPENDENT CONSULTANT
LOS ANGELES, CALIFORNIA

M. R. DUBMAN

ROCKETDYNE
A DIVISION OF NORTH AMERICAN ROCKWELL CORPORATION
CANOGA PARK, CALIFORNIA

INTRODUCTION AND SUMMARY

Let $X'(t) = [X_1(t), \ldots, X_p(t)]$ denote a real p-variate continuous parameter $(-\infty < t < \infty)$ time series. The time series $X(t)$ is *not* required to be stationary. Subject to mild regularity conditions on $X(t)$, a $p \times p$ Hermitian matrix-valued stochastic process $\hat{S}_t(\omega_0)$ is defined as a particular functional of the time series $X(t)$. It is demonstrated that $\hat{S}_t(\omega_0)$ may be considered to be a *time-varying* spectral density matrix estimator at frequency ω_0 of the time series $X(t)$. By studying properties of $\hat{S}_t(\omega_0)$, one in effect conducts a time-varying spectral analysis of $X(t)$. In applications, a time-varying spectral analysis is a procedure for discerning nonstationary characteristics of $X(t)$. In this connection, it is important to know the properties of $\hat{S}_t(\omega_0)$ on the *null-hypothesis* that $X(t)$ is stationary. A general complex Wishart matrix process is rigorously defined, and it is demonstrated that with $X(t)$ stationary and Gaussian, $\hat{S}_t(\omega_0)$ may be regarded as a special type of complex Wishart matrix process. This paper summarizes (without proofs) some detailed explicit distributional results pertaining to complex Wishart matrix processes and to time-varying spectral estimators on the null-hypothesis that $X(t)$ is stationary Gaussian. We remark that the restriction to continuous parameter

[1] Research supported by the United States Navy through the Office of Naval Research under Contract Nonr-4557(00). Reproduction in whole or in part permitted for any purposes of the United States Government.

[2] Additional support for preparation of the paper was provided, for the first author, by TRW, Inc. and, for the second author, by NASA under Contract NAS8-18734A.

time adhered to in this paper is not essential. Only the usual modifications are required to translate definitions and results from continuous to discrete parameter time.

1. THE MULTIVARIATE COMPLEX GAUSSIAN DISTRIBUTION

A p-variate complex Gaussian random variable $\xi' = [Z_1, Z_2, \ldots, Z_p]$ is a p-tuple of complex random variables $Z_j = X_j + iY_j$ such that the vector of real and imaginary parts $\eta' = [X_1, Y_1, \ldots, X_p, Y_p]$ is $2p$-variate Gaussian distributed with a covariance matrix

$$\Sigma_\eta \equiv E(\eta - E\eta)(\eta - E\eta)'$$
$$= \left\| \begin{bmatrix} E(X_j - \mu_{xj})(X_k - \mu_{xk}) & E(X_j - \mu_{xj})(Y_k - \mu_{yk}) \\ E(Y_j - \mu_{yj})(X_k - \mu_{xk}) & E(Y_j - \mu_{yj})(Y_k - \mu_{yk}) \end{bmatrix} \right\| \tag{1.1a}$$

of the special form where the 2×2 submatrices

$$\begin{bmatrix} E(X_j - \mu_{xj})(X_k - \mu_{xk}) & E(X_j - \mu_{xj})(Y_k - \mu_{yk}) \\ E(Y_j - \mu_{yj})(X_k - \mu_{xk}) & E(Y_j - \mu_{yj})(Y_k - \mu_{yk}) \end{bmatrix}$$
$$= \begin{cases} \dfrac{\sigma_k^2}{2} \begin{bmatrix} 1 & 0 \\ 0 & 1 \end{bmatrix} & \text{if } j = k \\ \dfrac{\sigma_j \sigma_k}{2} \begin{bmatrix} \alpha_{jk} & -\beta_{jk} \\ \beta_{jk} & \alpha_{jk} \end{bmatrix} & \text{if } j \neq k. \end{cases} \tag{1.1b}$$

In (1.1), $j, k = 1, \ldots, p$ and $E\eta' \equiv [\mu_{x1}, \mu_{y1}, \ldots, \mu_{xp}, \mu_{yp}]$. Let $\mu_\xi' = E\xi' = [\mu_{x1} + i\mu_{y1}, \ldots, \mu_{xp} + i\mu_{yp}]$, and

$$\Sigma_\xi \equiv E(\xi - \mu_\xi)\overline{(\xi - \mu_\xi)'} = \|E(Z_j - EZ_j)\overline{(Z_k - EZ_k)}\| \equiv \|\sigma_{jk}\| \tag{1.2}$$

where

$$\sigma_{jk} \equiv \begin{matrix} \sigma_k^2 & \text{if } j = k \\ (\alpha_{jk} + i\beta_{jk})\sigma_j\sigma_k & \text{if } j \neq k. \end{matrix} \tag{1.3}$$

If Σ_η is nonsingular, then Σ_ξ is nonsingular, and the probability density function of the $2p$-variate Gaussian random variable η is given by

$$p(\eta) \equiv p(\xi) = (\pi^p |\Sigma_\xi|)^{-1} \exp[-\overline{(\xi - \mu_\xi)}'\Sigma_\xi^{-1}(\xi - \mu_\xi)]. \tag{1.4}$$

The distribution of the random variable ξ specified above is called the *multivariate complex Gaussian distribution*, and its probability density function (in the case in which Σ_ξ is nonsingular) is given by (1.4). *Complex Gaussian multivariate analysis* concerns itself with the distributional theory of functions of multivariate complex Gaussian distributed random variables. Collected below for later reference are some results pertaining to the multivariate complex Gaussian distribution itself and some results of complex multivariate analysis.

Let ξ denote a zero mean p-variate complex Gaussian random variable with Hermitian covariance matrix Σ_ξ. The matrix Σ_ξ is permitted to be singular. Let $u' \equiv [u_1, u_2, \ldots, u_p]$ and $v' \equiv [v_1, v_2, \ldots, v_p]$. Then the characteristic function of $(\xi, \bar{\xi})$ can be shown to be

$$\begin{aligned} E \exp[i(u'\xi + v'\bar{\xi})] &= E \exp[i(u_1 Z_1 + \cdots + u_p Z_p + v_1 \bar{Z}_1 + \cdots + v_p \bar{Z}_p)] \\ &= \exp(-u'\Sigma_\xi v). \end{aligned} \tag{1.5}$$

Let $Z_1, Z_2, \ldots, Z_s, \ldots, Z_M$ denote M complex random variables that are jointly M-variate complex Gaussian distributed with zero mean and $M \times M$ Hermitian covariance matrix $\Sigma \equiv \|\sigma_{ss'}\|$. The matrix Σ is permitted to be singular, so that in particular some of the complex random variables Z_s, $s = 1, \ldots, M$ could be identical. Let j_s, $s = 1, \ldots, M$ take on values 0 or 1, and let $Z_s^{(0)} = Z_s$, $Z_s^{(1)} = \bar{Z}_s$. From the characteristic function (1.5), one obtains

$$EZ_1^{(j_1)} Z_2^{(j_2)} \cdots Z_s^{(j_s)} \cdots Z_M^{(j_M)} = 0 \qquad \text{if} \quad \sum_{s=1}^{M} j_s \neq \tfrac{1}{2}M; \tag{1.6}$$

that is, the Mth moment expressed in (1.6) vanishes if the number of conjugated random variables is not the same as the number of unconjugated random variables. Now, let $M = 2m$; then the Mth moment

$$EZ_1 Z_2 \cdots Z_m \bar{Z}_{m+1} \bar{Z}_{m+2} \cdots \bar{Z}_M = \begin{vmatrix} \sigma_{1,m+1} & \sigma_{1,m+2} & \cdots & \sigma_{1M} \\ \sigma_{2,m+1} & \sigma_{2,m+2} & \cdots & \sigma_{2M} \\ \vdots & \vdots & & \vdots \\ \sigma_{m,m+1} & \sigma_{m,m+2} & \cdots & \sigma_{mM} \end{vmatrix}^{+} \tag{1.7}$$

where the expression on the right-hand side of (1.7) is an $m \times m$ permanent. (The theory of permanents is discussed by Aitken [1].) For example, if $m = 2$ and $M = 4$,

$$EZ_1 Z_2 \bar{Z}_3 \bar{Z}_4 = \begin{vmatrix} \sigma_{13} & \sigma_{14} \\ \sigma_{23} & \sigma_{24} \end{vmatrix}^{+} = \sigma_{13}\sigma_{24} + \sigma_{14}\sigma_{23}. \tag{1.8}$$

2. THE CENTRAL COMPLEX WISHART DISTRIBUTION AND RELATED DISTRIBUTIONS

The following results are given by Goodman [5]. Let $\xi_1, \xi_2, \ldots, \xi_n$ be independent and identically distributed p-variate complex Gaussian random variables with Hermitian covariance matrix Σ_ξ, and define

$$A \equiv \|A_{jk}\| = \|A_{jkR} + iA_{jkI}\| \equiv \sum_{s=1}^{n} \xi_s \bar{\xi}_s'. \tag{2.1}$$

If the ξ_s have zero means, then the joint distribution of the distinct elements of the matrix A is called a $p \times p$ *central complex Wishart distribution* with parameters n (degrees of freedom) and Σ_ξ. The characteristic function of the random variables $A_{11}, \ldots, A_{pp}, 2A_{12R}, 2A_{12I}, \ldots, 2A_{p-1,pR}, 2A_{p-1,pI}$ is

$$C_W(\Theta) \equiv E \exp[i \operatorname{tr}(A\Theta)] = |I - i\Sigma_\xi \Theta|^{-n} \tag{2.2}$$

where $\Theta = \|\theta_{jk}\|$ and $\theta_{kj} = \bar{\theta}_{jk}$ with $\theta_{jk} = \theta_{jkR} + i\theta_{jkI}$ for $j, k = 1, \ldots, p$. It is important to point out that (2.2) holds even when Σ_ξ is singular and/or $n < p$. In the case in which Σ_ξ is nonsingular and $n \geq p$, the probability density function of the central complex Wishart distribution is given by

$$p_W(A) = \frac{|A|^{n-p}}{I(\Sigma_\xi)} \exp[-\operatorname{tr}(\Sigma_\xi^{-1}A)] \tag{2.3a}$$

where

$$I(\Sigma_\xi) \equiv \pi^{p(p-1)/2}\Gamma(n) \cdots \Gamma(n-p+1)|\Sigma_\xi|^n. \tag{2.3b}$$

The density $p_W(A)$ is defined over the domain D_A where A is Hermitian nonnegative definite. The probability density function $p_W(A)$ given by (2.3) is often the starting point in deriving the distributions of functions of the elements of a complex Wishart distributed matrix (see Goodman [5]).

3. THE NONCENTRAL COMPLEX WISHART DISTRIBUTION

Let $\xi_1, \xi_2, \ldots, \xi_n$ be independent p-variate complex Gaussian random variables with mean values $\mu_s \equiv E\xi_s$, $s = 1, \ldots, n$, and common Hermitian covariance matrix $\Sigma_\xi = E(\xi_s - \mu_s)(\overline{\xi_s - \mu_s})'$. Then the joint distribution of the distinct elements of the $p \times p$ matrix A defined by (2.1) is called a $p \times p$ *noncentral complex Wishart distribution* with parameters n (degrees of freedom), Σ_ξ, and $T \equiv \sum_{s=1}^{n} \mu_s \bar{\mu}_s'$ (noncentrality parameter).

Let $t \leq p$ denote the rank of the matrix T. When $t = 0$, the distribution of A is central complex Wishart. When $t = 1$ (the *linear case*), $n \geq p$, and Σ_ξ is nonsingular, the probability density function of A is given by (Khatri [7])

$$p(A) = \frac{|A|^{n-p}}{I(\Sigma_\xi)} \exp[-\operatorname{tr}(\Sigma_\xi^{-1}A)] \exp[-\operatorname{tr}(\Sigma_\xi^{-1}T)]\ {}_0F_1(n; \operatorname{tr}\{\Sigma_\xi^{-1}A\Sigma_\xi^{-1}T\}) \tag{3.1}$$

where $I(\Sigma_\xi)$ is defined by (2.3b) and ${}_0F_1(a; z)$ is the hypergeometric function

$$ {}_0F_1(a; z) = \sum_{k=0}^{\infty} \frac{\Gamma(a)}{\Gamma(a+k)} \frac{z^k}{k!}. \tag{3.2} $$

The following theorem is needed to obtain a result stated in the next section.

Theorem 3.1. *When $t = 2$ (planar case) and Σ_ξ is nonsingular, the probability density function of a 2×2 noncentral complex Wishart distributed matrix A is*

$$ p(A) = \frac{|A|^{n-2}}{\pi|\Sigma_\xi|^n} \exp[-\operatorname{tr}(\Sigma_\xi^{-1}A)] \exp[-\operatorname{tr}(\Sigma_\xi^{-1}T)] \cdot \sum_{k=0}^{\infty} \frac{|\Sigma_\xi^{-1}A\Sigma_\xi^{-1}T|^k}{\Gamma(n-1+k)\Gamma(n+2k)k!} \, {}_0F_1(n+2k; \operatorname{tr}\{\Sigma_\xi^{-1}A\Sigma_\xi^{-1}T\}). \tag{3.3} $$

We note here that an expression for the probability density function of the general noncentral complex Wishart distribution has been given by James [6] in terms of a Bessel-type (${}_0F_1$) hypergeometric function of matrix argument. We also note that Theorem 3.1 is the complex Gaussian version of the $p = t = 2$ case of Anderson and Girshick [2]. A similar result holds for $p \geq t = 2$.

4. THE JOINT DISTRIBUTION OF TWO CORRELATED CENTRAL COMPLEX WISHART MATRICES (THE BIVARIATE 2 × 2 COMPLEX WISHART DISTRIBUTION)

Let $\xi_j' = [\xi_{1j}'; \xi_{2j}'] = [Z_{1j}, Z_{2j}; Z_{3j}, Z_{4j}]$, $j = 1, \ldots, n$, denote independent and identically distributed zero mean 4-variate complex Gaussian random variables with Hermitian positive definite covariance matrix

$$ \Sigma \equiv E\xi_j\bar{\xi}_j' = E\begin{bmatrix} \xi_{1j} \\ \xi_{2j} \end{bmatrix}[\bar{\xi}_{1j}'; \bar{\xi}_{2j}'] = \left[\begin{array}{c|c} \Sigma_{11} & \Sigma_{12} \\ \hline \Sigma_{21} & \Sigma_{22} \end{array}\right], \qquad j = 1, \ldots, n. \tag{4.1} $$

Let

$$ A_{11} \equiv \sum_{j=1}^{n} \xi_{1j}\bar{\xi}_{1j}' \qquad \text{and} \qquad A_{22} \equiv \sum_{j=1}^{n} \xi_{2j}\bar{\xi}_{2j}'. \tag{4.2} $$

The matrices A_{11} and A_{22} are each 2×2 complex Wishart distributed with distributional parameters n, Σ_{11}, and n, Σ_{22}, respectively. Using Theorem 3.1

and the fact that the conditional distribution of A_{11} given A_{22} is noncentral complex Wishart, we obtain:

Theorem 4.1. *When $n \geq 2$, the joint probability density function $p(A_{11}, A_{22})$ of A_{11} and A_{22} is given by*

$$p(A_{11}, A_{22}) = \frac{|A_{11}|^{n-2}|A_{22}|^{n-2}}{\pi^2\Gamma(n)\Gamma(n-1)|\Sigma|^n} \exp[-\mathrm{tr}(\Sigma^{11}A_{11})] \exp[-\mathrm{tr}(\Sigma^{22}A_{22})]$$

$$\cdot \sum_{k=0}^{\infty} \frac{|\Sigma^{21}A_{11}\Sigma^{12}A_{22}|^k}{\Gamma(n-1+k)\Gamma(n+2k)k!} {}_0F_1(n+2k; \mathrm{tr}\{\Sigma^{21}A_{11}\Sigma^{12}A_{22}\}) \tag{4.3}$$

where $\|\Sigma^{jk}\| \equiv \Sigma^{-1}$.

5. THE MULTIVARIATE COMPLEX WISHART DISTRIBUTION

The joint distribution of the random matrices A_{11} and A_{22} which is given by Theorem 4.1 can be regarded as a particular case of the *multivariate complex Wishart distribution* which we define as follows. Let $\xi'_{\alpha j} = [Z_{1\alpha j}, \ldots, Z_{p\alpha j}]$, where $\alpha = 1, \ldots, N$ and $j = 1, \ldots, n$, be p-variate complex Gaussian random variables such that $\xi_j' \equiv [\xi'_{1j}; \ldots; \xi'_{Nj}]$, $j = 1, 2, \ldots, n$, are independent and identically distributed zero mean pN-variate complex Gaussian random variables with Hermitian covariance matrix

$$\Sigma \equiv E\xi_j\bar{\xi}_j' = E\begin{bmatrix} \xi_{1j} \\ \vdots \\ \xi_{Nj} \end{bmatrix} [\bar{\xi}'_{1j}; \ldots; \bar{\xi}'_{Nj}] \equiv \|\Sigma_{\alpha\beta}\|, \qquad j = 1, \ldots, n, \tag{5.1}$$

where $\Sigma_{\alpha\beta} \equiv \|E\xi_{\alpha j}\bar{\xi}'_{\beta j}\|$. Let

$$A_{\alpha\alpha} \equiv \sum_{j=1}^{n} \xi_{\alpha j}\bar{\xi}'_{\alpha j}, \qquad \alpha = 1, \ldots, N. \tag{5.2}$$

Each of the matrices $A_{\alpha\alpha}$ is $p \times p$ complex Wishart distributed with parameters n and $\Sigma_{\alpha\alpha}$. Their joint distribution (i.e., the joint distribution of the distinct real and imaginary parts of $A_{11}, \ldots, A_{NN}$) is called an *N-variate $p \times p$ complex Wishart distribution* with parameters n (degrees of freedom) and Σ. Note that the $A_{\alpha\alpha}$ are the $p \times p$ matrices which lie along the diagonal of the partitioned $pN \times pN$ matrix

$$A \equiv \|A_{\alpha\beta}\| \equiv \left\| \sum_{j=1}^{n} \xi_{\alpha j}\bar{\xi}'_{\beta j} \right\|, \tag{5.3}$$

and A is complex Wishart distributed with parameters n and Σ. Thus, multivariate complex Wishart distributions arise as marginal distributions of larger (univariate) complex Wishart random matrices. From this observation and from the known general form (2.2) of the characteristic function of a complex Wishart distribution, we immediately obtain the following result.

Let

$$A_{\alpha\alpha} = \|A_{\alpha\alpha;\, kk'}\|, \qquad k, k' = 1, \ldots, p; \quad \alpha = 1, \ldots, N, \tag{5.4}$$

where $A_{11}, \ldots, A_{NN}$ are N-variate $p \times p$ complex Wishart distributed with parameters n and Σ. Then the joint characteristic function of the random variables $A_{\alpha\alpha;\, kk}$, $2A_{\alpha\alpha;\, kk'R}$, $2A_{\alpha\alpha;\, kk'I}$, where $k < k'$; $k, k' = 1, \ldots, p$; and $\alpha = 1, \ldots, N$ is given by

$$\begin{aligned} C_W(\Theta_{11}, \ldots, \Theta_{NN}) &\equiv E \exp[i \operatorname{tr}(A_{11}\Theta_{11} + \cdots + A_{NN}\Theta_{NN})] \\ &= |I_{pN} - i\Sigma\Theta|^{-n}. \end{aligned} \tag{5.5}$$

Here I_{pN} is the $pN \times pN$ identity matrix and $\Theta \equiv \operatorname{diag}(\Theta_{11}, \ldots, \Theta_{NN})$ is a $pN \times pN$ matrix with $p \times p$ Hermitian blocks $\Theta_{\alpha\alpha}$ down the diagonal and with zeros elsewhere. This result holds if Σ is singular and/or $n < p$.

Using the terminology introduced above, we can describe the joint distribution of the random matrices A_{11} and A_{22} defined at the beginning of Section 4 as a bivariate 2×2 complex Wishart distribution. Theorem 4.1 gives the probability density function of this distribution in the nonsingular case. For comparison, we record here the $p = 1$ version of this result (i.e., the probability density function of the bivariate 1×1 complex Wishart distribution) which is given by Goodman [3]. Let $A = \|a_{jk}\|$ be a 2×2 central complex Wishart distributed matrix with distributional parameters $n \geq 1$ and Hermitian positive definite covariance matrix $\Sigma = \|\sigma_{jk}\|$. Then the joint probability density function $p(a_{11}, a_{22})$ of a_{11} and a_{22} is given by

$$p(a_{11}, a_{22}) = \frac{(a_{11}a_{22})^{n-1}}{\Gamma^2(n)|\Sigma|^n} \exp[-(\sigma^{11}a_{11} + \sigma^{22}a_{22})]\, {}_0F_1(n; |\sigma^{12}|^2 a_{11}a_{22}) \tag{5.6a}$$

where

$$\begin{bmatrix} \sigma^{11} & \sigma^{12} \\ \sigma^{21} & \sigma^{22} \end{bmatrix} \equiv \Sigma^{-1} = |\Sigma|^{-1} \begin{bmatrix} \sigma_{22} & -\sigma_{12} \\ -\sigma_{21} & \sigma_{11} \end{bmatrix}. \tag{5.6b}$$

6. COMPLEX WISHART PROCESSES

Let $\xi_s(t)$, $s = 1, \ldots, n$, denote (n) p-variate continuous parameter $(-\infty < t < \infty)$ stochastic processes which are: (i) zero mean weakly stationary, (ii) complex Gaussian, (iii) independent, and (iv) identically distributed. Condition (ii) means that for every choice of times $t_1, \ldots, t_N$, the random variables $[\xi_s'(t_1), \ldots, \xi_s'(t_N)]$ are pN-variate complex Gaussian distributed in the sense of Section 1. As a consequence of (i) and (ii), the processes $\xi_s(t)$ are strictly stationary, and their finite dimensional distributions are completely determined by their matrix-valued covariance functions $R_{\xi_s}(\tau) \equiv E\xi_s(t+\tau)\overline{\xi_s(t)}'$. Also, (iv) is equivalent to the equality of $R_{\xi_s}(\tau)$ for all τ and $s = 1, \ldots, n$. We denote the common covariance function of the $\xi_s(t)$ by

$$R_\xi(\tau) \equiv E\xi_s(t+\tau)\overline{\xi_s(t)}' \equiv \|R_{\xi;jk}(\tau)\|, \qquad s = 1, \ldots, n. \tag{6.1}$$

For each t in $-\infty < t < \infty$, we now let $A(t)$ denote the random $p \times p$ Hermitian matrix

$$A(t) \equiv \sum_{s=1}^{n} \xi_s(t)\overline{\xi_s(t)}' \equiv \|A_{jk}(t)\|. \tag{6.2}$$

Letting t vary, one obtains in this manner an Hermitian-matrix-valued stochastic process $A(t)$, $-\infty < t < \infty$, which is called a $(p \times p)$ *complex Wishart* (*matrix*) *process* with parameters n (degrees of freedom) and matrix covariance function $R_\xi(\tau)$.

The above definition of a complex Wishart process is a natural generalization to stochastic processes of the definition (see Section 2) of a complex Wishart distributed random matrix. We note, in fact, that a complex Wishart process is strictly stationary and that its first order distributions are complex Wishart with parameters n and $R_\xi(0)$.

In the special case $p = 1$, a complex Wishart process is real-valued (nonnegative), and its first order distribution is chi-squared with $2n$ degrees of freedom. It may be shown that the class of 1×1 complex Wishart processes contains as *proper* subclasses two types of processes which have been considered in the literature. These are the "chi-squared," or squared "generalized Rayleigh," processes with an even number of degrees of freedom (Silverman [12], Miller *et al.* [8]) and the "squared envelopes" of stationary Gaussian noise (Rice [11]).

7. A PARTICULAR CLASS OF COMPLEX WISHART PROCESSES

In this section, we introduce special complex Wishart processes that are ideal counterparts of time-varying spectral density matrix estimators for multiple stationary Gaussian time series.

Let $X'(t) = [X_1(t), \ldots, X_p(t)]$ be a real zero mean continuous parameter $(-\infty < t < \infty)$ multiple stationary Gaussian time series. Under appropriate regularity conditions (mean square continuity, etc.) $X(t)$ has the spectral representation

$$X(t) = \int_{-\infty}^{\infty} e^{i\omega t}\, d\zeta(\omega) \tag{7.1}$$

where $\zeta'(\omega) = [Z_1(\omega), \ldots, Z_p(\omega)]$ and the increments $d\zeta'(\omega) = [dZ_1(\omega), \ldots, dZ_p(\omega)]$, $-\infty < \omega < \infty$ possess the properties: (i) $d\zeta(-\omega) = \overline{d\zeta(\omega)}$, and (ii) $d\zeta(\omega)$ for $0 < \omega < \infty$ are independent zero mean p-variate complex Gaussian random variables (in the sense of Section 1) with Hermitian nonnegative definite covariance matrix

$$Ed\zeta(\omega)\,\overline{d\zeta(\omega)}' = \|s_{jk}(\omega)\|\,d\omega \equiv S(\omega)\,d\omega. \tag{7.2}$$

The matrix $S(\omega)$ is called the *spectral density matrix* at frequency ω of the time series $X(t)$.

Now consider $2M+1$ positive frequencies ω_m, $m = -M, \ldots, M$, equally spaced an interval $b > 0$ apart with $\omega_{-M} < \cdots < \omega_0 < \cdots < \omega_M$; that is, $\omega_m = \omega_0 + mb$, $m = -M, \ldots, M$. The ω_m are the center frequencies of the intervals $(\omega_m - \frac{1}{2}b, \omega_m + \frac{1}{2}b]$ which comprise a partition of the frequency band $(\omega_0 - \frac{1}{2}B, \omega_0 + \frac{1}{2}B]$, with $B \equiv (2M+1)b$, into $2M+1$ nonoverlapping subbands of equal length b. We assume that $\omega_0 - \frac{1}{2}B > 0$. Let $G(\omega)$ be a real-valued, even, continuous function of ω which is not identically zero, but which vanishes outside the interval $-\frac{1}{2}b \le \omega \le \frac{1}{2}b$, and consider the complex-valued processes

$$\zeta_m(t) \equiv \int_{-\infty}^{\infty} G(\omega - \omega_m)e^{i\omega t}\,d\zeta(\omega), \qquad m = -M, \ldots, M. \tag{7.3}$$

Because of the properties of the function $G(\omega)$ and of the increments $d\zeta(\omega)$ stated above, it follows that the processes $\zeta_m(t)$ are independent zero mean multiple stationary complex Gaussian time series. *We assume now and henceforth that* $S(\omega) = S(\omega_0)$ *for* $\omega_0 - \frac{1}{2}B < \omega \le \omega_0 + \frac{1}{2}B$, *where* $S(\omega_0)$ *is nonsingular*. The matrix-valued covariance function of $\zeta_m(t)$ is then given by

$$R_{\zeta_m}(\tau) \equiv E\zeta_m(t+\tau)\overline{\zeta_m(t)}' = S(\omega_0)\int_{\omega_m - b/2}^{\omega_m + b/2} G^2(\omega - \omega_m)e^{i\omega\tau}\,d\omega. \tag{7.4}$$

It is obvious from (7.4), and from the properties of $G(\omega)$ and $S(\omega_0)$, that the processes $\zeta_m(t)$ are not identically distributed. Consider, however, the processes $\xi_m(t) \equiv \zeta_m(t)\exp(-i\omega_m t)$, $m = -M, \ldots, M$ obtained by "heterodyning" the $\zeta_m(t)$. The $\xi_m(t)$ satisfy the conditions (i)–(iii) of Section 6 and, in addition, from (7.4), one has

$$R_{\xi_m}(\tau) \equiv E\xi_m(t+\tau)\overline{\xi_m(t)}' = R_{\zeta_m}(\tau)\exp(-i\omega_m\tau) = S(\omega_0)g(\tau) \tag{7.5}$$

where

$$g(\tau) \equiv \int_{-b/2}^{b/2} G^2(\omega)e^{i\omega\tau}\,d\omega = 2\int_0^{b/2} G^2(\omega)\cos\omega\tau\,d\omega. \tag{7.6}$$

Consequently, the $\zeta_m(t)$ processes are identically distributed; i.e., they also satisfy condition (iv) of Section 6. Now consider the $p \times p$ Hermitian matrix-valued process

$$C(t) \equiv \sum_{m=-M}^{M} \zeta_m(t)\overline{\zeta_m(t)}' \equiv \|c_{jk}(t)\|. \tag{7.7a}$$

Since

$$C(t) = \sum_{m=-M}^{M} \xi_m(t)\overline{\xi_m(t)}', \tag{7.7b}$$

it follows that $C(t)$ is a complex Wishart process. The parameters of $C(t)$ as a complex Wishart process are $n = 2M + 1$ and $R_\xi(\tau) = S(\omega_0)g(\tau)$.

We note that the function $g(\tau)$ is an autocovariance function since it is the Fourier (cosine) transform of $G^2(\omega)$. By the Riemann-Lebesgue lemma, one has $g(\tau) \to 0$ as $|\tau| \to \infty$ which implies that $R_\xi(\tau) \to 0$ as $|\tau| \to \infty$. Since $g(\tau)$ is an even function of τ, one has $R_\xi(-\tau) \equiv R_\xi(\tau)$, or equivalently $R_\xi(\tau) = \overline{R_\xi(\tau)}'$. This Hermitian symmetry of the covariance function $R_\xi(\tau)$ of the complex Wishart process $C(t)$ implies that the processes $\xi_m(t)$ have the following special covariance properties.

Let $\xi_{jm}(t)$ be the jth component of $\xi_m(t)$ so that $R_\xi(\tau) \equiv \|R_{\xi;\, jk}(\tau)\| = \|E\xi_{jm}(t+\tau)\overline{\xi_{km}(t)}\|$. Also let $\xi_{jmR}(t)$ and $\xi_{jmI}(t)$ denote the real and imaginary parts, respectively, of $\xi_{jm}(t)$. Then the stochastic processes $\xi_{jmR}(t)$ and $\xi_{jmI}(t)$ are independent. In particular

$$E\xi_{jmR}(t+\tau)\xi_{jmI}(t) = 0. \tag{7.8a}$$

Also

$$E\xi_{jmR}(t+\tau)\xi_{jmR}(t) = E\xi_{jmI}(t+\tau)\xi_{jmI}(t) = \tfrac{1}{2}R_{\xi;jj}(\tau), \tag{7.8b}$$

and

$$\begin{aligned} E\xi_{jmR}(t+\tau)\xi_{kmR}(t) &= E\xi_{jmI}(t+\tau)\xi_{kmI}(t) = \tfrac{1}{2}R_{\xi;jkR}(\tau) \\ -E\xi_{jmR}(t+\tau)\xi_{kmI}(t) &= E\xi_{jmI}(t+\tau)\xi_{kmR}(t) = \tfrac{1}{2}R_{\xi;jkI}(\tau). \end{aligned} \tag{7.8c}$$

Comparing (7.8) with (1.1), we observe that the $\xi_m(t)$ have covariance properties as stochastic processes that are analogous to the covariance properties of complex Gaussian distributed random variables ξ. In this connection, the matrix covariance function $R_\xi(\tau)$ plays a role analogous to a Hermitian covariance matrix Σ_ξ.

In relation to the comment made at the close of Section 6, we remark that in the special case $p = 1$, the processes $C(t)$ as defined above are "chi-squared" processes. Such processes $C(t)$ may also be characterized as *sums* of independent realizations of "squared envelopes" of stationary Gaussian noise.

8. TIME-VARYING SPECTRAL ESTIMATORS

In this section, $X'(t) = [X_1(t), \ldots, X_p(t)]$ is taken to be a real p-variate continuous parameter time series. The definitions which follow do not require that the time series be stationary, or even have zero mean, although it is assumed that the sample functions of $X(t)$ are integrable over finite-time intervals.

We first introduce certain linear functionals of $X(t)$ which are finite-sample counterparts of the $\zeta_m(t)$, given by (7.3), in the special case of stationary-time series $X(t)$ that were considered in Section 7. For this purpose, let ω_0, b, and T be fixed positive constants and M a fixed positive integer. Also let ω_m, $m = -M, \ldots, M$, denote the frequencies defined above, and let $K(\tau)$ be a real-valued, even, integrable function of τ which vanishes outside the interval $-T \leq \tau \leq T$. We set

$$K_m(\tau) \equiv \tfrac{1}{2}K(\tau)\exp(-i\omega_m \tau), \tag{8.1}$$

and define

$$\Delta_t \zeta(\omega_m) \equiv \int_{-\infty}^{\infty} K_m(\tau)X(t+\tau)\,d\tau. \tag{8.2}$$

In (8.1) and (8.2), and in subsequent equations, m ranges over $-M, \ldots, M$; t in $-\infty < t < \infty$; and τ in $-\infty < \tau < \infty$. Note that since $K(\tau)$ vanishes for $|\tau| > T$, so does the "kernel" $K_m(\tau)$. Thus, for each t the random variables defined by (8.2) are integral averages of the finite realization $X(s)$, $t - T \leq s \leq t + T$, of length $2T$ and centered at time t, where the averaging kernel in (8.2) is independent of t. In the language of communications engineering, we say that $\Delta_t \zeta(\omega_m)$ is obtained by passing $X(t)$ through a linear time-invariant filter with impulse response function $K_m(\tau)$. It is intended that $K(\tau)$ be chosen so that if $X(t)$ is stationary Gaussian as described in Section 7, then $\Delta_t \zeta(\omega_m)$ approximate $\zeta_m(t)$ defined by (7.3).

To see how $K(\tau)$ should be chosen, introduce the spectral representation of $X(t+\tau)$ given by (7.1) into (8.2). Interchanging the order of integration, one obtains

$$\Delta_t \zeta(\omega_m) = \int_{-\infty}^{\infty} F_m(\omega)e^{i\omega t}\,d\zeta(\omega) \tag{8.3}$$

with

$$F_m(\omega) \equiv \int_{-\infty}^{\infty} K_m(\tau)e^{i\omega\tau}\,d\tau = F(\omega - \omega_m) \tag{8.4a}$$

where

$$F(\omega) \equiv \tfrac{1}{2}\int_{-\infty}^{\infty} K(\tau)e^{i\omega\tau}\,d\tau = \int_0^T K(\tau)\cos\omega\tau\,d\tau. \tag{8.4b}$$

Upon considering (8.4) and comparing (8.3) with (7.3), one notes that $\Delta_t \zeta(\omega_m) = \zeta_m(t)$ if $F(\omega) = G(\omega)$. Since $K(\tau)$ is a time-limited function and $G(\omega)$ a band-limited function, it is not possible to choose a $K(\tau)$ so that exact equality of $F(\omega)$ and $G(\omega)$ will result. However, if the sample length $2T$ is sufficiently long, it is possible to "design" an $F(\omega)$ which is a good approximation to $G(\omega)$. (See Parzen [10], Ormsby [9], and Goodman [4].) Furthermore, under suitable regularity conditions on $S(\omega)$, $-\infty < \omega < \infty$, the $\Delta_t \zeta(\omega_m)$ and $\zeta_m(t)$ are also approximately equal (in a mean square sense).

Returning now to the general case of a possibly nonstationary $X(t)$ and Eqs. (8.1) and (8.2), we define

$$\hat{S}_t(\omega_0) \equiv \|\hat{s}_{t;jk}(\omega_0)\| \equiv (2M+1)^{-1} \sum_{m=-M}^{M} \Delta_t \zeta(\omega_m) \overline{\Delta_t \zeta(\omega_m)'}. \tag{8.5}$$

For ω_0 and t fixed, $\hat{S}_t(\omega_0)$ is called a *sample spectral density matrix* of $X(t)$ corresponding to frequency ω_0 and time t. Keeping ω_0 fixed and letting t vary, one obtains an Hermitian-matrix-valued stochastic process which we call a *time-varying sample spectral density matrix process* (corresponding to frequency ω_0). Similar terminology is applied to the elements $\hat{s}_{t;\,jk}(\omega_0)$ and to functions of these elements.

In the theory of multiple stationary time series, various functions of the elements of spectral density matrices play important roles, especially those functions which arise in describing linear relationships between components of the time series. If $\hat{S}(\omega) = \|\hat{s}_{jk}(\omega)\|$ is an estimator of a spectral density matrix $S(\omega) = \|s_{jk}(\omega)\|$ obtained from a finite-length sample in some suitable manner (e.g., by the method outlined above), then functions of the $s_{jk}(\omega)$ are usually estimated by taking the same functions of the $\hat{s}_{jk}(\omega)$. By analogy, we define time-varying estimators of functions of a spectral density matrix by taking the same functions of the elements $\hat{s}_{t;\,jk}(\omega_0)$ of a time-varying sample spectral density matrix $\hat{S}_t(\omega_0)$. An example of interest in applications is as follows. For any $j, k = 1, \ldots, p$ with $j \neq k$ let

$$\hat{\gamma}_{t;jk}(\omega_0) = \{\hat{s}_{t;jj}(\omega_0)\hat{s}_{t;kk}(\omega_0)\}^{-1} |\hat{s}_{t;jk}(\omega_0)|^2. \tag{8.6}$$

Equation (8.6) gives the *time-varying sample coherence* (at frequency ω_0) between the components $X_j(t)$ and $X_k(t)$ of the time series $X(t)$. It is a time-varying finite-sample counterpart of the coherence between two jointly weakly stationary time series.

9. DISTRIBUTIONAL RESULTS PERTAINING TO TIME-VARYING SPECTRAL ESTIMATORS

In Section 8, we considered a real p-variate continuous parameter time series $X(t)$ and introduced time-varying sample spectral density matrices

$\hat{S}_t(\omega_0)$. This was done by using formulas which yield estimators of the spectral density matrix of a zero mean stationary time series and applying them to the finite realizations $X(s)$, $t - T \leq s \leq t + T$ of fixed length $2T$ but varying midpoint t.

In the present section, we consider properties of the process $\hat{S}_t(\omega_0)$ under the null hypothesis that the time series $X(t)$ is zero mean stationary Gaussian as described in Section 7. With reference to Sections 7 and 8, we employ in this consideration the approximation that $\Delta_t\, \zeta(\omega_m) \doteq \zeta_m(t)$, and take as ideal counterparts of $\hat{S}_t(\omega_0)$ the process $(2M + 1)^{-1}C(t)$ where $C(t)$ is given by (7.7). Using the idealization stated above, the process $(2M + 1)\hat{S}_t(\omega_0)$ is then the special type of complex Wishart process $C(t)$ described in Section 7. First, we present in summary form some results concerning the finite-dimensional distributions, moments and spectral densities of a general (see Section 6) complex Wishart process. Corresponding results for the process $C(t)$ are then obtained upon appropriate specialization.

The following theorem characterizes the finite dimensional distributions of a general complex Wishart process in terms of its degrees-of-freedom parameter n and its covariance-function parameter $R_\xi(\tau)$.

Theorem 9.1. *Let $A(t) = \|A_{jk}(t)\|$ be a $p \times p$ complex Wishart process with n degrees of freedom and covariance-function parameter $R_\xi(\tau) = \|R_{\xi;\, jk}(\tau)\|$. Then for any choice of times $t_1, \ldots, t_N$, the random matrices $A(t_1), \ldots, A(t_N)$ are jointly distributed as the N-variate $p \times p$ complex Wishart distribution with n degrees of freedom and Hermitian-covariance-matrix parameter*

$$\Sigma \equiv \|\Sigma_{\alpha\beta}\| \equiv \|R_\xi(t_\alpha - t_\beta)\|; \qquad \alpha, \beta = 1, \ldots, N. \tag{9.1}$$

The joint characteristic function of the random variables

$$A_{jj}(t_\alpha), \quad 2A_{jkR}(t_\alpha), \quad 2A_{jkI}(t_\alpha); \qquad j < k; \;\; j, k = 1, \ldots, p; \;\; \alpha = 1, \ldots, N \tag{9.2}$$

is given by (5.5) where Σ is defined by (9.1); I_{pN} is the $pN \times pN$ identity matrix; $\Theta \equiv \operatorname{diag}(\Theta_{11}, \ldots, \Theta_{NN})$ is a $pN \times pN$ matrix with $p \times p$ Hermitian blocks down the diagonal and with zeros elsewhere; and $A_{\alpha\alpha} \equiv A(t_\alpha)$ for $\alpha = 1, \ldots, N$.

The previous theorem and Eq. (1.7) enable moments to be calculated. In particular, for any choice of times t, $t + \tau$, we obtain

$$EA_{j_1k_1}(t) = nR_{\xi;j_1k_1}(0), \tag{9.3a}$$

and also

$$\begin{aligned} &\operatorname{Cov}\{A_{j_1k_1}(t + \tau), A_{j_2k_2}(t)\} \\ &\quad \equiv E\{A_{j_1k_1}(t + \tau) - EA_{j_1k_1}(t + \tau)\}\overline{\{A_{j_2k_2}(t) - EA_{j_2k_2}(t)\}} \\ &\quad = nR_{\xi;j_1j_2}(\tau)\overline{R_{\xi;k_1k_2}(\tau)}. \end{aligned} \tag{9.3b}$$

In (9.3), the indices j_1, k_1, j_2, k_2 range over the integers $1, 2, \ldots, p$. In the absolutely continuous case, i.e., in the case in which

$$R_{\xi; jk}(\tau) = \int_{-\infty}^{\infty} e^{i\omega\tau} s_{\xi; jk}(\omega)\, d\omega, \qquad -\infty < \tau < \infty; \quad j, k = 1, 2, \ldots, p \tag{9.4}$$

with $s_{\xi;\, jk}(\omega)$ integrable functions, one has in (9.3)

$$nR_{\xi; j_1 j_2}(\tau)\overline{R_{\xi; k_1 k_2}(\tau)} = \int_{-\infty}^{\infty} e^{i\omega\tau}\left[n \int_{-\infty}^{\infty} s_{\xi; j_1 j_2}(\omega + \omega')\overline{s_{\xi; k_1 k_2}(\omega')}\, d\omega'\right] d\omega \tag{9.5}$$

so that the cross-spectral density between $A_{j_1 k_1}(t)$ and $A_{j_2 k_2}(t)$ is given by the term in brackets in (9.5).

To specialize the above results to the process $C(t)$, one takes, in accordance with Section 7, $n = 2M + 1$ and $R_\xi(\tau) = S(\omega_0) g(\tau)$. For example, the cross-spectral density between $c_{j_1 k_1}(t)$ and $c_{j_2 k_2}(t)$ is then given by the bracketed term in (9.5) with $s_{\xi;\, j_1 j_2}(\omega + \omega') = s_{j_1 j_2}(\omega_0) G^2(\omega + \omega')$ and $s_{\xi;\, k_1 k_2}(\omega') = s_{k_1 k_2}(\omega_0) G^2(\omega')$.

Now consider the $C(t)$ process in the case $p = 2$ with $n \geq 2$ and $S(\omega_0)$ nonsingular. From Theorem 9.1, the random matrices $C(t)$ and $C(t + \tau)$ are jointly bivariate 2×2 complex Wishart distributed (see (4.3)) with the 4×4 parameter matrix

$$\Sigma(\tau) = \left[\begin{array}{c|c} g(0)S(\omega_0) & g(\tau)S(\omega_0) \\ \hline g(\tau)S(\omega_0) & g(0)S(\omega_0) \end{array}\right]. \tag{9.6}$$

It is easily verified from (7.6) and the properties of $G(\omega)$ that $g(0) \geq |g(\tau)|$ with equality pertaining if and only if $\tau = 0$. Thus, for $\tau \neq 0$ the matrix $\Sigma(\tau)$ is nonsingular. For the joint distribution of $C(t)$ and $C(t + \tau)$, the specific parameter values in (4.3) then are

$$\begin{aligned} \Sigma^{11} &= \Sigma^{22} = g(0)[g^2(0) - g^2(\tau)]^{-1} S^{-1}(\omega_0) \\ \Sigma^{12} &= \Sigma^{21} = -g(\tau)[g^2(0) - g^2(\tau)]^{-1} S^{-1}(\omega_0) \\ |\Sigma| &= [g^2(0) - g^2(\tau)]^2 |S(\omega_0)|^2. \end{aligned} \tag{9.7}$$

A general goal in the study of time-varying spectral analysis is to investigate "derived processes," i.e., processes that are functions of the elements of a time-varying sample spectral density matrix process (e.g., sample coherence). The joint distribution of $C(t)$ and $C(t + \tau)$ given above provides a basis for achieving some results in the direction of this goal. The following results pertain to sample coherence. Let $\hat{\gamma}_1 \equiv \hat{\gamma}(t)$ and $\hat{\gamma}_2 \equiv \hat{\gamma}(t + \tau)$ denote sample coherences computed from $C(t)$ and $C(t + \tau)$, respectively; i.e., with reference to (7.7)

$$\hat{\gamma}_1 \equiv \hat{\gamma}(t) \equiv \frac{|c_{12}(t)|^2}{c_{11}(t) c_{22}(t)}, \qquad \hat{\gamma}_2 \equiv \hat{\gamma}(t + \tau). \tag{9.8}$$

The joint distribution of the real random variables $\hat{\gamma}_1 = \hat{\gamma}(t)$ and $\hat{\gamma}_2 = \hat{\gamma}(t + \tau)$ is the second order finite dimensional distribution, for lag τ, of a time-varying sample coherence process. An expression for the probability density function of this joint distribution (in the special case of zero population coherence) is given below.

$$p(\hat{\gamma}_1, \hat{\gamma}_2) = \sum_{k_1, k_2 = 0}^{\infty} K(f(\tau); k_1, k_2)\beta(\hat{\gamma}_1; k_1 + 1, n - 1 + k_2) \times \beta(\hat{\gamma}_2; k_1 + 1, n - 1 + k_2) \tag{9.9}$$

where

$$f(\tau) \equiv g^2(\tau)/g^2(0), \qquad \beta(x; p, q) = \Gamma(p + q)\Gamma^{-1}(p)\Gamma^{-1}(q)x^{p-1}(1 - x)^{q-1}$$

is the classical beta density, and $K(f(\tau); k_1, k_2)$ is given by

$$\sum_{k_3, k_4 = 0}^{\infty} \frac{\Gamma(n - 1 + k_2)\Gamma^2(n + k_1 + k_2 + k_3)\Gamma^2(n + k_1 + k_2 + k_4) \times [1 - f(\tau)]^{2n}[f(\tau)]^{2k_1 + 2k_2 + k_3 + k_4}}{\Gamma(n)\Gamma(n - 1)\Gamma^2(n + k_1 + k_2)\Gamma(n + 2k_1 + 2k_2 + k_3 + k_4)k_2!k_3!k_4!} \tag{9.10}$$

Since $g(\tau)$ tends to zero as τ approaches ∞, it follows (from the above equations) that

$$\lim_{\tau \to \infty} p(\hat{\gamma}_1, \hat{\gamma}_2) = \beta(\hat{\gamma}_1; 1, n - 1)\beta(\hat{\gamma}_2; 1, n - 1). \tag{9.11}$$

Since $\hat{\gamma}(t)$ is a strictly stationary process, one may use (9.11) to obtain

$$E\hat{\gamma}(t) = E\hat{\gamma}_1 = \int_0^1 \hat{\gamma}_1 \beta(\hat{\gamma}_1; 1, n - 1)\, d\hat{\gamma}_1 = n^{-1}. \tag{9.12}$$

More generally, one notes that $p(\hat{\gamma}_1, \hat{\gamma}_2)$ given by (9.9) is a mixture of products of beta densities. Thus moments are easily calculated. In particular, the autocovariance function (about the mean) of the time-varying sample coherence process $\hat{\gamma}(t)$ is given by

$$R_{\hat{\gamma}}(\tau) \equiv [E\hat{\gamma}_1\hat{\gamma}_2] - n^{-2} = \left[\sum_{k_1, k_2 = 0}^{\infty} K(f(\tau); k_1, k_2)\left(\frac{k_1 + 1}{n + k_1 + k_2}\right)^2\right] - n^{-2}. \tag{9.13}$$

REFERENCES

1. Aitken, A. C. (1956). "Determinants and Matrices," 8th ed. Wiley (Interscience), New York.
2. Anderson, T. W., and Girshick, M. A. (1944). Some extensions of the Wishart distribution. *Ann. Math. Statist.* **15** 345–357.

3. GOODMAN, N. R. (1957). On the joint estimation of the spectra, cospectrum and quadrature spectrum of a two-dimensional stationary Gaussian process. Sci. Paper No. 10. Engi. Statistics Lab., New York Univ., New York; Thesis, Princeton Univ., Princeton, New Jersey.
4. GOODMAN, N. R. (1960). Measuring amplitude and phase. *J. Franklin Inst.* **270** 437–450.
5. GOODMAN, N. R. (1963). Statistical analysis based on a certain multivariate complex Gaussian distribution (an introduction). *Ann. Math. Statist.* **34** 152–177.
6. JAMES, A. T. (1964). Distributions of matrix variates and latent roots derived from normal samples. *Ann. Math. Statist.* **35** 475–501.
7. KHATRI, C. G. (1965). Classical statistical analysis based on a certain multivariate complex Gaussian distribution. *Ann. Math. Statist.* **36** 98–114.
8. MILLER, K. S., BERNSTEIN, R. I., and BLUMENSON, L. E. (1958). Generalized Rayleigh processes. *Quartly. Appl. Math.* **16** 137–145.
9. ORMSBY, J. F. A. (1961). Design of numerical filters with applications to missile data processing. *J. Assoc. Comput. Mach.* **8** 440–466.
10. PARZEN, E. (1961). Mathematical considerations in the estimation of spectra. *Technometrics* **3** 167–190.
11. RICE, S. O. (1944, 1945). Mathematical analysis of random noise. *Bell System Tech. J.* **23** 282–332; **24** 46–156 [Reprinted in "Selected Papers on Noise and Stochastic Processes" (N. Wax, ed.). Dover, New York, 1954].
12. SILVERMAN, R. A. (1958). The fluctuation rate of the chi process. *IRE Trans. Information Theory* **IT-4** 30–34.

Stochastic Differential Equations in Statistical Estimation Problems[1]

G. KALLIANPUR and C. STRIEBEL

DEPARTMENT OF MATHEMATICS
UNIVERSITY OF MINNESOTA
MINNEAPOLIS, MINNESOTA

1. INTRODUCTION

The estimation problem considered in this paper can be described as follows: $\mathbf{x}(t, \eta)$, $0 \leq t \leq T$ called the "system process" is a stochastic process on a known probability space $(\Omega_X, \mathscr{B}_X, P_X)$ $(\eta \in \Omega_X)$ which takes values in R^n. It is assumed that direct observation of the system process is not possible or convenient, but data concerning $\mathbf{x}(t)$ is provided by observations on an m-dimensional process $\mathbf{z}(t)$ given by

$$\mathbf{z}(\tau) = \int_0^\tau \mathbf{h}(u, \mathbf{x}(u))\, du + \mathbf{y}(\tau), \qquad 0 \leq \tau \leq T \tag{1.1}$$

where the "noise" process $\mathbf{y}(t)$ is Gaussian, has independent increments and is independent of $\mathbf{x}(t)$. The available data, represented by $\mathscr{F}^t = \mathscr{B}[\mathbf{z}(\tau), 0 \leq \tau \leq t]$, the σ-field generated by the family $\mathbf{z}(\tau)$ $(0 \leq \tau \leq t)$, is to be used in estimating some given functional

$$g(\eta) \equiv G[\mathbf{x}(\tau, \eta), \quad 0 \leq \tau \leq T] \tag{1.2}$$

of the system process. The precise conditions to be satisfied by $\mathbf{h}$ will be stated later. The space Ω_X on which the system process is defined corresponds to the parameter space in the usual Bayes approach to the theory of estimation. Thus the process $\mathbf{x}(t)$ may be regarded as the unknown parameter and P_X the a priori distribution. If, as we shall always assume, g is an integrable random variable its least-squares estimate based on $\mathscr{F}^t$ is the conditional expectation $E[g \mid \mathscr{F}^t]$ (which for brevity, we write as $E^t(g)$). By suitably

[1] Work supported by the United States Air Force Office of Aerospace Research Grant No. AF-AFOSR-885-65, and by NSF Grant No. GP–7490.

choosing g, it can be seen that this problem includes smoothing, prediction, and filtering. A "Bayes" formula for $E^t(g)$ is obtained in Theorem 2.1. This is a central result from a theoretical point of view since the results of Sections 5 and 6 follow from it. However, while such a formula might be considered satisfactory for fixed t, if the data is coming in continuously, we require an estimate which can be continuously revised to take into account the new data. A practical method of describing the estimate or filter which depends continuously on time is furnished by a stochastic differential equation. To achieve this, we have to specialize to Markov system processes.

Both these problems (discussed in Sections 2 and 5) have been investigated by us in two earlier papers. In the work of Kallianpur and Striebel [6] the formula is derived for $E^t(g)$ when $\mathbf{x}(t)$ and $\mathbf{z}(t)$ are one dimensional, $\mathbf{h}(t, x) \equiv x$ and $\mathbf{y}(t)$ is a one dimensional standard Wiener process. Here in Section 2, we give the extension to vector valued processes and with nonlinear h as in (1.1). In Section 5, we consider the model (1.1) with $\mathbf{x}(t)$ Markov but assume both system and observation processes to be one dimensional. The main theorems of this section give conditions under which the conditional expectation $E^t[f(x(t))]$ satisfies a stochastic differential equation of Ito type whenever f belongs to the domain of the extended infinitesimal generator of $x(t)$. The proofs of these results being lengthy and rather formidable have been omitted since they would greatly overburden the paper. For the special case $h(t, x) = x$, these details are to be found in our second paper [7] which has been submitted for publication. However, in order to give the reader some idea of how we proceed, we have collected in Sections 3 and 4 the concepts and auxiliary results which are found essential in establishing these results.

As our only application of the theorems of Section 5, we give a rigorous derivation of the important results of Kalman and Bucy on linear filtering [8]. Although the Kalman-Bucy theory is by now familiar to engineers working in problems of stochastic estimation and control and has even found its way into textbooks in this field, we do not know of a published proof that is completely satisfactory. Another reason for including it is the hope that it will attract the interest of probabilists and statisticians.

Of the literature on the problems considered in this paper, we mention only the few that have a direct bearing: the paper of Wonham [14] which treats special cases; the short note by Bucy [1], and the recent paper by Kushner [9]. The last mentioned paper derives the stochastic differential equations for $E^t[f(\mathbf{x}(t)]$ when $\mathbf{x}(t)$ is the solution of a diffusion equation under conditions which seem more stringent than ours. To our knowledge the work that comes closest to ours is a recent paper, in two parts, by Liptzer and Shiryaev [10]. Without studying it carefully, it is difficult to compare their results with ours. They consider a model in which the system process is the (unobservable) component of a two-dimensional diffusion process. Their paper also contains a discussion of the Kalman-Bucy results and discusses several examples.

2. A BAYES FORMULA FOR THE CONDITIONAL EXPECTATION $E[g \mid \mathbf{z}(\tau), 0 \le \tau \le \mathbf{t}]$

The authors [6] have obtained a formula for the conditional expectation $E[g \mid z(\tau), 0 \le \tau \le t]$ when both the system and the observation process are one-dimensional. In this section, we present the vector-valued version of that result. Only a sketch of the proof is given and the auxiliary results that point the way to the proof are stated. We have elaborated only on those aspects of the argument in which the vector-valued situation presents features absent from the scalar case while details, mostly of a tedious nature, have been omitted. The reader interested in a meticulous construction of the proof of Theorem 2.1 will find these complementary details in our paper cited above.

We begin with a brief explanation of notation. The vector $\mathbf{a}'$ denotes the transpose of the row vector $\mathbf{a}$ in R^m. The coordinates of $\mathbf{a}$ with respect to some fixed basis will be denoted by a_j $(j = 1, \ldots, m)$ and the inner product in R^m by (,). We shall write $\|\mathbf{a}\|^2 = \sum_{j=1}^{m} a_j^{\,2}$.

Let $\xi(t)$ be a process of independent increments with $E\xi(t) = 0$ and variance operator

$$E[\xi(t)]'[\xi(t)] = \mathbf{A}(t) \qquad (0 \le t \le T), \tag{2.1}$$

where $\mathbf{A}(t) = [A_{ij}(t)]$ $(i, j = 1, \ldots, m)$. We shall adopt the following convenient notation due to Skorokhod [12]. If $\mathbf{a}(t)$ is a measurable function such that

$$\int_0^T \sum_{i,j} a_i(t) a_j(t)\, dA_{ij}(t) < \infty, \tag{2.2}$$

the integral

$$\int_0^T (\mathbf{a}(t), d\xi(t)) = \sum_i \int_0^T a_i(t)\, d\xi_i(t) \tag{2.3}$$

is defined as in the scalar case. We then have

$$E \int_0^T (\mathbf{a}(t), d\xi(t)) = 0 \tag{2.4}$$

and

$$E\left[\int_0^T (\mathbf{a}(t), d\xi(t))\right]^2 = \int_0^T \sum_{i,j} a_i(t) a_j(t)\, dA_{ij}(t). \tag{2.5}$$

The notation for the integral given on the left-hand side of (2.3) is Skorokhod's [12] and enables us to write the formulas in a more compact form.

Let us now precisely describe the model for the observation process introduced in the last section. First, we make the following assumptions:

$$\mathbf{y}(t), \qquad t \in [0, T] \qquad (\mathbf{y}(0) = 0) \tag{2.6}$$

is a separable, m-vector valued Gaussian process of independent increments such that

$$E\mathbf{y}(t) \equiv 0, \tag{2.7}$$

and

$$E[\mathbf{y}(t)]'[\mathbf{y}(t)] = \mathbf{F}(t), \tag{2.8}$$

where $\mathbf{F}(t)$ is a continuous function of t, and $\mathbf{F}(t) \neq 0$ for each $t > 0$.

$$\mathbf{x}(t, \eta) \text{ is an } n\text{-vector valued, jointly measurable stochastic process} \tag{2.9}$$

defined on a probability space $(\Omega_X, \mathscr{B}_X, P_X)$ $(0 \leq t \leq T, \eta \in \Omega_X)$.

$$\text{The } \mathbf{x}(t) \text{ and } \mathbf{y}(t) \text{ processes are independent.} \tag{2.10}$$

From (2.8), it follows that $\mu(t) = \operatorname{tr} \mathbf{F}(t)$ is also continuous in t. Since $\mathbf{F}(t)$ is a positive semidefinite operator in R^m, the following statements are verified easily.

$$\mu(t) \text{ is a nondecreasing function of } t, \tag{2.11}$$

and

$$\mu(t) > 0 \qquad \text{for} \quad t > 0. \tag{2.12}$$

$$F_{ij}(t) \text{ is absolutely continuous with respect to } \mu(t) \quad (i, j = 1, \ldots, m) \tag{2.13}$$

and the derivative of the matrix function

$$d/\mathbf{F}d\mu(t) = \hat{\mathbf{F}}(t) \tag{2.14}$$

where

$$\hat{\mathbf{F}}(t) \text{ is a symmetric, positive semidefinite operator in } R^m. \tag{2.15}$$

With respect to some fixed basis in R^m, let $\lambda_j(t)$ be the eigenvalues with corresponding orthonormal eigenvectors $\mathbf{e}_j(t)$ $(j = 1, \ldots, m)$ of $\hat{\mathbf{F}}(t)$. Clearly $\lambda_j(t) \geq 0$, and we may assume $\lambda_1(t) \geq \cdots \geq \lambda_m(t) \geq 0$. Since the λ_j's are the roots of a determinantal equation whose coefficients are measurable functions of t, it follows that the eigenvalues λ_j, and consequently, the eigenvectors $\mathbf{e}_j(t)$ are Borel-measurable functions of t.

Let $\xi_j(t)$ $(j = 1, \ldots, m)$ be one-dimensional, mutually independent Gaussian processes with independent increments with

$$E\xi_j(t) \equiv 0 \qquad \text{and} \qquad E\xi_j^2(t) = \mu(t).$$

Although the main result of this section can be proved without the following additional assumption on $\mu(t)$, we make it nevertheless because it is easier to verify the various steps in the proof by comparing with the proof given in detail by Kallianpur and Striebel [6] for the one-dimensional case.

$$\mu(t) \text{ is an absolutely continuous function of } t \tag{2.16}$$

with $\mu'(t) > 0$ for $(t > 0)$. Let

$$\mathbf{h}(t, \mathbf{x}): \quad [0, T] \times R^n \to R^m \tag{2.17}$$

be a Borel-measurable function of $(t, \mathbf{x})$. Abusing the notation somewhat, we shall write $\mathbf{h}(u, \eta)$ for $\mathbf{h}(u, \mathbf{x}(u, \eta))$. The conditions to be satisfied by the process $\mathbf{h}(u, \eta)$ are as follows.

There exists a jointly measurable m-vector valued process $\mathbf{p}(u, \eta)$ such that for $0 \le u \le T$

$$\mathbf{h}(u, \eta) = \sum_{j=1}^{m} p_j(u, \eta)(\lambda_j(u))^{1/2}\mathbf{e}_j(u)\mu'(u) \qquad \text{a.s.} \quad P_X. \tag{2.18}$$

$$\int_0^T \|\mathbf{p}(u, \eta)\|^2 \mu'(u)\, du < \infty \qquad \text{a.s.} \quad P_X. \tag{2.19}$$

Almost surely P_X

$$p_j(u, \eta) = 0 \qquad \text{for all} \quad u \text{ in } [0, T] \qquad \text{for which} \quad \lambda_j(u) = 0. \tag{2.20}$$

When this happens, we shall set

$$\frac{p_j(u, \eta)}{(\lambda_j(u))^{1/2}} = 0.$$

The observation process $\mathbf{z}(t)$ takes values in R^m and is defined by

$$\mathbf{z}(t) = \int_0^t \mathbf{h}(u, \mathbf{x}(u, \eta))\, du + \mathbf{y}(t), \qquad 0 \le t \le T \tag{2.21}$$

or

$$d\mathbf{z}(t) = \mathbf{h}(t, \mathbf{x}(t, \eta))\, dt + d\mathbf{y}(t). \tag{2.21'}$$

Observe that from (2.6) and (2.21), $\mathbf{z}(0) = 0$. It is easy to see that (2.18) is equivalent to the relation

$$(\mathbf{h}(u, \eta), \mathbf{e}_j(u)) = (\lambda_j(u))^{1/2} p_j(u, \eta)\mu'(u), \qquad j = 1, \cdots, m. \tag{2.22}$$

Let us now set

$$w_j(\tau) = \int_0^\tau (\mu'(u))^{-1/2}\, d\xi_j(u) \tag{2.23}$$

and

$$\hat{z}_j(\tau) = \int_0^\tau \left(\frac{\mathbf{e}_j(u)}{(\lambda_j(u)\mu'(u))^{1/2}}, d\mathbf{z}(u) \right). \tag{2.24}$$

Then $w_j(\tau)$ $(0 \le \tau \le T)$ $(j = 1, \ldots, m)$ are independent standard Wiener processes and, we have from (2.21) and

$$\mathbf{y}(t) = \sum_{j=1}^m \int_0^t (\lambda_j(u))^{1/2} \mathbf{e}_j(u)\, d\xi_j(u)$$

that

$$d\hat{z}_j(u) = (\mu'(u))^{1/2} p_j(u, \eta)\, du + dw_j(u), \qquad 0 \le u \le T, \quad j = 1, \ldots, m. \tag{2.25}$$

The arguments used by Kallianpur and Striebel [6] can now be applied to vector valued system and observation processes related by model (2.21) or (2.25). Theorem 2.1 and its corollaries are based on two results stated below. The first of these constitutes a general version of Bayes' theorem.[2] The second is an extension due to Skorokhod [12] of a theorem of Cameron and Graves (see [6] for reference). Note that the definition of the integral in (2.24) is clear from (2.3) and (2.21′).

Lemma 2.1. (i) *On the probability space* $(\Omega, \mathscr{A}, P)$, *let* $g(\omega)$ *be an integrable random variable measurable with respect to a sub* σ*-field* $\mathscr{A}_X$, *and let* $Q(A, \omega)$ *be a version of the conditional probability*

$$Q(A, \omega) = E(I_A | \mathscr{A}_X) \qquad \text{a.s.} \tag{2.26}$$

for $A \in \mathscr{A}_Z$, *a sub* σ*-field of* $\mathscr{A}$. *Then* φ_g *defined by*

$$\varphi_g(A) = \int g(\omega) Q(A, \omega) P(d\omega) \tag{2.27}$$

is a finite signed measure on $(\Omega, \mathscr{A}_Z)$. *It is absolutely continuous with respect to* P_Z $(\varphi_g \ll P_Z)$, *the restriction of* P *to* $\mathscr{A}_Z$ *with Radon-Nikodym derivative is given by*

$$E(g | \mathscr{A}_Z) = d\varphi_g / dP_Z \qquad \text{a.s. } P_Z. \tag{2.28}$$

(ii) *Suppose that the following conditions are fulfilled.*

$$\textit{The conditional probabilities } Q(A, \omega) \textit{ are regular} \tag{2.29}$$

(*see Loève* [11], p. 137).

$$\mathscr{A}_Z \textit{ is generated by a countable family of sets.} \tag{2.30}$$

There exists a probability Λ *on* $(\Omega, \mathscr{A}_Z)$ *such that*

$$Q(\cdot, \omega) \ll \Lambda \textit{ for } \omega \in \Omega' \textit{ where } P(\Omega') = 1. \tag{2.31}$$

Then

$$P_Z \ll \Lambda, \tag{2.32}$$

[2] See [6].

there exists a function

$$q(\omega', \omega) \text{ which is measurable on } (\Omega \times \Omega, \mathscr{A}_Z \times \mathscr{A}_X) \tag{2.33}$$

and satisfies

$$q(\omega', \omega) = (dQ/d\Lambda)(\cdot, \omega)(\omega') \quad \text{a.e.} \quad \Lambda \times P, \tag{2.34}$$

$$0 < \int q(\omega', \omega) P(d\omega) < \infty \quad \text{a.s.} \quad P_Z \tag{2.35}$$

and

$$E(g \mid \mathscr{A}_Z) = \frac{\int g(\omega) q(\omega', \omega) P(d\omega)}{\int q(\omega', \omega) P(d\omega)} \quad \text{a.s.} \quad P_Z \tag{2.36}$$

for g $\mathscr{A}_X$*-measurable and integrable.*

Lemma 2.2 [12]. *Let* $\mathbf{y}(t)$ $(0 \le t \le T)$ *be as in* (2.6)–(2.8), *and* $\mathbf{y}^{(1)}(t)$ *be such that*

$$\mathbf{y}^{(1)}(t) = \mathbf{y}(t) + \mathbf{a}(t) \tag{2.37}$$

where the nonrandom mean function $\mathbf{a}$ *satisfies*

$$\mathbf{a}(t) = \int_0^t \sum_{j=1}^m p_j(u)(\lambda_j(u))^{1/2} \mathbf{e}_j(u) \mu'(u)\, du, \tag{2.38}$$

$$\int_0^T \|\mathbf{p}(u)\|^2 \mu'(u)\, du < \infty \tag{2.39}$$

where $p_j(u)$ *are Borel-measurable functions and* $\mu(u)$, $\lambda_j(u)$, $\mathbf{e}_j(u)$, *and* $\mathbf{y}(t)$ *have been defined earlier.*

If $P_\mathbf{y}$ and $P_{\mathbf{y}^{(1)}}$ denote the respective probability measures then,

$$P_{\mathbf{y}^{(1)}} \ll P_\mathbf{y}$$

with Radon-Nikodym derivative given by

$$\exp\left\{\sum_{j=1}^m \int_0^t \left(\frac{p_j(u)}{(\lambda_j(u))^{1/2}} \mathbf{e}_j(u), d\mathbf{y}(u)\right) - \tfrac{1}{2} \sum_{j=1}^m \int_0^t p_j{}^2(u) \mu'(u)\, du\right\}. \tag{2.40}$$

In applying the Lemmas 2.1 and 2.2 to deduce Theorem 2.1, the following probability structure is assumed.

Let $(R^m)^{[0,t]}$ be the space of all m-vector valued functions $\mathbf{z}(\tau)$ $(0 \le \tau \le t)$, $\mathscr{B}_m^{[0,t]}$ the product σ-field in $(R^m)^{[0,t]}$, defined in the usual manner, and let $C_m[0, T]$ be the space of all continuous functions on $[0, T]$ taking values in R^m. Define

$$W_m = C_m[0, T], \qquad \mathscr{B}_{W_m} = W_m \cap \mathscr{B}_m^{[0,t]}, \qquad Z_m = C_m[0, t],$$
$$\mathscr{B}_{Z_m} = Z_m \cap \mathscr{B}_m^{[0,t]} \qquad (0 < t \le T). \tag{2.41}$$

Let P_{W_m} be a standard (m-dimensional) Wiener measure on $(W_m, \mathscr{B}_{W_m})$ and $(\Omega_X, \mathscr{B}_X, P_X)$ be the probability space in (2.9). Elements of Ω_X and W_m will be denoted by η and $\mathbf{w}$, respectively. We then take

$$(\Omega, \mathscr{A}, P) = (\Omega_X \times W_m, \mathscr{B}_X \times \mathscr{B}_{W_m}, P_X \times P_{W_m}). \tag{2.42}$$

Consider the transformations

$$\Phi: \quad (\Omega, \mathscr{A}) \to (\Omega_X, \mathscr{B}_X) \tag{2.43}$$

defined by

$$\Phi(\eta, \mathbf{w}) = \eta \tag{2.44}$$

and

$$\boldsymbol{\theta}: \quad (\Omega, \mathscr{A}) \to (Z_m, \mathscr{B}_{Z_m}) \tag{2.45}$$

defined by

$$\theta_j(\eta, \mathbf{w})(\tau) = \theta_j{}^*(\eta)(\tau) + w_j(\tau), \qquad 0 \le \tau \le t \tag{2.46}$$

where $\boldsymbol{\theta}^*$ is given by

$$\theta_j{}^*(\eta)(\tau) = \int_0^\tau (\mu'(u))^{1/2} p_j(u, \eta)\, du \qquad \text{for} \quad 0 \le \tau \le t \quad \text{and} \quad j = 1, \ldots, m \tag{2.47}$$

if

$$\sum_{j=1}^m \int_0^t p_j{}^2(u, \eta)\mu'(u)\, du < \infty,$$

and $\theta_j{}^*(\eta)(\tau) = 0$ for $0 \le \tau \le t$ and $j = 1, \ldots, m$ if

$$\sum_{j=1}^m \int_0^t p_j{}^2(u, \eta)\mu'(u)\, du = \infty.$$

The σ-fields $\mathscr{A}_X$ and $\mathscr{A}_Z$ are then defined by

$$\mathscr{A}_X = \Phi^{-1}(\mathscr{B}_X), \qquad \mathscr{A}_Z = \boldsymbol{\theta}^{-1}(\mathscr{B}_{Z_m}). \tag{2.48}$$

Lastly, we identify

$$Q(A, \omega) = P_{\boldsymbol{\theta}^*[\Phi(\omega)]}(\boldsymbol{\theta} A) \tag{2.49}$$

and

$$\Lambda(A) = P_{W_m} \psi^{-1}(\boldsymbol{\theta} A) \qquad (A \in \mathscr{A}_Z) \tag{2.50}$$

where ψ is defined on W_m by

$$[\psi(\mathbf{w})](\tau) = \mathbf{w}(\tau), \qquad 0 \le \tau \le t. \tag{2.51}$$

The methods of [6] now yield:

Theorem 2.1. *Let the assumptions* (2.6)–(2.10) *and* (2.16)–(2.20) *hold. Then for any integrable random variable* $g(\eta)$ *defined on* $(\Omega_X, \mathscr{B}_X, P_X)$, *we have the formula*

$$E[g \mid \mathbf{z}(\tau), 0 \le \tau \le t]$$

$$= \frac{\int g(\eta)\left\{\exp\left[\int_0^t \sum_{j=1}^m \left(\frac{\hat{h}_j(u,\eta)\mathbf{e}_j(u)}{\mu'(\mu)\lambda_j(u)}, d\mathbf{z}(u)\right) - \frac{1}{2}\int_0^t \sum_{j=1}^m \frac{\hat{h}_j^2(u,\eta)}{\mu'(u)\lambda_j(u)}\,du\right]\right\}P_X(d\eta)}{\int \exp\left[\int_0^t \sum_{j=1}^m \left(\frac{\hat{h}_j(u,\eta)\mathbf{e}_j(u)}{\mu'(u)\lambda_j(u)}, d\mathbf{z}(u)\right) - \frac{1}{2}\int_0^t \sum_{j=1}^m \frac{\hat{h}_j^2(u,\eta)}{\mu'(u)\lambda_j(u)}\,du\right]P_X(d\eta)} \tag{2.52}$$

where the denominator is positive a.s., *and* $\hat{h}_j(u, \eta) = (\mathbf{h}(u, \eta), \mathbf{e}_j(u))$. *It is also understood that the summation on the right-hand side of* (2.52) *is taken over those indices* j *for which* $\lambda_j(u) > 0$.

Corollary to Theorem 2.1. *Suppose there is an integer* r, $1 \le r \le m$, *such that for* $j = 1, \ldots, r$

$$\lambda_j(u) > 0 \quad \textit{for} \quad 0 \le u \le T \quad \textit{and for} \quad j = r+1, \ldots, m,$$
$$\lambda_j(u) = 0 \quad \textit{for} \quad 0 \le u \le T. \tag{2.53}$$

Then formula (2.52) *holds with the sum on the right-hand side expression extending from* $j = 1$ *to* r. *It is possible to cast the formula in a more compact form in the case of full rank, i.e., when* $r = m$.

Theorem 2.2. *Let the assumptions of Theorem* 2.1 *hold. Furthermore, suppose that the matrix function* $\hat{\mathbf{F}}(t)$ *is invertible for* $0 \le t \le T$. *Then*

$$E[g \mid \mathbf{z}(\tau), 0 \le \tau \le t]$$

$$= \frac{\int g(\eta)\{\exp[\int_0^t([\mu'(u)\hat{\mathbf{F}}(u)]^{-1}\mathbf{h}(u,\eta), d\mathbf{z}(u)) - \frac{1}{2}\int_0^t([\mu'(u)\hat{\mathbf{F}}(u)]^{-1}\mathbf{h}(u,\eta), \mathbf{h}(u,\eta))\,du]\}P_X(d\eta)}{\int \exp[\int_0^t([\mu'(u)\hat{\mathbf{F}}(u)]^{-1}\mathbf{h}(u,\eta), d\mathbf{z}(u)) - \frac{1}{2}\int_0^t([\mu'(u)\hat{\mathbf{F}}(u)]^{-1}\mathbf{h}(u,\eta), \mathbf{h}(u,\eta))\,du]P_X(d\eta)}. \tag{2.54}$$

If the "noise" in model (2.21) *is an m-dimensional, standard Wiener process, i.e., if* $\mathbf{y}(t) = \mathbf{w}(t) = (w_1(t), \ldots, w_m(t))$ *where the* w_j*'s are independent, standard one-dimensional Wiener processes, then the right-hand side of* (2.54) *takes on an even simpler form since* $[\mu'(u)\hat{\mathbf{F}}(u)]^{-1} = I$, *the identity matrix.*

3. STOCHASTIC INTEGRALS AND DIFFERENTIALS OF ITO TYPE

Since the stochastic integral of Ito [5] is a basic tool used in the solution of the problems considered in this paper, it seems desirable to list some of its important properties. We state a very important result on stochastic differentials also due to Ito which might be looked upon as a "change of variables" formula for an Ito integral. The reader is referred to the book by Gikhman and Skorokhod [4] for proofs and details. See also Skorokhod [13].

We shall be concerned with stochastic integrals defined with respect to the system

$$(\Omega, \mathscr{A}, P), \quad \mathscr{F}_t, \quad w(t, \omega), \qquad 0 \le t \le T, \quad \omega \in \Omega \tag{3.1}$$

where $(\Omega, \mathscr{A}, P)$ is an arbitrary probability space. It will be assumed that the $\mathscr{F}_t$ are complete with respect to P, that

$$\mathscr{F}_{t_1} \subset \mathscr{F}_{t_2} \subset \bar{\mathscr{A}} \qquad \text{for} \quad 0 \le t_1 \le t_2 \le T, \tag{3.2}$$

and that $w(t, \omega)$ is a Wiener process such that

$$w(t, \cdot) \text{ is } \mathscr{F}_t\text{-measurable for} \quad 0 \le t \le T, \tag{3.3}$$

and for $0 \le t \le T$

$$\mathscr{F}_t \text{ is independent of } w(v) - w(t) \qquad \text{for} \quad t \le v \le T. \tag{3.4}$$

The notation $\bar{\mathscr{A}}$ indicates the completion of the σ-field with respect to P. We shall consider two classes of processes defined on $(\Omega, \mathscr{A}, P)$. Class $\mathscr{M}_1$ consists of those processes $a(t, \omega)$, $0 \le t \le T$, $\omega \in \Omega$ which satisfy the following conditions

$$a(t, \omega) \text{ is measurable on} \quad ([0, T] \times \Omega, \overline{\mathscr{B}_{[0, T]} \times \mathscr{A}}, \mu \times P) \tag{3.5}$$

where $\mathscr{B}_{[0, T]}$ is the family of Borel subsets of the interval $[0, T]$, and μ is Lebesgue measure on $[0, T]$,

$$a(t, \cdot) \quad \text{is} \quad \mathscr{F}_t\text{-measurable} \qquad \text{a.e.} \quad \mu, \tag{3.6}$$

and

$$\int_0^T |a(t, \omega)| \, dt < \infty \qquad \text{a.s.} \quad P. \tag{3.7}$$

The class $\mathscr{M}_2$ is defined to consist of those processes $b(t, \omega)$ $(0 \le t \le T, \omega \in \Omega)$ which satisfy (3.5), (3.6), and

$$\int_0^T [b(t, \omega)]^2 \, dt < \infty \qquad \text{a.s.} \quad P. \tag{3.8}$$

The stochastic integral $\int_0^T b(t, \omega) \, dw(t, \omega)$ is defined for $b \in \mathscr{M}_2$ as follows:

(i) If $b \in \mathscr{M}_2$ is a step function

$$b(t, \omega) = b_i(\omega) \qquad \text{for} \quad t_i \le t < t_{i+1} \tag{3.9}$$

where

$$0 = t_0 < t_1 < \cdots < t_m = T, \tag{3.10}$$

then define

$$\int_0^T b(t, \omega)\, dw(t, \omega) = \sum_{i=0}^{m-1} b_i(\omega)\{w(t_{i+1}, \omega) - w(t_i, \omega)\} \qquad \text{a.s.} \quad P. \tag{3.11}$$

(ii) If $b \in \mathcal{M}_2$, there exist step functions $b_n \in \mathcal{M}_2$, $n = 1, 2, \ldots$, such that

$$\int_0^T [b_n(t) - b(t)]^2\, dt \to 0 \tag{3.12}$$

in probability and the integrals

$$\int_0^T b_n(t)\, dw(t) \tag{3.13}$$

converge in probability to a random variable. We then define

$$\int_0^T b(t)\, dw(t) = \underset{n\to\infty}{\text{prob lim}} \int_0^T b_n(t)\, dw(t). \tag{3.14}$$

The following lemma states some of the familiar properties of the Ito integral.

Lemma 3.1. (i) *If $b_n \in \mathcal{M}_2$ $n = 0, 1, 2, \ldots$, and*

$$\int_0^T [b_n(t) - b_0(t)]^2\, dt \to 0 \qquad \textit{in probability} \tag{3.15}$$

then

$$\int_0^T b_n(t)\, dw(t) \to \int_0^T b_0(t)\, dw(t) \qquad \textit{in probability}. \tag{3.16}$$

(ii) *If $b_1, b_2 \in \mathcal{M}_2$ and α_1, α_2 are real numbers then*

$$\int_0^T [\alpha_1 b_1(t) + \alpha_2 b_2(t)]\, dw(t)$$

$$= \alpha_1 \int_0^T b_1(t)\, dw(t) + \alpha_2 \int_0^T b_2(t)\, dw(t) \qquad \text{a.s.} \quad P. \tag{3.17}$$

(iii) *If $b \in \mathcal{M}_2$ and $\int_s^t E^{\mathcal{F}_s}[b^2(u)]\, du < \infty$* a.s. *for $0 \le s \le u \le t \le T$, then*

$$E^{\mathcal{F}_s}\left\{\int_s^t b(u)\, dw(u)\right\} = 0 \tag{3.18}$$

and

$$E^{\mathcal{F}_s}\left\{\left[\int_s^t b(u)\, dw(u)\right]^2\right\} = \int_s^t E^{\mathcal{F}_s}[b^2(u)]\, du \qquad \text{a.s.} \quad P. \tag{3.19}$$

Integrals on the restricted range $[s, t]$ as in (3.19) are obtained by considering functions $b \in \mathcal{M}_2$ for which

$$b(u, \omega) = 0 \qquad \text{for} \quad 0 \le u < s \quad \text{and} \quad t < u \le T. \tag{3.20}$$

In addition to the properties mentioned above, the proofs of the principal theorems of Section 5 require results of a rather specialized nature concerning Ito integrals in which the integrand process depends on two probability parameters. More precisely, the situation is as follows.

Let $(\Omega_X, \mathscr{B}_X, P_X)$ be a probability space and define

$$(\tilde{\Omega}, \tilde{\mathscr{A}}, \tilde{P}) = (\Omega_X \times \Omega, \mathscr{B}_X \times \mathscr{A}, P_X \times P), \tag{3.21}$$

$$\tilde{\mathscr{F}}_t = \overline{\mathscr{B}_X \times \mathscr{F}_t} \qquad (0 \le t \le T). \tag{3.22}$$

The product system

$$(\tilde{\Omega}, \tilde{\mathscr{A}}, \tilde{P}), \quad \tilde{\mathscr{F}}_t, \quad w(t, \tilde{\omega}) \qquad 0 \le t \le T, \quad \tilde{\omega} \in \tilde{\Omega} \tag{3.23}$$

satisfies the conditions (3.2)–(3.4) where $w(t)$ on $\tilde{\Omega}$ is defined by

$$w(t, \tilde{\omega}) = w(t, \eta, \omega) = w(t, \omega). \tag{3.24}$$

Let $\tilde{\mathscr{M}}_1$ and $\tilde{\mathscr{M}}_2$ be the classes of processes for the product system (3.21) defined by (3.5)–(3.7), and (3.5), (3.6), and (3.8), respectively. The following results (of which Lemma 3.3 (ii) appears to be new) are Fubini-type theorems about the Ito stochastic integral (see Kallianpur and Striebel [7]).

Lemma 3.2. *If* $a \in \tilde{\mathscr{M}}_i$

$$\int_0^T \left| \int_{\Omega_X} a(u, \eta, \omega) P_X(d\eta) \right|^i du < \infty \qquad \text{a.s.} \quad P \tag{3.25}$$

and either

$$a(u, \eta, \omega) \ge 0 \qquad \text{a.e.} \quad \mu \times P \tag{3.26}$$

or

$$\int_{\Omega_X} |a(u, \eta, \omega)| P_X(d\eta) < \infty \qquad \text{a.e.} \quad \mu \times P, \tag{3.27}$$

then

$$\int_{\Omega_X} a(u, \eta, \omega) P_X(d\eta) \in \mathscr{M}_i \qquad \textit{for} \quad i = 1, 2. \tag{3.28}$$

Lemma 3.3. (i) *If* $a \in \tilde{\mathscr{M}}_1$ *and*

$$\int_0^T \int_{\Omega_X} |a(t, \eta, \omega)| P_X(d\eta)\, dt < \infty \qquad \text{a.s.} \quad P, \tag{3.29}$$

then

$$\int_{\Omega_X} a(t, \eta, \omega) P_X(d\eta) \in \mathscr{M}_1 \tag{3.30}$$

$$\int_{\Omega_X} \int_0^T a(t, \eta, \omega)\, dt P_X(d\eta) = \int_0^T \int_{\Omega_X} a(t, \eta, \omega) P_X(d\eta)\, dt \qquad \text{a.s.} \quad P. \tag{3.31}$$

(ii) *Let* $b \in \tilde{\mathcal{M}}_2$ *satisfy*

$$\int_s^t \left[\int_{\Omega_X} |b(u, \eta, \omega)| P_X(d\eta)\right]^2 du < \infty \qquad \text{a.s.} \quad P \tag{3.32}$$

and

$$\int_{\Omega_X} \left\{\int_s^t E^{\mathscr{F}_s}[b^2(u, \eta, \omega)]\, du\right\}^{1/2} P_X(d\eta) < \infty \qquad \text{a.s.} \quad P. \tag{3.33}$$

Then

$$\int_{\Omega_X} b(u, \eta, \omega) P_X(d\eta) \in \mathcal{M}_2 \tag{3.34}$$

and

$$\int_s^t \left[\int_{\Omega_X} b(u, \eta, \omega) P_X(d\eta)\right] dw(u, \omega)$$

$$= \int_{\Omega_X} \left[\int_s^t b(u, \eta, \omega)\, dw(u, \omega)\right] P_X(d\eta) \qquad \text{a.s.} \quad P \tag{3.35}$$

and the integrals in (3.35) *are finite* a.s. P.

It is with the help of Lemma 3.3 that we are able to obtain the stochastic differentials for the process referred to in Section 2.

We now turn to Ito's definition of a stochastic differential ([5], p. 187). A process $\zeta(t)$ defined on $(\Omega, \mathscr{A}, P)$ [or $(\tilde{\Omega}, \tilde{\mathscr{A}}, \tilde{P})$] has a stochastic differential of Ito type

$$d\zeta(t) = a(t)\, dt + b(t)\, dw(t), \qquad 0 \le t \le T \tag{3.36}$$

provided

$$a \in \mathcal{M}_1 \qquad (\text{or } \tilde{\mathcal{M}}_1) \tag{3.37}$$

$$b \in \mathcal{M}_2 \qquad (\text{or } \tilde{\mathcal{M}}_2), \tag{3.38}$$

and

$$\zeta(t) - \zeta(s) = \int_s^t a(u)\, du + \int_s^t b(u)\, dw(u) \qquad \text{a.s.} \quad P \quad (\text{or } \tilde{P}) \tag{3.39}$$

for all $0 \le s < t \le T$.

The following result of Ito's ([3], p. 222) is used extensively in the proofs of the theorems of Sections 5 and 6.

Lemma 3.4. *Assume that the processes* $\zeta_i(t)$ $(i = 1, 2, \ldots, n)$ *have differentials*

$$d\zeta_i(t) = a_i(t)\, dt + b_i(t)\, dw(t), \qquad 0 \le t \le T. \tag{3.40}$$

Let $\Gamma(x)$ be a real-valued function of the n-vector $x = (x_1, \ldots, x_n)$ defined on an open subset G of R^n which contains almost surely all points $(\zeta_1(t), \ldots, \zeta_n(t))(0 \le t \le T)$. Furthermore, suppose that

$$\frac{\partial^2 \Gamma(x)}{\partial x_i \, \partial x_j} \tag{3.41}$$

is continuous on G for $i, j = 1, 2, \ldots, n$. Let

$$\xi(t) = \Gamma(\zeta(t))$$

where

$$\zeta(t) = [\zeta_1(t), \ldots, \zeta_n(t)]. \tag{3.42}$$

Then $\xi(t)$ has a differential

$$d\xi(t) = A(t)\, dt + B(t)\, dw(t), \qquad 0 \le t \le T \tag{3.43}$$

where

$$A(t) = \sum_i a_i(t) \frac{\partial \Gamma}{\partial x_i}(\zeta(t)) + \frac{1}{2} \sum_{i,j} \frac{\partial^2 \Gamma(\zeta(t))}{\partial x_i \, \partial x_j} b_i(t) b_j(t) \tag{3.44}$$

and

$$B(t) = \sum_i \frac{\partial \Gamma(\zeta(t))}{\partial x_i} b_i(t). \tag{3.45}$$

4. MARKOV PROCESSES WITH EXTENDED INFINITESIMAL GENERATOR

In this section, it will be assumed that $x(t, \eta)$, $0 \le t \le T$, $\eta \in \Omega_X$, is a Markov process. We will say that $x(t, \eta)$ has jointly measurable transition probabilities provided it has regular transition probabilities

$$P[x(t) \in B \mid x(s) = x] = P(s, x; t, B) \tag{4.1}$$

(x real and $0 \le s \le t \le T$) which are jointly measurable in (s, x, t) for all Borel sets of the real line $B \in \mathscr{B}_R$. We will be concerned with the generalized semigroup (in the sense of Loève [11], p. 568) $P_s{}^t$ $(0 \le s \le t \le T)$ defined by

$$(P_s^t f)(x) = \int_{-\infty}^{\infty} f(y) P(s, x; t, dy) \tag{4.2}$$

on the Banach space with sup norm of bounded measurable functions of a real variable; i.e., for $f \in B(R, \mathscr{B}_R)$. The generalized semigroup property which corresponds to the Chapman-Kolmogorov equation for Markov processes, is given by

$$P_s{}^t = P_s{}^u P_u{}^t \qquad (0 \le s \le u \le t \le T). \tag{4.3}$$

We suppose that $\{P_s{}^t\}$ has a generalized infinitesimal generator G_t $(0 \le t \le T)$ defined on a domain $\mathscr{D} \subset B(R, \mathscr{B}_R)$. Specifically, it is assumed that for $0 \le t \le T$, G_t is a linear operator with domain $\mathscr{D}$ and range $B(R, \mathscr{B}_R)$ which satisfies

$$\sup_{\substack{-\infty < x < \infty \\ 0 \le t \le T}} |(G_t f)(x)| < \infty \tag{4.4}$$

and

$$\sup_{\substack{-\infty < x < \infty \\ 0 \le t \le T}} \left| G_t f(x) - \frac{(P_t^{[t+h]} f - f)(x)}{h} \right| \to 0 \tag{4.5}$$

as $h \to 0$ for all $f \in \mathscr{D}$, where

$$\begin{aligned} [t+h] &= t+h \qquad \text{if} \quad t+h \le T \\ &= T \qquad \text{if} \quad t+h > T. \end{aligned} \tag{4.6}$$

It can be shown that if $x(t)$ is a measurable Markov process with jointly measurable transition probabilities (4.1), then for $f \in \mathscr{D}$

$$(G_t f)(x) \tag{4.7}$$

is jointly measurable in (t, x) and

$$(P_s^t f - f)(x) = \int_s^t (P_s{}^u G_u f)(x)\, du \qquad (0 \le s \le t \le T) \quad (-\infty < x < \infty). \tag{4.8}$$

For purposes of application, we need to obtain stochastic differential equations for $E^t[f(x(t))]$ for certain unbounded functions f. The most natural class, say $\mathscr{D}^*$, of functions for which we can derive the basic stochastic differential equation is defined as follows. Here, $\mathscr{D}^*$ is the class of Borel measurable functions f which satisfy

$$E|f(x(t))| < \infty \qquad \text{for each} \quad t; \tag{4.9}$$

there exists a (t, x) Borel-measurable function $(G_t{}^* f)(x)$ such that

$$\int_0^T E\,|(G_t{}^* f)(x(t))|\, dt < \infty, \tag{4.10}$$

and for $0 \le s < t \le T$

$$(P_s^t f)(x(s)) - f(x(s)) = \int_s^t (P_s{}^u G_u{}^* f)(x(u))\, du \qquad \text{a.s.} \quad P_X. \tag{4.11}$$

We shall call $G_t{}^*$ the extended infinitesimal generator of the process $x(t)$. It is easy to see that $\mathscr{D}^*$ contains $\mathscr{D}$. The definition of a generalized or extended infinitesimal generator of a vector-valued Markov process presents no difficulties.

5. ITO STOCHASTIC DIFFERENTIAL EQUATION FOR $E^t[f(x(t))]$

In this section, we make the following assumptions concerning the process $x(t, \eta)$, $0 \leq t \leq T$, $\eta \in \Omega_X$.

$$x(t, \eta) \text{ is a jointly measurable Markov process.} \tag{5.1}$$

$$x(t, \eta) \text{ has regular transition probabilities} \tag{5.2}$$

given by (4.1) which are jointly measurable.

$$x(t, \eta) \text{ has an extended generator } G_t^* \text{ with domain } \mathcal{D}^*. \tag{5.3}$$

Furthermore, let $h(t, x)$ be a real valued, Borel-measurable function of (t, x) satisfying the following conditions:

$$\int_0^T E[h(t, x(t))]^4 \, dt < \infty; \tag{5.4}$$

there exists a $\Delta > 0$ such that

$$E\left[\exp\left[16 \int_t^{t+\Delta} h^2(u, x(u)) \, du\right]\right] < \infty \tag{5.5}$$

for all t for which $0 \leq t \leq T - \Delta$.

Theorem 5.1. *Let $x(t, \eta)$ satisfy* (5.1)–(5.5), *and let $f \in \mathcal{D}^*$ satisfy*

$$\int_0^T E[f^4(x(t))] \, dt < \infty, \tag{5.6}$$

and

$$\int_0^T E\left\{h(t, x(t))\left[f(x(T)) - \int_t^T G_u^* f(x(u)) \, du\right]\right\}^4 du < \infty. \tag{5.7}$$

Then the process $E^t[f(x(t))]$ on $(\Omega, \mathscr{A}, P)$ has a stochastic differential

$$\begin{aligned} dE^t[f(x(t))] = {} & E^t[(G_t^* f)(x(t))] \, dt \\ & + \{E^t[h(t, x(t)) \cdot f(x(t))] - E^t[h(t, x(t))] \\ & \cdot E^t[f(x(t))]\} \\ & \cdot \{dz(t) - E^t[h(t, x(t))] \, dt\}. \end{aligned} \tag{5.8}$$

Condition (5.5) can be replaced by a stronger, but more easily verifiable, condition. Then, for functions f in $\mathcal{D}$, the above result assumes the following particularly simple form.

Theorem 5.2. *Suppose $x(t, \eta)$ satisfies* (5.1), (5.2), *and the following condition.*

There exists a positive number c such that for all t in $[0, T]$

$$E[\exp(ch^2(t, x(t)))] \leq M < \infty, \tag{5.9}$$

where M does not depend on t. Then for $f \in \mathscr{D}$, $E^t[f(x(t))]$ *satisfies the stochastic equation* (5.8).

Proof. By use of Jensen's convexity inequality ([11], p. 159), it is easy to see that (5.9) implies that condition (5.5) holds with Δ such that $0 < \Delta < c/16$. Moreover, it follows that for every positive integer n, $E|h(t, x(t))|^n$ is finite for all t in $[0, T]$ and that

$$\int_0^T E\,|h(t, x(t))|^n \, dt < \infty. \tag{5.10}$$

In particular, (5.4) holds and since $f \in \mathscr{D}$, f and $G_t f$ are bounded functions. Hence, conditions (5.6)–(5.7) are all satisfied and Eq. (5.8) follows.

In many important applications the process $x(t, \eta)$ is supposed to be a dynamical system. In probabilistic terms this means that the temporal development of the process is described by a stochastic differential equation. Accordingly, we shall assume that $x(t)$ $(0 \leq t \leq T)$ is the solution of the Ito stochastic differential equation

$$dx(t) = m[t, x(t)]\, dt + \sigma[t, x(t)]\, dB(t), \qquad 0 \leq t \leq T, \tag{5.11}$$

or equivalently, of the equation

$$x(t) = x(s) + \int_s^t m[u, x(u)]\, du + \int_s^t \sigma[u, x(u)]\, dB(u) \qquad (0 \leq s < t \leq T). \tag{5.12}$$

Here $B(t)$ is a standard Wiener process and $x(0) = x_0$, a given initial random variable. The coefficients m and σ are Baire functions of (u, ξ) which will be assumed to satisfy the following conditions:

$$|m(u, \xi)| \leq K(1 + \xi^2)^{1/2} \qquad (-\infty < \xi < \infty, 0 \leq u \leq T) \tag{5.13}$$

$$|m(u, \xi_2) - m(u, \xi_1)| \leq K|\xi_1 - \xi_2| \tag{5.14}$$

$$0 < \sigma(u, \xi) \leq K \tag{5.15}$$

and

$$|\sigma(u, \xi_2) - \sigma(u, \xi_1)| \leq K|\xi_1 - \xi_2|. \tag{5.16}$$

Under these conditions, it is well known ([2], Chapter VI) that $x(t)$ is a Markov process and is the unique solution of (5.11) almost all of whose sample functions are continuous.

The probability space on which Eqs. (5.11) and (5.12) hold is, of course, that of the system process $(\Omega_X, \mathscr{B}_X, P_X)$.

Lemma 5.1. *Let $x(t)$ be the solution of* (5.11) *where $m(t, x)$ and $\sigma(t, x)$ satisfy* (5.13)–(5.16) *Furthermore, suppose that the initial value $x(0)$ satisfies*

$$E[\exp(c_0 x^2(0))] < \infty \qquad \text{for some} \quad c_0 > 0. \tag{5.17}$$

Then the functions of the form

$$f(x) = x^n p(x) \tag{5.18}$$

where n is any nonnegative integer and p, p', and p'' are bounded continuous functions, belong to $\mathscr{D}^*$. The extended infinitesimal generator $G_t{}^*$ is given by

$$(G_t{}^* f)(x) = m(t, x) f'(x) + 1/2\sigma^2(t, x) f''(x). \tag{5.19}$$

With the aid of the above lemma and Theorem 5.1, we can derive stochastic differential equations for the conditional moments of $x(t)$ and, if so desired, a stochastic differential equation for the conditional characteristic function of $x(t)$.

Theorem 5.3. *Let $x(t)$ be the solution of the Eq.* (5.11), *and let the conditions* (5.4), (5.5), *and* (5.13)–(5.17) *be satisfied. Then if p, p', and p'' are bounded and continuous and n is a nonnegative integer, $E^t[x^n(t)p(x(t))]$ has a stochastic differential of Ito type*

$$\begin{aligned} dE^t[x^n(t)p(x(t))] = {} & E^t[(G_t{}^* x^n p)(x(t))]\, dt \\ & + \{E^t[x^n(t)h(t, x(t))p(x(t))] \\ & - E^t[x^n(t)p(x(t))]E^t[h(t, x(t))]\} \\ & \cdot \{dz(t) - E^t[h(t, x(t))]\, dt\}, \qquad 0 \le t \le T \end{aligned} \tag{5.20}$$

where $G_t{}^*$ is given by (5.19).

6. THE LINEAR FILTER: THE KALMAN-BUCY THEORY

We shall now consider the important special case of the linear filter, i.e., when the observation process is given by

$$dz(t) = k(t)x(t)\, dt + dw(t) \qquad (0 \le t \le T), \quad z(0) = 0, \tag{6.1}$$

where

$$k(t) \text{ is a continuous function of } t. \tag{6.2}$$

Theorem 6.1. *Suppose the system process $x(t)$ satisfies the stochastic differential equation* (5.11) *whose coefficients $m(t, x)$ and $\sigma(t, x)$ satisfy the conditions* (5.13)–(5.16). *Let the initial value $x(0)$ satisfy* (5.17). *If the observation process is defined by* (6.1), *then*

$$dE^t[x^n(t)p(x(t))] = E^t[(G_t{}^*x^np)(x(t))]\,dt + k(t)\{E^t[x^{n+1}(t)p(x(t))] - E^t[x^n(t)p(x(t))]\cdot E^t[x(t)]\} \cdot\{dz(t) - k(t)E^t[x(t)]\,dt\}. \tag{6.3}$$

Now let us specialize to the case in which $x(t)$ is a Gaussian process which is the solution of the equation

$$dx(t) = m(t)x(t)\,dt + \sigma(t)\,dB(t) \qquad (0 \le t \le T) \tag{6.4}$$

where

$$x(0) = x_0, \qquad \text{a Gaussian random variable,} \tag{6.5}$$

and

$m(t)$ and $\sigma(t)$ are Baire functions and $\sigma(t)$ is bounded and nonnegative. (6.6)

For the process $x(t)$ satisfying (6.4)–(6.6), the following corollary is easily deduced from Theorem 6.1.

Corollary to Theorem 6.1. *Suppose that the assumptions* (6.1), (6.2), *and* (6.4)–(6.6) *hold for the processes $z(t)$ and $x(t)$. Then*

$$dE^t[x(t)] = m(t)E^t[x(t)]\,dt + k(t)\{E^t[x^2(t)] - (E^t[x(t)])^2\}\{dz(t) - k(t)E^t[x(t)]\,dt\} \tag{6.7}$$

and, for $n \ge 2$

$$dE^t[x^n(t)] = \{nm(t)E^t[x^n(t)] + \tfrac{1}{2}\sigma^2(t)n(n-1)E^t[(x(t))^{n-2}]\}\,dt + k(t)\{E^t[x^{n+1}(t)] - E^t[x^n(t)]E^t[x(t)]\} \cdot\{dz(t) - k(t)E^t[x(t)]\,dt\}. \tag{6.8}$$

This corollary, together with Ito's lemma given in Section 3 enables us to obtain a rigorous derivation of the basic result first obtained by Kalman and Bucy [8].

For convenience, let us first set

$$\hat{x}(t) = E^t[x(t)], \qquad \text{and} \qquad R(t) = E^t[x^2(t)] - [\hat{x}(t)]^2. \tag{6.9}$$

Theorem 6.2. *The process $\hat{x}(t)$ $(0 \le t \le T)$ is Gaussian and satisfies the stochastic differential equation*

$$d\hat{x}(t) = m(t)\hat{x}(t)\,dt + k(t)R(t)\{dz(t) - k(t)\hat{x}(t)\,dt\} \qquad (0 \le t \le T), \qquad \hat{x}(0) = Ex_0 \tag{6.10}$$

where $R(t)$ satisfies the Riccati equation

$$dR(t)/dt = \sigma^2(t) + 2m(t)R(t) - k^2(t)R^2(t). \tag{6.11}$$

Before proving the result, we need the following lemmas.

Lemma 6.1. *Let t be fixed* ($0 < t \leq T$), *and let* $0 \leq t_1 < \cdots < t_n \leq t$. *Then the conditional distribution of $x(t)$ given $z(t_1), \ldots, z(t_n)$ is Gaussian.*

Proof. For real constants $c_0, c_1, \ldots, c_n$, define the random variable

$$\xi = c_0 x(t) + c_1 z(t_1) + \cdots + c_n z(t_n).$$

Setting

$$y_j = \int_0^{t_j} k(u)x(u)\, du, \; w_j = w(t_j), \qquad \xi' = c_0 x(t) + \sum_{j=1}^{n} c_j y_j,$$

and

$$\xi'' = \sum_{j=1}^{n} c_j w_j,$$

we have

$$\xi = \xi' + \xi'',$$

where ξ' and ξ'' are clearly independent. The random variable ξ'' is Gaussian since w is a Gaussian process. From (6.4), a separable version of the $x(t)$ process (we consider only separable versions here) is a.s. sample continuous, i.e.; almost all of its sample functions are continuous. Hence by taking an appropriate sequence of subdivisions of the interval $[0, t]$, it is seen that ξ' is the almost sure limit of a sequence of random variables each of which is a finite linear combination of the random variables of the family $\{x(u), 0 \leq u \leq t\}$. Since x is Gaussian, it follows that ξ' is Gaussian. Hence ξ is Gaussian. Since the constants $c_0, \ldots, c_n$ are arbitrary, we have the joint normality of $\{x(t), z(t_1), \ldots, z(t_n)\}$. The conclusion of the lemma follows immediately.

Lemma 6.2. *The conditional distribution of $x(t)$ given $\mathscr{F}_t$ $(=\mathscr{B}(z(\tau), 0 \leq \tau \leq t))$ is Gaussian with mean $\hat{x}(t)$ and variance $R(t)$ given by* (6.9).

Proof. It follows from (6.1) that a separable version of $z(t)$ is almost surely sample continuous. Let $\{D_n\}$ $(n = 1, 2, \ldots)$ be a sequence of finite partitions of $[0, t]$ such that $D_n \subset D_{n+1}$ for each n and $\bigcup_{n=1}^{\infty} D_n$ is dense in $[0, t]$. Now let $\mathscr{F}_t^n = \mathscr{B}[z(\tau), \tau \in D_n]$. Then $\mathscr{F}_t^n \subset \mathscr{F}_t^{n+1}$. From the martingale convergence theorem and the a.s. sample continuity of the z process, it follows that

$$\lim_{n\to\infty} P\{x(t) \in B \mid \mathscr{F}_t^n\} = P\{x(t) \in B \mid \mathscr{F}_t\} \qquad \text{a.s.,} \tag{6.12}$$

for every Borel set B. By Lemma 6.1, the left-hand side probabilities in (6.10) are Gaussian. Lemma 6.2 follows.

Lemma 6.3. *The process $\hat{x}(t)$ $(0 \leq t \leq T)$ is Gaussian.*

Proof. The joint normality of the random variables $\hat{x}(v_1), \ldots, \hat{x}(v_p)$ $(0 \leq v_1 < \cdots < v_p \leq T)$ is shown by proceeding essentially as in the preceding two lemmas.

Proof of Theorem 6.2. Equation (6.10) is nothing but Eq. (6.7) of the Corollary to Theorem 6.1. What remains to be established is that $R(t)$ is the nonrandom function of t which is the solution of (6.11). From (6.9), $R(t)$ is the difference of the two stochastic processes $E^t[x^2(t)]$ and $[\hat{x}(t)]^2$. Taking $n = 2$ in (6.8), we obtain

$$\begin{aligned} dE^t[x^2(t)] = \{2m(t)E^t[x^2(t)] + \sigma^2(t)\}\, dt \\ + k(t)\{E^t[x^3(t)] - E^t[x^2(t)]\hat{x}(t)\} \\ \times \{dz(t) - k(t)\hat{x}(t)\, dt\}. \end{aligned} \tag{6.13}$$

Since the conditional distribution of $x(t)$ given $\mathscr{F}_t$ is Gaussian with mean $\hat{x}(t)$ and variance $R(t)$ (Lemma 6.2), we have

$$E^t[x^3(t)] = [\hat{x}(t)]^3 + 3[\hat{x}(t)]R(t).$$

Hence

$$\begin{aligned} E^t[x^3(t)] - E^t[x^2(t)]\hat{x}(t) &= [\hat{x}(t)]^3 + 3[\hat{x}(t)]R(t) - \hat{x}(t) \\ &\quad \times [R(t) + \{\hat{x}(t)\}^2] \\ &= 2\hat{x}(t)R(t). \end{aligned}$$

From Eq. (6.13), we then obtain the following stochastic differential for $E^t[x^2(t)]$

$$\begin{aligned} dE^t[x^2(t)] = \{2m(t)E^t[x^2(t)] + \sigma^2(t)\}\, dt \\ + 2k(t)R(t)\hat{x}(t)\{dz(t) - k(t)\hat{x}(t)\, dt\}. \end{aligned} \tag{6.14}$$

From (6.10) and applying Ito's lemma to $[\hat{x}(t)]^2$, we have

$$\begin{aligned} d[\hat{x}(t)]^2 = \{2m(t)[\hat{x}(t)]^2 + k^2(t)R^2(t)\}\, dt + 2k(t)R(t)\hat{x}(t) \\ \times \{dz(t) - k(t)\hat{x}(t)\, dt\}. \end{aligned} \tag{6.15}$$

Finally, from Ito's lemma applied to

$$R(t) = E^t[x^2(t)] - [\hat{x}(t)]^2$$

and from (6.14) and (6.15), it follows that $R(t)$ has the following stochastic differential from which, however, the random term is absent.

$$dR(t) = \{2m(t)R(t) + \sigma^2(t) - k^2(t)R^2(t)\}\, dt \qquad (0 \leq t \leq T). \tag{6.16}$$

Hence $R(t)$ is, almost surely, a nonrandom function of $t (0 \leq t \leq T)$ satisfying the ordinary differential equation (6.11). The proof of Theorem 6.2 is complete.

In view of (6.10), it follows that $\hat{x}(t)$ is a Gaussian process which is, almost surely, sample continuous.

REFERENCES

1. BUCY, R. S. (1965). Nonlinear filtering theory. *IEEE Trans. Automatic Control* **10**.
2. DOOB, J. L. (1952). "Stochastic Processes." Wiley, New York.
3. DYNKIN, E. B. (1965). "Markov Processes—I," English transl. Springer, Berlin.
4. GIKHMAN, I. I., and SKOROKHOD, A. V. (1965). "Vvedeniye v Teoriyu Sluchainikh Protsessov." Moscow.
5. ITO, K. (1961). "Lectures on Stochastic Processes." Tata Inst. of Fundamental Res., Bombay.
6. KALLIANPUR, G., and STRIEBEL, C. (1968). Estimation of stochastic processes: Arbitrary system process with additive white noise observation errors. *Ann. Math. Statist.* **39**.
7. KALLIANPUR, G., and STRIEBEL, C., Stochastic differential equations occurring in the estimation of continuous parameter stochastic processes. To be published.
8. KALMAN, R. E., and BUCY, R. S. (1961). New results in linear filtering and prediction theory. *J. Basic Engrg.* **83**.
9. KUSHNER, H. J. (1967). Dynamical equations for optimal nonlinear filtering. *J. Differential Equations* **3**.
10. LIPTZER, R. S., and SHIRYAEV, A. N., Nonlinear filtering of Markov diffusion processes, I and II. *Trudy* M.I.A.N. **104**. To be published.
11. LOEVE, M. (1963). "Probability Theory," 3rd ed. Van Nostrand, Princeton, New Jersey.
12. SKOROKHOD, A. V. (1964). "Sluchainie Protsessi s Nezavisimimi Prirasheniyami." Moscow.
13. SKOROKHOD, A. V. (1965). "Studies in the Theory of Random Processes," English transl. Addison-Wesley, Reading, Massachusetts.
14. WONHAM, W. M. (1965). Some applications of stochastic differential equations to optimal nonlinear filtering. *SIAM J. Control* **2**.

Multiple Time Series Modeling[1]

EMANUEL PARZEN

DEPARTMENT OF STATISTICS
STANFORD UNIVERSITY
STANFORD, CALIFORNIA

1. INTRODUCTION

Empirical multiple time series analysis is concerned with finding relations among r time series $X_1(\cdot), \ldots, X_r(\cdot)$, given finite samples

$$\{X_1(t), t = 1, 2, \ldots, T\}, \ldots, \{X_r(t), t = 1, 2, \ldots, T\}. \tag{1.1}$$

Multiple time series modeling could be equivalently defined as multivariate analysis of a sample of dependent (rather than independent) random vectors

$$\mathbf{X}(t) = \begin{bmatrix} X_1(t) \\ \vdots \\ X_r(t) \end{bmatrix}. \tag{1.2}$$

We call $\mathbf{X}(\cdot) = \{\mathbf{X}(t), t = 0, \pm 1, \pm 2, \ldots\}$ a multiple time series.

The point of view that a multiple time series is a series of vectors (rather than a vector of series) seems useful for mathematical statistical investigations of the distribution of various sample statistics.

Point One. For premathematical statistical investigations of the *specification of the models* to be fitted, it may be essential to first model each component by itself.

This paper seeks to provide a general framework for the theory and practice of multivariate analysis of time series. It seeks to compare:

(1) Spectral approaches to finding relations among time series.

(2) Time domain or innovations approaches to finding relations among time series.

[1] Research supported by the Office of Naval Research under contract Nonr-225(80) and by the U.S. Army Research Office under grant DA-ARO(D)-31-124-G726. Reproduction in whole or in part permitted for any purpose of the United States Government.

The paper also seeks to focus attention on:

(3) Innovations approaches to cross-spectral estimation.

(4) The problem of multivariate analysis of the joint innovations covariance matrix and the sampling properties of its estimators.

2. INNOVATION APPROACHES TO MODELING

When we admit the possibility that our vector samples $\mathbf{X}(1), \ldots, \mathbf{X}(T)$ are not independent, and seek to build stochastic dynamic models, the statistical inference problem could be conceived as one of estimating

$$m_j(t) = E[X_j(t)], \tag{2.1}$$

$$K_{jk}(s, t) = \operatorname{Cov}[X_j(s), X_k(t)]; \tag{2.2}$$

these means and covariances specify the probability law of the observations when it is assumed to be multivariate normal. In order that there will not be as many or more parameters as observations, one must assume models which restrict $m_j(\cdot)$ and $K_{jk}(\cdot, \cdot)$, since otherwise statistical inference is impossible.

A multiple time series $\mathbf{X}(\cdot)$ is called *covariance stationary* [see Parzen (1962), Chapter 3] if for each index j and k, there is a function $R_{jk}(v)$ of $v = 0, \pm 1, \ldots,$ such that

$$\operatorname{Cov}[X_j(s), X_k(t)] = R_{jk}(t - s). \tag{2.3}$$

The r by r matrix

$$\mathbf{R}(v) = \begin{bmatrix} R_{11}(v) & \cdots & R_{1r}(v) \\ \vdots & \cdots & \vdots \\ R_{r1}(v) & \cdots & R_{rr}(v) \end{bmatrix}, \qquad R_{hj}(v) = \operatorname{Cov}[X_h(t), X_j(t+v)], \tag{2.4}$$

is called the *covariance matrix* $\mathbf{R}(\cdot)$ of the *covariance stationary multiple* time series $\{\mathbf{X}(t), t = 1, 2, \ldots, T\}$.

The sample statistics appropriate for inferring models for covariance stationary time series are often interpretable even for nonstationary time series [either as time varying statistics, as in Priestley (1965), or through transformations to stationarity, as in Parzen (1967a) or Whittle (1963b)]. Therefore, we assume that the multiple time series $\mathbf{X}(\cdot)$ being discussed is covariance stationary.

Let us briefly review models for a univariate stationary time series $X(\cdot)$; its covariance function $R(v)$ has spectral representation

$$R(v) = \int_{-\pi}^{\pi} \cos v\omega \, dF(\omega). \tag{2.5}$$

When seeking to model a time series $X(\cdot)$ with given covariance function $R(\cdot)$ and spectral distribution function $F(\cdot)$, in principle one may treat separately the three types of distribution functions into which $F(\cdot)$ may be decomposed:

$$F(\omega) = F_{\mathrm{d}}(\omega) + F_{\mathrm{ac}}(\omega) + F_{\mathrm{sc}}(\omega); \tag{2.6}$$

in words, $F(\cdot)$ is the sum of three distribution functions which are, respectively, discrete (or purely discontinuous), absolutely continuous, and singular continuous.

Observed time series are assumed to have a *mixed spectrum*, in the sense that: (i) the singular continuous part of the spectral distribution function vanishes, (ii) the discrete part has only a finite number of jumps, and (iii) the absolutely continuous part has a spectral density function $f(\omega)$ satisfying

$$\int_{-\pi}^{\pi} \log f(\omega)\, d\omega > -\infty. \tag{2.7}$$

Note that $f(\omega)$ is an even nonnegative function such that

$$F_{\mathrm{ac}}(\omega) = \int_{-\pi}^{\omega} f(\omega')\, d\omega'. \tag{2.8}$$

We call $m(t) = E[X(t)]$ the mean value function of $X(\cdot)$. It may be shown that $X(t) - m(t)$ may be written as the sum of two time series,

$$X(t) - m(t) = X_{\mathrm{d}}(t) + X_{\mathrm{c}}(t) \tag{2.9}$$

satisfying

$$X_{\mathrm{d}}(t) = A_0 + \sum_{j=1}^{r} \{A_j \cos \lambda_j t + B_j \sin \lambda_j t\} \tag{2.10}$$

where A_0, A_j, B_j are uncorrelated random variables, and λ_j are frequencies in the band $0 < \lambda_j \leq \pi$, while

$$X_{\mathrm{c}}(t) = \eta(t) + b_1\eta(t-1) + b_2\eta(t-2) + \cdots \tag{2.11}$$

where $\{b_v\}$ are constants such that $\sum b_v^2 < \infty$ and $\{\eta(v)\}$ are uncorrelated random variables.

The *probability distribution* of A_0, A_j, B_j cannot be estimated from a single realization of $X(\cdot)$, or even of $X_{\mathrm{d}}(\cdot)$; all one can hope to estimate is the value of these variables in the realization observed. Thus A_0, A_j, B_j can be treated as *constants* (rather than random variables) for purposes of statistical inference and $X_{\mathrm{d}}(\cdot)$ can be treated as part of the mean value function of $X(\cdot)$. The mean value function of $X(\cdot)$ has to be eliminated by some detrending procedure (which could involve spectral analysis) in order to do statistical inference on $X_{\mathrm{c}}(\cdot)$, the "fluctuation" part of $X(\cdot)$.

Point Two. In multiple time series modeling, we can assume that we are dealing with zero mean jointly covariance stationary time series $X_j(\cdot)$, each satisfying (7), and therefore satisfying a model of the form

$$X_j(t) = \eta_j(t) + b_1^{(j)}\eta_j(t-1) + b_2^{(j)}\eta_j(t-2) + \cdots. \tag{2.12}$$

To understand the meaning of the random variables $\eta_j(t)$, let us hereafter consider *normal* time series $\{X(t)\}$. One can associate with a univariate series $X(\cdot)$ a series of successive conditional expectations (or minimum mean-square error predictors)

$$X^*(t) = E[X(t) \mid X(t-1), X(t-2), \ldots], \tag{2.13}$$

and conditional variances (or mean-square prediction errors)

$$\tilde{\sigma}_t^2 = \operatorname{Var}[X(t) \mid X(t-1), X(t-2), \ldots] = E[\,|X(t) - X^*(t)|^2]. \tag{2.14}$$

For nonnormal time series, the notion of projection is used in place of conditional expectation [see Rozanov (1967)].

The one-step prediction error, denoted

$$\eta(t) = X(t) - X^*(t) \qquad \text{or} \qquad \tilde{X}(t) = X(t) - X^*(t), \tag{2.15}$$

is called the *innovation* at time t. The successive innovations $\eta(t)$ are a sequence of uncorrelated (independent when $X(\cdot)$ is normal, as assumed here) random variables,

$$E[\eta(s)\eta(t)] = 0 \qquad \text{if} \quad s \neq t. \tag{2.16}$$

An uncorrelated sequence $\eta(\cdot)$ is called *white noise*; if all variances are equal, it is called stationary white noise.

Writing $X(t)$ as an infinite series in $\eta(t), \eta(t-1), \ldots$, is one way of expressing the time series $X(\cdot)$ as the output of a filter whose input is white noise $\eta(\cdot)$

$$\eta(\cdot) \text{—}\boxed{\text{filter } \Phi}\text{—} X(\cdot) = \Phi[\eta(\cdot)].$$

By representing a time series as the output of a filter whose input is *innovation* white noise, we are able to conveniently solve estimation (prediction, signal extraction) problems and simulation problems for the time series.

For a univariate time series $X(\cdot)$ which is assumed to be normal, covariance stationary, have zero means, and nondeterministic [in the sense that it satisfies model (11)], the modeling problem can be solved by estimating either:

(i) its covariance function $R(v)$, or
(ii) its spectral density function $f(\omega)$, or
(iii) its innovation variance $\tilde{\sigma}^2$ and the filter $\Phi[\cdot]$ which transforms $\eta(\cdot)$ to $X(\cdot)$.

Point Three. Approach (iii) is the most satisfactory for two reasons: (1) as the answer we seek since it is the most convenient form for prediction and control; (2) as the most suitable means of obtaining (ii) [the details of how to do this are discussed in Section 5].

Point Four. For a multiple stationary normal time series two types of innovation approaches to modeling can be considered:

(i) the individual innovation approach, and
(ii) the joint innovation approach.

The *individual innovations*, denoted $\eta_j(t)$, are defined in terms of the predictors of each series given its own past

$$X_j^*(t) = E[X_j(t) \mid X_j(s), s < t] \tag{2.17}$$

by

$$\eta_j(t) = X_j(t) - X_j^*(t). \tag{2.18}$$

Equation (12) is a representation of $X_j(t)$ in terms of its individual innovations.

The joint innovations, denoted $\boldsymbol{\eta}_j(t)$, are defined in terms of the predictors, denoted $\mathbf{X}_j^*(t)$, of each series given the pasts of *all* of them; in symbols

$$\mathbf{X}_j^*(t) = E[X_j(t) | X_k(s), s < t, \quad \text{and} \quad k = 1, 2, \ldots, r] \tag{2.19}$$

and

$$\boldsymbol{\eta}_j(t) = X_j(t) - \mathbf{X}_j^*(t). \tag{2.20}$$

The joint innovation multiple time series, denoted $\boldsymbol{\eta}(\cdot)$, and defined by $\boldsymbol{\eta}(\cdot)' = (\boldsymbol{\eta}_1(\cdot), \ldots, \boldsymbol{\eta}_r(\cdot))$, is multiple white noise in the sense that

$$E[\boldsymbol{\eta}(s)\boldsymbol{\eta}'(t)] = 0 \qquad \text{for} \quad s \neq t, \tag{2.21}$$

and therefore is described by the innovation covariance matrix

$$\tilde{\Sigma} = E[\boldsymbol{\eta}(t)\boldsymbol{\eta}'(t)]. \tag{2.22}$$

The joint innovation approach models $\mathbf{X}(\cdot)$ by estimating: (i) the innovation covariance matrix $\tilde{\Sigma}$, and (ii) the multi input-multi output filter which transforms the joint innovations $\boldsymbol{\eta}(\cdot)$ to the observed multiple time series $\mathbf{X}(\cdot)$.

The individual innovation approach models $\mathbf{X}(\cdot)$ by estimating: (i) each individual innovation series $\eta_j(\cdot)$ and the filter transforming $\eta_j(\cdot)$ to $X_j(\cdot)$, (ii) the multiple time series [denoted $\boldsymbol{\eta}_{\text{ind}}(t)$ and defined by $\boldsymbol{\eta}_{\text{ind}}(\cdot)' = (\eta_1(\cdot), \ldots, \eta_r(\cdot))$] of individual innovations in terms of their joint innovations [to be denoted $\boldsymbol{\varepsilon}(\cdot)$ and called the *innovation innovations*] and the multi input-multi output filter which transforms $\boldsymbol{\varepsilon}(\cdot)$ to $\boldsymbol{\eta}_{\text{ind}}(\cdot)$.

Point Five. To estimate the joint innovation structure of a multiple time series, we fit it by a *sufficiently long* joint autoregressive scheme. Probabilistic justification of such fits is provided by the work of Masani [see, for example, Masani's review paper (1966), Sect. 13].

A zero mean covariance stationary multiple time series $\mathbf{X}(\cdot)$ is called a *joint autoregressive scheme of order m* if the *infinite memory* predictor $\mathbf{X}^*(t)$ can be expressed as a linear combination of $\mathbf{X}(t-1), \ldots, \mathbf{X}(t-m)$

$$\mathbf{X}^*(t) = A(1)\mathbf{X}(t-1) + \cdots + A(m)\mathbf{X}(t-m). \tag{2.23}$$

When the multiple time series $\mathbf{X}(\cdot)$ is known to be a joint autoregressive scheme of order m, the autoregressive matrix coefficients $A(1), \ldots, A(m)$ are estimated from a sample $\{\mathbf{X}(t), t = 1, 2, \ldots, T\}$ of size T by the solutions $\hat{A}(1), \ldots, \hat{A}(m)$ of a system of equations called the multiple Yule-Walker equations:

$$\sum_{j=1}^{m} \hat{A}(j)\mathbf{R}_T(j-k) = \mathbf{R}_T(-k), \qquad k = 1, 2, \ldots, m, \tag{2.24}$$

where $\mathbf{R}_T(v)$ is the sample covariance matrix defined in the next section.

The Yule-Walker equations are suggested by the fact that the matrix coefficients $A(1), \ldots, A(m)$ of the finite memory predictor in (23) satisfy the *normal* equations

$$E[\mathbf{X}^*(t)\mathbf{X}'(t-k)] = E[\mathbf{X}(t)\mathbf{X}'(t-k)], \qquad k = 1, 2, \ldots, m \tag{2.25}$$

or

$$\sum_{j=1}^{m} A(j)\mathbf{R}(j-k) = \mathbf{R}(-k), \qquad k = 1, 2, \ldots, m. \tag{2.26}$$

The prediction error covariance matrix $\tilde{\Sigma}$ satisfies

$$\tilde{\Sigma} = [\{\mathbf{X}(t) - \mathbf{X}^*(t)\}\mathbf{X}'(t)] = \mathbf{R}(0) - \sum_{j=1}^{m} A(j)\mathbf{R}(j); \tag{2.27}$$

the natural estimator of $\tilde{\Sigma}$ is

$$\hat{\tilde{\Sigma}} = \mathbf{R}_T(0) - \sum_{j=1}^{m} \hat{A}(j)\mathbf{R}_T(j). \tag{2.28}$$

It is important to note that the *computation* of $\hat{A}(1), \ldots, \hat{A}(m), \hat{\tilde{\Sigma}}$ is most conveniently done *recursively* [as in Whittle (1963a,b), Jones (1964), or Robinson (1967)].

From the work of Wold (1954), Mann and Wald (1943), and Whittle (1953), we know the properties of the autoregressive coefficient estimator $\hat{A}(1), \ldots, \hat{A}(m)$; indeed, their properties are very similar to those of estimators of multivariate regression coefficients [as given, for example, in Kendall and Stuart (1966), p. 275].

What has not been explicitly proved in the literature, but seems plausible (and basic to the innovation approach to modeling), is that $(T-m)\,\hat{\tilde{\Sigma}}$ is approximately distributed as the Wishart distribution of dimension r, degrees of freedom $T-m$, and covariance matrix $\tilde{\Sigma}$. In Section 3, we shall make the point that multivariate analysis of $\hat{\tilde{\Sigma}}$ is an important tool of multiple time series modeling.

3. SPECTRAL APPROACHES TO MODELING

The spectral approach to multiple stationary time series analysis assumes that each component is nondeterministic, and in addition assumes that the covariance matrix $\mathbf{R}(\cdot)$ is absolutely summable in the sense that

$$\sum_{v} |R_{hj}(v)| < \infty \qquad \text{for} \quad h, j = 1, 2, \ldots, r, \tag{3.1}$$

so that an explicit formula can be given for the spectral density matrix

$$\mathbf{f}(\omega) = (2\pi)^{-1} \sum_{v=-\infty}^{\infty} e^{-iv\omega}\mathbf{R}(v) \tag{3.2}$$

or

$$\mathbf{f}(\omega) = \begin{bmatrix} f_{11}(\omega) & \cdots & f_{1r}(\omega) \\ \cdots & \cdots & \cdots \\ f_{r1}(\omega) & \cdots & f_{rr}(\omega)' \end{bmatrix}, \qquad f_{hj}(\omega) = (2\pi)^{-1} \sum_{v=-\infty}^{\infty} e^{-iv\omega} R_{hj}(v); \tag{3.3}$$

in terms of $\mathbf{f}(\omega)$, we have a Fourier representation for $\mathbf{R}(v)$

$$\mathbf{R}(v) = \int_{-\pi}^{\pi} e^{iv\omega}\mathbf{f}(\omega)\, d\omega. \tag{3.4}$$

One calls $\mathbf{f}(\omega)$ the *spectral density matrix* of the covariance stationary multiple time series $\mathbf{X}(\cdot)$ [for further discussion see Rozanov (1967), Granger (1964), Jenkins and Watts (1968)].

Point Six. There are *three kinds* of sample statistics in multiple time series modeling, which one should use simultaneously and between which one should know how to transform quickly. The three kinds of sample statistics are:

(i) the sample covariance matrix,
(ii) a matrix of estimated spectral densities,
(iii) various innovations and sample autoregressive coefficients.

The sample covariance matrix is defined by

$$\mathbf{R}_T(v) = T^{-1} \sum_{t=1}^{T-v} \mathbf{X}(t)\mathbf{X}'(t+v), \qquad \text{for} \quad v = 0, 1, \ldots, T-1. \tag{3.5}$$

When the multiple time series $\mathbf{X}(\cdot)$ has zero means and is covariance stationary, one regards $\mathbf{R}_T(v)$ as an estimate of the value of the covariance matrix $\mathbf{R}(v)$. Since $\mathbf{R}(-v) = \mathbf{R}'(v)$, we define $\mathbf{R}_T(-v) = \mathbf{R}_T'(v)$.

It should be noted that in the course of our discussion of estimated spectral densities, it will be seen that, in practice, one should *rarely* use (5) to *compute* $\mathbf{R}_T(v)$, and one should *not usually* use (5) to even *define* $\mathbf{R}_T(v)$ for "detrended" time series.

While the sample covariance matrix $\mathbf{R}_T(v)$ is of interest to determine the lags v at which the components of $\mathbf{R}_T(v)$ are significantly nonzero, *for time series modeling* $\mathbf{R}_T(\cdot)$ *needs to be transformed either to spectral density estimates or autoregressive coefficient estimates.*

A matrix $\hat{\mathbf{f}}(\omega)$ of estimated spectral densities $\hat{f}_{hj}(\omega)$ is denoted

$$\hat{\mathbf{f}}(\omega) = \begin{bmatrix} \hat{f}_{11}(\omega) & \hat{f}_{12}(\omega) & \cdots & \hat{f}_{1r}(\omega) \\ \hat{f}_{21}(\omega) & \hat{f}_{22}(\omega) & \cdots & \hat{f}_{2r}(\omega) \\ \cdots & \cdots & \cdots & \cdots \\ \hat{f}_{r1}(\omega) & \hat{f}_{r2}(\omega) & \cdots & \hat{f}_{rr}(\omega) \end{bmatrix}. \tag{3.6}$$

Point Seven. The spectral approach to multivariate analysis of time series may be defined to be concerned with the relations among time series that can be inferred statistically from the matrix of estimated spectral densities [as well as probabilistically from the matrix of true spectral densities; for example, see Koopmans (1964)].

We briefly describe ways of forming estimated spectra $\hat{\mathbf{f}}(\omega)$ [for a tabular presentation of these remarks see Parzen (1968)]. First, form the *sample Fourier transform*

$$\mathbf{Z}(\omega) = \sum_{t=1}^{T} e^{-i\omega t}\mathbf{X}(t) \tag{3.7}$$

at specified frequencies ω (we prefer $0, 2\pi/2T, \ldots, (2T-1)(2\pi/2T)$). Second, at these frequencies form the *sample spectral density* matrix by the formula

$$\mathbf{f}_T(\omega) = (2\pi T)^{-1}\mathbf{Z}(\omega)Z'(-\omega) \tag{3.8}$$

which satisfies the relations

$$\mathbf{R}_T(v) = \int_{-\pi}^{\pi} e^{iv\omega}\mathbf{f}_T(\omega)\, d\omega, \tag{3.9}$$

$$\mathbf{f}_T(\omega) = (2\pi)^{-1} \sum_{|v|<T} e^{-iv\omega}\mathbf{R}_T(v). \tag{3.10}$$

Third, form estimators of $\mathbf{f}(\omega)$ by averaging adjacent values of $\mathbf{f}_T(\omega)$; this averaging process is computationally faster if the averages one considers are of the form

$$\hat{\mathbf{f}}(k(2\pi/T)) = \Sigma K_T((j-k)(2\pi/T))\mathbf{f}_T(j(2\pi/T)), \tag{3.11}$$

which we call *filtered* sample spectral density functions.

An alternative third step, which seems to me the most convenient (and because of Fast Fourier Transform techniques perhaps faster) way to compute $\hat{\mathbf{f}}(\cdot)$, is via the method of covariance averages [compare Parzen (1967b) or Jenkins (1965)]

$$\hat{\mathbf{f}}(\omega) = (2\pi)^{-1} \sum_{|v|<T} e^{-iv\omega} k(v/M)\mathbf{R}_T(v) \tag{3.12}$$

in terms of a suitable *kernel* $k(\cdot)$ and constant M called the *truncation point.* We prefer (12) to (11) since one can readily compute $\mathbf{R}_T(v)$ for $v = 0, 1, \ldots, T-1$ (through the fast Fourier transform) by the formula

$$\mathbf{R}_T(v) = (2\pi/2T) \sum_{k=0}^{2T-1} \exp(ivk(2\pi/2T)\mathbf{f}_T(k(2\pi/2T)). \tag{3.13}$$

For the proof of (13), compare Gentleman and Sande (1966), p. 573.

To interpret estimated spectra, one has to take account of both their variability and their bias. The basic approximation on variability [which was first noted by Goodman (1963) and proved by Wahba (1968) and Brillinger (1970)] is that an estimated spectral density matrix $\hat{\mathbf{f}}(\omega)$ of form (12), or equivalently (11), has the following approximate distribution: $\nu\hat{\mathbf{f}}(\omega)$ has a complex Wishart distribution of dimension r, degrees of freedom ν, and covariance matrix $\mathbf{f}(\omega)$, where

$$\nu^{-1} = (M/T) \int_{-\infty}^{\infty} k^2(u)\, du. \tag{3.14}$$

By identifying the distribution of $\hat{\mathbf{f}}(\omega)$ with the Wishart distribution, one reduces to *standard problems of multivariate analysis* the problem of finding the distribution of various statistics derived from $\hat{\mathbf{f}}(\omega)$.

To conclude this section, we note that the foregoing computational path seems especially appropriate when one cannot assume the observed time series to have zero mean (no trend), and desires to *detrend* the series $\mathbf{X}(\cdot)$ by passing each component $X_j(\cdot)$ through a filter to form a detrended series ${}_dX_j(\cdot)$

$${}_dX_j(t) = \sum_{\alpha=-m}^{n} X_j(t-\alpha)w_j(\alpha). \tag{3.15}$$

However, the Fourier transform ${}_d\mathbf{Z}_j(\cdot)$ can be formed [without first forming ${}_d\mathbf{X}(\cdot)$] directly from the Fourier transform $\mathbf{Z}(\cdot)$ by

$${}_dZ_j(\omega) = Z_j(\omega)W_j(\omega) \tag{3.16}$$

where

$$W_j(\omega) = \sum_{\alpha} w_j(\alpha)\exp(i\omega\alpha). \tag{3.17}$$

Furthermore, to form ${}_d\mathbf{X}(\cdot)$ as a function of time, one need only *invert the Fourier transform* of ${}_d\mathbf{X}(\cdot)$. The sample spectral density matrix and sample covariance matrix of a detrended multiple time series ${}_d\mathbf{X}(\cdot)$ seem to me to be best computed by

$$\mathbf{f}_T(\omega) = (2\pi T)^{-1}\, {}_d\mathbf{Z}(\omega)\, {}_d\mathbf{Z}'(-\omega) \tag{3.18}$$

and (13), respectively. I must admit that as yet I have no practical experience with comparisons of formula (18) with more "direct" methods of calculation.

4. RELATIONS BETWEEN TIME SERIES

Given two jointly stationary zero mean multiple time series $\mathbf{X}(\cdot)$ and $\mathbf{Y}(\cdot)$, there are a variety of *relation filters*. To regard $\mathbf{X}(\cdot)$ as the independent variable is to regard it as the input of a filter whose output, denoted $\mathbf{Y}^*(\cdot)$, provides a representation of $\mathbf{Y}(\cdot)$ as a sum of two terms

$$\mathbf{Y}(t) = \mathbf{Y}^*(t) + \boldsymbol{\varepsilon}(t), \qquad \boldsymbol{\varepsilon}(t) = \mathbf{Y}(t) - \mathbf{Y}^*(t). \tag{4.1}$$

Point Eight. It is most meaningful to define $\mathbf{Y}^*(t)$ as a minimum mean-square error linear predictor of $\mathbf{Y}(t)$ given a specified past of the $\mathbf{X}(\cdot)$ series [for example $\{\mathbf{X}(s), s = 0, \pm 1, \pm 2, \ldots\}$ or $\{\mathbf{X}(s), s \leq t\}$]. In other words, $E[|\mathbf{Y}(t) - \mathbf{Y}^*(t)|^2]$ is a minimum among all possible linear functionals of the specified values of $\mathbf{X}(\cdot)$. Then $\boldsymbol{\varepsilon}(\cdot)$ is the *error series*, characterized by the *normal property* (for each $t = 0, \pm 1, \pm 2, \ldots$)

$$E[\mathbf{X}(s)\boldsymbol{\varepsilon}'(t)] = 0 \quad \text{for all indices } s \text{ such that } \mathbf{X}(s) \text{ is part of the memory used to form } \mathbf{Y}^*(t). \tag{4.2}$$

In addition to specifying the past of $\mathbf{X}(\cdot)$ used to form $\mathbf{Y}^*(t)$ as a linear predictor of $\mathbf{Y}(t)$, one may specify "matrix restraints" on the form of $\mathbf{Y}^*(t)$ of the type considered by Brillinger (1969).

The system which transforms $\mathbf{X}(\cdot)$ to $\mathbf{Y}^*(\cdot)$ is a filter which, when $\mathbf{X}(\cdot)$ and $\mathbf{Y}(\cdot)$ are jointly covariance stationary, is time invariant. The spectral representation of this filter is a matrix function of ω, denoted $\mathbf{B}_{Y^*}(\omega)$ and called the *filter transfer* function, best described by assuming that the filter is an infinite moving average

$$\mathbf{Y}^*(t) = \sum_{k=-\infty}^{\infty} \boldsymbol{\beta}(k)\mathbf{X}(t-k) \tag{4.3}$$

where $\{\boldsymbol{\beta}(k), k = 0, \pm 1, \ldots\}$ is a sequence of matrices called the *filter response* function. The filter transfer function is defined by

$$\mathbf{B}_{Y^*}(\omega) = \sum_{k=-\infty}^{\infty} e^{-i\omega k}\boldsymbol{\beta}(k). \tag{4.4}$$

The relation between $\mathbf{Y}(\cdot)$ and $\mathbf{X}(\cdot)$ is resolved into a *deterministic dynamic system* represented by the relation filter with filter transfer function $\mathbf{B}_{Y*}(\cdot)$ and a *stochastic driving function* represented by the error series $\boldsymbol{\varepsilon}(\cdot)$ with spectral density matrix denoted by $\tilde{\mathbf{f}}_{Y*}(\omega)$.

When $\mathbf{Y}^*(t)$ is a function of all values of $\mathbf{X}(\cdot)$ in the sense that

$$\mathbf{Y}^*(t) = E[\mathbf{Y}(t) \mid \mathbf{X}(s), s = 0, \pm 1, \ldots], \tag{4.5}$$

we call $\tilde{\mathbf{f}}_{Y*}(\omega)$ the *partial spectral density* matrix of $\mathbf{Y}(\cdot)$, given $\mathbf{X}(\cdot)$.

Point Nine. The spectral theory of multivariate analysis of time series has been mainly concerned with finding: (i) Formulas for $\mathbf{B}_{Y*}(\omega)$ and $\tilde{\mathbf{f}}_{Y*}(\omega)$ in terms of the joint spectral density matrix of the $\mathbf{X}(\cdot)$ and $\mathbf{Y}(\cdot)$ multiple time series

$$\mathbf{f}(\omega) = \begin{bmatrix} \mathbf{f}_{XX}(\omega) & \mathbf{f}_{XY}(\omega) \\ \mathbf{f}_{YX}(\omega) & \mathbf{f}_{YY}(\omega) \end{bmatrix}, \tag{4.6}$$

and (ii) The sampling properties of the natural estimators $\hat{\mathbf{B}}_{Y*}(\omega)$ and $\hat{\tilde{\mathbf{f}}}_{Y*}(\omega)$ formed from an estimated spectral density matrix

$$\hat{\mathbf{f}}(\omega) = \begin{bmatrix} \hat{\mathbf{f}}_{XX}(\omega) & \hat{\mathbf{f}}_{XY}(\omega) \\ \hat{\mathbf{f}}_{YX}(\omega) & \hat{\mathbf{f}}_{YY}(\omega) \end{bmatrix} = \begin{bmatrix} \hat{\mathbf{f}}_{XX}(\omega) & \hat{\mathbf{f}}_{XY}(\omega) \\ \hat{\mathbf{f}}'_{XY}(\omega) & \hat{\mathbf{f}}_{YY}(\omega) \end{bmatrix} \tag{4.7}$$

under the assumption that for a suitable number v of degrees of freedom $v\hat{\mathbf{f}}(\omega)$ obeys a complex Wishart distribution of v degrees of freedom and covariance matrix $\mathbf{f}(\omega)$.

For example, by the usual matrix pivoting procedures used to solve normal equations, one can transform [see Parzen (1967b)] an estimated spectral density matrix (6) to a partitioned matrix

$$\begin{bmatrix} \hat{\mathbf{f}}_{XX}^{-1}(\omega) & \hat{\mathbf{B}}'_{Y*}(\omega) \\ -\hat{\mathbf{B}}_{Y*}(\omega) & \hat{\tilde{\mathbf{f}}}_{Y*}(\omega) \end{bmatrix} \tag{4.8}$$

where

$$\begin{aligned} \hat{\mathbf{B}}_{Y*}(\omega) &= \hat{\mathbf{f}}_{YX}(\omega)\hat{\mathbf{f}}_{XX}^{-1}(\omega) \\ \hat{\tilde{\mathbf{f}}}_{Y*}(\omega) &= \hat{\mathbf{f}}_{YY}(\omega) - \hat{\mathbf{B}}_{Y*}(\omega)\hat{\mathbf{f}}_{XY}(\omega) \\ &= \hat{\mathbf{f}}_{YY}(\omega) - \hat{\mathbf{f}}_{YX}(\omega)\hat{\mathbf{f}}_{XX}^{-1}(\omega)\hat{\mathbf{f}}'_{YX}(\omega) \end{aligned} \tag{4.9}$$

are natural estimators of the regression transfer function and error spectrum, respectively, for $\mathbf{Y}^*(\cdot)$ defined by (5); for the multivariate analogue of (9) see Anderson (1958).

The work that has been done on estimating relations between time series in terms of $\mathbf{B}_{Y*}(\omega)$ and $\mathbf{f}_{Y*}(\omega)$ leaves open a number of problems and issues which it is the *major aim* of this paper to point out:

(1) One would like to describe in the time domain the filter which $\hat{\mathbf{B}}_{Y*}(\omega)$ estimates in the frequency domain; one way of doing this is to write

$$\hat{\mathbf{B}}_{Y*}(\omega) = \sum_{k=-m}^{n} \boldsymbol{\beta}(k) e^{-i\omega k} + \{\hat{\mathbf{B}}_{Y*}(\omega) - \mathbf{B}_Y(\omega)\} \tag{4.10}$$

where m, n, and $\boldsymbol{\beta}(k)$ are to be estimated and the "errors" $\hat{\mathbf{B}}_{Y*}(\omega) - \mathbf{B}_Y(\omega)$ are approximately normal with zero means and asymptotic variances that can be estimated; often the "errors" at different frequencies can be shown to be asymptotically independent. Pioneering and elegant work on this problem has been done by Hannan [Hannan (1963, 1965, 1967), Hamon and Hannan (1963)]. From (10), one estimates the coefficients $\boldsymbol{\beta}(k)$ by regression analysis.

(2) One would like to describe (model) in terms of a time domain filter with white noise input the error series $\boldsymbol{\varepsilon}(\cdot)$ whose spectral density matrix $\tilde{\mathbf{f}}_{Y*}(\omega)$ is estimated by $\hat{\tilde{\mathbf{f}}}_{Y*}(\omega)$.

(3) The sampling theory of the usual spectral estimators (namely, smoothed sample spectral densities) is based entirely on variability theory [for example, Rosenblatt (1959), Goodman (1963)] and ignores the fact that estimation of cross-spectra by the usual method of smoothed sample spectral densities is subject to serious bias errors [Akaike and Yamanouchi (1963), Nettheim (1966), Parzen (1967b), Tick (1967)]. I believe that it can be shown that spectral estimators which have "minimum" bias and variability can be found by fitting long enough autoregressive schemes. In this paper, we indicate several "autoregression approaches" to cross-spectral estimation and to fitting time domain models to time series.

(4) The relations between time series which can be inferred from estimated spectra are not "causal" unless the relations are between time series physically measured at the input and output, respectively, of a causal filter. Causal relations can be fitted only through "innovations" which can be found by fitting long autoregressive schemes. In other words, for finding relations between two arbitrary time series, spectral methods suffer from the drawback that they work directly only for predictors whose memory involves the future as well as the past. They cannot easily be used to estimate the error spectrum, and (more importantly) the filter transfer function from $\mathbf{X}(\cdot)$ to $\mathbf{Y}^*(\cdot)$, for cases such as the following

$$\begin{aligned} \mathbf{Y}^*(t) &= E[\mathbf{Y}(t) \mid \mathbf{X}(s), s < t], \\ \mathbf{Y}^*(t) &= E[\mathbf{Y}(t) \mid \mathbf{X}(s), s < t \quad \text{and} \quad \mathbf{Y}(s), s < t], \\ \mathbf{Y}^*(t) &= E[\mathbf{Y}(t) \mid \mathbf{X}(s), s \le t \quad \text{and} \quad \mathbf{Y}(s), s < t]. \end{aligned} \tag{4.11}$$

Autoregressive methods seem to provide directly estimators of these semi-infinite memory predictors.

To the multiple time series

$$\begin{bmatrix} \mathbf{X}(t) \\ \mathbf{Y}(t) \end{bmatrix}, \tag{4.12}$$

one can fit a sufficiently long autoregressive scheme

$$\begin{bmatrix} \mathbf{X}(t) \\ \mathbf{Y}(t) \end{bmatrix} = A(1)\begin{bmatrix} \mathbf{X}(t-1) \\ \mathbf{Y}(t-1) \end{bmatrix} + \cdots + A(m)\begin{bmatrix} \mathbf{X}(t-m) \\ \mathbf{Y}(t-m) \end{bmatrix} + \eta(t) \tag{4.13}$$

where $\eta(t)$ is multiple white noise. Writing

$$A(j) = \begin{bmatrix} A_{XX}(j) & A_{XY}(j) \\ A_{YX}(j) & A_{YY}(j) \end{bmatrix}, \qquad \eta(t) = \begin{bmatrix} \eta_X(t) \\ \eta_Y(t) \end{bmatrix}, \tag{4.14}$$

one obtains a relation between the $\mathbf{X}(\cdot)$ and $\mathbf{Y}(\cdot)$ series

$$\begin{aligned} \mathbf{Y}(t) - A_{YY}(1)\mathbf{Y}(t-1) - \cdots - A_{YY}(m)\mathbf{Y}(t-m) \\ = A_{YX}(1)\mathbf{X}(t-1) - \cdots - A_{YX}(m)\mathbf{X}(t-m) + \eta_Y(t). \end{aligned} \tag{4.15}$$

We next show how to add $\mathbf{X}(t)$ to the relation (15). Given $\mathbf{X}(t)$, and the past of $\mathbf{X}(\cdot)$ and $\mathbf{Y}(\cdot)$ up to $t-1$, one can form

$$\begin{aligned} \eta_X(t) &= \mathbf{X}(t) - \mathbf{X}^*(t) \\ &= \mathbf{X}(t) - A_{XX}(1)\mathbf{X}(t-1) - \cdots - A_{XX}(m)\mathbf{X}(t-m) \\ &\quad - A_{XY}(1)\mathbf{Y}(t-1) - \cdots - A_{XY}(m)\mathbf{Y}(t-m). \end{aligned} \tag{4.16}$$

Next, from $\eta_X(t)$ and the innovation covariance matrix $\tilde{\Sigma}$, one can form a predictor $\eta_Y{}^*(t)$ of $\eta_Y(t)$. To write $\eta_Y{}^*(t)$ explicitly, partition $\tilde{\Sigma}$

$$\tilde{\Sigma} = \begin{bmatrix} \tilde{\Sigma}_{XX} & \tilde{\Sigma}_{XY} \\ \tilde{\Sigma}_{YX} & \tilde{\Sigma}_{YY} \end{bmatrix}. \tag{4.17}$$

Then

$$\eta_Y^*(t) = \tilde{\Sigma}_{YX}\tilde{\Sigma}_{XX}^{-1}\eta_X(t). \tag{4.18}$$

In (15) substitute $\eta_Y{}^*(t)$, given by (18), for $\eta_Y(t)$; one thus obtains the formula

$$\begin{aligned} &E[\mathbf{Y}(t) \mid \mathbf{X}(s), s \le t \quad \text{and} \quad \mathbf{Y}(s), s < t] \\ &\quad = A_{YY}(1)\mathbf{Y}(t-1) + \cdots + A_{YY}(m)\mathbf{Y}(t-m) \\ &\qquad + A_{YX}(1)\mathbf{X}(t-1) + \cdots + A_{YX}(m)\mathbf{X}(t-m) + \eta_Y{}^*(t). \end{aligned} \tag{4.19}$$

One often seeks a parsimonious parameterization of the filter with output $\mathbf{Y}^*(\cdot)$. It might be sought through stepwise regression among predictor formulas of the form

$$\begin{aligned} \mathbf{Y}^*(t) = C_{YY}(1)\mathbf{Y}(t-1) + \cdots + C_{YY}(m)\mathbf{Y}(t-m) \\ + C_{YX}(1)\mathbf{X}(t-1) + \cdots + C_{YX}(m)\mathbf{X}(t-m) \\ + C_{Y\eta_Y}(1)\eta_Y(t-1) + \cdots + C_{Y\eta_Y}(m)\eta_Y(t-m). \end{aligned} \tag{4.20}$$

Once a relation of form (20) has been fitted, it can be computed recursively.

The foregoing models correspond to time domain versions of predictor formulas for $\mathbf{Y}(t)$ in which no rank constraints are imposed on the matrix coefficients. It would be of interest to develop time domain versions of the results of Brillinger (1969) on predictors with rank restraints.

(5) A final point, which seems to me the most important: multivariate analysis of the joint innovation covariance matrix

$$\tilde{\Sigma} = E[\boldsymbol{\eta}(t)\boldsymbol{\eta}'(t)] \tag{4.21}$$

provides interesting relations among components of the time series. The use of regression analysis of $\tilde{\Sigma}$ was discussed in Eqs. (17)–(19). The eigenvalues and eigenvectors of $\tilde{\Sigma}$ seem worth being routinely computed and examined to indicate ways of reducing the dimensionality of the data vector. The canonical correlations between η_X and η_Y seem to have meaningful interpretations, such as for testing for lack of correlation between $\mathbf{X}(\cdot)$ and $\mathbf{Y}(\cdot)$.

5. AUTOREGRESSIVE APPROACH TO A SINGLE TIME SERIES

When modeling a single time series $X(\cdot)$, one is interested in describing the innovation to series filter [which transforms the innovation $\eta(\cdot)$ to $X(\cdot)$] in *time domain* terms.

Any filter can be approximately expressed as a combination of autoregressive and moving average terms

$$\begin{aligned} X(t) + a_1 X(t-1) + \cdots + a_m X(t-m) \\ = \eta(t) + b_1\eta(t-1) + \cdots + b_q\eta(t-q), \end{aligned} \tag{5.1}$$

one regards the orders m and q, as well as the coefficients $a_1, \ldots, a_m, b_1, \ldots, b_q$ as parameters to be estimated. In this formula, it is usual to think of $\eta(\cdot)$ as a white noise series. A minor point of this paper is: We always require $\eta(\cdot)$ to be the innovation series of $X(\cdot)$.

It turns out that assuming the model for $X(\cdot)$ to be of the form (1) is equivalent to assuming a *model for the one-step linear predictor* $X^*(t)$ of the form

$$\begin{aligned} X^*(t) = a_1 X(t-1) + \cdots + a_m X(t-m) \\ + b_1\eta(t-1) + \cdots + b_q\eta(t-q). \end{aligned} \tag{5.2}$$

When $X^*(t)$ satisfies model (2) with: (i) $b_1 = \cdots = b_q = 0$, we call $X(\cdot)$ an *autoregressive* scheme of order m, (ii) $a_1 = \cdots = a_m = 0$, we call $X(\cdot)$ a *moving average* scheme of order q, (iii) some a's and some b's nonzero, we call $X(\cdot)$ a *mixed* scheme.

In other words, the usual models considered for stationary time series can be formulated equivalently as models for the predictors $X^*(t)$.

In modeling time series, our aim is to obtain a parsimonious parameterization of the form (2). There are available several methods for estimating the parameters of the mixed scheme (2) [see Box and Jenkins (1969), Durbin (1959, 1960), Walker (1961, 1962, 1967), Philips (1966), Hannan (1969)]. Possibly a new variant is the following method.

First, fit $X(\cdot)$ by a long autoregressive scheme

$$X(t) = c_1 X(t-1) + \cdots + c_M X(t-M) + \eta(t). \tag{5.3}$$

Efficient estimators $\hat{c}_1, \ldots, \hat{c}_M$ of the coefficients of autoregressive scheme can be computed (at little computational costs by recursive methods).

Second, consider the transfer function

$$C(z) = 1 - c_1 z - c_2 z^2 - \cdots - c_M z^M \tag{5.4}$$

and form its estimator

$$\hat{C}(z) = 1 - \hat{c}_1 z - \hat{c}_2 z^2 - \cdots - \hat{c}_M z^M. \tag{5.5}$$

Third, note that the transfer functions which we seek to estimate

$$A(z) = 1 - a_1 z - \cdots - a_m z^m, \qquad B(z) = 1 + b_1 z + \cdots + b_q z_q \tag{5.6}$$

are related to $C(z)$ by

$$(C(z))^{-1} = B(z)/A(z) \qquad \text{or} \qquad C(z) = A(z)/B(z). \tag{5.7}$$

The parameters of $A(z)$ and $B(z)$ are to be estimated (by nonlinear least squares) from

$$\hat{C}(e^{i\omega}) = A(e^{i\omega})/B(e^{i\omega}) + \text{error}(e^{i\omega}) \tag{5.8}$$

where the error term is a time series (regarded as a function of the index ω) defined by

$$\text{error}(e^{i\omega}) = \hat{C}(e^{i\omega}) - C(e^{i\omega}). \tag{5.9}$$

Point Ten. It can be shown that the error series (9) can be regarded as asymptotically uncorrelated at different frequencies and with variance

$$\text{Var}[\hat{C}(e^{i\omega})] = (M/T)|C(e^{i\omega})|^2 \tag{5.10}$$

which is easily estimated.

To motivate (10), let us note that one may regard the estimated autoregressive coefficients

$$\hat{c}_1, \hat{c}_2, \ldots, \hat{c}_M \tag{5.11}$$

as a "covariance stationary time series" with means $c_1, \ldots, c_M$, and spectral density function

$$f_C(\omega) = (2\pi)^{-1} T^{-1} |C(e^{i\omega})|^2. \tag{5.12}$$

By the theory of the periodogram

$$E\,|\,\hat{C}(e^{i\omega}) - C(e^{i\omega})|^2 = E\left|\sum_{k=1}^{M} (\hat{c}_k - c_k)e^{i\omega k}\right|^2$$
$$= 2\pi M f_C(\omega) = (M/T)\;|C(e^{i\omega})|^2 \qquad (5.13)$$

and the values $\hat{C}\,(e^{i\omega})$ at different frequencies are asymptotically uncorrelated.

Point Eleven. Fitting a suitably long autoregressive scheme to a univariate stationary time series is a possible method of spectral density estimation [especially when one assumes that there are no lines in the spectrum].

The usual type of estimator of the normalized spectral density $\bar{f}(\omega)$ [where $\bar{f}(\omega) = f(\omega)/R(0)$] of a stationary time series is a filtered sample spectral density of the form

$$\bar{f}_{T,M}(\omega) = 2\pi^{-1} \sum_{|v|<T} \cos v\omega k(v/M)\rho_T(v) \qquad (5.14)$$

where M is a suitable integer (called the *truncation* point) and $k(\cdot)$ is a suitable kernel. There is an extensive literature on how to choose M and $k(u)$ [see Parzen (1967b,c)].

It appears that an alternative estimator which is bias free and has similar variability is the autoregressive spectral estimator, defined by

$$\hat{\bar{f}}_M(\omega) = 2\pi^{-1}\hat{\bar{\sigma}}_M{}^2 \left|1 - \sum_{k=1}^{M} \hat{c}_k\, e^{-i\omega k}\right|^{-2}. \qquad (5.15)$$

While the idea of estimating the spectral density by first fitting an autoregressive scheme has been alluded to in the literature, there has been no treatment of its asymptotic variance. A variability theory is now being developed by Parzen (1970). The properties of (15) are discussed at the end of the next section in the context of the multivariate case.

Finally, we briefly discuss the question of how to determine the order M of a suitably long autoregressive scheme to fit to a sample $\{X(t), t = 1, 2, \ldots, T\}$ of a zero mean covariance stationary time series.

For each order m, one can recursively form: (i) estimators $\hat{a}_{1,m}, \ldots, \hat{a}_{m,m}$ of the coefficients of the predictor of finite memory m

$$E[X(t)\,|\,X(t-1), \ldots, X(t-m)] = a_{1,m}X(t-1) + \cdots + a_{m,m}X(t-m), \qquad (5.16)$$

and (ii) the sample innovation variance of order m

$$\hat{\bar{\sigma}}_m{}^2 = \{\rho_T(0) - \hat{a}_{1,m}\,\rho_T(1) - \cdots - \hat{a}_{m,m}\,\rho_T(m)\}R_T(0) \qquad (5.17)$$

where $\rho_T(v)$ is the sample correlation function. Define

$$\lambda_m = -T\log\hat{\bar{\sigma}}_m{}^2; \qquad (5.18)$$

it is increasing as a function of $m = 1, 2, \ldots, T-1$, and asymptotes to $\lambda_\infty = -T \log \tilde{\sigma}_\infty^2$, where $\tilde{\sigma}_\infty^2$ is the infinite memory prediction error variance.

A procedure for choosing an appropriate order M such that $X(\cdot)$ can be regarded as an autoregressive scheme of order M is: Choose M to be the smallest value of m such that $\lambda_\infty - \lambda_m$ is less than the 95% significance value of the chi-square distribution with $T - m$ degrees of freedom. Extensive investigation is needed on the theory and application of this procedure.

This suggestion can be roughly justified by the theory of likelihood ratio tests of the hypothesis that the series satisfies an autoregressive scheme of order m versus the alternative hypothesis that it satisfies an autoregressive scheme of order $T-1$ [see Whittle (1952) or Whittle's appendix to Wold (1954)].

It seems to me also justified from the likelihood point of view since the likelihood of the data under the parameters $\hat{a}_{1,M}, \ldots, \hat{a}_{M,M}$ can be considered to be not "significantly" different from the maximum liklihood of the data (which is a monotone function of λ_∞).

6. MULTIPLE SPECTRAL DENSITY ESTIMATION

In this section, we discuss autoregressive approaches to estimating the spectral density matrix

$$\mathbf{f}(\omega) = \begin{bmatrix} f_{11}(\omega) & \cdots & f_{1r}(\omega) \\ \cdots & \cdots & \cdots \\ f_{r1}(\omega) & \cdots & f_{rr}(\omega) \end{bmatrix}. \tag{6.1}$$

Traditionally, one estimates $\mathbf{f}(\omega)$ by estimating each entry $f_{hj}(\omega)$ by a filtered sample cross-spectral density

$$\hat{f}_{hj;\,T,\,M}(\omega) = 2\pi^{-1} \sum_{|v|<T} e^{-iv\omega} k(v/M) R_{hj;\,T}(v), \tag{6.2}$$

where $R_{hj;T}$ is the sample cross-covariance function. Except for ease of developing the distribution theory of the estimator $\hat{\mathbf{f}}(\omega)$, there seems to be no reason why one should use the *same* truncation point for each component $f_{hj}(\omega)$.

A method of letting the data determine an appropriate truncation point for each component is to estimate it via a sample analog of the formula

$$\begin{aligned} f_{hj}(\omega) = {} & \tfrac{1}{2}\{f_{X_h+X_j}(\omega) - f_{X_h}(\omega) - f_{X_j}(\omega)\} \\ & + \tfrac{1}{2}i\{f_{X_h+iX_j}(\omega) - f_{X_h}(\omega) - f_{X_j}(\omega)\}. \end{aligned} \tag{6.3}$$

Each univariate spectral density which appears in this formula could be estimated by autoregressive spectral estimation although further research is needed on the theory of the complex valued univariate series $X_h(\cdot) + iX_j(\cdot)$.

In the literature of empirical spectral analysis, remarks are frequently made about the value of prewhitening or prefiltering. It has long been my view that *prewhitening is of value but only when guided by model building.* An important approach to estimation of the spectral density matrix which could be said to use prewhitening is as follows.

First, generate the *individual* innovations $\eta_j(\cdot)$ of each time series $X_j(\cdot)$ by fitting to it a suitably long autoregressive scheme

$$\eta_j(t) = X_j(t) - c_1^{(j)} X_j(t-1) - \cdots - c_{M_j}^{(j)} X_j(t-M_j). \tag{6.4}$$

Second, by some method of spectral density matrix estimation form estimators of the spectral density matrix $\{f_{\eta_h \eta_j}(\omega)\}$ of the multiple time series of individual innovations.

Third, estimate $f_{X_h X_j}(\omega)$ by

$$\begin{aligned} \hat{f}_{X_h X_j}(\omega) = \hat{f}_{\eta_h \eta_j}(\omega)\{1 - c_1^{(h)} e^{-i\omega} - \cdots - c_{M_h}^{(h)} e^{-i\omega M_h}\}^{-1} \\ \times \{1 - c_1^{(j)} e^{i\omega} - \cdots - c_{M_j}^{(j)} e^{i\omega M_j}\}^{-1}. \end{aligned} \tag{6.5}$$

A method of spectral density matrix estimation whose value remains to be investigated is via the *joint autoregressive estimator* which is formed by first fitting a vector autoregressive scheme to the multiple time series $\mathbf{X}(\cdot)$. To conclude, we describe the main features of this approach.

In the notation introduced in Section 2, the joint autoregressive cross-spectral density matrix estimator is defined by

$$\hat{\mathbf{f}}_M(\omega) = (2\pi)^{-1}\{\hat{A}'(\omega)\,\hat{\hat{\Sigma}}^{-1}\,\hat{A}(-\omega)\}^{-1} \tag{6.6}$$

where

$$\hat{A}(\omega) = I - \hat{A}(1)e^{-i\omega} - \cdots - \hat{A}(M)e^{-i\omega M}. \tag{6.7}$$

The order M used would be determined by a goodness of fit test for joint autoregressive schemes fitted to a multiple time series [see Whittle (1953)]. Here we are interested only in the *variability* of the estimator $\bar{f}_M(\omega)$ under the assumption that $\mathbf{X}(\cdot)$ is a zero mean stationary multiple time series satisfying a joint autoregressive scheme of order M.

Research is in progress to prove (as rigorously as possible) that for $0 < \omega < \pi$, with

$$v = (T/M)(1/2), \tag{6.8}$$

$v\hat{\mathbf{f}}_M(\omega)$ has a complex Wishart distribution of dimension r, degrees of freedom v, and covariance matrix $\mathbf{f}(\omega)$.

The interpretation of this result is that the variability properties of the autoregressive cross-spectral estimator $\hat{\mathbf{f}}_M(\omega)$ are the same as those of the filtered sample spectral density matrix with *rectangular* kernel

$$\begin{aligned} k(u) &= 1, \qquad 0 \le |u| \le 1 \\ &= 0, \qquad |u| > 1 \end{aligned} \tag{6.9}$$

for which $\int_{-\infty}^{\infty} k^2(u)\,du = 2$.

Some advantages of the autoregressive cross-spectral estimator seem to me to be:

(1) No window is involved in forming $\hat{\mathbf{f}}_M(\omega)$, so we avoid a debate as to the choice of window.

(2) The truncation point M can be chosen on the basis that the multiple time series $\mathbf{X}(\cdot)$ passes a goodness of fit test for obeying a joint autoregressive scheme of order M.

(3) Under the assumption that the multiple time series $\mathbf{X}(\cdot)$ obeys a joint autoregressive scheme of order M, the autoregressive cross-spectral estimator has much smaller bias than filtered sample cross-spectral density estimators.

(4) Autoregressive cross-spectral estimators are easily *updated* for additional observations, and therefore lend themselves to adaptive estimation [compare Jones (1966)].

REFERENCES

AKAIKE, H., and YAMANOUCHI, Y. (1963). On the statistical estimation of frequency response function. *Ann. Inst. Statist. Math.* **14** 23–56.

ANDERSON, T. W. (1958). "Introduction to Multivariate Statistical Analysis." Wiley, New York.

BOX, G. M., and JENKINS, G. M. (1969). "Statistical Models for Forecasting and Control." Holden-Day, San Francisco, California.

BRILLINGER, D. R. (1969). The canonical analysis of stationary time series. *In* "Multivariate Analysis—II" (P. R. Krishnaiah, ed.). Academic Press, New York.

BRILLINGER, D. R. (1970). "An Introduction to the Frequency Analysis of Vector-Valued Time Series." Holt, New York. To be published.

DURBIN, J. (1959). Efficient estimation of parameters in moving-average models. *Biometrika* **46** 306–316.

DURBIN, J. (1960). The fitting of time-series models. *Rev. Internat. Stat. Inst.* **28** 233–244.

GENTLEMAN, W. M., and SANDE, G. (1966). Fast Fourier transforms—for fun and profit. *Proc. Fall Joint Comput. Conf.*, 1966, pp. 563–578.

GOODMAN, N. R. (1963). Statistical analysis based on a certain multivariate complex Gaussian distribution (an introduction). *Ann. Math. Statist.* **34** 152–177.

GRANGER, C. W. J. (1964). "Spectral Analysis of Economic Time Series." Princeton Univ. Press, Princeton, New Jersey.

HAMON, B. V., and HANNAN, E. J. (1963). Estimating relations between time series. *J. Geophys. Res.* **68** 6033–6041.

HANNAN, E. J. (1963). Regression for time series. *In* "Time Series Analysis" (M. Rosenblatt, ed.). Wiley, New York.

HANNAN, E. J. (1965). The estimation of relationships involving distributed lags. *Econometrica* **33** 206–224.

HANNAN, E. J. (1967). The estimation of a lagged regression relation. *Biometrika* **54** 409–418.

HANNAN, E. J. (1969). The estimation of mixed moving-average autoregressive systems. Tech. Rept. No. 109. Statist. Dept., John Hopkins Univ., Baltimore, Maryland.

JENKINS, G. M. (1965). A survey of spectral analysis. *Appl. Statist.* **14** 2–32.

JENKINS, G. M., and WATTS, D. (1968). "Spectrum Analysis and Its Applications." Holden-Day, San Francisco, California.

JONES, R. H. (1964). Prediction of multivariate time series. *J. Appl. Meteorol.* **3** 285–289.

JONES, R. H. (1966). Exponential smoothing for multivariate time series. *J. Roy. Statist. Soc. Ser. B* **28** 241–251.

KENDALL, M. G., and STUART, A. (1966). "The Advanced Theory of Statistics," Vol. 3. Griffin, London.

KOOPMANS, L. (1964). On the multivariate analysis of weakly stationary stochastic processes. *Ann. Math. Statist.* **35** 1765–1780.

MANN, H. B., and WALD, A. (1943). On the statistical treatment of linear stochastic difference equations. *Econometrica* **11** 173–220.

MASANI, P. (1966). Recent trends in multivariate prediction theory. *In* "Multivariate Analysis" (P. R. Krishnaiah, ed.), pp. 351–382. Academic Press, New York.

NETTHEIM, N. (1966). The estimation of coherence. Ph.D. Thesis, Statist. Dept., Stanford Univ., Stanford, California.

PARZEN, E. (1962). "Stochastic Processes." Holden-Day, San Francisco, California.

PARZEN, E. (1967a). The role of spectral analysis in time series analysis. *Rev. Inst. Internat. Statist.* **35** 125–141.

PARZEN, E. (1967b). On empirical multiple time series analysis. *Proc. Fifth Berkeley Symp. Math. Statist. Prob.* **1** (L. LeCam and J. Neyman, eds.), pp. 305–340. Univ. of California Press, Berkeley, California.

PARZEN, E. (1967c). "Time Series Analysis Papers." Holden-Day, San Francisco, California.

PARZEN, E. (1968). Statistical spectral analysis (Single-channel case) in 1968. Tech. Rept. No. 11. Statist. Dept., Stanford Univ., Stanford, California.

PARZEN, E. (1970). "Empirical Time Series Analysis." Holden-Day, San Francisco, California.

PHILIPS, A. W. (1966). Estimation of systems of difference equations with moving average disturbances. *Econometric Soc. Meeting, San Francisco, December* 1966.

PRIESTLEY, M. (1965). Evolutionary spectra and non-stationary processes. *J. Roy. Statist. Soc. Ser. B* **27** 204–237.

ROBINSON, E. A. (1967). "Multichannel Time Series Analysis with Digital Computer Programs." Holden-Day, San Francisco, California.

ROSENBLATT, M. (1959). Statistical analysis of stochastic processes with stationary residuals. *In* "Probability and Statistics" (Cramér Vol.), (U. Grenander, ed.), pp. 300–330. Wiley, New York.

ROZANOV, YU. A. (1967). "Stationary Stochastic Processes." Holden-Day, San Francisco, California.

TICK, L. J. (1967). Estimation of coherency. *In* "Advanced Seminar on Spectral Analysis of Time Series" (B. Harris, ed.). Wiley, New York.

WAHBA, G. (1968). On the distribution of some statistics useful in the analysis of jointly stationary time series. *Ann. Math. Statist.* **39** 1849–1862.

WALKER, A. M. (1961). Large sample estimation of parameters for moving-average models. *Biometrika* **48** 343–357.

WALKER, A. M. (1962). Large-sample estimation of parameters for autoregressive processes with moving-average residuals. *Biometrika* **49** 117–131.

WALKER, A. M. (1967). Some tests of separate families of hypotheses in time series analysis. *Biometrika* **54** 39–68.

WHITTLE, P. (1952). Tests of fit in time series. *Biometrika* **39** 309–318.

WHITTLE, P. (1953). The analysis of multiple stationary time series. *J. Roy. Statist. Soc. Ser. B* **15** 125–139.

WHITTLE, P. (1963a). On the fitting of multivariate autoregressions, and the approximate canonical factorization of a spectral density matrix. *Biometrika* **50** 129–134.

WHITTLE, P. (1963b). "Prediction and Regulation." English Univ. Press, London.

WOLD, H. (1954). "A Study in the Analysis of Stationary Time Series," 2nd ed. Almquist and Wicksell, Uppsala.

Representation Theory of Multidimensional Generalized Random Fields[1]

M. M. RAO

DEPARTMENT OF MATHEMATICS
CARNEGIE-MELLON UNIVERSITY
PITTSBURGH, PENNSYLVANIA

INTRODUCTION

Let $\mathscr{K}$ denote the Schwartz space of infinitely differentiable scalar functions on the euclidean n-space R^n, $n \geq 1$, vanishing off compact sets. If $\tilde{C}^N$ is the space of (complex) random N-vectors on a fixed probability space (Ω, Σ, P), then a linear map $F : \mathscr{K} \mapsto \tilde{C}^N$ is termed a *generalized N-dimensional random field* (process if $n = 1$) if F is also continuous in the sense that for any $\{f_n\} \subset \mathscr{K}$, $f_n \to 0$ in the topology of $\mathscr{K}$, implies $F(f_n) \to 0$ in probability [9]. Also if F has two moments finite, let $m(f) = E(F(f))$ and $B(f_1, f_2) = \text{cov}(F(f_1), F(f_2))$. If $m(\cdot)$ and $B(\cdot, \cdot)$ are invariant under translations, i.e., $m(f) = m(\tau_h f)$ and $B(f_1, f_2) = B(\tau_h f_1, \tau_h f_2)$ for all f, f_1, f_2 in $\mathscr{K}$ and $h \in R^n$ where $(\tau_h f)(x) = f(x + h)$, then $F(\cdot)$ is said to be a *homogeneous* or *stationary* random field [12]. The basic representation theory of stationary random fields has been considered in detail by Itô [12] and Yaglom [19]. However, in the multiplicity theory of ordinary (= nongeneralized) random processes, Cramér has recently shown ([2], Theorem 3) that for any spectral type sequence (as defined by Cramér [2]) there exists a harmonizable process with the given spectral type as its sequence and he has pointed out that the theory of stationary processes alone is insufficient for such a study. Other problems in which stationarity is an undesirable restriction can easily be cited.

This paper is motivated by such considerations. Its purpose is to present a general representation theory for a large class of (nonstationary) multidimensional generalized random fields (defined below), which always include the harmonizable ones, with a view to considering the multiplicity theory later for the generalized random processes, thereby extending the known work [2, 14]. However, the representation theorems given here also have

[1] This research was supported by the NSF grants GP-8777 and GP-7678.

important applications in general filtering and prediction problems. Some of the results extend certain aspects of the work of Yaglom [19] and Itô [12, 13], including the locally homogeneous case, as well as some recent work in [15], to the multidimensional case. The n-dimensional representation theory itself can be considered to have its real beginnings in [3].

A brief outline of the results is as follows. After giving the needed concepts as preliminaries in the next section, the covariance structure of second order generalized random fields on certain general test spaces, virtually without further restrictions, is considered in Section 2. This will complete and complement the remarks in [15], among others. Section 3 contains the main (integral) representation theory of the paper, and in Section 4 certain local classes of random fields and their representations are given. These two sections contain the essence of this paper. In the fifth (and last) section, the isotropic and harmonizable random fields are discussed. The work presented in this paper provides an extended study of the theory of mth order increments ([11], p. 291) of generalized processes though it will not be considered here.

1. PRELIMINARIES

Various concepts of the generalized random fields will be stated he e precisely, discussing their interrelations.

There are (at least) three definitions of generalized random fields due respectively to Gel'fand [9], Itô [12], and Ullrich [17] (cf. also [7]), and a fourth one due to Urbanik [18], which was then shown to be essentially the same as that of [9]. The first three are as follows.

Definition 1.1. (a) [9]. *A linear map $F: \mathscr{K} \mapsto \tilde{C}$, the space of complex random variables, is a generalized random field (grf) if $\{f_m\} \subset \mathscr{K}$, $f_m \to 0$ in $\mathscr{K}$ (i.e., all f_m vanish outside of a bounded set in R^n and tend to zero, together with their derivatives of all orders, uniformly) implies $F(f_m) \to 0$ in probability.*

(b) [12]. *A linear map $F: \mathscr{K} \mapsto L^2(P)$, the space of square integrable random variables on (Ω, Σ, P), is a grf if $\{f_m\} \subset \mathscr{K}$, $f_m \to 0$ in $\mathscr{K}$ implies $F(f_m) \to 0$ in $L^2(P)$.*

(c) [17]. *A map $F: (\Omega, \Sigma) \mapsto (\mathscr{K}^*, \mathscr{B})$ is a grf if it is measurable. Here $\mathscr{K}^*$ is the adjoint space of $\mathscr{K}$, and $\mathscr{B}$ is the Borel field of sets of $\mathscr{K}^*$, i.e., $\mathscr{B}$ is the σ-field generated by sets of the form $\{l \in \mathscr{K}^* : \mathrm{Re}(l(f)) < c_1, \mathrm{Im}(l(f)) < c_2\}$ where c_1, c_2 vary on reals and f varies in $\mathscr{K}$.*

The definition of a grf in [18] is different but the work there shows that it essentially coincides with that of [9]. On the other hand, the following statement holds when the definitions are comparable. (For the theory of Schwartz spaces, see Schwartz [16], Friedman [8], Gel'fand and Šilov [10].)

Lemma 1.2. *If the grf F, as defined in* (a), (b), *or* (c) *above, has two moments finite, then the three definitions coincide.*

Proof. It was noted in ([17], p. 278) that (b) ⇒ (c) ⇒ (a). Recall that in (a) and (c) the existence of moments was not postulated. If F has two finite moments then a category argument, pointed out by Dudley ([5], p. 776; cf. also [4], p. 114), shows that (a) ⇒ (b), as desired. (With regard to the implications (b) ⇒ (c) ⇒ (a), George Chi has expanded and completed the discussion of [17] in his thesis at Carnegie-Mellon University, 1969.) See also [7, Prop. III.4.2].

Since only second order grf's are considered in this paper, any of the equivalent definitions (a)–(c) can be interchangeably considered, though (a) will be used for the most part. *Hereafter a random field stands for a second order grf.* It may be noted, in passing, that the above definition of a grf makes sense if $\mathscr{K}$ is replaced by any test space treated by Gel'fand and Šilov [10]. This will be considered in more detail in Section 3.

If $F : \mathscr{K} \mapsto L^2(P)$ is a grf, let $m(\cdot)$ and $B(\cdot, \cdot)$ be its mean and covariance functionals. If τ_h is the translation operator on $\mathscr{K}$, then F is *stationary* if $m(\tau_h f) = m(f)$ and $B(\tau_h f, \tau_n g) = B(f, g)$ for all $f, g \in \mathscr{K}$ and $h \in R^n$. If F is a stationary grf then by [12] and [19], its covariance function admits the following representation (the overbar denotes complex conjugate):

$$B(f, g) = \int_{R^n} \hat{f}(t)\bar{\hat{g}}(t)\, d\mu(t), \qquad f, g \in \mathscr{K}, \tag{1.1}$$

where $\hat{f}$, $\hat{g}$ are the Fourier transforms of f, g, and μ is a (positive) tempered measure, i.e., a measure on the Borel sets of R^n such that $\int_{R^n} d\mu/(1 + |x|^2)^k < \infty$ for some integer $k \geq 0$. This result is a consequence of the Bochner-Schwartz theorem for the representation of the positive definite translation invariant hermitean functional B on $\mathscr{K} \times \mathscr{K}$ (cf. Gel'fand and Vilenkin [11], Theorem 6, p. 169). In view of the discussion in the Introduction, a general class of grf's, subsuming (1.1), will be defined. This class for the ordinary random processes was introduced by Cramér [1]. It will be called *class* (c) and is defined, in the present context, as follows.

Definition 1.3. *Let* $F : \mathscr{K} \mapsto \tilde{C}$ *be a second order* grf *with zero mean and* $B(\cdot, \cdot)$ *as its covariance functionals. Then F is said to be of* class (c) *relative to a covariance function* $\rho(\cdot, \cdot)$ *and a complex Borel function* $g(\cdot, \cdot)$ *on* $R^n \times R^n$, *with the properties* (i) ρ *generates a tempered measure* $\tilde{\rho}$ (*called* tempered covariance *for short*) *on the Borel field of* $R^n \times R^n$, *i.e.*,

$$\int_{R^n} \int_{R^n} \frac{|d^2\rho(x, y)|}{[(1 + |x|^2)(1 + |y|^2)]^{k/2}} < \infty \qquad (|x| = \textit{euclidean length of } x),$$

for some integer $k \geq 0$, *and* (ii) $\int_{R^n} \int_{R^n} g(t, x)\overline{g(s, x)}\, d^2\rho(t, s) = b(x)$ *exists for each* $x \in R^n$ *where* $b(\cdot)$ *is bounded on bounded sets of* R^n *such that* $B(\cdot, \cdot)$ *can be expressed as*

$$B(u, v) = \int_{R^n} \int_{R^n} \tilde{u}(t)\bar{\tilde{v}}(s)\, d^2\rho(t, s), \qquad u, v \in \mathscr{K}, \tag{1.2}$$

where $\tilde{u}(t) = \int_{R^n} g(t, x)u(x)\, dx$ *and similarly* $\tilde{v}$. *If in this representation* $g(t, x) = e^{it \cdot x}$, *where* $t \cdot x$ *is the scalar product in* R^n, *then the* grf F *is termed a* generalized harmonizable random field. *In these cases* $B(\cdot, \cdot)$ *is said to be, respectively, of* class (c) *or* harmonizable *covariance. The corresponding tempered measure* $\tilde{\rho}$ *is called the* spectral measure *of* F.

As an example, if ρ is of bounded variation on each bounded rectangle of $R^n \times R^n$, in the sense of ([1], p. 332), then $\tilde{\rho}$ is tempered.

A linear map $F = (F_1, \ldots, F_k) : \mathscr{K} \mapsto \tilde{C}^k$ is termed a *multidimensional* grf relative to $g_i(\cdot, \cdot)$ and $(\rho_{ij}, i, j = 1, \ldots, k)$, a positive definite matrix of tempered covariances ρ_{ij}, whenever $E(F(f_1)) = 0$, $B(f_1, f_2) = (B_{ij}(f_1, f_2)) = (E(F_i(f_1)\overline{F_j(f_2)}), i, j = 1, \ldots, k)$, and

$$B_{ij}(u, v) = \int_{R^n} \int_{R^n} \tilde{u}_i(t)\bar{\tilde{v}}_j(s)\, d^2\rho_{ij}(t, s), \qquad u, v \in \mathscr{K} \tag{1.3}$$

with

$$\tilde{u}_i(t) = \int_{R^n} u(x)g_i(t, x)\, dx, \qquad \tilde{v}_j(s) = \int_{R^n} v(x)g_j(s, x)\, dx.$$

In what follows it will be assumed for simplicity that $g_i(\cdot, \cdot) = g(\cdot, \cdot)$, $i = 1, \ldots, k$, and in that case the above definition can be stated as: A multidimensional grf $F = (F_1, \ldots, F_k)$ on $\mathscr{K}$ is said to be of *class* (c) or *harmonizable* according as the one dimensional field $F_a = \sum_{i=1}^k a_i F_i$ is respectively of class (c) or harmonizable, where $a = (a_1, \ldots, a_k)$ is an arbitrary vector of scalars. This observation enables one to obtain the multidimensional representation theorems from the one-dimensional case with an easy argument. Consequently, the latter case will first be considered in greater detail and then the general case will be deduced. It may be noted in passing that a multidimensional F is of class (c) or harmonizable implies that each one of its components has the same property.

It is also important to note that if the grf F is considered *on the space* $\mathscr{K}$, *or on any test space* Φ *containing* $\mathscr{K}$ *as a dense subset, then* $g(\cdot, \cdot)$ *can be any bounded Baire function for the theory here, satisfying* (1.2) *or* (1.3), *and* $g(\cdot, x)$ *need not be square integrable on* R^n *relative to* ρ *as assumed above*, unless $\tilde{\rho}(R^n \times R^n) < \infty$, in which the condition is automatic. *Thus* $g(\cdot, \cdot)$ *may depend on the test space in the generalization of the theory*. [This means that the first half of condition (ii) of Definition 1.3 can be dropped in $\mathscr{K}$ and in spaces Φ with $\mathscr{K}$ as a dense subset! It will be used *only* in (3.15) below.]

For the representation theory, the following concept of random measure, of not necessarily orthogonal values, is needed.

Definition 1.4. *If $\mathscr{B}$ is the Borel field of R^n, and $Z(\cdot) : \mathscr{B} \mapsto L^2(P)$ is a map, then it is said to be a (general)* random measure *whenever the following three conditions hold:*

(i) *For any bounded $A \in \mathscr{B}$, $E(Z(A)) = 0$,*

(ii) *A, $A_i \in \mathscr{B}$, $A = \bigcup_{i=1}^{\infty} A_i$, A_i disjoint and A_i, A are bounded implies $Z(A) = \sum_{i=1}^{\infty} Z(A_i)$, the series converging in $L^2(P)$,*

(iii) *there is a tempered covariance $\rho(\cdot, \cdot)$ on $R^n \times R^n$ such that for any bounded A, B in $\mathscr{B}$,*

$$E(Z(A)\overline{Z(B)}) = \int_A \int_B d^2\rho(x, y). \tag{1.4}$$

If (iii) *above is replaced by* (iii′) *below, then $Z(\cdot)$ is said to have* orthogonal values:

(iii′) *There is a tempered measure $\sigma(\cdot)$ such that $\rho(x, y) = \sigma(x)$, if $x = y$, and $=0$, if $x \neq y$ there, i.e., $E(Z(A)\overline{Z(B)}) = \sigma(A \cap B)$ for each bounded A, B in $\mathscr{B}$.* [Here σ stands for both the point and set functions, and the context makes this clear.]

To gain some insight into the tempered measures, the following remark, stated as a lemma, will be useful.

Lemma 1.5. *If σ on $\mathscr{B}$, the Borel field in R^n, is a tempered measure then $A \in \mathscr{B}$, bounded, implies $\sigma(A) < \infty$. On the other hand, if σ is a function of bounded variation on every bounded set and $\sigma(t)/|t|^k \to 0$ as $|t| \to \infty$ for some integer $k \geq 0$, then $\sigma(\cdot)$ defines a tempered measure on $\mathscr{B}$.*

Proof. If $\sigma(\cdot)$ is tempered, then, by definition, there is an integer $k \geq 0$ such that

$$\mu(A) = \int_A \frac{d\sigma(t)}{(1 + |t|^2)^k} \tag{1.5}$$

defines a finite measure on $\mathscr{B}$. If $A \in \mathscr{B}$ is bounded, then (1.5) implies (since μ and σ are equivalent) $d\mu(t)/d\sigma = (1 + |t|^2)^{-k}$, so that on A there exists $\alpha_A > 0$ $(\alpha_A = \inf_{t \in A}(1 + |t|^2)^{-k})$ satisfying $\alpha_A \leq d\mu(t)/d\sigma \leq 1$. So $(d\sigma/d\mu)(t) = (1 + |t|^2)^k \leq \alpha_A^{-1}$ on A. Thus

$$\sigma(A) = \int_A (1 + |t|^2)^k \, d\mu \leq \alpha_A^{-1}\mu(A) < \infty. \tag{1.6}$$

On the other hand $[\sigma(t)/|t|^k] \to 0$, for some (finite) integer $k \geq 0$, implies clearly $\int_{R^n} d\sigma(t)/(1 + |t|^2)^p < \infty$ for some integer $p > 0$; and $\sigma(\cdot)$ thus determines a tempered measure on $\mathscr{B}$, as desired.

Since a tempered measure depends on the integer (index) k, it follows that each grf (of class (c)) also depends on k, and as k varies one can consider the different classes of these random fields. This classification, motivated by that of Itô ([12], p. 214), clarifies the structure of these random fields.

Let $F = (F_1, \ldots, F_N)$ be an N-vector grf of class (c) relative to a $g(\cdot, \cdot)$ and a covariance matrix $\rho = (\rho_{ij})$ of its definition. Then since each ρ_{ij}, is a tempered covariance with a parameter k_{ij}, let $k^0 = \max(k_{ij} : k_{ij} \geq 0, i, j = 1, \ldots, N)$ and $k_0 = \max(k_{ij} : k_{ij} \leq 0)$. Then $k_0 \leq 0 \leq k_0$, and let $S(k)$ be the set of grf's of class (c), the parameters of whose tempered covariances determine k_0 and k^0, with $k = k_0$ for $k \leq 0$ and $k = k^0$ for $k > 0$. Then for any integer $k \geq 0$, one has

$$\cdots \subset S(-k) \subset S(-k+1) \subset \cdots \subset S(0) \subset \cdots \subset S(k) \subset \cdots. \tag{1.7}$$

The set $S(0)$ is sometimes termed the grf's of "zero order." It is clear that similar classifications hold for the harmonizable and stationary cases also. In view of (1.6) and (1.7), it suffices to consider, for the representation theory, the set $S(k)$ for some fixed but arbitrary $k \geq 0$.

2. COVARIANCE STRUCTURE

In this section the structure of the covariance functionals of second order grf's will be discussed without too many restrictions. This will complete and extend some results in [15], and will also throw further light on the class (c) random fields, besides having some independent interest.

Proposition 2.1. *Let F be a second order grf on $\mathscr{K}(N)$, with zero mean and covariance $B(\cdot, \cdot)$ where $\mathscr{K}(N)$ is the Schwartz space on the compact rectangle $N \subset R^n$ (or equivalently B has compact support and $F: \mathscr{K}(N) \mapsto L^2(P)$). Then there exists a continuous hermitean positive definite function h on $N \times N$ and an integer $m \geq 0$ such that*

$$B(f, g) = \int_N \int_N h(x, y) D^\alpha f(x) \overline{D^\alpha g}(y)\, dx\, dy, \qquad f, g \in \mathscr{K}(N) \tag{2.1}$$

where

$$D^\alpha = \frac{\partial^{|\alpha|}}{\partial x_1^{\alpha_1} \cdots \partial x_n^{\alpha_n}},$$

with $\alpha_i \geq 0$, $\alpha_1 + \cdots + \alpha_n = |\alpha| \leq m$ and $\alpha = (\alpha_1, \ldots, \alpha_n)$.

Proof. By definition, $B(\cdot, \cdot)$ is a continuous bilinear functional on $\mathscr{K}(N) \times \mathscr{K}(N)$. Hence by the Kernel Theorem of Schwartz (cf. [11]), there is a continuous linear functional G on $\mathscr{K}_2(N \times N)$ such that $B(f, g) = G(f\bar{g})$ where $(fg)(x, y) = f(x)g(y)$ for $f, g \in \mathscr{K}(N)$ so that $fg \in \mathscr{K}_2(N \times N)$, and linear combinations of such products are dense in the latter space. However (Gel'fand and Šilov [10], p. 114; or Friedman [8], p. 40), there exists an essentially bounded measurable h on $N \times N$ and an integer $m \geq 0$ such that (2.1) holds. By increasing the m one step if necessary (i.e., integrating by parts again), $h(\cdot, \cdot)$ can be taken actually continuous. Since $B(\cdot, \cdot)$ is a positive definite hermitean functional (taking f, g as arbitrary polynomials in $\mathscr{K}(N)$), it follows immediately that $h(\cdot, \cdot)$ is, moreover, an hermitean positive definite function, as desired.

Remark. This result is essentially known (e.g., see [11], p. 20). The proposition, however, motivates a more general case considered below. (Theorem 1 of [15] should have been stated as in the above proposition. By oversight, it was stated there somewhat less precisely.)

Let $\mathscr{K}(M_r)$ be the test space of Gel'fand and Šilov [10], containing the space $\mathscr{K}$. A linear map $F: \mathscr{K}(M_r) \mapsto L^2(P)$ is then a grf if it is continuous in the sense that $f_n \in \mathscr{K}(M_r), f_n \to 0$ in $\mathscr{K}(M_r)$ implies $F(f_n) \to 0$ in probability. The topology of $\mathscr{K}$ is stronger than that of $\mathscr{K}(M_r)$, and the spaces (and their topologies) coincide when the weights $\{M_r(\cdot), r \geq 1\}$ satisfy certain conditions. Thus the $\mathscr{K}(M_r)$ spaces afford greater flexibility for applications and so their definitions will briefly be recalled here.

The sequence $\{M_r(\cdot)\uparrow\}$ on R^n with values in $[1, \infty]$ is a set of functions, called weights, and $\mathscr{K}(M_r) = \{f | f$ on R^n are infinitely differentiable scalar functions such that $(M_r D^\alpha f)(\cdot)$ are bounded and continuous for $|\alpha| \leq r\}$. The linear space $\mathscr{K}(M_r)$ is endowed with the topology by finite collections of norms

$$\|f\|_r = \sup\{\sup[M_r(x)|D^\alpha f(x)| : x \in R^n], \quad |\alpha| \leq r\}, \qquad 1 \leq r < \infty$$

(see [10], and [8]). If $f \in \mathscr{K}(M_r)$ are *fast decreasing*, i.e., $|x|^m |D^\alpha f(x)| \to 0$ as $|x| \to \infty$, for any integer $m \geq 0$, and $M_r(x) = (1 + |x|)^r$, then $\mathscr{K}(M_r)$ is denoted by $\mathscr{S}$, called the (Schwartz) space of Fourier transforms. A condition on $\{M_r\}$, denoted by $(\mathscr{N})$, is important in this study, and it holds automatically for both $\mathscr{K}(N)$ and $\mathscr{S}$, where $N \subset R^n$ is compact. This can be stated as follows.

$(\mathscr{N})$: For each $p \geq 1$, there is a $p' > p$ such that if $m_{pp'}(x) = (M_p(x)/M_{p'}(x))$, then $m_{pp'}(\cdot)$ is Lebesgue integrable on R^n and $m_{pp'}(x) \to 0$ as $|x| \to \infty$.

It is known that the spaces $\mathscr{K}(M_r)$ where $\{M_r\}$ satisfies $(\mathscr{N})$ are "nuclear" spaces (hence the designation "$\mathscr{N}$"), and these are perfect and separable spaces containing functions of bounded supports as dense subsets. (See [10] and [11] for a proof of this result and for the properties of nuclear spaces.)

Proposition 2.2. *Let $F : \mathscr{K}(M_r) \mapsto L^2(P)$ be a grf, and let $\{M_r\}$ satisfy $(\mathscr{N})$. Then the covariance functional $B(\cdot, \cdot)$ of F can be represented as*

$$B(f, g) = \sum_{|\alpha|+|\beta| \leq r} \int_{R^n} \int_{R^n} M_r(x)M_r(y)h_{\alpha,\beta}(x, y)D^\alpha f(x)D^\beta g(y)\, dx\, dy, \quad (2.2)$$

for all $f, g \in \mathscr{K}(M_r)$ and some $r \geq 1$ and essentially bounded measurable functions $h_{\alpha,\beta}(\cdot, \cdot)$, on $R^n \times R^n$, which may be chosen hermitean.

Remark. If R^n is replaced by N, a compact set in R^n, and $M_r \equiv 1$ on N (and $= +\infty$ elsewhere), then this reduces to Proposition 2.1 since in that case (with integration by parts), one can also take $h(\cdot, \cdot)$ continuous (and positive definite).

Proof. As noted above, $\mathscr{K}(M_r)$ is a nuclear space. So by the Abstract Kernel Theorem ([11], p. 75), there are integers $p_0, p_1 \geq 1$ such that

$$B(u, v) = \sum_{k=1}^{\infty} \lambda_k (u, u_k)_{p_0} \overline{l_k(v)}, \qquad u, v \in \mathscr{K}(M_r) \quad (2.3)$$

where $\{u_k\}$ and $\{l_k\}$ are orthonormal bases in the spaces $\mathscr{H}_{p_0} \supset \mathscr{K}(M_r)$ and the adjoint space $\mathscr{H}^*_{p_1}$, and $\lambda_k \geq 0$, $\sum_{k=1}^{\infty} \lambda_k < \infty$. This follows from the fact that, in the Abstract Kernel Theorem, the Hilbert-Schmidt operator can actually be taken to be nuclear. (In fact, using the arguments of [11], p. 63 and also p. 40, property (2), the proof of the Kernel Theorem on p. 74 of [11] yields this result immediately.) Here the space $\mathscr{H}_{p_i}$ $(i = 0, 1)$ is the completion of $\mathscr{K}(M_r)$ under the norm $\|f\|_{p_i} = [(f, f)_{p_i}]^{1/2}$, where the inner product is defined by

$$(f, g)_{p_i} = \sum_{|\alpha| \leq p_i} \int_{R^n} [M_{p_i}(x)]^2 \overline{D^\alpha g(x)} D^\alpha f(x)\, dx, \quad (2.4)$$

for f, g in $\mathscr{K}(M_r)$. From this, generalizing an important special case of ([11], p. 78), it will be shown that there is a continuous linear functional G on $\mathscr{K}_2(M_r) = \mathscr{K}(M_r) \times \mathscr{K}(M_r)$ such that $B(f, g) = G(f\bar{g})$ so that the argument can be reduced to the preceding proposition.

For each $f \in \mathscr{K}_2(M_r)$ define a linear functional $l_k \times u_k$ on this space by the equation

$$(l_k \times u_k, f) = (l_k, (f, u_k)_{p_0})_{p_1} \quad (2.5)$$

where $v_k(y) = (f(\cdot, y), u_k)_{p_0}$ is defined for all $y \in R^n$. From the form of (2.4), it is seen that $v_k \in \mathscr{K}(M_r)$ so that $l_k \times u_k$ is well defined by (2.5). Moreover, using Schwarz inequality and the fact that $\|u_k\|_{p_0} = 1 = \|l_k\|_p$, one has

$$\begin{aligned} |(l_k \times u_k, f)| &= |(l_k, v_k)_{p_1}| \leq \|l_k\|_{p_1} \|v_k\|_{p_1} \\ &= \|v_k\|_{p_1} \leq \|u_k\|_{p_0} \cdot \|f\|_{p_0 p_1} = \|f\|_{p_0 p_1}, \end{aligned} \quad (2.6)$$

where

$$\|f\|_p^2 = \sum_{|\alpha| \le p} \sum_{|\beta| \le p} \int_{R^n} \int_{R^n} M_p^2(x) M_p^2(y) |D^{\alpha+\beta} f(x, y)|^2 \, dx \, dy.$$

Since $f \in \mathscr{K}_2(M_r)$, the above $\|f\|_{p_0 p_1} < \infty$ so that $l_k \times u^k \in [\mathscr{K}_2(M_r)]^*$. From the facts $\lambda_k \ge 0$, $\sum_{k=1}^{\infty} \lambda_k < \infty$, it follows that $\sum_{k=1}^{\infty} \lambda_k(l_k \times u_k, f)$ converges for each $f \in \mathscr{K}_2(M_r)$ and if $G = \sum_{k=1}^{\infty} \lambda_k(l_k \times u_k, \cdot)$, then $G \in [\mathscr{K}_2(M_r)]^*$. So (2.3) can be written as

$$B(u, v) = G(u\bar{v}), \qquad u, v \in \mathscr{K}(M_r) \tag{2.7}$$

where $uv(x, y) = u(x)v(y)$ and $uv \in \mathscr{K}_2(M_r)$. Thus, it remains to obtain (2.2).

The fact that the cartesian product of nuclear spaces is also nuclear implies $\mathscr{K}_2(M_r)$ is nuclear. So $G \in [\mathscr{K}_2(M_r)]^*$ can be characterized. In fact, as a consequence of Theorem 2 of ([10], p. 113) or Theorem 11 of ([8], p. 40), there exists an integer $r \ge 1$ and essentially bounded measurable $h_{\alpha,\beta}(\cdot, \cdot)$ on $R^n \times R^n$ such that

$$\begin{aligned} B(f, g) &= G(f\bar{g}) \\ &= \sum_{|\alpha|+|\beta| \le r} \int_{R^n} \int_{R^n} M_r(x) M_r(y) h_{\alpha,\beta}(x, y) D^\alpha f(x) \overline{D^\beta g(y)} \, dx \, dy. \end{aligned} \tag{2.8}$$

However, finite functions (=functions of bounded support) are dense in $\mathscr{K}(M_r)$ implies finite linear combinations of $f \cdot g$ of such elements are dense in $\mathscr{K}_2(M_r)$. With this, it is easily seen by a proper choice of f, g (or by averaging h's) that $h_{\alpha,\beta}$ can be chosen symmetric for each α, β such that (2.8) remains positive if $f = g$. Thus (2.2) holds and the proof is finished.

A simple extension of this result can be given for certain strict inductive limit (cf. [8]) spaces as follows.

Proposition 2.3. *Let Φ be a test space on R^n which is either $\mathscr{K}(M_r)$ or a strict inductive limit sequence of such spaces, i.e.,*

$$\mathscr{K}^1(M_r) \subset \mathscr{K}^2(M_r) \subset \cdots \subset \mathscr{K}^m(M_r) \subset \cdots,$$

and $\Phi = s \varinjlim \mathscr{K}^m(M_r)$. If $\{M_r\}$ satisfies $(\mathscr{N})$, then every continuous covariance $B(\cdot, \cdot)$ on $\Phi \times \Phi$ can be expressed as

$$B(f, g) = G(f\bar{g}), \qquad f, g \in \Phi, \tag{2.9}$$

where G on $\Phi_2 = \Phi \times \Phi$ is a continuous linear functional.

Proof. The standard results on inductive limit topology imply that B is continuous on Φ_2 if and only if it is continuous on each $\mathscr{K}_2^m(M_r) = \mathscr{K}^m(M_r) \times \mathscr{K}^m(M_r)$ when it is restricted. But by the proof of the above proposition, the restriction $B_m = B \,|\, \mathscr{K}_2^m(M_r)$ can be represented as a $G_m \in (\mathscr{K}_2^m(M_r))^*$

satisfying (2.9) (see Eq. (2.7)). Since B_m and $B_{m'}$ coincide on common domains for $m \neq m'$, the same is true of G_m and $G_{m'}$, i.e., they are compatible. But by the theory of (strict) inductive limits (cf., e.g., [8] or [10]), there exists a $G \in (\Phi_2)^*$ such that $G_m = G \mid \mathscr{K}_2{}^m(M_r)$. Hence (2.9) follows, as stated.

As a consequence of the above two propositions, one has:

Corollary 2.4. *Let* Φ *be as in Proposition* 2.3, *and* B *be a continuous covariance on* $\Phi_2 = \Phi \times \Phi$. *Then there exist essentially bounded measurable (hermitean) functions* $h_{\alpha,\beta}$, *and for each* m, *an integer* $p_m \geq 1$ *with*

$$B(f, g) = \sum_{|\alpha| + |\beta| \leq p_m} \int_{R^n} \int_{R^n} M_{p_m}(x) M_{p_m}(y) h_{\alpha,\beta}(x, y) D^\alpha f(x) \overline{D^\beta g(y)}\, dx\, dy, \tag{2.10}$$

for all $f, g \in \mathscr{K}^m(M_r)$ *and the series contains only a finite number of terms for each* $m < \infty$.

The point here is, due to (2.9) and "compatibility," $h_{\alpha,\beta}$ can be chosen independently of m.

Definition 2.5. *If* $m = 0$ *in* (2.1) (*or equivalently* $r = 0$ *in* (2.2)) *and* h *is continuous, then the covariance functional* B *on* $\mathscr{K}(M_r) \times \mathscr{K}(M_r)$ *is said to be of* function type (*or also of* "*zero order*"). *Also the* grf $F : \mathscr{K}(M_r) \mapsto L^2(P)$ *is said to be of* function type *if its covariance functional is.*

This definition is motivated by the terminology of ([8], p. 29), and this says that in Proposition 2.1 there will be only zero order derivatives whenever B is of *function type.*

The above results make it clear that for any further study the class of covariance functionals must be somewhat restricted. Also for certain applications (e.g., filtering and prediction theories), a formula such as (2.2) involving no derivatives will be of interest. For these and other reasons, the (general) class (c) grf's and their integral representations will be studied in the next two sections. It should be noted, however, that the above propositions show the general structure of covariances of second order grf's on $\mathscr{K}(M_r)$. This will be used in the last section of this paper.

3. REPRESENTATION THEORY

In this section integral representation of second order grf's of class (c) will be given. As in the above section, such grf's will be considered on certain test spaces including $\mathscr{K}$ and $\mathscr{S}$. The added generality is useful for applications.

Recall that Φ is a test space if it is either a complete countably normed space (e.g., $\mathscr{K}(M_r)$ of the preceding section) or a countable union of such spaces (e.g., the space $\mathscr{K}$) and if $f_m \in \Phi$, $f_m \to 0$ in the topology of Φ, then $_m(x) \to 0$ pointwise in R^n. Let $F : \Phi \mapsto L^2(P)$ be a grf, as in Definition 1.1(a).

Clearly, the corresponding definitions of class (c) and harmonizable (or homogeneous) cases can be formulated here in exactly the same way (as in Definition 1.3). This observation will be utilized below. [For a theory of these spaces, see [10], Chapitre 2; [8], Chapter 2.]

Theorem 3.1. *Let Φ be a test space on R^n of continuous functions and let $F:\Phi\mapsto L^2(P)$ be a grf with zero mean and covariance $B(\cdot,\ \cdot)$. Suppose F is of class* (c) *relative to a $g(\cdot,\ \cdot)$ and a tempered covariance ρ, and let the g-transforms of all functions in Φ exist (i.e., $f\in\Phi$ implies $\tilde{f}(t)=\int_{R^n} g(t,x)f(x)\,dx$ exists). Then there exists a random measure $Z(\cdot)$ relative to ρ, such that the following representation holds uniquely*

$$F(f)=\int_{R^n}\tilde{f}(t)\,dZ(t),\qquad f\in\Phi, \tag{3.1}$$

where $\tilde{f}$ is the g-transform of f and

$$B(u,v)=\int_{R^n}\int_{R^n}\tilde{u}(t)\bar{\tilde{v}}(s)\,d^2\rho(t,s)\qquad \textit{for}\quad u,v\in\Phi.$$

The stochastic integral in (3.1) *is defined in the mean square sense. On the other hand, if $g(\cdot,\ \cdot)$ and ρ are given with the properties of Definition* 1.3, *and $Z(\cdot)$ is a random measure, on the Borel field $\mathscr{B}$ of R^n, relative to ρ, and $\mathscr{K}\subset\Phi$ is dense, then the functional F defined by* (3.1), *is a grf of class* (c) *on $\mathscr{K}$ and has a unique continuous extension to Φ.*

Remark. In particular if $\Phi=\mathscr{S}$, then F above is called a "random tempered distribution" (cf. [4], [5a]), and the above result thus gives integral representations of such distributions if they are of class (c). Another class of random distributions (called "substationary" ones and investigated by Dudley) were considered in ([4] and [5a]) from a different viewpoint which is, in a sense, more similar in spirit to the work in [18].

Proof. The proof will be given in steps so that subsequently similar arguments can be shortened.

I. Suppose the grf $F:\Phi\mapsto L^2(P)$ is of class (c), $E(F(f))=0$, and $B(f_1,f_2)=E(F(f_1)\overline{F(f_2)})$. For simplicity, let $B(\cdot,\ \cdot)$ be (strictly) positive definite so that $B(f,f)=0$ implies $f=0$ and the continuity of F implies clearly that of B. Now introduce an inner product in Φ:

$$(f_1,f_2)=B(f_1,f_2)=\int_{R^n}\int_{R^n}\tilde{f}_1(t)\bar{\tilde{f}}_2(s)\,d^2\rho(t,s),\qquad f_i\in\Phi. \tag{3.2}$$

II. Let $\mathscr{H}_0=\mathrm{sp}\{F(f):f\in\Phi\}\subset L^2(P)$ be the linear span and let $\mathscr{H}$ be its completion in $L^2(P)$ relative to the usual inner product $(X,Y)=E(X\bar{Y})$ for $X,\ Y\in L^2(P)$. It then follows from the equation

$$(F(f_1),F(f_2))=B(f_1,f_2)=(f_1,f_2), \tag{3.3}$$

that the map: $f_1 \mapsto F(f_1)$ is an isometry of Φ onto $\mathscr{H}_0$. If $L^2(\rho)$ is the completion of Φ in the norm induced by (3.2), then the isometric map $f \mapsto F(f)$ considered above has a unique extension to $L^2(\rho)$ onto $\mathscr{H}$. If $A \in \mathscr{B}$ is bounded then (cf. Lemma 1.5) its indicator $\mathscr{X}_A \in L^2(\rho)$. Let $Z(A) \in \mathscr{H}$ be the corresponding element (by isometry) to $\mathscr{X}_A$. Then $Z(\cdot): \mathscr{B} \mapsto \mathscr{H}$ is a random measure relative to ρ. For, it is clear that $Z(\cdot)$ is additive for disjoint sets in $\mathscr{B}$. To see countable additivity, let $A, A_i \in \mathscr{B}$, $A = \bigcup_{i=1}^{\infty} A_i$, and $A_i \cap A_j = \emptyset$ for $i \neq j$ and A be bounded. Then, using the obvious notation,

$$\left\| Z(A) - \sum_{i=1}^{n} Z(A_i) \right\| = \left\| \mathscr{X}_A - \sum_{i=1}^{n} \mathscr{X}_{A_i} \right\|$$

$$= \left\| \mathscr{X}_{\underset{i \geq n}{\cup A_i}} \right\| = \tilde{\rho}\left(\bigcup_{i \geq n} (A_i \times A_i) \right) \leq \tilde{\rho}(A \times A) < \infty,$$

where $\tilde{\rho}$ is the measure determined by ρ. It follows that, as $n \to \infty$, the right-hand side tends to zero, so that $Z(A) = \sum_{i=1}^{\infty} Z(A_i)$, the series converging in $L^2(P)$. Finally, if S_1, S_2 in $\mathscr{B}$ are bounded, then

$$E(Z(S_1)\overline{Z(S_2)}) = (\mathscr{X}_{S_1}, \mathscr{X}_{S_2}) = \int_{S_1} \int_{S_2} d^2\rho(x, y),$$

so that $Z(\cdot): \mathscr{B} \mapsto \mathscr{H}$ is a random measure relative to ρ.

III. If $\tilde{\Phi} = \{\tilde{f}: f \in \Phi\}$, then $\tilde{\Phi} \subset L^2(\rho)$ and is dense in the latter. This is immediate since $f_1, f_2 \in \Phi$, then

$$(\tilde{f}_1, \tilde{f}_2) = \int_{R^n} \int_{R^n} \tilde{f}_1(t)\bar{\tilde{f}}_2(s)\, d^2\rho(t, s) = B(f_1, f_2) = (f_1, f_2) \tag{3.4}$$

by (3.2). Thus the map: $f \mapsto \tilde{f}$ is an isometry and the measurable $\tilde{f}$ now are in $L^2(\rho)$. The density of Φ in $L^2(\rho)$ implies that of $\tilde{\Phi} \subset L^2(\rho)$. Consequently, $\tilde{f} \in \tilde{\Phi}$ can be approximated in $L^2(\rho)$-norm by step functions $\tilde{f}_m$ where

$$\tilde{f}_m = \sum_{i=1}^{m} a_{m_i} \mathscr{X}_{A_i} \in L^2(\rho), \qquad \|\tilde{f} - \tilde{f}_m\| \to 0 \quad \text{as} \quad m \to \infty.$$

But Eqs. (3.3) and (3.4) imply that $f \mapsto F(f)$ is also an isometry, and hence if $f_m \in L^2(\rho)$ corresponds to $\tilde{f}_m$ and $F(f_m)$ is defined by

$$F(f_m) = \sum_{i=1}^{m} a_{m_i} Z(A_i) = \int_{R^n} \tilde{f}_n(t)\, dZ(t),$$

then $\|f - f_m\| \to 0$ and so $\{F(f_m)\} \subset \mathscr{H}$ is a (norm) Cauchy sequence. Thus

$$F(f_m) = \int_{R^n} \tilde{f}_m(t)\, dZ(t), \tag{3.5}$$

is well defined for all $\tilde{f}_m \in L^2(\rho)$ which are step functions. But the Cauchy sequence $\{F(f_m)\}$ has a unique limit in $\mathscr{H}$, which is denoted by $F(f)$ where f

is the strong limit of the f_m-sequence and $\tilde{f}$ is the limit of $\tilde{f}_m$, it follows that the density and isometry imply

$$F(f) = \int_{R^n} \tilde{f}(t)\, dZ(t), \qquad f \in \Phi,$$

uniquely. This proves (3.1).

IV. The random field F given by (3.1) defines a class (c) grf. Let $Z(\cdot)$, ρ and $g(\cdot, \cdot)$ be as in the converse hypothesis. Since F on Φ given by (3.1) is clearly linear, only the continuity need be shown. It is easy to see that $B(f, g) = \int_{R^n} \int_{R^n} \tilde{f}(t)\bar{\tilde{g}}(s)\, d^2\rho(t, s)$, $f, g \in \Phi$, so that it is of class (c) if it is continuous. However, for $f_m \in \mathscr{K} \subset \Phi$, $f_m \to 0$ in $\mathscr{K}$ implies $\{f_m\}$ is supported on a compact set and the f_m tend to zero uniformly there. Since $g(\cdot, \cdot)$ is bounded on bounded sets it follows that $\tilde{f}_m \to 0$ a.e. and boundedly. An interchange of limit and integral being permissible, it results from this argument that $B(f_m, f_m) \to 0$ so that $F(f_m) \to 0$ in $\mathscr{H}$. Hence by Definition 1.1(b), F is continuous on $\mathscr{K}$. But by hypothesis $\mathscr{K} \subset \Phi$ and its topology is stronger than that of Φ. So F is continuous on $\mathscr{K}$ in the topology of Φ also, and since $\mathscr{K}$ is dense in Φ, F has a unique continuous extension to Φ. Thus, F on Φ is a grf of class (c).

This completes the proof of the theorem.

Some consequences of this result will now be noted.

Corollary 3.2. *Let $\Phi = \mathscr{K}$ and $F : \Phi \mapsto L^2(P)$ is a* grf *of class* (c) *relative to a tempered covariance ρ and a $g(\cdot, \cdot)$. Then there is a random measure $Z(\cdot) : \mathscr{B} \mapsto L^2(P)$ relative to ρ such that*

$$F(f) = \int_{R^n} \tilde{f}(t)\, dZ(t) = \int_{R^n} \int_{R^n} f(x) g(t, x)\, dx\, dZ(t), \qquad f \in \mathscr{K}, \quad (3.6)$$

uniquely. Conversely a functional F defined on $\mathscr{K}$ by (3.6) *with $Z(\cdot)$, $g(\cdot, \cdot)$, and ρ is a grf of class* (c) *relative to $g(\cdot, \cdot)$ and ρ.*

This result was proved in this form in [15]. Recall that if $g(t, x) = e^{it \cdot x}$ in the definition of class (c), then it is a harmonizable class. For such a class the following representation obtains from the theorem.

Corollary 3.3. *Let $\mathscr{K} \subset \Phi \subset \mathscr{S}$, be a test space, the inclusions being both algebraic and topological. If $F : \Phi \mapsto L^2(P)$ is a grf which is harmonizable relative to a tempered covariance ρ, then there exists a random measure $Z(\cdot) : \mathscr{B} \mapsto L^2(P)$ relative to ρ such that*

$$F(f) = \int_{R^n} \hat{f}(t)\, dZ(t) = \int_{R^n} \int_{R^n} e^{it \cdot x} f(x)\, dx\, dZ(t), \qquad f \in \Phi, \quad (3.7)$$

uniquely. Conversely, F defined on Φ by (3.7) *with $Z(\cdot)$ and ρ is a generalized harmonizable random field relative to ρ.*

This result follows from the theorem since $\Phi \subset \mathscr{S}$ and Fourier transform on $\mathscr{S}$ is an isomorphism onto, and the hypothesis there is satisfied. If $\Phi = \mathscr{K}$ and $\tilde{\rho}(R^n \times R^n) < \infty$, this result was given in [15], and the latter condition is now seen to be unnecessary.

The next result similarly improves upon one given in [15].

Proposition 3.4. *Let Φ be a test space which is either a $\mathscr{K}(M_r)$ or a strict inductive limit of such a sequence (with the same $\{M_r\}$) where $\{M_r\}$ satisfies $(\mathscr{N})$. If $F : \Phi \mapsto L^2(P)$ is a grf of class* (c) *relative to a $g(\cdot, \cdot)$ and a tempered covariance ρ, let F have orthogonal values [i.e., $F(f_1)$ and $F(f_2)$ are orthogonal random variables if $f_1 \cdot f_2 = 0$]. Then ρ actually concentrates on $x = y$, and thus determines a tempered measure $\sigma(\cdot)$ on the Borel field $\mathscr{B}$ of R^n, and there exists a random measure, with orthogonal values, $Z(\cdot) : \mathscr{B} \mapsto L^2(P)$ relative to σ, such that*

$$F(f) = \int_{R^n} \tilde{f}(t)\, dZ(t) = \int_{R^n} \int_{R^n} f(x) g(t, x)\, dx\, dZ(t), \qquad f \in \Phi, \tag{3.8}$$

uniquely. Conversely, F on Φ defined by (3.8) *relative to $g(\cdot, \cdot)$, $Z(\cdot)$, and $\sigma(\cdot)$ is a grf of class* (c) *with orthogonal values.*

Proof. Let F be a grf of class (c) with $B(\cdot, \cdot)$ as its covariance. Then

$$B(u, v) = \int_{R^n} \int_{R^n} \tilde{u}(t)\bar{\tilde{v}}(s)\, d^2\rho(t, s), \qquad u, v \in \Phi. \tag{3.9}$$

Also the hypothesis on Φ implies, by Proposition 2.3, that

$$B(u, v) = G(u\bar{v}), \qquad u, v \in \Phi, \tag{3.10}$$

for some $G \in \Phi_2{}^*$. Since F has orthogonal values and $\{M_r\}$ satisfies $(\mathscr{N})$, it follows, as in ([11], p. 287), that any $f \in \Phi \times \Phi$ which vanishes in a neighborhood of $x = y$ satisfies $G(f) = 0$. This is a consequence of the fact that an f vanishing in a neighborhood of $x = y$ can be approximated by linear combinations of uv which similarly vanish near $x = y$. Thus, G "concentrates" on the diagonal $x = y$. Since $G_m = G \mid \mathscr{K}_2{}^m(M_r)$ has the same property for each m, by Corollary 2.4, Eqs. (3.9) and (3.10), one has, on using the definition of g-transform of u, v,

$$\int_{R^n} \int_{R^n} u(x)\bar{v}(y) \int_{R^n} \int_{R^n} g(t, x)\overline{g(s, y)}\, d^2\rho(t, s)\, dx\, dy$$

$$= \sum_{|\alpha| + |\beta| \le p_m} \int_{R^m} \int_{R^m} M_{p_m}(x) M_{p_m}(y) h_{\alpha, \beta}(x, y) D^\alpha u(x) \overline{D^\beta u(y)}\, dx\, dy, \tag{3.11}$$

for $u, v \in \mathscr{K}^m(M_r)$. However, that G_m concentrates on the diagonal $x = y$ implies (by proper choice of u, v) that in the right-hand side, $h_{\alpha,\beta}(x, y)$ vanishes on any set disjoint from any neighborhood of $x = y$.

Thus, Eq. (3.11) implies that ρ concentrates also on $x = y$. If this were false, the left-hand side integral would be different from zero, for some m, for (s, t) in a set A which is disjoint from a neighborhood of $x = y$ when u, v are nontrivial functions with their supports in the appropriate sections of A in R^n. Since by the preceding paragraph, $h_{\alpha,\beta}(\cdot, \cdot)$ vanishes on A, the right-hand side must vanish, and this contradicts Eq. (3.11). Thus, $\rho(x, y) = \sigma(x)$ if $x = y$, and $=0$ if $x \neq y$. This means

$$\tilde{\rho}(A_1 \times A_2) = \int_{A_1} \int_{A_2} |d^2\rho(x, y)| = \int_{A_1 \cap A_2} d\rho(x, x) = \sigma(A_1 \cap A_2), \quad (3.12)$$

and the temperedness of $\tilde{\rho}$ implies that of σ.

With this, the remaining proof on the existence of the orthogonal random measure $Z(\cdot)$, relative to σ, and the integral representation (3.8), follows as in Theorem 3.1, giving the direct part of the proposition.

Conversely, (3.8) immediately implies $F(\cdot)$ is a grf on $\mathscr{K}^m(M_r)$ with orthogonal values for each m. Since Φ is the inductive limit, this implies (cf. [8], p. 20) that F is a grf on Φ itself. This completes the proof.

Corollary 3.5. *Let Φ be as in the above proposition. Let F on Φ be a grf of class* (c) *relative to $g(\cdot, \cdot)$ and a tempered covariance ρ which concentrates on $x = y$, $(=\sigma$, say). If, moreover, F is stationary, then there exists a random measure, with orthogonal values, $Z(\cdot) : \mathscr{B} \mapsto L^2(P)$, relative to the tempered σ, such that* (*uniquely*)

$$F(f) = \int_{R^n} \hat{f}(t)\, dZ(t), \qquad f \in \Phi, \quad (3.13)$$

and necessarily $g(t, x) = e^{it\cdot x}$($\hat{f}$ is the Fourier transform of f). On the other hand, Eq. (3.13) *always defines a stationary grf F on Φ.*

Remark. The preceding result shows that ρ concentrates on $x = y$ if, moreover, F has orthogonal values. However, by the Bochner-Schwartz theorem $\rho(\cdot)$ concentrates on $x = y$ even if F does not have orthogonal values, provided $\Phi = \mathscr{K}$, and F is stationary. Since the spaces here are more general for which the Bochner-Schwartz theorem is not available, the result complements certain known cases.

Proof. By the theorem $F(f) = \int_{R^n} \hat{f}(t)\, dZ(t)$, where Z relative to $\rho(=\sigma)$ now has orthogonal values since $E(Z(A)\overline{Z(B)}) = \sigma(A \cap B)$. Thus, the covariance functional of F is given by

$$B(u, v) = \int_{R^n} \tilde{u}(t)\bar{\tilde{v}}(t)\, d\sigma(t), \qquad u, v \in \Phi. \quad (3.14)$$

It suffices to consider the case that $\Phi = \mathscr{K}^m(M_r)$ for a fixed m. By the stationarity of F, $B(\tau_h u, \tau_h v) = B(u, v)$, $h \in R^n$. This equation and (3.14) imply the following equation upon rearrangement.

$$\int_{R^n}\int_{R^n} u(x)\overline{v(y)}\left[\int_{R^n} g(t, x)\overline{g(t, y)}\, d\sigma(t)\right] dx\, dy$$

$$= \int_{R^n}\int_{R^n} u(x)\overline{v(y)}\left[\int_{R^n} g(t, x-h)\overline{g(t, y-h)}\, d\sigma(t)\right] dx\, dy, \quad (3.15)$$

for all u, v in $\mathscr{K}^m(M_r)$. Consequently, the middle terms can be identified. Thus letting $W_A(x, y) = \int_{R^n} \overline{g(t, x)}g(t, y)\, d\sigma_A(t)$, where $A \subset R^n$ is compact and σ_A is the restriction of σ to A, it follows that $W_A(\cdot, \cdot)$ is a positive definite hermitean function on $R^n \times R^n$ and (3.15) yields $W_A(x, y) = W_A(x - h, y - h)$ for all $h \in R^n$. Hence, it follows that $W_A(x, y) = W_A(x - y)$, and by Bochner's theorem, adopted to the present context, it follows that there is a tempered measure $\tilde{\sigma}$, uniquely, such that whenever $x, y \in R^n$, $x - y \in A \subset R^n$, compact,

$$W_A(x - y) = \int_{R^n} e^{it\cdot(x-y)}\, d\tilde{\sigma}_A(t) \quad (3.16)$$

where $\tilde{\sigma}_A = \tilde{\sigma}(\cdot \cap A)$, is the restriction of $\tilde{\sigma}$ to A. By the uniqueness of such a representation $\sigma = \tilde{\sigma}$ and $g(t, x) = e^{it\cdot x}$ here. Hence, $\tilde{f} = \hat{f}$ for each f of compact support in $\mathscr{K}^m(M_r)$, and since F is continuous the result holds on $\mathscr{K}^m(M_r)$, and therefore also on the space Φ. The last part is immediate.

The following result is a consequence of the present considerations and extends ([12], Theorem 4.2) to class (c).

Proposition 3.6. *The class of all zero order grf's $F: \Phi \mapsto L^2(P)$, where Φ is as in Proposition* 3.4, *which are of class* (c), *harmonizable, stationary or of orthogonal valued in class* (c), *and the class of all ordinary random fields of the corresponding classes are the same.*

Proof. Let $\mathscr{C}_0$ be the ordinary class and $\mathscr{C}^0$ the generalized class in each category. If $X(\cdot) \in \mathscr{C}_0$ then $F(f) = \int_{R^n} f(t)X(t)\, dt$ defines an $F \in \mathscr{C}^0$ so $\mathscr{C}_0 \subset \mathscr{C}^0$ always. On the other hand, if

$$B(f_1, f_2) = \int_{R^n}\int_{R^n} \tilde{f}_1(t)\bar{\tilde{f}}_2(s)\, d^2\rho(t, s) = E(F(f_1)\overline{F(f_2)})$$

for a grf of class (c), relative to ρ of order zero, so that $\tilde{\rho}(R^n \times R^n) < \infty$, let $Y(t) = \int_{R^n} g(t, \lambda)\, dZ(\lambda)$ where $Z(\cdot)$ is given by Theorem 3.1, for F, relative to ρ. Hence, $Y \in \mathscr{C}_0$ ([1]). Similar argument applies to the other cases also.

Remark. While the ordinary harmonizable and stationary cases demand that $\tilde{\rho}$ be a finite measure, the class (c) of [1] demands only that ρ be of bounded variation on every finite domain with a certain uniform bound. Thus certain "positive order" classes for grf's and ordinary random functions of class (c) can also be identified.

The main result on the multidimensional representation theorem, based on Theorem 3.1, will now be presented and this is essential for later work.

Theorem 3.7. *Let Φ be a test space as in Theorem* 3.1. *If $F = (F_1, \ldots, F_k)$ is a k-dimensional grf on Φ of class* (c) (*cf. Definition* 1.3 *and the following*) *relative to a $g(\cdot, \cdot)$ and a positive definite matrix $\rho = (\rho_{ij}, i, j = 1, \ldots, k)$ of tempered covariances ρ_{ij}, then there exists a random vector measure $Z = (Z_1, \ldots, Z_k)$ on the Borel sets of R^n relative to ρ such that*

$$F(f) = \int_{R^n} \tilde{f}(t)\, dZ(t), \qquad f \in \Phi, \tag{3.17}$$

uniquely, where $\tilde{f}$ is the g-transform as usual. Conversely, if $g(\cdot, \cdot)$, ρ, and a random vector measure Z (*relative to ρ*) *are given, then* (3.17) *defines a k-dimensional generalized random field on Φ, of class* (c), *relative to $g(\cdot, \cdot)$ and ρ.*

To prove this theorem, it is only necessary to pick an arbitrary, but fixed, vector $a = (a_1, \ldots, a_k) \in R^k$, and consider $F_a = \sum_{i=1}^k a_i F_i$. Then F_a is a one-dimensional grf of class (c) on Φ [and it depends on a linearly] relative to $g(\cdot, \cdot)$ and the tempered covariance $r_a(\cdot, \cdot) = (a, \rho_a) = (\rho_a, a)$. Then Theorem 3.1 yields

$$F_a(f) = \int_{R^n} \tilde{f}(t)\, dZ_a(t), \qquad f \in \Phi, \tag{3.18}$$

and since $a \in R^k$ is arbitrary, (3.18) implies (3.17) easily. The converse part is similarly obtained.

The following result for multidimensional harmonizable random fields is an immediate consequence of the above theorem and is stated for reference.

Theorem 3.8. *Let $\mathcal{K} \subset \Phi \subset \mathcal{S}$ be an in Corollary* 3.3, *and F on Φ be a k-dimensional generalized harmonizable random field relative to a positive definite matrix $\rho = (\rho_{ij})$ of tempered covariances. Then there exists a random vector measure Z relative to ρ on the Borel sets of R^n such that*

$$F(f) = \int_{R^n} \hat{f}(t)\, dZ(t), \qquad f \in \Phi, \tag{3.19}$$

uniquely where $\hat{f}$ is the Fourier transform of f. Conversely the formula (3.19) *defines a k-dimensional generalized harmonizable random field F relative to ρ on Φ.*

If each of the covariances $\rho_{ij}(\cdot, \cdot)$ concentrates on $x = y$ in the above result, then the F so obtained is a stationary grf and conversely (cf. [12], [19]).

The above results will be used in studying local properties of certain grf's in the next section.

4. LOCAL CLASSES OF RANDOM FIELDS

Instead of assuming that a grf on Φ is of class (c), one can assume such a property only on certain subspaces of Φ and then investigate the structure of such functionals. For stationary grf's such local properties were investigated by Yaglom [19]. These results will be generalized to certain locally class (c) grf's which include the locally harmonizable cases. The treatment here is not included so much for generality as to understand the problem, formulated in [19].

Definition 4.1. *If* Φ *is a test space,* $\Phi_1 = \{f \in \Phi : \int_{R^n} f(x)\,dx = 0\}$, *and* F *is a* grf *on* $\Phi_1 \mapsto L^2(P)$, *it is said to be* locally class (c) *whenever* F *verifies the following property: If* τ_h *is a translation operator* $T_h = I - \tau_h$ *so that* $T_h \Phi = \Phi_h = \{T_h f : f \in \Phi\} \subset \Phi_1$, *and* F_h *is the restriction of* F *to* Φ_h, *then for any* $h_1, \ldots, h_k$ *in* R^n, *the set* $(F_{h_i}, i = 1, \ldots, k)$ *forms a k-dimensional* grf *of class* (c) *on* Φ *relative to a fixed* $g(\cdot, \cdot)$ *and a positive definite matrix* $(\rho_{h_i h_j}, i, j = 1, \ldots, k)$ *of tempered covariances. If* $g(t, x) = e^{it \cdot x}$ *here, then* F *is said to be* locally harmonizable *and, moreover, if* $\rho_{h_i h_j}$ *concentrates on* $x = y$, *then it is* locally stationary.

As remarked in [19], the above concept is an abstraction of the ordinary random process whose increments are mutually class (c), harmonizable, or stationary without the whole process satisfying the same condition.

A subclass of locally class (c) grf's will be considered below and an integ al representation will be obtained for it. The restriction comes from the additional conditions imposed on $g(\cdot, \cdot)$ in the definition which, however, are satisfied for the harmonizable case.

Theorem 4.2. *Let* $F : \Phi \mapsto L^2(P)$ *be a grf, locally class* (c) *relative to* $g(\cdot, \cdot)$. *where* Φ *is a test space, as in Theorem* 3.1, *on which the g-transforms exist, Suppose* $g(t, x - y) = g(t, x)\overline{\beta(t, y)}$ *for all* t, x, y *in* R^n, *and that* (i) $\partial g(s, 0)/\partial x_k \neq 0$ *for* $s_k \neq 0$, (ii) $\partial \beta(s, r)/\partial s_k = \alpha_k(s, r) r_k$, *and* $\alpha_k(0, y) = \alpha_k \neq 0$, α_k *being independent of* r. *Here* s_k, r_k *are the* kth *components of* s, r *in* R^n. *Then there exists a tempered covariance* ρ *on the Borel field of* $R^n - \{0\} \times R^n - \{0\}$, *such that for some* p (p *is the index of temperedness in the definition of class* (c))

$$\int_{R^n - \{0\}} \int_{R^n - \{0\}} \frac{|x|\,|y|\,|d^2 \rho(x, y)|}{[(1 + |x|^2)(1 + |y|^2)]^{(p+1)/2}} < \infty, \tag{4.1}$$

and that there exists a random measure $Z(\cdot)$ *on the Borel field of* $R^n - \{0\}$ *relative to* ρ *and a second order random vector* $\alpha = (\alpha_1, \ldots, \alpha_n)$ *satisfying* $E(\alpha) = 0$, *and* $E(\alpha_i \overline{Z(A)}) = 0$, $i = 1, \ldots, n$, *for bounded* $A \in \mathscr{B}$, *in terms of which one has the following representation*

$$F(f) = \int_{R^n - \{0\}} \tilde{f}(t)\, dZ(t) + (\alpha, \tilde{\nabla} \tilde{f}(0)), \qquad f \in \Phi_1 \tag{4.2}$$

uniquely, where $(\cdot, \cdot)$ *is the inner product,* $\tilde{\nabla} = (-\alpha_k^{-1} \cdot \partial/\partial x_k, k = 1, \ldots, n)$ *and* $\tilde{f}$ *is the g-transform. On the other hand, a map* F *given by* (4.2) *is a grf, locally class* (c), *on* Φ_1 *relative to* g.

As noted before, the restrictions are satisfied if $g(t, x) = e^{it \cdot x}$ and then $\alpha_k = i$, for all k. Hence, the above result implies the following:

Theorem 4.3. *Let $\mathscr{K} \subset \Phi \subset \mathscr{S}$ be a test space as in Corollary* 3.3. *If F on Φ is a generalized harmonizable random field then there exists* (i) *a tempered covariance ρ on $R^n - \{0\} \times R^n - \{0\}$ satisfying* (4.1), (ii) *a random measure Z on the Borel field of $R^n - \{0\}$, relative to ρ, and* (iii) *a second order random vector $\alpha = (\alpha_1, \ldots, \alpha_n)$ with mean zero and each of whose components is uncorrelated with $Z(\cdot)$, in terms of which one has a unique representation as:*

$$F(f) = \int_{R^n - \{0\}} \hat{f}(t)\, dZ(t) + i(\alpha, \nabla \hat{f}(0)), \qquad f \in \Phi, \tag{4.3}$$

where $\nabla = (\partial/\partial x_1, \ldots, \partial/\partial x_n)$ and $\hat{f}$ is the Fourier transform of f. Conversely, (4.3) *defines a locally harmonizable random field, relative to the tempered covariance ρ, on Φ_1.*

In order to prove Theorem 4.2, the covariance functional of locally class (c), grf should be considered. This is a key step in the proof, and the argument here follows [19], of which it is an extension. The result is stated separately in:

Proposition 4.4. *Let F on Φ be a grf as in Theorem* 4.2 *and let B be its covariance functional. Then there is a tempered covariance ρ on $R^n - \{0\} \times R^n - \{0\}$ satisfying* (4.1) *and a positive definite matrix A such that for $f_i \in \Phi_1$, $i = 1, 2$,*

$$B(f_1, f_2) = \int_{R^n - \{0\}} \int_{R^n - \{0\}} \tilde{f}_1(t) \bar{\tilde{f}}_2(s)\, d^2\rho(t, s) + (A\tilde{\nabla}\tilde{f}_1(0), \tilde{\nabla}\tilde{f}_2(0)), \tag{4.4}$$

where the $\tilde{\nabla}$ was defined earlier. Conversely, (4.4) *defines a covariance functional of some locally class* (c) *grf on Φ_1.*

Proof. Let $F = (F_{r_1}, \ldots, F_{r_k})$ where $F_r(f) = F(T_r f), f \in \Phi$, and $T_r = I - \tau_r$, τ_r being the translation operator, $r \in R^n$. Then by hypothesis F is a multidimensional grf of class (c) for each k, and hence by Theorem 3.7, its covariance functional $B(\cdot, \cdot) = (B_{ij}(\cdot, \cdot))$ is given by

$$B_{ij}(f_1, f_2) = \int_{R^n} \int_{R^n} \widetilde{T_{r_i} f_1}(t) \overline{\widetilde{T_{r_j} f_2}}(s)\, d^2\rho_{r_i r_j}(t, s), \tag{4.5}$$

where $(\rho_{r_i r_j})$ is a positive definite matrix of tempered covariances. Since $\tau_{r_1}\tau_{r_2} = \tau_{r_2}\tau_{r_1}$ for any r_1, r_2 in R^n, it follows that for $f \in \Phi$

$$F_{r_1' + r_1''}(f) = F_{r_1'}(f) + F_{r_1''}(\tau_{r_1'} f) = F_{r_1''}(f) + F_{r_1'}(\tau_{r_1''} f). \tag{4.6}$$

Substituting (4.6) into (4.5) with $r_1 = r_1' + r_2''$ and simplifying, one gets $(\rho_{r_1 r_2}(\cdot, \cdot) \equiv \rho(\cdot, \cdot; r_1, r_2)$ below)

$$\int_{R^n} \int_{R^n} \widetilde{T_{r_1''} f_1}(t) \overline{\overline{f_2}}(s) \rho(dt\, ds; r_1', r_2) = \int_{R^n} \int_{R^n} \widetilde{T_{r_1'} f_1}(t) \overline{\overline{f_2}}(s) \rho(dt\, ds; r_1'', r_2) \tag{4.7}$$

and similarly for $r_2 = r_2' + r_2''$

$$\int_{R^n}\int_{R^n} \tilde{f}_1(t)\overline{\widetilde{T_{r_2''} f_2}(s)}\rho(dt\,ds; r_1, r_2') = \int_{R^n}\int_{R^n} \tilde{f}_1(t)\overline{\widetilde{T_{r_2'} f_2}(s)}\rho(dt\,ds; r_1, r_2''). \tag{4.8}$$

Since r_i' and r_2'' are arbitrary in (4.7) and (4.8), one can substitute various r's in these equations, replace f_1 by $T_{r_1'}\ f_1, f_2$ by $T_{r_2''}\ f_2$ suitably, and simplify to get

$$\begin{aligned}\int_{R^n}\int_{R^n} &\widetilde{T_{r_1''} f_1}(t)\overline{\widetilde{T_{r_2''} f_2}(s)}\rho(dt\,ds; r_1', r_2') \\ &= \int_{R^n}\int_{R^n} \widetilde{T_{r_1'} f_1}(t)\overline{\widetilde{T_{r_2'} f_2}(s)}\rho(dt\,ds; r_1'', r_2'').\end{aligned} \tag{4.9}$$

Note that $T_0 = 0$. Now if A, B are bounded Borel sets in $R^n - \{0\}$, define $\tilde{\rho}$ by

$$\tilde{\rho}(A \times B) = \int_A\int_B \frac{\tilde{f}_1(t)\bar{\tilde{f}}_2(s)}{\widetilde{T_{r_1} f_1}(t)\overline{\widetilde{T_{r_2} f_2}(s)}}\,\rho(dt\,ds; r_1, r_2), \qquad f_i \in \Phi. \tag{4.10}$$

If $r_1 \neq 0$, $r_2 \neq 0$, then $\tilde{\rho}$ is a well-defined measure and, by (4.9), it does not depend on r_1 and r_2. At this point the hypothesis on $g(\cdot, \cdot)$ will be used to show that $\tilde{\rho}$ does not also depend on f_1, f_2 and that it gives the required tempered covariance ρ satisfying (4.1).

Thus by the multiplicative hypothesis on $g(\cdot, \cdot)$, it follows that $\widetilde{T_r f}(s) = (1 - \overline{\beta(s, r)})\tilde{f}(s)$. Substituting this in (4.10), one has

$$\tilde{\rho}(A \times B) = \int_A\int_B \frac{\rho(dt\ ds; r_1, r_2)}{(1 - \overline{\beta(s, r_1)})(1 - \beta(t, r_2))} \tag{4.11}$$

so that $\tilde{\rho}$ does not depend on f_1, f_2. Note that if $A, B \subset R^n - \{0\}$ and $r_1 \neq 0$, $r_2 \neq 0$, then $\tilde{\rho}$ is well defined. The differentiability hypothesis on β and the temperedness of $\rho_{r_1\,r_2}$ implies, after a small computation, that $\tilde{\rho}$ verifies (4.1) also with $p \geq 0$ as the index of temperedness of $\rho(\cdot, \cdot, r_1, r_2)$. Writing ρ for the covariance that determines $\tilde{\rho}$ by (4.11), and using (4.10), one has from (4.5) (i.e., ρ is the point function corresponding to the set function $\tilde{\rho}$),

$$\begin{aligned}E(F(T_{r_1} f_1)\overline{F(T_{r_2} f_2)}) &= \int_{R^n}\int_{R^n} \tilde{f}_1(t)\overline{\tilde{f}_2}(s)\rho(ds\,dt; r_1, r_2) \\ &= \int_{R^n - \{0\}}\int_{R^n - \{0\}} \widetilde{T_{r_1} f_1}(t)\overline{\widetilde{T_{r_2} f_2}(s)}\rho(dt\,ds) \\ &\quad + \tilde{f}_1(0)\bar{\tilde{f}}_2(0)\rho(0, 0; r_1, r_2).\end{aligned} \tag{4.12}$$

From (4.6) and (4.7), one can see easily, as in [19], that $\rho(x, y; \cdot, \cdot)$ is a positive definite bilinear form so that it can be expressed as (Ar_1, r_2) for some hermitean positive definite matrix A. But the hypothesis on the partial derivatives of β implies, after a computation,

$$\tilde{f}_1(0)\tilde{f}_2(0)(Ar_1, r_2) = (A\tilde{\nabla}\tilde{f}_1(0), \tilde{\nabla}\tilde{f}_2(0)). \tag{4.13}$$

Thus (4.12) and (4.13) yield, for $f_i \in \Phi$,

$$B(T_{r_1} f_1, T_{r_2} f_2) = \int_{R^n - \{0\}} \int_{R^n - \{0\}} \widetilde{T_{r_1} f_1}(t)\overline{\widetilde{T_{r_2} f_2}}(s)\rho(dt\, ds) + (A\tilde{\nabla}\tilde{f}_1(0), \tilde{\nabla}\tilde{f}_2(0)). \tag{4.14}$$

However, as r_1 varies in R^n, $sp\{T_{r_1} f : f \in \Phi, r \in R^n\} = \Phi_2$ is dense in Φ_1. Since by the bilinearity of B, it follows that (4.14) holds on Φ_2 and, by its continuity, on Φ_1. Thus (4.4) holds, and the proof is complete since the last part is easy.

Proof of Theorem 4.2. The proof here is, in essence, similar to that of Theorem 3.1, and a modification is needed only to use the form of the covariance functional of (4.4) above. Thus, suppose the grf F on Φ is of class (c) locally, relative to $g(\cdot, \cdot)$ of the hypothesis, with zero mean and covariance B. Again for simplicity, let $B(\cdot, \cdot)$ be (strictly) positive definite and ρ be the tempered covariance of Proposition 4.4. If $L^2(\rho) \supset \Phi_1$ is the completion of Φ_1 under the norm given by the inner product

$$(f_1, f_2) = B(f_1, f_2) = (\tilde{f}_1, \tilde{f}_2), \tag{4.15}$$

and $\mathscr{H}$ is the completion in $L^2(P)$ of the set $\{F(f) : f \in \Phi_1\}$, then it follows that the maps $f \mapsto F(f)$ and $f \mapsto \tilde{f}$ are isometries between $L^2(\rho)$ and $\mathscr{H}$, and in $L^2(\rho)$ so that $\tilde{\Phi}_1 = \{\tilde{f} : f \in \Phi_1\} \subset L^2(\rho)$ is dense in the latter.

Let $A \in \mathscr{B}$ be such that $\mathscr{X}_A \in L^2(\rho)$ and let $Z(A) \in \mathscr{H}$ be the corresponding element. It can be seen, as in Theorem 3.1, that $Z(\cdot) : \mathscr{B} \mapsto \mathscr{H}$ is a random measure relative to ρ. Also it may be assumed that the original probability space is rich enough (as otherwise it can be enlarged by adjunction) so that one may choose a second order random vector $\alpha = (\alpha_1, \ldots, \alpha_n)$ on Ω, with zero means and covariance matrix A of (4.4), which is uncorrelated with Z.

Let $\tilde{f} \in \tilde{\Phi}_1 \subset L^2(\rho)$. Choose a simple $\tilde{f}_m$ in $L^2(\rho)$ such that $\tilde{f}_m \to \tilde{f}$ in mean and also a sequence $\{\beta_m{}^k\}$ in $L^2(\rho)$ which tends in mean to the kth component of $\tilde{\nabla}\tilde{f}(0)$. Because of the hypothesis on $g(\cdot, \cdot)$, it is seen that such a sequence can be constructed (using certain modifications of the method of [19], which holds essentially verbatim if $g(t, x) = e^{it \cdot x}$) so that if $\tilde{f}_{0m} = \tilde{f}_m + \beta_m{}^k \in L^2(\rho)$, then the corresponding element in $\mathscr{H}$ can be defined by

$$F(f_{0m}) = \int_{R^n - \{0\}} \tilde{f}_{0m}(t)\, dZ(t) + \sum_{k=1}^{n} \beta_m{}^k \alpha_k, \tag{4.16}$$

where $f_{0m} \leftrightarrow \tilde{f}_{0m}$ correspond to each other by the isometry. Since (4.16) is just (4.2) on $\Phi_2 \subset \Phi_1$ in the above notation, the continuity of F implies that the result holds as $m \to \infty$ in (4.16) (see the slightly more detailed argument in the proof of Theorem 3.1 in such a situation) yielding

$$F(f) = \int_{R^n - \{0\}} \tilde{f}(t)\, dZ(t) + (\alpha, \tilde{\nabla}\tilde{f}(0)), \qquad f \in \Phi_1. \tag{4.17}$$

This proves (4.2) and since the remaining parts are proved exactly as in Theorem 3.1, the proof is complete.

The most important consequence of this result is Theorem 4.3 which follows by setting $g(t, x) = e^{it \cdot x}$ in the above. The interesting point here is that Yaglom's representation [19] of the locally homogeneous random fields on the space $\mathscr{K}$ extends to the somewhat more general spaces and, more interestingly, to the locally harmonizable case as here.

The multidimensional extension of Theorem 4.3 will now be stated. Similar statements can be made for locally class (c) case and others also. The proof follows from an earlier remark and the details, therefore, will be omitted.

Theorem 4.5. *Let $F = (F_1, \ldots, F_N)$ be a multidimensional generalized locally harmonizable random field on Φ_1 where $\mathscr{K} \subset \Phi \subset \mathscr{S}$. Then there is a positive definite matrix $\rho = (\rho_{ij})$ of tempered covariances ρ_{ij} each satisfying* (4.1) *and a random vector measure $Z = (Z_1, \ldots, Z_N)$ relative to ρ on the Borel field $\mathscr{B}$, of $R^n - \{0\}$, and an $N \times n$ matrix $\alpha = (\alpha_{ij}, i = 1, \ldots, n, j = 1, \ldots, N)$ of second order random variables with means zero, $E(\alpha_{ij}\overline{Z(A)}) = 0$, $A \in \mathscr{B}$ bounded, such that the following representation holds uniquely*

$$F(f) = \int_{R^n - \{0\}} \hat{f}(t)\, dZ(t) + i\alpha\nabla\hat{f}(0), \qquad f \in \Phi_1. \tag{4.18}$$

Conversely, a functional F defined by (4.18) *relative to a ρ, $Z(\cdot)$, and α as above, defines an N-dimensional generalized locally harmonizable random field, relative to ρ, on Φ_1.*

5. ISOTROPIC AND HARMONIZABLE FIELDS

After introducing the isotropic random fields, a few properties of a random field which is both isotropic and harmonizable will be considered and then a characterization of a class of harmonizable covariance functionals will be considered in this section. The treatment here will be brief and it generalizes or complements some aspects of [13], [19], and [15].

Let $\mathscr{G}$ be the class of all orthogonal matrices on R^n. If $F : \Phi \mapsto L^2(P)$ is a grf and $m(f) = E(F(f))$, $B(f_1, f_2) = \operatorname{cov}(F(f_1), F(f_2))$, then F is said to be *isotropic* whenever $m(\sigma_u f) = m(f)$ and $B(\sigma_u f_1, \sigma_u f_2) = B(f_1, f_2)$ for all $u \in \mathscr{G}$ where $(\sigma_u f)(x) = f(ux)$, $f \in \Phi$. The following simple characterization holds:

Proposition 5.1. *Let $F : \Phi \mapsto L^2(P)$ be a grf of class* (c) *relative to a $g(\cdot, \cdot)$ and a tempered covariance ρ, where Φ is a test space, as in Theorem* 3.1, *whose* *g-transforms exist. Suppose* $g(ut, x) = g(t, u^*x)$ *for all* $u \in \mathcal{G}$ *where* u^* *is the adjoint of* u. *Then* F *is isotropic if and only if* ρ *is invariant under* $\mathcal{G}$, *i.e.,* $\rho(ux, uy) = \rho(x, y)$ *for* $x, y \in R^n$, *and* $u \in \mathcal{G}$.

Proof. By definition, for f_1, f_2 in Φ, the covariance $B(\cdot, \cdot)$ of F is representable as

$$B(f_1, f_2) = \int_{R^n} \int_{R^n} \tilde{f}_1(s)\overline{\tilde{f}_2(t)}\, d^2\rho(s, t). \tag{5.1}$$

However, for $u \in \mathcal{G}$, $i = 1, 2$,

$$\widetilde{\sigma_u f_i}(s) = \int_{R^n} f_i(ux)g(s, x)\, dx$$

$$= \int_{R^n} f_i(x)g(s, u^*x)\, dx \tag{5.2}$$

since $u^{-1} = u^*$. Consequently $B(\sigma_u f_1, \sigma_u f_2) = B(f_1, f_2)$ yields

$$\int_{R^n} \int_{R^n} \widetilde{\sigma_u f_1}(s)\overline{\widetilde{\sigma_u f_2}(t)}\, d^2\rho(s, t)$$

$$= \int_{R^n} \int_{R^n} f_1(x)\overline{f_2(y)}\left[\int_{R^n} \int_{R^n} g(us, x)\overline{g(ut, y)}\, d^2\rho(s, t)\right] dx\, dy$$

$$= \int_{R^n} \int_{R^n} \tilde{f}_1(s)\overline{\tilde{f}_2(t)}\, d^2\rho(us, ut) = B(f_1, f_2).$$

However $\tilde{\Phi} = \{\tilde{f} : f \in \Phi\} \subset L^2(\rho)$ is dense as seen in the proof of Theorem 3.1 so that using (5.1) for $B(f_1, f_2)$ on the right-hand side, it follows that $\rho(us, ut) = \rho(s, t)$. The converse is immediate from definitions.

Taking $g(t, x) = e^{it \cdot x}$ in the above, the following result obtains:

Corollary 5.2. *Let* $\mathcal{K} \subset \Phi \subset \mathcal{S}$. *Let* F *be a generalized harmonizable random field on* Φ *relative to a tempered covariance* ρ. *Then* F *is isotropic if and only if* ρ *is invariant under the action of the orthogonal group* $\mathcal{G}$.

Remark. The above corollary and proposition admit of straightforward multidimensional extensions.

An ordinary harmonizable covariance was characterized in [15]. Utilizing the same idea, a characterization of function type harmonizable covariance can be given as follows.

Proposition 5.3. *Let* $\Phi = \mathcal{K}$, *and suppose that* F *on* Φ *is a grf with zero mean and covariance functional* $B(\cdot, \cdot)$ *of function type. Then* $B(\cdot, \cdot)$ *is harmonizable (relative to some tempered covariance* ρ*) if and only if there exists a sequence* $\{B_m(\cdot, \cdot)\}$ *of covariances such that the following three conditions hold:*

(i) *$B_m(f_1, f_2) \to B(f_1, f_2)$ uniformly on $\Phi \times \Phi$ as $m \to \infty$,*

(ii) *B_m has its support contained in a compact rectangle E_m where $E_m \subset E_{m+1}$ and $R^n \times R^n = \bigcup_{m=1}^{\infty} E_m$,*

(iii) *if $h_m(\cdot, \cdot)$ is the continuous covariance function corresponding to B_m by formula (2.1), then each of the eigenfunctions $\{\varphi_i^m\}$ of h_m is a Fourier transform of some function G_i^m of bounded variation in R^n with support in $\{x \in R^n : (x, y) \in E_m\}$.*

Proof. Suppose B is harmonizable. Then by definition there is a tempered covariance ρ such that

$$B(f_1, f_2) = \int_{R^n} \hat{f}_1(t)\bar{\hat{f}}_2(s)\, d^2\rho(t, s), \qquad f_1, f_2 \in \Phi. \tag{5.3}$$

If $\rho_m = \rho \mid E_m$, the restriction of ρ to E_m and B_m is the corresponding covariance functional, then B_m has compact support and $B_m \to B$ uniformly in $\Phi \times \Phi$ (cf. also the argument of Proposition 2.3). Thus (i) and (ii) hold. For (iii), consider B_m. By hypothesis B, and hence B_m,is of function type. Hence by Proposition 2.1, there exists a positive definite continuous $h_m(\cdot, \cdot)$ such that

$$B_m(f, g) = \iint_{E_m} h_m(x, y) f(x)\overline{g(y)}\, dx\, dy. \tag{5.4}$$

Consequently, (5.3) and (5.4) imply for B_m

$$\iint_{E_m} f(x)\overline{g(y)} \left[h_m(x, y) - \int_{R^n}\int_{R^n} e^{i(t \cdot x - s \cdot y)}\, d^2\rho_m(t, s) \right] dx\, dy = 0. \tag{5.5}$$

Since f, g in Φ are arbitrary it follows from (5.5) that $h_m(x, y)$ actually defines a harmonizable covariance function relative to ρ_m. Then by ([15], Theorem 5), h_m satisfies (iii).

To prove the converse, let (i)–(iii) hold. Then (iii) implies (by the corresponding part of [15] and (5.5)) that B_m is harmonizable for each m. Since ρ_m determines a regular measure and $B_m \to B$ uniformly on $\Phi \times \Phi$, by (i) and (ii), Eq. (5.3) obtains by an application of a theorem Alexandroff's ([6], p. 316); since $\rho_m \to \rho$ on every compact set in $R^n \times R^n$, it follows that ρ is a covariance function of bounded variation on each such set and that B is harmonizable. This completes the proof.

Remark. It will be of interest to obtain a characterization of $B(\cdot, \cdot)$ above without assuming that it is of function type. In [15] it was assumed that $\tilde{\rho}(R^n \times R^n) < \infty$, in the definition of generalized harmonizability, and this corresponds to "zero order" in terms of this paper. The former is, therefore, more restrictive than the treatment of the harmonizable case in this paper.

Some results of Urbanik ([18], p. 323), and their extensions to harmonizable processes, indicate that the following general kind of characterization holds: A grf F of second order is harmonizable if and only if there is an integer $k \geq 0$, such that F is the (distributional) derivative of kth order of a continuous (ordinary) process with harmonizable kth increments. However, this is not very satisfactory for applications and a better characterization will be of interest. The theory of kth increments of class (c) or harmonizable can now be treated along the lines of [11] though it will not be considered in this paper.

ACKNOWLEDGMENT

I would like to thank Professor A. M. Yaglom for some helpful comments on this paper.

REFERENCES

1. Cramér, H. (1951). A contribution to the theory of stochastic processes. *Proc. Second Berkeley Symp. Math. Statist. Prob.* (J. Neyman, ed.), pp. 329–339. Univ. California Press, Berkeley, California.
2. Cramér, H. (1964). Stochastic processes as curves in Hilbert space. *Teor. Veroyatnost. i Primenen* **9** 169–179 (English translation).
3. Cramér, H. (1940). On the theory of stationary random processes. *Ann. Math.* **41** 215–230.
4. Deo, C. M. (1965). Prediction theory of non-stationary random processes. *Sankhyā Ser. A* **27** 113–132.
5. Dudley, R. M. (1965). Gaussian processes on several parameters. *Ann. Math. Statist.* **36** 771–788.
5a. Dudley, R. M. (1965). Fourier analysis of sub-stationary processes with a finite moment. *Trans. Amer. Math. Soc.* **118** 360–375.
6. Dunford, N., and Schwartz, J. T. (1958). "Linear Operators, Part I: General Theory." Wiley (Interscience), New York.
7. Fernique, X. (1967). Processus linéaire, processus généralisés. *Ann. Inst. Fourier (Grenoble)* **17** 1–92.
8. Friedman, A. (1963). "Generalized Functions and Partial Differential Equations." Prentice-Hall, Englewood Cliffs, New Jersey.
9. Gel'fand, I. M. (1955). Generalized random processes. *Dokl. Akad. Nauk. SSSR* **100** 853–856 (in Russian).
10. Gel'fand, I. M., and Šilov, G. E. (1964). "Les Distributions, tome 2: Espaces Fondamentaux." Dunod, Paris.
11. Gel'fand, I. M., and Vilenkin, N. Ya. (1964). "Generalized Functions," Vol. 4. Academic Press, New York.
12. Itô, K. (1954). Stationary random distributions. *Mem. Coll. Sci. Univ. Kyoto Ser. A* **28** 209–223
13. Itô, K. (1956). Isotropic random current. *Proc. Third Berkeley Symp. Math. Statist. Prob.* **2** (J. Neyman, ed.), pp. 125–132. Univ. California Press, Berkeley, California.
14. Kallianpur, G., and Mandrekar, V. (1965). Multiplicity and representation theory of purely nondeterministic stochastic processes. *Teor. Veroyatnost. i Primenen.* **10** 553–581 (English translation).

15. Rao, M. M. (1967). Characterization and extension of generalized harmonizable random fields. *Proc. Nat. Acad. Sci. U.S.A.* **58** 1213–1219.
16. Schwartz, L. (1957). "Théorie des Distributions," Vol.s 1 and 2, 2nd ed. Hermann, Paris.
17. Ullrich, M. (1957). Some theorems on random Schwartz distributions. *Trans. First Prague Conf., Information Theory, Statistical Decision Functions, and Random Processes*, pp. 273–291. Publ. House Czech. Acad. Sci., Prague.
18. Urbanik, K. (1958). Generalized stochastic processes. *Studia Math.* **16** 268–334.
19. Yaglom, A. M. (1957). Some classes of random fields in n-dimensional space related to stationary random processes. *Teor. Veroyatnost. i Primenen* **2** 273–320 (English translation).

On a New Class of Estimates

YU. A. ROZANOV

STEKLOV MATHEMATICAL INSTITUTE
ACADEMY OF SCIENCES OF THE USSR
MOSCOW, USSR

We assume that we have a parameter θ, the possible values of which form a set Θ and require an estimate of the unknown value $\theta \in \Theta$ by observation of the random quantity of the form $\xi = \phi(\theta, \Delta)$, where ϕ is some function, and Δ a random quantity with unknown probability distribution P. Moreover, not only the parametric space Θ but also the spaces of values of the quantities ξ or Δ are, generally speaking, arbitrary.

In this situation, it is possible to proceed in the following manner. Guided by these or other a priori considerations, it is possible to take a certain probability distribution Q and, by convention, having assumed it to be the probability distribution of the random quantity Δ, to construct these or other estimates of the unknown parameter $\theta \in \Theta$, satisfying these or other properties with respect to this distribution Q. Let us say that this can be an estimate of Bayes type

$$\hat{\theta} = \int_{\Theta} \theta \pi(d\theta/\xi),$$

where $\pi(d\theta/\xi)$ is the a posteriori distribution calculated under the assumption that the quantity Δ has the distribution Q; this can be the estimate constructed according to the fictitious (i.e., hypothetical) relationship of likelihood

$$L(\theta, x) = Q_{\xi}(\theta, dx)/dx$$

of the density of the distribution of the quantity $\phi(\theta, \Delta)$ with respect to some measure dx (calculated under the assumption that the quantity Δ has the distribution Q), and so on.

On proceeding in this way, the question soon arises about the corresponding properties of these estimates with respect to the true (but unknown) distribution P. This question is considered below for one important case when it is required to estimate the unknown function $\theta = \theta(t)$ of $t \in T$ by observation of the random process of the form

$$\xi(t) = \theta(t) + \Delta(t), \qquad t \in T, \tag{1}$$

where T is a certain set on the real axis, $\Delta(t)$ is a stationary process with null mean and unknown spectral density $f(\lambda)$, and the functional parameter $\theta = \theta(t)$ lies in some set Θ.

We choose a hypothetical spectral density $g(\lambda)$, and let us consider the estimate $\hat{\theta} = \hat{\theta}(t)$, which turns out to be the best linear unbiased estimate with respect to the spectral density $g(\lambda)$. Namely, let $L_T(g)$ be the Hilbert space of the functions $\phi(\lambda)$ with scalar product

$$\langle \phi, \psi \rangle_g = \int \phi(\lambda)\overline{\psi(\lambda)}g(\lambda)\, d\lambda, \tag{2}$$

being the closure of the space of all functions $\phi(\lambda)$ of the form

$$\phi(\lambda) = \sum_{k=1}^{n} c_k e^{i\lambda t_k},$$

where $t_1, \ldots, t_n \in T$ and $c_1, \ldots, c_n$ are real coefficients. In the case in which all linear unbiased estimates turn out to be degenerate, each function $\theta = \theta(t)$ of $t \in T$ is uniquely representable in the form (see e.g., Rozanov [1])

$$\theta(t) = \int e^{-i\lambda t}\phi_\theta(\lambda)g(\lambda)\, d\lambda, \qquad t \in T, \tag{3}$$

where $\phi_\theta(\lambda) \in L_T(g)$. Let $L_{T,\Theta}$ denote the subspace spanned by all functions $\phi_\theta(\lambda)$ corresponding, by formula (3), to the functions $\theta(t) \in \Theta$. Finally, let $\phi(\lambda, t)$ denote the projection of the element $e^{i\lambda t} \in L_T(g)$ on the subspace $L_{T,\Theta}$. Then the indicated estimate $\hat{\theta} = \hat{\theta}(t)$, $t \in T$, verifies the following spectral representation:

$$\hat{\theta}(t) = \int \phi(\lambda, t)\Phi(d\lambda), \tag{4}$$

whereby $\Phi(d\lambda)$ one could, for instance, understand the spectral stochastic measure of the harmonizable random process of the form

$$\xi(t) = \int e^{i\lambda t}\overline{\phi_\theta(\lambda)}g(\lambda)\, d\lambda + \Delta(t), \qquad -\infty < t < \infty,$$

which coincides with the observable process on the set T. Moreover, the formula (4) itself makes sense with respect to the true distribution P of the stationary process $\Delta(t)$ (with respect to the true spectral density $f(\lambda)$), if, for example,

$$L_T(g) \subseteq L_T(f) \tag{5}$$

which is satisfied, say, for

$$g(\lambda) \geq h \cdot f(\lambda) \tag{6}$$

(where h is some constant).

We remark that without loss of generality, it is possible to consider the parametric space Θ as a finite dimensional linear space, which we will do from now on. The problem of estimation of the functional parameter $\theta \in \Theta$ reduces to the problem of estimation of the "regression coefficients" $\alpha_1, \ldots, \alpha_N$ in the expansion of the function $\theta(t) \in \Theta$ with respect to some basis $\theta_1(t), \ldots, \theta_N(t) \in \Theta$:

$$\theta(t) = \sum_{k=1}^{N} \alpha_k \theta_k(t). \tag{7}$$

If $\phi_k(\lambda) \in L_T(g)$ are functions in the representation (3) for the basis elements $\theta_k(t) \in \Theta$, $k = 1, \ldots, N$, then the best linear unbiased estimates $\hat{\alpha}_1, \ldots, \hat{\alpha}_N$ for the unknown coefficients $\alpha_1, \ldots, \alpha_N$ in the expansion (7) (with respect to the hypothetical spectral density $g(\lambda)$) are representable in the form

$$\hat{\alpha}_k = \int \psi_k(\lambda)\Phi(d\lambda), \qquad k = 1, \ldots, N, \tag{8}$$

where $\psi_1(\lambda), \ldots, \psi_N(\lambda) \in L_{T,\Theta}$ is the dual system to the elements $\phi_1, \ldots, \phi_N$, forming a basis in the subspace $L_{T,\Theta}$. Namely

$$\psi_k(\lambda) = \sum_{j=1}^{N} \sigma_{kj} \phi_j(\lambda), \qquad k = 1, \ldots, N, \tag{9}$$

where the matrix $\{\sigma_{kj}\}$ is inverse to the matrix of elements $\langle \phi_k, \phi_j \rangle_g$; $k, j = 1, \ldots, N$, and coincides with the correlation matrix of the linear unbiased estimates $\hat{\alpha}_1, \ldots, \hat{\alpha}_N$ ($\{\sigma_{kj}\}$ is minimal among the correlation matrices of any other arbitrary linear unbiased estimates under the assumption that $g(\lambda)$ is the spectral density of the stationary process $\Delta(t)$).

Let us note that in the case $g(\lambda) \equiv 1$ we are dealing with the usual least-squares estimates, but for $g(\lambda) = f(\lambda)$ with actually the best linear unbiased estimates. In the case, in which T is the interval $[0, \tau]$ and

$$g(\lambda) = |Q(i\lambda)|^{-2} \tag{10}$$

(where $Q(z)$ is a polynomial), the indicated estimates $\hat{\alpha}_1, \ldots, \hat{\alpha}_k$ may be obtained as functions of τ from the solution of ordinary differential equations; they asymptotically (as $\tau \to \infty$) coincide with the least-squares estimates obtained for the random process of the form

$$Q(d/dt)\xi(t) = \sum_{k=1}^{N} \alpha_k[Q(d/dt)\theta_k(t)] + Q(d/dt)\,\Delta(t), \qquad 0 \leq t \leq \tau.$$

We also note that if the trajectories of the observable random process $\xi(t)$, $0 \le t \le \tau$ belong to the space $L_T{}^*(g)$ of functions $x = x(t)$ of t of the form

$$x(t) = \int e^{-i\lambda t}\phi(\lambda)g(\lambda)\, d\lambda, \qquad 0 \le t \le \tau$$

(where $\phi(\lambda) \in L_T(g)$), in which the scalar product is $\langle x, y\rangle_g \equiv \langle \phi, \psi\rangle_g$, then the indicated estimates $\hat{\alpha}_1, \ldots, \hat{\alpha}_n$ minimize the expression

$$\left\| \xi - \sum_{k=1}^{n} \alpha_k \theta_k \right\|_g^2$$

and in this sense, they are the estimates of least squares. It is worthwhile to note that $\xi(t) \in L_T{}^*(g)$ when, and only when, A^*A is a nuclear (or trace class) operator, where A is an operator from $L_T(g)$ to $L_T(f)$ of the form $A\phi(\lambda) = \phi(\lambda)$, $\phi \in L_T(g)$ and A^* is the adjoint operator to A. We turn to the general case, assuming that the process $\xi(t)$ is observable on the interval $0 \le t \le \tau$, and the unknown spectral density $f(\lambda)$ is bounded.

Theorem 1. *For consistency (as $\tau \to \infty$) of the linear unbiased estimates $\hat{\alpha}_1, \ldots, \hat{\alpha}_n$ of the form* (8), *it is necessary and sufficient that either*

$$\int_0^\infty [\theta(t)]^2\, dt = \infty$$

or for an arbitrary extension of the square-integrable function $\theta(t)$, to $-\infty < t < \infty$, the following condition holds:

$$\int_{-\infty}^{\infty} \frac{|\tilde{\theta}(\lambda)|^2}{g(\lambda)}\, d\lambda = \infty, \tag{11}$$

where $\tilde{\theta}(\lambda)$ is the Fourier transform of $\theta(t)$, $-\infty < t < \infty$.

In particular, for the hypothetical spectral density $g(\lambda) \equiv 1$, corresponding to the estimates of least squares, the necessary and sufficient condition for consistency is that

$$\int_0^\infty [\theta(t)]^2\, dt = \infty. \tag{12}$$

This says, in particular, that the estimates $\hat{\alpha}_1, \ldots, \hat{\alpha}_N$ constructed for the hypothetical density $g(\lambda)$ of the form (10) may be more preferable than the usual least squares estimates when $\int_0^\infty [\theta(t)]^2\, dt < \infty$.

We now assume that a somewhat stronger condition is satisfied than that of consistency. Namely, we will suppose that, for some n and $c > 0$,

$$f(\lambda) \ge c(1 + \lambda^2)^{-n} \tag{13}$$

($f(\lambda)$ is the true spectral density), and for each derivative $\theta_k^{(m)}(t)$, $0 \le m \le n$

($k = 1, \ldots, N$), there exists a nondegenerate matrix regression measure $\{M_{kj}^{(m)}(d\lambda)\}$. The elements $M_{kj}^{(m)}(d\lambda)$ are determined by the relation

$$\lim_{\tau\to\infty} \frac{\int_0^\tau \theta_k^{(m)}(t+h)\theta_j^{(m)}(t)\,dt}{\left(\int_0^\tau \theta_k^{(m)}(t)^2\,dt\right)^{1/2}\cdot\left(\int_0^\tau \theta_j^{(m)}(t)^2\,dt\right)^{1/2}} = \int_0^\infty e^{i\lambda h} M_{kj}^{(m)}(d\lambda)$$

(cf. Grenander and Rosenblatt [2]). We remark that the existence of all $\{M_{kj}^{(m)}(d\lambda)\}$, $m = 0, \ldots, n$, is equivalent to the existence of the regression measure $M_{kj}^{(Q)}(d\lambda)$ for the functions $Q(d/dt)\theta(t)$, where $Q(z)$ is a certain polynomial of degree n with roots in the right half-plane. And so, as in the work of Grenander and Rosenblatt [2], for $\{M_{kj}^{Q}(d\lambda)\}$, it is possible to determine the so-called elements of the regression spectra $\Lambda_1, \ldots, \Lambda_N$.

The following result holds (cf. Kholevo [3]).

Theorem 2. *With the above hypothesis, for asymptotic efficiency of the estimates of the form* (8), *it is sufficient that the ratio $f(\lambda)/g(\lambda)$ be constant for each of the elements of the spectra $\Lambda_1, \ldots, \Lambda_N$.*

As examples show, in the case of continuous t, the existence of the regression measure for the functions $\theta_k(t)$ only (even concentrated at the single point $\lambda = 0$) is still insufficient for asymptotic efficiency of the estimates of the form (8), and, in particular, of the least-squares estimates (cf. Grenander and Rosenblatt [2], where the case of discrete time t is considered, and the spectral density $f(\lambda)$ satisfies the condition $f(\lambda) \geq c$).

REFERENCES

1. ROZANOV, YU. A. (1968). Infinite-dimensional Gaussian distributions. *Publications of the V. A. Steklov Math. Inst.*, Acad. of Sci., USSR, Vol. 108, Moscow.
2. GRENANDER, U., and ROSENBLATT, M. (1957). "Statistical Analysis of Stationary Time Series." Wiley, New York.
3. KHOLEVO, A. S. (1969). On estimates of the regression coefficients (in Russian). *Teor. Veroyatnost. i Primenen.* **14**, 1.

Multidimensional Stochastic Approximation

L. SCHMETTERER

MATHEMATICISCHES INSTITUT
UNIVERSITY OF VIENNA
VIENNA, AUSTRIA

1. INTRODUCTION

The theory of multidimensional stochastic approximation (msa) has much in common with that of one-dimensional stochastic approximation. I do not know of any basic results of the one-dimensional theory which cannot be generalized to higher dimensions without any difficulties. All theorems which are given in this paper are multidimensional generalizations of known one-dimensional results or slight extensions of existing multidimensional theorems. It is not intended to point out many details but rather to give an outline of the current research in msa.

The first results on the multidimensional case were obtained by Blum [1]. They are concerned with generalizations of the procedure of Robbins-Monro (determination of a root of an equation of the form $M(x) = \alpha$ where M is an unknown function) and of the procedure of Kiefer-Wolfowitz (determination of an extremum of an unknown function). We shall consider slight generalizations of these two procedures. Many of the results that follow may easily be carried over to an infinite-dimensional Hilbert-space or even to a Banach space.

Inspired by the methods of stochastics approximation, the author [2] has recently considered a (nonstochastic) approximation procedure concerning equations with compact operators in a Banach space. We shall not dwell on all of these generalizations. Let us only mention that stochastic approximation in abstract spaces has already been considered by Block [3], Dvoretzky [4], and Schmetterer [5, 6]. We also exclude all problems that are concerned with the relation between stochastic approximation and nonlinear regression when. the regression function is known. The reader who is interested in these topics may consult the interesting monograph by Albert and Gardner [7].

2. NOTATIONS

We denote by R_n the n-dimensional Euclidean space, and by $\mathfrak{D}_n$ the σ-algebra of all Borel-subsets of R_n where $n \geq 1$. If $x = (x_1 \cdots x_n)$ is an element of R_n, then the symbol $\|x\| = (x_1{}^2 + \cdots + x_n{}^2)^{1/2}$ indicates the norm of x. If $y = (y_1 \cdots y_n)$ is also an element of R_n, then $x'y = y'x = \sum_{i=1}^n x_i y_i$ denotes the inner product of x and y. If M is a $k \times k$ matrix, then $\|M\|$ is defined by

$$\sup_{\substack{\|x\| \leq 1 \\ x \in R_k}} Mx.$$

Let a be any real number. Then, a^+ denotes max $(a, 0)$. Let $x = (\xi_{ik})$ be a matrix (or a vector) of random variables ξ_{ik} (over some probability field) such that $E(\xi_{ik})$ exists. Then the symbol $E(x)$ indicates the matrix (or the vector) $(E(\xi_{ik}))$.

3. SOME AUXILIARY RESULTS

At first let us formulate a very simple but useful statement.

Lemma 3.1. *Let $\{d_i\}$ be a sequence of real numbers which satisfy for $i = 1, 2, \ldots$ the condition, $0 < d_i < 1$. Assume, furthermore, that*

$$\sum_{i=1}^{\infty} d_i = \infty. \tag{3.1}$$

It follows that

$$\lim_{n\to\infty} \sum_{i=1}^{n} d_i \prod_{j=i+1}^{n} (1 - d_j) = 1 \qquad \textit{where} \quad \prod_{l}^{k} = 1 \quad \textit{as} \quad l > k.$$

For the proof, the relation

$$\sum_{i=1}^{n} d_i \prod_{j=i+1}^{n} (1 - d_j) = -\prod_{i=1}^{n} (1 - d_i) + 1$$

is used together with (3.1).

We immediately obtain the following corollary.

Corollary 3.2. *Suppose that the conditions of Lemma* 1 *are satisfied. Furthermore, assume that*

$$\lim_{i\to\infty} d_i = 0. \tag{3.2}$$

Then, the infinite triangular matrix (a_{ij}) where

$$a_{ni} = d_i \prod_{j=i+1}^{n} (1 - d_j), \qquad 1 \leq i \leq n, \quad a_{ni} = 0, \quad i > n$$

defines a regular summability procedure. This is still true if the definition of a_{ni} *for* $1 \le i \le n$ *is slightly altered, namely*

$$a_{ni} = d_i \prod_{j=i+1}^{n} (1 - d_i + o(d_j)).$$

Using Lemma 3.1, it is possible to obtain the following result:

Lemma 3.3. *Let* $\{\alpha_n\}$ *and* $\{\beta_n\}$ *be bounded sequences of real numbers such that* $\underline{\lim}\ \alpha_n > 0$ *and* $\underline{\lim}_{n\to\infty} \beta_n \ge 0$. *Let* $\{d_i\}$ *be one sequence of positive numbers which satisfy* (3.1) *and* (3.2), *and let* $\{e_i\}$ *be another sequence of positive numbers. Define* $d_{n+1}/d_n = 1 - \delta_n$ *and* $e_n/e_{n+1} = 1 + \varepsilon_n$, $n \ge 1$, *and assume that*

$$\varepsilon_n - \delta_n = o(d_n) \tag{3.3}$$

and

$$\varepsilon_n \delta_n = o(d_n). \tag{3.4}$$

If $b_i \ge 0$, $i \ge 1$, *and if*

$$b_{n+1} \le b_n(1 - \alpha_n d_n) + \beta_n e_n \tag{3.5}$$

for every $n \ge 1$, *then*

$$\overline{\lim_{n\to\infty}}\ (d_n/e_n)b_n \le \overline{\lim}\ \beta_n(\underline{\lim}\ \alpha_n)^{-1}. \tag{3.6}$$

If condition (3.3) *is replaced by*

$$\varepsilon_n - \delta_n = \gamma d_n + o(d_n) \tag{3.7}$$

where $\underline{\lim}_{n\to\infty} \alpha_n - \gamma > 0$, *then*

$$\overline{\lim_{n\to\infty}}\ (d_n/e_n)b_n \le \overline{\lim}\ \beta_n(\underline{\lim}\ \alpha_n - \gamma)^{-1}. \tag{3.8}$$

Proof. Let $\varepsilon > 0$ be an arbitrary small number such that $\underline{\lim}\ \alpha_n > 2\varepsilon > 0$. It follows from (3.5) that there exists a natural number n_0 such that

$$b_{n+1} \le b_n(1 - (\underline{\lim}\ \alpha_n - \varepsilon)d_n) + (\overline{\lim}\ \beta_n + \varepsilon)e_n$$

whenever $n \ge n_0$. Introducing the notation $f_n = (d_n/e_n)b_n$, $n \ge n_0$, one obtains the relation

$$f_{n+1} \le f_n \frac{e_n}{d_n}\frac{d_{n+1}}{e_{n+1}} (1 - (\underline{\lim}\ \alpha_n - \varepsilon)d_n) + (\overline{\lim}\ \beta_n + \varepsilon)e_n \frac{d_{n+1}}{e_{n+1}}.$$

It follows from the assumptions using (3.3) and (3.4) that

$$f_{n+1} \le f_n(1 - (\underline{\lim}\ \alpha_n - \varepsilon)d_n + o(d_n)) + (\overline{\lim}\ \beta_n + \varepsilon)d_n + o(d_n).$$

Therefore, it can be seen that for $n \geq n_1 \geq n_0$

$$f_n \leq f_{n_1} \prod_{i=n_1}^{n-1} (1 - (\underline{\lim}\, \alpha_n - 2\varepsilon)d_i)$$
$$+ \sum_{i=n_1}^{n-1} (\overline{\lim}\, \beta_i + 2\varepsilon)d_i \prod_{j=i+1}^{n-1} (1 - (\underline{\lim}\, \alpha_n - 2\varepsilon)d_j).$$

It is trivial that f_{n_1} is finite. The relation (3.6) follows now immediately by (3.1) and by application of Lemma 3.1. The statement (3.8) is deduced in the same way.

Later we will use the following:

Corollary 3.4. *Let C and K be positive real numbers. Let $\{d_i\}$ be a sequence of real numbers which satisfy the conditions* (3.1), (3.2), *and* $0 < 1 - Kd_i$, $i = 1, 2, \ldots$. *Let $b_n \geq 0$ and assume that for $n \geq 1$, the relation*

$$b_{n+1} \leq b_n(1 - Kd_n) + Cd_n^2$$

holds. If

$$d_n/d_{n+1} = 1 + o(d_n),$$

then

$$\overline{\lim}\, d_n^{-1} b_n \leq CK^{-1}.$$

If

$$d_n/d_{n+1} = 1 + \gamma d_n + o(d_n)$$

where $K - \gamma > 0$, then

$$\overline{\lim}\, d_n^{-1} b_n \leq C(K - \gamma)^{-1}.$$

Next, we note a lemma that follows from the martingale theorem and is a slight extension of a known statement (Blum [1], Fabian [8]).

Lemma 3.5. *Let $\{V_n\}$ be a sequence of random variables such that $E(V_1)$ exists. Let A be a real number and suppose that $V_n \geq A$. Furthermore, assume that $\Sigma_{n=1}^{\infty} E([E(V_{n+1} - V_n) \mid V_1, \ldots, V_n]^+)$ converges. Then the sequence $\{V_n\}$ converges with probability* 1. *Furthermore,*

$$\sum_{n=1}^{\infty} E(|E(V_{n+1} - V_n) \mid V_1, \ldots, V_n)| < \infty.$$

Finally, we need the following known result (cf., for instance, Sacks [9]).

Lemma 3.6. *Let U_{ni}, $1 \leq i \leq n$, $n = 1, 2, \ldots$ be random vectors satisfying the following conditions:*

$$E(U_{ni} \mid U_{n1}, \ldots, U_{ni-1}) = 0, \qquad 1 \leq i \leq n, \quad n \geq 1 \tag{3.9}$$

with probability 1; *the covariance matrix* $K_{ni} = E(U_{ni} U'_{ni})$ *exists for every* $1 \leq i \leq n$ *and* $n \geq 1$;

$$\lim_{n\to\infty} \sum_{i=1}^{n} E(\|K_{ni} - M_{ni}\|) = 0 \tag{3.10}$$

where

$$M_{ni} = E(U_{ni} U'_{ni} \mid U_{n1}, \ldots, U_{ni-1});$$

$$\sup_{n} \sum_{i=1}^{n} E(\|U_{ni}\|^2) < \infty; \tag{3.11}$$

for every $\varepsilon > 0$

$$\lim_{n\to\infty} \sum_{i=1}^{n} E(\|U_{ni}\|^2 c_{\{\|U_{ni}\| \geq \varepsilon\}}) = 0 \tag{3.12}$$

where c_M *denotes the indicator function of the set* M. *If*

$$\left\| \sum_{i=1}^{n} K_{ni} - \mathfrak{R} \right\| \to 0, \tag{3.13}$$

then $U_n = \sum_{i=1}^{n} U_{ni}$ *is asymptotically normally distributed with mean* 0 *and covariance matrix* $\mathfrak{R}$.

4. SOME THEOREMS

At first we shall demonstrate an almost immediate multidimensional generalization of a one-dimensional result of Comer [10].

Theorem 4.1. *Let* a_n *be a sequence of positive real numbers satisfying*

$$\sum_{i=1}^{\infty} a_i = \infty. \tag{4.1}$$

Let x_n *and* y_n *be k-dimensional random vectors such that*

$$x_{n+1} = x_n - a_n y_n \tag{4.2}$$

for every $n \geq 1$. *Furthermore, for every* $n \geq 1$, *let* M_n *be a* $(\mathfrak{D}_k, \mathfrak{D}_k)$*-measurable mapping from* R_k *to* R_k. *Assume that* $E(\|y_n - M_n(x_n)\|^2)$ *exists for every* $n \geq 1$, *and that there exists a real* $C > 0$ *such that*

$$E(\|y_n - M_n(x_n)\|^2) \leq C, \qquad n \geq 1. \tag{4.3}$$

Furthermore, suppose that there exists a $K > 0$ *which satisfies*

$$a_i < K^{-1}, \tag{4.4}$$

such that for every $n \geq 1$ *and* $x \in R_k$, *the inequality*

$$\|x - a_n M_n(x)\| \leq (1 - Ka_n)\|x\| \tag{4.5}$$

holds. If $E(\|x_1\|^2)$ *exists, then* $E(\|x_n\|^2)$ *exists for every* $n \geq 2$. *Furthermore*

$$(E(\|x_n\|^2))^{1/2} \leq C^{1/2}K^{-1} + ((E(\|x_1\|^2))^{1/2} - C^{1/2}K^{-1})\prod_{i=1}^{n-1}(1 - Ka_i).$$

It follows that

$$\overline{\lim_{n\to\infty}}\,(E(\|x_n\|^2))^{1/2} \leq C^{1/2}K^{-1}.$$

The proof is very simple. It follows from (4.2) and (4.5) that $\|x_{m+1}\| \leq (1 - Ka_m)\,\|x_m\| + a_m\,\|y_m - M_m(x_m)\|$. An application of Minkovski's inequality gives

$$(E(\|x_{m+1}\|^2))^{1/2} \leq (1 - Ka_m)(E(\|x_m\|^2))^{1/2} + a_m(E(\|y_m - M_m(x_m)\|^2))^{1/2}.$$

Using this inequality for $m = 1, \ldots, n-1$, one obtains by (4.3)

$$(E(\|x_n\|^2))^{1/2} \leq (E(\|x_1\|^2))^{1/2}\prod_{i=1}^{n-1}(1 - Ka_i) + C^{1/2}\sum_{i=1}^{n-1} a_i \prod_{j=i+1}^{n-1}(1 - Ka_j).$$

The statements of the theorem follow from Lemma 3.1 using (4.1) and (4.4).

Remark. There always exists a real number $K > 0$ such that (4.5) is satisfied if the following conditions hold: There exist real numbers C_i, $i = 1, 2$ which satisfy $0 < C_i \leq C_2$ such that

$$C_1\,\|x\|^2 \leq x'M_n(x) \qquad \text{and} \qquad \|M_n(x)\| \leq C_2\,\|x\|, \qquad n \geq 1,$$

for $x \in R_k$; the inequality

$$\inf_n(1 - (1 + a_n^2C_2^2 - 2a_n C_1)^{1/2})a_n^{-1} > 0 \tag{4.6}$$

holds.

The condition (4.6) is, for instance, satisfied if $\lim_{n\to\infty} a_n = 0$ and the infimum is taken for sufficiently large n only.

The conditions of Theorem 1 are too weak to permit statements about the convergence of the sequence $\{x_n\}$. Under somewhat more stringent conditions—the most important being (4.8)—it is possible to demonstrate a strong law of large numbers and a central limit theorem for the sequence $\{x_n\}$. At first, we formulate a lemma that is an immediate generalization of a result given by Gladyšev [11].

Lemma 4.2. *Let* $\{a_n\}$ *be a sequence of positive real numbers such that*

$$\sum_{n=1}^{\infty} a_n^2 < \infty. \tag{4.7}$$

Let x_n *and* y_n *be k-dimensional random vectors which satisfy the condition* (4.2) *for every* $n \geq 1$. *Let* M_n *be a* $(\mathfrak{D}_k, \mathfrak{D}_k)$*-measurable mapping from* R_k *to* R_k. *Assume that*

$$E(y_n \mid x_1, \ldots, x_n) = M_n(x_n) \tag{4.8}$$

with probability 1. *Let a, b, c be nonnegative real numbers and suppose that*

$$E(\|y_n\|^2 \mid x_1, \ldots, x_n) \le a + b\,\|x_n\| + c\,\|x_n\|^2 \tag{4.9}$$

with probability 1. *Suppose further that for every* $x \in R_k$ *and every* $n \ge 1$

$$x'M_n(x) \ge 0. \tag{4.10}$$

If x_1 *is chosen in such a way that* $E(\|x_1\|^2)$ *exists, then the sequence* $\{\|x_n\|\}$ *converges with probability* 1, *and the sequence* $(E\,\|x_n\|^2)$ *converges also.*

Proof. Introducing the notation $z_n = y_n - M_n(x_n)$, it follows from (4.8) that

$$E(z_n \mid x_1, \ldots, x_n) = 0 \tag{4.11}$$

with probability 1. From (4.2) and (4.10), one easily obtains the inequality

$$\|x_{n+1}\|^2 \le \|x_n\|^2 - 2a_n x_n' z_n + a_n^2\,\|y_n\|^2. \tag{4.12}$$

Next, we show that $E(\|x_n\|^2)$ is uniformly bounded for $n \ge 1$. The condition (4.9) implies that positive real numbers A_1, B_1 exist such that

$$E(\|y_n\|^2 \mid x_1, \ldots, x_n) \le A_1 + B_1\,\|x_n\|^2 \tag{4.13}$$

with probability 1. It follows from (4.12), (4.11), and (4.13) that

$$E(\|x_{n+1}\|^2) \le E(\|x_n\|^2) + a_n^2(A_1 + B_1 E(\|x_n\|^2))$$

for $n \ge 1$. This proves that $E(\|x_n\|^2)$ is finite for $n \ge 2$. Moreover

$$E(\|x_{n+1}\|^2) \le E(\|x_1\|^2)\prod_{i=1}^{n}(1 + a_i^2 B_1) + A_1 \sum_{i=1}^{n} a_i^2 \prod_{j=i+1}^{n}(1 + a_j^2 B_1).$$

The condition (4.7) implies that $D = \prod_{i=1}^{\infty}(1 + a_i^2 B_1) < \infty$. It follows without any difficulty that

$$E(\|x_{n+1}\|^2) \le (E(\|x_1\|^2) + A_1 B_1^{-1})D - A_1 B_1^{-1}. \tag{4.14}$$

Now using (4.12) and (4.13), we get

$$(E(\|x_{n+1}\|^2 - \|x_n\|^2) \mid x_1, \ldots, x_n))^+ \le a_n^2(A_1 + B_1\,\|x_n\|^2),$$

and also

$$(E(\|x_{n+1}\|^2 - \|x_n\|^2) \,|\, (\|x_1\|^2, \ldots, \|x_n\|^2))^+ \le a_n^2(A_1 + B_1\,\|x_n\|^2)$$

with probability 1. It follows easily from (4.14) that

$$\sum_{n=1}^{\infty} E[(E(\|x_{n+1}\|^2 - \|x_n\|^2) \,|\, \|x_1\|^2, \ldots, \|x_n\|^2))^+]$$

$$\le DB_1(E(\|x_1\|^2) + A_1 B_1^{-1}) \sum_{n=1}^{\infty} a_n^2.$$

Applying Lemma 3.5, we get the statements of the present lemma.

Remark 1. It is not difficult to see that the condition $E(\|x_1\|^2) < \infty$ can be omitted if only the first statement of Lemma 4.2 is retained.

Now, we can formulate the following:

Theorem 4.3. *Suppose that all the assumptions of Lemma* 4.2 *are satisfied. Furthermore, assume that* (4.1) *holds and that the following condition is satisfied: There exists for every* $\eta > 0$ *a* $\delta > 0$ *such that for* $n = 1, 2, \ldots$

$$\inf_{\eta < \|x\| < \eta^{-1}} x' M_n(x) \geq \delta. \tag{4.15}$$

Then $\{x_n\}$ *converges to* 0[1] *with probability* 1.

Proof. From (4.2), it follows immediately that

$$\|x_{n+1}\|^2 = \|x_1\|^2 - 2\sum_{i=1}^{n} a_i x_i' M_i(x_i) - 2\sum_{i=1}^{n} a_i x_i' z_i + \sum_{i=1}^{n} a_i^2 \|y_i\|^2 \tag{4.16}$$

Using (4.11), (4.13), and (4.14), from (4.16), we get

$$2\sum_{i=1}^{n} a_i E(x_i' M_i(x_i)) \leq E(\|x_1\|^2) - E(\|x_{n+1}\|^2)$$
$$+ \sum_{i=1}^{n} a_i^2 (E(\|x_1\|^2) + A_1 B_1^{-1}) B_1 D).$$

It follows that the series $\sum_{i=1}^{\infty} a_i E(x_i' M_i(x_i))$ is (absolutely) convergent, and the condition (4.1) implies that $\underline{\lim}_{i\to\infty} E(x_i' M_i(x_i)) = 0$. Therefore, there exists an increasing sequence $\{n_k\}$ of natural numbers such that $x_{n_k}' M_{n_k}(x_{n_k})$ converges to 0 with probability 1: Now, applying the Lemma 4.2, the statement of the theorem follows from (4.15).

Remark 2. A somewhat weaker theorem can also be deduced from a result by Derman and Sacks [12] concerning the multidimensional process of Dvoretzky.

Remark 3. Choosing $M_n(x) = M(x)$ for every $x \in R_k$ and $n = 1, 2, \ldots,$ Theorem 4.3 gives an essentially known result about the multidimensional analog of the Robbins-Monro process.

Remark 4. Theorem 4.3 also contains, as a special case, a convergence theorem for the multidimensional analog of the Kiefer-Wolfowitz process. Let M be a Borel-measurable mapping from R_k to R_1. Let $e_i = (0, \ldots, 1, \ldots, 0)$

[1] Here, 0 denotes, of course, the k-dimensional null vector. We do not repeat this convention.

be the ith unit vector for $1 \leq i \leq k$, and define for $x \in R_k$ and real $y \neq 0$ the k-dimensional vector

$$\delta(x, y) = \left(\frac{M(x + ye_1) - M(x - ye_1)}{2y}, \ldots, \frac{M(x + ye_k) - M(x - ye_k)}{2y}\right).$$

Let $\{c_n\}$ be a sequence of positive numbers and define $M_n(x) = \delta(x, c_n)$ for $n \geq 1$ and for every $x \in R_k$. But it should be pointed out particularly that the condition (4.15) is not very useful in this context and should undergo a modification (cf. Theorem 4.4).

We shall state a convergence theorem for the Kiefer-Wolfowitz process which is a slight modification of Blum's theorem [1]. Because the proof is very similar to that given by Blum and has, moreover, much in common with the proof of Theorem 4.3, we suppress it here.

Theorem 4.4. *Let M be a Borel-measurable function from R_k to R_1 such that all first partial derivatives exist in R_k. Denote the (k-dimensional) vector of the first partial derivatives by D. Suppose that D satisfies a Lipschitz-condition with constant K, that is, $\|D(x) - D(y)\| \leq K\|x - y\|$, $x, y \in R_k$. Assume that*

$$\inf_{\|x\| \geq \varepsilon} M(x) > 0 \qquad \text{and} \qquad \inf_{\|x\| \geq \varepsilon} \|D(x)\| > 0$$

are satisfied for every $\varepsilon > 0$. Let $\{a_n\}$ be a sequence of real positive numbers. Let x_n and y_n be k-dimensional random vectors which satisfy, for every $n \geq 1$, the relation $x_{n+1} = x_n - a_n y_n$. Let $\{c_n\}$ be a sequence of positive numbers, and assume that $E(y_n \mid x_1, \ldots, x_n) = \delta(x_n, c_n)$.[2] *Furthermore, suppose that there exists a $C > 0$ such that $E(\|y_n - \delta(x_n, c_n)\|^2) \leq Cc_n^{-2}$. If*

$$\lim_{n\to\infty} c_n = 0, \qquad \sum_{n=1}^{\infty} a_n = \infty, \qquad \sum_{n=1}^{\infty} a_n c_n^2 < \infty, \qquad \sum_{n=1}^{\infty} (a_n^2/c_n^2) < \infty,$$

then $\{x_n\}$ converges to 0 with probability 1.

It is not difficult to prove convergence theorems that convey a more detailed statement about the speed of the convergence. We quote as a pattern the following result.

Theorem 4.5. *Let $\{a_n\}$ be a sequence of positive numbers satisfying the condition* (4.1) *and the following:*

$$\lim_{n\to\infty} a_n = 0 \tag{4.17}$$

$$a_n/a_{n+1} = 1 + o(a_n). \tag{4.18}$$

Let x_n and y_n be k-dimensional random vectors for every $n \geq 1$ which satisfy the relation (4.2). *Assume that $E(\|x_1\|^2) < \infty$. For every n, let M_n be a*

[2] This notation is explained in Remark 4.

$(\mathfrak{D}_k, \mathfrak{D}_k)$-measurable mapping from R_k to R_k such that (4.8) *with probability* 1 *and* (4.3) *are satisfied. Furthermore, assume that there exist a real $K > 0$ and nonnegative numbers A, B such that*

$$x'M_n(x) \geq K\|x\|^2 \tag{4.19}$$

and

$$\|M_n(x)\| \leq A\|x\| + B \tag{4.20}$$

for every $x \in R_k$ and every $n \geq 1$. It follows from (4.20), *that there exist nonnegative numbers A_1, B_1 such that for every $x \in R_k$ and $n \geq 1$*

$$\|M_n(x)\|^2 \leq A_1\|x\|^2 + B_1. \tag{4.21}$$

Introducing the notation $b_n = E(|x_n\|^2)$, the following statement holds:

$$\overline{\lim_{n\to\infty}}\, a_n^{-1}b_n \leq (B_1 + C)/2K \tag{4.22}$$

If the condition (4.18) *is replaced by*

$$a_n/a_{n+1} = 1 + \gamma a_n + o(a_n) \tag{4.23}$$

where γ is a positive number which satisfies $2K - \gamma > 0$, then the statement (4.22) *holds in the following form:*

$$\overline{\lim_{n\to\infty}}\, a_n^{-1}b_n \leq (B_1 + C)/(2K - \gamma). \tag{4.24}$$

A proof follows almost immediately from Corollary 3.4. To see this, it is enough to observe that from (4.2), (4.8), (4.3), (4.19), and (4.21), the inequality

$$E(\|x_{n+1}\|^2) \leq E(\|x_n\|^2)(1 - 2a_n K + a_n^2 A_1) + a_n^2(B_1 + C)$$

can be deduced for every $n \geq 1$. Therefore, for every small $\varepsilon > 0$ and all sufficiently large n, the inequality

$$b_{n+1} \leq b_n(1 - 2a_n(K - \varepsilon)) + a_n^2(B_1 + C)$$

holds and the statements (4.22) resp. (4.24) follow.

Remark 5. If $a_n = an^{-1}$, $n \geq 1$, and

$$a > 1/2K, \tag{4.25}$$

then $a_n/a_{n+1} = (n + 1)/n = 1 + a^{-1}a_n$. Equation (4.25) implies that the condition (4.23) is satisfied with $\gamma = 1/a$. It follows that $b_n = O(1/n)$ if a_n is chosen in the above mentioned manner. This is a well-known result.

While Theorem 4.5 is essentially one of the Robbins-Monro type, the following results are concerned with a modification of the Kiefer-Wolfowitz process which is due to Fabian [13].

Theorem 4.6. *Suppose that the following assumptions are satisfied: M is a Borel-measurable function from R_k to R_1; all first partial derivatives of M exist in R_k; there exists an integer $l \geq 1$ such that $\partial^{2l+1}M/\partial x_j^{2l+1}$, $1 \leq j \leq k$, is defined in an open neighborhood $\mathfrak{A}$ of the zero element of R_k*

$$\sup_{\substack{x \in \mathfrak{A} \\ 1 \leq j \leq k}} \left| \frac{\partial^{2l+1} M(x)}{\partial x_j^{2l+1}} \right| = G < \infty \tag{4.26}$$

the function $\partial M/\partial x_j$, $1 \leq j \leq k$ is uniformly continuous in $R_k - \mathfrak{A}/2$.[3]

Furthermore, let u_i, $1 \leq i \leq l$, be real numbers satisfying

$$0 < u_1 < u_2 < \cdots < u_l \leq 1. \tag{4.27}$$

Define

$$U = \begin{pmatrix} u_1 & u_2 & \cdots & u_l \\ u_1{}^3 & u_2{}^3 & \cdots & u_l{}^3 \\ \cdot & \cdot & \cdots & \cdot \\ u_1^{2l-1} & u_2^{2l-1} & \cdots & u_l^{2l-1} \end{pmatrix}$$

and

$$v = U^{-1} e_{1,l} \tag{4.28}$$

$e_{1,l}$ being the l-dimensional unit vector $(1, 0, \ldots, 0)$.

Let $\{c_n\}$ be a sequence of positive numbers. Define

$$M_n(x) = \sum_{i=1}^{l} u_i v_i \, \delta(x, c_n u_i) \tag{4.29}$$

for every $x \in R_k$ and every $n \geq 1$. Furthermore, let y_{ni}, $n \geq 1$, $1 \leq i \leq l$ be k-dimensional random vectors. Define $y_n = \sum_{i=1}^{l} v_i y_{ni}$. Let $\{a_n\}$ be a sequence of positive numbers and let $\{x_n\}$ be a sequence of k-dimensional random vectors which, for every $n \geq 1$, satisfy the relation

$$x_{n+1} = x_n - a_n y_n \tag{4.30}$$

Furthermore, suppose that the following conditions are fulfilled: For every fixed n and $1 \leq i \leq l$, the components of the vectors y_{ni} given $x_1, \ldots, x_n$ are (conditionally) independent;

$$E(y_{ni} \mid x_1, \ldots, x_n) = u_i \, \delta(x_n, c_n u_i) \tag{4.31}$$

with probability 1; there exists an $C > 0$ such that for every $n \geq 1$ and every i with $1 \leq i \leq l$

$$E[\|y_{ni} - u_i \, \delta(x, c_n u_i)\|^2 \mid x_1, \ldots, x_n] \leq C c_n^{-2}; \tag{4.32}$$

[3] Of course, $\mathfrak{A}/2$ is the set that is defined by $\{x : x = y/2, y \in \mathfrak{A}\}$.

the k-dimensional vector D of the first partial derivatives of M satisfies the conditions

$$x' D(x) \geq K \|x\|^2 \tag{4.33}$$

for every $x \in R_k$ and some $K > 0$; there exist nonnegative numbers A, B such that

$$\|D(x)\| \leq A \|x\| + B \tag{4.34}$$

for every $x \in R_k$.

If the sequences $\{a_n\}$ and $\{c_n\}$ satisfy the conditions

$$c_n = o(1) \tag{4.35}$$

$$\sum_{n=1}^{\infty} a_n = \infty \tag{4.36}$$

$$a_n = O(c_n^{4l+2}) \tag{4.37}$$

$$c_n / c_{n+1} = 1 + o(a_n), \tag{4.38}$$

then $\overline{\lim}_{n \to \infty} c^{-4l} E(\|x_n\|^2)$ is bounded.

This conclusion remains valid if the condition (4.38) *is replaced by*

$$c_n / c_{n+1} = 1 + \gamma a_n + o(a_n) \tag{4.39}$$

where

$$K > 2l\gamma. \tag{4.40}$$

Proof. It follows from (4.29) that

$$M_n(x) = \sum_{i=1}^{l} u_i v_i D(x) + \sum_{i=1}^{l} u_i v_i V_n^{(i)}(x) \tag{4.41}$$

where $V_n^{(i)}(x)$ is defined by

$$\left(\frac{\partial M(x + \vartheta_{in}^{(1)} c_n u_i e_1)}{\partial x_1}, \ldots, \frac{\partial M(x + \vartheta_{in}^{(k)} c_n u_i e_k)}{\partial x_k} \right) - D(x)$$

with $-1 < \vartheta_{in}^{(j)} < 1$, $1 \leq j \leq k$. From (4.27) and (4.35), it can be deduced that

$$\|V_n^{(i)}(x)\| = o(1) \tag{4.42}$$

uniformly in $R_k - \mathfrak{A}/2$ for $i = 1, \ldots, l$. Let ρ be the radius of the largest open sphere with center 0 which is contained in $\mathfrak{A}/2$. Using (4.41) from (4.28), (4.33), and (4.42), we get for $x \in R_k - \mathfrak{A}/2$

$$x' M_n(x) \geq K \|x\|^2 \left(1 - \frac{o(1)}{K\rho} \right)$$

or

$$x' M_n(x) \geq K \|x\|^2 (1 - o(1)) \tag{4.43}$$

where o does not depend on x.

Furthermore using (4.41) from (4.34), we get

$$\|M_n(x)\| \leq A\,\|x\| + B + o(1) \tag{4.44}$$

uniformly for $x \in R_k - \mathfrak{A}/2$.

On the other hand, we get

$$M_n(x) = D(x) + F_n(x)c_n^{2l} \tag{4.45}$$

for every $x \in \mathfrak{A}/2$ where F_n is uniformly bounded on $\mathfrak{A}/2$ for all sufficiently large n. This follows easily from an application of Taylor's theorem up to order $2l+1$ to the mapping $c \to \sum_{i=1}^{l} cu_i v_i\, \delta(x, cu_i)$ using (4.28) and (4.35).

It turns out that

$$\|F_n(x)\| \leq G_1, \qquad x \in \mathfrak{A}/2 \tag{4.46}$$

where

$$G_1 = kG((2l+1)!)^{-1} \sum_{i=1}^{l} |v_i| u_i^{2l+1}. \tag{4.47}$$

Using (4.33) from (4.45), we get $x'M_n(x) \geq K\|x\|^2 - \|x\|\;\|F_n(x)\|\, c_n^{2l}$. It follows easily from (4.45) that

$$x'M_n(x) \geq (K-\eta)\,\|x\|^2 - G_1{}^2 c_n^{4l}(4\eta)^{-1} \tag{4.48}$$

for every $x \in \mathfrak{A}/2$ and every η with $0 < \eta < K$.

Furthermore, it follows from (4.45), using (4.34), that

$$\|M_n(x)\| \leq A\,\|x\| + B + G_1 c_n^{2l} \tag{4.49}$$

for every $x \in \mathfrak{A}/2$.

We introduce the notation $b_n = E(\|x_n\|^2)$. It follows from (4.30)–(4.32), (4.43), (4.44), (4.48), and (4.49) that

$$b_{n+1} \leq b_n + Cc_n^{-2}a_n{}^2 \sum_{i=1}^{l} v_i{}^2 + a_n{}^2(3A^2 b_n + 3B^2 + 3G_1{}^2 c_n^{4l} + o(1))$$
$$- 2a_n((K - \eta + o(1))b_n - G_1{}^2 c_n^{4l}(4\eta)^{-1}).$$

From (4.37), there follows the existence of an $L > 0$ such that $a_n \leq Lc_n^{4l+2}$, $n \geq 1$. With the help of this and of (4.35), we get

$$b_{n+1} \leq b_n(1 - 2a_n((K-\eta) + o(1)) + L_1 a_n c_n^{4l} + a_n\, o(c_n^{4l})$$

where

$$L_1 = LC \sum_{i=1}^{l} v_i{}^2 + G_1{}^2(2\eta)^{-1}.$$

After multiplication by c_{n+1}^{-4l} and using (4.38), an application of Lemma 3.3 yields

$$\overline{\lim_{n\to\infty}}\, c_n^{-4l} b_n \leq \inf_{0<\eta<K} L_1/2(K-\eta) \tag{4.50}$$

if (4.38) is satisfied. If (4.38) is replaced by (4.39) together with (4.40), then

$$\overline{\lim_{n\to\infty}}\, c_n^{-4l} b_n \le \inf_{0<\eta<K-2l\gamma} L_1/2(K-\eta-2l\gamma). \tag{4.51}$$

We consider a special case of Theorem 4.6: Let a and c be positive numbers and choose $a_n = an^{-1}$ and $c_n = cn^{-1/2(2l+1)}$. It follows that (4.39) is satisfied with $\gamma = 1/(4l+2)a$. If $a > l/(2l+1)K$, then $E(\|x_n\|^2) = O(1/n^{2l/(2l+1)})$. This special case has been systematically investigated by Fabian [14]. Many similar results in this direction can be obtained. Finally, let me mention that Fabian [14, 15] has also attacked the problem of the optimal choice of $u_1, \ldots, u_l$.

We conclude with a result on the asymptotic distribution of the sequence $\{x_n\}$ defined by (4.30). It generalizes somewhat known theorems given by Sacks [9] and Fabian [16]. We use the notation of Theorem 4.6 and consider the process defined by (4.30).

Theorem 4.7. *Suppose that*

$$x_n \to 0 \tag{4.52}$$

with probability 1. *Assume that all first and second partial derivatives of M exist in $\mathfrak{U}$ and are continuous at* 0. *Let $D(0) = 0$.*

Denote the matrix of the second partial derivatives at 0 *by H. Assume that H is positive definite. Furthermore, suppose that $\partial^{2l+1}M/\partial x_j^{2l+1}$, $1 \le j \le k$, exists and is continuous at* 0. *Denote the eigenvalues of H by $\lambda_1, \ldots, \lambda_k$ and define $\lambda = \min_j \lambda_j$. Assume that* (4.35) *and* (4.36) *are satisfied.*

Furthermore, suppose that there exists an $L > 0$ such that

$$a_n = Lc_n^{4l+2}, \qquad n \ge 1. \tag{4.53}$$

Assume that (4.38) *or alternatively* (4.39) *are satisfied. If this last condition holds, then suppose that the relation*

$$2l\gamma < \lambda \tag{4.54}$$

is valid. Suppose that (4.31) *is satisfied. Denote $c_n(y_n - M_n(x_n))$ by V_n. Let $\mathfrak{W}$ be a positive definite $k \times k$-matrix. Assume that*

$$\|\mathfrak{W} - E(V_n V_n' \mid x_1, \ldots, x_n)\| \to 0 \tag{4.55}$$

with probability 1. *Suppose that there exists a $C > 0$ such that for every $n \ge 1$*

$$\|E(V_n V_n' \mid x_1, \ldots, x_n)\| \le C \tag{4.56}$$

with probability 1. *Furthermore, assume that*

$$\lim_{n\to\infty} E(\|V_n\|^2 c_{\{\|V_n\|^2 \ge \varepsilon a_n^{-1}\}}) = 0 \tag{4.57}$$

for every $\varepsilon > 0$.

Let Q be an orthogonal matrix such that

$$Q'HQ = \Lambda = \begin{pmatrix} \lambda_1 & 0 & \cdots & 0 \\ 0 & \lambda_2 & \cdots & 0 \\ \cdot & \cdot & \cdots & \cdot \\ 0 & 0 & \cdots & \lambda_k \end{pmatrix}.$$

Denote the $k \times k$ unit-matrix by I, and define

$$\begin{pmatrix} \lambda_1{}^* & 0 & \cdots & 0 \\ 0 & \lambda_2{}^* & \cdots & 0 \\ \cdot & \cdot & \cdots & \cdot \\ 0 & 0 & \cdots & \lambda_k{}^* \end{pmatrix} = \Lambda^* = \Lambda$$

if (4.38) *holds, and* $\Lambda^* - \Lambda - 2l\gamma I$ *if* (4.39) *and* (4.54) *hold.*

Then $c_n^{-2l} x_n$ *is asymptotically normally distributed with mean* $-AQ\Lambda^{*-1} Q' D^{(2l+1)}$ *and covariance matrix*[4]

$$LQ[(Q'\mathfrak{W}Q)_{rs}/(\lambda_r^* + \lambda_s^*)]_{1 \le r, s \le k} Q'$$

where $D^{(2l+1)}$ *denotes the vector of the* $(2l+1)$*th partial derivatives of* M *at* 0, *and where*

$$A = ((2l+1)!)^{-1} \sum_{i=1}^{l} v_i u_i^{2l+1}.$$

Proof. It follows easily from the assumptions and from (4.45) that for every $x \in \mathfrak{A}$ and for every $n \geq 1$, the equality

$$M_n(x) = H(x)x + c_n^{2l} A m_n(x) \tag{4.58}$$

holds where $H(x)$ is a $k \times k$-matrix and $m_n(x)$ is a k-dimensional vector which satisfy the following conditions:

$$H(x) = H + J(x) \tag{4.59}$$

where

$$\lim_{\|x\| \to 0} \|J(x)\| = 0, \tag{4.60}$$

and

$$m_n(x) = D^{(2l+1)} + k_n(x) \tag{4.61}$$

where

$$\lim_{\substack{\|x\| \to 0 \\ n \to \infty}} \|k_n(x)\| = 0. \tag{4.62}$$

It follows from (4.52) that

$$x_{n+1} = x_n - (a_n/c_n) V_n - a_n H(x_n) x_n - a_n c_n^{2l} A m_n(x_n)$$

[4] If $\mathfrak{M}$ is an arbitrary $k \times k$-matrix, then we denote its rsth element by $\mathfrak{M}_{rs}$, $1 \leq r, s \leq k$.

for all sufficiently large n with probability 1 or

$$x_{n+1} = (I - a_n H(x_n))x_n - a_n c_n^{2l} A m_n(x_n) - (a_n/c_n)V_n.$$

Introducing the notation $w_n = Q'x_n$, $n \geq 1$, we get

$$w_{n+1} = (I - a_n Q'H(x_n)Q)w_n - a_n c_n^{2l} AQ'm_n(x_n) - (a_n/c_n)Q'V_n. \quad (4.63)$$

It follows from (4.52), (4.59), and (4.60) that

$$\|Q'H(x_n)Q - \Lambda\| \to 0 \quad (4.64)$$

with probability 1.

Define $w_n^* = c_n^{-2l} w_n$, $n \geq 1$. Then from (4.63), we get

$$w_{n+1}^* = (I - a_n K(x_n))w_n^* - a_n c_n^{2l} c_{n+1}^{-2l} AQ'm_n(x_n) - a_n c_n^{-1} c_{n+1}^{-2l} Q'V_n \quad (4.65)$$

where $\|K(x_n) - \Lambda^*\| \to 0$ with probability 1.

Define a sequence of k-dimensional random vectors $\{u_n^*\}$ by the recursion

$$u_{n+1}^* = (I - a_n K(x_n))u_n^* - a_n c_n^{-1} c_{n+1}^{-2l} Q'V_n. \quad (4.66)$$

It follows from (4.65) that

$$w_{n+1}^* - u_{n+1}^* = (I - a_n K(x_n))(w_n^* - u_n^*) - a_n c_n^{2l} c_{n+1}^{-2l} AQ'm_n(x_n). \quad (4.67)$$

It is not difficult to see that $\|w_n^* - u_n^*\|$ is bounded with probability 1. From (4.35), (4.36), (4.61), and (4.62), the definition of $K(x_n)$ and (4.38) or (4.39) and (4.54), we therefore get by applying Corollary 3.2 to the components of the vector equations (4.67) that $w_n^* - u_n^*$ converges to $-A\Lambda^{*-1}Q'D^{(2l+1)}$ with probability 1.

Therefore, it is enough to prove that the sequence $\{u_n^*\}$ is asymptotically normally distributed with mean 0 and covariance matrix

$$L[(Q'\mathfrak{W}Q)_{rs}/(\lambda_r^* + \lambda_s^*)]_{1 \leq r,\, s \leq k}.$$

By a similar consideration it turns out that $\{u_n^*\}$ can be replaced by a sequence $\{t_n\}$ which is defined by the recursion

$$t_{n+1} = (I - a_n \Lambda^*)t_n - a_n c_n^{-1} c_{n+1}^{-2l} Q'V_n, \qquad t_1 = 0.$$

It follows without any difficulty from (4.31) that for every $n \geq 1$ $E(t_n' Q'V_n \mid t_1, \ldots, t_n) = 0$ with probability 1. Using this from (4.56), we get by a repetition of the proof of Theorem 4.6 that $c_n^{-4l} E(\|c_n^{2l} t_n\|^2)$ is uniformly bounded. It follows that t_n is bounded in probability. Therefore, the relations

$$u_{n+1}^* - t_{n+1} = (I - a_n K(x_n))(u_n^* - t_n) + a_n(\Lambda^* - K(x_n))t_n$$

lead in a very similar manner as above to the conclusion that $u_n^* - t_n$ converges to 0 in probability. Due to (4.53) and (4.38) or (4.39), it is also enough to consider a sequence $\{t_n\}$ defined by

$$t_{n+1} = (I - a_n \Lambda^*)t_n - L^{1/2} a_n^{1/2} Q'V_n$$

where $t_1 = 0$. It follows that

$$t_{n+1} = -L^{1/2} \sum_{i=1}^{n} a_i^{1/2} \prod_{j=i+1}^{n} (I - a_j \Lambda^*) Q' V_i .$$

We apply Lemma 3.6 with

$$U_{ni} = a_i^{1/2} \prod_{j=i+1}^{n} (I - a_j \Lambda^*) Q' V_i .$$

The condition (3.9) is satisfied. This follows from the definition of V_n and from (4.31). Using the notation of Lemma 3.6 from

$$a_n \to 0, \tag{4.68}$$

we get

$$M_{ni} = \left(a_i \prod_{j=i+1}^{n} (1 - a_j(\lambda_r^* + \lambda_s^*) + o(a_j)) \right.$$
$$\left. (Q'E(V_i V_i' \mid U_{n1}, \ldots, U_{ni-1})Q)_{rs} \right)_{1 \le r, s \le k} .$$

The assumption (4.36) together with (4.68) permits us to apply Corollary 3.2, and from (4.55) we get

$$\left\| \sum_{i=1}^{n} M_{ni} - [(Q'\mathfrak{W}Q)_{rs}/(\lambda_r^* + \lambda_s^*)]_{1 \le r, s \le k} \right\| \to 0 \tag{4.69}$$

with probability 1. It follows easily from (4.55) and (4.56) that

$$\|\mathfrak{W} - E(V_n V_n')\| \to 0.$$

Therefore, Eq. (4.69) remains valid if M_{ni} is replaced by K_{ni}. Again using (4.56), we conclude from the bounded convergence theorem that (3.10) is satisfied. Furthermore, Eq. (3.13) turns out to be valid if $\mathfrak{R}$ is replaced by

$$[(Q'\mathfrak{W}Q)_{rs}/(\lambda_r^* + \lambda_s^*)]_{1 \le r, s \le k} .$$

It follows in a similar way that (3.11) is satisfied. Finally (3.12) follows from (4.57) by once more applying the Corollary 3.2. This proves the statement of the theorem.

REFERENCES

1. Blum, J. R. (1954). Multidimensional stochastic approximation methods. *Ann. Math. Statist.* **25** 737–744.
2. Schmetterer, L. (1968). Über ein Iterationsverfahren. *Arch. Math.* (*Basel*) **19** 195–200.
3. Block, H. D. (1957). On stochastic approximation. ONR Rept. Cornell Univ. Ithaca, New York.

4. DVORETZKY, A. (1956). On stochastic approximation. *Proc. Third Berkeley Symp. Math. Statist. Prob.* (J. Neyman, ed.), **I** pp. 39–55.
5. SCHMETTERER, L. (1958). Sur l'itération stochastique, Le Calcul des Probabilités et ses Applications. *Colloq. Intern. Centre Nat. Rech. Sci.* (*Paris*) **87** 55–63.
6. SCHMETTERER, L. (1961). Stochastic approximation. *Proc. Fourth Berkeley Symp. Math. Statist. Prob.* (J. Neyman ed.), **I** pp. 587–609.
7. ALBERT, A., and GARDNER, L., JR. (1967). "Stochastic Approximation and Non-linear Regression." M.I.T.-Press, Cambridge, Massachusetts.
8. FABIAN, V. (1960). Stochastic approximation methods. *Czechoslovak Math. J.* **10** 123–159.
9. SACKS, J. (1958). Asymptotic distribution of stochastic approximation procedures. *Ann. Math. Statist.* **29** 373–405.
10. COMER, J. R. (1964). Some stochastic approximation procedures for use in process control. *Ann. Math. Statist.* **35** 1136–1146.
11. GLADYŠEV, E. G. (1965). On stochastic approximation. *Teor. Veroyatnost. i Primenen* **10** 297–300.
12. DERMAN, C., and SACKS, J. (1959). On Dvoretzky's stochastic approximation theorem. *Ann. Math. Statist.* **30** 601–606.
13. FABIAN, V. (1967). Stochastic approximation of minima with improved asymptotic speed. *Ann. Math. Statist.* **38** 191–200.
14. FABIAN, V. (1967). On the choice of design in stochastic approximation methods. RM-185. Michigan State Univ., East Lansing, Michigan.
15. FABIAN, V. (1967). Stochastic approximation for smooth functions. RM-203. Michigan State Univ., East Lansing, Michigan.
16. FABIAN, V. (1967). On asymptotic normality in stochastic approximation. RM-198. Michigan State Univ., East Lansing, Michigan.

PART VI

Decision Procedures

Optimal Allocation of Observations when Comparing Several Treatments with a Control[1]

ROBERT E. BECHHOFER

DEPARTMENT OF OPERATIONS RESEARCH
CORNELL UNIVERSITY
ITHACA, NEW YORK

1. INTRODUCTION AND SUMMARY

Let $\Pi_0, \Pi_1, \ldots, \Pi_p$ be $p+1$ normal populations with unknown population means $\mu_0, \mu_1, \ldots, \mu_p$ and population variances $\sigma_0^2, \sigma_1^2, \ldots, \sigma_p^2$. We define $\theta_i = \sigma_i^2/\sigma_0^2$ $(1 \leqq i \leqq p)$, and assume that the θ_i are known. We shall refer to Π_0 as the "control" population and Π_i $(1 \leqq i \leqq p)$ as the ith "test" population. Based on N_i independent observations X_{ij} $(j = 1, 2, \ldots, N_i)$ from Π_i $(i = 0, 1, \ldots, p)$, where $N = \sum_{i=0}^{p} N_i$ is specified prior to experimentation, it is desired to make an exact joint confidence statement concerning the p differences $\mu_i - \mu_0$ $(1 \leqq i \leqq p)$.

A correct solution to this problem was first given by Dunnett [1] who considered the special case $\sigma_i^2 = \sigma^2$ (say) $(0 \leqq i \leqq p)$ where σ^2 may be known or unknown. For the situation in which $N_0 = N_1 = \cdots = N_p$, he provided tables of constants to be used when making one-sided or two-sided comparisons with joint confidence coefficient either 0.95 or 0.99. (The constants for the one-sided comparisons were exact and yielded the specified confidence coefficient, while the corresponding constants for the two-sided comparisons were approximate, and yielded slightly more than the specified confidence coefficient. In a later paper (Dunnett [2]), he provided exact constants which, for the two-sided comparisons, yielded the specified confidence coefficient.)

For the same case $\sigma_i^2 = \sigma^2$ $(0 \leqq i \leqq p)$, Dunnett also raised the question of the optimal (in the sense of maximizing the confidence coefficient for fixed N) allocation of observations between the control and the treatments when

[1] This research was supported by the U.S. Army Research Office-Durham under Contract DA-31-124-ARO-D-474 and the Office of Naval Research under Contract N-onr-401(53). Reproduction in whole or in part is permitted for any purpose of the United States Government.

$N_1 = N_2 = \cdots = N_p$ and one-sided comparisons are to be made. Based on numerical calculations of the effect of different allocations on the confidence coefficient, he concluded that if the experimenter is working with a joint confidence coefficient in the neighborhood of 0.95 or greater, and if $N_1 = N_2 = \cdots = N_p$, then the experiment should be designed so that $N_0 = N_1\sqrt{p}$. (This result had been recommended earlier. See, for example, Fieller [3] and Finney [4], p. 319.)

The purpose of the present paper is to consider the general case in which the σ_i^2 $(0 \leqq i \leqq p)$ are known, and one-sided comparisons are to be made. We investigate the question of the optimal allocation of observations, and give an exact formula for choosing the N_i $(0 \leqq i \leqq p)$ as a function of (i) the number of "test" populations p, (ii) the known values of the σ_i^2 $(0 \leqq i \leqq p)$, (iii) the total sample size $N = \sum_{i=0}^{p} N_i$ available for experimentation, and (iv) a specified "yardstick" d associated with the width of the confidence intervals. It is shown, as a corollary of our general result (see Theorem 1 and Corollary 2 of Section 5), that if $\sigma_0^2 = \sigma_1^2 = \cdots = \sigma_p^2$, then in the limit (as N and/or $d \to \infty$) we should choose $N_1 = N_2 = \cdots = N_p$ and $N_0 = N_1\sqrt{p}$.

2. STATEMENT OF THE PROBLEM

As above, we consider N_i independent observations X_{ij} $(j = 1, 2, \ldots, N_i)$ from Π_i $(i = 0, 1, \ldots, p)$, and let $\bar{X}_i = \sum_{j=1}^{N_i} X_{ij}/N_i$ $(0 \leqq i \leqq p)$. We assume that the σ_i^2 $(i = 0, 1, \ldots, p)$ are given, and that (initially) the N_i $(i = 0, 1, \ldots, p)$ are fixed. We let $N = \sum_{i=0}^{p} N_i$, and write

$$\theta_i = \sigma_i^2/\sigma_0^2 \qquad (1 \leqq i \leqq p), \qquad \gamma_i = N_i/N \qquad (0 \leqq i \leqq p). \tag{1}$$

For $1 \leqq i \leqq p$, we define

$$Z_i = [(\bar{X}_0 - \bar{X}_i) - (\mu_0 - \mu_i)]\left(\frac{\sigma_0^2}{N_0} + \frac{\sigma_i^2}{N_i}\right)^{-1/2}, \tag{2}$$

and consider

$$P\{Z_i < d'_{\alpha,p} \quad (i = 1, 2, \ldots, p)\} = 1 - \alpha \tag{3}$$

which is a function of $d'_{\alpha,p}$ alone. We note that the Z_i have a p-variate normal distribution with $E\{Z_i\} = 0$, $\mathrm{Var}\{Z_i\} = 1$, and for $i \neq j$

$$\mathrm{Corr}\{Z_i, Z_j\} = \rho_{ij} = [(1 + \theta_i\gamma_0/\gamma_i)(1 + \theta_j\gamma_0/\gamma_j)]^{-1/2}. \tag{4}$$

Assuming that $d'_{\alpha,p}$ has been calculated, Eqs. (2) and (3) permit one to make joint lower (or equivalently upper) confidence interval estimates, with confidence coefficient $1 - \alpha$, of the p differences $\mu_0 - \mu_i$ since

$$P\left\{\bar{X}_0 - \bar{X}_i - d'_{\alpha,p}\left(\frac{\sigma_0^2}{N_0} + \frac{\sigma_i^2}{N_i}\right)^{1/2} < \mu_0 - \mu_i \quad (i = 1, 2, \ldots, p)\right\} = 1 - \alpha. \tag{5}$$

Suppose now that for ($1 \leqq i \leqq p$) we set

$$d'_{\alpha,p}\left(\frac{\sigma_0^2}{N_0} + \frac{\sigma_i^2}{N_i}\right)^{1/2} = d, \tag{6}$$

where we regard d as a specified "yardstick." Next, we define

$$\lambda = d\sqrt{N}/\sigma_0, \tag{7}$$

and then (3) can be written as

$$P\left\{Z_i < \lambda\left(\frac{1}{\gamma_0} + \frac{\theta_i}{\gamma_i}\right)^{-1/2} \quad (i = 1, 2, \ldots, p)\right\} \tag{8}$$

where λ is a pure number, the θ_i are the known variance ratios, and γ_i ($0 \leqq i \leqq p$) is the proportion of the total number of observations taken from Π_i.

For fixed p, λ, and values of the θ_i ($1 \leqq i \leqq p$), we wish to choose the γ_i $\left(\sum_{i=0}^{p} \gamma_i = 1\right)$ so as to maximize (8); we call this choice of the γ_i the *optimal allocation* and denote it by $\hat{\gamma} = (\hat{\gamma}_0, \hat{\gamma}_1, \ldots, \hat{\gamma}_p)$. The main purpose of the present paper is to derive an explicit formula for determining $\hat{\gamma}$, and to study the behavior of $\hat{\gamma}$ as a function of λ. In Section 8, we show how this information would be used by a practitioner when designing his experiment.

Remark 1. One could consider a more general formulation of the problem which would involve replacing $d'_{\alpha,p}$ in (6) by $d'^{(i)}_{\alpha,p}$ ($1 \leqq i \leqq p$), and optimizing simultaneously with respect to the $d'^{(i)}_{\alpha,p}$ and the γ_i. An exact solution for this general formulation would be quite difficult to obtain. It can be shown that the exact solution for the general formulation coincides with the exact solution for the restricted formulation only if $\theta_i = \theta$ ($1 \leqq i \leqq p$). Thus the results that we obtain in this paper are optimal for the restricted formulation (6), but are not globally optimal for the more general formulation unless the $\theta_i = \theta$ condition holds.

3. AN ALTERNATIVE EXPRESSION FOR THE PROBABILITY

In our derivation it will be convenient to work with an alternative expression for (8). In terms of the symbols already defined, (5) can be rewritten as

$$P\left\{\frac{N_0^{1/2}(\bar{X}_0 - \mu_0)}{\sigma_0}\left(\frac{N_i}{N_0}\frac{\sigma_0^2}{\sigma_i^2}\right)^{1/2} - \frac{d\sqrt{N}}{\sigma_0}\left(\frac{N_i}{N}\frac{\sigma_0^2}{\sigma_i^2}\right)^{1/2}\right.$$
$$\left.< \frac{N_i^{1/2}(\bar{X}_i - \mu_i)}{\sigma_i} \quad (i = 1, 2, \ldots, p)\right\}$$
$$= P\left\{\left(\frac{Y_0}{\gamma_0^{1/2}} - \lambda\right)\left(\frac{\gamma_i}{\theta_i}\right)^{1/2} < Y_i \quad (i = 1, 2, \ldots, p)\right\}$$
$$= \int_{-\infty}^{\infty} \prod_{i=1}^{p} \left\{1 - F\left[\left(\frac{x}{\gamma_0^{1/2}} - \lambda\right)\left(\frac{\gamma_i}{\theta_i}\right)^{1/2}\right]\right\} f(x)\, dx \tag{9}$$

where $F(\cdot)$ is the standard normal distribution function, and $f(\cdot)$ is the corresponding density function. Because of (6), we are requiring that

$$\frac{\gamma_1}{\theta_1} = \frac{\gamma_2}{\theta_2} = \cdots = \frac{\gamma_p}{\theta_p} = \frac{1 - \gamma_0}{\sum_{i=1}^{p} \theta_i}. \tag{10}$$

Using (10), we see that (9) reduces to

$$g(\gamma) = \int_{-\infty}^{\infty} F^p\left[\left(\frac{x}{\sqrt{\gamma}} + \lambda\right)\left(\frac{1-\gamma}{\beta}\right)^{1/2}\right] f(x)\, dx \tag{11}$$

where for simplicity of notation, we have written $\gamma = \gamma_0$ and $\beta = \sum_{i=1}^{p} \theta_i$. We note (by writing $g(\gamma) = \int_{-\infty}^{0} + \int_0^{\infty}$) that $\lim_{\gamma\to 0} g(\gamma) = \frac{1}{2}$, and $\lim_{\gamma\to 1} g(\gamma) = (\frac{1}{2})^p$.

4. EVALUATION AND STUDY OF THE DERIVATIVE $g'(\gamma)$

Direct calculation yields

$$g'(\gamma) = \int_{-\infty}^{\infty} pF^{p-1}\left[\left(\frac{x}{\sqrt{\gamma}} + \lambda\right)\left(\frac{1-\gamma}{\beta}\right)^{1/2}\right] f\left[\left(\frac{x}{\sqrt{\gamma}} + \lambda\right)\left(\frac{1-\gamma}{\beta}\right)^{1/2}\right]$$
$$\cdot \frac{-1}{2[\beta(1-\gamma)]^{1/2}}\left[\frac{x}{\gamma^{3/2}} + \lambda\right] f(x)\, dx. \tag{12}$$

Making the change of variables $y = (\lambda + x/\sqrt{\gamma})((1-\gamma)/\beta)^{1/2}$, we see that (12) can be expressed as

$$g'(\gamma) = \frac{-p}{2(1-\gamma)^{3/2}}\left(\frac{\beta}{\gamma}\right)^{1/2} A + \frac{p\lambda}{2\gamma^{1/2}} B \tag{13}$$

where

$$A = \int_{-\infty}^{\infty} yF^{p-1}(y) f(y) f^*(y)\, dy, \tag{14}$$

$$B = \int_{-\infty}^{\infty} F^{p-1}(y) f(y) f^*(y)\, dy, \tag{15}$$

and $f^*(y)$ denotes $f\{\sqrt{\gamma}[y(\beta/(1-\gamma))^{1/2}-\lambda]\}$.

We now evaluate A and B. Integrating by parts in A with $U = f^*(y)F^{p-1}(y)$, $dV = yf(y)\,dy$, we find that

$$A = -\frac{\beta\gamma}{1-\gamma}A + \gamma\left(\frac{\beta}{1-\gamma}\right)^{1/2}\lambda B + (p-1)C \tag{16}$$

where

$$C = \int_{-\infty}^{\infty} F^{p-2}(y)f^2(y)f^*(y)\,dy. \tag{17}$$

Thus,

$$A = \frac{\gamma[\beta(1-\gamma)]^{1/2}\lambda}{1-\gamma+\gamma\beta}B + \frac{(p-1)(1-\gamma)}{1-\gamma+\gamma\beta}C, \tag{18}$$

and it remains to evaluate (15) and (17). Direct calculation followed by a change of variables yield

$$B = \left(\frac{1-\gamma}{1-\gamma+\gamma\beta}\right)^{1/2} f\left[\lambda\left(\frac{\gamma(1-\gamma)}{1-\gamma+\gamma\beta}\right)^{1/2}\right]\cdot D \tag{19}$$

$$C = \left(\frac{1-\gamma}{2(1-\gamma)+\gamma\beta}\right)^{1/2}(2\pi)^{-1/2} f\left[\lambda\left(\frac{2\gamma(1-\gamma)}{2(1-\gamma)+\gamma\beta}\right)^{1/2}\right]\cdot E \tag{20}$$

where

$$D = \int_{-\infty}^{\infty} f(z)F^{p-1}\left[\left(\frac{1-\gamma}{1-\gamma+\gamma\beta}\right)^{1/2} z + \frac{\gamma(\beta(1-\gamma))^{1/2}}{1-\gamma+\gamma\beta}\lambda\right]dz$$

$$= P\left\{\frac{Y_i - \left(\dfrac{1-\gamma}{1-\gamma+\gamma\beta}\right)^{1/2} Y_0}{\left(1+\dfrac{1-\gamma}{1-\gamma+\gamma\beta}\right)^{1/2}} < \frac{\lambda\gamma(\beta(1-\gamma))^{1/2}}{([1-\gamma+\gamma\beta][2(1-\gamma)+\gamma\beta])^{1/2}} \quad (i = 1, 2, \ldots, p-1)\right\}$$

$$= F_{p-1}\left\{\tau \,\middle|\, \frac{1-\gamma}{2(1-\gamma)+\gamma\beta}\right\}, \tag{21}$$

and

$$E = \int_{-\infty}^{\infty} f(z)F^{p-2}\left[\left(\frac{1-\gamma}{2(1-\gamma)+\gamma\beta}\right)^{1/2} z + \frac{\gamma(\beta(1-\gamma))^{1/2}}{2(1-\gamma)+\gamma\beta}\lambda\right]dz$$

$$= F_{p-2}\left\{\tau\left(\frac{1-\gamma+\gamma\beta}{3(1-\gamma)+\gamma\beta}\right)^{1/2} \,\middle|\, \frac{1-\gamma}{3(1-\gamma)+\gamma\beta}\right\}; \tag{22}$$

here $F_n(x \mid \rho)$ is the equicoordinate n-variate standard normal distribution function with $\rho_{ij} = \rho$ ($i \neq j$; $i, j = 1, 2, \ldots, n$), and

$$\tau = \lambda\gamma\left(\frac{\beta(1-\gamma)}{[1-\gamma+\gamma\beta][2(1-\gamma)+\gamma\beta]}\right)^{1/2}. \tag{23}$$

Combining (13) and (18)–(20), we have

$$g'(\gamma) = \frac{ph(\gamma, \lambda)}{2(1-\gamma+\gamma\beta)[\gamma(1-\gamma)]^{1/2}} f\left[\tau\left(\frac{2(1-\gamma)+\gamma\beta}{\gamma\beta}\right)^{1/2}\right] \tag{24}$$

where

$$h(\gamma, \lambda) = \frac{t(\gamma)\lambda D}{(1-\gamma+\gamma\beta)^{1/2}} - \frac{(p-1)f(\tau)[\beta(1-\gamma)]^{1/2}E}{(2(1-\gamma)+\gamma\beta)^{1/2}} \tag{25}$$

and

$$t(\gamma) = (1-\beta)\gamma^2 - 2\gamma + 1. \tag{26}$$

The sign of $g'(\gamma)$ depends on $h(\gamma, \lambda)$. Note that

$$\lim_{\gamma \to 0} h(\gamma, \lambda) \begin{Bmatrix} > \\ = \\ < \end{Bmatrix} 0 \qquad \text{for} \quad \lambda \begin{Bmatrix} > \\ = \\ < \end{Bmatrix} \lambda_p^*(\beta) \tag{27}$$

where

$$\lambda_p^*(\beta) = \tfrac{1}{2}[p(p-1)](\beta/\pi)^{1/2} F_{p-2}(0 \mid 1/3), \tag{28}$$

since $F_{p-1}(0 \mid 1/2) = p^{-1}$. Also,

$$\lim_{\gamma \to 1} h(\gamma, \lambda) < 0 \qquad \text{for} \quad \lambda > 0. \tag{29}$$

Remark 2. It is known (see e.g., Gupta [5], Section 6) that $F_0(0 \mid 1/3) = 1$, $F_1(0 \mid 1/3) = 1/2$, $F_2(0 \mid 1/3) = (1/4) + (1/2\pi) \arcsin(1/3)$, and $F_3(0 \mid 1/3) = (1/8) + (3/4\pi) \arcsin(1/3)$; $F_n(0 \mid 1/3)$ has been computed for $n = 1(1)12$, and is given by Gupta ([5], Table II, p. 817).

For $\lambda > \lambda_p^*(\beta)$, we wish to determine the maximum of $g(\gamma)$ for $0 < \gamma < 1$ by setting $g'(\gamma) = 0$. For fixed $p \geqq 2$, $\beta > 0$, $\tau > 0$, the equation $g'(\gamma) = 0$ will have a root $\hat{\gamma}$ only if $t(\hat{\gamma}) > 0$; from (24) it follows that there exists a unique root $\hat{\gamma}$ with $0 < \hat{\gamma} < (1 + \sqrt{\beta})^{-1}$. As $\lambda \to \lambda_p^*(\beta)$, we have $\hat{\gamma} \to 0$ ($\hat{\gamma} = 0$ for $0 < \lambda \leqq \lambda_p^*(\beta)$), while as $\lambda \to \infty$, we have $\hat{\gamma} \to (1 + \sqrt{\beta})^{-1}$. For $p = 1$ the unique root is $\hat{\gamma} = (1 + \sqrt{\beta})^{-1}$ for all $\lambda > 0$.

5. SUMMARY OF RESULTS, AND FUNDAMENTAL THEOREM

We now summarize the behavior of $g(\gamma)$ for $0 < \gamma < 1$ and fixed λ ($0 < \lambda < \infty$), $p \geqq 2$, and $\beta > 0$.

(a) For all λ, the function g is continuous in γ with $\lim_{\gamma \to 0} g(\gamma) = 1/2$ and $\lim_{\gamma \to 1} g(\gamma) = 1/2^p$.

(b) For $0 < \lambda < \lambda_p^*(\beta)$, g is strictly decreasing in γ for $0 < \gamma < 1$.

(c) For $\lambda = \lambda_p^*(\beta)$, g has a maximum at $\gamma = \hat{\gamma} = 0$ where $g'(0) = 0$; g is strictly decreasing in γ for $0 < \gamma < 1$.

(d) For $\lambda_p^*(\beta) < \lambda < \infty$, g has a maximum at $\hat{\gamma} > 0$ where $g'(\hat{\gamma}) = 0$; g is strictly increasing in γ for $0 < \gamma < \hat{\gamma}$, and strictly decreasing in γ for $\hat{\gamma} < \gamma < 1$.

(e) For $0 < \lambda < \lambda_p^*(\beta)$, we have $\hat{\gamma} = 0$ and $g(\hat{\gamma}) = 1/2$.

(f) For $\lambda_p^*(\beta) \leqq \lambda < \infty$, $\hat{\gamma}$ is strictly increasing in λ. When $\lambda = \lambda_p^*(\beta)$, we have $\hat{\gamma} = 0$, while as $\lambda \to \infty$, we have $\hat{\gamma} \to (1 + \sqrt{\beta})^{-1}$.

(g) For $\lambda_p^*(\beta) \leqq \lambda < \infty$, $g(\gamma)$ is strictly increasing in λ. When $\lambda = \lambda_p^*(\beta)$, we have $g(\hat{\gamma}) = 1/2$, while as $\lambda \to \infty$ we have $g(\hat{\gamma}) \to 1$.

The function $g(\gamma_0)$ is graphed versus γ_0 for selected λ in Fig. 1. Our basic results concerning optimal allocation are summarized in Theorem 1.

Theorem 1. *For fixed* λ $(0 < \lambda \leqq \lambda_p^*(\beta))$, *the optimal allocation on the "control" is* $\hat{\gamma}_0 = 0$, *while for fixed* λ $(\lambda_p^*(\beta) < \lambda < \infty)$, *the optimal allocation on the "control" is the unique root* $\hat{\gamma}_0$ $(0 < \hat{\gamma}_0 < 1/(1 + \sqrt{\beta}))$ *of the equation*

$$[(1-\beta)\gamma^2 - 2\gamma + 1]\tau F_{p-1}\left\{\tau \,\middle|\, \frac{1-\gamma}{2(1-\gamma)+\gamma\beta}\right\}$$

$$- \frac{(p-1)\gamma(1-\gamma)\beta}{2(1-\gamma)+\gamma\beta} f(\tau) F_{p-2}\left\{\tau\left(\frac{1-\gamma+\gamma\beta}{3(1-\gamma)+\gamma\beta}\right)^{1/2} \,\middle|\, \frac{1-\gamma}{3(1-\gamma)+\gamma\beta}\right\} = 0, \tag{30}$$

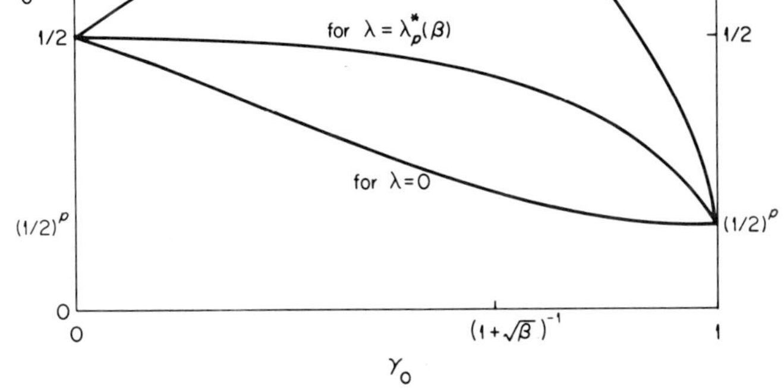

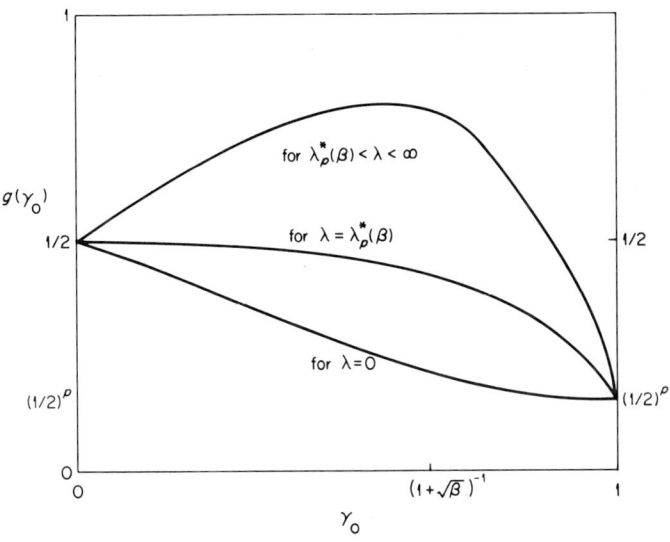

Fig. 1. Graph of $g(\gamma_0)$ versus γ_0 for selected λ.

where τ is defined by (23). *For fixed* λ $(0 < \lambda < \infty)$, *the optimal allocation on the ith "test"* $(1 \leqq i \leqq p)$ *is*

$$\hat{\gamma}_i = \theta_i(1 - \hat{\gamma}_0)/\beta. \tag{31}$$

In the above, $\hat{\gamma} = (\hat{\gamma}_0, \hat{\gamma}_1, \ldots, \hat{\gamma}_p)$ *is a function of* $p \geqq 2$ *and* $\beta = \sum_{i=1}^{p} \theta_i = \sum_{i=1}^{p} \sigma_i^2/\sigma_0^2 > 0$ (*as well, of course, as* λ).

Corollary 1. *For the setup of Theorem* 1, *we have in the limit* (*as* $\lambda \to \infty$) *that*

$$\hat{\gamma}_0 = (1 + \sqrt{\beta})^{-1}, \qquad \hat{\gamma}_i = \theta_i/\sqrt{\beta}(1 + \sqrt{\beta}) \qquad (1 \leqq i \leqq p). \tag{32}$$

Corollary 2. *For the setup of Theorem* 1, *we have in the limit* (*as* $\lambda \to \infty$) *that*

$$\frac{\text{proportion on the "control"}}{\text{proportion on the } i\text{th "test"}} = \frac{\sqrt{\beta}}{\theta_i} \qquad (1 \leqq i \leqq p); \tag{33}$$

if $\theta_i = 1$ $(1 \leqq i \leqq p)$, *i.e., if* $\sigma_0^2 = \sigma_1^2 = \cdots = \sigma_p^2$, *then the right-hand side of* (33) *reduces to* $\sqrt{p}$.

Remark 3. The $\theta_i = 1$ $(1 \leqq i \leqq p)$ case of Corollary 2 leads to the recommendation of Dunnett ([1], p. 1107).

Remark 4. The result of Corollary 1 can be obtained directly in a very simple way if one notes that for $\lambda \to \infty$ the probability (8) does not depend, to the first order, on the ρ_{ij} (4). Thus, maximizing (8) is equivalent to minimizing $1/\gamma_0 + \theta_i/\gamma_i$, which is to be done subject to (10) and $\sum_{i=0}^{p} \gamma_i = 1$.[2]

Remark 5. For $p = 1$ the probability (8) is maximized by the well-known optimal allocation $\hat{\gamma}_0 = \hat{\gamma}_1/\sqrt{\theta_1}$ which holds *uniformly* in λ $(0 < \lambda < \infty)$.

6. BARYCENTRIC REPRESENTATION OF THE OPTIMAL ALLOCATION

For $p = 2$, we can represent the allocation $\gamma = (\gamma_0, \gamma_1, \gamma_2)$ conveniently in barycentric coordinates. Referring to Fig. 2, we see that any point in the interior of or on the perimeter of the triangle ABC represents a possible allocation. As a consequence of (10), we limit consideration to allocations which

[2] Mantel [6] obtained the result (32) from a conjecture that it should follow from the approach of this last sentence. Mantel's formulation was that of determining the allocation for which all treatment-control comparisons would have equal variance, with this common variance at a minimum.

lie along the line segment DA. The optimal allocations occur along the line segment DF. The point D is associated with the allocation which is optimal for $(0 < \lambda \leqq \lambda_p^*(\beta))$, while the point F is associated with the limiting optimal allocation for $\lambda \to \infty$. The $\hat{\gamma}_0$-coordinate of the optimal allocation $\hat{\gamma}$ is the solution of (30), while $\hat{\gamma}_i = \theta_i(1 - \hat{\gamma}_0)/(\theta_1 + \theta_2)$ for $i = 1, 2$. The $\hat{\gamma}_0$-coordinate of $\hat{\gamma}$ is strictly increasing in λ for $\lambda_p^*(\beta) \leqq \lambda < \infty$.

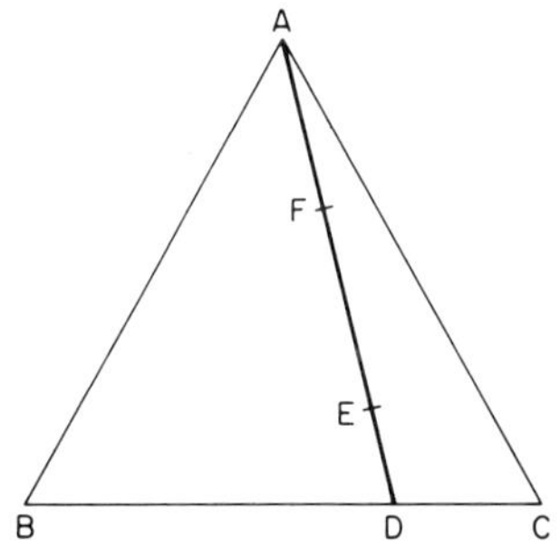

Fig. 2. Optimal allocation in barycentric coordinates for $p = 2$.

Coordinates of points $\gamma = (\gamma_0, \gamma_1, \gamma_2)$
$A = (1, 0, 0)$;
$B = (0, 1, 0)$;
$C = (0, 0, 1)$;
$D = (\theta_1 + \theta_2)^{-1}(0, \theta_1, \theta_2)$;
$E = (\hat{\gamma}_0, \hat{\gamma}_1, \hat{\gamma}_2)$;
$$F = \frac{((\theta_1 + \theta_2)^{1/2}, \theta_1, \theta_2)}{((\theta_1 + \theta_2)^{1/2} + \theta_1 + \theta_2)}.$$

7. COMPUTATION OF THE OPTIMAL ALLOCATION

From Theorem 1, it is clear that the optimal allocation $\hat{\gamma} = (\hat{\gamma}_0, \hat{\gamma}_1, \ldots, \hat{\gamma}_p)$ can be computed by tabling $\hat{\gamma}_0$ as a function of λ for fixed p and β. Such computations would depend on extended versions of tables such as those by Gupta [5] and Milton [7] which deal with equicoordinate percentage points and equal correlations ρ_{ij} for $i \neq j$, both of which are required for our problem. We plan to supply such tables in a later paper.

For $p = 2$, Eq. (30) simplifies considerably, and we obtain

$$\{(1 - \beta)\gamma^2 - 2\gamma + 1\}\tau F(\tau) - \frac{\gamma(1 - \gamma)\beta}{2(1 - \gamma) + \gamma\beta} f(\tau) = 0 \tag{34}$$

which involves only the univariate $F(\cdot)$ and $f(\cdot)$. We have computed the solution to (34) for $\beta = 2$ (i.e., for $({\sigma_1}^2 + {\sigma_2}^2)/{\sigma_0}^2 = 2$ which holds, in particular, when ${\sigma_0}^2 = {\sigma_1}^2 = {\sigma_2}^2$) and selected values of λ, in order to indicate the optimal allocations, and the associated maximum probabilities for various choices of λ. An abbreviated table of these results is given in Table I. The entries for $\hat{\gamma}_0$ are correct to five significant figures while those for $\hat{P}$ are correct to within ± 2 in the fifth decimal place.

TABLE I

Optimal Allocation on the Control ($\hat{\gamma}_0$), and Associated Maximum Probability ($\hat{P}$) for Selected λ when $p = 2$ and $\beta = 2$

λ	$\hat{\gamma}_0$	$\hat{P}$	λ	$\hat{\gamma}_0$	$\hat{P}$
0	0	0.5	3.50	0.38330	0.87084
			3.75	0.38786	0.89295
⋮	⋮	⋮	4.00	0.39172	0.91217
			4.25	0.39496	0.92867
$(2/\pi)^{1/2}$	0	0.5	4.50	0.39772	0.94266
1.00	0.13150	0.51959	4.75	0.40010	0.95438
1.25	0.21690	0.55598	5.00	0.40212	0.96404
1.50	0.26694	0.59647	5.25	0.40386	0.97200
1.75	0.29970	0.63728	5.50	0.40534	0.97840
2.00	0.32276	0.67799	5.75	0.40664	0.98352
2.25	0.33976	0.71611	6.00	0.40774	0.98755
2.50	0.35276	0.75259	6.50	0.40952	0.99311
2.75	0.36296	0.78651	7.00	0.41084	0.99631
3.00	0.37114	0.81762	7.50	0.41180	0.99813
3.25	0.37880	0.84575	8.00	0.41252	0.99909
			9.00	0.41340	0.99980
			10.00	0.41384	0.99997
			∞	$(1+\sqrt{2})^{-1}$	1

8. USE OF THE TABLES

Tables of $\hat{\gamma}_0$ and the associated $\hat{P}$ as a function of λ for fixed p and β would be used as follows by a practitioner when he is designing his experiment: p and the σ_i^2 $(0 \leqq i \leqq p)$ are given as data of the problem; these determine the θ_i $(1 \leqq i \leqq p)$ and hence β. The experimenter *specifies* d (his "yardstick") and N, the total number of observations available for experimentation, which together determine $\lambda = \sqrt{N}\, d/\sigma_0$. Then p, β and λ determine $\hat{\gamma}_0$ (and hence $\hat{\gamma}$) and the associated $\hat{P}$. If $\hat{P}$ is too low (high) for the experimenter's requirements, he can increase (decrease) $\hat{P}$ by increasing (decreasing) N and/or by increasing (decreasing) d.

Remark 6. In practice, one would never choose $\hat{\gamma}_0 = 0$ (the optimal allocation of Theorem 1 for $0 < \lambda \leqq \lambda_p^*(\beta)$), but rather, one would approximate this allocation by (say) $\hat{\gamma}_0 = N^{-1}$. And since the N_i $(0 \leqq i \leqq p)$ are integers, the $\hat{\gamma}_i$ $(0 \leqq i \leqq p)$ must also be approximated. For large N, these approximations should be quite close.

9. GENERALIZATIONS

It would be desirable to obtain results analogous to those given in the present paper for the problem of two-sided comparisons, i.e., optimal allocation for the problem described by Dunnett [2]. It would also be interesting to study in detail the more general formulation described in Remark 1. It is planned to carry out such studies in a later paper.

ACKNOWLEDGMENTS

The writer is indebted to Dr. Milton Sobel who called his attention to the relation between certain multivariate normal integrals. He also wishes to acknowledge the helpful discussions with Messrs. Vijay Bawa and Vijay Marathe who also assisted in checking certain of the calculations. Mr. Bawa and Mr. Dominique Nocturne computed the entries in Table I.

REFERENCES

1. DUNNETT, C. W. (1955). A multiple comparison procedure for comparing several treatments with a control. *J. Amer. Statist. Assoc.* **50** 1096–1121.
2. DUNNETT, C. W. (1964). New tables for multiple comparisons with a control. *Biometrics* **20** 482–491.
3. FIELLER, E. C. (1947). Some remarks on the statistical background in bio-assay. *Analyst* **72** 37–43.
4. FINNEY, D. J. (1952). "Statistical Methods in Biological Assay." Hafner Publ., New York.
5. GUPTA, S. S. (1963). Probability integrals of multivariate normal and multivariate *t*. *Ann. Math. Statist.* **34** 792–828.
6. MANTEL, N. (1968). Personal communication.
7. MILTON, R. C. (1963). Tables of the equally correlated multivariate normal probability integral. Tech. Rept. No. 27. Dept. of Statist., Univ. of Minnesota, Minneapolis, Minnesota.

Some Selection and Ranking Procedures for Multivariate Normal Populations[1]

SHANTI S. GUPTA and S. PANCHAPAKESAN

DEPARTMENT OF STATISTICS
PURDUE UNIVERSITY
LAFAYETTE, INDIANA

1. INTRODUCTION AND SUMMARY

This paper deals with several problems of selection and ranking for multivariate normal populations. Certain associated selection procedures for the univariate populations are also studied. Most of the work on selection and ranking has been concerned with the parameters of the univariate populations; recently there has been some work on selection procedures for restricted families of probability distributions [3, 4]. During the last few years, some papers have been written about the selection and ranking procedures for the multivariate normal populations. These papers have been concerned with the selection of multivariate normal populations in terms of (i) the distance functions $\boldsymbol{\mu}_i'\Sigma_i^{-1}\boldsymbol{\mu}_i'$ [1, 15, 19] where the π_i, the ith population, is $N_p(\boldsymbol{\mu}_i, \Sigma_i)$; (ii) the linear combinations of components of the mean vector and elements of the covariance matrix [22, 24]; and (iii) the generalized variance [8, 9]. Some other problems such as selection with respect to the means from the correlated normal populations have been investigated by Gnanadesikan [8]. The problem of selection in terms of the cell probabilities in a multinomial population has been investigated by Bechhofer *et al.* [6], Cacoullos and Sobel [7], and Gupta and Nagel [16]. In many of the multivariate problems of selection and ranking, certain probability integrals arise; these and other related topics are discussed by Gupta [11, 12].

Generally, problems of selection and ranking have been formulated in the following two types: (i) selecting a fixed number t of "best" populations using an indifference zone approach [5]; (ii) selecting a subset of random

[1]This research was supported in part by the Aerospace Research Laboratories Contract AF33(615)67C1244. Reproduction in whole or in part is permitted for any purposes of the United States Government.

size from k populations such that the selected subset includes the "best" population with a specified probability $P^*(k^{-1} < P^* < 1)$ [10, 14]. It is this latter subset selection formulation that we are concerned with throughout the present paper. The general nature of the investigations on subset-selection problems is to assume k populations with distribution functions $F(x; \boldsymbol{\theta}_i)$, $i = 1, 2, \ldots, k$ where $\boldsymbol{\theta}_i$ is a vector of population parameters. The selection is based on a well-defined scalar function $\psi_i = \psi(\boldsymbol{\theta}_i)$, $i = 1, 2, \ldots, k$. Each $\boldsymbol{\theta}_i$ may be completely unknown or partly unknown; the functional form $\psi(\boldsymbol{\theta}_i)$ is known. The ordered ψ_i are denoted by $\psi_{[1]} \leq \psi_{[2]} \leq \cdots \leq \psi_{[k]}$. Of course, the correct pairing of the unordered and ordered ψ's is not known. For a specified probability $P^*(k^{-1} < P^* < 1)$, we wish to define a selection Procedure R such that $P\{\text{CS} \mid R\} \geq P^*$ for all possible configurations of $\boldsymbol{\theta}_1, \boldsymbol{\theta}_2, \ldots, \boldsymbol{\theta}_k$ where CS stands for a correct selection which means selection of any subset containing the population associated with $\psi_{[k]}(\psi_{[1]})$. Thus, mathematically, we are interested in defining a selection rule R such that

$$\inf_{\Omega} P\{\text{CS} \mid R\} = P^* \tag{1.1}$$

where Ω is the space of the vectors $\boldsymbol{\theta}_1, \boldsymbol{\theta}_2, \ldots, \boldsymbol{\theta}_k$. After proposing the procedure, more or less heuristically, one is interested in studying its efficiency in terms of the expected size of the subset and other related criteria.

Section 2 of this paper deals with the selection problem for the largest and smallest multiple correlation coefficient in k p-variate normal populations. The multiple correlation coefficient is a measure of the dependence of one variable on the remaining ones and is used in studies connected with behavioral sciences. The contents of Section 2 form a substantial part of the paper. In this section selection procedures are considered for the conditional as well as the unconditional case. Exact, as well as asymptotic theory results are given. Section 3 deals with k p-variate normal populations in which the interest is in selection in terms of $|\Sigma|/|\Sigma_{11}| = |\Sigma_{22} - \Sigma_{21}\Sigma_{11}^{-1}\Sigma_{12}|$ where Σ_{11}, Σ_{12}, and Σ_{22} are the covariance matrices corresponding to a partition of the p variables into two sets of q_1 and q_2 variables, $q_1 + q_2 = p$. Then the criterion represents the conditional generalized variance of the q_2 set when the q_1 set is held fixed (see Anderson [2], Rao [27]). Section 4 deals with the description of two tables. Table I at the end of the paper gives the values of c_1 and d_1 $(0 < c_1, d_1 < 1)$ such that $P\{F_i \geq c_1 F_{\max}\} = P^*$ and $P\{d_1 F_i \leq F_{\min}\} = P^*$ where $F_{\max}(F_{\min})$ is the largest (smallest) of k central independent and identical F variables, $F_1, F_2, \ldots, F_k$. Table II deals, similarly, with the distribution of $R_i^2/R_{\max}^2$ and $R_i^2/R_{\min}^2$ where $R_1, R_2, \ldots, R_k$ are sample multiple correlation coefficients which are independent and identically distributed with the population multiple correlation coefficient $\rho = 0$. Both these tables are relevant for the various selection and ranking procedures proposed in this paper. But they are of wider applicability such as in hypothesis testing since they both give the distribution under the null case.

2. SELECTION WITH RESPECT TO MULTIPLE CORRELATION COEFFICIENT

Let $\mathbf{X}_i' = (X_{i1}, X_{i2}, \ldots, X_{ip})$, $i = 1, 2, \ldots, k$ be random vectors with p-variate normal distributions with unknown mean vectors $\boldsymbol{\mu}_i$ and unknown positive definite covariance matrices Σ_i. The multiple correlation coefficient between, say, X_{i1} and $X_{i2}, \ldots, X_{ip}$ denoted by $\rho_{1\cdot 2\ldots p}^{(i)} \equiv \rho_i$, is defined by

$$1 - \rho_i^2 = \frac{|\Sigma_i|}{\sigma_{i11}\,|\Sigma_{i(11)}|},$$

where σ_{i11} is the leading element of Σ_i and $\Sigma_{i(11)}$ is the matrix obtained from Σ_i by deleting the first row and first column. This ρ_i (taken to be the positive square root of ρ_i^2) is the maximum of the correlation between X_{i1} and a linear combination of $X_{i2}, \ldots, X_{ip}$ over all possible linear combinations and as such is a measure of the dependence of X_{i1} on $X_{i2}, \ldots, X_{ip}$. So it is meaningful to rank the k populations on the basis of the values of ρ_i, $i = 1, 2, \ldots, k$. Let $0 \le \rho_{[1]} \le \rho_{[2]} \le \cdots \le \rho_{[k]} < 1$ be the ordered ρ's. We are interested in selecting a nonempty subset of the k populations which will include the population associated with $\rho_{[k]}$ (or $\rho_{[1]}$) with probability which is at least $P^*(k^{-1} < P^* < 1)$.

Now $R_{1\cdot 23\ldots p}^{(i)} \equiv R_i$, the sample multiple correlation coefficient between X_{i1} and $X_{i2}, \ldots, X_{ip}$ is defined analogous to ρ_i by replacing Σ_i by the sample covariance matrix S_i in the definition of ρ_i. Two cases arise: (i) the case in which $X_{i2}, \ldots, X_{ip}$ are fixed, called the conditional case; (ii) the case in which $X_{i2}, \ldots, X_{ip}$ are random, called the unconditional case.

Subset Selection for the Population Associated with $\rho_{[k]}$

(i) **Unconditional Case.** Based on R_i^2 obtained from a sample of size $n > p$ from π_i, the ith population ($i = 1, 2, \ldots, k$), we propose the following procedure

$$\mathscr{R}_1 : \text{Select } \pi_i \text{ iff } R_i^2 \ge c \max_{1 \le j \le k} R_j^2,$$

where $0 < c = c(k, P^*, p, n) < 1$ is chosen so that the probability requirement (1.1) is satisfied.

Let $R_{(i)}^2$ be the sample R^2 from the population associated with $\rho_{[i]}^2$ and CS denote "a correct selection," i.e. selection of the population associated with $\rho_{[k]}$ in the present case. Then, letting $\lambda_i = \rho_i^2$, $i = 1, 2, \ldots, k$,

$$P(\mathrm{CS} \mid \mathscr{R}_1) = P\left(R_{(k)}^2 \geq c \max_{1 \leq j \leq k} R_{(j)}^2 \right)$$
$$= P(R_{(j)}^2 \leq R_{(k)}^2 / c, \quad j = 1, 2, \ldots, k-1)$$
$$= \int_0^1 \prod_{j=1}^{k-1} F_{\lambda_{[j]}}(x/c) \, dF_{\lambda_{[k]}}(x), \tag{2.1}$$

where $F_{\lambda_{[i]}}(x)$ is the cdf of the distribution of $R_{(i)}^2$, $i = 1, 2, \ldots, k$. We know that the density $f_\lambda(x)$ of R^2 is given by

$$f_\lambda(x) = \sum_{j=0}^{\infty} b(x; q+j, m) w(q, m; \lambda, j) \tag{2.2}$$

where

$$q = \tfrac{1}{2}(p-1) \qquad m = \tfrac{1}{2}(n-p)$$

$$b(x; q+j, m) = \frac{\Gamma(q+j+m)}{\Gamma(q+j)\Gamma(m)} x^{q+j-1}(1-x)^{m-1}, \qquad 0 \leq x \leq 1$$
$$w(q, m; \lambda, j) \equiv w(\lambda, j) = \frac{\Gamma(q+m+j)}{\Gamma(q+m)} (1-\lambda)^{q+m} \frac{\lambda^j}{j!}, \qquad 0 \leq \lambda \leq 1 \tag{2.3}$$
$$= \frac{(q+m)}{(q+m+j)(q+m+j+1)} b(\lambda, j+1, q+m+1)$$

Theorem 2.1. *Let Ω represent the space of the parameter vector $\boldsymbol{\rho} = (\rho_1, \rho_2, \ldots, \rho_k)$. Then*

$$\inf_{\Omega} P(\mathrm{CS} \mid \mathscr{R}_1) = \int_0^1 F^{k-1}(x/c) \, dF(x), \tag{2.4}$$

where $F(x) \equiv F_0(x)$ is the cdf of R^2 in the unconditional case in which $\rho^2 = 0$ and the corresponding density is given by

$$f_0(x) = \frac{\Gamma(q+m)}{\Gamma(q)\Gamma(m)} x^{q-1}(1-x)^{m-1}, \qquad 0 \leq x \leq 1, \quad q > 0, \quad m > 0. \tag{2.5}$$

In order to prove Theorem 2.1, we need the following lemmas.

Lemma 2.1. *Let the random variable X have a density function $p_\lambda(x)$ given by*

$$p_\lambda(x) = \sum_{j=0}^{\infty} g_j(x) W(\lambda, j), \qquad \lambda \text{ real} \tag{2.6}$$

where $g_j(x)$ is a sequence of density functions for $j = 0, 1, 2, \ldots,$ and $W(\lambda, j) \geq 0$ for all λ, and j and $\sum_{j=0}^{\infty} W(\lambda, j) = 1$. Let us assume that (i) *$g_j(x)$ is totally positive of order* 2 *(abbreviated* TP_2*), i.e.,*

$$\begin{vmatrix} g_{j_1}(x_1) & g_{j_1}(x_2) \\ g_{j_2}(x_1) & g_{j_2}(x_2) \end{vmatrix} \geq 0 \qquad \textit{for} \quad j_1 < j_2 \quad \textit{and} \quad x_1 < x_2,$$

and (ii) $W(\lambda, j)$ *is* TP_2. *Then* $p_\lambda(x)$ *is also* TP_2.

Proof. The proof follows immediately from the basic composition formula of Pólya and Szegö (see Karlin [21, p. 17]) which in this case is

$$\begin{vmatrix} p_{\lambda_1}(x_1) & p_{\lambda_1}(x_2) \\ p_{\lambda_2}(x_1) & p_{\lambda_2}(x_2) \end{vmatrix} = \sum_{j_1 < j_2} \begin{vmatrix} g_{j_1}(x_1) & g_{j_1}(x_2) \\ g_{j_2}(x_1) & g_{j_2}(x_2) \end{vmatrix} \begin{vmatrix} W(\lambda_1, j_1) & W(\lambda_1, j_2) \\ W(\lambda_2, j_1) & W(\lambda_2, j_2) \end{vmatrix} \tag{2.7}$$

for $x_1 < x_2$ and $\lambda_1 < \lambda_2$.

Remark 1. If the density function $p_\lambda(x)$ of a r.v. X is TP_2, then it has a monotone likelihood ratio (MLR) in x, and consequently the distribution of X is stochastically increasing in λ, i.e., the cdf of X is decreasing in λ.

Remark 2. Lemma 2.1 stated in terms of MLR is a modified form of Theorem 3 by Lehmann [25].

Lemma 2.2. *The density* $f_\lambda(x)$ *given by* (2.2) *has* MLR *in* x, *and the distribution of* R^2 *is stochastically increasing in* λ.

The proof is omitted since it involves only simple and routine verification of the conditions of Lemma 2.1.

Lemma 2.3. *Using our previous notation, let*

$$A(\lambda) = \int_0^1 F_\lambda^{k-1}(x/c) f_\lambda(x)\, dx, \qquad 0 < c < 1.$$

Then, $A(\lambda)$ *is increasing in* λ $(0 \le \lambda < 1)$.

Proof. We need only to show that the condition (2.52) of Theorem 2.5 given toward the end of this section is satisfied for $q_1 = q + m$, and

$$g_j(x) = \begin{cases} b(x; q+j, m), & 0 \le x \le 1 \\ 0, & \text{elsewhere} \end{cases}, \quad j = 0, 1, 2, \ldots .$$

For $x \ge c$, the condition is obviously satisfied. For $x < c$, $G_j(x) = I_x(q+j, m)$, where $I_x(q+j, m)$ is the incomplete beta function defined by

$$I_x(q+j, m) = \int_0^x b(t; q+j, m)\, dt, \qquad 0 \le x \le 1. \tag{2.8}$$

For $x < c$, using the relation

$$\begin{aligned} I_x(p+1, q) - I_x(p, q) &= -\frac{\Gamma(p+q)}{\Gamma(p+1)\Gamma(q)} x^p (1-x)^q \\ &= -\frac{1-x}{p+q} b(x; p+1, q), \end{aligned} \tag{2.9}$$

the left-hand side of the condition (2.52) can be written after some simplifications in the form

$$\sum_{i=0}^{l} \frac{(q_1)_i(q_1)_{l-i}\Gamma(q+i+m)\Gamma(q+l-i+m) \times x^{2q+l-1}(1-x)^{m-1}[1-(x/c)]^{m-1}}{i!\,(l-i)!\{\Gamma(m)\}^2\Gamma(q+i+1)\Gamma(q+l-i+1)c^q} T_i,$$

where

$$T_i = c^{-i}\left[\frac{x(1-c)}{c}(q+i)(q+l-i+m) - m\left(1-\frac{x}{c}\right)(l-2i)\right].$$

For $l > 0$, it can easily be verified that $T_i + T_{l-i} > 0$ for $i = 0, 1, \ldots, [\frac{1}{2}(l-1)]$ where $[a]$ denotes the integral part of a and that $T_{l/2} > 0$ where l is even. The proof is completed by verifying the condition (2.52) directly for $l = 0$. Now we complete the proof of Theorem 2.1.

$$\begin{aligned} P(\text{CS}\,|\,\mathscr{R}_1) &= \int_0^1 \prod_{j=1}^{k-1} F_{\lambda_{[j]}}(x/c)\,dF_{\lambda_{[k]}}(x) \\ &\geq \int_0^1 F_{\lambda_{[k]}}^{k-1}(x/c)\,dF_{\lambda_{[k]}}(x), \qquad \text{by Lemma 2.} \\ &\geq \int_0^1 F^{k-1}(x/c)\,dF(x), \qquad \text{by Lemma 2.3.} \end{aligned} \tag{2.10}$$

This completes the proof of Theorem 2.1.

Corollary 2.1. *The constant c defining the procedure* $\mathscr{R}_1$ *is given by*

$$\int_0^1 F^{k-1}(x/c)\,dF(x) = P^*. \tag{2.11}$$

(ii) **Conditional Case.** In this case, the density of R^2 is given by

$$h_\lambda(x) = \sum_{j=0}^{\infty} b(x; q+j, m)(e^{-m\lambda}(m\lambda)^j/j!), \qquad 0 \leq x \leq 1. \tag{2.12}$$

Let $H_\lambda(x)$ denote the corresponding cdf. To select a subset containing the population associated with $\rho_{[k]}$, we propose the procedure

$$\mathscr{R}_2: \quad \text{Select } \pi_i \text{ iff } R_i^2 \geq c' \max_{1\leq j\leq k} R_j^2,$$

where $0 < c' = c'(k, P^*, p, n) < 1$ is chosen so as to satisfy the probability requirement (1.1). Procedure $\mathscr{R}_2$ is of the same type as $\mathscr{R}_1$, but called differently in order to differentiate the conditional and the unconditional cases. We see that

$$P(\text{CS}\,|\,\mathscr{R}_2) = \int_0^1 \prod_{j=1}^{k-1} H_{\lambda_{[j]}}(x/c)\,dH_{\lambda_{[j]}}(x). \tag{2.13}$$

Lemma 2.4. *The conditional density of R^2, namely, $h_\lambda(x)$ has* MLR *in x.*

Proof. In Lemma 2.1, set $g_j(x) = b(x; q+j, m)$ and $W(\lambda, j) = e^{-m\lambda}(m\lambda)^j/j!$. Then the proof follows by verifying the two conditions of Lemma 2.1. Consequently, $H_\lambda(x)$ is nonincreasing in λ.

Now we state, without proof, as Lemma 2.5, the relevant part of Theorem 3.1 by Gupta and Studden [19].

Lemma 2.5. *Let $g_j(x), j = 0, 1, 2, \ldots$ be a sequence of density functions on the interval $[0, \infty)$, and define for $\lambda > 0$*

$$f_\lambda(x) = \sum_{j=0}^{\infty} (e^{-\lambda}\lambda^j/j!)g_j(x), \qquad x \geq 0. \tag{2.14}$$

For a fixed integer $k \geq 2$ and $0 < c < 1$, let $I(\lambda) = \int_0^\infty F_\lambda^{k-1}(x/c)f_\lambda(x)\,dx$. Then $I(\lambda)$ is nondecreasing in λ if for each integer $l \geq 0$

$$\sum_{i=0}^{l} (i!\,(l-i)!)^{-1}\{[G_{i+1}(x/c) - G_i(x/c)]g_{l-i}(x) - c^{-1}g_i(x/c)[G_{l-i+1}(x) - G_{l-i}(x)]\} \geq 0, \tag{2.15}$$

and $I(\lambda)$ is strictly increasing in λ if strict inequality holds in (2.15) *for some l.*

Lemma 2.6. *Let $B(\lambda) = \int_0^1 H_\lambda^{k-1}(x/c)\,dH_\lambda(x)$, $0 < c < 1$. Then $B(\lambda)$ is increasing in λ.*

Proof. Since $h_\lambda(x)$ is given by (2.14) with $g_j(x) = b(x; q+j, m)$, the beta density, the left-hand side of (2.15) vanishes for $x \geq c$. For $x < c$, using the relation (2.9), the left-hand side of (2.15) can be written, after some simplifications, in the form

$$\sum_{i=0}^{l} \frac{(1-x)^{m-1}(1-(x/c))^{m-1}\Gamma(q+i+m)\Gamma(q+l-i+m)}{i!\,(l-i)!\,\{\Gamma(m)\}^2\Gamma(q+i+1)\Gamma(q+l-i+1)c^{q+1}}\,T_i,$$

where $T_i = c^{-i}\{(1-c)(q+l-i) - (1-x)(l-2i)\}$. When l is even $T_{l/2} > 0$. For $l > 0$, it can be easily verified that $T_i + T_{l-i} > 0$. The proof is completed by verifying the condition (2.15) directly for $l = 0$.

Theorem 2.2. *Let Ω represent the space of the parameter vector $\boldsymbol{\rho} = (\rho_1, \rho_2, \ldots, \rho_k)$. Then*

$$\inf_{\Omega} P(\text{CS} \mid \mathscr{R}_2) = \int_0^1 H^{k-1}(x/c')\,dH(x), \tag{2.16}$$

where $H(x) \equiv H_0(x)$ is the distribution of R^2 in the conditional case when $\rho^2 = 0$. The corresponding density is given by

$$h_0(x) = \frac{\Gamma(q+m)}{\Gamma(q)\Gamma(m)} x^{q-1}(1-x)^{m-1}, \qquad 0 \leq x \leq 1. \tag{2.17}$$

Proof. The proof follows from Lemmas 2.4 and 2.6 on lines similar to that of Theorem 2.1.

Corollary 2.2. *The constant c' defining Procedure $\mathcal{R}_2$ satisfies the equation*

$$\int_0^1 H^{k-1}(x/c')\, dH(x) = P^*. \tag{2.18}$$

We note that the distribution of R^2 when $\rho^2 = 0$ is the same in the conditional as well as the unconditional case. Thus Eqs. (2.11) and (2.18) are the same and $c' = c$. We can rewrite Eqs. (2.11) and (2.18) as

$$\int_0^c I_{x/c}^{k-1}(q, m) b(x; q, m)\, dx + 1 - I_c(q, m) = P^*. \tag{2.19}$$

When q and m are integers, (2.19) can be written in the form

$$1 - P^* = I_c(q, m) - \int_0^c \left[\sum_{t=q}^{q+m-1} \binom{q+m-1}{t} \left(\frac{x}{c}\right)^t \left(1 - \frac{x}{c}\right)^{q+m-1-t} \right]^{k-1} \times \frac{\Gamma(q+m)}{\Gamma(q)\Gamma(m)} x^{q-1}(1-x)^{m-1}\, dx. \tag{2.20}$$

Let $A(q, m, k, c)$ denote the integral on the right-hand side of (2.20). Then, putting $y = 1 - (x/c)$ and $l = k - 1$

$$\begin{aligned} A(q, m, k, c) &= \frac{\Gamma(q+m)}{\Gamma(q)\Gamma(m)} c^q (1-c)^{m-1} \int_0^1 \left[\sum_{t=q}^{q+m-1} \binom{q+m-1}{t} y^{q+m-1-t}(1-y)^t \right]^l \\ &\qquad \times (1-y)^{q-1} \left[1 + \frac{cy}{1-c} \right]^{m-1} dy \\ &= \frac{\Gamma(q+m)}{\Gamma(q)\Gamma(m)} c^q (1-c)^{m-1} \int_0^1 \left[\sum_{r=0}^{l(q+m-1)} C(r, l; q+m-1, q) y^r \right] \\ &\qquad \times (1-y)^{q-1} \left[1 + \frac{cy}{1-c} \right]^{m-1} dy \end{aligned}$$

where $C(r, l; n, j)$ is the coefficient of y^r in the expansion of

$$\left[\sum_{t=j}^{n} \binom{n}{t} (1-y)^t y^{n-t} \right]^l.$$

The coefficients $C(r, l, n, j)$ are given by the following recursive relations:

$$C(r, 1; n, j) = \begin{cases} 1, & r = 0 \\ 0, & 1 \le r \le n - j \\ \binom{n}{r} \sum_{t=0}^{n-j} (-1)^{r-t} \binom{r}{t}, & n - j + 1 \le r \le n \end{cases} \tag{2.21}$$

and for $p > 1$

$$C(r, p; n, j) = \begin{cases} 1, & r = 0 \\ 0, & 1 \le r \le n - j \\ \displaystyle\sum_{t=\max(n-j+1,\, r-np+n)}^{\min(r,n)} C(t, 1; n, j)C(r-t, p-1; n, j) \\ \qquad + C(r, p-1; n, j)\,[1 - \varepsilon(r - np + n - 1)],^{2} & n - j + 1 \le r \le np \end{cases} \tag{2.22}$$

$$\begin{aligned} A(q, m, k, c) &= \frac{\Gamma(q+m)}{\Gamma(q)\Gamma(m)} c^q (1-c)^{m-1} \\ &\quad \times \sum_{r=0}^{l(q+m-1)} \sum_{\alpha=0}^{m-1} \binom{m-1}{\alpha} \left(\frac{c}{1-c}\right)^{\alpha} C(r, l; q+m-1, q) \int_0^1 z^{\alpha+r}(1-z)^{q-1}\, dz \\ &= \frac{c^q(1-c)^{m-1}}{\Gamma(q)\Gamma(m)} \Gamma(q+m) \\ &\quad \times \sum_{r=0}^{l(q+m-1)} \sum_{\alpha=0}^{m-1} \binom{m-1}{\alpha} \left(\frac{c}{1-c}\right)^{\alpha} C(r, l; q+m-1, q) \frac{\Gamma(\alpha+r+1)\Gamma(q)}{\Gamma(\alpha+r+1+q)}. \\ &= c^q(1-c)^{m-1} \\ &\quad \times \sum_{r=0}^{l(q+m-1)} \sum_{\alpha=0}^{m-1} \left(\frac{c}{1-c}\right)^{\alpha} \frac{\Gamma(q+m)\Gamma(\alpha+r+1)C(r, l; q+m-1, q)}{\Gamma(\alpha+1)\Gamma(m-\alpha)\Gamma(\alpha+r+1+q)} \end{aligned}$$

Thus, if q and m are integers, c is given by

$$\begin{aligned} 1 - P^* &= I_c(q, m) - c^q(1-c)^{m-1}\Gamma(q+m) \\ &\quad \times \sum_{r=0}^{l(q+m-1)} \sum_{\alpha=0}^{m-1} \left(\frac{c}{1-c}\right)^{\alpha} \frac{\Gamma(\alpha+r+1)C(r, l; q+m-1, q)}{\Gamma(\alpha+1)\Gamma(m-\alpha)\Gamma(\alpha+r+1+q)}. \end{aligned} \tag{2.23}$$

Asymptotic Results

When p is fixed and $m \to \infty$ (i.e., $n \to \infty$), the asymptotic distribution of nR^2 is the noncentral χ^2 with $(p-1)$ degrees of freedom and noncentrality parameter $n\rho^2$ both in the conditional and unconditional cases. Then, for our procedure $\mathcal{R}$ (which stands for $\mathcal{R}_1$ or $\mathcal{R}_2$), namely, $\mathcal{R}$: Select π_i iff $R_i^2 \ge c \max_{1 \le j \le k} R_j^2$, we get

$$P(\text{CS} \mid \mathcal{R}) = \int_0^\infty \prod_{j=1}^{k-1} G_{n\rho^2_{[j]},\, p-1}(x/c)\, dG_{n\rho^2_{[k]},\, p-1}(x), \tag{2.24}$$

[2] $\varepsilon(u) = 1$ if $u \ge 0$ and 0 if $u < 0$.

where $G_{\mu,\nu}(x)$ is the cdf of the noncentral χ^2 with ν df and noncentrality parameter μ. In this case the infimum of $P(\text{CS} \mid \mathcal{R})$ takes place when $\rho_{[1]}^2 = \cdots = \rho_{[k]}^2 = 0$ (for detailed discussion see Gupta and Studden [19]). Hence c must satisfy the equation

$$\int_0^\infty G_{p-1}^{k-1}(x/c)\, dG_{p-1}(x) = P^*, \tag{2.25}$$

where $G_\nu(x)$ is the cdf of the central χ^2 with ν df. For selected values of k, p, and P^*, the c-values are tabulated by Gupta [13].

Selection Procedures Based on a Transform of R^2

The transform of R^2, which we are concerned with here, is $R^2/(1 - R^2) = R^{*2}$ (say). The exact distribution of R^{*2} in the unconditional case has the density

$$u_\lambda(x) = \sum_{j=0}^\infty \frac{\Gamma(q+j+m)}{\Gamma(q+j)\Gamma(m)} \frac{x^{q+j-1}}{(1+x)^{q+j+m}} \frac{\Gamma(q+m+j)\lambda^j}{\Gamma(q+m)j!}(1-\lambda)^{q+m}, \qquad x \geq 0. \tag{2.26}$$

Then, for selecting a subset containing the population with $\rho_{[k]}$, we propose the procedure

$$\mathcal{R}_3: \qquad \text{Select } \pi_i \text{ iff } \quad R_i^{*2} \geq c_1 \max_{1 \leq j \leq k} R_j^{*2},$$

$$\text{where} \quad 0 < c_1 = c_1(k, P^*, q, m) < 1$$

is chosen to satisfy the probability requirement (1.1). Then, denoting $R_{(j)}^2/(1 - R_{(j)}^2)$ by $R_{(j)}^{*2}$ ($R_{(j)}^{*2}$ corresponds to the population $\rho_{[j]}$), we have

$$\begin{aligned} P(\text{CS} \mid \mathcal{R}_3) &= P(R_{(k)}^{*2} \geq c_1 R_{(j)}^{*2}, \quad j = 1, 2, \ldots, k-1) \\ &= \int_0^\infty \prod_{j=1}^{\infty} U_{\lambda_{[j]}}(x/c_1)\, dU_{\lambda_{[k]}}(x), \end{aligned}$$

where $U_\lambda(x)$ is the cdf corresponding to $u_\lambda(x)$.

Theorem 2.3. *Let Ω represent the space of the parameter vector $\boldsymbol{\rho} = (\rho_1, \rho_2, \ldots, \rho_k)$. Then*

$$\inf_\Omega P(\text{CS} \mid \mathcal{R}_3) = \int_0^\infty F_{2q,2m}^{k-1}(x/c_1)\, dF_{2q,2m}(x), \tag{2.27}$$

where $F_{2q,2m}(x)$ is the cdf of the central F random variable with $2q$ and $2m$ df.

Proof.

$$P(\mathrm{CS} \mid \mathscr{R}_3) = \int_0^\infty \prod_{j=1}^{\infty} U_{\lambda_{[j]}}(x/c_1)\, dU_{\lambda_{[k]}}(x)$$

$$\geq \int_0^\infty U_{\lambda_{[k]}}^{k-1}(x/c_1)\, dU_{\lambda_{[k]}}(x).$$

The last integral above can be shown to be increasing in $\lambda_{[k]}$. To this end, we need only show that the condition (2.52) of Theorem 2.5 is satisfied for $q_1 = q + m$ and for

$$g_j(x) = \frac{\Gamma(q+m+j)}{\Gamma(m)\Gamma(q+j)} \frac{x^{q+j-1}}{(1+x)^{q+j+m}}, \qquad x \geq 0, \quad q, m > 0.$$

Using the fact that

$$G_{j+1}(x) - G_j(x) = -\frac{\Gamma(q+m+j)x^{q+j}}{\Gamma(m)\Gamma(q+j+1)(1+x)^{q+m+j}},$$

it can be shown that the left-hand side of (2.52) is

$$\sum_{i=0}^{l} \frac{(q_1)_i (q_1)_{l-i} \Gamma(q+m+i)\Gamma(q+l-i+m)c^m x^{2q+l-1} m}{i!\,(l-i)!\,\{\Gamma(m)\}^2 \Gamma(q+i)\Gamma(q+l-i)(c+x)^{q+m}(1+x)^{q+m}} T_i,$$

where

$$T_i = \frac{2i - l}{(c+x)^i (1+x)^{l-i}}.$$

It is easily verified that for $l > 0$, $T_i + T_{l-i} > 0$ for $i = 0, 1, \ldots, [(l-1)/2]$ and that $T_{l/2} = 0$ for l even. For $l = 0$, the condition is directly verified. Hence, we conclude that

$$\inf_{\Omega} P(\mathrm{CS} \mid \mathscr{R}_3) = \int_0^\infty F_{2q,2m}^{k-1}(x/c_1)\, dF_{2q,2m}(x),$$

since $U_\lambda(x)$ for $\lambda = 0$ is the cdf of a constant multiple of a random variable which has the central F distribution with $2q$ and $2m$ df.

Corollary 2.3. *The constant c_1 defining $\mathscr{R}_3$ is given by*

$$\int_0^\infty F_{2q,2m}^{k-1}(x/c_1)\, dF_{2q,2m}(x) = P^*. \tag{2.28}$$

If we assume that q and m are integers, i.e., that p and n are odd, we can write (2.28) as

$$P^* = \int_0^\infty \left[(1-t)^q \left\{1 + \frac{(q)_1}{1!} t + \cdots + \frac{(q)_{m'}}{m'!} t^{m'}\right\}\right]^{k-1}$$

$$\times \frac{\Gamma(q+m)c_1(2q)^q(2m)^m(c_1 z)^{q-1}}{\Gamma(q)\Gamma(m)(2m+2qc_1 z)^{m+q}}\, dz \tag{2.29}$$

where $t = m/(m+qz)$, $m' = m - 1$ and $(q)_j = q(q+1)\cdots(q+j-1)$. By changing the variable of integration from z to t, we get after some simplifications

$$P^* = \int_0^1 \frac{\Gamma(q+m)t^{m-1}(1-t)^{qk-1}}{c_1{}^m\Gamma(q)\Gamma(m)\left\{1+\dfrac{1-c_1}{c_1}t\right\}^{m+q}} \left\{1+\frac{(q)_1}{1!}t+\cdots+\frac{(q)_{m'}t^{m'}}{m'!}\right\}^{k-1} dt. \tag{2.30}$$

If we expand

$$\left[1+\frac{(q)_1}{1!}t+\cdots+\frac{(q)_{m'}t^{m'}}{m'!}\right]^r$$

in powers of t as $\sum_{j=0}^{r(m-1)} a(r,j)t^j$, the coefficients $a(r,j)$ are given by the following recursive relations:

$$a(1,j) = \begin{cases} 1, & j=0 \\ \dfrac{(q)_j}{j!}, & 1 \le j \le m' \end{cases} \tag{2.31}$$

and for $r > 1$

$$a(r,j) = \begin{cases} 1, & j=0 \\ \displaystyle\sum_{s=\max(j-(r-1)m',\,0)}^{\min(m',j)} a(1,s)a(r-1,j-s), & 1 \le j \le rm'. \end{cases} \tag{2.32}$$

Using the above expansion and also the binomial expansion of $(1-t)^{qk-1}$ in (2.30), setting $t(1-c_1)/c_1 = \xi$ and integrating term by term, we obtain

$$P^* = \frac{\Gamma(q+m)}{\Gamma(q)\Gamma(m)(1-c)^m} \times \sum_{\alpha=0}^{qk-1} \sum_{j=0}^{(k-1)m'} (-1)^\alpha \binom{qk-1}{\alpha} a(k-1,j) \left(\frac{c_1}{1-c_1}\right)^{\alpha+j} K(c_1,m,q,\alpha,j) \tag{2.33}$$

where

$$K(c,m,q,\alpha,j) = \begin{cases} \dfrac{\Gamma(m+\alpha+j)\Gamma(q-\alpha-j)}{\Gamma(m+q)} I_{1-c}(m+\alpha+j,\, q-\alpha-j), & q > \alpha+j \\ \displaystyle\sum_{l=1}^{m+q-1} \binom{m+q-1}{l} (-1)^l \frac{\{1-c^l\}}{l} - \log c, & q = \alpha+j \\ \displaystyle\sum_{\substack{l=0 \\ l \ne \alpha+j-q}}^{m+\alpha+j-1} \binom{m+\alpha+j-1}{l} (-1)^l \frac{\{1-c^{l-\alpha-j+q}\}}{l-\alpha-j+q} \\ \qquad + \dbinom{m+\alpha+j-1}{\alpha+j-q} (-1)^{\alpha+j-q+1} \log c, & q < \alpha+j \end{cases} \tag{2.34}$$

In the conditional case, the density of $R^2/(1 - R^2)$ is given by

$$v_\lambda(x) = \sum_{j=0}^{\infty} \frac{\Gamma(q+j+m)}{\Gamma(q+j)\Gamma(m)} \frac{x^{q+j-1} e^{-m\lambda}(m\lambda)^j}{(1+x)^{q+j+m} j!}, \qquad x \geq 0. \tag{2.35}$$

We propose the following Procedure $\mathcal{R}_4$ based on $R_i^{*2} = R_i^2/(1 - R_i^2)$, $i = 1, 2, \ldots, k$.

$$\mathcal{R}_4: \quad \text{Select } \pi_i \text{ iff } \quad R_i^{*2} \geq c_2 \max_{1 \leq j \leq k} R_j^{*2},$$

where $0 < c_2 = c_2(k, P^*, q, m) < 1$ is chosen so that the probability requirement (1.1) is satisfied.

Theorem 2.4. *Let Ω represent the space of the parameter vector $\boldsymbol{\rho} = (\rho_1, \rho_2, \ldots, \rho_k)$. Then*

$$\inf_{\Omega} P(\text{CS} \mid \mathcal{R}_4) = \int_0^\infty F_{2q,2m}^{k-1}(x/c_2)\, dF_{2q,2m}(x),$$

where $F_{2q,2m}(x)$ is the cdf of central F with 2q and 2m df.

Proof.

$$P(\text{CS} \mid \mathcal{R}_4) = P(R_{(k)}^{*2} \geq c_2 R_{(j)}^{*2}, \quad j = 1, 2, \ldots, k-1)$$

$$= \int_0^\infty \prod_{j=1}^{k-1} V_{\lambda_{[j]}}(x/c_2)\, dV_{\lambda_{[k]}}(x),$$

where $\quad V_{\lambda_{[j]}}(x) \quad$ is the cdf of $\quad R_{(j)}^{*2}$

$$\geq \int_0^\infty V_{\lambda_{[k]}}^{k-1}(x/c_2)\, dV_{\lambda_{[k]}}(x),$$

because $V_\lambda(x)$ is stochastically increasing in λ by Lemma 2.1.

The last integral above has been shown by Gupta and Studden [19] to attain its infimum at $\lambda_{[k]} = 0$. This completes the proof of Theorem 2.4.

Corollary 2.4. *The constant c_2 defining Procedure $\mathcal{R}_2$ is given by*

$$\int_0^\infty F_{2q,2m}^{k-1}(x/c_2)\, dF_{2q,2m}(x) = P^*. \tag{2.36}$$

From (2.28) and (2.36), it is clear that $c_1 = c_2$. These constants are tabulated in Table I. Thus the constants needed both for the conditional case and the unconditional case are the same.

Selection of a Subset Containing the Population Associated with $\rho_{[1]}$

As in the case of $\rho_{[k]}$, we will discuss the conditional and the unconditional cases. For the unconditional case, we propose the procedure

$$\mathcal{R}_5: \quad \text{Select } \pi_i \text{ iff } \quad R_i^2 \leq d^{-1} \min_{1 \leq j \leq k} R_j^2,$$

where $0 < d = d(k, P^*, q, m) < 1$ has to be chosen so that the probability requirement (1.1) is satisfied. Then we have

$$\begin{aligned} P\{\mathrm{CS} \mid \mathscr{R}_5\} &= \int_0^1 \prod_{j=2}^{k} [1 - F_{\lambda_{[j]}}(xd)]\, dF_{\lambda_{[1]}}(x) \\ &\geq \int_0^1 [1 - F_{\lambda_{[1]}}(xd)]^{k-1}\, dF_{\lambda_{[1]}}(x), \qquad \text{by Lemma 2.2} \\ &\geq \int_0^1 [1 - F(xd)]^{k-1}\, dF(x), \end{aligned} \tag{2.37}$$

since the condition (2.52) of Theorem 2.5 is satisfied in this case.

The constant d defining Procedure $\mathscr{R}_5$ is given by

$$\int_0^1 I_{1-xd}^{k-1}(m, q) b(x; q, m)\, dx = P^*. \tag{2.38}$$

In the conditional case, Procedure $\mathscr{R}_6$ selects π_i iff $R_i^2 \leq (d')^{-1} \min_{1 \leq j \leq k} R_j^2$, $0 < d' = d : (k, P^*; q, m) < 1$.

$$\begin{aligned} P(\mathrm{CS} \mid \mathscr{R}_6) &= \int_0^1 \prod_{j=2}^{k} [1 - H_{\lambda_{[j]}}(xd')]\, dH_{\lambda_{[1]}}(x) \\ &\geq \int_0^1 [1 - H_{\lambda_{[1]}}(xd')]^{k-1}\, dH_{\lambda_{[1]}}(x), \end{aligned} \tag{2.39}$$

by stochastic ordering of H_λ.

In order to obtain the infimum over $0 \leq \lambda_{[1]} < 1$, we state, without proof, the following lemma, which is essentially a restatement of the relevant part of Theorem 3.1 by Gupta and Studden [19].

Lemma 2.7. *Let $f_\lambda(x)$ be the density function of the form defined in Lemma 2.5. Also define $J(\lambda) = \int_0^\infty [1 - F_\lambda(xd)]^{k-1} f_\lambda(x)\, dx$. Then $J(\lambda)$ is nondecreasing in λ if the condition* (2.15) *of Lemma* 2.5 *is satisfied, and $J(\lambda)$ is strictly increasing if strict inequality holds in* (2.15) *for some l.*

Now using Lemma 2.4 and the fact that the condition (2.15) is satisfied for the density $h_\lambda(x)$, we obtain

$$P(\mathrm{CS} \mid \mathscr{R}_6) \geq \int_0^1 [1 - H(xd')]^{k-1}\, dH(x).$$

Hence the constant d' defining Procedure $\mathscr{R}_6$ is given by

$$\int_0^1 [1 - H(xd')]^{k-1}\, dH(x) = P^*, \tag{2.40}$$

which is the same as (2.38) with d' in the place of d. Thus, as in the case of $\rho_{[k]}$, given k, q, m, and P^*, the constants d and d' of Procedures $\mathscr{R}_5$ and $\mathscr{R}_6$, respectively, are the same.

If we now assume that q and m are integers, we can write (2.38) as

$$P^* = \frac{\Gamma(q+m)}{\Gamma(q)\Gamma(m)} \int_0^1 \left[\sum_{t=0}^{q-1} \binom{q+m-1}{t} (xd)^t (1-xd)^{q+m-1-t}\right]^{k-1} \times x^{q-1}(1-x)^{m-1}\,dx.$$

Setting $y = 1 - xd$ and $l = k - 1$, we obtain

$$P^* = \frac{\Gamma(q+m)}{\Gamma(q)\Gamma(m)d^{q+m-1}} \int_{1-d}^1 \left[\sum_{r=0}^{l(q+m-1)} C'(r, l; q+m-1, q) y^r\right] \times (1-y)^{q-1}\{y-(1-d)\}^{m-1}\,dy \tag{2.41}$$

where $C'(r, p; n, j)$ is the coefficient of y^r in the expansion of

$$\left[\sum_{t=0}^{j-1} \binom{n}{t} (1-y)^t y^{n-t}\right]^p$$

and is given by the following relations:

$$C'(r, 1; n, j) = \begin{cases} 0, & 0 \le r \le n-j \\ \displaystyle\sum_{k=0}^{j-1-n+r} (-1)^k \binom{n}{n-r+k}\binom{n-r+k}{k}, & n-j+1 \le r \le n. \end{cases} \tag{2.42}$$

and for $p > 1$

$$C'(r, p; n, j) = \begin{cases} 0, & 0 \le r \le (n-j+1)p-1 \\ \displaystyle\sum_{s=\max(n-j+1,\, r-n(p-1))}^{\min(n,\, r-(p-1)(n-j+1))} C'(s, 1; n, j)C'(r-s, p-1; n, j), & (n-j+1)p \le r \le np. \end{cases} \tag{2.43}$$

Expanding $\{y-(1-d)\}^{m-1}$ in powers of y and integrating term by term, (2.41) yields

$$P^* = \frac{\Gamma(q+m)}{\Gamma(q)\Gamma(m)d^{q+m-1}} \times \sum_{r=0}^{l(q+m-1)} \sum_{\alpha=0}^{m-1} (-1)^{m-1-\alpha} \binom{m-1}{\alpha} (1-d)^{m-1-\alpha} C'(r, l; q+m-1, q) \times \frac{\Gamma(q)\Gamma(r+\alpha+1)}{\Gamma(q+r+\alpha+1)} I_d(q, r+\alpha+1). \tag{2.44}$$

When p is fixed and $m \to \infty$, we can use the asymptotic distribution of nR^2 and similar to (2.25), we will have

$$\int_0^\infty [1 - G_{p-1}(xd)]^{k-1} \, dG_{p-1}(x) = P^*, \tag{2.45}$$

where $G_\nu(x)$ is the cdf of the central χ^2 with ν df. For selected values of k, p, and P^*, d-values are given by Gupta and Sobel [18].

Procedure $\mathscr{R}_7$ corresponding to $\mathscr{R}_3$ is

$$\text{“Select } \pi_i \text{ iff } R_i^{*2} \le d_1^{-1} \min_{1 \le j \le k} R_j^{*2},\text{”}$$

where $0 < d_1 = d_1(k, P^*, q, m) < 1$ is chosen so that the probability requirement (1.1) is satisfied. Then

$$P(\mathrm{CS} \mid \mathscr{R}_7) \ge \int_0^\infty [1 - U_{\lambda_{[1]}}(xd_1)]^{k-1} \, dU_{\lambda_{[1]}}(x)$$

and this integral attains its infimum at $\lambda_{[1]} = 0$ since the condition (2.52) of Theorem 2.5 is satisfied. So the constant d_1 defining the procedure is given by

$$\int_0^\infty [1 - F_{2q,\,2m}(xd_1)]^{k-1} f_{2q,\,2m}(x) = P^*. \tag{2.46}$$

It is easy to see that $1 - F_{2q,\,2m}(xd_1) = F_{2m,\,2q}(x^{-1}d_1^{-1})$ and $f_{2q,\,2m}(x^{-1}) = x^2 f_{2m,2q}(x)$. Thus (2.46) becomes

$$P^* = \int_0^\infty F_{2m,\,2q}^{k-1}(x^{-1}d_1^{-1}) f_{2m,\,2q}(x^{-1}) x^{-2} \, dx = \int_0^\infty F_{2m,\,2q}^{k-1}(y/d_1) f_{2m,\,2q}(y) \, dy. \tag{2.47}$$

Thus for a given set of q, m, k, and P^*, the constant d_1 of Procedure $\mathscr{R}_7$ is the same as the constant c_1 of $\mathscr{R}_3$ with q and m interchanged.

For the conditional case, Procedure $\mathscr{R}_8$ for selecting a subset containing the population associated with $\rho_{[1]}$ is as follows:

$$\text{Select } \pi_i \text{ iff } R_i^{*2} \ge d_2^{-1} \min_{1 \le j \le k} R_j^{*2},$$

where $d_2 = d_2(k, P^*, q, m) \in (0, 1)$.

$$P(\mathrm{CS} \mid \mathscr{R}_8) \ge \int_0^\infty [1 - V_{\lambda_{[k]}}(xd_2)]^{k-1} \, dV_{\lambda_{[k]}}(x)$$

and this integral attains its infimum at $\lambda_{[k]} = 0$ (see Gupta and Studden [19]). Thus the constant d_2 defining the procedure is given by

$$\int_0^\infty [1 - F_{2q,\,2m}(xd_2)]^{k-1} \, dF_{2q,\,2m}(x) = P^*, \tag{2.48}$$

which is the same as (2.46) with d_2 instead of d_1. Hence, for given P^*, k, q, and m, $d_1 = d_2$.

Some Remarks on Procedures $\mathscr{R}_3$, $\mathscr{R}_4$, $\mathscr{R}_7$, and $\mathscr{R}_8$

As we remarked earlier the constants c_1 and c_2 defining Procedures $\mathscr{R}_3$ and $\mathscr{R}_4$, respectively, are equal. So are the constants d_1 and d_2 defining $\mathscr{R}_7$ and $\mathscr{R}_8$, respectively. These constants, c_1 and d_1, are useful in a wider sense. Suppose we have k F-populations with common df $2q$ and $2m$ and noncentrality parameters δ_i, $i = 1, 2, \ldots, k$. If we are interested in selecting a nonempty subset including the population associated with $\delta_{[k]}$ or $\delta_{[1]}$, we will take observations $x_1, x_2, \ldots, x_k$, one from each population and use the procedure

$$\text{Select } \pi_i \text{ iff } x_i \geq c_1 \max_{1 \leq j \leq k} x_j, \qquad 0 < c_1 < 1 \quad \text{or}$$

$$\text{Select } \pi_i \text{ iff } x_i \leq d_1^{-1} \min_{1 \leq j \leq k} x_j, \qquad 0 < d_1 < 1.$$

For both rules given above, the infimum of the probability of a correct selection takes place when $\delta_{[1]} = \delta_{[2]} = \cdots = \delta_{[k]} = 0$. So the constants c_1 and d_1 will be given by Eqs. (2.28) and (2.46), respectively.

Furthermore, let $Y_1, Y_2, \ldots, Y_k$ be k independent random variables, each distributed as central F with df $2q$ and $2m$. Define

$$Z_1 = \max\left\{\frac{Y_1}{Y_k}, \frac{Y_2}{Y_k}, \ldots, \frac{Y_{k-1}}{Y_k}\right\} \quad \text{and} \quad Z_2 = \min\left\{\frac{Y_1}{Y_k}, \frac{Y_2}{Y_k}, \ldots, \frac{Y_{k-1}}{Y_k}\right\}.$$

Then for a given P^*, (2.28) gives c_1, which is the reciprocal of the $100P^*$ percentage point of the distribution of Z_1 and (2.46) provides d_1, which is the $100(1 - P^*)$ percentage point of the distribution of Z_2.

A Result Concerning the Monotonicity Behavior of Two Probability Integrals

Let $g_j(x)$, $j = 0, 1, 2, \ldots$ be a sequence of density functions on the interval $[0, \infty)$, and define

$$f_\lambda(x) = \sum_{j=0}^{\infty} \frac{\Gamma(q_1 + j)}{\Gamma(q_1)} \frac{\lambda^j}{j!} (1 - \lambda)^{q_1} g_j(x), \qquad x \geq 0, \quad 0 \leq \lambda < 1. \quad (2.49)$$

For a fixed integer $k \geq 2$ and $0 < c < 1$, let

$$A(\lambda) = \int_0^\infty [F_\lambda(x/c)]^{k-1} f_\lambda(x)\, dx \quad (2.50)$$

and

$$B(\lambda) = \int_0^\infty [1 - F_\lambda(cx)]^{k-1} f_\lambda(x)\, dx. \quad (2.51)$$

Theorem 2.5. (i) *If for each integer* $l \geq 0$

$$\sum_{i=0}^{l} \frac{(q_1)_i (q_1)_{l-i}}{i!(l-i)!} \{(q_1+i)[G_{i+1}(x/c) - G_i(x/c)]g_{l-i}(x)$$
$$- c^{-1}(q_1 + l - i) g_i(x/c)[G_{l-i+1}(x) - G_{l-i}(x)]\} \geq 0 \quad (2.52)$$

where $(q_1)_s = q_1(q_1+1)\cdots(q_1+s-1)$, *and* $G_j(x)$ *is the cdf corresponding to* $g_j(x)$, *then the functions* $A(\lambda)$ *and* $B(\lambda)$ *defined in* (2.50) *and* (2.51) *are nondecreasing in* λ.

(ii) *If strict inequality holds in* (2.52) *for some integer* l, *then* $A(\lambda)$ *and* $B(\lambda)$ *are strictly increasing in* λ.

Proof. This theorem is similar to that of Gupta and Studden [19] with

$$f_\lambda(x) = \sum_{j=0}^{\infty} \frac{e^{-\lambda}\lambda^j}{j!} g_j(x), \qquad x \geq 0, \quad \lambda \geq 0.$$

The proof of the present theorem is exactly on the same lines, therefore, we omit the details and indicate only the major steps involved in the case of $A(\lambda)$. The case of $B(\lambda)$ is analogous to that of $A(\lambda)$.

Inserting the expression for $f_\lambda(x)$ from (2.49) in (2.50), we get

$$A(\lambda) = (1-\lambda)^{q_1 k} \sum_{\alpha=0}^{\infty} a_\alpha \lambda^\alpha \quad (2.53)$$

where

$$\alpha!\, a_\alpha = \sum_{A(\alpha)} \binom{\alpha}{\alpha_1 \cdots \alpha_k} \int_0^\infty \left\{ \prod_{i=1}^{k-1} G_{\alpha_i}(x/c)(q_1)_{\alpha_i} \right\} g_{\alpha_k}(x)(q_1)_{\alpha_k}\, dx, \quad (2.54)$$

where for each integer $\alpha \geq 0$, $A(\alpha)$ denotes the set of k-tuples $(\alpha_1, \alpha_2, \ldots, \alpha_k)$ where α_i $(i = 1, \ldots, k)$ are nonnegative integers and $\sum_{i=1}^{k} \alpha_i = \alpha$ and $\binom{\alpha}{\alpha_1 \cdots \alpha_k}$ denotes the multinomial coefficient $\alpha!/(\alpha_1! \cdots \alpha_k!)$. Differentiation of $A(\lambda)$ in (2.53) shows that $A(\lambda)$ is nondecreasing in λ provided that

$$(\alpha+1)a_{\alpha+1} - (\alpha + q_1 k)a_\alpha \geq 0, \qquad \alpha = 0, 1, 2, \ldots, \quad (2.55)$$

and $A(\lambda)$ is strictly increasing in λ if strict inequality holds in (2.55) for some α.

Now using

$$\binom{\alpha+1}{\alpha_1 \cdots \alpha_k} = \binom{\alpha}{\alpha_1 - 1\ \alpha_2 \cdots \alpha_k} + \binom{\alpha}{\alpha_1\ \alpha_2 - 1 \cdots \alpha_k} + \cdots$$
$$+ \binom{\alpha}{\alpha_1\ \alpha_2 \cdots \alpha_{k-1}\ \alpha_k - 1},$$

we obtain

$$(\alpha+1)!\,a_{\alpha+1} = \sum_{A(\alpha)} \binom{\alpha}{\alpha_1 \cdots \alpha_k} \Bigg[\sum_{j=1}^{k-1} \int_0^\infty G_{\alpha_j+1}\left(\frac{x}{c}\right)(q_1)_{\alpha_j+1} \left\{ \prod_{\substack{i=1\\ i\neq j}}^{k-1} G_{\alpha_i}\left(\frac{x}{c}\right)(q_1)_{\alpha_i} \right\}$$

$$\times\, g_{\alpha_k}(x)(q_1)_{\alpha_k}\, dx$$

$$+ \int_0^\infty \left\{ \prod_{i=1}^{k-1} G_{\alpha_i}\left(\frac{x}{c}\right)(q_1)_{\alpha_i} \right\} g_{\alpha_k+1}(x)(q_1)_{\alpha_k+1}\, dx \Bigg]. \tag{2.56}$$

Using

$$\int_0^\infty \prod_{i=1}^{k-1} G_{\alpha_i}\left(\frac{x}{c}\right) g_{\alpha_k+1}(x)\, dx$$

$$= \int_0^\infty \prod_{i=1}^{k-1} G_{\alpha_i}\left(\frac{x}{c}\right) g_{\alpha_k}(x)\, dx - \int_0^\infty \frac{d}{dx}\left[\prod_{i=1}^{k-1} G_{\alpha_i}\left(\frac{x}{c}\right)\right][G_{\alpha_k+1}(x) - G_{\alpha_k}(x)]\, dx \tag{2.57}$$

which can be easily verified, we obtain after some simplifications

$$(\alpha+1)!\,a_{\alpha+1} - (q_1 k + \alpha)\alpha!\,a_\alpha$$

$$= \sum_{A(\alpha)} \binom{\alpha}{\alpha_1 \cdots \alpha_k} \Bigg[\sum_{j=1}^{k-1} \int_0^\infty \left\{ \prod_{\substack{i=1\\ i\neq j}}^{k-1} G_{\alpha_i}\left(\frac{x}{c}\right)(q_1)_{\alpha_i} \right\}$$

$$\times \left\{ \left[G_{\alpha_j+1}\left(\frac{x}{c}\right) - G_{\alpha_j}\left(\frac{x}{c}\right) \right] g_{\alpha_k}(x)(q_1)_{\alpha_j+1}(q_1)_{\alpha_k} \right.$$

$$\left. - c^{-1}[G_{\alpha_k+1}(x) - G_{\alpha_k}(x)]\, g_{\alpha_j}\left(\frac{x}{c}\right)(q_1)_{\alpha_j}(q_1)_{\alpha_k+1} \right\} dx \Bigg]. \tag{2.58}$$

We now interchange the summations and fix $\alpha_i (i = 1, \ldots, k-1, i \neq j)$ and sum over α_j and α_k with $\alpha_j + \alpha_k = l$ to show that

$$\alpha!\,[(\alpha+1)a_{\alpha+1} - (q_1 k + \alpha)a_\alpha] \geq 0 \tag{2.59}$$

provided that (2.52) holds. This completes the proof of the theorem.

Properties of the Selection Rules $\mathcal{R}_i$ of Section 2

Procedures $\mathcal{R}_1, \mathcal{R}_2, \ldots, \mathcal{R}_8$ of this section select a nonempty subset of random size S which is just large enough to guarantee the probability requirement (1.1); and S is an integer-valued random variable which takes values 1 through k inclusive. The efficiency of these procedures can be studied in terms of: (i) $p_{[i]}$, the probability of selecting the population associated with $\rho_{[i]}$, $i = 1, 2, \ldots, k$; (ii) $E_{\boldsymbol{\rho}}(S)$, the expected size of the selected subset; and (iii) $E_{\boldsymbol{\rho}}(S) - P\{\text{CS} \mid \mathscr{R}\}$.

Monotonicity property of these procedures is proved in the following theorem.

Theorem 2.6. *For Procedures $\mathscr{R}_1$ through $\mathscr{R}_4$, $p_1 \le p_2 \le \cdots \le p_k$ and for Procedures $\mathscr{R}_5$ through $\mathscr{R}_8$, $p_1 \ge p_2 \ge \cdots \ge p_k$.*

Proof. We prove the theorem for $\mathscr{R}_1$. The proof is similar for $\mathscr{R}_2$ through $\mathscr{R}_4$ and by obvious modifications, the proof follows for $\mathscr{R}_5$ through $\mathscr{R}_8$. Now, for $\mathscr{R}_1$,

$$p_i = \int_0^1 \left[\prod_{\substack{j=1 \\ j \ne i}}^{k} F_{\lambda_{[j]}}(x/c)\right] f_{\lambda_{[i]}}(x)\,dx, \qquad i = 1, 2, \ldots, k. \tag{2.60}$$

It is enough if we show that $p_k \ge p_{k-1}$. Now

$$\begin{aligned} p_k &= \int_0^1 \left\{\prod_{j=1}^{k-2} F_{\lambda_{[j]}}(x/c)\right\} F_{\lambda_{[k-1]}}(x/c) f_{\lambda_{[k]}}(x)\,dx \\ &\ge \int_0^1 \left\{\prod_{j=1}^{k-2} F_{\lambda_{[j]}}(x/c)\right\} F_{\lambda}(x/c) f_{\lambda_{[k]}}(x)\,dx, \qquad \text{for} \quad \lambda \ge \lambda_{[k-1]}. \end{aligned}$$

Application of the lemma [26, p. 74] shows that the integral on the right-hand side of the above inequality is nondecreasing in $\rho_{[k]}$. Therefore

$$p_k \ge \int_0^1 \left\{\prod_{j=1}^{k-2} F_{\lambda_{[j]}}(x/c)\right\} F_{\lambda}(x/c) f_{\lambda_{[k-1]}}(x)\,dx$$

and since this is true for any value of $\lambda \ge \lambda_{[k-1]}$, we can take $\lambda = \lambda_{[k]}$, and obtain

$$p_k \ge \int_0^1 \left\{\prod_{j=1}^{k-2} F_{\lambda_{[j]}}(x/c)\right\} F_{\lambda_{[k]}}(x/c) f_{\lambda_{[k-1]}}(x)\,dx = p_{k-1}.$$

The expected size of the selected subset satisfies the following inequalities:

$$kp_1 \le E_{\boldsymbol{\rho}}(S) \le kp_k \qquad \text{for} \quad \mathscr{R}_1 \quad \text{through} \quad \mathscr{R}_4 \tag{2.61}$$

$$kp_1 \ge E_{\boldsymbol{\rho}}(S) \ge kp_k \qquad \text{for} \quad \mathscr{R}_5 \quad \text{through} \quad \mathscr{R}_8. \tag{2.62}$$

Let $S' = S - P\{\text{CS} \mid \mathscr{R}\}$. Then, for $\mathscr{R}_1$ through $\mathscr{R}_4$, $E(S') = \sum_{i=1}^{k-1} p_i$. For $\mathscr{R}_1$, p_i is given by (2.60) and

$$\frac{\partial p_i}{\partial \rho_{[k]}} = \int_0^1 \left\{\prod_{\substack{j=1 \\ j \ne i}}^{k-1} F_{\lambda_{[j]}}(x/c)\right\} \frac{\partial F_{\lambda_{[k]}}(x/c)}{\partial \rho_{[k]}}\,dF_{\lambda_{[i]}}(x), \qquad i = 1, 2, \ldots, k-1,$$

is less than or equal to 0 since $F_{\lambda_{[k]}}(x)$ is decreasing in $\rho_{[k]}$. Therefore, p_i decreases in $\rho_{[k]}$ for $i = 1, \ldots, k-1$. Consequently, $E(S')$ decreases in $\rho_{[k]}$.

We can show[3] that $\sup E(S')$ is attained when $\rho_{[1]} = \rho_{[2]} = \cdots = \rho_{[k]}$. Thus, we have

$$\sup_{\Omega} E_{\boldsymbol{\rho}}(S') = \sup_{\Omega_0} E_{\rho}(S'), \qquad \text{where} \quad \Omega_0 = \{\boldsymbol{\rho} \mid \boldsymbol{\rho} = (\rho, \rho, \ldots, \rho)\}. \tag{2.63}$$

Equation (2.63) holds also for $\mathscr{R}_5$ through $\mathscr{R}_8$.

3. SELECTION OF THE MULTIVARIATE NORMAL POPULATIONS WITH RESPECT TO CONDITIONAL GENERALIZED VARIANCE

Let us consider k p-variate normal populations $\pi_1, \pi_2, \ldots, \pi_k$, where π_i is $N_p(\boldsymbol{\mu}_i, \Sigma_i)$, $i = 1, \ldots, k$. We consider a partition of the p variables into two sets of q_1 and q_2 components, respectively, where $q_1 + q_2 = p$. The corresponding partition of Σ_i is denoted by

$$\Sigma_i = \begin{pmatrix} \Sigma_{11}^{(i)} & \Sigma_{12}^{(i)} \\ \Sigma_{21}^{(i)} & \Sigma_{22}^{(i)} \end{pmatrix}, \qquad i = 1, 2, \ldots, k.$$

Here Σ_i, $\Sigma_{11}^{(i)}$, $\Sigma_{22}^{(i)}$ $(i = 1, 2, \ldots, k)$ are all assumed to be positive definite. We are interested in selecting a subset containing the population associated with the smallest $|\Sigma_i|/|\Sigma_{11}^{(i)}| \equiv |\Sigma_{22}^{(i)} - \Sigma_{21}^{(i)} \Sigma_{11}^{(i)^{-1}} \Sigma_{12}^{(i)}| = \sigma_i$, say. In other words, if we consider for each population the conditional distribution of the q_2 set when the q_1 set is fixed, then our criterion of ranking is the conditional generalized variance. This provides a justification for the choice of the criterion.

If the observations are taken on the variables of the q_2 set, holding the variables of the q_1 set fixed, then the problem reduces to selecting in terms of the generalized variance for the conditional normal distributions with dimensionality q_2. This problem has already been solved by Gnanadesikan [8]. Now we discuss the unconditional case in which all the p variables are random and observations are taken on all of them.

Let S_i be the sample covariance matrix from π_i based on n observations, $i = 1, 2, \ldots, k$. Furthermore, let the partition of S_i be denoted by

$$S_i = \begin{pmatrix} S_{11}^{(i)} & S_{12}^{(i)} \\ S_{21}^{(i)} & S_{22}^{(i)} \end{pmatrix}, \qquad i = 1, 2, \ldots, k,$$

and $s_i = |S_i|/|S_{11}^{(i)}| \equiv |S_{22}^{(i)} - S_{21}^{(i)} S_{11}^{(i)^{-1}} S_{12}^{(i)}|$. We propose the following Procedure $\mathscr{R}$.

$$\mathscr{R}: \quad \text{Select } \pi_i \ \text{ iff } s_i \le D^{-1} \min_{1 \le j \le k} s_j,$$

[3] For a sufficient condition see Gupta and Panchapakesan (1969) in the *Proc. of the Duke Univ. Symp. on Computer Simulation Experiments.*

where $0 < D = D(k, P^*, n, q_1, q_2) < 1$ is chosen so as to satisfy the probability requirement (1.1).

Theorem 3.1. *Let Ω be the space of the covariance matrices $\Sigma_1, \Sigma_2, \ldots, \Sigma_k$ of k p-variate normal populations. Then*

$$\inf_{\Omega} P\{\text{CS} \mid \mathcal{R}\} = \int_0^\infty [1 - G(Dx)]^{k-1}\, dG(x), \tag{3.1}$$

where $G(x)$ is the cdf of the independent and identically distributed random variables $\eta_1, \ldots, \eta_k$, where η_j is the product of q_2 independent χ^2 variables with df $n - q_1 - 1, n - q_1 - 2, \ldots, n - q_1 - q_2$, respectively.

Proof. Denoting the jth largest σ_i by $\sigma_{[j]}$ and the s_j associated with $\sigma_{[j]}$ by $s_{(j)}$, we have

$$\begin{aligned} P\{\text{CS} \mid \mathcal{R}\} &= P\{s_{(1)} \leq D^{-1} s_{(j)},\quad j = 2, 3, \ldots, k\} \\ &= P\left\{\frac{s_{(j)}}{\sigma_{[j]}} \geq D \frac{s_{(1)}}{\sigma_{[1]}} \frac{\sigma_{[1]}}{\sigma_{[j]}},\quad j = 2, \ldots, k\right\} \\ &\geq P\left\{\frac{s_{(j)}}{\sigma_{[j]}} \geq D \frac{s_{(1)}}{\sigma_{[1]}},\quad j = 2, \ldots, k\right\} \\ &= P\{A_j \geq DA_1,\ j = 2, \ldots, k\} \quad \text{where } A_j = \frac{s_{(j)}}{\sigma_{[j]}},\quad j = 1, \ldots, k. \end{aligned}$$

We know that

$$S_{22}^{(i)} - S_{21}^{(i)} S_{11}^{(i)^{-1}} S_{12}^{(i)} \sim W_{q_2}(n - 1 - q_1, \Sigma_{22}^{(i)} - \Sigma_{21}^{(i)} \Sigma_{11}^{(i)^{-1}} \Sigma_{12}^{(i)}),$$

and hence A_i is distributed as the product of q_2 independent χ^2 variables with df $n - q_1 - 1, \ldots, n - q_1 - q_2$, respectively. Thus A_j, $j = 1, 2, \ldots, k$ are independent and identically distributed with cdf $G(x)$.

Corollary 3.1. *The constant D defining Procedure $\mathcal{R}$ is given by*

$$\int_0^\infty [1 - G(Dx)]^{k-1}\, dG(x) = P^*. \tag{3.2}$$

The constant D satisfying (3.2) is the $100(1 - P^*)$ percentage point of $\eta_{\min} = \min(\eta_2/\eta_1, \ldots, \eta_k/\eta_1)$. The exact distribution of η_i is unknown for $q_2 > 2$. When $q_2 > 2$, an approximation suggested by Hoel [20] could be used. A detailed discussion of this approximation has been given by Gnanadesikan [8]. For $q_2 = 2$, $2\eta_i^{1/2}$ is distributed as a χ^2 variable with $2(n - q_1 - 2)$ df, and hence in this case $D^{1/2}$ is the lower $100(1 - P^*)$ percentage point of

$$F_{\min} = \min\{\chi_{v,2}^2/\chi_{v,1}^2, \ldots, \chi_{v,k}^2/\chi_{v,1}^2\},$$

where $\chi_{v,i}^2$, $i = 1, 2, \ldots, k$ are independent central χ^2 variables each with $v = 2(n - q_1 - 2)$ df. Thus we can state the following theorem.

Theorem 3.2. *When* $q_2 = 2$, $k > 1$

$$\inf_{\Omega} P\{CS \mid \mathscr{R}\} = P\{F_{\min} \geq D^{1/2}\}. \tag{3.4}$$

As remarked by Gnanadesikan [8], the constant D is related to the constant of the procedure discussed by Gupta and Sobel [17], which has been tabulated by Gupta and Sobel [18] and Krishnaiah and Armitage [23].

When $k = 2$ and $q_2 = 2$, obviously $D^{1/2}$ is the $100(1 - P^*)$ percentage point of the central F variable with $(2n - 2q_1 - 4, 2n - 2q_1 - 4)$ df.

We now prove the monotonicity property of Procedure $\mathscr{R}$.

Theorem 3.3. *If p_i denotes the probability of including the population associated with $\sigma_{[i]}$, then $p_i \geq p_j$ if $i < j$.*

Proof. $p_i = P\{s_{(i)} \leq D^{-1} s_{(l)},\quad l = 1, 2, \ldots, k\}$

$$= P\left\{\frac{s_{(i)}}{\sigma_{[i]}} \leq D^{-1} \frac{\sigma_{[l]}}{\sigma_{[i]}} \frac{s_{(l)}}{\sigma_{[l]}},\quad l = 1, 2, \ldots, k\right\}$$

$$= P\left\{A_i \leq D^{-1} \frac{\sigma_{[l]}}{\sigma_{[i]}} A_l,\quad l = 1, 2, \ldots, k\right\}.$$

Similarly,

$$p_j = P\left\{A_j \leq D^{-1} \frac{\sigma_{[l]}}{\sigma_{[j]}} A_l,\quad l = 1, 2, \ldots, k\right\}.$$

Since A_l, $l = 1, 2, \ldots, k$ are iid random variables and their common distribution does not involve σ_l's, and since $\sigma_{[l]}/\sigma_{[i]} \geq \sigma_{[l]}/\sigma_{[j]}$, $l = 1, 2, \ldots, k$, we obtain $p_i \geq p_j$.

4. DESCRIPTION OF TABLES

Table I gives values of constants necessary for Procedures $\mathscr{R}_3$, $\mathscr{R}_4$, $\mathscr{R}_7$, and $\mathscr{R}_8$. The constants for $\mathscr{R}_3$ and $\mathscr{R}_4$ are the same and so are the constants for $\mathscr{R}_7$ and $\mathscr{R}_8$. Tables range over $k = 2(1)5$ and $P^* = 0.75$, 0.90, 0.95, and 0.99. For $\mathscr{R}_3$ and $\mathscr{R}_4$, the constants $c_1 = c_2$ are directly readable for specified $q = \frac{1}{2}(p - 1)$ and $m = \frac{1}{2}(n - p)$. For Procedures $\mathscr{R}_7$ and $\mathscr{R}_8$, the values $d_1 = d_2$ have to be obtained from Table I by interchanging the values of q and m. The constant c_1 is the solution of (2.28). For computational purposes, Eq. (2.33) was used to solve for c_1.

Table II gives values of $c = c'$ for Procedures $\mathscr{R}_1$ and $\mathscr{R}_2$ based on R^2 to select the subset containing the population with $\rho_{[k]}$. Tables range over $k = 2(1)5$ and $P^* = 0.75$, 0.90, 0.95, and 0.99. The constant $c = c'$ is the solution of (2.11) or (2.19). For computational purposes, Eq. (2.23) was used to solve for $c = c'$.

TABLE I[a–c]

Values of the Constants for Procedures $\mathscr{R}_3(c_1)$, $\mathscr{R}_4(c_2)$, $\mathscr{R}_7(d_1)$, *and* $\mathscr{R}_8(d_2)$

$k=2$

q \ m	1	2	3	4	5	6	7	8
1	2.4867 (3) 3.0066 (2) 4.1222 (2) 1.9548 (1)	5.2940 (3) 3.0525 (2) 7.0383 (2) 2.5680 (1)	6.8360 (3) 3.7366 (2) 8.2871 (2) 2.8065 (1)	7.6400 (3) 4.1035 (2) 8.9587 (2) 2.9323 (1)	8.1290 (3) 4.3298 (2) 9.3746 (2) 3.0097 (1)	8.4560 (3) 4.4826 (2) 9.6567 (2) 3.0622 (1)	8.6900 (3) 4.5926 (2) 9.8604 (2) 3.1000 (1)	8.8660 (3) 4.6756 (2) 1.0014 (1) 3.1286 (1)
2	5.2940 (3) 3.0525 (2) 7.0383 (2) 2.5680 (1)	2.1570 (2) 7.1916 (2) 1.3183 (1) 3.4925 (1)	3.2095 (2) 9.4110 (2) 1.6190 (1) 3.8816 (1)	3.8543 (2) 1.0729 (1) 1.7935 (1) 4.0964 (1)	4.2792 (2) 1.1594 (1) 1.9069 (1) 4.2327 (1)	4.5781 (2) 1.2203 (1) 1.9864 (1) 4.3269 (1)	4.7992 (2) 1.2654 (1) 2.0451 (1) 4.3960 (1)	4.9690 (2) 1.3001 (1) 2.0903 (1) 4.4488 (1)
3	6.8353 (3) 3.7366 (2) 8.2871 (2) 2.8065 (1)	3.2096 (2) 9.4109 (2) 1.6190 (1) 3.8816 (1)	5.1008 (2) 1.2714 (1) 2.0306 (1) 4.3534 (1)	6.3604 (2) 1.4777 (1) 2.2789 (1) 4.6209 (1)	7.2352 (2) 1.6176 (1) 2.4446 (1) 4.7938 (1)	7.8725 (2) 1.7185 (1) 2.5630 (1) 4.9150 (1)	8.3559 (2) 1.7946 (1) 2.6519 (1) 5.0047 (1)	8.7344 (2) 1.8540 (1) 2.7210 (1) 5.0739 (1)
4	7.6401 (3) 4.1036 (2) 8.9587 (2) 2.9323 (1)	3.8543 (2) 1.0729 (1) 1.7935 (1) 4.0964 (1)	6.3604 (2) 1.4777 (1) 2.2789 (1) 4.6209 (1)	8.1157 (2) 1.7385 (1) 2.5791 (1) 4.9236 (1)	9.3760 (2) 1.9194 (1) 2.7831 (1) 5.1219 (1)	1.0317 (1) 2.0519 (1) 2.9309 (1) 5.2623 (1)	1.1043 (1) 2.1532 (1) 3.0429 (1) 5.3671 (1)	1.1620 (1) 2.2331 (1) 3.1308 (1) 5.4484 (1)
5	8.1286 (3) 4.3298 (2) 9.3747 (2) 3.0097 (1)	4.2792 (2) 1.1594 (1) 1.9069 (1) 4.2327 (1)	7.2352 (2) 1.6176 (1) 2.4446 (1) 4.7938 (1)	9.3760 (2) 1.9194 (1) 2.7831 (1) 5.1219 (1)				
6	8.4557 (3) 4.4827 (2) 9.6568 (2) 3.0622 (1)	4.5781 (2) 1.2203 (1) 1.9864 (1) 4.3269 (1)	7.8725 (2) 1.7185 (1) 2.5630 (1) 4.9150 (1)	1.0317 (1) 2.0520 (1) 2.9309 (1) 5.2623 (1)				
7	8.6900 (3) 4.5927 (2) 9.8604 (2) 3.1000 (1)	4.7992 (2) 1.2654 (1) 2.0451 (1) 4.3960 (1)	8.3559 (2) 1.7946 (1) 2.6519 (1) 5.0047 (1)	1.1043 (1) 2.1532 (1) 3.0429 (1) 5.3671 (1)				
8	8.8659 (3) 4.6756 (2) 1.0014 (1) 3.1286 (1)	4.9691 (2) 1.3001 (1) 2.0903 (1) 4.4487 (1)	8.7344 (2) 1.8540 (1) 2.7210 (1) 5.0739 (1)	1.1620 (1) 2.2331 (1) 3.1308 (1) 5.4484 (1)				

$k = 3$

q \ m	1	2	3	4	5	6	7	8
1	9.0500 (4) 7.0579 (3) 1.8811 (2) 8.4314 (2)	3.1383 (3) 1.7622 (2) 3.9626 (2) 1.3550 (1)	4.2460 (3) 2.2752 (2) 4.9377 (2) 1.5733 (1)	4.8400 (3) 2.5568 (2) 5.4745 (2) 1.6915 (1)	5.2055 (3) 2.7322 (2) 5.8103 (2) 1.7652 (1)	5.4524 (3) 2.8513 (2) 6.0392 (2) 1.8155 (1)	5.6302 (3) 2.9375 (2) 6.2050 (2) 1.8519 (1)	5.7643 (3) 3.0026 (2) 6.3306 (2) 1.8794 (1)
2	2.6290 (3) 1.4934 (2) 3.3966 (2) 1.1979 (1)	1.4154 (2) 4.5506 (2) 8.1345 (2) 2.0451 (1)	2.2570 (2) 6.3957 (2) 1.0738 (1) 2.4437 (1)	2.7904 (2) 7.5320 (2) 1.2305 (1) 2.6723 (1)	3.1472 (2) 8.2895 (2) 1.3341 (1) 2.8202 (1)	3.4003 (2) 8.8276 (2) 1.4074 (1) 2.9235 (1)	3.5886 (2) 9.2285 (2) 1.4620 (1) 2.9998 (1)	3.7340 (2) 9.5384 (2) 1.5041 (1) 3.0584 (1)
3	3.4078 (3) 1.8462 (2) 4.0568 (2) 1.3415 (1)	2.1582 (2) 6.1120 (2) 1.0277 (1) 2.3553 (1)	3.7150 (2) 8.9373 (2) 1.3948 (1) 2.8564 (1)	4.7965 (2) 1.0779 (1) 1.6259 (1) 3.1529 (1)	5.5615 (2) 1.2053 (1) 1.7835 (1) 3.3489 (1)	6.1243 (2) 1.2983 (1) 1.8974 (1) 3.4881 (1)	6.5542 (2) 1.3689 (1) 1.9837 (1) 3.5921 (1)	6.8925 (2) 1.4244 (1) 2.0511 (1) 3.6728 (1)
4	3.8132 (3) 2.0353 (2) 4.4129 (2) 1.4182 (1)	2.6174 (2) 7.0528 (2) 1.1542 (1) 2.5312 (1)	4.7053 (2) 1.0560 (1) 1.5932 (1) 3.0982 (1)	6.2376 (2) 1.2926 (1) 1.8775 (1) 3.4407 (1)	7.3618 (2) 1.4605 (1) 2.0753 (1) 3.6706 (1)	8.2110 (2) 1.5852 (1) 2.2206 (1) 3.8357 (1)	8.8714 (2) 1.6813 (1) 2.3318 (1) 3.9603 (1)	9.3990 (2) 1.7576 (1) 2.4196 (1) 4.0576 (1)
5	4.0590 (3) 2.1518 (2) 4.6336 (2) 1.4658 (1)	2.9208 (2) 7.6740 (2) 1.2371 (1) 2.6444 (1)	5.3987 (2) 1.1672 (1) 1.7274 (1) 3.2575 (1)	7.2850 (2) 1.4436 (1) 2.0513 (1) 3.6334 (1)				
6	4.2235 (3) 2.2304 (2) 4.7833 (2) 1.4982 (1)	3.1344 (2) 8.1128 (2) 1.2956 (1) 2.7234 (1)	5.9064 (2) 1.2480 (1) 1.8241 (1) 3.3704 (1)	8.0728 (2) 1.5553 (1) 2.1784 (1) 3.7716 (1)				
7	4.3413 (3) 2.2870 (2) 4.8914 (2) 1.5216 (1)	3.2924 (2) 8.4386 (2) 1.3389 (1) 2.7817 (1)	6.2923 (2) 1.3092 (1) 1.8971 (1) 3.4548 (1)	9.6830 (2) 1.6411 (1) 2.2756 (1) 3.3759 (1)				
8	4.4297 (3) 2.3296 (2) 4.9731 (2) 1.5393 (1)	3.4139 (2) 8.6899 (2) 1.3724 (1) 2.8265 (1)	6.5949 (2) 1.3571 (1) 1.9541 (1) 3.5203 (1)	9.1698 (2) 1.7090 (1) 2.3521 (1) 3.9574 (1)				

TABLE I^{a-c} (*continued*)

$k=4$

q \ m	1	2	3	4	5	6	7	8
1	5.9490 (4)	2.3670 (3)	3.3067 (3)	3.8216 (3)	4.1419 (3)	4.3597 (3)	4.5172 (3)	4.6364 (3)
	4.5910 (3)	1.3156 (2)	1.7590 (2)	2.0069 (2)	2.1626 (2)	2.2691 (2)	2.3463 (2)	2.4048 (2)
	1.2145 (2)	2.9307 (2)	3.7871 (2)	4.2672 (2)	4.5701 (2)	4.7775 (2)	4.9283 (2)	5.0426 (2)
	5.3430 (2)	9.7883 (2)	1.1806 (1)	1.2919 (1)	1.3619 (1)	1.4099 (1)	1.4448 (1)	1.4712 (1)
2	1.7486 (3)	1.1166 (2)	1.8592 (2)	2.3412 (2)	2.6672 (2)	2.8999 (2)	3.0739 (2)	3.2084 (2)
	9.8820 (3)	3.5345 (2)	5.1926 (2)	6.2388 (2)	6.9441 (2)	7.4484 (2)	7.8257 (2)	8.1183 (2)
	2.2370 (2)	6.2529 (2)	8.6307 (2)	1.0097 (1)	1.1079 (1)	1.1778 (1)	1.2300 (1)	1.2704 (1)
	7.8003 (2)	1.5397 (1)	1.9241 (1)	2.1500 (1)	2.2979 (1)	2.4020 (1)	2.4792 (1)	2.5387 (1)
3	2.2696 (3)	1.7219 (2)	3.1121 (2)	4.1044 (2)	4.8150 (2)	5.3420 (2)	5.7460 (2)	6.0650 (2)
	1.2258 (2)	4.8022 (2)	7.3698 (2)	9.0894 (2)	1.0295 (1)	1.1182 (1)	1.1859 (1)	1.2392 (1)
	2.6852 (2)	7.9956 (2)	1.1388 (1)	1.3583 (1)	1.5099 (1)	1.6204 (1)	1.7045 (1)	1.7705 (1)
	8.8086 (2)	1.7988 (1)	2.2885 (1)	2.5862 (1)	2.7857 (1)	2.9286 (1)	3.0360 (1)	3.1196 (1)
4	2.5406 (3)	2.0979 (2)	3.9719 (2)	5.3880 (2)	6.4410 (2)	7.2430 (2)	7.8702 (2)	8.3730 (2)
	1.3532 (2)	5.5712 (2)	8.7742 (2)	1.0999 (1)	1.2601 (1)	1.3800 (1)	1.4730 (1)	1.5471 (1)
	2.9271 (2)	9.0329 (2)	1.3112 (1)	1.5831 (1)	1.7750 (1)	1.9172 (1)	2.0266 (1)	2.1134 (1)
	9.3498 (2)	1.9473 (1)	2.5051 (1)	2.8518 (1)	3.0879 (1)	3.2591 (1)	3.3890 (1)	3.4909 (1)
5	2.7048 (3)	2.3466 (2)	4.5767 (2)	6.3275 (2)				
	1.4316 (2)	6.0805 (2)	9.7429 (2)	1.2352 (1)				
	3.0771 (2)	9.7159 (2)	1.4285 (1)	1.7395 (1)				
	9.6862 (2)	2.0435 (1)	2.6489 (1)	3.0312 (1)				
6	2.8147 (3)	2.5219 (2)	5.0205 (2)	7.0360 (2)				
	1.4845 (2)	6.4409 (2)	1.0448 (1)	1.3357 (1)				
	3.1789 (2)	1.0199 (1)	1.5134 (1)	1.8546 (1)				
	9.9151 (2)	2.1109 (1)	2.7515 (1)	3.1609 (1)				
7	2.8934 (3)	2.6515 (2)	5.3580 (2)	7.5870 (2)				
	1.5226 (2)	6.7089 (2)	1.0984 (1)	1.4131 (1)				
	3.2523 (2)	1.0557 (1)	1.5777 (1)	1.9428 (1)				
	1.0081 (1)	2.1608 (1)	2.8285 (1)	3.2591 (1)				
8	2.9524 (3)	2.7512 (2)	5.6232 (2)	8.0260 (2)				
	1.5513 (2)	6.9157 (2)	1.1405 (1)	1.4746 (1)				
	3.3078 (2)	1.0834 (1)	1.6279 (1)	2.0125 (1)				
	1.0206 (1)	2.1992 (1)	2.8883 (1)	3.3361 (1)				

$k = 5$

q \ m	1	2	3	4	5	6	7	8
1	4.5000 (4) 3.4003 (3) 8.9608 (3) 3.9061 (2)	1.9550 (3) 1.0807 (2) 2.3950 (2) 7.8984 (2)	2.8000 (3) 1.4836 (2) 3.1806 (2) 9.8000 (2)	3.2711 (3) 1.7124 (2) 3.6276 (2) 1.0866 (1)	3.5667 (3) 1.8572 (2) 3.9116 (2) 1.1540 (1)	3.7687 (3) 1.9566 (2) 4.1069 (2) 1.2004 (1)	3.9153 (3) 2.0289 (2) 4.2491 (2) 1.2342 (1)	4 0261 (3) 2.0838 (2) 4.3573 (2) 2.8043 (1)
2	1.3099 (3) 7.3835 (3) 1.6675 (2) 5.7813 (2)	9.4700 (3) 2.9706 (2) 5.2240 (2) 1.2714 (1)	1.6280 (2) 4.5087 (2) 7.4508 (2) 1.6418 (1)	2.0783 (2) 5.4973 (2) 8.8501 (2) 1.8636 (1)	2.3855 (2) 6.1696 (2) 9.7945 (2) 2.0102 (1)	2.6060 (2) 6.6528 (2) 1.0471 (1) 2.1139 (1)	2.7713 (2) 7.0155 (2) 1.0978 (1) 2.1911 (1)	2.3995 (2) 7.2973 (2) 1.1371 (1) 2.2507 (1)
3	1.7014 (3) 9.1752 (3) 2.0066 (2) 6.5562 (2)	1.4704 (2) 4.0636 (2) 6.7270 (2) 1.4973 (1)	2.7537 (2) 6.4597 (2) 9.9237 (2) 1.9726 (1)	3.6885 (2) 8.0976 (2) 1.2034 (1) 2.2675 (1)	4.3645 (2) 9.2577 (2) 1.3507 (1) 2.4671 (1)	4.8681 (2) 1.0115 (1) 1.4587 (1) 2.6110 (1)	5.2560 (2) 1.0773 (1) 1.5412 (1) 2.7195 (1)	5.5630 (2) 1.1292 (1) 1.6061 (1)
4	1.9049 (3) 1.0135 (2) 2.1898 (2) 6.9731 (2)	1.7965 (2) 4.7294 (2) 7.6260 (2) 1.6277 (1)	3.5313 (2) 7.7268 (2) 1.1481 (1) 2.1709 (1)					
5	2.0282 (3) 1.0726 (2) 2.3033 (2) 7.2325 (2)	2.0125 (2) 5.1712 (2) 8.2196 (2) 1.7124 (1)	4.0800 (2) 8.6039 (2) 1.2545 (1) 2.3033 (1)					
6	2.1107 (3) 1.1125 (2) 2.3804 (2) 7.4092 (2)	2.1647 (2) 5.4843 (2) 8.6396 (2) 1.7720 (1)	4.4830 (2) 9.2442 (2) 1.3317 (1) 2.3980 (1)					
7	2.1697 (3) 1.1411 (2) 2.4360 (2) 7.5371 (2)	2.2773 (2) 5.7172 (2) 8.9520 (2) 1.8161 (1)	4.7905 (2) 9.7312 (2) 1.3902 (1) 2.4692 (1)					
8	2.2141 (3) 1.1628 (2) 2.4780 (2) 7.6340 (2)	2.3639 (2) 5.8970 (2) 9.1933 (2) 1.8500 (1)	5.0315 (2) 1.0114 (1) 1.4360 (1) 2.5247 (1)					

[a] The four entries in each cell refer to $P^* = 0.99, 0.95, 0.90, 0.75$ from top to bottom.

[b] The number in the parentheses refers to the power of 10^{-1} by which each entry should be multiplied to get the appropriate constant.

[c] For fixed k, P^*, q, and m, the table gives the values of $c_1 = c_2$, satisfying

$$P\left\{F_k \geq c_1 \max_{1 \leq j \leq k-1} F_j\right\} = \int_0^\infty \left[F_{2q,\,2m}\left(\frac{x}{c_1}\right)\right]^{k-1} dF_{2q,\,2m}(x) = P^*$$

where F_i, $i = 1, 2, \ldots, k$ are iid central F random variables with $2q$ and $2m$ degrees of freedom. Values of $d_1 = d_2$ are given by $d_1(k, P^*, q, m) = c_1(k, P^*, m, q)$.

TABLE II.[a–c]
Values of the Constants for Procedures $\mathscr{R}_1(c)$ and $\mathscr{R}_2(c')$

q \ m	k = 2				k = 3			
	1	2	3	4	1	2	3	4
1	2.0000 (2)	1.5056 (2)	1.3406 (2)	1.2580 (2)	1.5000 (2)	1.0748 (2)	9.3740 (3)	8.6980 (3)
	1.0000 (1)	7.6461 (2)	6.8524 (2)	6.4546 (2)	7.5000 (2)	5.4418 (2)	4.7705 (2)	4.4390 (2)
	2.0000 (1)	1.5609 (1)	1.4111 (1)	1.3359 (1)	1.5000 (1)	1.1064 (1)	9.7642 (2)	9.1204 (2)
	5.0000 (1)	4.1886 (1)	3.9030 (1)	3.7593 (1)	3.7500 (1)	2.9226 (1)	2.6385 (1)	2.4964 (1)
2	1.4142 (1)	1.0804 (1)	9.4690 (2)	8.7430 (2)	1.2247 (1)	9.0170 (2)	7.7620 (2)	7.0910 (2)
	3.1623 (1)	2.5000 (1)	2.2284 (1)	2.0794 (1)	2.7386 (1)	2.0788 (1)	1.8156 (1)	1.6732 (1)
	4.4722 (1)	3.6409 (1)	3.2930 (1)	3.1009 (1)	3.8730 (1)	3.0165 (1)	2.6673 (1)	2.4768 (1)
	7.0711 (1)	6.1904 (1)	5.8072 (1)	5.5934 (1)	6.1237 (1)	5.0723 (1)	4.6216 (1)	4.3715 (1)
3	2.7144 (1)	2.1511 (1)	1.8970 (1)	1.7496 (1)	2.4662 (1)	1.8982 (1)	1.6480 (1)	1.5051 (1)
	4.6416 (1)	3.8195 (1)	3.4375 (1)	3.2133 (1)	4.2171 (1)	3.3596 (1)	2.9700 (1)	2.7442 (1)
	5.8480 (1)	4.9497 (1)	4.5237 (1)	4.2717 (1)	5.3133 (1)	4.3412 (1)	3.8897 (1)	3.6255 (1)
	7.9370 (1)	7.1533 (1)	6.7690 (1)	6.5392 (1)	7.2112 (1)	6.2227 (1)	5.7420 (1)	5.4557 (1)
4	3.7606 (1)	3.0771 (1)	2.7413 (1)	2.5368 (1)	3.4997 (1)	2.7953 (1)	2.4566 (1)	2.2530 (1)
	5.6234 (1)	4.7713 (1)	4.3406 (1)	4.0748 (1)	5.2332 (1)	4.3227 (1)	3.8713 (1)	3.5959 (1)
	6.6874 (1)	5.8200 (1)	5.3737 (1)	5.0961 (1)	6.2233 (1)	5.2609 (1)	4.7736 (1)	4.4735 (1)
	8.4090 (1)	7.7242 (1)	7.3620 (1)	7.1346 (1)	7.8254 (1)	6.9370 (1)	6.4689 (1)	6.1755 (1)

q \ m	$k=4$: 1	$k=4$: 2	$k=4$: 3	$k=4$: 4	$k=5$: 1	$k=5$: 2	$k=5$: 3	$k=5$: 4
1	1.3332 (2) 6.6667 (2) 1.3333 (1) 3.3333 (1)	9.2370 (3) 4.6728 (2) 9.4890 (2) 2.4951 (1)	7.9410 (3) 4.0357 (2) 8.2447 (2) 2.2123 (1)	7.3100 (3) 3.7244 (2) 7.6344 (2) 2.0720 (1)	1.2500 (2) 6.2500 (2) 1.2500 (1) 3.1250 (1)	8.4460 (3) 4.2707 (2) 8.6676 (2) 2.2744 (1)	7.1820 (3) 3.6472 (2) 7.4441 (2) 1.9909 (1)	6.5700 (3) 3.3446 (2) 6.8482 (2) 1.8510 (1)
2	1.1547 (1) 2.5820 (1) 3.6515 (1) 5.7735 (1)	8.3040 (2) 1.9120 (1) 2.7713 (1) 4.6444 (1)	7.0650 (2) 1.6490 (1) 2.4177 (1) 4.1659 (1)	6.4072 (2) 1.5079 (1) 2.2264 (1) 3.9019 (1)	1.1180 (1) 2.5000 (1) 3.5355 (1) 5.5902 (1)	7.9052 (2) 1.8193 (1) 2.6354 (1) 4.4097 (1)	6.6677 (2) 1.5546 (1) 2.2772 (1) 3.9131 (1)	6.0150 (2) 1.4136 (1) 2.0845 (1) 3.6404 (1)
3	2.3712 (1) 4.0548 (1) 5.1087 (1) 6.9336 (1)	1.7925 (1) 3.1692 (1) 4.0915 (1) 5.8501 (1)	1.5410 (1) 2.7719 (1) 3.6243 (1) 5.3270 (1)	1.3985 (1) 2.5434 (1) 3.3528 (1) 5.0167 (1)	2.3208 (1) 3.9685 (1) 5.0000 (1) 6.7861 (1)	1.7321 (1) 3.0609 (1) 3.9500 (1) 5.6411 (1)	1.4785 (1) 2.6568 (1) 3.4710 (1) 5.0909 (1)	1.3356 (1) 2.4256 (1) 3.1941 (1) 4.7656 (1)
4	3.3981 (1) 5.0814 (1) 6.0427 (1) 7.5984 (1)	2.6749 (1) 4.1328 (1) 5.0259 (1) 6.6142 (1)	2.3309 (1) 3.6673 (1) 4.5158 (1) 6.0980 (1)	2.1257 (1) 3.3851 (1) 4.2034 (1) 5.7755 (1)	3.3437 (1) 5.0000 (1) 5.9460 (1) 7.4768 (1)	2.6052 (1) 4.0234 (1) 4.8913 (1) 6.4309 (1)	2.2565 (1) 3.5471 (1) 4.3649 (1) 5.8840 (1)	2.0495 (1) 3.2597 (1) 4.0439 (1) 5.5432 (1)

[a] For fixed k, P^*, q, and m, the table gives the values of $c = c'$ satisfying

$$P\left\{X_k \geq c \max_{1 \leq j \leq k-1} X_j\right\} = \int_0^1 I_{x/c}^{k-1}(q, m) b(x; q, m)\, dx = P^*$$

where X_i, $i = i, 2, \ldots, k$ are iid beta random variables with parameters q and m, and $I_x(q, m)$ and $b(x; q, m)$ as cdf and density, respectively.

[b] The four entries in each cell refer to $P^* = 0.99, 0.95, 0.90, 0.75$ from top to bottom.

[c] The number in the parentheses refers to the power of 10^{-1} by which each entry should be multiplied to get the constant c.

ACKNOWLEDGMENTS

The authors wish to thank Professor C. G. Khatri for some helpful discussions and Mrs. A. Barron for computational assistance.

REFERENCES

1. ALAM, K., and RIZVI, M. H. (1966). Selection from multivariate normal populations. *Ann. Inst. Statist. Math.* **18** 307–318.
2. ANDERSON, T. W. (1958). "Introduction to Multivariate Statistical Analysis." Wiley, New York.
3. BARLOW, R. E., and GUPTA, S. S. (1967). Selection procedures for restricted families of probability distributions. Mimeo. Ser. No. 132. Dept. of Statist., Purdue Univ., Lafayette, Indiana. To appear in *Ann. Math. Statist.* (1969).
4. BARLOW, R. E., GUPTA, S. S., and PANCHAPAKESAN, S. (1967). On the distribution of the maximum and minimum of ratios of order statistics. Mimeo. Ser. No. 133. Dept. of Statist., Purdue Univ., Lafayette, Indiana. *Ann. Math. Statist.* (1969).
5. BECHHOFER, R. E. (1954). A single-sample multiple decision procedure for ranking means of normal populations with known variances. *Ann. Math. Statist.* **25** 16–39.
6. BECHHOFER, R. E., ELMAGHRABY, S., and MORSE, N. (1959). A single-sample multiple decision procedure for selecting the multinomial event which has the highest probability. *Ann. Math. Statist.* **30** 102–119.
7. CACOULLOS, T., and SOBEL, M. (1966). An inverse sampling procedure for selecting the most probable event in a multinomial distribution. *In* "Multivariate Analysis" (P. R. Krishnaiah, ed.), pp. 423–455. Academic Press, New York.
8. GNANADESIKAN, M. (1966). Some selection and ranking procedures for multivariate normal populations. Ph.D. Thesis, Dept. of Statist., Purdue Univ., Lafayette, Indiana.
9. GNANADESIKAN, M., and GUPTA, S. S. (1969). Selection procedures for multivariate normal distributions in terms of measures of dispersion. *Technometrics.* To be published.
10. GUPTA, S. S. (1956). On a decision rule for a problem in ranking means. Mimeo. Ser. No. 150. Inst. of Statist., Univ. of North Carolina, Chapel Hill, North Carolina.
11. GUPTA, S. S. (1963). Probability integrals of the multivariate normal and multivariate t. *Ann. Math. Statist.* **34** 792–828.
12. GUPTA, S. S. (1963). Bibliography on the multivariate normal integrals and related topics. *Ann. Math. Statist.* **34** 829–838.
13. GUPTA, S. S. (1963). On a selection and ranking procedure for gamma populations. *Ann. Inst. Statist. Math.* **14** 199–216.
14. GUPTA, S. S. (1965). On some multiple decision (selection and ranking) rules. *Technometrics* **7** 225–245.
15. GUPTA, S. S. (1966). On some selection and ranking procedures for multivariate normal populations using distance functions. *In* "Multivariate Analysis" (P. R. Krishnaiah, ed.), pp. 457–475. Academic Press, New York.
16. GUPTA, S. S., and NAGEL, K. (1967). On selection and ranking procedures and order statistics from the multinomial distribution. *Sankhyā Ser. B* **29** 1–34.
17. GUPTA, S. S., and SOBEL, M. (1962). On selecting a subset containing the population with the smallest variance. *Biometrika* **49** 495–507.
18. GUPTA, S. S., and SOBEL, M. (1962). On the smallest of several correlated F statistics. *Biometrika* **49** 509–523.

19. GUPTA, S. S., and STUDDEN, W. J. (1969). On some selection and ranking procedures with applications to multivariate populations. *In* "Essays in Probability and Statistics" (R. C. Bose *et al.*, eds.). Univ. of North Carolina Press, Chapel Hill, North Carolina.
20. HOEL, P. G. (1937). A significance test for component analysis. *Ann. Math. Statist.* **8** 149–158.
21. KARLIN, S. (1968). "Total Positivity," Vol. 1. Stanford Univ. Press, Stanford, California.
22. KRISHNAIAH, P. R. (1967). Selection procedures based on covariance matrices of multivariate normal populations. *In* "Blanch Anniversary Vol.," pp. 147–160. Aerospace Res. Labs., Wright-Patterson Air Force Base, Ohio.
23. KRISHNAIAH, P. R., and ARMITAGE, J. V. (1964). Tables for the studentized smallest chi-square, with tables and applications. ARL 64-218. Aerospace Res. Labs., Wright-Patterson Air Force Base, Ohio.
24. KRISHNAIAH, P. R., and RIZVI, M. H. (1966). Some procedures for selection of multivariate normal populations better than a control. *In* "Multivariate Analysis" (P. R. Krishnaiah, ed.), pp. 477–490. Academic Press, New York.
25. LEHMANN, E. L. (1955). Ordered families of distributions. *Ann. Math. Statist.* **26** 399–419.
26. LEHMANN, E. L. (1959). "Testing Statistical Hypotheses." Wiley, New York.
27. RAO, C. R. (1965). "Linear Statistical Inference and Its Applications." Wiley, New York.

Decision Theoretic Approach to Some Multivariate Problems[1]

HERMAN RUBIN

DEPARTMENT OF STATISTICS
PURDUE UNIVERSITY
LAFAYETTE, INDIANA

INTRODUCTION

There are many problems in multivariate analysis which can profitably be approached in a decision-theoretic manner. In fact, many of them must be so treated if they are to be other than results in theoretical mathematical statistics. This includes many which are not now so treated. The author makes no claim that the approaches in this paper are good ones; in fact, the precise formulation of any applied decision-theoretic problem must *not* be made by the statistician but rather by the user. In some cases, no procedure is suggested. However, it is hoped that this work may suggest approaches which are more appropriate.

There is a deliberate omission of all references in this paper. These references would be to results in theoretical mathematical statistics which this author does not wish to urge on the reader as giving good practical procedures. Much further development is needed by mathematical statisticians with knowledge of the problems of application before this can be done, and the applicability of such procedures must be carefully circumscribed. In fact, there is a considerable misuse of statistical procedures by people who have no idea of the situations in which they are appropriate. Except for routine situations, such as occur in industrial quality control, adjustment of good observations to be compatible with known conditions, etc., it is necessary to apply statistical procedures with intelligence.

It is at least somewhat annoying that researchers will frequently use procedures, the applicability of which depends heavily on assumptions which they do not understand, and which they would probably not be willing to

[1] This research was partly supported by the Office of Naval Research Contract N00014-67-A-0226-0008. Reproduction in whole or in part is permitted for any purpose of the United States Government.

make if the assumptions were understood, and they object strenuously to being asked for some idea of the parameter values. As is also noted in Section 5, they use the results of a statistical investigation even though an understanding of the problem would clearly indicate otherwise.

1. INCLUSION OF VARIABLES IN A REGRESSION

Here the problem is complicated by possible structure in the space of variables, as well as the purpose of the regression. If the purpose of the regression is merely prediction, and the variables themselves have no structure, an appropriate loss function might be of the form

$$L(w,b) = E_w(y - b'x)^2, \tag{1}$$

where the expectation is on the future distribution of the observations. Now if M is the total moment matrix of the observed x's, m the moments vector of y with x, the residuals are normal, and the regression coefficients are a priori normal (μ, Σ), and the variance of the residuals is known, the Bayes estimator is

$$\hat{b} = \mu + (\sigma^2\Sigma^{-1} + M)^{-1}(m - M\mu). \tag{2}$$

All of this is well known. Normality of the residuals is not too important. However, in general the a priori distribution is not normal and σ^2 is not known. Of course, we have the well-known asymptotic results, but with reasonable sample sizes (say $<10^7$), there is reason to doubt the effectiveness of asymptotic approximations with the number of explanatory variables being on the order of 1000 or even 100. That Σ may be ill-conditioned is of no consequence, since

$$(\sigma^2\Sigma^{-1} + M)^{-1} = (\sigma^2 I + \Sigma M)^{-1}\Sigma \tag{3}$$

is a well-behaved function of Σ; in fact, (3) or

$$(\sigma^2\Sigma^{-1} + M)^{-1} = \Sigma^{1/2}(\sigma^2 I + \Sigma^{1/2}M\Sigma^{1/2})^{-1}\Sigma^{1/2} \tag{4}$$

enables (2) to be used even for certain infinite dimensional problems. Of course, none of this is relevant if there are, say, 10 explanatory variables and 1,000,000 observations. However, in many educational and psychological situations, there are 50–500 explanatory variables, and in meterological situations, 10,000 variables may not be too many.

Another problem which must be faced is that of computational cost. A frequently overlooked point is that the theory of rational behavior under uncertainty assumes zero cost of computation and zero computing time. If we consider a problem with 10^6 observations and 10^4 explanatory variables, and endow our computer with a multiply plus add time of 2 μsec, it would take about 28,000 hr (about 3.2 yr) to even compute the moments. The computation of the regression coefficients by (2) would take about 100 hr of computer time if Σ^{-1} were given, and less than 400 hr if Σ were given. However, if the number of variables were reduced to 1000, the moment time decreases to 280 hr and the computation time to 0.4 hr.

A practical problem with fitting large-scale regressions is the problem of multicollinearity. This is *not* due to chance, but is due to the fact that, in practice, the explanatory variables are highly related.

Because of these considerations, one may ask if standard procedures, such as stepwise choice of variables, can be modified to take into account decision-theoretic considerations. The prediction error is

$$\mu = (\beta_1{}^* - \hat{\beta}_1{}^*)'x_1 + \beta_2'(x_2 - M_{21}M_{11}^{-1}x_1) + v, \tag{5}$$

where x_1 is the included vector, x_2 the excluded vector, and v the residual. If a Bayes procedure is used to obtain $\hat{\beta}_1{}^*$, the various terms are orthogonal, and

$$\rho = E[(\beta_1{}^* - \hat{\beta}_1{}^*)'H_{11}(\beta_1{}^* - \beta_1{}^*) + \beta_2'H_{22}^*\beta_2 + \sigma^2]. \tag{6}$$

What can be done without using prior information? If we use standard regression techniques

$$E((\beta_1{}^* - \hat{\beta}_1{}^*)'H_{11}(\beta_1{}^* - \hat{\beta}_1{}^*)) = (\sigma^2 + \beta_2'\overline{M}_{22}^*\beta_2) \operatorname{tr} H_{11}M_{11}^{-1},$$

or we may rewrite (6) as

$$\rho = (\sigma^2 + \beta_2'\overline{M}_{22} + \beta_2)(1 + \operatorname{tr} H_{11}M_{11}^{-1}) + \beta_2'(H_{22}^* - \overline{M}_{22}^*)\beta_2. \tag{7}$$

We even have an unbiased estimator of the "variance" term in (7).

It is clear that we are likely to believe $\beta_2'\overline{M}_{22}^*\beta_2$ is "small," but nothing can be said without using some prior information about the last term in (7). From this we can get the general hint, however, that if a predictor is going to be considerably more variable in the future, it is desirable to include it even though it may not have been too important in the past. Of course, it is not the variability of the variable which counts, but it is the variability of its residual from the sample regression on the predictors included, that matters. Also several variables would have to be considered simultaneously.

Another thing that can be done is to use the methods of Stein and others to reduce the mean squared error of the estimates. It is hard to say how this would work in practice.

The next problem is which variables to include in the regression. If there are at most 20 predictors under consideration and a high-speed computer is available, all regressions can be computed cheaply, but the user will have to instruct the computer carefully so that storage of results and handling of output do not become unreasonable. It is very dangerous to eliminate variables; let the correlation matrix be

y	x_1	x_2
1.0	0.7	0
0.7	1.0	−0.7
0	−0.7	1.0

now x_2 has 0 correlation with y, but $R^2 = 0.49$ if only x_1 is used, and is 0.9608 if both are used.

Nor should one wish to include variables which give large increases in R^2 immediately. Let the correlation matrix be

y	x_1	x_2	x_3
1.0	0.7	0.7	0.84
0.7	1.0	0	0.6
0.7	0	1.0	0.6
0.84	0.6	0.6	1.0

The optimal regression is $y = 0.7x_1 + 0.7x_2$ with $R^2 = 0.98$; the best single variable, of course, is x_3 with $R^2 = 0.7056$; x_1 (or x_2) and x_3 gives $R^2 = 0.7656$. It might even be possible to reject as insignificant all variables individually which might improve the prediction, but the total set might give considerable improvement. This can be very easily seen if we change the last row of the correlation matrix to (0.98 0.7 0.7 1.0); the best single variable yields $R^2 = 0.9604$, the best two, $R^2 = 0.98$, two including the best one, $R^2 = 0.960784$.

The author would suggest, therefore, that if not more than n ($20 \leq n \leq 50$, depending on the value of the problem) predictors, it might be useful to compute all regressions, possibly using a Stein-type modification, and to take that one for which the estimated prediction error, taking into account degrees of freedom, is smallest.

However, one would expect that the user should be prepared to give prior information which should enable better procedures to be devised. Also, it is rare that follow-up studies are made of the uses of regression; this should be done. As to what should be done with large numbers of predictors, I suspect that modifications of the preceding procedures could be used, but the computational costs mount rapidly.

It is even possible, say in polynomial regressions, that the number of variables available may be infinite, in which case it is necessary to finitize the number of terms in order to compute. We now have a risk function which can be approximately written as

$$\rho = W(\hat{\beta} - \beta) + R(\hat{\beta}), \tag{8}$$

the first term being the prediction error and the second term due to the inconvenience or cost of computation. The term R can be a very complicated function; for example, the sequence $\{nab^{n-1}\}$ in a polynomial regression is cheaper than its first 5 terms, and the sequence $\{ab^n/(n+1)\}$ is cheaper than its first 20 terms.

Furthermore, the multicollinearity problem is very bad for polynomial regression, which may require us to add a term of an extremely involved analytic nature to (8). Thus, we need means of estimation which, at some stage, take into account both the complexity term and the computational cost term. With large amounts of data, this can be very difficult; the complexity term, is likely to lead to regressions nonlinear in the parameters, and possibly a complete recalculation of moments at each stage. Multicollinearity may also require calculation of residuals and moment computations. Since, except for error control problems, the moment computation is likely to be considerably costlier than any other single phase, we may have a very expensive computational situation. There is the further problem of the assessment, particularly by a computer program, of the possibility of nearby values of $\hat{\beta}$ with $R(\hat{\beta})$ small. The function R will always be discontinuous everywhere that it is finite if β is infinite dimensional, but it is lower semicontinuous. As the examples cited show, these discontinuities may be very complicated.

2. "SCIENTIFIC" PURPOSE OF A REGRESSION–STRUCTURAL INFERENCE

Here the loss function might be of the form (8), but the complexity term is much more important. The inclusion of many variables not functionally related, which before could not be seriously entertained, now can be of low cost. For example, if there is a "natural" enumeration of variables, $\{nab^{n-1}\}$ and $\{ab^{n-1}/n\}$ are likely to be of "complexity" between 2 and 10. Furthermore, R is much harder to evaluate. Too much complexity may make it difficult for theoretical models to be formulated which will advance the field; too little may not provide a good enough fit, or may leave out important variables. This would indicate the possibility that the risk may depend on $\hat{\beta}$ and β in a much more complicated manner. Note also that the complexity term is quite time dependent; if the current theoretical model takes into account all but one of the variables included in a regression, the complexity is low. We should remember that telescopic data would readily refute Kepler's laws at any reasonable significance level, yet these confirm Newtonian gravitation, which fits extremely well. There are also some relatively simple physical problems which have not yet been satisfactorily treated although much good data is available.

Occasionally, the hypothesis that certain elements of β are zero will have positive probability; in this case relatively simple Bayes or approximately Bayes procedures may suffice for large samples. Generally this will not be so. However, the prior distribution is likely to concentrate near the "simple" regressions. Again, followup of the results will be quite useful.

Similar comments apply to nonregression type problems of structural estimation, such as simultaneous equation models. There is the further effect here that certain incorrect assumptions may improve estimation substantially, but increase bias only slightly.

3. DISCRIMINANT ANALYSIS

If we consider the case of linear discriminant analysis among several groups each assumed normal with constant known covariance matrix, we find ourselves almost exactly in the prediction situation for regression. However, if there are more than three groups, the results of Stein would indicate that it might be possible to do somewhat better than standard regression techniques would indicate. Also, if there is sufficient information for good separation of the groups, deviations from normality can be very important even for linear discriminant functions.

If the covariance matrix is unknown, the problem is much more complicated. Even if the present procedures are admissible when there are more degrees of freedom than needed for estimation of the covariance matrix, they are probably worse than other reasonable procedures except for parts of the parameter space which would be considered highly unlikely. Here nonnormality is even more troublesome.

For those problems where the number of predictors is large and the amount of data is small, some prior knowledge must be used. Unfortunately, these situations are very common.

4. FACTOR ANALYSIS

In this case the aim is usually scientific, although occasionally estimates of factor scores are used for prediction purposes. All of the remarks of Section 2 apply to the assignment of number of factors, simple structure, and so forth. The standard model

$$y_i = \Lambda x_i + u_i \tag{9}$$

assumes the u's to be normal, independent of each other, and independent of the x's. The specific distribution assumptions are relatively unimportant if the estimates are normalized entirely on $\hat{\Lambda}$; that is, if the y's are not normalized to have unit variance, the x's are not assumed to be uncorrelated or to have unit variance, and no assumptions are made involving the moments of x's and u's other than each u_{ij} is uncorrelated with everything else, then the asymptotic theory is relatively simple. The above relaxation of assumptions also makes comparability of different samples easy.

5. LOOKING AT THE DATA

In most statistical problems, the tendency is to select a technique and "let the data speak for themselves." There are certainly dangers in "looking at the data"; the dangers in the other direction can be even greater. Of course, in complicated problems, it may be necessary to program the computer carefully so that the data can be looked at intelligently.

For example, suppose a regression of college grades on several criteria shows a negative coefficient for a mathematical aptitude score, there being no other criterion of a similar type in the list. Then for predicting college grades approximately, this regression should be used (assuming large samples and few predictors), but anyone who, on the basis of such a study, would suggest using the regression for college entrance purposes or who would conclude that the score does not reflect mathematical aptitude, amply fulfills Disraeli's opinion of statisticians.

For another example, suppose that the following results are obtained on a common final examination of a many-section course, the instructors being evaluated as of two types, and the students being rated before the course in equal groups as good, average, and poor, the figures being average numerical grades.

	A	*B*
Good	118	115
Average	102	120
Poor	100	70

Any policy decision on these numbers alone is dangerous, even assuming that sampling errors are small. However, a typical investigator, noting that the mean in the A group is significantly greater than that in the B group, would jump to the conclusion that A-type teachers should be used. This type of "statistical" behavior is unfortunately becoming very common in many fields.

Selecting a Subset Containing at Least One of the t Best Populations[1]

MILTON SOBEL

IMPERIAL COLLEGE
LONDON, ENGLAND

DEPARTMENT OF STATISTICS[2]
UNIVERSITY OF MINNESOTA
MINNEAPOLIS, MINNESOTA

1. INTRODUCTION

The goal considered is to select from k populations a subset containing at least one of the t best populations for given t and k $(1 \leq t \leq k)$ on the basis of a common fixed sample size n from each of the k populations $\pi_1, \pi_2, \ldots, \pi_k$. A correct selection (CS) is defined as the selection of any subset which contains at least one population π_i whose parameter value θ_i is among the t largest parameter values. Three procedures R, R', and R_m (and a truncated form for each) are constructed, all satisfying the same basic probability requirement, namely that the probability of a correct selection (PCS) is at least P^* whenever the t best populations are at a distance (defined below) of at least δ^* from the remaining $k - t$ populations; here $\delta^* \geq 0$ and $P^* < 1$ are specified. For the special case $t = 1$, the problem is related to the problems treated by Gupta [4] and Desu and Sobel [3], and comparisons are made. Under an additional assumption (related to a monotone likelihood ratio assumption) the truncated version R_T' of Procedure R' is minimax among all the procedures considered, in the sense that it minimizes the maximum of the expected subset size. These procedures select a subset which is either of fixed size or of random size depending on the values of P^*, δ^*, etc. Hence, they can be regarded as an attempt to relate the fixed subset-size approach and the random subset-size approach in the ranking and selection problem. Numerical illustrations and tables for comparing the procedures are included.

[1] Part of this work was done while on a John S. Guggenheim award, and part was done under a National Institute of Health special research fellowship.

[2] Present Address.

The asymptotic ($P^* \to 1$) efficiency of Procedure R_m is shown to be zero relative to that of Procedure R.

2. NOTATION, ASSUMPTIONS, AND REQUIREMENT

Let X_{ij} ($j = 1, 2, \ldots, n$) denote the random sample from π_i ($i = 1, 2, \ldots, k$); observations between and within populations are all (mutually) independent. Let $F_i = F(x; \theta_i)$ denote the distribution (cdf) of X_{ij} which is known except for the value of the scalar parameter θ_i. All θ_i belong to a common open interval Θ, which may be infinite, and larger θ-values are regarded as better. The ordered θ-values and associated vector $\boldsymbol{\theta}$ are given respectively by

$$\theta_{[1]} \le \theta_{[2]} \le \cdots \le \theta_{[k]}; \qquad \boldsymbol{\theta} = (\theta_{[1]}, \theta_{[2]}, \ldots, \theta_{[k]}). \tag{2.1}$$

No a priori information is assumed about the correct pairing of the π_i and $\theta_{[j]}$ ($i, j = 1, 2, \ldots, k$).

A given distance function $\delta(\theta_2, \theta_1)$ measures the distance between populations with parameters $\theta_1 \le \theta_2$; it is assumed to be (i) nonnegative, (ii) equal to 0 if and only if $\theta_1 = \theta_2$, (iii) increasing in θ_2 for fixed θ_1 and decreasing in θ_1 for fixed θ_2. Then $\delta_t = \delta(\theta_{[k-t+1]}, \theta_{[k-t]})$ measures the distance between the t best populations and the remaining $k - t$ worst populations. In a location parameter problem, we take $\delta(\theta_2, \theta_1) = \theta_2 - \theta_1 \ge 0$. Let $\delta^* \ge 0$ and $P^* < 1$ denote specified constants; let Ω denote the set of all $\boldsymbol{\theta}$ and $\Omega(\delta^*)$ denote the subset of Ω on which $\delta_t \ge \delta^*$.

Under Procedures R and R', we select a subset of size at least s, and it is assumed that $s \le k - t$; this assumption on s avoids the trivial case in which the subset necessarily (i.e., with probability one) contains at least one of the t best populations. Later we consider truncated tests in which the subset size is at most $k - t + 1$.

A lower bound for the specified P^* needs some discussion. If we only considered one value of s, we would assume that $P^* > P(s) = 1 - \binom{k-t}{s}/\binom{k}{s}$, but we consider different s-values ($1 \le s \le k - t$). Although it is sufficient to assume that $P^* > P(1) = t/k$, it is more convenient (and more practical) to assume that $P^* > P(k - t) = 1 - \binom{k}{t}^{-1}$; this enables us to use the full range $1 \le s \le k - t$ for s. For any t ($1 \leqq t < k$), this implies that $P^* > (k - 1)/k \geqq \frac{1}{2}$.

Our basic probability requirement for Procedure R (as well as for Procedures R', R_m, and R_0, all defined later) is

$$\text{PCS} \ge P^* \qquad \text{for all} \quad \boldsymbol{\theta} \in \Omega(\delta^*). \tag{2.2}$$

A statistic T is chosen depending on the given family $F(x; \theta)$; $\theta \in \Theta$, and the procedures are based on the observations only through the k values of T. Let $G_{\theta_i}(x)$ denote the cdf of T_i from population π_i ($i = 1, 2, \ldots, k$), and let $T_{[1]} \le T_{[2]} \le \cdots \le T_{[k]}$ denote ordered T-values.

Assumption 1. Here T is chosen so that the family of cdf's $\{G_\theta(x);\ \theta \in \Theta\}$ is a stochastically increasing family of absolutely continuous cdf's, i.e., for $\theta_1 \le \theta_2$, $G_{\theta_1}(x) \ge G_{\theta_2}(x)$ for all x and the distributions $G_\theta(x)$ are distinct for different θ values. We also assume that the derivative $G_\theta{}'(x)$ with respect to θ exists in Θ.

Assumption 2. For $x_1 \le x_2$ and $\theta_1 \le \theta_2$ (both in Θ)

$$G'_{\theta_1}(x_2)\, d_x G_{\theta_2}(x_1) - G'_{\theta_1}(x_1)\, d_x G_{\theta_2}(x_2) \ge 0, \tag{2.3}$$

where d_x denotes the differential element with respect to x.

It should be noted that for a location-parameter problem, the assumption (2.3) is equivalent to assuming a monotone likelihood ratio (mlr) property for $G_\theta(x)$. If the mlr property (or Assumption 2) holds in a location-parameter problem, then we can drop Assumption 1 since the mlr property implies the stochastically increasing property. Assumption 2 is used in this paper only to show that the maximum of the expected subset-size occurs at a vector $\boldsymbol{\theta}$ with equal components. Although it is not assumed that T is sufficient for θ, it will be understood that if a sufficient statistic exists, then T will be some function of it.

For convenience, we write $G_i(x)$ instead of $G_{\theta_{[i]}}(x)$ and omit the limits $-\infty$ to ∞ on integrals throughout this paper.

3. PROCEDURE R AND ITS PCS-FUNCTION

An ordered set of pairs (r, b_r) $(r = 1, 2, \ldots, k - t)$ with $0 \le b_r < \infty$ for $r < k - t$ and $b_{k-t} = \infty$ is constructed as a function of k, t, P^*, and δ^*. We investigate the infimum $Q(r, b_r)$ of the PCS for $\boldsymbol{\theta} \in \Omega(\delta^*)$ for the rule based on putting π_i in the selected subset if, and only if, $T_i \ge T_{[k-r+1]} - b_r$. Thus, each pair corresponds to a rule, and part of our procedure is to decide on the value s of the integer r to be used.

Procedure *R*. "Construct the ordered set (r, b_r), and use it to select an integer s as described in this section. Then put π_i in the selected subset if and only if

$$T_i \ge T_{[k-s+1]} - a_s, \tag{3.1}$$

where a_s (with $0 \le a_s \le b_s$) is determined by using the equality sign in (2.2). If the pair $(s = 1, a_1 = 0)$ already satisfies (2.2), then we use a fixed subset-size procedure and put in the selected subset only the population with the largest T-value."

For the normal location-parameter problem with common $\sigma^2 = 1$, the latter part of the procedure above applies when n is large enough so that

$$1 - \int \Phi^t(x - \delta^* \sqrt{n})\, d\Phi^{k-t}(x) \ge P^*. \tag{3.2}$$

For $t = 1$, the left side of (3.2) reduces to the well-known form

$$\int \Phi^{k-1}(x + \delta^* \sqrt{n})\, d\Phi(x) \tag{3.3}$$

which is given by Bechhofer [1].

The procedure (3.1) is given in an additive form without assuming a location-parameter problem since this form is useful in other cases also. When θ is a scale parameter however, it is preferable to change to the multiplicative form of the procedure; an example of this is given in Section 9.

To derive the PCS (and in the next section its infimum), we need more notation. Let the lower set $\theta_{[1]}, \theta_{[2]}, \ldots, \theta_{[k-t]}$ be denoted as the L-set and call the values in this set L-values; the remaining upper values form the U-set. Let $C_j^{(\gamma, U)}$ denote a particular combination of j of the θ-values not including $\theta_{[\gamma]}$ or any of the values in the U-set. Let C_{j+t+1} denote the union of $C_j^{(\gamma, U)}$ and $\theta_{[\gamma]}$ and the U-set, and let $\bar{C}_{j+t+1}$ denote the complement of C_{j+t+1}. Let $S_j^{(\gamma, U)}$ and $S_j^{(U)}$ denote the set of all combinations $C_j^{(\gamma, U)}$ and $C_j^{(U)}$, respectively; the empty set must be taken into account when $j = 0$.

Let $T_{(i)}$ denote the statistic arising from the population associated with $\theta_{[i]}$ $(i = 1, 2, \ldots, k)$; the L-set and U-set terminology can also be used here according to whether $i \leq k - t$ or $i \geq k - t + 1$. A correct selection (CS) fails to occur if, and only if, all the $T_{(i)}$ for $i \geq k - t + 1$ are less than $T_{[k-s+1]} - a_s$. If we first hold $T_{[k-s+1]}$ fixed (call it x), and then integrate over the possible values of x and sum over the possible origins of x, we find that under Procedure R with fixed $r = s$ the $P\{\text{CS}; \boldsymbol{\theta}, R\} = \text{PCS}$ is given by

$$\text{PCS} = 1 - \sum_{i=1}^{k-1} \sum_{S_{k-s-t}^{(i,U)}} \int \prod_{\alpha=k-t+1}^{k} G_\alpha(x - a_s) \prod_{\beta \in C_{k-s-t}^{(i,U)}} G_\beta(x) \times \prod_{\gamma \in \bar{C}_{k-s+1}} [1 - G_\gamma(x)]\, dG_i(x). \tag{3.4}$$

Integrating by parts and letting $H_{k-s-t+1}(x)$ denote the cdf of the $(k - s - t + 1)$st order statistic in the L-set of size $k - t$, gives the PCS in the alternative form

$$\text{PCS} = \int H_{k-s-t+1}(x)\, d\left\{ \prod_{\alpha=k-t+1}^{k} G_\alpha(x - a_s) \right\}, \tag{3.5}$$

where

$$H_{k-s-t+1}(x) = \sum_{j=k-s-t+1}^{k-t} \sum_{S_j^{(U)}} \prod_{\beta \in C_j^{(U)}} G_\beta(x) \prod_{\gamma \in \bar{C}_{j+t}} [1 - G_\gamma(x)]. \tag{3.6}$$

In the next section, we shall find the infimum of the PCS for $\boldsymbol{\theta} \in \Omega(\delta^*)$, and denote it by $Q(s, a_s; \theta)$ since it depends only on $\theta_{[k-t+1]} = \theta$ (say); let

$Q(r, a_r; \theta)$ denote the corresponding quantity for any integer r ($1 \le r \le k - t$). We now use the quantity $Q(r, a_r)$ defined as the inf $Q(r, a_r; \theta)$ for $\theta \in \Theta$ to define the constants b_r needed to make Procedure R explicit. For each r, we define b_r as the smallest value of b for which

$$Q(r, b) \ge Q(r + 1, 0), \tag{3.7}$$

where $Q(k - t + 1, 0) = 1$, by definition. It is easy to see that such a smallest $b \ge 0$ must exist for each r, and that it is finite for $r < k - t$ and infinite for $r = k - t$. For $r = k - t$, this is clear since the root of $Q(k - t, b) = Q(k - t + 1, 0) = 1$ is $b = \infty$; for $r < k - t$, we use $Q(r, 0) \le Q(r + 1, 0) < Q(r, \infty) = 1$. Since $Q(r, b)$ is nondecreasing in b, the inequality (3.7) holds for all $b \ge$ the smallest value $b_r \geqq 0$ that satisfies (3.7). Actually in most applications, $Q(r, b)$ is continuous and strictly increasing in b for each r; then we write (3.7) with an equality sign and b_r is the unique root of this equation.

Finally, we define the integer s as the smallest value of r for which

$$Q(r, b_r) \ge P^*. \tag{3.8}$$

Since the values of $Q(r, b_r)$ increase to one as r increases from 1 to $k - t$, it follows that such an s-value (with $1 \leqq s \leqq k - t$) must exist.

4. INFIMUM OF THE PCS UNDER PROCEDURE *R*

Consider the configuration, i.e., the set of vectors $\boldsymbol{\theta}$, for which

$$\theta_{[1]} = \theta_{[k-t]} = \theta' \quad \text{(say)} \quad \text{and} \quad \theta_{[k-t+1]} = \theta_{[k]} = \theta \quad \text{(say)}, \tag{4.1}$$

where $\theta \ge \theta'$ are both in Θ. We wish to show first that the vectors $\boldsymbol{\theta} \in \Omega$ at which the PCS approaches or attains its infimum have the structure (4.1). Then we show that the PCS in the subspace (4.1) is decreasing in θ' for fixed θ. It follows that the $\boldsymbol{\theta}$ satisfying both (4.1) and $\delta_t = \delta^*$ form the so-called least favorable configuration for our problem; the set of $\boldsymbol{\theta}$ satisfying (4.1) alone is called the generalized least favorable (GLF) configuration. In terms of the functions $Q(s, a_s; \theta)$ and $Q(s, a_s)$, these results can be written as

$$\inf_{\boldsymbol{\theta} \in \Omega(\delta^*)} P\{\text{CS}\,; \boldsymbol{\theta}\} = \inf_{\theta \in \Theta} Q(s, a_s\,; \theta) = Q(s, a_s); \tag{4.2}$$

actually, $Q(s, a_s; \theta)$ can be regarded either as a function of θ alone as in (4.2) (since θ' is determined by setting $\delta_t(\theta, \theta') = \delta^*$) or as a function of θ and θ' in which case it is the $P\{\text{CS; GLF}, R\}$.

To start the proof, we use (3.4) and note that $G_\alpha(x - a_s)$ is decreasing in $\theta_{[\alpha]}$ so that the PCS is increasing, and we can at once set all the $\theta_{[\alpha]}$ with $\alpha \ge k - t + 1$ equal to $\theta_{[k-t+1]} = \theta$ (say) to minimize the PCS. Let $Q_1(s, a_s; \boldsymbol{\theta})$ denote the PCS with the differential in (3.5) replaced by $dG_\alpha{}'(x - a_s)$. Differentiating (3.5) with respect to any θ-value in the L-set (say, $\theta_{[1]}$), we find that all combinations C_j containing $\theta_{[1]}$ for $j > k - s - t + 1$ yield a term that is canceled by the term containing the same combination $C_{j-1}^{(1)}$, except that $\theta_{[1]}$ is removed. Hence, only terms with combinations $C_{k-s-t+1}$ (i.e., with size exactly $k - s - t + 1$) containing $\theta_{[1]}$ remain. Thus, letting Q' and G' denote derivatives with respect to $\theta_{[1]}$,

$$Q_1'(s, a_s; \boldsymbol{\theta})$$

$$= \sum_{S_{k-s-t}^{(1,U)}} \int G_1'(x) \prod_{\beta \in C_{k-s-t}^{(1,U)}} G_\beta(x) \prod_{\gamma \in \bar{C}_{k-s+1}} [1 - G_\gamma(x)]\, dG_\theta^t(x - a_s). \tag{4.3}$$

Since $G_1'(x)$ is nonpositive by Assumption 1, we further minimize the PCS by increasing $\theta_{[1]}$. A similar argument holds for all θ-values in the L-set. Hence, we set all of the L-values equal to $\theta_{[k-t]} = \theta'$ (say).

The resulting value of the PCS for any GLF-configuration (4.1) is given by

$$\text{P}\{\text{CS; GLF}\}$$

$$= \sum_{j=k-s-t+1}^{k-t} \binom{k-t}{j} \int G_{\theta'}^j(x)[1 - G_{\theta'}(x)]^{k-t-j}\, dG_\theta^t(x - a_s)$$

$$= \int I_{G_{\theta'}(x-a_s)}(k - s - t + 1, s)\, dG_\theta^t(x), \tag{4.4}$$

where $I_y(p,q)$ denotes the usual incomplete beta function. It is clear from (4.4), since $G_{\theta'}(x)$ is decreasing in θ' by Assumption 1, that the minimum of the PCS in $\Omega(\delta^*)$ is obtained by setting $\delta_t(\theta, \theta') = \delta^*$.

We complete this section by giving some useful alternative expressions for the $P\{\text{CS; GLF}\}$ under Procedure R. Integrating the last member of (4.4) gives

$$Q(s, a_s; \theta) = s\binom{k-t}{s} \int [1 - G_\theta^t(x - a_s)] G_{\theta'}^{k-s-t}(x)[1 - G_{\theta'}(x)]^{s-1}\, dG_{\theta'}(x). \tag{4.5}$$

If θ is a location parameter with $\theta - \theta' = \delta$ and $G_0(x) = G(x)$ is symmetrical about zero, then we use the notation $Q_L(s, a_s; \delta)$, and we obtain from (4.5)

$$Q_L(s, a_s; \delta) = s\binom{k-t}{s} \int \{1 - [1 - G(x + a_s + \delta)]^t\}$$

$$\times\, G^{s-1}(x)[1 - G(x)]^{k-s-t}\, dG(x)$$

$$= s\binom{k-t}{s} \sum_{j=1}^{t} (-1)^{j-1} \binom{t}{j}$$

$$\times \int G^j(x + a_s + \delta) G^{s-1}(x)[1 - G(x)]^{k-s-t}\, dG(x); \quad (4.6)$$

the latter expression is useful when t is small and tables of the integral therein are available.

For small values of s, a more useful expression is obtained by expanding the power of the square bracket in (4.4) in increasing powers α of $G_{\theta'}(x)$, setting $i + \alpha = j$ and summing on i for fixed j. Using the well-known identity

$$\sum_{h=i}^{j} (-1)^j \binom{j}{h} = (-1)^i \binom{j-1}{i-1}, \tag{4.7}$$

we obtain after simplification

$$Q(s, a_s; \theta) = s\binom{k-t}{s} \sum_{i=0}^{s-1} \frac{(-1)^i \binom{s-1}{i}}{k-s-t+1+i} \int G_{\theta'}^{k-s-t+1+i}(x + a_s)\, dG_\theta^t(x) \tag{4.8}$$

If θ is a location parameter with $\theta - \theta' = \delta$ and $G(x)$ is symmetrical about zero, then (4.8) gives

$$Q_L(s, a_s; \delta)$$
$$= s\binom{k-t}{s} \sum_{i=0}^{s-1} \frac{(-1)^i \binom{s-1}{i}}{k-s-t+1+i} \int G^{k-s-t+1+i}(x + a_s + \delta)\, dG^t(x). \tag{4.9}$$

For the special case $\delta^* = 0$ and $t = 1$ in the normal location-parameter problem, Eqs. (4.6) and (4.9) reduce to the result of Gupta [4] if we set $s = 1$. Tables and numerical illustrations based on these formulas are given in Section 7.

5. THE EXPECTED SUBSET SIZE FOR PROCEDURE R; PROCEDURES R_0 AND R'

After deriving an expression for the expected subset size $E\{S; \theta\}$ for the equal parameter (EP) configuration under Procedure R, we use the result to define a Procedure R' by defining new constants b_r'. Later, we show that the maximum of $E\{S; \boldsymbol{\theta}\}$ over all of Ω lies at some vector $\boldsymbol{\theta}$ with equal components. For $t > 1$, truncated versions R_T and R_T' of R and R' are defined in a later section by restricting the subset size S so that $S \leqq k - t + 1$; Procedure R_T' (which reduces to R' for $t = 1$) is then a minimax solution for our problem among all procedures given either by a rule like that in (3.1) or by a fixed subset-size rule.

Any population π_i is put in the selected subset if, and only if, either (i) it gives rise to one of the s largest T-values or (ii) it gives rise to a T-value (strictly) between $T_{[k-s+1]}$ and $T_{[k-s+1]} - a_s$. Hence, for the EP-configuration under Procedure R

$$E\{S;\theta\} = kP\{\pi_1 \in \text{selected subset}\}$$
$$= k\left\{s/k + s\binom{k-1}{s}\int [G_\theta(x) - G_\theta(x - a_s)]\right.$$
$$\left.\times\, G_\theta^{k-s-1}(x)[1 - G_\theta(x)]^{s-1}\, dG_\theta(x)\right\}. \qquad (5.1)$$

Integrating by parts and using the fact that x refers to the $(k-s)$th order statistic in a set of size $k-1$, we obtain

$$E\{S;\theta\} = k\sum_{j=k-s}^{k-1}\binom{k-1}{j}\int G_\theta{}^j(x)[1 - G_\theta(x)]^{k-j-1}\, dG_\theta(x - a_s)$$
$$= ks\binom{k-1}{s}\int I_{G\theta(x)}(k-s, s)\, dG_\theta(x - a_s)$$
$$= ks\binom{k-1}{s}\int [1 - G_\theta(x - a_s)]G_\theta^{k-s-1}(x)[1 - G_\theta(x)]^{s-1}\, dG_\theta(x). \qquad (5.2)$$

If θ is a location parameter and $G_0(x) = G(x)$ is symmetric about zero, then the result does not depend on θ, and we have

$$E_L\{S\} = ks\binom{k-1}{s}\int G(x + a_s)G^{s-1}(x)[1 - G(x)]^{k-s-1}\, dG(x). \quad (5.3)$$

From (5.2) or (5.3) the value is s for $a_s = 0$, k for $a_s = \infty$, and nondecreasing in a_s. In (5.3), it is continuous in a_s, and in (5.2) the same property holds for each θ.

Before defining Procedure R', we introduce the fixed subset-size Procedure R_0 with the same assumptions on δ^* and P^*. This is a special case of the above, and we need only set $a_s = 0$ in the above. Under Procedure R_0, we find the smallest s for which $Q_0(s, t; \theta) \geqq P^*$ or equivalently by (4.5) for which

$$s\binom{k-t}{s}\int G_{\theta'}^t(x)G_{\theta'}^{k-s-t}(x)[1 - G_{\theta'}(x)]^{s-1}\, dG_{\theta'}(x) \le 1 - P^*. \qquad (5.4)$$

As in the work of Desu and Sobel [3], we do not restrict ourselves to integer values of s but we consider the average of two adjacent integers, denoted by $\bar{s}$ or by $(s, s+1; 0)$, which corresponds to a randomized Procedure R_0 that attains a PCS of exactly P^*.

To define Procedure R', we replace s by r and a_s by b' in the derivation of (5.2) and (5.3) and write the left members of these temporarily as $E\{S; r, \theta\}$.

For each $r(1 \leqq r \leqq k - t)$, we define b_r' to be the smallest b'-value for which

$$\max_{\theta \in \Theta} E\{S; r, \theta\} \geq r + 1. \tag{5.5}$$

Since for each $\theta \in \Theta$, $E\{S; r, \theta\}$ increases from r to k as b' increases, the same property holds for the left member of (5.5). Since $1 \leqq r \leqq k - t \leqq k - 1$, it follows that a smallest finite value b_r' of b satisfying (5.5) must exist, except possibly when $r = k - t = k - 1$; in the latter case b'_{k-1} may be ∞ but a'_{k-1} will still be finite. Since the left-hand side of (5.5) is nondecreasing in b', the inequality (5.4) remains satisfied for all $b' \geq b_r'$. Actually in most applications, the left-hand side of (5.5) is continuous and strictly increasing in b' for each r so that we can write (5.5) with an equality sign and b_r' is the unique root of this equation.

Applying these new constants b_r' as in Procedure R, we again define s as the r-value in the first pair (r, b_r') that satisfies (2.2). Since the $Q(r, b_r')$-values increase to one as r increases to $k - t$, it follows that such a value of s must exist. We now define Procedure R' *either* as given by (3.1) with the above s-value and an a_s'-value satisfying (2.2) with equality, *or* as the fixed subset-size Procedure R_0 based on $(s, s + 1; 0)$, whichever gives the smallest maximum $E\{S; s, \theta\}$. Although Procedures R and R' are identical for many values of k, t, P^*, and δ^*, Tables I and II (see Section 7) show that this is not always the case. In particular, if Procedure R' as outlined above terminates with the pair $(s, 0)$ and $Q(s, 0) > P^*$, then we randomize between $(s - 1, 0)$ and $(s, 0)$ to attain a PCS of exactly P^*.

It should be noted that max $E\{S; s, \theta\}$ over all $\boldsymbol{\theta} \in \Omega$ is nonincreasing in δ^* and $1 - P^*$ and is, in fact, continuous in these quantities. It should also be noted that the constants b_r' do not depend on δ^* as in the case of the b_r, and in the normal location-parameter problem the use of the quantities $B_r' = b_r'\sqrt{n}$ and $\lambda = \delta^*\sqrt{n}$ makes the problem independent of n.

After deriving an expression for $E\{S; \boldsymbol{\theta}\}$, we shall show that it is maximized at a vector $\boldsymbol{\theta}$ with equal components. This is done by proving a stronger result, namely that for any b $(s \leq b \leq k)$, $P\{S \geq b\}$ is maximized at a vector $\boldsymbol{\theta}$ with equal components. This implies our result and for the special case $t = 1$, $\delta^* = 0$, it implies Theorem 1 of Gupta [4].

The population associated with $\theta_{[i]}$, whose statistic $T_{(i)}$ has cdf $G_i(x)$, is put into the selected subset if, and only if, the $(k - s)$th order statistic among the remaining $k - 1$ values of T is at most equal to $T_{(i)} + a_s$. Using the standard method of characteristic random variables, we obtain

$$\begin{aligned} E\{S; \boldsymbol{\theta}\} &= \sum_{i=1}^{k} P\{\pi_i \in \text{selected subset}\} \\ &= \sum_{i=1}^{k} \int H_{k-s}^{(i)}(x + a_s)\, dG_i(x) = \sum_{i=1}^{k} \int H_{k-s}^{i}(x)\, dG_i(x - a_s), \end{aligned} \tag{5.6}$$

where $H_{k-s}^{(i)}(x)$, the cdf of the above-mentioned order statistic, is given by

$$H_{k-s}^{(i)}(x) = \sum_{j=k-s}^{k-1} \sum_{S_j^{(i)}} \prod_{\alpha \in C_j^{(i)}} G_\alpha(x) \prod_{\beta \in \bar{C}_{j+1}} [1 - G_\beta(x)]. \tag{5.7}$$

To get an expression for $P\{S \geqq b\}$, we first fix the value $T_{[k-s+1]}$ (call it x) and the population (or cdf $G(x)$) giving rise to it. Then the event $S \geqq b$ takes place if, and only if, the number j of populations with T-values between $x - a_s$ and x is at least $b - s$. Hence, we obtain

$$P\{S \geqq b\} = \sum_{i=1}^{k} \sum_{j=b-s}^{k-s} \sum_{(S_j^{(i)}, S_{s-1}^{(i)})} \int \prod_{\alpha \in C_j^{(i)}} [G_\alpha(x) - G_\alpha(x - a_s)]$$
$$\times \prod_{\beta \in C_{s-1}^{(i)}} [1 - G_\beta(x)] \prod_{\gamma \in \bar{C}_{j+s}} G_\gamma(x - a_s)\, dG_i(x), \tag{5.8}$$

where the inner summation is over all combinations of pairs of disjoint subsets of size j and $s - 1$ (for the first and second product, respectively), neither containing the subscript i.

Lemma 1. *The derivative $W_\theta(1)$ of $P\{S \geqq b\}$ with respect to $\theta_{[1]}$ can be written as a sum of integrals, each of the form*

$$\int \prod [G_\alpha(x) - G_\alpha(x - a_s)] \prod [1 - G_\beta(x)] \prod G_\gamma(x - a_s)$$
$$\times \{G_1'(x)\, dG_j(x - a_s) - G_1'(x - a_s)\, dG_j(x - a_s)\}, \tag{5.9}$$

where $j \neq 1$. The number of such terms N is $s\binom{k-1}{s}\binom{k-s-1}{b-s-1}$.

Proof. Consider values of j in (5.8) from $j = m$ to $j = k - s$, with particular attention to m and $m + 1$. We wish to show that telescopic cancellations take place and that only $j = m$ contributes to the derivative. Our plan is to integrate by parts all those terms ending in $dG_1(x)$ (i.e., with $i = 1$); the terms arising from this are called new terms, and the terms corresponding to $i > 1$ are called old terms. After some cancellation, we set up a 1–1 correspondence between old terms denoted by T_j and new terms denoted by T_j^*.

For $j = m + 1$, we get new terms of the form

$$T_{m+1}^* = -\int G_1(x) \prod_{\alpha \in C_m^{(1,\alpha_0)}} [G_\alpha(x) - G_\alpha(x - a_s)]$$
$$\times \prod_{\beta \in C_{s-1}^{(1,\alpha_0)}} [1 - G_\beta(x)] \prod G_\gamma(x - a_s)\, d[G_{\alpha_0}(x) - G_{\alpha_0}(x - a_s)] \tag{5.10}$$

and old terms of the form

$$T_{m+1} = \int [G_1(x) - G_1(x - a_s)] \prod_{\alpha \in C_m^{(1,\alpha_0)}} [G_\alpha(x) - G_\alpha(x - a_s)]$$
$$\times \prod_{\beta \in C_{s-1}^{(1,\alpha_0)}} [1 - G_\beta(x)] \prod G_\gamma(x - a_s)\, dG_{\alpha_0}(x), \tag{5.11}$$

and the partial cancellation between these two is clear. Since $m+1$ is a possible value of j, the third product in (5.8) is not empty for $j=m$, and this gives rise to new terms of the form

$$T_m^* = -\int G_1(x) \prod_{\alpha \in C_m^{(1,\alpha_0)}} [G_\alpha(x) - G_\alpha(x-a_s)] \times \prod_{\beta \in C_{s-1}^{(1,\alpha_0)}} [1 - G_\beta(x)] \prod_{\gamma \in \bar{C}_{m+s+1}} G_\gamma(x-a_s)\, dG_{\alpha_0}(x-a_s) \quad (5.12)$$

which cancels the remainder in (5.10). Since the third product in (5.8) is not empty, we also get old terms of the form

$$T_m = \int \prod_{\alpha \in C_m^{(1,\alpha_0)}} [G_\alpha(x) - G_\alpha(x-a_s)] \prod_{\beta \in C_{s-1}^{(1,\alpha_0)}} [1 - G_\beta(x)] G_1(x-a_s) \times \prod_{\gamma \in \bar{C}_{m+s+1}} G_\gamma(x-a_s)\, dG_{\alpha_0}(x); \quad (5.13)$$

all of these cancel against the appropriate part of T_{m+1} in (5.11).

We do not use the old terms of the form (5.13) for $j=m+1$ as these are needed to cancel against terms for $j=m+2$; it suffices to note that, for the maximum value $k-s$ of j, the third product in (5.8) is empty.

For $s>1$ and $j=m+1$, we also get new terms of the form

$$T_{m+1}^* = \int G_1(x) \prod_{\alpha \in C_{m+1}^{(1,\beta_0)}} [G_\alpha(x) - G_\alpha(x-a_s)] \times \prod_{\beta \in C_{s-2}^{(1,\beta_0)}} [1 - G_\beta(x)] \prod_{\gamma \in \bar{C}_{s+m+1}} G_\gamma(x-a_s)\, dG_{\beta_0}(x) \quad (5.14)$$

for $2 \leqq \beta_0 \leqq k$, but these cancel against old terms with $j=m+1$ and $1-G_1(x)$ in the second product in (5.8). The latter cancellation leaves terms that do not depend on $\theta_{[1]}$ and vanish in the derivative. The same type of cancellation takes place for $j=m$ between new and old terms.

Summing up, and making use of the 1–1 correspondence that holds between the old and new terms, the only terms that remain after the above cancellations are the old terms for $j=m$

$$T_m = \int [G_1(x) - G_1(x-a_s)] \prod_{\alpha \in C_{m-1}^{(1,\alpha_0)}} [G_\alpha(x) - G_\alpha(x-a_s)] \times \prod_{\beta \in C_{s-1}^{(1,\alpha_0)}} [1 - G_\beta(x)] \prod_{\gamma \in \bar{C}_{m+s}} G_\gamma(x-a_s)\, dG_{\alpha_0}(x), \quad (5.15)$$

and the new terms for $j=m$

$$T_m^* = -\int G_1(x) \prod_{\alpha \in C_{m-1}^{(1,\alpha_0)}} [G_\alpha(x) - G_\alpha(x-a_s)] \prod_{\beta \in C_{s-1}^{(1,\alpha_0)}} [1 - G_\beta(x)] \times \prod_{\gamma \in \bar{C}_{m+s}} G_\gamma(x-a_s)\, d[G_{\alpha_0}(x) - G_{\alpha_0}(x-a_s)]. \quad (5.16)$$

The sum of the terms in (5.15) and (5.16), after further cancellation and taking the derivative with respect to $\theta_{[1]}$, gives the final result

$$W_{\boldsymbol{\theta}}(1) = \sum_{i=2}^{k-1} \sum_{(S_{b-s-1}^{(1,i)}, S_{s-1}^{(1,i)})} \int \prod_{\alpha \in C_{b-s-1}^{(1,i)}} [G_\alpha(x) - G_\alpha(x - a_s)]$$

$$\times \prod_{\beta \in C_{s-1}^{(1,i)}} [1 - G_\beta(x)] \prod_{\gamma \in \bar{C}_b} G_\gamma(x - a_s)$$

$$\times \{G_1'(x)\, dG_i(x - a_s) - G_1'(x - a_s)\, dG_i(x)\}. \tag{5.17}$$

The number N of terms in (5.17) is easily seen (from (5.17) itself or from the discussion centering on (5.11) and (5.13)) to be

$$N = (k-1)\binom{k-2}{b-s-1}\binom{k-b+s-1}{s-1} = s\binom{k-1}{s}\binom{k-s-1}{b-s-1}. \tag{5.18}$$

In particular for $b = s$, the derivative is zero, as it should be since $P\{S \geqq s\} = 1$.

We now wish to show that for any $b (s \leq b \leq k)$ and for

$$\theta_{[1]} = \theta_{[2]} = \cdots = \theta_{[k_1]} = \theta \qquad \text{(say)},$$

$P\{S \geq b\}$ is a nondecreasing function of θ for any integer k_1 $(1 \leqq k_1 \leqq k)$. Let $W_\theta(k_1)$ denote the derivative with respect to θ, and let $W(1 \mid \theta_{[1]} = \theta_{[2]} = \cdots = \theta_{[k]} = \theta)$ denote the value of $W_\theta(1)$ when the $\theta_{[i]}$ $(1 \leqq i \leqq k_1)$ are set equal to θ.

Lemma 2. *For any integer* k_1 $(1 \leqq k_1 \leqq k)$

$$W_\theta(k_1) = k_1 W(1 \mid \theta_{[1]} = \theta_{[2]} = \cdots = \theta_{[k]} = \theta) \geqq 0. \tag{5.19}$$

Proof. By Assumption 2 and (5.17), it follows that $W_\theta(1) \geqq 0$. In differentiating (5.8) with respect to θ, we can differentiate with respect to each $\theta_{[i]}$ separately $(1 \leqq i \leqq k_1)$, holding all the other θ's fixed and then sum the results. Because of the symmetry of (5.8) in all the θ's, it follows that each of these k_1 differentiations gives the same result since we set $\theta_{[i]} = \theta$ $(1 \leqq i \leqq k_1)$, after differentiation. Hence, we merely have to multiply $W_\theta(1)$ by k_1 and set the k_1 smallest θ-values equal to θ. Since $W_\theta(1) \geqq 0$, the lemma follows.

We note that for $k_1 > 1$ some of the expressions in braces (see (5.17)) may vanish when we set $\theta_{[i]} = \theta$ $(1 \leqq i \leqq k_1)$, but for $k_1 < k$, there will be at least one term for which the expression in braces does not vanish.

From Lemma 2, we obtain the desired:

Theorem 1. *For any* b $(1 \leqq b \leqq k)$, $P\{S \geqq b\}$ *has its maximum under Procedure* R *(as well as* R' *and* R_M*) at some vector* $\boldsymbol{\theta}$ *with equal components.*

Proof. Step by step, we can increase $P\{S \geqq b\}$ first by increasing $\theta_{[1]}$ to $\theta_{[2]}$, then by increasing the common value θ of $\theta_{[1]} = \theta_{[2]}$ to $\theta_{[3]}$, etc. This proves the theorem.

Corollary 1. *For any integers k, t, s $(1 \leqq s \leqq k-t)$, $E\{S;\boldsymbol{\theta}\}$ has its maximum under Procedure R (as well as R' and R_m) at some vector $\boldsymbol{\theta}$ with equal components.*

Proof. It is easily verified that

$$E\{S;\boldsymbol{\theta}\} = \sum_{j=1}^{k} jP\{S=j\} = \sum_{j=s+1}^{k} P\{S \geqq j\} + sP\{S \geqq s\}. \tag{5.20}$$

It follows from Theorem 1 that each term in the last part of (5.20) is maximized at some $\boldsymbol{\theta}$ with equal components. If the maximum of the sum was not at such a vector, we could easily increase it as in the proof of Theorem 1; this proves the corollary.

Another corollary to Theorem 1 is given in Section 6. In the location-parameter problem, the resulting value for the maximum of $E\{S;\boldsymbol{\theta}\}$, which we denote by $E\{S;\theta\} = E_L\{S\}$, is independent of θ and is clearly the overall maximum. In other cases, we have reduced the problem of finding the maximum to a one-dimensional problem.

The expression (5.6) simplifies considerably in the GLF and LF-configurations, and the resulting expressions are needed for Tables I and II. From (5.6) and (5.7), we obtain

$$E\{S;\mathrm{GLF}\} = t\int J_{x,\theta,\theta'}(s,t)\,dG_\theta(x-a_s)$$
$$+ (k-t)\int J_{x,\theta,\theta'}(s,t+1)\,dG_{\theta'}(x-a_s), \tag{5.21}$$

where in terms of $B(y,n;p) = \binom{n}{y}p^y(1-p)^{n-y}$, we can write

$$J_{x,\theta,\theta'}(s,t) = \sum_{j=k-s}^{k-1}\ \sum_{i=j-t+1}^{\min(j,k-t)} B(i,k-t;G_{\theta'}(x))B(j-i,t-1;G_\theta(x)); \tag{5.22}$$

in particular, for $s=1$ and any t

$$J_{x,\theta,\theta'}(1,t) = G_{\theta'}^{k-t}(x)G_\theta^{t-1}(x). \tag{5.23}$$

An integration by parts gives for the first integral I_1 in (5.21) (not including the factor t)

$$I_1 = 1-(t-1)\sum_{j=1}^{t-1}\int G_\theta(x-a_s)B(k-s-j,k-t;G_{\theta'}(x))$$
$$\times B(j-1,t-2;G_\theta(x))\,dG_\theta(x) - (k-t)\sum_{j=0}^{t-1}\int G_\theta(x-a_s)$$
$$\times B(k-s-j-1,k-t-1;G_{\theta'}(x))B(j,t-1;G_\theta(x))\,dG_{\theta'}(x). \tag{5.24}$$

For the second integral I_2 in (5.21), we use (5.24) replacing t by $t+1$ and the first factor $G_\theta(x-a_s)$ in each integrand by $G_{\theta'}(x-a_s)$. For $t=1$, we get further reduction, and we note that the first term in (5.21) is the PCS $= Q(s,a_s;\theta)$, which by definition of a_s equals P^* in the LF-configuration. Hence, for the location-parameter problem with $t = 1$, $\delta_1(\theta, \theta') = \delta^*$ and $G(x)$ symmetrical about zero, we obtain from (5.21) and (5.24)

$$E\{S; \text{LF}\} = P^* + (k-1)(s-1)\binom{k-2}{s-1}\int G(x+a_s) \times G^{s-2}(x)[1-G(x)]^{k-s-1}\,dG(x) + s\binom{k-1}{s}\int G(x+a_s-\delta^*)G^{k-s-1}(x+a_s)[1-G(x+a_s)]^{s-1}\,dG(x). \tag{5.25}$$

Unless δ^* is close to zero, the second integral in (5.25) is quite small, and by neglecting it we obtain a lower bound for $E\{S; LF\}$ which is usually greater than the lower bound s. We also obtain the upper bound kP^* by comparing (5.3) with (4.5) for $t = 1$. Hence for $t = 1$, any s $(1 \leqq s \leqq k-1)$ and any δ^*

$$s \leqq E\{S; \text{LF}\} < E\{S; \text{EP}\} \leqq kP^*. \tag{5.26}$$

Gupta [4] pointed out that for $s = 1$ equality is attained at the upper bound in (5.26), and since we use a fixed subset-size rule for δ^* sufficiently large [see (3.2)], equality is also attained at the lower bound in (5.26).

6. TRUNCATED VERSION OF THE RSS PROCEDURES FOR $t > 1$

Although we assumed that $s \leq k - t$, we have not assumed any upper bound for the subset size S under the random subset-size (RSS) Procedures R, R', and R_M; (Procedure R_M is defined in a later section). We refer to an RSS procedure as truncated if, whenever $S \geqq k - t + 1$, we put in the selected subset only those populations with the $k - t + 1$ largest T-values. Truncation is only concerned with the case $t > 1$ since the procedure is unchanged for $t = 1$. The truncated procedures are denoted by R_T, R_T', and R_{MT}, respectively. Truncation does not affect the PCS or $Q(s, a_s; \theta)$ values and can only reduce the value of $E\{S; \boldsymbol{\theta}\}$, the reduction being small unless $\lambda = \delta^*\sqrt{n}$ is close to zero or P^* is close to one. The maximum of $E\{S; \boldsymbol{\theta}\}$ is at most $k - t + 1$ under truncation.

Let $E\{S_T; \theta\}$ denote the maximum expected subset size under Procedure R_T, and let $\Delta(\theta) = E\{S; \theta\} - E\{S_T; \theta\}$. For $t \geqq 2$, a simple analysis of the probabilities of getting $S = k - t + 2, k - t + 3, \ldots, k$ gives for the amount $\Delta(\theta)$ to be subtracted from (5.2) to get $E\{S_T; \theta\}$,

$$\Delta(\theta) = k\binom{k-1}{s-1}\sum_{j=0}^{t-2}\binom{k-s}{j}(t-1-j)\int[1-G_\theta(x)]^{s-1}$$
$$\times G_\theta^{j}(x-a_s)[G_\theta(x)-G_\theta(x-a_s)]^{k-s-j}\,dG_\theta(x)$$
$$= k\binom{k-1}{s-1}\sum_{i=t-1}^{k-s}\binom{k-s}{i}C_{t,i}\int G_\theta^{i}(x-a_s)$$
$$\times G_\theta^{k-s-i}(x)[1-G_\theta(x)]^{s-1}\,dG_\theta(x), \qquad (6.1)$$

where $C_{t,i} = \sum_{j=0}^{t-2}(-1)^{i-j}\binom{i}{j}$. For $t = 2$ in the normal location-parameter problem, we get for $\Delta_L(\theta) = \Delta_L$ from the first expression in (6.1)

$$\Delta_L = k\binom{k-1}{s-1}\sum_{j=0}^{k-s}(-1)^j\binom{k-s}{j}\int\Phi^{k-s-j}(x+A_s)\Phi^{s-1+j}(x)\,d\Phi(x). \quad (6.2)$$

For a_s (or A_s) $= 0$ the value of $\Delta(\theta)$ (or Δ_L) is zero.

Procedure R_T' is defined in terms of R' just as R_T was defined in terms of R; truncation also applies to Procedure R_M defined in Section 7 and gives rise to R_{MT}. We now make use of the stronger result proved in Theorem 1 by giving another corollary to that theorem.

Corollary 2. *For any integers k, t, s $(1 \le s \le k-t)$, $E\{S_T; \boldsymbol{\theta}\}$ under Procedure R_T (as well at R_T' and R_{MT}) is maximized at a vector $\boldsymbol{\theta}$ whose components are all equal.*

Proof. Using the relation

$$E\{S_T;\boldsymbol{\theta}\} = \sum_{j=s}^{k-t} jP\{S=j\} + (k-t+1)P\{S \ge k-t+1\}.$$
$$= \sum_{j=s+1}^{k-t+1} P\{S \ge j\} + sP\{S \ge s\}, \qquad (6.3)$$

the result follows exactly as in Corollary 1.

As a result of the construction of R' and this corollary, the Procedure R_T' is minimax among all procedures based *either* on rules given by (3.1) *or* on a fixed subset-size procedure, or on any combination of these two.

In Table II $E_L\{S\}$-values for the normal location-parameter problem for $k = 5$, $t = 2$, and $P^* = 0.95$ are given for Procedures R_0, R, R', and R_M in truncated and untruncated form; Eqs. (5.2) and (6.2) were used in the preparation of this table.

7. NUMERICAL ILLUSTRATIONS

Suppose $k = 5$ normal populations with common variance $\sigma^2 = 1$ are given, and we wish to select a subset containing at least one of the $t = 2$ best populations. We shall use Procedure R with common sample size $n = 100$, and we require a PCS of at least $P^* = 0.92$ whenever $\delta_2 = \theta_{[4]} - \theta_{[3]} \geq \delta^* = 0.10$.

For $s = 1$ and $a_1 = 0$, we first find the value of

$$Q_L(1, 0) = \int \Phi^3(x + \lambda)\, d\Phi^2(x), \tag{7.1}$$

where $\lambda = \delta^* \sqrt{n} = 1$; this is computed to be $0.739 < P^*$, and hence we proceed to the next pair ($s = 2, a_2 = 0$). By (4.9), we obtain

$$\begin{aligned} Q_L(2, 0) &= 3 \int \Phi^2(x + \lambda)\, d\Phi^2(x) - 2 \int \Phi^3(x + \lambda)\, d\Phi^2(x) \\ &= 3(0.8025) - 2(0.7387) = 0.93 > P^*. \end{aligned} \tag{7.2}$$

Hence for Procedure R, we use $s = 1$ with some $a_1 > 0$. To find a_1, we need the root in h of

$$\int \Phi^3(x + h)\, d\Phi^2(x) = 0.92 \tag{7.3}$$

which is computed to be $h = 1.85$. Then $(a_1 + \delta^*)\sqrt{n} = 1.85$ implies that $a_1 = 0.085$. Thus Procedure R is: "Put π_i in the selected subset if, and only if, $\bar{x}_i \geq \bar{x}_{[5]} - 0.085$". By (5.3) the maximum of $E\{S; \boldsymbol{\theta}\}$ is

$$E_L\{S\} = 20 \int \Phi(x + 0.85)[1 - \Phi(x)]^3\, d\Phi(x) = 2.22. \tag{7.4}$$

To find Procedure R', we try $s = 1$ with the same constant $a_1' = 0.085$, and we also try $s = 2$ with $a_2' = 0$. By (5.5), we set $E_L\{S\} = s + 1 = 2$ to compute b_1', and find that $b_1'\sqrt{n} = 0.71$, so that $b_1' = 0.071$. Using (4.9), we find that $Q_L(1, 0.071) = 0.90 < 0.92$. It follows from this and (7.2) that Procedure R' is a fixed subset-size procedure randomizing between $s = 1$ (with $p = 0.056$) and $s = 2$ (with $1 - p = 0.944$), so that $\bar{s} = 1.944$.

For Procedure R_T, we use (6.2) to compute the correction Δ_L and find it to be 0.085, so that $E_L\{S_T\} = 2.22 - 0.085 = 2.135$.

Since $E_L\{S\} = \bar{s} = 1.944 < 2.135$ under Procedure R', it follows that Procedures R' and R_T' are the same.

In the above, the value $P^* = 0.92$ is not typical but was purposely found and used to show that R and R' (and also R_T and R_T') need not be the same; other examples of this are seen in Tables I and II.

To better understand the numerical comparisons below, we also introduce an RSS Procedure R_M which arbitrarily sets $s = t$. Since $s \leq k - t$ for our goal, Procedure R_M is defined only for $t \leq k - t$ or $t \leq k/2$. For $\delta^* = 0$ and $t = 1$, this procedure is identical with Procedure R_G of Gupta [4]; for $t = 1$ and

$\delta^* > 0$, the improvement of Procedure R_M over R_G is due only to the introduction of the indifference zone.

All the necessary formulas for Procedure R_M are special cases of the previous results, and we need not repeat them here. As in the case of Procedures R and R', we use a fixed subset size if the smallest constant a_t (or $A_t = a_t\sqrt{n}$) satisfying (2.2) is negative.

Tables I and II respectively present a numerical comparison of the $E_L\{S; \boldsymbol{\theta}\}$-values for the untruncated procedures for $t = 1$, and for both the truncated and untruncated procedures for $t = 2$. Let $R^* \succ R^{**}$ (in LF) mean that Procedure R^* is uniformly (in λ) at least as good as Procedure R^{**} in the LF-configuration. From the constructions, we have $R \succ R_M \succ R_G$ (in LF) and $R' \succ R$

TABLE I

Comparison of $E_L\{S\}$-Values for Untruncated Procedures under the Least Favorable (LF) and Equal Parameter (EP) Configurations. Normal Location-Parameter Problem with Common $\sigma^2 = 1$ $(k = 5,\ t = 1,\ P^* = 0.95, \lambda = \delta^*\sqrt{n},\ A_s = a_s\sqrt{n})$.

	λ-values					
Procedures	0	0.50	1.00	2.25	3.00	∞
R_G LF	4.75	4.72	4.60	3.82	3.05	1.00
R_G EP	4.75[a]	4.75[a]	4.75[a]	4.75[a]	4.75[a]	4.75[a]
A_s	3.055	3.055	3.055	3.055	3.055	3.055
s	1	1	1	1	1	1
R_0 LF	4.75	4.52	3.96	1.98	1.11	1.00
R_0 EP	4.75	4.52	3.96	1.98	1.11	1.00
A_s	0	0	0	0	0	0
$(s-1, s)$	(4, 5)	(4, 5)	(3, 4)	(1, 2)	(1, 2)	1
R_M LF	4.75	4.46	3.91	1.48	1.01	1.00
R_M EP	4.75	4.47	4.23	2.19	1.07	1.00
A_s	3.055	2.555	2.055	0.830	0.055	0[a]
s	1	1	1	1	1	1
R LF	4.75	4.44	3.87	1.48	1.01	1.00
R EP	4.75	4.45	3.92	2.19	1.07	1.00
A_s	0.962	0.462	0.619	0.830	0.055	0[a]
s	4	4	3	1	1	1
R' LF	4.75	4.44	3.87	1.98	1.01	1.00
R' EP	4.75	4.45	3.92	1.98	1.07	1.00
A_s	0.962	0.462	0.619	0	0.055	0[a]
s	4	4	3	(1, 2)[a]	1	1

[a] See text at end of Section 7 for explanation.

(in EP) for any t. It is conjectured that for $t = 1$, we have $R \succ R_0$ (in LF) and $R_M \succ R_0 \succ R_G$ (in LF), but this has not been proved, and some of these do not hold for $t = 2$.

TABLE II

Comparison of $E_L\{S\}$-Values for Truncated and Untruncated Procedures under the Equal Parameter (EP) Configuration. Normal Location-Parameter Problem with Common $\sigma^2 = 1$ ($k = 5$, $t = 2$, $P^* = 0.95$, $\lambda = \delta^*\sqrt{n}$, $A_s = a_s\sqrt{n}$).

	λ-values					
Procedures	0	0.25	0.50	1.00	3.00	∞
$R_0 = R_{0T}$	3.500	3.225	2.911	2.334	1.000	1.000
A_s	0	0	0	0	0	0
$(s-1, s)$	(3, 4)	(3, 4)	(2, 3)	(2, 3)	1	1
R_M	3.859	3.511	3.122	2.278	2.000	2.000
R_{MT}	3.581	3.352	3.051	2.276	2.000	2.000
A_s	1.165	0.915	0.665	0.165	0[a]	0[a]
s	2	2	2	2	2	2
R	3.599	3.217	3.122	2.278	1.000	1.000
R_T	3.507	3.203	3.051	2.276	1.000	1.000
A_s	0.383	0.133	0.665	0.165	0	0
s	3	3	2	2	1	1
R'	3.500	3.217	2.911	2.278	1.000	1.000
R_T'	3.500	3.203	2.911	2.276	1.000	1.000
A_s	0	0.133	0	0.165	0	0
s	(3, 4)	3	(2, 3)	2	1	1

[a] See text at end of Section 7 for explanation.

For the RSS Procedure R_G, the whole row in Table I is one procedure and the λ-values are to be regarded as true population values $\lambda = \delta\sqrt{n}$, where $\delta = \theta_{[k-t+1]} - \theta_{[k-t]} = \theta_{[5]} - \theta_{[4]}$. In all the other rows the λ-values arise from different specified δ^*-values, $\lambda = \delta^*\sqrt{n}$, and each cell refers to a different problem. Hence, each entry is to be compared with the whole first row and, in particular, with the entry above it in the first row. The FSS Procedure R_0 and, in one instance, R' randomize between the two integer values of s shown. Procedures R, R', and R_M all revert to an FSS Procedure if the constant A_1 is negative, as it will be for large λ.

8. ASYMPTOTIC EFFICIENCY OF PROCEDURE R RELATIVE TO PROCEDURE R_M

To better understand the improvement of Procedure R over Procedure R_M, we define an asymptotic relative efficiency as $P^* \to 1$ with δ^* and n both fixed. Although this definition can be stated more generally, we restrict this discussion to the normal location-parameter problem.

Our plan is to start with the first expression in (4.6) set equal to P^* and find an asymptotic ($P^* \to 1$) expression for A_s (or $B_s = A_s + \lambda$), and then use (5.3) to evaluate the maximum $E_L\{S\}$ of the expected subset size as $P^* \to 1$. In the final result, we merely set $s = k - t$ for Procedure R and set $s = t$ for Procedure R_M; the asymptotic relative efficiency of R with respect to R_M is defined as

$$\operatorname{eff}(R; R_M) = \lim_{P^* \to 1} \left[\frac{k - E_L\{S; R\}}{k - E_L\{S; R_M\}} \right]. \tag{8.1}$$

We prove that for $t < k - t$ (or $t < k/2$), this limit is ∞, thus showing that for P^* close to 1 the max $E_L\{S\}$ is smaller for Procedure R than for Procedure R_M. In particular for $t = 1$, this limit is ∞ for all $k \geq 3$. For $t = k - t$ the two procedures are identical since s takes on the same value $t = k - t$ under both procedures. For convenience, we write below A and B instead of A_s and B_s.

From (4.6), we obtain for the normal location-parameter problem

$$1 - P^* = \int \Phi^t(x - B)\, dG(x), \tag{8.2}$$

where

$$dG(x) = s\binom{k - t}{s} \Phi^{k-s-t}(x) \Phi^{s-1}(-x)\, d\Phi(x). \tag{8.3}$$

Letting $\approx$ (or ae) denote asymptotic ($P^* \to 1$) equivalence and using the usual o-notation, we write the right side of (8.2) in the form

$$\int_{-\theta B}^{\theta B} \Phi^t(x - B)\, dG(x) + o(\exp\{-(B\theta)^2/2\}) \tag{8.4}$$

where $(k - t)/(k - t + 1) < \theta^2 < 1$. Using the first term of the Laplace-Feller expansion for the integrated "tail" of the standard normal density $\varphi(x)$, we write the integral in (8.4) as

$$\int_{-\theta B}^{\theta B} \frac{\varphi^t(x - B)}{|B - x|^t}\, dG(x) \approx \frac{C}{B^t} \int_{-\theta B}^{\theta B} \varphi^t(x - B)\, dG(x) \tag{8.5}$$

$$\approx \frac{C}{B^t} \int \varphi^t(x - B)\, dG(x) + o(\exp\{-(B\theta)^2/2\}).$$

Hence neglecting the error term in (8.5), we have from (8.2), (8.4), and (8.5)

$$\frac{1}{B^t}\int [\varphi^t(x-B)\varphi(x)]\Phi^{k-s-t}(x)\Phi^{s-1}(-x)\,dx \approx C(1-P^*), \tag{8.6}$$

where the same symbol C denotes different constants. Completing of the square in the brackets in (8.6) and letting u denote $1/(t+1)^{1/2}$, we obtain for the left member of (8.6)

$$\frac{\varphi(Bu(t)^{1/2})}{B^t}\int \Phi^{k-s-t}(yu+Btu^2)\Phi^{s-1}(-yu-Btu^2)\,d\Phi(y)$$

$$\approx \frac{\varphi(Bu(t)^{1/2})}{B^t}\left[\int_{-\theta tuB}^{\theta tuB}\Phi^{s-1}(-yu-Btu^2)\,d\Phi(y) + o(\exp\{-(\theta tuB)^2/2\})\right]. \tag{8.7}$$

Neglecting the error term for the Laplace-Feller expansion which does not depend on θ, we write the integral in (8.7) in the ae form

$$\int_{-\theta tuB}^{\theta tuB}\frac{\varphi^{s-1}(yu+tu^2B)}{|yu+tu^2B|^{s-1}}\,d\Phi(y)$$

$$\approx \frac{C}{B^{s-1}}\int \varphi^{s-1}(yu+tu^2B)\varphi(y)\,dy + o(\exp\{-(\theta tuB)^2/2\}) \tag{8.8}$$

$$= \frac{C}{B^{s-1}}\varphi(tuB[(s-1)/(s+t)]^{1/2}) + o(\exp\{-(\theta tuB)^2/2\}).$$

Since the error term in (8.5) is larger than that entering through (8.8) for all t, we have from (8.6), (8.7) and (8.8)

$$1-P^* \approx C\,\frac{\varphi(Bu(t)^{1/2})\varphi(tuB[(s-1)/(s+t)]^{1/2})}{B^{s+t-1}} + o(\exp\{-(B\theta)^2/2\}) \tag{8.9}$$

$$= \frac{C\varphi(B[st/(s+t)]^{1/2})}{B^{s+t-1}} + o(\exp\{-(B\theta)^2/2\}). \tag{8.10}$$

From (8.10) we obtain a main result

$$B = A+\lambda \approx [-2[(s+t)/st]\ln(1-P^*)]^{1/2} \tag{8.11}$$

From (5.3) for the normal location-parameter problem, the maximum of the expected subset size for any k, t, s and $\lambda = \delta^*(n)^{1/2}$ is given by

$$k - E_L\{S\,|\,EP\} = k\int \Phi(x-A)\,dG(x). \tag{8.12}$$

We use exactly the same analysis again except that $t=1$ and B is replaced by A, and obtain from (8.9)

$$k - E_L\{S\,|\,EP\} \approx \frac{C}{A^s}\varphi(A[s/(s+1)]^{1/2}). \tag{8.13}$$

The final result is obtained by substituting from (8.11) for A into (8.13), namely

$$k - E_L\{S \mid EP\} \approx \frac{C(1-P^*)^{(s+t)/t(s+1)} \exp\{\lambda[-2[s(s+t)/t(s+1)^2]\ln(1-P^*)]^{1/2}\}}{[-\ln(1-P^*)]^{s/2}} \tag{8.14}$$

For procedure R_M we set $s = t$ and for procedure R we set $s = k - t$, since the maximum value $k - t$ for s is attained under procedure R when P^* is close to unity. We note that $t \le k - t$ and hence $t \le k/2$. For $t > 1$ we use the power of $1 - P^*$ in (8.14) and note that $(s + t)/(s + 1)$ decreases in s; for $t = 1$ and $\lambda > 0$ we use the fact that $s/(s + 1)$ increases in s and it follows in both cases that the ratio (8.1) has the limiting value ∞. Hence for $1 < t < k/2$ with arbitrary $\lambda \ge 0$ and for $t = 1$ with $\lambda > 0$ the procedure R_M has asymptotic $(P^* \to 1)$ efficiency zero relative to R. For $t = 1$ with $\lambda = 0$ we get no result from (8.14) and it is easy to show that the maximum of $E_L\{S\} = kP^*$ for both $R_G = R_M$ and R, so that the limiting value and the exact value of (8.1) for any P^* is one. For $t = k - t$ the two procedures, R_M and R, are identical for P^* close to 1.

It is also possible and instructive to define another efficiency (eff_0) by letting δ^* $(\text{or } \lambda = \delta^*\sqrt{n}) \to 0$ with a fixed $P^* > 1 - \binom{k}{t}^{-1}$. The numerical results are different but the relative positions of the procedures in Table I remain the same. We restrict our attention to the normal case with $t = 1$ and define the asymptotic $(\lambda \to 0)$ efficiency of R_M with respect to R by

$$\text{eff}_0(R_M; R) = \lim_{\lambda \to 0}\left[\frac{kP^* - E_L(S; \text{LF}, R_M)}{kP^* - E_L(S; \text{LF}, R)}\right]. \tag{8.15}$$

From (5.27) with $s = k - 1$, we obtain the 2-term Taylor expansion

$$\begin{aligned} E_L\{S; \text{LF}, R\} &\approx kP^* - \lambda k(k-1)\int [1 - \Phi(x + A)]^{k-2}\varphi(x + A)\, d\Phi(x) \\ &\approx kP^* - \frac{\lambda k(k-1)}{\sqrt{2}}\,\varphi\!\left(\frac{A}{\sqrt{2}}\right)\left[1 - \Phi\!\left(\frac{y}{\sqrt{2}} + \frac{A}{2}\right)\right]^{k-2} d\Phi(y), \end{aligned} \tag{8.16}$$

where $A = A_{k-1}(P^*)$ is the root of

$$(k-1)\int \Phi(x + A)\Phi^{k-2}(x)\, d\Phi(x) = P^*. \tag{8.17}$$

Similarly for Procedure R_M, we set $s = t = 1$ in (5.27) to obtain

$$\begin{aligned} E_L\{S; \text{LF}, R_M\} &\approx kP^* - \lambda k(k-1)\int \Phi^{k-2}(x + A_1)\varphi(x + A_1)\, d\Phi(x) \\ &\approx kP^* - \frac{\lambda k(k-1)}{\sqrt{2}}\,\varphi\!\left(\frac{A_1}{\sqrt{2}}\right)\int \Phi^{k-2}\!\left(\frac{y}{\sqrt{2}} + \frac{A_1}{2}\right) d\Phi(y), \end{aligned} \tag{8.18}$$

where $A_1 = A_1(P^*)$ is the root of

$$(k-1)\int \Phi(x+A_1)[1-\Phi(x)]^{k-2}\,d\Phi(x) = P^*. \tag{8.19}$$

For $k = 5$ and $P^* = 0.95$, we obtain $4.75 - \lambda\ (0.4329)$ for (8.16), and $4.75 - \lambda\,(0.4097)$ for (8.18), so that (for these values of k and P^*) $\text{eff}_0(R_M; R_0) = 0.4097/0.4324 = 94.7\%$.

For Procedure R_0 with $t = 1$, fixed $P^* > (k-1)/k$, and λ small, the value of $\bar{s}$ needed to obtain equality in (2.2) is

$$\bar{s} = k - k(1-P^*)(1-\lambda k B)^{-1} \approx kP^* - \lambda k^2(1-P^*)B, \tag{8.20}$$

where $B = B(k)$ is a constant defined by

$$B = [(k-1)/2\sqrt{\pi}]\int \Phi^{k-2}(y/\sqrt{2})\,d\Phi(y). \tag{8.21}$$

For $k = 5$ and $P^* = 0.95$ this gives

$$\text{eff}_0(R_0; R) = 0.3635/0.4324 = 84.1\%. \tag{8.22}$$

It has not been shown that $\text{eff}_0(R_M, R) \leq 1$ for all $k \geq 2$ and all $P^* > (k-1)/k$ although this appears to be true by numerical investigation. It is easy to show that $0 \leq A \leq A_1$, and it follows that the above does hold for $k = 2$. For $k = 3$, the numerical values decrease monotonically from 99.0% at $P^* = 2/3$ to 86.6% at $P^* = 1$; for $k = 5$, they decrease from 97.3% at $P^* = 4/5$ to 79.1% at $P^* = 1$; this monotonicity has not been proved for $k > 2$.

We now derive the limiting ($P \to 1$) value of $\text{eff}_0(R_M, R)$ for any fixed k. For Procedure R, we integrate the first expression in (8.16) and use the Feller-Laplace expansion of the "tail" of the normal cdf to obtain for the asymptotic ($P^* \to 1$) form of the coefficient $C_1(R)$ of $-\lambda$

$$C_1(R) \approx (k-1)(1-P^*)A \approx (k-1)(1-P^*)\{-2[k/(k-1)]\ln(1-P^*)\}^{1/2}, \tag{8.23}$$

where the expression for A is obtained from (8.17) as in Section 8. For the Procedure R_M, Eq. (8.18) gives for $P^* \to 1$

$$\frac{1-P^*}{k-1} = \int \frac{[1-\Phi^{k-1}(x+A_1)]}{k-1}\,d\Phi(x) \approx \int \Phi(x+A_1)\,d\Phi(x)$$

$$= \Phi\left(\frac{A_1}{\sqrt{2}}\right)\cdot\frac{\varphi(A_1/\sqrt{2})}{A_1/\sqrt{2}}, \tag{8.24}$$

and it follows that $A_1 \approx [-\ln(1-P^*)]^{1/2}$. Hence the asymptotic ($P^* \to 1$) form of the coefficient $C_1(R_M)$ of $-\lambda$ is

$$C_1(R_M) \approx k(1-P^*)[-\ln(1-P^*)]^{1/2}. \tag{8.25}$$

Combining the results of (8.23) and (8.25) gives for any fixed $k \geq 2$

$$\lim_{P^* \to 1} \text{eff}_0(R_M, R) = [k/2(k-1)]^{1/2}, \tag{8.26}$$

which is less than or equal to 1 for all $k \geq 2$.

From (8.26), it follows that the monotonicity observed above for $k = 3$ and 5 will not hold for all k. In fact as $k \to \infty$, we note that $A_1 \to \infty$ and $A \to 0$, and hence $\text{eff}_0(R_M, R) \to 0$ for any fixed $P^* < 1$. Since $(8.26) \to \sqrt{2}/2 = 70.7\%$ as $k \to \infty$, it follows from continuity considerations that $\text{eff}_0(R_M, R)$ will not be strictly decreasing in P^* throughout the interval $[(k-1)/k, 1]$ for large values of k.

9. RELATED PROBLEMS

A. For a fixed subset-size procedure, it may happen that the subset size s is fixed by economic or other practical considerations, and we wish to determine the smallest t-value such that the infimum of the PCS is at least P^* in $\Omega(\delta^*)$. For the fixed s, define $\lambda_t > 0$ for $1 \leq t \leq k - s$ as the solution in $\lambda = (\theta - \theta')\sqrt{n}/\sigma = \delta^*\sqrt{n}/\sigma$ when we set both sides of (5.4) equal in the normal location-parameter problem; define $\lambda_0 = \infty$ and $\lambda_{k-s+1} = 0$. The first difference $\Delta_t = \Delta_t Q(s, t, k; \lambda)$ in t is positive since

$$\Delta_t = \binom{k-t-1}{s-1} \int \left[\left(\frac{k-t}{k-s-t} \right) \Phi(x) - \Phi(x-\lambda) \right]$$
$$\times \Phi^t(x-\lambda)[1-\Phi(x)]^{s-1} \, d\Phi^{k-s-t}(x) > 0 \tag{9.1}$$

and, since $Q(s, t, k; \lambda)$ is increasing in λ, it follows that the λ_t-values are decreasing with t. Then we compute $\lambda_c = \delta^*\sqrt{n}/\sigma$ and take as the solution the unique integer t for which

$$\lambda_{t-1} > \lambda_c \geq \lambda_t. \tag{9.2}$$

For comparisons, one could also find an average $\bar{t}$ of t and $t + 1$ using the same weights as are needed to make the infimum of the PCS over $\Omega(\delta^*)$ exactly equal to P^*.

B. The fixed subset-size Procedure R_0 is related to the procedures for two other problems R_1 and R_2 considered by Desu and Sobel [3], and we wish to show that the table by these authors [3] is also useful for our problem. Let R_1 and $Q_1(s, t, k; \delta^*)$ correspond to the problem of finding a subset containing the t best populations; let R_2 and $Q_2(s, t, k; \delta^*)$ correspond to the dual problem of finding a subset contained among the t best populations; let R_0 and $Q_0(s, t, k; \delta^*)$ correspond to the problem of this paper. For $t = 1$, comparing (5.4) above with (3.3) of Desu and Sobel [3], we have

$$Q_0(s, 1, k; \delta^*) = Q_1(s, 1, k; \delta^*) \tag{9.3}$$

and, in fact, the problems are identical, so that (9.3) also holds for all pairs (θ, θ') and without any assumptions.

Assuming a location-parameter problem and that $G_0(x)$ is symmetric about zero, we have for $s = 1$, by comparing (5.4) above with (3.3) of Desu and Sobel [3],

$$Q_0(1, t, k; \delta^*) = Q_1(k-1, k-t, k; \delta^*). \tag{9.4}$$

For $t \geq 1$, we can write $Q_0(s, t, k; \delta^*)$ in the form

$$Q_0(s, t, k; \delta^*) = 1 - \binom{k-t}{s} \int [1 - G(x - \delta^*)]^t [1 - G(x)]^{k-s-t} \, dG^s(x). \tag{9.5}$$

If we replace s by $k - s$ in the last term of (9.5), the result agrees with (3.3) of Desu and Sobel [3], and hence

$$Q_0(s, t, k; \delta^*) = 1 - Q_1(k - s, t, k; \delta^*). \tag{9.6}$$

Also, if we replace t by $k - t$ in the left member of (5.4), the result agrees with (8.1) of Desu and Sobel [3], and hence

$$Q_0(s, t, k, \delta^*) = 1 - Q_2(s, k - t, k; \delta^*). \tag{9.7}$$

It follows that for the normal location-parameter problem the table by Desu and Sobel [3] is also useful for this paper.

C. If we define the better population to be the one with the smaller θ-value, then the rule analogous to (3.1) is to put π_i in the selected subset if, and only if, $T_i \leq T_{[s]} + C_s$. In general, the results are different from those of Section 3, but for $\theta \geq \theta'$ using analogous methods, we obtain

$$P\{\text{CS}; \text{GLF}\} = 1 - s\binom{k-t}{s} \int [1 - G_{\theta'}(x + c_s)]^t \times G_\theta^{s-1}(x)[1 - G_\theta(x)]^{k-s-t} \, dG_\theta(x). \tag{9.8}$$

If θ is a location parameter and $G_0(x)$ is symmetrical about zero, then the problem is equivalent to the one already treated; in particular, Eq. (9.8) reduces to (4.5) and $c_s = a_s$.

D. To illustrate the multiplicative version of our Procedure R, we briefly consider the problem of selecting from k normal populations a subset containing at least one of the populations with the t smallest variances. Put π_i in the selected subset if, and only if, $T_i \leq c_s T_{[s]}$ where $c_s \geq 1$ and s both are to be determined as in Section 3. If the means are unknown, we use the sample variance for T; otherwise, we replaced $\overline{\overline{X}}_i$ by μ_i in the sample variance formula. Let $\delta_t = \sigma^2_{[t+1]}/\sigma^2_{[t]} > 1$ and let $\delta^* > 1$ be specified. As in (9.8), it can be shown that

$$P\{\text{CS}; \text{GLF}\} = 1 - s\binom{k-t}{s} \int_0^\infty [1 - G(xc_s\delta_t)]^t \times G^{s-1}(x)[1 - G(x)]^{k-s-t} \, dG(x), \tag{9.9}$$

where $G(x)$ can be taken as the cdf of the gamma density $x^{\nu/2}e^{-x}/\Gamma(\nu/2)$ for $x > 0$ (and zero, otherwise), and ν is the common number of degrees of freedom associated with each sample variance. For the special case $\nu = 2$, the equation determining c_s is easily shown to reduce to solving a polynomial of degree s. For the case $s = 1$ and $c_1 < 1$, we use a fixed subset-size rule in analogy with the corresponding instruction for Procedure R.

10. A LIKELIHOOD RATIO PROCEDURE, R_L

Another procedure is given as 7 Goal on page 88 of Bechhofer, Kiefer, and Sobel [2]; it is based on likelihoods and we denote it by R_L. We restrict our attention to the normal location-parameter problem with $t = 1$.

Let $y_i = \bar{x}_{[i]}$ denote the ordered sample means ($i = 1, 2, \ldots, k$). Under Procedure R_L the size S of the selected subset is the smallest integer j for which

$$\frac{\sum_{i=1}^{k-j} \exp\{-\lambda(y_k - y_i)\}}{\sum_{i=k-j+1}^{k} \exp\{-\lambda(y_k - y_i)\}} \leq \frac{1 - P^*}{P^*}. \tag{10.1}$$

For $j = k$ the left-hand side of (10.1) is zero, and hence $1 \leq S \leq k$. For $S = j$ the selected subset contains exactly those j populations which give rise to the j largest sample means. The form (10.1) is easily obtained from the derivation given by Bechhofer, Kiefer, and Sobel [2].

To obtain eff(R_L, R), we investigate the asymptotic ($P^* \to 1$) nature of Procedure R_L. Just as for the other procedures, $S \to k$ with probability 1 under Procedure R_L and we need only consider $P\{S = k\}$ and $P\{S = k - 1\}$. From (10.1) we note that $S = k$ if, and only if,

$$\sum_{i=2}^{k} \exp\{\lambda(y_i - y_1)\} < P^*/(1 - P^*). \tag{10.2}$$

For $k > 2$ consider the two events $\mathscr{E}_j$ ($j = 2, k$) defined by

$$\exp\{\lambda(y_j - y_1)\} < P^*/(k - 1)(1 - P^*); \tag{10.3}$$

for $k = 2$, we simply put in equality (or weak inequality) signs in the discussion below. Since $\mathscr{E}_k$ implies the event $S = k$, and the latter implies $\mathscr{E}_2$,

$$P\{\mathscr{E}_k\} < P\{S = k\} < P\{\mathscr{E}_2\}. \tag{10.4}$$

Letting $D = (1/\delta^*) \ln[P^*/(k - 1)(1 - P^*)]$, we obtain

$$\begin{aligned} P\{\mathscr{E}_k\} &= k \int [\Phi(x + D) - \Phi(x)]^{k-1} \, d\Phi(x) \\ &\approx k \int \{1 - \Phi(x) - [1 - \Phi(x + D)]\}^{k-1} \, d\Phi(x) \\ &\approx 1 - k(k - 1) \int [1 - \Phi(x)]^{k-2}[1 - \Phi(x + D)] \, d\Phi(x), \end{aligned} \tag{10.5}$$

since the remaining terms are negligible in comparison. As in (8.5), we replace $1 - \Phi(x + D)$ by $\varphi(x + D)/D$, obtaining

$$P\{\mathscr{E}_k\} \approx 1 - [k(k-1)/D\sqrt{2}]\varphi(D/\sqrt{2}) \int \Phi^{k-2}[(y/\sqrt{2}) + (D/2)]\, d\Phi(y)$$

$$\approx 1 - [k(k-1)/D\sqrt{2}]\varphi(D/\sqrt{2}) \approx 1 - (C/D)\exp\{-(D^2/4)\}. \quad (10.6)$$

Another analysis for $P\{\mathscr{E}_2\}$, somewhat similar, gives

$$P\{\mathscr{E}_2\} = 1 - k(k-1) \int \Phi(x - D)[1 - \Phi(x)]^{k-2}\, d\Phi(x)$$

$$= 1 - k \int [1 - \Phi(x + D)]^{k-1}\, d\Phi(x)$$

$$\approx 1 - (k/D^{k-1}) \int \varphi^{k-1}(x + D)\, d\Phi(x)$$

$$= 1 - (\sqrt{k}/D^{k-1})\varphi\{D[(k-1)/k]^{1/2}\}$$

$$\approx 1 - (C^1/D^{k-1})\exp\{-[(k-1)D^2/2k]\}. \quad (10.7)$$

Since

$$E\{S; R_L\} \approx kP\{S = k\} + (k-1)P\{S = k-1\} \approx k - [1 - P\{S = k\}]$$

it follows that for P^* sufficiently close to 1

$$(C^1/D^{k-1}) \exp\{-[(k-1)D^2/2k]\} < k - E\{S; R_L\}$$

$$< (C/D) \exp\{-(D^2/4)\}, \quad (10.8)$$

and both sides give the same result for $k = 2$. If we use the right-hand side of (10.8) as numerator in (8.1), and use (8.14) with $s = k - t$ as denominator for Procedure R, then we easily find that the limit ($P^* \to 1$) is zero. It is not necessary to show that the EP-configuration maximizes $E\{S; R_L\}$ since, if any other configuration gives a larger $E\{S; R_L\}$, then the same result holds a fortiori. It follows that Procedure R_L has asymptotic ($P^* \to 1$) efficiency zero relative to Procedure R.

REFERENCES

1. BECHHOFER, R. E. (1954). A single-sample multiple decision procedure for ranking means of normal populations with known variance. *Ann. Math. Statist.* **25** 16–39.
2. BECHHOFER, R. E., KIEFER, J., and SOBEL, M. (1968). "Sequential Ranking and Identification Procedures." Univ. of Chicago Press, Chicago, Illinois.
3. DESU, M. M., and SOBEL, M. (1968). A fixed subset-size approach to the selection problem. *Biometrika* **55** 401–410.
4. GUPTA, S. S. (1965). On some multiple decision (selection and ranking) rules. *Technometrics* **7** 225–245.

PART VII

Econometrics, Principal Components, Reliability, and Applications

On the Structure and Estimation of General Interdependent Systems

ANDERS ÅGREN and HERMAN O. WOLD

UNIVERSITY INSTITUTE OF STATISTICS
UPPSALA, SWEDEN

INTRODUCTION

Our paper takes up two aspects of general interdependent (GEID) systems:

(1) Graphic illustration of the GEID specification;
(2) Generalized versions of the fix-point (FP) estimation method.

It is only recently that the GEID approach has been launched [1–6]. Hence, it should be in order to give an introductory briefing of interdependent (ID) systems, with emphasis on the key differences between GEID systems and Classic ID (or CLID) systems. It is assumed that the reader is oriented about the classic theory of ID systems.[1]

A. Let us consider a multirelational stochastic model such that (a) the system in structural form is given by

$$y = \boldsymbol{\beta} y + \Gamma z + \delta, \tag{1}$$

say, with n endogenous variables y and m predetermined variables z; and (b) all structural relations are behavioral. Assumption (b) implies that the left-hand column vector $y = (y_1, \ldots, y_n)$ involves each of the current endogenous variables y_i once, and only once, and that matrix $\boldsymbol{\beta} = \|\beta_{ik}\|$ has mere zeros in the main diagonal,

$$\beta_{ik} = 0 \quad \text{for} \quad k = i; \qquad i = 1, \ldots, n.$$

For the reduced form of the system, we write

$$y = \Omega z + \varepsilon \tag{2}$$

[1] See Koopmans [7], Hood and Koopmans [8] and, for recent treatises, Malinvaud [9] and Christ [10].

where

$$\Omega = [I - \boldsymbol{\beta}]^{-1}\Gamma; \tag{3a}$$

$$\varepsilon = [I - \boldsymbol{\beta}]^{-1}\delta. \tag{3b}$$

In the applied work of such systems, it is desirable to make operative use of the behavioral relations (1) as well as the reduced form (2). Hence, it is desirable to specify the systematic parts of all relations (1)–(2) as predictors, i.e., as conditional expectations. For the structural form (1), this requires

$$E(y_i \mid y_p, z_q) = (\boldsymbol{\beta} y + \Gamma z)_i; \qquad i = 1, \ldots, n \tag{4}$$

where y_p, z_q stand for the variables y, z that occur in the right-hand member of the ith structural relation. For the reduced form (2), the requirement is

$$\begin{aligned} E(y_i \mid z_1, \ldots, z_m) &= (\Omega z)_i \\ &= ([I - \boldsymbol{\beta}]^{-1}\Gamma z)_i; \qquad i = 1, \ldots, n \end{aligned} \tag{5a}$$

or, more generally,

$$\begin{aligned} E(y_i \mid ([I - \boldsymbol{\beta}]^{-1}\Gamma z)_i) &= (\Omega z)_i \\ &= ([I - \boldsymbol{\beta}]^{-1}\Gamma z)_i; \qquad i = 1, \ldots, n. \end{aligned} \tag{5b}$$

B. A multirelational model (1) is called a causal chain (CC) system if matrix $\boldsymbol{\beta}$ is subdiagonal; that is, if

$$\beta_{ik} = 0 \qquad \text{for} \quad k \geq i; \qquad i = 1, \ldots, n. \tag{6}$$

A CC system (1), subject to suitable supplementary conditions, can be specified in accordance with (4) and (5) (see Wold [11]). At first sight, it might seem to be a radical restriction in the model design to satisfy both (4) and (5). For a CC system, the twofold specification is possible since (6) implies that the transformation that carries from the structural form (1) to the reduced form (2) is nothing other than a sequence of substitutions, and predictors that are subject to substitutions will—under fairly general supplementary conditions—remain predictors (Wold [11]).

C. If the endogenous variables y_i cannot be ordered so that condition (6) is satisfied, system (1) is called an ID system. For an ID system (1) it is, in general, not possible to satisfy both specifications (4) and (5) (see Wold [12]).

In a classic ID system (1), each current residual is assumed to be uncorrelated with all of the current predetermined variables; in symbols,

$$r(\delta_{it}, z_{kt}) = 0; \qquad i = 1, \ldots, n; \quad k = 1, \ldots, m \tag{7}$$

and for all time points t under consideration. Specification (7) is in line with (5a), inasmuch as (5a) implies (7), whereas (5b), in general, will not imply (7). Hence, we call (5a) the *classic* and (5b) the *general* predictor specification of an ID system (1).

In the classic literature of ID systems, the models are not specified in terms of predictors, as in (4) and (5). The classic ID systems are specified as involving "errors in equations." To spell out, they are specified as being exact,

$$y = \boldsymbol{\beta} y + \Gamma z$$

with reduced form

$$\begin{aligned} y &= \Omega z \\ &= [I - \boldsymbol{\beta}]^{-1} \Gamma z \end{aligned}$$

subject to residual error, say, δ and $\varepsilon = [I - \boldsymbol{\beta}]^{-1}\delta$, respectively, and the residuals are assumed to satisfy the noncorrelation relations (7). The classic approach of exact relations with superimposed residuals, called "errors in equations," thus, is in the nature of *apparent scatter*, as distinct from the approach of *genuine scatter*, where the relations are specified in terms of predictors (conditional expectations).[2] Evidently, the approach of apparent scatter is very stringent, too narrow to be realistic in econometrics and other social sciences. A main incentive for the GEID models was to break away from the approach of apparent scatter, designing the models in terms of genuine scatter. The first step in this direction is the REID approach, which is described next.

D. REID (Reformulated ID) Systems. Given a Classic ID system in structural form (1), we reformulate it as follows,

$$y = \boldsymbol{\beta} y^* + \Gamma z + \varepsilon \tag{8}$$

where matrices $\boldsymbol{\beta}$ and Γ are numerically the same as in (1), y^* to the right in (8) is the systematic part of y as given by the same relation, and the residuals δ are modified accordingly. The reformulation implies: (a) the system will have the same reduced form (2) as before; to repeat,

$$y = \Omega z + \varepsilon \tag{9a}$$

$$= [I - \boldsymbol{\beta}]^{-1} \Gamma z + \varepsilon \tag{9b}$$

and (b) the residuals will be the same in the structural and reduced forms. Statements (a) and (b) are readily verified, y^* being given by

$$y^* = \boldsymbol{\beta} y^* + \Gamma z \tag{10a}$$

$$= [I - \boldsymbol{\beta}]^{-1} \Gamma z \tag{10b}$$

and ε by

$$\varepsilon = \delta + \boldsymbol{\beta}(y - y^*) \tag{11a}$$

$$= \delta + \boldsymbol{\beta}\varepsilon \tag{11b}$$

$$= [I - \boldsymbol{\beta}]^{-1}\delta. \tag{11c}$$

[2] Whereas the distinction is of old standing, the terms apparent versus genuine scatter are new [13, 14], and designed to make for clarity in the haze around "errors in equations."

System (8) as specified by (5a) is called a REID (reformulated ID) system. The point of REID systems is that they allow predictor specification both for the structural form and for the reduced form. In symbols, the structural form (8) is specified by

$$y_i^* = E(y_i \mid y_p^*, z_q) = (\boldsymbol{\beta} y^* + \Gamma z)_i; \qquad i = 1, \ldots, n \tag{12}$$

and the reduced form by

$$y_i^* = E(y_i \mid z_1, \ldots, z_m) = (\Omega z)_i \tag{13a}$$

$$= ([I - \boldsymbol{\beta}]^{-1} \Gamma z)_i; \qquad i = 1, \ldots, n. \tag{13b}$$

E. GEID (General ID) Systems. These are formally the same as REID systems except that the predictor specification of the reduced form shifts from (5a) to the more general assumption (5b). Hence, GEID systems are given by formulas (8)–(12) with the predictor relation (12), which we repeat,

$$y_i^* = E(y_i \mid y_p^*, z_q) = (\boldsymbol{\beta} y^* + \Gamma z)_i; \qquad i = 1, \ldots, n \tag{14}$$

whereas the reduced form (9) is specified by the following predictor,

$$y_i^* = E(y_i \mid ([I - \boldsymbol{\beta}]^{-1} \Gamma z)_i) = (\Omega z)_i \tag{15a}$$

$$= ([I - \boldsymbol{\beta}]^{-1} \Gamma z)_i; \qquad i = 1, \ldots, n \tag{15b}$$

and not by the predictor (13a–b).

In REID and GEID systems the residual ε_i (for any $i = 1, \ldots, n$) is uncorrelated with those variables y_p^* and z_q that occur in the ith relation of the structural form. This key feature is an immediate implication of (12) and (14).

F. Given any REID or GEID system, the structural form (8) can be carried back to its classic form (1) by reversing the reformulation without numerical change in the parameters $\boldsymbol{\beta}$, Γ. For the ensuing classic ID system, as before, the predictor specification (4) of the structural form (1) will *not* hold, and the reduced form (2) will be subject to the predictor specification (5a) in the REID case, and (5b) in the GEID case.

G. The REID reformulation provides a predictor specification of the structural form of ID systems, and at the same time it is seen to provide the possibility of a cause-effect specification of the behavioral relations of the system. We see that the gain is bought at a price, for if we consider the effect variable y_i to the left in the ith structural relation of a REID (or GEID) system, the right-hand causal variables will not include the observed values y_p of the current endogenous variables, but instead their expected values y_p^*. As in classic ID systems, the right-hand causal variables will include the observed values of the predetermined variables z_q.

By the time the REID reformulation and the specification (12) were obtained [11, 12, 15], there were signs that the various techniques for the estimation of classic ID systems had become stuck when it came to large or moderately large systems (see Theil [16], Klein [17]). The root of the trouble was easy to see: All of the classic estimation techniques for ID systems start with ordinary least-squares (OLS) estimation of the reduced form; in ID systems each relation of the reduced form, in general, contains all of the predetermined variables $z_1, \ldots, z_m$; hence in systems of some size, the available observations will be outnumbered by the predetermined variables and their coefficients in the reduced form; OLS will run into the pitfall of "overfitting"; that is, OLS as applied to the reduced form will give residuals that are elusively small or altogether vanishing. This state of things suggested that the estimation procedure should avoid the reduced form and be based entirely on the structural form. Posed in this way, the problem of estimating the structural form becomes nonlinear, inasmuch as (8) involves the product $\boldsymbol{\beta} y^*$, where both factors are unknown and subject to estimation. The nonlinear nature of the problem suggests some iterative estimation procedure, and the first that came to mind was a simple device of iterative OLS regressions [1, 2], which is restated in Section 2.2. The procedure is called fix-point (FP) estimation because of the key property (10a) of the predictor y^* subject to estimation.

H. An example follows, somewhat stylicized for simplicity, but less drastic than some of the big ID systems that have been reported recently:

Let us consider an ID system (1) with 20 structural relations, each right-hand member with 2 current endogenous variables y_p and 2 predetermined variables z_q. Hence there are $n = 20$ endogenous variables y, and if we assume the predetermined variables z to be different in all relations, $m = 40$.

This system has a total of $(2 + 2) \times 20 = 80$ parameters $\boldsymbol{\beta}$, Γ.

Its classic specification involves $20 \times 40 = 800$ zero correlation assumptions (7).

The GEID specification (14) implies the zero correlations

$$r(\varepsilon_i, y_p^*) = r(\varepsilon_i, z_q) = 0; \qquad i = 1, \ldots, 20$$

in all $4 \times 20 = 80$ correlations, which is the same as the number of unknown parameters $\boldsymbol{\beta}$, Γ.

Comments. With regard to the parity in the numbers of parameters and zero correlation assumptions, the GEID approach is similar to OLS regression.

In Classic ID systems, the excess of the assumed residual zero correlations (7) over the number of available parameters $\boldsymbol{\beta}$, Γ is the cause behind the multiplicity of available estimation techniques for such models. In the 20-relations model just given as an illustration, any 4 predetermined variables z_k will make a set of instrumental variables for the estimation of a structural relation. For the estimation of the entire system this gives $\binom{40}{4}^{20}$ sets, an astronomic number $\approx 0.98 \times 10^{100}$, each set providing a consistent estimate for the 80 parameters $\boldsymbol{\beta}$, Γ.

I. Scope of the Present Paper

The REID and GEID specifications (12) make the model nonlinear. Given the product moment structure of the variables y_i, z_k, the situation raises problems about the *existence* and *uniqueness* of the parameters $\boldsymbol{\beta}$, Γ, and the expectations y_i^*.

The exact assessment of $\boldsymbol{\beta}$, Γ, y^* is complicated even in the smallest models. Lyttkens [3] has obtained exact solutions for some simple models, including Summers' two-relation models [18]. Here, the exact solution, in general, involves the solving of an algebraic equation of the 5th degree, giving 1 or 3 or 5 real solutions.

Section 1 of this paper gives a graphic illustration of the GEID specification of Summers' model. The existence of a solution $\boldsymbol{\beta}$, Γ, y^*, here, and in general GEID models, follows from the properties of projections onto closed subspaces. As to multiplicity of solutions, the situation presents analogies to (a) the assessment of the parameters of a moving average on the basis of its autocorrelation coefficients, [19], and (b) the iterative regression approach to principal components [2, 20].

Reference is made to a proximity theorem for ID systems to the effect that if the residual correlations are small of the order of magnitude Δ, then the bias of OLS regression as applied to the structural relations of the system is small of order Δ^2 (see Wold [13], Mosbaek and Wold [21]).

Another feature with a bearing upon the GEID specification: If the interdependence is weak—that is, if all parameters β_{ik} are small—there is no doubt about existence of the GEID specification, nor about convergence of the FP procedure; [21].

The FP (fix-point) estimation technique can be taken as a basis for modifications with a view to improve its performance in various respects. Section 2 reports a modified procedure called FFP (fractional fix-point) estimation, and gives brief reference to another approach, called RFP (recursive FFP) estimation. These techniques in many cases extend the scope and improve the performance of FP estimation with regard to convergence and speed of convergence. When they converge, they will give the same results as FP estimation, and in many cases the simple FP device will suffice.

The limited scope of this paper must be emphasized. The problem area is large, and research is in progress in several directions. Brief reference is made to some aspects not dealt with in the present paper.

ID Systems with Identities. This paper only deals with ID systems in which all relations are behavioral. A corresponding predictor specification of models that involve identities has recently been given by Lyttkens, [3].

Inversion of Instruments and Target Variables. On the classic specification (7) the allocation of current endogenous variables y to the right or to the left in a structural relation does not matter, numerically. This is not so on the GEID specification (see Wold [13]).

An important question which in essence is a matter for empirical research is whether in actual fact it is realistic to assume that instrument and target variables are reversible, as is done in Classic ID systems (again, see Wold [13]).

Empirical Applications. In the first phase of its development, the FP and GEID research has focused on theoretical aspects and on numerical work on artificial data. Research is in progress on empirical applications, and will be reported in due course.

J. Concluding Remarks

Any Verdict Yet? This is the motto of a symposium in Econometrica, held some years ago [22]. Does the GEID approach give an answer? Well, both GEID and the Classic ID approach have obvious advantages and disadvantages. Hence, it seems to us that the situation does not invite a choice but rather a compromising synthesis: Stick to the classic formulation (1), but with a grain of GEID salt. More specifically: Abandon (7); use some FP technique for parameter estimation; any structural relation (1) can then be used for autonomous prediction, subject to ancillary information about those predetermined variables z_q that are exogenous to the systems; disregard that the ensuing prediction is biased, inasmuch as (4) is not exactly valid but may be accepted as an approximation; disregard the conceptual contradiction that two variables y_{it}, y_{kt} interchange as cause and effect variables in two structural relations, accepting the contradiction as the result of an approximation that ignores short lags between causes and effects.

In conclusion, a comment (by H. W.) on Parzen's very interesting paper at this symposium [23]. With reference to Parzen's introductory remarks, page 2, it seems to me that ID systems are a clearcut case of multivariate analysis. There are many statisticians that have dealt with such systems without using the spectral approach. Maybe there is a difference here in philosophy about the general aims of the analysis. In any case, there is a rather clearcut distinction between two lines of approach, or perhaps better, two aspiration levels in time series analysis: (a) One which makes confidence analysis exclusively on the basis of past observations by way of standard errors and various devices of hypothesis testing; and (b) One which uses the past observations mainly for parameter estimation, and makes confidence analysis mainly by way of predictive tests, comparing the forecasts derived from the model with the actual course of events. Under (b) the primary thing is to ask for consistency of the parameter estimates. Only when consistency has been achieved is it meaningful to proceed to standard errors and hypothesis testing based on past observations. The present paper is a case in point. For any linear predictor—for example (5a)—OLS gives consistent estimates on the assumption of product moment ergodicity; that is, assuming that the observed product moments tend to the corresponding theoretical moments as the sample size increases indefinitely (see Wold [24]).

1. GRAPHIC INTERPRETATION OF INTERDEPENDENT SYSTEMS IN REID AND GEID SPECIFICATION[3]

The two-relation ID system studied by Summers [18] is suitable for purposes of illustration, being simple and yet sufficiently general to bring out key features of ID systems. We shall consider the REID and GEID versions of Summers' model, in **1.1** the special case of a just identified system, and in **1.2** the general case of an overidentified system. The notations are in accordance with formulas (1)–(16) in the Introduction.

1.1. Figure 1 refers to the REID or GEID system as defined by its structural form

$$\begin{aligned} y_1 &= \beta_{12} y_2^* + \gamma_{11} z_1 + \varepsilon_1 \\ y_2 &= \beta_{21} y_1^* + \gamma_{22} z_2 + \varepsilon_2 \end{aligned} \tag{1}$$

which has two relations, two predetermined variables, and is just identified. With 0 as origin, the coordinate axes z_1, z_2 are drawn in the plane P of the paper. The axes y_1, y_2 are in two other dimensions; hence the graph is four-dimensional. All four variables y_1, y_2, z_1, z_2 are normalized so as to have zero mean and unit standard deviation. Hence the vectors $0y_1$, $0y_2$, $0z_1$, $0z_2$ are taken to be of unit length. Since $0z_1$ and $0z_2$ are in the plane of the paper, it follows that these two vectors have the same length in the graph, whereas the lengths of $0y_1$ and $0y_2$ are distorted by the perpective.

The reduced form of system (1) takes the form

$$\begin{aligned} y_1 &= \omega_{11} z_1 + \omega_{12} z_2 + \varepsilon_1 \\ y_2 &= \omega_{21} z_1 + \omega_{22} z_2 + \varepsilon_2 . \end{aligned} \tag{2}$$

We note the fundamental formulas

$$\begin{aligned} y_1 &= y_1^* + \varepsilon_1 \\ y_2 &= y_2^* + \varepsilon_2 \end{aligned} \tag{3}$$

[3] By H. O. Wold.

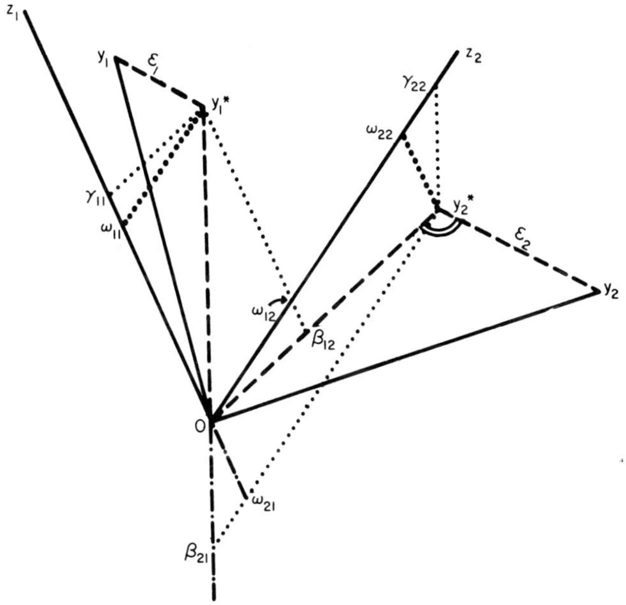

Fig. 1. Graphic illustration of system (1).

$$\begin{aligned} y_1^* &= \beta_{12} y_2^* + \gamma_{11} z_1 \\ y_2^* &= \beta_{21} y_1^* + \gamma_{22} z_2 . \end{aligned} \tag{4}$$

Relations (1)–(4) allow simple graphic interpretation. The following comments serve to elucidate the situation.

1.1.1. The coordinate axes of the observed variables y_1, y_2, z_1, z_2 are full-drawn lines. The broken lines refer to constructed variables: y_1^*, y_2^*, ε_1, ε_2. Stippled lines (dots and segments) indicate extensions of the coordinate axes to the negative side.

1.1.2. By (2) and (3), the variables y_1^*, y_2^* are linear combinations of z_1, z_2, and thus lie in the plane P of the paper.

1.1.3. As to (3), the graph marks 90° angles by ∢. For example, the vector $\varepsilon_1 = y_1 - y_1^*$ is orthogonal to the plane P and to the vector $0y_1^*$.

1.1.4. In accordance with 1.1.1 and 1.1.2, the graph shows that y_1^* and y_2^* generally have standard deviations smaller than unit.

1.1.5. The two relations (4) are illustrated by dotted lines projected from y_1^* and y_2^*, respectively. The coefficients β, γ come out as line segments from the origin 0 along the corresponding coordinate axes.

1.1.6. Similarly, the two relations (2) are illustrated by projections on the axes z_1, z_2; the requisite new lines are marked by small rings.

1.2. Figure 2 refers to Summers' model with four predetermined variables

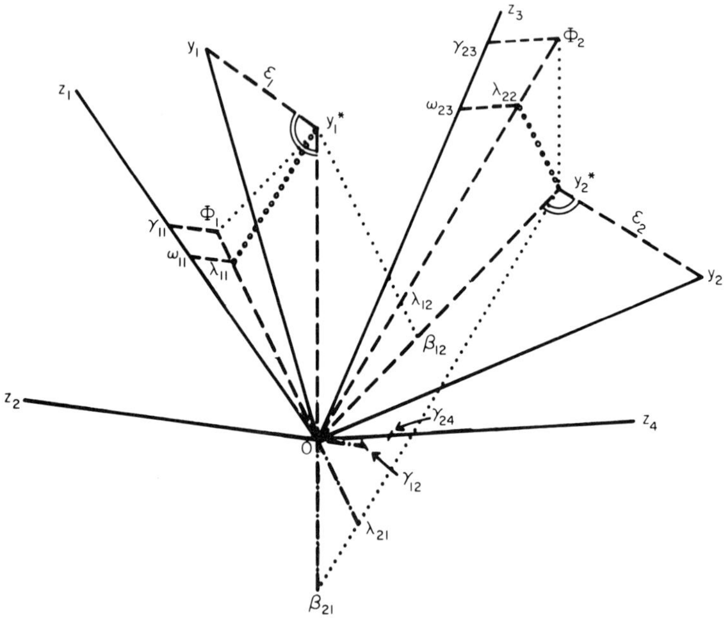

Fig. 2. Graphic illustration of system (5).

$$\begin{aligned} y_1 &= \beta_{12} y_2^* + \gamma_{11} z_1 + \gamma_{12} z_2 + \varepsilon_1 \\ y_2 &= \beta_{21} y_1^* + \gamma_{23} z_3 + \gamma_{24} z_4 + \varepsilon_2 \end{aligned} \tag{5}$$

and in reduced form

$$\begin{aligned} y_1 &= \omega_{11} z_1 + \omega_{12} z_2 + \omega_{13} z_3 + \omega_{14} z_4 + \varepsilon_1 \\ y_2 &= \omega_{21} z_1 + \omega_{22} z_2 + \omega_{23} z_3 + \omega_{24} z_4 + \varepsilon_2 \end{aligned} \tag{6}$$

Following Lyttkens' system of notations [3], we write

$$\begin{aligned} \Phi_1 &= \gamma_{11} z_1 + \gamma_{12} z_2 \\ \Phi_2 &= \gamma_{23} z_3 + \gamma_{24} z_4 \end{aligned} \tag{7}$$

which allows us to write the structural form as follows:

$$\begin{aligned} y_1 &= \beta_{12} y_2^* + \Phi_1 + \varepsilon_1 \\ y_2 &= \beta_{21} y_1^* + \Phi_2 + \varepsilon_2 \end{aligned} \tag{8}$$

and the reduced form as follows:

$$\begin{aligned} y_1 &= \lambda_{11}\Phi_1 + \lambda_{12}\Phi_2 + \varepsilon_1 \\ y_2 &= \lambda_{21}\Phi_1 + \lambda_{22}\Phi_2 + \varepsilon_2 . \end{aligned} \tag{9}$$

Figure 2 is drawn so as to have the coordinate axes Φ_1 and Φ_2 in the plane P of the paper. In general, none of the variables y_i, z_k will be in the plane P. Hence, the graph involves a total of 8 coordinate axes but only 6 dimensions, namely y_i, z_k. Some comments:

1.2.1. The variables Φ_1, Φ_2 are constructed and, therefore, are drawn as broken lines. In general, they are not of unit length.

In several respects, as noted in 1.2.2–1.2.5, Φ_1 and Φ_2 in Fig. 2 correspond to z_1 and z_2 in Fig. 1.

1.2.2. The predictors y_1^* and y_2^* are linear in Φ_1 and Φ_2 and therefore lie in the plane P of the paper.

1.2.3. As in Fig. 1, the residual vectors ε_1, ε_2 make 90° angles with the plane P.

1.2.4. Substituting z_i by Φ_i, the graphic illustration of the coefficients $\omega_{11}, \omega_{12}, \omega_{21}, \omega_{22}$ in Fig. 1 carries over to the coefficients $\lambda_{11}, \lambda_{12}, \lambda_{21}, \lambda_{22}$ in Fig. 2.

1.2.5. The interpretation of β_{12}, β_{21} is the same in the two graphs.

1.2.6. Turning to the differences between the two graphs, let P_{12} denote the plane spanned by the two vectors $0z_1$ and $0z_2$ in Fig. 2. Knowing from (7) that Φ_1 is linear in z_1 and z_2, the vector $0\Phi_1$ lies in P_{12}. This gives a graphic interpretation of λ_{11} and λ_{12} as projections of y_1^* on Φ_1 and Φ_2. Note that $0\Phi_1$ lies in the intersection between P_{12} and the plane P of the paper. Further note that the lines that measure γ_{11} and γ_{12} do not lie in P; hence, the magnitudes of γ_{11} and γ_{12} as given by the graph generally will be distorted by the perspective. Similarly, Φ_2 is linear in z_3 and z_4, which gives a graphic interpretation of λ_{23} and λ_{24}.

If we draw a vector $0\varepsilon_1$ from the origin 0 parallel to the residual vector ε_1, we may note in Fig. 2 that the vector $0\varepsilon_1$ is orthogonal to the vectors $0\Phi_1$ and $0\Phi_2$. The situation is similar for ε_2.

1.2.7. Making use of the relations

$$\begin{aligned} \omega_{11} &= \lambda_{11}\gamma_{11}; & \omega_{21} &= \lambda_{21}\gamma_{11} \\ \omega_{12} &= \lambda_{11}\gamma_{12}; & \omega_{22} &= \lambda_{21}\gamma_{12} \\ \omega_{13} &= \lambda_{12}\gamma_{23}; & \omega_{23} &= \lambda_{22}\gamma_{23} \\ \omega_{14} &= \lambda_{12}\gamma_{24}; & \omega_{24} &= \lambda_{22}\gamma_{24} \end{aligned} \tag{10}$$

which are implied by (6) and (9), Fig. 2 provides a graphic interpretation of the coefficients ω_{ik} of the reduced form (6). In order not to overburden the graph, Fig. 2 gives only the illustration of ω_{11} and ω_{23}.

1.3. Let us now compare the systems (1) and (5) in the light of the graphs.

1.3.1. In Fig. 1 the system is just identified, and then each residual ε_1, ε_2 is orthogonal to both z_1 and z_2.

1.3.2. In Fig. 2 the system is overidentified. Each ε_1, ε_2 will be orthogonal to both Φ_1 and Φ_2.

In Classic ID systems and in REID systems, each ε_1, ε_2 will be orthogonal to all z_1, z_2, z_3, z_4.

In the GEID specification, the residual ε_1 will be orthogonal to z_1 and z_2, but in general not to z_3 and z_4. As to this last feature, the zero correlation between ε_1 and Φ_2 leaves only one degree of freedom for the nonzero correlations between ε_1 and the two variables z_3 and z_4. As a consequence, the numerical specification of $r(\varepsilon_1, z_3)$ entails the numerical specification of $r(\varepsilon_1, z_4)$. For ε_2 and Φ_1, the situation is the same with regard to the nonzero correlations between ε_2 and z_1 and z_2.

1.3.3. Let us examine this last aspect of the graph a little more closely. The GEID specification determines the coefficients γ_{ik} (apart from plural solutions) and thereby determines Φ_1 and Φ_2, which fixes the plane P of the paper. The residual vector ε_1 is orthogonal to z_1 and z_2, and thereby orthogonal to Φ_1. Furthermore, the vector ε_1 is orthogonal to Φ_2. Hence, only one degree of freedom is left for the nonzero correlations between ε_1 and the two variables z_3 and z_4. To put it otherwise, once the plane P of the paper is fixed, the angles between the vector ε_1 and the two vectors z_3 and z_4 will be determined. These angles are nothing other than the correlation coefficients between ε_1 and z_3 and z_4; the two angles (correlation coefficients) are restricted, however, by the linear relation that expresses that Φ lies in the plane P_{34} spanned by z_3 and z_4.

Again the situation is similar for ε_2 and Φ_1.

1.4. The graphic interpretation readily extends to models with three relations. The vectors Φ_1, Φ_2, Φ_3 will then span an ordinary three-dimensional space, and y_1^*, y_2^*, y_3^* will be vectors in this space.

1.4.1. Most of the considerations in Sections 1.1–1.3 above carry over to the three-dimensional case, provided the $\boldsymbol{\beta}$ matrix is full,

$$\boldsymbol{\beta} = \begin{bmatrix} 0 & \beta_{12} & \beta_{13} \\ \beta_{21} & 0 & \beta_{23} \\ \beta_{31} & \beta_{32} & 0 \end{bmatrix}$$

that is, provided no coefficient β_{ik} is assumed a priori to be zero.

2. GENERAL INTERDEPENDENT SYSTEMS[4]

2.1. Introduction

Recently, a new iterative method for the estimation of econometric models was presented by Wold [1]. In a forthcoming monograph by Mosbaek and Wold an extensive study of the sampling properties of this new method, the fix-point (FP) method, will be presented [21]. This author took part in their project, and the results presented here are an outcome of more independent research in the course of their project. In their study Mosbaek and Wold found that some models caused serious convergence difficulties. This paper gives an explanation of these problems and suggests a modification of the original fix-point method which can be done to improve its behavior. This modification is called the fractional fix-point (FFP) method. A theorem which tells when convergence can be expected is given and some empirical illustrations to show the performance of the fractional fix-point method compared to the original method are presented. The results here reported draw from the work of Ågren [4]; more results will be published elsewhere.

2.2. The Fix-Point (FP) Method

The structural form of an interdependent system may be written

$$y_t = \boldsymbol{\beta} y_t + \Gamma z_t + \delta_t \tag{1}$$

where

- y_t is an $(n \times 1)$ column vector of endogenous variables,
- z_t is an $(m \times 1)$ column vector of predetermined variables,
- δ_t is an $(n \times 1)$ column vector of residuals,
- $\boldsymbol{\beta}$ is an $(n \times n)$ matrix of the coefficients of the endogenous variables;
- Γ is an $(n \times m)$ matrix of the coefficients of the predetermined variables.

Note that the elements of the main diagonal of $\boldsymbol{\beta}$ are all assumed to be 0. Some of the other elements of $\boldsymbol{\beta}$ may also be prescribed to be 0. As regards Γ, we have to assume that some elements are 0, otherwise the system will be under-identified.

Following Wold [1], we shall now rewrite the system in (1). If we solve for y_t (we assume that $I - \boldsymbol{\beta}$ is a nonsingular matrix), we obtain

$$y_t = (I - \boldsymbol{\beta})^{-1}\Gamma z_t + (I - \boldsymbol{\beta})^{-1}\delta_t. \tag{2}$$

We now introduce two new vectors defined as follows:

$$y_t^* = (I - \boldsymbol{\beta})^{-1}\Gamma z_t \qquad \text{and} \qquad \varepsilon_t = (I - \boldsymbol{\beta})^{-1}\delta_t. \tag{3}$$

[4] By A. Ågren.

Using this notation, we can rewrite Eq. (2)

$$y_t = y_t^* + \varepsilon_t, \tag{4}$$

and inserting this expression for y_t in the right-hand side of our original model in (1), we obtain

$$y_t = \boldsymbol{\beta} y_t^* + \Gamma z_t + \boldsymbol{\beta}\varepsilon_t + \delta_t. \tag{5}$$

But from the definition of δ_t in Eq. (3), we have

$$\boldsymbol{\beta}\varepsilon_t + \delta_t = \boldsymbol{\beta}\varepsilon_t + (I - \boldsymbol{\beta})\varepsilon_t = \varepsilon_t$$

which simplifies Eq. (5) to

$$y_t = \boldsymbol{\beta} y_t^* + \Gamma z_t + \varepsilon_t. \tag{6}$$

From (4) and (6), we see that

$$y_t^* = \boldsymbol{\beta} y_t^* + \Gamma z_t. \tag{7}$$

Now turning to the question of specification, we shall assume that our model is GEID[5] specified. This means that

$$E(y_{it} \mid y_{(i)t}^*, z_{(i)t}) = (\boldsymbol{\beta} y_t^* + \Gamma z_t)_i \tag{8}$$

where $y_{(i)t}^*$ and $z_{(i)t}$ mean those components of y_t^* and z_t which are in relation i. The column vector entry $(\boldsymbol{\beta} y_t^* + \Gamma z_t)_i$ makes the right-hand side in relation i. This is equivalent to saying that $(\boldsymbol{\beta} y_t^* + \Gamma z_t)_i$ is an *eo ipso* predictor of y_{it}. If the above assumption is fulfilled and if we know y_t^*, then the OLS (ordinary least squares) method will give consistent estimates of $\boldsymbol{\beta}$ and Γ. But the situation is not that simple since we cannot observe y_t^*. Hence, the fix-point method (the FP method) was suggested.

The FP procedure: Suppose that we have observations on y_t and z_t for $t = 1, \ldots, T$. The iteration process can be described by two steps.

(i) Suppose that iteration s has given the values $y_t^{*(s)}$. Then the least-squares method gives estimates $B^{(s)}$ and $G^{(s)}$ when applied to the system in Eq. (6) if y_t^* and z_t are substituted by $y_t^{*(s)}$ and z_t.

(ii) Having obtained $B^{(s)}$ and $G^{(s)}$, we obtain $y_t^{*(s+1)}$ from

$$y_t^{*(s+1)} = B^{(s)} y_t^{*(s)} + G^{(s)} z_t; \qquad t = 1, \ldots, T. \tag{9}$$

The procedure is continued until successive values of $B^{(s)}$ and $G^{(s)}$ do not differ from each other with more than the desired accuracy.

Comment 1. The start values can be chosen arbitrarily. A convenient choice is to let $y_t^{*(0)} = y_t$; $t = 1, \ldots, T$.

[5] GEID means general interdependent.

Comment 2. The FP-method requires that the model is written in such a way that each endogenous variable occurs once, and only once, on the left side of the equality signs. If the model is written with all its endogenous variables on one side and the predetermined variables on the other side then the variables must be rearranged before the FP method can be applied. Different rearrangements will generally provide different estimates. (This is also the case with OLS and TSLS.)

Comment 3. If the matrices $\boldsymbol{\beta}$ and Γ were known from the beginning, then the FP method would be identical to Jacobi's iterative method for solving a system of linear equations where $y_t{}^*$ is the unknown vector, $i = 1, \ldots, T$. Only step (ii) in the above description would then, of course, be necessary.

2.3. The Fractional Fix-Point (FFP) Method

The model and the specification of it are supposed to be exactly as in the previous section. The procedure for the fractional fix-point method will be:

(i) When the values of $y_t^{*(s)}$ have been obtained, $B^{(s)}$ and $G^{(s)}$ are obtained as for the FP method.

(ii) Then $y_t^{*(s+1)}$ is obtained from

$$y_t^{*(s+1)} = \alpha Y_t^{*(s+1)} + (1 - \alpha) y_t^{*(s)} \tag{10}$$

where

$$Y_t^{*(s+1)} = B^{(s)} y_t^{*(s)} + G^{(s)} z_t. \tag{11}$$

Here, α is a constant which is chosen in the interval (0, 2). A comparison between this method and the FP-method shows that the FP method is obtained as a special case when $\alpha = 1$.

As to the convergence of this method, some information is given by the following theorem (cf. Bellman [25], Varga [26]).

Theorem. *Let* $\boldsymbol{\beta} = (n \times n)$, $\Gamma = (n \times m)$, *and* $z = (m \times T)$ *be known constant matrices, where* $I - \boldsymbol{\beta}$ *is assumed to be nonsingular. Let* $u^{(0)} = (n \times T)$ *be an arbitrary matrix and apply the iteration procedure*

$$u^{(s+1)} = \alpha U^{(s+1)} + (1 - \alpha) u^{(s)}, \tag{12}$$

where

$$U^{(s+1)} = \boldsymbol{\beta} u^{(s)} + \Gamma z. \tag{13}$$

Then

$$\lim_{s \to \infty} u^{(s)} = u \qquad \text{and} \qquad u = \boldsymbol{\beta} u + \Gamma z \tag{14}$$

for any $u^{(0)}$ if, and only if, all the eigenvalues of

$$K = K(\alpha) = \alpha\boldsymbol{\beta} + (1 - \alpha)I \tag{15}$$

lie inside the unit circle in the complex plane. An α can be chosen such that this is the case if, and only if, the real parts of the eigenvalues of $\boldsymbol{\beta}$ are all less than 1.

Proof. First we can combine Eqs. (12) and (13) to give

$$u^{(s+1)} = [\alpha\boldsymbol{\beta} + (1 - \alpha)I]u^{(s)} + \alpha\Gamma z$$

or

$$u^{(s+1)} = Ku^{(s)} + \alpha\Gamma z \tag{16}$$

by using the definition of K in Eq. (15).

Now we want to find an expression of $u^{(s+n)}$ as a function of $u^{(s)}$. This must be of the form

$$u^{(s+n)} = K^n C + \alpha(I - K)^{-1}\Gamma z \tag{17}$$

since Eq. (16) is a difference equation of the first order. Putting $n = 0$, we infer

$$C = u^{(s)} - \alpha(I - K)^{-1}\Gamma z. \tag{18}$$

Hence, the solution is

$$u^{(s+n)} = K^n u^{(s)} + \alpha(I - K^n)(I - K)^{-1}\Gamma z. \tag{19}$$

Noticing that $\alpha(I - K)^{-1} = (I - \boldsymbol{\beta})^{-1}$, the solution can also be written

$$u^{(s+n)} = K^n u^{(s)} + (I - K^n)(I - \boldsymbol{\beta})^{-1}\Gamma z. \tag{19a}$$

A necessary and sufficient condition that the procedure will converge for any starting value $u^{(0)}$ is that $K^n \to 0$. This will be the case if, and only if, all the eigenvalues of K lie inside the unit circle. Hence, if this condition is fulfilled, we have

$$\lim_{n\to\infty} u^{(s+n)} = u = (I - \boldsymbol{\beta})^{-1}\Gamma z$$

and consequently

$$u = \boldsymbol{\beta}u + \Gamma z.$$

Now we shall prove the last statement of the theorem. To prove the necessity, we assume that one eigenvalue λ_1 of β has its real part greater than 1. Then the corresponding eigenvalue of $K(\alpha)$ will be $\gamma_1 = \alpha\lambda_1 + (1 - \alpha) = 1 + \alpha(x_1 - 1) + i\alpha y_1$, where $\lambda_1 = x_1 + iy_1$. We notice that for any choice of α in the interval (0, 2) it is impossible to get the real part of γ_1 less than 1. Hence, the absolute value of γ_1 is always greater than 1. This proves the necessity.

To prove the sufficiency, we assume that λ_2 has its real part less than 1. The eigenvalue λ_2 is transformed into $\gamma_2 = \alpha\lambda_2 + 1 - \alpha$, and we shall prove that α can be chosen such that $|\gamma_2| < 1$. But this is the same as proving that α can be chosen such that the circle

$$|\alpha z + 1 - \alpha| = 1 \quad \text{or} \quad |z + (1 - \alpha)/\alpha| = 1/\alpha$$

covers λ_2 (see Fig. 3). But this can always be done if α is small enough. If

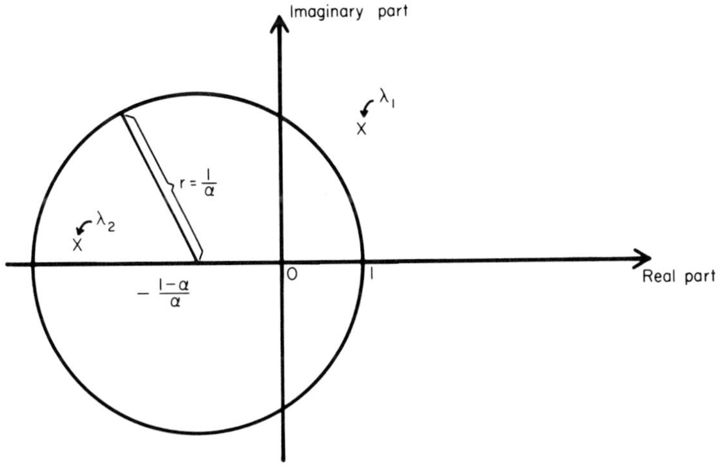

Fig. 3. Illustration of the second part of the proof.

there are many eigenvalues of β, we choose α small enough to make the circle cover all eigenvalues. This completes the proof.

Comment 1. Obviously, this theorem can be used only in an approximate sense since $\boldsymbol{\beta}$ and Γ are not constant matrices in the FP and FFP methods. However, the condition on the size of the eigenvalues of K gives us a hint for which values of α convergence could be expected. The numerical illustrations will throw more light on this problem area.

Comment 2. Our situation differs from that in the theorem also in another respect. From Eq. (19), we see that $u^{(s+n)}$ will tend to infinity if there is an eigenvalue of K greater than one. This cannot be the case in the FFP procedure since the variance of $y_i^{*(s)}$ is less than the variance of y_i. Nonconvergence will instead show up as a loop in the successive $y^{*(s)}$ values.

Comment 3. The FFP method can be regarded as the Jacobi method with a relaxation factor where the iteration matrix is adjusted in each step.

2.4. Choice of α

If we know the $\boldsymbol{\beta}$ matrix which we are going to find by the FFP method (it is possible to find a noniterative solution sometimes) then the choice of α is done in such a way that the spectral radius of $K(\alpha)$ is minimized. We shall have use of the following two definitions.

Definition 1. *The optimal α, α_{opt} is defined by*

$$\alpha_{\text{opt}} = \min_{\alpha} \rho(K(\alpha))$$

where $\rho(K(\alpha))$ denotes the spectral radius of $K(\alpha)$ for a given α.

Definition 2. *With reference to the theoretical model, $\alpha_{\max}$ is the upper limit of those α for which all eigenvalues of $K(\alpha)$ lie inside the unit circle.*

The optimal α_{opt} is best in the sense that the number of iterations needed to reach a desired accuracy is minimized. In the general situation, we do not know $\boldsymbol{\beta}$ in advance, and α must be chosen in another way. If it is chosen too small, the number of iterations will be too large but, on the other hand, if it is chosen too large, it might happen that the process will not converge at all. Practice has shown that $0.6 < \alpha < 0.8$ is a reasonable guess.

We shall now consider Summers' model [18]. It can be written

$$\begin{aligned} y_{1t} &= \beta_{12} y_{2t}^* + \gamma_{11} z_{1t} + \gamma_{12} z_{2t} + \varepsilon_{1t} \\ y_{2t} &= \beta_{21} y_{1t}^* + \gamma_{23} z_{3t} + \gamma_{24} z_{4t} + \varepsilon_{2t} \end{aligned} \tag{20}$$

and the matrix of particular interest for our convergence study is

$$\beta = \begin{bmatrix} 0 & \beta_{12} \\ \beta_{21} & 0 \end{bmatrix}. \tag{21}$$

The eigenvalues of β are $\pm(\beta_{12}\beta_{21})^{1/2}$. According to the theorem, the real parts of the eigenvalues must be less than 1 in order to have a possibility to choose an α that makes $\rho(K(\alpha)) < 1$. This requires that $-\infty < \beta_{12}\beta_{21} < 1$.

According to Eq. (15) $K(\alpha)$ is

$$K(\alpha) = \begin{bmatrix} 1-\alpha & \alpha\beta_{12} \\ \alpha\beta_{21} & 1-\alpha \end{bmatrix}. \tag{22}$$

and the eigenvalues of $K(\alpha)$ are

$$\begin{aligned} \lambda_1 &= 1 - \alpha + \alpha(\beta_{12}\beta_{21})^{1/2} \\ \lambda_2 &= 1 - \alpha - \alpha(\beta_{12}\beta_{21})^{1/2} \end{aligned} \tag{23}$$

Here we shall distinguish between two cases.

(I) $0 < \beta_{12}\beta_{21} < 1$.

To find α_{opt} in this case, we look at Fig. 4. It shows the two eigenvalues as functions of α.

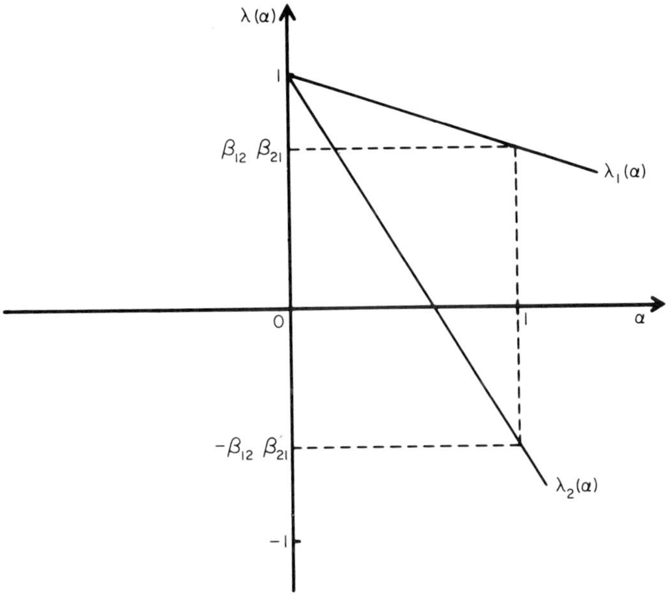

Fig. 4. The eigenvalues of $K(\alpha)$ in Summers' model (20).

For $\alpha < 1$, the spectral radius of $K(\alpha)$ equals $|\lambda_1(\alpha)|$, and for $\alpha > 1$, it is $|\lambda_2(\alpha)|$. Hence

$$\alpha_{opt} = 1. \tag{24}$$

Putting $\lambda_2(\alpha) = -1$, we find that

$$\alpha_{max} = 2/(1 + (\beta_{12}\beta_{21})^{1/2}). \tag{25}$$

(II) $\beta_{12}\beta_{21} \leq 0$.
In this case, we have

$$|\lambda_1|^2 = |\lambda_2|^2 = (1 - \alpha)^2 + \alpha^2\,|\beta_{12}\beta_{21}| \tag{26}$$

which should be less than 1. This condition gives

$$\alpha_{max} = 2/(1 + |\beta_{12}\beta_{21}|). \tag{27}$$

Minimizing the expression in Eq. (16) gives

$$\alpha_{opt} = 1/(1 + |\beta_{12}\beta_{21}|). \tag{28}$$

When the product of β_{12} and β_{21} is less than zero, we see that it is always possible to choose α in such a way that convergence can be obtained.

Illustration. One sample from each of two models, Model A and Model B will be considered. The models are:

Model A:

$$\begin{aligned} y_{1t} &= 0.5y_{2t}^* + 0.6591(z_{1t} + z_{2t}) + \varepsilon_{1t} \\ y_{2t} &= -3y_{1t}^* + 2.084(z_{3t} + z_{4t}) + \varepsilon_{2t} \end{aligned} \tag{29}$$

with

$$\begin{aligned} &\rho(z_1, z_3) = \rho(z_2, z_4) = 0.707 \\ &\rho(z_1, z_2) = \rho(z_1, z_4) = \rho(z_2, z_3) = \rho(z_3, z_4) = 0 \\ &\sigma^2(y_i) = \sigma^2(z_j) = 1, \qquad i = 1, 2; \qquad j = 1, 2, 3, 4 \\ &\sigma^2(\varepsilon_i) = 0.20, \qquad i = 1, 2 \end{aligned}$$

and

$$\rho(\varepsilon_i, z_j) = 0, \qquad \text{all} \quad i, j.$$

Model B:

$$\begin{aligned} y_{1t} &= y_{2t}^* + 0.8944(z_{1t} + z_{2t}) + \varepsilon_{1t} \\ y_{2t} &= -y_{1t}^* + 0.8944(z_{3t} + z_{4t}) + \varepsilon_{2t} \end{aligned} \tag{30}$$

with

$$\begin{aligned} &\rho(z_i, z_j) = 0, \qquad i \neq j, \qquad \text{all} \quad i, j, \\ &\sigma^2(y_i) = \sigma^2(z_j) = 1, \qquad i = 1, 2, \qquad j = 1, 2, 3, 4 \\ &\sigma^2(\varepsilon_i) = 0.20, \qquad i = 1, 2 \end{aligned}$$

and

$$\rho(\varepsilon_i, z_j) = 0, \qquad \text{all} \quad i, j.$$

The samples drawn from the two populations were of length 40. They were estimated for values of α ranging from 0.1 to 1.0 for Model A and from 0.2 to 1.4 for Model B. The iteration limit was fixed to 200 and the convergence criterion was put equal to 10^{-6}. The result is shown in Fig. 5. Note that $\alpha = 1$ gives the original FP method.

For Model A, we find that the minimum number of iterations required for convergence occurs when $\alpha = 0.3$ and nonconvergence occurs for $\alpha \geq 0.6$. The estimates of β_{12} and β_{21} were

$$b_{12} = 0.538 \qquad \text{and} \qquad b_{21} = -4.513 \tag{31}$$

which give the following estimates of $\alpha_{\max}$ and α_{opt}:

$$a_{\max} = 0.58; \qquad a_{\text{opt}} = 0.29. \tag{32}$$

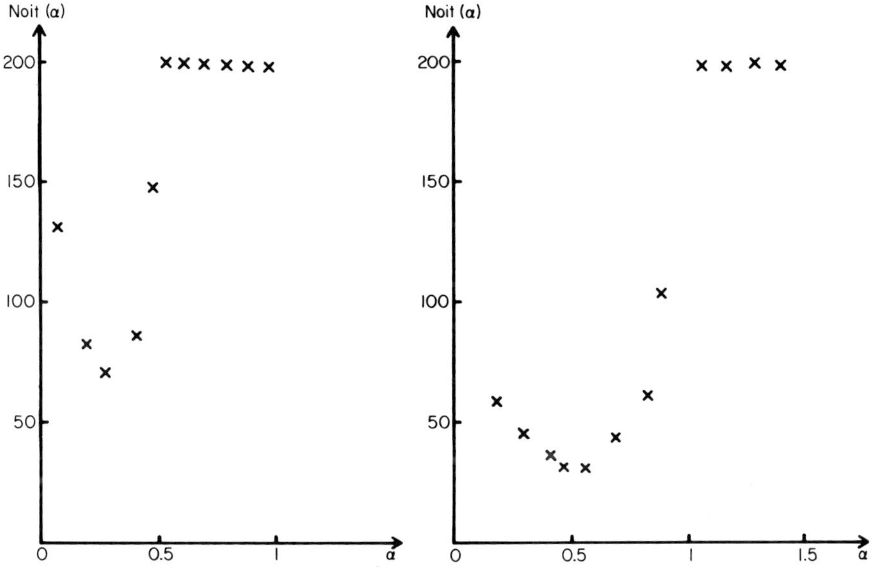

Fig. 5. Number of iterations (NOIT) for different α in Models A and B.

For Model B, the minimum number of iterations occurred when $\alpha = 0.5$ and $\alpha = 0.6$. This indicates that the best choice of α would have been somewhere between 0.5 and 0.6. Nonconvergence occurs for $\alpha \geq 1$. The estimates of β_{12} and β_{21} were

$$b_{12} = 1.233 \qquad \text{and} \qquad b_{21} = -0.782 \tag{33}$$

which give

$$a_{\max} = 1.02; \qquad a_{\text{opt}} = 0.51. \tag{34}$$

Comparing the results shown in the figure and the computed results in (32) and (34), we see that they agree very well. An increase of the iteration limit and a smaller step between the used α-values would probably have given a still better agreement.

These two examples do not indicate that the theory developed for a fixed iteration matrix cannot be applied in this case in which the iteration matrix is adjusted in each step.

Many more cases have been investigated, and when the start value $y_t^{*(0)}$ has been put equal to 0, convergence has been obtained even if $\alpha > a_{\max}$. But a decrease of the convergence criterion has made the convergence disappear. This phenomenon, called apparent convergence, has been investigated by Bodin [5].

2.5. Concluding Remarks

The theorem in Section 2.3 gives an explanation of the convergence difficulties encountered with the FP method. Combining the FP method with a relaxation factor leads to a better method, and it is often possible to get convergence when FP does not work.

Other iterative techniques have been suggested [5, 6], and Table I gives a brief description of the main differences between the different approaches. For brevity, we introduce P as a common notation for B and G. Then the methods differ in the calculation of $y^{*(s+1)}$ and $P^{(s+1)}$. The proxies $y^{*(s+1)}$ and $P^{(s+1)}$ are calculated component by component, and sometimes it is possible to use earlier computed components of $y^{*(s+1)}$ when calculating later components. In Table I we have marked xx when a vector is used throughout the calculation and x when a vector is partly used.

TABLE I
Modifications of the FP Method

Computation of	Case	$y_t^{*(s)}$	$y_t^{*(s+1)}$
$y_t^{*(s+1)}$	1	xx	
	2	x	x
	3		xx
$P^{(s+1)}$	A	xx	
	B	x	x

Both FP and FFP belong to Case 1–A. (Each number must be combined with either A or B.) Case 2–A is a method called the recursive fix-point method (R_1FP) [5, 6], and Case 2–B is called the recursive FP method, double sequence (RFP) [6]. Case 3–A is called the reduced fix-point method and has been suggested by Wold [2], but it has not been investigated very much as yet. We notice that both FP and FFP are based on the Jacobi method, whereas R_1FP and RFP are both based on the Gauss-Seidel method.

REFERENCES

1. WOLD, H. (1965). A fix-point theorem with econometric background. I-II. *Ark. Mat.* **6** 209–240.
2. WOLD, H. (1966). Nonlinear estimation by iterative least squares procedures. *In* "Research Papers in Statistics. Festschrift for J. Neyman" (F. N. David, ed.), pp. 411–444. Wiley, New York.
3. LYTTKENS, E. (1967). On the fix-point method and related problems; including an explicit treatment of the estimation problem of Girshick-Haavelmo's model. *Econometric Soc. Meeting, Blaricum, January* 1967.

4. Ågren, A. (1967). The fractional fix-point method. Licentiate Thesis, Univ. Inst. of Statist., Uppsala.
5. Bodin, L. (1968a). Studies of explicit and fractional fix-point estimation of interdependent systems. Licentiate Thesis, Univ. Inst. of Statist., Uppsala.
6. Bodin, L. (1968b). On modifications of the FP procedures. Seminar Paper, Univ. Inst. of Statist., Uppsala.
7. Koopmans, T. C., ed. (1950). "Statistical Inference in Dynamic Economic Models." Wiley, New York.
8. Hood, W. C., and Koopmans, T. C., eds. (1953). "Studies in Econometric Methods." Wiley, New York.
9. Malinvaud, E. (1964). "Méthodes Statistiques de l'Économétrie." Dunod, Paris.
10. Christ, C. (1966). "Econometric Models and Methods." Wiley, New York.
11. Wold, H. (1962). Unbiased predictors. *Proc. Fourth Berkeley Symp. Math. Statist. Prob.* (J. Neyman, ed.), **1** pp. 719–761. Univ. California Press, Berkeley, California.
12. Wold, H. (1960). Ends and means in econometric model building. Basic considerations reviewed. *In* "Probability and Statistics (The Harald Cramér Vol.)" (U. Grenander, ed.), pp. 355–434. Wiley, New York.
13. Wold, H. (1967). Nonexperimental statistical analysis from the general point of view of scientific method. *Bull. Internat. Statist. Inst.* **53** (In press).
14. Wold, H. (1968). Rev. of Christ [10]; *Rev. Intern. Statist. Inst.* **36** 100–103.
15. Wold, H. (1965). Toward a verdict on macroeconomic simultaneous equations. *In* "La semaine d'Étude sur le Role de l'Analyse Économétrique dans la Formulation de Plans de Développement" (P. Salviucci, ed.), pp. 115–166. Scripta Varia **28**. Pontifical Acad. of Sci., Vatican City.
16. Theil, H. (1958). "Economic Forecasts and Policy." North-Holland Publ., Amsterdam.
17. Klein, L. R. (1966). Problems in the estimation of interdependent systems. *In* "The Approach of Model Building in the Human Sciences" (R. Peltier and H. Wold, eds.), pp. 51–87. Trans. des Entretiens de Monaco, 1964. Centre Internat. d'Étude des Problèmes Humains, Monaco.
18. Summers, R. (1959). A capital intensive approach to the small sample properties of various simultaneous equation estimators. *Econometrica* **33** 1–41.
19. Wold, H. (1938). "A Study in the Analysis of Stationary Time Series." 2nd ed., 1954. Almqvist & Wiksell, Uppsala.
20. Lyttkens, E. (1966). On the fix-point property of Wold's iterative estimation method for principal components. *In* "Multivariate Analysis" (P. R. Krishnaiah, ed.). Academic Press, New York.
21. Mosbaek, E. J., and Wold, H. (1969). "Interdependent Systems. Structure and Estimation." North-Holland Publ., Amsterdam. (In press).
22. Christ, C. F. *et al.* (1960). Any verdict yet ? (Symposium.) *Econometrica* **28** 835–861.
23. Parzen, E. (1968). Multiple time series modelling. Tech. Rept. No. 22. Dept. of Statist., Stanford Univ., Stanford, California.
24. Wold, H. (1963). On the consistency of least squares regression. *Sankhyā Ser. A* **25**, 2, 211–215.
25. Bellman, R. (1960). "Introduction to Matrix Analysis." McGraw-Hill, New York.
26. Varga, R. S. (1962). "Matrix Iterative Analysis." Prentice-Hall, Englewood Cliffs, New Jersey.

Exploratory Techniques Involving Artificial Variables

ROLF E. BARGMANN

DEPARTMENT OF STATISTICS
UNIVERSITY OF GEORGIA
ATHENS, GEORGIA

1. INTRODUCTION

In his work with applied scientists, a statistician is frequently obliged to take the role of a cantankerous child. He must patiently explain the meaning of negative coefficients in a multiple regression equation. If you measure the same quantity, e.g., temperature, twice, once with great precision, and another time crudely, the latter may require a negative weight in a prediction equation even though both have high positive correlation with the criterion being predicted. In multivariate analysis, a conscientious statistician must refuse to report ideal indices or *ideal weighted total scores* until the scientist informs him of the use to which such an index or function is to be put. The perennial question which the impatient parent asks the teacher, " Where does my child stand in overall performance?" cannot be answered until the parent declares for what purpose he wants this information (predict success in *college*? predict success in *life*?).

The statistician does well to realize that, once a situation and all assumptions have been stated, he is called upon to construct some *artificial models* and, in multivariate analysis, *artificial mathematical combinations* of observable variates, which reflect assumptions and objectives of the study. Discriminant analysis, factor analysis, and some of the latent class models, are among the best developed and most easily interpretable models for this purpose.

This presentation is meant to be expository. There are few results reported here which have not been known to the serious student of multivariate analysis, for a decade or two. The emphasis here is on the *artificial* nature of all these constructs. There is a warning not to overinterpret or misconstrue such variables as being anything else. When we use such artificial constructs for conjecture regarding underlying mechanisms, we must not overlook the possibility that we may have, involuntarily, verified the very model which we conjectured in the first place, and modified, in a Hegelian sense, the facts to fit our theories.

2. DISCRIMINANT ANALYSIS

We may regard the *linear* discriminant function as an artificial variable [4] (in the sense of S. N. Roy [12], but with *parameters* introduced where he used *estimates*), a linear combination of observable response variables, $\mathbf{y}$,

$$z = \boldsymbol{\alpha}'\mathbf{y} \tag{1}$$

which, in terms of z, maximizes a *noncentrality parameter*

$$\theta = \boldsymbol{\alpha}'\boldsymbol{\Phi}'\mathbf{C}'[\mathbf{C}(\mathbf{A}'\mathbf{A})^{(-1)}\mathbf{C}']^{-1}\mathbf{C}\boldsymbol{\Phi}\boldsymbol{\alpha}/\boldsymbol{\alpha}'\boldsymbol{\Sigma}\boldsymbol{\alpha}. \tag{2}$$

Here, the notation is as follows (Roy [12]). The term $\mathbf{Y}$ is the $(n \times p)$ matrix of observation vectors on p variables;

$$\mathscr{E}(\mathbf{Y}) = \mathbf{A}\boldsymbol{\Phi} \tag{3}$$

$$\operatorname{var}(\mathbf{y}_i') = \boldsymbol{\Sigma} \tag{4}$$

$$\operatorname{cov}(\mathbf{y}_i, \mathbf{y}_j') = \mathbf{0} \tag{5}$$

where $\mathbf{y}_i'$ is the ith row of $\mathbf{Y}$, and $\mathbf{y}_i$ is the *same row*, written as a column vector. The term $(\mathbf{A}'\mathbf{A})^{(-1)}$ (*conditional inverse*) has been used, since the normal equations

$$\mathbf{A}'\mathbf{A}\hat{\boldsymbol{\Phi}} = \mathbf{A}'\mathbf{Y} \tag{6}$$

may be singular, and thus $\hat{\boldsymbol{\Phi}}$ may be a (*nonunique*) solution

$$\hat{\boldsymbol{\Phi}} = (\mathbf{A}'\mathbf{A})^{(-1)}\mathbf{A}'\mathbf{Y} \tag{7}$$

where $(\mathbf{A}'\mathbf{A})^{(-1)}$ is any matrix satisfying the defining relation (Bose [5])

$$(\mathbf{A}'\mathbf{A})(\mathbf{A}'\mathbf{A})^{(-1)}(\mathbf{A}'\mathbf{A}) = (\mathbf{A}'\mathbf{A}). \tag{8}$$

A general linear hypothesis is imposed,

$$\mathbf{C}\boldsymbol{\Phi} = \mathbf{0}, \tag{9}$$

which must be testable [5],

$$\mathbf{C}(\mathbf{A}'\mathbf{A})^{(-1)}\mathbf{A}'\mathbf{A} = \mathbf{C}, \tag{10}$$

and thus θ in Eq. (2) is unique. To use θ as a basis for the construction of a discriminant function, one must define groups between which one wishes to discriminate (or levels of a factor in a multifactor design). One must set up a null hypothesis assuming no differences between the groups thus defined (this may, of course, relate to one factor of an irregular factorial design [1]). With a grain of salt, in the union-intersection statistic [12]

$$c = ch_{\max}(\mathbf{E}^{-1}\mathbf{H}) \tag{11}$$

the associated (*right*) eigenvector

$$\mathbf{E}^{-1}\mathbf{Ha} = c\mathbf{a} \tag{12}$$

is a maximum-likelihood estimate of $\boldsymbol{\alpha}$. The restriction is, of course, that the maximum-likelihood estimates of the set of *all* right eigenvectors of

$$\boldsymbol{\Sigma}^{-1}\boldsymbol{\Theta} \tag{13}$$

is the set of *all* right eigenvectors of $\mathbf{E}^{-1}\mathbf{H}$, where

$$\boldsymbol{\Theta} = \boldsymbol{\Phi}'\mathbf{C}'[\mathbf{C}(\mathbf{A}'\mathbf{A})^{(-1)}\mathbf{C}']^{-1}\mathbf{C}\boldsymbol{\Phi}.$$

In the didactically useful notation (12), $\mathbf{E}$ denotes the matrix of sums of squares and products for error, and $\mathbf{H}$ the matrix of sums of squares and products for the hypothesis (see, e.g., Heck [6]).

If the first and second characteristic roots of $\mathbf{E}^{-1}\mathbf{H}$ are close to each other (a situation which, in extended practice, I have never encountered), any linear combination of the two associated eigenvectors may need to be considered as alternate estimates of the discriminant function.

The weights, $\mathbf{a}$, of this estimated discriminant function, are quite difficult to interpret except, perhaps, in the classical case of discrimination between two groups. Each element can be multiplied by the same, arbitrary, positive or negative, constant. As a crude form of a linear classification statistic, $\mathbf{a}'\mathbf{y}$ may have some limited use for *prediction when the criterion is categorized.* Even in this case, pairwise discrimination between any two groups or levels may be preferable. For interpretation of an artificial variable, however, we want *one*, and not *several*, discriminant functions. It is no coincidence that this linear function becomes Hotelling's "best predictable criterion" [8] in the multivariate, multiple-regression model [4].

The important observation is that $z = \boldsymbol{\alpha}'\mathbf{y}$ is an *artificial variable*, which may be called the *best linear discriminator* among the criterion groups. As such, it may be correlated against each observable response variable. Interestingly, the vector of estimated covariances between each observable variate and the best discriminator, is proportional to $\mathbf{u}$ where

$$\mathbf{HE}^{-1}\mathbf{u} = c\mathbf{u}, \tag{14}$$

i.e., $\mathbf{u}$ is the *left* eigenvector of Eq. (12). In the special case of two groups, or two levels of a factor, $\mathbf{u}$ is a vector of standardized mean differences, as would be expected logically. The estimated correlation between the ith response variable and the best discriminator

$$\text{est corr}(y_i, z) = (\mathbf{a}'\mathbf{E})_i/(e_{ii}\,\mathbf{a}'\mathbf{Ea})^{1/2}, \tag{15}$$

where $(\mathbf{a}'\mathbf{E})_i$ denotes the ith element of the row vector $\mathbf{a}'\mathbf{E}$, can thus give us information regarding the proximity of each response variable to the best discriminator. The following two examples illustrate the exploratory use of such a discriminant function. We used a program which performs a variety of univariate and multivariate analyses on sets of data [1].

Illustration I: Veterinary School Admission Study[1]

Seven educational tests were administered to 109 applicants for admission to the Veterinary School. After one year, these students were classified into four performance groups, based upon their total performance during the first year of study.

The estimate of the best linear discriminator for this factor (*Performance*) was obtained, and the following correlations were observed:

Correlation against Discriminant Function (all variables)

VARD	VASC	VAVE	SAVE	SAMA	PGPA	RATG
0.137	*0.293*	*0.332*	*−0.236*	*0.277*	*0.447*	*0.338*

Note that this approach makes *scaling* of the performance groups unnecessary. We do not really care what the distance between performance groups 1 and 2 is in relation to that between groups 2 and 3, and so forth. Here it is clear that the first variable VARD is further removed from the best discriminator than the others. It was thus eliminated at this stage. SAVE poses a problem, here, since in this instance the sign of the correlations is important (*high* performance groups had slightly *lower* scores on this test at the time of admission). Hence, SAVE was eliminated also. After the second run, SAMA was low, by comparison. After the third reduction, the following results were obtained:

Correlations against Discriminant Function (4 variables)

VASC	VAVE	PGPA	RATG
0.588	*0.235*	*0.874*	*0.457*

At this stage we could decide that we have chosen the best four variables in terms of their relation to the best linear discriminator, but now an unfortunate thing happened (which was indicated in the Introduction with reference to multiple regression): The weight of the discriminant function for variable VAVE was negative. There is some evidence, thus, that VAVE

[1] Courtesy of Dr. John Harris, Institute of Higher Education, University of Georgia, Athens, Georgia.

contributes to the discrimination in the same way, but in a cruder fashion, as the other three. A final analysis was thus performed on three variables:

Correlation against Discriminant Function
(3 variables)

VASC	PGPA	RATG
0.501	*0.876*	*0.675*

The *discriminant function* was

$$1.57(\text{VASC}) + 40.4(\text{PGPA}) + 11.7(\text{RATG}).$$

The disparity between the first and the other weights is due to the scale. PGPA and RATG had values, typically, between 1 and 5, whereas VASC ranged from 50 to 60 and had, thus, a considerably larger standard deviation.

The correlations between the selected variables are stated here for later reference (Section 5. Noncentrality and Factor Analysis):

Based on **E** *Matrix*
(all factors eliminated)

1	0.152	0.097
	1	0.044
		1

Based on (**H** + **E**) *Matrix*
(including the Performance Factor)

1	0.212	0.137
	1	0.472
		1

The last matrix shows that if a clearly significant difference is ignored and correlation analysis is performed (in this case wrongly) on the *total* or *combined* groups, a *relation* between PGPA and RATG is induced. This effect, frequently called *spurious* correlation or *correlation in widespread classes* is, of course, no correlation at all. It is a non-sense result, based on improper analysis. In a later section, however, we will show how one might deduce existence of nonhomogeneous samples from the *pattern* of such matrices.

Illustration 2: Gas Chromatograph Analysis

Seven mixtures of soft drinks were subjected to gas-chromatograph analysis. Relative areas under 24 observable peaks were recorded. In this case, scaling or a regression type analysis is clearly improper. There is not even a monotonic order between the 7 levels of this factor; it is, essentially, a *nominal scale* [14].

Correlations against Discriminant Function (all variables)

Peak:	1	2	3	4	5	6	7	8
	−0.072	−0.078	−0.010	−0.168	0.019	0.045	0.202	−0.110
Peak:	9	10	11	12	13	14	15	16
	−0.062	0.243	0.145	0.217	−0.155	−0.058	−0.092	−0.022
Peak:	17	18	19	20	21	22	23	24
	−0.020	−0.001	0.004	0.024	−0.123	−0.048	−0.042	−0.060

After several elimination stages, the following *nine* peaks were retained:

Correlations against Discriminant Function (9 variables)

Peak:	4	7	8	10	11	12	13	15	21
	−0.194	0.257	−0.136	0.289	0.176	0.294	−0.188	−0.104	−0.156

Since the peaks in the fractional distillation correspond to, possibly identifiable, volatile substances, one may deduce on what ingredients the seven mixtures differ most strongly. Furthermore, this example illustrates the use of discriminant analysis for pattern recognition.

During the past year, we made many studies in entomology (On what variables do irradiated flies differ most significantly?), food science (coffee flavors as related to peaks in the gas-chromatograph), education and psychology (test selection and personality trait differences), and pharmaceutical research (Which physiological variables show most differential effects under different drugs?).

In each of these studies, I have repeatedly warned the users that this technique indicates leads for future work and that proof, even statistical proof of relation, is difficult to establish by such exploratory methods alone. In most of these studies, there was more than one criterion (several factors in a factorial design) and the designs were usually irregular, requiring an adjusted normal equation solution for estimation. Formulation in terms of general linear hypotheses (Eq. (2)) permits the analysis to be made, routinely, in these instances.

A word of warning is in order here as in *stepwise* regression. Stepwise *inclusion* of variables, in terms of largest multiple correlation is, of course, quite objectionable (alas, many of the stepwise computer programs perform this contradictory analysis). Even stepwise *exclusion* of the poorest predictors has its traps, inasmuch as the poorest *pair* may not include the poorest *single* variable. If high precision is required, only *one* variable should be excluded at each stage, then *two* at the next stage.

What about the *second* discriminant function or *second canonical variable*, i.e., the *eigenvector* associated with the *second* largest root? Several critics have told me that they could show examples in which plots of the first versus the second discriminant function (even using *weights* rather than *correlations*) show *clusters*. In most instances (anthropological measurements, neuron emission patterns) group or pattern differences were so striking at first sight that no statistical technique was needed for pattern recognition. I stated then, and repeat here, that any discrimination technique, however crude, could distinguish between an ant and a hippopotamus. If an anthropological illustration of the efficiency of a discriminant analysis technique is desired, I would suggest that discrimination between infant boys and infant girls (barring the obvious discriminator) would be an ideal test case.

The second discriminant function would qualify as best after elimination of the effect due to the first one. But the first one is an *artificial* variable. Furthermore, if there are only two groups, there is only one discriminant function. Why should one wish to interpret *residual* discrimination after elimination of an artifact? Is it not preferable to make a separate discriminant analysis (*first* eigenvector) on the observable variates which were eliminated because of their low correlation versus the total discriminant function? In this way, we can establish, regardless of the rank of the **H** matrix, a hierarchy of sets of variables, based on directly observable and, hence, interpretable measurements

3. THE FIRST PRINCIPAL COMPONENT

In contrast to factor analysis, which is concerned with dependence structures, and readily interpretable artificial variables (or rather, their correlations to observable ones), component analysis poses difficult questions. Its dependence on origin and scale of measurements makes it almost mandatory that a standardized metric be employed [11]. The correlation matrix employed in this case is, in effect, a standardized variance-covariance matrix. It is difficult to formulate any hypothesis or model in the population for which such a matrix is a sample estimate. Component analysis is strictly descriptive and has the interesting, deterministic, geometrical interpretation which Pearson [11] formulated (planes of closest fit, vectors of greatest concentration) in terms of Euclidean distances.

The well-known proportionality between the average square of differences between pairs of observations and the sample variance permits an interesting interpretation of the *first* principal component of the correlation or scaled covariance matrix: It is that artificial variable, that linear combination of observed ones, which maximizes the sum of squares of differences between pairs of experimental units:

$$z_i = \boldsymbol{\alpha}'\mathbf{y}_i/(\boldsymbol{\alpha}'\boldsymbol{\alpha})^{1/2}, \qquad i = 1, 2, \ldots, n \tag{16}$$

where $\boldsymbol{\alpha}$ is chosen in such a way that

$$\sum_{i<j}^{n}\sum (z_i - z_j)^2 \quad \text{is a maximum.} \tag{17}$$

It seems reasonable to employ this first principal component if experimental units (on each of which we have p responses) are to be *ordered*, in terms of an unspecified criterion. In standard units, the z_i are as far apart from each other as possible.

The eigenvector associated with the *smallest* characteristic root is, of course, the normal to the *plane of closest fit* [11]. I have not been convinced that a case can be made for the intermediate principal components, i.e., vectors associated with intermediate roots. The practice to misname techniques, even to give the name "factor analysis" to computer programs which in fact perform the, somewhat evasive, "component analysis" (e.g., in BMD and SSP 360) is deplorable and misleading. The two techniques are totally unrelated. Again it can be argued that variables which have the highest correlation against the first principal component contribute most strongly to *discrimination among individual experimental units.* Then, to facilitate interpretation, it is advisable to obtain, successively, sets of best discriminator variables, and to establish the *first* principal component in each *subset* of variables, rather than to attempt interpreting variables based on elimination of artifacts. Utterly arbitrary names, such as "Intensity" have been proposed for second principal components.

4. MODEL BUILDING INVOLVING LATENT CLASS ANALYSIS

The occurrence of a major event is frequently signaled by the occurrence of many small events, which can thus be used for diagnostic purposes. A few illustrations may serve to clarify such situations.

Breakdown of a Structure

The diagnostic events in this example would be certain symptoms, such as the presence of rust in critical sections, significant bending of certain parts, characteristic noises, occurrence of sudden shocks or vibration, and so forth. On the basis of such diagnostic information, we wish to determine whether there is an imminent danger of breakdown.

Military Posture of an Enemy

Diagnostic events for this situation would be abnormally large troop movements, threatening releases, increase in weapons testing, sudden increase in communications, withdrawal of diplomats, and so forth. On the strength of occurrence or nonoccurrence of such symptoms, one may wish to determine whether there is an impending danger of military action.

Medical Prognosis

Examples of diagnostic events would be the occurrence of insomnia, skin irritation, irregularities of speech, nervous tics, and so forth. Based upon these and other symptoms, there is indication for the imminence of a nervous breakdown.

In trying to formulate a mathematical model simulating such situations, one must try to consider the kind of reasoning process that is customarily employed by an expert attempting to arrive at a conclusion. He will, first of all, weigh the relative importance of each individual diagnostic event, on the basis of either previous experience, or some intuitive evaluation of the relevance of each diagnostic event to the major event. He will probably regard each individual diagnostic event in conjunction with another one, i.e., he may weigh the importance of *pairs* of events. If the number of diagnostic events is large, he may not be able to evaluate *all* paired combinations. As he proceeds to a consideration of event *triples*, and combinations of higher order, he will most certainly be limited to very few cases only. To all intents and purposes, a systematic evaluation of all *individual* events and of every *pair* of events would constitute a rather sound foundation for reaching a decision. One has thus some justification for restricting one's attention to only these combinations.

In many applications, the number of observations made on each diagnostic event may be relatively small. One may observe the occurrence of each diagnostic event once a week, for ten weeks. Thus, if there are 50 diagnostic events, only 500 individual observations will be available while, even under the above mentioned restrictions, $(50 \times 51)/2 = 1275$ parameters would have to be estimated. Since this cannot be done uniquely, further restrictive assumptions on the model must be imposed.

Such a restriction is available because of the *very process of selection* of diagnostic events. The expert who decides *which* diagnostic events are to be observed will usually be guided by some underlying assumption that the diagnostic event is related to the major event. He may not be able to say that the major event is the exclusive cause which determines the probability of outcome of the diagnostic events, but he may say that some *single* underlying cause is the major determiner—and, hopefully, this artificial underlying cause would be highly correlated with the desired major event. Thus, in the medical example, symptoms to be observed would have been selected in such a way that they are clearly and predominantly caused by some nervous irregularity which is highly correlated with, but not identical to, the likelihood of a nervous breakdown. Here is a distinction between our method and that proposed by Solomon [13].

If the presence of such an underlying principle is assumed to determine inclusion or exclusion of a diagnostic event in the set, one may assume the following model:

Let $p_{i|0}$ denote the probability of the ith diagnostic event occurring if the underlying artificial event is in state 0 (e.g., completely absent). Let $p_{i|1}$ be the probability that the ith diagnostic event occurs if the underlying major event is in state 1 (e.g., certain). Then

$$p_i = (1 - \pi)p_{i|0} + \pi p_{i|1}, \tag{18}$$

where π is the probability that the underlying event is in state 1, and $1 - \pi$ is the probability that it is in state 0. The term p_i denotes the probability that the ith diagnostic event occurs. This model is closely related to a special case of the latent class model [9, 10]. The assumption that the underlying major event is the *only* or *predominant* determiner of the outcome of the ith diagnostic event can be summarized in the *assumption* of *conditional independence:*

$$p_{ij|0} = p_{i|0}p_{j|0} \qquad \text{and} \qquad p_{ij|1} = p_{i|1}p_{j|1}, \tag{19}$$

where $p_{ij|0}$ denotes the probability that diagnostic events i and j occur simultaneously, given that the underlying event is in state 0. Thus, if p_{ij} denotes the probability that diagnostic events i and j occur simultaneously, this probability will be given as

$$p_{ij} = (1 - \pi)p_{i|0}p_{j|0} + \pi p_{i|1}p_{j|1}. \tag{20}$$

Hence, under the additional restriction, which may be called a restriction in the *selection* of diagnostic events, the model contains $2k + 1$ parameters (if k denotes the number of diagnostic events). However, only $2k$ parameters can be estimated and, as has been shown by Bargmann [3], barring additional assumptions regarding the parameters $p_{i|0}$, $p_{i|1}$, and π, no separate estimation will be possible. However, p_{ij} can always be estimated uniquely under this model.

We now introduce the notation:

$$b_i = (\pi - \pi^2)^{1/2}(p_{i|0} - p_{i|1}), \tag{21}$$

which is combined into the column vector

$$\mathbf{b} = (\pi - \pi^2)^{1/2}(\mathbf{p}_0 - \mathbf{p}_1).$$

Let n be the number of experimental units (which may be less than p); then

$$n\boldsymbol{\Sigma} = \mathbf{D}_u + \mathbf{bb}', \tag{22}$$

where $\mathbf{D}_u$ is a diagonal matrix. Since the elements of the correlation matrix $\mathbf{R}$ are

$$\rho_{ij} = n\sigma_{ij}/(n\sigma_{ii}n\sigma_{jj})^{1/2},$$

we can write the correlation matrix in the form

$$\mathbf{R} = \mathbf{D}_\eta + \boldsymbol{\varphi}\boldsymbol{\varphi}', \tag{23}$$

and this is a matrix which exhibits *dependence of the first degree*, or, in other words, a correlation matrix requiring one factor, in terms of factor analysis. Here

$$\eta_i = u_i/(p_i - p_i^2) \qquad \text{and} \qquad \varphi_i = b_i/(p_i - p_i^2)^{1/2}.$$

It is well known that the maximum-likelihood estimate of $\boldsymbol{\varphi}$, assuming normality, is the vector $\mathbf{f}$ which satisfies the relation:

$$(\mathbf{R} - \mathbf{f}\mathbf{f}')\mathbf{D}_{1/(1-f^2)}\mathbf{f} = \mathbf{f}, \tag{24}$$

where $\mathbf{R}$ is the sample correlation matrix, and $\mathbf{D}_{1/(1-f^2)}$ denotes a diagonal matrix with elements $1/(1 - f_i^2)$ along the principal diagonal. Equation (24) can be expressed in the convenient computational form

$$f_i = \left[\sum_{j\neq i} r_{ij} f_j/(1 - f_j^2)\right] \Big/ \left[\sum_{j\neq i} f_j^2/(1 - f_j^2)\right]. \tag{25}$$

One starts with a convenient first guess of $\mathbf{f}$ (preferably *centroid*) and iterates according to Eq. (25). The vector $\mathbf{f}$, obtained in the final iteration, is then a vector of correlations (estimates) between each observable or diagnostic variable and the theoretical *major event*. The use of this approach for pattern recognition and classification should be obvious. One collects *calibration patterns*, i.e., status of diagnostic events when the major event was known to be in (or shortly afterward assumed) a known state. From each of these patterns one can obtain estimates of the variance-covariance matrix, subject to the above restrictions. This matrix is not only nonsingular, but it is most easily inverted. Hence the distance or, more precisely the likelihood, of a sample pattern from each calibration pattern can be calculated, rapidly; there is never a double sum. Again I wish to emphasize here that the *major event* has been introduced as an artifact, a device which has enabled us to obtain unique solutions in otherwise singular and nonunique cases. The uniqueness of this solution is based upon the validity of the assumption of systematic selection of diagnostic variables. Several illustrations, including estimation procedures in the presence of dependence between rows, have been stated by Bargmann [3].

5. NONCENTRALITY AND FACTOR ANALYSIS

Under the hypothesis that *partial* correlations between observable variates are zero, after the elimination of k artificial variables (or k *common factors*) $\mathbf{x}$, the covariance matrix will have the structure

$$\boldsymbol{\Sigma} = \mathbf{D} + \boldsymbol{\Lambda}\boldsymbol{\Lambda}' \tag{26}$$

where $\boldsymbol{\Lambda}$ is of order $p \times k$, and $\mathbf{D}$ is a diagonal matrix with unknown elements. The population correlation matrix has, of course, the same structure. Maximum-likelihood estimates of correlations between observable and artificial variates are easily obtainable.[2] Unlike the situation in component and discriminant analysis, the artificial variables are *not* linear combination of the observable ones, nor is there, implicitly or explicitly, a hierarchy of factors (as there is, in the case of component analysis and discriminant functions). There is merely a set of artificial variables which accounts for the dependence among the observable ones.

We now assume a general linear model as in Eq. (3), with conditions (4) and (5). The matrix $\mathbf{E}$ (defined in the paragraph following Eq. (13)) divided by degrees of freedom for error is, of course, an unbiased estimate of $\boldsymbol{\Sigma}$. The appropriate starting point for a factor analysis would be the correlation matrix derived from $\mathbf{E}$.

Suppose, however, that there exists a grouping in the data, unknown to us. Instead of observing a matrix $\mathbf{E}$, as we think, we observe a matrix $(\mathbf{H} + \mathbf{E})$ where

$$\mathscr{E}(\mathbf{H} + \mathbf{E}) = n_h \boldsymbol{\Sigma} + \boldsymbol{\Theta} \tag{27}$$

($\boldsymbol{\Theta}$ defined following Eq. (13), n_h = df for hypothesis). If there are m groups, $\boldsymbol{\Theta}$ will have rank $m - 1$, and can thus be written as $\boldsymbol{\Gamma}\boldsymbol{\Gamma}'$ where $\boldsymbol{\Gamma}$ is of order $p \times (m - 1)$. Thus, if the true $\boldsymbol{\Sigma}$ has a factor analysis structure with k factors, the correlation matrix derived from $(\mathbf{H} + \mathbf{E})$, involuntarily, would estimate a factor analysis structure of degree of dependence $k + m - 1$. This permits a most interesting interpretation of factors in terms of differences between latent groups. To illustrate, let $\boldsymbol{\Sigma}$ be diagonal and let there be, unknown to us, two samples in the total group. Then our $\mathbf{S}$ (an estimate of $\boldsymbol{\Sigma} + \boldsymbol{\Theta}$, since $n_h = 1$) would estimate a matrix

$$\mathbf{D} + \boldsymbol{\lambda}\boldsymbol{\lambda}' \tag{28}$$

where

$$\boldsymbol{\lambda} = \left(\frac{n_1 n_2}{(n_1 + n_2)(n_1 + n_2 - 1)}\right)^{1/2} (\boldsymbol{\mu}_1 - \boldsymbol{\mu}_2)$$

and n_1 and n_2 are sizes of the latent groups (of course, only proportions are important). The vector $\mathbf{f}$ (see Eqs. (24) and (25)) would then be an estimate proportional to the standardized group mean differences on each response variable, quite similar to the special example following Eq. (14).

If we express the data matrix $\mathbf{Y}$ in standard units (sample mean 0 and sample variance 1 in each column of $\mathbf{Y}$) we can use

$$z_i = \mathbf{f}'\mathbf{y}_i$$

[2] Currently, the most efficient and extensive computer programs for this are, to my knowledge, those of K. Jöreskog, Educational Testing Service, Princeton, New Jersey.

as an index, for each experimental unit, assigning the latter to latent group 1 or 2 according to the z_i-value, separating where a significant gap occurs in the ordered values. This weighting procedure is appropriate here, since the matrix **R** is symmetric, and thus the left eigenvector equals the right one. Again, this is a tentative assignment. The entries in **f** determine which of the response variables contribute significantly to the latent group difference. This seems to be an explanation why Factor Analysis is frequently successful as a tool for assigning experimental units to *clusters*.

In the case of three or more groups, the rank of $\boldsymbol{\Theta}$ is *greater* than 1, and hence the breakdown into groups becomes indeterminate. We thus encounter a *rotational* problem of a special kind, where *simple structure* may not be too useful. I did some experimenting with the stepwise maximum-likelihood procedure in factor analysis using, essentially, computer programs (*6.6.021*, *1* to *9* (1958), see also Bargmann [2]) which had been used as a compromise on the IBM 650, and as initial, and very close, first approximations in the later *maximum-determinant programs* (FCAN on 7094, (1962)). The criticism against the use of this technique is exactly the same as that directed against the second principal component, or the second discriminant function. As so many other statistical *explorers*, I find myself plotting *factor scores*, and I do not like it. Until much more evidence is available on the basis of demonstration studies and applications, no recommendations can be made. We should not be satisfied unless a representation can be suggested which permits interpretation in terms of physical concepts, not mathematical artifacts.

6. SUMMARY AND CONCLUSION

In the end of the preceding paragraph, I indicated a problem the solution of which is probably "just around the corner." Here I will enumerate some problems whose solution requires an amount of daring and intuition.

Exploratory techniques in multivariate analysis, such as discriminant, latent structure, and factor analysis, are useful if they are based on a clear understanding of the underlying physical model. In many cases, they do not help in the detection of latent variables and mechanisms, but are merely mirrors, showing our own ability or inability to include in a set of measurements variables relevant to one or a few common phenomena (see the principle of systematic selection in Section 4). The problem of sampling *measurements* or *variables* from an infinitely large universe of variables, has received attention in many treatises, ever since Hotelling's [7] famous discussion on the subject. Since human judgment and normative principles enter into the definition of a *universe of response variables*, a unique mathematical answer can probably never be found. And here I close the circle of my presentation; a statement of the *purpose* for which such a definition is made will have to precede the development of analytical techniques. Whichever course we take, we shall continue devising principles of constructing artificial variables, useful for throwing light on phenomena and mechanisms, but very dangerous and misleading if an eager interpreter tries to attach physical existence to them.

REFERENCES

1. Appelbaum, M., and Bargmann, R. E. (1967). A FORTRAN II program for MUDAID: Multivariate, univariate, and discriminant analysis of irregular data. Tech. Rept. NONR 1834(39). Univ. of Illinois, Urbana, Illinois.
2. Bargmann, R. E. (1962). Representative ordering and selection of variables. *Final Rept.*, III, HEW Cooperative Res. Project No. 1132, 2 vols. Virginia Polytech. Inst., Blacksburg, Virginia.
3. Bargmann, R. E. (1962). A method of classification based upon dependent 0-1 patterns. IBM Res. Rept. RC 677. IBM.
4. Bargmann, R. E. (1968). Interpretation and use of a generalized discriminant function. (Chapter 3). *In* "Essays in Probability and Statistics" (R. C. Bose *et al.*, eds.). Univ. of North Carolina Press, Chapel Hill, North Carolina.
5. Bose, R. C. (1956). "Lecture Notes, Design of Experiments." Univ. of North Carolina, Chapel Hill, North Carolina.
6. Heck, D. L. (1960). Charts of some upper percentage points of the distribution of the largest characteristic root. *Ann. Math. Statist.* **31** 625–642.
7. Hotelling, H. (1933). Analysis of a complex of statistical variables into principal components, Pt. II. *J. Educational Psychology* **24** 498–520.
8. Hotelling, H. (1936). Relations between two sets of variates. *Biometrika* **28** 321–377.
9. Lazarsfeld, P. F. (1950). The logical and mathematical foundation of latent structure analysis. *In* "Measurement and Prediction" (S. A. Stouffer *et al.*, eds.). Princeton Univ. Press, Princeton, New Jersey.
10. Madansky, A. (1958). Identification and estimation in latent class analysis. Ph.D. Thesis, Univ. of Chicago, Chicago, Illinois.
11. Pearson, K. (1901). On lines and planes of closest fit to systems of points in space. *Phil. Mag.* [6] **2** 559–572.
12. Roy, S. N. (1957). "Some Aspects of Multivariate Analysis." Wiley, New York.
13. Solomon, H. (1960). Classification procedure based on dichotomous response vectors. *In* "Contributions to Probability and Statistics" (I. Olkin *et al.*, eds.), pp. 414–423. Stanford Univ. Press, Stanford, California.
14. Young, L. L., Bargmann, R. E., and Powers, J. J. (1969). Correlation between gas chromatographic patterns and organoleptic evaluation of flavor. *J. Food Sci.* To be published.

On the Importance of Different Components in a Multicomponent System[1]

Z. W. BIRNBAUM

DEPARTMENT OF MATHEMATICS
UNIVERSITY OF WASHINGTON
SEATTLE, WASHINGTON

1. INTRODUCTION: DEFINITIONS AND NOTATIONS

1.1.

In a system whose performance depends on the performance of its components, some of these components may play a more important part than others. For example, if a system consists of n components in series, or of n components in parallel, one may be inclined to consider each component equally important for the performance of the system. In the system indicated in Fig. 1, however, component c_1 would seem intuitively more important

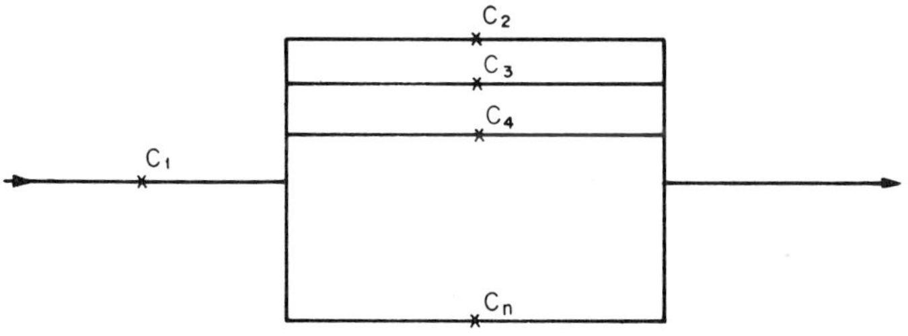

Fig. 1.

than $c_2, c_3, c_4, \ldots, c_n$. In the following, we propose a quantitative definition of this notion of importance and discuss some properties and applications of this concept.

[1] This research was supported by the Office of Naval Research. Reproduction in whole or part is permitted for any purpose of the United States Government.

1.2.

We assume that every device, whether it is a single component or a system consisting of components, can be in one and only one of two states: it functions or it fails.

When a system consists of components $c_1, c_2, \ldots, c_n$, we can ascribe to each of them a binary indicator variable

$$x_i = \begin{matrix} 1 & \text{when } c_i \text{ functions} \\ 0 & \text{when } c_i \text{ fails.} \end{matrix}$$

Each n-tuple of 0's or 1's

$$(x_1, x_2, \ldots, x_n) = \mathbf{x}$$

is called a *vector of component states* or in short a *state vector*. It can assume any one of the 2^n values represented by the vertices of the unit cube in n-dimensional space: $(0, 0, \ldots, 0), (1, 0, \ldots, 0), (1, 1, 0, \ldots, 0), \ldots, (1, 1, \ldots, 1)$. We shall use the following notations

$$\begin{array}{llll} \mathbf{x} \le \mathbf{y} & \text{when} & x_i \le y_i & \text{for} \quad i = 1, \ldots, n \\ \mathbf{x} = \mathbf{y} & \text{when} & x_i = y_i & \text{for} \quad i = 1, \ldots, n \\ \mathbf{x} < \mathbf{y} & \text{when} & \mathbf{x} \le \mathbf{y} & \text{and } \mathbf{x} \ne \mathbf{y} \end{array}$$

$$(0_k, \mathbf{x}) = (x_1, x_2, \ldots, x_{k-1}, 0, x_{k+1}, \ldots, x_n)$$
$$(1_k, \mathbf{x}) = (x_1, x_2, \ldots, x_{k-1}, 1, x_{k+1}, \ldots, x_n)$$
$$\mathbf{0} = (0, 0, \ldots, 0), \qquad \mathbf{1} = (1, 1, \ldots, 1).$$

We ascribe to the system a binary indicator variable

$$u = \begin{matrix} 1 & \text{when the system functions} \\ 0 & \text{when the system fails.} \end{matrix}$$

When the design of a system is known, then the state vector $\mathbf{x}$ determines the state of the system so that

$$u = \phi(\mathbf{x})$$

where ϕ is a function with values 0 or 1. This function ϕ is called the *structure function* of the system.

A structure function is called *coherent* [1] when it fulfills the conditions: $\phi(\mathbf{0}) = 0$, $\phi(\mathbf{x}) \le \phi(\mathbf{y})$ for $\mathbf{x} \le \mathbf{y}$, and $\phi(\mathbf{1}) = 1$. From now on we shall consider only coherent structure functions. One verifies immediately that $\phi(\mathbf{x})$ can be represented for every $j = 1, 2, \ldots, n$ in the form

$$\phi(\mathbf{x}) = x_j[\phi(1_j, \mathbf{x}) - \phi(0_j, \mathbf{x})] + \phi(0_j, \mathbf{x}) = x_j\,\delta_j(\mathbf{x}) + \mu_j(\mathbf{x}) \quad (1.2.1)$$

where

$$\delta_j(\mathbf{x}) = \phi(1_j, \mathbf{x}) - \phi(0_j, \mathbf{x}) = \partial\phi(\mathbf{x})/\partial x_j \tag{1.2.2}$$

$$\mu_j(\mathbf{x}) = \phi(0_j, \mathbf{x}), \tag{1.2.3}$$

and $\delta_j(\mathbf{x})$ as well as $\mu_j(\mathbf{x})$ do not depend on the state x_j of component c_j.

1.3.

If the state of c_j is determined by chance so that the value actually assumed by x_j is a binary random variable X_j with the probability distribution

$$\begin{aligned} P\{X_j = 1\} &= p_j \\ P\{X_j = 0\} &= q_j = 1 - p_j \end{aligned} \qquad j = 1, 2, \ldots, n \tag{1.3.1}$$

then p_j is called the *reliability* of c_j. In the following, we shall assume that $X_1, X_2, \ldots, X_n$ are totally independent. The n-tuple of component reliabilities determines a point

$$(p_1, p_2, \ldots, p_n) = \mathbf{p} \tag{1.3.2}$$

in the n-dimensional unit cube $\{(p_1, \ldots, p_n) : 0 \leq p_i \leq 1\} = J_n$.

For a given structure function $\phi(\mathbf{x})$, the values of component reliabilities $(p_1, \ldots, p_n) = \mathbf{p}$ determine the probability that the system will function

$$P\{\phi(\mathbf{x}) = 1 \mid \mathbf{p}\} = E[\phi(\mathbf{x}) \mid \mathbf{p}] = h_\phi(\mathbf{p}). \tag{1.3.3}$$

This function $h_\phi(\mathbf{p})$, defined on J_n, is the *reliability function* for ϕ.

There are situations when only the design of a system is known, i.e., $\phi(\mathbf{x})$ is given, but no information is available about the component reliabilities. We shall consider the relative importance of various components in such situations and shall call it *structural importance.*

In other instances, both the structure function ϕ and the component reliabilities $\mathbf{p}$ are known. The concept of importance which will be introduced for these situations will be referred to as *reliability importance.*

A third, substantially more complicated way of considering the importance of components will be mentioned briefly in Section 6.

2. STRUCTURAL IMPORTANCE

2.1.

A component c_j is *relevant* for structure ϕ *at* the *state vector* (vertex of unit cube) $\mathbf{x}$ when

$$\delta_j(\mathbf{x}) = \phi(1_j, \mathbf{x}) - \phi(0_j, \mathbf{x}) = 1; \tag{2.1.1}$$

and c_j is *relevant at* $\mathbf{x}$ *for the functioning of* ϕ when

$$(1 - x_j)\,\delta_j(\mathbf{x}) = 1 \tag{2.1.2}$$

and c_j is *relevant at* $\mathbf{x}$ *for the failure of* ϕ when

$$x_j\,\delta_j(\mathbf{x}) = 1. \tag{2.1.3}$$

Clearly, if c_j is relevant at $\mathbf{x}$ then it is relevant either for functioning or for failure, depending on whether the vertex $\mathbf{x}$ has its coordinate x_j equal to 0 or to 1.

We define the *structural importance* of c_j *for the functioning* of ϕ as

$$I_j(\phi, 1) = 2^{-n} \sum_{(\mathbf{x})} (1 - x_j)\,\delta_j(\mathbf{x}) \tag{2.1.4}$$

where the sum is extended over all 2^n vertices of the unit cube (state vectors), and similarly the *structural importance of* c_j *for failure of* ϕ as

$$I_j(\phi, 0) = 2^{-n} \sum_{(\mathbf{x})} x_j\,\delta_j(\mathbf{x}). \tag{2.1.5}$$

Finally, the *structural importance* of c_j for ϕ is defined as

$$I_j(\phi) = I_j(\phi, 0) + I_j(\phi, 1) = 2^{-n} \sum_{(\mathbf{x})} \delta_j(\mathbf{x}). \tag{2.1.6}$$

One verifies that if c_j is relevant at $\mathbf{x}$ for the functioning of ϕ, then c_j is relevant at $(1_j, \mathbf{x})$ for failure, and if c_j is relevant at $\mathbf{x}$ for failure of ϕ, then it is relevant at $(0_j, \mathbf{x})$ for functioning. There is, therefore, a one-to-one correspondence between those vertices (state vectors) at which c_j is relevant for functioning, and those at which it is relevant for failure, hence the number of either kind of vertices is the same, and from (2.1.4), (2.1.5), (2.1.6) follows

$$I_j(\phi, 1) = I_j(\phi, 0) = \tfrac{1}{2} I_j(\phi). \tag{2.1.7}$$

There is, therefore, no purpose in distinguishing between structural importance for functioning and for failure. We shall see, however, that for reliability importance a similar distinction is meaningful.

2.2. Examples

2.2.1. The *k*-out-of-*n* structures. A structure $\phi(\mathbf{x})$ with n components is called "k-out-of-n" when it functions whenever at least k of its components function. One verifies that for such ϕ

$$I_j(\phi) = 2^{-n} \cdot 2\binom{n-1}{k-1}, \qquad j = 1, 2, \ldots, n. \tag{2.2.1.1}$$

All components have the same structural importance, and this importance is greatest for $k = \frac{1}{2}n$ if n is even, and for $k = [\frac{1}{2}n]$ and $k = [\frac{1}{2}n] + 1$ if n is odd.

The importance of every component is smallest in the case of n components in series (n-out-of-n structure) and of n components in parallel (1-out-of-n structure) when $I_j(\phi) = 2^{-n} \cdot 2$.

2.2.2. k components in series, in series with $n - k$ in parallel. Let

$$\phi(\mathbf{x}) = x_1 x_2 \cdots x_k \cdot [1 - (1 - x_{k+1}) \cdots (1 - x_n)]. \qquad (2.2.2.1)$$

This structure may be represented by the diagram in Fig. 2. One computes

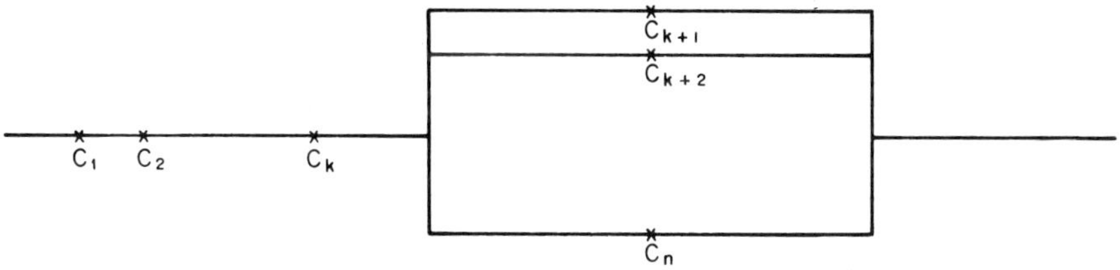

Fig. 2.

by (1.2.2)

$$\delta_j = \prod_{\substack{r=1 \\ r \neq j}}^{k} x_r \left[1 - \prod_{t=k+1}^{n} (1 - x_t)\right] \qquad \text{for} \quad j = 1, \ldots, k \qquad (2.2.2.2)$$

$$\delta_j = \prod_{r=1}^{k} x_r \prod_{\substack{t=k+1 \\ t \neq j}}^{n} (1 - x_t) \qquad \text{for} \quad j = k+1, \ldots, n \qquad (2.2.2.3)$$

hence

$$I_j(\phi) = 2 \cdot 2^{-n}(2^{n-k} - 1) = 2(2^{-k} - 2^{-n}) \qquad \text{for} \quad j = 1, \ldots, k \qquad (2.2.2.4)$$

$$I_j(\phi) = 2 \cdot 2^{-n} \qquad \text{for} \quad j = k+1, \ldots, n. \qquad (2.2.2.5)$$

We see that $c_1, \ldots, c_k$ each have importance $2(2^{-k} - 2^{-n})$, much greater than the importance $2 \cdot 2^{-n}$ of each of $c_{k+1}, \ldots, c_n$. In particular, for $k = 1$ we obtain the structure in Fig. 1 and have $I_1(\phi) = 1 - 2^{-n+1}$, $I_2(\phi) = \cdots = I_n(\phi) = 2^{-n+1}$, which agrees with what one would intuitively expect.

3. RELIABILITY IMPORTANCE

3.1.

From (1.2.1) and (1.3.3), one obtains immediately for the reliability function the expression

$$h_\phi(\mathbf{p}) = p_j E[\delta_j(\mathbf{X})] E + [\mu_j(\mathbf{X})] \qquad (3.1.1)$$

for every $j = 1, 2, \ldots, n$, and from (3.1.1) and (1.2.1) follows

$$\partial h_\phi(\mathbf{p})/\partial p_j = E[\delta_j(\mathbf{X})] = E[\partial\phi(\mathbf{X})/\partial X_j], \qquad j = 1, 2, \ldots, n. \tag{3.1.2}$$

It is known [3] that for coherent structures $\partial h_\phi(\mathbf{p})/\partial p_j \geq 0$, $j = 1, 2, \ldots, n$.

One also proves by straightforward algebra [2] the identity

$$\operatorname{cov}[X_j, \phi(\mathbf{X})] = p_j(1 - p_j)E[\delta_j(\mathbf{X})], \qquad j = 1, 2, \ldots, n. \tag{3.1.3}$$

3.2.

We define the *reliability importance* of c_j *for the functioning of* ϕ as

$$R_j(\phi, 1; \mathbf{p}) = P\{\phi(\mathbf{X}) = 1 \mid X_j = 1; \mathbf{p}\} - P\{\phi(\mathbf{X}) = 1; \mathbf{p}\} \tag{3.2.1}$$

and, similarly, the *reliability importance* of c_j *for failure of* ϕ as

$$R_j(\phi, 0; \mathbf{p}) = P\{\phi(\mathbf{X}) = 0 \mid X_j = 0; \mathbf{p}\} - P\{\phi(\mathbf{X}) = 0; \mathbf{p}\} \tag{3.2.2}$$

and the *reliability importance* of c_j for ϕ as

$$R_j(\phi; \mathbf{p}) = R_j(\phi, 1; \mathbf{p}) + R_j(\phi, 0; \mathbf{p}). \tag{3.2.3}$$

The following identities will be used frequently:

$$R_j(\phi, 1; \mathbf{p}) = (1 - p_j)\frac{\partial h(\mathbf{p})}{\partial p_j} = E[(1 - X_j)\,\delta_j(\mathbf{X})] \tag{3.2.4}$$

$$R_j(\phi, 0; \mathbf{p}) = p_j\frac{\partial h(\mathbf{p})}{\partial p_j} = E[X_j\,\delta_j(\mathbf{X})] \tag{3.2.5}$$

$$R_j(\phi; \mathbf{p}) = \frac{\partial h(\mathbf{p})}{\partial p_j} = E[\delta_j(\mathbf{X})] \tag{3.2.6}$$

Proof. Using (3.1.3)

$$\begin{aligned} P\{\phi(\mathbf{X}) = 1 \mid X_j = 1\} &= \frac{P\{\phi(\mathbf{X}) = X_j = 1\}}{P\{X_j = 1\}} = \frac{E[X_j\phi(\mathbf{X})]}{p_j} \\ &= \frac{\operatorname{cov}[X_j, \phi(\mathbf{X})] + E(X_j)E[\phi(\mathbf{X})]}{p_j} \\ &= (1 - p_j)E[\delta_j(\mathbf{X})] + E[\phi(\mathbf{X})], \end{aligned}$$

and from (3.2.1) and (1.3.3), one obtains (3.2.4). A similar argument yields (3.2.5), and (3.2.6) follows by adding (3.2.4) and (3.2.5).

3.3.

If nothing is known about the reliabilities of the components and, for lack of better knowledge, it is assumed that all vertices $\mathbf{x}$ are equally probable, i.e., each has probability 2^{-n}, then (3.2.4), (3.2.5), and (3.2.6) reduce to (2.1.4), (2.1.5), and (2.1.6), the corresponding structural importances.

3.4. Examples

3.4.1. The *k*-out-of-*n* structures. For a k-out-of-n structure, we have $\delta_j(\mathbf{x}) = \phi(1_j, \mathbf{x}) - \phi(0_j, \mathbf{x}) = 1$ if and only if exactly $k-1$ of the $n-1$ components different from c_j function. Therefore,

$$R_j(\phi; \mathbf{p}) = \sum p_{j_1} p_{j_2} \cdots p_{j_{k-1}} (1 - p_{j_k})(1 - p_{j_{k+1}}) \cdots (1 - p_{j_{n-1}}) \quad (3.4.1.1)$$

where the sum is extended over all permutations $(j_1, j_2, \ldots, j_{n-1})$ of the subscripts $(1, 2, \ldots, j-1, j+1, \ldots, n)$.

3.4.2. Parallel components. For $k = 1$, one obtains from (3.4.1.1)

$$R_j(\phi, \mathbf{p}) = \prod_{i \neq j}^{n} (1 - p_i) = \frac{\prod_{i=1}^{n}(1 - p_i)}{1 - p_j} \quad (3.4.2.1)$$

hence

$$R_j(\phi, 1, \mathbf{p}) = \prod_{i=1}^{n} (1 - p_i) \quad (3.4.2.2)$$

and

$$R_j(\phi, 0, \mathbf{p}) = p_j \prod_{i \neq j}^{n} (1 - p_j) = \frac{p_j}{1 - p_j} \prod_{i=1}^{n} (1 - p_i). \quad (3.4.2.3)$$

From (3.4.2.1), one sees that the component with the greatest reliability p_j has the highest reliability importance; from (3.4.2.2), that all components are equally important for functioning; and from (3.4.2.3) that the component with the greatest reliability p_j has also the highest reliability importance for failure.

3.4.3. Components in series. One obtains from (3.4.1.1) for $k = n$

$$R_j(\phi, \mathbf{p}) = \prod_{i \neq j}^{n} p_i = p_j^{-1} \prod_{i=1}^{n} p_i \quad (3.4.3.1)$$

hence

$$R_j(\phi, 1, \mathbf{p}) = \frac{1 - p_j}{p_j} \prod_{i=1}^{n} p_i \quad (3.4.3.2)$$

and

$$R_j(\phi, 0, \mathbf{p}) = \prod_{i=1}^{n} p_i. \quad (3.4.3.3)$$

One sees that here all components have the same reliability importance for failure, and that the most reliable component has the smallest reliability importance and the smallest reliability importance for functioning.

3.4.4. *k* components in series, in series with *n* − *k* in parallel. For the structure function (2.2.2.1), one computes

$$R_j(\phi, \mathbf{p}) = p_j^{-1} \prod_{r=1}^{k} p_r \left[1 - \prod_{t=k+1}^{n} (1 - p_t)\right], \qquad \text{if } j = 1, 2, \ldots, k,$$

$$R_j(\phi, \mathbf{p}) = \prod_{r=1}^{k} p_r (1 - p_j)^{-1} \prod_{t=k+1}^{n} (1 - p_t), \qquad \text{if } j = k + 1, \ldots, n, \tag{3.4.4.1}$$

and corresponding expressions are immediately obtained for $R(\phi, 1, \mathbf{p})$ and $R(\phi, 0, \mathbf{p})$.

The special case $k = 1$ which corresponds to Fig. 1 yields for $j = 1$

$$R_1(\phi, \mathbf{p}) = 1 - \prod_{t=2}^{n} (1 - p_t)$$

$$R_1(\phi, 1, \mathbf{p}) = p_1 \left[1 - \prod_{t=2}^{n} (1 - p_t)\right]$$

$$R_1(\phi, 0, \mathbf{p}) = (1 - p_1) \left[1 - \prod_{t=2}^{n} (1 - p_t)\right],$$

and for $j = 2, \ldots, n$

$$R_j(\phi, \mathbf{p}) = \frac{p_1}{1 - p_j} \prod_{t=2}^{n} (1 - p_t)$$

$$R_j(\phi, 1, \mathbf{p}) = p_1 \prod_{t=2}^{n} (1 - p_t)$$

$$R_j(\phi, 0, \mathbf{p}) = \frac{p_1 p_j}{1 - p_j} \prod_{t=2}^{n} (1 - p_t).$$

4. STRUCTURES WITH MODULES

4.1.

In designing multicomponent systems one often proceeds step-by-step, first constructing a system of fewer components and then replacing some of these components by subsystems, known as *modules*, each consisting of several components. Some properties of coherent systems constructed of coherent modules have been studied in [3]. For our present purpose, we shall use the following definitions.

Let

$$\phi(\mathbf{x}) = \phi(x_1, x_2, \ldots, x_n) = x_1\, \delta_{x_1}(\phi; \mathbf{x}) + \mu_{x_1}(\phi; \mathbf{x}) \tag{4.1.1}$$

and

$$\psi(\mathbf{y}) = \psi(y_1, y_2, \ldots, y_m) \tag{4.1.2}$$

be two coherent structures. We shall say that the structure

$$\begin{aligned}\chi(y_1, y_2, \ldots, y_m, x_2, \ldots, x_n) &= \phi[\psi(y_1, \ldots, y_m), x_2, \ldots, x_n] = \phi[\psi_1(\mathbf{y}), \mathbf{x}] \\ &= \psi(\mathbf{y})\, \delta_{x_1}[\phi; \mathbf{x}] + \mu_{x_1}[\phi; \mathbf{x}] \end{aligned}\tag{4.1.3}$$

was obtained by replacing component x_1 in $\phi(\mathbf{x})$ by the module $\psi(\mathbf{y})$.

4.2.

From (4.1.3), one obtains

$$\begin{aligned}\delta_{y_1}(\chi; y_1, \ldots, y_m, x_2, \ldots, x_n) &= \chi(1, y_2, \ldots, y_m, x_2, \ldots, x_n) \\ &\quad - \chi(0, y_2, \ldots, y_m, x_2, \ldots, x_n) \\ &= [\psi(1_1, \mathbf{y}) - \psi(0_1, \mathbf{y})]\, \delta_{x_1}(\phi; \mathbf{x}) \\ &= \delta_{y_1}(\psi; \mathbf{y}) \cdot \delta_{x_1}(\phi; \mathbf{x}).\end{aligned}$$

From the identity so obtained

$$\delta_{y_1}(\chi) = \delta_{x_1}(\phi; \mathbf{x})\, \delta_{y_1}(\psi; \mathbf{y}) \tag{4.2.1}$$

and from (3.2.6) follows

$$R_{y_1}(\chi; y_1, \ldots, y_m, x_2, \ldots, x_n) = R_{x_1}(\phi; \mathbf{x}) \cdot R_{y_1}(\psi; \mathbf{y}). \tag{4.2.2}$$

This "chain-rule" property (which could also have been obtained by the chain rule for differentiation using $E[\delta_j(\mathbf{x})] = \partial h(\mathbf{p})/\partial p_j$ makes it possible to compute the importance of each component of a module ψ for the entire system χ, and to repeat this step-by-step as modules are substituted for components. The computation of $R_{y_1}(\chi, 1; y_1, \ldots, y_m, x_2, \ldots, x_n)$ and of $R_{y_1}(\chi, 0; y_1, \ldots, y_m, x_2, \ldots, x_n)$ is then a simple matter, according to (3.2.4) and (3.2.5).

5. AN APPLICATION

If components with known reliabilities $(p_1, \ldots, p_n) = \mathbf{p}$ are available, and the known structure $\phi(\mathbf{x})$ has the reliability $h(\mathbf{p}) = E[\phi(\mathbf{X}); \mathbf{p}]$, then the problem may arise to decide on which components additional research and development should be done to improve their reliabilities, so that the greatest gain is achieved in system reliability.

Let us assume that improving the reliability of c_j from p_j to $p_j + \Delta_j$ can be achieved at cost $\lambda_j(p_j) \cdot \Delta_j$, for $j = 1, \ldots, n$. In practical situations $\lambda_j(p_j)$ will be an increasing function, such that

$$\lambda_j(0) = 0, \qquad \lambda_j(p) \underset{p \to 1}{\to} \infty.$$

The total cost of improving all components will be

$$C(\mathbf{p}, \mathbf{\Delta}) = \sum_{j=1}^{n} \lambda_j(p_j)\, \Delta_j, \tag{5.1}$$

and the gain in system reliability per unit of cost

$$\frac{h_\phi(\mathbf{p} + \mathbf{\Delta}) - h_\phi(\mathbf{p})}{C(\mathbf{p}, \mathbf{\Delta})}. \tag{5.2}$$

We shall look for the direction of steepest ascent of this gain in the following sense.

Let

$$\Delta_j = \alpha_j\, t, \qquad j = 1, 2, \ldots, n \tag{5.3}$$

with

$$\sum_{j=1}^{n} \alpha_j{}^2 = 1. \tag{5.4}$$

We wish to determine the vector of direction cosines $(\alpha_1, \ldots, \alpha_j, \ldots, \alpha_n) = \boldsymbol{\alpha}$ so that, for all Δ_j small, (5.2) is maximized. Since (5.2) now is

$$\frac{h_\phi(\mathbf{p} + \boldsymbol{\alpha} t) - h_\phi(\mathbf{p})}{t \sum_{j=1}^{n} \lambda_j(p_j)\alpha_j} \underset{t \to 0}{\longrightarrow} \frac{dh(\mathbf{p} + \boldsymbol{\alpha} t)/dt\,|_{t=0}}{\sum_{j=1}^{n} \lambda_j(p_j)\alpha_j},$$

our problem becomes to maximize

$$\frac{\sum_{j=1}^{n} (\partial h(p)/\partial p_j)\alpha_j}{\sum_{j=1}^{n} \lambda_j(p_j)\alpha_j} = \frac{\sum_{j=1}^{n} R_j(\phi, \mathbf{p})\alpha_j}{\sum_{j=1}^{n} \lambda_j(p_j)\alpha_j} = Q(\alpha)$$

under the restriction (5.4). It can be seen that the maximum of $Q(\alpha)$ is attained by selecting that component c_{j_0} for which the importance-to-cost ratio $R_j(\phi, \mathbf{p})/\lambda_j(p_j)$ is maximum, and setting $\alpha_{j_0} = 1$, $\alpha_j = 0$ for $j \neq j_0$. For, writing $R_j(\phi, \mathbf{p}) = R_j$, $\lambda_j(p_j) = \lambda_j$ and assuming without loss of generality $j_0 = 1$, one has $R_1/\lambda_1 > R_j/\lambda_j$ for $j = 2, \ldots, n$, and

$$Q(\boldsymbol{\alpha}) = \frac{R_1\alpha_1 + \sum_{j=2}^{n} R_j\alpha_j}{\sum_{j=1}^{n} \lambda_j\alpha_j} < \frac{R_1\alpha_1 + \sum_{j=2}^{n}(R_1/\lambda_1)\lambda_j\alpha_j}{\sum_{j=1}^{n} \lambda_j\alpha_j} = \frac{R_1}{\lambda_1} = Q(1, 0, \ldots, 0).$$

The practical conclusion is that work on improving component reliability need only be done on one component at a time, but that in this process one may have to change from one component to another according to which of the ratios $R_j(\phi, \mathbf{p})/\lambda_j(p_j)$ becomes the largest.

6. CONCLUDING REMARKS

6.1.

We have considered situations in which only the structure function $\phi(\mathbf{x})$ of the system was known, and situations in which also the reliabilities $\mathbf{p} = (p_1, p_2, \ldots, p_n)$ of the components were known, and for each of these situations we proposed a quantitative definition of importance of components. A third possibility should be considered when the coherent structure ϕ is known and each component c_i has a life length T_i, with a known probability distribution $F_i(t) = P\{T_i \leq t\}$. Under these assumptions the system has a life-length [4] T, with a probability distribution $P\{T \leq t\} = F(t)$ which depends on ϕ and on all the $F_i(T)$, $i = 1, 2, \ldots, n$. Again, intuitively some of the components are more important than others for the life distribution $F(t)$, and their importance depends on their location within the structure as well as on all the life distributions. To our knowledge, a study of the problem arising in this context has not even been initiated.

6.2.

Under some circumstances, it may be of interest to consider a property of components which one could call the Bays'ean importance. For example, when a complicated system fails, it may be of interest to make a guess which component has "caused" the failure, and for this purpose one may consider the quantities

$$P\{X_j = 0 \mid \phi(\mathbf{X}) = 0\}, \qquad j = 1, 2, \ldots, n.$$

These quantities indicate how "important" the different components are for the failure of the system. The mathematics of these quantities seems to be quite straightforward.

ACKNOWLEDGMENT

The author wishes to express his appreciation to Dr. J. D. Esary for many helpful discussions.

REFERENCES

1. Birnbaum, Z. W., Esary, J. D., and Saunders, S. C. (1961). Multicomponent systems and structures and their reliabilities. *Technometrics* **3** 55–77.

2. Esary, J. D.,and Proschan, F. (1963). Coherent structures of nonidentical components. *Technometrics* **5** 191–209.
3. Birnbaum, Z. W., and Esary, J. D. (1965). Modules of coherent binary systems. *SIAM* (*Soc. Indust. Appl. Math.*) *J.* **13** 444–462.
4. Esary, J. D., and Marshall, A. W. (1964). System structure and the existence of a system life. *Technometrics* **6** 459–462.

Data Analytic Methods in Multivariate Statistical Analysis

R. GNANADESIKAN and M. B. WILK

BELL TELEPHONE LABORATORIES, INCORPORATED
MURRAY HILL, NEW JERSEY

SUMMARY

This paper concerns multivariate statistical techniques, concepts, and data-based interpretations relevant to five general objectives in the analysis of multiresponse data: (i) reduction of dimensionality; (ii) development and study of multivariate relationships; (iii) multidimensional classification; (iv) assessment of statistical models; and (v) summarization and exposure.

The coverage includes a review of some relevant published work and also of some new procedures. Specifically, the new statistical methods discussed are: a generalization of linear principal components analysis for detecting and describing nonlinear relations among the responses; the use of regression procedures for multidimensional classification when there are certain systematic variations (due perhaps to experimental artifacts) among the known replicate observations of each category or group; and a technique of joint plotting of the component order statistics of multivariate observations for purposes of intercomparing the marginal distributions of the components.

Illustrative examples of use of the techniques are given.

1. INTRODUCTION

In a general sense, data—by its very nature—is always multivariate since it involves observations associated with various facets of a particular background or environment. Even in a narrow sense, when only a single type of response is to be analyzed, the analysis often leads to a multivariate situation. For example, in multiple regression, or in a more general model fitting involving a single dependent variable, one often is faced with correlations among the estimated coefficients, and analyzing the correlation structure for possible reparameterizations of the problem is not an uncommon venture.

The present paper is largely limited to those multiresponse problems which might, in their primitive form, be loosely designated as the analysis of n points in p-space, i.e., when each of n "objects" or experimental units, which may be classified or identified by various extraneous variables, has associated with it a p-dimensional vector of responses. Though one can generally behave as though the observations from object to object are statistically independent, the observed components within each response vector will usually be statistically related.

The orientation of this paper is that of statistical data analysis, concerned mainly with providing insightful descriptions of the informational content of the data.

The paper is organized according to five general objectives in analyzing multiresponse data and deals with concepts, techniques, and data-based interpretations in that framework. No coverage is given to distribution theory results, optimality properties, mathematical proofs, or detailed algorithms.

Everyone is well aware that multivariate analysis of data can be a most difficult and frustrating problem, far more so than uniresponse situations. Reasons for this include the following:

(1) It seems very difficult to know or to develop an understanding of what one really wants to do. Much iteration and interaction is required. This is also true in the uniresponse case in real problems. Perhaps in the multiresponse case, one is simply raising that difficulty to the pth power.

(2) Once a multiresponse view is adopted, there is no obvious "natural" value of p, the dimensionality of response. For any experimental unit, it is always possible to record an almost indefinitely large list of attributes. Any selection from this is usually accomplished using background information, preliminary analysis, informal criteria, and experimental insight. On the other hand, the number of objects or replications, n, will always have some upper bound. Hence n will often be less than p, or at least not much greater. These dimensionality considerations can become most crucial in determining what analyses or insights can be attained.

(3) Multivariate data analysis involves prodigious arithmetic and data manipulation. Even with modern high-speed computing, many techniques are severely limited in practice as to number of dimensions, p, or number of observations, n, or both.

(4) Pictures and graphs play a key role in data analysis, but with multiresponse data, elementary plots of the raw data cannot easily be made. This keeps one from obtaining the realistic primitive stimuli as to what to do, or what models to try, which often motivate uniresponse analyses.

(5) Last, but of great importance and consequence, points in p-space, unlike those on a line, do not have a unique linear ordering, which sometimes

seems to be almost a basic human requirement. Most formal models and their motivation grasp almost desperately for this feature—something to optimize or things to order. This is no sin unless in the desperation to achieve the comfort of linear ordering, one closes one's mind to the nature of the problem and the guidance which the data may contain.

The main coverage of the paper is in five sections, limited to the following objectives:

(1) Reduction of Dimensionality (Section 2);
(2) Development and Study of Multivariate Relationships (Section 3);
(3) Multidimensional Classification (Section 4);
(4) Assessment of Statistical Models (Section 5);
(5) Summarization and Exposure (Section 6).

No specific attention is given here to analysis of time series data, either univariate or multivariate.

2. REDUCTION OF DIMENSIONALITY

2.1. General

The issue in reduction of dimensionality in analyzing multiresponse situations is between attainment of simplicity for understanding, visualization and interpretation, on the one hand, and retention of sufficient detail for adequate representation, on the other hand.

Reduction of dimensionality can lead to parsimony of description or of measurement or of both. It may also encourage consideration of meaningful physical relationships between the variables, as for example, summarizing (mass, volume)–data in terms of density = mass/volume.

By some criteria of relevance, the experimenter always makes a drastic reduction of the dimensionality of the observations to be made. Such reduction may be based on: (1) exclusion prior to the experiment; (2) exclusion of features by specific experimental judgment; (3) general statistical techniques, such as principal components analysis, use of distance functions of general utility, and methods for recognizing and handling nonlinear singularities; and/or (4) specific properties of the problem which indicate choice of a particular real-valued function for analysis, e.g., relative weights for assigning an overall grade in matriculation examinations.

The first two of these lead to a reduction of measurement in that the number of variables to be observed is diminished. The last two, in general, will not lead to reducing current measurements but may do so for future measurements by showing that a subset of the variables is adequate.

From the point of view of description, too severe a reduction may be bad. Meaningful statistical analysis will be possible only when there has not been excessive elimination. Clearly, a dominant consideration in the use of statistical procedures for the reduction of dimensionality is the interpretability of the lower dimensional representations. For instance, the use of principal components *per se* does not necessarily yield directly interpretable measures, whereas a reasonable choice of a distance function will sometimes permit interpretation.

Circumstances under which one may be interested in reducing dimensionality of multiple response data include: (1) Exploratory situations in data analysis, for example in psychological testing results or survey questionnaire data, especially where there is ignorance of what is important in the measurement planning. Here, one may want to screen out redundant coordinates or to try to find more insightful ones as a preliminary to further analysis or data collection. (2) Where one hopes to stabilize "scales" of measurement when a similar property is described by each of several coordinates, for example, several measures of size of a biological organism. Here, the aim is to compound the various measurements into a fewer number which will exhibit more stable statistical properties. (3) The compounding of multiple information as an aid in significance assessment. Specifically, one may hope that small departures from null conditions may be evidenced on each of several jointly observed responses. Then, one might try to integrate these noncentralities into a smaller dimensional space wherein their existence may be more sensitively indicated. One particular technique which has received some usage is the univariate analysis of variance applied to principal components. (4) The preliminary specification of a space which is to be used as a basis for eventual discrimination or classification procedures. For example, the raw information per object available as a basis for talker identification consists of a 15,000-dimensional vector which characterizes each utterance. This array must be condensed as a preliminary to further classification analysis. (5) Where one is interested in detection of possible functional dependencies among observations in high-dimensional space. This purpose is perhaps the least well defined but nevertheless is prevalent, interesting, and important.

Many problems and issues exist in this general area of transformation of coordinates and reduction of dimensionality. These are problems of concept as to what one hopes to achieve, of techniques or methods to exhibit information which may be in the data, of how to interpret the results of application of available techniques, and of mathematical or algorithmic questions related to implementation. Specifically, if one develops a transformed or derived set of (reduced) coordinates, then there is the question of whether these can be given some meaning or interpretation that will aid understanding of the actual problem. Similarly, it may or may not be true that derived coordinates, or approximations to these, will be directly observable. Sometimes such observability may occur with gains in efficiency and simplicity of both experiment and analysis.

Another problem in this area is that of the commensurability of the original coordinates and of how this issue may affect a derived set of coordinates. Apparently, this is not a problem in principle since there is no difficulty in dealing with functions of variables having different units. However, if the functions themselves are to be determined or influenced by the data, as for example in principal components analysis, then some confusion may exist.

Almost exclusively, statistical methodology, in looking for a reduced set of coordinates, has considered derived coordinates which are just linear transforms of the original coordinates. Virtually all nonlinear analysis of multiresponse data has come from experimental insight and scientific theory and not from statistical data analysis. But, it is clearly essential that the statistical data analyst must develop techniques, linear and nonlinear, appropriate to these needs.

A review is now given of various techniques useful in the problem of reducing dimensionality. First, a brief outline is given of classical linear principal components and factor analysis. Then some discussion is given of the methods of multidimensional scaling, developed by Shepard (1962a,b) and Kruskal (1964a,b). Next, work of Shepard and Carroll (1966) is mentioned on finding parametric nonlinear representations, in lower dimensions, for multiresponse data arrays. Finally, some recent research of the present authors on detection of nonlinear singularities and on generalized nonlinear principal components analysis will be outlined.

2.2. Linear Reduction of Dimensionality

The basic idea of principal components analysis is to describe the dispersion of an array of n points in p-dimensional space by introducing a new set of orthogonal linear coordinates so that the sample variances of the given points with respect to these derived coordinates are in decreasing order of magnitude. Thus, the first principal component is such that the projections of the given points onto it have maximum variance among all possible linear coordinates; the second principal component has maximum variance subject to being orthogonal to the first; and so on.

This technique, mentioned by Karl Pearson (1901) and developed by Hotelling (1933), is perhaps the most widely used multivariate method, both directly as applied to the sample covariance matrix or correlation matrix and indirectly in various guises under the general term of factor analysis.

One geometric interpretation of principal components is as follows: The inverse of the sample covariance matrix may be employed as the matrix of a quadratic form which defines a family of concentric ellipsoids centered on the sample center of gravity. The principal components transformation of the data are just the projections of the observations onto the principal axes of this family.

Example 1. The basic idea is illustrated, for the 2-dimensional case, in Fig. 1 taken from Seal (1964). The original coordinates, (X_1, X_2), are first transformed by a shift of origin to the center of gravity yielding (X_1', X_2'). Then a

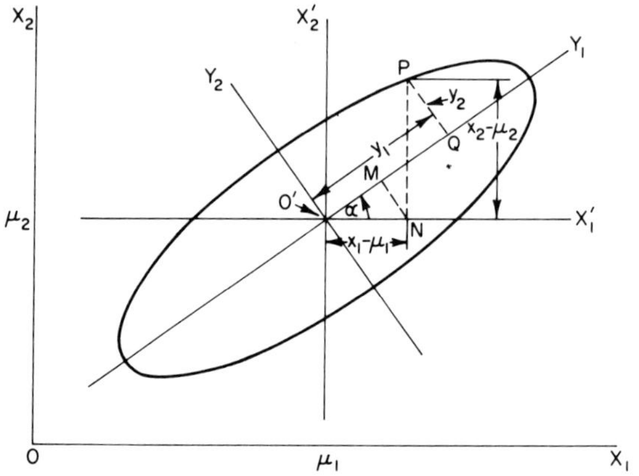

Fig. 1.

rigid rotation about the new origin leads to the principal components, Y_1 and Y_2.

Algebraically, the principal components analysis involves finding the eigenvalues and eigenvectors of the sample covariance matrix. The ranked eigenvalues are, in fact, just the sample variances of the linear combinations of the original variables specified by the eigenvectors.

These descriptions have been in terms of the covariance matrix. Clearly, if one standardizes each coordinate by dividing by the sample standard deviations, then the covariance matrix of the standardized variables is just the correlation matrix of the original variables. Thus the above discussion applies also to principal components analysis of the correlation matrix.

If the sample size, n, is not greater than the dimensionality, p, then the sample covariance matrix will be singular, corresponding to the fact that all n points will lie on a hyperplane of dimension less than p. Within that linear subspace, one can define a dispersion matrix and find its principal components. This will be reflected in the eigenvalue analysis of the singular covariance matrix, in that some of the eigenvalues will be zero. The eigenvectors corresponding to the nonzero eigenvalues will give the projections of the observations onto orthogonal coordinates within the linear subspace containing the observations.

In the principal components coordinate system the new variables have zero sample correlation, have sample variances ranging from maximum to minimum and with sum equal to that of the original variables.

One hope in the case of principal components analysis is that the bulk of the observations will be near a linear subspace, and thence that one can employ a new coordinate system of reduced dimension. Generally, interest would be in those coordinates along which the data show their greatest variability. However, while the eigenvector corresponding to the largest eigenvalue, for example, provides the projection of each point onto the first principal component, the equation of the first principal component coordinate is given by the conjunction of the equations of planes defined by the remaining eigenvectors. More generally, if most of the variability of a p-dimensional sample is confined to a q-dimensional linear subspace, that subspace is described by the $(p - q)$ eigenvectors which correspond to the $(p - q)$ "small" eigenvalues. For purposes of interpretation—detection or specification of constraints on, or redundancy of, the observed variables—it may often be the relations which define near constancy (i.e., those specified by the smallest eigenvalues) which are of greatest interest.

The interpretation of magnitude and separation of eigenvalues from a sample covariance matrix is considerably complicated by the sampling variation and statistical interdependence as exhibited even by the eigenvalues of a covariance matrix calculated from observations from a spherical normal distribution. Further discussion of this is given in Section 6.2.

Clearly, principal components are *not* invariant under linear transformation, including separate scaling, of the original coordinates. Thus, the principal components of the covariance matrix are not the same as those of the correlation matrix or of some other scaling according to measures of "importance." Note, however, that the principal components of the correlation matrix are invariant under separate scaling of the original variables. There does not seem to be any *general* elementary rationale to motivate the choice of scaling of the variables as a preliminary to principal components analysis on the resulting covariance matrix.

An important exception regarding invariance occurs when the observations are confined to a linear subspace. In this case, the specification of the singularities is unique under nonsingular linear transformation of the variables. One might expect that, loosely speaking, similar near-uniqueness would hold when the data have a "near-singular" structure.

When the multiresponse observation is observed in connection with known design or regression variables, then one will usually wish to express the responses as functions of the design variables and, possibly, augment that analysis by a principal components transformation of the multivariate residuals from the fit. This last analysis may help to describe statistical correlations in the errors of the combined original variables or aid in indicating inadequacies in the fit of the response variables by the design variables. Note that even the existence of an exact linear singularity among the multivariate residuals will *not* imply a linear or near-linear singularity among the "unadjusted" observations.

2.3. Nonmetric Reduction of Dimensionality

A technique of multidimensional scaling was developed by Shepard (1962a,b) and further refined by Kruskal (1964a,b), in connection with the following problem: Given a matrix of "similarities" among n objects, e.g., the proportion of times one stimulus is identified as another in a series of n stimuli, can one find a Euclidean space in which the interpoint distances of the representations of the n objects are, to a satisfactory degree, monotonically related to the similarities? For a high-enough dimension this is always achievable. The problem is to find a low-dimensional space within which this is achieved to a reasonable approximation. The above references describe computer algorithms for multidimensional scaling.

These ideas are directly relevant to reduction of dimensionality for a body of multiresponse data. Indeed, if n observed points in p-space are located close to a q-dimensional linear subspace, then the use of the interpoint Euclidean distances of the points as the elements of a similarity matrix in multidimensional scaling could lead to a "solution" in q-space, in correspondence with the results of a principal components analysis of the original covariance matrix.

However, if the n points in p-space are located close to certain kinds of *curved* q-dimensional subspaces, then multidimensional scaling may produce a solution in q-space which would not necessarily be indicated by the linear principal components analysis or usual factor analysis. The point is that multidimensional scaling attempts to preserve the monotone relation of distances and, if the distances along the curved q-dimensional subspace are reasonably monotone with the Euclidean distances, then the procedure will recognize the lower dimensional curved space.

Example 2. The data [cf. Ekman (1954)] used by Shepard (1962b) involved similarity ratings of every pair among fourteen color stimuli which varied primarily in hue. The similarity ratings from each subject were scaled to go from 0 ("no similarity at all") to 1 ("identical"), and a 14×14 matrix of mean similarity ratings was computed and treated by Ekman (1954) as a correlation matrix for purposes of a factor analysis, which led to a five-factor description. The five factors were identified as violet, blue, green, yellow, and red. On the other hand, as mentioned by Shepard (1962b), intuition and the familiar concept of the "color circle" might suggest the reasonableness of a two-factor (or perhaps even a one-factor) solution.

Figure 2a, taken from Shepard (1962b), shows the two-dimensional solution obtained by a multidimensional scaling algorithm. The multidimensional

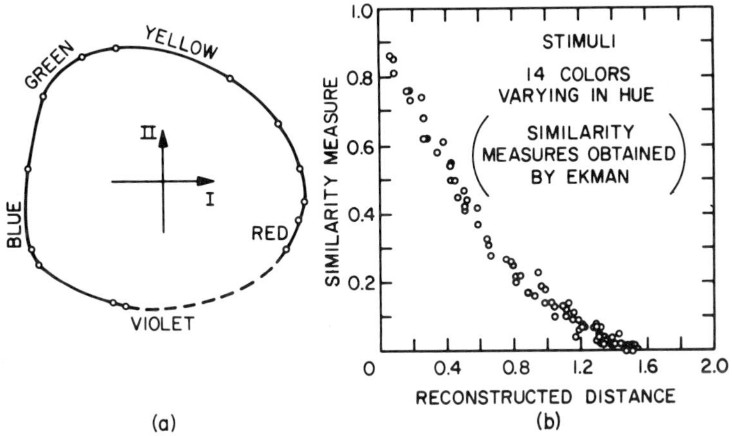

Fig. 2. Multidimensional scaling example (Shepard, 1962b).

scaling solution, of course, merely consists of the coordinate representation of the fourteen points and the smooth line was drawn through the points by Shepard to emphasize the similarity of the configuration to the color circle.

Figure 2b is a scatter plot of the original measures of similarity versus the interpoint distances in the two-dimensional solution shown in Fig. 2a. The monotone relation between similarity and interpoint distance evidenced in this plot is, of course, a constraint of the multidimensional scaling procedure. The greater the observed similarity between two stimuli the smaller is the distance between the two points representing the stimuli.

A modification of the scaling approach, due to Shepard and Carroll (1966), is directed toward improving the recognition of near singularities of a nonlinear nature among multidimensional observations. This modification focuses attention mainly on retaining the monotone relationship between interpoint distances and similarities only for nearby points rather than for all the points. Shepard and Carroll (1966) have also considered maximizing an index of continuity, so as to find a representation of the original p-dimensional points in terms of $q(< p)$ new coordinates which are "smoothly" related to the old. Applications of these procedures are also described by Shepard and Carroll (1966).

These scaling ideas and procedures are imaginative and insightful. The procedures have limitations in practical application in that they involve extensive iteration on $n(n-1)/2$ quantities—the interpoint similarities or distances. Also, the solution space they produce does not have an analytic description which is simply interpretable in terms of the original response space.

These scaling procedures all depend upon the use of an index of achievement—defined as the minimum "stress"—as an informal basis for assessing the comparative adequacy of the successive dimensions employed. This index is to be used with appropriate judgment relative to meaningfulness of interpretation in the subject matter area.

Example 3. The data, from an experiment of Rothkopf (1957) [see also Shepard (1963), Kruskal (1964a)], was from 598 subjects who were asked to judge whether or not pairs of successively presented Morse code signals were

	A	B	C	D	E	F	G	H	I	J	K	L	M	N	O	P	Q	R
A	92	04	06	13	03	14	10	13	45	05	22	03	25	34	06	06	09	35
B	05	84	37	31	05	28	17	21	05	19	34	40	06	10	12	22	25	16
C	04	38	87	17	04	29	13	07	11	19	24	35	14	03	09	51	34	24
D	08	62	17	88	07	23	40	36	09	13	81	56	08	07	09	27	09	45
E	06	13	14	06	97	02	04	04	17	01	05	06	04	04	05	01	05	10
F	04	51	33	19	02	90	10	29	05	33	16	50	07	06	10	42	12	35
G	09	18	27	38	01	14	90	06	05	22	33	16	14	13	52	52	23	21
H	03	45	23	25	09	32	08	87	10	10	09	29	05	08	08	14	08	17
I	64	07	07	13	10	08	06	12	93	03	05	16	13	30	07	03	05	19
J	07	09	38	09	02	24	18	05	04	85	22	31	08	03	21	63	47	11
K	05	24	38	73	01	17	25	11	05	27	91	33	10	12	31	14	31	22
L	02	69	43	45	10	24	12	26	09	30	27	86	06	02	09	37	36	28
M	24	12	05	14	07	17	29	08	08	11	23	08	96	62	11	10	15	20
N	31	04	13	30	08	12	10	16	13	03	16	08	59	93	05	09	05	28
O	07	07	20	06	05	09	76	07	02	39	26	10	04	08	86	37	35	10
P	05	22	33	12	05	36	22	12	03	78	14	46	05	06	21	83	43	23
Q	08	20	38	11	04	15	10	05	02	27	23	26	07	06	22	51	91	11
R	13	14	16	23	05	34	26	15	07	12	21	37	14	12	12	29	08	37
S	17	24	05	30	11	26	05	59	16	03	13	10	05	17	06	06	03	18
T	13	10	01	05	46	03	06	06	14	06	14	07	06	05	06	11	04	04
U	14	29	12	32	04	32	11	34	21	07	44	32	11	13	06	20	12	40
V	05	17	24	16	09	29	06	39	05	11	26	43	04	01	09	17	10	17
W	09	21	30	22	09	36	25	15	04	25	29	18	15	06	26	20	25	61
X	07	64	45	19	03	28	11	06	01	35	50	42	10	08	24	32	61	10
Y	09	23	62	15	04	26	22	09	01	30	12	14	05	06	14	30	52	05
Z	03	46	45	18	02	22	17	10	07	23	21	51	11	02	15	59	72	14
1	02	05	10	03	03	05	13	04	02	29	05	14	09	07	14	30	28	09
2	07	14	22	05	04	20	13	03	25	26	09	14	02	03	17	37	28	06
3	03	08	21	05	04	32	06	12	02	23	06	13	05	02	05	37	19	09
4	06	19	19	12	08	25	14	16	07	21	13	19	03	03	02	17	29	11
5	08	45	15	14	02	45	04	67	07	14	04	41	02	00	04	13	07	09
6	07	80	30	17	04	23	04	14	02	11	11	27	06	02	07	16	30	11
7	06	33	22	14	05	25	06	04	06	24	13	32	07	06	07	36	39	12
8	03	23	40	06	03	15	15	06	02	33	10	14	03	06	14	12	45	02
9	03	14	23	03	01	06	14	05	02	30	06	07	16	11	10	31	32	05
Ø	09	03	11	02	05	07	14	04	05	30	08	03	02	03	25	21	29	02

	S	T	U	V	W	X	Y	Z	1	2	3	4	5	6	7	8	9	Ø
A	23	06	37	13	17	12	07	03	02	07	05	05	08	06	05	05	02	03
B	18	02	18	34	08	84	30	42	12	17	14	40	32	74	43	17	04	04
C	14	06	06	11	14	32	82	38	13	15	31	14	10	30	28	24	18	12
D	29	06	17	20	27	40	15	33	03	09	05	11	09	19	08	10	05	06
E	07	67	03	03	02	05	06	05	04	03	05	03	05	02	04	02	03	03
F	14	02	21	27	25	19	27	13	08	16	47	25	26	24	21	05	05	05
G	05	03	15	14	32	21	23	39	15	14	05	10	04	10	17	23	20	11
H	37	04	36	59	09	33	14	11	03	09	15	43	70	35	17	04	03	03
I	35	16	10	05	08	02	05	07	02	05	08	09	06	08	05	02	04	05
J	02	07	09	09	09	22	32	28	67	66	33	15	07	11	28	29	26	23
K	02	02	23	17	33	63	16	18	05	09	17	08	08	18	14	13	05	06
L	12	05	16	19	20	31	25	59	12	13	17	15	26	29	36	16	07	03
M	07	09	13	04	21	09	18	08	05	07	06	06	05	07	11	07	10	04
N	12	10	16	04	12	04	06	11	05	02	03	04	04	06	02	02	10	02
O	03	04	11	14	25	35	27	27	19	17	07	07	06	18	14	11	20	12
P	09	04	12	19	19	19	41	30	34	44	24	11	15	17	24	23	25	13
Q	02	03	06	14	12	37	50	63	34	32	17	12	09	27	40	58	37	24
R	16	02	23	23	62	14	12	13	07	10	13	04	07	12	07	09	01	02
S	96	09	56	24	12	10	06	07	08	02	02	15	28	09	05	05	05	02
T	07	96	08	05	04	02	02	06	05	05	03	03	03	08	07	06	14	06
U	51	06	93	57	34	17	09	11	06	06	16	34	10	09	09	07	04	03
V	11	06	32	92	17	57	35	10	10	14	29	79	44	36	25	10	01	05
W	12	04	19	20	86	22	25	22	10	22	19	16	05	09	11	06	03	07
X	12	03	12	17	21	91	48	26	12	20	24	27	16	57	29	16	17	06
Y	07	04	06	13	21	44	86	23	26	44	40	15	11	26	22	33	23	16
Z	04	03	09	11	12	36	42	87	16	21	27	09	10	25	66	47	15	15
1	04	02	03	12	14	17	19	22	84	63	13	08	10	08	19	32	57	55
2	05	03	06	10	11	17	30	13	62	89	54	20	05	14	20	21	16	11
3	07	06	04	16	06	22	25	12	18	64	86	31	23	41	16	17	08	10
4	09	03	17	55	08	37	24	03	05	26	44	89	42	44	32	10	03	03
5	27	02	14	45	07	45	10	10	14	10	30	69	90	42	24	10	06	05
6	14	03	12	30	09	58	38	39	15	14	26	24	17	86	65	14	05	14
7	06	02	03	13	09	30	30	50	22	29	18	15	12	61	85	70	20	13
8	06	04	06	07	05	24	35	50	42	29	16	16	09	30	60	89	61	26
9	06	07	06	03	08	11	21	24	57	39	09	12	04	11	42	56	91	78
Ø	03	04	05	03	02	12	15	20	50	26	09	11	05	22	17	52	81	94

Fig. 3a.

the same. Thirty-six signals were employed: twenty-six for the letters of the alphabet and ten for the digits, 0 through 9. Figure 3a is a matrix of percentages of times that a signal corresponding to the row label was identified as being the same as the signal corresponding to the column label. The averages of each pair of symmetrically situated off-diagonal elements of this matrix may be used as input measures of similarity between the corresponding pair in the thirty-six signals.

Figure 3b, taken from Kruskal (1964a), shows the minimum stress achieved by the multidimensional scaling solution plotted against the number of dimensions employed for that solution. As recommended by Kruskal (1964a), a stress value of 20% would be considered as corresponding to a "poor" fit, 10% would indicate a "fair" fit, 5% a "good" one and 2.5% would correspond to an "excellent" fit. Also, as a general rule, both Shepard and Kruskal recommend that the choice of dimensionality for the scaling solution be based on the location of an "elbow" on a plot such as the one in Fig. 3b. Thus, one might feel that a choice of $p = 2$ in this example would, from the point of view of the index of achievement, be between fair and poor, and if not the value of 5 for p, one should at least consider the value 3.

However, the two-dimensional solution obtained and interpreted by Shepard (1963) is shown in Fig. 3c. The vertical axis in this solution is seen to cor-

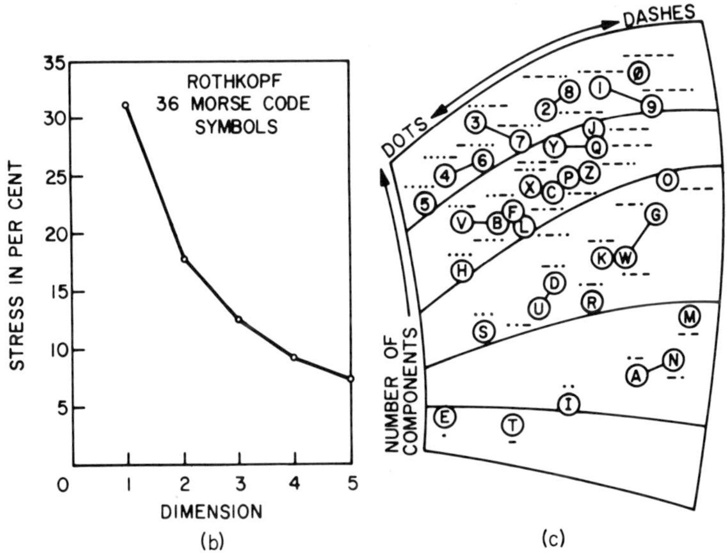

Fig. 3b, c. Multidimensional scaling example (Shepard, 1963; Kruskal, 1964).

respond to the number of components in the Morse code symbol (i.e., the total number of dots and dashes) while the horizontal axis characterizes the composition of the symbol (i.e., the ratio of the number of dots to the number of dashes). As Kruskal (1964a) points out, the fact that Shepard could not extract additional interpretable structure by going to three dimensions would suggest that $p = 2$ instead of $p = 3$ would be a better choice for this problem regardless of any contraindication from Fig. 3b. Interpretability and simplicity are important in data analysis and any rigid inference of optimal dimensionality, in the light of the observed values of a numerical index of goodness-of-fit, may not be productive.

2.4. Nonlinear Singularities

The problem of reduction in dimensionality concerns the recognition of lower dimensional, possibly nonlinear, subspaces near which the multiresponse observations may, statistically speaking, lie. This is, of course, not a well defined concept—but then neither is the notion of "fitting a curve" to a scatter plot of y against x.

The difficulties in the problem are mainly due to the fact that in the analysis of high-dimensional data, there are not available the informal, mainly graphical, internal comparisons procedures—such as scatter plots—which guide so much of single-response, and some two-response, data analysis.

So far as near-linear singularities in a body of data are concerned, these may be statistically indicated by principal components analysis (but see Section 6.6 for further discussion of possible effects of outliers). However, nonlinear singularities will not necessarily be indicated by principal components, and one might not be able to infer their existence even from all possible two-dimensional scatter plot representations of the data.

Example 4. The C-shaped configuration shown in Fig. 4a, is an oversimplified example of data configurations which may not be revealed by

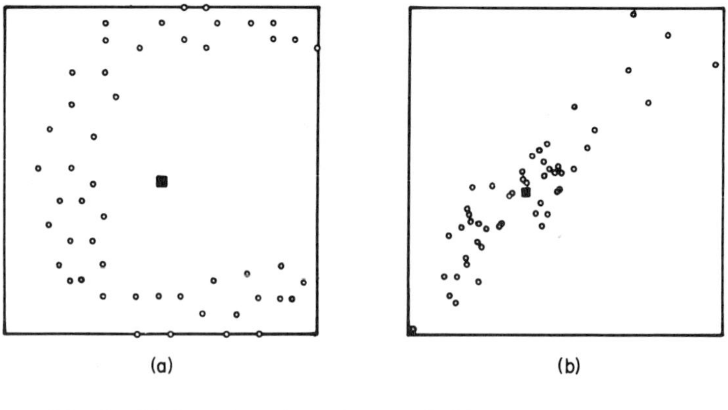

(a) (b)

Fig. 4. (a) Curved configuration and (b) bivariate normal scatter.

classical linear principal components analysis. Clearly, the three-dimensional analogue of this, namely a cup-shaped configuration of data, might not be revealed even by a combination of principal components analysis in three-space and two-dimensional marginal scatter plots. Example 5 discusses such an example.

Figure 4b is a plot of fifty computer-generated random bivariate normal samples with an underlying positive correlation coefficient. This is, therefore, an example of typical normal distributional scatter when $p = 2$.

The filled-in squares in Figs. 4a and 4b are the centers of gravity of the data.

One elementary technique for detecting the existence of curved configurations, such as the one considered in Example 4, involves the computation of the squared generalized distances (using the inverse of the sample covariance matrix) of each point from the center of gravity. For a typical multivariate normal scatter (cf. Fig. 4b), either throughout p dimensions or mainly on a linear subspace, these distances will have approximately a gamma distribution and on an appropriately selected gamma probability plot (Wilk *et al.*, 1962a), using shape parameter values in the neighborhood of $p/2$, they will tend to show as a linear configuration oriented toward the origin. But for curved singularity, such as the illustration, it is clear that there will be a deficiency of small distances. This will show on the gamma plot by the configuration being oriented toward a nonzero intercept at the "small" end.

Example 5. The following simulated three-dimensional example illustrates some of these ideas and procedures. Sixty-one triads were obtained by appending a standard normal deviate to each of the coordinates of points on the surface of a specified paraboloid. The array of data so obtained is given in Fig. 5a. Figures 5b–5d show the three different two-dimensional marginal scatter plots of these data. None of these data displays is suggestive of the observations in three dimensions lying "near" a curved subspace.

The inverse of the sample covariance matrix, **S**, of these observations was employed to compute the generalized squared distance of each of the 61 points from their centroid. A gamma probability plot of the ordered squared distances is shown in Fig. 5e. The value of the shape parameter used for this plot was $\eta = 3/2$.

The configuration which has a nonzero intercept shows clearly the "deficiency" of small values, indicating a "hole" in the data. Investigation of the nature of the indicated peculiarity may be pursued further by using the methods discussed below.

This simple-minded idea, of course, will not be indicative when the surface has several bends, such as a sinusoidal shape. Furthermore, if a peculiarity is indicated, the probability plot does not tell very much about its nature.

Some recent work of the present authors, useful for the analysis of multi-

-2.732	6.557	25.507	-3.452	2.948	25.591
-5.264	5.253	24.200	-7.261	6.959	26.789
-5.103	5.986	26.446	-2.370	3.617	25.510
-3.335	5.888	23.947	-4.181	4.530	29.118
-5.420	5.607	25.321	-2.360	3.916	24.879
-3.261	7.697	27.479	-5.297	5.802	29.073
-4.607	6.651	26.518	-1.585	2.524	26.954
-4.236	4.220	24.416	-3.267	4.402	28.899
-4.947	5.363	26.918	-1.187	3.257	26.100
-2.189	5.881	26.282	-2.095	6.931	27.269
-2.913	5.953	26.962	-4.800	3.339	27.011
-4.838	5.909	25.196	-5.602	5.322	28.759
-3.448	5.610	27.489	-1.478	1.644	26.057
-0.990	5.391	25.667	-5.151	4.481	27.583
-6.116	6.326	30.189	-0.694	3.408	24.997
-2.715	4.645	25.613	-5.687	4.766	29.640
-5.849	6.876	26.070	-1.733	3.932	26.198
0.162	5.521	25.027	-6.154	4.932	29.631
-5.360	5.494	28.675	-3.823	3.784	25.123
-1.740	4.070	27.311	-2.588	4.923	28.343
-2.975	6.716	27.999	-3.237	3.648	26.249
-4.220	3.853	26.396	-5.740	4.537	30.277
-6.306	4.573	25.715	-0.709	1.542	27.240
-1.972	5.615	24.900	-6.568	5.335	29.631
-4.497	5.314	27.978	-1.669	1.501	25.413
-2.005	3.352	24.599	-7.690	4.578	30.863
-3.809	5.421	28.794	0.837	1.271	25.303
-2.081	3.795	25.542	-5.832	7.020	28.915
-4.907	7.120	27.449	-0.405	3.669	27.587
-0.742	2.800	26.394	-3.019	3.752	29.665
-2.750	2.233	27.669			

Fig. 5a. Table of data.

dimensional linear or nonlinear singularities, constitutes a generalization of classical linear principal components analysis.

If one has near-linear singularity of the data, what one wishes to do is to determine that linear coordinate system which is most nearly in concordance with the data configuration. Then, the expression of the data in the new coordinate system is simpler in that the effective description can be given by use of fewer coordinates. This is accomplished by linear principal components analysis.

If one has near-nonlinear singularity of the data, what one wishes to do is to determine that *nonlinear* coordinate system which is most nearly in agreement with the data configuration, just as in the linear case. Given a class of possible nonlinear coordinates, the task is to select that one along which the data variance is maximum, then obtain another, uncorrelated with the first, along which the variance is next largest, and so on. For any class of coordinates which consists of an unspecified linear combination of arbitrary *functions* of the original coordinates, the solution to this problem is simply an enlarged eigenvalue-eigenvector problem. The following trivial two-dimensional artificial examples provide illustrations.

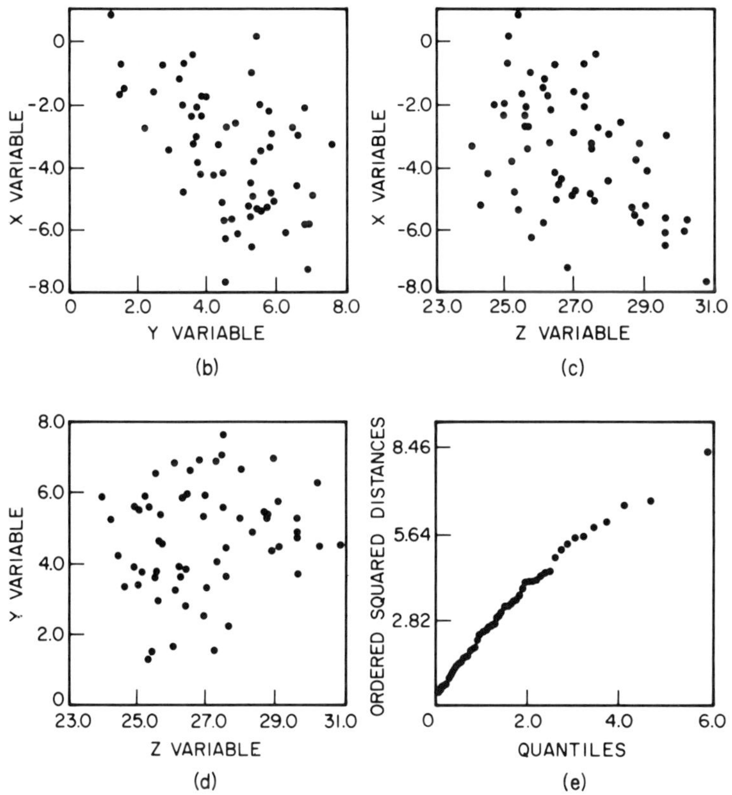

Fig. 5b–e. Cup shaped data with noise. (e) Gamma plot of generalized squared distances ($N = 61, \eta = 1.5$).

Example 6. The data consisted of 41 points lying on the parabola, $Y_2 = 2 + 4Y_1 + 4Y_1^2$, with $Y_1 = -1.5(0.05)0.5$. A quadratic principal components analysis was applied to this data and the dimension of the enlarged eigenvalue problem was, therefore, $2p + \frac{1}{2}[p(p-1)] = 5$ since $p = 2$. The resulting eigenvalues and eigenvectors are shown in Fig. 6a. The largest eigenvalue is seen to be over 2000 while the smallest which is "known" to be zero is computed as 9×10^{-6}.

Each eigenvector provides a nonlinear (quadratic in this case) coordinate in

CHARACTERISTIC ROOTS

2163.634	219.915	2.258	2.223	0.000009

CHARACTERISTIC VECTORS

−.002513	.246077	.508757	−.442445	.696310
.169321	.011882	.758811	.604229	−.174076
−.094253	.932909	−.212548	.274991	.0000004
.044843	−.243106	.319056	.593499	.696311
.980015	.099425	−.135640	−.106239	.0000003

(a)

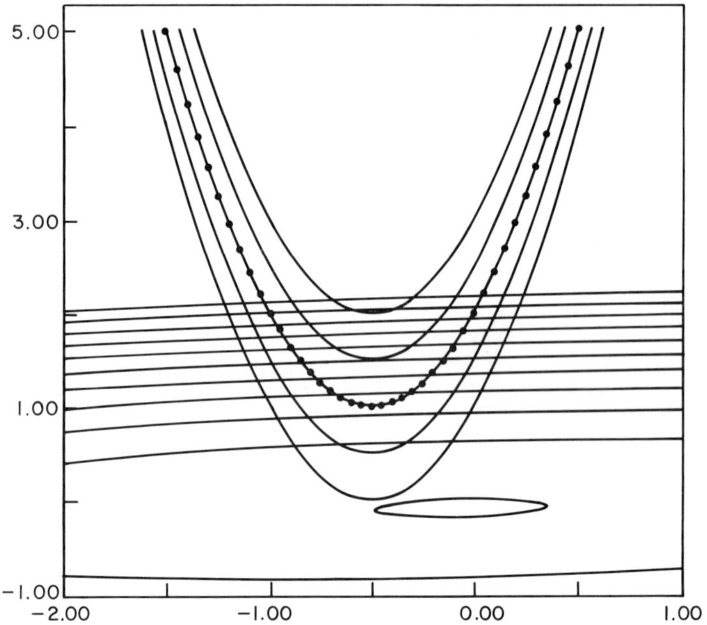

(b)

Fig. 6. Generalized principal components for nonlinear singularities. (a) Eigenanalysis; (b) coordinates from the largest and smallest eigenvalues.

the original space, and Fig. 6b shows the coordinates determined by the eigenvectors corresponding to the smallest and largest of the five eigenvalues. The parabolic corodinate is from the smallest eigenvalue and the flat elliptic coordinate is from the largest. In the absence of statistical errors in the data, one of the parabolas (viz., the middle one) passes exactly through the points.

Example 7. The effect of "error" on the technique is indicated by modifying the data of Example 6 by adding $N(0, 1/16)$ random components to each of the two coordinates of each point. The results of an eigenanalysis, comparable to the one in Example 6, are shown in Fig. 7a. It is seen that, while the largest eigenvalue is still about 2000, the smallest one is now 1.081. Figure 7b shows the data and the quadratic coordinates defined by the eigenvectors

CHARACTERISTIC ROOTS

1969.563	285.938	5.717	2.034	1.081

CHARACTERISTIC VECTORS

−.010915	.260105	−.269383	.610264	.698023
.172863	.012363	.189273	.761768	−.594853
−.106665	.930317	.301394	−.146763	−.103707
.062983	−.230187	.892766	.062053	.377047
.977064	.117118	−.061142	−.147978	.077413

(a)

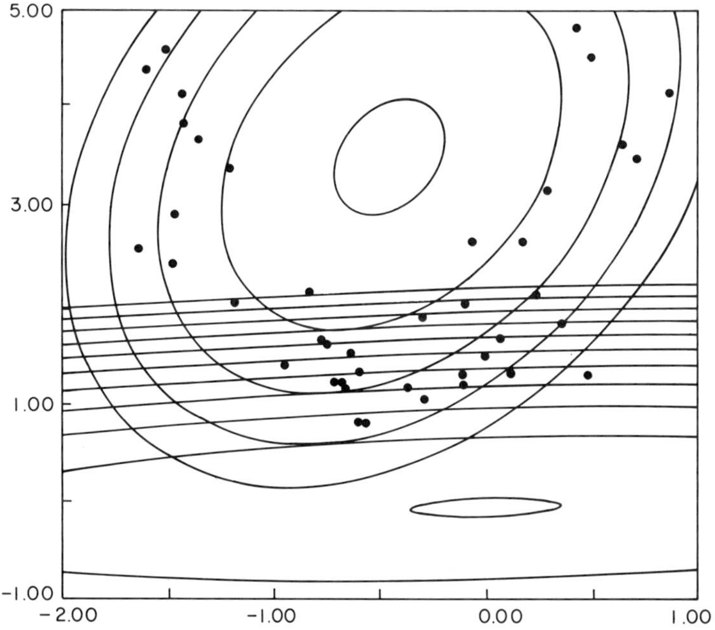

(b)

Fig. 7. Generalized principal components for nonlinear singularities. (a) Eigenanalysis; (b) coordinates from the largest and smallest eigenvalues.

corresponding to the smallest and largest eigenvalues. The smallest eigenvalue now leads to an elliptical coordinate system due to the influence of the statistical errors.

The illustration of the technique of generalized principal components in this example and in the preceding one is trivial since $p = 2$ for both cases. With $p = 3$, more interesting possibilities begin to arise since the points may then lie on ($q =$) 1- or 2-dimensional curved subspaces. Example 8 below is a case with $p = 3$ and $q = 2$. The purpose of Examples 6 and 7 is to illustrate the basic concept of nonlinear coordinate transformations and the analytical and algorithmic aspects of the method which, of course, are valid for any value of p. The method is not crucial for two- or three-dimensional problems which lend themselves to graphical representation and study.

With the above formulation in terms of eigenvectors, there is a unity among all proposed classes of coordinate systems which involve a linear combination of functions of the given response coordinates. However, to see the problem of nonlinear singularities in a broader context of nonlinear coordinate systems, one can formulate the question in function-fitting terms. Thus, in the linear case, the eigenvector corresponding to the smallest eigenvalue essentially determines a plane of closest fit, where closeness is measured by the sum of squares of perpendicular distances. The next eigenvector then gives the next closest fit among all planes orthogonal to the first, and so on. This, indeed, was Karl Pearson's (1901) formulation leading to the linear principal components.

In the same vein, the generalization of principal components described above may be viewed as the process of finding the specific member of the class of coordinates considered (limited to linear combinations of functions of the response variables) which is closest to the observed points; then determining the next closest member among those uncorrelated with the first, and so on.

Example 8. The data, shown in Fig. 8a, consists of nineteen points lying on the surface of the sphere, $X^2 + Y^2 + Z^2 = 25$. Thus, in this example, $p = 3$ and $q = 2$.

A quadratic principal components analysis, involving an eigenanalysis of dimension 9, yields the eigenvalues and eigenvectors shown in Fig. 8b. The largest eigenvalue is seen to be about 121 while the smallest, which in the absence of "noise" in the data is zero, was computed to be less in value than 10^{-7} and hence shown as being zero. Also shown at the bottom of Fig. 8b is the equation of the sphere on which the data lie as determined by the eigenvector for the zero (smallest) eigenvalue. With the error-free data, the original sphere is recovered. Since $p = 3$, it is possible to represent stereoscopically the data of this example and the fitted sphere, in a three-dimensional display,

X	Y	Z
-5.0	0.0	0.0
-4.0	1.0	±2.828
-3.0	0.5	±3.969
-2.0	4.0	±2.236
-1.0	0.0	±4.899
0.0	3.0	±4.000
1.0	2.0	±4.472
2.0	4.0	±2.236
3.0	3.3	±2.261
4.0	2.4	±1.800

Fig. 8a. Table of data.

EIGENVALUES

120.6	110.3	46.7	7.9	3.5	.99	.012	.0001	.0000

EIGENVECTORS

-.0144	.2475	.1644	.1978	-.0947	.8889	.2650	-.0555	.0000
-.0126	.1277	-.1095	.0302	-.1039	.1724	-.5201	.8121	-.0001
.1282	.0041	.0460	.0601	-.1108	.1694	-.7941	-.5534	.0001
-.2107	.3401	.5415	.6013	-.2455	-.3520	-.0153	.0274	-.0000
-.2381	.5366	.3906	-.6238	.3219	-.0262	-.0932	-.0251	.0000
.0811	.3229	-.2310	-.3379	-.8312	-.1004	.1225	-.0747	.0000
-.6309	-.4115	.1335	-.1401	-.2210	.1023	-.0510	-.0045	.5774
-.0578	.4891	-.5320	.2461	.2516	-.0749	.0048	-.1075	.5774
.6886	-.0776	.3985	-.1061	-.0306	-.0274	.0462	.1121	.5773

Equation obtained by GPCA

$$0.577x^2 + 0.577y^2 + 0.577z^2 = 14.4$$

Fig. 8b. Eigenanalysis for GPC.

which can be obtained by using current capabilities in computer software and graphical aids.

In utilizing polynomial principal components, such as the quadratic one illustrated in Examples 6–8, the hope is that these will respond to local nonlinearities. For a problem in p-space, a quadratic principal components analysis will involve the eigenvector solution for a $(2p + \frac{1}{2}[p(p-1)])$-dimensional matrix, so that a nontrivial solution could be obtained only if $n > 2p + \frac{1}{2}[p(p-1)]$; thus for $p = 8$, n must exceed 44.

The magnitude of the eigenvector computation grows rapidly both with the degree of the polynomial coordinate system considered and with the dimension of the response. Thus, using a cubic coordinate system with $p = 5$ would require $n > 55$.

One advantage of viewing generalized principal components analysis in the framework of function fitting is that the latter area is one that has received considerable attention in statistics, both conceptually and methodologically, under categories such as linear and nonlinear regression. The available methodology of these familiar areas may be relevant for further extending the usefulness of the generalized principal components approach. For instance, with a projected class of coordinates which involves arbitrary functions of the response variables, with some unspecified coefficients which may occur *nonlinearly*, the mathematical problem is still just that of finding members of the class which give the closest fit, and nonlinear-fitting ideas and procedures may prove useful. The eigenvector algorithms used earlier cannot be applied simply to yield the solution although one might apply them iteratively to develop a solution.

3. MULTIVARIATE RELATIONSHIPS

3.1. General

One may distinguish among multivariate relationships as between dependencies involving only the multivariate responses and dependencies of the response vector on extraneous design or regression variables.

3.2. Internal Dependencies

The recognition or description of internal dependencies overlaps in obvious ways with both the objectives and techniques discussed under reduction of dimensionality. The familiar techniques of partial and multiple correlation analysis are also relevant in this area. A pictorial technique of displaying association, which can at times be useful, has been discussed by Anderson (1960) under the name *Glyphs*.

3.3. Relation to Extraneous Variables

The classical technique for investigating and specifying dependence of multiresponse observations on design characteristics or extraneous variables is so-called multivariate multiple regression. The usual descriptions involve the separate regressions of each of the multivariate responses on a common design matrix, yielding a matrix of regression coefficients having certain joint statistical properties.

Extensions of this basic fitting procedure are possible though they have not received much attention. For instance, one might carry out fitting for the various responses in terms of partially similar design matrices, so that some but not all the regression coefficients would be of the same nature. However, the general problems of joint interpretation of these descriptive relationships are very difficult even in the simple case, and hence it is not surprising that little emphasis has gone into more general formulations. Discussion of some generalizations is given by Roy *et al.* (1968).

Perhaps the most important issue in adapting a multivariate view in multiresponse regression situations, whether or not with a common design matrix, is the recognition that the estimated regression coefficients may be statistically dependent because of the intercorrelations of the responses. Such a recognition may play an important role in the subsequent analysis and interpretation of the results. This is illustrated in an example in Section 6.3, taken from Wilk and Gnanadesikan (1964).

Canonical correlation, developed by Hotelling (1936), is another classical technique of developing relations between two sets of variables. Given a set of variables, **Y**, and another set, **X**, the basic idea is to find the two linear combinations, one of the Y-variables and one of the X-variables, which have maximal correlation; then among the two sets of linear combinations orthogonal to those already determined, to select those of maximal correlation, and so on.

The algorithms for determining the canonical correlations and variates involve eigenvalues and eigenvectors of matrices derived from the partitioned covariance matrix of the combined set of variables.

The canonical correlations indicate the interdependence of the pairs of canonical variates. The interest in such analyses usually focuses on the nature of the canonical variates. These may be of use as a preliminary to classification or as a stimulus to insight toward better or simpler coordinates or variables.

A useful analytic device is to represent the observations in terms of their canonical variate values and to show these graphically in a scatter plot of the pairs of canonical variates. This displays the canonical correlations while permitting the possible existence of aberrant values or peculiar relationships to exhibit themselves.

Example 9. The use of the pairwise canonical variate plots is illustrated with data from a questionnaire study, which was concerned with assessing employees' readership and attitudes toward one of the internal general informational publications of their company.

Figure 9a shows a plot for the two canonical variates corresponding to the largest canonical correlation, derived from the answers of 645 employees to two subsets consisting of four questions each. One subset consisted of four questions pertaining to the expectations of the respondent regarding the publication while the other subset was concerned with his evaluation of the actual performance of the publication. Each of the eight questions was answered on a six-point scale and, as indicated on Fig. 9a, the observed largest canonical correlation was 0.4023. The striking features about the configuration are the "bunching" of points on the right-hand boundary of, and the vertical striations evidenced in, the plot. A subsequent inspection of the data, stimulated by these indications of peculiarities, revealed that a large proportion of the respondents tended to use only the higher values of their six-point scale when dealing with their expectations and only the middle values of the scale when it came to evaluating the performance of the publication. Such tendencies would lead to the peculiarities indicated in the plot of canonical variates although one could detect their existence by other methods of displaying the data as well.

Figure 9b shows a plot derived from a canonical correlation analysis of two other subsets of questions in the same study. Each subset consisted of fourteen

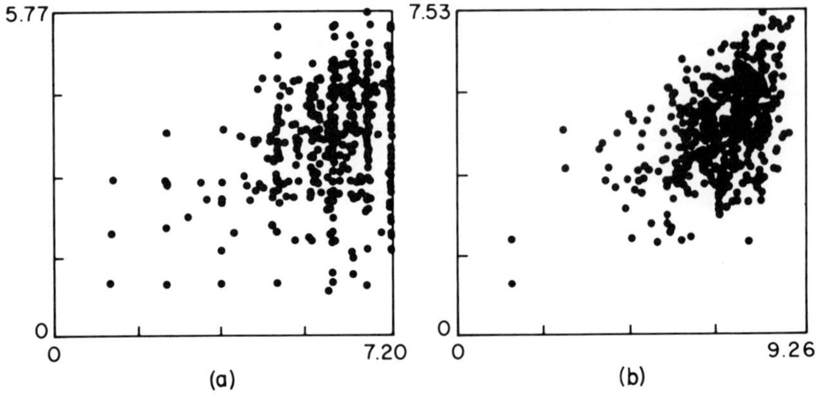

Fig. 9. Pairwise plot of canonical variates. (a) Canonical correlation = 0.4023, $N = 645$, $p_1 = 4$, $p_2 = 4$; (b) canonical correlation = 0.4833, $N = 580$, $p_1 = 14$, $p_2 = 14$.

questions and answers from 580 respondents were used in the analysis. The observed value of the largest canonical correlation was 0.4833. The configuration suggests possible asymmetry in, and departure from normality of, the joint distribution of the canonical variates, with the scatter of the points appearing to be bounded above by a straight line parallel to a "diagonal line" drawn through the configuration. There is also a mild suggestion of two outliers in the lower left-hand corner of the plot.

3.4. Factor Analysis

One model underlying factor analysis is the joint linear dependence of the responses on a set of so-called factors, fewer in number than the dimensionality of response. If these factors were directly observed, then this model would simply be a multivariate multiple regression model. The difficulty is that these postulated factors are neither known nor measurable directly and must be inferred in some way from the responses themselves.

A wide variety of algorithms exist for performing factor analysis. Several examples of use of factor analysis in analyzing data have been published with varying amounts of success in such issues as interpretability or simplicity. A comprehensive discussion of concepts and methods of factor analysis is given by Harman (1967).

4. MULTIDIMENSIONAL CLASSIFICATION

4.1. General Types of Problems

Classification is a broad area with many varieties of interests, objectives, and concepts—many not tightly defined. Loosely speaking, the concern is with categorization—either with respect to a known structure or to infer a structure. Typically such problems are multidimensional in their primitive form.

Perhaps the simplest guise of the classification problem is the situation in which one wishes to make a binary choice—either this item belongs or it does not. An extension of this is the problem of classification into one of several categories or identification with one of several species. Sometimes the problem is one of finding meaningful groupings of objects based on observed multiresponse properties, i.e., the definition of clusters or groups from a body of data.

Distinctions will usually exist in regard to the kind and amount of background information in individual problems. For example, given a set of fingerprints of some unknown person, it is one problem to check on whether they do or do not correspond to a specific individual. It is quite another problem to attempt to determine to which one, if any, of a large population of alternative possibilities the unknown might correspond. Clearly, the strategy of the procedures may differ. Indeed, the characteristics used may be quite dissimilar.

From a data analytic view, the main problems of classification do not appear to be ones of optimal decision strategy given a space and a set of statistical assumptions regarding the observations. Those issues seem to be quite secondary relative to the challenges of appropriately formulating the problem, or of choosing an effective space for discrimination. Like most scientific problems, this one is iterative in nature.

The primitive input to many classification problems is often of unwieldy character or magnitude. For instance, in one approach to the problem of identification of talkers on the basis of speech spectrogram records, the basic input from a single utterance of a word is an approximately 15,000-dimensional observation, classified in a 57×275 matrix. For elementary practical reasons, this is beyond direct use in classification. Moreover, it is inefficient in terms of performance to use the 15,000-dimensional space for discrimination, because many of its coordinates are just "noise." Here redundancy is inherent, but it is not obvious where it is or how to deal with it. The primary task is to find an effective condensation to a discrimination space of dimension at least two orders of magnitude smaller. In the work of the present authors on this problem, no usable subject matter was available for guidance, and the approach has been empirical, guided by internal analysis of the data. Effective representations have been obtained in 20 dimensions.

4.2. Basic Role of a Distance Measure

Given a discrimination space, the fundamental issue in classification comes down to choosing a measure of distance to be used. Theoretical formulations have, by and large, been confined to the derivation of specific distance measures to satisfy narrowly defined optimality criteria under a body of assumptions, which are usually beyond empirical check by the data on hand. For instance, the optimal Bayes discriminant function minimizes expected loss, using prior probabilities, as well as other distributional assumptions.

From the point of view of data analysis, the prescription of a distance function will generally be a trial and error task in which the use of some general techniques needs to be aided by insight, intuition, and good luck.

Fisher (1938) defined the so-called discriminant function as that linear combination of a multiple response which shows the greatest ratio of variance between two groups to that within the groups. A generalization of this to the case of several groups is described by Rao (1952).

The general formulation leads to determining the eigenvalues and eigenvectors of $\mathbf{W}^{-1}\mathbf{B}$, where $\mathbf{B}$ is the sample covariance matrix among group means, and $\mathbf{W}$ is the pooled covariance matrix within groups. In general, if there are g groups and the problem is p-dimensional, then the number of positive eigenvalues will be a number, k, equal to the smaller of $(g - 1)$ and p. This is a consequence of the fact that if g is less than p, then the g group means are contained in a $(g - 1)$-dimensional hyperplane.

The eigenvectors associated with the k positive eigenvalues define a space within which the original observations may be represented. Any subset of these eigenvectors may be used to determine a distance for classification purposes. Thus, for example, one might choose to use the space spanned by the two "largest" eigenvectors of $\mathbf{W}^{-1}\mathbf{B}$ and to employ Euclidean distance for classification. If one uses the entire set of k eigenvector coordinates in this way, the resulting distance measure is equivalent to using a quadratic form in the original p-variate space with $\mathbf{W}^{-1}$, as its matrix. Using more or less of the k eigenvectors in classification may or may not be an improvement.

Using generalized distance, i.e., quadratic forms whose compounding matrix is $\mathbf{W}^{-1}$, has the merit of conceptual geometric simplicity, avoidance of eigenvector computations and of transformation to an unfamiliar space, and it may perform as well as any subset of the k eigenvectors. On the other hand, the computation of the eigenvectors may lead to reduction in dimensionality of the problem, perhaps some insight and, sometimes, using a subset might improve the classification process.

One form of the classification process may be roughly phrased as follows: Given g group locations and an unknown, u, associate u with that center to which it is nearest in terms of some distance measure. However, in some situations, there may be an arbitrary change in the observed vector, for artifactual reasons, from observation to observation on the same individual. Then a modified view of the above classification problem is in order. For example, in repeated utterances of a word by the same talker, the general level of the jointly observed energies may shift because of changed proximity to the microphone. Thus, one observation may lead to the vector, $\mathbf{x}$, and the next to $\mathbf{x} + \mathbf{c}$, where all the components of the vector, $\mathbf{c}$, are equal but unknown. When such possibilities exist, it is no longer wise or proper to classify the unknown with the group to whose center it is closest. Now, each group is represented, in concept, not by a point, but by the line joining the group center, $\mathbf{x}$, and the point, $\mathbf{x} + \mathbf{c}$, for any $\mathbf{c}$. The proper classification is then in terms of shortest generalized distance to such lines. A version of this problem has been considered by Burnaby (1966) and by Rao (1966).

Similarly, one may need to allow for possible joint scale change, or even higher order change, affecting all the coordinates of the multiresponse vector identically. If both scale and origin are artifactual, then each group is defined as a plane and classification is in terms of shortest generalized distances to these group planes.

The problem may be cast in a more familiar and suggestive form. In place of regarding a group location as a point in p-space, consider marking each of its individual coordinate values on a line, to be used as abscissa. Using the corresponding coordinates of the unknown as ordinates, one can now make a scatter plot. Clearly, perfect correspondence would lead to a linear configuration with unit slope and passing through the origin. If the unknown is a member of the group, one expects a good linear configuration and indeed, the appropriate quadratic form in the residuals of the observations, from the line of slope 1 through the origin, is just the generalized distance in the p-dimensional space between the unknown, u, and the group location.

A joint additive shift and common scale change would show as a nonzero intercept and a slope not equal to unity. The classification would now be based on the minimum residual quadratic form from the generalized linear least-squares regression of the coordinates of the unknown on those of the centroid of the proposed group.

Example 10. The approach is illustrated by application to data from the talker-identification problem. One summary employed in this problem consisted of a 57-dimensional vector of energies for characterizing each utterance of a given word by each talker.

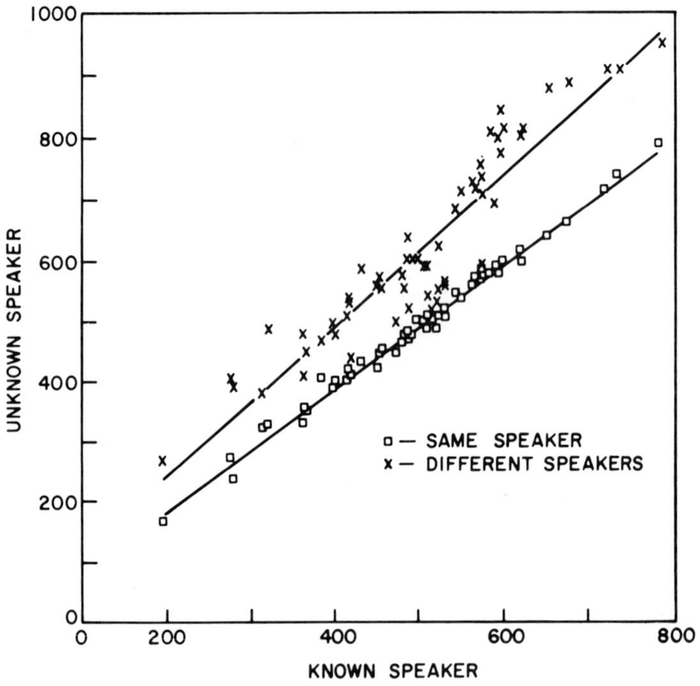

Fig. 10. Linear regression of unknown versus known; SSRES for same is 8257.9; SSRES for different is 180747.

Figure 10 shows a scatter plot of the values of the 57 components for two "unknown" utterances of a word against their corresponding values in the average of four "known" utterances of the same word by a specific talker. One of the unknowns was chosen from the same talker and the points for this are shown as squares, while the other was from another talker and the corresponding points are shown in Fig. 10 as asterisks. Also shown in Fig. 10 are the least-squares linear fits to the two sets of points.

The existence, in this data, of shift and scale artifacts of the type discussed above is evident in this plot. The configuration of the squares, while quite linear, has both a nonzero intercept and a slope smaller than unity. The configuration of the asterisks exhibits poor linearity, with considerably more scatter about the linear fit. A comparison of the two configurations suggests the possible utility of a classification procedure based on a quadratic form in the residuals from a linear least-squares fit. In the present example, the sums of squares of the residuals, for instance, turn out to be about 8260 for the configuration of the squares and over 18,000 for that of the asterisks.

This approach has a number of attractions. First, it involves familiar regression ideas. Second, it permits a graphical representation. Third, largely as a consequence of the second point, the procedure enables the use of a flexible internal comparisons process, in that the data itself may help to suggest the nature of the possible corrections which may be desirable, such as the detection of coordinate outliers or the form of the regression which ought to be used.

In this approach, there can be additional methodological problems when *both* the covariance matrix and the regression function need to be estimated from the data. In that case, some iterative process is possible, if necessary. There are also problems of strategy and implementation.

4.3. Recognition of Groups

A complement of the kinds of classification problems discussed above is recognizing and constituting groups or clusters in a body of multiresponse data.

One graphical technique which may be tried is that of Glyphs [cf. Anderson (1960)]. Another technique which is often valuable in recognizing groups is to make scatter plots of the points using pairs of eigenvectors as coordinates. This technique is illustrated next by application to the talker-identification problem.

Example 11. This example, also pertaining to the talker-identification problem, involves data from 10 talkers each of whom repeated a given word 6 times, [cf. Becker *et al.* (1965)]. Figure 11 shows a two-dimensional representation of the 60 resultant utterances on coordinates which are obtained from the eigenvectors corresponding to the two largest eigenvalues of a $\mathbf{W}^{-1}\mathbf{B}$ matrix calculated from a 16-dimensional summary associated with each utterance. The utterances are labeled by the ten digits, 0 through 9, to correspond to the talker with whom they are known to be associated.

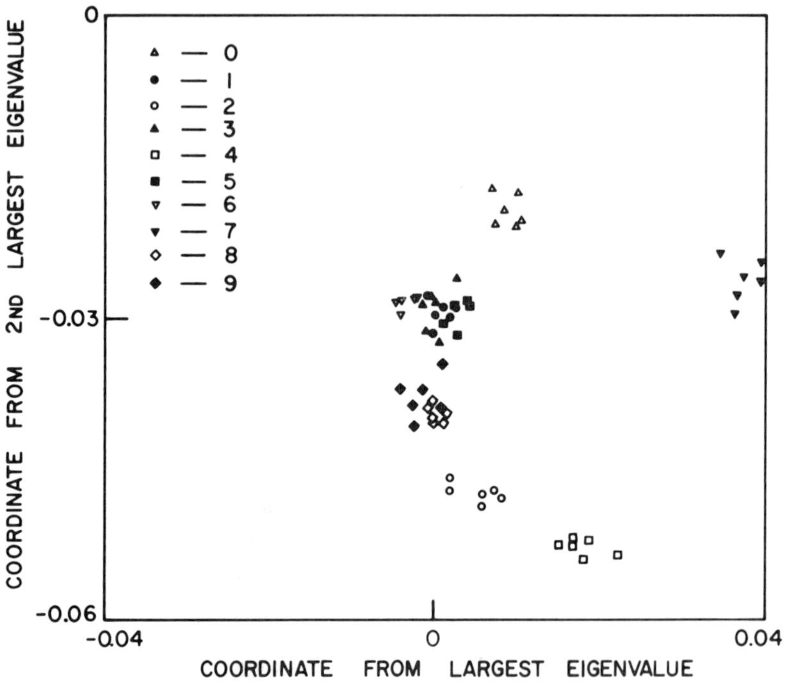

Fig. 11. Discriminant coordinates plot.

The clustering of the points in Fig. 11 corresponds generally to the known categorization of the utterances and indicates the clear separations of and among talkers 0, 2, 4, and 7, as well as the considerable overlap of talkers 1, 3, 5, and 6. Such plots are also useful for suggesting metrics for classification purposes and for indicating stray or outlying observations.

The grouping problem is currently receiving substantial attention under the general name of cluster analysis [see Ball (1965), Friedman and Rubin (1967), Johnson (1967), Neely (1967)]. In these techniques clusters are determined by the iterative seeking of neighborhoods defined in terms of some metric. [See Hartigan (1967) for a discussion of a method of clustering which does not involve a metric].

In addition to the choice of metric, the two main conceptual problems in most cluster-seeking techniques are the dimensionality of the space within which to define clusters, and the number of clusters one is to have. A major problem in implementation, reminiscent of stepwise and steered regression, is the development of practical algorithms for achieving solutions.

4.4. Control Techniques

Multivariable quality control is another form of the classification problem. A technique using the Hotelling T^2-statistic was suggested by Hotelling (1947) for use in quality control judgments. Jackson (1956) has suggested a bivariate graphical implementation of this with plotted points appearing in an elliptical frame defined by the Hotelling T^2-statistic.

5. ASSESSMENT OF MULTIVARIATE STATISTICAL MODELS

5.1. General

Formal multivariate statistical theory and methods have been mainly directed toward the assessment of specific aspects of a narrowly defined model. Typically, the multivariate procedures for assessment have developed by mathematical analogy with univariate models. The assessment of models is certainly a legitimate concern of statistical data analysis. However, multivariate problems are presumably ones that would benefit from a joint view of the responses. Such situations must, in general, be quite complex. It is far from clear that productive understanding of these complex problems will be aided by formal assessment of a narrow and tight model.

The complaint is not with the objective of assessing the adequacy of multivariate models, but rather with the limited viewpoint on, and utility of, the range of models which have been put forth as the focus for multivaıiate statistical methods and data analysis.

Since material in this area is well organized and accessible, what follows is just a quick overview of some standard aspects of multivariate model assessments.

5.2. Multivariate Analysis of Variance

The general multivariate linear model is a well-known example of an extension to multiresponse situations by analogy with the uniresponse case. Starting from such a mathematically analogous model, various theories and methods have been proposed of estimating the specific parameters that occur in the model and of testing linear hypotheses concerning them. The more classical of these theories are based, by and large, on a multivariate normal distributional assumption, either implicitly or explicitly. More recently some tests of a nonparametric nature, avoiding the normality assumption, have been put forth for the usual null hypotheses [cf. for example Puri and Sen (1966), Tamura (1966)]. These distribution-free procedures, being solely directed toward the objectives of testing a narrowly specified hypothesis, have the drawback of many nonparametric methods in that the statistics involved have little value as summaries of interesting structure of the data. Some recent work on robust estimation [e.g. Gentleman (1965)], on the other hand, is directed to achieving meaningful estimates with robust properties under certain kinds of departures from normality.

Features common to all of the above-mentioned approaches to multivariate analysis of variance are that their conceptualization and development depends on a few mathematically well-defined parameters and that the questions asked are rather narrow, formulated in terms of these parameters as problems of estimation or testing.

The problem of comparisons and assessments of treatment factors and their relationships, when the response is multivariate in character, is intrinsically complicated by the difficulty that there is, in general, no unique linear ordering for vectors. One method of approach is to associate a measure of size with each vector and make the assessments in terms of its values. Examples of this are Hotelling's T^2 (1931), Mahalanobis's D^2 (1930), Fisher's discriminant function (1938), and the use by the present authors of a quadratic form for internal comparisons among single-degree-of-freedom contrast vectors (Wilk and Gnanadesikan, 1961, 1964).

Another approach has been to attempt the reduction of dimensionality through the use of a transformation motivated by the data. As an extreme example of this, one can formally ignore the correlational structure of the responses; analyze the data separately in terms of each response; and, finally, intuitively integrate the conclusions arrived at from the separate analyses. A variant of this approach is initially to perform a principal components transformation and follow with uniresponse analyses of variance on each of the principal components which, in number of important ones from the standpoint of accounting for over-all variability in the data, will usually be fewer than the number of original responses. While this technique may be useful in some problems, it might be difficult to interpret the results.

The definition of treatment effects and interactions is, of course, multidimensional when multivariate responses are observed. For formal statistical assessments of the multidimensional treatment effects, various analogs of univariate procedures have been proposed.

Perhaps the area that has received most attention is that of tests of significance of the null hypothesis of no effects against the completely general alternative. Apart from questions of the real value of such tests, there are other complexities that arise. If one takes invariance under nonsingular linear transformations as a necessary characteristic, one is led to tests that depend on the roots of certain determinantal equations. Among procedures which have been suggested are: (i) the likelihood-ratio test, based on the product of the roots of a determinantal equation (Wilks, 1932); (ii) the sum-of-the-roots test (Lawley, 1938; Hotelling, 1947); (iii) the largest-root test (Roy, 1939); and (iv) the combined consideration of the smallest and largest roots (Tukey, 1949). Usable distribution theory, under the null hypothesis, is available for the largest-root test (Roy, 1945) and for some particular cases of the likelihood-ratio test and the sum-of-the-roots test [see Anderson (1958)]. Asymptotic distribution theory is available both for the likelihood-ratio test and the sum-of-the-roots test [see Anderson (1958), Schatzoff (1966)]. Some tabulations of percentage points for these tests of significance are given by Anderson (1958), Heck (1960), Pillai (1960), and Schatzoff (1966).

Some fragmentary and preliminary work has been done on criteria for choice, in particular cases, among these characteristic-root test procedures [see for example Das Gupta *et al.* (1964), Mikhail (1965), Pillai and Jayachandran (1967), Roy *et al.* (1968)]. The present state of knowledge concerning the operating characteristics of the various test procedures proposed is not sufficiently detailed to be of use in choosing among them for a specific application.

The statistics that are used for multivariate tests are complex derivatives from the data and do not generally have significant value as summaries of informational content. It would, therefore, be useful to generate data with underlying structure and to study the utility of the different multiresponse test statistics for uncovering such structures. Preliminary results from such a Monte Carlo approach indicate that the use of several criteria is important for gaining different insights into a body of multiresponse data (Roy *et al.*, 1968).

Procedures for formal confidence estimation and multivariate multiple comparisons have been proposed [see Krishnaiah (1965), Roy and Gnanadesikan (1957), Roy *et al.* (1968)].

A class of "step-down" procedures, including confidence estimation and tests of significance, has been proposed by Roy (1958) and by Dempster (1963). These techniques involve consideration of the marginal behavior of one of the responses taken together with a hierarchical sequence of conditional behaviors of each of the other responses. Conclusions drawn may depend on the order of consideration of the responses, and fruitful areas of application are those where a meaningful order for the responses exists, for example, successive measurements in a learning process. The step-down procedures require only univariate mathematical results.

In the multiresponse case, one can have a situation in which the number of responses exceeds the number of degrees of freedom available for the estimation of error and, for the two-sample location hypothesis in this high-dimensional case, Dempster (1958) has proposed a test.

In summary, when the data is multiresponse in character, what is available by way of statistical techniques for the assessment of models is very limited even from the standpoint of theory and more so from the standpoint of practice.

6. SUMMARIZATION AND EXPOSURE

6.1. General

The main business of statistical data analysis is the description and communication of the informational content of a body of data. This process requires summarization—perhaps in terms of a simple graph or perhaps using a complex mathematical model. The process also requires exposure—the presentation of the data in such a way as to facilitate the assessment of the summarization and to aid detection of the unanticipated. A simple example of this two-pronged process is that of fitting a straight line to y versus x data and plotting the residuals in a variety of ways—against x, against y, perhaps against values of some extraneous variable such as time, and probability plotting the residuals.

Such processes of data analysis are directed toward description, communication, development of insight, and toward detecting unanticipated as well as anticipated peculiarities. Even for the problem of assessing the adequacy of a very specific model, the essential features are to summarize the data in terms of the model and to expose what is left in some cogent way as an indicator of adequacy.

Though statistical and mathematical models, theories and ideas are of key importance in this process, one cannot expect that formal theories of inference can subsume the direction of this flexible and iterative process. Some further general discussion is given by Tukey and Wilk (1966).

Indeed, in the analysis of uniresponse data the actual usage made of many statistical methods does not closely correspond to their usual theoretical justification. Still, applied statisticians have managed to adapt these methods productively. The extension of formal uniresponse problems and theory to multiresponse situations, however, has not produced many methods which are directly adaptable in applied work, even for *ad hoc* purposes.

Some general problem areas of summarization and exposure can be distinguished, together with a few techniques. An attempt is now made to review these.

6.2. Study of an Unstructured Multiresponse Sample

In uniresponse data analysis, through one means or another, one is often interested in examining a body of data *as if* it were an unstructured collection or sample. In such cases, the class of techniques loosely called probability plotting methods can be very useful [see Wilk and Gnanadesikan (1968)].

For multiresponse data, there does not seem to be any extension of the usual uniresponse quantile versus quantile plots. Even more basically, there is no convenient graphical representation, for $p \geq 3$, of a multivariate histogram or empirical distribution function.

Still, some things *can* be done to give some insights into multivariate data distributions.

(1) Two-dimensional scatter plotting of the original data is a powerful tool for studying cohesiveness, separation within the sample, possible outliers and general shape. Presumably with direct interaction graphical display to be available in the near future, one could sweep through a series of various two-dimensional projections in addition to those on to the original coordinate planes.

Three-dimensional stereoscopic projections of multiresponse data may now be easily obtained, and there are also available techniques for viewing the rotation of such three-dimensional displays in real time.

In addition, one can also prepare movies of the three-dimensional stereoscopic projections of a rotating four-dimensional array of data.

(2) One-dimensional probability plotting of each original coordinate separately will generally be of use, in conjunction with other multivariate analyses. A natural base for such plotting will often be the normal distribution. Such plots may indicate the desirability of marginal transformations or of more insightful kinds of probability plots.

(3) Computation of linear or generalized principal components may aid in describing the data distribution, if in fact the observed points are re-expressed in the new coordinates and the representations with respect to each derived coordinate are treated as a one-dimensional sample. Then, probability plotting analyses may be applied to these derived samples.

(4) The use of one, or preferably several, distance functions to convert the multiresponse data to single numbers, followed by the probability plotting of these, can be very effective. A common useful class of distance functions is that of positive semidefinite quadratic forms, $\mathbf{x}'\mathbf{A}\mathbf{x}$, where the vector, $\mathbf{x}$, and matrix, $\mathbf{A}$, may both be some functions of the response vector, $\mathbf{y}$. Methodology for developing an estimated gamma probability plot for such an application has been suggested by Wilk and Gnanadesikan (1961, 1964).

(5) Another version of probability plotting for the multivariate case is the joint plotting of component order statistics, a technique which does not seem to have been considered heretofore. Specifically, one can form, from the multivariate sample, the separate marginal order statistics. One can now group the corresponding order statistics to define the coordinates of a set of points. Two- and three-dimensional projections of these points may be graphically

displayed. For any number of dimensions, further summary statistical analyses of these combined order statistics may be carried out by fitting that straight line to the points that minimizes the sum of squares of perpendicular deviations.

The motivation for this procedure is that if, in the original coordinate system, the marginal distributions are the same up to scale and origin parameters, then one would expect that, irrespective of correlations among the variates, the combined order statistics will produce a linear configuration. This then is a method for intercomparison of the distributions of the components of the multivariate observation, and this technique will be referred to as *component probability plotting*.

For the case of two variates, it is apparent that when there is perfect positive correlation, the component probability plot as defined above will be an exact linear configuration. As the correlation decreases the scatter about a linear configuration would be expected to increase. A convenient measure of such scatter is the minimum orthogonal sum of squares.

This procedure does not, of course, depend on any specific distributional assumptions. It is rather addressed to the assessment of the composite hypothesis that the marginal distributions are the same up to location and scale. Negative indication from this analysis may suggest the need for a nonlinear transformation on one or more of the coordinates. Experience with the technique indicates that it is relatively robust with respect to correlations among the components.

Example 12. Fifty random samples of a trivariate ($p = 3$) stochastic variable were generated. Two of the components were drawn from standard normal populations and the third was standard exponential. All three were statistically independent. The fifty triads were as follows: (−0.627, 0.035, 1.327), (0.472, −1.058, 0.506), (−0.665, 1.617, 0.854), (−0.817, −1.452, 1.025), (−1.899, 1.069, 0.178), (−0.161, −0.591, 0.721), (−0.119, 0.988, 2.193), (−0.472, 1.445, 1.240), (0.190, 0.599, 0.397), (−1.482, 0.260, 1.471), (−0.704, −0.318, 1.387), (−0.281, 0.803, 0.822), (−0.460, 1.011, 0.203), (−1.783, 0.594, 1.237), (−0.645, 0.053, 0.759), (−0.920, −0.203, 1.057), (1.843, −0.387, 0.005), (2.699, −2.010, 0.168), (−0.621, −0.787, 1.466), (−0.374, −1.708, 0.883), (−0.102, 1.009, 4.107), (0.151, 0.022, 0.423), (−2.318, 0.315, 0.069), (0.201, 0.388, 0.666), (0.663, −0.898, 0.502), (−1.192, −0.035, 1.777), (0.097, −0.602, 4.360), (−0.128, −0.611, 1.920), (0.603, 0.698, 1.646), (0.254, 0.899, 0.066), (0.206, −0.870, 3.066), (0.230, 0.149, 0.144), (0.057, −0.420, 0.582), (−1.278, 0.168, 1.415), (−0.462, −1.466, 1.808), (0.381, −0.451, 0.495), (0.290, 0.264, 0.510), (1.323, 1.453, 0.243), (−1.001, 0.122, 0.716), (−0.583, −1.134, 0.877), (1.919, 2.652, 0.134), (−0.681, −1.283, 2.915), (1.264, −1.169, 0.361), (−0.887, 0.368, 0.102),

(2.378, −0.048, 0.061), (−0.005, −1.581, 8.026), (−0.036, −2.215, 1.915), (0.564, −0.978, 0.301), (−1.563, 1.179, 0.104), (−1.477, −0.226, 0.969).

After forming the order statistics of each component separately, two-dimensional plots of the order statistics of one component against those of another (i.e., component probability plots) were made. The resulting three plots are shown in Figs. 12a, 12b, and 12c. Also shown on each plot is the line of fit which minimizes the orthogonal sum of squares. It is seen that Fig. 12a,

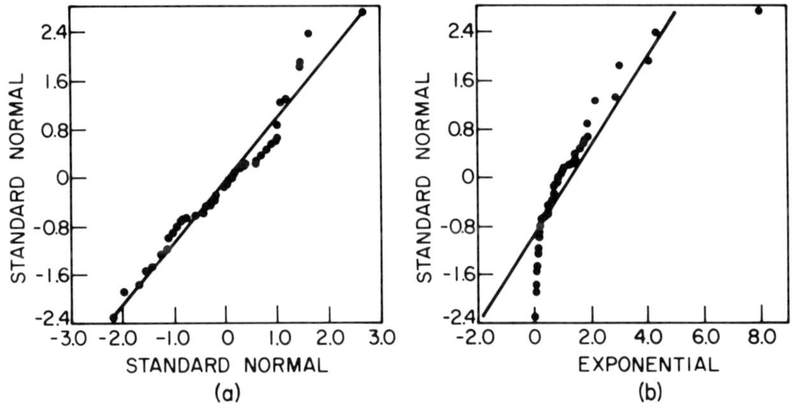

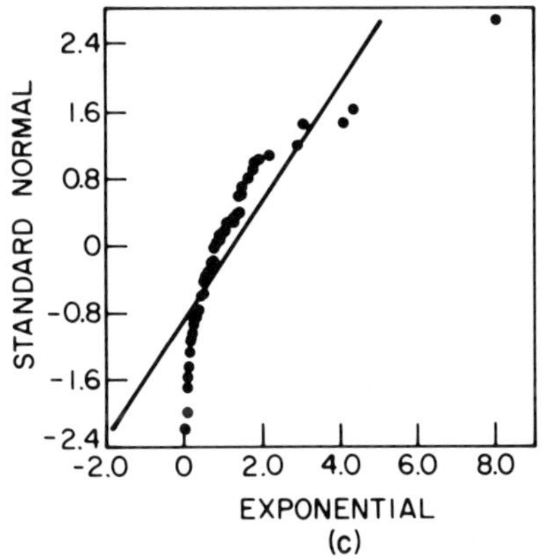

Fig. 12. Component probability plots. (a) Min. orthogonal SS = 0.022; (b) min. orthogonal SS = 0.162; (c) min. orthogonal SS = 0.207.

which derives from the two components with the same marginal distributions, exhibits a good linear configuration. Figures 12b and 12c, in which the two components do not have the same marginal distributions, exhibit considerable nonlinearity.

A graphical view of all three components jointly may be obtained by the use of a stereoscopic representation—a technique which is attainable with modern computing and graphical output procedures.

An associated problem in the analysis of an unstructured multivariate sample is the joint evaluation of the eigenvalues of the sample covariance or correlation matrices. As mentioned earlier, such considerations may play a key role in possible reduction of dimensionality. The adequate assessment of specific sample eigenvalue results is not, however, an elementary task. The fact is that even for large samples from spherical multivariate distributions, the sample eigenvalues may exhibit substantial variability.

Example 13. This example is based on some Monte Carlo experiments given by Munk and Wilk (1967). Two hundred samples of a 49-dimensional vector of independent standard normal components were drawn and the eigenvalues of the sample covariance matrix were obtained. Figure 13 shows a plot of the cumulative proportion of the number of sample eigenvalues versus the ordered eigenvalues.

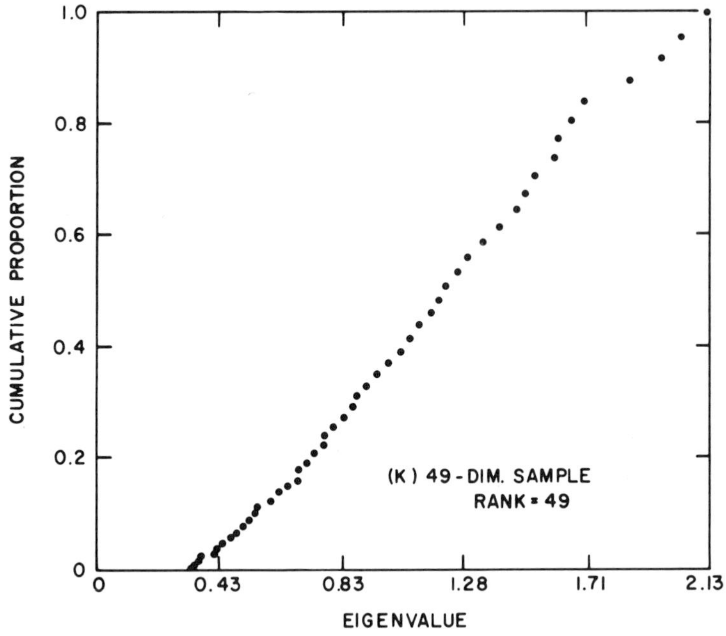

Fig. 13.

Although the population eigenvalues are all equal to unity, in the sample one sees a variation from about 0.3 to 2.13.

This and other similar experiences would tend to suggest caution in the interpretation of magnitudes of and separations among individual eigenvalues.

It would be useful to develop techniques for the probability plotting of ordered sample eigenvalues against their respective expected values under a null model of independent normal components. The computation of the required plotting positions is presently cumbersome and good computable approximations would be of value.

6.3. Comparison of Several Multiresponse Samples

Many situations require the presentation of data from several identified groups for comparative purposes. In the uniresponse case, it will often be useful to supplement the computation of Student's t, or an F statistic, with a normal probability plot of the several samples all on the same graph.

In the multiresponse case, Hotelling's T^2 can be computed for two groups, and one or more versions of an analysis of variance for several groups may be employed. However, such analyses are typically not sufficiently revealing. They need to be augmented by various plots: two-dimensional scatter plots; various marginal probability plots with all groups plotted on the same graph; pairwise eigenvector plots jointly for all groups; and other adaptations including the use of glyphs.

An internal comparisons method for the analysis of a collection of single-degree-of-freedom multiresponse contrast vectors—as from a 2^n multiresponse experiment—has been suggested by Wilk and Gnanadesikan (1961, 1964). The procedure involves the gamma probability plotting of quadratic forms in the elements of the contrast vectors, using an appropriately estimated shape parameter. One value of such a multivariate approach is that the sensitivity of the analysis may be improved.

Example 14. The data is from a study of factors affecting PICTUREPHONE^R quality [Gabbe and Wilk (1960), see also Wilk and Gnanadesikan (1964)], organized as a $\frac{1}{2}$-replicate of a 2^9 factorial in a split-plot design, with $p = 8$ responses per experimental unit. Each response involved a subjective assessment of picture quality.

Figures 14a–14d illustrate how multiresponse analysis can importantly augment the separate uniresponse analyses. Figures 14a–14c are typical of the eight $\chi^2(1)$ probability plots of the squared contrasts for the separate responses. Some of these plots (e.g., Figs. 14a and 14c) suggest the existence of one or two real effects. On the other hand Fig. 14d, based on a multiple response analysis (using the identity matrix for compounding the multiresponse contrasts), indicates seven or eight possible real effects.

Such internal comparison techniques have the advantage of providing both summarization of informational content and exposure of inadequacy of null assumptions and other peculiarities in a single graphical presentation. The

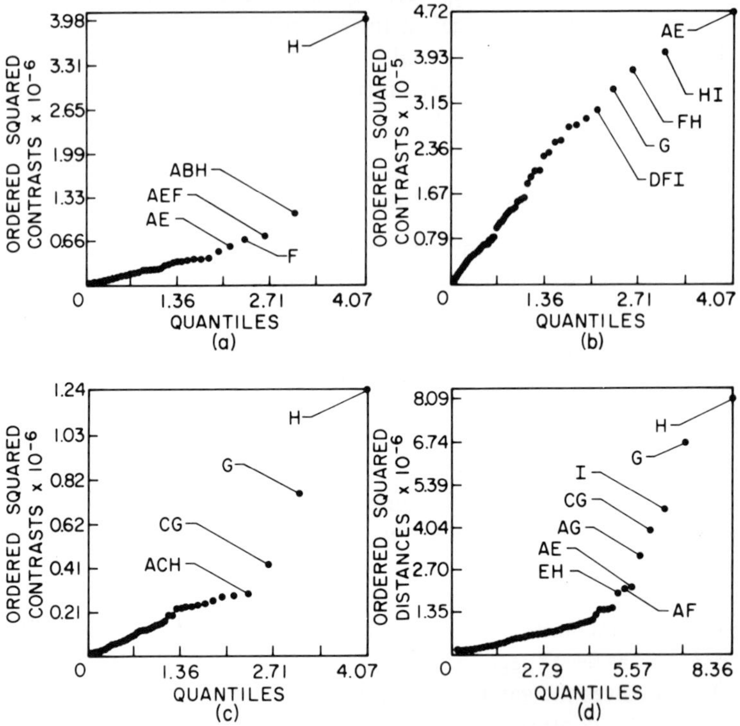

Fig. 14. Internal comparisons gamma plots. (a) Gamma plot of squared contrasts Response 2, $N = 115$, $\eta = 0.5$; (b) gamma plot of squared contrasts Response 3, $N = 115$, $\eta = 0.5$; (c) gamma plot of squared contrasts Response 5, $N = 115$, $\eta = 0.5$; (d) multivariate gamma plot of squared distances $N = 115$, $\eta = 2.404$.

following Table I shows a categorization of orthogonal analysis of variance situations according to the multiplicity of response and the degrees of freedom decomposition of the design.

Example 14 illustrates the use of the multiresponse method (Cell IV) for assessing a collection of single-degree-of-freedom vectors. Example 15 illustrates a technique [cf. Gnanadesikan and Lee (1968)] for the case of Cell V.

Example 15. This example is based on computer-generated trivariate normal data which simulate the results of a 5×6 cross-classified experiment with four replications per cell. The data for fifteen of the thirty cells had one covariance structure while for the remaining cells, they had another. The geometric means of the nonzero eigenvalues of the within-cell covariance matrices were computed and a gamma probability plot obtained [cf. Gnanadesikan and Lee (1968) for a description and discussion of the technique] for the thirty values of the function. The shape parameter required for the plot

TABLE I
Internal Comparisons Probability Plotting Methods

DF decomp. of design	Response structure: Uniresponse	Response structure: Multiresponse
All 1 df contrasts	(I) Full-normal and/or half-normal	(IV) Gamma plot of squared distances (estimated η)
All $\nu(>1)$ df groupings	(II) Gamma plot with shape parameter $\eta = \nu/2$	(V) Gamma plots of eigenvalue functions (estimated η)
Mixed df groupings	(III) Generalized probability plotting using conditional expected values	(VI) ?

was estimated from the data based on an order statistics formulation [see Wilk *et al.* (1962b)]. Figure 15 shows this gamma plot. Each of the points is labeled 1 or 2 according to whether it derives from a cell with one or the other of the covariance structures employed.

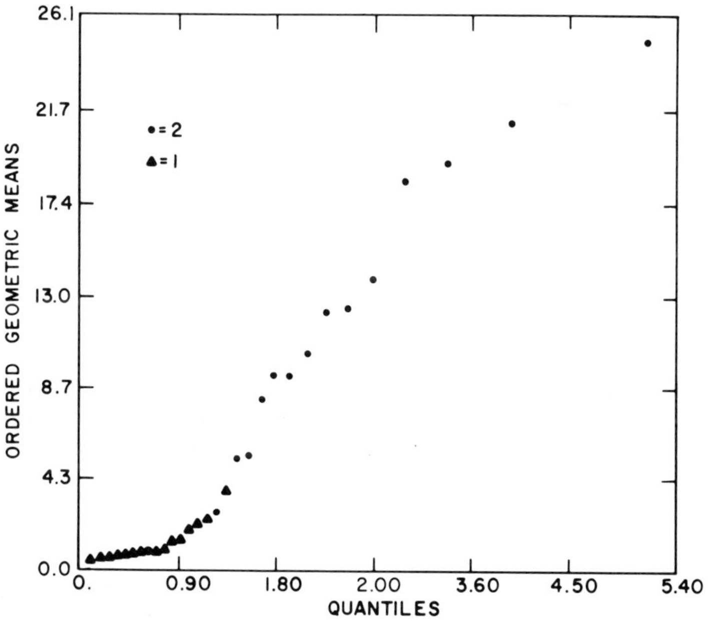

Fig. 15. Gamma plot of geometric means of eigenvalues $N = 30$, $\eta = 1.514$.

The configuration is suggestive of two intersecting straightlines each of which consists of points that correspond to the cells with a common covariance structure. An analogous analysis using the sum of eigenvalues, in place of the geometric mean, gave similar results.

Many of the formal techniques of uniresponse and multiresponse analyses of variance are developed under the assumption (often unverified in practice) of homoschedasticity of errors. It is known, for instance, that tests for homogeneity of means are critically dependent on this assumption, and such tests in themselves provide no assessment of the validity of this assumption. Informal probability plotting methods, such as the one here illustrated, may be useful for such an assessment. Typically, in these probability plots, the existence of several pieces of straight lines in the configuration would be indicative of groupings which are internally homoschedastic but, as a collection, are heteroschedastic.

6.4. Recognition of Groups or Relations

Mention has been made earlier of multiresponse cluster analysis and of search for relations. However, not all techniques can be used on all data; guidance and selection are needed. Sometimes this comes from prespecified objectives, but often there is a need for general data-descriptive procedures to stimulate analysis. The problem is to display multiresponse data so as to suggest the existence of nonlinear singularities or clusters, or outliers, or some such.

For bivariate representations, a suggestion due to Rao (1952) seems a worthwhile one—namely, to display the data using a linearly transformed scale so that the sample covariance configurations are circular. The advantage of this is that the statistical metric of the plot is now Euclidean, i.e., points on a circle are equidistant from the center instead of points on an ellipse being equidistant from the center. Because of the human ability to "recognize" circles this is advantageous in informal assessment of relationships.

For $p > 2$, one might make such displays for various two-dimensional projections. However, the informal exploration of multiresponse data for groupings and relationships must depend, more than the uniresponse case, on the use of analytical arithmetic techniques in conjunction with graphical ones. Relevant techniques are: linear and generalized principal components analysis, multidimensional scaling, cluster analysis, the use of glyphs, and the iterative employment of pairwise eigenvector plots.

6.5. Exposing Inadequacy of Fit

One of the most insightful processes for exposure in analysis of uniresponse data is the study of residuals in a variety of ways, especially through plotting.

The development of this kind of analysis for multivariate situations is very difficult but probably even more needful than in the uniresponse case. The point is that multiresponse models or modes of summarization are inherently more complex, and ways in which the data can depart from the model are infinitely more varied than in the univariate case. Consequently, it is even more essential to have informal, informative exposure procedures.

Given some summarizing fit to a body of multiresponse data, there exists, in principle, a vector of multivariate residuals between the data and the fit; but, more than in the univariate case, there is the important issue of how to express these multivariate residuals. Though experience is still rudimentary on these matters, some things can be done.

Under the assumptions underlying the summarizing fit, it will usually be true that one expects the multivariate residuals to behave like an unstructured multivariate sample with certain characteristics, such as having a centroid at the origin. Consequently, those methods applicable to the study of an unstructured multivariate sample may be useful for analysis of multivariate residuals, including the use of marginal probability plots and of component probability plotting and analysis. Such analyses are of interest for detection of outliers and, more subtly, for the detection of possible need for transformation or for suggesting appropriate modification of the model.

Another mode of study of multivariate residuals is their linear or generalized principal components analysis. A two-dimensional plot of the residuals, linearly transformed according to pairs of eigenvectors (say, those two corresponding to the two largest eigenvalues), and labeled in various ways—such as by time if it is a factor—may be useful. If most of the variability in, say, a 5-dimensional vector is associated with two principal components, then it may be informative to plot the projections on each of the three remaining eigenvectors against the distance from the centroid of each of the projected points in the two-dimensional plane associated with the two largest eigenvalues. This may show a certain kind of multidimensional inadequacy of fit: namely, whether the magnitude of the residuals in the coordinates of the smaller eigenvalues is related to the clustering of the points in the two-dimensional space of the two eigenvectors corresponding to the largest two eigenvalues.

6.6. Outliers in Principal Components Analysis

In one form or another, principal components analysis is a widely used multivariate technique. It is of interest, therefore, to inquire as to the possible effects of outlying observations on sample principal components. Some indication of such effects is given in the following example.

Example 16. Twenty-five simulated samples were drawn from a 5-dimensional spherical standard normal distribution. The eigenanalysis of the

EIGENVALUES

1.62	1.41	0.89	0.53	0.47

EIGENVECTORS

0.03	0.54	0.70	-0.46	0.05
-0.41	-0.32	-0.19	-0.65	0.51
-0.87	-0.04	0.22	0.19	-0.39
0.0	0.36	-0.55	-0.48	-0.59
-0.27	0.69	-0.35	0.31	0.49

(a)

EIGENVALUES

3.39	1.57	1.03	0.63	0.51

EIGENVECTORS

0.12	-0.11	0.88	0.11	-0.43
-0.07	0.46	-0.29	-0.21	-0.80
-0.09	0.86	0.32	-0.02	0.40
-0.15	-0.16	0.18	-0.95	0.11
-0.97	-0.11	0.07	0.18	-0.05

(b)

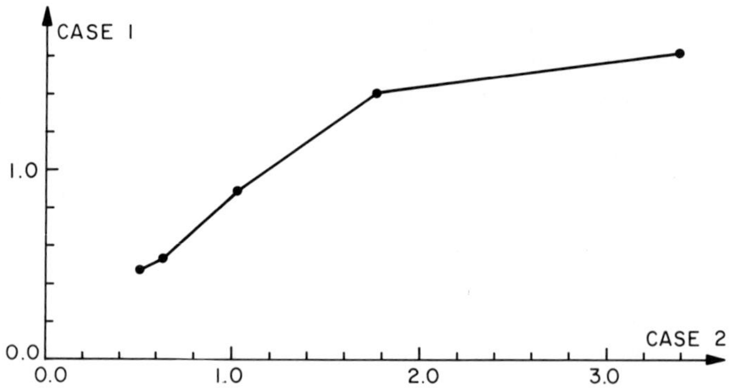

(c)

Fig. 16. (a) Eigenanalysis for case 1 (without outlier); (b) eigenanalysis for case 2 (with outlier); (c) eigenvalues—case 1 versus case 2.

sample covariance matrix is shown in Fig. 16a. The eigenvalues range from 0.47 to 1.62.

Then the value 7 was added to one of the components of one of the samples to simulate an outlier. The eigenanalysis from this changed data is shown in Fig. 16b. The eigenvalues now range from 0.51 to 3.39. Each of the eigenvectors shows considerable perturbation due to the single outlier.

A graphical representation for the comparison of the eigenvalues in Figs. 16a and 16b is given in Fig. 16c, which shows a plot of the corresponding ordered eigenvalues, with the abscissa corresponding to the eigenanalysis with the outlier and the ordinate to the one without the outlier. The effect of the outlier on the largest eigenvalue is clearly evident from this plot.

This and other examples in preliminary investigations of the present authors indicate a real and important need for caution with respect to the potential perturbations which outliers may effect in eigenanalyses.

7. CONCLUDING REMARKS

Most will agree that the area of multivariate analysis is both difficult and important. Some have reacted with understandable frustration to multivariate methods, asserting that they are a fraud, or unproductive, or otherwise useless, or misguided.

Most theoretical work in multivariate analysis has dealt with distribution theory and inferential procedures for the extension of quite specific formal univariate problems, such as how to test the hypothesis of equality of two means. The resulting methods are, indeed, only of little use in multidimensional data analysis.

Some suggestions as to reasons for the difficulties of multivariate analysis were given at the outset of this paper. Briefly, some of these are: understanding and formulating objectives, the difficulty of getting primitive informal graphical presentations to use as guidance and stimulus, the technological difficulties of computing and handling of the data, and the instinctive human uneasiness in some situations when some of the properties of linear ordering are lacking.

It is not overly optimistic to assert that some aids are on their way. Certainly, raw computing power has grown astronomically in recent years. Graphical display devices are now relatively cheap and widely available. Much more data-analytic software is to be expected in the immediate future. Admittedly, the technology of data analysis is still in a very primitive state, but there are reasons to be hopeful of substantial advances.

One of the most important strategies of data analysis is, and has always been, graphical presentation and pictorialization. Man is a geometric animal and seems to need and want pictures for parsimony and to stimulate insight. Thus, among the exciting potential tools of data analysis are graphical real-time interaction devices and microfilm facilities. However, one should realize that, for the multiresponse situation, even more than in the uniresponse case, simplicity of results and of understanding will typically require substantial complexity in statistical analysis.

ACKNOWLEDGMENT

The authors wish to thank J. L. Warner for his assistance in organizing the presentation of the examples.

REFERENCES

1. ANDERSON, E. (1960). A semigraphical method for the analysis of complex problems. *Technometrics* **2** 387–392.
2. ANDERSON, T. W. (1958). "Introduction to Multivariate Statistical Analysis." Wiley, New York.
3. BALL, G. H. (1965). Data analysis in the social sciences—what about details? *AFIPS Conf. Proc., Fall Joint Comput. Conf.* **27** pp. 533–560.
4. BECKER, M. H., GNANADESIKAN, R., MATHEWS, M. V., PINKHAM, R. S., PRUZANSKY, S., and WILK, M. B. (1965). Comparisons of some statistical distance measures for talker identification. Unpublished work.
5. BURNABY, T. P. (1966). Growth invariant discriminant functions and generalized distances. *Biometrics* **22** 96–110.
6. DAS GUPTA, S., ANDERSON, T. W., and MUDHOLKAR, G. S. (1964). Monotonicity of the power functions of some tests of the multivariate linear hypothesis. *Ann. Math. Statist.* **35** 200–205.
7. DEMPSTER, A. P. (1958). A high dimensional two sample significance test. *Ann. Math. Statist.* **29** 995–1010.
8. DEMPSTER, A. P. (1963). Multivariate theory for general stepwise methods. *Ann. Math. Statist.* **34** 873–883.
9. EKMAN, G. (1954). Dimensions of color vision. *J. Psychology* **38** 467–474.
10. FISHER, R. A. (1938). The statistical utilization of multiple measurements. *Ann. Eugenics* **8** 376–386.
11. FRIEDMAN, H. P., and RUBIN, J. (1967). On some invariant criteria for grouping data. *J. Amer. Statist. Assoc.* **62** 1159–1178.

11a. GABBE, J. D., and WILK, M. B. (1960). A study of some factors affecting the quality of television pictures. Unpublished work.

12. GENTLEMAN, W. M. (1965). Robust estimation of multivariate location by minimizing *p*th power deviations. Unpublished work.
13. GNANADESIKAN, R., and LEE, E. T. (1968). A graphical internal comparison method for simultaneous assessments of multiple equal-degree-of-freedom groupings in multi-response experimental data. Unpublished work.
14. HARMAN, H. H. (1967). "Modern Factor Analysis," 2nd ed. Univ. of Chicago Press, Chicago, Illinois.
15. HARTIGAN, J. A. (1967). Representation of similarity matrices by trees. *J. Amer. Statist. Assoc.* **62** 1140–1158.
16. HECK, D. L. (1960). Charts of some upper percentage points of the distribution of the largest characteristic root. *Ann. Math. Statist.* **31** 625–642.

17. HOTELLING, H. (1931). The generalization of Student's ratio. *Ann. Math. Statist.* **2** 360–378.
18. HOTELLING, H. (1933). Analysis of a complex of statistical variables into principal components. *J. Educational Psychology* **24** 417–441, 498–520.
19. HOTELLING, H. (1936). Relations between two sets of variates. *Biometrika* **28** 321–377.
20. HOTELLING, H. (1947). Multivariate quality control, illustrated by the air testing of sample bombsights. *In* "Techniques of Statistical Analysis" (C. Eisenhart *et al.*, eds.), pp. 111–184. McGraw-Hill, New York.
21. JACKSON, J. E. (1956). Quality control methods for two related variables. *Ind. Qual. Cont.* **12** 2–6.
22. JOHNSON, S. C. (1967). Hierarchical clustering schemes. *Psychometrika* **32** 241–254.
23. KRISHNAIAH, P. R. (1965). Multiple comparison tests in multiresponse experiments. *Sankhyā Ser. A* **27** 65–72.
24. KRUSKAL, J. B. (1964a). Multidimensional scaling by optimizing goodness of fit to a nonmetric hypothesis. *Psychometrika* **29** 1–27.
25. KRUSKAL, J. B. (1964b). Nonmetric multidimensional scaling: A numerical method. *Psychometrika* **29** 115–129.
26. LAWLEY, D. N. (1938). A generalization of Fisher's *z* test. *Biometrika* **30** 180–187.
27. MAHALANOBIS, P. C. (1930). On tests and measures of group divergence. *J. Asiatic Soc. Bengal* **26** 541–588.
28. MIKHAIL, N. N. (1965). A comparison of tests of the Wilks-Lawley hypothesis in multivariate analysis. *Biometrika* **52** 149–156.
29. MUNK, J. F., and WILK, M. B. (1967). Detecting outliers in a two-way table, I: Statistical properties of residuals. Unpublished work.
30. NEELY, P. M. (1967). Towards a theory of classification. Unpublished work.
31. PEARSON, K. (1901). On lines and planes of closest fit to systems of points in space. *Phil. Mag.* [6] **2** 559–572.
32. PILLAI, K. C. S. (1960). "Statistical Tables for Tests of Multivariate Hypotheses." The Statist. Center, Univ. of the Philippines, Manila.
33. PILLAI, K. C. S., and JAYACHANDRAN, K. (1967). Power comparisons of tests of two multivariate hypotheses based on four criteria. *Biometrika* **54** 195–210.
34. PURI, M. L., and SEN, P. K. (1966). On a class of multivariate multi-sample rank order tests. *Sankhyā Ser. A* **28** 353–376.
35. RAO, C. R. (1952). "Advanced Statistical Methods in Biometric Research." Wiley, New York.
36. RAO, C. R. (1966). Discriminant function between composite hypotheses and related problems. *Biometrika* **53** 339–345.
37. ROTHKOPF, E. Z. (1957). A measure of stimulus similarity and errors in some paired-associate learning tasks. *J. Experimental Psychology* **53** 94–101.
38. ROY, S. N. (1939). *p*-statistics or some generalizations in analysis of variance appropriate to multivariate problems. *Sankhyā* **4** 381–396.
39. ROY, S. N. (1945). The individual sampling distribution of the maximum, minimum and any intermediate of the '*p*'-statistics on the null hypothesis. *Sankhyā* **7** 133–158.
40. ROY, J. (1958). Step-down procedure in multivariate analysis. *Ann. Math. Statist.* **29** 1177–1187.
41. ROY, S. N., and GNANADESIKAN, R. (1957). Further contributions to multivariate confidence bounds. *Biometrika* **44** 399–410.
42. ROY, S. N., GNANADESIKAN, R., and SRIVASTAVA, J. N. (1968). "Analysis and Design of Certain Quantitative Multiresponse Experiments." Pergamon Press, Oxford. To be published.

43. SCHATZOFF, M. (1966). Exact distributions of Wilks' likelihood ratio criterion. *Biometrika* **53** 347–358.
44. SEAL, H. L. (1964). "Multivariate Statistical Analysis for Biologists." Methuen, London.
45. SHEPARD, R. N. (1962a). The analysis of proximities: Multidimensional scaling with an unknown distance function. I. *Psychometrika* **27** 125–140.
46. SHEPARD, R. N. (1962b). The analysis of proximities: Multidimensional scaling with an unknown distance function. II. *Psychometrika* **27** 219–246.
47. SHEPARD, R. N. (1963). Analysis of proximities as a technique for the study of information processing in man. *Human Factors* **5** 33–48.
48. SHEPARD, R. N., and CARROLL, J. D. (1966). Parametric representation of nonlinear data structures. *In* "Multivariate Analysis" (P. R. Krishnaiah, ed.), pp. 561–592. Academic Press, New York.
49. TAMURA, R. (1966). Multivariate nonparametric several-sample tests. *Ann. Math. Statist.* **37** 611–618.
50. TUKEY, J. W. (1949). Dyadic ANOVA, an analysis of variance for vectors. *Human Biology* **21** 65–110.
51. TUKEY, J. W., and WILK, M. B. (1966). Data analysis and statistics: An expository overview. *AFIPS Conf. Proc., Fall Joint Comput. Conf.* **29** 695–709.
52. WILK, M. B., and GNANADESIKAN, R. (1961). Graphical analysis of multiresponse experimental data using ordered distances. *Proc. Nat. Acad. Sci. U.S.A.* **47** 1209–1212.
53. WILK, M. B., and GNANADESIKAN, R. (1964). Graphical methods for internal comparisons in multiresponse experiments. *Ann. Math. Statist.* **35** 613–631.
54. WILK, M. B., and GNANADESIKAN, R. (1968). Probability plotting methods for the analysis of data. *Biometrika* **55** 1–17.
55. WILK, M. B., GNANADESIKAN, R., and HUYETT, M. J. (1962a). Probability plots for the gamma distribution. *Technometrics* **4** 1–20.
56. WILK, M. B., GNANADESIKAN, R., and HUYETT, M. J. (1962b). Estimation of parameters of the gamma distribution using order statistics. *Biometrika* **49** 525–545.
57. WILKS, S. S. (1932). Certain generalizations in the analysis of variance. *Biometrika* **24** 471–494.

Geometrical Models and Badness-of-Fit Functions

JOSEPH B. KRUSKAL
and J. DOUGLAS CARROLL[1]

BELL TELEPHONE LABORATORIES, INCORPORATED
MURRAY HILL, NEW JERSEY

1. GEOMETRICAL MODELS AND BADNESS-OF-FIT FUNCTIONS

Geometrical models are models such as tree structure, parametric mapping, multidimensional scaling, multidimensional unfolding, and factor analysis. Four of these models are discussed in this paper. For each a brief description will be given as well as a brief discussion of its demonstrated utility.

One good way to do model fitting is through badness-of-fit or goodness-of-fit functions. The model allows for data values and for parameter values. Somehow or other a badness-of-fit or a goodness-of-fit function is devised which measures or evaluates how well the parameter values in question match the data values being considered. By definition, the best fitting parameter values are those which optimize this function. The central question in this approach is how to choose the badness-of-fit or goodness-of-fit function. This is the problem on which attention is focused here. Our approach is not theoretical but rather through illustration. For each of the geometrical models we discuss, we describe at least one and sometimes several alternative functions that can be or have been used, and discuss advantages and disadvantages.

Statisticians are most accustomed to thinking of badness-of-fit and goodness-of-fit functions for models which have an explicit stochastic element. For example, consider the method of maximum likelihood. Likelihood is a goodness-of-fit function which can be defined only in terms of an explicit stochastic or probabilistic model. While statisticians are also accustomed to badness-of-fit functions where no stochastic element is present, they are sometimes disparaging. For example, consider the familiar method of least squares. Here the sum of squares is the badness-of-fit function, and can be defined without recourse to any explicit stochastic element. However, there is

[1] Carroll acted as co-author for the sections on multidimensional scaling and on multidimensional unfolding.

a strong tradition of "justifying" least squares by some underlying stochastic model, and many least squares applications are traditionally derived in this way. Without such justification, statisticians sometimes feel unsatisfied.

I certainly have no quarrel with stochastic models, nor do I deny their great value. However, I would argue that they present a more sophisticated approach which requires a much greater knowledge of the situation. In many instances it is neither practical nor useful to attempt this level of sophistication. Consequently, I believe that the use of badness-of-fit functions, where no stochastic element is explicitly present in the model, is a perfectly well-justified procedure when greater detail and sophistication is either impractical or unjustified by the current state of knowledge. I suggest that least square fitting (for example the simple average of several observations) was used long before probabilistic models, and that its use was valuable and fully justified.

None of the models discussed in this paper contain an explicit stochastic element. Using the terminology of Professor Wold's paper in this symposium, the stochastic element is always "apparent" rather than "genuine." Typically, the model describes or constrains the central value of some measurement but says nothing about its variability or its probability distribution function. Hopefully more detailed models will be built in the future, but no one should be deterred from work in this area simply because they are not yet available.

The use of badness-of-fit functions (or goodness-of-fit functions) immediately leads to a substantial computing problem. Somehow or other, the parameter values which optimize the function must be found. This is not always a simple matter and can sometimes be quite challenging indeed. I believe that much more general use should be made of the numerical method of iterative improvement. While it has the disadvantage of being computationally slower than alternative methods in many simple situations, it has the great advantage of flexibility and uniformity. The same method, with relatively minor alterations to fit the situation, can be used in an amazingly wide variety of situations. This encourages the user to suit the model and the badness-of-fit function to his situation. This is much better than tailoring the experiment to match an available technique of analysis, and making assumptions merely because they are convenient. Of course, when a particular technique of analysis becomes sufficiently valuable and widespread, it is desirable to introduce some specific method of calculation which saves computer time. However, it is most important that this be done within the context of a flexible framework, so that the user of this technique is not locked into the exact version which is now most popular, but instead is free without undue programming effort (at the cost primarily of computer time) to use a variation of the technique whenever that seems helpful.

Frank Yates has long emphasized the value of iterative methods in connection with irregular designs which result from missing data. Such designs can be handled very gracefully and with little effort in this framework although they sometimes require great effort within other familiar and less flexible frameworks. Some of the very interesting statistical programs at Rothamsted make full use of this advantage, which can be of great practical importance.

2. TREE STRUCTURE MODEL

Tree structure is a very common and important conception. For example, consider the familiar evolutionary tree for some group of animal species. At the top is the common ancestor. Proceeding through time this species gives rise by divergence to other species, which in turn give rise to still further species, and so on till the present day. This model applies not only to plants and animals but to other things as well, for example, languages and written documents. By way of illustration, David Kendall has told me of a study by Gweneth Whitteridge (exact reference not known) in which many existing manuscripts of the "Romance of the Rose" are compared. It is assumed that there is one original version of the story. Spontaneous "mutation" by means of copying errors gave rise to new versions. The object of the study was to disentangle the tree structure relationship between the known manuscripts. Of course both here and in connection with animal species, allowance must be made for extinction or loss of some lines which cannot be observed today.

A model which is precisely equivalent to tree structure but which has a different surface appearance is hierarchical clustering. By this is meant the assignment of the species or other objects into clusters, and then the assignment of these clusters into clusters, and so on up a hierarchy until at the very top everything is in one large single cluster. It is easy to see that tree structure and hierarchical clustering are equivalent. If the tree structure is given, the hierarchical clustering can easily be formed. First, make a cluster of each group of "brothers" at the lowest level, then make a higher level cluster of each group of first cousins, then a still higher level cluster of each group of second cousins, and so on up the line. Conversely, if a hierarchical clustering is given, a tree is easily formed by reversing this process. Once it is seen that tree structure also covers hierarchical clustering, many new applications of this model come to mind. For example, most library classification schemes (such as the Dewey decimal system and the Library of Congress classification system) are of this type. When tree structure is used in this way, there may be no variable which clearly corresponds to time in the evolutionary tree situation though some variable such as "degree of generality" might be constructed to serve this role. We shall call such a variable timelike, and distinguish different applications according to whether there *is* or *is not* a preexisting timelike variable.

So far the tree structure we have been dicussing is entirely combinatorial in structure. Thus parameters in the usual sense do not enter at all. However. when we speak of model fitting, we explicitly want to include the possibility that the model fitted may include combinatorial aspects over which the badness-of-fit function must be optimized, as well as the possibility of ordinary real-valued parameters. Another version of the tree structure model is important where there is a timelike variable. One particular version of this model, which we shall discuss more fully below, requires that every node of the tree be labeled with a nonnegative real number (called the *node value*), and that this parameter have the value zero for all the terminal (bottom) nodes of the tree. Also, the value at any node must be greater than or equal to the value at all nodes below it in the tree (closer to the terminal nodes). If the bottom nodes of the tree represent species which all still exist, then these assumptions seem very appropriate, where the node value indicates how many years ago the divergence below it took place.

Still another variation on the tree structure model was introduced in a biological context by Fitch and Margoliash (1967) and could also be used in connection with situations like that of the "Romance of the Rose." (However, their explanation is not too clear.) Suppose it is natural to measure just how different two manuscripts of the same story are by counting the specific points at which well-defined distinctions occur. If each leg of the tree represents a copying operation during which one or more errors occurred, then that leg can be given a length according to the number of errors which it carries. Presumably, the total distance between two documents would (at least approximately) be the sum of the lengths of the legs along the path which connects them. (Precise equality breaks down if some error occurs more than once independently, or if some error is canceled by a second error which reverses the first.) In contexts like this, it is natural to form a tree structure in which each edge is labeled by a nonnegative real number (the *edge value*). Any variable for which this model seems appropriate will be called *distancelike*. Furthermore, depending on circumstances, the structure might or might not include indication as to which nodes come prior to other nodes. (If priority is part of the structure, and if there is one common ancestor which is prior to all the other nodes of the tree, and if, in addition, the length of every path from the common ancestor to every bottom node is the same, then "timelike" and "distancelike" become equivalent.) Very likely several other variations of the tree structure model can be devised which are appropriate to other circumstances.

There are two major types of data which are often used for tree structure and hierarchical clustering. One type consists of a matrix of dissimilarities or similarities, which shows for each pair of objects how different or how much alike they are. (Dissimilarities may be timelike, distancelike, both, or neither.) The second type of data is what I call a score matrix. Each row corresponds to one object, and each column corresponds to some variable which can be measured. The elements in the matrix, of course, consist of the scores or values of the variables for the objects. It is also useful to think of this matrix as a set of row vectors or points. Each object corresponds to one such vector or point, and the coordinates of that point are the values of the variables.

It is possible, starting from either type of data, to create the other type. For example, starting from a score matrix considered as a set of points, it is easy to calculate a matrix of distances between the points, thereby obtaining a matrix of dissimilarities between the objects. Conversely, starting with the matrix of dissimilarities, it is possible through the use of multidimensional scaling to find a set of points in some space which can then be read off as a score matrix. Because of these conversion procedures, it is possible to use any method which accepts one type of data with the other type of data. Unfortunately, this has resulted in a good deal of confusion in the literature. There are published papers in which the method of clustering the author describes is based essentially on one form of data but which the author describes as applying to the other form of the data, because he has used a preprocessing step which amounts to a conversion of data type. In this paper we limit ourselves to tree structure obtained from a matrix of dissimilarities.

A very interesting paper by Hartigan (1967) uses the badness-of-fit approach to get tree structure from timelike dissimilarities. His method of defining the badness-of-fit function is elegantly simple. The arguments of this function are the dissimilarities, the combinatorial tree structure, and the values at the nodes of the tree. The data consists of a symmetric matrix of dissimilarities with zeros down the diagonal. (In application to evolutionary trees, each dissimilarity might be an independent estimate of how long ago the last common ancestor lived.) To define the badness-of-fit function, Hartigan first defines a *tree matrix* from the tree structure and the node values. For each pair of bottom (terminal) nodes, the entry in the tree matrix is found by taking the node value at the lowest common ancestor node. If the tree and the node values represent true evolutionary history, then this procedure would yield values which correspond to the measurements we are supposing. Since the tree matrix and the data matrix are of the same size, Hartigan defines his badness-of-fit function as the sum of squares of the differences between the corresponding elements of these two matrices. As simple as this conception may seem, I believe that it is the first approach to tree structure and hierarchical clustering which uses the badness-of-fit function with input data which is a matrix of similarities of dissimilarities.

The computational problem of optimizing the badness-of-fit function is especially nasty in this case because it involves a search over the combinatorial space of trees. When the right combinatorial tree is known, it is a relatively simple matter to find the best node values. However, the process of finding the right tree is very difficult. Hartigan does not have a procedure which is guaranteed to produce the very best tree. However, he does have a procedure (implemented as a working computer program) which is capable of doing very well indeed. This is an important accomplishment. In addition, his method should be readily applicable to optimizing many other functions over the space of trees.

The use of tree structure is a fundamental human intellectual activity, as we can see in biological taxonomy, in library classifications, and in almost any systematically arranged body of information. In most cases, it is true, these tree structures are imposed as a result of direct inspection or by trial and error. It should come as no surprise, however, that there is a substantial need for automatic methods to accomplish this kind of classification; and indeed, a great many papers have been published in numerous fields presenting methods for doing this. Many of these are statistically quite naive. The author simply presents a method which he had used and which he considers workable. Little is said about the properties of the method or how it compares with other methods. Indeed, the author may not clearly be aware that there are many other methods. Besides the work I have already mentioned, some very interesting work has been published by the following authors as cited in the bibliography: Ball (1965), Gower (1967), Johnson (1967), Rohlf (1967), Sokal and Sneath (1963), Sokal and Rohlf (1962), and Wylie (1967). It is very clear from the published work that automatic methods have already made a very significant contribution. It is even clearer that the field is wide open for further improvement.

3. PARAMETRIC MAPPING

Parametric mapping was first introduced in the second half of a paper by Shepard and Carroll (1966). In order to avoid repetition with their paper I will make my description of this method brief. However, there are some new and useful remarks which can be made. Furthermore, it is possible to make the presentation more elegant and streamlined in certain ways, at this time.

Parametric mapping involves two euclidian spaces. I shall call one of them the high-dimensional space and the other the low-dimensional space. All that is required, however, is that the high-dimensional space have more dimensions than the low-dimensional space. The input data consists of a collection of points in the high-dimensional space. Typically this arises from a score matrix, where each object corresponds to one point. The coordinates of the point are the measurements or scores of that object on the several variables. The conceptual basis for parametric mapping is that all possible objects of the sort being studied can be represented as points in this space, and that these points lie in some limited region which takes the form of a possibly curved subspace of fewer dimensions. For example, the object points might all lie on the surface of some sphere, or on some torus, or on the surface of some less regular figure. The general object of parametric mapping is to open out this curved surface onto a flat surface of the same dimensionality. Thus the low-dimensional space serves as the platform onto which the curved region is to be flattened out.

Such a flattening out is, of course, a mapping between the region of high-dimensional space and some suitable region of low-dimensional space. In order to reconstruct such a mapping, which is assumed to exist, some assumptions must be made about its nature. Rather than use the more conventional assumptions which are characteristic of statistical regression theory, parametric mapping uses the primary assumption that this mapping is "smooth." However, the "smoothness" of the mapping is not symmetric. A mapping from A to B may be smooth while the inverse mapping from B to A may be quite the opposite. For example, if we cut open a circle and straighten it out, that mapping is not at all smooth because the cutting open is discontinuous in a bad way. However, the reverse operation of bending a line segment into a circle does not violate continuity at all. For this reason parametric mapping assumes smoothness of the mapping in one particular direction: namely from the low-dimensional space into the high-dimensional space. Indeed, the decision to measure continuity or smoothness in this direction was an important step in getting this method to work. While Carroll had experimented earlier with continuity in this direction, Carroll and Shepard subsequently were using continuity measured in the reverse direction and could not get their procedure to work as well as they wanted. I urged them to turn the notion around and this eventually led to a successful result.

Smoothness or continuity of a mapping from a region in one euclidian space to a region in another is a familiar mathematical idea. However, in practice parametric mapping does not have available whole regions, but merely discrete sets of points from the region. The mapping, in fact, is represented entirely by a set of labeled points in the low-dimensional space which correspond to a labeled set of points in the high-dimensional space. Therefore, it is essential to be able to measure something like continuity or smoothness for mapping of finite sets of points. Fortunately, Douglas Carroll had developed just such a notion in his doctoral thesis. In fact, it was the availability of this notion which was one of the central forces leading to the development of parametric mapping. As a mathematician, I can testify that mathematicians find it awkward to accept the notion of *degree* of continuity. After all, in mathematics a function either is continuous or it is not. For those who resist the description of Carroll's index as a measure of continuity, I suggest that they recognize that something new and important has come along and that it is not essential to use the word continuity in labeling it. Unfortunately, no generally acceptable name has yet been proposed.

In the following development, I make some small changes from the original presentation. I conceive of these as perfections of the original idea, and I believe that Carroll and Shepard approve the spirit of these changes. To start with, I shall call their index a *discontinuity index* because larger values indicate less continuous mappings, and smaller values more continuous mappings. The index is defined in such a way that any *similarity* mapping (which is the geometrical term for a mapping in which all distances change by a single constant multiplier) receives the smallest possible value (namely, one), and that no other mapping receives this value. (The index could be considered as a measurement of how much the mapping departs from being a similarity, and could be called a "dissimilarity index." However, I dislike this name for several reasons.)

The essential idea of continuity is that small changes in the argument should not lead to very large changes in the value of the function. Suppose we consider the function at two points. One way to measure how sharply the function has changed in response to the change in the argument is to divide the distance between the two function values by the distance between the two argument values. If we use D to represent distances in the high-dimensional space and d to represent distances in the low-dimensional space, then this ratio is D/d. (Our use of D and d reverses Carroll's convention.) The larger this ratio, the more discontinuous the function is. This is the fundamental idea of the discontinuity index. However, the index actually used will have certain normalizing scale factors, which modify in an essential way this rather simple notion. Thus, the index eventually used will be invariant under uniform contraction or expansion of the array of argument points and also of the array of function points.

At this point let us make a slight change and consider the square of this ratio. Basically, this is for historical reasons. However, new generality to be introduced in a moment means that this change is not really important. The next step is to take some sort of average of these ratios. In more recent work, Carroll and Shepard have considered using averages in some more general sense. However, at this time let us restrict consideration to ordinary weighted averages. The question then arises as to what weights to use. Basically, their notion is to give less weight to pairs of argument points which are far apart. This suggests the consideration of a weight something like d^{-1} or some power of it. Carroll and Shepard demonstrate that in order to assure certain desirable properties, the weights must have the form of some power of d. This leads to a possible index of this form

$$\frac{\sum (D/d)^2(d^{-1})^P}{\sum (d^{-1})^P}. \tag{1}$$

Generalizing this a little and making some minor alterations in order to assure further desirable properties which I shall state in a moment, this leads to the following index

$$\left[N^{-1} \sum \frac{D^{2a}}{d^{2b}}\right] \frac{[N^{-1} \sum d^{2c}]^{b/c}}{[N^{-1} \sum D^{2h}]^{a/h}}, \tag{2}$$

where $N = n(n - 1)/2$ is the number of pairs of points over which the summation extends.

The first factor in square brackets is the heart of this index. The parameters a and b which appear there simply generalize slightly what we started from. The ratio which follows serves to give the index certain desirable properties (i) to (iv) which we discuss in the next few paragraphs. (i) The index is invariant under changes of scale in both the low-dimensional space and the high-dimensional space. This is because if we expand or contract the whole configuration of points in either space, all the distances in that space increase or decrease by some fixed factor, and this factor cancels out in the index of discontinuity. The use of the multiplier N^{-1} in each of the square brackets is relatively minor. However, (ii) its presence makes this index behave well in certain limiting cases which are of particular interest, namely when c and $h \to 0$. We shall be discussing these cases a little later.

Now Carroll and Shepard introduce an important new principle which they call the *principle of similitude*. A perfectly smooth mapping would presumably be one in which the distances of one space are equal to or proportional to the distances in the other. (Such mappings are called "similarities" in geometry.) In general, a similarity mapping will not be possible because of the constraint that the distances arise from points in a specified space. However, if these constraints are removed, the principle of similitude asserts that the index should achieve its optimum value where the distances in the two spaces are proportional to one another. The principle of similitude can be invoked in two ways. First, the distances D can be considered as fixed and the distances d as free from all constraint. Second, conversely, the distances d can be considered as fixed and the distances D as free from all constraint. Of course, the first of these is the one which seems appropriate in the present circumstances. However, with the thought in mind that the same index could be used in other circumstances, it is natural to require both kinds of similitude to hold in order that a single elegant index may serve many purposes.

Let us consider the earlier of these two principles of similitude. It requires that if the D's are given, then the optimum d's must be proportional to D's. To find out what the optimum values of the d's are, we first take the logarithm of the index for mathematical convenience, and differentiate. On setting the derivatives equal to zero and simplifying, we find that

$$\frac{b}{c}\frac{D^{2a}}{d^{2b+2c}} = \frac{\sum (D^{2a}/d^{2b})}{\sum d^{2c}} = \text{constant.}$$

Clearly, if (D/d) is to be constant, it is necessary and sufficient that $a - b = c$. Similarly, the second principle of similitude yields that $a - b = h$. Using the parameter values given by this means, the index of discontinuity becomes

$$\left[N^{-1} \sum \frac{D^{2a}}{d^{2b}}\right] \frac{\left[N^{-1} \sum d^{2(a-b)}\right]^{b/(a-b)}}{\left[N^{-1} \sum D^{2(a-b)}\right]^{a/(a-b)}}. \tag{3}$$

Of course, (iii) this index satisfies both similitude principles. It also has some further desirable properties which come along as a byproduct. It is, of course, desirable that the index have an absolute meaning in different situations so that its value may be used to judge how smooth the mapping is. A necessary minimum step toward this is that the smoothest mappings available, namely similarities, should yield the same minimum value for this discontinuity index in all circumstances. It is easy to see (iv) that the last form of the index has value one for a similarity mapping. Furthermore, an application of the Minskowski inequality shows that this index is always greater than or equal to one.

Carroll and Shepard had some really dramatic successes with parametric mapping of synthetic data. For example, their method is able to tear open a circle (which is in two dimensions) and unroll it flat in one dimension; their method is able to cut open a sphere (which is in three dimensions) most of the way around its equator and flatten it out in two dimensions; and their method is able to double cut a torus imbedded in four dimensions and open it out as a slightly curved square in two dimensions. For details, see their paper. Furthermore, their method has been of definite value for real data. For example, Kurt Enslein has related during discussion of a previous paper how he has used parametric mapping with considerable success although in a manner slightly different from that which was originally intended. Other examples could be quoted.

Nevertheless, parametric mapping has not lived up to the high promise it first showed with synthetic data. I believe that there are two principal reasons for this. First of all, when the points are scattered irregularly on the curved surface in high-dimensional space, then the recovered configuration is undesirably irregular. For example, when Carroll and Shepard used 62 points regularly spaced on the sphere, along with a considerable number of points at random on the sphere, parametric mapping opened up this configuration in two dimensions. However, the locations of these 62 regular points were quite a bit distorted from the positions they occupied if no random points were used. They did not form a very regular appearance in this situation. The second reason is that the value of the index has been hard to interpret. Hopefully, once the index has been optimized by finding the configuration which makes it smallest, its resulting value will be a measure of how far the mapping departs from smoothness, and how well this whole model fits the data. Unfortunately, it has not turned out to be possible to match the values of the index with any realistic measure of how well the data fit the model, or how smooth the mapping is in any other sense. In my opinion, it is these two problems which have prevented parametric mapping from gaining wider use and acceptance.

Can these troubles be traced down to the discontinuity index that is being used? In my opinion they can, and furthermore, I believe that a relatively simple cure is available. For a variety of reasons Carroll and Shepard have concentrated most of their experiments on the parameter values $a = 1$ and $b = 2$. However, this involves the fourth powers of d in the denominator of the main factor of the index. I believe that this is a very strong force against the possibility of small distances and that this distorts the appropriate reconstruction. I believe that a more natural index would result if $a = 1$ and $b = 1$ were used, and I have been urging Carroll and Shepard to experiment with these values for some time.

Unfortunately, their index did not contain the factor N^{-1} in the square brackets (among other differences from the present form). As a result, the limiting behavior of their index when $a \to b$ was bad, and so the index was not really defined in this case. As a practical reflection of this, their computer program could not be used in this case. They have since modified their program to handle this case by special means. I hope that experiments will soon be done to see whether this change does in fact improve the results of parametric mapping.

Furthermore, it appears to me at this time that moving in the direction of still lower indices might help even more. For this reason I would like to propose the use of $a = \frac{1}{2}$ and $b = 1$, or $a = \frac{1}{2}$ and $b = \frac{1}{2}$. When these are put into the formula above, it reduces to particularly simple forms.

Perhaps it is worth noting the form of the above index in the limiting case when $a \to b$. Consider the scale factor which is in the numerator of the fraction. Its logarithm is

$$b\,\frac{\log[N^{-1}\sum d^{2(a-b)}]}{a-b}.$$

Applying l'Hospital's rule, we differentiate the numerator and denominator separately with respect to a. The denominator disappears, and we obtain

$$b\,\frac{N^{-1}\sum d^{2(a-b)}(2\log d)}{N^{-1}\sum d^{2(a-b)}}.$$

It is easy to see what this approaches as $a \to b$. Exponentiating, we get

$$[\prod d]^{2b/N}.$$

(Note that this is the $2b$ power of the geometric mean of the distances.) Therefore, in the case $a = b$, the discontinuity index becomes

$$[N^{-1} \sum (D/d)^{2b}] \frac{[\prod d]^{2b/N}}{[\prod D]^{2b/N}}.$$

(This limiting case of the index of discontinuity was first pointed out by J. P. Benzecrí in conversations with Carroll.)

4. MULTIDIMENSIONAL SCALING

Multidimensional scaling is a data analysis technique which constructs a configuration of points in space from some kind of information about the distances between the points. At least this is the definition we personally like to use. In this paper, I would like to be very brief in discussing multidimensional scaling because I have introduced it primarily as a platform for discussing multidimensional unfolding. However, we do have a few remarks about the badness-of-fit functions in the scaling case.

The fundamental conception of scaling is that the object can be represented as points in space in such a way that the similarity or dissimilarity between objects is directly related to the distances between the objects. This conception, first clearly stated by Shepard (1962), appears in most major approaches, including Guttman (1968), Lingoes (1966), Torgerson (1965), and Young and Torgerson (1967). Suppose this conception holds in some particular situation and we wish to devise a badness-of-fit function to measure how well any given configuration matches some given data. One very natural approach is to start by finding the distance between each pair of points and making a scatter diagram of distances versus dissimilarities. Since a direct relationship is expected between these two quantities, it is natural to do a regression of distance on dissimilarity and measure how bad the fit is by using the residual sum of squares from the regression. In fact, this is exactly the approach to multidimensional scaling which I have used [see Kruskal (1964a,b) and subsequent unpublished documents]. By using different kinds of regression, we obtain different kinds of multidimensional scaling. For example, let us start with an almost trivial type of regression, namely where the regression curve is a straight line of slope 1 through the origin. In other words, the family of regression functions has only one element, the identity function. In this case, the regression sum of squares reduces to

$$\sum (d_{ij} - \delta_{ij})^2. \tag{1}$$

This quantity can be used as is as a very natural badness-of-fit function although I generally prefer to make the trivial alteration of taking its square root (so as to improve interpretability). Scaling of this kind I refer to as *simple scaling*. Before going on to other types of regression and their associated types of scaling, let us consider several variations on simple scaling. Suppose that the dissimilarities δ_{ij} are conceived to be noisy measurements of the distances d_{ij}. If the standard deviation of the measurement error is the same for all the measurements, then the simple expression used above seems very appropriate. Other assumptions about the standard deviations would lead to other relatively simple expressions. For example, suppose the standard deviation of measurement is proportional to d_{ij}. In that case, it would be very natural to use either of the following expressions for the badness-of-fit function

$$\left(\sum \frac{(d_{ij} - \delta_{ij})^2}{d_{ij}^2}\right)^{1/2} \quad \text{or} \quad \left(\sum \frac{(d_{ij} - \delta_{ij})^2}{\delta_{ij}^2}\right)^{1/2}. \tag{2}$$

This is closely related to what McGee (1966) calls "elastic scaling." Similarly, if the standard deviation is proportional to the square root of d_{ij} (for example, when the measurements are Poisson variables), then it would be natural to use expressions like the following:

$$\left(\sum \frac{(d_{ij} - \delta_{ij})^2}{d_{ij}}\right)^{1/2} \quad \text{or} \quad \left(\sum \frac{(d_{ij} - \delta_{ij})^2}{\delta_{ij}}\right)^{1/2}. \tag{3}$$

Obviously, still other error structures could be accommodated just as easily.

Now consider other kinds of regression. Several possibilities, all within the general category of polynomial regression, can be treated simultaneously. First, consider linear regression without any constant term. This generalizes the method above by permitting an arbitrary slope for the regression line. Next, consider linear regression with constant term permitted and finally consider general polynomial regression (of some fixed degree). In all these cases a problem arises which did not arise in simple scaling. To use an expression like the one above as the badness-of-fit function would not work. To see this, consider any given configuration of points and the associated residual sum of squares analogous to (1) above. By simply shrinking the configuration uniformly, all the distances are made to shrink by a single constant factor, say k. For the kinds of regression we are talking about, this would result in the residual sum of squares shrinking by k^2. Thus by shrinking the configuration arbitrarily far, we could reduce the regression sum of squares arbitrarily close to zero. However, it is clear that we do not wish to rate a configuration as matching the data very well simply because the configuration is very small. Obviously, a badness-of-fit function of this kind is not appropriate. The cure, however, is quite simple. Clearly, we need a scale factor to provide invariance of the badness-of-fit function under changes of scale of the configuration. Many scale factors come easily to mind. We shall mention only two at this point, both of which we have used at various times. They are

$$\sum d_{ij}^2 \qquad \text{or} \qquad \sum (d_{ij} - \bar{d})^2 \tag{4}$$

where $\bar{d}$ is the arithmetic average of all the d_{ij}. (Later, we consider some of the most natural further alternatives, and show that they yield the same minimizing configurations as these.) Use of these scale factors leads to the following two badness-of-fit functions:

$$\left(\frac{\sum [d_{ij} - p(\delta_{ij})]^2}{\sum d_{ij}^2}\right)^{1/2} \qquad \text{or} \qquad \left(\frac{\sum [d_{ij} - p(\delta_{ij})]^2}{\sum (d_{ij} - \bar{d})^2}\right)^{1/2} \tag{5}$$

where p is the regression function. In several of my scaling programs, I refer to these expressions as "stress formula one" and "stress formula two," respectively. Historically, stress formula one was the only badness-of-fit function used for some time. Stress formula two has been in use more recently and I now tend to recommend it. For any given configuration, of course, stress formula two yields a substantially larger value than stress formula one, perhaps twice as large in many cases. However, in typical multidimensional scaling applications, minimizing stress formula two typically yields very similar configurations to minimizing stress formula one. Thus in this sense it makes little difference which of these formulas is used in typical scaling applications. However, it will turn out in the next section that this choice, unimportant in the case of scaling, can be very important in other contexts.

Suppose the dissimilarities are merely ordinal rather than numerical. For example, suppose the data from one subject indicate which pair of objects is most similar, which pair next most similar, etc. It would, of course, be perfectly feasible to assign rank values to the pairs (by any one of several familiar schemes) and then to use, say, polynomial regression. Even though I consider this in practice a perfectly reasonable procedure, a theoretical criticism can be raised that the data are being used numerically when, in fact, they simply consist of rank order information. An alternative procedure is not to use polynomial regression (which requires the use of numerical dissimilarities) but to use some kind of regression which makes use of the dissimilarities merely in their ordinal character. Least-squares monotone regression fills this bill perfectly.

While monotone regression is not yet too well known among statisticians, it is certainly worthy of wider consideration. It is perfectly analogous to the more familiar types of regression. It has previously been used, for example, to test the hypothesis that the means of several populations are ranked in a certain a priori order, and also to test the hypothesis that the population means are all equal given that they are ranked in a certain order. As far as I know, the concept was first introduced by van Eeden (1957a,b) though she certainly did not use this name. References to other uses of this concept are given by Kruskal (1964b). Let me simply comment at this time that rapid practical algorithms exist for performing least-squares monotone regression. I have implemented one of these and used it extensively on computers. When this kind of regression is employed, the scaling is usually referred to as *nonmetric* or *monotone*. In practice, it is one of the most widely used forms although I personally consider that the other types of scaling have at least equal interest. Let me simply note in passing that at least one other kind of regression has been used. Shepard (in press) used negative exponential regression functions on one occasion.

Now we consider some measures of badness-of-fit which are very natural alternatives to stress, but which turn out after analysis to yield nothing really new. We thank Myron Wish for stimulating this material by asking some important questions. For simplicity, we shall restrict our discussion to alternatives which are associated with the use of scale factor 2. However, analogous alternatives associated with scale factor 1 can easily be developed in the same way. For generality, we shall not limit the development to badness-of-fit measures actually based on regression. Rather, we represent the fitted values (which can come from regression or otherwise) by $\hat{d}_{ij}$ or just plain $\hat{d}$ without the subscripts. As will shortly become clear, this approach includes a great many least-squares regression techniques.

To simplify the following discussion, we introduce a deliberate notational ambiguity. We have already used d to mean d_{ij}. We shall also use d to represent a vector whose components are $d_{12}, d_{13}, \ldots, d_{n-1,n}$. Similarly, we shall use $\hat{d}$ ambiguously to represent a vector whose components are $\hat{d}_{ij}$; and we shall use $\bar{d}$ ambiguously to represent a vector whose components are all equal to each other and to the average of the d_{ij}. This ambiguity should cause no real confusion.

As generalized, the problem is to find a configuration of points whose distances are d, and to find numbers $\hat{d}$ which satisfy some given constraint (such a monotonicity or polynomiality over the data), such that d and the $\hat{d}$ jointly optimize a badness-of-fit measure. The badness-of-fit measure introduced earlier, and called stress, now reappears slightly altered as

$$S_A = \left(\frac{\sum (d - \hat{d})^2}{\sum (d - \bar{d})^2}\right)^{1/2} = \frac{\|d - \hat{d}\|}{\|d - \bar{d}\|} \qquad \text{(alternative } A\text{)},$$

where $\| \ \|$ indicates the ordinary euclidian length of a vector. The mathematical equivalence between this approach and the one given earlier (through the use of regression) will be made clear in a moment. Two natural alternatives arise simply by substituting the two obvious alternative scale factors

$$S_B = \left(\frac{\sum (d - \hat{d})^2}{\sum (\hat{d} - \bar{\hat{d}})^2}\right)^{1/2} = \frac{\|d - \hat{d}\|}{\|\hat{d} - \bar{\hat{d}}\|} \qquad \text{(alternative } B\text{)},$$

$$S_C = \frac{[\sum (d - \hat{d})^2]^{1/2}}{[\sum (d - \bar{d})^2]^{1/4}[\sum (\hat{d} - \bar{\hat{d}})^2]^{1/4}} = \frac{\|d - \hat{d}\|}{(\|d - \bar{d}\| \cdot \|\hat{d} - \bar{\hat{d}}\|)^{1/2}} \qquad \text{(alternative } C\text{)}$$

where $\bar{\hat{d}}$ is the average of the $\hat{d}_{ij}$, and also ambiguously a vector whose components all have this value. (It will soon turn out that in most situations of interest, $\bar{\hat{d}} = \bar{d}$. This is true for most kinds of regression, of course.) Another natural alternative, this time a *goodness*-of-fit, is simply the correlation coefficient between d and $\hat{d}$,

$$S_D = \frac{\sum (d - \bar{d})(\hat{d} - \bar{\hat{d}})}{(\sum (d - \bar{d})^2)^{1/2}(\sum (\hat{d} - \bar{\hat{d}})^2)^{1/2}} = \frac{(d - \bar{d}) \cdot (\hat{d} - \bar{\hat{d}})}{\|d - \bar{d}\| \, \|\hat{d} - \bar{\hat{d}}\|} \qquad \text{(alternative } D\text{)},$$

where the last numerator is the dot product (scalar product) of the two factors.

The first mathematical task is to show that minimizing S_A comes to the same thing as minimizing stress. Now

$$\min_{\text{configurations}, \hat{d}} (S_A) = \min_{\text{configurations}} [\min_{\hat{d}} S_A]$$
$$= \min_{\text{configurations}} \left[\|d - \bar{d}\|^{-1} \min_{\hat{d}} \|d - \hat{d}\| \right].$$

Now consider the inner minimization for a fixed configuration. This is precisely the same as least-squares regression (since the inner norm is simply the square root of the residual sum of squares) if the constraint set for $\hat{d}$ consists of all possible such vectors which could be generated by all possible regression functions. Thus for any desired type of least-squares regression, minimizing S_A with the right constraint set for $\hat{d}$ is the same as minimizing stress with $\hat{d}$ given by regression.

To obtain equivalence of the four alternatives A, B, C, D, it is necessary to make a mild assumption about the constraint set for $\hat{d}$. Phrased in terms of regression language, this assumption is that the regression method is at least as rich as linear regression with nonnegative slope. In other words, if the regression can yield values $\hat{d}_{ij}$, then it can also yield values $a + b\hat{d}_{ij}$ for any number a and any nonnegative number b. Phrased in terms of the constraint set, this assumption says that the constraint set is closed under addition of constant vectors and under scalar multiplications by nonnegative numbers, that is, if $\hat{d}$ is in the constraint set, and if a is any constant vector (vector whose components are all equal to each other) and b is any nonnegative number, then $a + b\hat{d}$ is in the constraint set. (Actually, either of two somewhat weaker conditions would suffice, but this condition simplifies the discussion.)

For alternatives A, B, C, the value of $\bar{\hat{d}}$ affects the values S_A, S_B, S_C only through $\|d - \hat{d}\|$. For alternative D, the value $\bar{\hat{d}}$ does not affect S_D at all.

Consequently, it is easy to show (for the first three alternatives) or may be assumed without real loss of generality (for the fourth alternative) that $\bar{\hat{d}} = \bar{d}$. (This relies on the above assumptions about the constraint set.) From now on, this fact will be assumed.

We wish to show that alternatives A, B, C, and D all yield the same optimum configuration. Let us consider the four quantities, S_A, S_B, S_C, S_D as functions of the vectors d and $\hat{d}$. (Strictly speaking, they are functions of the underlying configuration and $\hat{d}$. However, we shall find it convenient to let d stand for the configuration which gives rise to it.) Thus we can write $S_A(d, \hat{d})$, etc. Now

$$\min_{d,\hat{d}} S_A(d, \hat{d}) = \min_d \left[\min_{\hat{d}} S_A(d, \hat{d})\right].$$

Let

$$S_A(d) = \min_{\hat{d}} S_A(d, \hat{d}).$$

We introduce similar notation for alternatives B and C. (Alternative D is handled differently.)

It turns out that for $\hat{d}$ to minimize $S_A(d, \hat{d})$ with d fixed, $\hat{d} - \bar{d}$ must have just the right length (and likewise for B and C). This length, which we call the *proper* length, can be written in a simple way. In fact, let θ be the angle between $d - \bar{d}$ and $\hat{d} - \bar{d}$. Then the proper length for $\hat{d} - \bar{d}$ is

$$\|d - \bar{d}\| \cos\theta \qquad \text{(alternative } A\text{)},$$
$$\|d - \bar{d}\| / \cos\theta \qquad \text{(alternative } B\text{)},$$
$$\|d - \bar{d}\| \qquad \text{(alternative } C\text{)}.$$

We shall prove this shortly. First, let us see what it yields. Clearly, the minimization which defines $S_A(d)$ leads to the same resulting value if $\hat{d} - \bar{d}$ is required to have the proper length (as well as $\hat{d}$ being in the constraint set). However, when d and $\hat{d}$ are such that $\hat{d} - \bar{d}$ has the *proper length* (and $\hat{d}$ is in the constraint set), *then* $S_A(d, \hat{d})$ and $S_B(d, \hat{d})$ both equal $\sin\theta$, while $S_C(d, \hat{d})$ equals $(2(1 - \cos\theta))^{1/2}$. But $S_D(d, \hat{d})$ equals $\cos\theta$. From this, it is clear that the four alternatives all achieve optimum values at the same configuration. Furthermore, alternatives A and B yield the same value, and the identity $\sin^2\theta + \cos^2\theta = 1$ yields a simple relationship between that value and the value from alternative D, namely ${S_A}^2 = {S_B}^2 = 1 - {S_D}^2$. For alternative C, by simple algebra, we have $S_D = 1 - \frac{1}{2}{S_C}^2$.

It remains to prove the facts about proper length. Let d and $\hat{d}$ be given with $\hat{d}$ in the constraint set. Let S_p mean any one of S_A, S_B, S_C (the nature of the parameter p will be seen shortly). Consider

$$S_p(d, x(\hat{d} - \bar{d}) + \bar{d}) = S_p(x)$$

as a function of x. Suppose the length of $\hat{d} - \bar{d}$ is already adjusted so that $\|d - \bar{d}\| = \|\hat{d} - \bar{d}\| \cos\theta$, in other words, so that $\hat{d} - d$ is perpendicular to $d - \bar{d}$. (It is helpful to make a diagram with d, $\hat{d}$, $\bar{d}$ as the vertices of a right triangle.) Then treating $(d - \bar{d})$ and $(\hat{d} - \bar{d})$ as constant

$$S_p(x) = \frac{\|x(\hat{d} - \bar{d}) - (d - \bar{d})\|}{\|d - \bar{d}\|^{1-p}\|x(\hat{d} - \bar{d})\|^p}$$

$$= \frac{\|x(\hat{d} - d) + (x - 1)(d - \bar{d})\|}{\|d - \bar{d}\|^{1-p}\|x(\hat{d} - \bar{d})\|^p}$$

$$= \frac{(x^2\|\hat{d} - d\|^2 + (x - 1)^2\|d - \bar{d}\|^2)^{1/2}}{\|d - \bar{d}\|^{1-p}x^p\|\hat{d} - d\|^p}$$

(the simplification in the numerator was possible because of the assumed perpendicularity of $\hat{d} - d$ and $d - \bar{d}$). To get alternatives A, B, and C, we let p take on values 0, 1, and $\frac{1}{2}$, respectively.

Let the length of $\hat{d} - \bar{d}$ be represented by L. Then $\|d - \bar{d}\| = L\cos\theta$ and $\|\hat{d} - d\| = L\sin\theta$ (by elementary trigonometry). Making these substitutions yields

$$S_p(x) = \frac{(x^2L^2\sin^2\theta + (x - 1)^2L^2\cos^2\theta)^{1/2}}{L^{1-p}(\cos\theta)^{1-p}x^pL^p} = \frac{(x^2\sin^2\theta + (x - 1)^2\cos^2\theta)^{1/2}}{(\cos\theta)^{1-p}x^p}$$

Differentiating $S_p(x)$ with respect to x, setting the resultant expression to zero, and solving, we find the optimum values of x to be $\cos^2\theta$, 1, and $\cos\theta$ for the three alternatives, respectively. Since the initial length of $\hat{d} - \bar{d}$ was $\|d - \bar{d}\|/\cos\theta$, the "adjusted" length for the three alternatives (after multiplication by the appropriate value of x) are as stated earlier. Furthermore, substitution of these values of x into the expression for $S_p(x)$, with appropriate values of p (followed by simplification utilizing appropriate trigonometric identities), yields the value of S_A, S_B, and S_C [$\sin\theta$, $\sin\theta$, and $(2(1 - \cos\theta))^{1/2}$] stated earlier.

Analogous developments are possible when the scale factors are $\sum d^2$, $\sum \hat{d}^2$, or $(\sum d^2 \sum \hat{d}^2)^{1/2}$ (for scale factors of type 1). The relations are, in fact, simpler to derive. In this case, the $\bar{d}$ vector is replaced by the zero vector, and we assume only that the constraint set for $\hat{d}$ is closed under multiplication by a positive constant (that is, we may drop the additive constant a from our assumption about the "richness" of the regression procedure). Now θ is simply the angle between d and $\hat{d}$. Clearly, in this case, the analog of the correlation measure used for alternative D is

$$\frac{\sum d\hat{d}}{(\sum d^2 \sum \hat{d}^2)^{1/2}} = \frac{d \cdot \hat{d}}{\|d\| \cdot \|\hat{d}\|}.$$

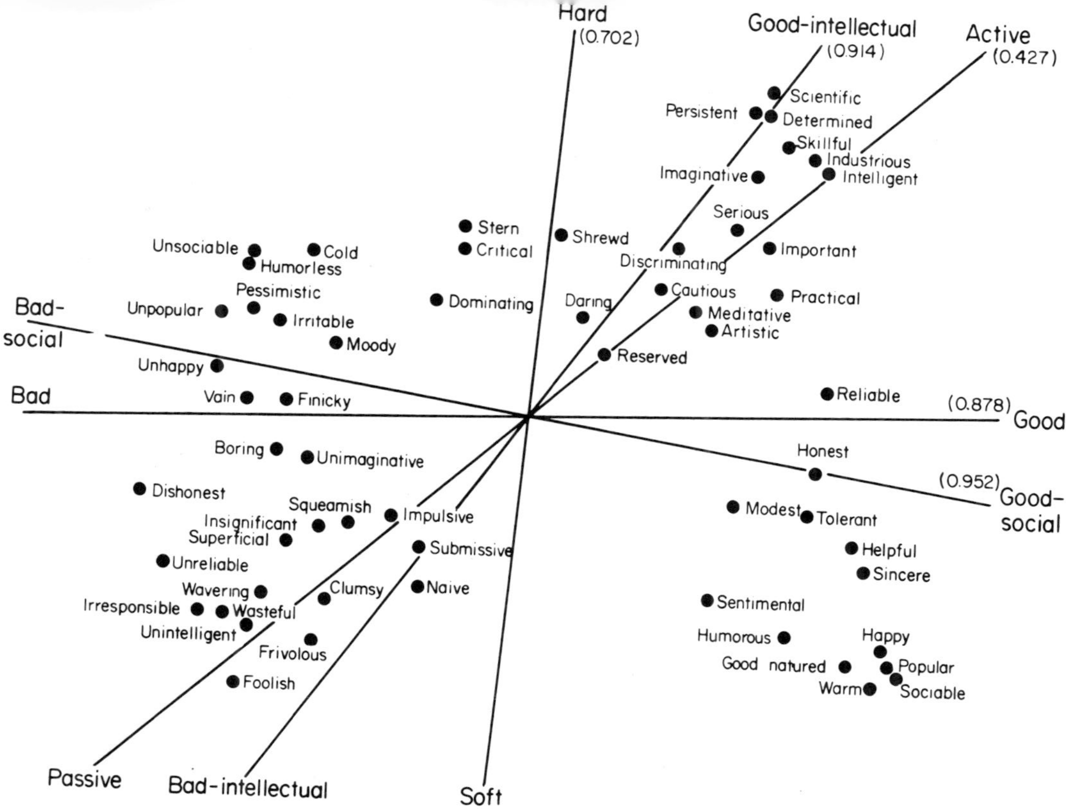

Fig. 1. Two-dimensional configuration of 60 traits showing best-fitting axis for five properties: *good-bad*; *hard-soft*; *active-passive*; *social desirability*; *intellectual desirability*. Each number in parentheses indicates correlation between projections on best fitting axis and property values.

I would like to give one recent and very interesting application of scaling. Rosenberg and his collaborators (1968) worked with 64 adjectives which are used to describe people, such as "intelligent," "lazy," "sociable." Each subject was asked to group these into several groups so that each group could plausibly be used to describe a single person. After many subjects had completed this task, a primary measure of similarity was derived by seeing how often each pair of adjectives was grouped together. From the matrix of similarities, a secondary measure of disassociation was derived as the squared euclidian distance between rows of the matrix. When the disassociations were scaled in 2 dimensions, Fig. 1 resulted. This presents a very satisfying picture which indicates that an important part of the common cultural meaning of these adjectives can be described in terms of two coordinates.

In a separate experiment *using new subjects*, the subjects were asked to rate each of the adjectives on a single scale such as "intelligence—high or low" or "active—passive." Five such scales were distributed among the subjects in this experiment. (Each subject handled only one scale.) For each scale, the median of the subjects' responses was used as the group rating for that adjective. These group ratings from each scale were then regressed linearly against the two-dimensional configuration coordinates. The arrows in Fig. 1 indicate the direction of ascent of the resulting linear functions. The numbers on the arrows indicate the value of the multiple correlation coefficients for that linear regression. The excellent concordance of two different experiments presents very convincing evidence that an important culturally common element of semantic meaning has in fact been extracted for this collection of adjectives.

Rosenberg and his collaborators used nonmetric scaling and did their scalings in three dimensions, two dimensions, and one dimension. The scatter diagrams from each of the scalings are shown in Fig. 2. We see from

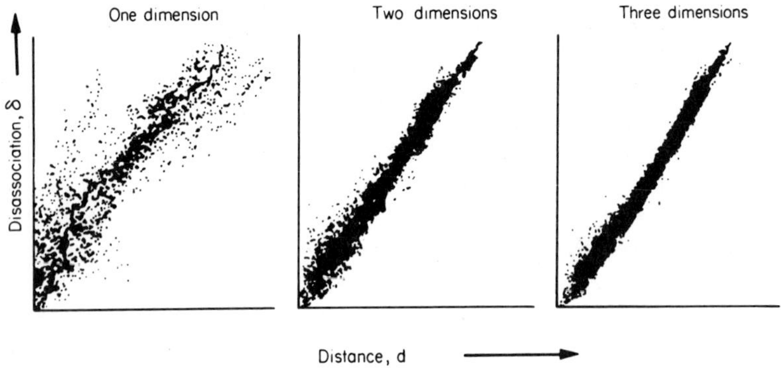

Fig. 2. Scattergrams of d versus δ (disassociation) for solutions in one-, two-, and three-dimensional spaces.

these figures that simple scaling could have been used without distorting the situation and that in fact simple scaling might do slightly better in providing the exact configuration. However, I doubt that any great difference would result in a situation like this one.

5. MULTIDIMENSIONAL UNFOLDING

Unfolding was invented by Coombs (1950) and later generalized to the multidimensional case by Bennett and Hays (1960). Unfolding has always been thought to be closely related to multidimensional scaling. The view of unfolding that we discuss here enhances this relationship so strongly that both models can be and are handled by a single computer program in a natural unified way. The distinction arises simply through the use of slightly different options. A typical situation for which unfolding seems appropriate is one in which several judges or subjects rank several stimuli or objects in order of preference. Thus, each judge assigns to all the objects a score or ranking indicating how well he prefers that object in comparison to all the others. Formally speaking, such data constitute a score matrix in which judges are substituted for variables.

Our particular version of multidimensional unfolding is based on the following model. A single euclidian space is used. Each object and each judge is represented by one point in that space. It is supposed that all judges perceive the objects in a similar common manner and that the location of the object point corresponds to how the object is perceived. However, each judge has an ideal kind of object which, if it existed, would be located at that judge's point. The judge points are sometimes called ideal points because they represent the ideal objects of the judges. A further key assumption, which is what brings unfolding into such a close relationship with scaling, is that each judge ranks the objects in accordance with how far they are from his ideal point. The farther a real object is from his ideal object, the less he likes it. (A slight generalization which is sometimes used is to permit each judge to have an antiideal rather than an ideal object. Thus his point could indicate the kind of object he likes least rather than the kind of object he likes most.)

A classic example which shows why unfolding is a very natural kind of model is the situation in which coffee has been sweetened by different amounts of sugar, and different judges decide how well they like these different cups of coffee. Presumably, the judges would agree fairly well as to how sweet the different cups of coffee are. However, each judge would presumably have his own ideal degree of sweetness, and downgrade the other cups according to how much they differed from his ideal. This would lead, of course, to a one-dimensional unfolding. If we now introduce cream into the coffee as well, we could easily get a two-dimensional unfolding. By introducing different types of coffee and different kinds of cream and milk, and perhaps even different kinds of sweetness, the situation could become quite multidimensional. Of course, it is easy to imagine situations in which a judge would have more than one ideal point. Thus, in some ways the model we are using is a fairly limited one. Indeed, one of the authors (Carroll) has worked in another context with models in which the judge's preference function is permitted to depend in a much more flexible way on the position of the object point than we permit here. However, that approach has one great simplification that the present one does not; namely, it supposes that the objects have *already* been placed in a perceptual space by some technique, such as scaling. Thus, the positions of the objects are not free to change during his computations: only the subject's preference functions may change. By contrast, the approach to be described now does not presuppose that the perceptual space is understood in advance, so the objects must be placed in their correct positions by the computation. While quite a number of interesting applications have been made of one-dimensional unfolding, very little has been done yet with multidimensional unfolding, presumably because of the great methodological difficulties it has offered. However, there are several people working actively on this problem now, and I am optimistic that in the not too distant future, practical methods will be available and useful results will be forthcoming.

Given a configuration of judges and objects, and given the data, how shall we measure the badness-of-fit? One approach is to copy the method we have used before with multidimensional scaling. For the moment, consider only one judge. Make a scatter diagram of the distances (from his ideal point to all the object points) versus the rankings of scores he has assigned to the objects. If the configuration matches the data well, then low preference will correspond to large distances and high preference to small distances. To measure the deviation from the situation, it is very natural to perform a regression (of some kind) of distance on preference score, and use the residual sum of squares. If the preference scores are simply ordinal rankings, then it seems appropriate to use monotone descending regression. If the scores are actual numerical preferences, other kinds of regression would also be natural, such as linear or polynomial regression (though we might like to restrict the polynomials used to be monotone descending over the relevant region). Once a particular type of regression has been settled upon, we see that it is necessary to divide the residual sum of squares by a suitable scale factor, for the same reason that the same operation was necessary in multidimensional scaling, namely to provide invariance if the configuration is uniformly expanded or contracted.

At this point, we have a separate badness-of-fit function for each judge. Now the question is how to combine them. Originally, based on nothing more than programming convenience, I took the square root of each judge's badness-of-fit, and then averaged across judges.

Before proceeding, let us stop and consider why an alternative badness-of-fit function is not acceptable. Why are the scatter diagrams for the different judges split apart and separate regressions performed (as we have described above)? Why not use a single composite diagram for all judges, and perform a single regression which includes all judges? (We restrict ourselves throughout the following discussion to the use of monotone regression. This is important, since the use of other kinds of regression changes the picture quite substantially.) It turns out that it is vital to split the scatter diagrams and perform a separate regression for each judge. Otherwise, it is always possible to obtain a configuration of zero stress regardless of what data is used. This configuration can be described as follows. First, among the scores provided by all judges for all objects, find the smallest value. We refer to the object and the judge that go with that score as the distinguished object and the distinguished judge. This pair should be farther apart in the final solution than any other object-judge pair. Now represent all the objects except the distinguished object by the same point. Similarly, represent all the judges except the distinguished judge by some other single point. Using each of these points as a center, draw the circle which goes through the other point. On the circle containing the common object point, place the distinguished object point, and on the circle containing the common judge point, place the distinguished judge point. This insures that all the distances from a judge point to an object point are the same, with the exception of the distance from the distinguished judge point to the distinguished object point. Now make sure that the distinguished object point and the distinguished judge point have been placed on the circles in such a way that their distance is larger than the distance between the common object point and the common judge point. Using the distances from this configuration, monotone regression will result in a perfect fit. The residual sum of squares will be zero. While this configuration seems to require at least two dimensions, it can be reduced to one dimension by allowing the distinguished object and judge to move around their respective circles until they both lie on the straight line defined by the common object and common judge point. (There is one partial exception to this statement. If the secondary approach to monotone regression is being used, and if the highest score which was picked out is tied with other scores of the same size, then this statement will not hold.) Regardless of which scale factor is used, the badness-of-fit function in this case will turn out to be zero. Thus when monotone regression is used, it is necessary to split the scatter diagrams and perform separate regressions in order for the badness-of-fit function to satisfy the most elementary requirements of common sense. (This mathematical state of affairs was discovered empirically several years ago by Kruskal in an attempt to perform nonmetric scaling in a situation which closely resembles unfolding, namely where the only dissimilarities which have been observed are between objects of two different types and no dissimilarities have been observed between the objects of each type.)

Now let us consider what scale factor to use in the individual badness-of-fit function for each judge. We restrict our attention to the two discussed previously, namely, $\sum d^2$ and $\sum (d - \bar{d})^2$. Again recalling that our analysis is restricted to the use of monotone regression, we point out that the first scale factor cannot be used. To see this, consider the special configuration described above. (Alternatively, consider a simpler configuration in one dimension in which all objects are at one point and all judges at another.) Even though we split the scatter diagrams and perform separate regressions, as decided above, the residual sum of squares from each of these separate regressions is zero. If we use the first scale factor, then the denominator in each of the individual badness-of-fit functions is strictly positive. Consequently, the configuration has an overall stress of zero, which rules out the first scale factor. (This argument rules out the first scale factor regardless of whether splitting is done.) However, the second scale factor is zero for each judge except the distinguished judge. Consequently, with one exception, the individual badness-of-fit values are 0/0. While this is not a positively reassuring sign, it does suggest that a computation which seeks to minimize the overall badness-of-fit will avoid this kind of configuration.

As an interesting historical note, the option of using the second scale factor and the option of splitting the regressions were added to the program by Kruskal at different times, for reasons having no connection with unfolding. When the possibility of doing unfolding was realized, Jih-Jie Chang and the authors started testing the unfolding application of version 4 of M-D-SCAL empirically.

Of course, the first step in empirical testing is to use synthetic data. Thirty random object points in the plane were generated and fifteen random judge points. (We actually used 45 points from Coombs and Kao (1960), who had generated them for a very similar purpose.) The distances between the judge points and the object points were calculated. The rank order of these distances were fed into the program as data. Figure 3 shows the original configuration, and also the recovered configuration after it has been rotated[2] to best fit with the original. We see from this that the reconstruction is excellent. Two further tests were done by adding different amounts of random error to the distances before taking their rank orders. Each distance was altered by adding to it a pseudorandom normal deviate. The standard deviation of these deviates was chosen by comparison with the standard deviation of the 450

[2] Here and subsequently, the program actually used found the best linear transformation, not the best orthogonal rotation. However, except where noted, the transformation was close to an orthogonal rotation. The "best" transformation means the one which minimizes the sum of squared distances, and hence the measure of agreement described below.

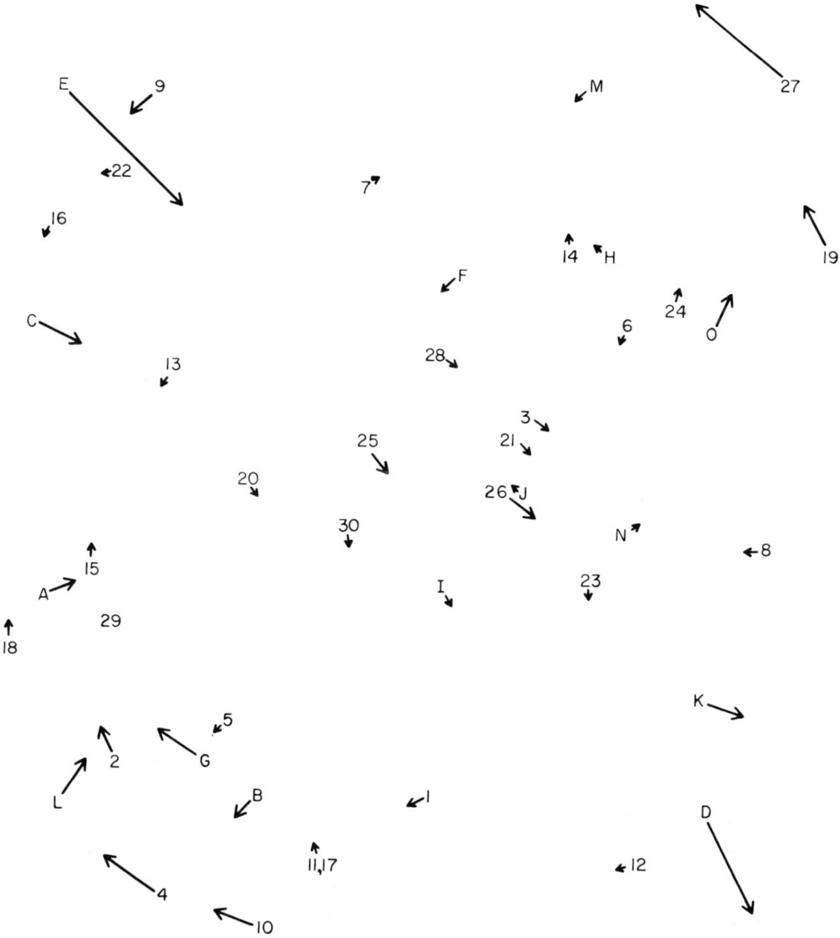

Fig. 3. Original artificial configuration of 30 "stimuli" and 15 "judges," as shown by the numbers and letters, respectively, with reconstructed configuration shown by arrowheads. Preference data based on the original configuration were "unfolded" by a generalized multidimensional scaling program, version 4 of M-D-SCAL, to reconstruct configuration. Reconstructed configuration was then rotated to best fit with original configuration. (Stress = *0.044*, measure of agreement = *0.993*.)

distances themselves. In the low-noise case, the standard deviation for the random deviates was 0.5 times the standard deviation of the original distances, while in the high-noise case it was 0.71 times that standard deviation. Figures 4 and 5 show the reconstructions in the same way that the previous figure did. Although the noise certainly reduces the accuracy of the reconstruction

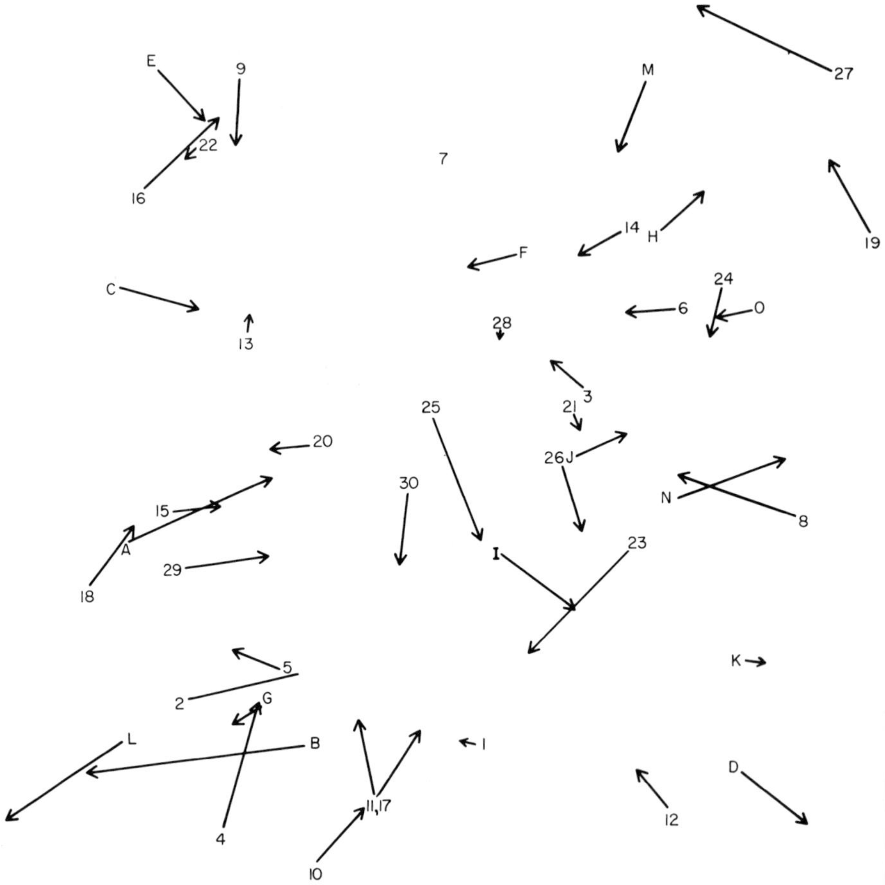

Fig. 4. Same original configuration as in Fig. 3. However, synthetic data were altered by independent random "errors" before "unfolding" was applied. Standard deviation of errors is 0.5 times standard deviation of preference values. (Stress $=0.28$, measure of agreement $=0.961$.)

quite substantially, the low-noise reconstruction still remains quite good. It should be noted that Fig. 5 resulted from a calculation in which the true original configuration was used as the starting configuration. Unfortunately, the one solution we obtained without this help was a local minimum which looked considerably worse than Fig. 5. (Presumably, a solution equivalent to Fig. 5 could be obtained by trying several different starting configurations, and would distinguish itself as best by having the lowest stress value.) This suggests that the computational method could be improved, but supports the definition of stress.

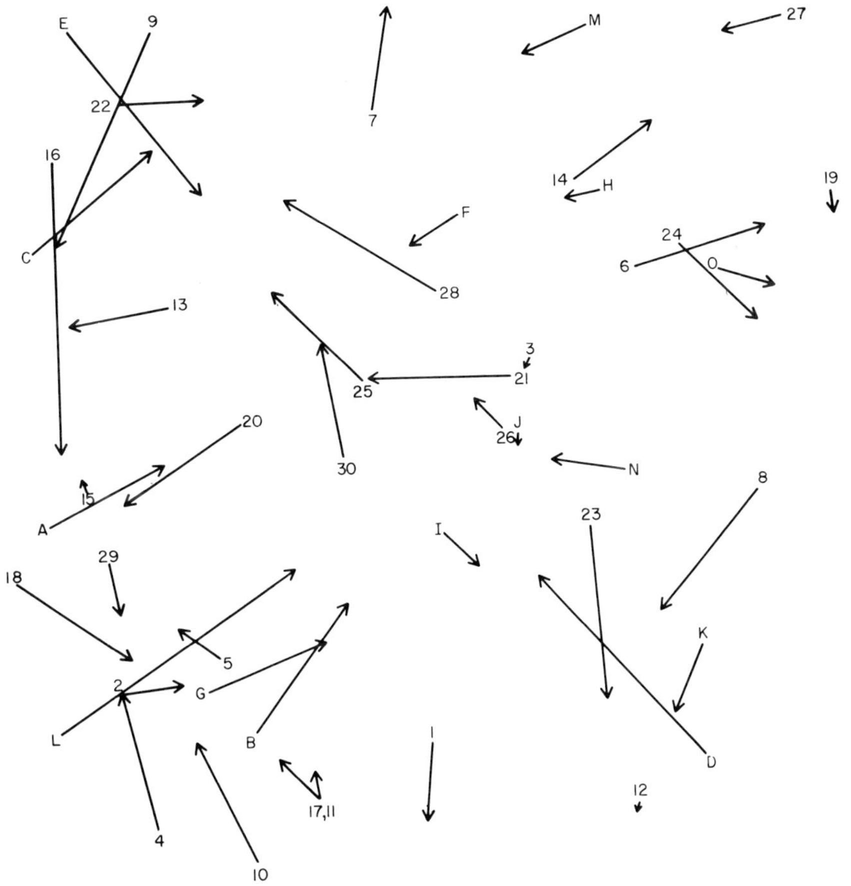

Fig. 5. Same as Fig. 4, except that standard deviation of errors is 0.71 times standard deviation of preference values (Stress = *0.36*, measure of agreement = *0.925*).

The stress values associated with Figs. 3, 4, and 5 are 0.044, 0.28, and 0.36. The stress of the other solution to the high-noise case is 0.39. The accuracy with which the original configuration has been reconstructed may be summarized numerically by the "measure of agreement" $[1 - (\sum d_i^2)/(\sum d_{i0}^2)]^{1/2}$, where d_i is the distance between the original position of the point i and the reconstructed position of point i (after rotation), while d_{i0} is the distance between the original position of point i and the centroid of the configuration. Figures 3, 4, and 5 yielded values of 0.993, 0.961, and 0.925. The other solution to the high-noise case yielded 0.726.

Suppose the judge points all lie well outside the region which contains the object points. Then the distance from an object point to a single judge point is almost completely along a line from the region of space containing the object points through the judge point. In other words, when the judge points are far out, this model becomes very like (and ordinally identical to) the vector model which underlies factor analysis. (In the vector model, it is the projections of the stimulus points on each judge vector which are compared

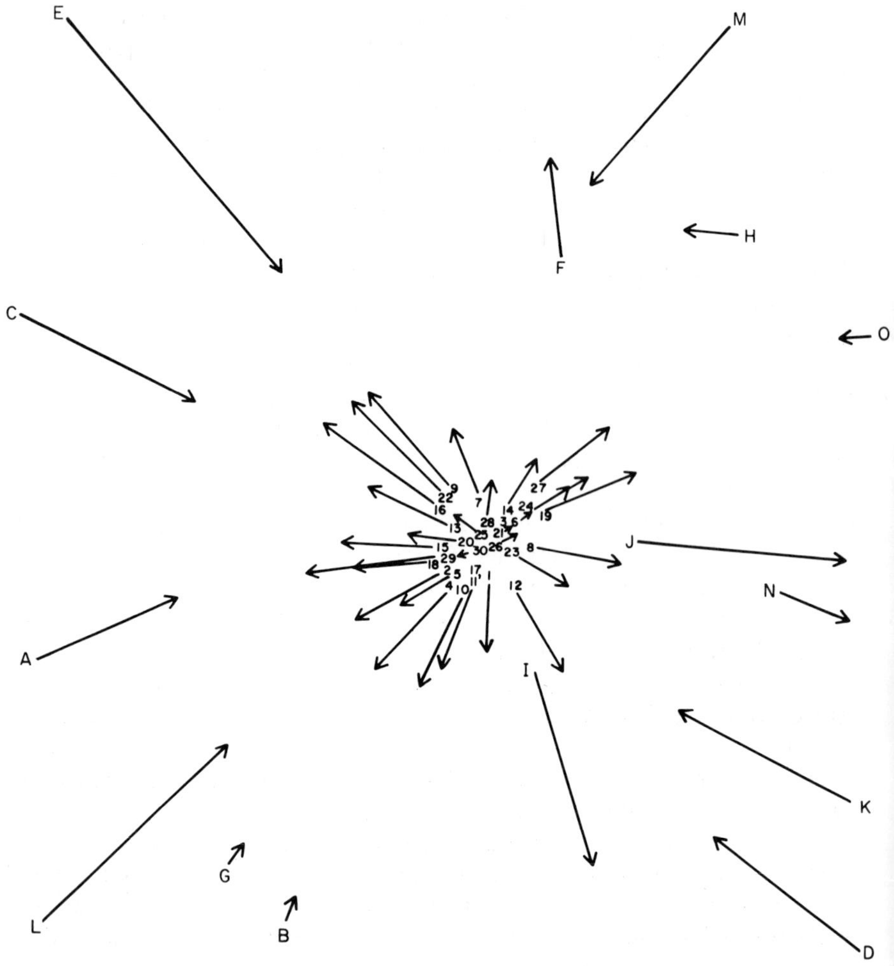

Fig. 6. Same as Fig. 3, except that original configuration was changed so that synthetic data approximated data arising from a vector model. The actual change involved merely moving each judge point 10 times as far from the origin. (Stress = *0.040*, measure of agreement = *0.883*.)

with the data.) In order to test the computational value of this approach under these circumstances, the original 15 judge points were all multiplied by a factor of 10 so as to place almost all of them well outside the region of the object points. Distances from the judge points to the object points were computed (no noise was added), and the program was tried once again. The reconstruction is shown in Fig. 6, whose stress and measure of agreement are 0.040 and 0.883.

It is immediately clear that while relatively large errors have occurred in the radial distance of the judge points, the angle at which they lie is quite good. Since in the vector model only the angle is recovered, the use of this approach for vector model situations seems encouraging. Furthermore, a little thought shows that when monotone regression is being used, the radial distance of remote judge points cannot be reconstructed very well because once the judge point is sufficiently far out, further radial motion does not change the rank order of the distances to that judge point at all. For these reasons, we decided to measure the agreement between our solution and the original configuration as if we were dealing with a vector model, in a manner which is entirely insensitive to radial distance of the judge points. Unfortunately, there is no way to do this which is as elegant as the single measure of agreement used above, nor is there any standard measure.

What we actually did was to bring the reconstructed solution into best agreement with the original configuration in a certain sense explained below. The results are shown in Fig. 7, where the reconstructed judge vectors and the original judge vectors are shown as radial lines of fixed length. For the stimulus points alone, the measure of agreement described above is 0.9977. For the judge vectors, the cosine of the angle between the reconstructed vector and the original vector averages to 0.9986. Thus in the vector model sense, the reconstruction is excellent.

To bring the reconstruction into agreement with the original configuration as shown in Fig. 7, we found the best linear transformation in terms of the stimulus points alone. We then applied to the judge vectors the appropriate companion transformation for the vector model situation (namely, the inverse adjoint transformation).

The next step of course was to use real data. So far we have experimented primarily with two sets of data. One set which comes from a book by Newcomb (1961) was drawn to our attention by Terry Gleason who is at the University of Michigan, where he has been working on an approach quite similar to the one we have been describing. In essence, the data simply consist of rankings provided by 17 fraternity men on how well they like all the others. This ranking process was repeated once each week for many weeks. The other set of data was collected by Peter Bricker, Sandra Pruzansky, and Barbara McDermott of Bell Telephone Laboratories. Various

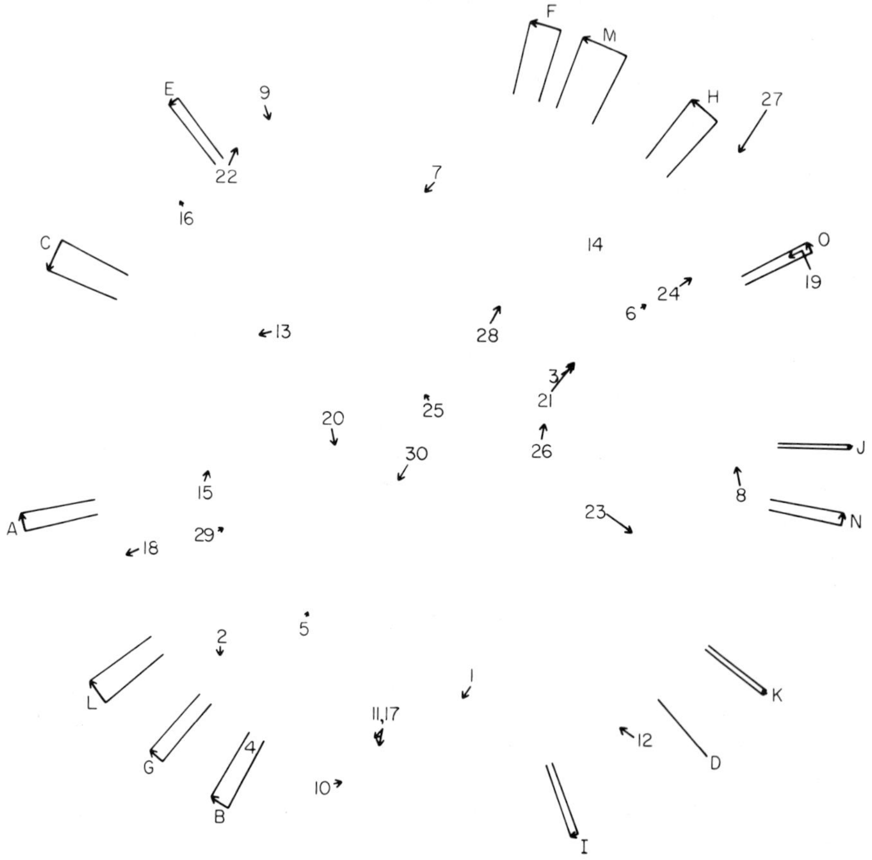

Fig. 7. Same as Fig. 6, except that stimuli alone were rotated (actually, linearly transformed) to best fit with original stimuli. Appropriate companion transformation (inverse adjoint) was applied to judge vectors. Judge vectors are shown as having fixed common length, since actual length is immaterial in vector model if monotone regression is used. (Stress = *0.040*, measure of agreement for stimuli alone = *0.9977*, average cosine of angle between original and reconstructed judge vectors = *0.9986*).

synthetic sounds for possible use to replace the telephone bell were ranked according to pleasantness by many subjects. The data pertain to 12 sounds and 49 subjects. It rapidly became clear when working with this data that the badness-of-fit function in use was not, in fact, acceptable, despite its success with synthetic data. Among other problems was the fact that there always appeared to be one or a few judges for whom the individual badness-of-fit values have an absolute *maximum* value, namely 1. If the data is edited by removing these judges, then the same phenomenon again happens with other judges. After some thought it appeared that at least part of the difficulty resulted from the way the individual badness-of-fit values were combined into the overall badness-of-fit. Starting from the ratio of the sum of squares, we first took the square root and then averaged. It appeared that as the configuration was changing during the computation, this method of combining the individual badness-of-fit values gave too much weight to the further decrease in those which were already quite small, and paid insufficient attention to reducing the large values. To rectify this situation, it was decided to change from

$$n^{-1} \sum \left(\frac{\sum (d - \hat{d})^2}{\sum (d - \bar{d})^2} \right)^{1/2}$$

to

$$\left(n^{-1} \sum \frac{\sum (d - \hat{d})^2}{\sum (d - \bar{d})^2} \right)^{1/2}.$$

This makes the larger badness-of-fit values contribute much more substantially to the overall value, and certainly alters the balance. This helps a good deal, and the method works much better after this change. However, we still do not feel that we have produced a successful practical application of unfolding.

We believe that the method may now be good enough to be successful with some data in some cases, even though we do not have such examples. In addition to Terry Gleason, whom we have mentioned, there are other people following approaches quite like this one. This is clearly within the spirit of the times. Louis Guttman and James Lingoes have one or more programs which do something similar. Young has modified the TØRSCA program (Young and Torgerson, 1967) for similar purposes, and Green and Carmone have used it. It should be noted, however, that Young does not split the regression by judges (rather, all the judges are pooled in the same regression), and uses a badness-of-fit measure equivalent to the older definition of stress. As discussed above, a degenerate solution with technically perfect fit always exists in any number of dimensions. His procedure is evidently saved from converging to a degenerate solution because he starts with a very good, rationally generated starting configuration, and iterates into a nearby local minimum which substantively speaking is a good solution. Also, Roskam (1968) in the Netherlands has just completed a doctoral thesis which contains interesting work that is again closely related. He appears to have avoided one difficulty because he averaged the ratios rather than their square roots right from the beginning. However, as far as we can judge, he has been having exactly the same problems we have at this stage. From what we have learned about these various approaches, we feel that all of them are vulnerable to one of the two kinds of theoretical degeneracies discussed earlier, and avoid them in practice (if at all) by use of "rational" starting configurations.

Our personal belief is that our badness-of-fit function is still not the right one to use in this situation. We are looking for some mathematically satisfying way of changing it which would appear to provide a way out. So far we have not been able to find it. We tend to see the practical behavior and the 0/0 situation described above as both stemming from the same source. While waiting for the mathematical situation to improve and some stroke of inspiration to come along, we have been doing further experimentation. Since version 4 of M-D-SCAL permits polynomial regression of specified degree, with or without constant term, there is a lot of experimentation possible. Also, when a badness-of-fit function is somewhat inadequate but not totally without merit, its weaknesses can sometimes be overcome by starting the iterative computation with a good starting configuration. For example, it may happen that the badness-of-fit function has a local minimum at the configuration which is really most desirable, even though its global minimum is undesirable. This also leads to many possibilities for empirical work. However, we will not take up space describing the fragmentary observations. It suffices to say that what we have is not yet a working method, but we have considerable optimism for the future.

Acknowledgments

The authors are pleased to acknowledge the very valuable contribution of Mrs. Jih-Jie Chang to the analysis of the artificial unfolding data. We are also grateful to Myron Wish, whose penetrating questions stimulated several of the developments in this paper. Mrs. Carolyn Brown was also very helpful in a number of ways.

REFERENCES

Ball, G. (1965). Data analysis in the social sciences: what about the details?. *Joint Comput. Conf. Proc., Fall, 1965* **27** Pt. 1, pp. 533–559.

Bennett, J. F., and Hays, W. L. (1960). Multidimensional unfolding: determining the dimensionality of ranked preference data. *Psychometrika* **25** 27–43.

Coombs, C. H., and Kao, R. C. (1960). On a connection between factor analysis and multidimensional unfolding. *Psychometrika* **25** 219–231.

Coombs, C. H. (1950). Psychological scaling without a unit of measurement. *Psychological Rev.* **57** 148–158.

Fitch, W. M., and Margoliash, E. (1967). Construction of phylogenetic trees. *Science* **155** 279–284.

Gower, J. C. (1967). Comparison of some methods of cluster analysis. *Biometrics* **23** 623–637.

Green, P., and Carmone, F. J. (1968). An empirical comparison of nonmetric unfolding techniques. Unpublished paper.

GUTTMAN, L. (1968). A general nonmetric technique for finding the smallest coordinate space for a configuration of points. *Psychometrika* **33**. To be published.

HARTIGAN, J. A. (1967). Representation of similarity matrices by trees. *J. Amer. Statist. Assoc.* **62** 1140–1158.

JOHNSON, S. C. (1967). Hierarchical clustering schemes. *Psychometrika* **32** 241–254.

KRUSKAL, J. B. (1964a). Multidimensional scaling by optimizing goodness of fit to a nonmetric hypothesis. *Psychometrika* **29** 1–27.

KRUSKAL, J. B. (1964b). Nonmetric multidimensional scaling: a numerical method. *Psychometrika* **29** 115–129.

LINGOES, J. C. (1966). Recent computational advances in nonmetric methodology for the behavioral sciences. *Proc. Internat. Symp.: Mathematical and Computational Methods in Social Sciences.* Rome: International Computation Centre, pp. 1–38.

MCGEE, V. E. (1966). The multidimensional analysis of "elastic" distances. *British J. Math. Statist. Psychology* **19** 181–196.

NEWCOMB, T. N. (1961). "The Acquaintance Process." Holt, New York.

ROHLF, J. (1967). Correlated characters in numerical taxonomy. *Systematic Zoology* **16** 109–126.

ROHLF, J., and FISHER, D. (1968). The co-phenetic correlation coefficient as an index of structure in taxonomic data. *Systematic Zoology*. To be published.

ROSENBERG, S., NELSON, C., and VIVEKANANTHAN, P. S. (1968). A multidimensional approach to the structure of personality impressions. *J. Personality Social Psychology* **9** 283–294.

ROSKAM, E. I. (1968). Metric analysis of ordinal data in psychology: models and numerical methods for metric analysis of conjoint ordinal data in psychology. Ph.D. Thesis, Katholieke Univ. te Nijmegen.

SHEPARD, R. N. (1962). The analysis of proximities: multidimensional scaling with an unknown distance function, Pts. I and II. *Psychometrika* **27** 125–140, 219–246.

SHEPARD, R. N. (in press). Psychological representation of speech sounds. *In* "Human Communication: A Unified View" (E. E. David and P. B. Denes, eds.). McGraw-Hill, New York.

SHEPARD, R. N., and CARROLL, J. D. (1966). Parametric representation of nonlinear data structures. *In* "Multivariate Analysis." (P. R. Krishnaiah, ed.), pp. 561–592. Academic Press, New York.

SOKAL, R. R., and ROHLF, J. (1962). The comparison of dendrograms by objective methods. *Taxon.* **11** 33–40.

SOKAL, R. R., and SNEATH, P. H. A. (1963). "Principles of Numerical Taxonomy." Freeman, San Francisco, California.

TORGERSON, W. S. (1965). Multidimensional scaling of similarity. *Psychometrika* **30** 379–393.

WYLIE, D. (1967). Latent partition analysis. *Psychometrika* **32** 183–193.

YOUNG, F. W., and TORGERSON, W. S. (1967). TØRSCA, a Fortran IV program for Shepard-Kruskal multidimensional scaling analysis. *Behavioral Sci.* **12** 498.

VAN EEDEN, C. (1957a). Maximum likelihood estimation of partially or completely ordered parameters, I. *Nederl. Akad. Wetensch. Proc.* Ser. **A60** 128–136.

VAN EEDEN, C. (1957b). Note on two methods for estimating ordered parameters of probability distributions. *Nederl. Akad. Wetensch. Proc.* Ser. **A60** 506–512.

Optimality of Principal Components

MASASHI OKAMOTO

DEPARTMENT OF STATISTICS
IOWA STATE UNIVERSITY
AMES, IOWA

DEPARTMENT OF APPLIED MATHEMATICS[1]
OSAKA UNIVERSITY
OSAKA, JAPAN

1. INTRODUCTION

The notion of principal components of a sample was introduced by Pearson [6] as a statistical tool to reduce multivariate data encountered in applied statistical research into a smaller dimensionality. He defined a "plane of closest fit" as a subspace which minimizes the sum of squares of the distances from each point contained in the data. The term "principal components" was applied by Hotelling [4] to a random vector, which can be regarded as a generalization of the older notion applied to a sample.

Various ways of characterization or interpretations of principal components of a sample as well as of a random vector have been presented since by several authors (Anderson [1], Wilks [10], Rao [7, 8], Darroch [3], Takeuchi and Masuda [9], Okamoto and Kanazawa [5]). Since all of them are stated in terms of minimization or maximization, they may be called optimal properties, which we shall classify into three categorics: variation, information loss, and correlation optimality.

The present paper surveys and unifies theories on optimality of principal components with the following two new contributions: (i) In some cases, it simultaneously considers all the eigenvalues of a matrix which characterize the performance of a feasible solution of the minimization or maximization problem. This is a more general treatment of the problem than in literature since the trace, the Euclidean norm, or the determinant of a matrix as used quite often is each an increasing function of the eigenvalues arranged in order of magnitude. (ii) In each case, it determines all optimum solutions of the problem, whereas any paper published so far states only a sufficient condition of an optimum solution.

[1] Present address.

2. LEMMAS IN MATRIX THEORY

First, we shall state the following fundamental lemma in matrix theory.

Lemma 2.1. *Let A be a real symmetric $p \times p$ matrix. Then there exists a pair of $p \times p$ matrices Λ and V which satisfy*

$$AV = V\Lambda, \qquad V'V = I_p, \qquad \Lambda \text{ is diagonal,} \tag{2.1}$$

where I_p stands for an identity $p \times p$ matrix. The diagonal elements $\lambda_1, \ldots, \lambda_p$ of Λ are the roots of the determinantal equation in λ

$$|A - \lambda I_p| = 0 \tag{2.2}$$

with identical numbers of multiplicity. Thus, under the restriction that $\lambda_1 \geq \lambda_2 \geq \cdots \geq \lambda_p$, the matrix Λ is determined uniquely, whereas V is determined uniquely except for a post-factor

$$S = \begin{bmatrix} S_1 & & 0 \\ & \ddots & \\ 0 & & S_t \end{bmatrix}, \qquad S_i \in O(m_i), \quad i = 1, \ldots, t, \tag{2.3}$$

where t is the number of different eigenvalues of A, $m_1, \ldots, m_t$ denote the numbers of multiplicity of them and $O(m)$ stands for the set of all orthogonal matrices of order p.

Definition. *The diagonal elements $\lambda_1, \ldots, \lambda_p$ of Λ are called eigenvalues of the matrix A. Any $p \times 1$ vector v satisfying $Av = \lambda_i v$ for some $i = 1, \ldots, p$ is called an eigenvector of A associated with λ_i.*

Let $v_1, \ldots, v_p$ be the columns of the matrix V. Since the first equation of (2.1) is equivalent to

$$Av_i = \lambda_i v_i \qquad \text{for} \quad i = 1, \ldots, p, \tag{2.4}$$

the set $\{v_1, \ldots, v_p\}$ is an orthonormal set of eigenvectors of A associated with $\lambda_1, \ldots, \lambda_p$.

Definition. *For a real symmetric matrix A of order p, we denote by $\lambda_i(A)$ the* i*th largest eigenvalue of A, $i = 1, \ldots, p$. We write simply λ_i if there is no fear of ambiguity. For any $k = 1, \ldots, p$, an orthonormal set of eigenvectors $\{v_1, \ldots, v_k\}$ of A associated with $\lambda_1, \ldots, \lambda_k$ (or $\lambda_p, \ldots, \lambda_{p-k+1}$) will be called first* (*or last*) *k eigenvectors of A.*

Lemmas 2.2–2.5 are well known (see, for example, Rao [8] or Bellman [2] for Lemma 2.5) except for an explicit statement of a necessary and sufficient condition that the bounds are attained.

Lemma 2.2.

$$\sup_x x'Ax/x'x = \lambda_1(A),$$

where the left-hand side denotes the supremum over all real $p \times 1$ vectors x. The supremum is attained iff x is a first eigenvector of A. Dually,

$$\inf_x x'Ax/x'x = \lambda_p(A)$$

and the infimum is attained iff x is a last eigenvector of A.

Lemma 2.3. *For any $k = 1, 2, \ldots, p-1$, let $\{v_1, \ldots, v_k\}$ be a set of first k eigenvectors of A. Then*

$$\sup_{\substack{v_i'x=0\\ i=1,\ldots,k}} \frac{x'Ax}{x'x} = \lambda_{k+1}(A).$$

The supremum is attained iff x is an eigenvector of A associated with $\lambda_{k+1}(A)$. Dually, if $\{v_1, \ldots, v_k\}$ is a set of last k eigenvectors of A, then

$$\inf_{\substack{v_i'x=0\\ i=1,\ldots,k}} \frac{x'Ax}{x'x} = \lambda_{p-k}(A),$$

and the infimum is attained iff x is an eigenvector of A associated with $\lambda_{p-k}(A)$.

Lemma 2.4 (The Courant-Fischer min-max theorem).

$$\inf_L \sup_{L'x=0} x'Ax/x'x = \lambda_{k+1}(A), \tag{2.5}$$

where "inf" *denotes the infimum with respect to a $p \times k$ matrix L, while* "sup" *denotes the supremum with respect to a $p \times 1$ vector x satisfying $L'x = 0$. The infimum is attained when L consists of first k eigenvectors of A. Equation* (2.5) *also holds true when L is, at most, of rank k with any number of columns.*

Lemma 2.5. *If A and B are real symmetric matrices, and if B is nonnegative definite, then*

$$\lambda_i(A + B) \geq \lambda_i(A) \qquad \text{for any } i. \tag{2.6}$$

A necessary and sufficient condition that the equality sign holds simultaneously in (2.6) *is that $B = 0$.*

Lemma 2.6. *Let P be a $p \times k$ matrix ($k \leq p$) such that $P'P = I_k$. Then*

(i) *It holds that*

$$\lambda_i(P'AP) \leq \lambda_i(A) \qquad \text{for any} \quad i = 1, \ldots, k. \tag{2.7}$$

(ii) *A necessary and sufficient condition that the equality sign in* (2.7) *holds for all i simultaneously is that*

$$P = V_k Q,$$

where V_k is a $p \times k$ matrix consisting of first k eigenvectors of A and $Q \in O(k)$.

Proof. (i) By Lemma 2.4, there exists for each i a $p \times (i-1)$ matrix L such that

$$\sup_{L'x=0} x'Ax/x'x = \lambda_i(A).$$

Now

$$\sup_{L'x=0} x'Ax/x'x \geq \sup_{\substack{L'x=0 \\ x=Py}} x'Ax/x'x = \sup_{L'Py=0} (Py)'A(Py)/(Py)'(Py)$$

$$= \sup_{(P'L)'y=0} y'(P'AP)y/y'y \geq \lambda_i(P'AP),$$

since $P'L$ is a $k \times (i-1)$ matrix. This proves (i).

(ii) *Sufficiency.* If $P = V_k Q$, then it follows that

$$\lambda_i(P'AP) = \lambda_i(Q'\Lambda_k Q) = \lambda_i(\Lambda_k) = \lambda_i \qquad \text{for each} \quad i,$$

where Λ_k is the diagonal matrix with the diagonal elements $\lambda_1, \ldots, \lambda_k$.

Necessity. Assume that $\lambda_i(P'AP) = \lambda_i(A)$ for all i. Then there exists $Q \in O(k)$ such that $\Lambda_k = QP'APQ'$. Since $A = V \Lambda V'$, we have

$$\Lambda_k = QP'V \Lambda V'PQ' = R' \Lambda R, \tag{2.8}$$

where we have put $R = V'PQ'$. Now

$$R'R = QP'VV'PQ' = I_k. \tag{2.9}$$

If we write $R = (r_1, \ldots, r_k)$, then (2.8) and (2.9) imply

$$r_i' \Lambda r_i = \lambda_i, \qquad r_i' r_j = \delta_{ij}, \qquad i, j = 1, \ldots, k.$$

By Lemmas 2.2 and 2.3, we know that $\{r_1, \ldots, r_k\}$ is a set of first k eigenvectors of Λ, and hence R is represented by first k columns of a matrix S given in (2.3). Define $V_k = VR$, then $P = VRQ = V_k Q$ and $V_k = (Vr_1, \ldots, Vr_k)$ consists of first k eigenvectors of A.

Lemma 2.7. *If A is nonnegative definite, and if T is a $p \times k$ ($k \leq p$) matrix such that all diagonal elements of $T'T$ are unity, then*

(i) $|T'AT| \leq \prod_{i=1}^{k} \lambda_i$.

(ii) *Assume $r(A) \geq k$. A necessary and sufficient condition that the equality sign holds in* (i) *is that*

$$T = V_k Q$$

with the same V_k and Q defined in Lemma 2.6.

Proof. (i) Let $\delta_1 \geq \cdots \geq \delta_k$ be the eigenvalues of $T'T$ and $u_1, \ldots, u_k$ be corresponding orthonormal eigenvectors. Write

$$\Delta = \begin{bmatrix} \delta_1 & & 0 \\ & \ddots & \\ 0 & & \delta_k \end{bmatrix} \qquad \text{and} \qquad U = (u_1, \ldots, u_k).$$

Then it holds that $T'TU = U\Delta$. If $\delta_k = 0$, we can easily show (i). Suppose, therefore, that $\delta_k > 0$ and define $G = U\Delta^{-1/2}$, $P = TG$. Since

$$\delta_1 + \cdots + \delta_k = \operatorname{tr}(T'T) = k,$$

we have

$$\left(\prod_{i=1}^{k} \delta_i\right)^{1/k} \leq k^{-1} \sum_{i=1}^{k} \delta_i = 1.$$

Thus

$$|P'AP| = |G'T'ATG| = |G|^2 |T'AT| = \left(\prod_{i=1}^{k} \delta_i\right)^{-1} |T'AT| \geq |T'AT|. \tag{2.10}$$

Since

$$P'P = G'T'TG = \Delta^{-1/2} U'T'TU \Delta^{-1/2} = I_k,$$

Lemma 2.6 implies

$$|P'AP| = \prod_{i=1}^{k} \lambda_i(P'AP) \leq \prod_{i=1}^{k} \lambda_i(A). \tag{2.11}$$

This and (2.10) prove (i).

(ii) *Sufficiency.* If $T = V_k Q$, then

$$|T'AT| = |Q'V_k'AV_kQ| = |V_k'AV_k| = |\Lambda_k| = \prod_{i=1}^{k} \lambda_i .$$

Necessity. We assume $|T'AT| = \prod_i \lambda_i$, then it follows from (2.10) and (2.11) that $\delta_i = 1$ for any i, and

$$\lambda_i(P'AP) = \lambda_i(A) \qquad \text{for any } i. \tag{2.12}$$

Hence, $\Delta = I_k$, and we may suppose $U = I_k$, which implies in turn $G = I_k$ and $T = P$. From (2.12) and Lemma 2.8, we have $P = V_k Q$.

Definition. *For any matrix A, let $M(A)$ denote the linear space (or manifold) spanned by the columns of A. If A has n rows, then $M(A)$ is conceived as a subspace of R^n. For any two subspaces M_1 and M_2 of R^n, we denote by $[M_1, M_2]$ the linear subspace generated by M_1 and M_2.*

The following lemma will be obvious.

Lemma 2.8. *If for three matrices A, B, and C, it holds that $A = B + C$ and $r(A) \geq r(B) + r(C)$, then*

$$M(A) = [M(B), M(C)] = [M^{\perp}(B), M^{\perp}(C)], \tag{2.13}$$

where $M^{\perp}$ stands for the orthocomplement subspace taken in the space $M(A)$.

Lemma 2.9.[2] *If A, B, and $A - B$ are real symmetric and nonnegative definite matrices, and if B is, at most, of rank k, then*

(i) *it holds that*

$$\lambda_i(A - B) \geq \lambda_{k+i}(A) \qquad \text{for any } i, \tag{2.14}$$

where $\lambda_j(A) = 0$ for $j > p$.

(ii) *A necessary and sufficient condition that the equality sign in* (2.14) *holds simultaneously for all i is that*

$$B = \lambda_1(A)v_1v_1' + \cdots + \lambda_k(A)v_k v_k', \tag{2.15}$$

where $v_1, \ldots, v_k$ is a set of first k eigenvectors of A.

Proof. Put $C = A - B$.

(i) By Lemma 2.4, there exists for each i a $p \times (i - 1)$ matrix L such that

$$\lambda_i(C) = \sup_{L'x=0} \frac{x'Cx}{x'x}. \tag{2.16}$$

The right-hand side, however, is not smaller than

$$\sup_{\substack{L'x=0\\ B'x=0}} \frac{x'(A-B)x}{x'x} = \sup_{(B,L)'x=0} \frac{x'Ax}{x'x} \geq \lambda_{k+i}(A),$$

since the matrix (B, L) is, at most, of rank $k + i - 1$.

(ii) *Sufficiency.* Let $\{v_1, \ldots, v_p\}$ be an augmented set of orthonormal eigenvectors of A, then we have $A = \sum_{i=1}^{p} \lambda_i v_i v_i'$. The assumption (2.15) implies then

$$C = \sum_{i=k+1}^{p} \lambda_i v_i v_i',$$

which means that C has the eigenvalues $\lambda_{k+1}, \ldots, \lambda_p$ together with k zeroes.

Necessity is obvious if A has the rank $r = r(A) \leq k$. Suppose that $r > k$ and that C has the eigenvalues $\lambda_{k+1}, \ldots, \lambda_p$ together with k zeroes. Let $\{v_{k+1}, \ldots, v_r\}$ be a set of first $r - k$ eigenvectors of C, then we have

$$C = \lambda_{k+1}v_{k+1}v_{k+1}' + \cdots + \lambda_r v_r v_r'. \tag{2.17}$$

Since $r(A) = r$, $r(B) \leq k$ and $r(C) = r - k$, from Lemma 2.8, it follows that

$$M(A) = [M(B), M(C)] = [M^{\perp}(B), M^{\perp}(C)].$$

[2] Though this lemma is identical with Lemma 2.3 of Okamoto and Kanazawa [5], a simplified proof will be given here, the necessity part of which has been suggested to the author by Dr. K. Isii, Osaka University.

Since $v_i \in M(C) \subset M(A)$, there exists $u_i \in M^{\perp}(C)$ such that $v_i + u_i \in M^{\perp}(B)$ for $i = k+1, \ldots, r$. Let $\| \ \|$ denote the Euclidean norm of the vector. Since $v_r + u_r$ belongs to $M^{\perp}(B) \subset M(A)$, it is orthogonal to any set of last $p - r$ eigenvectors of A. By the dual part of Lemma 2.3, we find that

$$\begin{aligned} \lambda_r \|v_r + u_r\|^2 &\le (v_r + u_r)' A (v_r + u_r) \\ &= (v_r + u_r)' C (v_r + u_r) \qquad \text{since} \quad B(v_r + u_r) = 0 \\ &= v_r' C v_r \qquad \text{since} \quad C u_r = 0 \\ &= \lambda_r \|v_r\|^2 \le \lambda_r \|v_r + u_r\|^2. \end{aligned}$$

Therefore, all equality signs should hold, and hence $u_r = 0$, and in turn

$$v_r' A v_r = \lambda_r \|v_r\|^2.$$

By the dual part of Lemma 2.5, v_r is found to be an eigenvector of A associated with λ_r.

Next, we shall consider v_{r-1}. Since $v_{r-1} \perp v_r$ from the definition and $u_{r-1} \perp M(C) \ni v_r$, it follows that $v_{r-1} + u_{r-1} \perp v_r$. Moreover, $v_{r-1} + u_{r-1}$ is orthogonal to any set of last $p - r$ eigenvectors of A. Therefore, using Lemma 2.3, we have

$$\lambda_{r-1} \|v_{r-1} + u_{r-1}\|^2 \le (v_{r-1} + u_{r-1})' A (v_{r-1} + u_{r-1}).$$

The right-hand side can be shown to be not greater than

$$\lambda_{r-1} \|v_{r-1}\|^2 \le \lambda_{r-1} \|v_{r-1} + u_{r-1}\|^2$$

in a way similar to v_r. Thus, $u_{r-1} = 0$, and hence

$$v_{r-1}' A v_{r-1} = \lambda_{r-1} \|v_{r-1}\|^2.$$

Thus v_{r-1} is an eigenvector of A associated with λ_{r-1}.

By mathematical induction, we can conclude that $v_{k+1}, \ldots, v_r$ is a set of orthonormal eigenvectors of A associated with $\lambda_{k+1}, \ldots, \lambda_r$. Now let $v_1, \ldots, v_r$ be an augmented set of first r eigenvectors of A, then it follows that

$$A = \lambda_1 v_1 v_1' + \cdots + \lambda_r v_r v_r'. \tag{2.18}$$

From (2.17) and (2.18), we obtain (2.15).

3. DEFINITION OF PRINCIPAL COMPONENTS

3.1. Principal Components of a Random Vector

Let x be a random $p \times 1$ vector with mean vector $\mu = E(x)$ and covariance matrix $\Sigma = V(x) = E(x - \mu)(x - \mu)'$. Let $\lambda_1 \ge \lambda_2 \ge \cdots \ge \lambda_p$ (≥ 0) be the eigenvalues of Σ, and $\gamma_1, \ldots, \gamma_p$ be a set of orthonormal $p \times 1$ eigenvectors of Σ associated with $\lambda_1, \ldots, \lambda_p$, respectively.

Definition. *For $i = 1, \ldots, p$, the random variable $\xi_i = \gamma_i'(x - \mu)$ will be called an* ith *principal component of x.*

If we write

$$\xi = \begin{bmatrix} \xi_1 \\ \vdots \\ \xi_p \end{bmatrix}, \qquad \Lambda = \begin{bmatrix} \lambda_1 & & 0 \\ & \ddots & \\ 0 & & \lambda_p \end{bmatrix} \qquad \text{and} \qquad \Gamma = (\gamma_1, \ldots, \gamma_p),$$

then we have

$$\xi = \Gamma'(x - \mu) \tag{3.1}$$

and

$$\Sigma\Gamma = \Gamma\,\Lambda, \qquad \Gamma'\Gamma = I_p, \qquad \Lambda \text{ is diagonal.} \tag{3.2}$$

Then from Lemma 2.1, we have the following:

Theorem 3.1. *Principal components of x are unique except for a pre-factor S' of the type* (2.3) *applied to ξ.*

From (3.1) and (3.2), we can easily obtain the following property of principal components:

$$E(\xi) = 0 \qquad \text{and} \qquad V(\xi) = \Lambda, \tag{3.3}$$

or

$$E(\xi_i) = 0, \qquad \mathrm{Cov}(\xi_i, \xi_j) = \lambda_i \delta_{ij} \qquad i, j = 1, \ldots, p.$$

3.2. Principal Components of a Sample

Let $x_1, \ldots, x_N$ be a sample of $p \times 1$ vectors of size N. This is not necessarily a random sample drawn from a certain population, and it is regarded simply as numerical data. The $p \times N$ matrix

$$X = (x_1, \ldots, x_N)$$

will be called the sample matrix or data matrix. Define the sample mean vector

$$E_s(X) = N^{-1} \sum_{\alpha=1}^{N} x_\alpha = \bar{x} = \hat{\mu} \qquad \text{(say)}$$

and the sample covariance matrix

$$V_s(X) = N^{-1} \sum_{\alpha=1}^{N} (x_\alpha - \bar{x})(x_\alpha - \bar{x})' = \hat{\Sigma} \qquad \text{(say).}$$

Let $\hat{\lambda}_1 \geq \hat{\lambda}_2 \geq \cdots \geq \hat{\lambda}_p$ (≥ 0) be the eigenvalues of $\hat{\Sigma}$ and $\hat{\gamma}_1, \ldots, \hat{\gamma}_p$, be a set of orthonormal eigenvectors of $\hat{\Sigma}$ associated with $\hat{\lambda}_1, \ldots, \hat{\lambda}_p$, respectively.

Definition. *For any real $p \times 1$ vector x and $i = 1, \ldots, p$, the scalar $\xi_i = \hat{\gamma}_i{}'(x - \hat{\mu})$ will be called an* ith *sample principal component of x.*

If we write

$$\xi = \begin{bmatrix} \xi_1 \\ \vdots \\ \xi_p \end{bmatrix}, \qquad \hat{\Lambda} = \begin{bmatrix} \hat{\lambda}_1 & & 0 \\ & \ddots & \\ 0 & & \hat{\lambda}_p \end{bmatrix} \qquad \text{and} \qquad \hat{\Gamma} = (\hat{\gamma}_1, \ldots, \hat{\gamma}_p),$$

then we have

$$\xi = \hat{\Gamma}'(x - \hat{\mu}) \tag{3.4}$$

and

$$\hat{\Sigma}\hat{\Gamma} = \hat{\Gamma}\hat{\Lambda}, \qquad \hat{\Gamma}'\hat{\Gamma} = I_p, \qquad \hat{\Lambda} \text{ is diagonal.} \tag{3.5}$$

If we denote by $\xi_{i\alpha} = \hat{\gamma}_i{}'(x_\alpha - \hat{\mu})$ the ith sample principal component of x_α for $i = 1, \ldots, p$; $\alpha = 1, \ldots, N$, and let $\Xi = (\xi_{i\alpha})$, a $p \times N$ matrix, then we have, similarly as in (3.3), that

$$E_s(\Xi) = 0 \qquad \text{and} \qquad V_s(\Xi) = \hat{\Lambda}. \tag{3.6}$$

Now we have the following theorem which implies that the notion of principal components of data is a special case of that of a random vector, and hence we have only to consider the latter in the next section.

Theorem 3.2. *If for a given sample matrix $X = (x_1, \ldots, x_N)$, we define a random $p \times 1$ vector x by the probability distribution*

$$\Pr\{x = x_\alpha\} = N^{-1} \qquad \textit{for} \quad \alpha = 1, \ldots, N,$$

then the sample principal components of x_α, $\alpha = 1, \ldots, N$ are the αth *values taken by the principal components of the random vector x.*

Proof. The mean vector of x is given by

$$\mu = E(x) = \sum_{\alpha=1}^{N} x_\alpha \Pr\{x = x_\alpha\} = N^{-1} \sum_{\alpha=1}^{N} x_\alpha = \hat{\mu},$$

while the covariance matrix is

$$\begin{aligned} \Sigma &= E(x - E(x))(x - E(x))' \\ &= \sum_{\alpha=1}^{N} (x_\alpha - \hat{\mu})(x_\alpha - \hat{\mu})' \Pr\{x = x_\alpha\} \\ &= N^{-1} \sum_{\alpha=1}^{N} (x_\alpha - \hat{\mu})(x_\alpha - \hat{\mu})' = \hat{\Sigma}. \end{aligned}$$

Thus $\hat{\Lambda} = \Lambda$, while $\hat{\Gamma} = \Gamma$ with a suitable choice of a postfactor S mentioned in Lemma 2.1. The principal components of the random vector x are given by

$$\xi = \Gamma'(x - \mu) = \hat{\Gamma}'(x - \hat{\mu}),$$

which obeys the probability distribution

$$\Pr\{\xi = \xi_\alpha\} = N^{-1} \qquad \text{for} \quad \alpha = 1, \ldots, N,$$

where $\xi_\alpha = \hat{\Gamma}'(x_\alpha - \hat{\mu})$ is the sample principal components of x_α. This completes the proof.

4. OPTIMALITY OF PRINCIPAL COMPONENTS

4.1. Variation Optimality

Theorem 4.1.

(i) *Consider the following problem:*

Maximize $\quad \mathrm{Var}(\gamma' x)$
Subject to the condition: γ is a $p \times 1$
vector with unit length, i.e., $\gamma'\gamma = 1$.

The solution γ is an eigenvector of Σ associated with γ_1.

(ii) *For fixed $k = 1, 2, \ldots, p - 1$ let $\{\gamma_1, \ldots, \gamma_k\}$ be a set of first k eigenvectors of Σ. Consider the problem:*

Maximize $\quad \mathrm{Var}(\gamma' x)$
Subject to the condition: γ is a $p \times 1$ vector with
unit length satisfying $\mathrm{Cov}(\gamma' x, \gamma_i' x) = 0 \quad$ for $\quad i = 1, \ldots, k$.

The solution γ is an eigenvector of Σ associated with λ_{k+1} and orthogonal to $\gamma_1, \ldots, \gamma_k$.

Proof. Since $\mathrm{Var}(\gamma' x) = \gamma' \Sigma \gamma$, (i) is reduced to Lemma 2.2. Similarly (ii) follows from Lemma 2.3 since $\mathrm{Cov}(\gamma' x, \gamma_i' x) = \gamma' \Sigma \gamma_i = \lambda_i \gamma' \gamma_i$.

Theorem 4.2. *The solution of the problem: For fixed $k = 1, \ldots, p$*

Maximize $\quad |V(T'x)|$
Subject to the condition: T is a $p \times k$ matrix
and all diagonal elements of $T'T$ are unity

is written as $T = \Gamma_k Q$, where Γ_k is a $p \times k$ matrix consisting of $\gamma_1, \ldots, \gamma_k$, a set of first k eigenvectors of Σ, and $Q \in O(k)$.

Proof. By Lemma 2.7, the determinant of the matrix $V(T'x) = T' \Sigma T$ is maximized iff $T = \Gamma_k Q$, where $\Gamma_k = (\gamma_1, \ldots, \gamma_k)$ consists of first k eigenvectors of Σ and $Q \in O(k)$.

Similarly, from Lemma 2.6, we obtain the following:

Theorem 4.3. *The solution of the problem: For fixed $k = 1, \ldots, p$*

Maximize simultaneously all the eigenvalues of $V(T'x)$
Subject to the condition: T is a $p \times k$ matrix such that $T'T = I_k$

is $T = \Gamma_k Q$ *as in Theorem* 4.2.

Remark. In this theorem we cannot replace the condition $T'T = I_k$ by the one in the previous theorem, i.e., that all diagonal elements of $T'T$ are unity. For instance, if $T = (\gamma_1, \ldots, \gamma_1)$, then the eigenvalues of $V(T'x)$ are $k\lambda_1$ and $k-1$ zeros.

4.2. Information Loss Optimality

If we want to approximate the given random $p \times 1$ vector x by a linear form $Ay + b$ of some random $k \times 1$ vector y, then the error of approximation or information loss may be measured by the mean square error matrix $E(x - Ay - b)(x - Ay - b)'$ or rather by its eigenvalues, p in number. The following theorem has been proved by Okamoto and Kanazawa [5] in the special case in which $E(x) = 0$ and $b = 0$.

Theorem 4.4. *Consider the following problem: For fixed* $k = 1, \ldots, p$

Minimize simultaneously all the eigenvalues of

$$E(x - Ay - b)(x - Ay - b)'$$

Subject to the condition: A is a $p \times k$ matrix,
b is a $p \times 1$ vector and y is a random $k \times 1$ vector.

The solution is given by

$$Ay + b = \gamma_1 \xi_1 + \cdots + \gamma_k \xi_k + \mu. \tag{4.1}$$

The following two theorems can be obtained as corollaries.

Theorem 4.5 (Darroch [3]). *For fixed* $k = 1, \ldots, p$ *the problem:*

Minimize $\operatorname{tr} E(x - Ay - b)(x - Ay - b)'$
Subject to the same condition as in Theorem 4.4

has the solution (4.1).

Theorem 4.6 (Rao [7]). *For fixed* $k = 1, \ldots, p$ *the problem:*

Minimize $\|E(x - AT'x - b)(x - AT'x - b)'\|$,
where $\| \ \|$ denotes the norm of a matrix
Subject to the condition: A and T are
$p \times k$ matrices and b is a $p \times 1$ vector

has the solution $AT'x + b = \gamma_1 \xi_1 + \cdots + \gamma_k \xi_k + \mu$.

4.3. Correlation Optimality

Theorem 4.7. *Assume rank* $(\Sigma) \geq k$ *for fixed* $k = 1, \ldots, p$. *Then the problem:*

Maximize $\sum_{i=1}^{p} \mathrm{Var}(x_i) R^2(x_i, y)$,
where R denotes the multiple correlation coefficient
Subject to the condition: y is a random
$k \times 1$ vector with $E(y) = 0$

has a solution $y = (\xi_1, \ldots, \xi_k)'$. *The solution is unique except for a pre-factor* L, *a* $k \times k$ *nonsingular matrix.*

First, we need the following lemma which is essentially contained in the proof of the main theorem of Okamoto and Kanazawa [5].

Lemma 4.1. *Let* x *and* y *be random* $p \times 1$ *and* $k \times 1$ *vectors, respectively, satisfying* $E(x) = 0$, $E(y) = 0$, $E(xx') = \Sigma$, $E(yy') = I_k$, *and* $E(xy') = B$. *Denote by* $\lambda_1 \geq \cdots \geq \lambda_k$ *the first* k *eigenvalues of* Σ, *where we assume* $\lambda_k > 0$, *and by* $\gamma_1, \ldots, \gamma_k$ *a set of first* k *eigenvectors of* Σ. *Then a necessary and sufficient condition that*

$$BB' = \lambda_1 \gamma_1 \gamma_1' + \cdots + \lambda_k \gamma_k \gamma_k' \tag{4.2}$$

is that there exists $Q_1 \in O(k)$ *such that*

$$B = (\lambda_1^{1/2} \gamma_1, \ldots, \lambda_k^{1/2} \gamma_k) Q_1$$

and

$$y = Q_1'(\gamma_1/\lambda_1^{1/2}, \ldots, \gamma_k/\lambda_k^{1/2})' x.$$

Proof of Theorem 4.7. When $E(y) = 0$, the multiple correlation coefficient is defined by

$$R^2(x_i, y) = E(x_i y')[V(y)]^{-1} E(y x_i)/\mathrm{Var}(x_i). \tag{4.3}$$

Since this is invariant under any nonsingular linear transformation of y, we may assume that $V(y) = I_k$. Define $B = E(xy')$, then

$$\sum_{i=1}^{p} \mathrm{Var}(x_i) R^2(x_i, y) = \sum_{i=1}^{p} E(x_i y') E(y x_i) = \mathrm{tr}(BB').$$

Since $\Sigma - BB' = V(x - By)$ is nonnegative definite, from Lemma 2.9 we have

$$\mathrm{tr}(\Sigma - BB') = \sum_{i=1}^{p} \lambda_i(\Sigma - BB') \geq \sum_{i=1}^{p} \lambda_{k+i} = \sum_{i=k+1}^{p} \lambda_i.$$

On the other hand,

$$\mathrm{tr}(\Sigma - BB') = \mathrm{tr}(\Sigma) - \mathrm{tr}(BB') = \sum_{i=1}^{p} \lambda_i - \mathrm{tr}(BB'),$$

and hence

$$\operatorname{tr}(BB') \leq \sum_{i=1}^{k} \lambda_i .$$

But Lemma 2.9 implies that the equality sign holds iff

$$BB' = \lambda_1 \gamma_1 \gamma_1' + \cdots + \lambda_k \gamma_k \gamma_k'.$$

Thus, using Lemma 4.1, we have

$$\begin{aligned} y &= Q_1'(\gamma_1/\lambda_1^{1/2}, \ldots, \gamma_k/\lambda_k^{1/2})'x = Q_1'(\xi_1/\lambda_1^{1/2}, \ldots, \xi_k/\lambda_k^{1/2})' \\ &= L(\xi_1, \ldots, \xi_k)', \end{aligned}$$

where L is a $k \times k$ nonsingular matrix.

REFERENCES

1. ANDERSON, T. W. (1958). "An Introduction to Multivariate Statistical Analysis." Wiley, New York.
2. BELLMAN, R. (1960). "Introduction to Matrix Analysis." McGraw-Hill, New York.
3. DARROCH, J. N. (1965). An optimal property of principal components. *Ann. Math. Statist.* **36** 1579–1582.
4. HOTELLING, H. (1933). Analysis of a complex statistical variables into principal components. *J. Educational Psychology* **26** 417–441, 498–520.
5. OKAMOTO, M., and KANAZAWA, M. (1968). Minimization of eigenvalues of a matrix and optimality of principal components. *Ann. Math. Statist.* **39** 859–863.
6. PEARSON, K. (1901). On lines and planes of closest fit to systems of points in space. *Phil. Mag.* **2** 559–572.
7. RAO, C. R. (1964). The use and interpretation of principal component analysis in applied research. *Sankhyā Ser. A* **26** 329–358.
8. RAO, C. R. (1965). "Linear Statistical Inference and Its Applications." Wiley, New York.
9. TAKEUCHI, K., and MASUDA, T. (1966). On principal component analysis and factor analysis (in Japanese). *Management Sci.* **9** 141–176.
10. WILKS, S. S. (1960). Multidimensional statistical scatter. "Contributions to Probability and Statistics" (I. Olkin *et al.*, eds.), pp. 486–503. Stanford Univ. Press, Stanford, California.

Information Theory and the Statistical Estimation of Econometric Relations

GERHARD TINTNER

DEPARTMENT OF ECONOMICS
UNIVERSITY OF SOUTHERN CALIFORNIA
LOS ANGELES, CALIFORNIA

M. V. RAMA SASTRY

GRADUATE SCHOOL OF BUSINESS ADMINISTRATION
UNIVERSITY OF WASHINGTON
SEATTLE, WASHINGTON

INTRODUCTION

Historically, the statistical application of information theory was started with the works of Wiener [21] on cybernetics. It was later applied by Shannon (see Shannon and Weaer [15]) to communication theory. Applications of information theory to the problems of economics were considered by Theil [16] and Tintner [18]. The purpose of this article is to show that certain statistical estimation procedures are optimum in the sense of information theory. The procedures considered are: least squares, weighted regression, maximum likelihood, two-stage least squares, and k-class estimators.

1. THEORY OF INFORMATION

Every number may be written as a dyadic fraction. Hence, a set E_N of real numbers with N elements contains the information, defined by

$$I(E_N) = \log_2 N. \tag{1}$$

This definition of information due to Hartley [5] obeys the following obvious relations:

(a) $I(E_{NM}) = I(E_N) + I(E_M)$;
(b) $I(E_N) < I(E_{N+1})$;
(c) $I(E_2) = 1$.

Let $E_1, E_2, \ldots, E_n$ be disjoint sets, and let $E = E_1 + E_2 + \cdots + E_n$. Assume that E_k has N_k elements and

$$p_k = N_k/N. \tag{2}$$

Then a measure of average information to which set E_k, an element of E belongs, is

$$H(P) = \sum_{k=1}^{n} p_k \log_2(p_k)^{-1}. \tag{3}$$

Shannon [15] deduced this formula for the entropy of the probability distribution $P = (p_1, p_2, \ldots, p_n)$, which gives the amount of information contained in a single observation of a random variable X which assumes values $x_1, x_2, \ldots, x_n$ with probabilities $P(X = x_k) = p_k$. Shannon's concept of information satisfies the following postulates (see, for example, Rényi [14]). Let π denote the set of all finite, discrete probability distributions $P = (p_1, p_2, \ldots, p_k)$.

$$p_k \geq 0, \qquad k = 1, 2, \ldots, n, \qquad \text{and} \qquad \sum_{k=1}^{n} p_k = 1.$$

Define a function $I(P) = I(p_1, \ldots, p_n)$ for all $P \in \pi$ which satisfies the following conditions:

(a) $I(p, 1-p)$ is a continuous function of p for $0 \leq p \leq 1$ and $I(\frac{1}{2}, \frac{1}{2}) = 1$.
(b) $I(p_1, \ldots, p_n)$ is a symmetric function of the probabilities.
(c) If $0 \leqq \theta < 1$, we have

$$I(p_1, p_2, \ldots, p_{n-1}, \theta p_n, (1-\theta)p_n) = I(p_1, p_2, \ldots, p_n) + p_n I(\theta, 1-\theta).$$

Then $I(P) = H(P)$.

Shannon's measure of information has one limitation that with this measure any condensation of the data results in loss of information whereas some condensation is possible with Fisher's measure without loss of information. See Kempthorne [7] and Kullback [11] for further discussion.

Kullback [10] obtained a generalized entropy known as the discrimination information. This measure could be defined as follows. Let $f_i(x)$ be density function with respect to λ, $i = 1, 2$. If H_i, $i = 1, 2$ is the hypothesis that x is from the statistical population with density f_i, then the mean information per observation from the density f_2 for discrimination in favor of the hypothesis of the second against the first population is

$$I(2:1) = \int f_2(x) \log f_2(x)/f_1(x)\, d\lambda. \tag{4}$$

The integral is taken over the whole space of the random variable. A measure of divergence between the two hypotheses could be expressed as

$$J(1, 2) = I(1:2) + I(2:1) = \int [f_1(x) - f_2(x)] \log f_1(x)/f_2(x)\, d\lambda. \tag{5}$$

This measure of divergence does not satisfy the triangle inequality property of a distance or metric as defined in topology, and hence was not termed as a distance.

Now using natural logarithms, let us define the divergence of two populations with probability distributions $f_1(x_1, x_2, \ldots, x_k)$ and $f_2(x_1, x_2, \ldots, x_k)$

$$J = \int [f_1 - f_2] \log_e f_1/f_2\, dx \tag{6}$$

where $dx = dx_1, dx_2, \ldots, dx_k$ and the integral is taken over the whole space of the random variables $x_1, x_2, \ldots, x_k$. Let

$$y_i = y_i(x_1, x_2, \ldots, x_k), \qquad i = 1, 2, \ldots, r \leq k \tag{7}$$

be linear transformations of the random variables $x_1, x_2, \ldots, x_k$. Then the distribution of y is $g_1(y)$ for the first population and $g_2(y)$ for the second population. The divergence is

$$J' = \int (g_1 - g_2) \log_e(g_1/g_2)\, dy, \tag{8}$$

where the integral is taken over the whole space of the random variables $y_1, y_2, \ldots, y_r$, and we define $dy = dy_1, dy_2, \ldots, dy_r$. In multivariate analysis, we want to maximize the relative efficiency of J' compared with J, namely the quantity J'/J.

2. DISCRIMINANT FUNCTION AND WEIGHTED REGRESSION

Let y be a linear discriminant function,

$$y = b_1 x_1 + b_2 x_2 + \cdots + b_k x_k = b'X. \tag{9}$$

Let Σ_1 and Σ_2 be the covariance matrices of the two normal populations with zero means. Then we have

$$J = \tfrac{1}{2} \operatorname{tr} \Sigma_1 \Sigma_2^{-1} + \tfrac{1}{2} \operatorname{tr} \Sigma_2 \Sigma_1^{-1} - k \tag{10}$$

$$J' = \tfrac{1}{2}(b'\Sigma_1 b)(b'\Sigma_2 b)^{-1} + \tfrac{1}{2}(b'\Sigma_2 b)(b'\Sigma_1 b)^{-1} - 1 \tag{11}$$

where tr means trace. Maximizing the ratio J'/J leads to the equation

$$(\Sigma_1 - L\,\Sigma_2)\hat{b} = 0, \tag{12}$$

where L is a Lagrange multiplier. For a maximum we have to choose the smallest or the largest root of the determinantal equation:

$$|\Sigma_1 - L\Sigma_2| = 0. \tag{13}$$

All roots of this equation are real and positive. Each root λ_i is associated with a vector b_i and the linear discriminant function $y_i = b_i'X$. The discriminant function $\hat{y} = \hat{b}'X$ discriminates optimally between the populations, in the sense of information theory.

With the method of weighted regression (Tintner [17, 18]), we assume that we have a set of variables consisting of a systematic part and superimposed errors of observations. Let A be the variance-covariance matrix of the observations and V be the variance-covariance matrix of errors. We replace (13) by $(A - \lambda V)b = 0$, and choose the smallest root of the determinantal equation corresponding to (13): $|A - \lambda V| = 0$ in order to derive the weighted regression equation $y - b'X = 0$ where the elements of the vector X denote the systematic parts of our variables. Recently, Tintner [19] established the relationship between Mahalanobis distance and weighted regression.

3. MULTIPLE REGRESSION

Suppose an economic relation is expressed as a multiple regression equation. The model is

$$y = X\beta + z, \tag{14}$$

where z is a vector of independent normal variates with zero mean and variance σ^2, X is a matrix of p fixed variates with rank p. Consider the hypothesis $H_1 : \beta = \beta^{(1)}$ against $H_2 : \beta = \beta^{(2)}$. Then Kullback ([10], p. 213) obtained the divergence

$$J(1, 2) = (\beta^{(1)} - \beta^{(2)})'S(\beta^{(1)} - \beta^{(2)})/\sigma^2 \tag{15}$$

where $S = X'X$. The minimum information statistic of Kullback is defined as the minimum of $I(1:2)$, where

$$I(1:2) = \int f_1(x) \log f_1(x)/f_2(x)\, d\lambda(x) \tag{16}$$

for given $f_2(x)$ and all $f_1(x)$ such that:

$$\theta = \int T(x) f_1(x)\, d\lambda(x)$$

and $T(x)$ is a measurable statistic. For the null hypothesis $\beta^{(2)} = 0$, the divergence based upon the minimum information statistic becomes

$$\hat{J}(H_1, H_2) = \frac{\hat{\beta}^{(1)\prime} S \hat{\beta}^{(1)}}{\hat{\sigma}^2}. \tag{17}$$

In Eq. (17) $\hat{\sigma}^2$ is an estimate of σ^2 whereas in Eq. (15), no such estimate was used. The term $\hat{\beta}^{(1)}$ can be obtained from the normal equations:

$$S\hat{\beta}^{(1)} = X'y. \tag{18}$$

The linear regression $\hat{y} = \hat{\beta} X$ is optimal in the sense of the minimum information statistic.

It is interesting to note that $\hat{J}(H_1, H_2)$ is closely related to the statistic:

$$(p\hat{\sigma}^2)^{-1}\hat{\beta}^{(1)\prime}S\hat{\beta}^{(1)} \tag{19}$$

which arises in the likelihood ratio test of the null hypothesis $\beta^{(2)} = 0$, and is distributed as F with p and $n - p$ degrees of freedom. Kullback ([10], p. 94) has already shown the existence of a relation between the minimum discrimination information statistic and the likelihood ratio. A similar relationship could exist between $J(H_1, H_2)$ and the likelihood ratio test.

4. LIMITED INFORMATION MAXIMUM LIKELIHOOD

In general, an econometric model can be expressed as a system of linear equations (cf. Johnston [6])

$$AY_t + BX_t = U_t, \qquad t = 1, 2, \ldots, T, \tag{20}$$

where A is a $G \times G$ matrix of coefficients of endogenous variables, and B is a $G \times K$ matrix of coefficients of predetermined variables (exogenous or lagged endogenous); Y_t, X_t, and U_t are column vectors of G, K, and G elements, respectively. The assumptions about the probability distribution of the disturbance terms are

$$E(U_t) = 0 \qquad \text{for all } t$$

$$E(U_t U_t') = \Phi, \qquad \text{a } G \times G \text{ symmetric variance-covariance matrix.}$$

Consider the first equation of this model,

$$\alpha_1 Y_t + \beta_1 X_t = u_{1t}, \tag{21}$$

where α_1 and β_1 are the first rows of the matrices A and B, respectively. More explicitly Eq. (21) could be written as

$$\alpha_{11}y_{1t} + \alpha_{12}y_{2t} + \cdots + \alpha_{1G_1}y_{G_1t} + \beta_{11}x_{1t} + \beta_{12}x_{2t} + \cdots + \beta_{1K_1}x_{K_1t} = u_{1t}. \tag{22}$$

Let us denote the linear combination of G_1 endogenous variables which appear in Eq. (22) by a single symbol, namely,

$$\tilde{y}_t = \alpha_{11}y_{1t} + \alpha_{12}y_{2t} + \cdots + \alpha_{1G_1}y_{G_1t}. \tag{23}$$

Let X_1 represent the vector of K_1 exogenous variables which appear in Eq. (22). Then vector X in Eq. (20) could be subdivided into

$$X = (X_1, X_2), \tag{24}$$

where X_2 is the vector of $(K - K_1)$ excluded predetermined variables. Now we can express the relation (23) as

$$u_1 = \tilde{y} - (X_1 X_2)\begin{pmatrix}\beta_1\\ \beta_2\end{pmatrix} \tag{25}$$

and, in particular, we wish to test the null hypothesis

$$H_1:\quad \beta = \beta^1 = \begin{pmatrix}\beta_1{}^1\\ \beta_2{}^1\end{pmatrix}$$

against

$$H_2:\quad \beta = \beta^2 = \begin{pmatrix}\beta_1{}^2\\ 0\end{pmatrix}.$$

The least variance ratio principle due to Anderson and Rubin [2] states that the α coefficients in the definition of $\tilde{y}$ should be so chosen that the ratio of the residual variance, when $\tilde{y}$ is regressed on X_1 to that when $\tilde{y}$ is regressed on X, is made as small as possible. This means the addition of the "excluded" predetermined variables X_2 should make a minimal improvement in the explained sum of squares in $\tilde{y}$. The sum of squares in $\tilde{y}$ is

$$\tilde{y}'\tilde{y} = \alpha_1 Y_1' Y_1 \alpha_1', \tag{26}$$

where Y_1 is the matrix of observations on the endogenous variables which actually appear in our relation. If we regress $\tilde{y}$ on X_1, the residual sum of squares is

$$\alpha_1 Y_1' Y_1 \alpha_1' - \alpha_1 Y_1' X_1 (X_1' X_1)^{-1} X_1' Y_1 \alpha_1' = \alpha_1 W_1 \alpha_1' \tag{27}$$

where

$$W_1 = Y_1' Y_1 - Y_1' X_1 (X_1' X_1)^{-1} X_1' Y_1.$$

If we regress $\tilde{y}$ on X, the residual sum of squares is given by

$$\alpha_1 W \alpha_1' \tag{28}$$

where

$$W = Y_1' Y_1 - Y_1' X (X' X)^{-1} X Y_1.$$

According to the least-variance ratio principle, we minimize the ratio

$$l = \alpha_1 W_1 \alpha_1' / \alpha_1 W \alpha_1'. \tag{29}$$

Differentiating l with respect to vector α_1 and equating to zero gives

$$(W_1 - lW)\alpha_1' = 0 \tag{30}$$

which has a nontrivial solution for α_1 only if the determinantal equation

$$|W_1 - lW| = 0 \tag{31}$$

is satisfied. The smallest root of Eq. (31), say $\hat{l}$ is obtained, and when it is substituted in Eq. (30), the estimates $\hat{\alpha}_1$ are determined by the relation

$$(W_1 - \hat{l}W)\hat{\alpha}_1' = 0. \tag{32}$$

The estimates of the predetermined variables of Eq. (22) are given by regressing $\tilde{y}(= Y_1\hat{\alpha}_1')$ on X_1

$$\hat{\beta}_1 = -\hat{\alpha}_1 Y_1'X_1(X_1'X_1)^{-1}. \tag{33}$$

The estimates of the parameters of Eq. (22) are thus estimated in two steps. The first step consists of obtaining a discriminant function, and we have shown that such a function discriminates between two populations optimally in the sense of information. The second step of obtaining the estimates is the same as obtaining the minimum discriminant information statistic when we have a two-partition linear subhypothesis.

5. TWO-STAGE LEAST SQUARES

Consider again Eq. (22). Normalizing it,

$$y_{1t} = \alpha_{12}y_{2t} + \alpha_{13}y_{3t} + \cdots + \alpha_{1G_1}y_{G_1t} + \beta_{11}x_{1t} + \beta_{12}x_{2t} + \cdots + \beta_{1K_1}X_{K_1t} + u_{1t}, \qquad t = 1, 2, \ldots, T \tag{34}$$

or in matrix form

$$y_1 = Y_2\alpha_2' + X_1\beta_1' + U_1. \tag{35}$$

The basic idea of two-stage least-squares estimation (cf. Basmann [3]) is to replace the endogenous variables $y_2, y_3, \ldots, y_{G_1}$ by their least-squares estimates, $\hat{Y}_2$

$$\hat{Y}_2 = (\hat{y}_2, \hat{y}_3, \ldots, \hat{y}_{G_1}) = X(X'X)^{-1}X'Y_2.$$

In other words we are replacing Y_2 in Eq. (35) by the minimum discrimination information statistic $\hat{Y}_2$. Now we consider regression of y_1 on $\hat{Y}_2$ and X_1 to obtain the two-stage least-squares estimates, $\hat{\alpha}_2$ and $\hat{\beta}_1$. This is a multiple regression discussed in Section 2.

If we denote V for the matrix of reduced form residuals for $(G_1 - 1)$ endogenous variables appearing on the right-hand side of (35), we can write the two-stage least-squares estimates of (35) as follows:

$$\begin{pmatrix} \hat{\alpha}_2' \\ \hat{\beta}_1' \end{pmatrix} = \begin{pmatrix} Y_2'Y_2 - V'V & Y_2'X_1 \\ X_1'Y_2 & X_1'X_1 \end{pmatrix}^{-1} \begin{pmatrix} Y_2' & -V' \\ X_1' & \end{pmatrix} y_1. \tag{36}$$

Theil has developed the k-class estimators from (36) by defining

$$\begin{pmatrix} \hat{\alpha}_2' \\ \hat{\beta}_1' \end{pmatrix}_k = \begin{pmatrix} Y_2'Y_2 - kV'V & Y_2'X_1 \\ X_1'Y_2 & X_1'X_1 \end{pmatrix}^{-1} \begin{pmatrix} Y_2' & -kV' \\ X_1' & \end{pmatrix} y_1 \tag{37}$$

Two-stage least squares corresponds to $k = 1$ since Eq. (37) reduces to (36). If $k = \hat{l}$ where $\hat{l}$ is the smallest root of Eq. (31), we have the limited information maximum likelihood estimates. If $k = 0$, we have the ordinary least-squares estimates.

6. MULTICOLLINEARITY AND USE OF PRINCIPAL COMPONENTS

One of the major obstacles in the estimation of econometric relations is multicollinearity (cf. Tintner [20], Klein and Nakamura [8], Chipman [4]). Frisch [4a] took the view that the variables in economic relations are composed of two parts, a systematic or "true" part and an "error" component. In case there is a high intercorrelation between the so-called independent variables in a regression equation, the least squares estimates will probably be dominated by the error terms. Linear dependence between the independent variables may also lead to singular or near singular moment matrix of the explanatory variables. Consider two-stage least-squares estimation. We are interested in obtaining consistent estimates of the parameters in an equation like Eq. (35) which is a part of a system of simultaneous equations. As a first step, we need to obtain the reduced form or solve Eq. (36) in which $(X'X)^{-1}$ is involved. Practical experience with reasonably large systems of econometric relations indicate that any linear dependence in the predetermined variables could lead to singularity or near singularity of $(X'X)$.

Kloek and Mennes [9] suggested a solution to the above problem by means of the use of principal components of the predetermined variables. One of the four variants of their techniques is as follows: Define V as the $(T \times G_1)$ matrix of least squares estimated disturbances in that part of the reduced form that corresponds to Y_2:

$$V = Y_2 - X(X'X)^{-1}X'Y_2. \tag{38}$$

Replace V by V_1

$$V_1 = Y_2 - Z(Z'Z)^{-1}Z'Y_2, \tag{39}$$

where

$$Z = [X_1 \quad F_1]. \tag{40}$$

The term F_1 represents the first k principal components (to be used as instrumental variables) of the "excluded" predetermined variables (X_2). In order to derive these principal components, we need the correlation matrix of the variables and its characteristic vectors. Suppose all the predetermined variables are normalized such that $\xi_j'\xi_j = 1$ and $\xi_j'l = 0$ where ξ_j is a column of X, and l a column of T unit elements. Then $X_2'X_2$ is a correlation matrix instead of a product matrix. Now the characteristic equation to be solved is

$$(X_2{}'X_2 - \lambda I)\delta = 0, \tag{41}$$

with λ being the characteristic root and δ the corresponding characteristic vector. Define

$$P = X_2{}'X_2 . \tag{42}$$

Then the determinantal Eq. of (41) could be written as

$$|P - \lambda I| = 0. \tag{43}$$

Kullback ([10], p. 199) has obtained the results

$$I(1:2) = -\tfrac{1}{2} \log |P| \tag{44}$$

and

$$J(1:2) = \tfrac{1}{2} \operatorname{tr} P^{-1} - (k/2) = (1 - \lambda_1)/2\lambda_1 + \cdots + (1 - \lambda_k)/2\lambda_k, \tag{45}$$

where λ's are roots of Eq. (43).

REFERENCES

1. ANDERSON, T. W. (1958). "An Introduction to Multivariate Statistical Analysis." Wiley, New York.
2. ANDERSON, T. W., and RUBIN, H. (1960). Estimation of the parameters of a single equation in a complete system of stochastic equations. *Ann. Math. Statist.* **55** 650–659.
3. BASMANN, R. L. (1957). A generalized classical method of linear estimation of coefficients in a structural equation. *Econometrica* **25** 77–83.
4. CHIPMAN, J. S. (1964). On least squares with insufficient observations. *J. Amer. Statist. Assoc.* **59** 1078–1111.

4a. FRISCH, R. (1934). "Statistical Confluence Analysis by Means of Complete Regression Systems." University Economics Inst., Oslo.

5. HARTLEY, R. V. L. (1928). Transmission of information. *Bell System Tech. J.* **7** 535.
6. JOHNSTON, J. (1963). "Econometric Models." McGraw-Hill, New York.
7. KEMPTHORNE, O. (1966). Some aspects of experimental inference. *J. Amer. Statist. Assoc.* **61** 11–34.
8. KLEIN, L. R., and NAKAMURA, N. (1962). Singularity in the equation systems of econometrics. *Internat. Economic Rev.* **3** No. 3, 274–299.
9. KLOEK, T., and MENNES, L. B. M. (1960). Simultaneous equations based on principal components of predetermined variables. *Econometrica* **28** 45–61.
10. KULLBACK, S. (1959). "Information Theory and Statistics." Wiley, New York.
11. KULLBACK, S. (1967). The two concepts of information. *J. Amer. Statist. Assoc.* **62** 685–686.
12. RAO, C. R. (1965). "Linear Statistical Inference and Its Applications." Wiley, New York.
13. RENYI, A. (1962.). "Wahrscheinilichkeitsre Chnung." Deut. Verlag. Wiss., Berlin
14. RENYI, A. (1965). On the foundations of information theory. *Rev. Inst. Internat. Statist.* **33** No. 1, 1–14.

15. SHANNON, C. E., and WEAER, W. (1949). "The Mathematical Theory of Communication." Univ. of Illinois Press, Urbana, Illinois.
16. THEIL, H. (1967). "Economics and Information Theory." Rand McNally, Chicago, Illinois.
17. TINTNER, G. (1952). "Econometrics." Wiley, New York.
18. TINTNER, G. (1960). Application of the theory of information to the problem of weighted regression. Onore De Corrado Gini, Vol. 1, p. 29. Rome Inst. De Statist. Univ., Dgli Studi, Rome.
19. TINTNER, G. (1963). A Note on the relation between Mahalanobis distance and weighted regression. "Contributions to Statistics" (C. R. Rao *et al.*, eds.), pp. 481–484. Statist. Publ. Soc., Calcutta.
20. TINTNER, G. (1945). A note on rank, multicollinearity and multiple regression. *Ann. Math. Statist.* **16** 304–308.
21. WIENER, N. (1948). "Cybernetics." Wiley, New York.